The Greenhill NAPOLEONIC Wars Data Book

The Greenhill NAPOLEONIC Wars Data Book

DIGBY SMITH

GREENHILL BOOKS, LONDON
STACKPOLE BOOKS, PENNSYLVANIA

The Greenhill Napoleonic Wars Data Book
first published 1998 by Greenhill Books, Lionel Leventhal Limited,
Park House, 1 Russell Gardens, London NW11 9NN
and
Stackpole Books, 5067 Ritter Road, Mechanicsburg, PA 17055, USA

British Library Cataloguing in Publication Data
Smith, Digby George
The Greenhill Napoleonic Wars Data Book: actions and losses
in personnel, colours, standards and artillery, 1792-1815
1. Napoleonic Wars, 1800-1815
I. Title II. Napolenic Wars Data Book
940.2'7

ISBN 1-85367-276-9

Library of Congress Cataloging-in-Publication Data
Smith, Digby George
The Greenhill Napoleonic Wars Data Book: actions and losses in
personnel, colours, standards and artillery, 1792-1815 / by Digby Smith
p. cm.
Includes bibliographical references (p.) and index.
ISBN 1-85367-276-9
1. France—History—Revolution, 1789-1799—Campaigns—
Participation, French—Sources. 2. Napoleonic Wars, 1800-1815—
Campaigns—Participation, French—Sources. 3. France—History,
Military—1789-1815—Sources. 4. France—History, Naval—
19th century—Sources. 5. Napoleonic Wars, 1800-1815—Equipment
and supplies—Sources. 6. France. Armée—Military life—Sources.
I. Title.
DC220.S63 1998 97-39991
944.04—DC21 CIP

Designed by David Gibbons, DAG Publications Ltd
Printed and bound in Singapore

CONTENTS

ACKNOWLEDGEMENTS

Completing a work of this scope and detail has been a massive and absorbing task. Despite having been actively engaged in studying the Napoleonic military era (1805–1815) closely for over 20 years, the task of resolving the many uncertainties in the battle participation of the various nations, even for this well-documented period, has absorbed much time. This is the largest and most complex book that I have produced to date and without having committed the last few years to full time, solid research and presentation this work would never have been written.

The much-neglected Revolutionary Wars (1792–1801), with hundreds of engagements and patchy documentation, presented an even greater challenge; and was a task which I doubt I could have completed without the helpful assistance of many friends and acquaintances. Their advice led to numerous literary 'mining expeditions'; some more, some less profitable. What did emerge, however, was the realization that this period contains a large number of fascinating actions every bit as dynamic as any in the subsequent Napoleonic era. Perhaps the best of these is the odyssey of the Russians under Suvorov in northern Italy and Switzerland in 1799. There are still areas in which material has proved elusive, particularly concerning the French in 1794, 1795 and 1797, but sufficient data is available to give an insight into the course of military events throughout 23 of the most fascinating years in the political and military history of Europe and learn many surprising aspects of the operations – particularly of Napoleon Bonaparte in the earlier years of his military and political career.

Among those who have assisted me most in my researches are Alfred Umhey, Peter Hofschröer, Jörg Titze and – above all – Markus Gärtner who placed his entire, comprehensive collection at my disposal. Also extremely helpful were Mike Cox and George Nafziger who both obtained obscure and inaccessible information on my behalf. Margaret and Peter Roth were invaluable in turning my material into a presentable typescript and my wife has been most tolerant in allowing me to cover our dining room, lounge and bedroom with my papers over the last few years.

Particular thanks are also due to the Greenhill team of expert readers and editors who kindly took the time to read the working manuscript and to correct some of my errors and omissions. These include John Elting, Paddy Griffith, Paul Chamberlain, Dave Hollins, Philip Haythornthwaite, Charles Esdaile, George Nafziger, Jonathan North and the painstaking Gerald Napier.

The following archives, museums and libraries have proved to be of immense value in my search for military historical data over the last 30 years:

GREAT BRITAIN

London:

The National Army Museum (and its library) houses a considerable collection of artifacts, uniforms, portraits, uniform plates and books covering the British Army.

The Victoria and Albert Museum includes many rare and valuable books on military history and uniforms of many armies.

The National Maritime Museum is a source of excellent details of the history of the Royal Navy.

The Polish Institute and Sikorski Museum contains much literature and many items of uniform of the Napoleonic era. Mr Fiedler, the assistant curator, is incredibly helpful.

The Monaco Information Centre will provide information on the archives of the Napoleonic Museum, Principality of Monaco.

Much very finely detailed data on the British Army may be found in the *Journal of the Society for Army Historical Research*.

All existing regimental museums in Great Britain may be found in Terence Wise's excellent *Guide to Military Museums*. These museums are each a treasure trove to the serious researcher.

AUSTRIA

Graz: In the castle is a large collection of weapons and equipment of the Napoleonic era.

Innsbruck: The *Zeughausmuseum* (arsenal) contains a wealth of exhibits mainly relating to the 1805–1809 period.

The *Bergiselmuseum*, built on the hill south of the city on which so much fighting took place in 1809, houses the museum of the Austrian Jägers and contains some items of the period 1805–1815.

Vienna: The *Heeresgeschichtliches Museum* displays a splendid collection of uniforms, weapons, colours and standards including the period 1792–1815. This institution produces a series of extremely well-researched booklets on various campaigns and actions of this and other periods.

The *Aspern museum:* a small but very high-quality collection of battlefield relics.

DENMARK

Copenhagen: *Tøjhusmuseet* has an extensive collection of contemporary colour plates of Danish uniforms.

FRANCE

Paris: The *Musée de l'Armée* contains an unequalled and very extensive collection of uniforms, weapons, colours, standards, harness and horse furniture of the Napoleonic era, including items from some of the Napoleonic satellite kingdoms.

Strasbourg: The city museum has an extensive collection of uniforms, weapons and colours.

Vincennes: The home of the French military archives; extremely detailed and extensive records.

GERMANY

Bad Wildungen: *Wehrhistorisches und Jagdmuseum.* An astounding collection of uniforms, weapons, colours and standards mainly centred on the armies of Hessen-Kassel and Westfalia. The curator, Herr Grosse-Löscher, is most helpful.

Berlin: *Deutsches Historisches Museum.* Many weapons and uniforms of the period as well as uniform and battle plates.

The *Staatliche Museen Preussischer Kulturbesitz* holds an unequalled collection of colour and black and white uniform plates and costumes.

Brunswick: *Braunschweigisches Landesmuseum.* Excellent for Brunswick troops.

Celle: The *Bomann-Museum* is excellent for the Hanoverian Army and the King's German Legion.

Coburg: The *Herzoglich Sachsen Coburg und Gotha'sche Hauptverwaltung* contains much on the Ducal Saxon contingents.

Darmstadt: *Hessisches Staatsarchiv.* Excellent for Hessen-Darmstadt; good for some other minor German states.

The *Hessisches Staats- und Universitätsbibliothek* houses an excellent and wide ranging collection of illustrated works in colour, mainly on German states' military forces but also including rare works on Spain ca 1800 and Poland ca 1780.

Dresden: The *Militärbibliothek Dresden* holds the united collections of the old West and East German armies and is strongly recommended.

Düsseldorf: The *Nordrhein-Westfälisches Hauptstaatsarchiv* is good for documents on the Grand Duchy of Berg.

The *Hauptstaatsarchiv* is also good for documents on the Grand Duchy of Berg and they may be found filed under 'Local Government'.

Fulda: The *Hessische Landesbibliothek* has an interesting collection on the bishopric of Fulda and some items on Hessen-Kassel.

Göttingen: The *Niedersächsische Staats- und Universitäts-Bibliothek* includes an excellent collection of rare works covering the wars of 1792–1815.

Hamburg: The *Staatsarchiv der Freien und Hansestadt* is home to one of the three copies of the brothers Cornelius and Christian Suhr's famous *Uniformen alle in Hamburg zwischen 1806 und 1813 gewesenene Truppen.* A collection of hundreds of hand-coloured uniforms plates of all troops who passed through the city during this period.

The *Museum für Hamburgische Geschichte* is good for Russian, French and allied troops (colour plates), 1813–14.

Altonaer Museum – a collection of 21 naive contemporary watercolours of Danish troops ca 1809 by FWC von Prangen.

Hannover: The *Niedersächsisches Hauptstaatsarchiv* is excellent for the Hanoverian Army, the King's German Legion and some Westfalian documents.

Historisches Museum am Hohen Ufer is an excellent source for the Hanoverian Army and the King's German Legion and holds many uniforms.

Ingolstadt: The *Bayerisches Armeemuseum* holds a fine collection of Bavarian uniforms, colours, standards and weapons.

Kaub: The *Blüchermuseum* is a small but excellent collection of Blücher memorabilia and a selection of shakos (mainly French) ca 1810–1814.

Koblenz: The *Landeshauptarchiv* is good for data on German electoral troops (Köln, Mainz, Trier).

Cologne: *Historisches Archiv.* Some data on the troops of the Electorate of Cologne.

Krefeld: The *Archiv der Stadt Krefeld* has some data on the Grand Duchy of Berg.

Mainz: *Stadtarchiv.* Very good for the troops of the Electorate of Mainz, including colourplates. Much information on the various sieges.

Mannheim: The *Stadtarchiv* is good for the siege and surrender of the city in 1795.

Marburg: *Hessisches Staatsarchiv.* Excellent for Hessen-Kassel.

Munich: The *Bayerisches Hauptstaatsarchiv*: Excellent for the Bavarian Army.

Rastatt: *Wehrgeschichtliches Museum.* Excellent for a wide range of uniforms, weapons, colours, standards and books on the armies of Baden, Württemberg, Bavaria and the Austrian 'Reichskontingente'.

Schrozberg-Bartenstein: The *Militär-Museum* is excellent for a narrow range of items on the local troops and the 1er Regiment Étranger.

Stuttgart: The *Hauptstaatsarchiv Stuttgart* is good for the Württemberg Army.

Trier: *Stadtbibliothek/Stadtarchiv.* Some data on the troops of the Electorate of Trier. A colour and a standard are held in the town museum.

Weilburg: *Heimat- und Bergbaumuseum der Stadt Weilburg/Lahn* has some weapons, drums and uniform plates relating to the Nassauers in Spain and at Waterloo.

THE NETHERLANDS

Den Haag: The *Koninklijke Landmacht* is good for the armies of the United Provinces, the Batavian Republic and the Kingdom of the Netherlands.

Leiden: The *Koninklijk Nederlands Leger-en Wapenmuseum* holds a small but high-quality collection on the period 1792–1815.

PORTUGAL

Lisbon: *Museo Militar.* An excellent collection of contemporary uniforms and equipment.

RUSSIA

St Petersburg: *The Hermitage Museum* holds a vast collection of contemporary items.

Borodino: The museum has a small but high quality collection of artifacts from 1812, including many captured cannon barrels.

Moscow: *The Kremlin* contains hundreds of captured cannon barrels.

SPAIN

Madrid: *The Military Museum* contains much original material (uniforms) from the period.

SWEDEN

Stockholm: The *Armémuseum* has a small but very high-quality collection of uniforms and weapons, 1792–1815.

SWITZERLAND

Bâsle: *The Historical Museum* has a collection of contemporary items, including the uniform of an officer of the Regiment de Roll in British service, ca 1812.

Geneva: *Museum for the Swiss in Foreign Service.* An impressive collection including a highly detailed series of watercolours showing the Regiment de Meuron in Dutch service, ca 1790, and in British service 1795–1805.

Morges: The *Musée Militaire Vaudois* has an excellent collection on Swiss regiments in French service.

Neuchâtel: *The Historical Museum*: contains an extensive, high-quality collection of contemporary uniforms, weapons and equipment of several armies.

St Maurice: The museum has a small but high-quality collection.

Valais: *Musée Militaire du Valais.* This houses an excellent collection of uniforms, weapons, colours and standards of the Swiss regiments in foreign service and includes the uniforms of a fusilier, Helvetian Legion, 1800, and a captain of the Stosstrupp-grenadier-Bataillon Nr 11, ca 1810.

Zürich: *Schweizerisches Landesmuseum.* An excellent source for Swiss regiments in foreign service and for the Suvorov's campaign in Switzerland in 1799.

I would like to extend my thanks to all those with whom I have corresponded over many years, generally and specifically, whilst researching this fascinating period of history, and to those who have directly contributed to the present work and assisted in its completion. Inevitably this book will not answer every question and will contain errors and mistakes that have been overlooked in such a complex undertaking. I would therefore be grateful for further information and this may be addressed to me via my publisher.

Digby Smith
Hanau, 1998

INTRODUCTION

This work lists over 2,000 skirmishes, raids, ambushes, clashes, battles, blockades, sieges and capitulations which took place in and around Europe and in Egypt between the years 1792 and 1815. For each action I provide as detailed an entry as possible on the participation and losses of units involved. The details given in the entries include the date and precise location of each action, who won, the names of the opposing commanders, the actual regiments which took part in the fighting (ie fired shots at the enemy and took casualties), the totals involved on each side, the losses incurred in killed, wounded, missing and the loss of any trophies (cannon, colours and standards). Where considered appropriate I have also included a brief comment to highlight significant events, errors or consequences of the action concerned. All such comments reflect my own opinions and serve to place the action in context. An exception to these rules are the so-called 'skeleton actions' – indicated by the alpha code 'XX', which were either part of the French civil war in the Vendée or did not involve the main protagonist, France. For these actions only the totals involved and the losses incurred are given. I have made a conscious and determined attempt to emphasize the participation of the many minor contingents from the smaller nations of Europe which fought on both sides of these epic struggles and highlight their oft neglected role in this dramatic and wide-ranging conflict.

The detail on participants in 'normal' actions usually goes down to battalion/squadron/battery level. It must, however, be stressed that this book is *not* a collection of Orders of Battle (OOBs). An OOB – or a return or parade state – is a highly detailed statement of the exact strengths and status of all component parts of an army or formation at a given point in time. Inevitably, OOBs changed frequently and radically. It would be impossible to take an OOB for 1 May 1792 and expect it to be valid for 30 April or 2 May of the same year. It is in fact a 'snap shot' of the formation usually giving the number of field officers, junior (commissioned) officers, non-commissioned officers (NCOs), drummers, buglers, trumpeters, bandsmen, surgeons and privates present and fit for duty, sick, wounded, detached and missing.

In this work the data consists of information on those regiments which were actually engaged with the enemy during the action in question. Only when it has not been possible to find this information have I had to resort to including the more general and less accurate OOBs. This is the case with the revolutionary French armies in 1793–95 and 1797. The records of the French armies of this era were very incomplete due, in large part, to the disruptions of the amalgams (the fusion of the old, royalist, regiments with the newer national guard and volunteer formations) and of the Terror during which scores of senior officers were denounced for 'cowardice' or treason, tried, condemned and executed by Robespierre's government.

It must also be pointed out that there are very few absolutely reliable totals of combatants and of casualty figures during this, or any other period including the Vietnam war and the Gulf war. The various sources used have to be carefully evaluated for their fidelity. The British, Prussian, Austrian and minor German states' statistics are highly detailed, comprehensive and generally accepted as being faithful records. Russian records are usually rounded up or down to the nearest thousand; French figures for the revolutionary period are patchy and incomplete, and later figures – including Napoleon's own – are notoriously inaccurate and seem often to have been intended for French public consumption only.

Even in the best cases, where faithfulness and accuracy were high priorities, considerable margins of error may inadvertently have crept into the records. Records of battle losses were made in the following way: at the first possible opportunity the regiments would gather together and the platoon/company sergeants would parade their men, call the roll of those present and try to elicit the fate of those missing. The results would be collated at regimental level then at brigade, division, corps and army level.

For the victors, usually left in possession of the battlefield, this task was relatively easy. They had the added advantage that they could count the dead and wounded of both sides left on the battlefield and the prisoners that they had made. They thus had the basis to produce a relatively accurate statement of events *if they so chose.*

The vanquished, often in partial or complete disorganization, had a much more difficult task. The Spanish armies of the period 1808–1813, for instance, frequently suffered crushing defeats at French hands and records are understandably sparse. Even in the best cases, the records contained a potentially large unknown in the numbers who could only be recorded as 'wounded' or 'missing'. A high proportion of the wounded in those days inevitably died within the next days or weeks. Many of the missing were actually dead, wounded and not yet so identified, or off marauding, or had deserted or been captured.

Even if the reported figures are correct and accurate statistics another issue must be addressed when we come to determining how to interpret the available data. Those killed in action present fewer problems than those listed as 'wounded' and 'captured'. These two categories present a dilemma and it is very difficult to determine whether all the wounded are still with their own side after a defeat or whether all those noted as captured by the victors are the unwounded prisoners or whether that figure includes enemy wounded captured in the aftermath of the battle.

This book has been designed to permit the reader easy access to any desired action and includes an alphabetical index of the actions detailed for quick reference. The main listing of the actions is, however, entirely chronological. The chronological layout of the work gives a clear overview of the range and intensity of the military activity in time and permits one to place events in the context of conflict in Europe as a whole and in direct relation to other campaigns. All too frequently the consequences of an action in one theatre of war brought far reaching changes to the course of events in another.

Once having found a particular action, it is likely that the reader will then wish to follow the entire chain of events in any selected campaign from start to finish. Each action is therefore equipped with 'Last action' and 'Next action' links giving the names and dates of the actions flanking the one that the reader has chosen. This means that even in an incredibly active year such as 1809, when all of Europe was up in arms, the reader may quite simply skip along through the related actions of any desired campaign, ignoring other events if desired. Using the book in this way is facilitated by the two-letter alpha code to the left of each action's entry. This code identifies the theatre of the war in which the action took place. NL for instance identifies not only those actions which took place within the borders of the present-day Kingdom of Netherlands but also those which were related to the main events despite having actually taken place in Belgium, France or Germany as the tide of the war ebbed and flowed through the region.

Similarly IN (Italy, north) will include actions in southern France, Switzerland, Austria and parts of the ex-Yugoslavia. DV (Danube Valley) will range through southern Germany, Austria and the Czech and Slovak republics.

It must be remembered, moreover, that during the period under review, the political map of Europe bore almost no resemblance to the modern picture. Germany, Italy, Austria, Russia, Scandinavia and Turkey were radically different as was the whole of eastern Europe.

The many tiny states which made up present-day Germany each had their own army, many only since the creation of the Confederation of the Rhine in 1806. Many of these states grew out of the territory of others which were absorbed by their neighbours and vanished from the political map over the period 1800–1805. Many of these had maintained their own armed contingents.

Some of the more far reaching examples of these changes include the abolition of the Electorates of Köln (Cologne), Mainz and Trier, the creation of the ephemeral Kingdom of Westfalia, the Grand Duchies of Berg and Frankfurt and the temporary abolition of Hessen-Kassel and Hanover.

A similar situation developed in the Italian peninsula with the Kingdom of Italy absorbing archaic duchies and principalities until a partial reversion to the old order in 1815.

Several of the sieges during this period (eg Mainz, Danzig, Colberg, Hamburg) have justified books of their own in the past; for purposes of uniformity and to give emphasis on the end result, they have been shown as single-action entries and placed at the date of final capitulation.

Most naval actions involving only one ship on each side have been excluded as they were of little strategic consequence to a naval war decided by fleet actions. Colonial conflicts have not been included and international treaties and conventions have only been included if they were militarily significant.

Names of commanders and towns were often spelt in various ways in the period under review (eg Clerfait, Clerfayt, Clerfaye). I have decided to spell them as they appear in the majority of the sources consulted and used this to act as a guide and standard. The major cities' names have been anglicised (Rome, Vienna, Munich, Venice, Genoa, Naples) to ease quick recognition.

ALPHA CODES

AD	Adriatic
CH	Switzerland
DK	Denmark
DV	Danube Valley
EC	Central Spain
EE	Eastern Spain
EG	Northwestern Spain (Galicia)
EM	Spain, Madrid & area
EN	Northern Spain
EW	Western Spain
FC	France, Champagne
FE	Eastern France
FJ	France, Jura region
FN	Northern France
FP	Pyrenees
FS	Southern France
FW	Western France
GB	Great Britain
GN	Northern Germany
IM	Central Italy
IN	Northern Italy
IS	Southern Italy
MD	Mediterranean
MR	Middle Rhine
NL	Netherlands
OP	East Prussia
PN	Northern Portugal
PM	Central Portugal
PS	Southern Portugal (1808–1814)
PS	Prussia/Silesia (1806–1807 only)
RM	Russia, main body, Moscow
RN	Russia, north flank guard
RS	Russia, south flank guard
RL	Russia, Latvia
SX	Saxony
TY	Tyrol
UR	Upper Rhine
WW	Warsaw
XX	Skeleton actions; not involving France, or being Vendée civil war
YE	Egypt
ZZ	Naval actions

Table of Comparative British, Prussian, Austrian and Russian Commanders' Titles at the Various Command Levels. (1.)

Command Level	*British*	*French*	*Prussian*	*Austrian*	*Russian (4.)*
Army	Field Marshal or General	Maréchal (2.) Maréchal de l'Empire (3.)	Feldmarschall	Generalissimo or Feldmarschall	Field Marshal
Corps	Lieutenant General	Général (2.) Maréchal de l'Empire (3.) or Général en Chef	General der Infanterie or General der Kavallerie or Generalleutnant	Feldzeugmeister or General der Kavallerie or General der Infanterie	General of Infantry or General of Cavalry
Division	Lieutenant General or Major General	Général (2.) Général de Division (3.) Maréchal de camp (2.)	Generalleutnant	Feldmarschalleutnant	Lieutenant General or Major General
Brigade	Brigadier General or Colonel	Général de Brigade (3).	Generalmajor	Generalmajor or Oberst	Major General or Colonel
Regiment	Colonel or Lieutenant Colonel	Colonel (2.) and (3.)	Oberst	Oberst or Oberstleutnant	Colonel or Lieutenant Colonel

Notes
1. = there was always a certain flexibility concerning which rank commanded which formation; these rules are not 'carved in stone'.
2. = Ranks used in the Revolutionary Wars.
3. = Ranks used in the Napoleonic Wars.
4. = Particularly in 1812, 1813 and 1814, major generals in the battered Russian armies commanded corps and divisions as well as brigades.

ABBREVIATIONS USED IN THE TEXT

ArtR	Artillery regiment
bn/Bn	battalion (general) / a particular Battalion eg 4th, an infantry unit of 600–1,000 men
bns/Bns	as above but plural
Brand	Brandenburg, a Prussian provincial regimental designation
Brig/BG	Brigadier General
bties	batteries
bty	battery (an artillery unit of from 6–12 guns)
CavR	Cavalry Regiment
ChàCh	Chasseurs à Cheval: mounted rifles - not usually armed with rifled weapons
ChàP	Chasseurs à Pied: rifles - in the French army; not usually armed with rifled weapons in this era
Chass	Chasseurs
ChLL	Chevaux Légèrs Lanciers: light horse lancers regiment
ChLR	Chevaux Légèrs Regiment: light horse
Col	Colonel
Coy/coy	company: a unit of about 100 men
CuirR	Cuirassier Regiment: heavy cavalry often wearing armoured breast and backplates
DB	Demi-Brigade
DBdeLé	Demi-Brigade-Légère: a French light infantry unit usually of three battalions
DBdeLi	Demi-Brigade de Ligne: a French line infantry unit, usually of three battalions
det	Detachment
DragR	Dragoon Regiment: originally mounted infantry; in this era light cavalry
EH	Erzherzog (Archduke): a rank in the Austrian nobility
Elb	German title of the Elbe infantry Regiment
FAB	Foot Artillery Battery
FM	Field Marshal or Feld-Marschall
FML	Feld Marschalleutnant: an Austrian rank below FM and FZM
Füs	Füsilier (or Fusileer): originally 'light infantry' style; infantry regiments armed with lighter, shorter muskets than the rest of the 'line infantry'. The designation for the centre companies of French line infantry regiments
FZM	Feldzeugmeister: an Austrian rank below that of FM
GdB	Général de Brigade: a French rank equating to Brigadier General
GdC	General der Cavallerie (General of Cavalry): a rank in the Austrian, Russian and Prussian armies
GdD	Général de Division: a French rank equating to the British Major General or the Austrian Feldmarschalleutnant
GdI	General der Infanterie: a rank in the Austrian, Russian and Prussian armies
GdK	General der Kavallerie: see GdC
GdN	Garde Nationale: French national guard formations; not part of the infantry of the regular army
Gds	Guards
GL	Generalleutnant: equivalent to Lieutenant General; senior to a Major General
GM	General Major: equivalent to Major General; senior to a Brigadier General
Gren	Grenadiers
Gren à Ch	Grenadiers à Cheval, horse grenadiers
Gren à P	Grenadiers à Pied, foot grenadiers
GrenR	Grenadier Regiment
GzIR	Grenz-Infanterie-Regiment: Border Infantry Regiments of the Austrian army, from the areas in Romania and the ex-Yugoslavia
HAB	Horse Artillery Battery
HusR	Hussar Regiment: light cavalry of Hungarian origin
IR	Infantry Regiment
JgR	Jäger Regiment
JzPf	Jäger-zu-Pferde: mounted rifles, not normally armed with rifled weapons in this era

KürR	Kürassier-Regiment: the German equivalent of Cuirassiers
LDR	Light Dragoon Regiment, light cavalry
LG	Leib-Garde or Life Guards; Lieutenant General
LIR	Line Infantry Regiment, 'heavy' infantry units, usually of 1-5 battalions
LtCol	Lieutenant Colonel
LtI	Light Infantry, units of smaller, more agile men, often armed with lighter muskets than the line and trained in open-order fighting (skirmishing)
LWCR	Landwehr-Cavallerie-Regiment: a German innovation of the period 1813–1815; units raised for the duration of the war; not part of the Line cavalry
LWIR	the infantry equivalent of LWCR, often poorly armed, clothed and trained
LWKR	Landwehr-Kavallerie-Regiment. See LWCR
M	Marshal, the highest French military rank during the Napoleonic period.
MCR	Militia Cavalry Regiment
MdC	Maréchal de Camp (Field marshal), a French and Spanish title of the Revolutionary period
MG	Major General; senior to a Brigadier, usually in command of a division (two or more brigades)
MIR	Militia Infantry Regiment
MtdRR	Mounted Rifle Regiment; light cavalry; not usually armed with rifled weapons in this era
MuskR	MusketierR, a Russian designation for standard line infantry
NatFd	National-Feld-Battalion or Regiment; a Bavarian designation for a home guard unit which volunteered for service outside Bavaria
NatKR	National-Kavallerie-Regiment: a Prussian innovation of the years 1813–14 for non-regular cavalry regiments
Obst	Oberst, German equivalent of Colonel. Obstlt: Oberstleutnant, German equivalent of Lieutenant Colonel
Ostpr	Ostpreussisch - East Prussian, a Prussian provincial regimental designation
Pomm	Pommersches - Pommeranian, a Prussian provincial regimental designation
PosB	Position Battery, a Russian heavy artillery battery (12 pdr guns).
Prov	Provisional
Pv	Provisional
RAdm	Rear Admiral
RIdLi	Régiment Infanterie de Ligne, French line infantry regiment
RILé	Régiment Infanterie Légère, French light infantry regiment
ResIR	Reserve Infantry Regiment
Schl	Schlesisches - Silesian, a Prussian provincial regimental designation
Tp	Troop
UlR	Ulan regiment - lancers
Westpr	West Prussian; a Prussian provincial designation
vac	Vacant, not having a colonel-in-chief
1er, 1ère, 2e, etc	Premier, Première, Deuxième, etc: 1st, 2nd etc (in French unit titles, masculine and feminine forms)
1a, etc	Prima, etc: 1st (in Italian unit titles)
(2)	number of battalions, eg, GdN Haute-Vienne (2) = two bns of the Garde Nationale de la Haute-Vienne. GdN Haute-Vienne (2e) = 2nd Battalion of Garde Nationale de la Haute-Vienne

The REVOLUTIONARY WARS

1792–1801

1792

1792 THE ACTIONS

NL Mons (Quaregnon village), 28–29 April 1792, clash

A town in south Belgium, 20 km south-southeast of Brussels, on Routes A7/E9/E19/E42, N6 and N40.

An Austrian victory over the French.

(Last action – this was the opening clash of the campaign; next action – Tournay, 29 April.)

French Forces GL Biron commanding:

Infantry 1er RIdLi (1 bn); 18e RIdLi (1 bn); 49e RIdLi (1 bn); 68e RIdLi (1 bn); 74e RIdLi (1 bn); 89e RIdLi (1 bn); GdN Paris (2e Bn); Aisne (1er Bn); Seine-Inférieure (1er Bn).

Cavalry 5e DragR (2 sqns); 6e DragR (2 sqns); 3e CavR (3 sqns); 3e HusR (3 sqns). 30 cannon, 6 howitzers.

French totals 9 bns, 10 sqns, 36 guns, 7,500 men.

French losses 400 dead, wounded and captured, 5 guns, 1 howitzer several ammunition waggons, 63 carts.

Austrian Forces FML Beaulieu commanding: Gren Bn Briey (1 bn); Le Loup Jägers (3 coys); O'Donnell Freikorps (2nd Bn); IR Bender Nr 41(⅓ bn); IR Sztáray Nr 33 (1st and 2nd Bns); Émigrés (2 coys); DragR Coburg Nr 37 (3 sqns), Degelmann Ulans (3 sqns); Le Loup Jägers (2 sqns); Émigrés (3 sqns).

Austrian totals 4⅓ bns, 5 coys, 11 sqns, 18 guns, ca 5,000 men.

Austrian losses 10 dead, 20 wounded.

Comment This was the first French raid and was a total failure. FML Beaulieu did not exploit his victory.

Sources Kriege F II, Chuquet, Schulz, Wrede.

NL Tournay (Marquain Village), 29 April 1792, clash

A town in south Belgium, 25 km east of Lille, on Routes A16/E42, N7 and N50.

An Austrian victory over the French.

(Last action – Mons, 28 and 29 April; next action – Bavay, 17 May 1792.)

French Forces Gen Th Dillon commanding: 24e RIdLi (1 bn); 56e RIdLi (1 bn); 90e RIdLi (1 bn); GdN Seine-et-Oise (1 coy); 6e ChàCh (2 sqns); 1er, 8e and 13e CavR (2 sqns each); 6 x 4 pdr guns.

French totals 3 bns, 1 coy, 8 sqns, 6 guns; 5,000 men.

French losses 150 captured, 4 guns.

Austrian Forces GM Happoncourt commanding: IR Clerfayt Nr 9 (1 bn); IR D'Alton Nr 15 (⅔ bn); IR de Ligne Nr 30 (⅓ bn); ChLR Latour Nr 31 (4 sqns); 6 guns.

Austrian totals 2 bns, 4 sqns, 6 guns ca 2,600 men.

Austrian losses None.

Comments The French troops panicked; Gen Dillon was wounded by them when he tried to restore order and was murdered by the mob in Lille. The Austrians did not exploit their victory.

Sources Kriege F II, Chuquet, Schulz, Wrede.

NL Bavay, 17 May 1792, clash

A French village near the Belgian border 12 km West of Maubeuge, on Route N543.

An Austrian victory over the French.

(Last action – Tournay, 29 April; next action – Rumégies, 19 May.)

French Forces 49e RIdLi (½ bn); 10e ChàP (½ bn); 3e HusR (½ sqn).

French total ca 1,200 men.

French losses ca 1,160 infantry captured.

Austrian Forces Obst Fischer commanding: Briey Grenadiers (1 bn); IR D'Alton Nr 15 (1st Bn); IR Württemberg Nr 38 (1st Bn); IR Murray Nr 55 (1st Bn); Le Loup Jägers (1 bn); DragR Coburg Nr 37 (2 sqns); HusR Blankenstein Nr 16 (2 sqns); Degelmann Ulans (2 sqns); 6 guns.

Austrian totals 5 bns, 6 sqns, 3,600 infantry, 500 cavalry, 6 guns.

Austrian losses None.

Comments The village surrendered after a few cannon shots; the French cavalry fled. This small operation was the first 'offensive-defensive' of the Austrian commander, the Herzog Albert of Sachsen-Teschen.

Sources Kriege F II, Chuquet, Schulz, Wrede.

NL Rumégies, 19 May 1792, clash

A village in southwest Belgium, 15 km southwest of Tournay.

An Austrian victory over the French.

(Last action – Bavay, 17 May; next action – Florennes 23 May.)

French Forces 400 National Guards, 40 dragoons.

French losses 40 men dead, wounded and captured.

Austrian Forces Obstlt Owerland commanding: IR Clerfayt Nr 9 (2 coys); ChLR Latour Nr 31 (20 men); 1 gun, ca 250 men.

Austrian losses Not known, very slight.

Comment Another successful Austrian raid which further lowered French morale.

Sources Kriege F II, Chuquet, Schulz, Wrede.

NL Florennes, 23 May 1792, clash

A village in southern Belgium 20 km southeast of Charleroi, on Route N98.

An Austrian victory over the French.

(Last action – Bavay, 17 May; next action – La Grisuelle 27 May.)

French Forces: Gen Lafayette's Advanced Guard Gen Gouvion commanding: 55e RIdLi (1 bn); 83e RIdLi (1 bn); Grenadiers (¾ bn); GdN Marne (2e Bn); Côte-d'Or (2e Bn); 9e RILé (1 bn); 3e ChàCh (2 sqns); 11e ChàCh (2 sqns); 6e HusR (½ sqn); 1 x HAB of 8 guns.

French totals 5¾ bns, 4½ sqns, 8 guns; ca 5,000 men.

French losses 111 dead, wounded and captured; 3 guns.

Austrian Forces GM Sztáray commanding:

Dandini Jägers (6½ coys); IR Sztáray Nr 33 (5 coys); IR Stuart Nr 18 (5 coys); IR Esterházy Nr 34 (4 coys); Grenadier Bn Morzin (6 coys); DragR Coburg Nr 37 (2 sqns); HusR Wurmser Nr 30 (2 sqns); 6 guns.

Austrian totals 26½ coys, 4 sqns, 6 guns, ca 3,000 men.

Austrian losses 7 dead, 22 wounded.

Comment Following the Austrian raid on Bavay on 17 May 1792, this was their second 'spoiling attack' to keep their French opponents off balance.

Sources Kriege F II, Chuquet, Schulz, Wrede.

NL La Grisuelle, 11 June 1792, skirmish

A village in northern France about 5 km north of Maubeuge, on Route N2.

An Austrian victory over the French.

(Last action – Florennes 23 May; next action – Menin, 17 June.)

French Forces Gen Gouvion commanding:

9e and 10e ChàP (2 bns); GdN Meurthe (4e Bn); Côte-d'Or (2e Bn); 3e and 11e ChàCh (2 sqns each); 2e HusR (2 sqns).

French totals 4 bns, 6 sqns, 6 guns, ca 4,000 men.

French losses 500 dead and wounded, 30 prisoners; Gen Gouvion killed in action.

Austrian Forces FZM Clerfayt commanding: 10 bns including IR Hohenlohe Nr 17 (1st Bn); IR Sztáray Nr 33 (2 bns); IR Bender Nr 41 (2nd Bn) and IR Murray Nr 55 (1 bn); Tyroler-Scharfschützen (6 coys); Dandini Jäger (1 coy) HusR Blankenstein Nr 16 (6 sqns); DragR Koburg Nr 37 (6 sqns); Degelmann ULR (4 sqns).

Austrian totals 10 bns, 7 coys, 12 sqns, 12 guns ca 10,000 men.

Austrian losses 26 dead, 42 wounded, 9 missing.

Comment Yet another good example of how to dominate the battle area with repeated, small offensive raids on the enemy.

Sources Kriege F II, Chuquet, Schulz, Wrede.

NL Menin, 17 June 1792, capture of

A town in southwestern Belgium, 15 km north-northeast of Lille, on Routes N8 and N32.

A French victory over the Austrians.

(Last action – La Grisuelle, 11 June; next action – Courtray, 18 June.)

French Forces

The Avantgarde of the Armée du Nord Gen Jarry commanding: Chasseurs Belgiques (1 bn); Grenadiers (1 bn) 1er and 6e ChàCh (2 sqns each); 3e HusR (2 sqns).

French totals 2 bns, 6 sqns, 6 guns ca 1,500 men.

French losses Not known; slight.

Austrian Forces Hauptmann Morzin commanding: Freikorps Grün Laudon (1 coy); Steffanini Jägers (1 coy).

Austrian totals ca 200 men.

Austrian losses Not known, slight.

Comment This was the start of Marshal Luckner's offensive into Belgium; his targets were Gent and Brussels, the outnumbered Austrians could not stop him.

Sources Kriege F II, Chuquet, Schulz, Wrede.

NL Courtray, 18 June 1792, clash

A town in western Belgium, 40 km southwest of Gent, on Routes N36, N43, A14/E17 and N8.

A French victory over the Austrians.

(Last action – Menin 17 June; next action – Harlebeke 23 June.)

French Forces Gen Valence commanding:

Avantgarde Gen Jarry: Chasseurs Belgiques (1 bn); Grenadiers (1 bn); 1er and 6e ChàCh, 3e HusR (2 sqns each). **Totals** 2 bns, 6 sqns, 6 guns ca 1500 men. **The Reserve** (part of): Grenadiers (5 bns); 1er ChàP (1 bn); 1er and 2e Carabiniers R (2 sqns each).

Totals 6 bns, 6 sqns, 6 guns.

French totals 8 bns, 12 sqns, 12 guns, ca 10,500 men.

French losses Not known, slight.

Austrian Forces Obst Mylius commanding: IR Württemberg Nr 38 (1/6 bn); Grün-Loudon Freikorps (2/6 bn); Tyroler-Scharfschützen (2 coys); ChLR Latour Nr 31 (1 tp), (later 2 coys and 40 hussars from Tournay reinforced him).

Austrian totals ½ bn, 4 coys, 1 sqn; ca 760 men.

Austrian losses Not known, slight.

Comment The French Armeé du Nord continued to push on Gent, outnumbering Austrian forces in Western Belgium by about 2 : 1.

Sources Kriege F II, Chuquet, Schulz, Wrede.

NL Harlebeke, 23 June 1792, clash

A village in western Belgium 35 km southwest of Gent, on Route N43 towards Courtray.

An Austrian victory over the French.

(Last action – Courtray, 18 June; next action – Orchies, 15 July 1792.)

French Forces Gen Chatelet commanding: Reserve Armée du Nord: Grenadiers (5 bns), 1er ChàP (1 bn); 1er and 2e Carabiniers R (3 sqns each) 6 guns.

French totals 6 bns, 6 sqns, 6 guns ca 7,000 men.

French losses Not known; slight.

Austrian Forces FML Beaulieu commanding: IR Württemberg Nr 38 (1/6 bn); Grün-Loudon Freikorps (2/6 bn); Tyroler-Scharfschützen-Corps (2 coys). IR Bender Nr 41 (1 bn); Grenadier Bn Briey (1 bn); IR Josef Colloredo Nr 57 (2nd Bn); IR Sztáray Nr 33 (2 bns); IR Franz Ulrich Kinsky Nr 36 (1st Bn); Dandini Jägers (1 coy); ChLR Latour Nr 31 (2 sqns); HusR Blankenstein Nr 16 (4 sqns); Degelmann Freikorps Ulans (1 sqn); 2 x 6 pdr, 2 x 12 pdr cannon and 2 howitzers. Grenadier Bn Barthodeiszky (1 bn); IR d'Alton Nr 15 (2nd Bn); IR Clerfayt Nr 9 (1st Bn); IR Hohenlohe Nr 17 (1st Bn); Dandini Jäger (2 coys); Tyroler Scharfschützen-Corps (2 coys); HusR Wurmser Nr 30 (1 sqn); ChLR Latour Nr 31 (1½ sqn); Degelmann Freikorps Ulans (½ sqn); 1 x 6 pdr, 1 x 12 pdr cannon. 2 x howitzers.

Austrian totals 10½ bns 7 coys, 10 sqns, 6 guns, 4 howitzers, ca 11,050 men.

Austrian losses Not known; slight.

Comments The Austrian commander FML Baron Clerfayt, was able to achieve local superiority to defeat the French thrust. Luckner's men fell back to Courtray where the Austrians again attacked them on 29 June. This – and the failure of the Belgians to rise to the French revolutionary call – caused FM Luckner to withdraw to his previous positions around Lille.

Sources Kriege F II, Chuquet, Schulz, Wrede.

NL Orchies, 15 July 1792, clash

A small town in northwestern France, 20 km southeast of Lille, on Route D938.

An Austrian victory over the French.

(Last action – Harlebeke, 23 June 1792; next action – siege of Lille, 25 September 1792.)

French Forces About 600 men of various units of the Armée du Nord.

French losses ca 100 men dead, wounded and captured.

Austrian Forces FML Latour out of Tournay garrison commanding: 2⅔ bns, 2 light coys, 2 sqns, 6 guns, ca 3,000 men including IR Bender Nr 41 (1st Bn); Dandini Jäger (1 coy), Tyroler-Scharfschützen (1 coy).

Austrian losses 8 dead, 48 wounded. Major Dandini killed.

Comment After capturing Orchies, the Austrians returned to Tournay; the French reoccupied the village with 800 men from Douai. This was another successful Austrian pinprick designed to keep the French off balance.

Sources Kriege F II, Chuquet, Schulz, Wrede.

FC Sierck-les-Baines (or Oppach), 11 August 1792, clash

A village on the River Moselle 15 km northwest of Thionville on Route 153.

A Prussian victory over the French.

(Last action – this was the first action in the advance into Champagne; next action Aumetz, 19 August.)

French Forces Not known.

French totals Not known.

French losses 1 officer and 23 men dead and wounded, 31 captured, 1 gun, 1 colour.

Prussian Forces Prince von Hohenlohe commanding (part of the Advanced Guard): Jägers (2 coys); Füs Bn von Ernest (1 coy); HusR Wolffradt (5 sqns).

Prussian totals 3 coys, 5 sqns, ca 850 men.

Prussian losses Not known, slight.

Comment The French were surprised and overthrown

as the Duke of Brunswick slowly advanced. This was the opening action.

Sources Kriege F II, Chuquet, Schulz, Jany.

XX Dubienka, 18 August 1792, clash.

A town in 'Russian Poland' in the province of Lublin, on the River Bug, 100 km southwest of Lublin.

A Polish victory over the Russians.

Polish Forces GL Kosciuszko commanding: ca 6,000 men.

Polish losses About 1,000 dead, wounded and captured.

Russian Forces GM Kochowski commanding: ca 10,000 men.

Russian losses About 1,000 dead, wounded and captured; GM von Palmback killed in action.

Sources Schulz.

FC Fontoy (or Aumetz), 19 August 1792, clash

A village on the River Fensch, midway between Thionville and Longwy, on Route D16 in Lorraine, eastern France.

A Prussian victory over the French.

(Last action – Sierck, 11 August; next action – Longwy, 23 August.)

French Forces Gen Deprey-Crassier commanding: Grenadiers (2 coys); ChàCh (5 sqns).

French totals ca 600 men.

French losses 200 ChàCh killed and wounded, 24 captured.

Prussian Forces Part of Hohenlohe's Advanced Guard including HusR von Wolffradt (5 sqns).

Prussian totals Not known but superior to the French.

Prussian losses Very slight, not known exactly.

Sources Kriege FII Schulz.

FC Longwy, 23 August 1792, capitulation

A town in northeastern France 25 km east-southeast of Luxembourg, on the River Chiers.

An Austro-Prussian victory over the French.

(Last action – Fontoy, 19 August; next action – capitulation of Verdun, 2 September 1792.)

French Garrison Col Lavergne-Champlorier commanding: 34e RIdLi (1 bn); GdN Côte-d'Or (2e Bn), GdN Ardennes (3e and 4e Bns); 5e HusR (1 sqn).

French total 2,600 men, 71 guns.

French losses 71 guns, 4 colours, 4 standards, 500 muskets, large quantities of stores, and the town; the garrison were released on oath not to fight against the allies again during the war. Col Lavergne-Champlorier committed suicide after surrendering. Chuquet names Lavergne-Champlorier as the commandant, Minutoli gives 'de Vigne' and the Austrian general staff give 'Legrand'.

Prussian-Austrian Forces Duke of Brunswick commanding:

Austrian Troops* Graf Clerfayt, FML Freiherr Allvintzy, GM Freiherr von Jordis: Gren Bn Morzin (1 bn); Gren Bn Bathodeiszky (1 bn), IR Franz Ulrich Kinsky Nr 36 (1st and 2nd Bns). GM Smakers de Miremont: IR Hohenlohe Nr 17 (1st and 2nd Bns), IR Stuart Nr 18 (1st and 2nd Bns). GM von Boros: HusR Esterházy Nr 32 (10 sqns); DragR Coburg Nr 37 (2 sqns). HQ Staff Corps: Mahony Jäger (ex Dandini) (2 coys); Le Loup Jäger (6 coys); engineers (½ coy), pontonniers (1 coy). **Artillery Reserve** Major von Müller 2 x 3 pdr, 2 x 6 pdr, 8 x 12 pdr guns and 6 howitzers. Bombardierkorps – 13 men; 1st Feldartillerieregiment (1 coy); Feldzeugamt (20 men); Artilleriehandlanger and bespanner (287 men).

Austrian totals 8 bns, 9½ coys, 12 sqns, 48 guns, 13,731 men.

* each infantry battalion had 3 x light guns.

Prussian Troops GL von Schönfeld, GM Romberg: IR Herzog von Braunschweig Nr 21 (3 bns), IR von Woldeck Nr 41 (3 bns). GM von Borch : IR von Thadden Nr 3 (3 bns), IR von Romberg Nr 10 (3 bns). GL von Budberg, GM von Thadden: IR von Budberg Nr 9 (3 bns). Crown Prince of Prussia: IR Graf Hertzberg Nr 47 (3 bns). GM Herzog von Sachsen-Weimar: KürR Sachsen-Weimar Nr 6 (5 sqns). GM von Normann: DragR von Normann Nr 4 (5 sqns); DragR Anspach-Bayreuth Nr 5 (10 sqns). GM von Tschirschky: DragR von Lottum Nr 1 (5 sqns); DragR Tschirschky Nr 11 (5 sqns). GL von Koenitz, GM von Vietinghof: IR von Koenitz Nr 39 (3 bns); IR von Borcke Nr 31 (3 bns); IR von Vietinghof Nr 38 (Gren Bn).

Prussian totals 24½ bns, 18,200 infantry, 30 sqns, 4,000 cavalry, 48 regimental pieces, 40 heavy guns and howitzers (each infantry battalion had 2 light guns, each battery had 8 guns).

Allied losses None.

Comment The town was largely royalist in sympathy

and the small garrison was intimidated into surrendering.

Sources Kriege F II, Chuquet, Schulz, Jany, Wrede.

FC Verdun, 2 September 1792, capitulation

A fortified city in eastern France, on the River Meuse, 55 km west of Metz, at the junction of Routes N3 and D964.

A Prussian victory over the French.

(Last action – the capitulation of Longwy, 23 August 1792; next action – the blockade of Thionville, 3–5 September 1792.)

French garrison LtCol Beaurepaire commanding: 9e RIdLi (depot), GdN Mayenne-et-Loire (1 bn), Allier (1er Bn), Charente-Inférieure (det), Eure-et-Loire (det), Seine-et-Marne (depot), 44 gunners.

French total 4,128 men.

French losses LtCol Beaurepaire committed suicide. The garrison marched out with honours of war and with their regimental pieces but had to leave their colours and standards behind.

Prussian forces Duke of Brunswick commanding: as for the capitulation of Longwy, 23 August.

Prussian losses None.

Comment The French garrison surrendered after a token bombardment.

Sources Kriege F II, Chuquet, Schulz, Jany.

UR Thionville, 3–5 September 1792, blockade and bombardment of

A fortified city in eastern France on the River Moselle, 25 km north of Metz, at the junction of Routes N153, D1, D918 and motorway E25.

A French victory over the Austrians.

(Last action – the capitulation of Verdun, 2 September 1792; next action – the clash at La Croix au Bois, 14 September 1792.)

French Forces 103e RIdLi (2 bns); some National Guard battalions.

French total 3,000–4,000 men.

French losses Not known; very slight.

Austrian Besieging Forces FZM Hohenlohe commanding: FML Waldeck, GM Kollonitz, GM Schröder: GzIR Warasdiner (1 bn), IR Mittrowsky Nr 40 (2 bns); ChLR Kinsky Nr 7 (4 sqns), HusR Wurmser Nr 30 (4 sqns). FML d'Alton, GM Lilien, GM Einsiedel: IR d'Alton Nr 15 (1 bn), IR Josef Colloredo Nr 57 (1 bn), IR Franz Kinsky Nr 47 (1 bn), IR Carl Schröder Nr 7 (2 bns), IR de Vins Nr 37 (1 bn), HusR Wurmser Nr 30 (2 sqns), ChLR Kinsky Nr 7 (2 sqns). **The Reserve Artillery** FML Wallis, GM Werneck: IR Manfredini Nr 12 (2 bns), IR Stain Nr 50 (2 bns); DragR Erzherzog Josef Nr 26 (6 sqns); HusR Wurmser Nr 30 (2 sqns). 4 x howitzers, 4 x 12 pdr guns. **Émigré Corps of the Prince of Bourbon, M de Castries** Avantgarde infantry (2 coys); Chasseurs carabiniers (6 coys); Légion de la Normandie (7 coys); cavalry (2½ sqns). Brigade Picardie (2 bns); Brigade d'Auxerrois (2 bns); Reserve (9 coys). Cavalry (6 sqns); artillery (1 coy).

Austrian and Émigré totals 19 bns, 28½ sqns, ca 20,000 men.

Austrian losses ca 10 killed and wounded.

Comment The Austrians gambled that the fortress would surrender without a fight; they had no siege artillery.

Sources Kriege FII, Chuquet, Schulz, Wrede.

FC La Croix-au-Bois, 14 September 1792, clash

A village and defile in the Argonne mountains in northeastern France, 55 km east-northeast of Reims.

An Austrian victory over the French.

(Last action – the bombardment of Thionville 3–5 September 1792; next action – the clash at Montcheutin, 15 September 1792.)

French Forces GL Chazot commanding: including 29e, 71e, 83e, 98e and 99e RIdLi (1 bn each), 3 GdN bns, 13e DragR and 2e HusR (2 sqns each).

French total 8 bns, 5 sqns, 12 guns, ca 5,000 men.

French losses Not known but included 'some guns, limbers and waggons'.

Austrian Forces (commander unknown) Mahony Jägers (2 coys); Le Loup Jägers (6 coys); HusR Esterházy Nr 32 (2 sqns); 1 infantry bn.

Austrian totals 1 bn, 8 coys, 2 sqns, ca 1,700 men.

Austrian losses 32 dead, 65 wounded, 15 missing.

Comment The Austrians seized the abandoned, fortified defile and defeated the French counter attack thus securing their passage through the Argonne.

Sources Kriege FII, Chuquet, Schulz, Wrede.

FC Montcheutin, 15 September 1792, clash

A town in northeastern France, 5 km west of the River Aisne, 55 km east of Reims.

A Prussian victory over the French.

(Last action – the clash at La Croix au Bois, 14

September 1792; next action – Valmy, 20 September.)

French Forces GL Chazot commanding: 29e, 71e, 83e 98e, 99e RIdLi (1 bn each); 5e Gren Bn, 3 GdN bns; 12e ChàCh (3 sqns); 2e DragR (2 sqns); 8 or 9 guns.

French totals 9 bns, 5 sqns 8–9 guns ca 6,000 men.

French losses 283 prisoners, 4 guns, 36 waggons and a war chest.

Prussian Forces (commander unknown) Füs-Bn Ernest Nr 19 (1 bn); Feldjäger (1 bn); DragR von Schmettau Nr 2 (4 sqns); HusR von Köhler Nr 3 (2 sqns); HusR von Wolffradt Nr 6 (2 sqns); 1 x HAB.

Prussian totals 2 bns, 8 sqns, ca 2,600 men.

Prussian losses None.

Comment Chazot's men, demoralized by their defeat the previous day, panicked at the approach of the Prussian hussars. The French cavalry rode down their own grenadiers and the whole column fled to Autry.

Sources Chuquet, Schulz, Jany.

FC Valmy, 20 September 1792, cannonade of

A village in northeastern France, 33 km northeast of Chalons sur Marne.

French victory over the Prussians and Austrians.

(Last action – the clash at Montcheutin, 15 September 1792; next action – Speyer, 30 September.)

French Forces Generals Dumouriez and Kellermann commanding: GL Dumouriez Armée du Nord.

Avantgarde GL A Dillon, GdB la Marche, GdB Money; GdB Miaczynski: Free Company Ransonnet (1 coy); 6e RIdLi (1 bn); 8e RIdLi (1 bn); 9e Chass Bn (1 bn); 14e Chass Bn (1 bn); 5e HusR (3 sqns); 6e HusR (3 sqns); 3e ChàCh R (3 sqns); 12e ChàCh R (3 sqns). **Totals** 4 bns, 1 coy, 12 sqns. **Right Wing** GL Leveneur; GdB Dietmann, GdB Stettenhofen, GdB Stengel. 17e RIdLi (1 bn); GdN Meurthe (1er Bn); Saône-et-Loire (2e Bn); 43e RIdLi (1 bn); GdN Aisne (1er Bn); GdN de Paris (3e Bn); GdN Vienne (1er Bn); 94e RIdLi (1 bn); GdN Marne (1er Bn); GdN Sarthe (1er Bn); 3e, 7e, 15e, CavR (2 sqns each). **Flanqueurs de la droite** 54e RIdLi (gren coy); dets of various RIdLi (600 men); 55e RIdLi (1 coy); 1er HusR (3 sqns); 11e ChàCh (3 sqns). **Totals** 14 bns, 1 coy, 12 sqns. **Left Wing** GL Chazot, GdB Miranda, GdB Maltzen: 29e RIdLi (1 bn); GdN Allier* (1er Bn); GdN Charente (1er Bn); 71e RIdLi (1 bn); GdN Ardennes (4e Bn)**; Meurthe (5e Bn); 98e RIdLi (1 bn); GdN Seine-Inférieure (1er Bn); GdN Vosges (5e Bn); 99e RIdLi (1 bn); GdN Marne (2e Bn); GdN Nord (3e Bn); 21e and 23e CavR (2 sqns each); 13e DragR (2 sqns) **Flanqueurs de la gauche** 83e RIdLi (gren coy); dets of various RIdLi (600 men); 47e RIdLi (1 coy); 2e HusR (3 sqns); 6e ChàCh (3 sqns). **Totals** 14 bns, 1 coy, 12 sqns. **Reserve** Grenadiers (6 bns); 2e, 7e, 10e, and 12e DragR (2 sqns each). **Totals** 6 bns, 8 sqns.

Totals Armée du Nord 36 bns, 3 coys, 44 sqns.

* = at Verdun ** = at Longwy.

Armée du Centre GL Kellermann commanding:

Avantgarde Légion Kellermann (2 bns). **Détachement of Gen Depréz-Crassier** 1er RIdLi (1er Bn); Gren Bn (1 bn); 3e Hus R (3 sqns); DragR Nr 4 (2 sqns); 1e ChàCh R (3 sqns). **Détachement of Gen la Barolière** Grenadiers (1 bn); 8e, 9e and 10e ChàCh R (3 sqns each). **Totals** 5 bns, 17 sqns. **First Rank Gen Linch** (an Englishman). 1ère Brigade: 1er, 22e, 24e and 81e RIdLi (4 bns). 2e Brigade: 5e, 44e, 90e and 102e RIdLi (4 bns). **Cavalry** Gen Pully and the Duc de Chartres (Gen Égalité) resp. 1ère Brigade: 8e and 10 CavR (4 sqns). 2e Brigade: 14e and 17e DragR (4 sqns). **Totals** 8 bns, 8 sqns. **Second Rank Gen Muratel** 6e, 30e, 62e RIdLi (3 bns) GdN Seine-et-Loire (1er Bn); Moselle (2e Bn); Yonne (1er Bn); 4e and 19e CavR (3 sqns each); 1er DragR (2 sqns); 8e and10e ChàCh (2 sqns each); artillery (?). **Totals** 6 bns, 14 sqns. **Reserve** GL Valence 3e RIdLi (1 bn); Grenadiers (4 bns); GdN (1 bn); 1er and 2e Carabinier R (8 sqns); 17e CavR (2 sqns).

Totals 6 bns, 10 sqns.

French totals 61 bns, 3 coys, 93 sqns; ie 50,000 infantry, 2,000 cavalry, 60 guns (plus 2 light guns with each infantry battalion).

French losses 300 dead, wounded and missing.

Prussian Forces FM Duke of Brunswick commanding:

Avantgarde GL Erbprinz von Hohenlohe-Ingelfingen. 1st Brigade: GM von Wolffradt: IR Hohenlohe Nr 32 (3 bns). 2nd Brigade: GM Graf Hertzberg: IR von Kleist Nr 12 (3 bns). 3rd Brigade: GM von Kleist: Füs-Bn von Forcade Nr 10 (1 bn); Füs-Bn von Renouard Nr 2 (1 bn); Feldjäger (5 coys); DragR von Schmettau Nr (5 sqns); HusR von Wolffradt Nr 6 (10 sqns); 1 x 6 pdr foot bty (8 guns); 1 x HAB (9 guns). **Totals** 8 bns, 5 coys, 15 sqns, 17 guns plus 14 regimental pieces with the infantry battalions.

First Rank FM Duke of Brunswick 1st Division GL

von Schönfeld: 1st Brigade GM von Romberg: IR von Braunschweig Nr 21 (3 bns); IR Woldeck Nr 41 (3 bns). 2nd Brigade GM von Borch: IR von Thadden Nr 3 (3 bns); IR von Romberg Nr 10 (3 bns). 2nd Division GL von Budberg: 1st Brigade GM von Thadden: IR von Budberg Nr 9 (3 bns); IR von Schönfeld Nr 30 (3 bns). **Totals** 18 bns, 36 regimental pieces.

Second Rank GL l'Homme de Courbière 1st Division GL Kenitz: 1st Brigade GM von Vietinghof: IR von Koenitz Nr 39 (3 bns); IR von Borch Nr 31 (3 bns). 2nd Brigade Crownprince Friedrich Wilhelm: IR Graf Hertzberg Nr 47 (3 bns). 2nd Division GM von Wolframsdorf: 1st Brigade Oberst Ludwig, Prinz von Baden: IR von Wolframsdorf Nr 37 (3 bns); IR von Vietinghof Nr 38 (3 bns). **Totals** 15 bns, 30 regimental pieces. **Cavalry** GL Graf Lottum 1st Division GL Graf Kalckreuth: 1st Brigade GM Herzog von Sachsen-Weimar: KürR von Weimar Nr 6 (5 sqns). 2nd Brigade GM von Normann: DragR Anspach-Bayreuth Nr 5 (10 sqns); DragR von Normann Nr 4 (5 sqns). 2nd Division GL Prinz Ludwig von Württemberg: 1st Brigade GM von Tschirschky: DragR von Tschirschky Nr 11 (5 sqns); DragR von Lottum Nr 1 (5 sqns). 2nd Brigade GM von Ilow: KürR von Ilow Nr 7 (5 sqns). **Total** 35 sqns.

Corps of GM von Köhler Füs Bn von Müffling Nr 18 (1 bn); Füs Bn von Ernest Nr 19 (1 bn); HusR von Köhler Nr 3 (10 sqns); ½ x HAB (5 guns). **Totals** 2 bns, 10 sqns, 5 guns, 2 x 3 pdr regimental pieces. **Corps of GM von Eben** Füs Bn von Schencke Nr 1 (1 bn); Füs Bn von Legat Nr 20 (1 bn); HusR von Eben Nr 2 (10 sqns); ½ x HAB (4 guns). **Totals** 2 bns, 10 sqns, 4 guns and 2 x 3 pdr regimental pieces. **Reserve Artillery** Obst von Tempelhof: 2 x mortar bties each of 8 x 10 pdr mortars; 2 x 12 pdr bties each of 8 guns; 7 x 6 pdr bties each of 8 guns. **Totals** 72 guns and 16 mortars. The infantry battalion pieces were 6 pdrs.

Prussian totals 42 bns, 70 sqns 3,500 men.

Prussian losses 200 dead, wounded and missing.

Comment The Prussian King Friedrich Wilhelm II forced the army commander, the Duke of Brunswick, to undertake a daring outflanking move prior to the battle with an army short of food and ammunition and in hostile territory. The Duke, seeing himself outnumbered and ignoring the problems that the French faced with their half-trained masses, refused to fight and withdrew to Germany. This was the humiliating end to the allied invasion attempt.

An Austrian corps under FZM Graf Clerfayt and a French Émigré corps under the Prince de Bourbon did not reach the battlefield until the 'fighting' was over.

Sources Chuquet, Schulz, Jany.

IN Oneglia, 23 September, 1792 raid

A small port on the Italian coast, 50 km along the Riviera di Ponente east from Monaco at the junction of Routes 1/E80 and 28.

A French 'victory' over the Sardinians.

(Last action – This was the opening action; next action – Sospello 18 November.)

French Forces RAdm Truguet commanding: A battalion from Villa Franca.

French totals ca 800 men.

French losses Nil.

Sardinian Forces Commander unknown. Oneglia town militia.

Sardinian totals unknown.

Sardinian losses unknown.

Comment The French sacked the town, murdered some monks in a nearby abbey and returned to Villa Franca.

Sources Schulz, Brancaccio.

NL Lille, 25 September – 8 October, 1792 siege

A city in northwestern France on the River Deule, at the junction of motorways A25/E42, A1/E17 and A23.

A French victory over the Austrians.

(Last action – Orchies, 15 July 1792; next action – Wilheries and Elonges, 3 November.)

French Forces MdC Ruault commanding the garrison of the city: 15e RIdLi (1 bn); 85e RIdLi (2 bns); 86e RIdLi (1 bn); 100e RIdLi (1 bn); the depot of battalions of the RIdLi 24e, 44e, 56e, 90e; the depot squadrons of the 3e and 6e Cav Rs; GdN (1 bn); the depots of 3 National Guard bns.

French totals 10 bns, 3 sqns ca 10,000 men. Other reinforcements joined the garrison continuously during the 'siege' which was never really effective.

French losses Not known, probably 100–200 dead and wounded.

Austrian Forces FM Herzog von Sachsen-Teschen commanding: FML Latour, GM Wenkheim: Grenadier

Bn Leeuven (1 bn); Grenadier Bn Rousseau (1 bn); IR Sztáray Nr 33 (2 bns). FML Württemberg, GM Sztáray: Grenadier-Bn Pückler (1 bn); IR Clerfayt Nr 9 (1st Bn); IR d'Alton Nr 15 (2nd bn); IR Württemberg Nr 38 (1st bn). FML Beaulieu, GM Biela: IR de Ligne Nr 30 (1st Bn); IR Josef Colloredo Nr 57 (2nd bn); IR Murray Nr 55 (1st bn); O'Donell Freikorps (4 coys). GM Happoncourt: HusR Blankenstein Nr 16 (2 sqns); ChLR Latour Nr 31 (7 sqns). GM Lothringen: HusR Wurmser Nr 30 (2 sqns); Degelmann Freikorps Ulanen (6 sqns). Obst Lindenau: pontonniers (1 coy); engineers (1 coy).

Austrian totals 10½ bns, 6 coys, 18 sqns, 13,800 men and 52 guns, howitzers and mortars.

Austrian losses 43 dead, 161 wounded and 20 guns worn out or burst.

Comment The Austrians had no hope of taking the extremely strong and well-garrisoned fortress with such limited means. The whole exercise was a diversion to attract French forces away from the main allied army on the Rhine.

Sources Kriege FII, Chuquet, Schulz, Wrede.

UR Speyer, 30 September 1792, capture of

A town on the west bank of the Rhine, in southwestern Germany, 18 km west-southwest of Heidelberg, at the junction of Routes B39 and B9.

A French victory over the Austrians.

(Last action – this was the first action on the Upper Rhine; next action – the surrender of Mainz, 21 October.)

French Forces Armée du Rhin Gen Custine commanding. Column of Gen Munnier Avantgarde: GdN Jura (2e Bn); GdN Ain (2e Bn); 2e CavR (2 sqns). Main Body (4e Brigade): Grenadiers (1 bn); 32e and 82e RIdLi (2 bns); GdN Haute-Saône (2e Bn); GdN Jura (3e Bn). Right Flank Guard (Col Houchard) Volontaires Grenadiers (1 bn); 2e ChàCh (3 sqns); 2e CavR (2 sqns). **Column of Gen Blou** 3e Brigade: Grenadiers (1 bn); 3e, 57e, and 82e RIdLi (1er Bns); GdN Vosges (3e Bn); 4 x 8 pdr guns, 2 x 6 howitzers. **Column of Gen Neuwinger** Avantgarde (Gen Lafarelle): GdN des Vosges (4e Bn); 7 ChàCh (3 sqns); 9e and 19e CavR (2 sqns each). Main Body (1ère Brigade): 13e and 64e RIdLi (2 bns); GdN Jura (4e Bn); Vosges (1e Bn); 8 x 8 pdr guns, 4 x field mortars. 2e Brigade: 36e and 93e RIdLi (2 bns); GdN Rhône-et-Loire (3e Bn); Haut-Rhin (3e Bn).

French totals 22 bns, 14 sqns, 12 x 8 pdr guns, 2 x 6 inch howitzers, 4 x field mortars, ca 24,000 men.

French losses Not known; slight.

Allied Forces Obst Winkelmann commanding Kur-Mainz IR (2 bns); IR Gyulai Nr 32 (3e Bn); 194 infantry recruits; DragR Erzherzog Josef Nr 26 (1 sqn); 60 artillerymen, 4 guns, 1 howitzer.

Allied totals 3½ bns, (3,424 infantry), 1 sqn (124 cavalry) 60 artillery, ca 3,608 men.

Allied losses Unknown dead and wounded; 1,451 prisoners of the Kur-Mainz troops; 782 of Austrian IR Gyulai captured; 90 cavalry, 55 artillery and 168 reinforcement draftees captured as well as five colours (1 of IR Gyulai, 4 of the Kur-Mainz infantry). These were the first allied trophies to fall to the French Revolutionary armies and were sent in triumph to Paris.

Comment The Austrians would have got off in good order but they were trapped in a loop of the Rhine without boats or a bridge and, after a hard fight, had to capitulate.

Sources Kriege FII, Chuquet, Schulz, Wrede.

FC Verdun, 14 October 1792, surrender of

A fortified city in eastern France on the River Meuse, 55 km west of Metz, at the junction of Routes N3 and D964.

A French victory over the allies.

(Last action – the cannonade of Valmy, 20 September 1792; next action – the clash at Latour, 22 October 1792.)

Comment Following Valmy the allies were in retreat to the Netherlands and to Germany. The peaceful handover of Verdun was negotiated; there was no fighting and no casualties.

Sources Kriege FII, Chuquet, Schulz, Wrede.

UR Mainz, 21 October 1792, surrender of

A fortified city in Western Germany, on the west bank of the River Rhine, at its confluence with the River Main, on Routes A60 and B9.

A French victory over the imperial forces.

(Last action – the capture of Speyer 30 September 1792; next action – the capture of Frankfurt/Main, 22 October 1792.)

French Forces Gen Custine commanding See the capture of Speyer, 30 September 1792. The artillery park had now increased to 45 field guns and 8 howitzers. There was no siege artillery or engineer park.

French totals Estimates vary between 13,000 and 19,000 men.

French losses None.

Imperial Forces General Gymnich (Kur-Mainz) commanding Oberrheinische Kreiskompanie (60); Worms militia (37); the Prince Bishopric of Fulda (134); Nassau-Oranien (224); Nassau-Weilburg (62); Nassau-Usingen (114); Kur-Mainz Leibgarde (70); Landjäger (30); 50 Austrian recruiters, 23 men of the IR Gyulai Nr 32 , HusR Esterházy Nr 32 (153); Mainzer HusR (51); Artillery (63); University Student Volunteers (101); Mainzer Schützenkorps (70); armed peasants (200); tradesmen (700); armed citizens (1500) and the remnants of the four Mainz Infantry Regiments (Gymnich, Rüdt, Hatzfeld and Knorr - together 908 men) and 854 Austrian infantry convalescents.

Imperial total 5,404 men, 184 guns, 9 howitzers.

Imperial losses All artillery and stores in the city which was occupied by the French.

Comment The Austrian troops broke out eastwards over the Rhine and escaped; the Kur-Mainz and imperial kreis troops marched out with honours of war, promising not to fight against France or her allies for one year. The imperial city of Mainz had been abandoned by her allies due to lack of available forces in the area.

Sources Kriege FII, Chuquet, Schulz, Wrede.

UR Frankfurt am Main, 22 October 1792, capture

An imperial city on the north bank of the River Main, 32 km from its confluence with the River Rhine in Western Germany.

A French victory over the imperial forces.

(Last action - the capture of Mainz, 21 October 1792; next action the clash at Limburg, 10 November.)

French Forces Gen Neuwinger commanding The columns of Gen Neuwinger and Gen Monchard as had been used at the capture of Speyer (on 30 September) and at the capture of Mainz on 21 October.

French losses None.

Imperial Forces The Frankfurt town militia under the magistrate.

Imperial losses None.

Comment Frankfurt was a neutral city with no external imperial (Austrian) forces to defend it. No combat took place; the city surrendered.

Sources Ditfurth, Chuquet, Schulz.

FC Latour, 22 October 1792, clash

A village in southeastern Belgium 40 km west of Luxembourg.

A French victory over the Austrians.

(Last action - the handover of Verdun to the French on 14 October; next action - the clash at Virton, 23 October.)

French Forces - Gen Valence's Avantgarde of the Armée des Ardennes

Grenadiers (3 bns); GdN Charente-Inférieure (1er Bn); 2e and 5e DragR (4 sqns); 5e HusR (3 sqns).

French totals 3,500 infantry, 1,500 cavalry, 6 guns.

French losses Not known, very slight.

Austrian Forces Obstlt Lusignan commanding IR Bender Nr 41 (4 coys of 3rd Bn); Le Loup Jägers (4 coys); HusR Esterházy Nr 32 (1 sqn).

Austrian totals 800 infantry, 100 cavalry.

Austrian losses Not known, slight.

Comment Bad weather and war-weariness on both sides enabled the Austrians - although defeated - to remain in the area to fight again next day.

Sources Kriege FII, Chuquet, Schulz, Wrede.

FC Virton, 23 October 1792, clash

A village in southeastern Belgium, 40 km west of Luxembourg, on Route N82.

A French victory over the Austrians.

(Last action - the clash at Latour, 22 October 1792; next action - this was the last action of the campaign in the Champagne, 1792. On 22 October the fortress of Longwy had been peacefully handed over to the French.)

French and Austrian Forces As for the clash at Latour the previous day.

French losses Not known; slight.

Austrian losses 43 men, 11 horses.

Sources Kriege FII, Chuquet, Schulz, Wrede.

NL Wilheries and Elonges (or Thulin), 3 November 1792, clash

Two villages in southwest Belgium, 15 km west of Mons, on Route N51.

An Austrian victory over the French.

(Last action - Lille, 25 September - 8 October; next

action – Boussu, 4 November.)

French Forces (part of Gen Dumouriez's Avantgarde) GL Beurnonville commanding: Chasseurs Belgiques (1 bn); 2e HusR (2 sqns).

French totals ca 1,300 men.

French losses 200 dead and wounded, 50 captured.

Austrian Forces Freikorps O'Donell (1 bn); HusR Blankenstein Nr 16 (2 sqns); IR Bender Nr 41 (1 bn); IR Würzburg (1 bn).

Austrian totals 3 bns, 3 sqns, ca 3,400 men.

Austrian losses 17 dead and wounded.

Comment Although numerically superior (the French Avantgarde totalled about 22,000 men), the more experienced and better-disciplined Austrians managed to catch the French off guard and to defeat part of the enemy in isolation. The Chasseurs Belgiques battalion was caught in the open by the Austrian hussars and destroyed, leaving 200 dead and wounded and 50 captured. This was the opening action of Dumouriez's long-cherished invasion of Belgium.

Sources Kriege FII, Chuquet, Schulz, Wrede.

NL Boussu, 4 November 1792, clash

A village in southwestern Belgium, 12 km west of Mons, on Route N51.

A French victory over the Austrians.

(Last action – Wilheries and Elonges, 3 November; next action – Jemappes, 6 November.)

French Forces

Dumouriez's Avantgarde under GL Beurnonville: 2e and 6e Gren Bns (2 bns); 19e and 71e RIdLi (2 bns); GdN Paris (1er, 2e and 3e Bns); GdN de la Marne (1er Bn); Saint-Denis (1er Bn); 10e and 14e RILé (2 bns); 3 Free Companies (les Quatre-Nations, l'Égalité, les Cambrelots); 4 Belgian and Liègeois bns; 1er and 3e Bn francs (2 bns); 1er, 2e and 6e HusR; 3e, 6e, 11e and 12e ChàCh (3 sqns each = 21 sqns); 3e and 6e artillery coys.

French totals 17 bns, 3 coys, 21 sqns, 2 bties; ca 22,000 men and 12 guns including 6 x 12 pdrs, 6 x 6 pdrs and the usual battalion pieces.

French losses ca 120 dead and wounded.

Austrian Forces Freikorps O'Donell (2nd Bn); IR Bender Nr 41 (1st Bn); IR Würzburg (1 bn); Servisches Freikorps (1 coy); Jägers (1 coy); HusR Blankenstein Nr 16 (3 sqns); 6 regimental arty pieces, ca 3,100 men.

Austrian losses 150 dead, 200 captured.

Comment The superior French strength, and mainly their heavier and more numerous artillery decided the day. Dumouriez closed up to Mons on 5 November.

Sources Kriege FII, Chuquet, Schulz, Wrede.

NL Jemappes, 6 November 1792, battle

A village in southwestern Belgium, 4 km southwest of Mons, now a suburb of that town.

A French victory over the Austrians.

(Last action – Boussu, 4 November; next action – Mecheln, 16 November.)

French Forces Gen Dumouriez commanding 'Armée de la Belgique'.

(This was Dumouriez's private name for the 'Armée de l'Argonne' and was never officially recognized or adopted).

Right Wing Avantgarde GL Beurnonville, MdC Dampièrre, Cie des quatre nations (1 coy); Cie des Cambrelots (1 coy); 1ère Cie franche (1 coy); 3e Cie franche (1 coy); Légion Belgique (1 bn); 19e RIdLi (1 bn); Grenadiers (1er and 6e Bns); 10e and 14e ChàP (2 bns); GdN Paris (1er and 2e Bns); 1er, 2e and 6e HusR (9 sqns); 3e, ChàCh (3 sqns); 6e ChàCh (3 sqns); 12e ChàCh (2 sqns). **Flanqueurs de la gauche** Gen Maczynski: 99e RIdLi (1 bn); 5e ChàP (1 bn); 5e and 13e DragR (4 sqns). **Flanqueurs de la droite** Gen Stengel: 11e ChàP; GdN Ardennes (3e Bn); Cie des Clemendos (1 coy); 3e Drag (2 sqns); 7e DragR (2 sqns) 3 x HAB. **Left Wing** Gen Ferrand. **First Line 1ère Bde** GdB Drouet 17e Fédérés (1 bn); GdN Seine-Inférieure (5e Bn); Charente (1er Bn). **2e Bde** GdB Desforest: GdN Aisne (1er Bn); 1er RIdLi (1 bn); GdN de Ste Marguerite (1 bn). **3e Bde** Gen Ferrand: GdN Vendée (1er Bn); Meurthe (1er Bn); Deux-Sèvres (1er Bn). **5e Bde** GdN Gravilliers (1 bn); 29e RIdLi (2 bns); Côtes-du-Nord (1er Bn). **7e Bde** GdN Lombards (1 bn); 54e RIdLi (2e Bn); GdN Marne (2e Bn). **4e Bde** Gen Ihler: GdN Yonne (3e Bn); Côte-d'Or (1er Bn); Vienne (2e Bn). **6e Bde** GdN Eure-et-Loire (1er Bn); 49e RIdLi (1er Bn); 9e Fédérés (1 bn). **8e Bde** GdN Marne (3e Bn); 71e RIdLi (1er Bn); GdN St Denis (1 bn). **Second Line** Gen Blotterfière **9e Bde** GdN Républicaine (1 bn); 83e RIdLi (2 bns). **11e Bde** GdN Meurthe (5e Bn); 78e RIdLi (2 bns); GdN Meuse (4e Bn). **13e Bde** GdN Marne (1er Bn);

Mayenne-et-Loire (1er Bn); Eure (2e Bn). **15e Bde** GdN Seine-et-Oise (1er Bn); 98e RIdLi (1er Bn); GdN Seine-Inférieure (1er Bn). **10e Bde** Gen Stettenhofen: GdN Butte des Moulins (1 bn); 72e RIdLi (2 bns). **12e Bde** GdN Pas-de-Calais (1er Bn); 94e RIdLi (1er Bn); GdN Paris (9e Bn). **14e Bde** GdN Nièvre (1er Bn); Allier (1er Bn); Seine-et-Marne (1er Bn). **16e Bde** GdN Seine-et-Oise (3e Bn); 104e RIdLi (2 bns); GdN Grenadiers de Paris (1er Bn). **Reserve** Gen de Flers: Gendarmerie Nat (2 sqns); Grenadiers (? bns*).

French totals 63 bns*; 5 coys, 40,000 infantry; 27 sqns, 3,000 cavalry, 100 guns including 6 x 16 pdrs, 18 x 6 pdrs and some heavy howitzers. The 10–12,000 strong division of Gen d'Harville did not come up on the French right wing until the battle was over.

* = Chuquet does not specify how many grenadier battalions were in the reserve.

Chuquet's order of battle conflicts with Austrian and French general staff presentations but is the best available data.

French losses ca 650 dead, 1,300 wounded.

Austrian Forces FM Duke Albert of Sachsen-Teschen commanding:

Right Wing FML Lilien: Grün-Loudon-Freikorps and O'Donell-Freikorps (7 coys); Brigade of GM Erzherzog Karl: Gren Bn Morzin (1 bn); Gren Bn Barthodeiszky (1 bn); Brig Obst Keim: IR Bender Nr 41 (2 bns); HusR Blankenstein Nr 16 (3 sqns). **Centre** FZM Clerfayt Brig GM Mikoviny: Gren Bn Leeuven; Gren Bn Pückler; IR Würzburg (1 bn); DragR Coburg Nr 37 (4 sqns). **Left Wing** FML Beaulieu, Brigade of GM Jordis: IR Hohenlohe Nr 17 (1 bn); IR Stuart Nr 18 (2 bns); Servisches-Freikorps (5 coys); HusR Blankenstein Nr 16 (1 sqn). **Cavalry Reserve** GM Lamberg: DragR Coburg Nr 37 (4 sqns); ChLR Latour Nr 31 (2 sqns); HusR Esterházy Nr 32 (2 sqns). **Infantry Reserve** IR Hohenlohe Nr 17 (1 bn); IR Matheson Nr 42 (4 coys); Tyroler-Scharfschützen (5 coys).

Austrian totals 11 bns, 17 coys, 11,628 infantry, 16 sqns - 2168 cavalry, 14 x 12 pdrs, 6 x 7 pdr howitzers, 36 x 6 and 3 pdrs.

Austrian losses 305 dead, 513 wounded and missing, 423 captured, 5 guns.

Comment The heavily outnumbered Austrians held a fortified ridge with an impassable obstacle in their rear (the swampy flood plain of the River Hain) over which only one bridge was available for a withdrawal. Most Austrian casualties were caused by French canister, the Regiment Bender Nr 41 losing 14 officers and 400 men during the battle. Dumouriez missed the chance to destroy his opponents completely. The many raw French troops were difficult to control. Mons was surrendered without a fight on 7 November; the Austrians decided on the evacuation of Belgium. France went wild with joy at news of this victory which confirmed that their army could successfully act offensively as well as defensively as at Valmy. It has not been possible to clarify all details of the French order of battle here.

Sources Kriege FII, Chuquet, Schulz, Wrede.

NL Comines, Pont-Rouge and Warneton, 6 November 1792, clashes

Villages along the River Lys in western Belgium, ca 60 km southwest of Gent.

French victories over the Austrians.

(Last action - Boussu, 4 November; next action - Mecheln, 16 November.)

French Forces Gen La Marlière and MdC Champmorin of Gen Tricotel's corps commanding:.

Full details are not known; the following units have been identified: 14e RIdLi (1 bn); 22e RIdLi (1 bn); GdN Soissons (1 bn); Gendarmerie nat. (2e and 3e Foot Divisions); Volontaires de Bergues (1 bn); 'a local Belgian corps'; 3e DragR (? sqns).

French totals ca 2,500 men.

French losses 5 dead, 15 wounded.

Austrian Forces FML Graf Latour in overall command; in Warneton Major Wöstenrädt commanded IR de Ligne Nr 30 (2 coys) and UlR Degelmann (1 sqn). In the other posts and at Rousbrugge were IR Württemberg Nr 38 (1 coy) but the exact dispositions are not known.

Austrian losses 22 dead, ? wounded, 10 captured.

Comment Clerfayt had given orders for these right-wing outposts to concentrate to the rear and centre if seriously threatened and this is what they did.

Sources Kriege FII, Chuquet, Schulz, Wrede.

NL Menin, 6 November 1792, clash

A town in western Belgium, 50 km southwest of Ghent, on Routes N8 and N32.

A French victory over the Austrians.

(Last action – Boussu, 4 November; next action – Mecheln, 16 November.)

French Forces Col des Brunières commanding: 12e RIdLi (1 bn); GdN Gironde (1er Bn); plus other, unidentified units.

French total ca 2,200 men.

French losses 13 dead, 17 wounded.

Austrian Forces FML Graf Latour commanding: IR Württemberg Nr 38 (1 bn); IR De Ligne Nr 30 (1 bn); Freikorps Grün-Laudon (2 coys); Tyroler-Scharfschützen (2 coys); UlR Degelmann (1 sqn).

Austrian totals 2 bns, 4 coys, 1 sqn, ca 2,000 men.

Austrian losses 30 dead, ? wounded, 49 captured.

Comment This was the main feint attack undertaken by Gen Tricotel's 3,000-strong force on the Austrian right flank in Flanders to distract them from Dumouriez's main thrust at Jemappes. The Austrians fell back northeast on Courtray.

Sources Kriege FII, Chuquet, Schulz, Wrede.

NL Namur, 6 November – 2 December 1792, siege and capture of

A fortified city in southern Belgium, on the northern bank of the River Sambre, 62 km southeast of Brussels, on Routes N4, N80 and N90.

A French victory over the Austrians.

(Last action – Antwerp, 29 November; apart from some minor skirmishes around Trier on the Moselle River, this was the last action in the 1792 campaign.)

French Forces – the Armée des Ardennes GdD Valence commanding,
plus Gen Harville's Corps:

Avantgarde 13e RILé (1 bn); Chass de Ransonnette (1 coy); Chass de Rennes (1 coy); Grenadiers (4 bns); 56e RIdLi (1er Bn); GdN Jemappes (1er Bn); St-Amand (1er Bn); Paris (2e Bn); Somme (4e Bn); Fédérés (14e Bn); 4e HusR (3 sqns); 2e DragR (2 sqns). **Corps de Bataille 1ère Ligne** GL Le Veneur. **1ère Bde** GdN Saône-et-Loire (2e Bn); 17e RIdLi (1er Bn); GdN Mayenne (1er Bn). **2e Bde** GdN Paris (6e Bn); 25e RIdLi (1er Bn); GdN Sarthe (1er Bn). **3e Bde** GdN Meuse (4e Bn); 43eRIdLi (1er Bn); GdN Paris (10e Bn); 16e CavR (2 sqns); 23e CavR (2 sqns). **2e Ligne GL Diettmann 4e Bde** GdN Vosges (5e Bn); 45e RIdLi (1er Bn); GdN Théâtre-Français (1 bn). **5e Bde** GdN Bon-Conseil (1 bn); 58e RIdLi (2e Bn); GdN Meurthe (2e Bn). **6e Bde** GdN Nord (2e Bn); 47e RIdLi (1er Bn); GdN Meurthe (3e Bn); 7e and 18 CavRs (4 sqns); artillery park (153 men).

French totals 29 bns, 2 coys, 15,022 infantry, 13 sqns, 9,634 cavalry, 153 artillery (1 bty).

French losses Not known, slight.

Reserve Division GL d'Marville commanding:

Avantgarde Cie franche de Clermont (1 coy); Cie Franche de Boussard (1 coy); 68e RIdLi (2 bns); GdN Haute-Vienne (2e Bn); Loiret (1er Bn); Calvados (2e Bn); Ardennes (2e Bn); 6e HusR (2 sqns). **Right Brigade** GdN Hautes-Alpes (2e Bn); 18e RIdLi (2 bns); GdN Basses-Alpes (2e Bn); 12e DragR (½ sqn). **Left Brigade** GdN Gard (2e Bn); 16e RIdLi (1 bn); GdN Maine-et-Loire (2e Bn); Bouches-du-Rhône (1er Bn); 12e DragR (½ sqn). **Corps de Bataille 1ère Bde** GdN Nord (1er Bn); 14e RIdLi (1er Bn); GdN Yonne (2e Bn). **2e Bde** GdN Nord (6e Bn or 1er Cambrai); 45e RIdLi (2e Bn); GdN Pas de Calais (4e Bn). **3e Bde** GdN Ille-et-Vilaine (2e Bn); Charente (3e Bn); Fédérés (7e Bn); Seine-et-Oise (10e Bn); Artillery park (266 men). **Reserve** 1er, 21e and 24e CavRs (2 sqns each); 12e DragR (1 sqn).

Reserve Division totals 24 bns, 2 coys, 13,256 infantry, 8 sqns, 1,425 cavalry, 266 artillery – 2 bties.

Reserve Division losses Not known, very slight if any.

Austrian Garrison GM Moitelle commanding: IR Franz Ulrich Kinsky Nr 36 (2 bns); IR Vierset Nr 58 (2nd Bn); Le Loup Jägers (2 coys); HusR Esterházy Nr 32 (½ sqn); Artillery – 90 men.

Austrian total 2,599 men.

Austrian losses 850 men dead, wounded and deserted; the rest captured, 3 colours (Regiments Kinsky and Vierset).

Comment The IR Vierset was a Walloon regiment (ie recruited in Belgium) and suffered badly from desertion; there was very little fighting.

Sources Kriege FII, Chuquet, Schulz, Wrede.

UR Limburg, 10 November 1792, clash

A town on the River Lahn in western Germany, 42 km north of Wiesbaden, on Routes B8, B49, B417 and Autobahn A3/E35.

A French victory over the Prussians.

(Last action – Frankfurt 22 October; next action – recapture of Frankfurt, 2 December.)

French Forces Gen Houchard commanding the

Avantgarde of Custine's army: 2e and 7e ChàCh (? sqns); GdN 1er Bn Jura (1 bn); 1 x HAB.

French totals Not known.

French losses Not known.

Prussian Forces Gen von Vietinghof commanding: Gren Bn Kenitz; 1es Bn Borch.

Prussian totals ca 1,200 men.

Prussian losses 170 dead, wounded and missing, including 3 officers.

Comment This minor skirmish lasted one hour and was the last French success in this campaign on the upper Rhine.

Sources Kriege FII, Chuquet, Schulz, Jany.

NL Mecheln, 16 November 1792, surrender of

A town in western Belgium, 20 km south of Antwerp, on Routes N1, N14, N26 and motorway A1/E19.

A French victory over the Austrians.

(Last action – Jemappes 6 November; next action – Voroux les Liers, 27 November.)

French Forces Gen Stengel commanding: The Avantgarde of Gen Dumouriez's Armée de la Belgique (no exact details known).

French total 6,000 men.

French losses Not known, very slight.

Austrian Forces IR Württemberg Nr 38 (1 bn).

Austrian losses Not known, very slight.

Comment After a brief bombardment, the Austrian garrison capitulated and was allowed free withdrawal. The French captured an artillery foundry and large stocks of guns and powder.

Sources Kriege FII, Chuquet, Schulz, Wrede.

IN Sospello, 18 November 1792, clash

A village 20 km northeast of Nice on the French Riviera, on Route D2204.

A Sardinian victory over the French.

(Last action – Oneglia, 23 September; this was the last action of the 1792 campaign.)

French Forces Unknown.

French totals Unknown.

French losses Unknown.

Sardinian totals Unknown.

Sardinian losses Unknown.

Comment The French fell back to Lescarene, 12 km northeast of Nice and went into winter quarters. Both sides were sick of winter warfare.

Sources Schulz, Brancaccio.

NL Voroux-les-Liers, 27 November 1792, clash

A village in eastern Belgium, 4 km north of Liège, nowadays a suburb.

A French victory over the Austrians.

(Last action – Mecheln, 16 November; next action – Antwerp, 29 November.)

French Forces Gen Stengel commanding: The Avantgarde of the Armée de la Belgique – ca 8,000 men (no exact details known).

French losses Not known, slight.

Austrian Forces GM Sztáray commanding: 4 battalions, 4 guns, no exact details known.

Austrian losses 150 men dead, wounded and captured.

Comment Although the Austrian high command had resolved to evacuate the country, they still attempted to defend everything instead of concentrating their forces and moving decisively eastwards to good defensive positions with shorter lines of communication.

Sources Kriege FII, Chuquet, Schulz, Wrede.

NL Antwerp, 29 November 1792, clash

A city port in northern Belgium on the River Schelde.

A French victory over the Austrians.

(Last action – Voroux les Liers, 27 November; next action – Namur, 2 December.)

French Forces The Armée du Nord Gen La Bourdonnaye* commanding

Avantgarde Grenadiers (4 bns); Chass de l'Égalité (1 coy); Cie franche de Clemendos (1 coy); 2e RIdLi (1er Bn); 38e RIdLi (1er Bn), GdN Yonne (1er Bn); Meurthe (1er Bn); Moselle (1er Bn); Fédérés (9e Bn); 5e HusR (2 sqns); 5e ChàCh (3 sqns); HA (26 men). **Corps de Bataille Left Division** MdC Duval 74e RIdLi (1er Bn); 81e RIdLi (1er Bn), 89e RIdLi (2e Bn); GdN Manche (1er Bn); St Denis (1 bn); Côtes-du-Nord (1er Bn); Eure (2e Bn); St-Martin (1 bn); Deux-Sèvres (1er Bn); Somme (2e Bn); Fontaine de Grendle (1 bn); Seine-Inférieure (1er Bn). **Right Division** MdC Champmorin 71e RIdLi (2e Bn); 78e RIdLi (2 bns); 87e RIdLi 2e Bn); GdN Paris (4e Bn); Orne (2e Bn); Nord (7e Bn); Quatre Nations (1 bn); Eure (1er Bn); Nord (8e Bn); Marne (1er and 2e Bns); 13e CavR (2 sqns); 3e DragR (2 sqns); artillery park (260 men).

French totals 34 bns, 2 coys, 17,600 infantry, 9 sqns, 1,245 cavalry, 286 artillery, 2 bties.

French losses Very slight.

*replaced on 27th November by GL Miranda.

Austrian Forces Obst Molitor commanding: IR Hohenlohe Nr 17 (1st Bn); IR Vierset Nr 58 (2 coys); IR Würzburg (4 coys). Artillery (140 men).

Austrian losses 2 dead, 4 wounded, the rest captured, 57 cannon, 50 x 3 pdr regimental pieces, 3,150 muskets, 1,523 hundredweight of powder.

Comment It is unclear why a garrison was placed in Antwerp when the Austrians had already decided to evacuate the country; it was a useless squandering of scarce manpower.

Sources Kriege FII, Chuquet, Schulz, Wrede.

UR Frankfurt am Main, 2 December 1792, storm and capture of

A free, imperial city on the north bank of the River Main about 20 km east of its confluence with the Rhine.

An Allied victory over the French.

(Last action – the French capture of Frankfurt, 22 October; next action – apart from a minor skirmish near Wiesbaden on 14 December, this was the last action on the Upper Rhine in 1792.)

French Forces GdB van Helden commanding: 82e RIdLi (1er Bn); GdN Vosges (7e Bn); Bas-Rhin (5e Bn); Haute-Saône (10e Bn); 2 x 3 pdr guns.

French totals 1,800 infantry, 2 guns.

French losses 41 dead, 139 wounded, 1,153 captured, 2 guns, 2 colours.

Allied Forces GL von Biesenrodt (Hessen-Kassel) commanding: GM von Wurmb, GM von Hanstein: IR Kospoth (2 bns); Füs-Bn Lenz (1st Bn); R Garde zu Fuss (2 bns); Leib R (2 bns); Gren Bn Philippsthal (1 bn); Gren Bn Eschwege (1 bn); Garde-Gren-R (2 bns); Jägerkorps (2 coys); HusR (5 sqns); Garde du Corps (1 sqn); Carabiniers (3 sqns); ChLR * (4 sqns); DragR Kleist ** (1 sqn); 2 mortars**, 1 howitzer**, 6 x 12 pdr cannon**.

Allied totals 10 bns, 2 coys, 14 sqns, 3 guns, ca 11,000 men.

Allied losses 16 officers, 168 men dead and wounded Prince Carl von Hessen-Philippsthal killed.

Comment General Custine completely ignored van Helden's requests for reinforcements. The town populace overpowered the defenders, dismantled their guns and opened the gates to the Allies.

Sources Ditfurth, Jany, Schulz.

* = Hessen-Darmstadt troops.

** = Prussian troops.

UR Trier on the River Moselle, around December 1792, clashes.

On Routes B51, Autobahns A1/E44.

NB It has not been possible to identify the individual regiments of Gen Beurnonville's Armée de la Moselle who were involved in the individual clashes. The French aim was to destroy the Electorate of Trier.

The order of battle of the Armée de la Moselle in December 1792 was as follows

Avantgarde Gen la Barolière: 1er Light Inf (1 bn); Chass de l'Observatoire, (? coys); Légion de la Moselle (? coys); Cie franche de Humbert (1 coy); Cie franche de Guillaume (1 coy); Cie franche de Fischer (1 coy); GdN de St Maurice (1 bn); 1er and 2e Gren Bns; 62e and 96e RIdLi (? bns); GdN Vienne (1er Bn); Meuse (1er Bn); Indre-et-Lot (1er Bn).

Cavalry Gen Destournelle: Hus de la Mort; 3e HusR (? sqns); 10e ChàCh (? sqns); 4e DragR (? sqns); 11e and 19e CavR (? sqns); Sorbier's HA coy.

First Rank Gen Ligniville: (GdB Linch, Freytag, Landremont, Muratel and Legrange) 3e, 4e and 5e Gren Bns (3 bns); 1er, 5e, 17e, 22e, 24e, 44e, 54e, 58e, and 90e RIdLi (? bns); GdN Haut-Marne (1er Bn); Saône-et-Loire (1er Bn); Manche (3e and 4e Bns); Bn de Popincourt (1 bn); Bn des Sections armées (1 bn); Moselle (4e Bn); Seine-Inférieure (4e Bn); Meurthe (9e Bn); Fédérés (13e Bn); 4e and 10e CavR (? sqns); 14e and 17e DragR (? sqns).

Second Rank Gen Aboville: (GdB Delaage and Prilly) 30e, 53e, 55e, 74e, 89e and 102e RIdLi (? bns); GdN Haute-Marne (2e Bn); Moselle (3e Bn); Haute-Saône (4e Bn); Meurthe (4e, 6e and 8e Bns); Fédérés des 83e Département (? bns); Bn de Palloy or 3e Bn de la République (1 bn). **Reserve** Gen Pully: 1er and 2e Carabiniers (? sqns); 8e CavR (? sqns); 1er DragR (? sqns); 1er and 9e ChàCh (? sqns); 2e Division de Gendarmerie (? sqns). **Total** ca 20,000 men. No casualties are detailed.

The Austrian dispositions in the area at this time were as follows

FML Prince Hohenlohe-Kirchberg commanding: IR Gemmingen Nr 21: in Pellingen (a village 10 km southeast of Trier), 1 bn; at the Moselle bridge at Konz, 5 km southwest of Trier, 2 coys; in Trier, 4 coys and 1¾ ChL sqns; at Zerf (a village 16 km southeast of Trier), one troop ChL IR Klebek Nr 14; in Tawern (a village 10 km southwest of Trier), 2 coys; in Grevenmachern (a village 15 km upstream of Trier), 1 bn.

DragR Erzherzog Josef Nr 26: in Euren (2 km southwest of Trier), 1½ sqns; in Onsdorf (18 km southwest of Trier), 1 tp, in Saarburg (18 km south of Trier), ½ tp.

The Trier garrison was reinforced from the garrison of Luxembourg by IR Mittrowsky Nr 40 (2 bns); and IR Stain Nr 50 (2 bns); Gz IR Warasdiner-Kreutzer Nr 64 (1 bn) and Captain Andujar's 700-strong reinforcement draft which had broken out of Mainz.

The garrison of Luxembourg was IR Carl Schroeder Nr 7 (2 bns); IR Clerfayt Nr 9 (3d Bn); IR Manfredini Nr 12 (2 bns); IR Württemberg Nr 38 (3d Bn); IR Jellačič Nr 53 (1 bn); IR Murray Nr 55 (3d Bn); IR J Colloredo Nr 57 (1 bn); ChLR Kaiser Nr 1 (4 sqns); HusR Wurmser Nr 30 (8 sqns); 3rd Garrison R (4 coys); IR Anhalt-Zerbst (2 coys); DragR Anhalt-Zerbst (½ sqn).

On 4 December the Armée de la Moselle pushed its advance guard from Reinsfeld to the River Ruwer and Gen Humbert's Free Corps clashed with Austrian outposts at Tawern and Fellerich (2 km northwest of Tawern). Prince Hohenlohe's forces were now completely surrounded. On 6 December Humbert attacked Tawern again but was again beaten off and on the same day the brigades of Generals Lagrange and Destournelle plus 500 tirailleurs and 1,200 cavalry assaulted Pellingen whilst Beurnonville and the main body attacked the heights southwest of Trier. All assaults failed.

Hohenlohe brought IR J Colloredo Nr 57 (1 bn) from Luxembourg to Grevenmachern. On 7 December Beurnonville failed in another assault on the Grüneberg east of Trier and on 10 December his further attacks on Pellingen also failed.

Also on this day FML Beaulieu reinforced Trier. Pellingen with IR Nr 15 d'Alton (1 bn); IR Nr 37 de Vins (1 bn); Le Loup Jägers (1 coy); Limburg Volunteers (1 coy) and ChLR Kinsky Nr 7 (6 sqns) and Hohenlohe came down from Trier with IR Manfredini Nr 12 (2 bns); HusR Wurmser Nr 30 (6 sqns) and some 12pdr guns a total on site of 12 bns and 14 sqns.

GM Werneck commanded the Reserve at Grevenmachern: IR Matheson Nr 42 (1 bn), IR Murray Nr 55 (1 bn) and ChLR Latour Nr 31 (2 sqns). No casualties are known.

On 15 December the French momentarily captured Tawern; French forces involved included the Bn de Popincourt; 1er du Lot and 4e de la Seine-Inférieure.

On 17 December Beurnonville's starving army, dwindling daily from desertion, streamed off home; the operation was a complete failure.

Sources Kriege FII, Chuquet, Schulz, Wrede.

1793

FRENCH ORDERS OF BATTLE 1793

During 1793 and 1794 the data on the organizations of the individual French armies and their battle participation is extremely fragmentary and scarce. To help clarify matters we produce below the listings of the various regiments and battalions and their allocation to the armies concerned.

Armée du Nord

Infantry Grenadiers (5e Bn); **Infanterie de Ligne** 12e (2 bns); 13e–19e (1er Bns only); 22e (2 bns); 24e (2e Bn); 25e, 36e, 38e (2 bns each); 43e (1er Bn); 45e (2 bns); 47e (1er Bn); 49e (2 bns); 54e (1er Bn); 58e, 62e, 67e, 68e, 71e and 78e (1er Bns only); 81e (2e Bn); 83e, 89e and 90e (2 bns each); 94e (1er Bn); 98e (2 bns); 102e (1er Bn); 104e (2 bns); **Total** 51 bns.

Infanterie Légère 1er, 2e, 3e and 5e ('Free' company each only); 9e, 10e, 14e, 21e, 23e, 24e, 28e and 32e. **Total** 8 bns, 4 coys.

Garde Nationale Aisne (1er, 5e and 6e); Allier (1er); Basses-Alpes (2e); Ardennes (3e, 5e); Aube (3e); Bouches-du-Rhône (1er); Calvados (1er, 2e, 3e, 6e*, 10e); Charente (3e, 4e and 5e); Charente-Inférieure (1er); Corrèze (2e); Côte-d'Or (5e, 9e); Côtes-du-Nord (1er); Doubs (7e); Eure (1er); Evre (les deux) (1er, 2e); Finistère (1er, 2e); Gare (2e); Gers (7e); Gironde (1er); Bec d'Ambez (3e); Hérault (6e); Ille-et-Villaine (1er); Jura (6e); Loiret (1er); Lot (3e)*; Manche (1er, 2e); Marne (1er, 3e); Marne (haute) (1er, 3e); Mayenne (1er, 2e); Mayenne-et-Loire (2e); Meurthe (1er, 2e, 3e, 5e, 8e); Meuse (2e, 4e); Moselle (1er); Nièvre (2e); Nord (1er, 2e, 4e, 5e, 7e, 9e); Oise (1er, 2e, 3e, 5e, 6e); Orne (1er, 2e); Paris, 'Amis de la Patrie' (11e); Paris, 'Bon Consul' (7e); Paris, 'Commune et Areis' (1); Paris, 'Lombarde' (19e); Paris, 'Luxembourg' (1); Paris, 'Marguerittte' (9e)*; Paris, 'Molière' (16e); Paris, 'Popincourt' (1); Paris, 'Républicain' (17e); Paris, 'Theatre Français' (7e)*; Pas de Calais (1er, 2e, 4e, 5e, 6e, 7e, 8e, 9e, 10e); Rhin (haut) (2e, 5e, 6e); Rhône-et-Loire (5e); Sarthe (4e); Paris, 'Sections' Armée (1er, 2e, 4e, 5e, 6e*); Seine-et-Aisne (4e, 8e, 10e); Seine-et-Marne (1er, 2e); Seine Inférieure (6e, 7e, 9e, 10e, 11e); Somme (1er, 2e, 3e, 4e, 5e); Vienne (haute) (1er, 2e); Vosges (2e, 5e, 10e); Vendée (2e); Vienne (1er, 2e); Yonne (2e, 3e, 4e, 5e, 6e, 7e). **Total** 121 bns and 5 coys.

* = 1 coy only.

Fédérés Nationeaux (2e–17e Bns) **Total** 16 bns.

Volontaires de la Réserve 3e, 4e, 6e, 8e, 9e, 11e, 15e, 16e, 17e, 21e, 23e, 25e **Total** 12 bns.

Cavalry Carabiniers 1er and 2e; **Cavalry** 1er, 3e, 6e, 7e, 8e, 13e, 16e, 17e, 19e, 20e, 21e, 22e, 25e, 27e, 28e **Total** 17 regiments. **Hussars** 3e, 4e, 5e, 6e, 8e, 9e, 10e. **Total** 7 regiments. **Dragoons** 2e, 3e, 6e, 7e, 12e, 13e, 20e, and 'de la Manche' **Total** 8 regiments. **Chasseurs à Cheval** 3e, 5e, 6e, 13e, 16e, 17e, 21e, 23e **Total** 8 regiments.

The Armée du Nord was reinforced on 11 August 1793 by 11,000 men from the armies of the Rhine and Moselle RIdLi 36e and 67e (1er and 2e Bns each); 49e and 74e (1er Bns each); GdN Haut-Rhin (2e, 5e and 6e Bns); Vosges (2e, 11e); Jura (6e and 7e); Var and Gironde (4e Bns each); Seine-et-Oise (8e), Doubs (7e), 13e Fédérés (2e Bn); 83e Départements (3e Bn), Oise (6e Bn); Haute-Marne (3e Bn); Eure (3e); 5e HusR, 16e CavR. The reinforced army was divided into three corps: I or 'Corps de Cassel' of 25,000 men to fight the Hanoverians; II or 'Corps de Maubeuge' of 20,000 to observe FM Prince of Coburg's Austrians and III or 'Corps de la Camp de Madelaine' of 50,000 men to attack the Prince of Orange and the Duke of York.

French Armée du Rhin, Spring 1793
Gen Custine Commanding

Right Wing Gen Munnier: 3e RIdLi (1 bn); 27e RIdLi (1 bn); 30e RIdLi (1 bn); 32e RIdLi (1 bn); 46e RIdLi (1 bn); 93e RIdLi (1 bn); 96e RIdLi (1 bn); GdN Haute-Saône (1e and 2e Bns); Nièvre (2e Bn); Vosges (4e Bn); Seine-et-Oise (5e Bn); Bas-Rhin (3e Bn); Puy-de-Dôme (2e Bn); Doubs (1e and 3e Bns); Haut-Rhin (3e Bn); Ain (3e Bn); Grenadiers de l'Indre et Loire (3e Bn); Rhône-et-Loire (2e Bn). **Total** 20 bns.

Centre (at Mainz) Gen Custine: Grenadiers (1e, 2e, 3e and 4e Bns); 57e RIdLi (2 bns); 62e RIdLi (1 bn); 82e RIdLi (1 bn); GdN Jura (2e, 3e and 5e Bns); Ain (2e Bn); Haut-Rhin (4e Bn); Haute-Saône (9e and 10e Bns); Calvados (4e Bn); Meurthe (10e Bn); République (2e Bn); Chasseurs républicains (1er Bn); Vosges (3e, 7e and 8e Bns); Bas-Rhin (5e and 6e Bns); Fédérés Nationeaux (1er Bn); Seine-et-Oise (2e Bn); 14e CavR (3 sqns); 2e ChàCh (1 sqn); 7e ChàCh (4 sqns); 10e ChàCh (4 sqns). **Totals** 26 bns, 12 sqns.

Left Wing (at Bingen) Gen Neuwinger **1ère Brigade** GdB Houchard 7e Bn Lé (1 bn); 36e RIdLi (1 bn); 37e RIdLi (1 bn); GdN Jura (4e and 6e Bns); Haut-Rhin (2e

Bn); Saône-et-Loire (1er Bn); Vosges (1er and 2e Bns); 8e ChàCh (4 sqns). **2e Brigade** GdB Gilot 13e RIdLi (1 bn); 48e RIdLi (1 bn); Jura (1er, 7e and 9e Bns); Haut-Rhin (1er Bn); Bas-Rhin (1er Bn); Corrèze (1er Bn); Nièvre (3e Bn); **Cavalry** GdB Beaurevoir: 2e ChàCh (3 sqns); 2e CavR (3 sqns); 3e CavR (3 sqns); 9e CavR (3 sqns); 11e CavR (3 sqns); 12e CavR (3 sqns). **Totals** 18 bns, 22 sqns. **Reserve** Grenadiers (12 coys); 6e RILé (1 bn); 21e RIdLi (1 bn); des Vosges (6e, 10e and 13e Bns); de l'Eure (5e Bn); de Calvados (6e Bn); de Haute Saône (12e Bn); 22e CavR (3 sqns); 16e DragR (3 sqns); Hus de la Liberté (? sqn); Gendarmerie Nationale (? sqn) **Totals** 8 bns, 12 sqns, 2 tps.

Totals Armée du Rhin Spring 1793 72 bns, 12 coys, 43 sqns, 2 tps = 45,000 men.

Order of Battle of the Armée du Rhin, 30 October 1793

Avantgarde GdD Meynier: Chasseurs du Rhin, 6e and 12e RIdLi, GdN Corrèze (1er Bn); Jura (1er Bn); Grenadiers (1er and 2e Bns); Lot-et-Garonne (2e Bn); 48e and 105e RIdLi. GdB Loubat: 7e HusR, 8e and 10e ChàCh; 8e, 11e and 17e DragR. **Right Wing** Gen Dubois: Gen Michaud: 11e RILé 37e and 40e RIdLi; GdN Haute-Saône (3e and 7e Bn); Ain (5e Bn); Charente-Inférieure (3e Bn); Pyrénées-Orientales (1er Bn); Rhône-et-Loire (3e Bn); 1 free company. **Centre** Gens Munnier and Mequillet: 3e and 30e RIdLi, GdN Ain (1er and 3e Bns); Doubs (3e Bn); Jura (12e Bn); Gen Isambert: 46e RIdLi; GdN Bas-Rhin (3e Bn); Doubs (11e Bn); Puy-de-Dôme (2e Bn); Eure-et-Loire (2e Bn); Gen Dauriol: 93e RIdLi (2 bns); GdN Rhône-et-Loire (2e Grenadiers); Lot-et-Garonne (1er Bn); Seine-et-Oise (5e Bn). **Left Wing** Gen Ferey, Gen Desaix: 7e RILé, 13e and 27e RIdLi; GdN Vosges (1er Bn); Jura (4e Bn); Haut-Rhin (1er and 3e Bns); Indre-et-Loire (3e Bn); Indre (1er Bn); Rhône-et-Loire (2e Bn); Seine-et-Loire (4e Bn); Haute-Saône (1er Bn); Vosges (10e Bn); 7e ChàCh, 2e CavR (1 sqn); Gendarmes (1 sqn); Gen Ravel: 5e Artillery R; GdN Bas-Rhin (1er Bn); Ouvriers Pioniers (1 bn); Guides (22 men).

Totals Armée du Rhin 30 October 1793 57,369; present, fit for duty 42,420.

Source Chuquet.

Armée des Ardennes 1793

Infanterie de Ligne 13e, 43e, 94e (2e Bns each). **Total** 3 bns.

Infanterie Légère 11e*, 20e, 26e. **Total** 3 bns. **Garde Nationale battalions** Aisne (4e); Ardennes (6e); Aube (5e); Creuse (3e); Loire-et-Cher (2e); Marne (4e); Nord (6e, 8e); Norde (3e, 6e, 8e); Paris, 'Pont-neuf' (1); Saône-et-Loire (2e, 5e); Seine-et-Loire (2e, 5e); Seine-et-Oise (5e, 9e); Seine Inférieure (5e); Vendée (1er). **Total** 18 bns. **Volontaires de la Réserve** (2e Bn). **Infantry total** 24 bns, 1 coy. **Cavalry** 15e, 23e Regiments. **Dragoons** 5e, 10e. **Hussars** 2e, **Chasseurs à Cheval** 11e, 20e **Cavalry total** 7 Regiments.

* = 1 coy only.

Armée de la Moselle, 1793.

Infanterie de Ligne 1er (1er Bn); 2e (2e Bn); 5e (1er Bn); 8e, 17e, 18e, 19e (2e Bns each); 27e (1er Bn); 30e, 33e (2 bns each); 40e (2e Bn); 41e (1er Bn); 47e, 54e, 55e, 58e, 71e (2e Bns each); 81e (1er Bn); 96e, 99e (2 bns each); 100e (2e Bn); 103e (2 bns). **Total** 27 bns. **Infanterie Légère** 6e, 13e, 16e, 17e Bns. **Total** 4 bns. **Garde Nationale battalions** Ardennes (1er); Cher (1er, 2e); Côte-d'Or (3e); Creuse (1er); Loiret (2e, 3e); Lot (2e); Manche (3e); Marne (7e); Haute-Marne (2e); Meurthe (4e, 6e, 7e); Meuse (1er, 3e, 5e); Moselle (2e, 3e, 4e, 5e); Oise (4e); Orne (5e); Paris, 'Butte de Moulins' (1er Bn); Paris, 'de la République' (1er, 3e); Paris, 'St Margueritte' (9e); Paris, 'Sections Armée' (3e); Basses-Pyrénées (6e); Bas-Rhin (3e, 4e); Haut-Rhin (3e); Rhône-et-Loire (1er, 7e); Haute-Saône (1er, 4e); Saône-et-Loire (1er), Seine-et-Oise (6e), Var (4e), Vosges (1er, 6e), Yonne (1er). **Total** 42 bns. **Cavalry** 4e, 10e, 11e, 14e Regiments. Dragoons 1er, 11e, 14e. Hussars 2e; Chasseurs à Cheval 1er, 9e, 18e, 19e. **Total** 12 regiments.

Armée du Rhin

Infantry Grenadiers: 5e Bn. **Infanterie de Ligne** 3e, 21e (2 bns each); 24e (1er Bn); 27e, 37e (2e Bns each); 40e (1er Bn); 46e (2 bns); 48e (1er Bn); 55e (1er Bn); 75e (2 bns); 82e (2e Bn); 88e (1er Bn); 93e and 105e (2 bns each). **Infanterie Légère** 7e, 11e, 12e, 14e* **Total** 25 bns. **Garde Nationale battalions** Ain (1er, 3e, 5e, 8e); Allier (2e); Aube (2e); Charente-Inférieure (2e); Cher (3e); Corrèze (1er); Côte-d'Or (4e, 8e, 12e); Côtes-du-Nord (2e); Creuse (2e); Dordogne (1er, 2e); Doubs (1er–6e, 8e–12e, 14e); Drôme (5e, 6e, 7e, 8e); Eure (4e); Eure-et-Loire (2e); Gard (3e); Gironde (2e); Ille-et-Villaine (4e); Indre (2e); Jura (1er, 4e, 8e, 10e, 11e, 12e, 14e); Lot-et-Garonne (1er, 2e); Manche (4e);

Meurthe (9e, 11e); Meuse (6e); Mont Terrible (1er); Paris de la République (2e); Puy-de-Dôme (1er, 2e, 3e); Saône-et-Loire (3e, 4e, 6e); Basses-Pyrénées (7e, 8e); Pyrénées-Orientales (1er); Haut-Rhin (1er); Bas-Rhin (1er, 2e, 7e); Rhône-et-Loire (2e, 3e, 5e*); Haute-Saône (3e); Seine-et-Marne (5e); Seine-et-Oise (7e); Seine-Inférieure (4e); Vosges (4e, 7e, 8e, 9e, 11e, 13e, 14e). **Total** 79 bns and 1 coy.

Cavalry 2e, 9e, 12e, 18e. Dragoons 4e, 8e, 17e. Hussars 7e. Chasseurs à Cheval 2e, 4e, 8e, 10e. **Total Cavalry** 11 regiments.

* = 1 coy only.

The Armée des Pyrénées Orientales (East Pyrenees) 1793, 1794 and 1795

1er, 8e and 29e RILé; 3e, 5e, 7e, 10e, 17e, 20e, 27e, 28e, 35e, 39e, 53e, 61e, 70e, 79e, 80e, 122e, 130e and 147e RIdLi; six veteran companies (5e, 15e, 17e, 34e, 37e and 77e). 27e CavR, 14e and 15e Drag. 14e, 19e and 22e ChàCh, 1er HusR. Batteries of the 2e, 4e and 5e Artillery Regiments, the 5e Sapeurs and the following GdN battalions: Basses-Alpes 1er; Hautes-Alpes 1er; Ardèche 2e, 3e, 4e, 5e, 6e; Arriège 1er–7e; Aube 3e; Aude 1er- 9e; Bouches-du-Rhône 1er and 2e Grenadiers and 1 sqn dragoons; Cantal 1er; Corrèze 4e; Corse* 4e; Dordogne 6e and 8e; Drôme 3e and 9e; Gard 1er and 2e Grenadiers and 6 fusilier bns; Haute-Garonne 2e–10e; Gers 1er and 2e; Gironde 1er, 2e, 6e; Hérault 1er, 2e, 3e; de Montpellier, 1er and 2e Béziers, 1er and 2e de St Pons; 1er de Lodève and 30 dragoons; Haute-Loire 3e; Loire-Inférieure, Bn de Nantais; Lot 3e, 4e, 5e; Montblanc 1er–5e forming the 'Légion des Allobroges'; Moselle Chass à Pied bn; Hautes-Pyrénées 1er and 2e; Pyrénées-Orientales 1er–4e forming the 'Légion des Pyrénées-Orientales; Bn des Corbières, 150 Miqueletes de Collioure and 340 cavalry; Seine 3e; Tarn 1er, 3e, 4e and 240 cavalry; Vaucluse 1er ChàP, 5e Fusiliers; Haute-Vienne 3e and 5e.

The following irregular corps: Volontaires des Côtes Maritimes 1er–4e, 6e, 7e and 13e Bns; Légion de la Montagnes 1er–6e and 10e Bns; Vengeurs 1er Bn; Chasseurs Flanqueurs, 1er Bn.

Totals May 1793 10,800 field troops and 10,289 garrison troops.

* = There is some doubt that this unit was actually with the army.

Source Fervel.

Armée des Pyrénées Occidentales, (West Pyrenees) 1793

Infanterie de Ligne: 20e, 80e, 148e (2 bns each); **Infanterie Légère** 5e; **Garde Nationale** Aldudes (1); Dordogne (3e); Landes (3e); Lot-et-Garonne (4e); Paris, 'Louvre' (1); Compagnies franches (18 coys). **Cavalry** 18e DragR; Volontaires des Pyrénées Occidentales (later 12e HusR); Chasseurs Volontaires de Bayonne (later 24e ChàCh); 15 artillery coys.

1793 THE ACTIONS

UR Hochheim, 6 January 1793, clash

A village in the western German province of Hessen, on the north bank of the River Main, 4 km from its confluence with the Rhine.

An Allied victory over the French.

(Last action – Frankfurt, 2 December 1792; next action – Weiler/Waldalgasheim, 27 March.)

French Forces GdD Sédillon commanding part of Gen Custine's army: 8 combined grenadier bns, 13e RIdLi (2 bns); 56e RIdLi (1 bn); GdN Vosges (3e Bn); 16 guns

French totals ca 6,000 men.

French losses 100 killed, 300 wounded, 12 guns.

Allied Forces Prince von Hohenlohe commanding (Prussian King Friedrich Wilhelm II was also present) HusR Eben Nr 2 (5 sqns); HusR von Wolffradt Nr 6 (5 sqns); Jägerkorps* (1coy); Gren Bn von Känitz (1 bn); IR von Känitz Nr 39 (2 bns); IR von Manstein Nr 9 (2 bns); IR von Borch Nr 49 (1st Bn); Gren Bn vacant von Hessen-Philippsthal* (1 bn); Regt Garde-Gren* (2 bns); DragR Bayreuth Nr 5 (10 sqns); Leibdragoner-R* (3 sqns); 1½ HAB

Allied totals 8 bns, 18 sqns, 1½ HAB, ca 10,600 men.

Allied losses 12 killed, 3 officers and 65 men wounded.

* = Hessen-Kassel troops; the others were Prussians.

Sources Chuquet, Ditfurth, Jany.

MD Cagliari, 14 February 1793, clash

A port on the southern coast of the Italian island of Sardinia.

A Sardinian victory over the French.

This was the only action of note in the area.

French Forces R Adm La Touche commanding: Marseille Militia, Volontaires Nationales de Marseille

(1er and 2e Bns) and the following free corps: Martigues, Aix, Tarascon, l'Union, Luberon, Vaucluse (4,000 men); 26e, 42e and 52e DBdeLi (1 bn each) from Ajaccio in Corsica

French totals 6,700 men, 4 ships of the line, 5 frigates.

French losses Not exactly known; light.

Sardinian Forces Commander unknown: Swiss IR de Courten (2 bns); town militia and artillery

Sardinian total ca 4,000 men.

Sardinian losses Not known, light.

Comment The young Napoleon Bonaparte was captain in this landing and was almost lynched by the near-mutinous militia.

Sources Fortescue, Schultz.

NL Breda, 21–24 February 1793, capitulation

A fortified town in the Dutch province of North Brabant, 22 km southeast of Rotterdam, on Routes A16/E19 and A27/E311.

A French victory over the Dutch.

(This was the opening action; next action – Aldenhoven, 1 March).

French Forces GdB d'Arcon commanding the Division of the Right of the 'Armée de Hollande'. GdN Oise (3e Bn); Calvados (2e Bn); Charente (5e Bn); Loire-et-Cher (2e Bn); Volontaires de la Réserve (2e, 11e and 17e Bns); Fédérés (6e Bn); Gendarmes de Paris (2 bns); 8e HusR (200 men); 1 x FAB

French total 5,000 men, 8 guns.

French losses 25 killed and wounded.

Dutch Forces GM Count Bylandt commanding: 2,500 infantry and a dragoon regiment.

Dutch total 3,000 men.

Dutch losses Not known, light. The garrison went free, the French took 250 guns in the place. The French evacuated Breda on 3 April again.

Sources Chuquet, Dohna.

IN Levens, 28 February 1793, clash

A small town in the southern French Department of Alpes Maritimes, east of the River Vesubie, 20 km north of Nice on Route 19.

A French victory over the Sardinians.

(This was the opening action in this theatre; next action – Saorgio, 8 June).

French Forces GdG Biron commanding part of the Armée d'Italie. Exact details unknown.

French total 12,000 men.

French losses ca 800 killed and wounded.

Sardinian Forces LG Count de St André commanding. Exact details unknown.

Sardinian total ca 7,000 men and 6 guns.

Sardinian losses ca 800 men and 2 guns.

Sources Brancaccio, Schultz.

NL Aldenhoven (Eschweiler), 1 March 1793, clash

Two villages in the (then) Prussian province of the Rhine, 11 km northeast of Aachen on Route B56, just off Autobahn A44.

An Austrian victory over the French.

(Last action – Breda, 24 February; next action – Maastricht, 3 March.)

French Forces MdC de la Noue commanding Dumouriez' Reserve. GdB Stengel: 3e and 4e Grenadiers (2 bns); Bn Liègeois (1 bn); 14e Bn Ilé (1 bn); GdN Paris (2e Bn); 29e RIdLi (2 bns); 6e and 12e ChàCh

French total 7 bns, 6 sqns, 2 x FAB, ca 9,000 men and 12 guns.

French losses 2,000 killed and wounded, 300 captured, 7 guns, 2 colours (1 of 29e Li and one other).

Austrian Forces FM Duke Josias von Coburg-Saalfeld commanding: Gen EH Charles of Austria: DragR Latour Nr 31, HusR Esterházy Nr 32.

Austrian total 12 sqns, ca 1,000 men.

Austrian losses 50 killed and wounded.

Comment Only these two Austrian cavalry regiments were involved; the French army fell back west utterly demoralized. This victory caused the siege of Maastricht to be lifted.

Sources Chuquet, Wrede.

NL Maastricht, 21 February – 3 March 1793, failed siege

A fortress and town in the Dutch province of Limburg, on the south bank of the River Maas, on the German border, 24 km north of Liège on Route A2/E25.

An Austro-Dutch victory over the French.

(Last action – Aldenhoven, 1 March; next action – Geertruidenberg, 4 March.)

French Forces Gen Miranda commanding until 28 February thence Gen Valence, GdD Thouvenot, GdD Petitjean; exact details not known.

French total 10,000 men and 24 guns.

French losses Not known, light.

Austro-Dutch Forces GM Prince von Hessen commanding: troops included a corps of Émigrés under the Marquis d'Autichamp.

Austro-Dutch total 8,000 men 60 guns.

Austro-Dutch losses Not known, light.

Comment Due to the startling Austrian victory at Aldenhoven on 1 March the siege was lifted. The French withdrew to Tongres.

Sources Chuquet.

NL Geertruidenberg, 1–4 March 1793, siege and capitulation

A fortress in the west of the Dutch province of North Brabant, on the southern side of the Amer-Bergser-Maas canal, 17 km north of Breda, just west of Route A27/E311.

A French victory over the Dutch.

(Last action – Maastricht, 3 March; next action – Klundert, 4 March.)

French Forces GdD d'Arcon commanding the Division of the Right of Dumouriez 'Armée de Hollande' as for Breda, 21–24 February

French total 5,000 men and 18 guns.

French losses None.

Dutch Forces Gen Bedaulx commanding: LIR Hirzel (2 bns); 1 x DragR (2 sqns); 150 guns

Dutch total 2 bns, 2 sqns.

Dutch losses Not known, slight. Bedaulx (over 80 years old) capitulated with honours of war; the garrison went free. The French evacuated the place again on 2 April.

Sources Chuquet, Dohna.

NL Klundert, 1–4 March 1793, siege and capture

A small fortress in the western Dutch province of North Brabant, on the southern side of the Hollands Diep, 18 km northwest of Breda.

A French victory over the Dutch.

(Last action – Geertruidenberg, 4 March; next action – Tirlemont, 16 March.)

French Forces GdB Berneron commanding the Avantgarde of Dumouriez 'Armée de Hollande': GdN Aube (3e Bn); Finistère (1er Bn); Légion Batave (1er and 2e Bns); Drag Bataves (80 men)

French total 4 bns, 1 sqn, 6 guns, ca 4,000 men.

French losses Not known, very light.

Dutch Forces Capt Kropf commanding 2 coys infantry.

Dutch total 150 men, 54 guns, 2 mortars.

Dutch losses Capt Kropf and about 60 men killed, 73 captured.

Sources Chuquet.

NL Tirlemont (Gutzenhoven), 16 March 1793, clash

A village in the Belgian province of Liège on the Little Geete River, 5 km north of Neerwinden, between Tirlemont and St Trond. Not marked on modern maps.

A French victory over the Austrians.

(Last action – Klundert, 4 March; next action – Neerwinden, 18 March.)

French Forces Gen Dumouriez commanding part of the Armée du Nord. Exact details not known.

French totals 10,000 men, ? guns.

French losses ca 500 killed, wounded and missing.

Austrian Forces FM Archduke Charles commanding the Avantgarde GM von Rehbach: Karabinier R Kaiser Nr 6 (2 sqns). IRs Kheul Nr 10 (1st and 2nd Bns); Callenberg Nr 54 (2 bns); Gren Bn Nr 18 (1 bn); HusR Esterházy Nr 32 (2 sqns); UlR Schwarzenberg (4 sqns).

Austrian total 6,000 men, 6 guns, 2 mortars.

Austrian losses About 800 men killed, wounded and missing.

Comment This was the last successful French action in the invasion of Holland.

Sources Chuquet, Ditfurth, Wrede.

NL Neerwinden, 18 March 1793, battle

A village in the Belgian province of Liège, 42 km west of Liège city, 9 km southeast of Tirlemont, 20 km southwest of St Trond.

An Austrian victory over the French.

(Last action – Tirlemont, 16 March; next action – Löwen, 23 March.)

French Forces Gen Dumouriez commanding the Armée du Nord Exact details not known.

Avantgarde GdB La Marche 4,000 infantry, 1,000 cavalry. **Right Wing** GdD Valence: 18 bns, 7,000 men. (the divisions of Valence, Neuilly, le Veneur) and the Flanqueurs de droite. GdB Dampièrre (2,000 infantry, 1,000 cavalry). **Centre** Gen Égalité (the Duc de Chartres): 18 bns, 7,000 infantry, 1,000 cavalry, GdB Dietmann, GdB Thouvenot. **Corps de Réserve**

GdD Chancel 8 bns, 4,000 men. **Left Wing** GdD Miranda, GdB Ihler 7,000 men; GdD Champmorin - 5,000 infantry, 1,000 cavalry. **Flanqueurs de la gauche** GdB Miaczynski - 2,000 infantry, 1,000 cavalry.

French totals 40-45,000 men.

French losses 4,000 killed and wounded. (MdC Guiscard de Bar killed, 4 other generals wounded), 1,000 missing or captured, 30 guns.

Austrian Forces FM Prince Josias of Coburg commanding

Austrian Forces: Avantgarde Archduke Charles Obst Michaljevich: HusR Esterházy Nr 32 (1 sqn); Mahony Jägers (3 bns); Freikorps O'Donnell (1 bn); Freikorps Branovaczky (⅓ bn); Obstlt Prince Schwarzenberg: Tyroler-Scharfschützen (1⅓ bn); Freikorps O'Donnell (1 bn); Freikorps Branovaczky (⅓ bn); UlR (3 sqns); Obst Gruber: IR Sztáray Nr 59 (2 bns); Obst Devay: Gren-Bns Briey, Barthodeiszky, Pückler (3 bns); HusR Esterházy Nr 32 (6 sqns); Obst Mylius: Tyroler-Scharfschützen (⅓ bn); Freikorps Grün-Laudon (1 bn); HusR Esterházy Nr 32 (1 sqn). **Totals** 11 bns, 11 sqns. **1st Rank FZM Ferraris**, FML Prince von Württemberg: Carabinier R Herzog Albert Nr 5 (2 sqns); KürR Nassau Nr 14 (6 sqns); IR EH Carl Nr 3 (1 bn); IR Jordis Nr 59 (1 bn); IRs Kheul Nr 10, Wartensleben Nr 28, Brentano Nr 35 (2 bns each); KürR Kavanagh Nr 12 (6 sqns); CarabinierR Kaiser Nr 1 (2 sqns); **Totals** 8 bns, 16 sqns. **2nd Rank FZM Wenzel Colloredo**, FML Benjowsky, GM Hoditz: ChLR Karaczay Nr 18 (2 sqns); KürR Zeschwitz Nr 10 (6 sqns); IRs Callenberg Nr 54 and Brechainville Nr 25 (2 bns each); IRs d'Alton Nr 15 and Joseph Colloredo Nr 57 (1 bn each); DragR Coburg Nr 37 (2 sqns). **Totals** 6 bns, 10 sqns. **Reserve** FZM Clerfayt; FZM Allvintzy, GM Lützow: IRs Vierset Nr 58 and Murray Nr 55 (1 bn each); IRs de Ligne Nr 30, Württemberg Nr 38 and Esterházy Nr 34 (2 bns each); HusR Blankenstein Nr 16 (6 sqns); ChLR Latour Nr 31 (8 sqns); Gren Bns Morzin, Leeuven and Rousseau (3 bns). **Totals** 11 bns, 14 sqns.

Austrian totals 36 bns, 51 sqns.

Dutch Forces IRs Welderen (1 bn), Stokkar (2 bns); Waldeck (2 bns); May (1 bn).

Dutch totals 6 bns.

Allied totals 42 bns, 51 sqns, ca 43,000 men.

Allied losses 97 officers, 2,762 men and 779 horses killed, wounded and missing.

Comment The Austrians failed completely to follow up this victory; 6,000 French volunteers deserted after the action.

Sources Chuquet, Bodart, Wrede.

NL Pellenberg (Löwen), 23 March 1793, clash

A town in the Belgian province of Brabant, on the River Dyle, 30 km east of Brussels on Routes N2, N25 and N26.

An Austrian victory over the French.

(Last action - Neerwinden, 18 March; next action - Raismes, 8 May.)

French Forces Gen Dumouriez commanding the Armée du Nord as for Neerwinden.

French totals 22,000 men.

French losses ca 2,000 including MdC Conigliano-Clarenthal killed.

Austrian Forces FM Prince Josias von Coburg commanding the same forces as at Neerwinden

Austrian totals 38,000 men.

Austrian losses ca 900 men.

Sources Chuquet, Bodart, Witzleben.

UR Weiler (Waldalgasheim) 27 March 1793, clash

Two villages just west of the western German town of Bingen, on the west bank of the River Rhine, between Route B48 and Autobahn A61.

A Prussian-Hessian victory over the French.

(Last action - Hochheim, 6 January; next action - Alsheim, 30 March.)

French Forces GdD Neuwinger commanding 4 grenadier bns; GdN Corrèze (1er Bn); 2e CavR (1 sqn); 19e CavR (1 sqn); 6 guns.

French total ca 4,200 men and 6 guns.

French losses 80 killed, 131 wounded or captured. GdD Neuwinger captured, 6 guns.

Prussian-Hessian-Trier Forces Gen Erbprinz von Hohenlohe-Ingelfingen commanding:

Prussians Jägers (2 coys); Füs Bns von Thadden Nr 13, von Müffling Nr 18 and von Renouard Nr 2 (1 bn); HusR von Wolffradt Nr 6 (5 sqns); Combined CavR (5 sqns from various Drag and HusRs). **Hessen-Kassel** Jägers (2 coys); LtI Bn Lenz (2 coys); HusR (3 sqns); **Trier Jägers** (1 coy)

Allied totals ca 3,000 men and 2 guns.

Allied losses Not known exactly; very light.

Sources Chuquet, Ditfurth.

UR Alsheim, 30 March 1793, skirmish

A village in the western German province of Rheinhessen, 14 km north of Worms, just west of Route B9.

A Prussian victory over the French.

(Last action – Weiler, 27 March; next action – Arlon, 9 June.)

French Forces GdD Munnier commanding 3e and 4e Gren Bns (2 bns); GdN Haut-Rhin (1er Bn); 14e CavR (3 sqns); 10 ChàCh (1 sqn); 32e RIdLi (2 bns); 96e RIdLi (1 bn); GdN Vosges (4e Bn); 9e CavR (1 sqn)

French totals ca 4,600 men.

French losses 200 killed, 944 captured (many of these wounded), 4 guns. In a second clash a further 100 were killed and 50 captured.

Prussian-Hessian-Trier Forces GM von Eben commanding. Obst Szekuli: Prussian Füs Bn Wedel Nr 1 (1 bn); Combined CavR (5 sqns from various Drag and HusRs); DragR Bayreuth Nr 5 (3 sqns); **Trier Jägers** (1 coy); HusR von Wolffradt Nr 6 (8 sqns); LIR Hohenlohe Nr 17 (2 bns); **Hessen-Kassel** HusR (3 sqns) and Jägers (2 coys).

Allied totals ca 4,000 men.

Allied losses Not known exactly, very light.

Comment The French, already demoralised by their defeat at Weiler, blundered into an ambush.

Sources Chuquet, Ditfurth.

FP St Laurent de Cerdans, 17 April 1793, skirmish

A small mountain village in the French Eastern Pyrenees between the River Tech and the Spanish border, just south of Route 115.

A Spanish victory over the French.

(This was the opening action of the campaign; next action – Céret, 20 April).

French Forces (commander unknown) about 400 men

French losses Unknown.

Spanish Forces, Captain General Ricardo commanding: 6 battalions and 8 grenadier companies.

Spanish total ca 4,500 men.

Spanish losses Unknown but very light.

Comment This opened the invasion of France. The French garrison fled.

Source Schulz.

FP Céret, 20 April 1793, clash

A small town in southeastern France, on the south bank of the River Tech, at the junction of Routes 115, 615 and 618, about 8 km west of the motorway 9/E15.

A Spanish victory over the French.

(Last action – St Laurent de Cerdans, 17 April; next action – Mas d'Eu, 19 May.)

French Forces commander unknown): 1 infantry battalion and 1,000 Volontaires Nationales, 4 guns

French total ca 1,800 men

French losses 100–200 killed, wounded and missing, 200 drowned trying to escape across the Tech.

Spanish Forces Captain General Ricardo commanding: 6 battalions and 8 grenadier companies.

Spanish total ca 4,400 men.

Spanish losses Ricardo reported 17 wounded.

Comment The unsteady French troops panicked and fled.

Source Schulz.

NL Raismes, 8 May 1793, clash

A village in the northern French Département du Nord, 6 km northwest of Valenciennes, on Route A23, about 20 km south of the Belgian border.

An Allied victory over the French.

(Last action – Pellenberg, 23 March; next action – Tourcoing, 23 May.)

French Forces GdD Dampièrre commanding. Exact details not known

French totals ca 30,000 men.

French losses 1,500 killed, wounded and missing: Gen Dampièrre mortally wounded.

Allied Forces FM Prince Josias von Coburg commanding part of the Armée du Nord. **Austrian Forces** As at Neerwinden (18 March).

British Forces HRH The Duke of York commanding 1st and 2nd Foot Guards (3 bns).

Dutch Forces Prince Friedrich of Orange commanding 6 bns. IRs Welderen and May (1 bn each), Stokkar and Waldeck (2 bns each).

Allied totals 60,000 men (by no means all were engaged).

Allied losses 600 killed and wounded.

Prussian Forces GL von Knobelsdorff commanding: IRs von Köthen Nr 48, Kunitzky Nr 44, Kalckstein Nr 5, Knobelsdorff Nr 27 (3 bns each); Jägers (2 coys); LeibkürR Nr 3, Leib-Karabiniers Nr 11; HusR Gotz Nr 8 (1st Bn); 5 sqns each, 2 x 6 pdr FAB (16 guns).

Prussian Forces ca 11,000 men.

Prussian losses Not known exactly but very light.

Sources Chuquet, Schulz, Jany.

NL Tourcoing, 23 May 1793, skirmish

A fortified town in northern France up against the Belgian border, about 6 km northeast of Lille.

A French victory over the Dutch.

(Last action - Raismes, 8 May; next action - Famars, 23 May.)

French Forces Gen La Marlière commanding 2e and 12e RIdLi (2 bns each); 1er Bn Belges (1 bn); Gendarmes (400 men); 6e DragR (3 sqns)

French totals ca 5,000 men.

French losses Not known, light.

Dutch Forces Col Zeilenhard commanding 1 bn, 2 sqns, 2 guns

Dutch losses killed and wounded unknown, 400 captured (mostly cavalry) 1 gun exploded, 1 standard.

Sources Chuquet.

FP Mas d'Eu, 19 May 1793, clash

A small village in southeastern France, between the Rivers Tet and Tech, just south of Trouillas and west of motorway 9/E15, about 12 km southwest of Perpignan. Not shown on some modern maps.

A Spanish victory over the French.

(Last action - Céret, 20 April; next action - Fort les Bains, 3 June.)

French Forces GdB Deflers commanding: Exact details not known.

French totals Not known.

French losses 150 killed, 280 wounded, 3 x 6 pdr guns, 6 ammunition waggons.

Spanish Forces Capt Gen Ricardo commanding: 6 line battalions, 8 grenadier companies, 4 cavalry regiments and 30 companies of provincial militia.

Spanish total ca 7,000 men.

Spanish losses 34 killed.

Comment Following their defeat at Céret, the French would not stand here and fell back to Perpignan where, that night, an entire battalion of Volontaires Nationales declared that they would not fight against the Spanish and were disbanded. Ricardo did not pursue his beaten foe. He now decided to return south to capture Fort Bellegarde which commanded the road from Perpignan to Barcelona.

Source Schulz.

NL Famars, 23 May 1793, battle

A village in the northern French Département du Nord, 5 km south of Valenciennes.

An Allied victory over the French.

(Last action - Tourcoing, 23 May; next action - Condé, 12 July.)

French Forces GdD Lamarche commanding part of the Armée du Nord, exact details not known

French totals ca 27,000 men.

French losses ca 3,000 killed and wounded, 300 captured, 17 guns, 14 ammunition waggons, 3 colours.

Allied Forces

1st Main Column HRH The Duke of York commanding.

Austrian Troops IRs Sztáray Nr 33, Callenberg Nr 54, Hohenlohe Nr 17 and Stuart Nr 18 (2 bns each); KürR Nassau Nr 14, HusR Esterházy Nr 32 and ChLR Karaczay Nr 18 (6 sqns each); ChLR Kaiser Nr 1 (2 sqns). **British Troops** 1st, 2nd and 3rd Foot Guards; Guards Flankers (1 bn each); 11th, 15th and 16th LDR (2 sqns each). **Hanoverian Troops** R Garde (2 bns); Grenadiers (1st and 2nd Bns); 9th and 10th LDR (2 sqns each). **Artillery** 8 x 18 pdrs, 16 x 12 pdr guns, 5 x 10 pdr and 7 x 7 pdr howitzers, 2 x 6 pdr guns. Pioniers (2 coys)

2nd Main Column FZM Count Ferraris commanding: **Austrian Troops** Grenadiers (3 bns); IR Jordis Nr 59 (1 bn); HusR Barco Nr 35 (4 sqns). **British Troops** 1st/14th and 1st/53rd Foot (1 bn each). **Hanoverian Troops** Grenadiers (½ bn); IRs Nr 4 and Nr 10 (2 bns each); Leibgarde, 1st, 2nd and 4th CavRs (2 sqns each). **Artillery: Austrian** 6 x 18 pdr and 3 x 10 pdr guns and 4 x 7 pdr howitzers. **Hanoverian** 8 guns. Pioniers (1 coy).

1st Small Column Gen Count Colloredo commanding: **Austrian Troops** IRs Beaulieu Nr 31, Splényi Nr 51 and Colloredo Nr 56 (1 bn each); HusR Esterházy Nr 32 (2 sqns). **Hanoverian Troops** IR Nr 5 (2 bns); 5th and 7th CavRs (2 sqns) each. **Artillery** 2 x 12 pdr guns.

2nd Small Column GM Otto commanding (all Austrian troops). IRs EH Carl Nr 3 and Deutschmeister Nr 4 (1 bn each); KürR Zeschwitz Nr 10 (6 sqns); HusR Barco Nr 35 (4 sqns); UlR (2 sqns). **Artillery** 2 x 12 pdr and 4 x 6 pdr guns, 2 x 7 pdr howitzers.

Allied totals ca 53,000 men.

Allied losses ca 1,100 killed, wounded and missing: **Hanoverian losses** 22 killed, 61 wounded. **Austrian losses** 32 officers and 1,000 men.

Sources Chuquet, Ditfurth, Dohna, Bodart, Sichart, Witzleben, Fortescue.

XX Fontenay-le-Comte, 25 May 1793, battle

A town in the French Département de la Vendée, 100 km southeast of Nantes, at the junction of Routes N148 and D938; 50 km northwest of La Rochelle.

A Royalist victory over the Republicans.

(This was the first action in 1793; next action - Saumur, 11 June).

Republican Forces GdD Chalbos commanding. 14,000 men

Republican losses 4,000 men, 40 guns.

Royalist Forces Marquis de Lescure and 35,000 Vendéens

Royalist losses 1,000 men.

Sources Bodart, Schulz.

FP Fort les Bains, 23 May - 3 June 1793, bombardment and surrender

An outwork to the north of Fort Bellegarde in southeastern France between Le Boulou on the River Tech and the Spanish border. Just off motorway 9/E15.

A Spanish victory over the French.

(Last action - Mas d'Eu, 19 May; next action - Fort de la Garde, 5 June.)

French Garrison (commander unknown) - ca 350 men

French losses All captured.

Spanish Forces Capt Gen Ricardo commanding: exact details and losses unknown but including the émigré 'Bataillon Vallespir' who fought well.

Comment The fort surrendered after a bombardment from 16 guns was opened up at 1,200 paces range on 30 May. A French resupply convoy of 3,350 men was repulsed on 29 May.

Source Schulz.

FP Fort de la Garde, 5 June 1793, surrender

An outwork to the north of Fort Bellegarde in southeastern France between Le Boulou on the River Tech and the Spanish border. Just off motorway 9/E15.

A Spanish victory over the French.

(Last action - Fort les Bains, 23 May - 3 June; next action - Fort Bellegarde, 23 May - 24 June.)

French Garrison (commander unknown) 200 men

French losses All captured.

Spanish Forces Capt Gen Ricardo commanding.

Spanish totals and losses Unknown.

Comment The Spanish cut off the fort's water supply forcing the surrender and hastening the fall of Fort Bellegarde.

Source Schulz.

IN Saorgio (l'Aution), 8 June 1793, 1st clash

A village in the mountains of the southern French Département des Alpes Maritimes, on the River Roja, 40 km northeast of Nice on Route N204/E72.

A French victory over the Austro-Sardinians.

(Last action - Levens, 28 February; next action - 2nd Saorgio, 12 June.)

French Forces GdD Brunet commanding part of the Armée d'Italie. Exact details not known.

Sardinian Forces IRs Saluzzo, Sardegna, Lombardia; 1st and 3rd Gren Bns, LtI Légion, Cacciatore di Canale, R di Cacciatori (2 bns); Corpo Franco (2 coys). Provincial IRs di Vercelli, di Casale, di Acqui; Swiss IR Christ (2 bns each)

Sardinian totals 10 bns, 6 coys.

Sardinian losses Not known.

Sources Brancaccio, Schulz.

UR Arlon, 9 June 1793, clash

The capital town of the Belgian province of Luxembourg, 5 km west of the Luxembourg border, on Route N81/E25.

A French victory over the Austrians.

(Last action - Alsheim, 30 March; next action - Mainz, 23 July.)

French Forces GdD Delaage commanding part of the Armée de la Moselle. Exact details not known.

French totals 8,500 infantry, 1,000 cavalry.

French losses ca 900 killed and wounded.

Austrian Forces GM Schröder commanding IRs d'Alton Nr 15 (1st Bn); de Vins Nr 37 (3rd Bn); Franz Kinsky Nr 47 (3 bns); J Jellačič Nr 53 (3rd Bn); Murray Nr 55 (1 bn); ChLR Kinsky Nr 7 (6 sqns) and 2 other sqns

Austrian totals 7 bns, 8 sqns, ca 6,000 men.

Austrian losses 600 killed, wounded and captured, 5 guns, 4 ammunition waggons.

Sources Chuquet, Bodart, Schulz, Wrede.

XX Saumur, 11 June 1793, clash

A town in the French Département du Maine-et-Loire, on the left bank of the River Loire, 110 km east of Nantes on Route N147.

A Vendéen Royalist victory over the Republicans.

(Last action - Fontenay-le-Comte, 25 May; next action - Nantes, 29 June.)

Republican Forces GdB Menou commanding ca 8,000 men

Republican losses Not exactly known, light.

Sources Bodart, Schulz.

IN Saorgio (Cima di Raus), 12 June 1793, 2nd clash

A village in the southern French Département des Alpes Maritimes, on the River Roja, 40 km northeast of Nice, on the Route N204/E72.

An Austro-Sardinian victory over the French.

(Last action - 1st Saorgio, 8 June; next action - Epierre, 15 September.)

French Forces GdD Brunet commanding part of the Armée d'Italie. Exact details not known.

Sardinian Forces IRs Saluzzo, Sardegna, Lombardia, 1st, 3rd and 5th Gren Bns, R di Cacciatore, Provincial IRs di Casale and di Acqui; Swiss IR Christ.

Sardinian totals 10 bns.

Sardinian losses Not known.

Sources Brancaccio, Schulz.

FP Bellegarde, 23 May - 24 June 1793, siege and capture

A fortress in the southern French Département des Pyrénées Orientales, 30 km south of Perpignan, in the mountains beside Route 9 into Spain.

A Spanish victory over the French.

(Last action - Fort de la Garde, 5 June; next action - Niel, 17 July.)

French Garrison Col Boisbrulé commanding 1,536 men, 41 guns and 7 mortars. On 3 June the outwork Fort les Bains surrendered with 350 men and on 5 June Fort la Garde surrendered with 200 men

French losses 30 killed, 56 wounded, 1,450 captured.

Spanish Forces Capt Gen Don Ricardo commanding 6,000 men and 34 guns

Spanish losses Not known.

Sources Chuquet, Beaulac.

XX Nantes, 29 June 1793, battle

The capital of the French Département du Loire-Inférieure, at the estuary of the River Loire into the Bay of Biscay, on Routes N165/E60, N137/E3 and N149/E62.

A Republican victory over the Vendéen Royalists.

(Last action - Saumur, 11 June; next action - Châtillon-sur-Sèvre, 5 July.)

Republican Forces GdD Canclaux commanding: 12,000 men

Republican losses ca 2,000 killed and wounded.

Royalist Forces Cathelineau commanding 38,000 men

Royalist losses Cathelineau killed, 5,000 killed, wounded and missing.

Sources Chuquet.

XX Châtillon-sur-Sèvre, 5 July 1793, clash

A town in the French Département des Deux-Sèvres, 70 km southeast of Nantes, near Mauléon on Routes N149/E62 on modern maps.

A victory of the Vendéen Royalists over the Republicans.

(Last action - Nantes, 29 June; next action - Vihiers, 18 July.)

Republican Forces GdD Westermann commanding: 20,000 men

Republican losses 5,000 killed and wounded; GdB Chambon and GdB Lecomte killed.

Royalist Forces Marquis de la Roche-Jacquelin commanding 20,000 men

Royalist losses ca 2,000 killed, wounded and missing.

Sources Schulz, Fervel.

NL Condé, 8 April - 12 July 1793, blockade and capitulation

A fortified town in the northern French Département du Nord, on the River Schelde, 13 km northeast of Valenciennes.

An Allied victory over the French.

(Last action - Famars, 23 May; next action - Valenciennes, 27 July.)

French Garrison GdB Chancel commanding: 4 bns, 4 coys, 8 sqns

French total 4,300 men.

French losses killed and wounded not known; the rest marched out with honours of war, laid down their arms and went into captivity. 103 guns and all the colours and standards were taken.

Allied Forces FML Prince of Württemberg commanding:

Austrian Troops IRs d'Alton Nr 15 and Joseph Colloredo Nr 57 (1 bn each); 2 composite bns of IRs Murray Nr 55, de Ligne Nr 30, Vierset Nr 58 and Württemberg Nr 38; Tyroler Scharfschützen (4 coys); HusRs Saxe* and Berching*; CavR Royale Allemand* (2 sqns each); KürR Kavanagh Nr 12 (2 sqns)
Austrian totals ca 6,000 men.
Austrian losses Not known, light.
* = French Émigré troops.
Sources Chuquet, Fortescue, Bodart, Wrede.

FP Niel, 17 July 1793, skirmish
A village in the southern French Département des Pyrénées Orientales, 15 km south of Perpignan; not marked on many modern maps.
A French victory over the Spanish.
(Last action – Bellegarde, 24 June; next action – Puigcerda, 28 August.)
French Forces GdD de Flers commanding.
French total 12,000 men.
French losses 800 killed and wounded, 1 gun. 600 men deserted and two bns GdN were disbanded for trying to surrender en masse.
Spanish Forces Capt Gen Don Ricardo commanding.
Spanish total 15,000 men.
Spanish losses 31 killed, 131 wounded, 3 captured.
Sources Beaulac, Fervel.

XX Vihiers, 18 July, 1793 clash
A village in the western French Département du Maine-et-Loire, 35 km south of Angers, at the junction of Routes 25, 960 and 748, between Saumur and Cholet.
A Vendéen Royalist victory over the Republicans.
(Last action – Châtillon-sur-Sèvre, 5 July; next action – Lucon, 14 August.)
Republican Forces GdD Santerre commanding.
Republican total 14,000 men and 30 guns.
Republican losses 2,000 killed and wounded, 3,000 captured, 25 guns.
Royalist Forces Piron commanding ca 12,000 men
Royalist losses ca 1,000 killed and wounded.
Sources Bodart, Schulz.

UR Mainz, 10 April – 23 July 1793, siege and capitulation
A city in Germany, on the west bank of the Rhine, just north of the confluence with the River Main.
An Allied victory over the French.
(Last action – Arlon, 9 June; next action – Kettricher Hof, 20 August.)
French Garrison, GdD d'Oyre commanding 32e RIdLi (1 bn); 57e RIdLi (2 bns); 62e RIdLi (1 bn); 82e RIdLi (1 bn); 16e Bn Chasseurs (1 bn); Grenadiers (6 coys); Chasseurs Républicains (1er Bn); Légion des francs (5 coys); Grenadiers de l'Ardèche (1 bn); Grenadiers de Rhône-et-Loire (1 bn); Chasseurs de Rhône-et-Loire (1 bn); GdN Fédérés Nationeaux (1er Bn); Amis de la République (1er Bn); Calvados (4e and 6e Bns); Eure (5e Bn); Meurthe (10e Bn); Nièvre (3e Bn); Seine-et-Oise (2e Bn); Vosges (3e, 7e, 8e and 13e Bns); Ain (2e Bn); Jura (2e, 3e, 5, and 9e Bns); Bas-Rhin (1e, 5e and 6e Bns); Haute-Saône (2e, 9e, 10e, 11e, 12e Bns); 14e CavR 'Royal Piemont' (3 sqns); 7e ChàCh (4 sqns); detachments of the 2e, 8e and 10e ChàCh; cavalry of la Légion des francs (2 coys); 5e Artillery Regt; 2e Artillery Regt (HA Coy). Artillery Coy de Paris.
Total strength at the start of the siege 23,000 men with 312 guns. French losses 4,000 men dead and wounded (including GdD Blou de Chadenac and Meusnier de la Place, both killed). 18,675 men surrendered and were allowed to march off to France on condition that they did not fight against the allies for one year; they were at once sent to fight the French Royalists in the Vendée.
Allied Forces FM Duke of Brunswick commanding
Prussian Contingent Duke of Sachsen-Weimar KürR Sachsen-Weimar Nr 6 (5 sqns). **GL von Wolframsdorf** IR 'Wegner' Nr 30 (3 bns); IR 'Manstein' Nr 9 (3 bns); IR 'Thadden' Nr 3 (3 bns); IR Garde Nr 15 (3 bns). **Totals** 12 bns, 5 sqns. **GM von Kleist** IR 'Wolframsdorf' Nr 37 (2 bns); IR 'Vietinghof' Nr 38 (2 bns); IR 'Schladen' Nr 41 (3 bns). **Totals** 7 bns. **GM von Vietinghof** Gren Bn, Vietinghof (1 bn); IR Borcke Nr 49 (3 bns); IR Crousaz Nr 39 (3 bns); KürR Borstelll Nr 7 (5 sqns). **Obst von Rüchel** Füs Bn Thadden (1 bn); Füs Bn Legat (1 bn); Gren Bn Wolframsdorf (1 bn).
Prussian totals 29 bns, 10 sqns.
Austrian Contingent FML von Bruchlag. **Obst Graf von Heister** IR Gemmingen Nr 21 (2 bns); IR Bender Nr 41 (2 bns); IR Manfredini Nr 12 (2 bns); IR Wartensleben Nr 28 (1 bn); IR d'Alton Nr 15 (1 bn); IR Stuart Nr 18 (1 bn); IR Schröder Nr 26 (1 bn); HusR Wurmser Nr 30 (6 sqns); DragR Erzherzog Joseph Nr

26 (4 sqns). **Totals** 10 bns, 10 sqns, 6,000 men.

Saxon Contingent GL von Lind Gren Bn Christiani (1 bn); IR Churfürst Nr 1 (1 bn); IR Prinz Anton Nr 2 (1 bn); IR Prinz Clemens Nr 6 (1 bn); IR Sachsen-Gotha Nr 11 (1 bn); HusR Süssmilch (1 sqn); Karabiniers R (4 sqns); ChLR Kurland (4 sqns). **Totals** 5 bns, 9 sqns.

Contingent of Hessen-Kassel GL von Biesenrodt Garde-Gren-R (2 bns); Leib-R (2 bns); Gren-Bn Dinklage (1 bn); Leib-DragR (5 sqns). **Totals** 5 bns, 5 sqns.

Contingent of Hessen-Darmstadt Landgraf Ludwig X Leib-R (2 bns); IR Landgraf (1 bn); Leibgrenadier-Bns (2 bns); Jägers (¼ bn); ChLR (3 sqns). **Totals** 5¼ bns, 3 sqns.

Contingent of Kurpfalz-Bayern Combined IR (2 bns); combined Jäger-Bn (1 bn). **Total** 3 bns.

Allied totals 57¼ bns, 37 sqns, 36,850 men.

Allied losses 3,000 dead and wounded including GM von Wegner and 120 other officers.

Sources Ditfurth, Schulz, Wrede, Jany.

NL Valenciennes, 25 May – 27 July 1793, siege and storm

A fortified town in the northern French Département du Nord, on the River Schelde, 51 km southeast of Lille, 20 km south of the Belgian border.

An Allied victory over the French.

(Last action – Condé, 12 July; next action – Caesar's Camp, 7 August.)

French Garrison GdB Ferrand commanding:

29e RIdLi (2 bns); 73e and 87e RIdLi (1 bn each); GdN: Grenadiers de Paris (1er Bn); Deux-Sèvres (1er Bn); Seine-Inférieure (1er Bn); Eure (2e Bn); Parement de Valenciennes (2e Bn); Grenadiers de la Côte-d'Or (1 bn); Côte-d'Or (1er Bn); Loire-et-Cher (1er Bn); Charente (1er Bn); Mayenne-et-Loire (1er Bn); Nièvre (1er Bn); Gravilliers (1er Bn); Ardennes (4e Bn); 25e and 26e CavRs (1 sqn each); companies from 1er and 3e Artillery Rs; and of the Volunteer Artillery of Valenciennes (4 coys); Douay (1 coy) and Paris (8 coys)

French totals 17 bns, 2 sqns, 800 gunners: 9,000 men.

French losses 1,000 killed and died of sickness; the garrison marched out with honours of war and were released on condition that they did not fight against the Allies for one year.

Allied Forces HRH The Duke of York commanding:

English troops Grenadiers, 1st, 2nd and 3rd Foot Guards and Guards Flank Bn (1 bn each); 1st/14th, 1st/53rd Foot (1 bn each); 11th, 15th and 16th LDRs (2 sqns each).

English totals 7 bns, 6 sqns.

Austrian troops Walloon Freikorps: IRs Wartensleben Nr 28, Splényi Nr 51, Jordis Nr 59; Beaulieu Nr 31 (1 bn each); IRs M Wallis Nr 11, von Brentano Nr 35, and Brechainville Nr 25 (2 bns each); KürR Zeschwitz Nr 10 (6 sqns); HusR Blankenstein Nr 16 (2 sqns).

Austrian totals 11 bns, 8 sqns.

Hanoverian troops 1st Inf Bde GM von Diepenbroick: Garde (2 bns); Gren Bns Drieberg and Heimbruch (2 bns). 2nd Inf Bde GM von Hammerstein: IRs Bothmer Nr 4, Hammerstein Nr 6 and Taube Nr 11 (2 bns each). 3rd Inf Bde Obst von Klinkowström: IRs Hohorst Nr 5 and Diepenbroick Nr 10 (2 bns each); Gren Bn Wense (1 bn); LDRs Königin Nr 9 and Prinz von Wallis Nr 10 (2 sqns each).

1st Cavalry Bde GM von Dachenhausen: Leib-Garde and KürR Prinz Ernst Nr 2 (2 sqns each): 2nd Cavalry Brigade GM Graf von Oyenhausen: DragRs Ramdohr Nr 5 and Oyenhausen Nr 7 (2 sqns each). 3rd Cavalry Bde GM von dem Busche: KürRs Leib Nr 1 and von dem Busche Nr 4 (2 sqns each).

Hanoverian totals 15 bns, 16 sqns.

Allied totals 33 bns, 30 sqns.

Allied losses 1,300 killed and wounded.

Comment The populace of the town attacked the garrison as it left and hoisted the Bourbon colours over the city.

Sources Bodart, Chuquet, Schulz, Wrede, Fortescue, Sichart.

NL Caesar's Camp, 7 August 1793

An area in northern France, just northeast of Cambrai (at the crossing of Routes N42, N43 and N44, bounded by the Rivers Schelde, Sensée and Agache and the wood of Bourlon.

An Allied victory over the French.

(Last action – Valenciennes, 27 July; next action – Lincelles, 18 August.)

French Forces Gen Kilmaine commanding part of the Armée du Nord with reinforcements from the Armée du Rhin: 12e RILé (1 bn); 8e and 10e ChàCh, 11e DragR (3 sqns each) and 2 x HAB. The Armée de la Moselle sent Gen Pully and his corps from

Forbach. Other units were as follows: At Mouveaux: Légion Belgiques (2 bns); six Free Companies, 1 bn Volontaires, GdN Tourcoing (1ère Cie); Seine-Inférieure (10e Bn); 13e CavR (1 sqn); 1er HusR (1 sqn). At Wasquehal: GdN Somme (3e Bn); Grenadiers de Calvados (1ère Cie); Finistère (1ère Cie); Pas de Calais (½ coy); 13e ChàCh (½ sqn); 10e Hus (1 sqn). At Marque: Volontaires (10e Bn); 13e ChàCh (½ sqn). At Lazaro: 8e Free Bn (1 bn). At Wambrechis: GdN Pas de Calais (2e Bn). At Fives: GdN Loire (1er Bn); 6e DragR (½ sqn). At Barque bridge: Bataves (2 coys); ChàCh Bataves (2 sqns); Cie de Clemendo (1 coy). At Fleers: Liègeois (1er Bn); Cie Polytechnique (1 coy); GdN Gironde (1 bn); Paris (2 bns); 13e CavR, 3e DragR (½ sqn each). At the Château of M Dussart: Volontaires (13e Bn). At Helmes: GdN Loire-et-Cherie (2e Bn); Nationales (27e Bn); 3e DragR (½ sqn). At Marquelle: 9e RIdLi (1 bn). In Magdelaine suburb - 3e DragR (½ sqn). At Lincelles: GdN Côte-d'Or (1er Bn); Finistère (2e Bn). At Blaton: 12e RIdLi (2 coys); GdN ? (12e and 14e Bns). At Comines: GdN Lyons (2e and 4e Bns); 13e ChàCh (½ sqn). At Dierlemont: GdN Loire (1er Bn); 4e Bn Bataves (1 bn). At the Dierlemont locks: 15e RIdLi (1 bn). In the Invalides suburb: 52 dragoons, 12 cavalrymen. At Pont-à-Marque: 2,100 men. In Haubourdin, Lantes and Warnies - 200 infantry.

French totals 25,435 men.

French losses Killed and wounded not known; assumed light as the French withdrew before the blow fell. Two infantry battalions at Marquion were cut off by English cavalry and surrendered but Kilmaine brought up his entire cavalry and set them free again.

Allied Forces FM Prince Josias of Coburg commanding.

1st Column HRH The Duke of York. **English troops** 1st Brigade, GM Lake: 1st, 2nd and 3rd Foot Guards, Guards' Flank Bn (1 bn each), 1 x FAB. 2nd Brigade, GM Abercromby: 1/14th, 1/37th, 1/53rd Foot, Flank Bn (1 bn each), 1 x FAB; Cavalry GM Dundas: 11th, 15th and 16th LD (2 sqns each). **Hanoverian troops** Garde, 5th, 10th and 11th IRs (2 bns each); Leibgarde, 1st, 2nd, 4th and 5th CavRs (2 sqns each). **Total** 8 bns, 10 sqns, 1 x HAB, 2 x FABs.

2nd Column Austrian Troops FZM Count Colloredo; FML Terzy, GM Czernetzy: IRs Jordis Nr 59 and Murray Nr 55 (2 bns each); GM Hutton; IRs Stein Nr 50 and J Colloredo Nr 57 (2 bns each). FML Lilien, GM Prince Lothringen: DragR Coburg Nr 37 (6 sqns); CavR Royal Allemande* (2 sqns); KürR Nassau Nr 14; GM Borus HusR Barco Nr 35 (6 sqns each); Gz Scharfschützen (1 bn).

3rd Column FZM Count Clerfayt, FML Allvintzy, Prince Carl Auersperg: Grenadiers (11 bns); GM Otto: Gz Scharfschützen (1 bn); GzIR (1 bn); HusR Esterházy Nr 32 (8 sqns). Obst Prince Liechtenstein: ChLR Kinsky Nr 7 (6 sqns); ChLR Lobkowitz Nr 28 (2 sqns). 1 x 12 pdr FAB.

Allied totals 41 bns, 58 sqns, ca 43,000 men.

Allied losses Not exactly known, light. The French slipped away south without fighting seriously.

* = French Émigré unit.

Sources Bodart, Chuquet, Sichart, Witzleben, Ditfurth, Fortescue.

XX Lucon, 14 August, 1793 battle

A town in the western French Département de la Vendée, 28 km west of Fontenay-le-Comte, on Route 949, north of La Rochelle.

A Republican victory over the Vendéen Royalists.

(Last action - Vihiers, 18 July; next action - Chantonnay, 5 September.)

Republican Forces GdD Tuncq commanding 10,000 men.

Republican losses ca 500 killed and wounded.

Royalist Forces Gigot d'Elbée commanding 35,000 men and 17 guns

Royalist losses ca 5,000 killed, wounded and missing, 17 guns.

Sources Schulz.

NL Lincelles, 18 August 1793, clash

A village in the French Département du Nord, about 10 km west of Tourcoing and 13 km north of Lille.

An English victory over the French.

(Last action - Caesar's Camp, 7 August; next action - Rexpoede and Oost Cappel, 21 August.)

French Forces GdB Jourdan commanding. Exact details not known.

French totals 5,000 men, 12 guns.

French losses killed and wounded ca 600, 70 captured, 12 guns and limbers, 1 colour.

Dutch Forces The Prince of Orange: IRs Nassau and Waldeck (2 bns each).

English Forces Gen Lake commanding 1st, 2nd and 3rd Foot Guards.

English totals 3 bns, 1,100 men.

English losses 38 killed, 143 wounded.

Dutch losses Unknown.

Comment The Prince of Orange first attacked Lincelles and Blaton on his own; drove out the French and took 10 guns. A French counter-attack retook Lincelles. The Prince asked the Duke of York for help and then withdrew his forces. The Guards, unsupported, finally secured Lincelles.

Sources Fortescue, Ditfurth, Sichart, Chuquet.

UR Kettricher Hof, 20 August 1793, clash

A village on a hilltop about 8 km south of Pirmasens in southwestern Germany on the side road to Bitche.

A Prussian victory over the French.

(Last action – Mainz, 23 July; next action – Weissenburg Lines, 20 August.)

French Garrison GdB Lagoublaye commanding: 96e and 102e RIdLi (1 bn each); GdN la Manche (3e); Meurthe (9e); Compagnie franches des Bons Tireurs (1 coy); 4e CavR (4 sqns); 3 x 8 pdr guns, 1 mortar

French totals 4 bns, 1 coy, 4 sqns, 4 guns, ca 3,200 men.

French losses Killed and wounded not known, light, 3 guns, 3 limbers, all the baggage.

Prussian Forces Fussjägers; KürR von Borstell Nr 7; DragR Lottum Nr 2; HusR von Wolffradt Nr 6

Prussian total ca 1,900 men.

Prussian losses None.

Comment The French garrison fled at the first shot without putting up any resistance. By taking this post, the Prussians had cut communications between the French armies of the Rhine and of the Moselle.

Sources KGE Heft 16, Chuquet, Schulz, Jany.

UR Weissenburg Lines, 20 August 1793, 1st skirmish

A series of earthworks along the south side of the River Lauter, a western tributary of the River Rhine. Nowadays the border between Germany and France (Alsace-Lorraine).

An Allied victory over the French.

(Last action – Kettricher-Hof, 20 August; next action – Pirmasens, 14 September.)

French Forces GdB Illier commanding part of the Armée des Vosges (Gen Moreau): 3 bns, 6 sqns, 10 guns

French total ca 3,000 men.

French losses Killed and wounded unknown. GdB Illier killed by a Hessian Jäger, 3 officers and 100 men captured; 5 guns, 6 ammunition waggons.

Allied Forces FM Count Wurmser commanding (for full details see Weissenburg Lines, 13 October 1793)

4th Column FML Kavanagh **Hessen-Kassel troops** HusR (3 sqns); Jägers (2 coys); LtI Bn Lenz (2 coys). **Austrian troops** HusR EH Leopold Nr 17 (6 sqns); Seresaner (2 coys); IR Gyulai Nr 32 (1 bn); Freikorps Gyulai (1 bn); IR O Wallis Nr 29 (2 bns); DragR Kaiser Nr 3 (4 sqns). **French Émigré troops** IR Noble (1 bn); 1 x 12 pdr FAB. **Totals** 5 bns, 6 coys, 13 sqns, 12 guns. **Losses** 147 killed, wounded and missing.

Comment There followed a series of clashes and skirmishes along these lines on 21 and 27 August; 7, 11, 12, 14, 19, 20, 23 and 30 September, culminating in the major, successful Allied assault on 13 October.

Sources Chuquet, Ditfurth, von Baumbach, Wrede.

NL Rexpoede and Oost-Cappel, 21 August 1793, clash

Two villages in northern France, about 15 km southeast of Dunkirk on the English Channel coast just by the Belgian border, on Route N308.

An Allied victory over the French.

(Last action – Lincelles, 18 August; next action – Rosendael, 24 August.)

French Garrison Oost-Cappel; GdN Rhône (5e Bn); Somme (5e Bn); 4 guns, ca 1,600 men. Rexpoede: GdN Orne (1er Bn) under Maj Jacques Fromentin and 4 guns.

French totals 3 bns, ca 2,200 men and 8 guns.

French losses 150 killed and wounded, 150 captured, 1 colour, 11 guns (other units became involved in the fighting).

Allied Forces GL Freytag's Avantgarde; Obst Prüschenk commanding: Hanoverian Gren Bn (1 bn); Hessen-Kassel Jägers (2 coys); Grün-Laudon Freikorps (2 coys); 9th Hanoverian LDR (2 sqns); 1 x light 6 pdr FAB. **Dutch Forces** The Prince of Orange: IRs Nassau and Waldeck (2 bns each)

Allied totals 5 bns, 4 coys, 2 sqns, 1 x FAB, ca 5,200 men.

Allied losses Not known, very light.

Comment The 1er de l'Orne were raw new levies and fled, abandoning their commander.
Sources Fortescue, Ditfurth, Sichart, Chuquet.

NL Rosendael, 24 August 1793 clash
A village near the north French coast, about 2 km southeast of the Channel port of Dunkirk, just off Route E40.
An Allied victory over the French.
(Last action – Rexpoede and Oost Cappel, 21 August; next action – Cysoing, 28 August.)
French Forces Part of Dunkirk garrison, exact details not known
French totals ca 5,000 men.
French losses Not known, moderate.
Allied Forces GL von Wurmb commanding: 1st, 2nd and 3rd Foot Guards, Guards' Flank Bn (1 bn each). Austrians IRs J Colloredo Nr 57, Brentano Nr 35, W Colloredo Nr 56, Jordis Nr 59 (2 bns each) and Stuart Nr 18 (1 bn).
Allied totals ca 8,000 men.
Allied losses Light.
Sources Fortescue, Ditfurth, Sichart, Chuquet, Schulz.

NL Cysoing (Wervicq), 28 August 1793, clash
A village in western Belgium, close to the French border, on the River Lys, 6 km southeast of Menin.
An Austrian victory over the French.
(Last action – Rosendael, 24 August; next action – Hondschoote, 6 –8 September.)
French Forces Gen Dumesny commanding. Exact details not known.
French totals ca 8,000 men, 12 guns.
French losses Exact details not known.
Austrian Garrison FML Beaulieu commanding: IRs Württemberg Nr 38 and Clerfayt Nr 9 (2 bns each); Le Loup Jägers (1 bn); KürR Kavanagh Nr 12 (4 sqns)
Austrian totals 5 bns, 4 sqns, ca 5,000 men.
Austrian losses Not exactly known but very light.
Sources Chuquet, Wrede.

FP Puigcerda, 28 August 1793, clash
A small mountain town in the eastern Spanish Pyrenees, on Route 1313, just east of the Republic of Andorra.
A French victory over the Spanish.
(Last action – Niel, 17 July; next action – Peyrestortes, 17 September.)
French Forces Gen Dagobert with 6,500 men.
French losses Not known.
Spanish Forces Gen La Peña with 3 bns and 3 sqns
Spanish losses 19 officers and 346 men captured; other losses not known.
Sources Beaulac, Ferreira.

XX Chantonnay, 5 September 1793, clash
A town in the western French Département de la Vendée, 30 km east of La Roche-sur-Yon, just east of Route N137/E3.
A Vendéen Royalist victory over the Republicans.
(Last action – Lucon, 14 August; next action – Coron, 18 September.)
Republican Forces GdD Lecomte commanding 8,000 men
Republican losses ca 4,000 killed, wounded and missing.
Royalist Forces Gigot d'Elbée commanding 20,000 men
Royalist losses ca 500 killed, wounded and missing.
Sources Bodart, Schulz.

NL Hondschoote, 6–8 September, 1793 battle
A village in northern France, about 15 km southeast of Dunkirk on the English Channel coast, on a minor road running parallel to the Belgian border.
A French victory over the Allies.
(Last action – Cysoing, 28 August; next action – Dunkirk, 8 September.)
French Forces GdD Houchard's Armée du Nord. The columns of Generals Vandamme (3,600 men); Hédouville's Avantgarde (10,000); Jourdan's Corps de Bataille (10,000); Dumesny's Right Wing (9,000); Landrin's Left Wing (6,000) and Leclaire's Reserve (4,000).
French totals 42,600 men of these, Hédouville's 10,000 and Jourdan's 10,000 assaulted Hondschoote itself.
French losses ca 3,000 killed and wounded overall, losses at Hondschoote not exactly known.
Allied Forces LG Freytag commanding: Cavalry: Leibgarde, 1st, 2nd, 4th, 5th, 7th CavR, 9th and 10th LDRs (2 sqns each); Infantry: 1st, 2nd and 3rd Gren Bns, Garde, 4th, 5th, 6th, 10th, 11th IRs (2 bns each). **Austrian troops** IR Brentano Nr 35 (1 bn), Freikorps Grün-Laudon (1 bn). **Hessen-Kassel troops** IR Erbprinz (2 bns). **Dutch troops** Prince of Orange commanding 4 bns.

Allied totals 16 sqns, 23 bns, 12 guns, ca 17,500 men.

Allied losses 15 officers, 211 men killed; 52 officers, 1,092 men wounded, 28 officers, 933 men missing, 6 guns and 2 colours (5th IR). These were about 30% of the men involved. Gen Freytag was captured and wounded but then rescued. Austrian and Hessian losses not known but considerable.

Comment This three-day battle ended the siege of Dunkirk and was one of the first occasions on which the swarms of French skirmishers beat troops in line.

Sources Bodart, Fortescue, Chuquet, Sichart, Ditfurth.

NL Dunkirk, 24 August – 8 September 1793, failed siege

A fortified French port on the English Channel, between Calais and the Belgian border.

A French victory over the Allies.

(Last action – Hondschoote, 6–8 September; next action – Ypres, 8–9 September.)

French Garrison GdB Souham commanding.

French total 10,000 men.

French losses ca 1,000 killed and wounded, 14 guns, 2 mortars, 6 ammunition waggons, 17 colours and 3 standards.

Allied Forces FM HRH The Duke of York commanding:

British troops Gen Erskine, Gen Abercromby. 1st, 2nd and 3rd Foot Guards, Guards' Flank Bn, 1st/14th, 1st/37th, 1st/53rd, Flank Bn, Loyal Emigrants (1 bn each); Horse Guards (Blues), 1st (Royal) DragR, 2nd DragR (Greys); 2nd Drag Gds, 3rd Drag Gds, 6th Drag Gds (Inniskillings); 7th, 11th, 15th and 16th LDRs (2 sqns each).

Hanoverian troops GL von Freytag: 1st Bde: GM von Diepenbroick: Garde (2 bns); 2nd and 3rd Gren Bns. 2nd Bde GM von Hammerstein: 4th, 6th and 11th IR (2 bns each). 3rd Brigade: Obst von Klinkowström: 5th and 10th IRs (2 bns each), 1st Gren Bn. 1st Cavalry Bde: GM von Dachenhausen: Leibgarde, 2nd CavR (2 sqns each); 2nd Cavalry Bde: GM Graf von Oyenhausen: 5th and 7th CavRs (2 sqns each); 3rd Cavalry Bde: GM von dem Busche: 1st and 4th CavR, 9th and 10th LDRs (8 sqns).

Austrian troops FML Allvintzy: IRs Brentano Nr 35, J Colloredo Nr 57, W Colloredo Nr 56, Jordis Nr 59 (2 bns each); Stuart Nr 18, Sztáray Nr 33, Grün-Laudon, O'Donnell Freikorps (1 bn each); Jägers (2 coys); ChLR Karaczay Nr 18 (6 sqns); HusR Blankenstein Nr 16 (2 sqns).

Hessen-Kassel troops GL von Buttlar: Gren Bn Eschwege, Gren Bn Wurmb (1 bn each); IRs Kospoth, Prinz Carl, Lossberg, Erbprinz (2 bns each); Jägers (2 coys); Gendarmes, Carabiniers (3 sqns each); DragR Prinz Friedrich (5 sqns).

Allied totals 29,700 infantry, 5,400 cavalry, artillery not known.

Allied losses ca 2,000 men killed and wounded, 32 heavy guns. Austrian FML Count d'Alton was killed.

Comment The detachment of this Allied force (at British government insistence) to this strategically insignificant 'blockade' (Dunkirk's sea side remained open throughout) sabotaged any hope of defeating the French field armies in the Netherlands for this year and for many to come.

Sources Chuquet, Bodart, Fortescue, Ditfurth, Sichart, Wrede.

NL Ypres, 8–9 September 1793, clash

A fortified town in the Belgian province of West Flanders, on Route N8, midway between Ostende and Lille.

An Allied victory over the French.

(Last action – Dunkirk, 8 September; next action – Avesnes-le-Sec, 12 September.)

French Forces Part of the Armée du Nord; exact details not known.

French totals ca 15,000 men.

French losses Not known, moderate.

Allied Garrison Austrian Obst von Salis commanding: IR Stuart Nr 18 (2 bns); Freikorps O'Donnell (1 coy); 1 x FAB. **Hessen-Kassel troops** IRs Erbprinz, Prinz Karl and Lossberg (2 bns each); Gensd'armes (1 sqn); Hanoverian tps: Gards and 4th IR (1st Bns each); 10 LDR (2 sqns)

Allied total ca 12,000 men.

Allied losses Not known, light.

Sources Ditfurth, Sichart, Wrede.

NL Avesnes-le-Sec, 12 September 1793, clash

A village in the northern French Département du Nord, 6 km south of Bouchain.

An Austrian victory over the French.

(Last action – Ypres, 8–9 September; next action – Werwik, 13 September.)

French Forces GdB Claye (or Declaye) commanding.

Exact details not known but including the 10e HusR, 10e ChàCh and the Ch de Versailles

French totals 7,000 infantry, 4 sqns cavalry, 20 guns.

French losses 2,000 killed and wounded, 2,000 captured, 20 guns, 5 colours.

Austrian Forces Obst Prince Liechtenstein commanding: KürR Nassau Nr 5 (2 sqns); ChLR Kinsky Nr 7 (4 sqns); HusR Kaiser Nr 1 (3 sqns); HusR Royal-Allemand (1 sqn)

Austrian totals 2,000 cavalry.

Austrian losses ca 69 men killed and wounded. This was an outstandingly effective cavalry action.

Sources Chuquet, Fortescue, Wrede, Sichart.

NL Werwik, 13 September 1793, clash

A town in the western Belgian province of West Flanders, close to the French Border, 15 km southwest of Courtray, on the River Lys, 6 km southwest of Menin.

A French victory over the Dutch.

(Last action – Avesnes-le-Sec, 12 September; next action – Le Quesnoy, 13 September.)

French Forces GdD Dumesny commanding part of the Armée du Nord. Exact details not known.

French totals ca 30,000 men.

French losses ca 1,500 men. Some of the regiments which distinguished themselves were: GdN Paris (2e Bn); Batave (4e Bn); Gironde (2e) and the 6e ChàCh who took a colour.

Dutch Garrison The Prince of Hessen-Darmstadt commanding: Gren Bns van Buseck, van Tengnagel (1 bn each); IRs van Hirzel, van Gumoens (2 bns each); van Quadt, van Dopff (1 bn each) and five other bns; CavRs Gravemoer (2 sqns); Gardes DragR, Gardes te Paard, Hessen-Kassel (3 sqns each) and van Tuyll (2 sqns). **English troops** Loyal Emigrants (3 coys).

Dutch totals 13 bns, 3 coys, 10 sqns, ca 13,500 men.

Dutch losses Not exactly known but ca 3,100 men, several colours and 40 guns. The Prince of Hessen-Darmstadt was wounded. The Dutch field army was destroyed. There was no French follow up.

Sources Chuquet, Bodart, Schulz, Fortescue.

NL Le Quesnoy, 28 August – 13 September 1793, siege and capture

A fortified town in the northern French Département du Nord, 12 km southwest of Valenciennes.

An Allied victory over the French.

(Last action – Werwik, 13 September; next action – Menin, 12–13 September.)

French Garrison GdB Boulu commanding. Exact details not known.

French totals 5,000 men.

French losses 1,000 killed, others wounded; the rest (4,000) captured.

Allied Forces FZM Count Clerfayt commanding: FML Beaulieu: IRs Beaulieu Nr 31 (1 bn); IRs Klebek Nr 14, EH Carl Nr 3, Erbach Nr 42, Hohenlohe Nr 17, Deutschmeister Nr 4, Toscana Nr 23, Wartensleben Nr 28, M Wallis Nr 29, Stain Nr 50 (2 bns each); Gren Bns Watsch, Ulrich, Sinoth, Ulm, Attems (5 bns); ChLR Latour Nr 31 (4 sqns); HusR Barco Nr 35, HusR Bérchény*; HusR Saxe* (2 sqns each).

Allied totals 24 bns, 10 sqns, ca 18,000 men.

Allied losses 208 killed and wounded.

* = French Émigré regiments.

Sources Witzleben, Chuquet, Wrede.

NL Menin, 12 –13 September 1793, clash

A fortified town on the Franco-Belgian border, on the River Lys and on Routes N8 and N32, about 19 km north of Lille.

A French victory over the Dutch.

(Last action – Le Quesnoy, 13 September; next action – Menin, 15 September.)

French Forces Generals Hédouville and Ledru with two division of the Armée du Nord. Exact details not known

French totals ca 22,000 men.

French losses Not exactly known, light.

Dutch Forces Friedrich, Prince of Orange commanding: Gardes Dragonders, Gaardes te Paard (3 sqns each), Carabiniers, CavRs Orange Vriesland (1 sqn) and van Tuyll (3 sqns), Huz van Heeckeren (3 sqns), Huz van der Hoop (½ sqn), Hollandsche Gardes, Zwitsersche Gaardes, Gren Bns van Breijdenback and van Larreij. IRs 2nd Waldeck, Bedaulx, van Welderen, van Dopff, Gren Bns van Tengnagel, van Raesfeldt, van Rechteren, van Buseck, 5th IR Waldeck, Jagers de Anspachsche, Jagers van Bylandt and Grenadiers and Füsiliers (1 bn each). CavRs Hessen-Kassel and Hessen-Philippsthal (3 sqns each); van Bylandt and van der Duyn (2 sqns each); IRs Orange Gelderland, Nassau-Usingen, Hessen-Darmstadt, van Randwyck, Saxen-Gotha, De Perez,

De Thouars, De Schepper, von Wartensleben, van Brakel, 1st Waldeck, Markgraaf van Baden (1 bn each); IRs Stokkar, Hirzel and May (2 bns each) and Bedaulx (2nd coy)

Dutch totals ca 13,000 infantry, 1,800 cavalry.

Dutch losses 5 generals, 88 officers, 3,000 men killed, wounded and missing, 40 guns, several colours.

Comment The Dutch army was now in tatters and fell back north opening a gap between the Duke of York and Prince Coburg.

Sources Sichart, Schulz, de Bas, Bosscha.

UR Pirmasens, 14 September 1793, clash

A town in the (then) Bavarian Pfalz, 62 km west of Speyer, on Route B10, south of Kaiserslautern.

A Prussian victory over the French.

(Last action – Weissenburg Lines, 20 August; next action – Weissenburg Lines, 13 October.)

French Forces GdD Moreau commanding the 'Corps des Vosges': Left column GdB Lequoy: 9e ChàCh, 14e DragR (6 sqns). Right Column GdB Guillaume: Coy de Guillaume (270 men); 8e RIdLi (2e Bn); GdN Haute-Saône (4e Bn); 30e RIdLi (1er Bn). Centre Column Gen Freytag: GdN République (3e Bn); Observatoire (2e Bn); 3e Louvre; 1er RIdLi (1er Bn); 24e RIdLi (1 bn); 96e RIdLi (1 bn); 102e RIdLi (1 bn); GdN Haute-Saône (6e Bn); Manche (3er and 4e Bns); Moselle (2e Bn); Seine-Inférieure (4e Bn); Yonne (1er Bn-); Meurthe (9e Bn); Chass des Bons-Tireurs (1 coy); 4e CavR (3 sqns).

French totals 34,000 men, 36 guns.

French losses 1,788 killed and captured, 226 wounded, 19 guns, 29 ammunition waggons.

Prussian Forces FM the Duke of Brunswick; GL von Kalckstein: IR Prinz Heinrich Nr 35 (3 bns); IR Braunschweig Nr 19 (3 bns); Garde zu Fuss Nr 15 (2nd and 3rd Bns); GM Prinz zu Baden: IR Schladen Nr 41 (1st Bn); IR Wolframsdorf Nr 37 (2nd Bn); IR Borch Nr 49 (1st Bn); KürR von Borstell Nr 7 (4 sqns); HusR von Wolffradt Nr 6 (2 sqns); DragR Tschirschky Nr 11 (5 sqns), 5 x FAB, 1 x HAB.

Prussian totals 8,000 men and 58 guns.

Prussian losses 167 killed and wounded.

Comments There was no Prussian pursuit of the routed French thus no fruits of this victory were reaped.

Sources KGD Heft 16, Chuquet, Schulz, Jany.

NL Menin, 15 September 1793, skirmish

A fortified town on the Franco-Belgian border, on the River Lys and on Routes N8 and N32, about 19 km north of Lille.

An Allied victory over the French.

(Last action – Menin, 12–13 September; next action – Maubeuge, 16 October.)

French Garrison Gen Daendels commanding: GdN de Paris (1 bn); de la Gironde (1 bn); 21e CavR (1 sqn); 8e RIdLi (1 bn); Légion Belges (1 bn); Bataves (1 bn)

French totals ca 5,000 men.

French losses 400 killed and wounded, 2 guns, 8 limbers, 1 colour.

Allied Forces MG Count Erbach commanding: HusR Esterházy Nr 32 (4 sqns); ChLR Karaczay Nr 18 (2 sqns) and the Hessen-Kassel Regiment, von Lossberg.

Allied totals ca 1,600 men.

Allied losses ca 100 killed, wounded and missing.

Comment The Allies had now plugged the gap in their lines caused by the Dutch defeat here two days before; the French withdrew south to Lille and Cassel. British and Austrian troops occupied Menin and Wervicq.

Sources Chuquet, Wrede, Ditfurth.

IN Epierre, 15 September 1793, clash

A village in the southeastern French province of Savoy, 47 km southeast of Chambéry, in the valley of the River Arc, south of Lac Leman (Lake Geneva).

A French victory over the Sardinians.

(Last action – 2nd Saorgio, 12 June; next action – Gilette, 18 October.)

French Forces GdD Kellermann commanding part of the Armée d'Italie. Exact details not known; see order of battle.

French totals ca 8,000 men.

French losses About 500 men killed and wounded.

Sardinian Forces LG Gordon commanding. Exact details not known.

Sardinian totals ca 6,000 men.

Sardinian losses ca 1,000 killed, wounded and missing.

Sources Schulz, Brancaccio.

FP Peyrestortes, 17 September 1793, clash

A village in the southern French Département des

Pyrénées Orientales, 4 km northwest of Perpignan; not marked on modern maps.

A French victory over the Spanish.

(Last action – Puigcerda, 28 August; next action – Truillas, 22 September.)

French Forces GdB Davout commanding. No details known

French totals ca 8,000 men.

French losses ca 200 men killed and wounded.

Spanish Forces LG de Courten commanding. No details known.

Spanish totals ca 6,000 men.

Spanish losses 52 officers, 1,150 men killed, wounded and missing, 26 guns, 7 colours, 500 captured.

Comment Courten's initial assault on the French camp at Vernet succeeded but Davout's counter attack restored the situation when the Spanish cavalry fled the field.

Sources Beaulac, Fervel.

XX Saint-Fulgent, 22 September 1793, clash

A hamlet in the French Département de la Vendée, 45 km southeast of Nantes, on Route N137/E3.

A Royalist victory over the Republicans.

(Last action – Coron, 18 September; next action – Lyon, 9 October.)

Republican Forces GdB Mieszkowski commanding ca 6,000 men

Republican losses ca 3,000 killed, wounded and missing.

Royalist Forces Marquis de la Roche-Jacquelin commanding ca 11,000 men

Royalist losses ca 300 killed, wounded and missing.

Sources Schulz.

FP Truillas (Mas d'Eu), 22 September 1793, battle

A village in the southern French Département des Pyrénées Orientales, 10 km southwest of Perpignan, where Route 612 crosses the River Tech.

A Spanish victory over the French.

(Last action – Peyrestortes, 17 September; next action – Boulu, 30 October.)

French Forces GdD Dagobert commanding. GdB Goguet and LtCol d'Aoust; Gen Davout. Regiments included the 7e, 61e, 70e and 79 Li and the GdN Gers and Gard.

French total 22,000 men, ? guns.

French losses 3,000 killed and wounded, 1,500 captured, 10 guns. Dagobert reported only 1,500 killed and wounded.

Spanish Forces Capt Gen Don Ricardo commanding; Gen Courten; Gen Crespo, Gen Count de la Union, Gen Godoy. Further details unknown

Spanish totals 17,000 men.

Spanish losses ca 2,000 killed, wounded and missing.

Sources Beaulac, Schulz, Fervel.

FP Boulu, 3 October 1793, skirmish

A village in the southern French Département des Pyrénées Orientales, 22 km southwest of Perpignan, where the River Tech is crossed by Route D9 and A9/E15.

A Spanish victory over the French.

(Last action – Truillas, 22 September; next action – Villelongue, 7 December.)

French Forces GdD Davout commanding. Details unknown

French totals 16,000 men, ? guns.

French losses 400 killed, 800 wounded and 1,500 deserted.

Spanish Forces Capt Gen Don Ricardo commanding; LG Eslava. Further details unknown

Spanish totals 15,000 men, guns.

Spanish losses ca 300 killed and wounded.

Sources Beaulac, Fervel.

XX Lyon, 8 August 1793, siege and capture

The capital of the French Département de la Rhône, at the confluence of the Rivers Rhône and Saône, at the junction of Routes N7, N6 N83 and A47.

A Republican victory over the Royalists.

(Last action – Saint-Fulgent, 22 September; next action – Cholet, 17 October.)

Republican Forces Dubois-Crancé commanding 35,000 men.

Republican losses Unknown.

Royalist Garrison Gen Préci commanding ca 20,000 men

Royalist losses Unknown.

Comment The conquered city was subject to a reign of terror.

Sources Beaulac, Schulz.

UR Weissenburg Lines, 13 October 1793, clash

A town in Alsace-Lorraine (eastern France) on the

River Lauter, 59 km north of Strasbourg, on the border with Germany.

An Allied victory over the French.

(Last action – Pirmasens, 14 September; next action – Fort Louis, 14 November.)

French Forces GdD Carlen commanding the Armée du Rhin: **Avantgarde** GdD Meynier: GdB Isambert; 6e, 48e and 105e RIdLi (1 bn each); GdN Corrèze (1er); Jura (1 bn); Lot-et-Garonne (1 bn). GdB Ferette: 93e and 95e RIdLi (2 bns each). GdB Combez: Grenadiers (1er and 2e Bns); 8e, 11e and 17e DragR (3 sqns each); 7e HusR (3 sqns); 8e and 10e ChàCh (3 sqns each). **Right Wing** GdD Dubois GdB Michaud: 11e RILé, 37e, 40e and 79e RIdLi (1 bn each); GdN Haute-Saône (3e and 7e); Ain (5e); Charente-Inférieure (3e); Pyrénées-Orientales (1er); Rhône-et-Loire (3e); 1 x Compagnie franche. **GdB Legrand** 37e and 75e RIdLi (1 bn each); GdN Vosges (9e); Bas-Rhin (4e); Eure (4e); Jura (8e); Gendarmerie (1 sqn); 4e DragR (3 sqns); 2e ChàCh (4 sqns). **Centre** GdD Meuner GdB Vachot: 3e RIdLi (2 bns); GdN Doubs (1er); Ain (1er and 3e). GdD Mequellier: GdB Bauriolle: 30e RIdLi (1 bn); GdN Doubs (3e); Jura (12e); Haut-Rhin (3e). GdB Isambert: 46e RIdLi (2 bns); GdN Bas-Rhin (3e); Doubs (11e); Puy-de-Dôme (2e); Grenadiers Rhône-et-Loire (2e). **Left Wing** GdD Ferey GdB Desaix: 13e RIdLi (2 bns); 27e RIdLi (2e Bn); GdN Vosges (1er); Jura (4e); Haut-Rhin (1er); Indre-et-Loire (2e); GdB ? : 7 RILé (1 bn); GdN Rhône-et-Loire (2e); Saône-et-Loire (4e); Haute-Saône (1er); Vosges (10e); 2e CavR (1 sqn); 7e ChàCh (4 sqns); Gendarmerie (1 sqn). **Reserve** GdD Dettmann GdB Lafarelle 2e, 12e and 14e CavRs (3 sqns each); Gendarmerie (1 sqn); GdB ? : 9e and 19e CavRs (3 sqns each); Gendarmerie (2 sqns). GdB Ravel; 5e ArtR GdN Bas-Rhin (1er Bn); Ouvriers-pioniers (2 bns); Guides (½ sqn)

French totals 45,312 infantry, 6,278 cavalry, ? guns.

French losses ca 2,000 killed and wounded, 1,000 captured, 31 guns, 12 colours.

Allied Forces GdK Count Wurmser commanding. **1st Column** FML Prince von Waldeck **Avantgarde** GM von Lichtenberg: Wurmser Freikorps (8 coys); IR EH Ferdinand Nr 2 (1 bn); HusR Szeckler Nr 44 (2 sqns). **Main Body** GM von Funk: IR EH Ferdinand Nr 2 (2 bns); IR EH Carl Nr 3 (1 bn); Gren Bns Rödel and Zschok (1 bn each); HusR Wurmser Nr 30 (4 sqns); HusR Szeckler Nr 44 (2 sqns); DragR Waldeck Nr 39 (4 sqns). **2nd Column** FML Hotze: GM Jellačič, GM Jordis, GM Aufensees: IR Fürstenberg (Swabians, 2 bns); Swabian Gren Bn (1 bn); Serbian Freikorps Michailovich (5 coys); HusR Wurmser Nr 30 (4 sqns); DragR Württemberg (Swabians, 2 sqns). **3rd Column** FML Hotze GM Gyulai, GM Klenau: IRs Kaiser Nr 1 and Lacy Nr 22 (2 bns each); Gyulai Freikorps (1 bn); HusR EH Leopold Nr 17 (4 sqns); DragR Waldeck Nr 39 (2 sqns); Kurpfalz combined ChLR (3 sqns); Hessen-Kassel HusR (2 sqns). **4th Column** GM Mészáros **Avantgarde** Obst Sell von Pellegrini: IR Pellegrini Nr 49 (2 bns); Hessen-Kassel Jägers and Lt I Bn Lenz (2 coys). **Main Body** (GM Mészáros): Slovene Freikorps (1½ bns); IR Oliver Wallis Nr 29 and Gyulai Nr 32 (2 bns each); HusR EH Leopold Nr 17 (4 sqns); HusR Erdödy Nr 11 (2 sqns); DragR Kaiser Nr 3 (6 sqns). **5th Column** GM Brunner: IRs Terzy Nr 16 and Lattermann Nr 45 (1 bn each); KarabinierR Kaiser Nr 6 (6 sqns); HusR EH Leopold Nr 17 (2 sqns). **6th Column** GM Kospoth: IRs Huff Nr 8 and Preiss Nr 24 (2 bns each); IR Gemmingen Nr 21 (1 bn); Combined GzIR Siebenburger (2 bns); KürR Mack Nr 6 (6 sqns); HusR Erdödy Nr 11 (2 sqns). **7th Column** The Prince de Condé, GM Vioménil: IR Hohenlohe Nr 17 (2 bns); Infanterie Noble* (2 bns); Cavallerie Noble* (4 sqns); Chevaliers Dauphin* , Chevaliers de la Couronne*, Légion de Mirabeau'(2 sqns each).

Allied totals 33,599 infantry, 9,635 cavalry.

Allied losses 1,800 killed, wounded and missing.

Comment This was a major break-through for the Allies. The French withdrew south to Hagenau. It caused them to concentrate everything against the Allies to reset the strategic situation on the Upper Rhine under General Pichegru. They also brought up the Armée de la Moselle under General Hoche.

* = French Émigré units.

Sources Chuquet, Schulz, Ditfurth, Wrede.

NL Maubeuge, 30 September – 16 October 1793, failed siege

A fortified town in the French Département du Nord, 35 km east of Valenciennes, on the River Sambre, at the crossing of Route N62.

A French victory over the Allies.

(Last action – Menin, 15 September; next action – Wattignies, 15/16 October.)

French Garrison GdD Ferraud commanding. Exact details not known.

French total 20,000 men, guns.

French losses Not known.

Allied Forces FM Prince Josias of Coburg commanding Austrian Forces: IRs EH Carl Nr 3 (3 bns); Deutschmeister Nr 4 (2 bns); Schröder Nr 7 (3 bns); Klebek Nr 14 (2 bns); Kaunitz Nr 20 (1 bn); Brechainville Nr 25 (2 bns); Wartensleben Nr 28 (2 bns); De Ligne Nr 30 (1 bn); Esterházy Nr 34 (2 bns); Württemberg Nr 38 (2 bns); Murray Nr 55 (1 bn). Grenadier Bns (1 bn each); Attems, Brentano. Briey, Malovetz, Morzin, Mosel, Rosseau, Synoth. Mahony Jägers (6 coys), Freikorps O'Donnell (2 bns) Freikorps Grün Laudon (4 coys). Freikorps Branovaczky (4 coys); Tyroler Scharfschützen (6 coys); Carabinier R Herzog Albert Nr 5 (6 sqns); DragR Coburg Nr 37 (6 sqns); ChLR Latour Nr 31 (6 sqns); HusR Blankenstein Nr 16 (6 sqns); HusR Wurmser Nr 30 (6 sqns); HusR Esterházy Nr 32 (6 sqns).

Dutch Forces GL van Münster: Zwitsers van May (2 bns), Gren Bns van Reuss, van Plettenberg (1 bn each); IR Waldeck (2nd and 5th Bns); IR Oranien-Nassau (2 bns); IR Mecklenburg (2 bns), IR Hirzel (2 bns).

Allied total ca 60,000 men.

Allied losses Not known.

Comment The French vistory at Wattignies on 15/16 October forced the Allies to lift the siege.

Sources Bodart, Chuquet, Ditfurth, Fortescue, Sichart, Wrede.

NL Wattignies, 15/16 October 1793, battle

A village in the French Département du Nord, 9 km southeast of Maubeuge.

A French victory over the Allies.

(Last action - Maubeuge, 16 October; next action - Menin, 21/22 October.)

French Forces GdD Jourdan commanding the Armée du Nord (see orders of battle for details).

French total 60,000 men.

French losses ca 5,000 men killed, wounded and missing, 27 guns.

Austrian Forces FM Prince Josias of Coburg commanding; Generals Clerfayt, Haddik and Benjowsky; Gren Bns Adelstein Attems, Synoth, Ulrich, Ulm (5 bns); IRs M Wallis Nr 11, Hohenlohe Nr 17, Brechainville Nr 25, Esterházy Nr 34 and Württemberg Nr 38 (2 bns each); IRs Carl Schröder Nr 7, Klebek Nr 14 (3 bns each); IR Beaulieu Nr 31 (1st Bn) and IR U Kinsky Nr 6 (1 bn). CarabinierR H Albert Nr 5 and KürR Kavanagh Nr 12 (6 sqns each); HusR Barco Nr 35 (2 sqns)

Austrian totals 23 bns, 14 sqns, ca 30,000 men.

Austrian losses 2,500 killed and wounded, 500 captured.

Comment The Austrian commander now was too weak to hold his advanced line and withdrew over the Sambre, lifting the siege of Maubeuge.

Sources Chuquet, Schulz, Fortescue, Wrede, Sichart.

XX Cholet, 17 October 1793, battle

A town in the French Département de la Maine-et-Loire, 58 km southwest of Angers, 57 km southeast of Nantes on Route N160 and D249.

A Republican victory over the Vendéen Royalists.

(Last action - Lyon, 9 October; next action - Entrames, 27 October.)

Republican Forces GdD Léchelle commanding 25,000 men, ? guns.

Republican losses 4,000 killed and wounded.

Royalist Forces Gigot d'Elbée commanding 40,000 men, ? guns.

Royalist losses ca 8,000 killed, wounded and missing, 12 guns. Gigot d'Elbée and Marquis de Bonchamp killed.

Sources Schulz.

IN Gilette, 18 October 1793, skirmish

A hamlet in the French Alpes Maritimes, on the west side of the valley of the River Vesubie, about 22 km from the coast up Route N202 from Nice and Cannes.

A Sardinian victory over the French.

(Last action - Epierre, 15 September; next action - Utelles, 21 October.)

French Forces Part of the Armée d'Italie; exact details not known.

Sardinian Forces IRs Piemonte, Guardia and Aosta (2 bns each).

Sardinian losses Not known, light.

Sources Brancaccio, Phipps.

NL Menin, 21/22 October 1793, clash

A fortified town on the Franco-Belgian border, on the River Lys and on Routes N8 and N32, about 19 km north of Lille.

A French victory over the Allies.

(Last action – Wattignies, 15/16 October; next action – Halluin, 22 October.)

French Forces GdD Souham and part of the Armée du Nord. Exact details not known

French totals ca 10,000 men.

French losses Not exactly known; moderate.

Allied Garrison Gen Count Erbach commanding. **Hanoverian troops** Cavalry: LeibR, 4th CavR and 9th LDR (2 sqns each); Infantry: 1st, 2nd and 3rd Gren Bns (1 bn each); Garde R (2 bns). **Austrian troops** IR Kheul Nr 10 (2 bns); Kaunitz Nr 20 (3 coys); Clerfayt Nr 9 (1 bn); Sztáray Nr 33 (1 bn); **English troops** Loyal Emigrants (1 bn)

Allied totals 10 bns, 4 sqns, ca 8,000 men.

Allied losses Not known exactly; most of the 2nd Hanoverian Grenadier Bn were captured.

Sources Sichart, Wrede, Fortescue.

NL Halluin, 22 October 1793, clash

A village in the French Département du Nord, close to the Belgian border, about 6 km north of Tourcoing.

A French victory over the Allies.

(Last action – Menin, 21/22 October; next action – Furnes, 22 October.)

French Forces GdD Souham commanding part of the Armée du Nord. Exact details not known.

French totals ca 10,000 men.

French losses Not exactly known; light.

Allied Forces 2nd and 3rd Hanoverian Gren Bns; Loyal Emigrants (2 coys).

Allied totals 1,700 men.

Allied losses Not known exactly, moderate.

Sources Ditfurth, Sichart, Fortescue.

IN Utelles (Madonna de), 21 October 1793, skirmish

A mountain peak in the French Alpes Maritimes about 30 km north of Nice, between the Rivers Vesubie and Tinée.

A drawn match between the French and the Sardinians.

(Last action – Gilette, 18 October; next action – this was the last action of the campaign.)

French Forces Part of the Armée d'Italie. Exact details not known.

Sardinian Forces 5th Granatieri (2 bns).

Sardinian losses Not known, light.

Sources Brancaccio, Phipps.

NL Furnes (Veurne), 22 October 1793, clash

A fortified town in the Belgian province of West Flanders, near the Channel coast and the French border at the junction of Routes N8 and A18/E40.

A Hessian victory over the French.

(Last action – Halluin, 22 October; next action – Lannoy, 28 October.)

French Forces GdD Vandamme and part of Dunkirk garrison (Armée du Nord). Exact details not known.

French totals 12,000 men.

French losses Not known.

Hessen-Kassel Garrison GM von Schmied commanding: IR Kospoth (2 bns); DragR Prinz Friedrich (5 sqns) and 2 weak Austrian battalions, Loyal Emigrants

Hessen-Kassel totals ca 4,000 men.

Hessen-Kassel losses 120 killed and wounded.

Sources Ditfurth, Sichart, Fortescue.

XX Entrames, 27 October 1793, battle

A village in the western French Département du Mayenne, 8 km south of Laval. Not marked on modern maps.

A Vendéen Royalist victory over the Republicans.

(Last action – Cholet, 17 October; next action – Granville, 14/15 October.)

Republican Forces GdD Westermann commanding 25,000 men.

Republican losses 4,000 killed, wounded and missing; GdB Blosse killed.

Royalist Forces Marquis de la Roche-Jacquelin commanding 31,000 men

Royalist losses ca 2,100 killed and wounded.

Sources Schulz.

NL Lannoy, 28 October 1793, clash

A village in the French Département du Nord about 8 km east of Lille and 4 km southeast of Roubaix.

An Allied victory over the French.

(Last action – Furnes, 22 October; next action – Nieuwpoort, 30 October.)

French Forces Exact details not known

French totals ca 5,000 men.

French losses 2,000 killed, 1,700 captured.

Allied Forces MG Abercromby commanding: **English troops** 3rd Foot Guards, Guards' Flank Bn (1 bn each); 7LD, 15LD (1 sqn each). **Austrian troops** GM von Werneck, IR Sztáray Nr 33 (2 bns); O'Donnell Freikorps (1 bn).

Allied totals 4 bns, 2 sqns, ca 4,000 men.

Allied losses Not exactly known, very light.

Comment The English cavalry cut down the French infantry when they broke and fled. Another excellent cavalry action.

Sources Fortescue, Ditfurth, Sichart, Wrede.

NL Nieuwpoort, 23–30 October 1793, failed siege

A fortified Belgian coastal town, between Ostende and Dunkirk on Route N34.

An Allied victory over the French.

(Last action – Lannoy, 28 October; next action – Marchiennes, 30 October.)

French Forces GdD Vandamme with part of the Armée du Nord. Exact details not known; see order of battle

French totals 12,000 men.

French losses Not exactly known, light; 4 guns.

Allied Garrison Obst von Wurmb commanding: 1st/53rd Foot (English); Hessen-Kassel IR von Kospoth (2 bns) and DragR Prinz Friedrich (2 sqns) and 13 guns (including battalion 3 pdrs).

Allied totals 1,300 men on 23 October. This was increased over the next days by the following English troops: 1st/42nd and the light companies of the 19th, 27th and 57th Foot and the Hessian Gren Bn von Eschwege, IR Prinz Karl (1st Bn) and 20 Hanoverian gunners to a total of 3,000 men.

Allied losses 21 killed, 79 wounded.

Sources Fortescue, Ditfurth, Sichart.

NL Marchiennes, 29/30 October 1793, capture

A town in the French Département du Nord on the River Scarpe, 18 km northwest of Valenciennes.

An Allied victory over the French.

(Last action – Nieuwpoort, 30 October; this was the last action in the Netherlands in 1793.)

French Garrison ca 3,000 men and 12 guns

French losses ca 2,000 killed, wounded and captured, 12 guns.

Allied Forces G Kray, G Otto: IRs Kheul Nr 10 (2 bns); Kaunitz Nr 20 (2nd Bn); Wartensleben Nr 28 (3rd Bn); Beaulieu Nr 31 (1st Bn); HusR Esterházy Nr 32 (10 sqns).

Allied totals 8,000 men.

Allied losses ca 100 killed, wounded and missing.

Sources Chuquet, Ditfurth, Wrede, Sichart.

UR Fort Louis, 14 October – 14 November 1793, siege and capture

A fortress then on an island in the Rhine, 22 km east of Hagenau, 20 km west of Baden-Baden and now on the west bank of the River Rhine.

An Allied victory over the French.

(Last action – Weissenburg Lines, 13 October; next action – Bitsch, 17 November.)

French Garrison GdB Durand commanding: 37e and 40e RIdLi (1er Bns); GdN Saône-et-Loire (3e); Gard (3e); Vosges (12e); de Strasbourg (1er); 4e RILé (1 bn).

French total 4,500 men, 111 guns.

French losses All captured, together with 5 colours.

Allied Forces GM von Lauer commanding. Combined Bavarian IR (3 bns); Hessen-Darmstadt troops: Leib-R (1 bn); Leib-Gren Bn (1 bn); 1 Austrian Bn (not known); Szeckler HusR (2 sqns).

Allied total 4,700 men, 55 guns.

Allied losses Not known; light.

Sources Chuquet, Schulz, von Baumbach, Ditfurth, Wrede.

XX Granville, 14/15 November 1793, clash

A harbour town in the French Département de la Manche, 90 km south of Cherbourg, on the Gulf of St Malo, at the junction of Routes 673, 924 and 971.

A Republican victory over the Vendéen Royalists.

(Last action – Entrames, 27 October; next action – Antrain, 20/21 November.)

Republican Forces GdB Peyre commanding 5,000 men.

Republican losses 200 killed and wounded.

Royalist Forces Marquis de la Roche-Jacquelin commanding 25,000 men

Royalist losses 1,500 killed, wounded and missing.

Sources Bodart, Schulz.

UR Bitsch (Bitche), 17 November 1793, raid

An impregnable fortress in eastern France (Alsace-Lorraine) on Route N62, 34 km east of Sarreguemines and 29 km south of Zweibrücken.

A French victory over the Prussians.

(Last action – Fort Louis, 14 November; next action – Biesingen, 17 November.)

French Garrison GdB Babra commanding: GdN du Cher (2e Bn); 64 gunners.

French total 739 men.

French losses Killed and wounded unknown (very light); 63 captured.

Prussian Forces Obst von Wartensleben commanding 100 men each from regiments Gren-Garde (Rohdich) Nr 6; Prinz Heinrich Nr 35 (3rd Bn); Braunschweig Nr 21 (3rd Bn); Hohenlohe Nr 32 (3rd Bn); Romberg Nr 10 (3rd Bn); Schladen Nr 41 (1st Bn); Hertzberg Nr 47 (2nd Bn); Füs Bns Legat Nr 20 (75 men) and Thadden Nr 13 (75 men).

Prussian total 1,200 men.

Prussian losses 120 killed, 251 captured.

Comment A French traitor let the raiding party into the outer defences but they were then discovered and ejected with heavy loss. The traitor was subsequently shot.

Sources Ditfurth, von Baumbach, Jany.

UR Biesingen, 17 November 1793, clash

A village in western Germany about 18 km west of Zweibrücken on Route B423 towards Sarreguemines in France.

An Allied victory over the French.

(Last action – Bitsch, 17 November; next action – Kaiserslautern, 28–30 November.)

French Forces GdD Hoche commanding the divisions of: GdDs Taponnier (6 bns, 4 coys, 2 CavRs, 2 x FAB) and Huet (6 bns, 4 coys, 2 CavRs, 1 x FAB).

French totals 20,000 men.

French losses 760 killed and wounded, 42 captured.

Allied Forces GL Count von Kalkreuth commanding: Prussian troops: Gren Bn Christiani (1 bn); IRs Crousaz Nr 47 and Vietinghof Nr 38 (3 bns each); 1 x 12 pdr FAB; 1 x howitzer and 1 x mortar (1 bn each). 1 x FAB. ChLR Kurland and Karabiniers (5 sqns each). Obst Szekely's detachment Füs Bn von Wedel Nr 1, Kur-Trier Jägers (1 coy), 1 combined cavalry regiment (500 men). Saxon HusR (2 sqns), 3 guns

Allied totals 12 bns, 1 coy, 17 sqns. 4 x FAB, ca 13,000 men.

Allied losses 16 killed, 92 wounded.

Sources KGE Heft 16, Jany.

XX Antrain (Dol), 20/21 November 1793, battle

A hamlet in the French Département de l' Ille-et-Vilaine, 40 km north of Rennes on Route N175/E3.

A Vendéen Royalist victory over the Republicans.

(Last action – Granville, 14/15 November; next action – Le Mans, 13 December.)

Republican Forces GdD Rossignol commanding 25,000 men

Republican losses 8,000 killed, wounded and missing.

Royalist Forces Marquis de la Roche-Jacquelin commanding 20,000 men

Royalist losses 2,000 killed and wounded.

Sources Bodart, Schulz.

UR Kaiserslautern, 28–30 November 1793, battle

A town in western Germany, 50 km northwest of Speyer on Routes B37 and B270; just south of the Autobahn A6.

A Prussian victory over the French.

(Last action – Bitsch, 17 November; next action – Landau, 23 December.)

French Forces GdD Hoche commanding the Armée de la Moselle. GdD Ambert: GdB Olivier. Légion de la Moselle (1 bn and 4 sqns); 13e RIdLi (1 bn); 2e CarabinierR (4 sqns); 1 x HAB (6 guns). GdB Simon: 30e RIdLi (1er Bn); GdN République (3e Bn); Haute-Saône (4e Bn); Orne (5e Bn); Meurthe (4e Bn); 55e RIdLi (2e Bn). GdB Joinville: 99e RIdLi (2e Bn); GdN Joinville (1 bn); Grenadiers (1 bn); 1 x FAB (8 guns), engineers (½ coy). GdD Vincent Chass de Rheims (1 bn); 1er ChàCh (5 sqns); Gendarmerie (5 sqns); 1 x HAB (6 guns); 5e RIdLi (1er Bn); GdN République (1er Bn); Rhône-et-Loire (1er Bn); Moselle (4e Bn); Lot (1er Bn); 17e RIdLi (2e Bn); engineers (½ coy); 1 x FAB (8guns). GdD Huet GdB – ? –: Free companies: de l'Observatoire, Maurice and Billard (3 coys); 96e RIdLi (1 coy); 4e CavR (4 sqns); 9e ChàCh (4 sqns). GdB Morlot: 71e RIdLi (2e Bn); 81e RIdLi (1er Bn). GdN Haute-Marne (2e Bn); Ardennes (1er Bn); Meurthe (6e Bn); 44e RIdLi (1er Bn); 2 x FAB (16 guns). GdB Paillard: 58e RIdLi (2e Bn); 103e RIdLi (1er Bn); GdN Vosges (6e Bn); Rhône-et-Loire (1er Bn); Meurthe (7e Bn); Seine-et-Marne (2e Bn); engineers (½ coy). **Avantgarde** GdB Dubois: Free companies Metz, Guillaume, Gérard and Louvre (4 coys); 89e RIdLi (1 coy); 6e ChàCh (½ coy); 16e ChàCh (½ sqn); HusR de Jemappes (½ sqn); 7e HusR (1 sqn); 3e HusR (3 sqns); 1er DragR (4 sqns); 1er Carabiniers (4 sqns); 2 x HAB (12 guns). GdD Taponnier: GdB – ? –: Free companies 3e and 4e Louvre, Jemappes and Bons Tireurs (4 coys); 10e CavR and 14e DragR (4 sqns each); 1 x FAB (8 guns). GdB Lombard: 1er RIdLi (1er Bn); 8e RIdLi (2e Bn); 54e RIdLi (2e Bn); GdN Manche (3e Bn); Rhône-et-

Loire (7e Bn); Meuse (5e Bn); engineers (½ coy); 1 x FAB (8 guns).

French totals 29,115 infantry, 5,046 cavalry, 52 guns.

French losses 2,400 killed and wounded, 700 captured, 2 guns, 1 colour (RIdLi 99e).

Allied Forces The Duke of Brunswick commanding: GL von Kalckstein; IR Prinz Heinrich Nr 35, IR Braunschweig Nr 21 (3 bns each). GM von Roeder: IR Garde Nr 15 (2 bns); Gren Bn Rohdich (1 bn). GL von Schönfeld: KürR von Borstell Nr 7, DragR von Lottum Nr 1 (5 sqns each); Jägers (1 coy); Kur-Trier Jägers (1 coy); IR von Crousaz Nr 39 (3 bns); Füs Bn Legat Nr 20 (1 bn); HusR von Eben Nr 2 (2 sqns); 1 x HAB (8 guns); 1 x FAB (8 guns). GL Count von Kalckreuth: Prussian troops: Füs Bn Wedel Nr 1 (1 bn); IR von Kalckstein Nr 5 (3 bns); IR Braunschweig Nr 21 (3 bns); IR von Knobelsdorff Nr 27 (3 bns); IR von Vietinghof Nr 38 (2 bns); Gren Bn Rohdich (2e Bn); IR Garde Nr 15 (2nd Bn); DragR Voss Nr 11 (5 sqns); Saxon troops: IRs Kurfürst, Prinz Anton, Clemens and Gotha (1 bn each); Karabiniers; Leib-KürR; ChLR Kurland (5 sqns each). Obst Szekely's Avantgarde, Saxon HusR (2 sqns); Combined CavR (5 sqns); IR Vietinghof (2nd Bn). 2 guns; 4 x 6 pdr FAB (26 guns); 1 x 12 pdr FAB (8 guns); 1 x mortar battery (8 guns).

Allied totals 35¾ bns, 54 sqns, 10 batteries, ca 26,000 men.

Allied losses (killed and wounded) Prussians: 32 officers, 584 men; Saxons: 12 officers, 178 men.

Comment Once again, the Prussian king's insistence on a passive strategy against France meant that this victory was not followed up and the potential fruits were thus not harvested.

Sources Chuquet, Schulz, KGE Heft 16, Wagner.

FP Villelongue, 7 December 1793, clash

A village in the French Département des Pyrénées Orientales, 15 km east of Céret, in the mountains close to where the Route A9/E15 crosses the border into Spain.

A Spanish-Portuguese victory over the French.

(Last action – Boulu, 3 October; next action – Collioure, 20 December.)

French Forces GdB Daoust commanding. No details known

French totals 10,000 men, 40 guns.

French losses 340 killed and wounded, 312 missing, 26 guns, 2 colours, 2,000 muskets.

Spanish-Portuguese Forces Capt Gen Don Ricardo commanding. Forces included 6 x Portuguese infantry regiments, IRs 1 and 2, 1st of Olivenca, Cascais, Peniche and Freire de Andrade, 5,000 men with 22 guns. No other details known.

Spanish-Portuguese total 8,000 men.

Spanish-Portuguese losses 56 killed and wounded.

Sources Beaulac, Ferreira.

XX Le Mans, 13 December 1793, battle

Capital town of the French Département de la Sarthe, at the confluence of the Rivers Sarthe and Huisne and the junction of Routes A81/E50, A11 and N138/E402.

A Republican victory over the Vendéen Royalists.

(Last action – Antrain, 20/21 November; next action – Savenay, 23 December.)

Republican Forces GdDs Marceau and Kléber commanding: 25,000 men, ? guns.

Republican losses 2,000 men killed and wounded.

Royalist Forces Marquis de la Roche-Jacquelin commanding 25,000 men, ? guns.

Royalist losses 15,000 killed, wounded and missing.

Sources Schulz.

FS Toulon, 18 September – 18 December 1793, siege and capture

A major naval base and fortified city in the southern French Département du Var, 50 km southeast of Marseille on Route D8/A50.

A French Republican victory over the Royalists and the Allies. Apart from civil war, this was the only action of note in southern France.

Republican Forces GdD Dugommier commanding including Gen Carteaux' Corps from Marseilles (8,000), Gen Doppet's Corps from Lyon (25,000), the ex-garrison of Valenciennes and Gen La Poype's 6,000 men from the Armée d'Italie.

Republican total 32,000 men, (the highest level), 100 guns.

Republican losses 2,000 killed and wounded.

French Forces as at 11 December 1793 GdD Dugommier commanding: **Division de l'Est** GdD Lapoype: Légion Allobroges (1 bn); 59e RIdLi (2e Bn); 28e RIdLi (1 bn); 10e RIdLi (1er Bn); 35e RIdLi (2 bns); GdN Ardèche (2e and 4e Bns); Drôme (10e and 14e Bns); Arriège (1 coy); Chasseurs de l'Arriège (1 bn); Barjois (1er Bn); Vaucluse (2e and 4e Bns); Luberon (2e Bn);

Baurset (1 bn); Cotignac (1 coy); Côtes-Maritimes (7e Bn); Isère (3e and 4e Bns); Ambes (5e Bn); Apt (1er Bn); Hérault (4e Bn); Brignoles (2e Bn); Marseille (1er Bn); Montagne de Marseille (4e and 5e Bns); Montagne d'Aix (5e Bn); Var (7e Bn); Aveyron (2e Bn); Chasseurs de St-Hilaire (½ bn); Sans-Culottes (1er and 2e Bns); Bn des Landes (1 bn); Grenadiers des Bouches-du-Rhône (1 bn); Chasseurs de la Revolution (1 bn); Cie Franche de Senary (St Nazaire) (1 coy); Cie France de la Ciotat (½ coy); Cie du Luc (1 coy); Bn de la Union (1 bn); Pioniers (1 coy); Cie des Jacobins (½ coy); 5e Cie Franche (½ coy); GdN Montblanc (2e Bn). **Total** 18,530 men. **Division de l'Ouest Right Wing** 23e RIdLi (1 bn); 5e Gren Bn (1 bn). GdN Hautes-Alpes (5e Bn); Gard (1er Bn); Ardèche (1er Bn); Montagne (1 bn); Légion Allobroges (1 coy). Plaine de la Seyne: GdN Haute-Garonne (4e and 5e Bns); Côte-d'Or (2e Bn); Drôme (1er Bn); Aix (4e Bn); Marseille (Grenadiers and Chasseurs, 6e Bn); Chasseurs Allobroges (1 coy). Gen Le Ponnet: GdN Côte-d'Or (1 coy, 2nd Bn); Basses-Alpes (2e Bn: 1 coy; 3e Bn: 4 coys); Chasseurs Allobroges (2e Cie); Cie du Basset (½ coy); **Centre** GdN Drôme (9e Bn). **Left Wing** 59e RIdLi (1er Bn); GdN Bouches-du-Rhône (2e Bn); Drôme (12e Bn); Carpenteras (1er Bn); Vaucluse (5e Bn and Grenadiers of the 4e Bn); Montagne (6e Bn and Grenadiers of the 4e Bn); Isère (8e Bn); Ardèche (1 coy, 2e Bn); Arles (1 coy); Légion Allobroges (1 coy); Aubagne (½ bn); Chasseurs des Basses-Alpes (1 coy); Chasseurs de St Esprit (½ coy); Cie Franche de Marseilles (3e Cie). Cie Franche de la Seine (½ coy); Cie Franche de la Drôme (½ coy); Grenadiers de Luberon (½ coy); GdN Montblanc (3e Bn); Gironde (6e Bn); le Bandol: GdN Basses-Alpes (1 coy, 3e Bn, 1 coy, 5e Bn); Bandol (1 coy, 1er Bn); St Nazaire (1 bn); 59e RIdLi (½ coy); Bn d'Aubagne (½ coy).

Cavalry: 9e DragR (½ sqn); 15e DragR (2 sqns); ChàCh (½ sqn); Guides (½ sqn); Gendarmerie (½ sqn). Artillery: Right Wing: Canonniers de la Côte-d'Or; de la Lozère (½ coy together). Naval Artillery (4 coys); Line artillery (2 bns); Volunteer artillery (2 bns).

French totals 32,000 men, 100 guns.

French losses 2,000 men.

Royalist and Allied Forces MG Dundas commanding: GdN du Toulon (4 bns); Maclean's Chasseurs* (2 coys); IR Royal Louis* (6 coys). **British troops** 2nd/1st, 1st/11th, 1st/18th, 1st/25th, 1st/30th, 1st/69th Foot; Royal Marines and artillery, 8,000 men. **Neapolitan troops** IR Rey, IR Borgogna (2 bns each); IR Real Napoli (2nd Bn); IR Messapia (1st Bn); IR Real Macedonia (2 coys); 4,000 men. **Sardinian troops** IR Piemonte (2 bns); IR de Courten (Swiss) (2 bns); Cacciatori (1st Bn); Grenadiers (4th Bn); 2,000 men. **Spanish troops** IR Cordoba, Hibernia, Malaga, Mallorca, Betschart (Swiss) (2 bns each); Provincial infantry regiments Chinchilla and Mallorca. Marines (1 bn); 4,000 men

Allied totals ca 22,000 men plus a squadron of 12 ships of the line under Admiral Hood.

Allied losses ca 4,000 men.

Comment The British destroyed 14 French ships of the line in the harbour and took 15 others. This reinforced British naval mastery of the Mediterranean. Captain Napoleon Bonaparte managed the besiegers' artillery and caught the eye of his superiors. The Republicans organized a blood-bath among those of the populace who did not or could not escape with the Allies.

* = Émigré regiments raised by the British in September and taken into British service.

Sources Fortescue, Schulz.

FP Collioure, 20 December 1793, clash

A town in the French Département des Pyrénées Orientales, on the Mediterranean coast, 25 km southeast of Perpignan, on the coastal road Route 114.

A Spanish victory over the French.

(Last action – Villelongue, 7 December; next action – this was the last action of note in the Pyrenees in 1793.)

French Forces GdB Delatre commanding. No further details known.

French total 5,000 men, 100 guns.

French losses 4,000 killed, wounded and captured.

Spanish Forces LG de La Cuesta commanding. The force included six Portuguese regiments: IRs 1 and 2, 1st of Olivenca, Cascais, Peniche and Freire de Andrade.

Spanish total 8,000 men.

Spanish losses 300 killed, wounded and missing.

Sources Beaulac, Ferreira.

XX Savenay, 23 December 1793, clash

A town in the western French Département de la Loire-Inférieure, near the River Loire, 33 km northwest of Nantes. Not marked on many modern maps.

A Republican victory over the Vendéen Royalists.

(Last action - Le Mans, 13 December; this was the last action of 1793 in the Vendée.)

Republican Forces GdD Marceau commanding: 20,000 men

Republican losses 500 killed and wounded.

Royalist Forces Fleuriot commanding 7,000 men and 7 guns

Royalist losses 6,000 killed, wounded, missing; 7 guns.

Sources Schulz.

UR Landau, 20 August - 23 December 1793, failed blockade

A fortress in the western German state of the Pfalz, about 22 km west of Germersheim on the River Rhine, at the junction of Routes B10 and B38; just west of Autobahn A65.

A French victory over the Prussians.

(Last action - Kaiserslautern, 28–30 November; next action - Weissenburg Lines, 6 December - 9 February 1794.)

French Forces GdD Joseph-Marie Tenet de Laubadère: 3e and 55e RIdLi (1 bn each); GdN Seine-et-Marne (2e Bn); 22e CavR and 3e HusR (2 sqns each)

French totals ca 3,800 men.

French losses Not known.

Prussian Forces GL Erbprinz von Hohenlohe commanding: IRs Romberg Nr 10, Hohenlohe Nr 32, Hertzberg Nr 47 (3 bns each); Gren Bn Schladen (1 bn); IRs von Wegnern Nr 30, Kleist Nr 12, Wolframsdorf Nr 37, Thadden Nr 3, Manstein Nr 9 (3 bns each); 5 x 6 pdr FAB.

Prussian totals 25 bns, 40 x 6 pdrs.

Prussian losses Not known, very slight from action but heavier from sickness.

Comment With no siege artillery the Prussians were powerless to take the place. Hoche's relentless advance eastwards with the combined armies of the Rhine and Moselle forced the Prussians to withdraw.

Sources Chuquet, KGE Heft 16.

UR Weissenburg Lines, 6 December 1793 - 9 February 1794, clashes

A series of earthworks along the south side of the River Lauter, a western tributary of the River Rhine. Nowadays the border between Germany and France (Alsace-Lorraine).

French victories over the Allies.

(Last action - Kaiserslautern, 28–30 November; next action - these were the last actions in this theatre in this campaign.)

French Forces Gen Hoche commanding the Armée de la Moselle.

Division of GdD Lefebvre Detachments of the 6e, 7e, 12e, 13e, 16e, 17e, 18e and 19e RIdLi (1 bn); 40e RIdLi (2e Bn); 55e RIdLi (2e Bn); 96e RIdLi (1 coy); GdN Chasseurs de Rheims (1 bn); Légion de la Moselle (1 coy); GdN Chasseurs de la Meuse (1 coy); Free Corps Gérard (1 coy); Free Corps de l'Observatoire (1 coy); Free Corps de Billard (1 coy); Free Corps de Guillaume (1 coy); Sans-Culottes (2e Coy); GdN Chasseurs du Louvre (1e, 2e and 3e Coys); GdN Tirailleurs de Nancy (1 coy); Free Corps de Metz (1 coy); Free Corps de Saint-Maurice (1 coy); 102e RIdLi (2e Bn); GdN Haute-Saône (1e Bn); GdN Rhône-et-Loire (2e Bn); GdN Vosges (1e Bn); 1er ChàCh 'Alsace' (4 sqns); 26e Coy HA (1 bty); 30e Coy HA (1 bty). **Totals** 8 bns, 14 coys, 4 sqns, 2 bties. **Division of GdD Paillard** 89e RIdLi (1 coy); 5e RIdLi (1er Bn); GdN République (4e Bn); GdN Puy-de-Dôme (2e Bn); GdN Rhône-et-Loire (7e Bn); GdN Bas-Rhin (1 coy of the 5e Bn); HusR Nr 7 (½ sqn); 9e ChàCh (½ sqn); Gendarmes (1e and 2e Divisions). **Totals** 4 bns and 2 coys, 3 sqns. **Division of GdD Championnet** 30e RIdLi (2e Bn); 47e RIdLi (2e Bn); 71e RIdLi (2e Bn); 103e RIdLi (1er Bn); GdN Doubs (2e Bn); GdN Paris (9e and 19e Bns); GdN Haut-Rhin (3e Bn); GdN Meuse (5e Bn); GdN Cher (1er Bn); GdN Vosges (6e Bn); GdN Moselle (5e Bn); 4e CavR (3 sqns). **Totals** 12 bns, 3 sqns. **Division of GdD Moreau** 30e RIdLi (1er Bn); 44e RIdLi (1er Bn); 54e RIdLi (2e Bn), 81e RIdLi (1er Bn); 99e RIdLi (2e Bn); GdN Loiret (2e Bn); GdN Lot (1er Bn); GdN Ardennes (1er Bn); GdN Orbe (5e Bn); GdN Haute-Saône (4e and 6e Bns); 10e CavR (3 sqns); 9e ChàCh 'Lorraine' (4 sqns). **Totals** 11 bns, 7 sqns.

French totals 35 bns, 16 coys, 17 sqns, ca 35,000 men.

French losses Not exactly known.

Allied Forces:

Austrian Forces GdK Count Wurmser commanding: Grenadiers (5 bns); IRs Kaiser Nr 1 and Huff Nr 8 (2 bns each); Tercy Nr 16 (1 bn); Lacy Nr 22, Preuss Nr

24, Oliver Wallis Nr 29, Gyulai Nr 32, IR Thurn Nr 43 (2 bns each); Lattermann Nr 45 (1 bn); Pellegrini Nr 49 (2 bns); GzIR Slavonier (2nd and 3rd Combined Bns); GzIR Siebenburger Szeckler; GzIR Wallachen and Serbisches Freikorps (1 bn each); Wurmser Freikorps (⅓ bn). KarabinierR Kaiser Nr 6, KürR Mack Nr 20 (6 sqns each); DragR Kaiser Nr 3 (2 sqns); DragR Waldeck Nr 39, HusR EH Leopold (6 sqns each); HusR Erdödy Nr 11 (4 sqns); Wurmser Freikorps Hus (2 sqns). **Austrian totals** 5 bns, 10 sqns, ca 5,800 men.

Prussian Forces GM von Rüchel: IRs von Kleist Nr 12, Wolframsdorf Nr 37, Hertzberg Nr 47 (8 bns); Jägers (2 coys); HusR von Wolffradt Nr 6 (3 sqns); 1½ x HAB, ½ x 6 pdr FAB.

Bavarian Forces GM count Minucci commanding: Combined IR (2 bns); Combined Jäger Bn (1 bn); Combined ChLR (4 sqns).

Hessen-Kassel troops LtI Bn Lenz (2 coys); Jägers (2 coys); HusR (3 sqns).

Hessen-Darmstadt troops Leib IR (2 bns); 2. Leib-Gren Bn (1 bn); 6 guns

Allied totals ca 38,000 men at the beginning of the action.

Allied losses Not exactly known; quite considerable due to sickness and desertion; 21 guns.

Comment Under pain of death the French generals were spurred on to clear the left bank of the Rhine. This led to a continuous series of clashes in the Vosges mountains culminating in the defeat of the Allies at Wörth on 22 December and - finally - at Geisberg on 26 December and their precipitate withdrawal over the Rhine. Data on French participation in individual actions is non-existent.

Sources Chuquet, Schulz, KGE Hefte 7 and 12, Ditfurth, Dohna, Jany, Wrede.

1794

1794 INTRODUCTION

It is regretted that it has not been possible to find very much detailed information on individual French regiments' battle participation and losses for 1794. This was possibly due to the disruptive effects of both The Terror and the first 'Amalgame' of the old line regiments with the new Garde Nationale and Volontaire battalions.

We reproduce herewith orders of battle for the Armies of the North, of the Sambre and Meuse, the Ardennes and of the Moselle as at least some basis for constructing events in the various theatres of war. At the beginning of the chapter on 1793 will be found further orders of battle for the French armies of the East and West Pyrenees, of the North and the Rhine (for spring and October) and the Ardennes.

Order of Battle of the Armée du Nord; 1 September 1794

Gen Pichegru commanding. **1st Division** GdD Souham. GdB Macdonald: 3e, 24e and 68e DBdeLi (3 bns each). GdB de Winter: 23e DBdeLi (3 bns); 1er BnLé (1 bn); 1er and 2e Tirailleurs (2 bns). 1er and 2e Carabiniers (4 sqns each); 5e ChàCh (6 sqns); 6e DragR (6 sqns), 3e and 9e HusR (4 sqns each). **Totals** 20,000 men, 6,000 horses. **2nd Division** GdD Moreau. GdB Vandamme: DBdeLi 16e (1 coy); 22e (2e Bn); 24e (2e Bn). GdN Bouches-du-Rhône and Calvados (1er bns each); Rhône-et-Loire (5e Bn), Corrèze (2e Bn); Ile-et-Vilaine (1er and 2e bns). GdB Laurent: DBdeLi 5e (2e Bn); 22e (1er Bn). GdN Lot (3e Bn); Seine-et-Oise (4e Bn); Finistère (1er Bn); Marne (1er and 3e bn); Indre-et-Loire (1er and 2e bns). 14e BnLé (1 bn); Chass du Mont Cassel (1 bn). 21e CavR (4 sqns); 2e HusR (2 sqns); 2e ChàCh (4 sqns). **Totals** 13,000 men, 1,943 horses. **3rd Division** GdD Lemaire. GdB Desenfans: 150e DBdeLi (3 bns); Seine-Inférieure (3 bns); 19e ChàCh (6 sqns). GdB Blondeau: DBde d'Allier and 90e DBdeLi (3 bns each); Tirailleurs du Mont des Chats (1 bn); 3e Chass francs (1 bn); 1er CavR (5 sqns). **Totals** 12,500 men, 2,068 horses. **4th Division** GdD Dépeaux. GdB Salme: 38e and 131e DBdeLi (3 bns each); Chass Tirailleurs (3e Bn); Chass francs (5e Bn); 19e CavR (4 sqns); 13e ChàCh (2 sqns). **Totals** 6,600 men, 1,213 horses. **5th Division** GdD Bonneau. GdB Compère: 183e DBdeLi (2 bns); Tirailleurs (5e Bn); GdB Noel: 107e and 154e DBdeLi (3 bns each). GdB Baillot: 163e and 183e DBdeLi (3 and 2 bns resp). 5e HusR (4 sqns); 2e DragR (5 sqns); 6e HusR (6 sqns) **Totals** 11,800 men, 2,311 horses **6th Division** GdD Delmas. GdB Daendels: 29e DBdeLi and DBde de Lombards (3 bns each) GdB Reynier 3e Lé (1 bn); 8e HusR (4 sqns) **Totals** 5,290 men, 819 horses. **Artillery Park** 5 x 24pdrs, 16 x 16pdrs, 30 x 12pdrs, 163 x 4pdrs (battalion guns); 37 x 8pdrs 31 x 6in and 14 x 8in howitzers, 10 mortars. **Total** 275 field guns.

Source Sabron.

Order of Battle of the Armée de la Sambre-et-Meuse

General Kléber commanding: **GdD Bernadotte** 21e DBdeLi (3e Bn); 71e and 72e DBdeLi (3 bns each); 32 Lé (1 bn); 13e CavR, 2e and 4e HusR, 7e DragR; 32e and 34e Gendarmerie divs. 2 x FAB. 1 coy sappers. **Total** 9,215 men. **GdD Duhesme** 93e, 111e and 123e DBdeLi (3 bns each); Chasseur-Volontaires (4e Bn). 2e Chass à Pied; 17e CavR. 1 coy sappers. **Totals** 7,663 men. **GdD Richard** Chass de Hainaut (1er Bn); 35e, 97e 127e and 128e DBdeLi (3 bns each); 12e and 16e ChàCh, 1 x FAB. **Totals** 9,961 men. **GdD Friant** 33e, 49e and 161e DBdeLi (3 bns each); 74e DBdeLi (2e Bn). GdN Somme (2e Bn), Vosges (3e Bn). 1 coy sappers **Totals** 8,769 men.

Order of Battle of the Armée de la Moselle; 19 February 1794

General Hoche commanding (replaced by Jourdan on 10 March).

Lefebvre's Division 1er ChàCh; detachments of 6e, 7e, 12e 13e, 16e, 17e, 18e and 19e RILé Ch de Reims (1 bn); Légion de la Moselle (infantry only) Ch de la Meuse; Compagnies franches de Gérard; de Guillaume; de l'Observatoire; de Billard; Sans-Culottes (2e Cie); 96e RIdLi (2e Chass Cie); Ch du Louvre (1er, 3e and 4e Cies); Tirailleurs de Nancy; Compagnies franches de Metz and de St Maurice; 40e, 55e and 102e RIdLi (2e Bns each); GdN Haute-Saône (1er Bn); Rhône-et-Loire (2e Bn); Vosges (1er Bn); 26e and 30e HABs.

Championnet's Division GdN Doubs (2e Bn); Paris (9e and 19e Bns), Haut-Rhin (3e Bn); Meuse (5e Bn); Cher (1er Bn); Moselle (5e Bn); Vosges (6e Bn); 30e, 47e and 71e RIdLi (2e Bns each); 103e RIdLi (1er Bn); 4e CavR.

Morlot's Division 1er RIdLi (1er Bn); 17e and 43e RIdLi (2e Bns); GdN Meurthe (6e and 7e bns); Moselle (4e Bn); Meuse (3e Bn); Haut-Rhin (1er Bn); Côte-d'Or (4e Bn); Bas-Rhin (3e Bn); Loiret and Puy-de-Dôme (3e Bns each) 1er and 14e DragRs.

Paillard's Division 5e RIdLi (1er Bn), 89e RIdLi (1/2 bn); GdN République (4e Bn); Puy-de-Dôme (2e Bn); Rhône-et-Loire (7e Bn); Bas-Rhin (5e Bn-); detachments of 7e HusR, 9eChàCh; 1er and 2e Gendarmerie divisions.

Moreau's Division RIdLis Nr 30e(1er Bn); 44e (1er Bn); 54e (2e Bn); 81e (1er Bn) and 99e (2e Bn); GdN Loiret (2e Bn); Lot (1er Bn); Ardennes (1er Bn); Orne (5e Bn); Haut-Saône (4e and 6e bns); 10e CavR; 9e ChàCh.

Desbureaux's Division 8e RIdLi (2e Bn); GdN Moselle (2e and 3e bns); Meurthe (4e Bn); Haute-Marne (2e Bn); Var (4e Bn); Meuse (1er Bn); Drôme (5e Bn); Haute-Saône(7e Bn); Seine-et-Oise (5e Bn); Seine-et-Marne (2e Bn).

Hatry's Division 13e and 24e RIdLi (1er Bns each); 13e RILé (2e Bn); 27e RIdLi (1er Bn); 33e and 103e RIdLi (2e Bns each); GdN Manche (4e Bn); Yonne (1er Bn); Cher (2e Bn); 8e DragR.

Detached: Légion de la Moselle (cavalry; 1er and 2e Carabiniers; 11e CavR; 3e HusR; GdN Paris (4e Bn).

Total strength 76,489 men; present and fit for duty - 47,665.

Sources Chuquet.

Armée des Ardennes 15 Floréal (4 May) 1794. Gen Desjardins commanding.

Division of Gen Miller GdB Richard, GdB Poncet: 4e Chass francs (340); 10e Lé (753); 15e Cie ArtLé (87); 16e ChàCh [2e Sqn 285 (sic)]; 7e DragR (459); 6e CavR (1 sqn - 138); 18e Li (1 bn - 815); 49e Li (1er Bn - 996); 68e Li (1er Bn - 744); 89e Li (1er Bn - 900); 68e Li (2e Bn - 807); GdN 2e Calvados (960); 2e Nièvre (844); 2e Haut-Rhin (952); 2e Mayenne et Loire (854); 3e Eure (950); 3e Haute-Marne (864); 5e Somme (789); 6e Oise (936); 3e ArtR (102). Total 14,075.

Division of Gen Fromentin GdB Soland, Duhesme: 4e HusR (478); 12e ChàCh (644); 1re Cie ArtLé (91); GdN 1er Saint-Denis (912); 5e Vosges (899); 10e Paris (892); 10e Seine-et-Oise (926); 47e Li (1er Bn - 870); 2e Vienne (926); 2e Meurthe (806); 56e Li (1er Bn - 871); 1er Orne (878); 32e Lé (878); 22e CavR (491); Gendarmerie (16); Artillery Park (98). Total 10,619.

Division of Gen Despeaux GdB Ransonnet: 6e Pas-de-Calais (875); Loiret (783); 4e Nord (816); 17e Li (1er Bn - 919); 3e Meurthe (865); Chass du Hainaut (1er Bn - 889); 25e Li (1er Bn - 791); 9e Nord (874); 6e CavR (1er Sqn - 127); 6e ArtR (30); 3e ArtR (53). Total - 7,042.

Grand total 31,736 men.

Source Dupuis.

The corps detached from the Armée du Rhin at Bliecastel, Homburg and Kaiserslautern 20 Floréal (9 May) 1794 GdD Offenstein, GdB Xaintrailles, GdB Argoust.

The Division du Haut-Rhin 10e Doubs (987); 6e Seine-et-Oise (1,101); 2e Puy-de-Dôme (866); 8e Doubs (921). **Division de Strasbourg** 5e Drôme (854); 7e Drôme (699); 11e Doubs (898). Trauvaux de la Ligne: 7e Haute-Saône (801); 4e Saône-et-Loire (501); 1er Creuse (724); 8e Ain (759). **3rd Division** 2e Allier (677); 2e Côtes-du-Nord (828). **4th Division** 1er Montagne (538); 9e Meurthe (640). **5th Division** 9e Vosges (674). **2nd Division** 3e Ain (848), 3e Rhône-et-Loire (765).

The Left Wing of the Armée de la Moselle 1er Prairial (20 May).

GdD Lefebvre: **Avantgarde** Légion Moselle (infantry - 33 officers + 484 men), 16e bn Lé (33 + 923); 13e DBdeLé (113 + 2,447); 80e DBdeLi (98 + 2,592); 5e Li (1er Bn: 30 + 787); 54e Li (2e Bn: 27 + 511); 81e Li (1er Bn: 31 + 627); 99e (2e Bn: 26 + 564); 5e Orne (32 + 502); 6e Haute-Saône (29 + 496); 1er Vosges (27 + 717); 3e HusR (det: 7 + 142); 1er ChàCh (52 + 515); 9e ChàCh (53 + 500); 18e ChàCh (det: 23 + 169); 19e ChàCh (det: 14 + 119). Gendarmerie (1re Division: 1 + 32). **Total** 629 officers, 12,172 men, 4,470 horses.

GdD Championnet 94e DBdeLi (98 + 2,597); 132e DBdeLi (94 + 2,503); 181e DBdeLi (99 + 2,591); 30e Li (1er Bn: 30 + 792); 4e Paris (33 + 697); 7e Rhône-et-Loire (35 + 600); 1er DragR (39 + 481); 4e CavR (41 + 319). **Total** 469 officers, 10,580 men, 768 horses.

GdD Morlot 1ère DBdeLi (89 + 2,280); 34e DBdeLi (90 + 2,888); 110e DBdeLi (87 + 2,532); 177e DBdeLi (89 + 2,698); 14e DragR (26 + 462); 10e CavR (30 + 278); Gendarmerie (1ère Division: 28 + 435). **Total** 439 officers, 11,573 men, 1,172 horses.

GdD Hatry 6e BnLé (28 + 339); 1er Bas-Rhin (32 + 817); 2e Loiret (33 + 513); 1er Creuse (33 + 679); 105e Li (1er Bn: 24 + 636); 2e Moselle (27 + 531); 4e Var (33 + 576); 33e Li (2e Bn: 36 + 854); 1er Lot-et-Garonne (36 + 556); 58e Li (2e Bn: 30 + 411); 4e Oise (32 + 650); 9e Meurthe (33 + 1,107); 27e Li (1er Bn: 29 + 1,100); 44e Li (1er Bn: 27 + 780). 3e Moselle (35 + 659); 3e Manche (26 + 448); 9e Doubs (28 + 469); 3e Côte-d'Or (34 + 481); 4e Meurthe (27 + 555); 11e DragR (36 + 940); 18e CavR (15 + 148); **Total** 634 officers, 13,149 men, 903 horses. 173e DBdeLi (103 + 2,528). Sapeurs, 8e Bn (24 + 1,083); Gendarmerie (2e Division: 1 + 23); Force publique (2 + 22). Guides (1 + 21). Artillery (23 + 1,028); gunners attached to the divisions (1,152). Total 169 officers, 6,200 men, 4,307 horses.

Grand Total 2,340 officers, 53,674 men, 8,620 horses.

Source Dupuis.

Armée de la Moselle 15 Prairial (3 June) 1794 cooperating under Jourdan with parts of the Armée du Nord and the Armée des Ardennes.

Division of General Hatry 11e DragR (420); 6e Seine-et-Oise (1,030); 3e Côte-d'Or (428); 9e Doubs (455); 3e Moselle (604); 44e Li, 1er Bn (768); 27e Li, 1er Bn (680); 9e Meurthe (563); 58e Li, 2e Bn (730); 1er Lot-et-Garonne (582); 33e Li, 2e Bn (789); 4e Var (554); 2e Moselle (771); 2e Loiret (582), 1er Bas-Rhin (789); 18e ChàCh (158); artillery (3e Cie lé – 93) **Total** 10,005.

Division of General Morlot 14e DragR (445); 110e DBdeLi (2,709); 34e DBde (2,354); 1ère DBdeLi (2,190); 10e CavR (416); 30e Cie artLé (96) **Total** 8,210.

Division of Gen Championnet 1er DragR (444); 18e DBdeLi (2,153); 94e DBdeLi (2,327); 59e DBdeLi (1,638); 4e CavR (398); 2e Cie artLé (90) **Total** 7,500.

Division of Gen Lefebvre 19e ChàCh (11); 9e ChàCh (341); 1er Vosges (717); 99e Li, 2e Bn (640); 54e Li, 2e Bn (423); 5e Li, 1er Bn (777); 149e DBdeLi (1,663); 80e DBdeLi (2,064); 13e DBdeLi (1,572); 16e Lé (380); Légion de la Moselle (410); 3e HusR (110); 18e ChàCh (126); 1er ChàCh (381); 19e Cie artLé (110) **Total** 9,925.

Detached corps Gendarmerie (45); 173e DBde (1,716); 177e DBdeLi (1,656); 132e DBdeLi (2,439) Sapeurs, 8e Bn (930); canonniers (435) **Total** 7,221.

Grand total 42,411. GdBs Leval, Jacopin, Legrand, Olivier, Simon, Chapsal, Bonnet, Grenier.

Source Dupuis.

The Division of Gen Desjardins (the right wing of the Armée du Nord) 3 June 1794.

32e Bn Lé (793); 1er Seine-et-Marne (748), 6e Haut-Rhin (734); 10e Paris (796); 10e Seine-et-Oise (779); 47e Li, 1er Bn (736); 2e Vienne (773); 2e Meurthe (677); 56e Li, 1er Bn (806); 1er Orne (802); 10e bn Lé (303); 2e Mayenne-et-Loire (626); 49e Li, 1er Bn (834); 2e Calvados (743); 71e DBdeLi, 1er Bn (823); 2e Bn (704); 3e Bn (662); 3e Eure (827); 68e Li, 2e Bn (446); 6e Oise (743); 3e Haute-Marne (777); 89e Li, 1er Bn (821); 2e Haut-Rhin (864); 4e Nord (772), 17e Li, 1er Bn (874); 6e Pas-de-Calais (816); 9e Nord (859); 25e Li, 1er Bn (694); 1er Loiret (822); 6e Paris (880); 19e Li, 1er Bn (664); 5e Vosges (785); 3e Meurthe (830); 74e Li, 2e Bn (788); 5e Oise (778); 2e Nièvre (609); 4e bn franc (782); 5e Somme (600); 34e Gend Div (275); 68e Li, 1er Bn (655); 123e DBdeLi, 1er Bn (880); 18e Li, 1er Bn (801); 5e Meurthe (720); 2e HusR (265); 4e HusR (476); 6e ChàCh (624); 12e ChàCh (616); 16e ChàCh (140); 7e DragR (471); 6e CavR (550); 17e CavR (342); 25e CavR (350); artLé, 1re, 12e and 15e Cies (270). **Total** 37,147.

Source Dupuis.

Armée des Ardennes 1er Messidor (9 June) 1794.

GdD Marceau At Dinant: GdN Pas-de-Calais (8e Bn, 838); 172e DBdeLi (2e Bn 859; 3e 876); GdN Nord (3e Bn, 882); Volontaires nationaux (2e Bn, 828); GdN Vendée (1er Bn, 846); 9e DBdeLi (2e Bn, 746; 3e Bn 767); 5e DragR (409); ArtLé (25) **Total** 7,067. At the bridge at Auveloix and in the wood there: 19e DBdeLi (1er Bn, 792); 172e DBdeLi (752); 11e ChàCh (306) **Total** 1,850.

GdD Mayer to the right of the bridge at Auveloix: GdN Nord (2e Bn, 721). On the heights of Insemont: 26e DBdeLi (1er Bn, 649; 2e Bn, 640; 3e Bn, 686). GdN Finistère (2e Bn, 805); Volontaires nationaux (19e Bn, 760); GdN Sarthe (1er Bn, 530); Seine-Inférieure (7e Bn, 890); 26e RILé (786); 10e DragR (200); 20e ChàCh (194); 23e CavR (338); artLé (59) **Total** 6,537. To the left of the bridge of Tamines: GdN Aisne (4e Bn, 911); 17e RILé (840) **Total** 1,751.

Grand total 18,747.

Source Dupuis.

1794 THE ACTIONS

FP Sans Culottes Camp, 5 February 1794, clash

A fortified hill position in southwestern France just north of the Spanish border, between Hendaye and Ainhoe.

A French victory over the Spanish.

(This was the opening action in the west Pyrenees in 1794: next action – Casa Fuorte, 3 June.)

French Forces Gen Dubouquet commanding part of the Armée des Pyrénées Occidentales. Exact details not known; see OOB at the start of 1793. The 39e and 147e DBdeLi and GdN Gironde (8e Bn-half) had just been sent to the east Pyrénées and were not present nor were the GdN Lot-et-Garonne (4e Bn) and a battalion formed of various Chasseur companies which had just been sent to the Armée de l'Ouest.

French losses 235 men killed, wounded and missing.

Spanish Forces Gen Urrutia with 13,000 infantry, 700 cavalry and artillery. Exact details not known.

Spanish losses 335 killed, wounded and missing.

Sources Beaulac, Schulz, Chuquet, Phipps.

NL Zandvoorde, 19 February 1794, skirmish

A village 3 km southeast of Ypres in the Belgian province of West Flanders.

A French victory over the Allies.

(Last action – this was the first action in 1794; next action – Le Cateau, 29 March.)

French Forces Part of the Armée du Nord; possibly a brigade.

French totals and losses Exact details not known; see the OOB at the start of 1794.

Allied Forces 4th Hanoverian LIR (1 bn); Baden GrenR (1 bn); York Rangers (1 coy).

Allied totals ca 850 men.

Allied losses Hanoverians 34, Badeners 35, York Rangers* 32 killed, wounded and missing.

* = Émigré unit.

Sources Sichart.

NL Le Cateau, 29 March 1794, skirmish

A town in the French Département du Nord, on the River Selle, 24 km southeast of Cambrai, on Route N43.

An Austrian victory over the French.

(Last action – Zandvoorde, 19 February; next action – ten Briel 6 April.)

French Forces GdD Chapuis commanding part of the Armée du Nord. Exact details not known; see the OOB at the start of 1794.

French totals 15,000 men.

French losses 1,200 killed, wounded and missing, 4 guns, 2 ammunition waggons.

Austrian Forces FML Baron von Kray commanding. IRs Kaiser Nr 1 (3 bns); EH Ferdinand Nr 2 (Grenadiers); Deutschmeister Nr 4 (1 bn); M Wallis Nr 11 (2 bns); Brechainville Nr 25 (2); Wartensleben Nr 28 (3 bns); Beaulieu Nr 31 (1 bn); S Gyulai Nr 32 (1 bn); A Esterházy Nr 34 (2 bns); Matheson Nr 42 (1 bn); Callenberg Nr 54 (3 bns); J Colloredo Nr 57 (2 bns). ChLR Kinsky Nr 7 (6 sqns); 4x FAB. Of these, only 7,000 came under fire.

Austrian losses ca 300 men.

Sources Bodart, Sichart, Wrede.

XX Raclawice, 4 April 1794, clash

A village in (then) Russian-Poland, 35 km northeast of Krakau, 14 km east of Miechów.

A Polish victory over the Russians.

(This was the first action of the Polish rebellion; next action – Warsaw, 17–19 April).

Polish Forces LG Kosciuszko commanding 6,000 men.

Polish losses ca 1,000 killed, wounded and missing.

Russian Forces GM Tormassow commanding 5,000 men.

Russian losses ca 2,000 killed, wounded and missing, 12 guns.

Sources Bodart, Jany, Gembarzewski, ÖMZ 1831 Vol 1.

IN Cerisiera, 6 April 1794, skirmish

A mountain village in the Alps between France and Italy near the Great Little Mont Cenis passes. Not to be found on modern maps.

An Austro-Sardinian victory over the French.

(This was the opening action of the campaign; next action – Saorgio 24 April).

French Forces The Army of Italy (part) Gen Massena commanding. Exact details and losses not known.

Austrian Forces IR EH Anton Nr 52 (1st and 2nd bns); Stabs-Dragoner (2 sqns).

Sardinian Forces Provincial IR di Mondovi (2nd Bn).

Sardinian totals ca 2,800 men.

Sardinian losses Not known, light.

Sources Schulz, Brancaccio, Wrede.

NL ten Briel, 6 April 1794, skirmish

A village 2 km south east of Ypres in the Belgian province of West Flanders.

A Hanoverian victory over the French.

(Last action – Le Cateau, 29 March; next action – Catillon, 17 April.)

French Forces Exact details not known; part of GdD Moreau's division of the Armée du Nord; possibly a brigade; see the OOB at the beginning of 1794.

French losses Not known.

Hanoverian Forces Grenadiers (3 bns); Garde IR (2 bns); 7th DragR and 9th LDR (2 sqns each); 6th IR (2 bns) 1 x HAB.

Hanoverian totals ca 2,800 men.

Hanoverian losses 1 killed, 49 wounded, 89 captured.

Sources Sichart.

NL Catillon, 17 April 1794, clash

A village in the French Département du Nord, 30 km southeast of Cambrai and on the River Sambre.

An Allied victory over the French.

(Last action – ten Briel, 6 April; next action – Landrecies, 19 April.)

French Forces GdD Pichegru commanding the divisions of Fromentin, Ballaud and Goguet.

French totals 60,000 men – see the OOB at the start of 1794.

French losses Over 2,000 killed, wounded and captured; 24 guns (11 taken by the two English columns).

Allied Forces FM Prince Josias von Coburg-Saalfeld commanding.

1st Column Prince von Hessen-Darmstadt 9 bns, 3 sqns.

2nd Column Allvintzy 12½ bns, 22 sqns.

3rd Column Emperor Franz II of Austria, FM Prince Josias von Coburg: 19½ bns, 30 sqns.

4th Column The Duke of York and **5th Column** LG Erskine: **English troops** 1st, 2nd and 3rd Footguards, Guards Flank Bn (1 bn each); Abercromby's Bde: 1st/14th, 1st/37th and 1st/53rd Foot (1 bn each). Cavalry; Harcourt's Bde: 1st, 5th and 6th DG (7 sqns); Mansel's Bde: Blues, 3rd DG, 1st D (Royals) (6 sqns); Laurie's Bde: Bays, Greys, Inniskilling DG (6 sqns) Ralph Dundas' Bde: 7th, 11th, 15th and 16th LD, (2 sqns each); Carabiniers (1 sqn). **Hessen-Kassel troops** GM von Hanstein: Grenadiers (1 bn); Garde-Grenadier and Leib-R (2 bns each). **Austrian troops** IR Kaunitz Nr 20 (3 bns). HusR EH Ferdinand Nr 32 (10 sqns) **Totals** 4th and 5th Columns: 27 bns 38 sqns.

Three further columns (6th – Graf von Haddik with 2 bns and 2 sqns; 7th – The Prince of Orange with a Dutch contingent (12½ bns and 15 sqns) and 8th Gen Geusau with 2⅓ bns and 2½ sqns. The Dutch demonstrated against the enemy line along the River Schelde from Crèvecoeur to Cambrai but did not get involved in the fighting and are not calculated in the figures here.

Allied totals 64 bns, 97 sqns ca 60,000 men.

Allied losses ca 1,000 killed, wounded and missing. Of these, the Austrians lost 627 killed and wounded. There was no pursuit (on Coburg's orders) no exploitation of the victory was attempted.

Sources Sichart, Wrede, Fortescue.

XX Warsaw (Warszawa), 17–19 April 1794, clash

The capital of (then) Russian Poland, on the River Vistula (Wisla).

A Polish victory over the Russians.

(Last action – Raclawice, 4 April; next action – Rawka, 6 June.)

Polish Forces 2,000 regular troops and about 10,000 citizens.

Polish losses Unknown.

Russian Forces LG Count Igelström commanding 5,000 men.

Russian losses 2,265 killed, 122 wounded.

Sources Bodart, Jany, Gembarzewski, ÖMZ 1831 Vol 1.

NL Landrecies, 19 April 1794, clash

A fortified town in the French Département du Nord, 26 km southeast of Valenciennes on the River Sambre, at the junction of Routes D934 and D959.

An Austro-Dutch victory over the French.

(Last action – Catillon, 17 April; next action – Villers-en-Cauchie, 24 April.)

French Forces Exact details not known; part of Pichegru's Armée du Nord. See the OOB at the beginning of 1794.

French totals 7,000 men.

French losses ca 2,000 men.

Austro-Dutch Forces Captain General The Erbprince of Orange commanding:

Dutch Forces Avantgarde Col Count van Bijlandt; Waldeck Jagers (1 coy); Jagers van Bijlandt, van

Béon, van Mathieu (3 coys each); IR Damas (6 coys). **1st Line** LG Prince von Hessen-Darmstadt, GM von Treba: GM van Oijen: Oranje Carabiniers (2 sqns); Garde Drag (2 sqns); Gardes te Paard (2 sqns); Béon and Damas CavR (1 sqn each). GM de Constant: Hollandsche Gardes, Swiss Gardes, Gren bns von Solms, Mollenbruiin and Panhuis, Veld bns van Welderen and von Wilcke (1 bn each); Swiss IR Schmidt (2 bns); IR Waldeck (1st bn); Gren bns von Reuss, van Raesfeldt, Hessen-Philipsthal and von Buseck (1 bn each). GM van der Duijn: Drag Rs Hessen-Kassel and van Bijlandt, HusRs van Heeckeren and Hessen-Philipsthal (2 sqns each). **2nd Line** GM von Geusau: GM von Haacke: IR Waldeck (5th bn); Swiss IR May (2 bns): Veld Bns von Wartensleben and Petit; Bn Walen Perez (1 bn each); Swiss IR Stockar (2 bns); Veld Bn Oranje-Gelderland. GM van Boetslaer: CavRs van Tuyll and Hoeuft van Oijen and HusR Timmermann (2 sqns each).

Dutch totals 23 bns, 16 coys, 22 sqns, ca 10,000 men.

Dutch losses ca 1,000 men. The Austrians (and many of the Dutch) involved did not come into action. The Dutch battalions were very weak, averaging about 220 men.

Sources Sabron, Fortescue, Sichart.

IN Saorgio, 24 April 1794, clash

A village in the French Département des Alpes Maritimes, 40 km northeast of Nice on the French Riviera on Route N204 in the valley of the River Roya.

A French victory over the Austro-Sardinians.

(Last action – Cerisiera, 6 April; next action – Col Ardente, 24 April.)

French Forces GdD Massena commanding the Armée d'Italie. Exact details not known.

French totals ca 20,000 men.

French losses 1,500 killed and wounded; GdB Beulé killed.

Austro-Sardinian Forces GL Colli commanding:

Austrian troops IRs Allvintzy Nr 19 (3 bns); Strassoldo Nr 27 (3rd bn); EH Anton Nr 52 (1st and 2nd bns); GzIR Carlstadt (2nd and 9th bns).

Austro-Sardinian totals ca 8,000 men.

Austro-Sardinian losses ca 2,800 killed, wounded and missing.

Sources Schulz, Wrede, Bodart.

IN Col Ardente, 24 April 1794, clash

A pass in the Alpes Maritimes, in the valley of the River Roya about 50 km northeast of Nice on the French Riviera.

A French victory over the Sardinians.

(Last action – Saorgio, 24 April; next action – Little St Bernard pass, 24 April.)

French Forces GdD Massena with Gen La Harpe's division of the Armée d'Italie. Exact details and losses not known.

Sardinian Forces Gen Colli commanding. Exact details and losses not known.

Sardinian totals 8,000 men.

Sardinian losses Not exactly known; light.

Sources Schulz, Brancaccio.

Comment French and German sources mention a 'Régiment Pignerol' of the Sardinian army as having been scattered and causing the Sardinian defeat but there was no regiment of that title or commander of that name in the army from 1790 to 1815 nor any free corps of that description.

IN Little St Bernard Pass, 24 April 1794, skirmish

An Alpine mountain pass between France and Italy now carrying Route N90 (Route 26 in Italy) from Albertville in France to Aosta in Italy.

A French victory over the Sardinians.

(Last action – Col Ardente, 24 April; next action – La Tuilla, 25 April.)

French Forces GdB Bagdelone commanding part of the Armée des Alpes. Exact details and losses not known.

Sardinian Forces Gen Duke of Monserrat commanding. Exact details and losses not known.

Sources Schulz.

NL Villers-en-Cauchie, 24 April 1794, clash

A village in the French Département du Nord, 15 km south of Valenciennes, near Montrecourt.

An Allied victory over the French.

(Last action – Landrecies, 19 April; next action – Le Cateau, 26 April.)

French Forces GdD Chappuis commanding part of the Armée du Nord 6 bns, 8 sqns.

French totals 7,000 men.

French losses 800 killed, 400 wounded, about 150 captured, 5 guns. See the OOB at the beginning of 1794.

Allied Forces Gen von Otto Austrian HusR EH

Leopold Nr 17 and English 15th LD (2 sqns each).

Allied losses Austrians: 10 killed and wounded, 10 missing. English: 58 men and 68 horses killed, 17 men and 23 horses wounded. This was yet another 'text book' cavalry success for the Allies.

Sources Fortescue, Sichart.

IN La Tuilla, 25 April 1794, skirmish

A village on the Italian side of the Little St Bernard pass, on Route 26 from Aosta.

A French victory over the Sardinians.

(Last action – Little St Bernard 24 April; next action – Briga, 27 April.)

French Forces GdB Bagdelone commanding part of the Armée des Alpes. Exact details not known.

Sardinian Forces the Duke de Monserrat commanding. Exact details not known.

Sardinian losses Killed, wounded and captured unknown; 1 gun.

Sources Schulz, Brancaccio.

NL Le Cateau (Troisvilles), 26 April 1794, battle

A town in the French Département du Nord, on the River Selle, 24 km southeast of Cambrai, on Route N43.

An Allied victory over the French.

(Last action – Villers-en-Cauchie, 24 April; next action – Courtray, 29 April 1794.)

French Forces GdD Fromentin and Chappuis of the Armée des Ardennes. See the OOB at the start of 1794.

French totals ca 40,000 men.

French losses ca 7,000 killed, wounded and missing, 40 guns, 50 ammunition waggons. Gen Chappuis was captured by Gen Otto's cavalry who rolled up the French line from their open flank.

Allied Forces FM Prince Josias von Coburg commanding:

Austrian troops IRs Deutschmeister Nr 4 (3 bns); M Wallis Nr 11 (2 bns); Brechainville Nr 25 (2 bns); Wartensleben Nr 28 (3 bns); Beaulieu Nr 31 (1 bn); Gyulai Nr 32 (2 bns); Esterházy Nr 34 (2 bns); Matheson Nr 42 (2 bns); Callenberg Nr 54 (3 bns); I Colloredo Nr 57 (2 bns). ChLR Kinsky Nr 7 (6 sqns).

The Duke of York's Corps (only the light troops and the cavalry shown were engaged) Gen von Otto: Austrian KürR von Zeschwitz Nr 10 (6 sqns). English regiments: MG Mansel: Blues, 3rd DG, 1st Drag (Royals) (2 sqns each); Col Vyse; 1st, 5th DG (3 sqns each). Avantgarde of the Allied left wing: Austrian HusR EH Leopold, English 7th, 11th and 16th LDR (2 sqns each).

Allied totals 22 bns, 32 sqns, ca 23,000 men.

Allied losses ca 2,500 killed, wounded and missing. MG Mansel killed.

Sources Bodart, Sichart, Fortescue, Ditfurth, Schulz.

NL Courtray, 26 April 1794, skirmish

A town in the Belgian province of West Flanders, just northeast of Lille in northern France, at the junction of Motorways A17, A19 and A14/E17.

A French victory over the Hanoverians.

(Last action – Le Cateau, 26 April; next action – Mouscron 26, 28/29 April.)

French Forces Part of Gen Pichegru's Armée du Nord. Exact details not known; possibly a brigade; See the OOB at the start of 1794.

French losses Not known.

Hanoverian Forces GdI von dem Bussche commanding: Hanoverian troops: 9th LDR (2 sqns); combined infantry detachment, (200 men); 14th IR (1 coy) ½ HAB. English troops (Émigrés): York Rangers (1 bn); Uhlans Britannique (2 sqns).

Hanoverian totals ca 1,500 men.

Hanoverian losses Hanoverians 42 killed, captured and wounded, 1 gun. Émigrés losses not known but light.

Source Sichart.

IN Briga, 27 April 1794, skirmish

A village in northwestern Italy, in the valley of the River Roya leading northwards to the Col di Tenda pass, just east of Route N204.

(Last action – La Tuilla, 25 April; next action – Little Mont Cenis, 14 May.)

French Forces Gen Massena commanding part of the Armée d'Italie. Exact details not known.

French totals 20,000 men.

French losses Unknown; light.

Sardinian Troops Gen Colli commanding: Corpo Franco (2 coys). Cacciatori di Pandini (1 coy). Provincial IR di Tortona, Guardia, 1st Grenadiers, Cacciatori (di Linea).

Sardinian totals 8,000 men.

Sardinian losses Not exactly known, 'heavy'.

Sources Brancaccio, Schulz.

NL Mouscron, 26, 28/29 April 1794, clash

A town in the western Belgian province of West Flanders, 10 km south of Courtray.

A French victory over the Austro-Hanoverians.

(Last action – Courtray, 26 April; next action – Menin, 27–30 April.)

French Forces GdD Souham commanding a reinforced division of the Armée du Nord. Exact details not known; see the OOB at the start of 1794.

French totals 28,000 men.

French losses ca 1,500 men, 6 guns.

Austro-Hanoverian Forces 26 April GM von Wangenheim (Hanover) then GM Graf von Oeynhausen commanding: On 26 April – 1st and 4th Hanoverian IRs (4 bns); 7th DragR (2 sqns); 5 heavy guns, Jägers (2 coys). On 28/29 April these forces were joined by 6th and 9th Hanoverian IRs (4 bns), Leibgarde and 4th CavR (2 sqns each). Two guns had left for Courtray.

Austro-Hanoverian totals 3,600 men.

Austro-Hanoverian losses On 26th: not known, very light. On 28th (the recapture of Mouscron) 116 men killed, wounded, missing.

Austro-Hanoverian Forces 28/29 April On the night of 28/29 April the following Austrian troops under FZM Clerfayt arrived: 7 bns, 10 sqns 12 x 12pdrs.

Austro-Hanoverian total Allied strength now 10,000 men including IRs Sztáray Nr 33 (2 bns); von Brentano Nr 35 (2 bns); HusR Blankenstein Nr 16 (2 sqns).

Austro-Hanoverian losses on 29 April: Austrians – 903 men and 11 guns (IR Sztáray Nr 33 lost 11 officers and 400 men). Hanoverians (all three days) 58 killed, 272 wounded, 527 missing, 5 colours (1 from 1st and 4 from 6th IR), 13 guns, 16 ammunition waggons.

Sources Sichart, Wrede.

NL Menin, 27–30 April 1794, siege and capture

A fortified town in the Belgian province of West Flanders, 11 km southwest of Courtray on Route N8 towards Ypres.

A French victory over the Allies.

(Last action – Mouscron, 26, 28/29 April; next action – Landrecies 21–30 April.)

French Forces GdD Moreau commanding; GdB Vandamme, part of the Armée du Nord; exact details not known: see the OOB at the start of 1794.

French totals 14,000 men.

French losses 500 killed and wounded, 7 guns (5 recovered on 1 May).

Allied Forces GM Baron von Hammerstein commanding: Hanoverians: Grenadiers (1 bn); 14th LtIR (2 bns); 1st CavR and 9 LDR (62 men); gunners (160 men) 1 x FAB; Hessen-Kassel troops IR Erbprinz (282 men); Austrian troops (17 gunners). English troops: Loyal Emigrants (1 bn).

Allied totals 2,423 men, 22 guns, 6 howitzers.

Allied losses Hanoverians – 38 killed, 123 wounded, 387 captured. Loyal Emigrants – 92 killed*, 87 wounded; 7 field pieces and 3 battalion guns were lost; 7 French guns were taken but 5 had to be abandoned due to lack of horses to move them. Austrian and Hessen-Kassel losses not known.

* the French massacred all Émigré soldiers as a matter of course.

Sources Sichart, Ditfurth, Fortescue.

NL Landrecies, 21–30 April 1794, siege and capture

A fortified town in the French Département du Nord, 26 km southeast of Valenciennes; on the River Sambre, at the junction of Routes D934 and D959.

An Allied victory over the French.

(Last action – Menin, 27–30 April; next action – Rousselaere, 4 May.)

French Garrison Exact details not known; see the OOB at the start of 1794.

French totals ca. 7,000 men.

French losses 2,000 killed or died of sickness, 5,000 captured.

Allied Forces* FM Josias von Coburg commanding:

Austrian troops IRs EH Carl Nr 3 (2 bns); Deutschmeister Nr 4 (1 bn); C Schröder Nr 7 (3 bns); M Wallis Nr 11 (2 bns); Klebek Nr 14 (1 bn); Kaunitz Nr 20 (1 bn); Brechainville Nr 25 (2 bns); Wartensleben Nr 28 (3 bns); Beaulieu Nr 31 (1 bn); S Gyulai Nr 32 (1 bn); Württemberg Nr 38 (2 bns); Matheson Nr 42 (1 bn); Splényi Nr 51 (1 bn); Callenberg Nr 54 (3 bns); J Colloredo Nr 57 (2 bns); Vierset (3 bns); Jordis Nr 59 (2 bns).

Austrian Cavalry Carabiniers Albert Nr 5 (6 sqns); ChLR Kinsky Nr 7 (6 sqns); KürR Kavanagh Nr 12 (6 sqns); ChLR Latour Nr 31 (8 sqns); HusRs Blankenstein Nr 16 (8 sqns); Esterházy Nr 32 (10 sqns) and Barco Nr 35 (4 sqns). DragR Royal Allemande*, HusR Saxe* and HusR Bercsény* (4 sqns each). The Prince of Orange commanded the Dutch Army (see the clash at Landrecies 19th April).

Austrian totals 20,000 men.

Austrian losses Not exactly known; light.

* Émigré regiments.

Sources Sichart, Bodart, Fortescue, Wrede.

FP Boulou, 30 April/1 May 1794, battle

A hamlet in the French Département des Pyrénées Orientales, on the River Tech, 22 km south of Perpignan; a fortified, entrenched camp.

A French victory over the Spaniards and Portuguese.

(This was the opening action in the east Pyrenees; next action – San Lorenzo de la Muga, 6 May).

French Forces GdD Dugommier commanding part of the Armée des Pyrénées Orientales, 30,000 men. Exact details not known; see OOB at start of 1793. Generals present included Augereau, Pérignon, Martin, Chabert, Point, Sauret, Victor, Labarre, Despinoy, Mirabel, Guieux.

French losses reported as '20 killed'.

Spanish and Portuguese Forces LG Count de la Union commanding: Gens Navarro, Curten, Vives, Prince de Montforte and the Portuguese contingent: Gen Forbes with IRs Nr 1, Nr 2, 1st of Olivenza; Cascais, Peniche and Freire de Andrade and 22 guns. Spanish troops included the Spanish and Walloon Guards but other details are not known.

Spanish totals ca 20,000 men.

Spanish losses 2,000 killed and wounded, 1,500 captured, 140 guns; all train and baggage.

Comment The Spanish forces were thinly spread over a long line; the concentrated French assault here broke through easily. This well-planned operation took back all the French territory which the Spanish had captured in 1793 except for Collioure and Fort Bellegarde. The Spanish army never recovered from this setback.

Sources Fervel.

NL Rousselaere (Roulers), 4 May 1794, skirmish

A town in the Belgian province of West Flanders, midway between Brugge and Lille on Route N32.

A Hanoverian victory over the French.

(Last action – Landrecies, 21–30 April; next action – Harlebeke, 5 May.)

French Forces Exact details not known; 7 sqns of the Armée du Nord, 1 x HAB.

French losses Over 100 killed, 2 captured; 2 guns, 1 howitzer, 1 ammunition waggon complete with teams.

Hanoverian Forces Obst von Linsingen commanding LeibCavR (1 sqn); 10th LDR (2 sqns).

Hanoverian losses 3 killed, 27 wounded.

Sources Sichart.

NL Harlebeke, 5 May 1794, skirmish

A village in the Belgian province of West Flanders, on the River Lys, 5 km northeast of Courtray on Route N43.

An Allied victory over the French.

(Last action – Rousselaere, 4 May; next action – Willems, 10 May.)

French Forces No exact details known; part of the garrison of Courtray.

French totals ca 5,000 men.

French losses Not known, light; see the OOB at the start of 1794.

Allied Forces Generals Clerfayt (Austrian) and GM von Düring (Hessen-Darmstadt) commanding.

Austrian troops Tyroler-Scharfschützen (3 coys).

Hessen-Darmstadt troops Jägers (2 coys); LtI Bn (1 bn); Leib-Grenadiers (2nd Bn), IR Landgraf (1st Bn); ChLR (4 sqns).

Allied totals 3 bns, 5 coys, 4 sqns.

Hessen-Darmstadt losses 3 killed; 18 wounded.

Sources Sichart, Wrede, Bigge.

FP San Lorenzo de la Muga, 6 May 1794, raid

An iron foundry and town on the Rio Muga in northern Catalonia, close to the French border and just west of Motorway A7/E15 and Route 11 between Perpignan and Barcelona.

A French victory over the Spanish.

(Last action – Boulou, 30 April/1 May; next action – San Lorenzo, 19 May.)

French Forces GdD Augereau's division of the Armée des Pyrénées Orientales: GdBs Guieux and Mirabel. No other details known. See OOB at the start of 1793.

French losses Not known.

Spanish Forces Two battalions of line infantry and about 1,000 Somatenes. No other details known.

Spanish losses Unknown, 7 guns.

Sources Fervel.

Comment This was the only military arsenal in

Catalonia but, despite being so vital and so close to the French border, it was very poorly protected.

NL Willems*, 10 May 1794, clash

A hamlet in the Belgian province of West Flanders, on the border with France, just northeast of Moescron.

An Allied victory over the French.

(Last action - Harlebeke, 5 May; next action - Baisieux, 10 May.)

French Forces GdD Pichegru with the main body of the Armée du Nord including Souham's division.

French totals ca 30,000 men.

French losses 1-2,000 killed and wounded, 400 captured, 13 guns. See the OOB at the start of 1794.

Allied Forces The Duke of York commanding: Blues, 2nd DG, 3rd DG, 6th DG; 1st, 2nd and 6th DragRs; 7th, 11th, 15th and 16th LD. Austrian Cavalry HusR EH Leopold (2 sqns).

Allied totals 25 sqns.

Allied losses British 30 men killed, 73 wounded; 90 horses killed, 140 wounded and missing.

Comment This was the first occasion on which French infantry successfully formed square on the field and resisted Allied cavalry charges. British artillery came up and hit them with grape. A subsequent charge by the 2nd Dragoons (Greys) broke one square, two others were then broken and cut down.

* = part of the battle of Courtray.

Sources Fortescue, Sichart, Wrede.

NL Baisieux, 10 May 1794, clash

A village in the French Département du Nord, 9 km southeast of Roubaix.

An Anglo-Austrian victory over the French.

(Last action - Willems, 10 May; next action - Courtray, 11 May.)

French Forces GdD Bonneau commanding a division of the Armée du Nord. Exact details not known; see the OOB at the start of 1794.

French totals 10,000 men.

French losses 3,000 killed and wounded, 500 captured, 13 guns.

Anglo-Austrian Forces HRH the Duke of York commanding: Austrian Cavalry; HusR EH Leopold (2 sqns). English cavalry: Blues, 1st, 3rd and 5th DGs, 1st, 7th, 11th, 16th LDs.

Anglo-Austrian total 16 sqns. Apparently no infantry came into action.

Anglo-Austrian losses 245 men killed and wounded, 80 men missing; 254 horses killed.

Sources Sichart, Fortescue, Wrede.

NL Courtray*, 11 May 1794, clash

A town in the Belgian province of West Flanders, on the River Lys, 42 km south of Brugge, at the junction of Motorways A19, A17 and A14/E17.

A French victory over the Anglo-Austrians.

(Last action - Baisieux, 10 May; next action - Ingelmunster, 10, 11, 12 May.)

French Forces GdD Pichegru commanding. Exact details not known but the troops included Souham's division and Vandamme's brigade. See the OOB at the start of 1794.

French totals 25,000 men.

French losses ca 1,000 killed and wounded.

Anglo-Austrian Forces FZM Count Clerfayt commanding: Hanoverian troops GM von Hammerstein: 3rd and 4th Grenadiers (2 bns), 10th LDR (3 sqns). Austrian troops FML Baron von Wenkheim: IRs Clerfayt Nr 9 (2 bns); Stuart Nr 18 (3rd Bn); Sztáray Nr 33 (2 bns); ChLR Latour Nr 31 (8 sqns); DragR Kaiser Nr 3.

Anglo-Austrian totals 7 bns, 12 + sqns, ca 8,500 men.

Anglo-Austrian losses ca 1,500 killed, wounded and missing. Baron von Wenkheim was killed in action.

* = part of the Battle of Courtray; 10, 11 and 12 May.

Sources Sichart, Fortescue, Wrede.

NL Ingelmunster*, 10, 11, 12 May 1794, clash

A village in the Belgian province of West Flanders, about 12 km north of Courtray, on the Mandel stream just west of Route N50 to Brugge.

A French victory over the Allies.

(Last action - Courtray, 11 May; next action - Grandreng, 13 May.)

French Forces GdB Vandamme with 8,000 infantry and 1,000 cavalry of Souham's division of the Armée du Nord with 15 x 12 pdr guns.

French losses Not known exactly; moderate. See the OOB at the start of 1794.

Allied Forces Hessen-Darmstadt; GM von Düring: Jägers (2 coys); LtI Bn (1 bn); Leib-Grenadiers (2nd Bn) IR Landgraf (1st Bn); ChLR (4 sqns) and 8 guns. Austrian Troops; FML Count von Sponek: IR Sztáray Nr 33** (2 bns), IR Callenberg Nr 54 (2nd Bn). and 2 guns.

Allied totals 4 bns, 2 coys, 4 sqns, 10 guns.

Allied losses Hessen-Darmstadt - 47, killed, 181 wounded, 3 captured, 2 battalion guns. Austrian Losses - not known.

* = part of the Battle of Courtray.

** = came up at the end of the action.

Sources Sichart, Bigge, Keim, Wrede.

NL Grandreng (Rouvroi), 13 May 1794, clash

A village in the Belgian province of Hainaut, 26 km southwest of Charleroi on Route N40, against the border with France.

An Allied victory over the French.

(Last action - Ingelmunster, 10, 11, 12 May; next action - Tourcoing 17/18 May.)

French Forces GdD Charbonnier commanding part of the Armée des Ardennes. Exact details not known; see the OOB at the start of 1794.

French totals ca 33,000 men.

French losses ca 4,000 killed, wounded and missing, 12 guns.

Allied Forces FZM Count Kaunitz commanding: IRs Beaulieu Nr 31 (1 bn); Esterházy Nr 34 (2 bns); U Kinsky Nr 36 (2 bns); KürR Nassau Nr 14 (6 sqns). HusR Barco Nr 35 (10 sqns).

Allied totals 5 bns, 16 sqns.

Allied losses ca 2,800 men killed, wounded and missing.

Sources Bodart, Wrede.

Comment This was the first French attempt to establish a foothold north of the River Sambre. It failed.

IN Little Mont Cenis, 14 May 1794, clash

A peak in the Alps just north of the Franco-Italian border and of Lake Mont Cenis, by Route N6 leading down into Turin in Italy.

A French victory over the Sardinians.

(Last action - Briga, 27 April; next action - Dego, 21 September.)

French Forces GdB Bagdelone commanding part of the Armée des Alpes. Exact details not known.

French totals 6,000 men.

French losses Not known.

Sardinian Forces Provincial IR di Mondovi (2nd Bn). Austrian troops: IR EH Anton Nr 52 (1st and 2nd Bns); Stabs-Dragoner (2 sqns).

Sardinian totals Unknown.

Sardinian losses Killed and wounded unknown, 'some hundreds' captured, 28 guns.

Sources Schulz.

NL Tourcoing, 17/18 May 1794, battle

A town in the French Département du Nord, just south of the Belgian border, 12 km northeast of Lille.

A French victory over the Allies.

(Last action - Grandreng, 13 May; next action - Tournay, 22 May.)

French Forces Gen Pichegru's Armée du Nord (commanded this day by GdD Souham); the divisions of GdD Osten at Pont-à-Marque (10,000 men); GdD Bonneau (20,000 men) at Sainghin, Pont-à-Tressin and Lannoy on the River Marque; GdD Souham (28,000 men) and GdD Moreau (22,000 men) south of the River Lys, between Courtray and Aalbeke. Thierry's brigade was at Mouscron, Compère's brigade at Tourcoing. Exact details not known.

French totals 82,000 men.

French losses 3,000 killed and wounded, 7 guns. GdB Pierquin was killed.

Allied Forces FM Prince Josias von Coburg commanding:

Austrian Troops Archduke Charles: Tyroler-Scharfschützen (4 coys); IRs EH Carl Nr 3 (2 bns); C Schröder Nr 7 (3 bns); M Wallis Nr 11 (2 bns); Kaunitz Nr 20 (3 bns); Gemmingen Nr 21 (1 bn); W Colloredo Nr 56 and J Colloredo Nr 57 (2 bns each); Grenadiers (3 bns); ChLR Karaczay (6 sqns); HusR Esterházy Nr 32 (10 sqns). **Totals** 18 bns, 4 coys, 16 sqns. **English Troops** The Duke of York - MG Abercromby: 1st, 2nd and 3rd Foot Guards, Guards' Flank Bn; 14th, 37th and 53rd Foot, their Flank Bn (1 bn each); 7th, 15th and 16th LD. (2 sqns each). **Totals** 8 bns, 6 sqns. **Hessen-Darmstadt Troops** Leib-Gren (1st Bn); IR Landgraf (1st Bn); LtI Bn (1 bn); Jägers (2 coys); ChLR (4 sqns) **Totals** 3 bns, 2 coys, 4 sqns. **Hessen-Kassel Troops** Gren Bn von Eschwege (1 bn); IR von Kospoth (2 bns); Füsiliers (1 bn); Jägers (2 coys); Carabiniers (3 sqns); Prinz Friedrich DragR (5 sqns). **Totals** 4 bns, 2 coys, 8 sqns. **Hanoverian Troops** GL von dem Bussche: 1stIR (2 bns); 1st and 4th Grenadiers (2 bns); 1st and 7th CavRs (2 sqns each); 9th and 10th LDRs (2 sqns each); Loyal Emigrants* (1 bn). **Totals** 5 bns, 8 sqns.

Allied totals 38 bns, 8 coys, 42 sqns; about 48,000 men (of the 74,000 present).

Allied losses 4,000 killed and wounded, 1,500 captured (including most of the 1st Hanoverian IR); 6 guns.

Comment This was the decisive action of the campaign in Flanders and was lost due to poor Allied cooperation and staff work. Only half the Allied troops came into action. The French did not exploit this victory.

* = attached English troops.

Sources Bodart, Sichard, Fortescue, Wrede, Has, Ditfurth.

FP San Lorenzo de la Muga, 19 May 1794, raid

An iron foundry and town on the Rio Muga in northern Catalonia, close to the French border, just west of the Motorway A7/E15 and Route 11 between Perpignan and Barcelona.

A French victory over the Spanish.

(Last action – San Lorenzo, 6 May; next action – Collioure, 2–26 May.)

French Forces GdD Augereau with 15,000 men of the Armée des Pyrénées Orientales. Exact details not known; see OOB at the start of 1793. In the Division de Cerdagne the GdN Pyrénées-Orientales and the 14e ChàCh distinguished themselves.

French losses 200 killed.

Spanish Forces ca 5,000 men.

Spanish losses Not known.

Sources Fervel, Beaulac.

NL Tournay (Pont-à-Chin), 22 May 1794, battle

A town in the Belgian province of Hainaut, on the River Schelde (Escaut), 80 km southwest of Brussels, at the junction of Motorways A8, A16/E42 and Route N7.

An Allied victory over the French.

(Last action – Tourcoing, 17/18 May; next action – Erquelinnes, 24 May.)

French Forces GdD Pichegru commanding the Armée du Nord. Exact details not known.

French totals ca 45,000; see the OOB at the start of 1794.

French losses 5,500 killed and wounded, 450 captured, 7 guns.

Allied Forces FM Prince Josias von Coburg commanding: **Austrian Troops** IRs M Wallis Nr 11 (2 bns); Stuart Nr 18 (3 bns); S Gyulai Nr 32 (3 bns); I Colloredo Nr 57 (2 bns); Jordis Nr 59 (2 bns); Grenadiers (4 bns); HusR Blankenstein Nr 16 (8 sqns); and Barco Nr 35 (10 sqns), 4 x FAB. **English Troops** MG Fox 14th, 37th and 53rd Foot, their Flank Bn (1 bn each), 1 x FAB. **Hanoverian Troops** von dem Bussche: Grenadiers (2nd Bn); 1st IR (200 men); 4th, 6th and 11th IRs (2 bns each); Jägers (2 coys); Leibgarde, 2nd, 4th, 5th and 7th CavRs (2 sqns each); 1 x FAB, 1 x HAB.

Allied totals 27, bns; 4 coys, 28 sqns; 6 x FAB, 1 x HAB ca 28,000 men.

Allied losses About 3,000 men in all. The Hanoverians lost 27 killed, 237 wounded, 154 men missing, 81 horses killed. The English and Austrians together lost 1,728 men killed and wounded, 565 men missing.

Sources Sichart, Fortescue, Ditfurth, Wrede.

UR Schifferstadt, 23 May 1794, skirmish

A village in southwestern Germany, on the River Rehbach, 8 km northwest of Speyer, just west of the River Rhine.

A French victory over the Austro-Prussians.

(This was the opening action on the upper Rhine in 1794; next action – Kaiserslautern, 23 May).

French Forces GdD Michaud commanding; GdD Desaix's division; exact details not known. This was part of the Armée du Rhin.

French totals 20,000 men.

French losses 500 killed and wounded.

Allied Forces GdI Prince von Hohenlohe commanding: **Prussian Troops** IRs von Manstein Nr 9, von Romberg Nr 10, Hohenlohe Nr 32 (3 bns each); von Schladen Nr 41, von Kunitzky Nr 44 (2 bns each); Füs Bns Renouard Nr 2 and Martini Nr 10 Jägers (2 coys); KürR Sachsen-Weimar Nr 6, Leibkarabiniers Nr 11, DragRs von Schmettau Nr 2 and von Katte Nr 4 (5 sqns each); HusR von Wolffradt Nr 6 (10 sqns) and von Goltz Nr 8 (2nd Bn; 5 sqns) 5 x FAB, 2 x HAB. **Austrian Troops** IRs Reisky Nr 13, W Schröder Nr 26, Strassoldo Nr 27; O Wallis Nr 29 (grenadiers only in each case) **Bavarian Troops** Combined ChLR (4 sqns); combined infantry regiment 2 bns.

Allied totals ca 30,000 men.

Allied losses 900 killed, wounded and captured.

Sources Jany, Schulz, Wrede.

UR Kaiserslautern, 23 May 1794, battle

A town in western Germany, on Route B37, Autobahn A6, about 55 km west of Ludwigshafen on the River Rhine.

A Prussian-Saxon victory over the French.

(Last action – Schifferstadt, 23 May; next action – Schänzel, 12 and 13 July.)

French Forces GdD Ambert commanding ca 5,000 men; exact details not known. This was part of the Armée du Rhin.

French losses ca 1,000 killed, wounded and missing, 17 guns, 2 colours.

Prussian-Saxon Forces FM Count Möllendorf commanding: Gen von Kalckreuth: Prussian IRs Crousaz Nr 39 (1st and 2nd Bns); von Hertzberg Nr 47 (Gren Bn); von Borch Nr 49 (3 bns); Saxon IRs von Lindt (1st Bn); von Langenau (2nd Bn); Prinz Max (1st Bn); and Prinz Xaver (2nd Bn); Prussian cavalry: DragR Anspach-Bayreuth Nr 5 (3 sqns). Saxon cavalry: KürR Kurfürst and ChLR Albrecht (4 sqns each); HusR (2 sqns). 2 x FAB, ½ x HAB; 1 x Saxon howitzer battery. Gen von Romberg: (Prussians): IRs Braunschweig Nr 21, Prinz Heinrich Nr 35 and von Köthen Nr 48 (3 bns each); Jägers (1 coy); HusR von Eben Nr 2, 1 x FAB. Gen von Knobelsdorff (Prussians): IRs von Thadden Nr 3, von Kalckstein Nr 5, von Kleist Nr 12 (3 bns each); Füs Bn von Thadden Nr 13 (1 bn); Jägers (1 coy); HusR von Eben Nr 2 (2 sqns); 1 x FAB. Gen Prince Louis von Württemberg (Prussians): KürLeibR Nr 3 and KürR von Borstell Nr 7 (5 sqns each); DragR von Lottum Nr 1 (5 sqns); 1 x FAB. Gen von Rüchel, (Prussians): IRs von Rüchel Nr 30 and von Wolframsdorff Nr 37 (3 bns each); Füs Bn Ernest Nr 19 (1 bn); Jägers (3 coys); HusR von Eben Nr 2 (3 sqns); DragR Voss Nr 11 (3 sqns); 2 x FAB, 1 x HAB. Gen von Kleist (Prussians): IRs von Knobelsdorff Nr 27 and Prinz Ferdinand Nr 34 (3 bns each); DragR Voss Nr 11 (2 sqns), 1 x FAB.

Prussian-Saxon totals 43 bns, 4 coys, 42 sqns, 10½ bties, ca 46,000 men.

Prussian-Saxon losses Prussians 110 killed, wounded and missing; Saxons unknown, very light.

Sources Jany, Schuster and Franke, Schulz.

NL Erquelinnes (Péchant), 24 May 1794, clash

A village in the Belgian province of Hainaut 27 km southwest of Charleroi.

An Austro-Dutch victory over the French.

(Last action – Tournay, 22 May; next action – Charleroi, 3 June.)

French Forces GdD Charbonnier commanding part of the Armée des Ardennes. Exact details not known.

French totals ca 30,000 men.

French losses ca 3,000 killed and wounded, 2,400 captured and missing, 32 guns, 40 ammunition waggons, 3 colours. See the OOB at the start of 1794.

Allied Forces FZM Count Kaunitz commanding. **Austrian Troops** IRs Beaulieu Nr 31 (1 bn); U Kinsky Nr 36 (2 bns); Jellačič (1 bn); Grenadiers (2 bns); HusR Kaiser Nr 2 (10 sqns); KürR Nassau Nr 6 (6 sqns); 4 x FAB. **Dutch Troops** The Prince of Orange commanding, Exact details not known; most of the units in the clash at Landrecies on 19 April were involved.

Allied totals ca 24,000 men.

Allied losses 400 killed and wounded, 250 captured.

Comment This was another French attempt to advance north of the River Sambre.

Sources Wrede, Fortescue, Dupuis.

FP Collioure, 2–26 May 1794, siege and capitulation

A fortified town in the southern French Département Roussillon, close to the Mediterranean coast and to the Spanish border on Route 114 about 30 km southeast of Perpignan.

A French victory over the Spanish.

(Last action – San Lorenzo, 19 May; next action – San Lorenzo, 23 August.)

French Forces GdD Dugommier with part of the Armée des Pyrénées Orientales including the divisions of GdDs Labarre and Sauret; six brigades; GdBs Micas, Pelletier, Causse, Pinon, Victor and the cavalry.

French total 14,000 men with 16 x 24pdrs, 6 x 12pdrs, 2 x 12-inch and 4 x 8-inch mortars. Exact details not known, see OOB at the start of 1793.

French losses ca 150 killed and wounded.

Spanish Garrison MdC Navarro commanding 7,000 men with 91 guns. The garrison included the Émigré Légion de la Reine.

Spanish losses 160 killed and wounded; the garrison were released on condition that they would not fight against France for the rest of the war unless exchanged for French prisoners. The émigrés were to be handed over to the French. They also lost 22 colours and 91 guns.

Comment The outwork, Fort St Elme, was abandoned on 25 May; the Légion de la Reine escaped in fishing boats before the surrender.

Sources Fervel, Schulz, Beaulac.

ZZ Ushant (Ouessant) 'The Glorious 1st of June', 1 June 1794, battle

An area in the approaches to the English Channel, 40–50 km west of Brest in the French province of Bretagne.

A British victory over the French.

The French Fleet, Rear Admiral Villaret-Joyeuse

Vessel	Guns	Status*
Montagne	120	L
Terrible	100	B
Révolutionnaire	100	B**
Républicaine	100	B
Indomptable	80	B
Jacobin	80	B
Juste	80	B, P
Sans Pareil	80	B, P
Scipion	80	B
Achille	74	B, P
Amerique	74	B, P
Conception	74	
Entreprenant	74	
Eole	74	
Gasparin	74	
Jemappes	74	B
Impetueux	74	B, P
Montagnard	74	B
Mont Blanc	74	
Mucius	74	B
Neptune	74	
Northumberland	74	B, P
Patriote	74	
Pelletier	74	
Tourville	74	
Tyrannicide	74	B
Trente-un-Mai	74	
Vengeur du Peuple	74	B, P, S

* Status after the battle; B = badly damaged; L = lightly damaged; P = taken as a prize; S = sunk
** = damaged on 28 May and towed to Rochefort.

The British Fleet, Admiral Lord Howe

Vessel	Guns	Status*
Queen Charlotte	100	B
Royal George	100	B
Royal Sovereign	100	B
Barfleur	98	
Glory	98	B
Impregnable	98	B
Queen	98	B
Caesar	80	
Gibraltar	80	
Alfred	74	
Audacious	74	B
Bellerophon	74	B
Brunswick	74	B
Culloden	74	
Defence	74	B
Invincible	74	
Leviathan	74	
Majestic	74	
Marlborough	74	B
Montagne	74	
Orion	74	B
Ramillies	74	
Russel	74	
Thunderer	74	
Tremendous	74	
Valiant	74	
Latona	38	
Phaeton	38	
Aquilon	32	
Niger	32	
Southampton	32	
Venus	32	
Pegasus	28	
Comet	Fireship	
Incendiary	Fireship	
Charon	Hospital ship	
Kingfisher	Sloop	
Rattler	Cutter	
Ranger	Cutter	

This was the only naval action of note in 1794.

Personnel Losses

French 4,270 killed and wounded***, 3,254 unwounded captured. **British** 290 killed, 858 wounded.

*** = of these, 580 wounded were captured.

Sources Pemsel, Clowes, James, Steel.

FP Casa Fuorte, 3 June 1794, clash

A fortified complex blocking the pass of Ispegui from the valley of the R. Bidassoa into the valley of the Aldudes, on the western Franco-Spanish border, 15 km west of St Jean-Pied-à-Port.

A French victory over the Spanish.

(Last action - Sans Culottes, 5 February; next action - Mount Calvari, 23 June.)

French Forces GdB Lavictoire with 2,300 men of GdD Mauco's division of the Armée des Pyrénées Occidentales including some battalions of Basque chasseurs.

French losses Not known; light.

Spanish Forces IR Zamora (1 bn); Aldudes Rifles (3 coys); Légion Royal (Émigrés; 1 bn).

Spanish totals ca 1,000 men.

Spanish losses 94 killed and wounded, 307 captured.

Comment French assaults on Ispéguy ridge (GdB Lefranc and 2,000 men) on this same day and the Maya ridge were also successful.

Sources Fervel, Schulz, Beaulac.

NL Charleroi (Gosselies), 3 June 1794, battle

A town in the Belgian province of Hainaut, on the River Sambre, 49 km south of Brussels.

An Austro-Dutch victory over the French.

(Last action - Erquelinnes, 24 May; next action - Vry-Bosch, 6 June.)

French Forces GdD Desjardins commanding part of the Armée des Ardennes. Exact details not known.

French total ca 27,000 men.

French losses 2,000 killed, wounded and captured, 1 x 12pdr gun. See the OOB at the start of 1794.

Austro-Dutch Forces The Prince of Orange commanding*: **Austrian Troops** IRs d'Alton Nr 15 (1 bn); Hohenlohe Nr 17 (2 bns); Kaunitz Nr 20 (3 bns); Gemmingen Nr 21 (1 bn); Ligne Nr 30 (3 bns); Beaulieu Nr 31 (1 bn); A Esterházy Nr 34 (2 bns); Splényi Nr 51 (1 bn); W Colloredo Nr 56 (1 bn); Grenadiers (3 bns); HusR Kaiser Nr 2 (10 sqns); ChLR Kinsky Nr 7 (6 sqns); KürR Kavanagh Nr 12 (6 sqns); KürR Nassau Nr 14 (6 sqns). **Dutch Troops** Exact details not known; part of the army which took part in the clash at Landrecies on 19 April.

Allied totals ca 28,000 men.

Allied losses 11 officers, 413 men, 108 horses killed and wounded.

* The Prince of Orange took over command from FZM Kaunitz on the eastern Allied flank on 30 May and was reinforced by 10,000 men. This action broke the French siege of the town and threw them back south over the River Sambre yet again, where they were joined by 45,000 men of the Armée de la Moselle under Gen Jourdan. The combined army was entitled that of the Sambre-et-Meuse.

Sources Sichart, Fortescue, Wrede, Dupuis.

NL Vry-Bosch, 6 June 1794, skirmish

A fortified outpost just north of Ypres on Route N8 in the western Belgian province of West Flanders.

An Allied victory over the French.

(Last action - Charleroi, 3 June; next action - Roulers, 10 June.)

French Forces Exact details unknown; probably a brigade of the Armée du Nord.

French losses Killed and wounded unknown; 30 captured. See the OOB at the start of 1794.

Allied Forces Gen von Hammerstein commanding: Grenadiers (3rd and 4th Bns); 14th IR (2 bns); LeibR (1 sqn); 11 guns. **English Troops**** 12thFoot (1 bn); Loyal Emigrants* (1 bn); Volontaires* (1 bn); 8th LD (3 sqns). **Hessen-Kassel Troops** Gendarmes (1 sqn).

Allied total 7 bns, 5 sqns, 11 guns, ca 5,500 men.

Allied losses ca 80. The Hanoverians lost 4 killed, 33 wounded and 9 captured.

* = Émigré units.

** = The 38th Foot (1 bn) came up in support after Vry-Bosch had been captured.

Comment This was the first of three unsuccessful Allied attempts to relieve Ypres.

Sources Fortescue, Sichart, Has.

XX Rawka (Szczekocyny), 6 June 1794

A village in (then) Russian Poland, 60 km north of Krakau.

A Russo-Prussian victory over the Poles.

(Last action - Warsaw, 17-19 April; next action - Krakau, 15 June.)

Russo-Prussian Forces Prussian GL von Favrat commanding 15½ bns, 27 sqns. Total 10,000 men. Russian GM Dennisoff commanding 12½ bns, 35 sqns, 5 Cossack Pulks, 26 guns. Total 6,000 men.

Russo-Prussian total 16,000 men.

Prussian losses 21 officers, 552 men killed and wounded.

Russian losses 9 officers, 315 men killed and wounded.

Polish Forces GL Kosciuszko commanding 26,000 men.

Polish losses 2,000 killed, 1,000 wounded, 7 guns.

Sources Bodart, Jany, Gembarzewski, ÖMZ 1831 Vol 1.

NL Roulers (Rousselaere), 10 June 1794, clash

A town in the Belgian province of West Flanders, 32 km southwest of Brugge on Route N32.

A French victory over the Allies.

(Last action – Vry-Bosch, 6 June; next action – Hooglede, 13 June.)

French Forces GdD Souham commanding part of the Armée du Nord.

French total ca 20,000 men (exact details not known); see the OOB at the start of 1794.

French losses ca 1,000 killed and wounded.

Allied Forces FZM Count Clerfayt commanding Austrian Troops: IRs EH Carl Nr 3 (2 bns); Grenadiers (2 bns); ChLR Latour Nr 31 (8 sqns); 2 x FAB. Hessen-Darmstadt troops: Leib-Grenadiers (1st Bn); IR Landgraf (1st Bn); Jägers (2 coys); LtI Bn (2 coys); ChLR (4 sqns), 1 x FAB.

Allied totals ca 20,000 men.

Allied losses About 600 killed and wounded, 400 captured (Hessian losses: 1 killed, 16 wounded).

Sources Fortescue, Wrede, Keim, Bigge.

Comment This was the second unsuccessful Allied attempt to relieve Ypres.

NL Hooglede, 13 June 1794, clash

A town in the Belgian province of West Flanders 14 km northwest of Courtray and 5 km northwest of Roulers.

A French victory over the Allies.

(Last action – Roulers, 10 June; next action – Fleurus, 16 June.)

French Forces GdD Macdonald and GdD Souham commanding part of the Armée du Nord; exact details not known.

French total 24,000 men.

French losses 1,300 killed, wounded and missing, 1 gun. See the OOB at the start of 1794.

Allied Forces FZM Count Clerfayt commanding; FML Sztáray, GM Kerpen (with 6 bns of the Austrian Army of the Sambre). **Austrian Troops** IRs EH Carl Nr 3 (2 bns); Sztáray Nr 33 (2 bns); Württemberg Nr 38 (2 bns); Grenadiers (2 bns); 3 x FAB. **Hanoverian Troops** Gen von Hammerstein: Grenadiers (1st, 3rd and 4th bns); 14th LtIR (2 bns); LeibR (2 sqns) 2 x FAB. **English Troops** 38th and 55th Foot, Loyal Emigrants* (1 bn each); 8th LD (2 sqns); **Hessen-Kassel Troops** Gendarmes (1 sqn).

Allied total ca 19,000 men.

Allied losses About 900 in all. The English lost 28 killed, 70 wounded and 13 missing; the Hanoverians lost 35 killed, 113 wounded and 5 missing.

* = Émigré troops.

Sources Fortescue, Sichart, Has.

Comment This was the third and last unsuccessful Allied attempt to relieve Ypres.

XX Krakau, 15 June 1794, capture

A town in the Austrian province of Galicia, now in Poland, on the River Vistula (Wisla), at the junction of Routes 4/E40 and 7/E77.

A Prussian victory over the Poles.

(Last action – Rawka, 6 June; next action – Demnicki, 18 July.)

Prussian Forces GM von Elsner commanding 6,000 men. Losses not known exactly; light.

Polish Garrison Stadnicki commanding 4,000 armed peasants.

Polish losses Not known exactly but light.

Sources Bodart, Jany, Gembarzewski, ÖMZ 1831 Vol 1.

NL Fleurus (Lambusart), 16 June 1794, battle

A village in the Belgian province of Hainaut, 8 km northeast of Charleroi on Route N29.

An Austro-Dutch victory over the French.

(Last action – Hooglede, 13 June; next action – Ypres, 1–17 June.)

French Forces GdD Jourdan with part of the Armées de la Sambre-et-Meuse, du Nord and de la Moselle. Exact details not known.

French total 73,000 men.

French losses 3,000 men, 8 guns, 40 ammunition waggons. See the OOB at the start of 1794.

Austro-Dutch Forces The Prince of Orange commanding: **Austrian Troops** Grenadiers (4 bns); IRs Hohenlohe Nr 17 (2 bns); Kaunitz Nr 20 (3 bns); De Vins Nr 37 (3rd bn); Matheson Nr 42 (2 bns); Splényi Nr 51 (1 bn); W Colloredo Nr 56 (2 bns); Jordis Nr 59 (2 bns); HusR Kaiser Nr 2 (10 sqns); CarabinierR Albert Nr 5 (6 sqns); ChLR Kinsky Nr 7 (6 sqns); KürR Royal Allemande* (4 sqns). 4 x FAB. **Dutch Troops** Col Baron von Raesfeldt: IR Stockar (2 bns); Grenadiers: Graf Solms, Raesfeldt, van Buseck, Hessen-Philipsthal (1 bn each) IR Waldeck (1st and 5th bns). Col Count Morzin: Grenadier bns Depricy, Adorian, Biedeskuty; GM von Horn: IRs Schmid (2 bns). Gren Bns van Panhuijs, Mollenbruyn and Orange Gelderland. GM Baron van Boetslaer: DragR Hessen-Philipsthal, CavR van Tuyll and HusR Timmermann (2 sqns each). GM Baron van der Duijn: CavR Hoeufft van Oijen and Légion de Béon* (1 sqn each); DragRs van Bylandt and Hessen-Kassel and HusR van Heeckeren (2 sqns each).

Allied totals ca 41,000 men.

Allied losses Austrians 2,200; Dutch 800 killed and wounded.

Comment This was the fifth defeated attempt by the French to advance north over the River Sambre.

* = Émigré unit.

Sources Sichart, Fortescue, Wrede, Dupuis.

NL Ypres, 1–17 June 1794, siege and capture

A fortified town in the Belgian province of West Flanders, 46 km southwest of Brugge, just southeast of the crossing of Routes N8 and N38.

A French victory over the Austro-Dutch.

(Last action – Fleurus, 16 June; next action – Gent, 24 June.)

French Forces GdD Pichegru commanding about 50,000 men of the Armée du Nord. Exact details not known.

French losses Not known; light. See the OOB at the start of 1794.

Allied Garrison Austrian GM von Salis commanding: Austrian troops: Freikorps O'Donnell (1 coy) IRs C Schröder Nr 7 (3rd bn); Stuart Nr 18 (2 bns); Callenberg Nr 54 (3rd bn). **Hessen-Kassel Troops** IRs Erbprinz, Prinz Karl, Lossberg (2 bns each), Gendarmes (Leib-Eskadron) 12 guns. Hessen-Kassel commander GM von Borcke, GM von Lengerke.

Allied total 7,000 men.

Allied losses 400 killed, the rest captured, 34 colours (30 Hessian, 4 Austrian), 12 field guns. The garrison marched out with honours of war and then laid down their weapons.

Comment Ypres was the key to the Belgian province of Flanders and the French now took over the entire area.

Sources Bodart, Wrede, Sabron, Has.

FP Mount Calvari, 23 June 1794, clash

A fortified French hill position of Vera, just inside the Spanish border on the northern side of the River Bidassoa, about 30 km southwest of Bayonne.

A French victory over the Spanish.

(Last action – Casa Fuorte 3 June; next action – Mount Arquinzu, 10 July.)

French Forces No details known.

French losses 30 killed, 200 wounded. See OOB of the Armée de Pyrénées Occidentales at the start of 1793.

Spanish Forces Capt Gen Don Ventura Caro commanding: 8,000 infantry, 500 cavalry and artillery.

Spanish losses 500 killed and wounded, 34 captured.

Sources Beaulac.

NL Gent, 24 June 1794, skirmish

A fortified town in the Belgian province of East Flanders, 47 km northwest of Brussels at the junction of Routes A10/E40 and A14/E17.

An Allied victory over the French.

(Last action – Ypres, 1–17 June; next action – Charleroi, 19–25 June.)

French Forces Part of Gen Pichegru's Armée du Nord. Exact details and losses not known. See the OOB at the start of 1794.

Allied Forces Austrian IR EH Carl Nr 3 (2 bns), Hessen-Darmstadt ChLR (1 sqn).

Allied losses Not known; light.

Sources Sichart, Bigge.

NL Charleroi, 19–25 June 1794, siege and capitulation

A fortified town in the Belgian province of Hainaut, on the River Sambre, 50 km south of Brussels.

A French victory over the Austrians.

(Last action – Gent 24 June; next action – Fleurus, 26 June.)

French Forces GdD Hatry commanding part of the Armée de la Sambre-et-Meuse. Exact details not known.

French total ca 11,000 men.

French losses Not known, light. See the OOB at the start of 1794 and for Fleurus, 26 June.

Austrian Garrison Oberst Reinach commanding: IRs d'Alton Nr 15 (1 bn); Gemmingen Nr 21 (1 bn); de Ligne Nr 30 (1 bn).

Austrian total ca 3,000 men.

Austrian losses ca 200 killed and wounded; the rest captured.

Sources Bodart, Wrede.

NL Fleurus, 26 June 1794, battle

A town in the Belgian province of Hainaut, 11 km northeast of Charleroi on Route N29.

A 'drawn match' between the French and the Austro-Dutch.

(Last action – Charleroi, 19–25 June; next action – Landrecies, 1–16 July.)

French Forces GdD Jourdan commanding: **Armée de la Moselle GdD Hatry** GdB Chapsal: 27e and 44e RIdLi (1er Bns each), GdN Seine-et-Oise (6e Bn); Côte-d'Or (3e Bn); Doubs (9e); Moselle (2e and 3e Bns); Meurthe (9e Bn); 11e DragR (3 sqns); 18e ChàCh (1 sqn); GdB Bonnet: 58e RIdLi (2e Bn); GdN Lot-et-Garonne (1er Bn); Var (4e Bn); Loiret (2e Bn); 33e RIdLi (2e Bn); 1 x FAB. **Total** 11,000 men. **GdD Morlot** GdB Olivier: 110e DBdeLi (3 bns); 14e DragR (3 sqns). GdB Simon: 1er and 34e DBdeLi (6 bns); 10e CavR (4 sqns); 1 x FAB. **Total** 8,600 men. **GdD Championnet** GdB Grenier: 18e DBdeLi (3 bns); 1er DragR (3 sqns). GdB Lerwant: 59e and 94e DBdeLi (6 bns); 4e CavR (3 sqns); 1 x FAB. **Total** 9,100 men. **GdD Lefeuvre** GdB Leval: 5e DBdeLi (1er Bn); 54e and 99e DBdesLi (2e Bns each); 9e ChàP (1 bn). GdB Jacopin: 13e, 80e and 149e DBdesLi (9 bns). GdB Sulzmann: 16e BnLé (1 bn) 1er ChàP (1 bn); 18e ChàP (1 bn); Légion de la Moselle. 1 x FAB. **Total** 8,800 men. Reserve Artillery – 2 x FAB.

Armée du Nord GdD Kléber GdD Duhesme GdB Schlatter; GdN Vosges (5e Bn); St Denis (1er Bn); 4e HusR (4 sqns); 12e ChàCh (5 sqns). GdB Fusier: 47e DBdeLi (3 bns); GdN Paris (10e Bn); Seine-et-Oise (10e Bn); Vienne (2e Bn). GdB Bernadotte: 32e BnLé (1 bn); 56e RIdLi (3 bns); GdN: Meurthe (2nd bn); Orne (1er Bn); 22e CavR (4 sqns). 1 x FAB. **Total** 10,000 men. **GdD Monaigue** GdB Richard: 10e BnLé (1 bn); 4e Ch Francs (1 bn); 7e DragR (4 sqns); 6e Cavalry and 16e ChàCh (1 sqn each). GdB Poncet: 18e and 49e RIdLi (1er Bns each); 68e RIdLi (1er and 2e Bns); 89e RIdLi (1er Bn). GdB Boisset: GdN Calvados (2e Bn); Nièvre (2e Bn); Haut-Rhin (2e Bn); Mayenne-et-Loire (2e Bn); Eure (3e Bn); Haut-Marne (3e Bn); Somme (5e Bn); Oise (6e Bn), 2 x FAB. **Total** 8,200 men.

Armée des Ardennes GdD Marceau GdB Lorges: 9e and 172e DBdeLi (3 bns each); GdN Nord (3e Bn); Pas-de-Calais (8e Bn), GdB Hardy: GdN Volontaires (2e Bn); Vendée (1er Bn); 11e ChàCh (4 sqns). 1 x FAB. **Total** 6,000 men. **GdD Mayer** GdB Prestal: 26e DBdeLi (3 bns); GdN Nord (2e Bn); Seine-Inférieur (7e Bn): GdB Lecourbe: 16e BnLé (1 bn) GdN Aisne (4e Bn); 20e ChàCh (2 sqns) 1 x FAB. **Total** 5,500 men. **GdB Daurier** 18e RIdLi (2e Bn); 72e DBdeLi (1er and 2e Bns); GdN Loiret (1er Bn); 17e CavR (4 sqns); 1 x FAB. **Total** 6,000 men. **GdD Dubois** GdB d'Hautpoul: 12e DragR (4 sqns); 2e HusR (2 sqns); 6e ChàCh (4 sqns) 1 x HAB. GdB Soland: 6e and 8e CavR (4 sqns each) 1 x HAB.

French total 2,300 sabres, 75,000 men.

French losses ca 5,000 men and 1 gun. 1 colour (2e Bn, 54e Li).

Austro-Dutch Forces FM Prince Josias von Coburg commanding. **1st Column Prince William of Orange. GL Prince von Waldeck (Dutch Troops)** Grenadiers van Buseck, de Briey, Adorian, van Panhuijs (4 bns); Schmid (1 bn); Orange Gelderland, Mollenbruyn (1 bn each) IR Waldeck (1st Bn). HusR van Heeckeren, Hessen-Philipsthal and Timmermann (2 sqns each); CavR van Tuyll (2 sqns). CavR Légion Bourbon* (2 sqns). **GdD Prince Friedrich of Orange (Dutch Troops)** Hollands Gaardes (1 bn); Grenadiers von Hessen-Philipsthal, van Solms, van Raesfeldt (3 bns); IRs de Petit (1 bn); May (Swiss; 2 bns); Waldeck (5th Bn); Gaardes Dragonders, Gaardes te Paard, Carabiniers Orange-Friesland; DragR van Bylandt, DragR Hessen-Kassel, Légion de Damas* (2 sqns each). **GM Count Riesch (Austrian and Émigré Troops)** IR Gyulai Nr 32 (2 bns); Légions de Damas*, Béon,*, Mathieu* (1 bn each); Légion de Béon* (2 sqns). **2nd Column LG Baron Quosdanovich (Austrian troops)** including: IRs Stain Nr 50 (2 bns); Erbach Nr 42 (1⅓ bns); Klebek Nr 14 (2 bns); Toscana Nr 23 (2 bns) and 16 guns. **3rd Column FML Prince Kaunitz (Austrian**

Troops) IRs Splényi Nr 51 (1 bn); Callenberg Nr 54 (2 bns); Kaunitz Nr 20 (2 bns); HusR Bercsény* ChL R Lobkowitz Nr 3 (3 sqns), 16 guns. **4th Column Archduke Charles (Austrian Troops)** 7⅓ bns, 16 sqns and 18 guns including: Grenadiers (4 bns); HusR Barco Nr 35 (10 sqns); KürR Anspach Nr 11 (6 sqns). **5th Column: Gen Beaulieu (Austrian Troops)** Grenadiers (3 bns); Tyroler-Scharfschützen (3 coys); Carneville and Slavonier Freikorps (2 bns each); IRs d'Alton Nr 15 (2 bns); F Kinsky Nr 47 (3 bns); de Vins Nr 37 (3rd bn); A Esterházy Nr 34 (2 bns); Gemmingen Nr 21 (1 bn); HusR Wurmser Nr 30 (4 sqns), HusR EH Leopold (2 sqns); KürR EH Franz Nr 29 (6 sqns); HusR EH Ferdinand Nr 32 (2 sqns); ChLR Karaczay Nr 4 (6 sqns); KürR Royal Allemande* (2 sqns) 18 guns.

Austro-Dutch totals 32,000 infantry, 14,000 cavalry.

Austro-Dutch losses ca 208 killed, 1,017 wounded, 361 captured, 1 mortar, 3 caissons, 1 standard.

* = Émigré regiments.

Comment By this stage of the war the court in Vienna was convinced that it was no longer worth the effort to try to keep their Netherlands provinces and it is suspected that Coburg gave up the chance of a victory here so as to be able to pull out eastwards.

Sources Bodart, Wrede, Fortescue, Sabron, Dupuis.

FP Mount Arquinzu, 10 July 1794, clash

A fortified Spanish hilltop in the western Pyrenees, 24 km northeast of Pamplona.

A French victory over the Spanish.

(Last action – Mount Calvari, 23 June; next action – Bastan valley, 23 July.)

French Forces GdB Digonet with 4,000 men including Latour d'Auvergne; all of the Armée des Pyrénées Occidentales. Exact details not known; see OOB at the start of 1793.

French losses Not known; light.

Spanish Forces IR Zamora (1 bn); Légion Royal (Émigrés; 1 bn).

Spanish losses 314 killed, wounded and missing. Marquis de St Simon, commander of the Légion Royal, was badly wounded and 49 of its members were captured and shot by the French.

Sources Beaulac.

UR Schänzel, 12 and 13 July 1794, clash

A hilltop in the southwestern German state of the Pfalz, 11 km southwest of Neustadt a.d. Weinstrasse, 22 km southeast of Kaiserslautern.

A French victory over the Prussians.

(Last action – Kaiserslautern, 23 May; next action – Edighofen, 13 July.)

French Forces GdD St Cyr of the Armée du Rhin: GdB Desgranges; GdB Siscé with 9,000 men. Exact details not known, but including the 11e DBdeLé and the 186e DBdeLi of 3 bns each.

French losses ca 180 killed, wounded and missing.

Prussian Forces GM von Pfau: IRs von Schladen Nr 41 and von Kunitzky Nr 44 (3 bns each), Gren Bn Romberg Nr 10 (1 bn); Füs Bn von Müffling Nr 18 (2 coys), Jägers (2 coys).

Prussian total ca 6,000 men and 14 guns.

Prussian losses Accounts vary widely; Schulz gives 104 killed, 497 wounded and 328 captured; Jomini states '2,400'; St Cyr 'over 1,000'. 9 guns were lost; GM von Pfau was killed.

Comment This French victory caused the Allies to fall back over the Rhine.

Sources Jany, Schulz.

NL Landrecies, 1–16 July 1794, siege and capture

A fortified town in the French Département du Nord, 26 km southeast of Valenciennes, on the River Sambre, at the junction of Routes D934 and D959.

A French victory over the Austrians.

(Last action – Fleurus, 26 June; next action – Nieuwpoort, 6–18 July.)

French Forces GdD Schérer with part of the Armée de la Sambre-et-Maas. Exact details not known, but present were the divisions of Schérer, Osten and one other. See the OOB for Fleurus, 26 June.

Austrian Garrison GM de Foulon: IRs Deutschmeister Nr 4 (3 bns).

Austrian total 1,900 men.

Austrian losses All captured.

Sources Wrede, Bodart.

NL Nieuwpoort, 6–18 July, siege and capitulation

A fortified port on the Belgian Channel coast; between Dunkirk and Ostende.

A French victory over the Allies.

(Last action – Landrecies, 1–16 July; next action – Le Quesnoy, 19 July – 16 August.)

French Forces GdD Moreau with 8,000 men of the Armée du Nord; exact details not known.

French losses Not known. See the OOB for Fleurus, 26 June.

Allied Garrison Gen von Diepenbroick commanding: 5th and 10th Hanoverian IRs (2 bns each), 27 gunners. **Austrians** 54 gunners and sappers; **Hessen-Kassel** Gendarmes (67 men); **English (Émigrés)** Loyal Emigrants (1 bn); Volontaires (2 coys); other English troops - 22 cavalrymen, 15 infantry; sailors (140 men).

Allied losses 160 killed and wounded (excluding the Émigrés some of whom escaped by ship but the vast majority were massacred by the French). The rest of the garrison was captured.

Sources Sichart, Fortescue.

XX Demnicki, 18 July 1794, clash

A village in northeastern Poland (now Russia) about 4 km south of Novgorod on the River Narew, 16 km northwest of Lomzá and 27 km northeast of Ostroleka.

A Prussian victory over the Poles.

(Last action - Krakau, 15 June; next action - Kobryn, 15 September.)

Prussian Forces GM von Günther.

Prussian total ca 18,000 men.

Prussian losses 'very light'.

Polish Forces Gen Kosciuszko and 6,000 men, mainly raw volunteers.

Polish losses Not known exactly, 'heavy'; 6 guns.

Sources Chodzko, KuKKM 3. Series, Vol IV, 1906.

FP Bastan Valley, 23 July 1794, invasion

A Spanish valley in the western Pyrenees through which now runs Route 121 from Pamplona north to Bayonne.

A French victory over the Spanish.

(Last action - Mount Arquinzu, 10 July; next action - San Marcial, 1 August.)

French Forces GdD Moncey with part of the Armée des Pyrénées Occidentales, in three columns: his own of 13 bns, 800 cavalry, 14 x 4pdr battalion pieces and 4 heavy guns. GdD Delaborde with 9 bns, GdD Frégeville with 9 bns and 2 sqns light cavalry.

French losses Not known, light.

Spanish Forces No details known.

Spanish losses Killed and wounded unknown, 200 captured, 4 guns.

Sources Beaulac.

FP San Marcial and Fuentarrabia, 1 August 1794, clash

A village on the Franco-Spanish border in the western Pyrenees, near the Bidassoa river, 5 km east of Brun. Not shown on modern maps.

A French victory over the Spanish.

(Last action - Bastan valley, 23 July; next action - San Sebastian, 2 August.)

French Forces GdD Moncey with the Armée des Pyrénées Occidentales.

French total ca 12,000 men. Exact details not known; see OOB at start of 1793.

French losses ca 600 men.

Spanish Garrison LG Don Vincente de los Reyes commanding. 2,000 men and 300 guns.

Spanish losses All captured complete with 5 colours.

Sources Beaulac.

FP San Sebastián, 2 August 1794, capitulation

A Spanish Biscayan port about 40 km southwest of Biarritz in France; on Motorway A1/E5.

A French victory over the Spanish.

(Last action - San Marcial and Fuentarrabia, 1 August; next action - Mezquiriz 15 October.)

French Forces GdD Moncey with 6,000 men of the Armée des Pyrénées Occidentales. Exact details not known; see OOB at the start of 1793. The divisions of Frégeville and Delaborde were involved.

French losses None.

Spanish Garrison 1,700 captured, 90 guns.

Sources Beaulac.

FP San Lorenzo de la Muga, 13 August 1794, clash

A hamlet in the northeastern Spanish province of Catalonia, 15 km northwest of Figueras, on the Rio Muga. Not shown on modern maps.

A French victory over the Spanish.

(Last action - Boulou, 30 April/1 May; next action - Bellegarde, 5 May - 17 September.)

French Forces GdD Augereau with part of the Armée des Pyrénées Orientales.

French total ca 10,000 men. Exact details not known, see OOB at the start of 1793.

French losses ca 800 men. GdB Mirabel killed.

Spanish Forces LG Count de la Union commanding 14,000 line troops and 6,000 provincial levies. Including the Spanish and Walloon Guards (3 bns each) and the Portuguese contingent under Gen

Forbes: 1st and 2nd IRs, 1st of Olivenza, Cascais, Peniche and Freire de Andrade (1 bn each).
Spanish losses 1,400 killed, wounded and missing.
Sources Beaulac, Schulz.

NL Le Quesnoy, 19 July – 16 August 1794, siege and capture
A fortified town in the French Département du Nord 12 km southeast of Valenciennes on Route D934.
A French victory over the Austrians.
(Last action – Nieuwpoort, 6–18 July; next action – Rijsbergen, 20 August.)
French Forces GdD Schérer with part of the Armée de la Sambre-et-Meuse; exact details not known, but present were the divisions of Schérer, Osten and one other, as for Valenciennes, 27 August and Condé on 29 August.
Austrian Garrison Obst le Blanc: IRs Mittrowsky Nr 40 (2nd bn); Murray Nr 55 (Grenadier bn).
Austrian total 2,400 men. All captured.
Sources Bodart, Fortescue, Sichart, Wrede.

NL Rijsbergen, 20 August 1794, skirmish
A village in North Brabant province in Holland, about 15 km south of Breda.
A Dutch victory over the French.
(Last action – Le Quesnoy, 19 July – 16 August; next action – Zelden Effen, 23 August.)
French Forces Part of the Armée du Nord; exact details not known. It consisted of a cavalry force of 600 hussars and dragoons with 1 gun.
French losses 2 dead, 20 wounded.
Dutch Forces Major van Klesberg commanding: HusR van Heeckeren (2 sqns). Jagers van Bylandt (det), Corps de Béon (Émigrés) (1 bn).
Dutch total ca 1,000 men.
Dutch losses ca 4 dead and 8 wounded.
Comment This minor action was part of a general French probing attack this day.
Sources Sabron.

NL Zelden Effen, 23 August 1794, skirmish
A village in the Dutch province of North Brabant, about 10 km south of Breda.
A French victory over the Dutch.
(Last action – Rijsbergen, 20 August; next action – Sluis, 17 July – 24 August.)
French Forces Exact details not known; 600 infantry with 3 guns.
French losses 6 killed and wounded, 3 captured.
Dutch Forces GM van Haacke commanding: Swiss IR May (1st bn); Jagers van Bylandt (2 coys; HusR van Heeckeren (2 sqns).
Dutch total ca 850 men.
Dutch losses Some wounded.
Comment This was part of Pichegru's advance north on 's-Hertogenbosch.
Sources Sabron, von Porbeck.

NL Sluis, 17 July – 24 August 1794, siege and capture
A port town in the Dutch province of Zeeland, 20 km southwest of Vlissingen (Flushing) and of the West Schelde estuary.
A French victory over the Dutch.
(Last action – Zelden Effen, 23 August; next action – Strijbeek, 27 August.)
French Forces GdD Moreau commanding (the 2nd Division of Pichegru's Armée du Nord). GdB Vandamme: 14e BnLé (1 bn); Chass du Mont Cassel (1 bn); 16e RIdLi (1er Bn); 22e RIdLi (2e Bn); 24e RIdLi (2e Bn); GdN Bouches-du-Rhône (1er Bn); Calvados (1er Bn); Rhône-et-Loire (5e Bn); Corrèze (2e Bn); Ile-et-Vilaine (1er and 2e Bns); 21e CavR (4 sqns). GdB Laurent: 5e RIdLi (2e Bn); 22e RIdLi (1er Bn); GdN Lot (3e Bn); Seine-et-Oise (4e Bn), Finistère (1er Bn); Marne (1er and 3e Bns); Indre-et-Loire (1er and 2e Bns); 2e HusR (2 sqns); 2e ChàCh (4 sqns). Detachments 1er and 6e Foot and of a Horse Artillery Regiment (60 men).
French totals 13,156 men and 1,943 horses.
French losses 120 dead and wounded.
Dutch and Hanoverian Forces GM W H van der Duijn commanding: Hanoverian IR Nr 11 (1 bn) and Nr 14 (1 bn); IR Hessen-Darmstadt (1 bn); MuskBn von Dopf (1 bn); depot of IR Douglas (1 coy); artillery (104 men); CavR van der Duijn (20 men); Hanoverian cavalry (6 troopers) IR Nijvenheim (60 men); IR Oranje-Nassau (2 coys).
Dutch and Hanoverian total 1,700 men, 17 x 18pdr guns, 15 x 24pdrs, 43 x 12pdrs, 26 x 6pdrs, 5 x 16 inch howitzers, 4 x 16 inch mortars.
Allied losses 15 dead, 32 wounded, 1,000 sick; all captured.
Sources Sabron, von Porbeck, Sichart.

NL Valenciennes, 27 August 1794, capitulation

A fortified town in the French Département du Nord 51 km southwest of Lille, at the junction of the Motorways A2/E19 and A23.

A French victory over the Austrians.

(Last action - Sluis, 24 August; next action - Condé, 29 August.)

French Forces GdD Schérer with part of the Armée de la Sambre-et-Meuse; exact details not known, but present were the divisions of Schérer, Osten and one other, as for Le Quesnoy on 16 August and Condé on 29 August.

Dutch Garrison IR Bosc de la Calmette (1 bn); IR van Plettenberg (1 bn).

Austrian Garrison GM von Cameller, IRs C Schröder Nr 7 (3 coys); de Ligne Nr 30 (2 bns); Callenberg Nr 54 (2nd bn); Murray Nr 55 (1 bn); Vierset Nr 58 (3rd bn).

Allied total 3,500 men.

Austrian losses Not exactly known but very light. They went back to Austria on condition that they would not fight against France for the duration of the war.

Sources Bodart, Wrede, Fortescue, Sichart, Sabron.

NL Condé, 29 August 1794, capitulation

A fortified town in the French Département du Nord, 13 km northeast of Valenciennes, on the River Escaut, just west of Route D935.

A French victory over the Austrians.

(Last action - Valenciennes, 27 August; next action - Breda, 6 September.)

French Forces GdD Schérer with part of the Armée de la Sambre-et-Meuse; Exact details not known but present were the divisions of Schérer, Osten and one other as for Le Quesnoy on 16 and Valenciennes on 27 August.

Austrian Garrison Obst Reyniac commanding: IR a Esterházy Nr 34 (3 coys); IR J Colloredo Nr 57 (1 bn), IR Beaulieu Nr 58 (1 bn).

Austrian total 1,500 men.

Austrian losses Not known exactly, very light. The garrison marched out with honours of war and went back to Austria on condition that they would not fight against France for one year.

Sources Bodart, Wrede, Fortescue, Sichart.

NL Breda, 6 September 1794, clash

A town in North Brabant province in Holland on the River Mark and at the junction of Motorways A16/E19, A27/E311 and A5/E312.

An Allied victory over the French.

(Last action - Condé, 29 August; next action - Boxtel, 14 September.)

French Forces Part of Pichegru's Armée du Nord, exact details not known.

French losses 150 dead and wounded, 6 captured.

Dutch Forces GM von Bentinck commanding the garrison of Breda: IR Waldeck (1er Bn), IR Wartensleben (1 bn); Swiss IR Stockar (2 bns) about 1,300 men.

Dutch losses 4 men of IR Waldeck.

Comment Although this sortie was a success, the Allies had to withdraw before the much stronger French Armée du Nord.

Sources Sabron, Sichart, Ditfurth.

NL Boxtel, 14/15 September 1794, clash

A village in the Dutch province of North Brabant, on the River Dommel, 11 km south of 's-Hertogenbosch.

A French victory over the Anglo-Hessians.

(Last action - Breda, 6 September; next action - Sprimont, 18 September.)

French Forces GdD Pichegru with part of the Armée du Nord. Exact details not known but about 12,000 men with 24 guns attacked the isolated salient of Boxtel itself.

French losses Not known, light.

Anglo-Hessian Forces GM Baron von Dalwigk: Hessen-Darmstadt troops: LeibGren Bn (1 bn) IR Landgraf (1 bn); Jägers (75 men); ChLR (1 sqn); British Émigré troops: Hompesch Jägers (2 coys); Hompesch HusR (2 sqns); Irwin HusR (2 sqns); 4 guns.

Anglo-Hessian total 1,115 men, 4 battalion guns.

Anglo-Hessian losses 693 Hessians, 204 Émigrés killed, wounded and captured*; 4 guns.

Comment The following English troops took part in a counter-attack on Boxtel next day (it failed): 12th, 33rd, 44th and 89th Foot under Gen Abercromby, together with these Hanoverians: Grenadiers (1st, 2nd and 3rd bns), Jägers (1 coy).

Sources Fortescue, Sichart, Bigge, Keim, Ditfurth.

* no Émigrés were taken prisoner; the French killed any they found.

XX Kobryn, 15 September 1794, skirmish

A town in western Russia, 48 km east of Brest-Litowsk

on the Border river with Poland (the River Bug); on Route M1/E30.

A Russian victory over the Poles.

(Last action – Demnicki, 18 July; next action – Krupczyce, 18 September.)

Russian Forces GM Stahl with 800 Don Cossacks and 10 sqns ChàCh.

Russian losses Not exactly known, very light.

Polish Forces The Avantgarde; 500 strong.

Polish losses 300 killed, 65 captured.

Sources Gembarzewski, ÖMZ 1831 Vol 1.

FP Bellegarde, 5 May – 17 September 1794, blockade and capitulation

A fortress on the Franco-Spanish border, in the mountains of the French Département des Pyrénées-Orientales, 30 km south of Perpignan, just off Motorway 9.

A French victory over the Spanish.

(Last action – San Lorenzo de la Muga, 13 August; next action – Campmany, 17–20 November.)

French Forces GdD Pérignon with part of the Armée des Pyrénées Orientales.

French total ca 10,000 men. Exact details not known, see OOB at the start of 1793.

French losses Not known, light.

Spanish Garrison Details unknown.

Spanish losses 1,000 men captured.

Sources Baulac, Schulz.

NL Sprimont, 18 September 1794, clash

A village in the Belgian province of Liège, 16 km south of that city on Route N30, near the River Ourthe.

A French victory over the Austrians.

(Last action – Boxtel, 14 September; next action – 's-Hertogenbosch, 10 October.)

French Forces GdD Schérer with part of the Armée des Ardennes. Exact details not known; see the OOB for Fleurus, 26 June.

French total ca 35,000 men.

French losses about 1,000 killed and wounded.

Austrian Forces FML Count Latour commanding; IRs Gemmingen Nr 21 (1 bn); de Vins Nr 37 (3rd bn); Murray Nr 55 (2nd bn); Jordis Nr 59 (2 bns).

Austrian total 5 bns 3 x FAB*.

Austrian losses 1,500 killed and wounded, 1,000 captured, 36 guns, 100 ammunition waggons.

* = Obviously only a fraction of Latour's 18,000 strong corps was actually engaged. Panic must have broken out to result in the heavy loss of artillery and material. FZM Clerfayt, who was nearby, did nothing to help his compatriot.

Sources Bodart, Fortescue, Sichart, Wrede.

XX Krupczyce, 18 September 1794, clash

An abbey east of Brest-Litowsk in eastern Poland, close to the River Bug, near Routes 2/E30 and 812.

A Russian victory over the Poles.

(Last action – Kobryn, 15 September; next action – Brest-Litowsk, 19 September.)

Russian Forces LG Count Suvorov, Gen Buxhowden, Gen Markoff, Gen Ruschitzky: 6,000 infantry, 3,000 cavalry, 8 guns.

Russian losses Russian sources: 125 killed, 200 wounded; Chodzko: '3,000–4,000'. Gen Ruschitzky wounded.

Polish Forces Gen Sierakowski with the main body of his army: 14,000 infantry (including 2,000 peasants armed only with scythes), 3,500 cavalry, 30 guns.

Polish losses Russian sources – 3,000 killed. Chodzko: '192 killed, 67 wounded'.

Sources ÖMZ 1831 Vol 1; Chodzko.

XX Brest-Litowsk, 19 September 1794, battle

A town in Russia, at the confluence of the Rivers Bug and Muhavec, on the Border with Poland, 208 km east of Warsaw; at the junction of Routes 2/E30 and M1/E30, M14 and A239.

A Russian victory over the Poles.

(Last action – Krupczyce, 18 September; next action – Labiszyn, 29–30 September.)

Russian Forces LG Count Suvorov: Gen Buxhowden, Gen Markoff, Gen Islenieff: 4,300 infantry, 3,700 cavalry, 18 guns.*

Russian losses ca 150 killed and 170 wounded.

* = This force included the Carabiniers, 4 Jäger bns, IR Smolensk, the Don Cossacks and a hussar regiment.

Polish Forces Gen Sierakowski, Gen Krasinsky: 10,000 infantry (including 2,000 armed with scythes), 4,000 cavalry; 30 guns.

Polish losses 3,000 killed, wounded and captured, 28 guns, 2 colours.

Sources Bodart, Jany, Gembarzewski, ÖMZ 1831 Vol 1, Chodzko.

UR Kaiserslautern, 17–20 September 1794, clash

A town in the southwestern German state of the Pfalz, 50 km northwest of Speyer on the River Rhine and on Route B37 just south of the Autobahn A6.

An Allied victory over the French.

(Last action – Schänzel, 12 and 13 July; next action – Mannheim, 25 December.)

French Forces GdD Schaal of the Armée du Rhin. GdD Meynier, GdB Sibaud, GdB Cavrois with ca 16,000 men. Exact details not known.

French losses About 1,000 killed and wounded, 3,100 captured, 4 guns and ammunition waggons, 3 colours.

Allied Forces GdI Prince von Hohenlohe. **Prussian Troops** IRs von Manstein Nr 9, von Romberg Nr 10, von Kunitzky Nr 44 (3 bns each); Füs Bns Martini Nr 10, von Bila Nr 2 and von Müffling Nr 18 (1 bn each); Jägers (5 coys); DragR von Katte Nr 4 and von Schmettau Nr 2 (5 sqns each); HusRs von Wolffradt Nr 6 and Blücher Nr 8 (5 sqns each). **Austrian Troops** FML Count Wartensleben. Gren Bns Diedrich and Weidenfeld (1 bn each); IR de Vins Nr 37 (1st bn); Serbian Freikorps (1 bn); Gyulai's Freikorps (1 bn) HusR Vécsey Nr 34 (6 sqns) DragR Waldeck Nr (6 sqns). **Hessen-Darmstadt Troops** GM Count Wittgenstein: LeibR (2 bns); LeibGren (2nd bn); IR Landgraf (2nd bn).

Allied losses:

Prussians 401 men, **Austrians** 645 men killed, wounded and missing. **Hessians** not known; very light.

Sources Jany, Wrede.

IN Dego, 21 September 1794, clash

A hamlet in the northwestern Italian province of Piedmont, on the River Bormida, 31 km northwest of Savona (on the Italian Riviera), on Route 29.

A French victory over the Austro-Sardinians.

(Last action – Little Mont Cenis, 14 May; next action – this was the last action in the campaign here.)

French Forces GdD Massena commanding the Armée d'Italie. Exact details not known.

French total 18,000 men.

French losses According to French sources: '80 killed, 80 wounded.' According to Austrian sources: '2,000 killed and wounded'.

Austro-Sardinian Forces FML Count Wallis. **Austrian Troops** IR EH Anton Nr 52 (1st and 2nd bns); Combined GzIR Carlstadt (2nd and 9th Bns); IR Allvintzy Nr 19 (3 bns); IR Strassoldo (3rd bn).

Austro-Sardinian total ca 8,000 men.

Austro-Sardinian losses According to French sources: 'over 1,000 killed, wounded and missing' According to Austrian sources: '175 killed and wounded, 28 missing'.

Sources Schulz.

XX Labiszyn, 29 and 30 September 1794, skirmish

A village and abbey on the River Netze (Notec) in Poland, about 20 km southwest of Bromberg (Bydgoszcz), near Inowraclaw.

A Polish victory over the Prussians.

(Last action – Brest-Litowsk, 19 September; next action – Bromberg, 2 October.)

Prussian Forces Obst von Szekely: Füs Bn Hinrichs Nr 17 (1 bn); HusR (3 sqns) 2 x HA guns.

Prussian total ca 800 men.

Prussian losses Not known, moderate.

Polish Forces Gen Dombrowski with 6,000 men.

Polish losses Not known; light.

Sources Jany.

XX Bromberg (Bydgoszcz), 2 October 1794, clash

A town in central Poland, on the west bank of the River Vistula, about 46 km west of Thorn (Torun); at the junction of Routes 5/E261, 10, 23 and 25.

A Polish victory over the Prussians.

(Last action – Labiszyn, 29 and 30 September; next action – Maciejowice, 10 October.)

Prussian Garrison Obst Szekely commanding: Füs Bn Hinrichs Nr 17 (1 bn); IR Pirch Nr 8 (depot bn).

Prussian total ca 1,000 men.

Prussian losses killed and wounded unknown; most captured. Obst Szekely mortally wounded.

Polish Forces Gen Dombrowski commanding ca 6,000 men.

Polish losses Not known, light.

Sources Jany.

NL 's-Hertogenbosch, 22 September – 10 October 1794, siege and capitulation

A complex of fortresses in the Dutch province of North Brabant, just south of the River Maas, 80 km southeast of Amsterdam and at the junction of Motorways A2/E25, A50 and A59.

A French victory over the Dutch.

(Last action – Sprimont, 18 September; next action – Venlo, 27 October.)

French Forces GdD Souham GdB Macdonald: 3e, 24e and 68e DBdesLi (3 bns each); 1er and 2e Carabiniers (4 sqns each); 5e ChàCh (4 sqns) 1 x FAB, ½ x HAB. GdB de Winter; 23e DBdeLi (3 bns); GdN Yonne (3 bns); 30e Gendarmerie Div (1 bn). 1er RILé (1 bn); 6e DragR (4 sqns); 9e HusR (4 sqns); 1 x FAB, ½ x HAB. GdB Jardon: 1er and 4e Tirailleurs (2 bns); 2e RILé (1 bn); 3e HusR (4 sqns); 1 gun. GdB Daendels: 29e DBdeLi (3 bns); DBde de Lombards (3 bns). GdB Delmas – no exact details known.

French total 29,000 men.

French losses Not known exactly but very light.

Dutch Garrison LG Wilhelm, Landgraf von Hessen-Philipsthal commanding: In the main fortress: Gren Bn Hessen-Philipsthal (1 bn); IR van Brakel (1 coy); Swiss IR de Gumoens (depot, 446 men); IR de Petit (depot, 131 men); detachments of the depots of IRs van Plettenberg, Bosc de la Calmette, Bedaulx and 2 sqns of DragR Hessen-Philipsthal. Émigré Légion de Béon (1 bn); 146 guns. **Total** ca 1,800 men. In the nearby **Fort Crèvecoeur, LtCol Tieboel** commanding: IRs van Brakel (30 men), Bedaulx (20 men); de Petit (9 men), des Villattes (11 men); de Gumoens (34 men); 30 gunners; Hessen-Darmstadt Füsilier- Bn. **Total** 462 men, 34 guns. **Losses** Tieboel surrendered his fort at the first demand. Hessen-Philipsthal capitulated and the Dutch and German troops went home on condition that they would not fight against France until exchanged. The Émigrés were excluded from this capitulation and all that were identified were either shot by the French in Fort Papenbriel or sent to France and guillotined. Estimates of those executed range from 83 to 408. Hessen-Philipsthal knew what fate awaited the Émigrés and was heavily criticized for such a weak defence.

Sources Sichart, Sabron, Bigge, Fortescue.

XX Maciejowice, 10 October 1794, battle

A village in Poland on the right bank of the River Vistula (Wisla) 80 km southeast of Warsaw, 15 km north of Kozienice; southeast of Czersk.

A Russian victory over the Poles.

(Last action – Bromberg, 2 October; next action – Kobilka, 23 October.)

Russian Forces LG Baron Fersen, Gen Denissoff: 18 bns, 50 sqns, ca 12,000 men, 36 guns.

Russian losses ca 800 killed and 1,500 wounded.

Polish Forces LG Kosciuszko Gens Sierakowski and Kniaczewicz, Kosinski: 10,000 soldiers and armed peasants.

Polish losses ca 6,000 killed, 1,600 wounded and captured including Gens Sierakowski, Kniaczewicz and Kosinski.

Sources Bodart, Jany, Gembarzewski, ÖMZ 1831 Vol 1.

FP Mezquiriz, 15 October 1794, clash

A hill range in the western Pyrenees 24 km northeast of Pamplona, in the area of Egui along the valley of the Rio Arga.

A French victory over the Spanish.

(Last action – San Sebastián, 2 August; next action – Orbaiceta, 15–17 October.)

French Forces GdD Delaborde with part of the Armée des Pyrénées Occidentales including 11 infantry and 2 grenadier bns, 640 dragoons and hussars. Exact details not known.

French losses Not known exactly; light.

Spanish Forces Gen Antonia Filianghiery with 4,000 men. No details known.

Spanish losses 200 killed, 724 captured.

Sources Beaulac.

FP Orbaiceta, 15–17 October 1794, clash

A hamlet in the Spanish province of Navarra, 37 km northeast of Pamplona, on the road to Roncesvalles in the western Pyrenees.

A French victory over the Spanish.

(Last action – Mezquiriz, 15 October; next action – Bergara, 7 November.)

French Forces GdD Moncey with part of the Armée des Pyrénées Occidentales.

French total ca 46,000 men. Exact details not known; see OOB at the start of 1793. They included Gens Digonet, Marbot, Roucher, Moraud, Castelpers, Delaborde, Dumas, Mauco, Leferron, Frégeville, Pinet.

French losses Not known exactly.

Spanish Forces LG the Duke of Ossuna, Gens Don Manuel Cagigal, Antonio Filianghiery, Frias, Marquis de la Canada Ibagniez. About 13,000 men in various positions; no details known.

Spanish losses ca 4,000 killed, wounded and missing, 50 guns.

Comment The French mounted a complex pincer movement designed to trap and destroy the various Spanish detachments who just managed to slip away although badly mauled.
Sources Beaulac.

XX Kobilka, 23 October 1794, clash
A village in Poland 25 km northeast of Warsaw.
A Russian victory over the Poles.
(Last action – Maciejowice 10 October; next action – Pioniki, 1 November.)
Russian Forces LG Count Suvorov BGs Stahl. GL Isleniеff, Potemkin and Schawitsch. BG Isejoff's Avantgarde: 800 cossacks; Main body – Perenjaslav ChàCh (10 sqns); Hussars, Dragoons and Carabiniers (56 sqns); Jägers (4 bns); Grenadiers and Fusiliers (9 bns), 16 guns.
Russian total ca 20,000 men.
Russian losses 'very light'.
Polish Forces Gen Mokronowsky 12,000 men.
Polish losses 4,000 killed, wounded and missing, 9 guns, 1 colour.
Sources Bodart, Jany, Gembarzewski, ÖMZ 1831 Vol 1.

NL Venlo, 27 October 1794, capitulation
A town in the Dutch province of Limburg on the River Maas, 25 km west of Krefeld.
A French victory over the Dutch.
(Last action – 's-Hertogenbosch, 10 October; next action – Maastricht, 4 November.)
French Forces GdB Laurent commanding: 5e DBdeLi (2e Bn); 22e DBdeLi (1er Bn); GdN Lot (3e Bn); Seine-et-Oise (4e Bn); Finistère (1er Bn); Marne (1er and 3e Bns); Indre-et-Loire (1er and 2e Bn); 2e HusR (2 sqns); 3e ChàCh (4 sqns); 1er and 6e ArtR (47 men).
French total 6,000 men.
French losses 50 officers and men.
Dutch/German Forces GM Pfister commanding: Gren Bn von Buseck (1 bn); Gren Bn van Panhuijs (1 bn); 2e IR Oranje (1 bn); IR Baden (2 bns); IR von Geusau (2e Bn); IR von Maniel (depot). Swiss IR von Lochmann (Hirzel) (depot); Jägercorps van Mathieu (det); artillery (130 men); pioneers (100).
Dutch/German total 1,580 (incl. 230 sick).
Allied losses 14 dead, 41 wounded, 14 missing, 33 deserted.
Comment The garrison marched out with honours of war and went to Breda after agreeing not to fight against the French again in this campaign.
Sources Sabron, Sichart, Fortescue.

XX Pioniki, 1 November 1794, capitulation
A village in Poland, on the River Narew, 120 km northeast of Warsaw.
A Prussian victory over the Poles.
(Last action – Kobilka, 23 October; next action – Praga, 4 November.)
Prussian Forces LG de Favrat.
Prussian total 10,000 men, ? guns.
Prussian losses None.
Polish Forces Gen Grabowski.
Polish total 1,700 men.
Polish losses All captured.
Sources Bodart, Jany, Gembarzewski, ÖMZ 1831 Vol 1.

NL Maastricht, 22 September to 4 November 1794, siege and capture
A fortified city on the west bank of the River Maas, in the Dutch province of Limburg, 30 km west of Aachen and 25 km north of Liège.
A French victory over the Austro-Dutch.
(Last action – Venlo, 27 October; next action – Nijmegen, 7 November.)
French Forces GdD Kléber: GdD Bernadotte GdB Boyer: 21e DBdeLi (3e Bn); 32e BnILé (1 bn), 71e and 72e DBdesLi (3 bns each); 13e CavR; 2e and 4e HusR, 7e DragR, 32e and 34e Gendarmerie divs, 2 x FAB, 1 engineer coy: 9,215 men. **GdD Richard** GdB Poncet, GdB Boisset: 1er ChàP; 35e, 97e, 127e and 128e DBdeLi (3 bns each); 12e and 16e ChàCh. 1 x FAB: 9,961 men. **GdD Duhesme** GdB Daurier: Vol Chass (4e Bn); 93e, 111e and 123e DBdeLi (3 bns each); 17e CavR, 2e ChàCh, engineers (1 coy); 7,663 men. **GdD Friant** GdB Brusette, GdB Gencij: 33e, 49e and 161e DBdeLi (3 bns each), 74e DBdeLi (2e Bn); GdN Somme (2e Bn), Vosges (3e Bn); engineers (1 coy): 8,769 men.
French total 35,608 men.
French losses 300 killed and wounded.
Dutch Garrison LG Prince Friedrich von Hessen-Kassel IRs Nassau-Usingen, von Wilcke (depot); DragR Hessen-Kassel (4 sqns); gunners (316 men); miners (173 men).
Austrian Troops IRs Kinsky Nr 36 (2e Bn), Stain Nr 50 (1 bn), Kheul Nr 19 (2 bns), M Wallis Nr 11 (2 bns), U Kinsky Nr 36 (2nd Bn); W Colloredo Nr 56 (2 bns).

Allied total 8,000 men, 344 guns.

Allied losses ca 500 killed and wounded, all the guns, 31 colours and standards. The garrison went free.

Sources Bodart, Sabron.

XX Praga, 4 November 1794

A suburb of Warsaw, capital of Poland, on the right bank of the river Vistula (Wisla).

A Russian victory over the Poles.

(Last action – Pioniki, 1 November; next action – Radosczyce, 18 November.)

Russian Forces LG Count Suvorov commanding 22,000 men.

Russian losses 580 killed, 960 wounded.

Polish Garrison LG Wawrzecki commanding 28,000 men, mostly armed peasants and citizens of the city.

Polish losses 8,000 of the garrison and 12,000 inhabitants almost all killed, 104 guns.

Sources Bodart, Jany, Gembarzewski, ÖMZ 1831, Vol 1.

NL Nijmegen, 1–7 November 1794, siege and capitulation

A fortified town in the Dutch province of Geldern, on the left bank of the River Waal, 16 km south of Arnhem; on Route A73/E31, A52 and N271.

A French victory over the Anglo-Dutch.

(Last action – Maastricht, 4 November; next action – Zevenbergen, 27 December.)

French Forces GdD Souham, GdD Macdonald 23e, 24e and 68e DBdeLi (3 bns each); GdN Yonne (3 bns); 1er BnILé (1 bn); 1er and 2e Carabiniers (4 sqns each), 9e HusR (2 sqns); 5e ChàCh (3 sqns); 30e DivGendarmerie (2 sqns). **GdD Jardon** 2e BnILé (1/2 bn); Tirailleurs (1er and 4e Bns and 1 coy 5e Bn); 5e DBdeLi (3 bns); Dijkwacht (1 bn); Loopgraafwacht (1 bn); 5e ChàCh (1 sqn), 3e HusR (3 sqns). **GdD de Winter** 107e and 154e DBdeLi (3 bns each); Tirailleurs (2e Bn); 6e HusR and 6e DragR (6 sqns). **GdD Baillot** 163e, 176e and 183e DBdeLi (3 bns each); 2e DragR (5 sqns); 13e DragR (6 sqns).

French total 25,000 men.

French losses Not known exactly; very light.

Anglo-Dutch Garrison GM Haak: LIRs Stuart and Bentinck (2 very weak bns each); and ca 120 British troops of various regiments and some Royal Navy sailors; IR van Randwijk (1 coy); IR de Gumoens (½ coy).

Anglo-Dutch total 1,220 men, guns.

Anglo-Dutch losses After marching out with honours of war, the garrison went into captivity.

Comment The following Allied troops evacuated the town on the night 6/7 November: English troops: 3rd, 8th, 27th, 28th, 42nd, 55th, 59th, 63rd and 78th Foot; 7th and 15th LD; Hanoverian troops: Leibgarde, 2nd, 7th, 9th and 10th CavRs (2 sqns each); Irwin Hus*, Rohan Hus*; Légion de Damas* (2 sqns); HusR Choiseul* (3 sqns); Hompesch Hus* (2 sqns). Dutch troops: IR de Gumoens (Swiss). The French destroyed the bridges and the rest of the garrison were captured.

Sources Bodart, Fortescue, Sabron.

* = Émigré troops.

FP Bergara, 7 November 1794, clash

A ridge in the western Pyrenees, to the south of Roncesvalles and Orbaiceta, between the Rio Urrobi and Rio Irati.

A French victory over the Spanish.

(Last action – Orbaiceta, 15–17 October; next action – this was the last action in the western Pyrenees in 1794.)

French Forces Part of the Armée des Pyrénées Occidentales (exact details not known) including GdD Frégeville's division and one other.

French totals and losses Not known.

Spanish Forces Marquis de Ruby commanding about 4,000 men; exact details not known.

Spanish losses 150 killed, 200 captured, 1 gun, 4 colours.

Sources Beaulac.

XX Radosczyce, 18 November 1794, capitulation

A town in the Polish province of Radom, 50 km southwest of Radom city, due south of Warsaw. Not marked on modern maps.

A Russian-Prussian victory over the Poles.

(Last action – Praga, 4 November; next action – Sochaczew, 23 November.)

Russo-Prussian Forces LG Baron Fersen commanding.

Russo-Prussian total 20,000 men, ? guns.

Russo-Prussian losses Not known exactly.

Polish Forces LG Wawrzecki commanding.

Polish total 12,000 men, guns.

Polish losses Not known exactly.

Comment The Poles were trapped and forced to

surrender; losses were very light on both sides.

Sources Bodart, Jany, Gembarzewski, ÖMZ 1831 Vol 1.

FP Campmany (Montagne Noire), 17–20 November 1794, battle

A mountain in the northeastern Spanish province of Catalonia, 12 km north of Figueras.

A French victory over the Spanish.

(Last action – Bellegarde, 17 September; next action – San Fernando, 28 November.)

French Forces GdD Dugommier with part of the Armée des Pyrénées Orientales. Exact details not known; see OOB at the start of 1793.

French total 35,000 men.

French losses ca 3,000.

Spanish Forces LG Count de la Union. Few details known; the regiments included the Spanish and Walloon guards (3 bns each); provincial levies and the Portuguese contingent under Gen Forbes (1st and 2nd IRs, 1st of Olivenza, Cascais, Peniche and Freire de Andrade all of one Battalion).

Spanish total 50,000 men.

Spanish losses ca 10,000 killed, wounded and missing, 30 guns.

Sources Bodart, Schulz.

XX Sochaczew, 23 November 1794, clash

A village (location unknown) somewhere in Poland.

A Prussian victory over the Russians.

(Last action – Radosczyce, 18 November. This was the last action of the Polish rebellion.)

Prussian Garrison: Maj von Schenck commanding 1 bn.

Prussian losses Not known, moderate.

Polish Forces Prince Poniatowski commanding 4,000 men.

Polish losses Not known, light.

Sources Jany.

FP San Fernando, 28 November 1794, capitulation

A fortress in the northeastern Spanish province of Catalonia, 8 km northeast of Figueras.

A French victory over the Spanish.

(Last action – Campmany, 20 November; next action – Rosas, 3 February 1795.)

French Forces GdD Pérignon with part of the Armée des Pyrénées Orientales. Exact details not known; see OOB at the start of 1793.

French total 20,000 men.

French losses None.

Spanish Garrison LG Count Valdes; no details known.

Spanish total 9,000 men and 171 guns.

Spanish losses All captured.

Sources Bodart, Schulz.

UR Mannheim (bridgehead), 25 December 1794, surrender

A fortified town in western Germany, just to the northeast of the confluence of the Rivers Rhine and Neckar, about 20 km west of Heidelberg.

A French victory over the Austrians.

(Last action – Kaiserslautern, 17–20 September. This was the last action on the upper Rhine in 1794.)

French Forces Exact details not known, but GdD Vachot had 15,000 men here.

French losses Not known but light.

Austrian Troops IRs Preiss Nr 24 (3 bns); W Schröder Nr 26 (grenadiers only); Gren Bn St Julien.

Austrian losses All captured.

Sources Wrede, Horsetzky.

NL Zevenbergen, 27 December 1794, capitulation

A town in the Dutch province of North Brabant, 22 km south of Rotterdam and 4 km south of the River Waal and Maas estuary (Hollands Diep).

A French victory over the Dutch.

(Last action – Nijmegen, 1–7 November; next action – Bommel, 10–28 December.)

French Forces GdB Blondeau commanding (of 3e Division (GdD Lemaire) Pichegru's Armée du Nord): 90e DBdeLi (3 bns); GdN Allier (3 bns), 1er CavR (4 sqns); 26e ArtLé (1 coy).

French totals ca 4,000 men.

French losses None.

Dutch Forces GM von Haacke commanding: Garde-Dragonders (19 men); DragR Hessen-Kassel (80 men); HusR van Heeckeren (1st Sqn – 111 men); Gren Bn van Buseck (62 men); IR Erfprins (2nd Bn – 178 men); IR Waldeck (5th Bn – 211 men); artillery (1 man).

Dutch total 662 men.

Dutch losses All captured; released on the parole not to fight again against France until exchanged.

Comment Blondeau's brigade trapped these motley Dutch units which had been driven out of their posts by a general assault by Pichegru's Armée du Nord.

Sources Sabron, von Porbeck.

NL Bommel, 10–28 December 1794, capture

A town in the Dutch province of Geldern, on the north side of the island formed by the Rivers Rhine and Maas (the 'Bommeler Ward'), 15 km north of 's-Hertogenbosch on Route A2/E25 and now called Zaltbommel.

A French victory over the Dutch.

(Last action – Zevenbergen, 27 December; next action – Grave, 29 December.)

French Forces GdD Delmas with part of the Armée du Nord; exact details not known but including the divisions of Lemaire, Bonneau and Moreau (the latter commanded by GdB Vandamme). See the OOB for Fleurus, 26 June.

French total 12,000 men.

French losses Not known.

Dutch Forces GL Prince Christian von Hessen-Darmstadt, GM Constant; GM van Haacke: IR Erfprinz (1st and 2nd Bns); Hollandsche gardes, Swiss gardes (1 bn each); Swiss IR May (4 coys); Gren Bns van Solms, van Panhuijs, van Raesfeldt (1 bn each); Swiss IR Lochmann (2 bns); IRs Oranje Friesland and De Luningh (1 bn each); Jagers von Löwenstein (2 coys); IR Hohenlohe-Bartenstein (1 bn); DeLega LtI Bn (1 bn); Landzaten (1 bn); DragRs Hessen-Kassel and van Bylandt (1 sqn each); CavR van Damas* and de Béon* (2 sqns); artillery, HusR van Heeckeren (1 sqn), Garde Dragonders (1tp); IR Waldeck (5th Bn).

Dutch total 5,000 men.

Dutch losses 1,600 killed, wounded and missing, 60 guns.

* = Émigrés.

Sources Bodart, Sabron, Sichart, Bigge.

NL Grave, 1–29 December 1794, siege and capture

A fortified town in the Dutch province of North Brabant, on the left bank of the River Maas, about 15 km southwest of Nijmegen, on Route N321 towards 's-Hertogenbosch.

A French victory over the Dutch.

(Last action – Bommel, 28 December; next action – Tuil, 29–30 December.)

French Forces GdB Salme with part of the Armée du Nord; exact details not know.

French total 3,000 men.

French losses 13 killed and wounded.

Dutch Garrison GM de Bons: IR Waldeck (2nd bn); Swiss IR May (4 coys and the depot), IR Hessen-Darmstadt (depot); Jagers van Bylandt (50 men), Jagers van Löwenstein (50 men), gunners (100 men).

Dutch total 1,500 men, 160 guns.

Dutch losses 8 killed, 6 wounded, 2 captured, 8 deserted during the siege. The rest capitulated.

Sources Bodart, Sabron, Sichart.

NL Tiel (Geldermalsen), 29/30 December 1794, clash

A town in the northern Dutch province of Gelderland, on the north bank of the River Waal, 35 km southwest of Arnhem, just south of the Motorway A15/E31.

An Allied victory over the French.

(Last action – Grave, 1–29 December; next action – Geertruidenberg, 31 December 1794 – 19 January 1795.)

French Forces GdB Daendels commanding: 3e BnLé (1 bn); 29e DBdeLi (3 bns); GdN Lombards (3 bns); 8e HusR (4 sqns) 1 x FAB.

French total ca 4,000 men.

French losses ca 600 killed, wounded and missing.

Allied Forces Gen D Dundas commanding: 19th, 27th, 28th, 33rd, 42nd and 80th Foot (1 bn each); Loyal Emigrants* (1 bn), Rohan Hus* (4 sqns); 11th and 15th LD (2 sqns each). **Hessen-Kassel Troops** Garde-Gren-R (2 bns); Gren Bns Lelong and von Wurmb (1 bn each) 2 x FAB.

Allied total ca 9,000 men.

Allied losses About 50 killed and wounded.

Comment Although a local success which drove the French back south of the frozen River Waal, the Allies had to bow to greater French numbers and withdraw past Arnhem and over the Rhine.

Sources Sabron, Fortescue, Sichart, Bigge, Has.

1795

1795 THE ACTIONS

Due to the continued lack of detailed participation of French regiments we are forced to refer to OOB such as the ones given here:

Armée de la Sambre-et-Meuse on 1 October 1795 around Mainz

GdD Lefebvre's Avantgarde.

GdB Leval, Jacopin and d'Hautpoul 10e & 13e DBdeLé, 8e, 90e & 119e DBdeLi, 1er, 6e & 9e ChàCh. **Total** 12,618 men; Location: between Selsheim and Niederliederbach. **GdD Tilly** GdB Duvingau and Lorges: 23e, 27e & 72e DBdeLi; GdN Yonne (3 bns each); 12e ChàCh. **Total** 9,861 men. Location: between Herdenheim and Helsheim. **GdD Grenier** GdB Simon, Olivier and Oswald: 110e & 173e DBdeLi, 112e & 172e DBdeLi (3 bns each); 19e ChàCh, 4e HusR. **Total** 11,150 men. Location: around Weilsbach on the river Main. **GdD Poncet** GdB Schlatter and Soult: 53e, 87e, 66e & 116e DBdeLi (3 bns each); 7e & 11e DragRs. **Total** 9,384 men. Location: on the right bank of the river Main, between Wickert and Wilbach. **GdD Championnet** GdB Legrand and Klein: 59e, 132e & 181e DBdeLi (3 bns each); 1er & 12e DragR. **Total** 9,816 men. Location: on the plateau west of Mainz. **GdD Bernadotte** GdB Daurier, Barbon: 21e DBdeLé, 71e, 111e & 123e DBdeLi (3 bns each); 2e HusR, 3e ChàCh. **Total** 8,223 men. Location: around Biberach and in front of Kassel. GdD Harville (Reserve Cavalry); 6e, 8e, 10e & 13e CavR (4 sqns each). **Total** 1,593 men. Location: around Langenheim and Marxheim. **Total Avantgarde** 63,615.

Around the fortress of Ehrenbreitstein (opposite Koblenz) and Newied were: **GdD Marceau's division** GdB Naleche and Hardy: 1re, 9e, 21e, 26e & 178e DBdeLi (3 bns each); 11e ChàCh, 31e Gendarmes (1 bn). **Total** 11,240 men. At Düsseldorf was **Collaud's division** GdB Bastoul, Schoemsel: 34e, 112e & 175e DBdeLi (3 bns each); 4 composite battalions; 2e & 14e DragRs. **Total** 8,911 men.

Around Luxembourg fortress was **Friant's division** (3,296 men) and at Aachen was **Morlot's division** (3,471 men).

The Armée des Pyrénées Orientales, 1793–1795

Regular troops: 1er, 8e & 29e RlLé; 3e, 5e, 7e, 10e, 17e, 20e, 27e, 28e, 35e, 39e, 53e, 61e, 70e, 79e, 80e, 122e, 130e & 174e RIdLi. Veterans: 5e, 15e, 17e, 34e, 37e & 77e Coys. 1er HusR; 14e, 19e & 22e ChàCh, 14e & 15e DragR, 27e CavR. Artillery batteries from the 2e, 4e & 5e Regiments; Sapeurs: 5e Bn.

Volontaires and Garde Nationale: Alpes-Basses (1er Gren Bn); Alpes-Hautes (1er Bn); Ardèche (2e, 3e, 4e, 5e & 6e Bns); Arriège (1er–7e Bns), Aube (3e Bn); Aude (1er–9e Bns); Bouches-du-Rhône (1er & 2e Gren Bns & 1 sqn dragoons); Cantal (1er Bn); Corrèze (4e Bn), Corse (4e Bn)*; Dordogne (6e & 8e Bns); Drôme (3e & 9e Bns); Garde (1er & 2e Grenadiers & 6 fusilier bns); Garonne (Haute) (2e–10e Bns); Gers (1er & 2e Bns); Gironde (1er, 2e & 6e Bns); Hérault (1er, 2e & 3e de Montpellier, 1er & 2e de Béziers, 1er & 2e de St Pons, 1er de Lodève & 30 dragoons); Loire (Haute) (3e Bn); Loire (Inférieure) (Bn de Nantais); Lot (3e, 4e & 5e Bns); Montblanc (1er–5e Bns, known as the 'Légion des Allobroges'); Moselle (1 bn Chasseurs à Pied); Pyrénées (Hautes) (1er & 2e Bns); Pyrénées Orientales (1er–4e Bns, known as the 'Légion des Pyrénées Orientales'; bn des Corbières, 150 Miqueletes, 340 cavalry); Seine (3e Bn); Tarn (1er, 3e & 4e Bns & 240 cavalry); Vauclause (1er ChàP; 5e Fusiliers); Vienne (Haute) (3e & 5e Bns).

Irregular Corps: Volontaires des côtes maritimes (1er, 2e, 3e, 4e, 6e, 7e & 13e Bns); Légion de la Montagne (1er–6e & 10e Bns); Vengeurs (1er Bn); Braconniers montagnardes (1er Bn); Chasseurs Flanqueurs (1er Bn). These Irregular Corps and the Chasseurs were the elite of the army.

Armée d'Italie

DBdesLi 4e, 5e, 6e, 9e, 11e, 12e, 13e, 14e, 18e, 19e, 25e, 30e, 32e, 33e, 39e, 40e, 43e, 45e, 51e, 55e, 57e, 58e, 61e, 63e, 64e, 69e, 75e, 79e, 85e, 88e, 93e. DBdesLé: 11e, 12e, 20e. DragRs: 3e, 5e, 8e, 9e, 15e, 18e, 20e. ChàCh: 10e, 13e, 15e, 19e, 22e, 24e, 25e. HusRs 1er & 7e bis.

* = there is some doubt if this unit was actually deployed.

Source: Fervel.

NL Heusden, 5–14 January 1795, capitulation

A fortified town in the Dutch province of North Brabant, 12km northwest of 's-Hertogenbosch and just south of the River Maas.

A French victory over the Dutch.

(Last action – Tuil, 29/30 December 1794; next action – Geertruidenberg, 19 January.)

French Forces GdB Daendel's brigade of GdD Delmas' 6th Division: 3e DBdeLé (1 bn); 29e DBdeLi (3 bns); GdN des Lombards (3 bns); 8e HusR (4 sqns); 1 x FAB.

French total ca 4,000 men.

French losses Not exactly known but very light.

Dutch Garrison Col Teutscher von Lisfeld commanding: Gren bn Mollenbruyn (1 bn); IR von Geusau (2nd bn); IR Sachsen-Gotha (2 bns); CavR van der Duijn (1 sqn); Landzaten* (1 coy); artillery (½ coy).

Dutch total 1,400 men.

Dutch losses All captured as well as 175 guns. The troops kept their personal weapons and their colours and standards and went home.

Sources Bodart, Sabron.

Comment The severe weather caused the defensive inundations to freeze over. The commandant was 'a man of little character and independence' who felt he had been abandoned by his army.

* Landzaten = a type of Landwehr.

Sources Sabron.

NL Geertruidenberg, 31 December 1794 – 19 January 1795, blockade and surrender

A fortress on the south side of the Rivers Waal and Maas estuary, 30 km west of 's-Hertogenbosch in Holland.

A French victory over the Dutch.

(Last action – Heusden, 14 January; next action – Luxembourg, 4 June.)

French Forces GdD Bonneau's 5th Division of Pichegru's Armée du Nord: GdB Compère: 183 DBde (2 bns); GdN Tirailleurs (5e Bn); 5e HusR (4 sqns); ½ x FAB. GdB Noël: 107e & 154e DBdes (3 bns each); 6e HusR (4 sqns); ½ x FAB. GdB Baillot: 163e DBde (3 bns); 183e DBde (1er & 2e Bns); 2e DragR (4 sqns); ½ x FAB.

French total ca 13,000 men.

French losses Not known but very slight.

Dutch Garrison Gen Bedaulx commanding: IRs Oranje Friesland (1 coy); von Wartensleben (2 bns); Jagers van Bijlandt (1 coy); Jagers von Waldeck (½ coy); Landzaten* (1 coy); gunners (½ coy).

Dutch total ca 950 men.

Dutch losses all captured and released on condition that they would not serve against France until exchanged.

Comment Gen Bedaulx was 82 years old. Morale was low and desertion high. By 19 January there were only 365 men available for duty.

Sources Sabron.

FP Rosas, 21 November 1794 – 3 February 1795, siege and capture

A fortified port in the northeastern Spanish province of Barcelona, on the Mediterranean coast, 43 km northeast of Girona.

A French victory over the Spanish.

(This was the opening action here in 1795; next action – Bascara, 14 June).

French Forces GdD Sauret commanding*: GdB Victor: 2,455 men; GdB Martin: 1,747 men. GdB Motte: 1,799 men. GdB Causse: 1,403 men. GdB Chabert: 2,118 men. GdB Guillot: 1,019 infantry, 123 cavalry. At Castillon: GdD Beaufort: 2,586 infantry and 211 cavalry.

French total 13,261 men.

French losses Not known exactly but light.

Spanish Garrison LG Don Izquierdo commanding.

Spanish total 4,000 men

Spanish losses 113 killed, 470 wounded, 1,160 sick; the garrison escaped by sea except for 300 who were captured.

Sources Bodart, Schultz, Fervel.

* = exact details unknown; see OOB of the Army of the East Pyrenees at the beginning of the 1795 chapter.

ZZ Genoa, 14 March 1795, sea battle

A fortified port city in northwestern Italy, on the Mediterranean coast.

An Anglo-Neapolitan victory over the French.

(This was the first naval action of note in 1795; next action – Quiberon Bay, 23 June).

French Forces Rear Admiral Martin commanding. *Ça Ira* (80), *Victoire* (80), *Mercure* (74), *Censeur* (74), *Vestale* (36), *Sans Culotte* (120), *Duquesne* (74); *Tonnant* (74) and other, unidentified ships.

French total 13 ships of the line with 490 guns, 9,520 men.

French losses *Ça Ira* & *Censeur* taken, 600 men killed and wounded, 1,000 captured.

English Forces Vice Admiral Hotham commanding:

The Van: *Captain* (74); *Bedford* (74); *Tancredi** (74); *Princess Royal* (98); *Agamemnon* (64). The Centre: *Illustrious* (74); *Courageux* (74); *Britannia* (100, flagship); *Egmont* (74); *Windsor Castle* (98). The Rear: *Diadem* (64); *St George* (98); *Terrible* (74); *Fortitude* (74). Frigates: *Minerva** (32); *Pilade** (32); *Lowestoft* (32); *Poulette* (26); *Inconstant* (36); *Meleager* (32); *Romulus* (36); Brigs etc: *Tarleton* (14); *Moselle* (18); *Fox* (cutter).

* = Neapolitan ships

Allied total 14 ships of the line, 557 guns, 8,810 men

Allied losses 400 killed and wounded. *Illustrious* was so badly damaged that she was destroyed after the action.

Sources Clowes, James, Steel.

NL Luxembourg 9 August 1794 – 7 June 1795, blockade and capitulation

The capital city of the Grand Duchy of Luxembourg, between Belgium, Germany and France.

A French victory over the Austrians.

(Last action – Geertruidenberg, 19 January; next action – Düsseldorf, 21 September.)

French Forces GdD Hatry commanding; exact details not known.

French total ca 3,300 men

French losses Not exactly known but light.

Austrian Garrison FM Baron von Bender commanding: IRs Huff Nr 8 (2 bns); Clerfayt Nr 9 (3rd bn); Württemberg Nr 38 (3rd bn); Mittrowsky Nr 40 (2 bns), DragR Toscana Nr 26 (6 sqns). Artillery, engineers, miners.

Austrian totals 6,000 men.

Austrian losses ca 1,200 killed, wounded and died of sickness. The garrison went free on condition that they would not fight against France until exchanged.

Sources Bodart; ÖMZ 1830 Heft 3. Wrede.

FP Bascara, 14 June 1795, clash

A town in the northeastern Spanish province of Catalonia on the right bank of the Rio Fluvia, 12 km south of Figueras.

A Spanish victory over the French.

(Last action – Rosas, 3 February; next action – Puigcerda, 26 July.)

French Forces GdD Schérer commanding the Armée des Pyrénées Orientales. Exact details unknown; see the OOB at the beginning of the 1795 chapter.

French totals 25,000 men.

French losses 2,500 men killed, wounded and captured, 4 guns.

Spanish Troops LG Count Urrutia commanding: Gen Taranco, Gen Cuesta and the Marquis de la Romana. Exact details not known but the regiments included the Spanish and Walloon Guards (3 bns each); Gen Forbes' Portuguese contingent (1st & 2nd IRs, 1st of Cascais, Olivenca, Peniche and Freire de Andrade) and a newly-raised Hussar Regiment.

Spanish totals 35,000 men.

Spanish losses 534 killed and wounded, 12 captured.

Sources Bodart, Schulz, Fervel.

ZZ Quiberon Bay (Lorient) 23 June 1795, sea battle

A French island off the coast of the Département de Morbihan, 15 km south of Lorient.

An English victory over the French.

(Last action – Genoa, 14 March; next action – Hyères, 13 July.)

French Forces Vice Admiral Villaret-Joyeuse commanding: *Alexandre** (74); *Formidable** (74); *Peuple* (120); *Mucius* (74); *Wattignies* (74); *Nestor* (74); *Tigre** (74); *Redoutable* (74); *Zélé* (74); *Fougueux* (74); *Jean Bart* (74); *Droits de l'Homme* (74) and other ships.

French total 12 ships of the line, 11 frigates, 1,400 guns, 9,000 men

French losses Not exactly known; in the 3 prizes 670 men were killed and wounded.

* = taken.

English Forces Vice Admiral Lord Bridport commanding: *Royal George* (100); *Queen Charlotte* (100); *Queen* (98); *London* (98); *Prince of Wales* (98); *Prince* (98); *Barfleur* (98); *Prince George* (98); *Sans Pareil* (80); *Valiant* (74); *Orion* (74); *Irresistible* (74); *Russell* (74); *Colossus* (74); *Révolutionnaire* (44); *Thalia* (36); *Nymphe* (36); *Aquilon* (32); *Astroea* (32); *Babet* (20); Fireships: *Megoera* (14) and *Incendiary* (14). Hospital ships: *Charon* (44) Luggers: *Argus* (14) and *Dolly*. Under Commodore Sir John Warren were also: *Robust* (74), *Thunderer* (74) and *Standard* (64)

English losses 31 killed, 113 wounded.

Comment Bridport unexpectedly broke off the action. Had he continued, it is likely that the entire French force would have been destroyed. Only *Queen Charlotte*, *Sans Pareil*, *Irresistible*, *Colossus*, *Orion*, *Russell*, *London* and *Royal George* were engaged.

Sources Clowes, James, Steel.

ZZ Hyères, 13 July 1795, naval battle

A group of islands off the French Mediterranean coast, about 25 km east of Toulon.

An Anglo-Neapolitan victory over the French.

(Last action - Quiberon Bay, 23 June; this was the last naval action of note in 1795.)

French Forces Rear Admiral Martin commanding: *Alcide*** (74), *Alceste* (36) and several other ships of the line and frigates including *Justice* (40)

French losses Not known exactly, certainly over 100 killed.

Anglo-Neapolitan Forces Vice Admiral Hotham commanding: *Britannia* (100); *Victory* (100); *Princess Royal* (98); *St George*; *Windsor Castle* (98); *Blenheim* (90); *Gibraltar* (80); *Captain* (74); *Fortitude* (74); *Bombay Castle* (74); *Saturn* (74); *Cumberland* (74); *Terrible* (74); *Defence* (74); *Egmont* (74); *Culloden* (74); *Bedford* (74); *Courageux* (74); *Audacious* (74); *Guiscardo** (74); *Samnita** (74); *Agamemnon* (64); *Diadem* (64); *Meleager* (32); *Cyclops* (28); *Ariadne* (24); *Comet* (14); *Eclair* (20); *Flèche* (20); *Moselle* (18); *Mutine* (12), *Resolution* (cutter).

Only *Victory*, *Cumberland*, *Blenheim*, *Culloden*, *Captain* and *Defence* were engaged

Anglo-Neapolitan losses 11 killed, 28 wounded.

Comment Hotham broke off the action much to the chagrin of his officers and men.

* = Neapolitan ships.

** = blew up on 13 July.

Sources Clowes, James, Steel.

XX Quiberon (Saint-Barbe, Penthièvre) 16 - 20 July 1795, clashes

A peninsula in northwestern France, jutting south into the Bay of Biscay towards the island of Belle-Ile, 43 km southeast of Lorient.

A French Republican victory over the French Royalistes and Émigrés in English service.

(This was the only action of note in the Vendée in 1795).

Republican Forces GdD Hoche commanding.

Republican total 13,000 men

Republican losses ca 500 killed and wounded.

Royalist and Emigré Forces Comte d'Hervilly, Comte de Puisaye and Marquis de Sombreuil.

Royalist and Emigré totals 17,000 men.

Royalist and Emigré losses 1,700 killed and wounded, 6,300 captured.

Comment Many 'Royalists' were Republicans captured in the the Netherlands and pressed into service. They deserted en masse and betrayed the details of the Royalist defences to the Republicans.

Sources Chuquet, Bodart.

FP Puigcerda, 26 July 1795, storming of

A Spanish town in the eastern Pyrenees, close to the border with France, on the Rio Segre, 33 km southeast of the Republic of Andorra.

A Spanish victory over the French.

(Last action - Bascara, 14 June; next action - Bellver, 27 July.)

French Garrison Commander unknown.

French totals 1,500 men, 7 guns.

French losses Some killed and wounded, the rest captured.

Spanish Forces LG de La Cuesta commanding: Gen Oquendo. Exact details of the troops involved not known; see the OOB at the beginning of the 1795 chapter.

Spanish total 7,000 men.

Spanish losses Not known, light.

Sources Bodart, Schultz, Fervel.

FP Bellver, 27 July 1795, capitulation

A Spanish town in the eastern Pyrenees, close to the border with France, on the Rio Segre, 25 km southeast of the Republic of Andorra.

(Last action - Puigcerda, 26 July; this was the last action of the Franco-Spanish war.)

French Garrison 1,000 men.

French losses All captured.

Spanish Forces LG de La Cuesta commanding: Exact details not known.

Spanish total 9,000 men.

Spanish losses Not known; very light.

Comment The Peace of Bâsle (22 July 1795) ended the war.

Sources Bodart, Schultz, Fervel.

MR Mannheim, 20 September 1795, capitulation

A fortified city in western Germany, northeast of the confluence of the Rivers Rhine and Neckar, at the junction of Routes B37 and B44.

A French victory over the Allies.

(Last action - Düsseldorf, 21 September; next action - Handschuhsheim, 24 September.)

French Forces GdD Pichegru's Armée du Haut-Rhin; exact details not known.

French totals 30,000 men.

French losses None.

Allied Garrison Bavarian GL Baron von Belderbusch commanding: Bavarians: Grenadiers (1st & 2nd bns); 3rd GrenR; FüsRs 2nd, 3rd, 10th, 11th, 12th & a combined regiment (8th & 9th); Zweibrücken Garde (1 bn) ChLR (2 regts); artillery (6 coys). Austrians: IR Mittrowsky Nr 40 (1 bn), 471 guns.

Allied total 9,200 men.

Allied losses None. The French and Bavarians negotiated an agreement whereby the fortress was handed over to the French. The outraged Austrians were faced with a fait accompli and had to withdraw north over the river Main because the French now held a crossing point over the Rhine.

Sources Bodart, Bezzel Vol 5, KGE Heft 9, 1889, ÖMZ 1832 Heft 2, Wrede.

MR Düsseldorf, 21 September 1795, capitulation

A fortified town on the east bank of the lower River Rhine in northwestern Germany at the junction of Routes B7 & B8, 30 km northeast of Köln.

A French victory over the Bavarians.

(Last action – this was the first action on the middle-Rhine in 1795; next action Mannheim, 20 September.)

French Forces GdD Lefebvre's division of GdD Jourdan's Armée du Sambre et Meuse. 9e, 80e 119e DBdeLi; 10e & 13e DBdeLé (3 bns each); 1er, 6e & 9e ChàCh (4 sqns each).

French total ca 12,600 men.

French losses Not exactly known but very light.

Bavarian Garrison Gen Count Hompesch commanding: 2,000 men with 168 guns

Bavarian losses Nil. The garrison was free to go on condition that they would not fight against France for one year.

Sources Bodart, Bezzel Vol 5.

MR Handschuhsheim, 24 September 1795, clash

A village in southwestern Germany, just north of Heidelberg on the River Neckar and east of Route B3.

An Austrian victory over the French.

(Last action – Mannheim, 20 September; next action – Höchst, 11/12 October.)

French Forces GdD Dufour commanding: two divisions of Pichegru's Armée du Haut-Rhin. His own (7th) with GdBs Dusirat and Cavrois and GdD Ambert's 6th (GdBs Davout and AdjGen Bertrand). Exact details not known.

French total ca 12,000 men.

French losses 1,000 killed, 500 captured (wounded not known). GdB Dusirat and GdD Dufour were wounded (Dufour was captured); 8 guns, 9 caissons and teams.

Austrian Forces FML Quosdanovich commanding: IRs EH Karl Nr 3, Kaunitz Nr 20 (2 bns each), Lattermann Nr 45 (1 bn); GzIR Warasdiner (1st Bn); GzIR Slavonier (1st & 2nd bns); IR Wartensleben Nr 28 (2 bns). GM Count Klenau: KürR Hohenzollern Nr 4 (6 sqns); DragR Kaiser Nr 3 (2 sqns); HusR Szeckler Nr 44 (6 sqns); DragR Allemand (Émigrés, 4 sqns).

Austrian total ca 8,000 men.

Austrian losses 35 men and 54 horses killed, 6 officers, 144 men, 78 horses wounded, 2 men and 3 horses missing.

Comment Klenau's cavalry caught Dufour's division in the open, scattered the six squadrons of French ChàCh and cut down the infantry.

Sources Bodart, Wrede, ÖMZ 1832, Heft 2.

MR Höchst, 11/12 October 1795, clash

A village in the western German province of Hessen, 12 km west of Frankfurt am Main, between Autobahn A66 and the River Main.

An Austrian victory over the French.

(Last action – Handschuhsheim, 24 September; next action – Niedernhausen, 13 October.)

French Forces GdD Kléber commanding part of the Armée de la Sambre-et-Meuse: 1 division (either Championnet's or Bernadotte's).

French total ca 10,000 men.

French losses ca 500 killed, wounded and missing.

Austrian Forces Part of FZM Count Clerfayt's Corps under GM Boros: Grün-Laudon Freikorps (3 coys); GzIR Warasdiner (6 coys), DragR Waldeck Nr 39 (2 sqns); Tyroler Scharfschützen (2 coys); IR Jordis Nr 59 (1 bn); Wurmser Freikorps (2 bns, 4 sqns).

Austrian total ca 5,500 men.

Austrian losses 24 men killed, 7 officers, 194 men wounded.

Comment The Austrians defended the lower reach of the River Nidda just north of its entry into the River Main. Repeated French assaults were repulsed with heavy loss. Bodart's details of this action are wildly wrong. Jourdan withdrew his forces to the west bank of the Rhine and abandoned the blockade of Mainz.

Sources Wrede ÖMZ 1832 Hefte 2 & 3, Bodart.

MR Niedernhausen, 13 October 1795, clash

A village in western Germany about 18 km north of Wiesbaden, just east of the Autobahn A3/E35 in the Taunus hills, north of the River Main and west of Frankfurt.

An Austrian victory over the French.

(Last action – Höchst, 12 October; next action – Mainz, 13 October.)

French Forces GdD Klein, GdB Boyer with the cavalry and rearguard of the divisions of GdDs Poncet and Grenier of Jourdan's Armée de la Sambre-et-Meuse; 6 bns, 3 CavRs, 3 guns.

French total ca 5,000 men.

French losses 334 killed and wounded, 134 missing, 5 guns, 31 waggons, 80 ammunition caissons.

Austrian Forces GM Baron Nauendorf commanding part of FZM Count Clerfayt's 'Observazionskorps': 2 bns infantry; HusR Blankenstein Nr 16 (4 sqns); DragR Würzburg (2 sqns); HusR Bercsény (2 sqns Émigrés); GM Boros with the other half of the Observazionskorps (see the clash at Höchst, 12 October for details).

Austrian total ca 8,000 men.

Comment Jourdan's retreating army could not find enough horses to move their massive train northwards through the Taunus hills; the Austrians scattered the rearguard and took much booty including the 3 guns of the French rearguard and 2 others.

Sources Wrede, ÖMZ 1832, Hefte 2, 3.

MR Mainz, 20 September – 13 October 1795, failed blockade

A fortified city in western Germany on the west bank of the River Rhine, opposite its confluence with the River Main, at the junction of Autobahns A60 and A63.

An Austro-Allied victory over the French.

(Last action – Niedernhausen, 13 October; next action – Steinbach, 15 October.)

French Forces GdD Jourdan's Armée de la Sambre-et-Meuse (see the OOB at the beginning of the 1795 chapter)

French losses Not known exactly; light.

Allied Garrison in March

Austro-Allied troops BGs Baron Aussess, Baron Cezkay, Count Alcaini: IRs Manfredini Nr 12 (2⅔ bns); Lacy Nr 22, Lattermann Nr 45 (1 bn each); Pellegrini Nr 49 (2 bns); Strassoldo Nr 27 (1 bn); O Wallis Nr 29 (2 bns); Wenkheim Nr 35 (1 bn). **Cologne contingent** (1⅚ bns). **Hessen-Darmstadt Troops:** BG Count Wittgenstein: LeibGren Bn (1 bn); LeibIR (2 bns); IR Landgraf (1 bn). **Kur-Mainz Troops:** GL Count Hatzfeld: IRs Gymnich, Riedt, Hatzfeld, Knorr (1 bn each). **Imperial contingents:** BG Count von Salm Solms-Braunfels (1⅚ bns); Pfalz-Zweibrücken, Bamberg, Liege, Boineburg, Riedel (1 bn each). **Austrian Troops** BG Baron Cezkay: GzIR Warasdiner (1st & 2nd bns): Wurmser Freikorps (10 coys); BG Mercandin: Vécsey Hus (2 sqns); Wurmser HusR Nr 30 (6 sqns): artillery, engineers, miners.

Austro-Allied total ca 19,000 men.

Austro-Allied losses Not known exactly but light.

Sources Geschichtliche Landeskunde, Mainz Vol VIII; Bezzel Vol 5; Wrede.

MR Steinbach, 15 October 1795, skirmish

A hamlet north of the Taunus hills in western central Germany, about 10 km north of Limburg-on-the-Lahn, between Routes B49/E44 and B54.

A French victory over the Austrians.

(Last action – Mainz, 13 October; next action – Ehrenbreitstein, 17 October.)

French Forces The rearguard of GdD Lefebvre's force (part of GdD Jourdan's Armée de la Sambre-et-Meuse). Exact details and losses not known.

Austrian Forces GM Haddik with part of FZM Count Clerfayt's 'Observazionskorps'; exact details not known [see Höchst (12 October) and Niedernhausen (13 October) for details]

Austrian losses 3 guns, 2 caissons, 92 men and 111 horses killed, wounded and missing.

Comment The French continued to withdraw northwest despite this local success.

Sources ÖMZ 1832 Hefte 2 and 3.

MR Ehrenbreitstein, 15 September – 17 October 1795, failed siege

A fortress in western Germany, on the east bank of the Rhine, overlooking the confluence with the Moselle.

An Austro-Allied victory over the French.

(Last action – Steinbach, 15 October; next action – Mannheim, 18 October.)

French Forces GdD Marceau's division of GdD Jourdan's Armée de la Sambre-et-Meuse. GdBs Naleche, Hardy: 1ère, 21e, 26e, 178e DBdeLi, 9e DBdeLé (3 bns each); 31e GensdarmeDiv (1 bn); 11e ChàCh.

French totals 11,240 men.

French losses Not known but light.

Austro-Allied Garrison Obstlt von Sechtern commanding: IR Murray Nr 55 (1 bn), 1 bn **Trier** infantry and 2 coys **Trier** Jägers, artillery and engineers.

Austrian total ca 2,600 men.

Austrian losses Not known exactly but very light.

Comment As Jourdan's army withdrew north from Mainz, they caused this siege to be lifted. Von Sechtern had conducted an aggressive defence.

Source: ÖMZ 1832 Heft 2.

MR Mannheim, 18 October 1795, clash

A fortified city in western Germany, northeast of the confluence of the Rivers Rhine and Neckar, at the junction of Routes B37 and B44.

An Austrian victory over the French.

(Last action – Ehrenbreitstein, 17 October; next action – Mainz, 29 October.)

French Forces GdD Pichegru commanding the Armée du Haut-Rhin: GdD Desaix's 7th Division (GdB Dusirat Cavrois); GdD Ambert's 6th Division [GdB Davout and Col Oudinot's 108e DBdeLi (3 bns)] and GdB Beaupuy's brigade of the 5th Division.

French total 12,000 men.

French losses 1,500 killed and wounded, 500 captured including General Oudinot; 3 guns, 5 ammunition waggons, all camp equipment, 1 colour.

Austrian Forces GdK Count Wurmser commanding: IRs EH Carl Nr 3 (3 bns); Kaunitz Nr 20, Gemmingen Nr 21, Brechainville Nr 25 (2 bns each); Wartensleben Nr 28 (3 bns); Benjowsky Nr 31 (1st bn). Gyulai Nr 32 (1 bn), Sztáray Nr 33 (2 bns), A Esterházy Nr 34 (3 bns), Grenadier Bns Kottulinsky, Wolzogen, Retz, Haydt, Bender, Dietrich, Bydeskuty, Fronius, Candiani and La Marseille; KürRs Mack Nr 20, Hohenzollern Nr 4, ChLRs Kinsky Nr 7, Latour Nr 31, DragR Kaiser Nr 3, HusRs Erdödy Nr 11, EH Ferdinand Nr 32, Szeckler Nr 44 (6 sqns each); GzIR Slavonier (2nd bn). Wurmser Freikorps (2 bns, 4 sqns).

Austrian total 17,000 men, 24 x 6pdrs, 12 x 12pdrs.

Austrian losses 8 officers, 103 men, 161 horses killed; 29 officers, 497 men, 244 horses wounded, 27 men and 29 horses missing, total: 37 officers, 672 men, 434 horses.

Comment The 108e DBde was practically destroyed and its colour was captured. The French camp before the city was captured. The Austrians laid siege to Mannheim.

Sources Bodart, Wrede, ÖMZ 1832, Heft 3; Bezzel, Vol 5.

MR Mainz, 29 October 1795, battle

A fortified city in western Germany, on the west bank of the River Rhine at its confluence with the River Main.

An Austro-Allied victory over the French.

(Last action – Mannheim, 18 October; next action – Pfeddersheim, 10 November.)

French Forces GdD Schaal commanding part of the Armée du Haut-Rhin: 8e Division GdD Courtot; 9e Division GdD St Cyr; GdB Duverger, GdB Houel and the 2e ChàCh; 10e Division GdD Mengeaud; 11e Division GdD Renault; GdD Poncet's division. Exact details not known.

French totals 52 bns, 23 sqns, 33,000 men.

French losses 3,000 killed and wounded, 1,800 captured including two generals, 138 guns, 494 vehicles.

Austro-Allied Forces FZM Count Clerfayt commanding: Wurmser Freikorps (6 coys); IRs Toscana Nr 23 (2 bns) ; Manfredini Nr 12 (3 bns); Klebek Nr 14 (3 bns), Hohenlohe Nr 17 (2 bns); Lacy Nr 22 (1 bn and 1 coy); O Wallis Nr 29 (2 bns); Strassoldo Nr 27 (1st Bn); Mittrowsky Nr 40 (3rd Bn); Pellegrini Nr 49 (2 bns), F Kinsky Nr 47 (3 bns), Sztáray Nr 33 (2), vac Wenkheim Nr 35 (2). Legion EH Carl (2 coys); Karabinier Rs Albert Nr 5 and Kaiser Nr 6, KürR Nassau Nr 14 (6 sqns each); DragR Waldeck Nr (1 sqn); UlR Keglevich (6 sqns), IR Bamberg, IR Liège (1 bn each); HusR Blankenstein Nr 16 (8 sqns), HusR Barco Nr 35 (2 sqns), GzIR Warasdin (1 bn); Gren Bns Ullrich; KürR Kavanagh Nr 12; HusR Vécsey Nr 34; HusR Wurmser Nr 30. HusR Bercsény*, Légion Bourbon,* GzIR Warasdiner (1st, 2nd, 3rd), Wallachen (1st). Artillery: 4 x FAB, 1 x HAB. **Electorate of Cologne Troops:** 1 x IR (1 bn). **Electorate of Mainz Troops:** Jägers (1 coy); IRs Hatzfeld, Gymnich and Ried (1 bn each); Hussars (1 sqn).

Austro-Allied totals ca 27,000 men.

Austro-Allied losses 1,400 killed and wounded (FML Baron von Schmerzing and GM Count Wolkenstein killed); 200 captured.

Sources Bodart, Wrede.

* = Émigré troops.

MR Pfeddersheim, 10 November 1795, clash

A hamlet in the western German province of Hessen 7 km west of the city of Worms on Route B47.

An Austrian victory over the French.

(Last action – Mainz, 29 October; next action – Mannheim, 22 November.)

French Forces GdD Pichegru commanding the Armée du Haut-Rhin: Exact details not known.

French totals 37,000 men.

French losses 1,100 killed and wounded, 300 captured.

Austrian Forces FZM Count Clerfayt commanding the same forces as for the clash at Mainz on 29 October plus the following grenadier bns: Frankenbusch, Ulm, Kreisen, Riera.

Austrian totals: 33,000 men.

Austrian losses: 600 killed and wounded.

Sources Bodart, Wrede.

MR Mannheim, 19 October–22 November 1795, siege and capture

A fortified city in western Germany, northeast of the confluence of the Rivers Rhine and Neckar, at the junction of Routes B37 and B44.

An Austrian victory over the French.

(Last action – Pfeddersheim, 10 November; this was the last action in 1795 in this theatre.)

French Garrison GdD Montaign commanding: part of Pichegru's Armée du Haut-Rhin. Exact details not known.

French totals 10,000 men.

French losses All captured.

Austrian Forces GdK Count Wurmser commanding: IRs EH Ferdinand Nr 2 (2 bns); EH Carl Nr 3 (3 bns); Kaunitz Nr 20 (2 bns); Gemmingen Nr 21 (3 bns); Brechainville Nr 25 and Wartensleben Nr 28 (3 bns each); Benjowsky Nr 31 (1st bn); S Gyulai Nr 32 A. Esterházy Nr 34 (3 bns each), Splényi Nr 51 (1st bn); I Jellačič Nr 53 (2 bns); Grenadier bns Wolzogen, Retz, Haydt, Bender, Dietrich, Bydeskuty, Fronius, Candiani, La Marseille. KürR Mack Nr 20; ChLR Kinsky; Nr 7 HusRs EH Ferdinand Nr 32 and Erdödy Nr 11 (6 sqns each); GzIR Slavonier (1st and 2nd bns).

Austrian total 25,000 men.

Austrian losses Not exactly known but at least 400 killed and wounded.

Sources Bodart, Wrede.

IN Loano, 23/24 November 1795, battle

A town in northwestern Italy, on the Gulf of Genoa, 30 km southwest of Savona on Route 1.

A French victory over the Austro-Sardinians.

(This was the only action of note in 1795 in Italy).

French Forces GdD Schérer commanding: 4e, 5e, 6e, 9e, 11e, 12e, 13e, 14e, 18e, 19e, 25e, 30e, 32e, 33e, 39e, 40e, 43e, 45e, 51e, 55e, 57e, 58e, 61e, 63e, 64e, 69e, 75e, 79e, 85e, 88e, 93e, DBdeLi; 11e, 12e and 20e DBdeLé. 3e, 5e, 8e, 9e, 15e, 18e, 20e DragR. 10e, 13e, 15e, 19e, 22e, 24e and 25e ChàCh. 1er and 7e bis HusR.

French total 25,000 men.

French losses 2,500 killed and wounded (GdD Charlet killed), 500 captured.

Austro-Sardinian Forces FML Baron de Vins commanding: Austrian troops: IRs Reisky Nr 13 (3 bns), Terzy Nr 16, Allvintzy Nr 19 (3 bns each); Thurn Nr 43 (2 bns); Belgiojoso Nr 44 (2 bns), Schmidtfeld Nr 48 (2 bns); EH Anton Nr 52 (1st and 2nd bns); Grenadier bn Strassoldo; UlR Mészáros (4 sqns). GzIR Carlstadt (1st bn). Sardinian troops: IRs Piemont (2 bns); 1st GrenR (1st bn); 3rd and 5th GrenRs (2 bns each); Cacciatori (2 bns); Provincial IR di Mondovi (2 bns).

Austro-Sardinian total 18,000 men.

Austro-Sardinian losses 3,000 killed and wounded, 4,000 captured, 48 guns, 5 colours.

Comment Snow forced both parties to withdraw from the mountains into the valleys for the winter.

Sources Bodart, Wrede, Brancaccio.

1796

FRENCH ORDER OF BATTLE 1796

Order of Battle of the Armée du Rhin et de la Moselle

On the Upper Rhine 8 June 1796 Gen Moreau commanding.

Right Wing Gen Férino commanding: **GdD Delaborde** GdBs Scissé, Nouvion, Jordy: 3e, 38e, 56e DBdeLi (3 bns each); 21e CavR (2 sqns). **Totals** 8,300 infantry, 174 cavalry. **GdD Tuncq** GdBs Tholmé, Paillard: 74e, 79e, 88e DBdeLi (3 bns each); 9e CavR (3 sqns); 12e CavR (2 sqns). **Totals** 7,437 infantry, 432 cavalry. **GdD Bourcier** GdB Sibaud: 26e DBdeLé, 62e, 109e DBdeLi (3 bns each); 11e CavR (3 sqns); 6e DragR (4 sqns). **Totals** 9,281 infantry, 690 cavalry.

The Centre Gen Désaix commanding. **GdD Delmas** GdBs Eckmeyer, Frimont: 16e DBdeLé, 50e, 68e DBdeLi (3 bns each); 2e CavR (2 sqns); 10e DragR, 7e HusR (3 sqns each); 8e HusR (2sqns). **Totals** 7,898 infantry, 865 cavalry. **GdD Beaupuy** GdBs Tharreau, Jobat, Ste Susanne: 3e DBdeLé, 10e, 93e, 103e DBdeLi (3 bns each); 17e, 19e DragRs (3 sqns each), 4e ChàCh (3 sqns); 9e ChàCh (4 sqns). **Totals** 14,565 infantry, 1,266 cavalry. **GdD Xaintrailles** GdB Forest: 17e, 97e DBdeLi (3 bns each), 1er and 2e Carabiniers (3 sqns each); 14e and 15e CavRs (2 sqns each). **Totals** 4,828 infantry, 962 cavalry.

Left Wing Gen St Cyr commanding. **GdD Duhesme** GdBs Lambert, Vandamme: 24e and 44e DBdeLi (2 bns each); 100e DBdeLi (3 bns); 3e CavR, 20e ChàCh (2 sqns each); 11e HusR (4 sqns). **Totals** 7,438 infantry, 895 cavalry. **GdD Taponnier** GdBs Laroche, Lecourbe: 21e DBdeLé, 31e, 84e, 106e DBdeLi (3 bns each), 18e CavR (2 sqns); 4e DragR, 2e ChàCh (4 sqns each); 9e HusR (3 sqns). **Totals** 11,823 infantry, 1,231 cavalry.

Army totals 71,581 infantry, 6,515 cavalry.

1796 THE ACTIONS

IN Voltri, 10 April 1796, skirmish

A small port on the northwestern Italian coast, 16 km west of Genoa and at the junction of Routes 1 and 456.

An Austrian victory over the French.

(This was the opening action of the campaign; next action – Montenotte, 11–12 April.)

French Forces Col Cervoni commanding: 70e DBdeLi (3 bns)* 99e DBdeLi (1er Bn)*.

French total ca 3,500 men.

French losses Killed and wounded unknown; 150 captured.

* = the Demibrigade numbers are those prior to the 2nd Amalgame of May 1796.

Austrian Forces FZM Baron Beaulieu commanding; IRs Terzy Nr 16, Allvintzy Nr 19 (1 bn each), Nádasdy Nr 39 (1st Bn), Reisky Nr 13, W Colloredo Nr 56, EH Anton Nr 52 (2 bns each); GzIR Carlstadt (1st and 9th Bn); UlR Mészáros (2 sqns).

Austrian total ca 10,000 men.

Austrian losses Not known exactly; very light.

Sources Kuhl, Wrede, Charrié.

IN Montenotte, 11–12 April 1796, clash

A village in the northwestern Italian province of Liguria, 19 km northwest of Savona (on the Gulf of Genoa) in the valley of the River Erro.

A French victory over the Austrians.

(Last action – Voltri, 10 April; next action – Millesimo, 13–14 April.)

French Forces Gen Bonaparte commanding: GdD Laharpe, GdD Massena, GdB Ménard and Cervoni; 1er DBdeLé (2 bns); 14e & 70e DBdeLi (3 bns each) 21e DBdeLi (2 bns); 99e DBdeLi (1er & 2e Bns); 8e DBdeLé (3 bns); 100e & 46e DBdeLi (3 bns each); Grenadiers (4 coys); Dragoons (100); 18 guns. The Demibrigade numbers are those valid prior to the 2nd Amalgame of May 1796.

French totals 14,000 men.

French losses 800 killed, wounded and missing.

Austrian Forces FML Count Argenteau commanding: IRs Terzy Nr 16 (3 bns); Allvintzy Nr 19 (2nd Bn); Gyulai Nr 32 (3 coys); Preiss Nr 24 (1 bn); Brechainville Nr 25 (3 bns); Stain Nr 50 (3rd Bn); EH Anton Nr 52 (2 bns).

Austrian total 9,000 men.

Austrian losses 2,500 (mostly captured as was 1st Bn Terzy); 12 guns.

Sources Bodart, Charrié, Kuhl, Wrede.

IN Millesimo (Cosseria), 13–14 April 1796, clash

A hamlet in the northwestern Italian province of Liguria, on the River Bormida, 23 km northwest of Savona, on Route 339. Cosseria is a ruined castle nearby.

A French victory over the Austro-Sardinians.

(Last action – Montenotte 11–12 April; next action – Dego, 14 April.)

French Forces Gen Bonaparte commanding: GdD Augereau 69e DBdeLi (2 bns); GdB Beyrand: 39e DBdeLi (3 bns): GdB Ménard 8e DBdeLé (1 bn). GdB Joubert: 3e DBdeLé & 51e DBdeLi (1 bn each). GdB Dommartin: 84e DBdeLi (2 bns) 45e, 46e & 100e DBdeLé (3 bns each). The Demibrigade numbers are those valid prior to the 2nd Amalgame of May 1796.

French totals 9,000 men.

French losses ca 700 killed and wounded. AdjGen Quesnel and Col Banel were killed, GdB Joubert wounded.

Austro-Sardinian Forces FML Provera commanding: IR Gyulai Nr 32 (7½ coys); Gren Bn Strassoldo, Sardinian 3rd Gren Bn (1 bn each).

Austro-Sardinian total 988 men (no guns).

Austro-Sardinian losses 96 killed and wounded, the rest captured.

Comment Bodart's quoted strengths probably included Austrian IR Belgiojoso Nr 44 which was in the area but not engaged. The losses of the Austrians were probably French reports for public consumption. This combat opened the way for Bonaparte to strike at the Sardinians, who were now isolated from their Austrian allies.

Sources Bodart, Kuhl, Charrié.

IN Dego, 14 April 1796, clash

A hamlet in the northwestern Italian province of Piedmont, on the River Bormida, 31 km northwest of Savona and on Route 30.

A French victory over the Austrians.

(Last action – Millesimo, 13–14 April; next action – Dego, 15 April.)

French Forces Gen Bonaparte commanding: GdD Laharpe, Massena: 1er DBdeLé, 14e, 21e, 69e, 70e & 99e DBdeLi (3 bns each), 1 élite bn.

French total ca 12,000 men.

French losses ca 1,500 killed and wounded. The Demibrigade numbers are those valid prior to the 2nd Amalgame of May 1796.

Austro-Sardinian Forces FML Count Argenteau commanding: Austrian IRs Stain Nr 50, Pellegrini Nr 49, Schröder Nr 26, Allvintzy Nr 19, Terzy Nr 16, Nádasdy Nr 39, Deutschmeister Nr 4 (1 bn each); Preiss Nr 24 (3 bns), EH Anton Nr 52 (2 bns). **Sardinian Troops** IRs La Marina (2 bns), Monferrat (1 bn).

Austro-Sardinian totals ca 5,700 men.

Austro-Sardinian losses ca 3,000, mostly captured.

Comment After this action the battalions of Stain, Pellegrini and Schröder ceased to exist; two battalions of Allvintzy, two EH Anton, 1 Deutschmeister were so reduced that they were pulled out of the line.

Sources Bodart, Kuhl, Wrede, Charrié.

IN Dego, 15 April 1796, clash

A hamlet in the northwest Italian province of Piedmont, on the River Bormida, 31 km northwest of Savona and on Route 30.

A French victory over the Austrians.

(Last action – Dego, 14 April; next action – Mondovi, 21 April.)

French Forces GdD Massena commanding: GdD Laharpe: 1er DBdeLé, 14e, 21e, 69e, 70e & 99e DBdeLi as for the day before plus 8e Lé and Dommartin's brigade and 22e ChàCh and 5e DragR (2 sqns each).

French total ca 15,000 men.

French losses 621 killed and wounded, 317 captured. The Demibrigade numbers are those valid prior to the 2nd Amalgame of May 1796.

Austrian Forces FML Vukassovich commanding: GzIR Carlstadt (1st & 2nd Bns); IRs Allvintzy Nr 19, Nádasdy Nr 39, Preiss Nr 24 (1 bn each).

Austrian total ca 3,500 men.

Austrian losses 670 killed and wounded, 1,087 captured.

Comment Vukassovich was unaware of the loss of Dego to the French the previous day but attacked at dawn and threw them out of the place. The French had set no sentries and were completely surprised. Massena had to call up reinforcements to retake Dego after a hard fight. The battalion of the IR Preiss was destroyed.

Sources Bodart, Wrede, Kuhl, Charrié.

IN Mondovi, 22 April 1796, clash

A town in the northwestern Italian province of Piemont, on the Rio Ellera at the crossing of Route 28, 28 km east of Cuneo.

A French victory over the Austro-Sardinians.

(Last action – Dego, 15 April (see comment below); next action – Lodi, 10 May.)

French Forces GdD Serrurier commanding: 19e, 39e, 45e, 46e, 56e DBdeLi (3 bns each) 1ère DBdeLé (1er Bn), 84e DBdeLi (3 bns); 5e & 20e DragR, 22e ChàCh (2 sqns each). These Demibrigade numbers are those valid prior to the 2nd Amalgame of May 1796.

French totals ca 15,000 men.

French losses Not known.

Austro-Sardinian Forces Gen Colli commanding: IRs Guardia (2 bns) Granatieri Real (1 bn) Grenadiers (1st Bn); Provincial IRs Tortona, Mondovi, Acqui, 2 bns each.

Austro-Sardinian totals ca 11,000 men. Austrian Troops: Stabs-DragR (6 sqns).

Austro-Sardinian losses Not known.

Comment It was this final clash of a series which broke the resistance of the Sardinians who, isolated from their defeated Austrian allies, now sued for peace with Bonaparte. The other actions were Ceva (16 April) and Bicocca and St Michele on 19 April. Bonaparte had achieved the conquest of Piedmont and the Austrians, after making a desperate lunge at Nice, evacuated the entire province of Lombardy.

Sources Kuhl, Wrede, Charrié.

IN Lodi, 10 May 1796, clash

A town in the northern Italian province of Lombardy, on the right bank of the River Adda, 30 km southeast of Milan, at the junction of Routes 9 and 235.

A French victory over the Austro-Sardinians.

(Last action – Mondovi, 22 April; next action – Borghetto, 30 May.)

French Forces Gen Bonaparte commanding: GdD Serrurier: 14e, 45e, 46e & 100e DBdeLi (3 bns each). These Demibrigade numbers are those prior to the 2nd Amalgame of May 1796. Cavalry details not known.

French totals 15,500 infantry, 2,000 cavalry.

French losses 900 killed and wounded.

Austro-Sardinian Forces FZM Baron Beaulieu commanding. IRs Deutschmeister Nr 4 (3rd Bn); Terzy Nr 16 (2 bns); Strassoldo Nr 27 (2nd & 3rd bns); Nádasdy Nr 39 (1st Bn); Belgiojoso Nr 44 (3rd Bn); Thurn Nr 43 (3 bns); GzIR Warasdin (9th Bn); UlR Mészáros (6 sqns); Neapolitan cavalry regiments Re and Regina (4 sqns each).

Austro-Sardinian totals 11 bns, 14 sqns, 14 guns ca 9,500 men.

Austro-Sardinian losses: 900 killed and wounded.

Sources Bodart, Kuhl, Charrié.

IN Borghetto, 30 May 1796, clash

A village in northeastern Italy in the province of Venezio, on the River Mincio, 25 km southwest of Verona; near Valeggio.

A French victory over the Austro-Neapolitans.

(Last action – Lodi, 10 May; next action – Milan, 29 June.)

French Forces Gen Bonaparte commanding the **Armée d'Italie following the Amalgame of April 1796** 1st Division of the Avantgarde: GdD Laharpe, GdB Pijon, Ménard: 11e, 16e DBdeLé, 21e, 70e DBdeLi (3 bns each) – 8,614 men. 2nd Division of the Avantgarde: GdD Meynier, GdB Joubert, Cervoni, Dommartin: 3e DBdeLé (2 bns), 84e, 99e DBdesLi (3 bns each); 4e Légion des Allobroges; 51e and 55e DBdeLi (1 bn each) – 9,526 men. 3rd Division (1ère du corps de bataille); GdD Augereau; GdB Banel, Beyrand, Rusca: 8e, 18e Lé (2 bns each); 39e, 69e DBdeLi (3 bns each); 14e DBdeLi (1 bn) – 10,117. 4th Division (2e du corps de bataille); GdD Serrurier; GdB Miollis, Pelletier, Fiorella; 19e, 46e, 56e DBdeLi (3 bns each) – 9,448 men. 5th Division (3e du corps de bataille); GdD Macquart; GdB Dallemagne, David; 22e DBdeLi (1 bn); 100e DBdeLi (3 bns) – 3,675 men. 6th Division (4e du corps de bataille); GdD Garnier, GdB Davin, Bizanet, Colomb. 20e DBdeLi (3 bns); 7ePvDBdeLi (2e Bn) – 3,426 men. 7th Division (1ère de la Côte) GdD Mouret, GdB Serviez, Gardanne, Verne: 83e DBdeLi (3 bns); 13e DBdeLi (1 bn); 10e PvDBdeLi (2 bns); grenadiers (1 bn) – 4,808 men. 8th Division (2e de la Côte); GdD Casabianca; GdB Parra, Guillot: 15e DBdeLé (3 bns); DBde de la Jura et Hérault (1 bn); dismounted cavalry (1 bn) – 3,125 men. 9th Division (3e de la Côte); GdB Casalta: 12e, 56e DBdeLi (1 bn each) – 1,045 men. Cavalry: 1st Division: GdD Stengel; GdB Beaumont: 1er HusR, 10e and 22e ChàCh (4 sqns each); 25e ChàCh (3 sqns); 5e, 20e DragR (3 sqns each) – 3,090 men. 2nd Division: GdD Kilmaine: 7e HusR (4 sqns); 13e HusR (3 sqns); 24e ChàCh (4 sqns); 8e, 15e DragR (3 sqns each) – 1,778 men. Reserve in Marseille and Toulon: 113e DBdeLi (1 bn). DBde de Lot-et-Landes (2 bns); Bn de Jemappes, Bn de Paris (1 bn each) – 1,900 men.

French totals 27,000 men.

French losses ca 500 killed and wounded.

Austro-Neapolitan Forces FZM Baron Beaulieu commanding: IRs Reisky Nr 13 (3 bns); Allvintzy Nr 19 (2 bns); Nádasdy Nr 39 (1st Bn) GzIR Carlstadt (9th Bn); Neapolitan cavalry regiments Regina and Principe (4 sqns each).

Austro-Neapolitan totals 7 bns, 8 sqns, ca 6,000 men.

Austro-Neapolitan losses 300 killed and wounded, 300 captured, 4 guns, 13 ammunition waggons.

Sources Bodart, Kühl, Krebs and Moris, Annex 93 Vol II.

MR Altenkirchen, 4 June 1796, clash

A town in central western Germany, in the Westerwald hills of the River Rhine, at the junction of Routes B8, B256 and B414, about 43 km north of Neuwied.

A French victory over the Austrians.

(This was the opening action of the middle Rhine in 1796; next action – Wetzlar, 15 June).

French Forces GdD Lefebvre commanding: the Army of the Sambre-et-Meuse (part of). Exact details not known; see OOB Würzburg, 3 September for detail.

French total ca 11,000 men.

French losses Not known exactly but light.

Austrian Forces FZM Duke Ferdinand of Württemberg commanding part of Archduke Charles' Army of the Lower Rhine. IRs Kaiser Nr 1 (1st, 2nd, 4th Bns); Jordis Nr 59 (2 bns); HusR Blankenstein Nr 16 (6 sqns), Tyroler Scharfschützen (10 coys).

Austrian total ca 6,500 men.

Austrian losses Not exactly known; 2 bns Jordis captured, 10 guns lost.

Comment: The Austrians withdrew southeast over the River Lahn. On 9 June the French blockaded the fortress of Ehrenbreitstein opposite the confluence of the Rivers Rhine and Moselle.

Sources Wrede, Kaim, EH Carl.

UR Maudach, 15 June 1796, clash

A village in southwestern Germany, 10 km northwest of Speyer on the River Rhine. Not shown on modern maps.

A French victory over the Austrians.

(This was the opening action on the Upper Rhine; next action – Kehl, 24 June).

French Forces GdD Desaix commanding the Centre of the Armée du Rhin et de la Moselle GdDs Delmas: 16e DBdeLé, 50e and 68e DBdeLi (3 bns each); 2e CavR, 10e DragR, 3e and 7e HusRs (2 sqns each); GdD Beaupuy: 3e and 10e DBdeLé, 10e, 93e and 103e DBdeLi (3 bns each); 17e and 19e DragRs; 4e and 9e ChàCh (2 sqns each); GdD Xaintrailles: 17e and 97e DBdeLi (3 bns each); 1er and 2e Carabiniers, 14e and 15e CavRs (2 sqns each).

French total ca 27,000 infantry, 3,000 cavalry.

French losses ca 600 men killed, wounded and missing.

Austrian Forces FML Petrasch's division: IRs Gemmingen Nr 21, Stain Nr 50, Erbach Nr 42, Splényi Nr 51, Benjowsky Nr 31, Brechainville Nr 25 (1 bn each). ChLRs Kaiser Nr 1, Kinsky Nr 7 and DragR Kaiser Nr 3 (6 sqns each).

Austrian total 11,000 men.

Austrian losses ca 1,800 men killed, wounded and missing.

Sources Dedon, Angeli, Wrede.

MR Wetzlar, 15 June 1796, clash

A town in the western central German state of Hessen, on the River Lahn, at the junction of Routes B49/E44 and B277, about 10 km west of Giessen.

An Austro-Allied victory over the French.

(Last action – Altenkirchen, 4 June; next action – Uckerath, 19 June.)

French Forces GdD Lefebvre commanding part of the Armée de la Sambre-et-Meuse. Exact details not known.

French total 11,000 men.

French losses 500 men, 7 guns, 1 colour.

Austro-Allied Forces FM Archduke Charles commanding the Army of the Lower Rhine. IRs Kaiser Nr 1 (3 bns), Clerfayt Nr 9 (1st Bn), Manfredini Nr 12 (3 bns), Hohenlohe Nr 17 (2 bns), Reisky Nr 13 (4 bns); KürR Nassau Nr 14 (6 sqns); HusR Vécsey Nr 34 (2 sqns); ChLR Karaczay Nr 18 (2 sqns); DragR Coburg Nr 37 (4 sqns). Grenadier bns Kreyssern, Ghenedegg, Ulm, Frankenbusch, Riera, Bydeskuty, Zegraedt. GzIR Slavonier (1st Bn); DragR Royal Allemand*; HusR Saxe*; HusR Bercsény*; **Gen v Zeschwitz's Saxon Cavalry**, ChLR, HusR.

Austo-Allied total ca 36,000 in all (not all were engaged).

Austro-Allied losses 400 killed, wounded and missing.

Comment Following this defeat, the French split their forces and withdrew: Jourdan westwards to his bridgehead at Neuwied on the Rhine and Kléber northwest to an entrenched camp at Düsseldorf, further down the Rhine.

Sources Wrede, EH Carl.

*= Emigré troops.

MR Uckerath, 19 June 1796, clash

A village in the 'Bergisches Land' hills in the western German province of Nordrhein-Westfalen, about 20 km east of Bonn on the River Rhine and on Route B8.

A drawn match between the French and the Austrians.

(Last action - Wetzlar, 15 June; next action - Neuwied 2 July.)

French Forces GdD Kléber commanding part of Jourdan's Armée de la Sambre-et-Meuse. GdB Bastoul, Laval Gren Bn, 83e, 96e DBdes Richepanse's cavalry division. Exact details not known; see OOB Würzburg, 3 September.

French total 24,000 men.

French losses 2,300 killed and wounded; 700 captured; 1 colour; of the 1er Bn/83e DBdeLi (actually an old colour of the 80e DBde).

Austrian Forces FZM Baron Kray commanding part of Archduke Charles' Army of the Lower Rhine. LIRs Kaiser Nr 1 (3 bns), Hohenlohe Nr 17 (2 bns), Splényi Nr 51 (1st Bn), Beaulieu Nr 58 (1st Bn), Murray Nr 55 (1 bn), Tyroler Scharfschützen (10 coys); HusR Barco Nr 35 (6 sqns); Grenadier bns Ghenedegg, Ulm, Schröckinger.

Austrian total 30,000 men (only those shown came into action).

Austrian losses 600 killed, wounded and missing.

Comment Kléber continued his withdrawal northwest to the entrenched camp at Düsseldorf on the Rhine. Archduke Charles now split his forces; leaving FZM Count Wartensleben between the Rhine, Lahn and Sieg rivers with 35,000 men, he took 50,000 south; detached 30,000 to garrison the fortress of Mainz and took 20,000 to join FZM Latour's Army of the Upper Rhine.

Sources Wrede, Bodart, EH Carl.

UR Kehl, 24 June 1796, clash

A town on the east bank of the River Rhine in southwestern Germany, opposite the French city of Strasbourg, on Route B36 and Autobahn B28/E52.

A French victory over the Allies.

(Last action - Maudach, 15 June; next action - Renchen, 28 June.)

French Forces Part of GdD Moreau's Armée du Rhin et de la Moselle, Adjutant General Abbatucci commanding; GdBs Decaen, Montrichard: 3e DBdeLé (2e Bn); 16e DBdeLé (1er Bn); 31e, 56e, 89e DBdeLi (3 bns each).

French total 10,065 men.

French losses ca 150 killed, wounded and missing.

Allied Forces The Swabian Regional Contingent (Schwäbisches-Kreis-Contingent) IRs Württemberg, Baden-Durlach, Fugger, Wolfegg (2 bns each); Hohenzollern KürR and Württemberg DragR (4 sqns each); artillery (2 x FAB).

Allied total ca 7,000 men.

Allied losses Over 700 killed, wounded and missing, 14 guns, 22 ammunition waggons.

Comment The French launched a Rhine crossing in overwhelming force. The imperial Kreistruppen fought well but then, together with the Émigré corps here, separated from their Austrian Allies and took little further active part in the campaign. On 29 July the Kreistruppen were disarmed by FM Fröhlich, on Archduke Charles' orders, in Biberach.

Sources Dedon, Strack von Weissenbusch.

UR Renchen, 28 June 1796, clash

A village in southwestern Germany 16 km east of Strasbourg on the River Rhine; on the River Rench and on Route B3.

A French victory over the Austrian Imperial troops.

(Last action - Kehl 24 June; next action - Rastatt, 5 July.)

French Forces GdD Desaix commanding part of the Armée du Rhin et de la Moselle 16e DBdeLé, 50e and 68e DBdeLi (3 bns each). 2e CavR, 10e DragR, 3e and 7e HusRs (2 sqns each). 3e and 10e DBdeLé, 10e, 93e, 103e DBdeLi (3 bns each). 17e and 19e DragRs, 4e and 9e ChàCh (2 sqns each). 17e and 97e DBdeLi (3 bns each); 1er and 2e Carabiniers, 14e and 15e CavRs (2 sqns each).

French total 25,000 men (only partially engaged).

French losses 200 men.

Imperial Troops FML Count Sztáray commanding: GMs Prince von Lothringen, Württemberg including Gyulai's Freikorps (2 bns); CarabinierR Albert Nr 5 (4 sqns). Württemberg Contingent: IRs Wolfey, Württemberg, Fürstenberg, Hohenzollern (2 bns each). IR

Salzburg (2 bns). Kurpfalz-Bayern Contingent: IRs Lamotte, Birkenfeld (1 bn each); Wexten and Feldjägers (2 bns each).

Imperial total 9,000 men.

Imperial losses 550 killed and wounded, 850 captured, 7 guns, 2 ammunition waggons.

Sources Dedon, Wrede, Angeli.

IN Milan, 16 May – 29 June 1796, siege and capture

A fortified town in northern Italy, the capital of the province of Lombardy, about 40 km south of Lake Como.

A French victory over the Austrians.

(Last action – Borghetto, 30 May; next action – Rivoli, 29 July.)

French Forces GdD Dupois commanding: exact details not known.

French totals 6,000 men.

French losses None.

Austrian Garrison IRs Nrs 5 & 6 (2 bns); Milan militia; gunners.

Austrian totals 2,000 men, 152 guns.

Austrian losses All captured.

Source Wrede.

MR Neuwied, 2 July 1796, clash

A village on the eastern bank of the River Rhine in central western Germany, about 18 km northwest of Koblenz and the confluence of the Rhine with the Moselle.

A French victory over the Allies.

(Last action – Uckerath, 19 June; next action – Giessen, 8 July.)

French Forces Part of GdD Jourdan's Armée de la Sambre-et-Meuse. Exact details, total and losses not known.

Allied Forces Gen Count Wittgenstein commanding part of the Army of the Lower Rhine: Austrian troops IRs Kaiser Nr 1 (1 bn); Strassoldo Nr 27 (1st Bn); Rohan Émigrés (1 bn). Carneville Freikorps (2 bns); Grenadier bn Kreyssern; Wurmser Freikorps (2 bns), Slavonier Freikorps (2 bns); DragR Coburg Nr 37 (6 sqns). **Hessen-Darmstadt Troops** GM von Fincke commanding: LeibR (1st Bn); IR Erbprinz (1st Bn); Leib-Gren-R (2nd Bn). **Münster Troops** DragR (4 sqns).

Allied total ca 8,000 men.

Allied losses Not exactly known but the Hessians lost 147 killed, wounded and missing, mostly the latter.

Comment This was the southern prong of Jourdan's invasion of Germany.

Sources Wrede, Keim, Beck.

UR Rastatt (Kuppenheim), 5 July 1796, clash

A town in the southwestern German province of Baden, about 8 km east of the River Rhine, at the junction of Routes B3 and B36 and on the River Murg, between Karlsruhe and Strasbourg.

A French victory over the Austrians.

(Last action – Renchen, 28 June; next action – Malsch, 9 July.)

French Forces GdD Taponnier; GdBs Laroche, Lecourbe: 21e DBdeLé, 31e, 84e, 106e DBdeLi (3 bns each); 18e Cav R (2 sqns); 4e DragR, 2e ChàCh (4 sqns each); 9e HusR (3 sqns). GdD Bourcier; GdB Sibaud: 26e DBdeLé, 62e, 109e DBdeLi (3 bns each); 11e CavR (3 sqns); 6e DragR (4 sqns).

French totals 19,000 infantry, 1,500 cavalry.

French losses Not exactly known but light.

Austrian Forces FML Prince zu Fürstenberg and FML Meszáros commanding: IRs d'Alton Nr 15 (3 bns), Pellegrini Nr 49 (2 bns); GrenBn Warren (1 bn); KürR Kaiser Nr 6 (2 sqns); KürR EH Franz Nr 29 (6 sqns); DragR EH Johann Nr 26 (4 sqns).

Austrian totals ca 6,000 men.

Austrian losses Killed and wounded unknown; 200 captured, 3 guns.

Comment Although both main armies were present, the French made no frontal assault but turned the Austrians' wings, thus the very limited combat involvement as the Austrians withdrew at once northeast to Ettlingen.

Sources Dedon, Wrede, Archduke Charles, von Angeli.

MR Giessen, 8 July 1796, clash and capture

A town in the central German province of Hessen, on the River Lahn and at the junction of Routes B3, B49/E40 and Autobahn A45.

A French victory over the Allies.

(Last action – Neuwied, 2 July; next action – Friedberg, 10 July.)

French Forces Part of GdD Jourdan's Armée de la Sambre-et-Meuse. Exact details not known.

French total ca 20,000 men.

French losses Not exactly known, but very light.

Austrian Forces GM Baron von Kienmayer

commanding part of the Army of the Lower Rhine: IRs Gyulai Nr 32 (1 bn). Freikorps Carneville (4 coys, 2 sqns); ChLR Latour Nr 31 (6 sqns); HusR Blankenstein Nr 16 (6 sqns); UlR Schwarzenberg Nr 2 (4 sqns) Grenadier bns Apfaltrern, Candiani; GzIR Warasdiner (3rd Bn).

Austrian total ca 4,500 men.

Austrian losses Not exactly known but light.

Comment The weak garrison was surprised and quickly pushed out of the town.

Sources Wrede, Keim.

UR Malsch (Ettlingen), 9 July 1796, battle

A village in the southwestern German state of Baden, 10 km east of Rastatt, just south of Autobahn A5/E35/E52.

A French victory over the Austrians.

(Last action – Rastatt, 5 July; next action – Cannstadt, 21 July.)

French Forces GdD Moreau commanding the Armée du Rhin et de la Moselle (see the Order of Battle at the beginning of the 1796 section).

French total 45 bns, 55 sqns (exact details unknown), 36,000 men.

French losses 2,000 killed and wounded, 400 captured.

Austrian Forces Archduke Charles commanding parts of the Armies of the Upper and Lower Rhine. IRs EH Carl Nr 3 (1 bn); C Schröder Nr 7 (2nd & 3rd bns); Manfredini Nr 12 (3 bns); Reisky Nr 13 (4 bns); d'Alton Nr 15 (3 bns); Nádasdy Nr 39 (3 bns); Kinsky Nr 47 (3 bns); Pellegrini Nr 49 (2 bns). KürR EH Franz Nr 29 (4 sqns); CarabinierR H Albert Nr 5 (4 sqns); KürR EH Johann Nr 26 (4 sqns); HusR Siebenburgen Nr 47 (6 sqns); DragR Waldeck Nr 39 (6 sqns). Grenadier bns Riera, Retz, Reisinger, Apfaltrern, Candiani.

Austrian total ca 32,000 men.

Austrian losses 1,300 killed and wounded, 1,300 captured.

Comment The Austrian assault against the French centre failed and St Cyr's outflanking move forced the weaker Austrians to withdraw east to Pforzheim on the River Nagold in the Black Forest hills.

Sources Dedon, Wrede, Bodart.

MR Friedberg, 10 July 1796, clash

A village in the western German state of Hessen, 28 km south of Giessen at the junction of Routes B3 and B275.

A French victory over the Austrians.

(Last action – Giessen, 8 July; next action – Sulzbach, 17 August.)

French Forces GdD Jourdan commanding the Armée de la Sambre-et-Meuse. Exact details not known.

French totals ca 30,000 men.

French losses 700 killed, wounded and missing.

Austrian Forces FZM Count Wartensleben commanding part of Archduke Charles' Army of the Lower Rhine. IRs Clerfayt Nr 9 (1st Bn); EH Ferdinand Nr 23 (2 bns); Stuart Nr 28 (2nd & 3rd bns); Württemberg Nr 38 (1st Bn). KürR Nassau Nr 14 (4 sqns); HusR EH Ferdinand Nr 32 (part); DragR Waldeck Nr 39 (6 sqns).

Austrian total ca 6,000 men.

Austrian losses 1,000 killed, wounded and missing.

Comment Jourdan, hearing of Moreau's victory against Archduke Charles' outposts on the 27 June Rhine crossing at Kehl, recrossed to the east bank of the river, attacked Wartensleben and pushed him south to the River Main.

Sources Wrede, Bodart.

UR Cannstadt, 21 July 1796, clash

A small town in southwestern Germany, on the east bank of the River Neckar, on Route B29, just east of Stuttgart.

A French victory over the Austrians.

(Last action – Malsch, 9 July; next action – Neresheim, 11 August.)

French Forces Part of GdD Moreau's Armée du Rhin et de la Moselle (see the Order of Battle at the beginning of the 1796 section). Exact details not known; total and losses not known.

Austrian Forces IRs EH Carl Nr 3 (1 bn); C Schröder Nr 7 (2nd & 3rd bns); Manfredini Nr 12 (3 bns); Kinsky Nr 47 (3 bns); KürR Hohenzollern Nr 4 (4 sqns); DragR Waldeck Nr 39 (4 sqns).

Austrian total ca 8,000 men.

Austrian losses Not exactly known but light.

Comment Archduke Charles continued his withdrawal eastwards towards Neresheim.

Sources Dedon, Wrede.

IN Rivoli, 29 July 1796, 1st clash

A village in northeastern Italy, 22 km northwest of

Verona, in the valley of the River Adige (Etsch), just east of Lake Garda, north of Pastrengo, just off the Autostrada A22.

An Austrian victory over the French.

(Last action - Milan, 16 May - 29 June; next action - Mantua, 4 July - 1 August.)

French Forces GdD Massena commanding: GdB Pijon: 70e and 152e DBdeLi (4 bns); 1ère DBdeLé (1 bn); GdB Saint-Hilaire: 118e and 119e DBdeLi (3 bns each). GdN Paris (1er Bn); GdB Ménard: 21e and 117e DBdeLi (4 bns); 32eDBdeLé (1 bn). 5e CavR (3 sqns); 9e DragR (4 sqns).

French total ca 10,000 men.

French losses 1,200 killed and wounded, 1,600 captured, 9 guns.

Austrian Forces FM Count Wurmser commanding: IRs Allvintzy Nr 19 (2 bns); Preiss Nr 24, Brechainville Nr 25, W Schröder Nr 26 (3 bns each); Deutschmeister Nr 4 (2 bns); Combined Carlstädter GzIR (3rd Bn). Gren Bn Gavasini; IR Huff Nr 8 (2 bns). HusR EH Josef Nr 2 (4 sqns).

Austrian total ca 22,000 men (of which only those shown above came into action).

Austrian losses ca 800 killed, wounded and missing.

Mantua, 4 July - 1 August 1796, failed siege

A fortress in northeastern Italy, on the River Mincio, at the junction of Routes 10, 62 and 420; 42 km south of Lake Garda.

An Austrian victory over the French.

(Last action - Rivoli, 29 July; next action - Lonato, 2/3 August.)

French Forces GdD Serrurier commanding: GdB Guyeux: 46e DBdeLi (2e Bn); 83e DBdeLi (3e Bn); 102e DBdeLi (1er Bn); 166e DBdeLi (1er and 2e bns); 170e DBdeLi (2e Bn). GdB Fiorella: 6e DBdeLé (3e Bn); 46e DBdeLi (1er and 3e bns); 51e DBdeLi (3 bns); 56e DBdeLi (1er Bn). GdB Pelletier: 19e DBdeLi (3 bns); 56e DBdeLi (2e and 3e bns); 102e DBdeLi (2e and 3e bns). 166e DBdeLi (3e Bn); GdN Mayenne-et-Loire (1er Bn). Artillery and sappers - 160. **Total** ca 6,000 men. **GdD Augereau** GdB Victor: 45e DBdeLi (1 bn); 69e DBdeLi (3 bns); 130e, 145e and 147e DBdeLi (3 bns each). GdB Banel: 39e and 105e DBdeLi (3 bns each); 5e PvDBdeLi (1 bn); 18e DBdeLé (1 bn); Légion des Allobroges (4e Bn). **Total** ca 6,000 men. **GdB Rusca** 4e PvDBdeLi (1 bn); 6e PvDBdeLi (3 bns); 15e PvDB-deLi (1 bn); 211e PvDBdeLi (3 bns); GdN Nyons (2 coys). **Total** ca 2,000 men. **GdD Macquart** GdB Davis: 22e DBdeLi (3 bns); GdB Nicolas: 104e DBdeLi (1 bn); GdB Dallemagne: 6e DBdeLé (1 bn); 20e DBdeLi (3e Bn); 121e DBdeLi (3 bns); Tirailleurs (1er Bn); GdN Saône-et-Loire (8e Bn). Sappers (6e Coy); artillery (70 men). **Total** ca 3,800 men. **GdD Garnier** GdB Davin: 20e DBdeLi (½ x 2e Bn); 109e DBdeLi (½ x 1er Bn); 209e DBdeLi (3e Bn). GdB Charton: 20e DBdeLi (1er Bn); 199e DBdeLi (3e Bn). GdB Serviez: 209e DBdeLi (1 coy 1er Bn); GdN Hérault (5e Bn). GdB Rambeaud: 20e DBdeLi (2e Bn); 15e DBdeLé (3 bns); GdN Haute-Vienne (gunners of 5e Bn); artillery (200 men). Gendarmes à P (69). **Total** ca 3,300 men. **GdD Massena (the Avantgarde, 1ère Division)** GdB Pijon: 70e and 152e DBdeLi (4 bns); 1ère DBdeLé (1 bn). GdB Saint-Hilaire; 118e and 119e DBdeLi (3 bns each). GdN Paris (1er Bn). GdB Ménard 21e and 117e DBdeLi (4 bns), 32e DBdeLé (1 bn). Gendarmes à P (32 men). **Total** ca 8,000 men. **Avantgarde 2e Division** GdB Cervoni: 1ère PvDBdeLi (1 bn); 84e and 101e DBdeLi (3 bns each); GdB Joubert: 99e and 109e DBdeLi (1 bn each); 13e PvDBdeLi (1 bn); GdN Ain (10e Bn). GdB Dommartin 3e and 16e DBdeLé, 55e DBdeLi, 14e PvDBdeLi (1 bn each). **Total** ca 9,300 men.

French total ca 36,000 men.

French losses Not known exactly: 898 captured, approximately 1,200 killed and wounded, 174 guns either abandoned or captured.

Austrian Garrison FML Count Canto d'Yrlès commanding: IRs Nádasdy Nr 39 (2 bns); Thurn Nr 43 (2 bns); combined GzIR Warasdiner (1 bn); combined GzIR Karlstädter (2 bns); IRs EH Anton Nr 52 (2 bns), Belgiojoso Nr 44 (3 bns); Pellegrini Nr 49 (1 bn); Preiss Nr 24 (1 bn); Stein Nr 50 (1 bn). 1st GarrisonR (1 coy); 2nd GarrisonR (2 bns) Mantua Landmiliz (2 coys); Freikorps Gyulai (1 bn). Stabs-dragonerR (2 sqns); HusR EH Josef Nr 2 (1 sqn); UlR Mészáros (½ sqn) sappers and miners (96 men); artillery (701 men).

Austrian total ca 13,753 men.

Austrian losses 372 died of sickness, 2 officers, 118 men killed, 14 officers, 381 men wounded, 1 officer and 73 men captured; 13 men deserted. The fortress had 179 fortress guns, 76 mortars and howitzers and 60 field guns.

Comment The French were forced to lift the siege in order to concentrate against FM Wurmser's relief column advancing south from Lake Garda and a secondary force under Quosdanovich. By 10 August all French siege works had been levelled, rations and forage in the fortress replenished and all captured French guns removed.

Sources Wrede, ÖMZ 1830, Heft 1, Fabry, Clausewitz.

IN Lonato, 2/3 August 1796, battle

A small, fortified town in northeastern Italy, 22 km southeast of Brescia; on Route 11, 5 km west of Desenzano del Garda at the southern end of Lake Garda. The action started at Gavardo on the River Chiese about 20 km northwest on Route 45b.

A French victory over the Austrians.

(Last action – Mantua, 4 July – 1 August; next action – Lonato, 4 August.)

French Forces GdD Bonaparte commanding. As for Mantua, 1 August but without Saint-Hilaire's and Rampon's brigades and Sauret's division.

French total 20,000 men.

French losses 2,000 killed, wounded and missing.

Austrian Forces FML Baron Quosdanovich commanding. IRs Kheul Nr 10, Reisky Nr 13, Klebek Nr 14, W Schröder Nr 26, A Esterházy Nr 34 (3 bns each); De Vins Nr 37 (1st and 3rd bns); Erbach Nr 42 (3 bns); J Jellačič Nr 53 (1st, 3rd and 4th bns); W Colloredo Nr 56 (3 bns); Gren Bns St Julien, Gavasini and Kottulinsky.

Austrian total 15,000 men.

Austrian losses 3,000 killed, wounded and captured. The 3rd Bn IR Nr 53 was captured; the Gren Bns St Julien and Gavasini suffered heavy losses; 20 guns were lost.

Comment Quosdanovich's force was isolated from Wurmser's main body by Lake Garda. They were both heading for Mantua to raise the siege. Having beaten Quosdanovich, Bonaparte now turned on Wurmser at Castiglione to the south.

Sources Wrede, Fabry, ÖMZ 1830, Volumes 1 and 2.

IN Lonato, 4 August 1796, capitulation

A small, fortified town in northeastern Italy, 22 km southeast of Brescia; on Route 11, 5 km west of Desenzano del Garda at the southern end of Lake Garda.

A French victory over the Austrians.

(Last action – Lonato 2/3 August; next action – Castiglione, 5 August.)

French Forces GdD Bonaparte commanding. Exact details not known; there was no combat, the Austrians were cut off and surrendered.

French total 1,200 men.

French losses Nil.

Austrian Forces Oberst Knorr commanding: IRs De Vins Nr 37 (1st Bn) and Erbach Nr 42 (1 bn).

Austrian total ca 2,000 men.

Austrian losses All captured together with 3 guns.

Sources Wrede, ÖMZ 1830 Heft 1. Fabry.

IN Castiglione delle Stiviere, 5 August 1796, battle

A town in northeastern Italy, 30 km northwest of the fortress of Mantua; on Route 236, at the junction with Route 567 coming south from Desenzano del Garda at the southern end of Lake Garda.

A French victory over the Austrians.

(Last action – Lonato, 4 August; next action – Rovereto, 4 September.)

French Forces GdD Bonaparte commanding. As for Mantua, 1 August but without Saint Hilaire's and Rampon's brigades and d'Allemagne's and Sauret's divisions.

French total 35,000 men.

French losses ca 1,100 men killed, wounded and missing.

Austrian Forces FM Count Wurmser commanding: IRs Deutschmeister Nr 4 (2 bns); Huff Nr 8 (2 bns); Reisky Nr 13 (3 bns); Allvintzy Nr 19 (1st Bn); Preiss Nr 24, Brechainville Nr 25 (2 bns each); Gren Bns Strassoldo; Vermatti; Combined GzIR Carlstadt (2nd and 9th bns); Combined GzIR Warasdin (9th Bn). HusR Erdödy Nr 11 (10 sqns).

Austrian total ca 15,500 men.

Austrian losses 2,000 killed and wounded, 1,000 captured, 20 guns. Gen Liptay wounded.

Comment This victory drove Wurmser away from Mantua; he fell back over the River Mincio and was not pursued. The French returned to the siege of Mantua.

Sources Wrede, ÖMZ 1830, Volumes 1 and 2.

UR Neresheim, 11 August 1796, battle

A village in the southwestern German state of Württemberg, 46 km northeast of Ulm and 19 km southwest of Nordlingen on Route B466.

A French victory over the Austrians.

(Last action – Cannstadt, 21 July; next action – Neumarkt, 22 August.)

French Forces GdD Moreau commanding the Armée du Rhin et de la Moselle (see the Order of Battle at the beginning of the 1796 section). Exact details not known.

French total 50,000 men.

French losses 1,200 killed and wounded, 1,200 captured.

Austrian Forces FM Archduke Charles commanding. IRs EH Carl Nr 3 (1 bn), C Schröder Nr 7 (2nd & 3rd bns), Manfredini Nr 12 (3 bns), Reisky Nr 13 (4 bns), d'Alton Nr 15 (2nd bn), de Ligne Nr 30 (1 bn), Nádasdy Nr 39 (3 bns), Kinsky Nr 47 (3 bns). KürR EH Franz Nr 29 (4 sqns); HusR EH Ferdinand Nr 32 (part); HusR Siebenburgen Nr 47 (6 sqns). Grenadier Bns Pietsch, Retz, Apfaltrern, Candiani. GzIR Slavonier (1st, 2nd, 3rd, 5th bns).

Austrian total ca 20,000 men.

Austrian losses 1,100 killed and wounded, 500 captured.

Comment Whilst drawing Moreau eastwards, Archduke Charles had sent word to Wartensleben at Frankfurt/Main (now 200 km to his northeast at Amberg) to march to join him so that they might unite and crush Moreau. Unfortunately, Wartensleben did not obey and the two Austrian army groups were still widely separated and Jourdan was closing in on Wartensleben. Archduke Charles withdrew eastwards over the Danube at Donauwörth and Dillingen. There was also a cavalry clash at Bopfingen this day involving the Austrian CarabinierR H Albert Nr 5 and the Siebenburgen HusR Nr 47.

Sources Wrede, Bodart, Dedon.

MR Sulzbach, 17 August 1796, clash

A village in the southeastern German state of Bavaria, 45 km east of Nürnberg at the junction of Routes B14 and B85.

A French victory over the Austrians.

(Last action – Friedberg, 10 July; next action – Amberg, 24 August.)

French Forces GdD Kléber commanding part of Jourdan's Armée de la Sambre-et-Meuse. Exact details not known.

French total ca 25,000 men.

French losses 1,000 killed and wounded, 700 captured.

Austrian Forces FML Baron Kray commanding part of the Army of the Lower Rhine: IR Clerfayt Nr 9 (1st Bn); ChLR Latour Nr 31 (6 sqns); HusR Vécsey Nr 34 (10 sqns). GzIR Warasdiner (2nd & 3rd bns).

Austrian total ca 8,000 men.

Austrian losses 900 killed and wounded, 200 captured.

Source Wrede.

UR Neumarkt (in der Oberpfalz), 22 August 1796, clash

A small town in southeastern Germany, midway between Nürnberg and Amberg, at the junction of Routes B8 and B299.

An Austrian victory over the French.

(Last action – Neresheim, 11 August; next action – Friedberg, 24 August.)

French Forces GdD Bernadotte commanding part of Jourdan's Armée de la Sambre-et-Meuse. Exact details, total and losses not known; see OOB at start of this chapter.

Austrian Forces Part of the Army of the Upper Rhine (Archduke Charles and Nauendorf): IRs Manfredini Nr 12 (3 bns), Sztáray Nr 33 (1 bn); KürR Kavanagh Nr 12 (4 sqns); Grenadier bns Apfaltrern; GzIR Slavonischer (3rd Bn).

Comment Unable to get Wartensleben to react to his orders to march south to join him, Archduke Charles moved north to unite with Wartensleben. In so doing he clashed with Bernadotte and pushed him back northwest. Charles also changed his lines of supply from the south to Eger, eastwards in Bohemia.

Source Wrede, Dedon.

MR Amberg, 24 August 1796, clash

A town in the southeastern German state of Bavaria, 55 km east of Nürnberg; on the River Vils and at the junction of Routes B85/E50 and B299.

An Austrian victory over the French.

(Last action – MR: Sulzbach, 17 August and UR: Neumarkt, 22 August; next action – Würzburg, 3 September.)

French Forces GdD Jourdan commanding. The Armée de la Sambre-et-Meuse: Regiments as for Würzburg on 3 September.

French total 34,000 men.

French losses 1,200 killed and wounded, 800 captured, 2 colours; possibly of the 23e DBdeLi (who lost 2 in 1796) or the 92e who lost 3.

Austrian Forces FM Archduke Charles commanding the Army of the Lower Rhine: IRs Clerfayt Nr 9 (1st Bn); Reisky Nr 13 (4 bns); Stuart Nr 28 (1st Bn); Sztáray Nr 33 (3 bns); Nádasdy Nr 39 (3 bns); Callenberg Nr 54 (3 bns); J Colloredo Nr 57 (3rd Bn); Beaulieu Nr 58 (1st Bn). Freikorps Carneville (4 coys, 2 sqns). KürR Kavanagh Nr 12 (6 sqns); KürR Nassau Nr 14 (6 sqns); KürR Mack Nr 20 (6 sqns); ChLR Latour Nr 31 (6 sqns); HusR Kaiser Nr 2 (8 sqns); HusR Vécsey Nr 34 (6 sqns); HusR Blankenstein Nr 16 (8 sqns); HusR Barco Nr 35 (8 sqns); UlR Schwarzenberg (6 sqns); ChLR Karaczay Nr 18 (2 sqns); ChLR Lobkowitz Nr 28 (6 sqns); ChLR Levenehr Nr 19 (6 sqns). Grenadier bns Kreyssern, Retz, Reisinger, Dietrich, Bydeskuty, Zegraedt. GzIR Warasdiner (2nd Bn).

Austrian total ca 40,000 men.

Austrian losses ca 400 killed and wounded.

Comment The union between Archduke Charles and Wartensleben at last took place during this clash. Jourdan withdrew northwest to Schweinfurt on the River Main whilst Moreau, instead of joining with him to fight the united Austrians, made a raid on Munich, deep in southeastern Bavaria.

Source Wrede, Charrié.

UR Friedberg, 24 August 1796, skirmish

A village in the southeastern German state of Bavaria, 5 km east of Augsburg on Route B300.

A French victory over the Austrians.

(Last action – Neumarkt, 22 August; next action – Geissenfeld, 1 September.)

French Forces GdD Moreau commanding the Armée du Rhin et de la Moselle (see the Order of Battle at the beginning of the 1796 section). Exact details not known.

French total 40,000 men.

French losses 400 men.

Austrian Forces FZM Count Latour commanding the Army of the Upper Rhine. IRs C Schröder Nr 7 (3 bns).

Austrian total ca 2,500 men.

Austrian losses 600 killed and wounded, 1,200 missing, 17 guns.

Comment Despite Archduke Charles' instructions to withdraw north on Ingolstadt, Latour fell back eastwards to protect the borders of Austria thereby giving Moreau the chance to interpose his army between the two Austrian forces. Luckily, Moreau failed to seize his chance despite this excellent local success.

Sources Wrede, Bodart, Dedon.

UR Geissenfeld, 1 September 1796, clash

Nowadays 'Geisenfeld'; A village in the southern German state of Bavaria on Route B300, about 15 km southeast of Ingolstadt on the River Danube.

A French victory over the Austrians.

(Last action – Friedberg, 24 August; next action – Kehl 18 September.)

French Forces GdD Moreau's Armée du Rhin et de la Moselle (see the Order of Battle at the beginning of the 1796 section). Exact details, total and losses not known.

Austrian Forces MG Nauendorf commanding part of the Army of the Upper Rhine: IRs d'Alton Nr 15 (3 bns); Stuart Nr 28 (1st Bn); Benjowsky Nr 31 (2nd Bn); Sztáray Nr 33 (1 bn); J Colloredo Nr. 57 (3rd Bn); KürR EH Franz Nr 29 (4 sqns). KürR EH Johann Nr 26 (4 sqns).

Austrian total ca 6,000 men.

Austrian losses Not exactly known, light.

Comment Nauendorf was supported by Latour here. Latour withdrew east in good order to Pfeffenhausen whilst Nauendorf stayed at Abensberg to cover Archduke Charles' rear. Moreau at last began to realise how exposed his position was and withdrew westwards on Ulm.

Sources Dedon, Wrede.

MR Würzburg, 3 September 1796, battle

A fortified town in the southeastern German state of Bavaria, on the right bank of the River Main and at the junction of Routes B8, B13, B19 and B27.

An Austrian victory over the French.

(Last action – Amberg, 24 August; next action – Mainz, 7 September.)

French Forces GdD Jourdan commanding the Armée de la Sambre-et-Meuse GdD Lefebvre 25e DBdeLé, 43e, 83e, 96e & 105e DBdeLi (3 bns each); 8e CuirR, 11e DragR (4 sqns each); 16e DragR (1 sqn); 1er & 9e ChàCh, 4e HusR (3 sqns each); 2 x FAB, 2 x HAB. **GdD Grenier** 20e DBdeLé, 16e & 67e DBdeLi (3 bns each); 23e DBdeLi (1er Bn); 1er & 2e DragR; 6e ChàCh. 1 x FAB, 1 x HAB. **GdD Championnet** 8e DBdeLé, 61e, 78e & 92e DBdeLi (3 bns each); 12eDragR; 12e ChàCh

(4 sqns each); 2 x FAB, 1 x HAB. **GdD Bernadotte** 9e, 37e, 49e & 88e DBdeLi (3 bns each); 7e & 14e DragR, 3e ChàCh (4 sqns each); 2e HusR (3 sqns). 1 x FAB, 2 x HAB. **The Reserve GdD Bonneau** 4e, 7e, 10e & 17e CuirR (4 sqns each); 2 x HAB.

French total 51 bns, 70 sqns ca 25,000 infantry and 5,000 cavalry, 11 batteries.

French losses 2,000 killed and wounded, 1,000 captured, 7 guns. The colour of 67e DBdeLi.

Austrian Forces FM Archduke Charles commanding the Army of the Lower Rhine: FML Hotze, GM Kienmayer GzIR Slavonier (3rd Bn); HusR Kaiser Nr 2 (8 sqns). GM Hiller: IRs Gemmingen Nr 21 (1 bn); Splényi Nr 51 (1st Bn). GM Carnisius: ChLR Levenehr Nr 19 (5 sqns). **FML Sztáray** GM Prince Johannes Liechtenstein: GzIR Slavonier (2nd Bn); O'Donnell Freikorps (1 bn); HusR Siebenburgen Nr 47 (6 sqns); DragR Coburg Nr 37, ChLR Levenehr Nr 19 (1 sqn each); CarabinierR Albert Nr 5 (2 sqns). **GM Montfraut** IR Callenberg Nr 54 (3 bns); GM Bartels: Bavarian IR (2 bns); GM Kaim Grenadier Bns Szénassy, Apfaltrern, Candiani. **FML Riesch** GM Prince von Württemberg: DragR Coburg Nr 37 (5 sqns); GM Spielberg: Münster DragR (2 sqns), HusR Nr 2 Kaiser (4 sqns). **FML Kray** GM Hohenlohe: HusR Barco Nr 35 (4 sqns). **GM Hadik** ChLR Karaczay Nr 18 (4 sqns); HusR Blankenstein Nr 16 (6 sqns). **GM von Sebottendorf** IR Sztáray Nr 33 (2 bns). **GM Prince of Orange** IR Kaiser Nr 1 (4 bns); **GM Staader** IR Clerfayt Nr 9 (1st Bn); IR Beaulieu Nr 58 (1st Bn). **The Reserve FML Wartensleben** GM Werneck, GM Kollowrath: Grenadier bns Ulm, Frankenbusch, Zegraedt, Riera. GM Schnellenberg: Grenadier bns Bydeskuty, Reisinger, Dietrich, Retz, Pietsch. GM Vogelsang: Grenadier bns Ghenedegg, Paulus, Kreyssern. GM Rosenberg: CarabinierRs Albert Nr 5 (4 sqns), Kaiser Nr 6 (6 sqns). GM Prince von Lothringen: KürR Zeschwitz Nr 10 (6 sqns); KürR Nassau Nr 14 (6 sqns). Also IRs Reisky Nr 13 (4 bns) and Kinsky Nr 47 (1st Bn).

Austrian total ca 17,000 men (in combat).

Austrian losses ca 1,200 killed and wounded, 300 captured.

Comment Total armies present on this day were numerically equal at 30,000 apiece. Archduke Charles pursued his beaten foe, marching on a more southern (and better) route and continually turning the French right flank and keeping Jourdan separated from Moreau - still far away to the south - and from the French force around Mainz. On 8 September Charles relieved both Mainz and Mannheim.

IN Rovereto, 4 September 1796, clash

A town in the northern Italian province of South Tyrol, 24 km south of Trient, on the east bank of the River Adige, at the junction of Routes 12, 46 and 240.

A French victory over the Austrians.

(Last action - Castiglione, 5 August; next action - Primolano, 7 September.)

French Forces GdD Bonaparte commanding. Exact details not known; as for Bassano, 6 November.

French total 20,000 men.

French losses 750 killed, wounded and missing.

Austrian Forces FML Baron Davidovich commanding (The Corps of the Tyrol); as for Bassano, 6 November.

Austrian total 10,000 men.

Austrian losses 3,000 men (mostly captured), 25 guns, 7 colours.

Source Wrede.

MR Mainz, 14 June - 7 September 1796, failed blockade

A fortified city in western central Germany, on the west bank of the River Rhine, opposite the confluence with the River Main.

An Allied victory over the French.

(Last action - Würzburg, 3 September; next action - Wiesbaden, 9 September.)

French Forces GdD Moreau and the Armée du Rhin et de la Moselle.

French total 36,000 men.

Garrison Troops Governor FML von Neu: **Hessen-Darmstadt Troops** LeibR (1 bn); IR Erbprinz (1 bn); IR Landgraf (1 bn); Leib-Gren-Bn (1 bn) **Electorate of Mainz Troops** IRs von Knorr; von Gymnich; von Ried; von Faber (1 bn each); artillery (140 men). **Electorate of Köln Troops** (1 bn), **Imperial Troops** IR Bamberg (1 bn). Oberrhein Kreis-Compagnie (1 coy). The Franconian-Bn, IR Lacy Nr 22 (1 bn).

Comment Archduke Charles' victory over Jourdan's Armée de la Sambre-et-Meuse at Würzburg on 3 September forced Moreau to lift the blockade.

Sources Wrede, Keim, Beck, Bodart.

IN Primolano, 7 September 1796, clash

A village in the northeastern Italian province of Venetia, on the River Brenta, 22 km north of Bassano, at the junction of Routes 47 and 50 bis.

A French victory over the Austrians.

(Last action – Rovereto, 4 September; next action – Bassano, 8 September.)

French Forces GdD Augereau commanding: GdB Rusca and Victor. 4e & 18e DBdeLé, 39e & 69e DBdeLi (3 bns each).

French total ca 8,200 men.

French losses Not known; light.

Austrian Forces, Obst Cavasini commanding: GzIR Karlstadt (9th Bn); GzIR Warasdiner (4th Bn); IR Erbach Nr 42 (1 bn); IR M Wallis Nr 11 (1 bn); IR Pellegrini Nr 49 (Grenadiers); HusR Erdödy Nr 11 (6 sqns).

Austrian totals ca 4,000 men.

Austrian losses Some killed and wounded, 1,500 captured (most of IR Wallis and Erbach) 5 guns.

Sources Wrede, Charrié.

IN Bassano, 8 September 1796, battle

A town in the northeastern Italian province of Venetia, on the River Brenta, 28 km northeast of Vicenza and on Route 47.

A French victory over the Austrians.

(Last action – Primolano, 7 September; next action – Cerea, 11 September.)

French Forces GdD Bonaparte commanding: 20,000 men including 5eDBdLi.

French losses 400 killed, wounded and missing.

Austrian Forces FM Count Wurmser commanding: IRs Schröder Nr 26 (2 bns); Jordis Nr 59 (3rd Bn); GzIR Banater (1st Bn); UlR Mészáros (6 sqns); HusR Erdödy Nr 11; HusR Wurmser Nr 30 (10 sqns each); Gren Bns Strassoldo, Bianchi, Gavasini and St Julien.

Austrian totals ca 11,000 men.

Austrian losses 600 killed and wounded, 2,000 captured, 30 guns, 8 colours, 200 limbers and ammunition waggons.

Comment Having won the battle, it was Bonaparte's ruthless pursuit which reaped the spoils when the Austrians had to abandon their artillery and baggage. Most of IR Jordis and Gren Bn Gavasini were captured; the units ceased to exist.

Source Wrede.

MR Wiesbaden, 9 September 1796, clash

A town in western central Germany, on the bank of the River Rhine just northwest of its confluence with the River Main; opposite Mainz.

An Allied victory over the French.

(Last action – Mainz, 7 September; next action – Limburg, 16 September.)

French Forces The rearguard of GdD Jourdan's Armée de la Sambre-et-Meuse. Exact details not known.

French total 1,500 men, 4 guns.

French losses 60 killed; wounded and missing not known.

Allied Forces 1st Column Obst Czock commanding 'Rothmäntel' of Wurmser Freikorps infantry (300 men); Wurmser Freikorps Husaren (2 sqns); IR Strassoldo Nr 27 (1 bn); IR Mittrowsky Nr 40 (1 bn); 4 x bn guns, 4 x 8 pdr howitzers. 2nd Column, MG von Mylius commanding: Kür-Köln-IR (1 bn); hussars (1 sqn); Kur-Mainz IR von Gymnich (1 bn); IR Kaiser Nr 1 (1 bn); IR U. Kinsky Nr 36 (1 bn); IR Hohenlohe Nr 17 (1 bn); 10 x bn guns, 4 x 8 pdr howitzers. 3rd Column GM Count von Wittgenstein commanding: Hessen-Darmstadt Scharfschützen (2 coys); Hussars (1½ sqns); Fränkisches Gren-Bn (1 bn). Hessen-Darmstadt troops: IR Landgraf (2nd Bn); LeibR (2nd Bn); IR Erbprinz (1st Bn). Austrian IR Lacy Nr 22 (1 bn); IR Callenberg Nr 54 (1 bn); 12 x bn guns; 3 x HA guns.

Allied total ca 12,000 men.

Allied losses Not known exactly but very light.

Sources Wrede, Keim, Beck.

IN Cerea, 11 September 1796, clash

A village in the northeastern Italian province of Venetia, 9 km west of Legnano on the River Adige; north of the River Po and on Route 10 towards Mantua.

An Austrian victory over the French.

(Last action – Bassano, 8 September; next action – Legnano, 12 September.)

French Forces GdD Massena commanding GdB Joubert, Dommartin. 1ère, 3e & 8e DBdeLé, 21e, 63e & 84e DBdeLi (3 bns each).

French total ca 6,600 men.

French losses ca 400 killed and wounded, 800 captured, 6 guns, 5 ammunition waggons.

Austrian Forces FM Count Wurmser commanding:

IRs Allvintzy Nr 19 (2 bns); Esterházy Nr 34 (3 bns); HusR EH Joseph Nr 17 (10 sqns).

Austrian totals ca 3,500 men.

Austrian losses Not exactly known; moderate.

Comment IR Esterházy suffered heavy losses here.

Sources Wrede, Bodart, Charrié.

IN Legnano, 12 September 1796, capitulation

A fortress town in the northern Italian province of Venetia, on the River Etsch (Adige), 40 km southeast of Verona; on Route 434, 33 km east of Mantua.

A French victory over the Austrians.

(Last action – Cerea, 11 September; next action – Mantua, 15 September.)

French Forces GdD Augereau commanding: GdB Rusca, Victor: 4e & 18e DBdeLé, 39e & 69e DbdeLi.

French total ca 8,000 men.

French losses None.

Austrian Garrison IR Brechainville Nr 25 (3 bns) ca 1,700 men.

Austrian losses All captured, 22 guns.

Comment 500 French prisoners in the town were released.

Sources Wrede, Bodart, Charrié.

IN Mantua (La Favorita and San Giorgio), 15 September 1796, clash

A village in the northern Italian province of Lombardy, 2 km northeast of the fortress town of Mantua on the River Mincio.

A French victory over the Austrians.

(Last action – Legnano, 12 September; next action – Fontaniva, 5 November.)

French Forces GdD Kilmaine commanding 4e, 5e, 6e, 18e, 19e, 39e, 45e, 63e & 64e DBdeLi (3 bns each except the 19e who had only the 1er & 2e bns present).

French total ca 17,000 men.

French losses ca 1,500 killed and wounded, 9 guns.

Austrian Forces FM Count Wurmser commanding: IRs Allvintzy Nr 19 (2 bns), Esterházy Nr 34 (3 bns), Schröder Nr 26 (2 bns), Jordis Nr 59 (3rd Bn), Huff Nr 8 (1 bn), Reisky Nr 13 (2½ bns), Preiss Nr 24 (2 bns), Strassoldo Nr 27 (2 bns), Brechainville Nr 25 (3 bns), UlR Mészáros (8 sqns), HusR Erdödy Nr 11 (6 sqns); Gren Bn Strassoldo (1 bn).

Austrian total ca 14,000 men.

Austrian losses 2,500 killed, wounded and captured, 11 guns, 3 colours.

Comment This was the culmination of the second attempt of the Austrians to relieve Mantua. Wurmser's corps was forced into the fortress.

Sources Bodart, Wrede, Charrié, von Kausler.

MR Limburg, 16 September 1796, clash

A town in the western Central German state of Hessen, on the River Lahn, about 80 km north of Mainz and northwest of Frankfurt/Main and just south of the Autobahn A3/E35.

An Austrian victory over the French.

(Last action – Wiesbaden, 9 September; next action – Ehrenbreitstein.)

French Forces GdD Jourdan's Armée de la Sambre-et-Meuse. Regiments as for the battle of Würzburg, 3 September.

French total ca 15,000 men (in combat).

French losses Not exactly known; moderate.

Austrian Forces FZM Baron Kray commanding part of the Army of the Lower Rhine. IRs Hohenlohe Nr 17 (3 bns); Sztáray Nr 33 (1 bn); Reisky Nr 13 (4 bns); Freikorps Carneville (4 coys, 2 sqn Hus). ChLR Latour Nr 31 (4 sqns). Grenadier bns Ghenedegg, Frankenbusch, Riera. GzIR Warasdiner (1st Bn).

Austrian total ca 11,000 men.

Austrian losses Not exactly known but light.

Comment Jourdan's right wing was scattered and he was forced to withdraw northwest on Düsseldorf; he recrossed to the west bank of the Rhine and resigned his command. Archduke Charles left FML Werneck with 30,000 men between the Rhine and the Sieg and turned south to deal with Moreau.

Source Wrede.

MR Ehrenbreitstein, 9 June – 17 September 1796, failed blockade

A fortress on the eastern bank of the River Rhine in Germany, overlooking its confluence with the River Moselle.

An Allied victory over the French.

(Last action – Limburg, 16 September; this was the last action on the middle Rhine in 1796.)

French Forces Exact details and losses not known.

Allied Garrison Obst von Sechtern commanding: **Kurcöln** (1 bn); minor contingents (1⅔ bns) **Kur-**

Trier troops: Infantry (2 bns); Jägers (2 coys) artillery and engineers.
Allied total ca 2,600 men.
Allied losses Not exactly known but light.
Source Keim, Angeli.

UR Kehl, 18 September 1796, clash
A town in the southwestern German state of Baden, on the east bank of the Rhine opposite Strasbourg; on Route B36.
A French victory over the Austrians.
(Last action - Geissenfeld, 1 September; next action - Biberach, 2 October.)
French Forces GdD Schauenburg commanding the garrison. 24e DBdeLi (1 bn); 68e DBdeLi (3 bns); 104e DBdeLi (remnants); 19e DragR (2 sqns).
French total 7,000 men.
French losses 1,200 killed and wounded, 800 captured.
Austrian Forces FML Petrasch commanding. IRs Manfredini Nr 12 (3 bns); d'Alton Nr 15 (3 bns).
Austrian total 5,000 men.
Austrian losses ca 2,000 killed, wounded and missing.
Comment Petrasch captured the bridgehead of Kehl but was thrown out in the subsequent French counterattack.
Sources Wrede, Bodart, Dedon.

UR Biberach, 2 October 1796, battle
A town in the southwestern German state of Württemberg, 35 km southwest of Ulm; on the River Riss and at the junction of Routes B30 and B312.
A French victory over the Austrians.
(Last action - Kehl, 18 September; next action - Emmendiengen, 19 October.)
French Forces GdD Moreau commanding the Armée du Rhin et de la Moselle (see the Order of Battle at the beginning of the 1796 section). Exact details not known.
French total ca 35,000 men.
French losses 500 killed and wounded.
Austrian Forces FZM Count Latour commanding: IRs Kaiser Nr 1 (3rd Bn); EH Carl Nr 3 (1 bn); C Schröder Nr 7 (2nd & 3rd bns); M Wallis Nr 11 (2 bns); EH Ferdinand Nr 23 (2 bns); Wenkheim Nr 35 (3 bns); Württemberg Nr 38 (1st Bn); Croatian Freikorps (2 bns); KürR EH Johann Nr 26 (6 sqns); HusR EH Ferdinand Nr 32 (part); KürR Anspach Nr 33 (6 sqns); Grenadier Bns Pietsch.
Austrian total ca 15,000 men.
Austrian losses 300 killed and wounded, 4,000 captured, 18 guns, 2 colours.
Comment With this victory Moreau secured an uninterrupted withdrawal westwards through the southern Black Forest hills.
Sources Wrede, Bodart, Dedon.

UR Emmendiengen, 19 October 1796, battle
A village in the southwest German state of Baden, on the River Elz, 14 km north of Freiburg, between the Autobahn A5/E35 and Route B3.
An Austrian victory over the French.
(Last action - Biberach, 2 October; next action Schliengen, 24 October.)
French Forces GdD Moreau commanding the Armée du Rhin et de la Moselle. Exact details not known. See OOB at the start of this chapter.
French total 32,000 men.
French losses 1,000 killed and wounded, 1,800 captured, 2 guns. GdD Beaupuy killed.
Austrian Forces FM Archduke Charles commanding: IRs EH Carl Nr 3 (1 bn); M Wallis Nr 11 (2 bns); Manfredini Nr 12 (3 bns); d'Alton Nr 15 (2nd Bn); Benjowsky Nr 31 (2nd Bn); Sztáray Nr 33 (1 bn); J Colloredo Nr 57 (3rd Bn). KürR Hohenzollern Nr 4 (4 sqns); ChLR Lobkowitz Nr 28 (6 sqns); DragR Kaiser Nr 3 (6 sqns), Grenadier bns Pietsch, Retz, Reisinger. GzIR Slavonier (1st Bn).
Austrian total ca 10,000 men (in action out of 28,000).
Austrian losses 1,000 killed, wounded and missing. FZM Count Wartensleben killed.
Sources Wrede, Bodart, Dedon.

UR Schliengen, 24 October 1796, battle
A village in the southwestern German state of Baden, on the right bank of the Rhine, 20 km north of Bâsle, east of Mulhouse and on Route B3.
An Austrian victory over the French.
(Last action - Emmendiengen, 19 October; next action - Kehl, 10 January 1797.)
French Forces GdD Moreau commanding the Armée du Rhin et de la Moselle (see the Order of Battle at the beginning of the 1796 section). Exact details not known.

French total 32,000 men.

French losses 1,200 men.

Austrian Forces FM Archduke Charles commanding: IRs EH Carl Nr 3 (1 bn); M Wallis Nr 11 (2 bns); Manfredini Nr 12 (3 bns); d'Alton Nr 15 (3 bns); Stuart Nr 18 (1st Bn); Kaunitz Nr 20 (2nd Bn); Wartensleben Nr 28 (3 bns); Benjowsky Nr 31 (2nd Bn); Pellegrini Nr 49 (2 bns); J Colloredo Nr 57 (3rd Bn). KürR Kavanagh Nr 12 (6 sqns); KürR Lothringen Nr 21 (6 sqns); DragR Waldeck Nr 39 (6 sqns); ChLR Modena Nr 13 (6 sqns); DragR Coburg Nr 37 (6 sqns). Grenadier bns Pietsch, Retz, Reisinger, Dietrich.

Austrian total ca 24,000 men in combat (out of 36,000).

Austrian losses 800 killed, wounded and missing.

Comment Moreau withdrew over the Rhine into France. The Austrians now laid siege to Kehl and Hüningen, the last two French bridgeheads east of this river. Moreau offered an armistice to Archduke Charles who was in favour of accepting it as he could then send troops into northern Italy to help relieve the besieged fortress of Mantua. The Austrian high command in Vienna vetoed the suggestion and while the Austrians were besieging these minor works, the French sent 14 Demibrigades from the Upper Rhine into Italy to support Bonaparte and capture Mantua.

Sources Wrede, Bodart, Dedon.

IN Fontaniva, 5 November 1796, clash

A village on the eastern bank of the River Brenta in northeastern Italy, on Route 53, about 18 km northeast of Vicenza and 20 km north of Padua.

An Austrian victory over the French.

(Last action – Mantua, 15 September; next action – Bassano, 6 November.)

French Forces GdD Massena's division: 19e DBdeLé, 85e & 93e DBdeLi (3 bns each).

French total ca 7,000 men.

French losses Not known.

Austrian Forces GM Baron Liptay commanding IR Splényi Nr 51 (2 bns); GzIR Banater (4th & 5th bns); HusR Wurmser Nr 30 (1 sqn); HusR Erdödy Nr 11 (1 sqn).

Austrian total ca 3,000 men.

Austrian losses 6 killed, 16 wounded, 6 captured, 21 horses.

Comment All French attempts to force a river crossing here on this day failed.

Sources Wrede, ÖMZ 1828, Heft 9.

IN Bassano, 6 November 1796, clash

A town in the northern Italian province of Venetia, on the River Brenta, 28 km northeast of Vicenza and on Route 47.

An Austrian victory over the French.

(Last action – Fontaniva, 5 November; next action – Cembra and Calliano, 2–7 November.)

French Forces GdD Bonaparte commanding the divisions of Augereau, Massena and the Reserve (GdD Macquart). 4e, 18e DBdeLé; 39e & 69e DBdeLi; 1ère, 3e & 8e DBdeLé, 21e, 51e & 84e DBdeLi; 5e DbdeLi.

French totals Augereau – ca 8,000 men, Massena – 9,000, Macquart – 2,500 = 19,500.

French losses ca 3,000 men killed, wounded and missing, 1 howitzer. 508 men were captured.

Austrian Forces FZM Baron Allvintzy commanding the 'Friaul Corps': IRs Kheul Nr 10 and Reisky Nr 13 (3 bns); Brechainville Nr 25 (3 bns); Gren Bn Strassoldo; GzIR Banalisten (2nd Bn); IR Splényi Nr 51 (2nd & 3rd bns); IR Gyulai Nr 32 (3 bns), Deutschmeister Nr 4 (3 bns); GzIR Banater (4th Bn); HusR Wurmser Nr 30 (6 sqns); Mahony Jäger (1 bn); HusR Erdödy Nr 11 (5 sqns); UlR Mészáros (4 sqns).

Austrian totals ca 28,000 men.

Austrian losses FML Provera's division 208 killed, 873 wounded, 109 captured. FML Quosdanovich's division: 326 killed, 858 wounded, 449 captured; 2 guns.

Comment Despite Bonaparte's presence, the Austrians repelled all his attempts to cross the Brenta here today. Most of the Grenz battalions were raw young troops, very poorly armed and equipped. The French withdrew to Verona. IR Splényi Nr 51 lost 657 men out of 2,200.

Sources Wrede, Bodart, ÖMZ 1828, Vol 3, Heft 9. Charrié.

IN Cembra and Calliano, 2–7 November 1796, skirmishes

Two villages in the northern Italian province of South Tyrol, the first on the River Avisio, 15 km northeast of Trient and southeast of Mezzo Lombardo; the latter on the River Etsch (Adige), 15 km south of Triente on Route 12.

Austrian victories over the French.

(Last action - Bassano, 6 November; next action - Caldiero, 12 November.)

French Forces GdD Vaubois commanding. 5e, 14e, 18e, 33e, 39e, 45e & 63e DBdeLi.

French total 10,500 men.

French losses 4,400 killed, wounded and missing, 6 guns, 8 ammunition waggons.

Austrian Forces FML Baron Davidovich commanding The Corps of The Tyrol: IRs Klebek Nr 14 (3 bns); Allvintzy Nr 19 (3rd Bn); Toscana Nr 23 (1 bn); Preiss Nr 24 (2 bns); Brechainville Nr 25 (1 bn); U Kinsky Nr 36 (3rd Bn); Nádasdy Nr 39 (2 bns); EH Anton Nr 52 (2 bns); GzIR Carlstadt (9th Bn); GzIR Warasdiner (9th Bn). Combined Hungarian IR (2 bns) IR J Jellačič Nr 53 (1st & 4th bns).

Austrian total ca 11,000 men.

Austrian losses 2,000 killed and wounded; 1,500 captured including most of IR Nádasdy.

Source Wrede.

IN Caldiero, 12 November 1796, battle

A village in the northeastern Italian province of Venetia, 15 km east of Verona on Route 11 towards Vicenza and just south of Motorway A4.

An Austrian victory over the French.

(Last action - Cembra and Calliano, 2-7 November; next action - Arcole, 15-17 November.)

French Forces GdD Bonaparte commanding: GdD Augereau: 13e, 64e, 69e DBdeLi. GdD Massena 19e, 85e, 93e DBdeLi (3 bns each).

French totals ca 24,000 men.

French losses 1,000 killed and wounded, 800 captured, 2 guns.

Austrian Forces FZM Baron Allvintzy commanding The Corps of the Friaul: IRs Deutschmeister Nr 4 (2 bns); U Kinsky Nr 36 (3rd Bn); Nádasdy Nr 39 (2 bns); J Colloredo Nr 57 (2nd Bn). GzIR Carlstadt (7th & 8th bns); GzIR Warasdiner (4th Bn); GzIR Banalisten (2nd, 3rd, 4th bns); GzIR Banater (2nd, 4th, 5th, 6th bns). HusR Erdödy Nr 11 (4 sqns); HusR Wurmser Nr 30 (2 sqns), UlR Mészáros (4 sqns).

Austrian total ca 12,000 men.

Austrian losses 950 killed and wounded, 350 captured; 3rd bn, GzIR Banalisten suffered heavy casualties here.

Sources Wrede, ÖMZ 1829.

IN Arcole, 15-17 November 1796, battle

A town in the northeastern Italian province of Venetia, on the River Alpon, 25 km southeast of Verona; due south of San Bonifacio.

A French victory over the Austrians.

(Last action - Caldiero, 12 November; next action - Rivoli, 17 November.)

French Forces GdD Bonaparte commanding: GdD Augereau: 4e & 18e DBdeLé, 39e & 69e DBdeLi. GdD Massena: 19e, 85e, 93e DBdeLi (3 bns each). GdD Macquart's Infantry Reserve and GdB Beaurevoir's Cavalry Reserve were present but not directly engaged.

French total 20,000 men.

French losses 1,200 killed, 2,300 wounded. Generals Robert, Verne, Elliot, Gardanne, Lebon, Muiront, Verdier and Vignolle killed.

Austrian Forces FZM Baron Allvintzy commanding: The Corps of the Friaul: IRs Deutschmeister Nr 4 and Preiss Nr 24 (2 bns each); U Kinsky Nr 36 (3rd Bn); J Jellačič Nr 53 (3rd & 4th bns); J Colloredo Nr 57 (2nd Bn); GzIR Carlstadt (6th, 7th bns); GzIR Banater (5th & 6th bns); GzIR Warasdiner (4th & 5th bns); GzIR Banalisten (2nd, 4th bns); IR Splényi Nr 51 (2nd & 3rd bns); GzIR Wallachen (3rd Bn). UlR Mészáros (4 sqns); StabsDragR (4 sqns).

Austrian totals ca 18,500 men.

Austrian losses 600 killed, 1,600 wounded, 4,000 captured, 11 guns, 4 ammunition waggons. GM Baron Brabeck killed.

Comment Despite repeated urging from FZM Allvintzy, FML Baron Davidovich did not move south out of the Tyrol to join him for this battle. The action was fought in flooded rice fields with mobility limited to the few roads and dykes. A single Grenz-Infanterie-Battalion held up all French attempts to force the bridge at Arcole for two days.

Sources Wrede, Bodart, Charrié, ÖMZ 1829, Heft 4.

IN Rivoli, 17 November 1796, 2nd clash

A village in the northeastern Italian province of Venetia, 22 km northwest of Verona; just off Autostrada A22/E45, east of Lake Garda.

An Austrian victory over the French.

(Last action - Arcole, 15-17 November; next action - Rivoli, 22 November.)

French Forces GdD Vaubois commanding: 14e, 18e, 33e, 39e, 45e & 63e DBdeLi.

French total 6,500 men.

French losses 800 killed and wounded, 1,000 captured (including Generals Fiorella and la Valette), 7 guns.

Austrian Forces FML Baron Davidovich commanding The Corps of The Tyrol: IRs Klebek Nr 14 (1st & 3rd bns); Allvintzy Nr 19 (3rd Bn); Preiss Nr 24 (2 bns); de Vins Nr 37 (2nd Bn); Lattermann Nr 45 (1 bn); Combined IR (out of IRs Nrs 27, 39, 52); Gren Bn Gavasini; HusR Erdödy Nr 11 (4 sqns); GzIR Carlstadt (3rd, 5th bns); GzIR Wallachen (2nd Bn).

Austrian total ca 8,500 men.

Austrian losses 300 killed and wounded, 300 captured.

Comment Vaubois' troops were in danger of being completely surrounded and cut off; the withdrawal became a rout.

Sources Wrede. ÖMZ 1829, Heft 5.

IN Rivoli, 22 November 1796, 3rd clash

A village in the northeastern Italian province of Venetia, 22 km northwest of Verona; just off Autostrada A22/E45, east of Lake Garda.

A French victory over the Austrians.

(Last action – Rivoli, 17 November; this was the last action of note in northern Italy in 1796.)

French Forces GdD Bonaparte commanding: The Army of Italy including: 14e, 18e, 33e, 39e, 45e, 63e DBdeLi and the divisions of Massena, Augereau, the infantry reserve and the 6,000 strong remnants of Vaubois' division.

French total 15,000 men.

French losses ca 200 killed and wounded.

Austrian Forces FML Baron Davidovich commanding 'The Corps of the Tyrol': IRs Allvintzy Nr 19 (3rd Bn); Preiss Nr 24 (2 bns); IR Klebek Nr 14 (1 bn); de Vins Nr 37 (2nd Bn); Gren Bn Gavasini; IR Lattermann Nr 45; Combined Hungarian IR (2 bns); HusR Erdödy Nr 11 (4 sqns); GzIR Carlstadt (3rd & 5th bns); GzIR Wallachen (2nd Bn).

Austrian totals ca 7,000 men.

Austrian losses 81 killed, 170 wounded, 608 captured, 3 guns and ammunition waggons, a pontoon bridging train of 14 pontoons.

Comment The French captured an Austrian officer with complete details of the Friaul and Tyrolean corps and their dangerously wide separation. Hearing of Vaubois' defeat at Rivoli on 17 November, Bonaparte at once decided to strike at Davidovich's isolated corps, leaving only a few squadrons to observe Allvintzy's withdrawal northeastwards on Vicenza. Davidovich had already evacuated the Rivoli position to withdraw north to safety but, learning that Allvintzy was now marching to his aid, he tried to reoccupy it. The French – in superior numbers – got there first and the Tyrolean corps was hotly pursued up the River Etsch, (Adige).

Sources Wrede; ÖMZ 1829, Heft 5.

1797

THE ACTIONS 1797

UR Kehl, 10 November 1796 – 9 January 1797, siege and capture

A town in the southwestern German state of Baden, on the east bank of the Rhine, opposite Strasbourg and on Route B36.

An Austrian victory over the French.

(This was the opening action on the Upper Rhine in 1797; next action – Hüningen, 1 February.)

French Garrison: GdD Desaix commanding. Exact details not known, but including 16e DBdeLé, 17e, 31e, 76e, 100e, 109e DBdeLi (3 bns each) and 9e HusR (4 Sqns).

French totals 20,000 men.

French losses 4,000 killed and wounded.

Austrian Forces FM EH Charles commanding: IRs EH Ferdinand Nr 2 (2 bns); EH Carl Nr 3 (1st Bn); Oranien Nr 15 (3 bns); Kaunitz Nr 20 (1st Bn); Toscana Nr 23 (2 bns); Wartensleben Nr 28 (3 bns); De Ligne Nr 30 (1 bn); Benjowsky Nr 31 (2 bns); Sztáray Nr 33 (3 bns); Nádasdy Nr 39 (3rd Bn); F Kinsky Nr 47 (3 bns); W Colloredo Nr 56 (3rd Bn). Grenadier Bns Ghenedegg, Pietsch, Retz, Reisinger, Dietrich, Bydeskuty, Leeuven, Apfaltrern, Candiani. Serbisches Freikorps (2 bns); DragRs Lothringen Nr 21 (6 sqns); Toscana Nr 26 (2 sqns). HusR Blankenstein Nr 16 (2 sqns). GzIR Warasdiner (3rd & 7th Bns), GzIR Slavonier (8th & 9th Bns). GzIR Banater (1st Bn). GzIR Siebenburger (2nd & 3rd Bns).

Austrian total ca 40,000 men.

Austrian losses 3,800 killed, died of sickness or wounded, 1,000 captured.

Sources Bodart, Wrede, Dedon.

IN Rivoli, 14–15 January 1797, battle

A village in northeastern Italy, 22 km northwest of Verona, just off the Autostrada A22/E45, east of Lake Garda, 48 km north of Mantua.

A French victory over the Austrians.

(Last action – this was the opening action of the campaign in northern Italy; next action – Mantua, 16 January.)

French Forces GdD Bonaparte commanding: DBdeLi: 4e, 5e, 6e, 9e, 11e, 12e, 13e, 14e, 18e, 19e, 25e, 29e, 30e, 32e, 33e, 39e, 40e, 43e, 45e, 51e, 55e, 57e, 58e, 61e, 63e, 64e, 69e, 75e, 79e, 85e, 88e, 93e. DBdeLé 11e, 12e, 20e, 22e, 29e. DragRs 3e, 5e, 8e, 9e, 15e, 18e, 20e. ChàCh 10e, 13e, 15e, 19e, 22e, 24e, 25e. HusRs 1er & 7 bis.

French total 18,000 infantry, 4,000 cavalry, 60 guns.

French losses 2,200 killed and wounded, 1,000 captured.

Austrian Forces FZM Baron von Allvintzy commanding: IRs Hoch-und-Deutschmeister Nr 4 (3 bns), Huff Nr 8 (3rd Bn), M Wallis Nr 11 (3rd Bn), Reisky Nr 13 (3 coys), Klebek Nr 14* (2 bns), Preiss Nr 24 (3 bns), Brechainville Nr 25 (1 bn), Strassoldo Nr 27 (1 bn), Nádasdy Nr 39 (3 bns), Erbach Nr 42 (2 bns); Callenberg Nr 54 (1st Bn); Grenadier Bn Khevenhüller; HusR Wurmser Nr 30 (2 sqns); StabsDragR (2 sqns); GzIR Carlstädter (4th, 5th, 7th, 9th Bns); GzIR Banalisten (5th Bn); GzIR Banater (2nd Bn); GzIR Walachen (2nd & 3rd Bns). Freikorps Gyulai (2 bns); Jägercorps Kurz* (1 bn). FML Marquis Provera's Corps (destined to go on to Mantua to break the siege): IRs Allvintzy Nr 19 (3rd Bn), Gyulai Nr 32 (3 bns), J Colloredo Nr 57 (3rd Bn), Wiener Freiwilligen (1 bn); HusR Erdödy Nr 11 (2 sqns); GzIR Warasdiner (4th, 5th, 9th Bns).

Austrian total 28,000 men, 90 guns.

Austrian losses 4,000 killed and wounded, 8,000 captured, 8 guns, 11 colours and standards (Bonaparte originally claimed 24).

* = these units were captured complete.

Comment Bonaparte's various accounts of this action are fanciful when it comes to the numbers of Austrians involved.

Sources Bodart, Wrede; ÖMZ 1832 Heft 2.

IN Mantua (La Favorita), 16 January 1797, battle

A fortress town in the northern Italian province of Lombardy, on the River Mincio, 130 km east of Milan and due south of Lake Garda.

A French victory over the Austrians.

(Last action – Rivoli, 14/15 January; next action – Mantua, 2 February.)

French Forces GdD Bonaparte commanding: DBdeLi 4e, 5e, 6e, 9e, 11e, 12e, 13e, 14e, 18e, 19e, 25e, 29e, 30e, 32e, 33e, 39e, 40e, 43e, 45e, 51e, 55e, 57e, 58e, 61e, 63e, 64e, 69e, 75e, 79e, 85e, 88e, 93e. DBdeLé 11e, 12e, 20e, 22e, 29e. DragRs 3e, 5e, 8e, 9e, 15e, 18e, 20e. ChàCh 10e, 13e, 15e, 19e, 22e, 24e, 25e. HusRs 1er & 7e bis. The whole army consisted of the divisions of Dumas, d'Allemagne, Augereau,

Massena, Joubert, Rey, Victor's infantry reserve, Dugna's cavalry reserve and Lannes' mobile column. Garrisons apart from these were GdD Gauthier in Coni, Ceva, Cherasco - 1,334; Marquart in Tortona and Allessandria - 1,295; Kilmaine in Milan, Piacenza, Bergamo and Bologna - 4,658 and Vaubois in Leghorn - 1,974.

French total ca 28,000 men.

French losses 1,200 killed and wounded, 800 captured.

Austrian Forces FM Count Wurmser commanding part of the fortress garrison: IRs Huff Nr 8 (2 bns), Kheul Nr 10 (3 bns), Reisky Nr 13 (3 bns), Preiss Nr 24 (3rd Bn), Brechainville Nr 25 (4 coys), W Schröder Nr 26 (3 bns), Thurn Nr 43 (2 bns), Belgiojoso Nr 44 (3 bns), Kerpen Nr 29 (3rd Bn); Grenadier bns Bianchi and Strassoldo. Croatisches Freikorps (1 bn); HusR Wurmser Nr 30 (4 sqns); UlR Mészáros (6 sqns), Stabs-Dragoner (4 sqns); GzIR Carlstädter (1st, 2nd & 6th Bns); GzIR Banalisten (1st Bn). **Total** ca 10,000 men. **FML Marquis Provera's Relief Column** IRs Allvintzy Nr 19 (3rd Bn), S Gyulai Nr 32 (3 bns); J Colloredo Nr 57 (3rd Bn); Wiener Freiwilliger (1 bn); GzIR Warasdiner (4th, 5th & 9th Bns); HusR Erdödy Nr 11 (2 sqns). **Total** 4,000 men.

Total Austrian losses 1,300 killed and wounded, 4,700 captured, 22 guns, 43 vehicles including a bridging train.

Comment Provera's long-awaited relief column had suffered considerable loss in the battle of Rivoli on 14/15 January. Bonaparte's victory here forced Provera to capitulate with 2,000 men. The third Austrian attempt to relieve the starving garrison had failed and the place capitulated on 2 February. Most of the Austrian relief force were half-trained, new recruits, hurriedly scraped together.

Sources Bodart, Wrede, ÖMZ 1832, Heft 2.

UR Hüningen, 27 November 1796 - 1 February 1797, siege and capture

A town in the eastern French province of Alsace-Lorraine, on the west bank of the Rhine, 4 km north of Bâsle on Route N66.

An Austrian victory over the French.

(Last action - Kehl, 9 January; next action - Diersheim, 20/21 April.)

French Garrison GdD Dufour commanding: Exact details not known.

French total 4,000 men.

French losses Not exactly known. GdB Abbatucci was killed and the bridgehead handed over to the Austrians.

Austrian Forces FZM Prince Fürstenberg commanding: IRs Kaiser Nr 1 (3 bns); Bender Nr 41 (2 bns), Kerpen Nr 43 (3 bns), GzIR Warasdiner (3rd & 7th Bns); GzIR Slavonier (8th & 9th Bns); GzIR Banater (1st Bn); GzIR Siebenburger (2nd & 3rd Bns); artillery and engineers.

Austrian total ca 10,000 men.

Austrian losses Not known exactly but light.

Sources Bodart, Wrede.

IN Mantua, 27 August 1796 - 2 February 1797, blockade and capitulation

A fortress town in the northern Italian province of Lombardy, on the River Mincio, 130 km east of Milan and due south of Lake Garda.

A French victory over the Austrians.

(Last action - Mantua, 16 January; next action - Valvassone, 16 March.)

French Forces GdDs Dumas and d'Allemagne commanding*: DBdeLi: 4e, 5e, 6e, 9e, 11e, 12e, 13e, 14e, 18e, 19e, 25e, 30e, 32e, 33e, 39e, 40e, 43e, 45e, 51e, 55e, 57e, 58e, 61e, 63e, 64e, 69e, 75e, 79e, 85e, 88e, 93e. DBdeLé 11e, 12e, 20e. DragRs 3e, 5e, 8e, 9e, 15e, 18e, 20e. ChàCh 10e, 13e, 15e, 19e, 22e, 24e, 25e. HusRs 1er & 7 bis.

French total 10,000 men.

French losses Not known exactly.

* = GdD Kilmaine was titular commander but, as he was sick, GdD d'Allemagne took over. Not all the regiments shown were present for the entire siege.

Austrian Garrison FM Count Wurmser commanding: IRs Huff Nr 8 (2 bns), Kheul Nr 10, Reisky Nr 13 (3 bns each), Preiss Nr 24 (3rd Bn), Brechainville Nr 25 (4 coys), W Schröder Nr 26 (3 bns), Thurn Nr 34 (2 bns), Belgiojoso Nr 44 (3 bns), Kerpen Nr 49 (3rd Bn); Grenadier bns Bianchi, Strassoldo (1 bn each); Croatischer Freikorps (1 bn); HusR Wurmser Nr 30; HusR EH Joseph (4 sqns each); HusR Erdödy Nr 11 (2 sqns); UlR Mészáros (6 sqns); Stabs-Dragoner (4 sqns); GzIR Carlstädter (1st, 2nd & 6th Bns); Mahony Jägers (1 bn), GzIR Banalisten (1st Bn). Artillery, engineers, sappers.

Austrian total 28,000 men.

Austrian losses since May 1796 - 16,333 killed,

wounded and died of sickness, 325 Austrian guns were captured; the 179 French guns there were recaptured.

Comment In respect for the extremely able defence of the fortress, Wurmser, his staff, 700 men and 6 guns marched out free. 20,000 men marched out with honours of war and went home on condition not to fight against France until exchanged.

Sources Bodart, Wrede.

IM Castel Bolognese, 3 February 1797, clash

A village in the northern Italian province of Romagna, on the River Senio, 40 km southeast of Bologna on Route 9.

A French victory over the Papal troops.

(This was the opening French action against the Vatican; next action – Ancona, 9 February).

French Forces GdD Victor commanding. Exact details not known; this force was part of Bonaparte's Armée d'Italie. This force included GdD Lannes' Grenadier Reserve.

French total 9,000 men.

French losses ca 100 killed and wounded.

Papal Forces LG Baron Colli commanding: Exact details not known.

Papal forces total 7,000 men, 14 guns.

Papal forces losses 800 killed and wounded, 1,200 captured; 14 guns, 8 caissons, 8 colours.

Sources Bodart, ÖMZ 1832, Heft 2.

IM Ancona, 9 February 1797, capitulation

A fortified port on the central Italian Adriatic coast, 200 km northeast of Rome.

A French victory over the Papal troops.

(Last action – Castel Bolognese, 3 February; this was the last action against the Vatican.)

French Forces GdD Victor commanding part of Bonaparte's Armée d'Italie.

French total 4,000 men.

French losses Nil.

Papal Garrison – 1,200 men, 120 guns.

Papal losses All captured.

Comment The Pope bought his peace with Bonaparte at a very heavy price in land, gold, works of art and treasures in the Treaty of Tolentino of 19 February. The Papal state was reduced to the Vatican city.

Sources Bodart, ÖMZ 1832 Heft 2.

ZZ Cape St Vincent, 14 February 1797, naval battle

A cape in the southern Portuguese province of the Algarve, 180 km southwest of Lisbon.

A British naval victory over the Spanish.

This was the only naval action of note in this region in 1797.

Spanish Fleet Admiral Conde de Cordoba: *Santissima Trinidad* (130); *San Nicholas* (80); *San Josef* (112); *Salvador del Mundo** (112); *San Isodoro* (80); *San Vincente*** (80); *Arrogante** (74); *Concepción* (112); *Conde de Regla* (112); *Mexicano* (112); *Principe de Asturias* (112); *Neptuno* (80); *Atlante* (74); *Bahama* (74); *Conquistador* (74); *Firme* (74); *Glorioso* (74); *Oriente* (74); *Pelayo* (74); *San Antonio* (74); *San Domingo* (74); *San Firmin* (74); *San Francisco de Paula* (74); *San Genaro* (74); *San Idelfonso* (74); *San Juan Nepomuceno* (74); *San Pablo* (74); *Soberano* (74); *Terrible* (74). *Gallardo** (74); *Santa Cecilia** (34).

Spanish total 34 ships of the line, 12 frigates, 1 Aviso, 2,610 guns, 15,000 men.

Spanish losses 5 ships taken (464 guns); 1,500 killed and wounded, 2,000 (including an Admiral) captured.

* = taken by the British.

** = destroyed after being taken.

British Forces Vice Admiral Sir John Jervis commanding: *Victory* (100); *Blenheim* (98); *Prince George* (98); *Orion* (74); *Barfleur* (98); *Colossus* (74); *Egmont* (74); *Goliath* (74); *Excellent* (74); *Namur* (90); *Britannia* (100); *Captain* (74); *Irresistible* (74); *Diadem* (64); *Culloden* (74).

British total 15 ships of the line, 5 frigates*, 2 Avisos* (1,422 guns), 9,000 men.

British losses ca 500 killed and wounded.

* = not engaged in the action; the frigates were: *Minerve* (38); *Southampton* (32); *Lively* (32); *Niger* (32); *Bonne Citoyenne* (20). The Avisos were *Raven* (18) and *Fox* (10).

Sources Bodart, Clowes, James.

IN Valvassone, 16 March 1797, clash

A village in the northeastern Italian province of Venetia 20 km southwest of Udine, west of the River Tagliamento and north of Route 13.

A French victory over the Austrians.

(Last action – Mantua, 2 February; next action – Gradisca, 17 March.)

French Forces GdD Bonaparte commanding: DBdeLi:

4e, 5e, 6e, 9e, 11e, 12e, 13e, 14e, 18e, 19e, 25e, 30e, 32e, 33e, 39e, 40e, 43e, 45e, 51e, 55e, 57e, 58e, 61e, 63e, 64e, 69e, 75e, 79e, 85e, 88e, 93e. DBdeLé, 11e, 12e, 20e. DragRs 3e, 5e, 8e, 9e, 15e, 18e, 20e. ChàCh: 10e, 13e, 15e, 19e, 22e, 24e, 25e; HusRs 1er & 7 bis.

French total ca 40,000 men.

French losses 500 killed and wounded.

Austrian Forces FM EH Charles commanding: IRs Nádasdy Nr 39 (3 bns); Neugebauer Nr 46 (10 coys); HusR Wurmser Nr 30 (6 sqns).

Austrian total ca 5,000 men.

Austrian losses 700 killed, wounded and missing, 6 guns.

Comment This was a rearguard action as the Austrians withdrew northeast into Austria following the fall of Mantua on 2 February.

Sources Bodart, Wrede.

IN Gradisca, 17 March 1797, capitulation

A town in northeastern Italy, on the River Isonzo, 14 km southwest of Görz; east of Route 56, south of Autostrada 351 and 12 km from the border with Slovenia.

A French victory over the Austrians.

(Last action – Valvassone, 16 March; next action – Salurn, 20 March.)

French Forces GdD Bernadotte commanding part of the Armée d'Italie; GdD Serrurier. Exact details not known.

French total 18,000 men.

French losses None.

Austrian Garrison IR Splényi Nr 51 (1 bn); Hoch- und Deutschmeister Nr 4 (3 bns).

Austrian total 2,500 men.

Austrian losses All captured, 10 guns, 8 colours.

Comment This detachment became cut off from Archduke Charles' main body and was forced to capitulate.

Sources Bodart, Wrede.

IN Salurn, 20 March 1797, clash

A village in the northern Italian province of South Tyrol, on the River Etsch (Adige) 31 km south of Bozen on Route 12.

A French victory over the Austrians.

(Last action – Gradisca, 17 March; next action – Tarvis (Saifnitz), 22/23 March.)

French Forces GdD Joubert commanding part of the Armée d'Italie; exact details not known.

French total ca 18,000 men.

French losses ca 200 killed and wounded.

Austrian Forces FML Baron von Kerpen commanding: IRs EH Anton Nr 52 (3 bns), J Jellačič Nr 53 (detachments), Jordis Nr 59 (2 bns); Stabs Dragoner R (3 sqns) and 5,000 Tyroler Aufgebot (a sort of Home Guard).

Austrian total ca 12,000 men.

Austrian losses 300 killed and wounded, 3,500 captured.

Comment Yet another rearguard action as the Austrians withdrew out of northern Italy.

Sources Bodart, Wrede.

IN Tarvis (Saifnitz), 22–23 March 1797, clash

A village in the northeastern Italian province of Friaul, close to the Austrian/Slovene border and 27 km southwest of Villach on Route 13.

A French victory over the Austrians.

(Last action – Salurn, 20 March; this was the last action of note in the campaign in northern Italy in 1797.)

French Forces GdD Massena commanding part of the Armée d'Italie; exact details not known.

French total 11,000 men.

French losses 1,200 killed and wounded.

Austrian Forces FM EH Charles commanding: IRs Klebek Nr 14* (3rd Bn), Fürstenberg Nr 36 (2 bns), Nádasdy Nr 39 (3 bns); EH Anton Nr 52* (4th Bn); Grenadier Bns Khevenhüller*, Rüdt. DragR Toscana Nr 26 (1 sqn); HusR Erdödy Nr 11 (4 sqns).

Austrian total 8,000 men.

Austrian losses 1,000 killed and wounded, 3,500 captured, 25 guns, 400 vehicles.

* units thus marked were captured.

Comment Peace was briefly concluded between France and Austria on 17 October 1797 and lasted until 9 April 1799. The repeated Austrian attempts to relieve Mantua – overhasty and ill-prepared – had exhausted their army.

Sources. Bodart, Wrede.

MR Neuwied (Heddesdorf), 18 April 1797, clash

A village in western Germany, on the eastern bank of the River Rhine, about 20 km northwest of Koblenz.

A French victory over the Austrians.

(This was the only action of note on the middle Rhine in 1797).

French Forces GdD Hoche commanding part of Joubert's Armée de la Sambre-et-Meuse; exact details not known.

French total 38,000 men.

French losses 2,000 killed, wounded and captured.

Austrian Forces FML Baron von Werneck commanding: IRs Clerfayt Nr 9 (1st Bn), Manfredini Nr 12 (3 bns), de Vins Nr 37 (2nd Bn); Grenadier Bn Zegraedt.

Austrian total of the 21,000 Austrians there, only the above-mentioned units came into action - ca 7,000 men.

Austrian losses ca 1,000 killed and wounded, 3,000 captured, 24 guns, 60 vehicles, 5 colours.

Comment The French caught the Austrians by surprise.

Sources Bodart, Wrede.

UR Diersheim, 20 & 21 April 1797, clash

A village in the southwestern German state of Baden, on the east bank of the Rhine, 6 km north of Kehl and west of Route B36.

A French victory over the Austrians.

(Last action - Hüningen, 1 February; this was the last action of note on the Upper Rhine in 1797.)

French Forces GdD Moreau commanding part of the Army of the Upper Rhine; exact details not known.

French total 40,000 infantry, 8,500 cavalry.

French losses ca 3,000 killed, wounded and missing.

Austrian Forces FZM Count Sztáray commanding: IRs Kaiser Nr 1 (3 bns); EH Carl Nr 3 (2 bns); C Schröder Nr 7 (3 bns); Manfredini Nr 12 (3 bns); Oranien Nr 15 (3 bns); Kaunitz Nr 20 (3 bns); Benjowsky Nr 31 (4 coys); de Vins Nr 37 (2nd Bn); Callenberg Nr 54 (3 bns); Beaulieu Nr 58 (1st Bn). Grenadier Bn Clawitz (1 bn); KürR Hohenzollern Nr 4 (6 sqns); DragR Toscana Nr 2 (2 sqns); GzIR Banater (3rd Bn).

Austrian total ca 24,000 men.

Austrian losses 2,700 killed and wounded, 200 captured, 13 guns, 50 vehicles, GM Von Immens killed.

Sources Bodart, Wrede.

ZZ Camperdown, 11 October 1797, naval battle

An area of sea off the northern Dutch coastal village of Camperduin, 20 km northwest of Alkmaar.

A British victory over the Dutch.

(This was the only naval action of note in the North Sea this year).

Dutch Forces Vice Admiral de Winter commanding: *Vryheid* (74); *Staten-Generaal* (74); *Brutus* (74); *Jupiter* (72); *Beschermer* (56); *Gelykeid* (68); *Herkules* (64); *Tjerk Hiddes Devries* (68); *Wassenaer* (64); *Batavier* (56); *Leyden* (68); *Mars* (44); *Cerberus* (68); *Haerlem* (68); *Alkmaar* (56); *Delft* (54); *Galatée* (18); *Daphne* (18); *Ajax* (18); *Waaksamheid* (24); *Minerva* (24); *Heldin* (32); *Ambuscade* (32); *Atalanta* (18); *Monnikendam* (44).

Dutch total 16 ships of the line, 5 frigates, 5 Avisos, 1,268 guns 10,600 men.

Dutch losses 9 ships of the line and 2 frigates captured, 540 killed and wounded, 660 - including 3 admirals - captured, 668 guns.

British Forces Admiral Duncan commanding: Left column: *Venerable* (74); *Ardent* (64); *Triumph* (74); *Bedford* (74); *Director* (64); *Lancaster* (64); *Belliqueux* (64); *Adamant* (50); *Isis (50).* Right column: *Monarch* (74); *Powerful* (74); *Monmouth* (64); *Russell* (74); *Montague* (74); *Veteran* (64); *Beaulieu* (40); *Agincourt* (64). Centre Group: *Active* (12); *Martin* (16); *King George* (12); *Rose* (10); *Circé* (28); *Diligent* (6); *Speculator* (8).

British totals 16 ships of the line, 2 frigates, 6 Avisos; 9,400 men, 1,198 guns.

British losses 200 killed and wounded, 800 captured.

Comment Duncan used the double attack column which Nelson was to employ at Trafalgar (21 October 1805) with such devastating effect against the Franco-Spanish fleet. The Centre Group was not engaged in the fighting.

Sources Alison, Bodart, Clowes, James.

1798

THE ACTIONS 1798

Order of Battle of the Neapolitan army 1798 The Guard (2 bns); the Line (2 bns each): Regiments; Re, Regina, Real Borbone, Real Farnere, Real Napoli; Real Palermo, Real Italiano. National Regiments (2 bns each); Campania, Puglia, Lucania, Sannio, Messapia, Calabria, Agrigento, Siracusa. Walloon regiments (2 bns each); Borgogna, Hainaut. Foreign regiments (2 bns each); Real Macedonia. Swiss regiments (2 bns each); Real Guardie Svizzere, Wirtz, Tschudy, Jauch. There were also provincial regiments, mobilized only in time of war with 1 battalion each. Cavalry: Regiments (4 sqns each); Re, Rossiglione, Napoli, Sicilia. Dragoons (4 sqns each): Regina, Tanragona, Borbone, Principe. Artillery: 1 regiment.

UR Mannheim, 25 January 1798, raid

A fortified city on the eastern bank of the River Rhine in southwestern Germany, at the confluence with the River Neckar and at the junction of Autobahns A650, A659 and Route B44.

A French victory over the Bavarians.

(This was the only action of note in this theatre in 1798.)

French Forces GdD Ambert's division: GdB Oudinot commanding: GdB Lecourbe: Grenadiers (2 bns); ChàCh (3 sqns) artillery (2 x FAB).

French total ca 3,000 men.

French losses 600 killed and wounded.

Bavarian Forces Obstlt von Karg commanding: Münster DragR (2 sqns), 1st Kurpfalzbayerischen FeldjägerR (4 coys); artillery (1 coy); 6th Kurpfalzbayerischen FüsR (½ coy).

Bavarian total ca 450 men; 4 x 6 pdr guns.

Bavarian losses 9 officers, 400 men captured, 13 wounded (2 died later).

Comment Oudinot ignored the existing armistice and rushed the tiny bridgehead on the west bank of the Rhine in a surprise attack. Although the garrison was quickly overwhelmed, they caused havoc in the assault columns of the French grenadiers with their artillery and managed to evacuate all 4 pieces into Mannheim.

Source Fahrmbacher.

NL Ostende, 20 May 1798, clash and capitulation

A port on the Belgian coast, 22 km west of Brugge.

A French victory over the English.

French Forces The garrison of Brugge.

French total 2,000 men. Exact details and losses not known.

British Forces MG Sir Eyre Coote commanding: 2nd Foot Guards (4 x lt coys); 3rd Foot Guards (4 x lt coys), 23rd Foot (grenadier and lt coys), 11th Foot (1 bn); 49th Foot (grenadier and lt coys); 17th LDR (9 men); artillery (100 men).

British total ca 1,100 men.

British losses 163 killed and wounded; over 1,100 captured, 6 guns.

Comment The aim of the raid was to blow up the locks on the Brugge canal in Ostende. This was accomplished but adverse weather prevented the re-embarkation of the group and they were forced to surrender. The 1st Foot Guards (4 x lt coys) got lost and did not take part in the action.

Sources Bodart, Fortescue.

ZZ Malta, 11 June 1798, capitulation

An island in the Mediterranean, 90 km south of Sicily.

A French victory over the Knights of St John.

French Forces GdD Bonaparte commanding the Armée de l'Orient aboard a convoy bound for the conquest of Egypt: DBdeLi: 6e, 9e, 13e, 18e, 19e (1er Bn); 25e, 32e, 41e, 61e, 69e, 75e, 80e, 85e, 88e. DBdesLé 2e, 4e, 5e, 11e, 12e, 16e, 17e, 18e, 20e, 21e, 22e, 26e, 27e, 29e. The cavalry are not listed as they did not come into action.

French total ca 28,000 men.

French losses None.

Maltese Garrison Grandmaster Count Hompesch, 4,000 militia [IR Malta; Grenadiers of the Grand Master (200 men); Cacciatore (1,200 men); Sailors (400 men)].

Comment The Knights capitulated and gave sovereignty of Malta, Gozo and Cumino to Bonaparte. A French garrison of 3,000 men was put in place. The French captured 1,200 guns and 30,000 muskets. The French garrison was 6e DBdeLi (2 bns); 19e DBdeLi (2e & 3e Bns); 41e & 80e DBdeLi (1 bn each). The Maltese troops were formed into the Légion Maltaise (2 bns) and taken to Egypt.

Sources Bodart, Charrié.

YE Alexandria, 2 July 1798, storm and capitulation

A fortified port city in the western Nile delta in Egypt.

A French victory over the Janissaries.

(This was the opening action in the Egyptian campaign; next action – Pyramids, 21 July).

French Forces GdD Bonaparte commanding the Armée de l'Orient: Exact details not known.

French losses Not exactly known, very light.

Janissary Garrison Koraim Pasha commanding 500 men.

Janissary losses Not known.

Comment Koraim Pasha ceded control of the town, forts and harbour to the French.

Sources Bodart, Herold.

YE Pyramids (Embaleh), 21 July 1798, battle

A town on the left bank of the Nile in Egypt, 3 km northwest of Cairo.

A French victory over the Egyptians.

(Last action – Alexandria, 2 July; next action – Aboukir Bay, 1 August.)

French Forces GdD Bonaparte commanding: **1st Division GdD Kléber (or Dugua)** GdB Damas: 2e DBdeLé (3 bns). GdB Verdier: 25e & 75e DBdeLi (3 bns each). **2nd Division GdD Bon** GdB Marmont. 4e DBdeLé (3 bns); GdB Rampon: 18e & 32e DBdeLi (3 bns each). **3rd Division GdD Reynier** GdB Fugière: 9e & 85e DBdeLi (3 bns each). GdB Legrange: Légion Maltaise (2 bns). **4th Division GdD Dessaix** GdB Belliard: 21e DBdeLé (3 bns). GdB Friant: 6e & 88e DBdeLi (3 bns each). **5th Division GdD Lannes**: GdB Veaux: 22e DBdeLé (3 bns). GdB Vial: 13e & 69e DBdeLi (3 bns each). **Cavalry GdD Dumas, GdD Dugua** GdB Léclere: HusR 7e bis (3 sqns); 3e DragR (2 sqns); GdB Mireur: 22e ChàCh (3 sqns); 20e DragR (2 sqns). GdB Murat: 14e DragR (3 sqns); 15e DragR (2 sqns); GdB Davout 18e DragR (4 sqns).

French total 20,000 men.

French losses 300 killed, wounded and missing.

Egyptian Forces Murad Bey commanding: 6,000 Mamelukes, 54,000 Arab irregulars (mostly cavalry).

Egyptian losses 2,000 Mamelukes killed, wounded and captured, 20 guns, 400 camels, all baggage and camp equipment.

Comment This action demonstrated the relative combat values of Bonaparte's seasoned, victorious troops drawn mainly from the Armée d'Italie and the loosely organized, ad hoc horde which they faced.

Sources Bodart, Herold.

ZZ Aboukir Bay, 1 August 1798, naval battle

A bay on the northern Egyptian coast, 21 km northeast of Alexandria.

An English victory over the French.

(Last action – Pyramids, 21 July; next action – Sediman, 7 October.)

French Forces Vice Admiral Comte Brueys commanding: ships of the line: *l'Orient*** (120); *Guerrier*** (74), *Conquerant** (74); *Spartiate** (74); *Aquilon** (74); *Peuple Souverain** (74), *Franklin** (80); *Tonnant** (80); *Heureux*** (74); *Mercure*** (74); *Guillaume Tell* (74), *Généreaux* (74), *Timoleon*** (74). Frigates: *Sérieuse*** (36); *l'Artemise*** (36); *Diane* (40); *Justice* (40).

French totals 1,200 guns, ca 7,000 crewmen.

French losses: Ships marked * were taken; ships marked ** destroyed; Admiral Brueys and 2,000 men killed, 1,100 wounded, 3,900 captured.

British Forces Rear Admiral Horatio Nelson commanding: Ships of the Line: *Vanguard* (74); *Culloden* (74); *Audacious* (74); *Zealous* (74); *Goliath* (74); *Theseus* (74); *Orion* (74); *Minotaur* (74); *Defence* (74); *Leander* (50); *Swiftsure* (74); *Alexander* (74); *Bellerophon* (74); *Majestic* (74); Frigate: *Mutine* (16).

British totals 1,028 guns, 8,000 crewmen.

British losses Admiral Nelson wounded; 218 killed, 678 wounded.

Comment Nelson had been chasing Bonaparte's task force around the Mediterranean for weeks. This crushing victory ensured British naval supremacy in this theatre for years. All French prisoners were put ashore. The French crews were weaker than normal on the day of the battle because many were on shore. HMS *Culloden* grounded and took no part in the battle; neither did HMS *Mutine* who stayed to guard her. The French transport fleet was safely in Alexandria harbour at this point so Bonaparte's mobility was preserved.

Sources Bodart, Clowes, James.

GB Castlebar, 27 August 1798, clash

A town in the Irish county of Connaught, 16 km inland from Clew Bay on the central western coast of the island.

A French victory over the English.

(This was the first action in Ireland; next action – Ballinamuk).

French Forces GdB Humbert: 70e DBdeLi (2e Bn), IRs

Lamourex, Lee, O'Meara, La Chatre, Feydur (about 1 coy each); 12e HusR (11 men) 3e ChàCh (½ sqn).

French total ca 1,200 men.

French losses Not exactly known but very light.

British Forces MG Lake: 6th Foot (1 coy); Lord Roden's Fencible Dragoons (1 sqn); Longford Militia, Kilkenny Militia (1 bn each); Fraser's Fencibles (½ bn); Galway Volunteers (1 coy); 6th DG (4 sqns); artillery.

British total ca 5,000 men.

British losses ca 400 men, 10 guns, 8 colours.

Comment Apart from the 6th Foot, the artillery (100 men) and Roden's Fencible Dragoons, the Anglo-Irish force panicked and fled. The quantity of colours claimed to have been taken seems most excessive for the regiments present.

Sources Fortescue, Bodart, Charrié.

GB Ballinamuk, 8 September 1798, capitulation

A town in Ireland, in the county of Connaught, 12 km northeast of Galway between Lough Corrib and Galway Bay on the western coast of the island.

An English victory over the French.

(Last action – Castlebar, 27 August. This was the last action in Ireland.)

French Forces GdB Humbert commanding: 70e DBdeLi (2e Bn); IRs Lamourex, Lee, O'Meara, La Chatre and Feydur (about 1 coy each); 12e HusR (11 men); 3e ChàCh (½ sqn); artillery.

French total ca 1,100 men.

French losses All captured, 12 guns, 1 colour (2e Bn, 70e DBde).

British Forces FM Lord Cornwallis commanding: 6th Foot (1 coy); Lord Roden's Fencible Dragoons (1 sqn); various Irish militia regiments; artillery.

British total ca 8,000 men.

British losses None.

Comment 250 Irish rebels were taken; 36 of these were hanged after drawing lots for the privilege. The colour of the 2e Bn, 70e DBdeLi (taken by Pte Toole of the Armagh Militia Regiment) may now be seen in St Patrick's Cathedral, Armagh.

Sources Fortescue, Bodart.

YE Sediman, 7 October 1798, clash

A small town in Egypt, 80 km southwest of Cairo.

A French victory over the Egyptians.

(Last action – Aboukir Bay, 1 August; this was the last action of note in Egypt in 1798.)

French Forces GdD Desaix commanding: 21e DBdeLé, 61e & 88e DBdeLi (3 bns each), 2 guns.

French total ca 2,900 men.

French losses 43 killed, 100 wounded.

Egyptian Forces Murad Bey commanding 4,000–5,000 Mameluke and Bedouin cavalry, 4 guns.

Egyptian losses ca 400 killed and wounded, 4 guns.

Sources Bodart, Herold.

ZZ Tory Island, 12 October 1798, naval clash

An island off the northwest coast of Ireland 75 km north of the Bay of Donegal.

An English victory over the French.

French Forces Commodore Bompart: *Hoche** (74), *Embuscade** (36); *Coquille** (36), *Bellone** (36); 5 other frigates [*Immortalité, Loire, Romain* (40 guns each); *Résolue* and *Semillante* (36 guns each)].

French total 1 ship of the line, 9 frigates, 410 guns, 4,000 crewmen.

French losses 4 ships taken, 425 killed and wounded, 1,870 captured.

* = taken by the British.

British Forces Commodore Sir J B Warren commanding: *Foudroyant* (80); *Canada* (74), *Robust* (74); *Anson* (44); *Magnanime* (44); *Amelia* (38); *Ethalion* (38), *Melampus* (36).

British totals 3 ships of line, 5 frigates; 434 guns; 3,000 men.

British losses 13 killed, 75 wounded.

Comment The ridiculously weak French invasion force met with the total disaster it deserved. Most of the other French frigates were caught and destroyed over the next two weeks. Only *Semillante* and *Romaine* reached Brest safely.

Sources Bodart, Clowes, James.

ZZ Minorca, 9 November 1798, capture

One of the Spanish Balearic Isles in the western Mediterranean.

A British victory over the Spanish.

Spanish Garrison Exact details not known but including one Swiss regiment.

Spanish total 3,500 men.

Spanish losses 14 gunboats.

British Forces Royal Navy: Commodore John Thomas Dickworth commanding: *Leviathan* (74), flagship. *Centaur* (74); *Argo* (44); *Dolphin* (44); *Aurora* (28); *Cormorant* (20); *Petrel* (16); *Ulysses* (44) (storeship);

Calcutta (24) (armed transport); *Coromandel* (24) (armed transport); *Constitution* (cutter) and several merchant transports. Army: Gen The Honourable Charles Stuart: 28th, 42nd, 58th and 90th Foot (1 bn each).

British total ca 3,000 men.

British losses None.

Sources Fortescue, Clowes, James.

IM Fermo, 25 November 1798, clash

A village in eastern central Italy, on Route 210 about 12 km from the coast, just south of the River Tenna, 55 km south of Ancona.

A French victory over the Neapolitans.

(This was the first action in the Neapolitan invasion of the Papal state. Next action - Civita Castellana, 4 December).

French Forces GdD Rusca commanding part of the Armée d'Italie.

French total 9 bns, 3 sqns: ca 8,000 men.

French losses Not exactly known; very light.

Neapolitan totals 12 bns, 6 sqns.

Neapolitan losses Not exactly known. The force disintegrated; many were captured along with all the artillery. The rest went home.

Comment The Neapolitan army had no experience of warfare (except the four cavalry regiments who had fought alongside the Austrians in 1796) and the French veterans had an easy victory.

Source Schulz Vol 5.

IM Civita Castellana, 4 December 1798, clash

A town in the central Italian province of Rome, 40 km north of the city, at the junction of Routes 3 and 311 and on the River Faleri Nova, west of Autostrada A1/E35.

A French victory over the Neapolitans.

(Last action - Fermo, 25 November; next action - Otricoli, 9 December.)

French Forces GdD Macdonald commanding a division of the Armée d'Italie.

French total 10,000 men.

French losses 500 killed and wounded.

Neapolitan Forces Gen Baron Mack commanding.

Neapolitan total 36 bns, 18 sqns; 26,000 men.

Neapolitan losses 2,500 killed, wounded and missing.

Sources Bodart, Schulz Vol 5.

IM Otricoli, 9 December 1798, clash

A village in central Italy in the province of Umbria, 60 km north of Rome.

A French victory over the Neapolitans.

(Last action - Civita Castellana, 4 December. This was the end of the campaign.)

French Forces GdD Championnet commanding part of the Armée d'Italie.

French total 6 bns, 3,500 men.

French losses 300 killed and wounded.

Neapolitan Forces Gen Metsch commanding.

Neapolitan total 4,500 men.

Neapolitan losses ca 200 killed and wounded, 4,000 captured, 5 guns.

Comment In all actions of this brief campaign, the Neapolitan forces involved disintegrated at first contact with the enemy. The impregnable fortress of Gaëta (garrison 3,000 men) surrendered as last Neapolitan stronghold on 30 December, without offering serious resistance to the French. The mainland part of the Neapolitan kingdom became the Parthenopian Republic.

Sources Bodart, Schulz Vol 5.

1799

THE ACTIONS 1799

IM Gaëta, 5 January 1799, capitulation

A fortress on the central western Italian coast, just off Route 213, about 60 km northwest of Naples.

A French victory over the Neapolitans.

(This was the opening action of the campaign in central Italy; next action - Naples, 14/15 June.)

French Forces GdB Rey commanding: exact details not known.

French total 4,000 men.

French losses None.

Neapolitan Garrison LG Chudi commanding: exact details not known.

Neapolitan total 3,600 men.

Neapolitan losses The officers went free; the men were prisoners of war.

Sources Bodart.

YE El Arish, 14–20 February 1799, blockade and capitulation

A village on the Egyptian Mediterranean coast, 170 km northeast of Suez.

A French victory over the Turks.

(Last action - this was the opening action of 1799 in Egypt; next action - Jaffa, 7 March.)

French Forces GdD Bonaparte commanding: GdD Kléber, GdB Verdier, GdB Damas (Junot from 10 March 1799): 2e DBdeLé (3 bns); 25e and 75e DBdeLi (1er and 2e Bns each). GdD Reynier GdB Lagrange: 9e DBdeLi (3 bns); 85e DBdeLi (1er and 2e Bns). GdD Bon: GdB Rampon, GdB Vial; 4e DBdeLé (1 bn); 18e DBdeLi (1er and 2e Bns); 32e DBdeLi (1er and 2e Bns). GdB Lannes: GdB Veaux, GdB Robin; 22e DBdeLé (1 bn); 13e DBdeLi, 69e DBdeLi (1er and 2e Bns each). 2 x FAB, 1 x HAB. Cavalry GdD Murat: 7e HusR bis; 22e ChàCh, 20e DragR (1 sqn each); 3e DragR (2 sqns); 14e and 18e DragRs (4 sqns each). Artillery Park 3 x FAB.

French total 13,000 men, 5 x FAB, 1 x HAB.

French losses Not exactly known, at least 391 killed and wounded.

Egyptian Garrison 1,500 Albanians, Moroccans and Mamelukes.

Egyptian losses 750 killed and wounded.

Comment The survivors of the garrison were incorporated into the French army. On the night of 14/15 February Reynier attacked part of the enemy camped outside the fortress (600 Mamelukes, Bedouin and Turkish cavalry and 1,200 Albanian infantry) and drove them off with a loss of 450 killed and wounded and 900 captured. French loss was 3 killed. On 18 February the French bombarded the fortress not doing it much damage at all but killing and wounding 388 of their own men.

Sources Bodart, Herold.

ZZ Corfu, 18 November 1798 – 2 March 1799, siege and capitulation

An island off the Albanian coast, at the mouth of the Adriatic Sea, opposite the heel of Italy.

A Russo-Turkish victory over the French.

(This was the only action of note in this region in 1799).

French Forces 6e DBdeLi (3e Bn); 79e DBdeLi (1er and 3e Bns); local levies (1 bn); artillery.

French total ca 4,000 men.

French losses Not known exactly. The colours of the French DBdes were taken as were the warships *Leander* (50) and *Brune* (28) in the harbour.

Russo-Turkish Forces Exact details, totals and losses unknown.

Comment *Leander* was originally a British ship taken by the French on 18 August 1798. The Tsar returned the vessel to the British.

CH Maienfeld (St Luciensteig), 6 March 1799, 1st clash

A small town in the eastern Swiss Canton of Graubünden, just south of the Principality of Liechtenstein, on Route 3/13 in the valley of the upper Rhine. St Luciensteig (now Luzisteig) is a mountain pass just north of the town.

A French victory over the Austrians.

(This was the opening action of the Swiss campaign; next action - Chur, 7 March).

French Forces GdD Massena commanding the Army of the Danube: Lecourbe's 3rd Division; GdB Loison: 36e and 38e DBdeLi (2 bns each); GdB Maynoni : 44e DBdeLi (3 bns); 76e DBdeLi (2 bns); 12e ChàCh (1 sqn); 3 x FAB; engineers (1/2 coy).

French total 5,000 men.

French losses 300 killed, wounded and missing.

Austrian Forces FML Baron von Auffenberg commanding: IRs Oranien Nr 15 (1st and 3rd Bns); Brechainville Nr 25 (3 bns).

Austrian total 4,200 men.

Austrian losses 400 killed and wounded, 1,450 captured, 12 guns, 4 ammunition waggons, 3 colours (IR Brechainville).

Comment The Austrians were scattered along the entire front with no adequate reserves and no aggressive patrolling.

Sources Bodart, Wrede, Günther R.

CH Chur, 7 March 1799, clash

A town in the eastern Swiss Canton of Graubünden, in the valley of the upper Rhine, on Motorway N13/E61, 14 km south of Maienfeld.

A French victory over the Austrians.

(Last action – Maienfeld, 6 March; next action – Feldkirch, 7 March.)

French Forces GdD Massena commanding the Army of the Danube: as for Maienfeld, 6 March.

French total 9,600 men.

French losses 100 killed and wounded.

Austrian Forces FML Baron von Auffenberg commanding: IRs Oranien Nr 15 (1st and 3rd Bns); Brechainville Nr 35 (1 bn).

Austrian total 2,400 men.

Austrian losses Killed and wounded unknown; 1,000 captured, 4 guns, 2 colours (IR 15).

Sources Bodart.

CH Feldkirch, 7 March 1799, 1st clash

A small town in the western Austrian province of Vorarlberg, just north of the principality of Liechtenstein and south of the Bodensee (Lake Constance).

A French victory over the Austrians.

(Last action – Chur 7 March; next action – Ponte d'Alto, 12 March.)

French Forces GdD Oudinot commanding: exact details not known.

French total 9,000 men.

French losses 200 killed, wounded and missing.

Austrian Forces FML Baron von Hotze commanding: IRs Kaunitz Nr 20 (3rd Bn), de Vins Nr 37 (3rd Bn); GzIRs Warasdiner-St Georger Nr 6 (2nd Bn), Broder Nr 7 (1st Bn), Peterwardeiner Nr 9 (3rd Bn).

Austrian total 6,000 men.

Austrian losses 1,100 (mostly captured), 4 guns.

Sources Bodart, Wrede, Günther.

YE Jaffa (Haifa), 7 March 1799, storm

A fortified port city on the Israeli Mediterranean coast, 55 km northwest of Jerusalem.

A French victory over the Turks.

(Last action – El Arish, 14 – 20 February; next action – Quena, 3 April.)

French Forces GdD Bonaparte commanding: GdD Kléber: 2e DBdeLé, 25e and 75e DBdeLi (3 bns each). GdD Reynier: 9e and 85e DBdeLi (3 bns each); Légion Maltaise (2 bns). GdD Bon: 4e DBdeLé, 18e and 32e DBdeLi (3 bns each). GdD Lannes, GdB Veaux, GdB Robin: 22e DBdeLé (1 bn); 13e and 69e DBdeLi (1er and 2e Bns each). Cavalry GdD Murat: 7e HusR bis; 22e ChàCh, 20 Drag (1 sqn each); 3e DragR (2 sqns); 14e DragR (3 sqns); 18e DragR (4 sqns); 5 x FAB, 1 x HAB.

French total 18,000 men.

French losses Not known, very light.

Turkish Garrison 4,600 men.

Turkish losses 2,000 were killed in the storm; the town was looted. Next day 2,600 survivors in the citadel surrendered. At Bonaparte's express orders these prisoners of war were all shot over the next few days: 8 March, 800; 9 March 600; 10 March, 1,041 shot. The fortress was well stocked with food so 'economy' was not a reason.

Sources Bodart, Herold.

CH Ponte d'Alto, 12 March 1799 clash

Now 'La Punt' a hamlet in eastern Switzerland, in the valley of the upper Inn on Route 27 through the Engadin.

A French victory over the Austrians.

(Last action – Feldkirch, 7 March; next action – Martinsbrück, 14 March.)

French Forces GdD Lecourbe commanding the 3rd Division, Army of the Danube: GdB Loison: 36e and 38e DBdeLi (2 bns each).

French total ca 2,600 men.

French losses 60 killed and wounded.

Austrian Forces GM Loudon commanding: IRs Brechainville Nr 25 (2 bns), de Vins Nr 37 (2 bns); GzIR Deutsch-Banater Nr 12 (1st Bn).

Austrian total ca 3,300 men.

Austrian losses 200 killed and wounded, 1,250 captured.

Comment Lecourbe outflanked the Austrian position via the Sertigpass and took them in rear. The Austrians withdrew over the Ofenpass to Sta Maria (on Route 28 to the east).

Sources Günther, Wrede.

CH Martinsbrück, 14 March 1799, first clash

Now Martina; a village in the Austrian province of the Tyrol, 4 km south of Finstermünz, on the Swiss border in the valley of the upper Inn, on Route 27.

A French victory over the Austrians.

(Last action - Ponte d'Alto, 12 March; next action - Martinsbrück, 17 March.)

French Forces GdD Lecourbe commanding the 3rd Division, Army of the Danube. GdB Loison: 36e and 38e DBdeLi (2 bns each). GdB Maynoni: 44e DBdeLi (3 bns); 76e DBdeLi (2 bns); 12e ChàCh (1 sqn); 2 x FAB. Engineers (½ coy).

French total ca 4,600 men.

French losses Not known. GdB Maynoni captured.

Austrian Forces GM Loudon commanding: IRs Brechainville Nr 25, de Vins Nr 37 (2 bns each), LtI Bn Munkátsy Nr 12 (1 bn); local Schützen (1 coy).

Austrian total ca 2,600 men.

Austrian losses Killed and wounded unknown, 610 captured. Günther claims that the 2e Bn, 38e DBdeLi captured three companies of Austrian grenadiers here, but the battalion to which they belonged is not identified and Wrede does not mention this event.

Sources Günther, Wrede.

CH Martinsbrück, 17 March 1799, second clash

Now Martina; a village in the Austrian province of the Tyrol, 4 km south of the Finstermünz pass, on the border with Switzerland and in the valley of the upper Inn, on Route 27.

An Austrian victory over the French.

(Last action - Martinsbrück, 14 March; next action - Tauffers, 25 March.)

French Forces GdD Lecourbe commanding the 3rd Division, Army of the Danube. GdB Loison: 36e and 38e DBdeLi (2 bns each). GdB Maynoni: 44e DBdeLi (3 bns); 76e DBdeLi (2 bns); 12e ChàCh (1 sqn); 2 x FAB. Engineers (½ coy).

French total ca 5,300 men.

French losses 12 killed, 130 wounded, 286 captured.

Austrian Forces GM Count Alcaini commanding: IRs Toscana Nr 23 (3 bns), Kinsky Nr 47 (3 bns); LtI Bn Munkátsy Nr 13 (1 bn) and 3 Landesschützenkompanien (Pfunds, Landeck and Laudeck), DragR EH Johann Nr 3 (1/2 sqn), HusR Erdödy Nr 9 (2 1/2 sqns).

Austrian total 6,500 men.

Austrian losses 200 killed, wounded and missing.

Comment Charrié states that the 3e DBdeLi lost the colour of its 2e Bn here.

Sources Bodart, Wrede, Charrié, Günther.

UR Ostrach, 21 March 1799, clash

A village in southwestern Germany, 18 km southeast of the town of Sigmaringen and 9 km south of the River Danube (Donau); (also known as Liptingen).

An Austrian victory over the French.

(Opening action; next action - Stockach, 25/26 March).

French Forces GdD Jourdan commanding the Armée du Rhin: Avantgarde: GdD Lefebvre (GdBs Soult, Mortier, Laval, Klein): 25e DBdeLé, 53e, 67e DBdeLi (3 bns each); 17e DragR, 1er ChàCh, 4e and 5e HusR (4 sqns each); 1 x FAB 1 x HAB. 1st Division GdD Ferino (GdBs Thar, Laboissière, Jacobin): 10e DBdeLé; 46e, 102e DBdeLi (3 bns each); 11e DragR, 6e ChàCh (4 and 5 sqns resp). 2nd Division GdD Souham (GdBs Decaen, Goulus); 2e DBdeLi (3 bns); 7e DBdeLi (2 bns); 83e DBdeLi (3 bns); 1er DragR (5 sqns); 6e DragR (4 sqns). 3rd Division GdD St Cyr: 1ère DBdeLé, 1ère DBdeLi (2 bns each); 108e DBdeLi (3 bns); 8e and 10e ChàCh, 2e DragR (4 sqns each). Cavalry Reserve GdD Hautpoul (GdBs Compère, Oswald) 1er, 2e, 4e, 6e, 7e, 8e, 23e, 25e CavRs.

French total 28,000 men.

French losses 400 killed, 1,600 wounded, 2,000 captured, 3 guns.

Austrian Forces FM Archduke Charles commanding: IRs Kaiser Nr 1 (2nd and 3rd Bns); EH Carl Nr 3, Schröder Nr 7 (3 bns each); Manfredini Nr 12 (4 coys); Lacy Nr 22 (3 bns); Benjowsky Nr 31 (1st and 2nd Bns); vacant Wenkheim Nr 35 (3 bns); Erbach Nr 42 (2 bns). Gren Bn Bojakowsky. KürRs EH Franz Nr 2 (1 sqn); Lothringen Nr 7, Hohenzollern Nr 8 (6 sqns each); DragRs Latour Nr 11, Kinsky Nr 12 (6 sqns each). HusRs Kaiser Nr 1, EH Ferdinand Nr 3 (8 sqns each), Vécsey Nr 4 (6 sqns), Mészáros Nr 10 (8 sqns); UlRs Merveldt Nr 1, Motschlitz Nr 2 (6 sqns each). GzIR Gradiskaner Nr 8 (1 bn).

Austrian total 26,000 men.

Austrian losses 500 killed, 1,100 wounded, 650 captured.

Sources Bodart, Wrede, Michaelovski-Danielevski.

CH Feldkirch, 23 March 1799, 2nd clash

A small town in the western Austrian province of Vorarlberg, just north of the Principality of Liecht-

enstein and south of the Bodensee (Lake Constance).
An Austrian victory over the French.
(Last action – Martinsbrück, 17 March; next action – Tauffers, 25 March.)
French Forces Part of the Army of the Danube: exact details not known but including GdD Dessole's command (see Tauffers, 25 March) and GdD Lecourbe's command (see Martinsbrück, 17 March).
French total 12,000 men.
French losses 3,000 killed and wounded.
Austrian Forces GM Baron von Jellačič commanding: IRs Kaunitz Nr 20 (3rd Bn); de Vins Nr 37 (3rd Bn); GzIRs Warasdiner-St Georger Nr 6 (2nd Bn); Broder Nr 7 (1st Bn); Peterwardeiner Nr 9 (3rd Bn).
Austrian total 5,500 men.
Austrian losses 900 killed, wounded and missing.
Sources Bodart, Wrede.

CH Tauffers, 25 March 1799, 1st clash
A hamlet in northern Italy (now Tauvers/Tubre) in South Tyrol, on Route 41, in the valley of the River Rum (a tributary of the Adige/Etsch), just north of the Swiss border and the Swiss town of Sta Maria.
A French victory over the Austrians.
(Last action – Feldkirch, 23 March; next action – Nauders, 25 March.)
French Forces GdD Dessoles commanding part of the Army of the Danube: 12e DBdeLé, 39e DBdeLi (2 bns each), 1 x FAB. GdB Lecci's Bde (Cisalpine troops): 3 bns, 1/2 sqn cavalry, 1 x FAB.
French total ca 5,000 men.
French losses 60 killed, 200 wounded.
Austrian Forces GM Baron von Loudon commanding: IRs Wallis Nr 11 (3rd Bn); De Ligne Nr 30 (1st Bn); Sztáray Nr 33 (2 bns), 13 x Landesschützenkompagnien (1,500 men).
Austrian total ca 6,500 men.
Austrian losses 600 killed and wounded, 4 colonels, 150 other officers, 4,500 men, 17 guns and 1 howitzer captured.
Comment FML Bellegarde had altered Loudon's dispositions here on 24 March; in so doing, he exposed the almost-dry river bed. The French advanced up the river (concealed from view of the defenders), took them in rear and the majority threw down their weapons and surrendered. Only Loudon and 409 men on the extreme north wing escaped. The entire action lasted only 30 minutes.
Sources Bodart, Günther, Wrede.

CH Nauders, 25 March 1799, clash
A small village in the upper valley of the River Inn, in the Engadin valley in southwestern Austria, on Route 815 on the way up to the Reschen Pass into Italy.
A French victory over the Austrians.
(Last action – Tauffers, 25 March; next action – Tauffers, 4 April.)
French Forces GdD Lecourbe commanding the 3rd Division, Army of the Danube: GdB Loison: 36e and 38e DBdeLi (2 bns each); GdB Maynoni: 44e DBdeLi (3 bns); 76e DBdeLi (2 bns); 12e ChàCh (1 sqn); 2 x FAB; engineers (½ coy).
French total 4,000 men.
French losses ca 300 men killed, wounded and missing.
Austrian Forces GM Count Alcaini commanding: IR F Kinsky Nr 47 (3 bns).
Austrian total ca 3,000 men.
Austrian losses 500 killed and wounded, 1,450 captured, 6 guns.
Sources Bodart, Wrede.

UR Stockach, 25/26 March 1799, battle
A town in southwestern Germany on Route B31 and Autobahn A98/E54, just northwest of the Bodensee (Lake Constance).
A French victory over the Austrians.
(Last action – Ostrach, 21 March; next action – Mannheim, 18 September.)
French Forces GdD Jourdan commanding the Armée du Rhin: **Avantgarde** GdD Lefebvre: GdBs Soult, Mortier, Laval, Klein: 25e, 53e, 67e DBdeLi (3 bns each); 17e DragR, 1er ChàCh, 4e, 5e HusR (4 sqns each), 2 x FAB,1 x HAB. **1st Division** GdD Ferino: GdBs Thar, Laboissière, Jacobin: 10e, 46e, 102e DBdeLi (3 bns each); 11e DragR, 6e ChàCh (4 sqns each); 3 x FAB; 1 x HAB. **2nd Division** GdD Souham; GdBs Decaen, Goulus: 2e, 83e DBdeLi (3 bns each); 7e DBdeLi (2 bns); 1er, 6e DragR (4 sqns each); 2 x FAB, 1 x HAB. **3rd Division** GdD St Cyr; GdBs Legrand, Daurier, Walther: 11e DBdeLé, 1e DBdeLi (2 bns each); 108e DBdeLi (3 bns), 2e DragR, 8e, 10e ChàCh (4 sqns each); 2 x FAB; 1 x HAB. **Cavalry Reserve** GdD d'Hautpoul: 1er, 2e, 4e, 6e, 7e, 8e, 23e,

25e CavRs (3,265 men). **Detached Flank Corps** GdD Vandamme: 8e, 50e DBdeLi (3 bns each); 1 x FAB.

French total 38,000 men.

French losses 400 killed, 1,600 wounded, 2,000 captured, 1 gun.

Austrian Forces FM Archduke Charles commanding: IRs Kaiser Nr 1 (2nd and 3rd Bns), EH Ferdinand Nr 2, EH Carl Nr 3, Schröder Nr 7, Manfredini Nr 12, Gemmingen Nr 21, Lacy Nr 22, Wallis Nr 29 (3 bns each), Benjowsky Nr 31 (1st and 2nd Bns), vacant Wenkheim Nr 35 (3 bns), Erbach Nr 42 (2 bns), Kerpen Nr 49 (3 bns). Grenadier Bns Teschner, Sebottendorf, Lippe, Juch, Tegetthof, Bojakowsky. Light Infantry Bns Radivojevich Nr 5, Rubenitz Nr 12. Wurmser Freikorps (2 bns). KürRs EH Franz Nr 2, Lothringen Nr 7, Hohenzollern Nr 8, Nassau Nr 9, Anspach Nr 11 (6 sqns each); DragRs Kronprinz Nr 2, Coburg Nr 6, Latour Nr 11, Kinsky Nr 12 (6 sqns each); HusRs Kaiser Nr 1, EH Ferdinand Nr 3 (8 sqns each), Vécsey Nr 4 (6 sqns); Mészáros Nr 10 (8 sqns); UlRs Merveldt Nr 1, Motschlitz Nr 2 (6 sqns each). GzIR Gradiskaner Nr 8, Roman-Banater Nr 13, 2nd Walachen (1 bn each).

Austrian total 46,000 men.

Austrian losses 500 killed, 2,400 wounded, 2,900 captured; 2 guns FZM Prince Fürstenberg killed.

Sources Bodart, Wrede, Michaelovski-Danielevski.

IN Pastrengo, 26 March 1799, clash

A village in northeastern Italy, on the western bank of the River Etsch (Adige), 18 km northwest of Verona, just east of Autostrada A22/E45.

A French victory over the Austrians.

(This was the opening action of the campaign; next action – Verona, 26 March).

French Forces GdD Schérer commanding: GdD Hatry: GdB Fresia: 21e DBdeLi (1 bn); 33e DBdeLi, 63e DBdeLi (3 bns each). 3rd Piemont IR (2 bns), (½ x FAB). GdD Montrichard; GdB Vignes and GdB Gardanne: 5e and 14e DBdeLi (3 bns each); 3e DBdeLi (2 bns); 45e DBdeLi (3 bns); Polish Volunteers (1 bn); Cavalry (1,900 men). 1 x FAB. GdD Victor: GdB Digeon, GdB Chamberlac: 56e, 92e, 99e DBdeLi (3 bns each); 1ère Légion Helvetique (1 bn); 2e Légion Polonaise. Cavalry (1,000 men); 1 x FAB. GdD Grenier: GdB Quesnel GdB Rister: 17e, 24e, 106e DBdeLi (3 bns each); 2e Légion Helvetique (1 bn); 1ère Légion Polonaise (1 bn); cavalry (450 men); 1 x FAB.

French total 22,400 men.

French losses ca 1,000 killed, wounded and missing.

Austrian Forces FML Baron von Elsnitz commanding: IRs Klebek Nr 14 (3 bns); W Schröder Nr 26 (2 bns); Fürstenberg Nr 36 (1st and 2nd Bns); Jellačič Nr 53 (1st and 2nd Bns), Jordis Nr 59 (3 bns); Gren Bn Stentsch; Hus vacant Nr 5 (8 sqns); GzIR Oguliner Nr 3, GzIR Warasdiner-Kreutzer Nr 5 (1 bn each).

Austrian total ca 11,000 men.

Austrian losses 2,000 killed and wounded, 1,500 captured, 12 guns, 2 pontoon bridges, 2 colours (possibly GrenzIRs). IR Schröder Nr 26 suffered very heavy losses.

Sources Bodart, Wrede, Clausewitz, Michaelovsky-Danielevsky.

IN Verona, 26 March 1799, clash

A fortified city in northern Italy, on the River Adige (Etsch) just east of Lake Garda and northeast of the junction of Autostrada A4/E7 and A22/E45.

A drawn match between the French and the Austrians.

(Last action – Pastrengo, 26 March; next action – Legnano, 26 March.)

French Forces GdD Moreau commanding: GdD Hatry: 21e DBdeLi (1 bn); 33e, 63e DBdeLi (3 bns); Cavalry (800 men); ½ x FAB. GdD Gauthier, GdB Miollis, GdB Vignolles: 16e DBdeLé, 3e DBdeLi, 21e DBdeLi (1 bn each); 1ère DBde Cisalpine (3 bns). Cavalry (700 men); ½ x FAB. **Sardinian Troops** 1a Mezza-Brig-Li (2nd Bn); 3a Mezza-Brig-Li (1st and 3rd Bns).

French and Sardinian total 14,500 men.

French and Sardinian losses 1,500 killed and wounded, 300 captured, 3 guns.

Austrian Forces FML Baron von Keim commanding: GM von Elsnitz: HusR vacant Nr 5 (8 sqns); Jg-Corps d'Aspre (10 coys); GzIR Oguliner Nr 13; GzIR Warasdiner-Kreutzer Nr 5 (1 bn each); GM Gottesheim: IRs Jellačič Nr 53, Jordis Nr 59 (3 bns each). GM Minkwitz; IRs W Schröder Nr 26 (3 bns), vacant Nr 48 (2 bns); Gren Bns Pers.

Austrian total 16,400 men.

Austrian losses 1,600 killed and wounded, 1,100 captured Generals Keim, Minkwitz and Liptay wounded.

Sources Bodart, Wrede, Clausewitz, Michaelovski-Danielevski.

IN Legnano, 26 March 1799, clash

A village in northeastern Italy, on the west bank of the River Adige (Etsch), 42 km east of Mantua.

An Austrian victory over the French.

(Last action - Verona, 26 March; next action - Perona, 30 March.)

French Forces GdD Montrichard commanding: GdB Vignes; GdB Gardanne: 3e, 5e, 14e, 45e DBdeLi (3 bns each). Polish Volunteers (1 bn); Cavalry (1,900 men); 1 x FAB.

French total 9,500 men.

French losses 2,000 killed and wounded, 600 captured, 14 guns, GdB Vignes killed.

Austrian Forces FML Baron von Kray commanding: GM Morzin: IRs Gyulai Nr 32 (2 bns); Mittrowsky Nr 40 (3 bns); Gren Bn Stentsch. GM Hohenzollern: DragRs Karacsay Nr 4 and Lobkowitz Nr 10 (6 sqns each). GM Liptay: IRs Klebek Nr 14 (3 bns); Fürstenberg Nr 36 (2 bns).

Austrian total ca 14,000 men.

Austrian losses 700 killed and wounded, 100 captured.

Sources Bodart, Wrede, Clausewitz.

IN Perona, 30 March 1799, clash

A village in northeastern Italy, on the eastern bank of the River Adige (Etsch), 5 km northwest of Verona on Route 12.

An Austrian victory over the French.

(Last action - Legnano, 26 March; next action - Magnano, 5 April.)

French Forces GdD Serrurier commanding: GdB Meyer: 1ère DBdeLi (1 bn), 18e, 29e, 30e DBdeLi (3 bns each); Grenadiers (2 coys); cavalry (4 sqns); 1/2 x FAB.

French total ca 7,000 men.

French losses 400 killed and wounded, 1,700 captured.

Austrian Forces FML Baron von Kray commanding: IRs Stuart Nr 18 (1 bn); Jordis Nr 59 (3 bns); HusR vacant Nr 5 and vacant Nr 7 (8 sqns each).

Austrian total 6,000 men.

Austrian losses 400 killed, wounded and missing.

Sources Bodart, Wrede, Clausewitz, Michaelovski-Danielevski.

YE Quena, 3 April 1799, massacre

A village on the River Nile in Egypt near Thebes.

An Egyptian victory over the French.

(Last action - Jaffa, 7 March; next action - Abaud, 3 April.)

French Forces Capt Morandi in the Nile cruiser *L'Italie* with 200 sailors, 61e DBdeLi (2 coys) and 300 sick and wounded.

French losses All killed.

Egyptian Forces Sherif Hassan and 2,000 infantry from Mecca.

Egyptian losses Not known; very light.

Source Herold.

YE Abaud, 3 April 1799, skirmish

A village on the right bank of the River Nile in Egypt.

A French victory over the Egyptians.

(Last action - Quena, 3 April; next action - Mount Tabor, 16 April.)

French Forces GdB Belliard and the 21e DBdeLé, 1 guns.

French total ca 1,000 men.

French losses 60 killed, 60 wounded.

Egyptian Forces 350 Mamelukes, 3,000 infantry from Mecca, 7 guns.

Egyptian losses 280 killed.

Source Herold.

CH Tauffers, 4 April 1799, 2nd clash

A hamlet in the northern Italian province of South Tyrol (now Tauvers/Tubre), on Route 41, in the valley of the River Rum (a tributary of the Adige/Etsch), just north of the Swiss border and the Swiss town of Sta Maria.

An Austrian victory over the French.

(Last action - Nauders, 25 March; next action - Remüs, 22 April.)

French Forces GdD Dessoles commanding part of the Army of the Danube: 12e DBdeLé, 39e DBdeLi (2 bns each), 1 x FAB. GdB Lecci's Cisalpine brigade: 3 bns, 1/2 sqn cavalry, 1 x FAB.

French total ca 4,600 men.

French losses Killed and wounded unknown, 400 captured, 3 guns, 14 caissons.

Austrian Forces FML Bellegarde commanding: IRs Clerfayt Nr 9 (2 bns); Wallis Nr 11 (1 bn-); Gyulai Nr 32 (1 bn); De Ligne Nr 30 (1st Bn); Sztáray Nr 33 (1 bn); Kray Nr 34 (3rd Bn); de Vins Nr 37 (2nd and 3rd Bns); Württemberg Nr 38 (1st Bn); LtI Bn Trautenberg Nr 6 (1 bn); Le Loup Jägers (1 bn), HusR Erdödy Nr 9 (2 sqns).

Austrian total ca 10,000 men.

Austrian losses 200 killed and wounded.

Comment It took Bellegarde ten days to mount his counterattack. Having succeeded he just sat and awaited events.

Sources Bodart, Günther, Wrede.

IN Magnano, 5 April 1799, battle

A village in northwestern Italy, about 8 km east of the River Ticino, 34 km northwest of Milan.

An Austrian victory over the French.

(Last action - Perona, 30 March; next action - Brescia, 21 April.)

French Forces GdD Schérer commanding: GdD Montrichard, GdB Gardanne: 3e DBdeLi (2 bns); 5e, 14e, 45e DBdeLi (3 bns each); Polish Volunteers (1 bn); cavalry (1,900 men); 1 x FAB. GdD Victor, GdB Digeon, GdB Chamberlac: 56e, 92e, 99e DBdeLi (3 bns each), 1ère Légion Helvetique, 2e Légion Polonaise (1 bn); cavalry (1,000 men); 1 x FAB. GdD Hatry, GdB Fresia: 21e DBdeLi (1 bn); 33e, 63e DBdeLi (3 bns each); 3rd Piemont IR (2 bns); cavalry (800 men); ½ x FAB. GdD Delmas; GdB Grandjean; GdB Dalesme: 26e, 31e, 93e DBdeLi (3 bns each); grenadiers (1 bn); cavalry (1,800 men); 1 x FAB. GdD Serrurier: GdB Meyer: 18e, 29e, 30e DBdeLi (3 bns each); 1ère DBdeLi (1 bn); grenadiers (2 coys); cavalry (850 men); ½ x FAB. GdD Grenier, GdB Quesnel, GdB Rister: 17e, 24e, 106e DBdeLi (3 bns each); 2e Légion Helvetique (1 bn); 1ère Légion Polonaise (1 bn each); cavalry (450 men); 1 x FAB.

French total 40,600 men.

French losses 3,500 killed and wounded, 4,500 captured, 18 guns, 40 vehicles, 7 colours including those of the 24e DBdeLi (1er and 2e Bns). The 1ère Légion Helvetique and one battalion 56e DBdeLi were captured. GdB Digeon, GdB Rynkiewicz killed.

Austrian Forces FML Baron von Kray commanding: FML Mercandin: GM Mittrowsky: IRs vacant Preiss Nr 24 and Frelich Nr 28 (3 bns each). FML Frelich GM Lusignan: IRs Thurn Nr 43, Reisky Nr 13 (3 bns each). GM Lattermann: IR Nádasdy Nr 39 (3 bns); Gren Bns Ficquelmont, Weber, Korherr. GM Döllar: Gren Bn Neny, HusR vacant Nr 7 (8 sqns). FML Keim: GM von Elsnitz: GzIR Oguliner Nr 3, Warasdiner-Kreutzer Nr 5, JgCorps d'Aspre (1 bn each); HusR vacant Nr 5 (8 sqns). GM Gottesheim IRs Jellačič Nr 53, Jordis Nr 59 (2 bns each). GM Minkwitz: IR W Schröder Nr 26 (3 bns), IR vacant Nr 48 (2 bns). FML Baron Kray, GM Morzin: IRs Gyulai Nr 32 (2 bns), Mittrowsky Nr 40 (3 bns); Gren Bn Stentsch. GM Liptay: IRs Klebek Nr 14 (3 bns), Fürstenberg Nr 36 (2 bns). FML Zoph, GM St Julien: IRs Allvintzy Nr 19 (1 bn), vacant Nr 34 (2 bns). GM Kavacsevics: IRs vacant Huff Nr 8 and GzIR Banater Nr 12 (2 bns each); combined Banater GzIR (4th Bn). NB sources quote GM Klenau's brigade as being between the Adige and the Po on the day of the battle and thus not present. Wrede, however, shows the following regiments as having participated: HusR vacant Wurmser Nr 8 (2 sqns); Szluiner GzIR Nr 4 (1 bn).

Austrian total 46,000 men.

Austrian losses 4,000 killed and wounded, 2,000 captured. FML Count Mercandin, GM von Kovacsevics killed.

Comment Schérer went into this battle without forming a reserve and was thus unable to react to crisis or opportunities effectively.

Sources Bodart, Wrede, Clausewitz. Michaelovski-Danielevski.

YE Mount Tabor, 16 April 1799, skirmish

A mountain in Israel 11 km southeast of Nazareth; west of the southern tip of the Sea of Galilee.

A French victory over the Turks.

(Last action - Abaud, 3 April; next action - Beni Adi, 1 May.)

French Forces GdD Bonaparte commanding: GdD Kléber: 2e DBdeLé, 25e and 75e DBdeLi (3 bns each), GdD Bon: 4e DBdeLé; 18e and 32e DBdeLé (3 bns each); 16e guns.

French total ca 4,000 men.

French losses 2 killed, 60 wounded.

Turkish Forces Abdallah, Pasha of Damascus commanding ca 25,000 cavalry and 2 guns.

Turkish losses 6 killed and wounded, 500 captured.

Sources Bodart, Herold.

IN Brescia, 21 April 1799, capitulation

A town in northern Italy, on Autostrada A4 between Lakes Garda in the east and Iseo in the west.

An Austro-Russian victory over the French.

(Last action - Magnano, 5 April; next action - Lecco, 26 April.)

French Garrison GdB Bouzet commanding.

French total 1,300 men, 46 guns.

French losses 100 killed, 330 captured, 2 colours.

Austro-Russian Forces FM Count Suvorov commanding:

Austrian Forces FML Ott commanding: IRs Klebek Nr 14 (3 bns), Allvintzy Nr 19 (1st and 2nd Bns), Nádasdy Nr 39 (3 bns); LtI Bn Mihanovic Nr 15 (1 bn); GzIR Banater Nr 12 (2nd Bn); GzIR Roman Banater Nr 13 (2nd Bn); IR Mittrowsky Nr 40 (2 bns).

Austrian total ca 8,500 men.

Austrian losses Nil.

Russian Forces Prince Bagration's Avantgarde; only the cossacks were involved: the Pulks of Denisoff, Grekoff and Moltschanoff.

Russian total ca 1,900 men.

Russian losses 4 killed, 14 wounded.

Sources Bodart, Wrede, Clausewitz, Mihailovski-Danielevski.

CH Remüs, 22 April 1799, 1st skirmish

A village (now Ramosch) in the Swiss Canton of Graubünden, on Route 27, 13 km southwest of the Finstermünz pass on the Austrian border.

A French victory over the Austrians.

(Last action – Tauffers, 4 April; next action – Remüs, 30 April.)

French Forces Half of GdD Lecourbe's 3rd Division, Army of the Danube: 44e DBdeLi (2 bns).

French total ca 1,300 men.

French losses 2 killed, 23 wounded, 1 officer captured.

Austrian Forces Maj Schmidt commanding: IR Neugebauer Nr 46 (LW Bn), 6 x Landesschützenkompagnien.

Austrian total ca 1,800 men.

Austrian losses 100 killed, 120 wounded, 475 captured.

Comment Bellegarde mounted this assault after being prodded into action by FM Suvorov. A snowstorm forced its cancellation but Schmidt's column (only part of the force concerned) did not receive this order and set off alone.

Sources Günther, Wrede.

IN Lecco, 26 April 1799, skirmish

A small, walled town in northwestern Italy, on the eastern bank of the River Adda 48 km north of Milan on Route 36, at the southern end of Lake Lecco.

A Russian victory over the French.

(Last action – Brescia, 21 April; next action – Vaprio and Cassano, 27/28 April.)

French Forces GdD Serrurier commanding: GdB Meyer: 18e, 29e DBdeLi (6 bns); cavalry (4 sqns).

French total 6 bns, 4 sqns; 5,000 men.

French losses Killed and wounded unknown; 100 captured.

Russian Forces GL Prince Bagration commanding Suvorov's Avantgarde: JgR Bagration (1 bn); Cossack Pulks of Denisoff, Grekoff and Moltschanoff. Gren Bn Dendrygin (1 bn); GrenR Rosenberg, MuskR Baranowski (1 bn each) under GL Schwiekowski.

Russian total ca 3,000 men.

Russian losses 385 killed and wounded. Prince Bagration wounded.

Comment With this action the Russians seized a bridge over the Adda intact. At this point GdD Moreau took over the French Armée d'Italie from the discredited Schérer. Less than half the French force was engaged.

Source Mihailowski-Danielewski.

IN Vaprio and Cassano, 27/28 April 1799, battle

A village in northwestern Italy, just west of the River Adda, on Route 11 ca 20 km east of Milan.

An Austro-Russian victory over the French.

(Last action – Lecco, 26 April; next action – Verderio, 28 April.)

French Forces GdD Moreau commanding: GdD Grenier: GdB Quesnel, GdB Rister: 17e, 24e, 106e DBdeLi (3 bns each); 2e Légion Helvetique, 1ère Légion Polonaise (1 bn each); cavalry (450 men); 1 x FAB. GdD Victor, GdB Chamberlac; GdB Argod: 56e DBdeLi (2 bns); 92e, 99e DBdeLi (3 bns); 2e Légion Polonaise (1 bn); cavalry (900 men); 1 x FAB. GdD Serrurier, GdB Meyer: 18e, 29e , 30e DBdeLi (3 bns each); 1ère DBdeLi (1 bn), grenadiers (2 coys). Cavalry (800 men); ½ x FAB. GdD Laboissière (ex-Fresia): 21e DBdeLi (1er Bn); 24e ChàCh (4 sqns); 33e DBdeLi (2 bns); 63e DBdeLi (2 bns).

French total 28,000 men.

French losses 2,500 killed and wounded, 5,000 captured, 27 guns, 12 vehicles, 3 colours (21e DBdeLi (1er Bn), 33e DBdeLi (3e Bn); 63e DBdeLi (2e Bn), GdB Argod killed. GdB Becker captured.

Austro-Russian Forces FM Count Suvorov commanding: **Austrian Troops** FML Ott at Vaprio: IRs Frelich Nr 28 (3 bns), Nádasdy Nr 39 (3 bns);

Gren Bns Weber, Neny; JgCorps d'Aspre (10 coys); HusR EH Joseph Nr 2 (8 sqns); Combined Banater GzIR (5th Bn). FML Zoph: IRs Mittrowsky Nr 19 (1 bn), Esterházy Nr 32 (1 bn), Allvintzy Nr 19 (1st and 2nd Bns); Combined GzIR Banater (6th Bn). Gren Bns Stentsch, Pers (1 bn each). At Cassano: GdK Baron Melas, FML Frelich: IR Stuart Nr 18 (2 bns), Thurn Nr 43 (3 bns), Reisky Nr 13 (3 bns). FML Kaim: IR Preiss Nr 24 (2 bn). **Russian Troops** Cossack Pulks of Denisoff, Grekoff and Moltschanoff.

Austro-Russian total 24,500 men.

Austro-Russian losses ca 2,000 killed, wounded and missing.

Comment As is so often the case, the various sources for the casualties here do not coincide. The results of the battle were that the French left a 2,400-man garrison in Milan and withdrew to the west; Grenier to Novara, Victor and Laboissière to Valenza.

Sources Bodart, Wrede, Michaelovski-Danielevski.

IN Verderio, 28 April 1799, clash

A hamlet in northwestern Italy about 1 km west of the River Adda, midway between Milan and Lecco, at the southern end of Lake Lecco.

An Austro-Russian victory over the French.

(Last action – Vaprio and Cassano, 27/28 April; next action – Peschiera, 6 May.)

French Forces GdB Serrurier commanding: 1ère DBdeLi (1 bn); 29e DBdeLi (3 bns); cavalry (6 sqns).

French total 4 bns, 6 sqns, 3,000 men.

French losses 252 killed, 2,700 captured (including those wounded), 8 guns.

Austro-Russian Forces FML Vukassovich commanding: IR EH Anton Nr 52 (2 bns); LtI Bn Rohan Nr 14, LtI Bn Mihanovic Nr 15 (1 bn each). Cossack Pulk Posdjäjeff; two other Austrian infantry regiments and one Austrian hussar regiment – unidentified.

Austro-Russian total 8½ bns, 8 sqns, 1 cossack regiment.

Austro-Russian losses Not exactly known; moderate.

Comment Russian general Rosenberg was approaching from the north with 12 more battalions of infantry. Serrurier capitulated after a sharp fight. The French officers (250) were allowed to return to France on condition that they would not fight against the Allies again in this campaign; the men were sent to Venice until they would be exchanged.

These French defeats on the Adda River gave Milan to the Austro-Russians. On 29 April Suvorov entered the city and dissolved the young Cisalpine Republic. The Italians rose against the other new Francophile republics throughout the peninsula.

Sources Wrede, Michaelovski-Danielevski.

CH Remüs, 30 April 1799, 2nd clash

A village (now Ramosch) in the Swiss canton of Graubünden, on Route 27, 13 km southwest of the Finstermünz pass on the Austrian border.

An Austrian victory over the French.

(Last action – Remüs 22 April; next action – Maienfeld, 1 May.)

French Forces GdD Lecourbe commanding the 3rd Division, Army of the Danube: as for Nauders, 25 March.

French total ca 4,000 men.

French losses 52 killed, 371 wounded and 87 missing GdB Demont wounded.

Austrian Forces FZM Count Bellegarde commanding: IRs Toscana Nr 23 (3 bns), Neugebauer Nr 46 (1 bn), F Kinsky Nr 47 (3 bns).

Austrian total ca 8,000 men.

Austrian losses 600 killed, 1,500 wounded, 600 captured.

Comment The incredible casualty figures are from Günther. Lecourbe abandoned the position.

Sources Bodart, Wrede, Günther.

CH Maienfeld (St Luciensteig), 1 May 1799, 2nd clash

A small town in the eastern Swiss Canton of Graubünden, just south of the Principality of Liechtenstein on Route 3/13 in the valley of the upper Rhine. St Luciensteig (now Luzisteig) is a mountain pass just north of the town.

A French victory over the Austrians.

(Last action – Remüs, 30 April; next action – Süs, 2 May.)

French Forces GdD Mesnard commanding. Exact details not known.

French total 8,000 men.

French losses 400.

Austrian Forces FML Baron von Hotze commanding: IRs Kaiser Nr 1 (2nd and 3rd Bns), Kaunitz Nr 20 (2nd Bn), de Vins Nr 37 (3 bns), Oranien Nr 15 (1st and 3rd Bns).

Austrian total 6,000 men.

Austrian losses 600 killed and wounded, 2,000 captured (9 coys of IR Oranien were taken).

Sources Bodart, Wrede.

YE Beni Adi, 1 May 1799, skirmish

A village 8 km west of the River Nile in Egypt, 30 km northwest of Asynt.

A French victory over the Egyptians.

(Last action - Mount Tabor, 16 April; next action - Acre, 17 March - 21 May.)

French Forces GdB Davout with 1,000 cavalry (exact regiments involved not known, but they would have been drawn from the 3e, 14e, 15e, 18e and 20e DragRs, 22e ChàCh and 7e bis HusR).

French losses 8 men killed.

Egyptian Forces 2,000 Egyptian Fellahin (peasant infantry).

Egyptian losses 'considerable'.

Source Herold.

CH Süs, 2 May 1799, skirmish

Now Susch, a hamlet in eastern Switzerland, in the upper Inn valley (the Engadin), at the junction of Routes 27 and 28.

An Austrian victory over the French.

(Last action - Maienfeld, 1 May; next action - Maienfeld, 14 May.)

French Forces GdD Lecourbe's 3rd Division, Army of the Danube: GdB Loison: 36e and 38e DBdeLi (2 bns each). GdB Demont: 44e DBdeLi (3 bns); 76e DBdeLi (2 bns). 2 x FAB, 12e ChàCh (1 sqn), engineers (1/2 coy).

French total ca,7,600 men.

French losses 20 killed, 172 wounded, 56 captured.

Austrian Forces Part of FML Bellegarde's division: IRs Clerfayt Nr 9 (2 bns), Brechainville Nr 25 (2 bns), Gyulai Nr 32 (1 bn), De Ligne Nr 30 (1st Bn), Sztáray Nr 33 (3 bns), Kray Nr 34 (3rd Bn); LtI Bn Trautenberg Nr 6 (1 bn); Le Loup Jägers (1 bn); HusR Erdödy Nr 9 (2 sqns); Gren Bn Görschen (1 bn).

Austrian total ca 12,000 men.

Austrian losses 'Slight'.

Comment Once again Suvorov had stung Bellegarde into action; Lecourbe evacuated Graubünden as the inhabitants rose against the French.

Sources Bodart, Wrede, Günther.

IN Peschiera, 6 May 1799, capitulation

A fortress at the southern tip of Lake Garda in northern Italy, on the River Mincio, 34 km north of Mantua.

An Austrian victory over the French.

(Last action - Verderio, 28 April; next action - Pizzighettone, 9-11 May.)

French Garrison Col Coutheaux commanding: 21e DBdeLi (3e Bn).

French total 1,200 men, 90 guns, 18 gunboats.

French losses 1 colour; the garrison was released on condition that they would not fight against the Allies again in this war; the guns, boats and other stores were captured.

Austrian Forces FZM Baron von Kray commanding: IRs vacant Huff Nr 8 (3rd Bn); Klebek Nr 14 (3 bns); Jellačič Nr 53 (3 bns); Jordis Nr 59 (1 bn). GzIR Oguliner Nr 3 (1 bn).

Austrian total ca 8,000 men.

Austrian losses None.

Sources Bodart, Wrede.

IN Pizzighettone, 9-11 May 1799, siege and capture

A village in northern Italy, at the point where Route 234 crosses the River Adda; about 20 km west of Cremona.

An Austrian victory over the French.

(Last action - Peschiera, 6 May; next action - Bassignana, 12 May.)

French Garrison 92e DBdeLi (3e Bn).

French total 1,500 men, 97 guns.

French losses all captured, the colour of the 3e Bn was also taken.

Austrian Forces FML Baron von Keim commanding: IRs vacant Preiss Nr 24 (2 bns); HusR vacant Nr 5 (8 sqns).

Austrian total ca 3,000 men.

Austrian losses None.

Sources Bodart, Wrede.

IN Bassignana, 12 May 1799, clash

A village in northwestern Italy, about 18 km northeast of Alessandria, between the Rivers Po and Tanaro.

A French victory over the Russians.

(Last action - Pizzighettone, 9-11 May; next action - Marengo, 16 May.)

French Forces GdD Moreau commanding: GdBs

Miollis, Vignolles: 16e DBdeLé (1 bn); 3e DBdeLi (2 bns); 21e DBdeLi (2 bns); 1ère DBde Cisalpine (3 bns). Cavalry (700 men); 1 x FAB. GdD Grenier; GdBs Quesnel, Rister: 17e DBdeLé, 24e, 106e DBdeLi (3 bns each); 2e Légion Helvetique, 1ère Légion Polonaise (1 bn each); cavalry (450 men); 1 x FAB. 63e DBdeLi (3 bns). **Sardinian Troops** 1a Mezza-Brig-Li (2nd Bn).

French total 12,000 men.

French losses ca 600 killed, wounded and missing. GdB Quesnel killed.

Russian Forces GdI Rosenberg commanding: MG Tschubaroff's Avantgarde: JgR Tschubaroff Nr 8 (2 bns), MuskR Jung-Baden (1 bn); MuskR Tyrtoff (2 coys); Cossack Pulk Semiornikoff; Gren Bn Sanajeff (2 coys). 1 x FAB.

Russian total ca 3,500 men.

Russian losses 333 killed, 659 wounded, 300 captured, 2 guns.

Comment Rosenberg ignored Suvorov's warnings not to cross the Po here and suffered these needless casualties before the main body arrived.

Sources Bodart, Michaelovski-Danielevski.

CH Maienfeld (St Luciensteig), 14 May 1799, 3rd clash

A small town in the eastern Swiss Canton of Graubünden, just south of the Principality of Liechtenstein, on Route 3/13 in the valley of the upper Rhine. St Luciensteig (now Luzisteig) is a mountain pass just north of the town.

An Austrian victory over the French.

(Last action – Süs, 2 May; next action – Frauenfeld, 25 May.)

French Forces GdD Mesnard commanding: as for Maienfeld, 1 May.

French total 8,000 men.

French losses 300 killed and wounded, 3,100 captured, 15 guns, 22 ammunition waggons, 1 colour.

Austrian Forces FML Baron von Hotze commanding: IRs Kaiser Nr 1 (2nd and 3rd Bns), Oranien Nr 15 (1st and 3rd Bns), Kaunitz Nr 20 (2nd Bn), Kerpen Nr 49 (3 bns). DragRs Modena Nr 5, Waldeck Nr 7 (6 sqns each).

Austrian total 10,000 men.

Austrian losses 100 killed, wounded and missing.

Comment This action scattered Mesnard's division. Bellegarde's Austrian division was in close support of Hotze here.

Sources Bodart, Wrede, Günther.

IN Marengo, 16 May 1799, clash

A village in northwestern Italy, just west of Alessandria on the River Tanaro.

An Austro-Russian victory over the French.

(Last action – Bassignana, 12 May; next action – Ferrara, 24 May.)

French Forces GdD Moreau commanding: GdD Victor: 56e DBdeLi (2 bns); 92e, 99e DBdeLi (3 bns each); 2e Légion Polonaise, one HusR (4 sqns). 1 x FAB.

French total 8,000 men.

French losses ca 500 killed, wounded and missing.

Austro-Russian Forces GM Prince von Bagration commanding. **Austrian Troops** FML Lusignan commanding: Avantgarde: GM Karaczay: IR Gyulai Nr 32 (2 bns); IR Frelich Nr 28 (2 bns); DragR Karaczay Nr 4 (6 sqns). Division of FML Frelich (commanded by Lusignan): Gren Bns Stentsch, Weber, Paar, Korherr; IR Stuart Nr 18 (2 bns); DragR Lobkowitz Nr 10 (6 sqns). **Total** ca 9,000 men. **Losses** 97 killed, 250 wounded. **Russian Troops** JgRs Bagration (2 bns); Gren Bns Rosenberg, Dendrygin, Lomonosoff, MuskR Baranowski (1 bn each); Cossack Pulks Grekoff, Posdjäjeff, Moltschanoff. **Total** ca 7,500 men. **Losses** 27 killed, 80 wounded.

Comment Moreau thought he was facing only minor enemy forces and sent Victor's division over the Tanaro, keeping Grenier's in reserve. When the Allies appeared in strength Victor fell back over the single bridge. Most of a complete French battalion was cut off and thrown into the river where many drowned.

Sources Bodart; Michaelovski-Danielevski.

YE Acre (Akka), 17 March – 21 May, failed siege

A fortified port-city on the Israeli coast, 125 km northwest of Jerusalem and just north of the Bay of Acre.

An Anglo-Turkish victory over the French.

(Last action – Beni Adi, 1 May; next action – Aboukir, 25 July.)

French Forces GdD Bonaparte commanding: GdD Kléber*: 2e DBdeLé, 25e and 75e DBdeLi (3 bns each). GdD Bon: 4e DBdeLé, 18e and 32e DBdeLi (3 bns each).

GdD Reynier: 9e DBdeLé, 85e DBdeLi (3 bns each); Légion Maltaise (2 bns). GdD Lannes: 22e DBdeLé (1 bn); 13e and 69e DBdeLi (1er and 2e Bns each).

French totals 12,000 men, ? guns.

French losses 4,000 killed and died of sickness; GdD Bon and GdBs Rambeaud and Caffarelli were killed, 23 field guns and a complete siege train.

Anglo-Turkish Garrison Jezzar Pasha commanding: Émigré French artillery officer Picard de Phélipeaux and 5,000 Turks and Mamelukes, supported by Commodore Sir Sydney Smith with a small squadron of ships including *Tigre* (74) and *Theseus* (74), some captured gunboats and about 200 Royal Marines and sailors.

Anglo-Turkish losses ca 2,000 killed and wounded.

* = Kléber's division was absent from the siege until 8 May.

Sources Bodart, Herold, Fortescue.

IN Ferrara, 24 May 1799, capitulation

A city in northeastern Italy, just south of the River Po and east of Autostrada A13.

An Austrian victory over the French.

(Last action – Marengo, 16 May; next action – Ravenna, 24 May.)

French Forces Col Lapouant commanding: 5e DBdeLi (3e Bn) and some Ligurian and Piemontese troops.

French total 1,500 men, 75 guns.

French losses After handing over all weapons the garrison was free to go on condition that they would not fight against the Allies for six months. The colour of the 3e Bn was also taken.

Austrian Forces GM Count Klenau commanding: LtI Bns Am Ende Nr 3, Bach Nr 4, GzIR 1st Banal Nr 10 (1 bn each). HusR Nauendorf Nr 8 (1 sqn).

Austrian total 3,000 men, 10 guns.

Austrian losses None.

Source Bodart.

IN Ravenna, 24 May 1799, capitulation

A fortified town in northeastern Italy, near the Adriatic coast at the junction of Routes 16, 253 and 309, north of the River Montone, 51 km north of Rimini.

An Austrian victory over the French.

(Last action – Ferrara, 24 May; next action – Milan, 24 May.)

French Garrison Exact details, totals and losses not known.

Austrian Forces Exact details, totals and losses not known.

Source Bodart.

IN Milan, 30 April – 24 May 1799, blockade and capitulation

A city in northern Italy, north of the River Po and south of Lake Como.

A major junction of several Autostrada.

An Austrian victory over the French.

(Last action – Ravenna, 24 May; next action – Modena, 12 June.)

French Garrison GdB Béchaud commanding. 10e DBdeLi (2e Bn), 56e DBdeLi (1er Bn).

French total 2,000 men, 119 guns.

French losses After handing over all weapons and swearing not to fight against the Allies for one year, the garrison was allowed to return to France. The colours of both battalions were taken.

Austrian Forces GM Count Hohenzoller-Hechingen commanding: IR vacant Preiss Nr 24 (2 bns); HusR vacant Nr 5 (8 sqns).

Austrian total ca 3,000 men.

Austrian losses 14 killed, 22 wounded.

Sources Bodart, Wrede, Michaelovski-Danielevski.

CH Frauenfeld, 25 May 1799, clash

A town in northern Switzerland, at the junction of Routes 1, 7 and 14, about 14 km northeast of Winterthur.

A French victory over the Austrians.

(Last action – Maienfeld, 14 May; next action – Winterthur, 27 May.)

French Forces GdD Massena commanding part of the Army of the Danube: Exact details not known.

French total 23,000 men.

French losses 230 killed and wounded, 570 captured.

Austrian Forces FML Baron von Hotze commanding: IRs Kaunitz Nr 20 (3 bns), Gemmingen Nr 21 (3 bns); DragR Kinsky Nr 12 (6 sqns). GzIR Deutsch-Banater Nr 12 (1st Bn).

Austrian total 6,000 men.

Austrian losses 750 killed and wounded, 1,450 captured, 2 guns, 1 colour. GM von Piacsek killed.

Source Bodart.

CH Winterthur, 27 May 1799, clash

A town in northern Switzerland, at the junction of

Routes 1, 7, 15; just south of Motorway N1/E17; 18 km northeast of Zürich.
An Austrian victory over the French.
(Last action - Frauenfeld, 25 May; next action - Muottental, 29 May.)
French Forces GdD Ney commanding part of the Army of the Danube. Exact details not known.
French total 7,000 men.
French losses 800 men, 4 guns.
Austrian Forces FML Baron von Hotze commanding: IRs Manfredini Nr 12 (3 bns), Gemmingen Nr 21 (2 coys), Bender Nr 41 (3 bns), vacant Nr 60 (3rd Bn); LtI Bn Strozzi Nr 1 (1 bn); DragR Waldeck Nr 7 (6 sqns); GzIR Ungarisch-Banater (1st Bn).
Austrian total 8,000 men.
Austrian losses 1,000 killed, wounded and missing.
Sources Bodart, Wrede.

CH Muottental, 29 May 1799, clash
A small town in central Switzerland, in the valley of the Muota stream, 13 km southeast of Schwyz and east of the Vierwaldstädtersee lake.
A French victory over the Austrians.
(Last action - Winterthur, 27 May; next action - Urseren, 29 May.)
French Forces GdD Lecourbe commanding the 3rd Division, Army of the Danube: 12e DBdeLé (3 bns); 6e DBdeLi (2 bns); 109e DBdeLi (3 bns), 3 x gren coys (from 38e, 76e and 109e DBdeLi).
French total ca 7,000 men.
French losses Not known but light.
Austrian Forces FM Rovéréa commanding the 'Légion Rovéréa' (800 Swiss peasants without training, discipline or organization): GzIR Broder Nr 7 (6 coys); UlR Motschlitz Nr 2 (30 men); local 'Landsturm-Schützen' from Glarus (300 men) and Schwyz (20 men); 14 gunners, 2 guns.
Austrian total ca 1,760 men.
Austrian losses 50 killed, 200 wounded, 200 captured, 2 guns.
Comment Rovéréa ignored Austrian advice to leave Muottental on 28 May after he had routed the 12e DBdeLé and taken 150 prisoners; Lecourbe mounted a rapid and determined counterattack.
Sources Wrede, Günther.

CH Urseren, 29 May 1799, clash
A mountain ridge in the central Swiss canton of Uri, just north the St Gotthard pass, at the junction of Routes 2/N2 and 19. Also known as the Teufelsbrücke.
An Austrian victory over the French.
(Last action - Muottental, 29 May; next action - Wasen, 31 May.)
French Forces GdB Loison commanding 36e and 38e DBdeLi (2 bns each); 76e DBdeLi (1 bn) - of the 3rd Division, Army of the Danube.
French total 3,300 men.
French losses 29 killed, 168 wounded, 467 captured including 2 coys of 1er Bn, 76e DBdeLi.
Austrian Forces Obst Count St Julien commanding: IRs de Vins Nr 37 (2 bns), Neugebauer Nr 46 (1 bn), Kerpen Nr 49 (3 bns); LtI Bn Munkátsy Nr 13 (1 bn).
Austrian total 6,300 men.
Austrian losses 200 killed, wounded and missing.
Sources Bodart, Wrede, Günther.

CH Wasen, 31 May 1799, clash
A village in central Switzerland, in the valley of the Hornbach stream, 30 km northeast of the city of Bern.
A French victory over the Austrians.
(Last action - Urseren, 29 May; next action - Zürich, 4 June.)
French Forces GdD Lecourbe commanding the 3rd Division Army of the Danube: GdB Loison: 36e and 38e DBdeLi (2 bns each). GdB Maynoni : 109e DBdeLi (3 bns); 76e DBdeLi (2 bns); 12e ChàCh (1 sqn); 2 x FAB; engineers (½ coy).
French total ca 8,000 men.
French losses 10 killed, 167 wounded.
Austrian Forces Obst Count St Julien commanding: IRs de Vins Nr 37 (2 bns), Bender Nr 41 (3 bns), F Kinsky Nr 47 (3 bns), vacant Nr 62 (2nd Bn). LtI Bn Munkátsy Nr 13 (1 bn); Ungarisch Banater GzIR (1st Bn).
Austrian total 8,000 men.
Austrian losses 120 killed, 650 wounded, 1,640 captured. The regiments de Vins, Bender and Kinsky suffered the heaviest losses.
Comment The incredible casualty figures are from Günther.
Sources Bodart, Wrede, Günther.

CH Zürich, 4 June 1799, first battle
A city in northern Switzerland, at the northern end of Lake Zürich and on the River Limmat.

An Austrian victory over the French.

(Last action - Wasen, 31 May; next action - Oberwald, 13/14 August.)

French Forces GdD Massena commanding the Army of the Danube: Exact details not known but probably as for the Second Battle of Zürich, 25/26 September: 3rd Division: 25e DBdeLé, 36e, 44e, 94e DBdeLi (3 bns each); 4th Division: 50e, 53e, 100e, 108e DBdeLi (3 bns each); 1er DragR (2 sqns) 8e ChàCh (4 sqns). 5th Division: 10e DBdeLé, 37e, 57e, 102e DBdeLi (3 bns each); 1ère DBde Helvetique (1 bn); Chass Helvetique (2 sqns); 9e HusR, 13e DragR (4 sqns each). 6th Division: 1ère DBdeLé (2 bns); 2e, 46e, DBdeLi (3 bns each); 17e DBdeLi (1 bn); 5e ChàCh (4 sqns). 7th Division: 103e DBdeLi (3 bns); 2e DBde Helvetique (1 bn); 7e HusR (3 sqns); 8e HusR (4 sqns); 23e ChàCh (4 sqns); 2e DragR (4 sqns); 102e DBdeLi (2 bns). Grenadier Reserve (3,500 men). 8th Division: 14e DBdeLé, 1ère DBdeLi (3 bns each); 1ère DBde Helvetique (1 bn); 4e DBde Helvetique (½ bn); 4e HusR (3 sqns). Reserve Artillery Park. 60 guns.

French total 45,000 men.

French losses 500 killed, 800 wounded; 300 captured; 28 guns. GdB Cherin killed. 150 other guns were taken when the French abandoned Zürich.

Austrian Forces FM Archduke Charles commanding: Left Wing FML Hotze: GM Jellačič : IRs Stein Nr 50 (3 bns), Kerpen Nr 49, Gemmingen Nr 21 (1 bn each); DragRs Modena Nr 5 (1 sqn), Waldeck Nr 7 (2 sqns). GM Petrasch: GzIR Peterwardeiner Nr 9 (3rd and 4th Bns); IR vacant Nr 60 (2 bns). GM Prince Joseph von Lothringen: IRs Gemmingen Nr 21, Kaiser Nr 1 (2 bns each); DragR Waldeck Nr 7 (2 sqns); UlR Motschlitz Nr 2 (1 sqn). GM Kempf: IR Bender Nr 41 (3 bns); IR Brechainville Nr 25 (2 coys); Obst Grünne: DragRs Kronprinz Nr 2 (6 sqns); Coburg Nr 6 (4 sqns); Waldeck Nr 7 (2 sqns). GM O'Reilly: GzIR Peterwardeiner Nr 9 (1 bn); IR Kaunitz Nr 20 (3 bns); DragR Coburg Nr 6 (2 sqns); GzHusR (2 sqns). The Centre: FZM Wallis: FML Prince Reuss: LtI Bn Strozzi Nr 1 (1 bn); IR Wenkheim Nr 35 (3 bns); GzHusR (8 sqns). FML Prince Anhalt-Köthen: Gren Bns Rüffer (ex Teschner), Sebottendorf, Fitz-Gibbons, Juch, Tegetthof, Bojakowsky. IR EH Ferdinand Nr 23 (2 bns). GM Lindenau: IRs EH Carl Nr 3, O Wallis Nr 11 (3 bns each). Prince von Hessen-Homburg; KürR Zeschwitz Nr 5 (4 sqns); DragRs Latour Nr 11, Kinsky Nr 12 (6 sqns each). GM Riesch: KürRs Nassau Nr 9, Mack Nr 10 (6 sqns each). The Right Wing Gen Nauendorff, GM Kienmayer: Tyroler Jäger (1 bn); Gz Scharfschützen (1 bn); LtI Bn Rubinitz; GzIR Deutsch-Banater Nr 12 (1 bn); HusR Mészáros Nr 10 (8 sqns); UlR Motschlitz Nr 2 (1 sqn). GM Simbschen: IRs Callenberg Nr 54 (3 bns), Manfredini Nr 12 (3 bns), EH Ferdinand Nr 2 (1 bn). Obst Mylius: IRs Lacy Nr 22, Schröder Nr 7 (3 bns each).

Austrian total ca 53,000 men.

Austrian losses 730 killed, 1,470 wounded, 2,200 captured. FZM Count Wallis killed.

Comment The casualty figures for both sides here are controversial and by no means well-based. Following the battle, Archduke Charles failed to follow up his beaten foe and thus lost all the potential fruits of his victory, much to the disgust of the Russian liaison officer, Generaladjutant Count Tolstoi.

Sources Bodart, Michaelovski-Danielevski, Wrede.

IN Modena, 12 June 1799, clash

A city in northeastern Italy, south of the River Po and between its tributaries the Panaro and the Secchia, 40 km northwest of Bologna.

A French victory over the Austrians.

(Last action - Milan, 24 May; next action - Tidone River 17 June.)

French Forces GdD Macdonald commanding: Avantgarde GdB Salm: 15e DBdeLé, 11e DBdeLi (2 bns each); 25e ChàCh (1 sqn); ½ x FAB. GdD Olivier: 12e, 30e, 73e DBdeLi (2 bns each); 7e ChàCh (3 sqns); 19e ChàCh (3 sqns); 1 x FAB. GdD Vatrin: 62e, 78e DBdeLi (3 bns each); 25e ChàCh (3 sqns); ½ x FAB. GdD Rusca 17e DBdeLé (2 bns); 55e DBdeLi (1 bn); 97e DBdeLi (2 bns); 16e DragR (4 sqns); 19e DragR (3 sqns); ½ x FAB. GdD Montrichard: 5e DBdeLé (2 bns); 3e DBdeLi (1 bn); 21e DBdeLi (2 bns); 68e DBdeLi (1 bn); 1er CavR (3 sqns); 12e DragR, 11e HusR (2 sqns each); 1er Cisalpine DragR (1 sqn), 1er Cisalpine HusR (3 sqns); 1 x FAB. GdB Dombrowski: 8e DBdeLé (1 bn); 1ère Légion Polonaise (5 bns); Polish Cavalry (200 men).

French total 29,000 men.

French losses 400 killed and wounded, 200 captured. GdB Forest killed, GdD Macdonald wounded.

Austrian Forces GM Count Hohenzollern-Hechingen commanding: IR Preiss Nr 24 (2 bns); IR Klebek Nr 14 (1 bn); HusR Nauendorf Nr 8 (8 sqns); JzPfR Bussy (6 sqns).

Austrian total 4,300 men.

Austrian losses 750 killed and wounded, 1,650 captured, 8 guns, 3 colours.

Sources Bodart, Wrede, Michaelovski-Danielevski.

IM Naples, 14/15 June 1799, capitulation

A major city port on the central western Italian coast; the forts of Rivigliano, Uovo, Nuovo and Castellamare were concerned. A British victory over the French.

(Next action - Naples, 29 June - 11 July)

Franco-Neapolitan Forces (commanders unknown).

Franco-Neapolitan total 2,800 men, mostly Neapolitan republican rebels.

British Forces Captain Edward Foote commanding the ships *Mutine* (14), *San Leone* (16) and *Perseus* (bomb).

British total 1,000 men.

British losses Not known but very light.

Comment Rear Admiral Horatio Nelson arrived on 24 June and the capitulation (allowing the garrison free passage to France) was totally ignored at his insistence. The credulous rebels were kept penned up in small transport ships in the harbour until King Ferdinand of Naples arrived on July 8 when they were all executed, including the women! Nelson also court-martialled and had hanged at the yard arm Prince Francesco Caracciolo, a renegade Neapolitan naval officer, much to the disgust of most of the Allied commanders present.

Sources Bodart, James, Clowes.

IN Tidone River, 17 June 1799, clash

A southern tributary of the River Po, entering the latter river west of Piacenza. The action took place just west of the point where Route 10 crosses the Tidone at Rottofreno.

An Allied victory over the French.

(Last action - Modena, 12 June; next action - Turin, 11-20 June.)

French Forces GdD Macdonald commanding. GdD Victor: 5e, 39e, 92e, 93e, 99e DBdeLi (2 bns each); 15e ChàCh (4 sqns). GdD Rusca: 17e DBdeLé (2 bns); 55e DBdeLi (1 bn); 97e DBdeLi (2 bns); 16e DragR (4 sqns); 19e DragR (3 sqns); ½ x FAB. GdB Salm (Avantgarde) 15e DBdeLé, 11e DBdeLi (2 bns each); 25e ChàCh (1 sqn); ½ x FAB. GdD Dombrowski: 1ère Légion Polonaise (5 bns, 2 sqns); 1 x FAB.

French total ca 19,000 men.

French losses 1,000 killed and wounded; 1,200 captured.

Allied Forces FM Prince Suvorov commanding: FML Ott's Austrian Avantgarde: Jg d'Aspre (1 bn); IR Nádasdy Nr 39 (3 bns); DragR Karaczay Nr 4 and Levenehr Nr 14 (6 sqns each); 1 x FAB. Gen Prince Constantine's Russian Contingent: Cossack Pulks Grekoff, Posdjäjeff, Semiornikoff, Moltschanoff. JgR Bagration (2 bns); Gren Bns Dendrygin, Lomonosoff, Sanajeff, Kalemin.

Allied total ca 15,000 men.

Allied losses Not known exactly.

Sources Michaelovski-Danielevski; Wrede.

IN Turin, 11-20 June 1799, siege and capture

A city in northwestern Italy, on the upper River Po, on Route 25 and Autostrada A32/E70 into France via the Mont Cenis pass.

An Austrian victory over the Franco-Sardinians.

(Last action - Tidone River, 17 June; next action - Trebbia River, 20 June.)

Franco-Sardinian Garrison GdB Fiorella commanding 107e DBdeLi (1er Bn) and other troops.

Franco-Sardinian total 3,000 men.

Franco-Sardinian losses 100 killed, 300 wounded. The commandant and his staff were captured; the men were let go on condition that they would not fight against the Allies until exchanged. The Allies captured 382 guns and 40,000 muskets and the colour of 107e as well as large quantities of military supplies.

Austrian Forces FML Baron von Keim commanding: IRs vacant Huff Nr 8 (3 bns), Frelich Nr 28 (2 bns); S Gyulai Nr 32 (3 bns); Fürstenberg Nr 36 (1st and 2nd Bns); EH Anton Nr 52 (1½ bns).

Austrian total 6,500 men, 126 siege guns.

Austrian losses 30 killed, 40 wounded.

Sources Bodart, Wrede, Michaelovski-Danielevski.

IN Trebbia River, 17-20 June 1799, battle

A southern tributary of the River Po, joining it at Piacenza in northern Italy.

An Austro-Russian victory over the French.

(Last action - Turin, 20 June; next action - Cassina Grossa, 20 June.)

French Forces GdD Macdonald commanding: Avantgarde GdB Salm: 15e DBdeLé, 11e DBdeLi (2 bns each); 25e ChàCh (1 sqn); ½ x FAB. GdD Vatrin: 62e, 78e

DBdeLi (3 bns each); 25e ChàCh (3 sqns); ½ x FAB. GdD Olivier: 12e, 30e DBdeLi (2 bns each); 73e DBdeLi (3 bns); 7e ChàCh (3 sqns); 19e ChàCh (3 sqns); 1 x FAB. GdD Rusca: 17e DBdeLé (2 bns); 55e DBdeLi (1 bn); 97e DBdeLi (2 bns); 16e DragR (4 sqns); 19e DragR (3 sqns); ½ x FAB. GdD Montrichard: 5e DBdeLé (2 bns); 3e DBdeLi (1 bn); 21e, 68e DBdeLi (1 bn each); 1er CavR (3 sqns); 12e DragR, 11e HusR (2 sqns each); 1er Cisalpine DragR (1 sqn), 1er Cisalpine HusR (3 sqns); 1 x FAB. GdB Dombrowsky: 1st Polish Legion [Gren Bn, Chass Bn, 3 x Fus Bns, CavR (2 sqns)]. Artillery Park 4 x FABs. GdD Victor: 5e, 39e, 92e, 93e, 99e DBdeLi (2 bns each); 15e ChàCh (4 sqns).

French total 33,000 men.

French losses 2,000 killed, 7,500* wounded, 7,000 captured; 7 guns, 8 colours: 55e DBdeLi (1); GdD Cambray killed.

* = almost all these wounded were captured in the hospital in Piacenza.

Austro-Russian Forces FM Count Suvorov commanding: **Austrian Troops** FML Gottesheim's Avantgarde (in the Left Hand Column): HusR EH Joseph Nr 2 (8 sqns); JgCorps d'Aspre (6 coys); GzIR Banater* Nr 6 (1 bn); LtI Bn Mihanovic Nr 15 (1 bn). FML Prince Liechtenstein (The Reserve) Gren Bns Mercandin, Weber, Ficquelmont, Korherr, Neny, Wouvermanns, Soudain; IR Frelich Nr 28 (3 bns); GM Morzin: IRs Nádasdy Nr 39 (3 bns), Mittrowsky Nr 40 (2 bns); DragR Württemberg Nr 8 (6 sqns); **Austro-Russian Troops** Right Hand Column – Prince Bagration's Avantgarde: JgR Bagration (2 bns); Combined Gren Bns Lomonosoff, Kalemin, Sanajeff, Dendrygin. Cossack Pulks of Grekoff and Posdjäjeff; Austrian Karaczay Nr 4 (6 sqns). Division of LG Schwiekowski: GrenR Rosenberg (2 bns); MuskRs Schwiekowski (2 bns), Dalheim (1 bn); Austrian DragR Lobkowitz Nr 10 (6 sqns). Centre Column: LG Förster MuskRs Förster (1 bn), Baranowski (1 bn); Tyrtoff (2 bns); Miloradovitch (2 bns); Jung-Baden (1 bn); Cossack Pulk Moltschanoff; Austrian DragoonR Levenehr Nr 14 (6 sqns).

* = it has not been possible to identify exactly which GzIR this should be; it was certainly NOT Nr 6.

Allied totals 20,000 Austrians, 17,000 Russians.

Allied losses Austrians: 10 officers, 244 men killed; 87 officers, 1,816 men wounded. Russians: 5 officers, 675 men killed; 3 generals, 44 officers, 675 men wounded. The Austrians also reported 3 officers and 497 men missing, mainly from IRs Nádasdy (166) and Frelich (158).

Sources Bodart, Wrede, Michaelovski-Danielevski.

IN Cassina Grossa, 20 June 1799, battle

A village in northwestern Italy, about 20 km east of Alessandria, towards Tortona. Also known as San Giuliano.

A French victory over the Austrians.

(Last action – Trebbia River, 20 June; next action – Alessandria, 22 July.)

French Forces GdD Moreau commanding: Exact details not known; see OOB for Trebbia River, 17–20 June.

French total 14,000 men.

French losses ca 1,000 killed, wounded and missing.

Austrian Forces FML Count Bellegarde commanding: IRs Stuart Nr 18 (1st and 3rd Bns), Allvintzy Nr 19 (2 bns), Frelich Nr 28 (3 bns), De Ligne Nr 30 (1st Bn), Fürstenberg Nr 36 (1st and 2nd Bns), Beaulieu Nr 58 (3 bns). Gren Bns Stentsch, Ficquelmont, Morzin, Korherr, Hohenfeld. LtI Bn Otto Nr 7, DragR EH Johann Nr 3 (6 sqns); HusR vacant Nr 5 (8 sqns); HusR Erdödy Nr 9 (? sqns); JzPf Bussy (4 sqns).

Austrian total 8,000 men.

Austrian losses 1,000 killed and wounded, 1,300 captured, 3 guns.

Sources Bodart, Wrede.

IM Naples (Fort St Elmo) 29 June – 11 July 1799, siege and capitulation

A major city port on the central western Italian coast.

An Allied victory over the French.

(Last action – Naples, 14/15 June; next action – Capua, 28 July.)

French Garrison GdB Méjan commanding.

French total ca 800 men.

French losses Not exactly known. The garrison was returned to Toulon on British ships.

Allied Forces Captain Troubridge (Royal Navy) commanding a force of British and Portuguese marines.

Allied total ca 1,600 men.

Allied losses 37 killed, 84 wounded.

Sources Clowes, James.

IN Alessandria, 22 June – 22 July 1799, siege and capture

A fortified town in northwestern Italy, on the

southern bank of the River Tanaro and southeast of the junction of Autostrada A21/E70 and A26; 82 km southwest of Milan.

An Austrian victory over the French.

(Last action - Cassina Grossa, 20 June; next action - Mantua, 28 July.)

French Garrison GdB Gardanne commanding: 24e DBdeLi (3e Bn); 39e DBdeLi (3e Bn); Sardinian Troops: 1a Mezza-Brig-Li (2nd and 3rd Bns); 1ère Légion Helvetique (1 bn).

French total 3,100 men, 105 guns.

French losses 400 killed and wounded, 2,700 captured (including 300 sick) 7,000 muskets, 6 colours: 24e DBdeLi (3e Bn); 39e DBdeLi (3e Bn).

Austrian Forces FML Count Bellegarde commanding: IRs vacant Huff Nr 8 (3 bns); Clerfayt Nr 9 (1st Bn); Reisky Nr 13 (3 bns); Stuart Nr 18 (1st and 3rd Bns); Frelich Nr 28 (3 bns); De Ligne Nr 30 (1st Bn); S Gyulai Nr 32 (3 bns); Sztáray Nr 33 (3 bns); Kray Nr 34 (3 bns); Fürstenberg Nr 36 (1st and 2nd Bns). Gren Bn Hohenfeld. JgCorps d'Aspre (10 coys). HusR vacant Nr 5 (8 sqns).

Austrian total ca 21,000 men.

Austrian losses ca 400 killed, wounded and missing.

Sources Bodart, Wrede.

YE Aboukir, 25 July 1799, clash

A fortified port on the Nile delta in Egypt, 21 km northeast of Alexandria.

A French victory over the Turks.

(Last action - Acre, 17 March; this was the last action in Egypt in 1799.)

French Forces GdD Bonaparte commanding: GdD Murat (Avantgarde): 3e and 14e DragRs and Guides à Ch (2 sqns each). GdD Destaing: 4e DBdeLé (1 bn); 61e DBdeLi (2 bns); 75e DBdeLi (1 bn). GdD Lanusse: 18e and 32e DBdeLi (3 bns each). GdD Lannes: 22e DBdeLé, 13e and 69e DBdeLi (3 bns each). GdD Kléber: 2e DBdeLé and 25e DBdeLi (3 bns each); 75e DBdeLi (2 bns).

French total 8,000 men.

French losses 1,100 killed and wounded.

Turkish Forces Mustafa Pasha commanding: 7,000 Mamelukes and Bedouin.

Turkish losses ca 5,000 killed, wounded and captured.

Comment The Turkish figures of '18,000 total and 12,000 casualties' quoted in Bodart would seem to be yet another of Bonaparte's beloved embroideries of the truth.

Sources Bodart, Herold.

IN Mantua, 8 April - 28 July 1799, blockade, siege and capture

A fortified city in northern Italy, on the River Mincio, at the junction of Routes 10, 62 and 420; 42 km south of Lake Garda.

An Austrian victory over the French and their allies.

(Last action - Alessandria, 22 July; next action - Novi, 15 August.)

French and Allied Garrison GdD Foissac-Latour commanding: 26e DBdeLi (2 coys); 31e DBdeLi (2 coys); 29e DBdeLi (1 bn); 45e DBdeLi (3e Bn), 93e DBdeLi (3e Bn); 1ère and 2e Légion Helvetique (2 coys each); 1ère DBde Cisalpine, 56e DBdeLi (1 bn); 2e Légion Polonaise (3 bns); 280 gunners.

French and Allied total 11,000 men.

French and Allied losses 3,100 killed or died of wounds and sickness or deserted; 657 guns. The French were allowed to return to France on condition that they would not fight against the Allies again in this war. The Poles (about 250) were kept back and returned to the regiments of the Austrian army in which they had originally served. The following colours were taken: 31e DBdeLi (3), 45e DBdeLi (3e Bn), 56e DBdeLi (2e Bn), 93e DBdeLi (3e Bn), Légion Polonaise, Légion Helvetique, 1ère DBde Cisalpine.

Austrian Forces FZM Baron von Kray commanding: IRs EH Maximilian Nr 4, vacant Huff Nr 8, Kheul Nr 10, Reisky Nr 13, Klebek Nr 14, Terzy Nr 16, Nádasdy Nr 39, Mittrowsky Nr 40, Thurn Nr 43 (3 bns each), Lattermann Nr 45 (2 bns), Vukassovich Nr 48, Jellačič Nr 53, Jordis Nr 59 (3 bns each). LtI Bn Am Ende Nr 3; JgCorps d'Aspre (10 coys); KürR Kavanagh Nr 12 (6 sqns); HusR vacant Nr 7 (1 sqn); HusR Nauendorf Nr 8 (8 sqns); Stabs-DragR (8 sqns); GzIR Szluiner Nr 4 (1 bn); GzIR 2nd Banal Nr 11 (1 bn).

Austrian total ca 32,000 men.

Austrian losses ca 2,100 killed, wounded and missing. NB not all these regiments were here throughout the blockade; most came up after the 4 July.

Sources Bodart, Wrede.

IM Capua, 28 July 1799, capitulation

A fortified town in western central Italy, on the south

bank of the River Volturno, 30 km north of Naples, at the junction of Routes 6 and 264.

An Allied victory over the French.

(Last action - Naples, 11 July; next action - Gaëta, 1 August.)

French Garrison GdB Girardon commanding: exact details not known.

French total 2,200 men.

French losses None; the garrison was allowed free passage back to France.

Allied Force Captain Troubridge (of the Royal Navy) commanding: a mixed force of British seamen and marines and Portuguese marines.

Allied total 1,600 men.

Allied losses None.

Sources Bodart, Clowes, James.

IM Gaëta, 1 August 1799, capitulation

A fortress on the central western Italian coast, just off Route 213, about 60 km northwest of Naples.

An Anglo-Neapolitan victory over the French.

(Last action - Gaëta, 5 January; next action - Rome, 29 September.)

French Garrison Exact details not known.

French total 1,500 men.

French losses Not exactly known but very light; the garrison was allowed to go free, except for Sicilian rebel subjects who were tried and executed by their compatriots.

Anglo-Neapolitan Forces Neapolitans: LG Salandra commanding: exact details not known.

Neapolitan total 6,000 men.

British Force Rear Admiral Horatio Nelson commanding: exact details not known; it did not come into action; it included *Foudroyant* (80) *Minerva* and *Minotaur* (74).

Sources Bodart, Clowes, James.

CH Oberwald, 13/14 August 1799, clash

A village in the Swiss valley of the Rhône, between Grimsel pass and the town of Brig in the valley of the River Rotten on Route 19, close to the Italian border.

A French victory over the Austrians.

(Last action - Zürich, 4 June; next action - Grimsel Pass, 14 August.)

French Forces GdD Thar commanding: 4 x French DBdes, 1 Swiss bn.

French total 6,000 men.

French losses 500 killed, wounded and missing.

Austrian Forces GM Prinz Rohan commanding: exact details not known but including: Lt Bn L Rohan Nr 14, IR EH Anton Nr 52 (1 bn); Le Loup Jägers (3 coys); HusR vacant Nr 7 (1 sqn).

Austrian total 6,000 men.

Austrian losses 3,000 men, 2 guns.

Sources Bodart, Michaelovski-Danielevski.

CH Grimsel Pass, 14 August 1799, skirmish

A mountain pass in central Switzerland over which Route 6 runs south from the Brienzer See (Lake) into the valley of the River Rotten where it joins Route 19.

A French victory over the Austrians.

(Last action - Oberwald, 13/14 August; next action - Schwyz, 14 August.)

French Forces GdB Gudin's Brigade: 25e DBdeLé (2 bns); Swiss (1 bn).

French total ca 2,400 men.

French losses 60 killed and wounded.

Austrian Forces Obst Strauch commanding: IR Neugebauer Nr 46 (4 coys); GzIR Deutsch-Banater Nr 12 (1st Bn).

Austrian total ca 2,600 men.

Austrian losses 400 killed and wounded, 500 captured.

Comment The astounding casualty figures are - as usual - from Günther (who used French figures). Wrede does, however, mention 'heavy losses' for IR Neugebauer. Michaelovski-Danielevski quotes the Austrian losses as '200 killed and wounded, 500 captured'. The French outflanked an apparently impregnable position and caught the Austrians by surprise. In other actions near here this day IR Wallis Nr 11 (2 bns); LtI Bn Siegenfeld Nr 10, the Carneville Freikorps (1 bn); GzIR Warasdiner-St Georger Nr 6 (1 bn); HusR Erdödy Nr 9 (1 sqn) were also badly mauled.

Sources Wrede, Günther; Michaelovski-Danielevski.

CH Schwyz, 14 August 1799, clash

A town in central Switzerland, just northeast of the Vierwaldstädtersee lake, at the junction of Routes 2, 8 and Autobahn N4/E60.

A French victory over the Austrians.

(Last action - Grimsel Pass, 14 August; next action - Amsteg, 14-16 August.)

French Forces GdD Lecourbe commanding part of the Army of the Danube: 3rd Division: exact details not known but including GdB Boivin: 84e DBdeLi (1st and 3rd Bns); 109e DBdeLi (3 bns). GdD Loison's Brigade: 76e DBdeLi (3 bns). 36e and 38e DBdeLi (2 bns each).

French total 12 bns, ca 12,000 men.

French losses 28 killed, 140 wounded.

Austrian Forces GM Baron Simbschen commanding: IR Kerpen Nr 49 (3 bns); IR Stain Nr 50 (1 bn); Swiss militia (800 men).

Austrian total ca 4,600 men.

Austrian losses 195 killed, 610 wounded, 13 officers and 1,000 men captured, 5 guns, 1 Swiss colour.

Comment The amazing casualty figures are from Günther. The French mounted an amphibious assault at Brunnen on the Urnersee lake with 8 grenadier companies. They subsequently sacked and burned Schwyz.

Sources Wrede, Günther, Bodart; Michaelovski-Danielevski.

IN Novi, 15 August 1799, battle

A town in northwestern Italy, 22 km southeast of Alessandria on the River Tanaro.

An Austro-Russian victory over the French.

(Last action – Mantua, 28 July; next action – Tortona, 11 September.)

French Forces GdD Joubert commanding: **Left Wing** GdD Pérignon: GdD Grouchy, GdB Grandjean: 26e DBdeLé (1 bn); 39e, 92e DBdeLi (2 bns each). GdB Charpentier: 93e and 99e DBdeLi (2 bns each). Col Rouget: 41e and 83e DBdeLi (élite coys only). GdD Lemoine: GdB Garreau: 5e DBdeLé (1 bn); 26e and 80e DBdeLi (2 bns each). GdB Serras 20e DBdeLé, 34e DBdeLi (2 bns each); 1er HusR (3 sqns). **The Reserve** GdB Clausel: 29e DBdeLé, 74e DBdeLi (2 bns each). GdB Partouneaux: 26e DBdeLé (1 bn); 105e DBdeLi (2 bns). GdD Richepanse: 1er, 3e and 18e CavRs, 12e DragR, 2e ChàCh (2 sqns each). **The Centre and Right Wing** GdD St Cyr, GdD Laboissière: GdB Quesnel: 17e DBdeLé, 63e DBdeLi. GdB Gardanne 18e DBdeLé, 21e DBdeLi (6 bns in all). 6e HusR (3 sqns). GdB Colli: 14e, 24e and 68e DBdeLi (2 bns each); Poles (1 bn). **Reserve** 3e and 106e DBdeLi (4 bns); GdB Guerin: 16e and 19e DragRs, 19e ChàCh (5 sqns). GdD Watrin, GdB Arnaud: 12e and 30e DBdeLi; GdB Petitot: 62e and 78e DBdeLi. **Avantgarde** GdB Calvin: 8e, 15e, 27e DBdeLé; 2e DBdeLi (10 bns); 25e ChàCh (2 sqns). GdD Dombrowsky: 17e and 55e DBdeLi, Polish Legion (5 bns, 1 sqn), 1ère DBde Cisalpine (2 bns). The details are after Jomini.

French total 35,000 men.

French losses 1,500 killed, 5,500 wounded, 4,500 captured and missing, 37 guns, 40 ammunition waggons, 8 colours. GdD Joubert killed. The colours taken included: 39e DBdeLi (2e Bn); 68e (1er Bn); 92e (1er Bn); 106e (1er Bn). Generals Pérignon, Grouchy, Colli and Partouneaux were captured.

Austro-Russian Forces FM Count Suvorov commanding. **Austrian Troops: The Corps of FZM Baron Kray** Divisions of FML Ott and Bellegarde; Brigades of Bellegarde, Gottesheim, Minkwitz, Seckendorff: IRs Nádasdy Nr 39, Mittrowsky Nr 40, Terzy Nr 16, Deutschmeister Nr 4 (3 bns each); Vukassovich Nr 48, Lattermann Nr 45, GzIR Oguliner Nr 3; GzIR Szluiner Nr 4 (2 bns each). IRs Sztáray Nr 33 (3 bns), Gyulai Nr 32, Oranien Nr 15, vacant Huff Nr 8 (2 bns each). DragRs Kaiser Nr 1, EH Johann Nr 3 (6 sqns each); HusR EH Joseph Nr 2 (8 sqns). **The Russian Corps of GdC Derfelden Avantgarde** Gen Bagration: JgR Bagration (2 bns); JgR Miller (2 bns); Combined Gren Bns Lemonosoff, Dendrygin, Sanajeff, Kalemin, Cossack Pulks Denisoff, Grekoff, Semiornikoff, Systschoff. **Austrian DragR** Karaczay Nr 4 (6 sqns). Gen Miloradovitch: MuskRs Dalheim, Jung-Baden, Miloradovitch (2 bns each). Gen Derfelden: GrenR Rosenberg, MuskRs Förster, Schwiekowski, Tyrtoff, Baranowski (2 bns each). **The Austrian Corps of FZM Melas** Division of FML Prince Liechtenstein, Brigades of GMs Lusignan, Loudon, Mittrowski, Nobili and Liechtenstein. Gren Bns Pertusi, Gerschen, Weissenwolf, Morzin, Schiaffenati, Paar, Hohenfeld, Weber. IRs Fürstenberg Nr 36, Stuart Nr 18 (2 bns); DragRs Lobkowitz Nr 10 (6 sqns), Levenehr Nr 14 (6 sqns); HusR vacant Nr 5 (6 sqns).

Austro-Russian total 35,000 men.

Austro-Russian losses ca 900 killed, 4,200 wounded, 1,400 captured and missing; 3 guns. This was one of the bloodiest battles of the era; Generals Tyrtoff, Gortschakoff and Tschubaroff were wounded.

Comment The sources relating to this action are often at variance over details.

Sources Bodart, Wrede, Charrié, Michaelovski-Danielevski, Jomini.

CH Amsteg, 14–16 August 1799, skirmish

A small village in central Switzerland, on Route 2 and Motorway N2/E9, about 12 km south of the Vierwaldstädtersee Lake, in the valley of the River Reuss.

A French victory over the Austrians.

(Last action – Schwyz, 14 August; next action – Zürich, 25/26 September.)

French Forces GdD Lecourbe commanding the 3rd Division, Army of the Danube: and Chabran's division as for Schwyz on 14 August including 109e DBdeLi (2 bns) and 4 coys of the 38e and 76e DBdeLi.

French total 8,000 men.

French losses 500 killed, wounded and missing.

Austrian Forces GM Baron von Simbschen commanding: IR vacant Nr 62 (2nd Bn); IR Kerpen Nr 49 (2 bns); GzIR Gradiskaner Nr 8 (1 bn); DragR Modena Nr 5 (2 sqns); IR Neugebauer NR 46 (1 bn); GzIR Deutsch-Banater Nr 12 (1st Bn).

Austrian total 4,400 men.

Austrian losses 2,300 killed, wounded and missing, 3 guns. This action ended Lecourbe's offensive; it left him in control of the upper reaches of the Rivers Rhine, Rhône and Reuss and the entrances into Italy and Graubünden. In the three days (14–16 August) the Austrians had lost over 7,500 men and 11 guns. French losses were about 1,500 men. These victories were mainly due to faulty Austrian dispositions which were fully exploited by the French.

Sources Bodart, Wrede, Günther, Michaelovski-Danielevski.

NL Groët-Keeten, 27 August 1799, clash

A village in northwestern Holland, 9 km south of the town of Den Helder on the northern tip of the peninsula of the province of Noord-Holland, at the end of Route N9. Not marked on modern maps.

An British victory over the Batavians.

(This was the opening action of this campaign; next action – Zyper Sluis, 10 September).

Batavian Forces GdD Daendels commanding: **Right Wing** GM Van Guerike: 5th and 7th DBdeLi (3 bns each); 2nd Jagers (1 bn); 1st and 2nd CavRs (4 and 2 sqns resp); 2nd HAB. Left Wing GM Zuilen-Van-Nyewelt: 1st DBdeLi (3 bns); 3rd DBdeLi (1st Bn); 4th DBdeLi (1st Bn); 6th DBdeLi (3rd Bn); 1st Jagers (1 bn); DragR (1 sqn).

Batavian total 11,000 men.

Batavian losses 1,400 men killed, wounded and missing.

British Forces LG Pulteney commanding: Coote's Brigade: 2nd, 27th, 29th, 69th, 85th Foot. Col Macdonald: 23rd, 55th Foot (1 bn each). 18th LDR (2 sqns) 650 artillery, 36 x 6 pdr guns, 20 x 12 pdrs, 30 x 24 pdrs. No Russians were involved in this action.

British total ca 8,000 men.

British losses 3 officers, 60 men killed (a further 20 men drowned in the landing), 24 officers, 380 men wounded.

Comment The British landing was supported by the guns of the fleet. Vice Admiral Andrew Mitchell commanding: *Ratsivan** (66); *Mistisloff** (74); *Monmouth* (64); *Ardent* (64); *Belliqueux* (64); *America* (64); *Overyssel* (44); *Veteran* (64); *Glatton* (54); *Isis* (50); *Romney* (50); *Melpomene* (44); *Latona* (38); *Shannon* (32); *Juno* (32); *Lutine* (32).

* = Russian ships.

On 28 August MG John Moore occupied den Helder capturing the town, the naval yard at Nieuwe Werk together with 97 guns, many naval stores and the following ships in the Nieuwe Diep: *Verwachting* (64); *Broederschap* (54); *Belle Antoinette* (44); *Constitutie* (44); *Duif* (44); *Expeditie* (44); *Hector* (44); *Unie* (44); *Heldin* (32); *Minerva* (24); *Alarm* (24); *Valk* (24); *Venus* (24); three Indiamen and a hulk. On 30 August, the Allied fleet forced the surrender of the following Batavian ships in the Vlieter under Vice Admiral Storij: *Washington* (70); *Cerberus* (68); *De Ruijter* (64); *Gelderland* (64); *Leijden* (68); *Utrecht* (68); *Batavier* (56); *Beschermer* (56); *Amphitrite* (44); *Mars* (44); *Embuscade* (34); *Galathée* (16). All these twelve ships were added to the Royal Navy; *Washington* as *Princess of Orange*, *Cerberus* as *Texel* and *Mars* as *Vlieter*. For this shameful event Storij and five of his captains were sacked and punished but they were really powerless to do anything as their crews mutinied and threw the charges of the guns overboard.

Sources Fortescue, James, Clowes, Michaelovski-Danielevski.

NL Zyper-Sluis, 10 September 1799, clash

A water control point on the drainage system in the northwestern Dutch province of Noord-Holland, 4 km east of Camperduin on the North Sea coast and northwest of Alkmaar.

A British victory over the Franco-Batavians.

(Last action – Groët-Keeten, 27 August; next action – Bergen, 19 September.)

Franco-Batavian Forces GdD Brune commanding: Batavians – as for Groët-Keeten on 27 August. French Forces: exact details not known; part of the divisions of Vandamme, Boudet, Gouvion, St Cyr and Barbou: 22e and 42e DBdeLi (3 bns each); 48e DBdeLi (1 bn and 3 gren coys); 49e DBdeLi (3 bns); 51e DBdeLi (1 bn); 54e DBdeLi (3 bns); 60e DBdeLi (1 bn); 72e DBdeLi (2 bns); 90e DBdeLi (3 bns); 98e DBdeLi (2 bns); 10e DragR, 4e ChàCh (4 sqns each); 5e ChàCh (1 sqn); 16e ChàCh (4 sqns); 5 x HAB, 2 x FAB.

Franco-Batavian total ca 21,000 men (14,000 Batavians, 7,000 French).

Franco-Batavian losses 2,000 killed, wounded and missing.

British Forces LG Sir Ralph Abercromby commanding: MG Manner's 9th Bde: 1/9th, 2/9th, 56th Foot, 7th LDR (2 sqns): MG Doyley's 1st Bde: 3/1st Foot Guards, Guard's Gren Bn. MG Burrard's 2nd Bde: 1/2nd Foot Guards, 1/3rd Foot Guards. Prince William's 8th Bde: 1/5th, 2/5th, 2/35th Foot; 11th LDR (2 sqns). MG Coote's 3rd Bde 2nd, 27th, 29th, 85th Foot. MG Don's 5th Bde: 1/7th, 2/17th, 1/40th, 2/40th Foot, 11th LDR (2 sqns): MG Moore's 4th Bde: 2/1st, 25th, 49th, 79th, 92nd Foot. MG Lord Cavan's 6th Bde: 1/20th, 2/20th, 63rd Foot. MG Lord Chatham's 7th Bde: 4th and 31st Foot (3 bns). Col Macdonald's Reserve: 23rd and 55th Foot; combined grens (1 bn); combined light coys (1 bn), 18th LDR (2 sqns).

British total 17,000 men.

British losses 200 killed, wounded and missing.

Sources Fortescue, James, Clowes, Michaelovski-Danielevski.

IN Tortona, 5 August – 11 September 1799, siege and capture

A small fortress in northwestern Italy, just southeast of the junction of Autostrada A7/E62 and A21/E70, 22 km east of Alessandria on the River Tanaro.

An Austrian victory over the French.

(Last action – Novi, 15 August; next action – Fossano, 16 September.)

French Garrison GdB Gast commanding: 63e DBdeLi (3e Bn).

French total 1,200 men, 75 guns.

French losses 100 killed or died of wounds or sickness. After marching out with honours of war, the rest laid down their weapons and were free to go. The battalion colour was taken but returned by FM Count Suvorov out of respect for their gallant defence.

Austrian Forces FML Count Alcaine commanding: IRs Allvintzy Nr 19, Frelich Nr 28 (3 bns each), De Ligne Nr 30 (1st Bn), Kray Nr 34 (3 bns); DragRs EH Johann Nr 3, Württemberg Nr 8 (6 sqns each); HusR vacant Nr 5 (8 sqns).

Austrian total ca 11,000 men.

Austrian losses Not exactly known but very light.

Comment This was one of the fruits of the Allied victory at Novi on 15 August.

Sources Bodart, Wrede.

IN Fossano, 16 September 1799, skirmish

A small town in northwestern Italy, on Route 231, 65 km south of Turin.

A French victory over the Austrians.

(Last action – Tortona, 11 September; next action – Savigliano, 18 September.)

French Forces GdD Grenier commanding: 17e DBdeLé (2 bn); 24e, 106e DBdeLi (3 bns each); 2e Légion Helvetique (1 bn); 1ère Légion Polonaise (1 bn); cavalry (4 sqns); 1 x FAB.

French total 8,000 men.

French losses ca 200 killed, wounded and missing.

Austrian Forces GM Baron von Gottesheim commanding: IRs vacant Huff Nr 8, Allvintzy Nr 19, Frelich Nr 28, S Gyulai Nr 32, Nádasdy Nr 39, Mittrowsky Nr 40 (3 bns each). Gren Bns Paar, Neny, Weissenwolf. LtI Bn Otto Nr 7, DragR Württemberg Nr 8 (6 sqns).

Austrian total ca 5,000 men.

Austrian losses 300 killed and wounded, 700 captured.

Sources Bodart, Wrede.

IN Savigliano, 18 September 1799, clash

A village in northwestern Italy, on the River Maira, about 50 km south of Turin on Route 20.

An Austrian victory over the French.

(Last action – Fossano, 16 September; next action – Bracco, 13 October.)

French Forces GdD Grenier commanding: 17e, 24e, 106e DBdeLi (3 bns each).

French total 7,500 men.

French losses 2,000 killed, wounded and missing, 2 guns.

Austrian Forces GdK Baron von Melas commanding: IRs Deutschmeister Nr 4 (3 bns); vacant Huff Nr 8 (2 bns); Kheul Nr 10, Reisky Nr 13, Klebek Nr 14 (3 bns each); Stuart Nr 18 (2 bns); Fürstenberg Nr 36 (1st and 2nd Bns), Nádasdy Nr 39 (3 bns); Gren Bns Paar, Stentsch, Weber, Soudain, Mercandin.

Austrian total ca 20,000 men.

Austrian losses 400 killed, wounded and missing.

Sources Bodart, Wrede.

UR Mannheim, 18 September 1799, clash

A city in southwestern Germany, just east of the confluence of the Rivers Rhine and Neckar, about 18 km northwest of Heidelberg.

An Austrian victory over the French.

(Last action - Stockach, 25/26 March; next action - Philippsburg, 16 November.)

French Forces, GdD Müller commanding part of the Army of the Rhine: see OOB for Stockach, 25/26 March.

French total 18,000 men.

French losses 1,600 killed and wounded, 1,900 captured, 23 guns, 20 vehicles, 2 colours.

Austrian Forces FM Archduke Charles commanding: IRs EH Ferdinand Nr 2, EH Carl Nr 3 (3 bns each); Schröder Nr 7 (2 coys); Wallis Nr 29 (3 bns). Grenadier Bns Rüffer, Sebottendorf, Fitz-Gibbons, Tegetthof, Bojakowsky. KürRs Kaiser Nr 1, Lothringen Nr 7 (6 sqns each); DragRs Anspach Nr 11, Kinsky Nr 12 (6 sqns each); HusR Vécsey Nr 4 (6 sqns). GzIRs Broder Nr 7 (1st & 2nd Bns); Deutsch-Banater Nr 12 (1st Bn).

Austrian total ca 18,000 men.

Austrian losses 1,300 killed, wounded and missing.

Sources Bodart, Wrede.

NL Bergen, 19 September 1799, battle

A village in northwestern Holland, 6 km northwest of Alkmaar and 6 km from the North Sea coast.

A Franco-Batavian victory over the Anglo-Russians.

(Last action - Zyper-Sluis, 10 September; next action - Egmond-aan-Zee, 2 October.)

Franco-Batavian Forces GdD Brune commanding: **Batavian Troops** GdD Daendels: 1st DBdeLi (3 bns); 3rd DBdeLi (1 bn); 4th DBdeLi (2 bns); 5th DBdeLi (3 bns); Jagers (1st and 2nd Bns); 2nd CavR (2 sqns); DragR (1 sqn); 1 x HAB, 3 x FAB. GdD Dumonceau: 2nd and 6th DBdeLi (3 bns each); 7th DBdeLi (2 bns); Jagers (3rd and 4th Bns); 1st CavR (4 sqns); 2nd CavR (2 sqns); HusR (4 sqns); 1 x HAB; 2 x FAB. **French Troops** the divisions of Vandamme, Boudet, Gouvion, St Cyr and Barbou: 22e and 42e DBdeLi (3 bns each); 48e DBdeLi (1 bn and 3 gren coys); 49e DBdeLi (3 bns); 51e DBdeLi (1 bn); 54e DBdeLi (3 bns); 60e DBdeLi (1 bn); 72e DBdeLi (2 bns); 90e DBdeLi (3 bns); 98e DBdeLi (2 bns); 10e DragR, 4e ChàCh (4 sqns each); 5e ChàCh (1 sqn); 16e ChàCh (4 sqns); 5 x HAB, 2 x FAB.

Franco-Batavian total ca 22,000 men.

Franco-Batavian losses 1,000 killed and wounded, 2,000 captured.

Anglo-Russian Forces FM the Duke of York commanding. **Right Hand Column (Russians)** LG Hermann: Gren Bn Timothejeff, Gren Bn Strick (1 bn each); GrenBn Scherebzoff, GrenR Benkendorff (2 bns each); MuskRs Fersen, Arbenjeff (2 bns each); Jägers (1 bn). LeibHusR (4 sqns). MG Manners' 9th Bde: 1 and 2/9th; 56th Foot, 7th LDR (2 sqns). **Second Column** LG David Dundas: 2nd Bde: MG D'Oyley: 3/1st Foot Guards, Guard's Gren Bn. MG Burrard 1/2nd Foot Guards, 1/3rd Foot Guards. Prince William's 8th Bde - 1/5th, 2/5th, 2/35th, 11th LDR (2 sqns). **Third Column** LG Pulteney: 3rd Bde MG Coote - 2nd, 27th, 29th, 85th Foot. 5th Bde MG Don: 1/7th, 2/17th, 1/40th, 2/40th; 11th LDR (2 sqns). **4th Column** Gen Abercromby: 4th Bde MG Moore: 2/1st, 25th, 49th, 79th, 92nd Foot. The following troops were not engaged: 6th Brigade MG Lord Cavan - 1/20th, 2/20th, 63rd Foot. 7th Bde MG Lord Chatham - 4th and 31st Foot (3 bns). Reserve, Col Macdonald 23rd and 55th Foot; Combined grens (1 bn), combined light coys (1 bn); 18th LDR (2 sqns) and the garrison of den Helder (1/35th and 69th Foot).

Anglo-Russian total 23,000 men.

Anglo-Russian losses British: 6 officers, 127 men killed; 44 officers, 397 men wounded; 840 men captured and missing. Russian: Gen Herrmann captured; GL Scherebzoff killed. 1 colour each of regiments Benkendorff and Arbenjeff captured; 43 officers, 1,749 men killed and missing, 50 officers, 1,225 men wounded.

Comment The Allied assault had been timed to start

at 6.00 am but the Russians set off at 2.00 am alone and were bloodily repulsed. Lack of Allied communication seems to have been the fault.

Sources Fortescue, James, Clowes, Michaelovski-Danielevski.

CH Zürich, 25/26 September 1799, second battle

A city in northern Switzerland, at the northern end of Lake Zürich and on the River Limmat.

A French victory over the Russians.

(Last action – Amsteg, 14–16 August; next action – Linth River, 25/26 September.)

French Forces GdD Massena commanding **The Army of the Danube** 5th Division GdD Lorges GdB Gazan, GdB Bontemps: 10e DBdeLé; 37e, 57e, 102e DBdeLi (3 bns each); 1ère DBde Helvetique (1 bn); Chass Helvetique (2 sqns); 9e HusR, 13e DragR (4 sqns each). 6th Division GdD Menard; GdB Quetard, GdB Heudelet: 1ère DBdeLé (2 bns); 2e, 46e DBdeLi (3 bns each); 17e DBdeLi (1 bn); 5e ChàCh (4 sqns). 7th Division GdD Klein GdB Goulus, GdB Roget: 103e DBdeLi (3 bns); 2e DBde Helvetique (1 bn); 7e HusR (3 sqns); 8e HusR (4 sqns); 23e ChàCh (4 sqns); 2e DragR (4 sqns); 102e DBdeLi (2 bns). GdB Humbert's Grenadier Reserve (3,500 men). Reserve Artillery Park (58 guns, 798 men). 8th Division GdD Mortier; GdB Bastout, GdB Nouvion, GdB Walther: 14e DBdeLé, 1ère DBdeLi, 23e DBdeLi (3 bns each); 1ère DBde Helvetique (1 bn); 4e DBde Helvetique (1/2 bn); 4e HusR (3 sqns). 4th Division GdD Mortier; GdB Drouet, GdB Brunet: 50e, 53e, 100e, 108e DBdeLi (3 bns each); 1er DragR (2 sqns); 8e ChàCh (4 sqns).

French total 33,500 men.

French losses ca 4,000 killed, wounded and missing.

Russian Forces LG Korsakov commanding: **GL Prince Gortschakoff** MuskR Tutschkoff (2 bns); Combined Gren Bns Selechoff, Rachmanoff, Potapoff. JgRs Titov Nr 5 (2 bns) Fok Nr 6 (1 bn); HusR Lykoschin (10 sqns); Ural Cossack Pulk Borodin (4 sqns); 10 Reserve Artillery guns. **Total** 6,214 men. GM Essen III: MuskR Essen III (2 bns); GrenR Sacken I (1 bn); DragR Schepeleff (1 sqn); Jägers (1 coys each from 5th and 6th Regts). **Total** ca 1,380 men. 6 Reserve Artillery guns. **LG Durasoff*; GM Markoff** Combined Gren Bn Treublut (1 bn); Ural Cossack Pulk Misinoff (3 sqns, 2 guns); MuskR Markoff (2 bns, 2 guns); Combined Gren Bn Schkapski (1 bn, 2 guns). **Total** ca 3,000 men. **The garrison of Zürich GM Schepeleff** DragR Schepeleff (4 sqns); 6 guns. On outpost duty along the River Limmat: GM Puschtschin: MuskR Durasoff (2 bns); MuskR Puschtschin (2 bns); Don Cossack Pulk Astachoff (4 sqns, 6 guns); Baranowski's TartarR (10 sqns, 8 guns); Don Cossack Pulk Kumtschatski (4 sqns). **Total ca 4,840 men. The Reserve LG Sacken** MuskRs Kosloff, Prczibyschewski, Ismailoff (2 bns each) **Total** ca 4,171 men.

Russian grand total 19,605* men.

Russian losses 2,800 killed, 3,200 wounded and captured, 2,000 unwounded captured, 26 guns, 407 vehicles, all baggage, 10 colours. Gens Sacken, Sergäjeff captured.

* = Durasoff's corps remained on the River Limmat during the action and was not involved.

Comment The Russian line cavalry and various other regiments were detached from the main body during the battle but KürR Woinoff came up in time to hold up the French pursuit late on 26 September. Estimates of the Russian losses vary from 3,000 – 8,000. No exact data is available except that 58 officers were killed, 54 wounded and captured, 60 missing. Another source states that 145 Russian officers were captured. Jomini claimed to have taken '100 guns'. As the entire force had only 110 guns (regimental and field) and as 28 were on the Rhine to the north, this claim is a wild over-estimation. The colours lost were: Durasoff – 3, Tutschkoff – 2, Markoff – 2, Prczibyschewski – 1, Ismailoff – 1, Rasumowski (in Uznach) – 1.

Sources Bodart, Michaelovski-Danielevski.

CH Linth River, 25–26 September 1799, clashes

A river in north-central Switzerland running northwest from the western end of Lake Walen into the southeastern end of Lake Zürich, also known as Schänis, Wesen.

French victories over the Austro-Russians.

(Last action – Zürich 25/26 September; next action – Näfels and Glarus, 25/26 September.)

French Forces. GdD Soult commanding the 3rd Division, Army of the Danube: GdB Mainoni, GdB Laval: 25e DBdeLé, 36e, 44e, 94e DBdeLi (3 bns each); 10e ChàCh (5 sqns); 2 x FAB. Col Lochet 94e DBdeLi (1 bn).

French total 11,000 men.

French losses ca 1,100 killed, wounded and missing.

Austrian Forces FML Hotze's Corps: FML Petrasch between Wesen and Uznach: IRs Bender Nr 41, Gemmingen Nr 21, Stein Nr 50 (3 bns each); vacant Nr 60 (2 bns); GzHusR (10 sqns). From Uznach to Meilen: FML Prince von Württemberg: DragR Waldeck Nr 7 (6 sqns); Swiss Bns Roverey, Bachmann (1 bn each). The flotilla on Lake Zürich: Obst Williams, 19 boats, 13 guns, 211 crew. **Russian Forces** at Rapperswyl MG Titoff with IR Rasumowski (2 bns).

Austro-Russian total ca 13,000 men.

Austrian losses Austrians and Swiss: killed and wounded unknown, 3,500 captured, 20 guns, 33 ammunition waggons, large quantities of stores, the colour of 2nd Bn IR Bender, 1 Swiss colour, the flotilla.

Russian losses 195 killed, 39 missing, 1 colour. Hotze and Obst Plunket killed.

Comment Soult's bold offensive easily pierced the thinly-held line of the River Linth; the Austrians were completely surprised. Hotze and Obst Plunket (his chief of staff) were killed early on 25 September and this demoralized the Austrians. They withdrew northeast into the upper Rhine valley; the Russians fell back north to Konstanz. This French success blocked off Suvorov's escape route to the Lake Constance.

Sources Bodart, Wrede; Michaelovsky-Danielevski.

CH Näfels and Glarus, 25/26 September 1799, clashes

Two towns in central northern Switzerland, in the valley of the Linth River on Route 17 running up to the western end of Lake Walen.

A French victory over the Austrians.

(Last action – Linth River, 25/26 September; next action – St Gotthard, 23–27 September.)

French Forces GdB Molitor (of Lecourbe's 2nd Division) commanding: 76e and 84e DBdeLi (3 bns each) plus one other battalion.

French total 7 bns, 6,000 men.

French losses Killed and wounded unknown, 1 bn of 76e DBde was captured in the Sernft valley (ca 900 men); this Demibrigade lost the colours of 1er and 2e Bns here.

Austrian Forces GM Baron Jellačič commanding part of FML Baron Lincken's corps: IRs Kaiser Nr 1 (1 bn), Kaunitz Nr 20 (2 bns); GzIR Peterwardeiner Nr 9 (2nd, 3rd, 4th Bns); GzIR Broder Nr 7 (1st Bn); LtI Bn Strozzi Nr 1 (1 bn); DragR Modena Nr 5 (3 sqns).

Austrian total ca 7,500 men.

Austrian losses Killed and wounded unknown, 500 captured.

Comment Austrian attempts to cross to the west bank of the Linth on 25 September were repulsed. Next day, hearing of Hotze's death and Petrasch's defeat on Lake Zürich, Jellačič withdrew along Lake Walen eastwards completely over the upper Rhine at Maienfeld.

Sources Bodart, Wrede, Charrié, Michaelovski-Danielevski.

CH St Gotthard, 23–27 September 1799, skirmishes

A mountain pass in southern Switzerland through which Route 2 passes and under which Motorway N2/E35 now runs from Andermatt in the north to Bellinzona in the southeast, also known as Teufelsbrücke.

An Austro-Russian victory over the French.

(Last action – Näfels and Glarus, 25/26 September; next action – Glarus and Schwanden, 27–29 September.)

French Forces GdD Lecourbe commanding the 3rd Division, Army of the Danube: GdB Gudin: 38e DBdeLi (2 bns); 67e DBdeLi (2 bns); 76e DBdeLi (3 bns); 109e DBdeLi (3 bns). GdB Loison: 36e DBdeLi (2 bns); 109e DBdeLi (3 bns).

French total 15,000 men (of whom 6,000 were actually engaged).

French losses 2,000 killed, wounded and missing, 10 guns, which were thrown into the River Reuss.

Austro-Russian Forces FM Prince Suvorov commanding: **Austrian Troops** IR Wallis Nr 11 (1st and 2nd Bns); LtI Bns Trautenberg Nr 6, Munkátsy Nr 13, Rohen Nr 14, Le Loup Jägers (1 bn each); GzIR Warasdiner-St Georger Nr 6 (2nd Bn). **Total** 4,500 men. **Losses** killed and wounded unknown, 200 captured. **Russian Troops** FM Prince Suvorov commanding: Avantgarde Prince Bagration: JgRs Bagration Nr 5, Miller Nr 6 (4 bns, 3 guns); Combined Gren Bns Lomonosoff, Dendrygin, Sanajeff, Kalemin (4 bns, 2 guns). Division of LG Schwiekowski: GrenR Rosenberg; MuskRs Schwiekowski, Baranowski, Kamenski (8 bns, 6 guns); Division of LG Förster: MuskRs Förster, Tyrtoff, Miloradovitch, Welezki (8 bns, 6 guns). Division of LG Rosenberg: JgR Kaschkin, MuskRs Rehbinder, Mansuroff, Fertsch (8 bns, 6 guns); 2 reserve guns. **Russian totals** 32 bns, 25 guns, 200 cossacks, c16,000 men. **Austrian Troops** Obst Strauch commanding: IR Neugebauer Nr 46 (1 bn); GzIR Deutsch-Banater Nr 12 (1st Bn). **Total** (actually in the combat) 6,700 men.

Austro-Russian losses 2,000 killed, wounded and missing.

Comment The Russians lost most men forcing the bridge over the River Reuss at Teufelsbrücke.

Sources Bodart, Wrede, Günther, Michaelovski-Danielevski.

CH Glarus and Schwanden, 27–29 September 1799, clash

Two towns in central northern Switzerland, on Route 17 in the Linth River valley, south of Lake Walensee.

A French victory over the Austrians.

(Last action – St Gotthard, 23–27 September; next action – Klöntal 30 September – 1 October.)

French Forces GdB Molitor (of Lecourbe's 2nd Division) commanding: 76e DBdeLi (2 bns); 84e DBdeLi (3 bns) plus 44e DBdeLi (2 bns) from Soult's 3rd Division. On 28 September 2e Bn, 25e DBdeLi arrived to support him.

French total ca 8,000 men.

French losses Not known exactly but light.

Austrian Forces FML Baron Lincken GM Baron Simbschen: IRs Kaiser Nr 1 (2 bn), Kaunitz Nr 20, vacant Nr 62; GzIR Peterwardeiner Nr 9 (1 bn each).

Austrian total ca 5,000 men.

Austrian losses Killed and wounded unknown, 300 captured.

Comment Molitor's victory over Jellačič on 25 September left him free to turn south to fight Lincken when he appeared out of the Sernft valley next day. Lincken's attitude was timid. Although Suvorov's column was now fighting its painful way northeast through the Muotta valley, looking for help from him to escape from the encircling French, Lincken did not know of the Russians' presence. Hearing of Jellačič's defeat, Lincken gave up the ghost and withdrew southeast to Ilanz in the valley of the upper Rhine in Graubünden. The French had achieved their strategic aim of preventing the junction of the Allied forces.

Sources Bodart, Wrede, Michaelovski-Danielevski.

IM Rome, 29 September 1799, capitulation

Capital city of modern Italy, in the centre of the peninsula.

An Anglo-Neapolitan victory over the French.

(Last action – Gaëta, 1 August; next action – Ancona, 13 November.)

French Garrison GdB Garnier commanding: exact details not known.

French total 4,500 men.

French losses None. The various French garrisons in Naples were returned to France, with their weapons and baggage, on British ships.

Anglo-Neapolitan Forces Neapolitan Troops LG Bourcard commanding: exact details not known.

Neapolitan total 4,000 men.

Neapolitan losses None.

British Forces Captain Louis commanding HMS *Minotaur.* Louis rowed up the Tiber in his barge and hoisted the British colours over the Capitol.

Comment The liberation of central Italy was in great part due to British naval power.

Sources Bodart, James, Clowes.

CH Klöntal, 30 September – 1 October 1799, clash

A valley and lake in central northern Switzerland, between the Pragel Pass in the southwest and the town of Netstall on Route 17 in the valley of the River Linth in the east.

An Austro-Russian victory over the French.

(Last action – Glarus and Schwanden, 27–29 September; next action – Muottental, 30 September – 1 October.)

French Forces GdB Molitor (of Lecourbe's 2nd Division) commanding: 76e DBdeLi (2 bns); 84e DBdeLi (3 bns) plus 25e DBdeLi (2e Bn) and 44e DBdeLi (2 bns) of Gazan's 3rd Division.

French total ca 6,500 men.

French losses ca 1,000 killed and wounded, 1,020 captured, 5 guns.

Austrian Forces GM Baron Auffenberg (of FML Baron Lincker's corps) commanding: IRs Brechainville Nr 25 (1 bn), Kerpen Nr 49 (3 bns); GzIR Gradiskaner Nr 8 (1 bn); DragR Modena Nr 5 (3 sqns); 1 Cossack sotnia (100 men).

Austrian total ca 2,100 men.

Austrian losses Not exactly known but light.

Russian Forces Prince Bagration commanding FM Suvorov's Avantgarde: JgRs Bagration Nr 5, Miller Nr

6 (2 bns each); combined Gren Bns Lomonosoff, Dendrygin, Sanajeff, Kalemin (1 bn each). Division of LG Schwiekowski: GrenR Rosenberg; MuskRs Schwiekowski, Baranowski, Kamenski (2 bns each); two dismounted Cossack Pulks.

Russian total 5,900 men.

Russian losses Not exactly known but light.

Comment The Russians knew that they were alone and in a mountainous trap; ragged, hungry, frozen, they fought with desperation and broke through into the Linth valley, pushing north onto Näfels.

Sources Bodart, Wrede, Michaelovski-Danielevski.

CH Muottental, 30 September–1 October 1799, clash

A valley in northern central Switzerland (in which runs the River Muotta) from the heights of the Alplerhorn in the southeast, to Schwyz and Brunnen on Lake Lucerne (Vierwaldstätter See) in the west.

A Russian victory over the French.

(Last action – Klöntal; 30 September – 1 October; next action – Netstall and Näfels, 1 October.)

French Forces GdD Massena commanding part of the Army of the Danube: GdD Gazan's 3rd Division: 25e DBdeLi (2 bns); 36e DBdeLi (3 bns); 94e DBdeLi (3 bns). GdD Mortier's 4th Division: 50e DBdeLi (3 bns); 53e and 100e DBdeLi (2 bns each); 108e DBdeLi (3 bns); 1er DragR (2 sqns); 8e ChàCh (4 sqns). From Lecourbe's 2nd Division: 67e DBdeLi (2 bns).

French total 1st Day – 8,000; 2nd Day – 15,000.

French losses 1st Day – 500 killed, 1,000 wounded, 100 drowned, 70 captured, 1 howitzer. 2nd Day – ca 1,000 killed and wounded, 1,000 captured, 5 guns.

Russian Forces LG Rosenberg commanding FM Suvorov's rearguard: Avantgarde MuskR Rehbinder (2 bns); JgR Kaschkin (2 bns). Cossack Pulks Kurnakoff, Denisoff*, Grekoff*, Posdjäjeff. Main Body: MuskRs Förster, Milarodowitsch, Welezki, Mansuroff*, Fertsch*, Tyrtoff* (2 bns each).

Russian total 1st Day – 4,000; 2nd Day – 7,000.

Russian losses 1st Day 'light'; 2nd Day – no information available.

Comment Suvorov, trapped in the Muotta valley, instructed Rosenberg to hold off the French at all costs while Bagration broke out to the east through the Klöntal. Despite the French superiority in numbers and in artillery (Suvorov's had been abandoned over the mountainous withdrawal) repeated bayonet charges threw them back. The captured guns were spiked and buried.

Sources Michaelovski-Danielevski, Bodart.

* = dismounted.

CH Netstall and Näfels, 1 October 1799, clash

Two villages in central northern Switzerland, on Route 17 in the valley of the River Linth, between Lake Walensee in the north and Glarus in the south.

An Austro-Russian victory over the French.

(Last action – Muottental, 30 September – 1 October; next action – Schwanden, 5 October.)

French Forces GdB Molitor's brigade of Lecourbe's 2nd Division: initially six unidentified battalions, two of whom lost colours. Later joined by GdD Gazan's (ex Soult's) 3rd Division: 25e, 36e, 44e, 94e DBdeLi, 10e ChàCh; the 3e DBde Helvetique was also involved.

French total Initially 3,000 men and 7 guns, later ca 10,000 men.

French losses 140 killed, 200 wounded, 406 captured, 2 guns, 2 colours (unidentified).

Austro-Russian Forces Prince Bagration commanding Suvorov's Avantgarde: JgRs Bagration and Miller (2 bns each); combined Gren Bns Lomonosoff, Dendrygin, Sanajeff, Kalemin (1 bn each); Austrian IR Kerpen Nr 49 (4 coys).

Austro-Russian total 5,800 men.

Austro-Russian losses Not exactly known; the French alleged 400 killed, 1,700 wounded, 200 captured.

Comment With this surprise night attack, Suvorov broke out of the Muottental trap into the Linth River valley. Molitor and Gazan were pushed back north to Näfels. That evening Suvorov ordered LG Rosenberg to abandon the Muottental and join him. Rosenberg fooled Massena into allowing him a 12-hour head start in his withdrawal over the difficult Pragel Pass. He joined Suvorov on 4 October and the battered Russian army withdrew south.

Sources Bodart, Wrede, Michaelovski-Danielevski.

NL Egmond-aan-Zee, 2 October 1799, battle

A village in the northwestern Dutch province of Noord-Holland; on the North Sea coast, 11 km west of Alkmaar.

An Anglo-Russian victory over the Franco-Batavians.

(Last action – Bergen, 19 September; next action – Castricum, 6 October.)

Franco-Batavian Forces GdD Brune commanding: As for Bergen, 19 September.

Franco-Batavian total 20,000 men.

Franco-Batavian losses 3,000 killed, wounded and missing, 7 guns.

Anglo-Russian Forces FM the Duke of York commanding: **Russians** LG Essen: 1st Column MG Emme: Jägers (1 coy); pioniers (50 men); combined Gren Bns Mitiuschin, Osipoff, Ogarjeff (1 bn each); 6 guns. MG Arbenjeff: GrenR Emme, GrenR Scherebzoff (2 bns each), 7 guns. 2nd Column Col Gladki: pioniers (25 men); GrenR Benkendorff (2 bns); Gren Bn Timothejeff (2 coys), 3 guns. 3rd Column GM Sedmorazki: pioniers (50 men); MuskR Sedmorazki (2 bns); combined Gren Bn Erikson (1 bn) Gren Bn Timothejeff (2 coys); 7 guns.

Russian total ca 9,000 men.

Russian losses 2 officers, 77 men killed; 16 officers, 372 men wounded.

British Forces The Duke of York commanding: as for Bergen, 19 September.

British total 21,000 men.

British losses 1,300 killed and wounded, 200 captured.

Sources Fortescue, Clowes, James, Michaelovski-Danielevski.

CH Schwanden, 5 October 1799, clash

A village in northern central Switzerland, on Route 17 in the valley of the River Linth at the confluence with the Sernft stream, 6 km south of Glarus.

A Russian victory over the French.

(Last action – Netstall and Näfels, 1 October; this was the last action in Suvorov's Swiss campaign.)

French Forces GdB Molitor's brigade of Lecourbe's 2nd Division: 76eDBdeLi (2 bns); 84e DBdeLi (3 bns) plus part of Gazan's 3rd Division: 25e DBdeLi (2e Bn); 44e DBdeLi (2 bns); 6 guns.

French total ca 5,000 men.

French losses Not known.

Russian Forces Prince Bagration commanding Suvorov's Avantgarde (now acting as rearguard): JgRs Bagration and Miller (2 bns each); combined Gren Bns Lemonosoff, Dendrygin, Sanajeff, Kalemin (1 bn each).

Russian total 1,800 men. The MuskR Welezki (2 bns) joined in later.

Russian losses Not known.

Comment The Russians firmly held off all French assaults and their army escaped over the Panixer pass southwards into the Rhine valley at Janz and thence to Chur; subsequently back to Russia. Of the 20,000 men who entered Switzerland, 15,000 reached Janz; all guns had been lost as had all the baggage. About 661 men had been killed, 1,317 wounded.

Sources Bodart; Michaelovski-Danielevski.

NL Castricum, 6 October 1799, battle

A village in the northwestern Dutch province of Noord-Holland, 12 km southwest of Alkmaar and 4 km inland from the North Sea coast.

A Franco-Batavian victory over the Anglo-Russians.

(Last action – Egmond-aan-Zee, 2 October; next action – Alkmaar, 18 October.)

Franco-Batavian Forces GdD Brune commanding: As for Bergen, 19 September.

Franco-Batavian total 24,000 men.

Franco-Batavian losses French: 1,100 killed and wounded, 42 captured. Batavians: 65 killed and wounded, 177 captured.

Anglo-Russian Forces FM the Duke of York commanding: **Russians** LG Essen: GrenR Benckendorff (2 bns); GrenR Emme (2 bns); MuskR Sedmorazki, JgR Sutgoff (2 bns); Combined Gren Bns Timothejeff, Strick, Osipoff, Ogarjeff, Erikson, Mitiuschin; pioniers (1 coy); Ural Cossacks (2 sqns).

Russian total ca 11,000 men.

Russian losses 9 officers, 374 men killed and missing; 26 officers, 709 men wounded, 8 guns taken **British Troops** As for Bergen, 19 September.

British total 21,000 men.

British losses 4 officers, 91 men killed; 36 officers, 696 men wounded, 19 officers, 593 men missing. Most losses were in Chatham's brigade.

Sources Fortescue, James. Clowes, Michaelovski-Danielevski.

IN Bracco, 13 October 1799, skirmish

A small village in northwestern Italy, in the coastal hills of the Gulf of Genoa, on Route 1 about 60 km east of Genoa.

A French victory over the Austrians.

(Last action – Savigliano, 18 September; next action – Novi, 24 October.)

French Forces GdD Watrin commanding. Exact details not known; probably: 12e and 30e DBdeLi; 62e and 78e DbdeLi.

French total 7,000 men.

French losses 100 killed, wounded and missing.

Austrian Forces GM Count Klenau commanding. Exact details not known.

Austrian total 5,000 men.

Austrian losses 1,200 men, mostly captured.

Sources Bodart, Wrede.

NL Alkmaar, 18 October 1799, convention

A town in the northwestern Dutch province of Noord-Holland, at the junction of Motorway A9 with Routes N9 and N242.

A Franco-Batavian victory over the Anglo-Russians.

(Last action – Castricum, 6 October; this was the last event in the campaign in the Netherlands in 1799.)

Comment The Duke of York agreed to evacuate Holland by 30 November, to restore the batteries of den Helder to their state as at the point of the Allied invasion and to hand back 8,000 Franco-Batavian prisoners of war.

Sources Fortescue, James, Clowes, Michaelovsi-Danielevski.

IN Novi, 24 October 1799, 1st clash

A village in northwestern Italy, 22 km southeast of Alessandria on the River Tanaro.

A French victory over the Austrians.

(Last action – Bracco, 13 October; next action – Centallo, 31 October.)

French Forces GdD Gouvion St Cyr commanding: exact details not known but including: 18e, 21e, 63e DBdeLi (6 bns). GdD Dombrowski, GdB Jablonowski: 3e DBdeLé (1 bn); 17e DBdeLé (2 coys); 55e DBdeLi (1 bn), 106e DBdeLi (3 bns); 1ère Légion Polonaise (5 bns), Polish CavR (2 sqns).

French total ca 12,000 men.

French losses 400 killed and wounded, 800 captured.

Austrian Forces GM von Karaczay commanding: IRs Frelich Nr 28 (3 bns), Kray Nr 34 (2nd Bn and grenadiers); DragR Württemberg Nr 8 (6 sqns); 1 x FAB.

Austrian total ca 5,000 men.

Austrian losses 300 killed and wounded, 1,000 captured, 4 guns.

Sources Bodart, Wrede.

IN Centallo, 31 October 1799, skirmish

A village in northwestern Italy, on Route 20 between Turin and Cuneo.

An Austrian victory over the French.

(Last action – Novi, 24 October; next action – Genola, 4 November.)

French Forces GdD Grenier commanding: 17e DBdeLé (2 bns); 24e, 106e DBdeLi (3 bns each); 2e Légion Helvetique; 1ère Légion Polonaise (1 bn each); cavalry (4 sqns); 1 x FAB.

French total 7,000 men.

French losses 1,000 killed, wounded and missing, 4 guns.

Austrian Forces GdK Baron von Melas commanding: IRs Reisky Nr 13, Terzy Nr 16 (3 bns each), Stuart Nr 18 (2 bns), Allvintzy Nr 19 (1st and 2nd Bns), EH Ferdinand Nr 23, Nádasdy Nr 39 (3 bns each); Gren Bns Hohenfeld, Weissenwolf, DragRs EH Johann Nr 3, Württemberg Nr 8 (6 sqns each); HusR EH Joseph Nr 2 (8 sqns).

Austrian total 15,000* men.

Austrian losses ca 200 killed, wounded and missing.

* = Obviously only part were engaged; exact details not known.

Sources Bodart, Wrede.

IN Genola, 4 November 1799, battle

A village in northwestern Italy, just east of Route 20, between Turin and Cuneo.

An Austrian victory over the French.

(Last action – Centallo, 31 October; next action – Novi, 6 November.)

French Forces GdD Championnet commanding the Army of Italy: exact details not known; see OOB for Novi, 15 August.

French total 15,000 men.

French losses 3,400 killed and wounded, 4,200 captured, 5 guns.

Austrian Forces GdK Baron von Melas commanding: IRs Reisky Nr 13, Terzy Nr 16 (3 bns each), Stuart Nr 18 (2 bns), Allvintzy Nr 19 (1st and 2nd Bns), EH Ferdinand Nr 23, Sztáray Nr 33, Nádasdy Nr 39 (3 bns each); Gren Bns Hohenfeld, Weissenwolf, DragRs EH Johann Nr 3, Württemberg Nr 8 (6 sqns each); HusR EH Joseph Nr 2 (8 sqns).

Austrian total 29,000 men.

Austrian losses 2,150 killed and wounded, 250

captured GM von Adorjan killed.
Sources Bodart, Wrede, Michaelovski-Danielevski.

IN Novi, 6 November 1799, 2nd clash
A village in northwestern Italy, 22 km southeast of Alessandria on the River Tanaro.
A French victory over the Austrians.
(Last action – Genola, 4 November; next action – Mondovi, 13 November.)
French Forces GdD Gouvion St Cyr commanding: exact details not known but including: GdB Jablonowski: 3e DBdeLé (1 bn); 17e DBdeLi (1 bn); 55e DBdeLi (1 bn), 106e DBdeLi (3 bns), GdD Dombrowski 1st Polish Legion [Gren Bn, Chass Bn, 3 x Fus Bns, CavR (2 sqns)].
French total ca 11,000 men.
French losses ca 400 killed, wounded and missing.
Austrian Forces FML Baron von Kray commanding: IRs Klebek Nr 14, Frelich Nr 28 (3 bns each); IR Belgiojoso Nr 44 (1 coy); Gren Bn Morzin, Weber, Stentsch, Mercandin. HusR vacant Nr 5 (8 sqns); JzPf Bussy (4 sqns).
Austrian total ca 12,000 men.
Austrian losses ca 1,000 men killed, wounded and missing, 5 guns.
Sources Bodart, Wrede.

IN Mondovi, 13 November 1799, skirmish
A village in northwestern Italy at the crossing of Route 28 over the River Ellera, about 27 km east of Cuneo.
An Austrian victory over the French.
(Last action – Novi, 6 November; next action – Torriglia, 16 November.)
French Forces GdD Championnet commanding part of the Army of Italy: exact details not known, see OOB for Novi, 15 August.
French total 9,000 men.
French losses 500 killed, wounded and missing.
Austrian Forces GdK Baron von Melas commanding: IRs Reisky Nr 13, Terzy Nr 16 (3 bns each); Stuart Nr 18 (2 bns); Allvintzy Nr 19 (1st and 2nd Bns); EH Ferdinand Nr 23, Sztáray Nr 33, Nádasdy Nr 39 (3 bns each); Gren Bns Hohenfeld, Weissenwolf. DragRs EH Johann Nr 3, Württemberg Nr 8 (6 sqns each); HusR EH Joseph Nr 2 (8 sqns).
Austrian total 14,000 men.
Austrian losses ca 500 men killed, wounded and missing.
Sources Bodart, Wrede.

IM Ancona, 14 October – 13 November 1799, siege and capture
A fortress-port on the central Italian Adriatic coast, on Route 16, 200 km northeast of Rome.
An Austro-Russo-Turkish victory over the French.
(Last action – Rome, 29 September; this was the last action of the campaign.)
French Garrison GdB Monnier commanding: 15e Pv DBdeLi (2 bns); 43e DBdeLi (1er and 3e Bns).
French total 2,800 men and about 1,000 local citizenry.
French losses ca 1,000 killed and wounded, 585 guns; the colours of the 15e Pv and 43e DBdes. 10 ships including: *Laharpe*, *Beyrand*, *Stengel*, *Rivoli*, *Cibelle* and *La Hoche*. The garrison marched out with honours of war and were allowed free passage to France on condition that they would not fight against the Allies until exchanged.
Austrian Forces FML Frelich commanding. IRs vacant Hohenlohe Nr 17 (3 bns); Strassoldo Nr 27 (1st and 2nd Bns plus grenadiers); Thurn Nr 43 (3 bns). JzPf Bussy (8 sqns). GzIR Liccaner Nr (1 bn); HusR Nauendorf Nr 8 (2 sqns).
Austrian total 8,000 men.
Austrian losses 35 killed, 176 wounded.
Russian Forces Rear Admiral Pustochkin commanding: ships of the line *St Michael* (74); *Simeon* and *Anna* (74); frigates *Navarchia*, *Ascension of Christ*, *Virgin of Kazan*; Avisos *Novokuplennaja*, *Count Suvorov*. The Russians manned two shore batteries in the siege.
Turkish Forces 1 ship of the line, 2 frigates, 1 corvette, 1 tartan. The Turks manned one shore battery in the siege and a battalion under Aga Omer. Local Insurgents under Lahoz – 6,000 men.
Turkish losses Unknown.
Comment Monnier would only capitulate to the Austrians and not to the Russians or Turks. Frelich signed the capitulation without the knowledge of his allies and hoisted the Austrian flag over the fortress. This led to the 'Affair of the Flags' which hastened the end of the allied alliance and the suspension of Frelich from the Austrian army.
Sources Bodart, Lehnert, Wrede.

UR Philippsburg, 16 November 1799, clash

A small town in southwestern Germany, just east of the River Rhine, between Karlsruhe and Speyer.

A French victory over the Austrians.

(Last action – Mannheim, 18 September; next action – Wiesloch, 3 December.)

French Forces GdD Lecourbe commanding the Army of the Rhine. The divisions of Laborde, Decaen, Ney, B d'Hilliers and d'Hautpoul's Cavalry Reserve; see OOB for Stockach, 25/26 March.

French total 15,000 men.

French losses 400 men.

Austrian Forces FML Prince Hohenlohe commanding: IRs Lacy Nr 22 (1 bn), vacant Wenkheim Nr 35 (3 bns); KürR EH Franz Nr 2 (6 sqns); HusRs Vécsey Nr 4 (6 sqns), Blankenstein Nr 6 (8 sqns), DragR Kronprinz Nr 2 (6 sqns); GzIRs Broder Nr 7; 2nd Walachen (1 bn each).

Austrian total 8,000 men.

Austrian losses 1,200 killed, wounded and missing.

Sources Bodart, Wrede.

IN Torriglia, 16 November 1799, clash

A village in northwest Italy, in the coastal hills of the Gulf of Genoa, on Route 45, about 24 km northeast of Genoa.

A French victory over the Austrians.

(Last action – Mondovi, 13 November; next action – Cuneo, 3 December.)

French Forces GdD Gouvion St Cyr commanding: exact details not known but including: GdD Dombrowski's 1st Polish Legion [Gren Bn, Chass Bn, 3 x Fus Bns, Cavalry (2 sqns)]. GdB Jablonowski: 3e DBdeLé (1 bn); 17e DBdeLi (1 bn); 55e DBdeLi (1 bn), 106e DBdeLi (3 bns).

French total ca 10,000 men.

French losses 200 killed, wounded and missing.

Austrian Forces GM Count Klenau commanding: exact details not known but including: IRs J Jellačič Nr 53 (3 bns), Brentano JgCorps (6 coys); GzIR Roman Banater Nr 13 (2nd Bn); Combined GzIR Banater (6th Bn).

Austrian total 4,000 men.

Austrian losses 400 killed and wounded, 1,800 captured.

Sources Bodart, Wrede.

IN Cuneo, 16 November – 3 December 1799, siege and capture

A fortified town in northwestern Italy, 75 km southwest of Turin, between the Rivers Vermenagne and Stura di Dimonte; at the junction of Routes 20, 22 and 564, on the way up to the Coldi Tenda and the French border.

An Austrian victory over the French.

(Last action – Torriglia, 16 November; this was the last action in the campaign.)

French Garrison, GdB Clément commanding: exact details unknown.

French total 3,000 men.

French losses Killed and wounded unknown; all the survivors captured, 187 guns, 14,000 cwt of powder.

Austrian Forces FML Prince Liechtenstein commanding: IRs Kheul Nr 10, Reisky Nr 13 (3 bns each), Stuart Nr 18 (1st and 3rd Bns), Vukassovich Nr 48 (3 bns); DragR Württemberg Nr 8 (6 sqns); HusR EH Joseph Nr 2 (8 sqns).

Austrian total 8,000 men.

Austrian losses Not known exactly but light.

Sources Bodart, Wrede.

UR Wiesloch, 3 December 1799, clash

A small town in southwestern Germany, east of the River Rhine, 15 km south of Heidelberg on the River Neckar.

An Austrian victory over the French.

(Last action – Philippsburg, 16 November; this was the last action on the Upper Rhine.)

French Forces GdD Lecourbe commanding part of the Army of the Rhine; the divisions of Laborde, Decaen, Ney, B d'Hilliers and d'Hautpoul's Cavalry Reserve. See OOB for Stockach, 25/26 March.

French total 17,000 men.

French losses 700 killed and wounded, 800 captured.

Austrian Forces FZM Count Sztáray IR vacant Wenkheim Nr 35 (3 bns); KürR Kaiser Nr 1 (6 sqns), KürR Albert Nr 3 (2 sqns); HusRs Kaiser Nr 1 (8 sqns), Blankenstein Nr 6 (6 sqns). DragR vacant Nr 13 (2 sqns). GzIR Deutsch-Banater Nr 12 (1st Bn).

Austrian total ca 5,000 men.

Austrian losses ca 500 killed, wounded and missing.

Sources Bodart, Wrede.

1800

FRENCH ORDERS OF BATTLE

The French Armée d'Italie, 5 April 1800
(After Belhomme, page 222. The numbers in brackets indicate men present).

Commander in Chief: GdD Massena

Corps of GdD Soult GdD Miollis: 5e Lé (600); 24e Li (800), 74e Li (1,100); 106e Li (1,700). GdD Gazan: GrenPiémontais (90); 30e Lé (500); 2e Li (1,600); 3e Li (1,300); 78e Li (1,300). GdD Marbot: 3e Lé (900); 62e Li (1,500); 63e Li (500); 97e (1,300). Reserve: 25e Lé (1,700); 92e Li (500). Garrison of Genoa: 41e, 73e, 93e Li (3,000); 2e Légion Polonaise (1,200).
Total of Soult's corps - 19,790.

Corps of GdD Suchet GdD Clausel: 20e Lé (853) 10e Li (1,409); 34e Li (1,122), 87e Li (460). GdD Pouget: 7e Lé (965); 11e Li (454); 99e (1,352). GdD Garnier: 33e Li (487); 39e (422); 68e (620); 55e (213); 104e (1,050). GdD Menard: 16e Lé (800); 30e Li (1,200); 105e Li (1,400) 1ère Légion Polonaise (800). Garrisons of Savona, Vintimille and Montalbais: 17e Lé and 14e Li.
Total of Suchet's corps - 15,607.

In Antibes Gen Monnier 8e & 16e Lé (3e Bns each); 1ère Légion Romaine (1,500).

The Corps of the Alps GdD Tharreau 15e, 28e Lé; 12e, 21e, 26e, 80e, 88e, 107e Li; Bn de patriotes piémontais (8,000).

Total Armée d'Italie 44,897.

Armée du Danube, Gen Moreau

The Corps of General Lecourbe GdD Vandamme: 1er Lé (2 bns); 36e, 93e, 94e Li. (9,623), GdD Lorges: 10e Lé, 37e, 84e, 109e Li (8,238); GdD Montrichard: 4 combined gren, bns, 38e, 67e Li (8,498).
Total of Lecourbe's Corps - 28,368.

The Corps of the Reserve GdD Delmas; 14e Lé, 46e, 50e, 57e, 108e Li (8,638); GdD Leclerc: 53e, 89e Li (6,035); GdD Richepanse: 4 combined gren. bns, 4e, 59e, 100e Li (6,848).

The Corps of GdD St Cyr GdD Baraguey: 12e Lé, 1er, 15e, 23e Li (8,340); GdD Tharrieu: 2e Lé, 42e, 51e, 101e Li (8,326); GdD Ney: 54e, 76e, 103e Li (7,270). GdD Salme: 16e Li (2,474).
Total of St Cyr's Corps - 26,410.

The Corps of GdD Ste Sauzanne GdD Collard: 48e Li (2,740); GdD Souhaut: 8e, 95e Li (4,687); GdD Legrand: 7e, 27e Li (5,286). GdD Delaborde: 19e, 65e Li, 2e Helvétique (2,573); GdD Montchoisy: 1re Lé, 9e, 28e, 44e, 102e (7,715); GdD Level (sic); 65e, 91e, 110e, 1er Helvétique (5,640). Garrisons du Rhin: 20e, 29e, 80e, 95e, 3e Helvétique, légions des francs du Nord et Polonaise (9,366).
Total of St Sauzanne's Corps - 15,286.

Total Armée du Danube 114,306.

The Armée de Réserve assembling at Dijon (this was the force with which Bonaparte was to invade north-western Italy over the Alps): GdD Chambarlhac: 24e Lé, 43e, 96e Li (5,288); GdD Watrins: 6e Lé, 22e, 40e Li (5,083); GdD Loison: 13e Lé; 58e, 60e Li (5,304); GdD Boudet: 9e Lé, 30e, 59e Li (5,316); GdD Monnier: 19e Lé; 70e, 72e Li (4,500); GdD Chabran: 3 DBdes from the (Armée) d'Orient (the two others did not return for some time) (3,500); Grenadiers and Chasseurs of the Consular Guard (800); Légion italienne (4,000) **Total** 33,791.

Total French infantry available in the Italian campaign 192,994 men.

Armée du Rhin, GdD Moreau commanding

At the end of April 1800 the organization was as follows:
Right Wing GdD Lecourbe in Zürich: GdD Vandamme: GdB Jardon, Laval, Molitor; 1ère DBdeLé, 36e, 83e, 94e DBdeLi, 8e HusR (9,632 infantry, 540 cavalry). GdD Lorges*: GdB Goullus, Bontemps: 10e DBdeLé, 37e, 84e, 109e DBdeLi, 9e HusR (8,238 infantry, 464 cavalry). GdD Montrichard, GdB Daultane: 10e DBdeLé, 38e, 67e DBdeLi (6,998 men); GdD Nansouty: combined grenadiers; 25e CavR, 11e DragR, 12e ChàCh. (1,500 infantry, 1,280 cavalry).
Centre GdD Giouvion St Cyr in Bâsle: GdD Baraguay

d'Hilliers: GdB Joba, Roussel, Sabathier: 12e DBdeLé, 1re, 15e, 23e DBdeLi, 2e HusR (8,340 infantry, 542 cavalry). GdD Tharreau: GdB Heudelet, Aubrée, Beauregard: 2e DBdeLé, 24e, 51e, 101e DBdeLi, 23e DragR, 16e ChàCh (8,326 infantry, 611 cavalry). GdD Ney: GdB Bonnet, Bonamy: 12e DBdeLé; 54e, 76e, 103e DBdeLi, 8e ChàCh (7,270 infantry, 569 cavalry). GdD Desbrulys: GdB Sahne, Saligny, Debilly: 16e DBdeLi, 12e, 17e CavR, 2e DragR, 5e ChàCh. (2,474 infantry, 1,616 cavalry) The 12e DBdeLé, 1ère & 101e DBdeLi were soon detached to the Armée d'Italie.

* = Lorges left the army on 13 May with the 1ère DBdeLé, 67e DBdeLi; 25e CavR and 2e ChàCh.

Left Wing GdD St Sauzanne in Strasbourg: GdD Collaud: GdB Lacoste, Girard-Vieux: 48e DBdeLi, 10e, 16e CavRs, 20e ChàCh (2,740 infantry, 981 cavalry). GdD Souham: GdB Decaën, Puthod: 8e, 95e DBdeLi, 7e CavR, 6e DragR, 1er ChàCh (4,687 infantry, 1,394 cavalry). GdD Legrand; GdB Boivin, Devent: 7e, 27e DBdeLi, 13e DragR, 6e ChàCh (5,286 infantry, 1,094 cavalry). GdD Delaborde. GdB Mercier, Thuring: 29e, 65e DBdeLi; 2e Helvétique; 4e, 19e CavR (2,573 infantry, 286 cavalry). The 29e DBdeLi was later transferred to Moncey's corps.

Reserve GdD Moreau: GdD Delmas: GdB Jacopin, Grandjean, Lorcet, Quétard, Boyer: 14e DBdeLé; 46e, 50e, 57e, 108e DBdeLi, 6e CavR, 11e ChàCh, 4e HusR (8,635 infantry, 1,031 cavalry). GdD Leclerc: GdB Bastoul, Walther, Desperrières: 14e DBdeLé, 53e, 89e DBdeLi, 10e, 23e ChàCh (6,035 infantry, 963 cavalry). GdD Richepanse: GdB Digonnet, Durutte: Combined grenadiers; 4e, 50e, 100e DBdeLi, 5e HusR, 13e CavR, 17e DragR (6,848 infantry, 1,187 cavalry). GdD d'Hautpoul: GdB Espagne; 1er, 2e Carabiniers GdB Dévrigny: 8e, 9e CavR (1,504 cavalry). Moreau thus had 89,585 infantry, 14,065 cavalry. There was also GdD Montchoisy's division in Switzerland: GdB Mainoni, Chabert: 1ère DBdeLé, 9e, 28e, 44e, 102e DBdeLi, 14e, 22e CavRs (7,715 infantry, 519 cavalry). The garrisons of the fortresses in Alsace and in Mainz were as follows: GdD Freytag: 29e, 95e DBdeLi, 3e Helvétique (2,935 men); GdD Gillot; 6e HusR, 1er DragR (750); GdD Châteauneuf-Raudon: 80e DBdeLi; Legion of the Danube (Poles) (3,430 men); 15e, 24e CavR (485); GdD Laroche: 20e DBdeLi, North French Legion (3,001); 16e CavR (91); GdD Leval: 65e, 91e, 110e DBdeLi; 1ère Helvétique (5,640); 3e HusR (426). The 29e & 91e DBdeLi were later transferred to the Armée d'Italie.

Armée du Rhin totals 52,778 infantry; 5,622 cavalry.

1800 THE ACTIONS

YE Heliopolis (Matarieh), 20 March 1800, battle

A town in northern Egypt, 11 km northeast of Cairo.

A French victory over the Turks.

(This was the only action of note in Egypt this year.)

French Forces GdD Kléber - Exact organization not known; including: 9e, 15e, 25e, 61e, 75e, 85e, 32e, 18e, 69e, 88e DBdeLi; 2e, 4e, 21e, 22e DBdeLé; Légion Nautique; Dromedary Corps, 3e, 14e, 15e, 18e, 20e DragRs; 22e ChàCh; 7e bis HusR; Légion Syrienne; Légion Maltaise.

French total ca 12,000 men.

French losses 600 killed and wounded.

Turkish Forces Grandvizier Yussuf Pasha commanding about 40,000 Mamelukes, Bedouin cavalry and Fellahin.

Turkish losses 8,000–9,000 killed, wounded and captured.

Sources Bodart, Herold.

IN Cadibona, 6 April 1800, clash

A village in northwestern Italy, 7 km northwest of the port-town of Savona on the Gulf of Genoa, just off Route 29.

An Austrian victory over the French.

(This was the opening action in northern Italy; next action – Monte Fascio, 7 April).

French Forces GdD Soult's Right Wing of the Armée d'Italie: GdD Marbot's 3rd Division GdB Gardanne: 3e DBdeLé (1 bn), 62e DBdeLi (3 bns). 97e DBdeLi (2 bns).

French total ca 3,800 men.

French losses ca 200 killed and wounded, 500 captured; 5 guns. GdB Seras captured.

Austrian Forces GdK Baron Melas commanding: FML Haddik's Division; MG Palffy, MG St Julien, MG Lattermann: IRs Reisky Nr 13, von Fürstenberg Nr 36, Nádasdy Nr 39, Splényi Nr 51 (3 bns each); Gren Bn Kleimayrn.

Austrian total ca 13,000 men.

Austrian losses ca 200 killed and wounded.

Comment This was the start of the Austrian operation to take Genoa and Savona.
Sources Wrede, Günther.

IN Monte Fascio, 7 April 1800, clash
A mountain in northwestern Italy, 15 km northeast of the port-city of Genoa.
A French victory over the Austrians.
(Last action - Cadibona, 6 April; next action - Monte Cenis, 7/8 April.)
French Forces GdD Soult commanding: GdD Miollis: 25e DBdeLé (2 bns); 93e DBdeLi (3 bns); another, unidentified DBde (4 bns).
French total 5,000 men.
French losses ca 200 killed and wounded.
Austrian Forces FML Baron von Ott commanding: IRs EH Anton Nr 53, EH Joseph Nr 55, Jordis Nr 59; GzIR Warasdiner-Kreuzer Nr 5.
Austrian total 7,000 men.
Austrian losses 58 killed, 178 wounded, 1,400 captured; GM Baron d'Aspre captured; the entire 2nd Bn, IR EH Joseph was taken.
Comment Monte Fascio dominated the valley of the River Bisagno and the road from Genoa to Piacenza. The French assault caught the Austrians napping.
Sources Wrede, Günther.

IN Monte Cenis, 7/8 April 1800, capture
A fortified post in the Alps in northwestern Italy, on the Franco-Italian border, just off Route 25 and south of the Mont Cenis pass.
(Last action - Monte Fascio, 7 April; next action - La Bochetta, 9 April.)
An Austrian victory over the French.
French Forces GdB Caffri commanding 15e DBdeLé of GdD Tharreau's Corps of the Alps.
French total 1,350 men.
French losses 1,344 men, 16 guns captured.
Austrian Force Major Metzko (of HusR vacant Nr 7) and 1,200 men.
Austrian losses Nil.
Comment The raid took place just before dawn; the French sentries were all asleep, not a shot was fired.
Sources Wrede, Günther, ÖMZ 1811, Heft 8; ÖMZ 1822, Heft 4 p 169.

IN La Bocchetta, 9 April 1800, clash
A mountain in northwestern Italy, 16 km north of the port-city of Genoa; just west of the source of the River Lemme.
An Austrian victory over the French.
(Last action - Monte Cenis, 7/8 April; next action - Sassello, 10 April.)
French Forces GdD Soult's Right Wing of the Armée d'Italie, GdD Gazan commanding: 1st Division including the 25e DBdeLé (2 bns); 3e DBdeLi (2 bns).
French total ca 3,500 men.
French losses ca 1,000 killed, wounded and missing.
Austrian Forces FML Count Hohenzollern commanding: IRs Allvintzy Nr 19 (3 bns); Kray Nr 34 (2 bns); vacant Nr 61 (2nd Bn); LtI Bn Munkátsy Nr 13 (1 bn); HusR vacant Nr 5 (2 sqns).
Austrian total ca 10,000 men.
Austrian losses ca 600 killed, wounded and missing; 2 mountain guns.
Comment Soult left Savona on 7 April (leaving a small garrison there) and fought his way eastwards to join Massena in Genoa.
Sources Wrede, Günther.

IN Sassello, 10 April 1800, clash
A hamlet in northwestern Italy, 30 km northwest of the port-city of Genoa, 22 km north of the port-town of Savona on Route 334.
An Austrian victory over the French.
(Last action - La Boccetta, 9 April; next action - Monte Settepani, 10–11 April.)
French Forces GdD Soult commanding the Right Wing of the Army of Italy: GdD Gazan's 1st Division: 25e DBdeLé (2 bns); 3e DBdeLi (2 bns) and two other DBdes (62e and 63e?).
French total 7,000 men.
French losses ca 2,000 killed, wounded and missing.
Austrian Forces FML Hohenzollern commanding: GM St Julien: IRs Reisky Nr 13, Stuart Nr 18 (3 bns each); Sztáray Nr 33 (1 bn); Vukassovich Nr 48 (3 bns).
Austrian total 20,000 men.
Austrian losses ca 1,000 killed, wounded and missing.
Comment The sources vary on this action. Günther (page 45) mentions that the IR Hoch-und-Deutschmeister Nr 3 (in fact this regiment was Nr 4) lost 2,000 men and 7 colours here this day; Wrede mentions no such loss and IR Nr 3 (EH Carl) was in Germany in 1800. No such losses of colours were

recorded for IR Nr 4 or for any of the other regiments involved.

Sources Wrede, Günther, Bodart, Belhomme.

IN Monte Settepani, 10/11 April 1800, clash

A mountain in northwestern Italy, 20 km southwest of the port-town of Savona on the Gulf of Genoa.

A French victory over the Austrians.

(Last action – Sassello, 10 April; next action – Verreira, 11 April.)

French Forces GdD Suchet commanding the Centre of the Armée d'Italie: GdD Fressinet: 3e DBdeLé (1 bn); 62e and 63e DBdeLi (3 bns).

French total ca 5,000 men.

French losses ca 200 killed and wounded.

Austrian Forces GM Ulm commanding: IRs Huff Nr 8 (3 bns); Oranien Nr 15 (2 bns); Jellačič Nr 53 (3 bns); J Colloredo Nr 57 (3 bns) Gren Bn Pertusy (1 bn).

Austrian total ca 10,000 men (only 3,000 in action).

Austrian losses 400 killed and wounded, 1 colour and 1,400 (of IR Nr 15) captured.

Sources Wrede, Günther.

IN Verreira, 11 April 1800, clash

A village in northwestern Italy, 14 km north of the port-town of Savona, just off Route 334.

A French victory over the Austrians.

(Last action – Monte Settepani, 10/11 April; next action – San Giacomo, 12 April.)

French Forces GdD Soult commanding the Right Wing of the Armée d'Italie: exact details not known.

French total ca 4,000 men.

French losses ca 300 killed and wounded.

Austrian Forces GM Count St Julien commanding: IRs Reisky Nr 13, Stuart Nr 18 (3 bns each); Sztáray Nr 33 (1 bn).

Austrian total ca 4,500 men.

Austrian losses 500 killed and wounded, 1,500 captured, 6 colours.

Sources Wrede, Günther.

IN San Giacomo, 12 April 1800, clash

A mountain in northwestern Italy, 12 km west of the port-town of Savona on the Gulf of Genoa.

An Austrian victory over the French.

(Last action – Verreira, 11 April; next action – Voltri, 18 April.)

French Forces GdD Suchet commanding the Centre of the Armée d'Italie: 7e DBdeLé (1 bn); 11e & 99e DBdeLi (1 & 3 bns resp).

French total ca 5,000 men.

French losses ca 1,000 killed, wounded and missing.

Austrian Forces FML Baron von Elsnitz commanding: IRs Huff Nr 8, von Terzy Nr 16; Sztáray Nr 33, Nádasdy Nr 39 (3 bns each); Gren Bns Pertusy, Piret, Khevenhüller, Görschen, Weissenwolf, St Julien.

Austrian total ca 12,000 men.

Austrian losses ca 800 killed, wounded and missing.

Sources Wrede, Günther, Belhomme.

IN Voltri, 18 April 1800, clash

A hamlet in northwestern Italy, on the Gulf of Genoa, 10 km west of the port-city of Genoa on Route 1.

An Austrian victory over the French.

(Last action – San Giacomo, 12 April; next action – Loano, 1 May.)

French Forces GdD Soult commanding the Right Wing of the Armée d'Italie. Exact details not known; see OOB for the Armée d'Italie at the beginning of this chapter.

French total 7,000 men.

French losses ca 2,000 killed, wounded and missing.

Austrian Forces GdK Baron Melas commanding: IRs Stuart Nr 18, Frelich Nr 28 (3 bns each), and others (unidentified).

Austrian total 14,000 men.

Austrian losses ca 1,000 killed, wounded and missing.

Comment Massena was now besieged in Genoa with FML Ott's force of 24,000 blockading the landward side and a British naval squadron sealing off communications by sea. Melas and FML Elsnitz now turned on Suchet.

Sources Wrede, Günther.

IN Loano, 1 May 1800, clash

A small port on the Gulf of Genoa in northwestern Italy, on Route 1 ca 28 km southwest of the port-town of Savona.

An Austrian victory over the French.

(Last action – Voltri, 18 April; next action – Monte Calvo, 7 May.)

French Forces GdD Suchet commanding the Centre of the Armée d'Italie: exact details not known, see OOB for the Armée d'Italie at the beginning of this chapter.

French losses Not known exactly but light.

Austrian Forces Gen Lattermann commanding; IRs Preiss Nr 24, Fürstenberg Nr 36; Gren Bn Paar.

Austrian total ca 5,000 men.

Austrian losses Not exactly known but light.

Comment This was part of an Austrian thrust along the coast towards France.

Sources Wrede, Günther.

UR Büsingen, 1 May 1800, clash

A village in the southwestern German state of Baden, on the right bank of the River Rhine, 4 km east of the Swiss town of Schaffhausen.

A French victory over the Austrians.

(This was the opening action of this campaign; next action – Hohentwiel, 1 May).

French Forces GdB Goulu commanding: 10e DBdeLé, 37e DbdeLi.

French total ca 6,000 men.

French losses ca 500 killed, wounded and missing.

Austrian Forces FML Prince von Lothringen commanding: IR Schröder Nr 7 (3 bns).

Austrian total 4,000 men.

Austrian losses 400 killed and wounded, 750 captured, 3 guns.

Comment There may well have been some Imperial 'Kreistruppen' present as well but details are not known.

Sources Wrede, Günther.

UR Hohentwiel, 1 May 1800, capitulation

A hill fortress in southwestern Germany, just west of the town of Singen, in the triangle formed by Route B33, B34, B314 and Autobahn A98/E54, just west of Lake Constance.

A French victory over the Württembergers.

(Last action – Büsingen, 1 May; next action – Engen and Stockach, 3 May.)

French Forces GdD Vandamme's division: GdB Jardon, Laval, Molitor: 1ère DBdeLé, 36e, 83e, 94e DBdeLi, 8e HusR.

French total 9,632 infantry, 540 cavalry.

French losses None.

Württemberg Garrison GM Georg von Bilfinger commanding: 106 men of the Garrison IR, 27 guns.

Württemberg losses The garrison were released: the French occupied the impregnable fortress.

Comment The Duke of Württemberg was enraged at this spineless action; the fortress had successfully survived 15 years of various sieges in the Thirty Years' War and could easily have been held. As it was, it was surrendered on the day the French appeared. The commandant and his deputy were court martialled and sentenced to life imprisonment.

Sources von Stadlinger, Wrede, Günther.

UR Engen and Stockach, 3 May 1800, battle

Villages in the southwest German state of Baden. Stockach is at the northwestern tip of the Lake Constance, at the junction of Routes B31, B14 and B313; Engen is 20 km west of Stockach at the junction of Routes B31 and B33.

A French victory over the Austrians.

(Last action – Hohentwiel, 1 May; next action – Mösskirch, 5 May.)

French Forces GdD Moreau commanding: exact details not known, see OOB Moreau's Armée du Rhin, April 1800 at the beginning of this chapter. The divisions of Lecourbe, Montrichard, Lorges, Vandamme, Delmas and Nansouty were present.

French total ca 84,000 men.

French losses 3,000 killed, wounded and missing.

Austrian Forces FZM Baron von Kray commanding: Prince von Lothringen: IRs EH Carl Nr 3; Schröder Nr 7 (3 bns each); Clerfayt Nr 9 (1st Bn); De Ligne Nr 30 (1 bn); Benjowsky Nr 31 (3 bns); Württemberg Nr 38 (1st and 2nd Bns); Bender Nr 41, Erbach Nr 42 (3 bns each); Kerpen Nr 49 (1st and 3rd Bns); Stain Nr 50 (1 bn); Callenberg Nr 54, Murray Nr 55 (3 bns each); Beaulieu Nr 58 (1st Bn). Gren Bns Rüffer, Papp, Tegethoff, Fleming, Wouvermanns. LtI Bn Radivojevich. KürRs Kaiser Nr 1, EH Franz Nr 2 (6 sqns each), Kinsky Nr 12. DragR Latour Nr 11; DragR Kronprinz Nr 2, HusR Mészáros Nr 10, UlR Merveldt Nr 1. KürRs Anspach Nr 11, Zezschwitz Nr 5, DragR Coburg Nr 6 (6 sqns each). GzIR Deutsch-Banater Nr 12 (1st Bn).

Austrian total ca 72,000 men.

Austrian losses 397 killed and wounded, 718 captured, 5 guns, 3 colours.

Sources Wrede, Günther.

UR Mösskirch, 5 May 1800, battle

A village in the southwest German state of Baden, 37 km northwest of the city of Konstanz on Lake Constance.

A French victory over the Austrians.

(Last action - Engen and Stockach, 3 May; next action - Biberach, 7 May.)

French Forces GdD Moreau commanding: exact details not known; certainly Lecourbe's division, Vandamme's, Montrichard's, Lorges' divisions and Nansouty's cavalry were present. See OOB at the beginning of the 1800 chapter.

French total ca 52,000 men.

French losses 3,000 killed, wounded and missing.

Austrian Forces FZM Baron Kray commanding: IRs EH Carl Nr 3 (3 bns); Clerfayt Nr 9 (1st Bn); De Ligne Nr 30 (1 bn); Benjowsky Nr 31 (3 bns); Württemberg Nr 38 (1st and 2nd Bns); Bender Nr 41, Erbach Nr 42, Callenberg Nr 54, Murray Nr 55 (3 bns each); Beaulieu Nr 58 (1st Bn). Gren Bns Rüffer, Papp, Tegethoff, Fleming, Wouvermanns. Wurmser Freikorps (2 bns, 2 sqns). KürR Kaiser Nr 1, EH Franz Nr 2, Nassau Nr 9, Lothringen Nr 7, Hohenzollern Nr 8, Kinsky Nr 12. DragR Latour Nr 11. HusR Mészáros Nr 10, UlR Motschlitz Nr 2 (6 sqns each). GzIR Deutsch-Banater Nr 12 (1st Bn).

Austrian total 48,000 men.

Austrian losses 2,400 killed and wounded, 1,600 captured, 5 guns.

Sources Wrede, Günther.

IN Montecalvo, 7 May 1800, clash

A mountain in northwestern Italy, just southwest of the port-town of Savona on the Gulf of Genoa.

An Austrian victory over the French.

(Last action - Loano, 1 May; next action - Monte Becco, 11 May.)

French Forces Gen Adjutant Cravey commanding: 34e and 68e DBdeLi of Suchet's Centre Corps of the Armée d'Italie.

French total 5,000 men.

French losses 200 killed and wounded, 1,500 captured, 1 colour (probably of 68e), Cravey was also taken.

Austrian Forces FML Baron von Elsnitz commanding: GM Lattermann: IRs Preuss Nr 24, Fürstenberg Nr 36; Gren Bn Paar.

Austrian total 5,000 men.

Austrian losses ca 200 men killed and wounded.

Comment The Austrian coastal thrust continued to near the French border. Crevey delayed his rearguard too long and was cut off. Clausel now abandoned the naturally very strong line of the River Roya and fell back towards Nice. Charrié gives the 11e Li of this Corps (Ponget's division) as losing a colour on this day at 'Oneille' but no such action has been traced. According to the same source neither the 34e nor 68e lost a colour this year.

Sources Wrede, Günther, Charrié.

UR Biberach, 9 May 1800, clash

A town in the southwest German state of Württemberg, 35 km southwest of Ulm/Danube, just northwest of the junction of Routes B30, B312 and B465.

A French victory over the Austrians.

(Last action - Mösskirch, 5 May; next action - Iller River, 5 June.)

French Forces GdD Gouvion St Cyr commanding. Exact details not known; see OOB at the beginning of the 1800 chapter.

French total 25,000 men.

French losses 2,000 killed, wounded and missing.

Austrian Forces FZM Baron von Kray commanding: IRs EH Carl Nr 3, Clerfayt Nr 9, Benjowsky Nr 31 (3 bns each), Württemberg Nr 38 (1st and 2nd Bns), Bender Nr 41, Erbach Nr 42, Callenberg Nr 54, Murray Nr 55 (3 bns each); Beaulieu Nr 51 (1st Bn), Gren Bns Rüffer, Tegethoff. KürRs Kaiser Nr 1, Lothringen Nr 7, Kinsky Nr 12 (6 sqns each); HusR Blankenstein Nr 6, Mészáros Nr 10, UlR Motschlitz Nr 2 (6 sqns each).

Austrian total 20,000 men.

Austrian losses 1,250 killed and wounded, 2,750 captured.

Sources Wrede, Günther.

IN Monte Becco, 11 May 1800, clash

A mountain in northwestern Italy, just northeast of the port-city of Genoa.

A French victory over the Austrians.

(Last action - Montecalvo, 7 May; next action - Monte Creto, 13 May.)

French Forces GdD Soult commanding: 25e DBdeLé (2 bns); 62e DBdeLi (3 bns).

French total 6,000 men.

French losses ca 500 men.

Austrian Forces GM Baron von Gottesheim commanding: IR Klebek Nr 14 (3 bns); HusR Nauendorf Nr 8 (6 sqns).

Austrian total 4,000 men.

Austrian losses 600 killed and wounded, 1,400 captured, 2 guns.
Comment This successful sally by the garrison of Genoa did much to raise their morale.
Sources Günther, Wrede.

IN Monte Creto, 13 May 1800, clash
A mountain in northwestern Italy, just northeast of the port-city of Genoa.
An Austrian victory over the French.
(Last action – Monte Becco, 11 May; next action – Savona, 15 May.)
French Forces GdD Soult commanding: 1st Column 3e DBdeLé, 2e, 3e, 24e, 62e DBdeLi – 2,400 men. 2nd Column GdD Gazan: 92e, 97e, 106e DBdeLi – 2,600 men.
French total 5,000 men.
French losses 1,000 men killed, wounded and missing. Soult was captured; GdB Perrin was killed. GdB Gauthier was badly wounded.
Austrian Forces FML Prince Hohenzollern commanding: IRs Kray Nr 34, Jellačič Nr 53, J Colloredo Nr 57 (3 bns each); IR vacant Nr 61 (2nd Bn).
Austrian total 7,000 men.
Austrian losses 650 killed, wounded and missing.
Comment This defeat caused the garrison's morale to collapse; many units were near to mutiny, food very short.
Sources Wrede, Günther.

IN Savona, 21 April – 15 May 1800, blockade and capitulation
A port-town in northwestern Italy, on the Gulf of Genoa, 50 km west of the port-city of Genoa.
An Austrian victory over the French.
(Last action – Monte Creto, 13 May; next action – Susa, 22 May.)
French Garrison GdB Buget commanding: 63e DBdeLi of Marbot's division of Soult's Right Wing of the Armée d'Italie.
French total 1,100 men.
French losses The garrison were prisoners of war; 146 guns were taken. Charrié quotes 2e Li as losing 1 colour here and the 73e Li as losing 2 colours.
Austrian Forces GM Count St Julien commanding: IR Hoch und Deutschmeister Nr 4 (2 bns). Gren Bn Sciaffinati (1 bn).
Austrian total 2,000 men.
Austrian losses Not known exactly; very light.
Sources Günther, Wrede, Charrié.

IN Susa (Gravières), 22 May 1800, skirmish
A small, walled town in northwestern Italy, in the valley of the River Dora Suzina, on Route 25, 38 km west of Turin and at the junction of the roads from France via the Mt Cenis Pass (25) and the Col de Montgenèvre (Route 24).
A French victory over the Austrians.
(Last action – Savona, 15 May; next action – Ivrea, 22–24 May.)
French Forces GdD Tharreau's Corps of the Alps. Exact details not known, see OOB at the beginning of the 1800 chapter.
French total 5,000 men, 12 guns.
French losses Not known.
Austrian Forces GM La Marseille commanding: IRs EH Anton Nr 52, EH Joseph Nr 55 (5 bns in all); HusR vacant Nr 7 (2 sqns); Piemontese IR Ivrea (1 bn).
Austrian total 3,919 men.
Austrian losses 175 killed and wounded.
Sources ÖMZ 1822 Vol IV, Wrede.

IN Ivrea, 22–24 May 1800, clash
A small town in the valley of the Dorea Baltea River in northwestern Italy, 37 km north of Turin, about 23 km south of Bard castle.
A French victory over the Austrians.
(Last action – Susa, 22 May; next action – Romano, 26 May.)
French Forces GdD Lannes commanding part of the Armée de Réserve. Exact details not known; losses not known. See OOB at the beginning of the 1800 chapter.
Austrian Forces GM de Briey commanding: parts of IRs M Wallis Nr 11 (1 bn), F Kinsky Nr 47 ($1^1/_2$ bns).
Austrian total ca 800 men, 14 guns.
Austrian losses 300 men killed, wounded and missing, 14 guns.
Sources ÖMZ 1822 Vol IX, Wrede.

IN Romano, 26 May 1800, clash
A village in the valley of the Dorea Baltea River in northwestern Italy, between Ivrea and Turin.
An Austrian victory over the French.
(Last action – Ivrea, 22–24 May; next action – Var River, 22–27 May.)

French Forces GdD Bonaparte commanding the Armée de Réserve: GdD Lannes, GdD Boudet, GdB Mâcon: 6e DBdeLé, 22e and 40e DBdeLi; 9e DBdeLé; 30e and 59e DbdeLi.

French total ca 12,000 men.

French losses ca 1,700 killed, wounded and missing.

Austrian Forces FML Count Haddik commanding: IRs M Wallis Nr 11 (2 bns); F Kinsky Nr 47 (1½ bns). MG Palfy, MG Pilati: DragR Lobkowitz Nr 10, DragR Kaiser Nr 1 (4 sqns).

Austrian total ca 5,000 men.

Austrian losses 348 men killed, wounded and missing, 216 horses. MG Palfy mortally wounded.

Comment After a hard fight the Austrians withdrew, unmolested, southwards towards Turin via Foglizzo, after their cavalry had cut down and scattered a column of French infantry.

Sources ÖMZ 1822, Vol IV, Wrede.

IN Var River, 22–27 May 1800, clashes

A river in southeastern France entering the Mediterranean between Nice and Cannes.

A series of drawn matches between the French and Austrians.

(Last action – Romano, 26 May; next action – Turbigo, 31 May.)

French Forces GdD Suchet commanding the Centre of the Armée d'Italie; 20e DBdeLé, 34e, 39e, 99e DBdeLi, 13e ChàCh (2 sqns) and other formations, exact details not known.

French total ca 7,000 men.

French losses Not known.

Austrian Forces FML Baron Elsnitz commanding: IRs Wallis Nr 11 (3rd Bn), Oranien Nr 15 (1 bn), von Preiss Nr 24 (3 bns); Gren Bns Paar, Sciaffinati, Weber, Kleimayrn, Pertusy, Piret, Khevenhüller, Weissenwolf, St Julien, Pers.

Austrian total ca 15,000 men.

Austrian losses Not known exactly; possibly 200 killed and wounded, 300 captured.

Comment Melas now abandoned his offensive at the news of Bonaparte's thrust over the Alps into Piemont and marched at once for Turin. This was the end of the Austrians' successes in northern Italy.

Sources Wrede, Günther.

IN Turbigo, 31 May 1800, clash

A small town in northwestern Italy, just east of the River Ticino and north of the Autostrada A4/E64 between Milan and Novara.

An Austrian victory over the French.

(Last action – Var River, 22–27 May; next action – Bard Castle, 2 June.)

French Forces GdD Murat commanding part of Bonaparte's Armée de Réserve: GdD Monnier: 19e DBdeLé, 70e, 72e DBdeLi and two other divisions (Moncey and Duhesme) exact details not known.

French total 12,000 men.

French losses Not exactly known but they must have been at least moderate.

Austrian Forces FML Vukassovich's division: GM Loudon, Obst Prince Victor Rohan: LtI Bns Trautenberg Nr 6, Siegenfeld Nr 9, Rohan Nr 14* (1 bn each); JzPf Bussy (6 sqns); DragR Württemberg Nr 8 (4 sqns); GzIR Warasdiner-Kreutzer Nr 6 (2 bns). Le Loup Jägers (1 bn).

Austrian total 5,346 men.

Austrian losses Not exactly known.

* = present in reserve but not engaged.

Comment A canal (parallel to the Ticino) runs through the town; the Austrians defended this obstacle against heavy odds and held up Murat's advance on Milan for a whole day.

Sources ÖMZ 1822 Vol IV, Günther, Wrede.

IN Bard Castle, 19 May – 2 June 1800, siege and capitulation

An almost impregnable fortress in the narrow valley of the upper Dorea Baltea River in northwestern Italy, on Route 26 (and now Autostrada A5/E25) between Aosta and Turin.

A French victory over the Austrians.

(Last action – Turbigo, 31 May; next action – Genoa, 4 June.)

French Forces GdD Berthier of Bonaparte's Armée de Réserve commanding: initially GdD Loison, later GdD Chabran with three demi-brigades of the old Armée de l'Orient out of Egypt.

French total Unknown.

French losses Not exactly known but at least 1,000 killed and wounded; many powder waggons destroyed.

Austrian Garrison Captain Bernkopf and 2 coys IR F. Kinsky Nr 47, 18 guns.

Austrian total ca 200 men.

Austrian losses Killed and wounded unknown; the

garrison were sent to France as prisoners of war.

Comment Fort Bard completely blocked Bonaparte's chosen invasion route to wheeled traffic. For 12 days he was unable to move his artillery and train past this obstacle. The progress of his invasion was thus much slower than he wished. Captain Bernkopf's energetic and aggressive defence continued until the castle walls were breached in several places.

Sources Wrede, ÖMZ 1822 Vol IV.

IN Genoa, 19 April – 4 June 1800, blockade and capitulation

A port-city in northwestern Italy on the Gulf of the same name and at the junction of Autostrada A10/E80 and A7/E25.

An Anglo-Austrian victory over the French.

(Last action – Bard Castle, 2 June; next action – Monte Nave, 5/6 June.)

French Garrison GdD Massena commanding 1st Division GdD Miollis: 3e and 8e DBdeLé, 21e, 62e, 63e, 74e, 78e DBdeLi – 4,500 men. 2nd Division GdD Gazan: 5e and 25e DBdeLé; 44e, 55e, 92e, 97e, 106e DBdeLi – 3,500 men. 3rd Division GdB Poinsot: 2e, 3e DBdeLi – 1,600 men; Genoese GdN (?).

French total 12,000 men.

French losses 4,000 killed or died of sickness. In recognition of their brave defence of the place, the garrison marched out with honours of war and those fit enough (about 4,000) marched off to France. The sick and wounded, guns and baggage were transported to France in British ships.

Austrian Forces FML Baron von Ott commanding: IRs Reisky Nr 13, Klebek Nr 14, von Terzy Nr 16, Stuart Nr 18, Allvintzy Nr 19, Kray Nr 34, Nádasdy Nr 39, Splényi Nr 51, Jellačič Nr 53; EH Joseph Nr 55; J Colloredo Nr 57, Jordis Nr 59; vacant Nr 61, all of 3 bns except 53 and 61 which had 1 bn each. LtI bns Bach Nr 3, Am Ende Nr 4, Schmelzern Nr 7, Mihanovic Nr 15. JzPf Bussy, HusR vacant Nr 5, Nauendorf Nr 8. GzIR Oguliner Nr 3, Warasdiner-Creutzer Nr 5 (2 bns each); 2nd Banal Nr 11 (1 bn).

Austrian total 24,000 men.

Austrian losses 2,500 killed and wounded, 3,500 captured.

British Naval Forces Admiral Lord Keith commanding: *Phaeton* (38) and some smaller vessels.

Comment This victory soured at once for the Austrians as Bonaparte had already crossed the Alps; on 22 June, Suchet re-occupied Genoa.

Sources Clowes, Günther, Wrede.

UR Iller River, 5 June 1800, clashes

A tributary of the River Danube in southwestern Germany, including the actions at Erolzheim and Illertissen, between Memmingen in the south and Ulm in the north at the confluence of Iller and Danube (Donau).

French victories over the Austrians.

(Last action – Biberach, 9 May; next action – Höchstädt, 18/19 June.)

French Forces GdD Moreau commanding: Right Wing GdD Lecourbe with the divisions of Gudin, Montrichard and Nansouty and Molitor's Flanqueurs de la Droite. Centre Moreau and the divisions of Grandjean, Leclerc, Decaën and Hautpoul. Left Wing GdD Grenier and the divisions of Baraguay d'Hilliers, Ney, Legrand, Fauconnet and Richepanse's Flanqueurs de la Gauche. Exactly which units were engaged is not known; see OOB at the beginning of this chapter.

French total ca 55,000 infantry, 2,780 cavalry.

French losses ca 700 killed and wounded, 300 captured.

Austrian Forces FZM Baron von Kray commanding: IRs EH Ferdinand Nr 2, EH Carl Nr 3, Benjowsky Nr 31, Bender Nr 41 (3 bns each), Beaulieu Nr 58 (1st Bn). Gren Bns Rüffer, Fleming, Wouvermanns, Wurmser Freikorps (2 bns); Tyroler-Scharfschützen (10 coys). KürRs Kaiser Nr 1, Zezschwitz Nr 5, Coburg Nr 6, Kinsky Nr 12 (6 sqns each). DragRs Kronprinz Nr 2, vacant Nr 13, GzIR Deutsch-Banater Nr 12 (1st Bn).

Austrian total ca 28,000 men.

Austrian losses 800 killed and wounded, 1,100 captured, 4 guns, 8 ammunition waggons.

Sources Wrede, Günther.

IN Monte Nave, 5/6 June 1800, clash

Also known as Monte Laution; a fortified mountain peak in the Maritime Alps in southeastern France up against the Italian border, south of Cuneo, northeast of Nice.

A French victory over the Austrians.

(Last action – Genoa, 4 June; next action – Casteggio, 9 June.)

French Forces GdD Suchet commanding the Centre of the Armée d'Italie: GdB Brunet. Exact details not known; losses light. See OOB at the beginning of the 1800 chapter.

Austrian Forces GM Gorrupp commanding: part of FML Baron von Elsnitz's division (MGs Ulm and Bellegarde): IRs Preiss Nr 24, Sztáray Nr 33 (3 bns each). GM Lattermann: Gren Bns Paar, Weber, Kleimayr (1 bn each).

Austrian total ca 7,000 men.

Austrian losses Killed and wounded unknown; the 2nd Bn IR Sztáray (600 men) was cut off and captured, 7 guns were taken. The regiments dissolved and fled.

Comment Following Bonaparte's invasion of Piemont, the Austrian high command in Italy (GdK Melas) was paralysed with shock and unable to form coherent decisions. This led to the Col di Tenda being poorly secured and the French poured through it to take this isolated post.

Sources Wrede, Günther.

IN Casteggio (Montebello), 9 June 1800, battle

A small town in northwestern Italy, at the junction of Routes 10 and 35, just south of the Autostrada A21/E70, midway between the port-city of Genoa and Milan.

A French victory over the Austrians.

(Last action – Monte Nave, 5/6 June; next action – Marengo, 14 June.)

French Forces GdD Bonaparte commanding the Armée de Réserve: GdD Lannes, exact details not known. GdD Victor; GdD Monnier: 19e DBdeLé, 70e, 72e DBdeLi; GdD Chambarlhac: 24e DBdeLé; 43e, 96e DBdeLi; GdD Gardanne, exact details not known.

French total ca 12,000 men.

French losses reported as '600 killed, wounded and missing'. Bodart gives 3,000.

Austrian Forces FML Ott commanding part of the force which had been besieging Genoa: FML Vogelsang; FML Schellenberg, FML O'Reilly: IRs Reisky Nr 13 (3 bns, mostly captured), Stuart Nr 18 (3 bns), Splényi Nr 51 (3 bns), Jellačič Nr 53 (3 bns*), J Colloredo Nr 57 (3 bns*). HusR EH Joseph Nr 2 (6 sqns); HusR Nauendorf Nr 8 (4 sqns); GzIR Ottocaner Nr 2 (3rd Bn*); GzIR Oguliner Nr 3 (2 bns). DragR Lobkowitz Nr 10 (4 sqns).

Austrian total ca 11,000 men.

Austrian losses 659 killed, 1,445 wounded, 2,171 captured, 2 guns.

* = suffered very heavy losses.

Comment FML Ott did not realize that he was facing the main body of Bonaparte's army or he would not have offered combat in such adverse circumstances. The Austrians withdrew westwards over the River Scrivia on Alessandria.

Sources Wrede, Bodart, ÖMZ 1823 Heft 8, Belhomme.

IN Marengo, 14 June 1800, battle

A village in northwestern Italy (Piemont province), 4 km east of Alessandria near the confluence of the Rivers Tanaro and Bormida.

A French victory over the Austrians.

(Last action – Casteggio, 9 June; this action ended the campaign in northwestern Italy.)

French Forces GdD Bonaparte commanding the Armée de Réserve. **I Corps GdD Victor** GdD Gardanne: 44e, 101e DBdeLi (3 bns each). GdD Chambarlhac: GdB Hebbin: 24e DBdeLé (3 bns); 43e DBdeLé (3 bns). GdB Rivaud: 96e DBdeLi (3 bns). **II Corps GdD Lannes** GdD Watrin; GdB Malher 6e DBdeLé, 49e DBdeLi (3 bns each). GdB Gency: 22e and 28e DBde (3 bns each). **III Corps GdD Desaix** GdD Monnier: GdB Carra-St Cyr: 19e DBdeLé (2 bns); 70e DBdeLi (3 bns); GdB Schilt: 72e DBdeLi (3 bns). GdD Boudet; GdB Musnier: 9e DBdeLé, 30 DBdeLi (3 bns each); GdB Gresneau. 59e DBdeLi (3 bns); Consular Guard (1 bn). **Cavalry: GdD Murat** GdB Champeaux: 1er, 8e and 9e DragRs (4, 4 and 3 sqns resp,). GdB Kellermann: 2e CavR (1 sqn); 20e CavR (3 sqns); 21e CavR ($^1/_2$ sqn). GdB Rivaud: 12e HusR (4 sqns); 21e ChàCh (4 sqns). **The Reserve** 6e DragR (4 sqns); 12e ChàCh (4 sqns); 1er HusR (1 sqn); 11e HusR (2 sqns); 3e CavR (2 sqns); Consular guard CavR (3 sqns).

French total 28,127 men.

French losses (after Berthier): 1,100 killed, 3,600 wounded, 900 captured and missing. GdD Desaix, GdB Champeaux killed.

Austrian Forces GdK Baron Melas commanding:.

1st Column: **Avantgarde Obst Frimont** Jg Bn Mariassy, LtI Bn Bach Nr 4, Am Ende Nr 3 (1 bn each); JzPfR Bussy; DragR Kaiser Nr 1 (2 sqns each); pioniers (1 coy) **Avantgarde totals** 832 infantry, 458 cavalry, 100 pioniers. **Main Body FML Haddik** GM Pilati: DragR Kaiser Nr 1 (3 sqns); DragR Karaczay Nr 4 (6 sqns). GM Bellegarde: IRs Jellačič Nr 53 (1 bn);

EH Anton Nr 52 (2 bns). GM St Julien: IR vacant M Wallis Nr 11 (3 bns). **Main Body totals** 3,677 infantry, 1,362 cavalry. **Division of FML Kaim** GM de Briey: IR F Kinsky Nr 47 ($2^1/_2$ bns); GM Knesevich: IR Toscana Nr 23 (3 bns). GM La Marseille: IR EH Josef Nr 63 (3 bns): **Divisional total**: 4,939 infantry. **Division of FML Morzin** GM Lattermann GM Weidenfeld: Gren Bns Paar, Pers, Sciaffinati, Weber, Czerwenka, Pertusy, Piret, Khevenhüller, Görschen, Weissenwolf, St Julien. Pioniers (400). **Divisional total** 4,786. **Division of FML Elsnitz** GM Nobili: DragRs EH Johann Nr 3 and Liechtenstein Nr 9 (6 sqns each). GM Nimptsch: HusR Erdödy Nr 9 (6 sqns). Grenadier Division.

1st Column total 13,795 infantry, ca 1,820 cavalry.

2nd (or Left) Column FML Ott. **Avantgarde** GM Gottesheim: Jg Bn Mariassy (1 coy); IR Fröhlich Nr 28 (1 bn); DragR Lobkowitz Nr 10 (2 sqns). 1 x HAB. **Avantgarde totals** 563 infantry, 248 cavalry. **Main Body: Division of FML Schellenberg** GM Retz: IRs Fröhlich Nr 28 (2 bns); Mittrowsky Nr 40 (3 bns); pioniers (1 coy); 2 x 12pdr guns. GM Sticker: IRs Splényi Nr 51 (2 bns), Josef Colloredo Nr 57 (3 bns); DragR Lobkowitz Nr 10 (4 sqns). **Divisional totals** 4,005 infantry, 492 cavalry, 100 pioniers. **Division of FML Vogelsang** GM Baron Ulm: IRs Stuart Nr 18 (3 bns); Hohenlohe Nr 17 (2 bns); **Total** 2,194 infantry.

2nd Column totals 6,762 infantry, 740 cavalry, 100 pioniers.

3rd (or Right) Column, FML O'Reilly Avantgarde Jg Bn Mariassy (1 coy); HusR Nauendorf Nr 8 ($3^1/_2$ sqns), HusR vacant Nr 5 (2 sqns). **Main Body** GzIRs Ottocaner Nr 2 (3rd Bn); Oguliner Nr 3 (2 bns); Warasdiner-Kreutzer Nr 5 (1st Bn); DragR Württemberg Nr 8 (1 sqn). 1 x HAB.

3rd Column totals 2,228 infantry, 769 cavalry.

Austrian Army totals 23,294 infantry, 5,202 cavalry, 600 pioniers, 92 guns.

Austrian losses 963 killed, 5,518 wounded, 2,921 captured; 13 guns taken (20 more abandoned in the River Bormida), 13 ammunition waggons. FML Count Haddick was mortally wounded, Generals Vogelsang, Lattermann, Count Bellegarde, la Marseille, Gottesheim and 238 officers were wounded.

Comment This was the bloodiest battle of the campaign; Melas, lightly wounded but confident of victory early in the day, left the battlefield at midday, abandoning his men to their destruction in Bonaparte's counterattack. His Chief of Staff, Zach, took over command. This victory gave the French the French 12 fortresses, 1,500 guns and considerable magazines and destroyed Austria's will to continue the war. It also gave Bonaparte the political weight he needed to return to Paris and confirm his position as the leader of the French. There was no point in continued Austrian resistance in the field after 14 June; Melas was surrounded by a far more numerous army and would have been defeated again to no purpose. He salvaged by negotiation whatever he could.

Sources Wrede, ÖMZ 1822, Heft 10, 1823 Heft 9, 1828, Heft 8, Günther.

UR Höchstädt, 18/19 June, clash

A town on the northern bank of the River Danube in southern Germany, on Route B16, 35 km northwest of Augsburg on the River Lech.

A French victory over the Austro-Allies.

(Last action – Iller River, 5 June; next action – Neuburg, 27 June.)

French Forces GdD Moreau commanding: exact details not known; see OOB at the beginning of the 1800 chapter.

French total ca 40,000 men.

French losses ca 1,000 men killed, wounded and missing.

Austro-Allied Forces FZM Count Sztáray commanding: FML von Hügel's **Württemberg Contingent**: GM Beulwitz: IRs Beulwitz, Seckendorf, Seeger (1 bn each); Füss-Jägers (3 coys); Garde du Corps (1 sqn); ChLR (3 sqns); Kontingents-Rs von Zobel, von Mylius, von Obernitz (1 bn each); 6 x 3 pdr guns, 8 x 6 pdr guns.

Austrian Troops KürR Albert Nr 3, Hohenzollern Nr 8 (6 sqns each); HusRs Vécsey Nr 4, Blankenstein Nr 6 (8 sqns each).

Austro-Allied total 10,000 men.

Austro-Allied losses 1,000 killed and wounded, 3,000 captured, 20 guns, 4 colours.

Sources Wrede, Günther.

UR Neuburg, 27 June 1800, clash

A town in the southern German state of Bavaria, on the southern bank of the River Danube, on Route 16 between Ingolstadt and Donauwörth.

A French victory over the Austrians.

(Last action – Höchstädt, 18/19 June; next action – Ampfing, 1 December.)

French Forces GdD Lecourbe commanding. Exact details not known; see OOB at the beginning of the 1800 chapter.

French total 11,000 men.

French losses 800 killed and wounded, 200 captured. Théophile Corret de Latour-d'Auvergne, 'First Grenadier of France' was killed here.

Austrian Forces FZM Baron von Kray commanding: IRs Wenkheim Nr 35, Erbach Nr 42 (3 bns each); KürRs Lothringen Nr 7, Hohenzollern Nr 8, Kinsky Nr 12 (6 sqns each). DragR Latour Nr 11 (6 sqns).

Austrian total ca 8,000 men.

Austrian losses 700 killed and wounded, 600 captured.

Comment There now followed an armistice (prompted by Bonaparte's decisive victory at Marengo in northern Italy on 14 June) until late November.

Sources Wrede, Günther.

ZZ Malta, early June 1798 – 5 September 1800, capture

An island in the Mediterranean, 90 km south of Sicily.

A British victory over the French.

This was the only 'naval' action of note in 1800.

French Garrison GdD Vaubois commanding: 6e DBdeLi (2e, 3e Bns); 19e DBdeLi (1er Bn); 80e DBdeLi (3e Bn); 7e DBdeLé; 41e DBdeLi (det); 23e DBdeLé (carabiniers).

French total 6,000 men.

French losses ca 2,000 died. The colour of the 19e DBdeLi was taken. The garrison marched out with honours of war and were returned to France on British ships together with their weapons and baggage. The warships *Athénian** (64), *Dégo** (64) and *Cartegénoise** (36) and several smaller vessels were also taken.

* = Maltese ships.

British Forces Captain George Martin commanding: *Northumberland* (74), *Généreux* (74), *Success* (32).

British totals and losses Not known; light.

Comment Towards the end of the blockade, the garrison were dying at a rate of over 100 per day due to starvation and sickness. Britain now took possession of the island.

Sources Clowes, Fortescue, Charrié.

UR Ampfing, 1 December 1800, clash

A village in the southeastern part of the southern German state of Bavaria, on the River Isen, just north of Route B12, 8 km west of Mühldorf, ca 60 km east of München (Munich).

An Austrian victory over the French.

(Last action – Neuburg, 27 June; next action – Hohenlinden, 3 December.)

French Forces GdD Moreau commanding. Part of the divisions of Delmas, Leclerc, Richepanse and d'Hautpoul. Exact details of participation not known, see OOB at the beginning of this chapter.

French total 35,000 men.

French losses 1,200 killed and wounded; 4 guns dismounted, 3 caissons exploded.

Austrian Forces FML Archduke Johann commanding: IRs EH Carl Nr 3, Clerfayt Nr 9, vacant Nr 60 (3 bns each); DragRs Waldeck Nr 7, Latour Nr 11 (6 sqns each); HusR Vécsey Nr 4 (6 sqns).

Austrian total 12,000 men.

Austrian losses 303 killed, 1,690 wounded, 1,077 captured.

Sources Wrede, Günther, Picard.

UR Hohenlinden, 3 December 1800, battle

A village in the southeastern part of the southern German state of Bavaria, 33 km east of the capital München, on Route B12/E552.

A French victory over the Austro-Bavarians.

(Last action – Ampfing, 1 December; next action – Rosenheim, 9 December.)

French Forces GdD Moreau commanding the Centre and Left Wing of the Armée du Rhin.

Centre: 1st Division GdD Grouchy, GdBs Boye and Grandjean: 46e, 57e and 108e DBdeLi (3 bns each); 6e CavR (3 sqns), 11e ChàCh (4 sqns); 4e HusR (4 sqns); 1 x HAB, 1 x FAB. Sappers (1 coy); 12 guns. **Divisional totals** ca 7,039 infantry, 1,380 cavalry. **2nd Division** GdD Richepense, GdBs Walther, Drouet, Lorcet, Sahuc: 8e, 27e and 48e DBdeLi (3 bns each); 14e DBdeLé (1er Bn); 10e CavR (3 sqns); 1er ChàCh, 20e ChàCh and 5e HusR (4 sqns each). 1 x FAB, 2 x HAB. Sappers (1 coy). **Divisional totals** 8,299 infantry, 2,204 cavalry, 14 guns. **3rd Division** GdD Decaen, GdBs Debilly, Durutte, Kniaziewicz: 4e, 100e DBdeLi (3 bns each), 14e DBdeLé (2 bns). Polish infantry (3 bns); 17e DragR, 6e and 10e ChàCh (4 sqns each); Polish Lancers (400 men). 1 x FAB, 1 x

HAB, Polish artillery (64 men). Sappers (1 coy). **Divisional totals** 7,850 infantry, 2,069 cavalry, 12 guns. **Cavalry Division** GdD d'Hautpoul, GdBs Espagne, La Coste: 57e DBdeLi (1 coy); Hus Volontaires (2 sqns); 1er and 2e Carabiniers (4 sqns each); 8e and 9e CavRs (3 sqns each); 1 x HAB. **Divisional totals** 87 infantry, 1,578 cavalry, 6 guns. Artillery Park 2 x FAB (6 guns, 346 men).

Centre totals 23,275 infantry, 7,250 cavalry, 50 guns.

Left Wing GdD Grenier: 1st Division GdD Legrand, GdBs Salligny, Sabatier, Bontems: 16e, 42e and 51e DBdeLi (3 bns each); 12e CavR (3 sqns); 5e and 16e ChàCh (4 sqns each) 1 x HAB, 1 x FAB. Sapeurs (1 coy). **Divisional totals** 6,374 infantry, 1,406 cavalry, 12 guns. **2nd Division** GdD Ney, GdBs Joba, Bonnet, Desperrières: 15e, 23e, 76e, 103e DBdeLi (3 bns each); combined grenadiers (1 bn); 19e CavR (3 sqns); 13e DragR, 8e ChàCh (4 sqns each); 1 x FAB, 2 x HAB, sappers (1 coy). **Divisional total** 8,315 infantry, 1,105 cavalry, 14 guns. **3rd Division** GdBs Bastoul and Fauconnet: 53e, 89e DBdeLi (3 bns each), 13e and 17e CavRs (3 sqns each); 2e DragR, 23e ChàCh (4 sqns each); 1 x FAB, 2 x HAB. **Divisional totals** 4,060 infantry, 2,044 cavalry, 16 guns. Artillery park: 3 x coys, 7 guns.

Left Wing total 18,749 infantry, 4,555 cavalry, 49 guns.

Right Wing GdD Lecourbe. **1st Division** GdD Molitor, GdB Jardon: 83e DBdeLi (3 bns) 1ère DBdeLé (1er Bn), 10e DBdeLé (1er and 3e Bns); 6e HusR (3 sqns); 7e HusR (4 sqns). Sappers (1 coy); 1 x HAB, 1 x FAB. **Divisional total** ca 5,240 infantry, 1,016 cavalry, 11 guns. **2nd Division** GdD Gudin, GdBs Laval, Puthod: 36e, 38e, 94e DBdeLi (3 bns each); 10e DBdeLé (2e Bn); 8e HusR (4 sqns); sappers (1 coy), 1 x HAB, 1 x FAB. **Divisional total** ca 7,588 infantry, 605 cavalry, 9 guns. **3rd Division** GdD Montrichard, GdBs Roussel, Schinner: 37e, 84e, 109e DBdeLi (3 bns each); 9e HusR (4 sqns); Sappers (1 coy); 2 x HAB, 1 x FAB. **Divisional total** ca 6,835 infantry, 413 cavalry, 13 guns. **Reserve Division** GdB Nansouty: 11e DragR, 23e ChàCh (4 sqns each); 1/2 x HAB **Divisional total** 881 cavalry, 3 guns. Artillery Park 147 gunners and artificers, 3 guns.

Right Wing totals 19,663 infantry, 2,915 cavalry, 36 guns.

Total Armée du Rhin 61,687 infantry, 14,720 cavalry, 135 guns.

French losses ca 2,500 killed and wounded.

Austro-Bavarian Forces FML Archduke Johann commanding: **Avantgarde** GM Meczery: UlR Motschlitz Nr 2 (8 sqns); Tyroler-Scharfschützen (10 coys); Wurmser Freikorps (12 coys); HusR Mészáros Nr 10 (8 sqns). LtI Bn Radivojevich Nr 5 (1 bn). **Right Wing** FZM Kienmayer: FML Schwarzenberg: GM Frenel: DragR Coburg Nr 6, KürR Mack Nr 10 (6 sqns each); Combined Siebenburg-Wallachische GzIR (1st Bn); GzIR Peterwardeiner Nr 4 (1 bn). GM Gavassini: IRs Clerfayt Nr 9; Gemmingen Nr 21 (2 bns each); De Ligne Nr 30 (1 bn); Murray Nr 55, Beaulieu Nr 58 (2 bns each). GM Candiani: IRs EH Ferdinand Nr 2 (3 bns), Württemberg Nr 38 (2 bns). FML EH Ferdinand GzIR Gradiskaner Nr 8 (1st Bn) GzIR Peterwardeiner Nr 9 (2nd Bn); IRs Wenkheim Nr 35, Stain Nr 50 (3 bns each); GM Vincent: DragR vacant Nr 13 (6 sqns); GM Weeber: KürR Kaiser Nr 1 (6 sqns). **Centre** FZM Baillet FML von Hessen-Homburg: GM O'Donnell: IRs Lacy Nr 22, O Wallis Nr 29 (3 bns each). GM Roschowsky. DragR EH Ferdinand Nr 2 (6 sqns). GM Dinnersberg: KürR Nassau Nr 9 (6 sqns). FML Hohenlohe: GM Majthany: IRs de Vins Nr 37, Brechainville Nr 25 (2 bns each). GM Esterházy: KürR Zezschwitz Nr 5, DragR La Tour Nr 11 (6 sqns each). **Left Wing** FZM Riesch: FML Merveldt: GM Klein IRs EH Carls Nr 3, W Colloredo Nr 56 (3 bns each). GM Görger: KürR Anspach Nr 11, DragR Waldeck Nr 7 (6 sqns each). FML Albert Gyulai: GM Leuwen: IRs Manfredini Nr 12, Kaunitz Nr 20 (3 bns each). GM Stahel: DragR Kinsky Nr 12, KürR EH Franz Nr 2 (6 sqns each). **The Reserve** FML Liechtenstein: GM Wolfskehl: HusR Vécsey Nr 4, KürR Albert Nr 3, KürR Lothringen Nr 7 (6 sqns each). FML Kollowrath: GM Spannochi: IR vacant Nr 60 (3 bns); Gren Bns Sebottendorf, Tegethoff, Wouvermanns, Eichler (1 bn each). GM Beyer: IR Benjowsky Nr 31 (3 bns): Gren Bns Eggerdes, De Ligne, Papp, Morwitz. GM Grünne: KürR Hohenzollern Nr 8 (6 sqns); HusR EH Ferdinand Nr 3 (8 sqns).

Austrian total ca 49,000 men.

Austrian losses 1,900 killed and wounded, 8,000 captured, 50 guns, 85 ammunition and baggage waggons.

The Bavarian Division 1st Brigade GM von Deroy: Gren Bn Reuss, LIRs Minucci, Stengel, Sprety, Schlossberg, Jg Bns Kessling, Metzen (1 bn each). 2nd Brigade: GM Wrede; Gren Bn Pompey, LIRs Buseck,

Dalwigk, Zoller, de la Motte, Jg Bn Preysing (1 bn each). Combined ChLR (6 sqns). Artillery 24 guns.

Bavarian total 9,221 men.

Bavarian losses 3 officers, 21 men, 32 horses killed; 7 officers, 83 men, 30 horses wounded, 37 officers, 1,544 men and 7 horses captured; 19 cannon; 5 howitzers, 44 ammunition waggons, 211 train horses captured.

Comment This battle sealed the fate of the 'Holy Roman Empire of German nations'.

Sources, Wrede, Günther, Bezzel, Picard.

UR Rosenheim, 9 December 1800, clash

A town in southeastern German, on the west bank of the River Inn on Route B15, 46 km southeast of München (Munich).

A French victory over the Austrians.

(Last action - Hohenlinden, 3 December; next action - Salzburg, 14 December.)

French Forces GdD Montrichard (of Gen Lecourbe's corps) commanding: 36e, 84e, 109e DBdeLi (3 bns each); 9e HusR (4 sqns); 8 guns.

French total ca 10,000 men.

French losses 110 men killed, wounded and missing.

Austrian Forces FZM Riesch commanding: FML Merveldt, GM Klein, GM Görger: IRs W Colloredo Nr 56, EH Carl Nr 3 (3 bns each); DragR Waldeck Nr 7, KürR Anspach Nr 11 (6 sqns each). FML Albert Gyulai, GM Leuwen, GM Stahel: IRs Manfredini Nr 12, Kaunitz Nr 20 (3 bns each); DragR Kinsky Nr 12, KürR EH Franz Nr 2 (6 sqns each). FML Condé's Émigré Corps: IRs Noble, Bourbon, Durand.

Austrian total ca 6,000 men.

Austrian losses 600 killed, wounded and captured, 5 guns dismounted.

Comment The Austrian units had suffered badly during and after the battle of Hohenlinden on 3 December and were short of food, ammunition and sleep.

Sources Wrede, Günter, Picard.

UR Salzburg, 14 December 1800, clash

Capital city of the Austrian province of the same name, on the River Salzach, up against the border with Germany and at the junction of Autobahns A8/E52, A10/E55/E60. The action took place north of the city, near the confluence of the Salzach with the Saalach.

An Austrian victory over the French.

(Last action - Rosenheim, 9 December; next action - Neumarkt, 16 December.)

French Forces GdD Lecourbe commanding part of the right wing of the Armée du Rhin: 2nd Division, GdD Gudin: 94e DBdeLi (3 bns); 36e DBdeLi (3 bns). GdD Montrichard: combined grenadiers (4 bns); 38e and 67e DBdeLi (3 bns each). GdB Nansouty: 11e DragR, 23e ChàCh (4 sqns each); 7e, 8e and 9e HusRs (4 sqns each). 2 x HAB, 3 x FAB.

French total ca 20,000 men, 30 guns.

French losses ca 1,000 killed, wounded and missing.

Austrian Forces FML Archduke Johann commanding: IRs Wenkheim Nr 35 (3 bns); de Vins Nr 37 (2nd Bn); vacant Nr 60 (2 bns), Gren Bns Rüffer, Papp KürRs Kaiser Nr 1 (6 sqns), Nassau Nr 9 (2 sqns), Mack Nr 10 (6 sqns); DragRs Waldeck Nr 7, Latour Nr 11 (6 sqns each). HusR Vécsey Nr 4 (8 sqns). KürR Anspach Nr 11 (6 sqns).

Austrian total 10,000 men.

Austrian losses 500 killed, wounded and captured, 5 guns.

Comment A hard-fought and successful rearguard action.

Sources Wrede, Günther, Picard.

UR Neumarkt, 16 December 1800, clash

A village in the northern Austrian province of Salzburg, about 27 km northeast of Salzburg city, just west of Route 1 and north of Lake Waller. The combat began at Strass, some kilometres to the southwest on Route 1.

A French victory over the Austrians.

(Last action - Salzburg, 14 December; next action - Frankenmarkt, 17 December.)

French Forces GdD Richepanse commanding the 2nd Division of the Centre of the Armée du Rhin: GdB Sahuc: 48e DBdeLi (3 bns). 1er ChàCh (4 sqns), 1 x FAB. GdB Lorcet: 8e DBdeLi (3 bns); 5e HusR (4 sqns); 1 x HAB.

French total ca 7,000 men.

French losses Not known but light.

Austrian Forces GM Löpper commanding: IR de Vins Nr 37 (2nd Bn); KürR Nassau Nr 9 (2 sqns). HusR Vécsey Nr 4 (2 sqns).

Austrian total 3,700 men.

Austrian losses 500 killed, wounded and missing.

Sources Wrede, Günther, Picard.

UR Frankenmarkt, 17 December 1800, clash

A hamlet in the northwestern Austrian province of Oberösterreich, 18 km west of Vöcklabruck, on Route 1, north of Lake Attersee and northeast of Salzburg city.

A French victory over the Austrians.

(Last action - Neumarkt, 16 December; next action - Schwanstadt, 18 December.)

French Forces GdD Richepanse commanding: GdB Digonnet, Durutte: Combined grenadiers; 4e, 50e, 100e DBdeLi, 13e CavR, 17e DragR, 5e HusR.

French total 6,000 men.

French losses Not exactly known; moderate.

Austrian Forces FML Baron von Kienmayer commanding: IR Wenkheim Nr 35 (3 bns).

Austrian total 4,000 men.

Austrian losses 2,650, mostly captured.

Sources Wrede, Günther, Picard.

UR Schwanstadt, 18 December 1800, clash

A hamlet in the northwestern Austrian province of Oberösterreich, 11 km northeast of Vöcklabruck on Route 1 towards Wels, at the junction with Route 135. Now called Schwanenstadt.

A French victory over the Austrians.

(Last action - Frankenmarkt, 17 December; next action - Vöcklabruck, 18 December.)

French Forces GdD Richepanse commanding: 10e CavR, 1er and 20e ChàCh, 5e HusR.

French total ca 2,000 men.

French losses Not exactly known; light.

Austrian Forces FML Count Riesch commanding: Lt Bn Steigentesch Nr 12 (1 bn); Freikorps Wurmser (2 bns, 2 sqns); Tyroler-Scharfschützen (10 coys); KürR Lothringen Nr 7 (6 sqns); DragR Waldeck Nr 7 (4 sqns); DragR Latour Nr 11 (2 sqns).

Austrian total 3,000 men.

Austrian losses 700 cavalrymen, mostly captured. A standard of KürR Lothringen was taken by the 20e ChàCh.

Comment Only the cavalry were seriously engaged and they had their backs to a river.

Sources Wrede, Günther, Picard.

UR Vöcklabruck, 18 December 1800

A small town in the Austrian province of Oberösterreich, at the junction of Routes 1 and 145 on the Dürre Ager river; just north of the Attersee lake.

A French victory over the Austrians.

(Last action - Schwanstadt, 18 December; next action - Lambach, 19 December.)

French Forces GdD Richepanse commanding the 2nd Division of the Centre of the Armée du Rhin: GdB Sahuc 48e DBdeLi (3 bns); 14e DBdeLé (1er Bn); 1er and 20e ChàCh.

French total ca 4,700 men.

French losses Not known but very light.

Austrian Forces GM Löpper commanding: IR de Vins Nr 37 (2nd Bn). GzIR Gradiskaner (3rd Bn); KürR Nassau Nr 9 (2 sqns); HusR Vécsey Nr 4 (2 sqns). 1 x HAB.

Austrian total ca 2,600 men.

Austrian losses Not exactly known but very heavy. Most of the infantry were captured (as was Gen Löpper) with 2 guns.

Comment The morale of the Austrians was now so low that they put up practically no fight.

Sources Wrede, Günther, Picard.

UR Lambach, 19 December 1800, clash

A small town in the northwestern Austrian province of Oberösterreich, 20 km northeast of Vöcklabruck on Route 1 towards Wels, at the junction with Route 144 and on the River Traun.

A French victory over the Austrians.

(Last action - Vöcklabruch, 18 December; next action - Kremsmünster, 19 December.)

French Forces GdD Richepanse commanding: GdB Sahuc, Sarrut: 14e DBdeLé, 27e DBdeLi, 1er and 20e ChàCh, 5e HusR.

French total 5,000 men.

French losses ca 500 killed, wounded and missing.

Austrian Forces GM v Mecséry commanding: IR Manfredini Nr 12 (3 bns), KürR Anspach Nr 2 (6 sqns); KürR EH Franz Nr 2 (6 sqns); KürR Mack Nr 10 (6 sqns). UlR Motschlitz Nr 2 (8 sqns).

Austrian total 3,000 men.

Austrian losses 1,450 men mostly of IR Manfredini; captured. The Austrian army was now disintegrating; 500 waggons of rations and forage were captured.

Sources Wrede, Günther, Picard.

UR Kremsmünster, 20 December 1800, clash

A small town and Benedictine monastery in the Austrian province of Oberösterreich, on the River

Krems at the junction of Routes 122 and 139; 27 km southwest of Linz on the Donau (Danube).

A French victory over the Austrians.

(Last action – Lambach, 19 December; this was (apart from minor skirmishes) the last action of this campaign.)

French Forces GL Lecourbe commanding: GdD Montrichard's 3rd Division, Right Wing of the Armée du Rhin: 109e DBdeLi (1er and 2e Bns); 7e and 9e HusRs (4 sqns each).

French total ca 2,300 men.

French losses Not known exactly; 'extremely light'.

Austrian Forces FML Schwarzenberg commanding: UlR Motschlitz Nr 2 (8 sqns); Tyroler Scharfschützen (10 coys); Wurmser Freikorps (12 coys). LtI Bn Radivojevich Nr 5 (1 bn); 6 guns.

Austrian total Not exactly known; all regiments very weak.

Austrian losses 1,200 captured, 4 guns.

Comment The Austrian army was by now so demoralized that it was incapable of serious resistance. Archduke Charles had arrived at Schwanenstadt on 17 December to take over command of the army from the incompetent Archduke John. He realised the hopelessness of the situation and concluded an armistice at Steyer on 22 December. Austria then concluded a separate peace with France at Luneville on 9 February 1801. French mopping up operations continued to harvest large quantities of prisoners, guns, materiel and stores. **Total** Austrian losses were put at 20,000 men, 147 guns, 400 caissons and over 7,000 other vehicles.

Sources Wrede, Günther, Picard.

IN Mincio River, 25/26 December 1800, battle

A river in northeastern Italy, running south out of lake Garda into the River Po; the area of the three villages Monzambano, Valeggio and Pozzolo between Lake Garda and the fortress city of Mantua.

A French victory over the Austrians.

(Last action – Marengo, 14 June; this was the last action of the campaign.)

French Forces GdD Brune commanding: the French army as at Marengo, 14 June.

French total 66,000 men, 160 guns.

French losses 4,000 killed, wounded and missing, 1 colour (of GdD Watrin's Division). GdB Calvin killed.

Austrian Forces GdK Count Bellegarde commanding: IRs: Hoch und Deutschmeister Nr 4 (2 bns*); M Wallis Nr 11 (3 bns); Oranien Nr 15 (1 bn); Terzy Nr 16 (2 bns); Hohenlohe Nr 17 (3 bns); Stuart Nr 18 (3 bns); Allvintzy Nr 19 (3 bns); Preiss Nr 24 (3 bns); Strassoldo Nr 27 (3 bns); Frelich Nr 28 (3 bns); S Gyulai Nr 32 (1 bn); Kray Nr 34 (1 bn); Fürstenberg Nr 36 (3 bns); Nádasdy Nr 39 (2 bns); Thurn Nr 40 (3 bns); F Kinsky Nr 47 (2 bns); Splényi Nr 51 (3 bns); Jellačič Nr 53 (2 bns); Gren Bns Reinwald, Weber, Kleimayrn, Pertusy, Piret, Hoffmeister, Riese, St Julien. LtI Bns Schmelzern Nr 7, Mihanovic Nr 15 (1 bn each); JzPf Bussy (6 sqns); HusR EH Joseph Nr 2, vacant Nr 7, Erdödy Nr 9. GzIR Oguliner Nr 3 (2 bns), Warasdiner-Kreutzer Nr 5 (2 bns); 2nd Banal Nr 11 (1 bn); HusR Nauendorf Nr 8 (2 sqns), Tiroler Freiwilligen Schützencorps (2 coys) Jäger Corps Kurz (5 coys) DragR Lobkowitz Nr 10 (4 sqns). DragR Karaczay Nr 4 (6 sqns). Jäger Corps d'Aspre (1bn).

Austrian totals 38,000 infantry, 12,000 cavalry, 100 guns.

Austrian losses 22 officers, 785 men killed; 144 officers, 3,258 men wounded; 83 officers, 3,984 men captured, 1 officer, 312 men missing: 657 horses killed, wounded and missing; 14 x 3 pdrs, 6 x 6 pdrs, 3 x 12 pdrs and 6 x 7 pdr howitzers.

* = suffered very heavy casualties.

Comment Following this defeat the Austrians withdrew eastwards over the River Adige (Etsch). The expected armistice between France and Austria came into force within a few days. Oudinot claimed that the Austrians lost 16,000 men (including 1,000 prisoners), 42 guns, 2 howitzers and three colours in the period 25–27 December 1800. He quoted French losses on 25 December as '900 killed and wounded'. The Austrian FML Kaim was killed, Gen Prince Karl Rohan wounded.

Sources Wrede, ÖMZ 1828 Vol III, Heft 8.

1801

1801 THE ACTIONS

YE Aboukir, 8 March 1801, clash

A fort on a bay of the same name on Egypt's Mediterranean coast, 21 km northeast of Alexandria.

A British victory over the French.

(This was the first action in Egypt in 1801; next action – Lake Mareotis, 13 March.)

French Forces GdD Friant commanding: 61e & 75e DBdeLi (1 bn each); 25e & 51e DBdeLi (½ bn each); 18e DragR (2sqns); 20e DragR (det).

French total 1,800 men, 15 guns.

French losses 350 killed, wounded and missing, 8 guns.

British Forces LG Sir Ralph Abercromby commanding: MG Ludlow: 1/2nd & 1/3rd Foot Guards (1 bn each). MG Coote 2/1st Foot (1 bn); 54th Foot (2 bns). Reserve MG Moore, BG Oakes: 23rd, 28th, 42nd, 58th (1 bn each); 40th (4 coys); Corsican Rangers (1 bn).

British total ca 8,000 men.

British losses 31 officers, 621 men killed, wounded and missing.

Comment GdD Menou (French commander in Egypt) knew the British had landed but instead of opposing them with sufficient force, he sent Friant with inadequate means and thus ensured his defeat.

Sources Fortescue, Herold, Bodart.

YE Lake Mareotis, 13 March 1801, clash

A lake in northern Egypt, southeast of Alexandria.

A British victory over the French.

(Last action – Aboukir, 8 March; next action – Alexandria, 21 March.)

French Forces GdD Lanusse commanding. GdB Silly: 4e DBdeLé (1 bn); 18e DBdeLi (3 bns); GdB Vanentin: 69e DBdeLi (2 bns); 88e DBdeLi (2 bns). GdD Friant. 61e & 75e DBdeLi (1 bn each); 25e & 51e DBdeLi (½ bn each) 18e DragR (2sqns), 22e ChàCh (2sqns).

French total ca 9,000 men, 21 guns.

French losses 500 killed, wounded and missing; 5 guns.

British Forces LG Sir Ralph Abercromby commanding: The Reserve MG Moore: BG Oakes: 23rd, 28th, 42nd, 58th Foot, Corsican Rangers (1 bn each); 40th Foot (4 coys). Guards Brigade MG Ludlow: 1/2nd & 1/3rd Foot Guards (2 bns). MG Coote: 2/1st Foot, 54th Foot (2 bns); 92nd Foot (1 bn). MG Cradock: 8th, 13th, 18th, 90th Foot (1 bn each). MG Lord Cavan: 50th & 79th Foot, Royal Marines (1 bn each). BG Doyle: 2nd, 30th, 44th & 89th Foot (1 bn each). BG John Stuart: Minorca R; De Roll's R; Dillon's R. Cavalry BG Finch: 11th LDR (1tp); 12th & 26th LDRs, Hompesch's LDR (4 sqns each).

British total ca 14,000 men & 16 guns (dragged by sailors).

British losses 1,300 killed and wounded mostly in the 90th & 92nd Foot who stormed the Mandora redoubt. Their descendant regiments carry this battle honour today.

Comment Heavy British losses were mainly caused by lack of artillery horse teams to move the guns and caissons.

Sources Fortescue, Bodart.

YE Alexandria, 21 March 1801, battle

A port city on the Egyptian Mediterranean coast, on the Nile Delta, 182 km northwest of Cairo.

A British victory over the French.

(Last action – Lake Mareotis; next action – Cairo, 27 June.)

French Forces GdD Menou commanding: **Right Wing** GdD Reynier*: GdB Damas: 13e DBdeLi (1er & 2eBns); 85e DBdeLi (1er & 2eBns). GdD Friant: 25e DBdeLi (1er & 2eBns); 61e DBdeLi (2 bns); 75e DBdeLi (1er & 2eBns). **The Centre** GdD Rampon, GdD Destaing: 21e DBdeLé (3 bns); 25e DBdeLi (2 coys); 32e DBdeLi (1er & 2eBns); 2e DBdeLé (3 coys). **Left Wing** GdD Lanusse: GdB Silly: 4e DBdeLé (1 bn); 18e DBdeLi (3 bns). GdB Valentin: 69e DBdeLi (2 bns); 88e DBdeLi (2 bns); Dromedary Corps (130 men). **Cavalry** GdB Roize, GdB Bron: 7e HusR bis (1 sqn); 22e ChàCh (1 sqn); GdB Boussard: 3e DragR (2 sqns); 14e & 18e DragR (4 sqns each); 20 DragR (1 sqn), 15e DragR (2 sqns).

French totals 9,600 infantry, 400 cavalry, 46 guns.

French losses 3,000 killed and wounded, 500 captured, 2 guns, 1 colour (that of the 21e DBdeLé). GdD Lanusse, GdB Baudot and Roize killed.

British Forces LG Sir Ralph Abercromby commanding: GM Ludlow 1st/2nd & 1st/3rd Guards (1 bn each). 1st Bde GM Coote: 2nd/1st (1 bn); 54th (2 bns) & 92nd (1 bn) Foot. 2nd Bde GM Cradock*: 8th, 13th, 18th & 90th Foot (1 bn each). 3rd Bde GM Lord Cavan*: 50th & 79th Foot (1 bn each). 4th Bde

BG Doyle*: 2nd, 30th, 44th & 89th Foot (1 bn each). 5th Bde BG Sir John Stuart: Minorca Regt, De Roll's and Dillon's (1 bn each). Reserve MG Moore: BG Oakes: 23rd, 28th, 42nd, 58th, Corsican Rangers (1 bn each); 40th Foot (4 coys). Cavalry Bde BG Finch: 11th LD (1tp); 12th & 26th LD; Hompesch's LD (4 sqns each). Artillery 700 men; 24 x light 6 pdrs, 4 x light 12 pdrs; 1 x medium 12 pdr, 6 x 5½ inch howitzers.

British totals 11,700 infantry, 300 cavalry, 35 guns.

British losses 243 killed, 1,253 wounded, 33 missing. Sir Ralph Abercromby killed.

Comment It was in this battle that the 28th Foot, attacked from both front and rear, won their famous 'back badge' which they still wear on the backs of their hats today. This battle decided the campaign in favour of the British.

Sources Fortescue, Bodart.

* = these troops were not engaged in the action but are included in the totals.

ZZ Copenhagen, 2 April 1801, naval battle

The capital of Denmark; the battle was fought in the Sound, east of the city.

A British victory over the Danes.

(This was the only naval action of note in this region in 1801).

Danish Forces Commodore Fischer commanding: *Dannebrog** (62); *Hjälperen* (?); *Jylland** (48); *Holsteen** (60), *Elephanten* (70); *Infödsretten** (64); *Aggershus** (20); *Haien** (20); *Valkyrien** (48); *Nyborg** (20), *Provesteen** (56); *Rendsborg** (20) *Kronborg** (20); *Själland** (74); *Charlotte Amalie** (26). Floating batteries *Söhesteen** (18); *Flaadeblatt* (18); *Svärdfisken** (20); one other; eleven gunboats and the guns of Trekroner Fort, Little Crown battery and Stricker's battery.

Danish total 370 guns, 6,000 men in the ships, floating batteries and gunboats, a further 66 guns and 1,500 men in the batteries and works on shore.

Danish losses 480 killed, 570 wounded, 2,000 captured and missing. All prisoners were returned on 12 April.

British Forces Sir Hyde Parker commanding. The part of the fleet which came into combat was commanded by Vice Admiral Lord Nelson: *Elephant* (74); *Dart* (28); *Arrow* (28); *Blanche* (36); *Alcmene* (32); *Amazon* (38); *Zephyr* (28); *Defiance* (74); *Monarch* (74); *Ganges* (74); *Glatton* (50); *Ardent* (64); *Edgar* (74); *Bellona*** (74); *Russel*** (74); *Isis* (50); *Polyphemus* (64); *Désirée* (36); *Jamaica* (24); *Agamemnon*** (64) and two gunboats.

British total 600 guns, 60 carronades, 9,000 men.

British losses 256 killed, 688 wounded.

Comment The British aim was to destroy the Baltic fleets of Denmark, Sweden and Russia and thus emasculate the 'Armed Neutrality'. Copenhagen was a close-run victory but achieved the desired result in that Sweden and Russia were bullied into abandoning their desire to fight the British. Nelson's popularity with the British people soared.

* = taken by the British. All prizes except *Holsteen* were burnt.

** = went aground on the Mittelgrund and took no part in the action.

Sources Clowes, James.

YE Cairo, 27 June 1801, capitulation

The capital city of Egypt, situated on the River Nile in northern Egypt.

An Anglo-Turkish victory over the French.

(Last action - Alexandria, 21 March; next action - Alexandria, 31 August.)

French Forces GdD Belliard commanding. Exact details not known.

French total 13,000 men.

French losses All captured.

British Forces LG Hutchinson commanding the troops as for the Battle of Alexandria, 21 March.

British losses Not exactly known but very light.

Turkish Forces Grand Vizier Yussuf Pasha commanding 9,000 irregulars.

Turkish losses Not exactly known but very light.

Sources Fortescue, Herold.

ZZ Algeciras, 5 July 1801, naval clash

A naval harbour town in southern Spain, 7 km west of Gibraltar.

A Franco-Spanish victory over the British.

(This was the first naval action of note in this area; next action - Algeciras, 12 July).

Franco-Spanish Forces Rear Admiral Linois commanding 3 ships of the line, 1 frigate, 5 gunboats and the guns of the port. *Formidable* (80); *Indomptable* (80); *Desaix* (74); *Muiron* (40).

Franco-Spanish totals 284 guns, 2,000 men.

Franco-Spanish losses 600 killed and wounded; 5 gunboats (50 guns) sunk.

British Forces Rear Admiral Saumarez commanding 6 ships of the line. *Caesar* (80); *Pompée* (74); *Spencer* (74); *Venerable* (74); *Hannibal* (74); *Audacious* (74).

British totals 450 guns, 3,000 men.

British losses *Hannibal* (74) taken; 373 killed and wounded, 600 captured.

Comment Hannibal went aground and could not be got off.

Sources Bodart, Clowes, James.

ZZ Algeciras, 12 July 1801, naval clash

A naval harbour town in southern Spain, 7 km west of Gibraltar.

A British victory over the Franco-Spaniards.

(Last action – Algeciras, 5 July; this was the last naval action of note in this region in 1801.)

Franco-Spanish Forces Vice Admiral Moreno commanding: Spanish ships: *Real Carlos* (112); *San Hermenegildo* (112); *San Fernando* (94); *Argonauta* (80); *San Augustin* (74); *Perla* (24); *Sabina* (44). French ships: *Formidable* (80); *Indomptable* (80); *St Antoine* (74); *Desaix* (74); *Liberté* (40); *Muiron* (40); *Valeur* (14).

Franco-Spanish totals 9 ships of the line, 3 frigates, 1 gunboat. 918 guns, 6,000 men.

Franco-Spanish losses 2,300 men killed and wounded, 500 captured. 1 French ship [*St Antoine* (74)], 2 Spanish ships of the line [*Real Carlos* (112), *San Hermenegildo* (112)] and the frigate *Perla* (24) taken. The Spanish ships were destroyed; *Real Carlos* and *San Hermenegildo* blew up with heavy loss of life.

British Forces Rear Admiral Saumarez commanding: *Caesar* (80); *Venerable* (74); *Superb* (74); *Spencer* (74); *Audacious* (74); *Thames* (32); *Carlotta* (Portuguese); *Calpe* (14); *Louisa* (8). 5 ships of the line, 2 frigates, 3 smaller vessels; 460 guns, 3,600 men.

British losses 200 killed and wounded.

Sources Bodart, Clowes, James.

ZZ Boulogne, 15 August 1801, naval clash

A harbour town in the northwestern French Département Pas de Calais, 110 km northwest of Arras.

A French victory over the British.

(This was the only naval action of note in this region in 1801).

French Forces Vice Admiral Latouche commanding: a flotilla of gunboats and small vessels.

French losses 10 killed, 30 wounded.

British Forces Vice Admiral Viscount Nelson commanding 3 ships of the line, 4 frigates, 70 gunboats and fireships and 4,000 men.

British losses 44 killed, 126 wounded.

Comment This was strictly a small boat raiding action to disrupt the French invasion preparations.

Sources Bodart, James, Clowes.

YE Alexandria, 17 August – 2 September 1801, siege and capitulation

A major, fortified harbour city on the Nile delta in northern Egypt 182 km northwest of Cairo.

A British victory over the French.

(Last action – Cairo, 27 June; this was the last action of the Egyptian campaign.)

French Forces GdD Menou commanding. Exact details not known.

French total 4,500 men and the following warships: *Causse* (64); *Egyptienne* (44); *Justice* (40); *Régénéree* (36) and two Venetian 32s.

British Forces LG Hutchinson commanding. The army as at the Battle of Alexandria plus: Ancient Irish Fencibles (1 bn); 20th Foot (2 bns) and drafts for the following regiments: 24th, 25th, 26th Foot, de Watteville's (Swiss); Chasseurs Britanniques, Löwenstein's Jägers.

Comment Under the terms of the capitulation all French troops and civilians in Egypt (ca 8,000 in all) were returned to France on British ships with their personal weapons and baggage. All cannon and all warships in Alexandria harbour were surrendered to the British.

Sources Bodart, Herold.

The NAPOLEONIC WARS

1805–1815

1805

1805 THE ACTIONS

DV Wertingen, 8 October 1805, clash

A small town in the southern German state of Bavaria, about 10 km south of the River Danube and about 40 km northwest of the town of Augsburg.

A French victory over the Austrians.

(This was the opening action of the Danube Valley campaign; next action – Günzburg, 9 October.)

French Forces Prince Murat's Cavalry Corps and Lannes' V Corps GdD Klein: GdB Fenerolz, GdB Fauconnet, GdB Millet: 1er, 14e, 20e and 26e DragRs. 16 sqns ca 3,000 men. GdD Lasalle, GdB Treilhard: 9e and 10e HusRs, 8 sqns ca 1,600 men. GdD Beaumont, Gdb Boyer, GdB Scalfort: 5e, 8e, 9e 12e and 16e DragR, 18 sqns, ca 2,400 men. 28e RILé (3 bns) and Oudinot's grenadiers (8 bns); 2HAB (12 guns).

French totals 42 sqns ca 4,000 men and 11 bns, ca 8,000 infantry, ca 12,000 men.

French losses About 24 officers and 150 men dead and wounded.

Austrian Forces FML Auffenberg's III Corps FML Baillet, GM Vogel, GM O'Donnell, GM Sinzendorf, GM Dinersberg: IR Kaunitz Nr 20 (4 bns); Grenadiers (4 bns); IR Chasteler Nr 64 (½ bn), Kür R Albert Nr 3 (8 sqns); ChLR Rosenberg Nr 6 (6 sqns). IR EH Ludwig Nr 8 (3 bns); IR Jellačič Nr 62 (4 bns). FML Hohenzollern, GM Hohenfeld, GM Weber, GM Rohan: IR Spork Nr 25 (5 bns); IR Württemberg Nr 38 (GrenBn); IR Reuss-Greitz Nr 55 (4 bns+Gren bn); IR Stuart Nr 18 (3 bns); ChLR Latour Nr 4 (2 sqns), HusR Palatine Nr 12 (4 sqns).

Austrian totals 26½ bns; 20 sqns, 24 guns, ca 5000 infantry and 400 cavalry (actually engaged.)

Austrian losses 400 dead and wounded, 2,900 (including 52 officers) captured; 6 guns, 6 colours (IR 38 & IR 5).

Comment The element of surprise achieved by the French over Auffenberg's isolated corps gave them this victory; several Austrian infantry battalions were cut down before they could form square or were surrounded and forced to surrender. The Austrians withdrew westwards towards Günzburg. It is not clear why FM Mack had sent this small force to such an isolated position.

Sources: Wrede, Schulz, Martinien, v Angeli, Krauss.

DV Günzburg, 9 October 1805, clash

A small town in the southern German state of Bavaria, just south of the river Danube, just north of the motorway A8/E52, at the crossing of routes B10 and B16.

A French victory over the Austrians.

(Last action – Wertingen, 8 October; next action – Haslach, 10 October.)

French Forces GdD Malher of M Ney's VI Corps commanding. GdB Labasse: 25e RILé (3 bns); 27e, 50e & 59e RIdLi (6 bns).

French totals 9 bns ca 8,000 infantry and 6 guns.

French losses ca 700 men.

Austrian Forces FML d'Aspre commanding: IR Kaunitz Nr 20 (4 bns), IR Württemberg Nr 38 (3 bns), IR Jellačič Nr 62 (1 bn), 6 guns, Jägers (1 bn); Gren Bns Stuart, Colloredo, Erbach and Kaunitz (4 bns), HusR Palatine Nr 12 (4 sqns), ChLR Rosenberg Nr6, UlR Schwarzenberg Nr2 (2 sqns each).

Austrian Totals 9 bns, 8 sqns, 6 guns ca 7,000 men.

Austrian Losses About 2,000 men including 1 general; (they fell mostly on IR Württemberg) and 6 guns.

Comment The 59e RIdLi finally stormed the bridge over the Danube, chasing after two large Austrian columns withdrawing towards Ulm. Auffenberg's command had been sharply defeated at Wertingen the day before this action by Murat's cavalry and Oudinot's grenadiers. FM Mack had aimed to cross the Danube here but had to abandon the plan. His continual reorganization of the troops on the battlefield sowed confusion and demoralization.

Sources Wrede, Schulz, Krauss, Martinien.

DV Haslach (Jungingen or Albeck), 11 October 1805, clash

A village in the southern German state of Württemberg, about 7 km northeast of the city of Ulm/Danube, on route B19 (nowadays absorbed by Kesselbronn).

A French victory over the Austrians.

(Last action – Günzburg, 9th October; next action – Memmingen, 13 October.)

French Forces GdD Dupont commanding the 1st Division of Ney's VI Corps: GdB Rouyer: GdB Marchand: 9e RILé (3 bns); 32e and 96e RIdLi (4 bns). GdB Tilly: 2e, 15e & 17e DragR; 26e ChàCh, 1er HusR (12 sqns).

French totals 7 bns, 5,350 infantry, 12 sqns, 2,169 cavalry, 18 guns.

French losses 1,500 dead and wounded, 900 captured, 11 guns, 18 ammunition waggons. Two French dragoon regiments suffered heavily. The eagles and guidons of the 15e and 17e Dragoons were lost, the former being taken by the Austrian ChLR Latour Nr 4.

Austrian Forces FML Prince Schwarzenberg commanding: (FM Baron Mack was present and was wounded), FML Klenau: IR EH Ludwig Nr 8 (4 bns); IR EH Rainer Nr 11 (4 bns); IR Manfredini Nr 12 (4 bns); IR Reuss-Plauen Nr 17 (3 bns); IR Kaunitz Nr 20 (4 bns); IR EH Max Nr 35 (5 bns); IR Fröhlich Nr 28 (3 bns); IR Kollowrath Nr 36 (4 bns); IR Froon Nr 54 (4 bns); IR Württemberg Nr 38 (3 bns); IR Spork Nr 25 (3½ bns); IR Erbach Nr 42 (4 bns); IR Kaiser Nr 1 (Gren Bn); IR Beaulieu Nr 58 (Gren Bn); IR Riese Nr 15 (4 bns). DragR Hohenlohe Nr 2 (8 sqns); KürR Hohenzollern Nr 8 (2 sqns); KürR Albert Nr 3 (8 sqns); ChLR Latour Nr 4 (8 sqns); KürR Mack Nr 6 (2 sqns).

Austrian Totals 49½ bns, 28 sqns, 30 guns = 25,000 men.

Austrian losses ca 1,100 dead and wounded, over 3,000 (IR Nr 35) captured, 5 colours, 2 regimental guns.

Comment Mack received subsequently (and believed) a report of an anti-Bonapartist revolution in Paris and felt himself secure because his enemy would be forced to retire. Ney had foreseen Dupont's perilous exposure but Murat (in command of his own cavalry and of the V and VI Corps at this point) refused to take his advice to reinforce this isolated division.

Sources Wrede, Schulz, Martinien, Bodart, Charrié.

DV Memmingen, 13 October 1805, capitulation

A town in the southern German state of Bavaria, about 5 km east of the River Iller and 55 km south of Ulm, next to the junction of motorways A7/E43 and A96/E54.

A French victory over the Austrians.

(Last action – Haslach, 11 October; next action – Elchingen, 14 October.)

French Forces Marshall Soult's IV Corps ca 20,000 men.

French losses 4 dead, 12 wounded.

Austrian Forces GM Count Spangen commanding IR Czartoryski Nr 9 (1st, 3rd, 4th and Gren Bns); IR Mittrowsky Nr 40 (5 bns); IR Beaulieu Nr 58 (1st Bn); HusR Palatin Nr 12 (2 sqns), 10 guns

Austrian totals 10 bns, 2 sqns, 8 x 3 pdr guns, ca 4,600 men, 9 colours.

Austrian losses All captured.

Comment This was yet another 'soft fruit' in Napoleon's whirlwind harvest. The Austrians were low on ammunition, completely outgunned and isolated and their morale had been sapped by FM Mack's chaotic orders and their growing lack of confidence in their nominal commander, Archduke Ferdinand, the 25-year old brother in law of the Emperor Francis.

Sources Wrede, Schulz, Martinien.

DV Elchingen, 14 October 1805, clash

A village in the southern German state of Bavaria, about 1 km north of the River Danube, and about 12 km northeast of the city of Ulm.

A French victory over the Austrians.

(Last action – Memmingen, 13 October; next action – Ulm, 15 October.)

French Forces Ney's VI Corps (ca 20,000 men) of which GdD Loison's and GdD Malher's commands came into action: GdB Villatte, GdB Roguet: 6e and 25e RILé; 27e, 39e, 50e, 69e and 76e RIdLi (7 bns). GdB Tilly's cavalry: 18e and 19e DragR, 10e ChàCh, 3e HusR (12 sqns), 18 guns.

French losses 54 officers and ca 800 men dead and wounded.

Austrian Forces FML Count Riesch commanding: GM Loudon, GM Mecsery IR Kaiser Nr 1 (1stBn); IR EH Ludwig Nr 8 (2 bns); IR Riese Nr 15 (4 bns) IR Erbach Nr 42 (1, 2, 4th and Gren Bns); KürR EH Franz Nr 2 (2 sqns); KürR Hohenzollern Nr 8 (3 sqns); ChLR Rosenberg Nr 6 (6 sqns) 12 guns.

Austrian totals 14 bns, 11 sqns, 12 guns, ca 8,000 men.

Austrian losses ca 6,000 men dead, wounded and captured (IRNr42), 4 guns, 4 colours.

Comment Once again, the lightning French advance bowled the Austrians over as the trap closed around Ulm. At least half the Austrian Reserve Artillery park was captured in the sunken road at Thalfingen. It was Riesch's task to protect the flank of the Austrian army by destroying the Danube bridges; in this he was frustrated. Ney received the title 'Duc d'Elchingen' for this action.

Sources Wrede, Schulz, Martinien.

DV Ulm, 15 October 1805, capitulation

A fortified city on the northern bank of the River Danube in the southern German state of Württemberg at the junction of routes B10, B19, B28 and B311.

A French victory over the Austrians.

(Last action – Elchingen, 14 October; next action – Langenau, 16 October.)

French Forces Emperor Napoleon I commanding: II, V, VI Corps, Ney's Cavalry and the Imperial Guard.

French totals ca 80,000 men.

French losses A few prisoners in a skirmish at one of the gates; all released later, 11 officers dead, 49 wounded, ca 130 men dead and wounded, mostly from the 50e RIdLi.

Austrian Forces FM Baron v Mack commanding. IRs Kaiser Nr 1 (5 bns); IR EH Carl Nr 3 (3 bns); IR EH Ludwig Nr 8 (3 bns); IR EH Rainer Nr 11 (4 bns); IR Manfredini Nr 12 (5 bns); IR Riese Nr 15 (4 bns); IR Auersperg Nr 24 (5 bns); IR Fröhlich Nr 28 (5 bns); IR Kollowrath Nr 36 (5 bns); IR Hildburghausen Nr 41 (5 bns); IR Froon Nr 54 (5 bns); IR J Colloredo Nr 57 (GrenBn); IR Chasteler Nr 64 (1 bn); KürR EH Franz Nr 2 (6 sqns); KürR Hohenzollern Nr 8 (2 sqns); DragR Hohenlohe Nr 2 (2 sqns); UlR Schwarzenberg Nr 2 (7 sqns); Kür Mack Nr 6 (1 sqn); HusR Blankenstein Nr 6 (¼ sqn).

Austrian totals 25 bns ca 20,000 infantry; 10 ¼ sqns, 3,273 cavalry, 59 field guns.

Austrian losses The entire Austrian force was captured; the officers were allowed to return home on condition that they would not serve against France until exchanged. Apart from the men and guns, the French took 300 ammunition waggons, 3,000 horses. Only 26 colours and standards were claimed to have been taken; many must have been smuggled away or hidden and lost. The Austrians reported 40 colours lost.

Comment This crushing blow stopped the Austrian campaign in its tracks and decided the war. The speed of Napoleon's advance, coupled with the torpor and timidity of his opponent provided history with perfect examples of how, and how not, to conduct war. Archduke Ferdinand and 12 Austrian cavalry squadrons broke out through the French army and escaped, although hotly pursued, to Bohemia. There were no heavy artillery pieces in Ulm and Mack's force was low on artillery and infantry ammunition. He was living in a world of his own, unaware of the state of the available artillery, the strength of the defences, the garrison needed to man them, the availability of rations and infantry ammunition.

Sources Wrede, Schulz, Krauss, Martinien.

DV Langenau, 16 October 1805, clash

A town in the southern German state of Württemberg, about 6 km north of the River Danube and 14 km northeast of Ulm.

A French victory over the Austrians.

(Last action – Ulm, 15 October; next action – Herbrechtingen, 17 October.)

French Forces GdD Tilly commanding the cavalry of Ney's VI Corps. Only the 1er HusR came into action.

French losses Not known – slight.

Austrian Forces FML Hohenzollern's Right Wing Division of Werneck's Reserve Corps: IR Württemberg Nr 38 (3 bns); IR J Colloredo Nr 57 (3 bns); Grenadiers (4 bns); KürR Albert Nr 3 (8 sqns), 6 guns.

Austrian totals 10 bns, 8 sqns, 6 guns ca 8,000 men.

Austrian losses Not exactly known, slight.

Sources Wrede, Schulz, Martinien, Krauss.

DV Herbrechtingen, 17 October 1805, clash

A town in the southern German state of Württemberg, on the River Brenz, on route B19 and about 30 km northeast of Ulm.

A French victory over the Austrians.

(Last action – Langenau, 16 October; next action – Neresheim and Nördlingen, 17 October.)

French Forces M Prince Murat's Cavalry Reserve Corps ca 8,000 men and GdD Dupont's division: 9e Lé , 32e and 96e Li; GdD Klein: DragR 1er, 2e, 4e 14e and 20e; 5 guns.

French losses Not known, Martinien shows no officer losses at all.

Austrian Forces GM Graf Sinzendorf commanding IR Stuart Nr 18 (4 bns); ChLR Rosenberg Nr 6 (6 sqns).

Austrian totals 4 bns, 6 sqns, 3 guns ca 5,000 men.

Austrian losses ca 2,500, mostly captured.

Sources Wrede, Schulz, Martinien, Krauss.

DV Nördlingen, 17 October 1805, clash

A small town in the southern German state of Bavaria, at the junction of routes B25, B29 and B466 and about 32 km north of Donauwörth on the River Danube.

(Last action - Herbrechtingen, 17 October; next action - Trochtelfingen, 18 October.)

French Forces M Murat commanding the Reserve Cavalry, GdD Nansouty and d'Hautpoul. 1er CuirR 1er and 26e DragR (12 sqns).

French totals 12 sqns in action.

French losses Not known; slight.

Austrian Forces Archduke Ferdinand and FML Schwarzenberg commanding: KürR Mack Nr 6 (8 sqns); ChLR Klenau Nr 5 (4 sqns).

Austrian totals 12 sqns, ca 1,200 cavalry.

Austrian losses Not known; slight.

Comment These 12 squadrons had escaped from Ulm and were closely pursued by Murat's cavalry as they made their way eastwards to Bohemia.

Sources Wrede, Krauss, Martinien, Schulz.

DV Neresheim, 17 October 1805, clash

A village in the southern German state of Württemberg, on route B466, about 15 km southwest of Nördlingen.

A French victory over the Austrians.

(Last action - Herbrechtingen, 16 October; next action - Trochtelfingen, 18 October.)

French Forces M Murat's Reserve Cavalry and GdD Dupont's infantry division of M Ney's VI Corps: 1er CuirR (4 sqns); 1er DragR (4 sqns).

French totals 8 sqns in action ca 900 men.

French losses Not known; slight.

Austrian Forces FML Werneck's Corps IR Reuss-Plauen Nr 17 (5 bns); HusR Palatin Nr 12 (8 sqns).

Austrian totals 5 bns, 8 sqns, 4 guns, ca 7,000 men.

Austrian losses Not known; slight.

Sources Wrede, Krauss, Martinien.

DV Trochtelfingen, 18 October 1805, capitulation

A small village in the southern German state of Württemberg about 8 km west of the town of Nördlingen on route B29.

A French victory over the Austrians.

(Last action - Neresheim, 17 October; next action - Oberhaus fortress, 25 October.)

French Forces Murat's Cavalry Reserve and Soult's IV Corps.

French totals ca 28,000 men.

French losses Nil.

Austrian Forces FML Werneck commanding IR Reuss-Plauen Nr 17 (5 bns); IR Kaunitz Nr 20 (5 bns); IR Spork Nr 25 (1st, 2nd and 3rd Bns); IR EH Max Nr 35 (5 coys); IR Erbach Nr 42 (400 men); Kür R EH Franz Nr 2 (2 sqns).

Austrian totals 13½ bns, 2 sqns, 28 guns, ca 15,000 men.

Austrian losses All captured plus 12 colours, 2 standards, 4 generals.

Comment The capitulation applied to all of Werneck's troops even if they were not in Trochtelfingen. Even most of the army Artillery Reserve at Kirchheim and Wallerstein surrendered. FML Graf Hohenzollern, with 10 squadrons of cavalry (originally part of Werneck's division) flatly refused to obey the order to surrender and successfully escaped.

Sources Wrede, Schulz, Krauss, Martinien.

IN Verona, 18 October 1805, clash

A town in northeastern Italy on the River Etsch (Adige) about 20 km east of the southern tip of Lake Garda close to the crossing of the motorways A4/E13 and A22/E6.

A French victory over the Austrians.

(This was the first action of this campaign; next action - Caldiero, 29-31 October.)

French Forces M Massena commanding: GdD Gardanne's 1st Division GdB Compère: 24 Voltigeur coys and 22e RILé (3 bns); 29e and 52e RIdLi (3 bns each).

French totals 13 bns, 15 guns.

French losses 150 dead, 300 wounded.

Austrian Forces FML Vukassovich commanding: IR Auffenberg Nr 37 (4 bns); GzIR Ottocaner Nr 2 (2ndBn and 1 coy); GzIR 2nd Banal Nr 11 (1 bn); HusR Erzherzog Ferdinand Nr 3 (1 sqn).

Austrian totals 6 bns, 1 coy, 1 sqn, 12 battalion guns.

Austrian losses 1,622 men dead, wounded and captured, 4 guns, 1 colour.

Comment Archduke Charles had given clear instructions that Vukassovich was not to get involved in a serious fight here. The Austrians held a low-lying tongue of land surrounded on three sides by the River Etsch whose French-held opposite banks dominated their position and were armed with field artillery. Vukassovich ignored this eminently sound advice and his men paid the price of his stupidity.

Sources Wrede, von Angeli, Martinien, Rüstow.

ZZ Trafalgar, 21 October 1805, sea battle

An area in the Atlantic Ocean about 80 km west of Cadiz and off Cape Trafalgar.

A British victory over the Spanish and French fleets. (This was the only naval action of any significance in 1805.)

The French Fleet Vice Admiral P Ch J B S Villeneuve.

(L = lightly damaged in the battle; B = badly damaged; S = sunk; P = taken as a prize).

Ship	Guns	Commander	State	Killed	Wounded
Bucentaure	80	Captain Jean Jacques Magendie	B, P	97	85
Formidable	80	Rear-Admiral P R M E Dumanoir le Pelley			
		Captain Jean Marie Letellier	L	22	45
Neptune	80	Commodore Esprit Tranquille Maistral	L	15	39
Indomptable	80	Commodore Jean Joseph Hubert	L (wrecked later) — all hands drowned.		
Algéciras	74	Rear-Admiral Charles Magon			
		Captain Gabriel Auguste Brouard	B, P	77	143
Pluton	74	Commodore Julien M Cosmao	L	60	132
Mont Blanc	74	Commodore G J Noel la Villegris	L	20	24
Intrépide	74	Commodore Louis Antoine Cyprian Infernet	B, P	half the crew lost	
Swiftsure	74	Captain C E L'Hospitalier Villemadrin	B, P	68	123
Aigle	74	Captain Pierre Paul Gourrège	B, P	two-thirds of crew lost	
Scipion	74	Captain Charles Berenger	L	17	22
Duguay-Trouin	74	Captain Claude Touffet	L	12	24
Berwick	74	Captain Jean Gilles Filhol Camas	P, S	all lost	
Argonaute	74	Captain Jacques Epron	B	55	137
Achille	74	Captain Gabriel de Nieport	P, S	480 casualties	
Redoubtable	74	Captain Jean Jacques Etienne Lucas	P, S	490	81
Fougueux	74	Captain Louis Baudoin	B, P	546 casualties	
Héros	74	Captain Jean, B J Remi Poulain	L	12	26

Also present were 5 frigates: *Cornélie*, *Hermione*, *Hortense*, *Rhin*, *Themis*; and 2 brigs, *Argus*, *Furet*.

The Spanish Fleet Admiral don Federico Gravina

(L = lightly damaged in the battle; B = badly damaged; S = sunk; P = taken as a prize).

Ship	Guns	Commander	State	Killed	Wounded
Santissima-		Rear-Admiral don B Hidalgo Césneros			
Trinidad	130	Commodore don Fransisco de Uriarte	B, P	216	116
Principe de	112	Admiral Gravina			
Asturias		Rear-Admiral don Antonio Escano	B	54	109
Santa Anna	112	Vice-Admiral don Ign Maria de Alava			
		Captain don Josef Guardoqui	B, P	104	137
Rayo	100	Commodore don Enrique Macdonell	L	4	14
Neptuno	80	Commodore don Cayetano Valdes	L, P	38	35
Argonauta	80	Commodore don Antonio Pareja	B, P	103	202
Bahama	74	Captain don Dioniscio Galiano	L, P	75	66
Montanez	74	Captain don Josef Salcedo	L	20	29
San Augustino	74	Captain don Felipe Xado Cagigal	B, P	184	201

Ship	Guns	Commander	State	Killed	Wounded
San Ildefonso	74	Captain don Josef Bargas	B, P	36	124
San Juan de Nepomuceno	74	Captain don Cosme Churruaca	B, P	103	131
Monarca	74	Captain don Teodora Argumosa	B, P	101	154
San Fransisco de Asis	74	Captain don Luis de Flores	L	5	12
San Justo	74	Captain don Miguel Gaston	L	-	7
San Leandro	64	Captain don Josef Quevedo	L	8	22

French and Spanish losses French Rear Admiral Charles Magon and Spanish Admiral Don Frederico Gravina killed, 2,600 officers and men killed and wounded, 4,400 captured. These included many of the French 2e, 16e, 67e, 70e, 79e and 93e RIdLi (whose 2nd Bn lost its eagle).

The British Fleet
(L = lightly damaged in the battle; B = badly damaged; S = sunk; P = taken as a prize).

Ship	Guns	Commander	State	Killed	Wounded
Victory	100	Vice-Admiral Horatio Nelson			
		Captain Thomas Masterman Hardy	B	57	75
Britannia	100	Rear-Admiral the Earl of Northesk			
		Captain Charles Bullen	L	10	40
Téméraire	98	Captain Eliab Harvey	B	47	76
Neptune	98	Captain Thomas F Freemantle	L	10	34
Conqueror	74	Captain Israel Pellew	L	3	9
Leviathan	74	Captain Henry W Bayntun	L	4	22
Ajax	74	Lieutenant John Pilford	L	2	2
Orion	74	Captain Edward Codrington	L	1	21
Minotaur	74	Captain Charles J M Mansfield	L	3	20
Spartiate	74	Captain Sir Charles Laforey	L	3	17
Agamemnon	64	Captain Sir Edward Berry	L	2	7
Africa	64	Captain Henry Digby	B	18	37

Rear or lee column – Vice Admiral Collingwood

Ship	Guns	Commander	State	Killed	Wounded
Royal Sovereign	100	Captain Edward Rotherham	B	47	97
Prince of Wales	98	Captain Richard Grindall	L	-	-
Dreadnought	98	Captain John Conn	L	7	26
Tonnant	80	Captain Charles Tyler	B	26	50
Mars	74	Captain George Duff	B	29	69
Belle Isle	74	Captain William Hargood	B	33	93
Bellerophon	74	Captain John Cooke	B	27	123
Colossus	74	Captain James N Morris	B	43	110
Achilles	74	Captain Richard King	L	13	59
Revenge	74	Captain Robert Moorsam	L	28	51
Swiftsure	74	Captain William G Rutherford	L	9	8
Defence	74	Captain George Hope	L	7	29
Thunderer	74	Lieutenant John Stockham	L	4	12
Defiance	74	Captain Philip C Durham	L	17	53
Polyphemus	64	Captain Richard Redmill	L	2	4

Also present were 4 frigates: *Euryalus* - Captain the Hon Henry Blackwood, *Naiad* - Captain Thomas Dundas, *Phoebe* - Captain the Hon Thomas Bladen Capel, *Sirius* - Captain William Prowse (36s); 1 schooner, *Pickle* (10) - Lieutenant John R Lapenotiere; and 1 cutter, *Entreprenante* (10) - Lieutenant John Power.

British Losses Vice-Admiral Nelson killed, 1,596 officers and men killed and wounded.

Comment Nelson had been chasing Villeneuve across the Atlantic and back again since 29 March. This victory gave Britain mastery of the seas for over a hundred years.

The French ships *Formidable, Duguay-Trouin, Mont Blanc* and *Scipion* under Admiral Dumanoir were caught on 4 November in the Bay of Biscay by Admiral Sir Richard Strachan with the 74s *Caesar, Hero, Courageux* and *Namur* and forced to surrender.

In 1808 the few surviving French ships in Cadiz were handed over to the British when the Spanish rose in revolt against the French.

Control of the sea allowed Britain to land an army in Portugal in 1808; the start of a campaign which extended into 1814 and bled France and her allies of hundreds of thousands of men and contributed in no minor way to Napoleon's eventual downfall.

It is a popular myth that Trafalgar saved Britain from invasion in 1805; this is patently not so. Bonaparte issued orders for the Grande Armée to concentrate from Boulogne (and various other locations) onto the Franco-German border opposite the Black Forest as early as mid-August 1805 and Ulm capitulated on 17 October.

Sources James, Clowes, Charrié.

DV Oberhaus Fort, (near Passau), 25 October 1805, storm

A fortified city in south eastern Germany, at the confluence of the Rivers Inn and Danube, at the junction of routes B8, B12 and B85, just east of motorway A3/E56.

An Austrian victory over the Bavarians.

(Last action - Trochtelfingen, 18 October; next action - Haag and Lambach, 31 October.)

Bavarian Garrison Invalides (2 coys).

Bavarian totals ca 180 men.

Bavarian losses All captured.

Austrian Forces Count Nostitz commanding GzIR Peterwardein Nr 9 (1 bn).

Austrian totals ca 600 men.

Austrian losses Not known, very slight.

Sources Wrede, von Angeli, Leyh.

IN Caldiero, 29–31 October 1805, battle

A small town in north eastern Italy, about a third of the way between Verona (in the west) and Vicenza, about 5 km north of the River Etsch (Adige), on Route 11 and just south of the motorway A4/E13.

A drawn match between the French and the Austrians.

(Last action - Verona, 18 October; next action - Forano, 2 November.)

French Forces M Massena commanding: **GdD Espagne's Avantgarde** Gren Bn (1 bn); 3e, 15e, 19e, 23e and 24e ChàCh (20 sqns). **1st Division** GdD Gardanne: GdB Compère, GdB Lechantin: 22e RILé (3 bns); 29e, 52e, 101e RIdLi (3 bns each). **2nd Division** GdD Verdier, GdB Digonnet, GdB Herbin: 23e RILé, 56e and 62e RIdLi (10 bns); 4e ChàCh (4 sqns). **3rd Division** GdD Molitor: GdB Lannay, GdB Valory: 5e, 23e, 60e and 79e RIdLi (15 bns). **4th Division** GdD Duhesme: GdB Goulus, GdB Camus: 14e RILé; 1er, 20e and 102e RIdLi (13 bns). Sera's 5th Division, Partouneaux's Reserve Division and the cavalry divisions of Mermet and Pully were not engaged. (Martinien shows losses also for 6e RIdLi, 29e DragR, 14e, and 25e ChàCh, the 2nd Italian LIR and the Italian artillery).

French totals 54 bns, 24 sqns, 30 guns ca 46,000 men.

French losses Massena only reported 'less dead than the Austrians, more wounded and fewer prisoners'. Archduke Charles estimated French loss to be about 8,000 men including 1,700 captured. The 5e RIdLi lost its eagle to IR Schröder Nr 7. Two other colours were also lost. This eagle is now in Vienna town hall.

Austrian Forces Archduke Charles commanding: **Right Wing** FML Baron Simbschen, GM v Soudain: IR Coburg Nr 22 (4 bns); IR Hohenlohe Nr 26 (4 bns). GM Chevalier Johnson: IR Strassoldo Nr 27 (4 bns); IR Sztáray Nr 33 (4 bns). GM Baron v Kottinlinsky: IR Schröder Nr 7 (3 bns): IR Lindenau Nr 29 (3 bns). GM Count O'Reilly: ChLR Kaiser Nr 1(8 sqns); HusR Kienmayer Nr 8 (8 sqns). **Right Wing totals** 22 bns, 16 sqns, 32 guns and 10 howitzers. **Centre GdC Arch-**

duke Charles, FML Count Argenteau Avantgarde GM Nordmann: GzIR Warasdiner-Kreutzer Nr 5 (2 bns); GzIR Gradiskaner Nr 8 (3 bns); HusR Erdödy Nr 9 (8 sqns). GM v Lippa: Gren Bns Anspach, Coburg, Hohenlohe, Lindenau and Strassoldo (5 bns). GM Prince Hohenlohe: Gren Bns Auffenberg, Davidovich, Sztáray (3 bns). **FML Baron von Vogelsang** GM Count H Colloredo: Gren Bns Esterházy, Franz, Splényi, St Julien, Vukassovich (5 bns). Obst von Croll: Gren Bns Bellegarde, Lattermann, Reisky, C Schröder (4 bns). **FML Prince Reuss-Plauen** GM v Wetzel: IR EH Ferdinand (4 bns). FML Count Argenteau, GM v Kalnassy: IR Vukassovich Nr 48 (3 bns). **FML Baron v Mittrowsky** GM v Zschock: IR W Colloredo Nr 56 (4 bns). GM v Michaljevich: IR Esterházy Nr 32 (3 bns); IR Splényi Nr 51 (3 bns). **FML Prince Josef v Lothringen** GM v Walthör: ULR EH Carl Nr 3 (8 sqns) GM v Révay: Hus R Stipsics Nr 10 (8 sqns) **Centre totals** 39 bns; 24 sqns; 18 guns and 6 howitzers. **Left Wing FML Baron v Davidovich Avantgarde** GM Count Radetsky; HusR Ott Nr 5 (8 sqns); GzIR Warasdiner-St Georger Nr 6 (3 bns). **FML Baron v Löwenberg** GM Baron v Löwenberg: IR EH Josef Nr 63 (3 bns). GM v Siegenthal: GzIR 1st Banal Nr 10 (3 bns). **Left Wing totals** 9 bns; 8 sqns; 18 guns and 8 howitzers.

Austrian totals 71 bns, 48 sqns, 58 guns, 24 howitzers, ca 49,000 men.

Austrian losses 5,700 killed and wounded.

Comment This was a hard-fought battle; Archduke Charles, on receipt of the news of the catastrophe of Ulm decided to fight a spoiling action to win time to organize his withdrawal. FML Rosenberg's division was off to the north of the battlefield and did not take part in this action.

Sources Wrede, von Angeli, Martinien, Rüstow.

DV Haag and Lambach, 31 October 1805, clashes

Two villages in the Austrian State of Oberösterreich; Lambach is on Route 1 on the River Traun 10 km upstream from Wels; Haag is about 20 km northwest of Lambach.

French victories over the Austrians.

(Last action – Oberhaus fortress (Passau); 25 October; next action – Strub Pass, 3 and 4 November.)

French Forces M Davout's III Corps; GdD Bisson's division. Only the 17e RIdLi (3 bns) came into action.

French totals ca 2,000 men.

French losses Slight; GdD Bisson was wounded and GdD Caffarelli took over.

Austrian Forces GM Schustek commanding: IR Gyulai Nr 60 (1st, 2nd and Gren Bns); Drag R Kaiser Nr 1 (2 sqns); HusR Kaiser Nr 1 (8 sqns).

Austrian totals 3 bns, 10 sqns, ca 4,000 men.

Austrian losses Not known, slight.

Comment Schustek's rearguard was being chased by the III and V Corps and was striving to join up with Kutusov's Russian corps.

Sources Wrede, Krauss, Martinien.

IN Forano, 2 November 1805, clash

A village in the hills about 20 km north of Caldiero.

A French victory over the Austrians.

(Last action – Caldiero 29-31 October; next action – S Pietro Engu, 4 November.)

French Forces G Solignac commanding: 4 gren bns; GM Serras with 6 coys and 2 sqns.

French totals ca 6,000 men, 12 guns.

French losses ca 600 killed and wounded.

Austrian Forces GM Hillinger commanding: GzIR 2nd Banal Nr 11 (3 bns); IR Davidovich Nr 34 (4 bns); Hus R EH Ferdinand Nr 2 (2 sqns).

Austrian totals 7 bns, 2 sqns, 14 battalion guns, ca 4,000 men.

Austrian losses 400 killed, 1,800 captured, 12 guns.

Comment GM Hillinger had been ordered to demonstrate at Veronetta but advanced too far, too rashly and was overwhelmed in detail. Only one battalion of GzIR 2nd Banal escaped.

Sources Wrede, von Angeli, Martinien, Schulz.

DV Strub Pass, 2–3 November 1805, clash

A pass between the Austrian provinces of Tyrol and Salzburg, on Route 312, about 5 km west of the town of Lofer.

An Austrian victory over the Bavarians.

(Last action – Haag and Lambach, 31 October; next action – Steyer, 4 November.)

Bavarian Forces GL Count Deroy, GM Minucci: Leib IR Nr 1 (2 bns); LIR Kurprinz Nr 2 (2 bns); 1st LtI Bn Metzen (1 bn); DragR Nr 1 Minucci (2 sqns). GM Marsigli: LIR Salern Nr 4 (2 bns); LIR Preysing Nr 5 (2 bns); 3rd LtI Bn Preysing (1 bn); DragR Nr 2 Taxis (3 sqns).

Bavarian totals 10 bns, 5 sqns, 24 guns, ca 7,500 men.

Bavarian losses Between 1,200 men and 1,800 dead, wounded and missing, 1 gun. Deroy wounded.

Austrian Forces GM Count St Julien commanding: IR Klebek Nr 14 (1st, 2nd and 3rd Bns - 3 coys each); IR Kerpen Nr 49 (4th Bn - 2 coys); DragR Melas Nr 6 (3 sqns); Tyroler Landmiliz (1stCoy); Salzburger Schützen (1 coy); St Johann, Kirchdorfer and Loferer Schützen (1 coy each); Kitzbühel Schützen (1st and 2nd Coys), 3 x 3 pdr guns.

Austrian totals ca 1,500 men.

Austrian losses up to 200 dead and wounded, 1 gun.

Comment On 1 November the Bavarian Obst Count Pompei had rushed and taken the passes at Bodenbichl, Stein and Knie between Reichenhall and Lofer. His advance was stopped there. The aim of blocking this pass was to stop the Bavarians cutting off FML Chasteler's Corps withdrawing eastwards through the Tyrol on Klagenfurt and to protect the northern flank of Archduke John's corps making for Villach. This successful defence owed much to the locals who rallied to the Austrian army.

Sources HGM 60, Wrede, Krauss, Leyh.

DV Steyer (nowadays Steyr) on the River Enns, 4 November 1805, clash

A village in the Austrian province of Oberösterreich, about 25 km south of Linz on the River Danube.

A French victory over the Austrians.

(Last action - Pass Strub, 3 November; next action - Mariazell, 8 November.)

French Forces M Davout's III Corps. GdD Caffarelli's division (ex GdD Bisson): 13e RILé (3 bns); 22e ChàCh (4 sqns).

French totals 3 bns, 4 sqns, ca 3,000 men.

French losses Not known, slight.

Austrian Forces FML Merveldt's Reserve Corps (ex Kienmayer): IR Colloredo Nr 57 (3 bns); IR Gyulai Nr 60 (1st, 2nd and Gren Bns).

Austrian totals 6 bns ca 4,000 men.

Austrian losses ca 2,000, mostly captured (IR Nr 57); 3 colours.

Comment This was the end of Merveldt's corps as an effective fight force.

Sources Wrede, Krauss, Martinien, Schulz.

DV Scharnitz and Leutasch, 4 November 1805, clash

Two fortified passes in the north of the Austrian province of the Tyrol, about 30 km north of Innsbruck on the way to Mittenwald in Bavaria. Scharnitz is on Route 177.

A French victory over the Austrians.

(Last action - Steyer/Enns, 4 November; next action - Amstetten, 5 November.)

French Forces at Scharnitz M Ney's VI Corps. GdD Loison, GdD Malher, GdB Marcognet, GdB Labasse: 25e RILé (3 bns); 27e RIdLi (2 bns); 50e RIdLi (2 bns). The 59e RIdLi did not come into action. 8 guns.

French totals at Scharnitz 7 bns, 8 guns, ca 6,000 men.

French losses at Scharnitz Estimated at about 800 dead and wounded.

French forces at Leutasch 69e RIdLi (2 bns); ca 1,500 men.

French losses at Leutasch 10 dead, 16 wounded.

Austrian Forces at Scharnitz Obstlt Swinburne commanding: IR EH Carl Nr 3 (1 bn, 295 men); IR EH Ludwig Nr 8 (1 bn, 588 men); 4 Militia coys (Innsbruck, Hötting, Seefeld and Sterzing; (594 men); 3 Scharfschützen coys (300 men); Stabs-Dragoner (20 men).

Austrian totals at Scharnitz 804 line troops, 894 Militia and Scharfschützen, 12 guns.

Austrian losses at Scharnitz ca 100 dead and wounded.

Austrian Forces at Leutasch Major Kraus commanding: IR Kinsky Nr 47 (1 bn, 600 men); 2 Militia coys (Telfser and Silzer - 336 men); 4 guns.

Austrian totals 936 men and 4 guns.

Austrian losses 13 dead, 20 wounded, all line troops captured, 4 guns.

Comment The French eventually broke through by overrunning the Leutasch and advancing south of Seefeld (Tyrol) thus outflanking the Scharnitz. On 5 November Ney occupied Innsbruck.

Sources HGM 60, Leyh, Wrede, Martinien.

IN S Pietro Engu, 4 November 1805, skirmish

A village in northeastern Italy (now called S Pietro in Gu) about 5 km west of the River Brenta, just north of route 53 and about 12 km northeast of Vicenza.

An Austrian victory over the French.

(Last action - Forano, 2 November; next action - Valvasone, 11 November.)

French Forces GdD Molitor commanding the 3rd Division and GdB Merlin's cavalry of Espagne's Avantgarde Division: 23e and 79e RIdLi (6 bns); 1

gren bn; 15e, 23e and 24e ChàCh (12 sqns).

French totals 7 bns, 12 sqns, 12 guns.

French losses Not known exactly.

Austrian Forces GM Frimont commanding the rearguard: GzIR Warasdiner-Kreutzer Nr 5 (3 bns); GzIR Ottocaner Nr 2 (1 bn); HusR Eh Ferdinand Nr 3 (2 sqns).

Austrian totals 4 bns, 2 sqns, 6 guns.

Austrian losses Not exactly known; 1 bn of GzIR Nr 5 was destroyed after holding out against very heavy odds.

Comment This was a successful Austrian rearguard action.

Sources von Angeli, Wrede, Schulz, Martinien.

DV Amstetten, 5 November 1805, clash

A town in the Austrian province of Oberösterreich, about 14 km south of the River Danube, midway between Enns and Ybbs on route 1 and just south of the motorway A1/E5.

A French victory over the Austrians and Russians.

(Last action – Scharnitz and Leutasch, 4 November; next action – Weyer, 7 November.)

French Forces M Murat: M Lanne's V Corps GdD Oudinot's combined grenadier battalions; 3e and 12e RILé; 9e and 10e HusRs (8 sqns).

French totals Not exactly known; at least 5 bns and 8 sqns.

French losses Not exactly known; slight.

Austro-Russian Forces Part of FML Kienmayer's Corps. GzIR Peterwardein Nr 9 (3 bns); KürR Lothringen Nr 7 (8 sqns); HusR Hessen-Homburg Nr 4 (8 sqns).

Austrian totals 3 bns, 16 sqns, ca 2,000 men, 6 guns.

Austrian losses Not exactly known; the GzIR Nr 9 was scattered; the two cavalry regiments withdrew in good order.

Russian Forces: Prince Bagration commanding the Russian rearguard: GrenR Kiev, MuskR Azov, 6th JgR (3 bns each); HusR Pavlograd (10 sqns); 2 guns.

Russian totals ca 6,500 men.

Russian losses ca 400 killed and wounded, 660 captured.

Comment The retreating Austrians were now very close to Kutusov's Russian army but the strain of repeated defeats was beginning to cause their cohesion to crack.

Sources Wrede, Martinien, Schulz.

DV Weyer, 7 November 1805, clash

A village in the Austrian province of Oberösterreich in a valley between the Rivers Enns and Ybbs on route 121 about 42 km south of Amstetten.

(Last action – Amstetten, 5 November; next action – Kufstein, 8 November.)

French Forces Marmont's II Corps.

French totals ca 20,000 men.

French losses Not known, slight.

Austrian totals 3 bns, 8 sqns.

Austrian losses Most of 1st and 2nd Bns IR 60 captured, 3 colours, 6 guns.

Comment There was practically no fight; the Austrian cavalry fled and the infantry were surrounded.

Sources Wrede, Martinien.

DV Kufstein, 8 November 1805, capitulation

A strong, natural fortress in the north of the Austrian province of Tyrol, on the east bank of the River Inn, just south of the German border on motorway A12/E45/E60.

A Bavarian victory over the Austrians.

(Last action – Weyer, 7 November; next action – Gross-Ramig, 8 November.)

Bavarian Forces GdB Mezzanelli commanding the 2nd Brigade: 4th LIR (2 bns); 5th LIR (2 bns); 5th LtI Bn (1 bn); 2nd DragR (4 sqns); 1 foot bty.

Bavarian losses Nil.

Austrian forces IR Klebek Nr 14 (4th Bn).

Austrian losses Nil, the garrison marched out with honours of war to Bohemia.

Comment Kufstein fortress was built on a sheer-sided rock and was in those days almost impregnable.

Sources Wrede, Bezzel, Leyh.

DV Gross-Ramig (Mariazell), 8 November 1805, clash

A village in the Austrian province of Steiermark on route 20 about 52 km south of St Pölten.

A French victory over the Austrians.

(Last action – Kufstein, 8 November; next action – Dürnstein, 11 November.)

French Forces GdB de Bierre commanding the Avantgarde of Davout's III Corps: 13e RILé, 108e RIdLi (2 bns each); 12e ChàCh (3 sqns); 2 guns.

French totals ca 3,800 men.

French losses Not known exactly but very light.

Austrian Forces Part of FML Merveldt's corps. IR Deutschmeister Nr 4 (4 bns); IR Colloredo Nr 57 (3 bns); IR Gyulai Nr 60 (GrenBn).

Austrian totals 8 bns, ca 4,000 men.

Austrian losses 2,000 mostly captured, 4 colours, 16 guns.

Comment By now the worn-out Austrian infantry was beginning to disintegrate under the relentless pursuit; their morale was low and ammunition running short.

Sources Wrede, Schulz, Martinien.

DV Dürnstein-Loiben, 11 November 1805, clash

A village on the north bank of the River Danube about 74 km west of Vienna, Austria; on route 3 and about 5 km west of Krems.

An Austro-Russian victory over the French.

(Last action – Gross-Ramig, 8 November; next action – Hollabrunn and Schöngraben, 16 November 1805.)

French Forces M Adolph Edouard Mortier commanding the VIII Corps. **2e Division** (of V Corps) GdD Gazan; GdB Graindorge, GdB Campana: 4e RILé (3 bns); 54e, 100e and 103e RIdLi (3 bns each); 4e DragR (3 sqns). Totals 9 bns, 3 sqns, 3 guns. **1ère Division** (of the VI Corps) GdD Dupont; GdB Marchand, GdB Rouyer: 9e RILé, 32e and 96e RIdLi (2 bns each); 1e HusR (3 sqns). **1ère Division totals** 6 bns, 3 sqns, 3 guns.

The Batavian Division (GdD Dumonceau) of Mortier's command did not get involved in the fighting.

French total in the clash: 15 bns, 6 sqns, 6 guns, ca 12,000 men.

French losses Not exactly known; Gazan's division was destroyed; estimates of French losses are ca 4,000 dead and wounded, 47 officers and 895 men captured, 5 guns. The eagle of the 4e RILé was lost as was the eagle and Guidon of the 4e DragR (taken by IR Moscow).

Austro-Russian Forces GI Kutusov, FML Schmidt: **1st Column** GdB Prince Bagration: GrenR Kiev; IR Azov; JgR Nr 6 (3 bns each); HusR Pavlograd (10 sqns). **2nd Column** GL von Essen: GrenR Little Russia; IR Apscheron; IR Smolensk (3 bns each); DragR Tschernigov (5 sqns). **3rd Column** GL Dochtorov: IR Butirsk (3 bns); IR Moscow (3 bns); JgR Nr 8 (1 bn); HusR Mariupol (10 sqns). **4th Column** GL Schepelev: IR Novgorod; IR Narva; IR Podolien (3 bns each). **5th Column** GL Freiherr von Maltitz: IR Viatka; IR Briansk; IR Yaroslav (3 bns each). **6th Column** GL Freiherr von Rosen (did not actually take part in the fighting): IR New Ingermannland; IR Vladimir; IR Galicia (3 bns each); DragR Twer; DragR Petersburg (5 sqns each). **Austrian Infantry Brigade** GM Graf Nostitz-Rieneck GzIR Brooder Nr 7; GzIR Peterwardeiner Nr 9 (2 bns each). **Austrian Cavalry Division** FML Fürst Hohenlohe: KürR Lothringen Nr 7; KürR Nassau-Usingen Nr 5 (8 sqns each); HusR Hessen-Homburg Nr 4 (6 sqns).

Allied totals 58 bns, 62 sqns, 14 artillery batteries, ca 24,000 men and 168 guns.

Allied losses 4,000 dead and wounded, FML Freiherr von Schmidt killed. 2 colours of MuskR Viatka taken by the 9eRILé.

Comment Mortier, ignoring Napoleon's strict advice, failed to ensure the security of his corps' left or northern flank and suffered a tactical defeat. Both sides claimed a victory. Schmidt's loss was very serious; his place was taken by Weyrother who was much less effective at Austerlitz than Schmidt would have been. The allies continued their withdrawal to the east.

Sources HGM 3, Wrede, Schulz, Martinien, Charrié.

IN Valvasone, 11 November 1805, clash

A village in northeastern Italy, about 3 km west of the River Tagliamento, a third of the way from Pordenone (in the west) to Udine and about 4 km north of Route 13.

An Austrian victory over the French.

(Last action – S Pietro Engu, 4 November; next action – Gorizia (Gradisca) 14 November.)

French Forces GdD Espagne commanding: **Avantgarde** 3e, 15e, 19e, 23e and 24e ChàCh 1 gren bn (20 sqns, 1 bn). **2nd Division** GdD Verdier: 4e ChàCh (4 sqns). **GdD Mermet's Dragoons** 23e, 30e DragR, (8 sqns).

French totals 1 bn, 32 sqns, 12 guns.

French losses Not known.

Austrian Forces Archduke Charles commanding: HusR Ott Nr 5 (8 sqns) HusR Erdödy Nr 9 (8 sqns); 6 guns.

Austrian totals 16 sqns, 6 guns, ca 1,200 men.

Austrian losses Not exactly known; moderate.

Comment Archduke Charles had just received news of the destruction of Merveldt's corps at Mariazell on 8th November and decided to withdraw to

Präwald, northeast of Trieste, a naturally very strong blocking position. This was a successful rearguard action.

Sources von Angeli, Wrede, Martinien.

DV Dornbirn, 13 November 1805, capitulation

A town in the Austrian province of Voralberg, just east of the motorway A14/E17, about 12 km south of Bregenz on the eastern end of Lake Constance.

A French victory over the Austrians.

(Last action - Dürnstein, 10 November; next action - Schöngraben, 17 November.)

French Forces M Augereau's VII Corps, 1st Infantry Division.

French totals ca 15,000 men.

French losses None.

Austrian Forces FML Jellačič commanding: IR Stain Nr 50 (3 bns); IR Beaulieu Nr 58 (GrenBn); IR Jellačič Nr 62 (3 bns); 2nd Jägers (1 bn) plus 1½ combined bns.

Austrian totals 9½ bns ca 4,000 men.

Austrian losses All 3 generals, 160 officers and 3,895 men were disarmed and allowed to march off to Bohemia on condition that they did not fight against France for one year, 7 colours.

Comment All the cavalry regiments which had been with Jellačič had already escaped to fight another day either at Austerlitz or Stecken.

Sources Wrede, Schulz, Martinien.

DV Hollabrunn and Schöngraben, 16 November 1805, clash

A village in the Austrian province of Niederösterreich, on Route 2/E84 about 4 km north of Hollabrunn and 50 km north of Vienna.

A French victory over the Austro-Russians.

(Last action - Dornbirn, 13 November; next action - Wischau, 25 November.)

French Forces M Joachim Murat commanding: **IV Corps M Soult: 3rd Division GdD Legrand** 3e RILé (3 bns); 18e and 75e RIdLi (2 bns each); Tirailleurs Corses (2 bns); Tirailleurs du Po (1 bn); 17e RILé (2 bns); 18e RILé (2 bns); 3e RIdLi (2 bns). **V Corps M Lannes: Grenadier Division GdD Oudinot** 10 combined grenadier battalions, part of GdD Suchet's 3rd Division: 40e RIdLi (2 bns). **2nd Division GdD Gazan** 4e RILé (3 bns); 58e, 100e and 103e RIdLi (3 bns each), also the 9e RILé, 9e, 13e and 81e RIdLi (3 bns each). **Reserve Cavalry: M Joachim Murat 1st Dragoon Division** GdD Klein 14e, 20e and 26e DragR (4 sqns each). **2nd Dragoon Division** GdD Walther: 11e, 13e and 22e DragR (4 sqns each).

French totals 48 bns, 20 sqns, 48 guns, ca 35,000 men.

French losses Reported as: '2,000 killed and wounded, 52 captured, 1 infantry colour'. GdD Oudinot was badly wounded.

Austro-Russian Forces GL Prince Bagration commanding:

Russians Gren R Kiev; IR Podolien, IR Azov, IR Narva, IR Novgorod, 6th Jägers, (3 bns each) DragR Tschernigov (5 sqns); HusR Pavlograd (10 sqns); 12 guns.

Austrians GM Count Nostitz: GzIR Peterwardein Nr 9 (4 coys); HusR Hessen-Homburg Nr 4 (8 sqns).

Allied totals 5,500 infantry, 1,500 cavalry, 12 guns.

Allied losses ca 3,000 including 1,800 captured, 4 guns and 100 baggage waggons.

Comment This action bought time enough for the Allies to unite Kutusov's 1st Russian Army and the remnants of the Austrian Danube Valley army with Buxhowden's 2nd Russian Army advancing from Galicia.

Sources Wrede, Martinien, Leyh, Charrié.

IN Gorizia (Gradisca), 16 November 1805, skirmish

A town on the Italian-Slovenian border, about 20 km north of the Gulf of Trieste on Route 56 just north of motorway 351, on the Isonzo (Soce) River.

An Austrian victory over the French.

(Last action - Valvasone, 11 November; next action - Flitscher-Klause, 19 November.)

French Forces M Massena commanding: GdD Molitor's 3rd Division: 79e RIdLi (3 bns). GdD Partouneaux's Reserve Division: 14e ChàCh (4 sqns).

French totals 3 bns, 4 sqns, 12 guns, ca 2,400 men.

French losses Not known, slight.

Austrian Forces FML Vincent commanding the rear-guard. GzIR Warasdiner-Kreutzer Nr 5 (2 bns); GzIR Gradiskaner Nr 8 (3 bns); HusR Ott Nr 5 (8 sqns); HusR Erdödy Nr 9 (8 sqns), 6 guns.

Austrian totals 5 bns, 16 sqns, 6 guns.

Austrian losses Not known, slight.

Comment FML Vincent beat back all French attempts to cross the Isonzo River here this day.

Sources Wrede, von Angeli, Martinien, Schulz.

IN Flitscher-Klause (Bovec), 19 November 1805, skirmish

A small town in the upper Isonzo (Soce) valley in Slovenia on a minor road from Gorizia (Gradisca) in the south to Tarvis in the north.

An Austrian victory over the French.

(Last action – Gorizia, 14 November; next action – Castelfranco Veneto, 24 November.)

French Forces GdB Lacour commanding four regiments of dragoons.

French totals Not known.

French losses Not known; Martinien shows no officer losses.

Austrian Forces GM Siegenthal commanding a brigade of Archduke John's army: IR de Ligne Nr 30 (2 bns).

Austrian totals 2 bns, 4 guns, ca 1,200 men.

Austrian losses Not known, slight.

Comment As in any combat in a mountain defile, it is possible for a small force to hold up a much larger one if conditions do not allow the latter to deploy and that is what happened here.

Sources Wrede, Martinien, von Angeli, Schulz.

IN Castelfranco Veneto, 24 November 1805, capitulation

A town in northeastern Italy, about 40 km northwest of Venice, between Vicenza and Treviso, just south of Route 53 on Route 307.

A French victory over the Austrians.

(Last action – Flitscher-Klause, 19 November; next action – Lippa, 6 December.)

French Forces GdD Reynier commanding the 2nd Division of Massena's army. 10e, 53e, 56e and 62e RIdLi, 1er Swiss IR.

French totals 11 bns, ca 8,000 men, 12 guns.

French losses Not known, 16 officers dead and wounded.

Austrian Forces Prince Rohan commanding: IR Duka Nr 38 (4 bns); IR Beaulieu Nr 58 (2nd and 4th Bns); KürR Kronprinz Nr 4 (8 sqns); ChLR Hohenzollern Nr 2 (1 sqn); 1 combined infantry bn, 1 combined cavalry sqn.

Austrian totals 8 bns, 9 sqns, 5 guns, ca 4,400 men.

Austrian losses Dead and wounded – unknown, almost all captured, 5 guns, 4 colours, Prince Rohan wounded.

Comment When Reynier's Division came up in the rear of the Austrians they were forced to surrender, after having marched all the way from Bavaria.

Sources ÖMZ 1822 and 1823, Schulz, Wrede.

DV Wischau (Rausnitz), 25 November 1805, clash

A village between Olmütz and Austerlitz in Moravia, now the Czech Republic, on Route 462.

A Russian victory over the French.

(Last action – Hollabrunn and Schöngraben, 16 November; next action – Austerlitz, 2 December.)

French Forces GdD Walther's division of Murat's Reserve Cavalry and GdD Lasalle's division of M Lanne's V Corps. 6e DragR (4 sqns); 11e DragR (4 sqns); 9e and 10e HusR (4 sqns each); 22e ChàCh (4 sqns), 12 guns.

French totals 20 sqns, 12 guns, ca 1,400 men.

French losses Not exactly known, the 11e DragR lost an eagle and guidon here.

Russian Forces GL Prince Bagration commanding the Advanced Guard: GM Dolgoruky, Ulanius and Tschaplitz: 6th Jägers (3 bns); IRs Alt-Ingermannland, Archangel and Pskov (9 bns); Leib KürR (5 sqns); DragR Twer (5 sqns); DragR St Petersburg (5 sqns); HusR Pavlograd (10 sqns); HusR Mariupol (10 sqns); Cossacks (8 sotnias).

Russian totals 12 bns, 35 sqns and 8 sotnias, 24 guns, ca 12,000 men.

Comment This minor Russian success further lulled the Allies into thinking that they would be able to deal quite easily with Napoleon whose army's strength had been considerable diminished and who was now at the end of very extended lines of communication.

Sources Wrede, Schulz, Martinien, Charrié, Leyh.

DV Austerlitz, 2 December 1805, battle

A small town in the south east of the Czech Republic (then known as Moravia) about 16 km east of Brno (then Brünn) on Route 51 south to Hodonin on the Czech-Hungarian border.

A French victory over the Austro-Russians.

(Last action – Wischau, 25 November; next action – Wonau, 2 December.)

French Forces Emperor Napoleon I commanding:

The Imperial Guard Marshals Mortier and Bessières 1er ChàP; ChàCh (4 sqns); GrenàCh (4 sqns); Mamelukes (½ sqn); Sailors (1 bn); artillery and engineers 12 guns, 3 bns, 8½ sqns.

I Corps M Bernadotte GdD Drouet GdB Frère and Werle: 94e and 95e RIdLi (4 bns). GdD Rivaud GdB Dumoulin and Pacthod: 45e and 54e RIdLi (4 bns). GdD Kellermann, GdB Picard and Marizy: 5e ChàCh; 2e, 4e and 5e HusR (16 sqns). Artillery and engineers 36 guns, 8 bns, 16 sqns.

III Corps M Davout GdD Caffarelli, GdB Demont, Debilly, Eppler: 13e RILé, 17e, 30e and 51e RIdLi (8 bns). GdD Friant, GdB Heudelet, Lochet, Grandeau: 15e RILé, 33e, 48e, 108e and 111e RIdLi (10 bns). GdD Viallannes: 2e ChàCh (4 sqns). Artillery and engineers 24 guns, 18 bns, 4 sqns.

IV Corps M Soult GdD St Hilaire, GdB Thiebault, Morand, Varé: 10e RILé, 14e, 36e, 43e and 55e RIdLi (10 bns). GdD Vandamme, GdB Schinner, Ferrey, Caudras: 24e RILé, 4e, 28e, 46e and 57e RIdLi (10 bns). GdD Legrand, GdB Levasseur, Merle, Brouard: 26e RILé, 3e, 18e and 75e RIdLi; Tirailleurs du Po (9 bns). GdD Suchet, GdB Becker, Valhubert, Claparède: 34e, 40e, 64e and 88e RIdLi (10 bns). GdD Margaron: 11e and 26e ChàCh, 8e HusR (12 sqns). Artillery and engineers 48 guns, 39 bns, 12 sqns.

V Corps M Lannes GdD Oudinot, GdB Laplanches-Mortières, Dupas, Ruffin: 10 combined grenadier bns. GdD Gazan, GdB Graindorge, Campana: 58e RIdLi (2 bns). GdD Lasalle, GdB Treilhard: 13e ChàCh, 9e and 10e HusR (12 sqns). Artillery and engineers 18 guns, 12 bns, 12 sqns.

VI Corps M Ney GdD Loison, GdB Villatte, Roguet: 39e RIdLi (3 bns). Reserve Cavalry M Prince Murat, GdD Nansouty, GdB Piston, Lahoussaye, St Germain: 1er and 2e Carabiniers, 3e, 9e and 12e Cuir R (20 sqns). GdD d'Hautpoul, GdB St Sulpice: 1er, 5e, 10e and 11e Cuir R (16 sqns). GdD Klein: 1er DragR (4 sqns). GdD Walther, GdB Sebastiani, Roget: 3e, 6e, 10e, 11e, 13e and 22e DragR (18 sqns). GdD Beaumont, GdB Boyer, Scalfort: 5e, 8e, 9e, 12e and16e DragR (18 sqns). GdD Bourcier, GdB Laplanche, Sahuc: 15e, 17e, 18e and 19e DragR (14 sqns). Artillery and engineers: 60 guns, 90 sqns.

Grande Armée totals 83 bns, 140½ sqns, 282 guns, ca 50,000 infantry, 15,000 cavalry.

French losses 14 generals, 80 staff officers and 514 officers killed and wounded, ca 10,000 men dead and wounded, the eagle and colour of the 4e RIdLi (1er Bn) was taken by the Russian Chevalier Guard.

Austro-Russian Forces Czar Alexander I of Russia commanding (Emperor Franz I of Austria also present):

FM Kutusov (regiments marked '*' are Austrian). The Avantgarde: FML Kienmayer GM Carneville: Wiener-Jäger* (2 coys); GzIR Broder Nr 7* (1 bn); GzIR 1st Szeckler Nr 14* (2 bns); GzIR 2nd Szeckler Nr 15* (2 bns). GM Stutterheim: ChLR O'Reilly Nr 3* (8 sqns); UlR Merveldt Nr 1* (¼ sqn). GM Count Nostitz: HusR Hessen-Homburg Nr 4* (8 sqns); UlR Schwarzenberg Nr 2* (½ sqn). GM Prince Moriz v Liechtenstein: HusR Szeckler Nr 11* (6 sqns); Sesajev Cossack R (5 sqns); Melentiev Cossacks (5 sqns); 2 x HAB*.

Avantgarde totals 5 bns and 2 coys, 3,400 infantry, 32¾ sqns, 2,940 cavalry, 12 guns.

GdI Count Buxhowden commanding: 1st Column GL Dochtorov, GM Lewis: 7th Jägers (3 bns); IR Neu-Ingermannland (3 bns); IR Jaroslav (3 bns). GM Urusov: IRs Vladimir, IR Briansk, IR Viatsky, IR Moscow, GrenR Kiev (3 bns each) Artillery **1st Column totals** 24 bns, 13,730 men. **2nd Column** LG Langeron, GM Alsufiev: 8th Jägers (2 bns); IRs Viborsky, Permskoy (3 bns each). GM Kamersky: IRs Kursky, Riasky, Fanagorsky (3 bns each); pioniers (1 coy). **2nd Column totals** 17 bns, 1 coy, 10,840 men. **3rd Column LG Przybyczewsky** GM Müller: Dennisoff Cossacks (5 sqns); 8th Jägers (1 bn); IRs Galitzin, Budersky, Podolsky, Narva, Asov (3 bns each); pioniers (1 coy). **3rd Column totals** 16 bns, 1 coy, 8,250 infantry, 5 sqns, 500 cavalry. **4th Column FM Count Kutusov**, **GL Miloradowitz**, GM Wodniansky: DragR EH Johann Nr 1* (2 sqns). GM Berg: IRs Novogrodky and Malorossisky (3 bns each); pioniers (2 coys). GM Repninsky: IRs Apscheron, Sonolenskoy (3 bns each); artillery reserve. **4th Column totals** 12 bns, 2 coys, 6,840 infantry, 2 sqns, 125 cavalry.

FML Count Kollowrath, **GM Rottermund** IR Salzburg Nr 23* (6 bns); IR Kaunitz Nr 20* (1 bn); IR Auersperg Nr 24* (1 bn). GM Jurscheck: IR's Kaiser Nr 1* (6th Bn); Czartorisky Nr 9* (2nd Bn); Lindenau Nr 29* (4th Bn); Württemberg Nr 38* (3rd Bn); Kerpen Nr 49* (6th Bn); Reuss-Greitz Nr 55* (6th Bn); Beaulieu Nr 58* (3rd Bn); Pioniers with 3 flying bridges (3 coys). **Totals** 15 bns, 3 coys, 11,250 men.

Cavalry Corps FM Prince M Liechtenstein, FM Prince Hohenlohe, GM Caramelli: KürR Nassau Nr 5* (8 sqns); KürR Lothringen Nr 7*(8 sqns). GM Weber: KürR Kaiser Nr 1* (6 sqns). **GL v Essen** GM Czepelov: Cossacks of the Guard (5 sqns); UlR Grand Prince Constantin (10 sqns); Leib-KürR (5 sqns); DragR Petersburg (5 sqns). **GL Kvarov** GM Penitzky: DragR Karkov (5 sqns); DragR Tschernigov (5 sqns); HusR Elisabethgrad (10 sqns); HAB.

Cavalry totals 69 sqns, 5,600 cavalry.

The Corps of the Right Wing GL Prince Bagration GM Dolgoruky; FM Ulanius; GM Czaplitz: Cossack Rs Isajev, Kuselev, Charsumkov and Malachov (5 sqns each); 5th and 6th Jägers (3 bns each); IR Archangelsk, IR Staroi Ingermannland, IR Pskov (3 bns each); HusR Pavlograd, HusR Mariupol (10 sqns each); DragR Twer (5 sqns); HAB.

Right Wing totals 15 bns, 8,500 infantry, 45 sqns, 4,500 cavalry.

The Russian Imperial Guard Grand Prince Constantin: GL Kollowretzov GM Jankowitz: Life Cossack R (2 sqns); Life HusR (5 sqns); Chevalier-Garde (5 sqns); Life Horse Guard (5 sqns); Life-Jäger (1 bn); IR Siemienovsky (2 bns); IR Preobrashenski (2 bns); IR Ismailovski (2 bns); Life Grenadiers (3 bns); Pioniers (1 coy).

Russian Imperial Guard totals 10 bns, 6,830 infantry, 17 sqns, 2,900 cavalry, 1 pionier coy. Artillery.

Austro-Russian grand totals 114 bns, 69,460 infantry, 173¾ sqns, 16,565 cavalry, 7 pionier coys, 252 guns (5 Russian batteries did not partake in the battle.)

Austro-Russian losses 16,000 dead and wounded* including GL Count Essen and GM Juerscheck; 7 other generals and 293 officers killed or wounded. 9 generals, 820 officers and ca 20,000 captured; 186*guns, 400 ammunition waggons and 45 colours and standards including the following Russian infantry colours: IR Azov - 3; IR Archangelsk - 1; IR Narva - 2; IR Podolie - 5; IR Kursk - 2; IR Perm - 1.

* Schulz gives 5,922 Austrians killed, wounded and missing; 21,000 Russians killed wounded and missing and 133 guns.

Comment This battle is considered by many experts to have been Napoleon's greatest. The immediate profits were the ending of this dramatic campaign on his terms; the end of the Third Coalition; the reduction and humbling of the Austrian Empire and the setting up of the Confederation of the Rhine at Austria's expense in 1806.

Sources Wrede, Martinien, Charrié, Schulz, Stutterheim.

DV Wonau, 2 December 1805, skirmish

A village in the centre of the Czech Republic (Bohemia in 1805) about 5 km south of Deutschbrod on the road to Iglau.

An Austrian victory over the Bavarians.

(Last action - Austerlitz, 2 December; next action - Stecken, 5 December.)

Bavarian Forces GL v Wrede commanding the 3rd and 5th Bavarian brigades. 2nd Lt Inf Bn (1 bn) ca 800 men.

Bavarian losses 8 officers and 145 men killed wounded and missing.

Austrian Forces FML Prince Schwarzenberg commanding: IR Reuss-Plauen Nr 17 (6th Bn); IR Gemmingen Nr 21 (4 bns); ChLR Rosenberg Nr 6 (6 sqns).

Austrian totals 5 bns, 6 sqns, 6 guns.

Austrian losses Not known, slight.

Comment Wrede had the task of keeping Napoleon's northern flank safe from interference from Archduke Ferdinand's corps around Czaslau. The Bavarians withdrew south to regroup.

Sources Wrede, Leyh, Schulz, Bezzel.

DV Stecken, 5 December 1805, clash

A village in the centre of the Czech Republic (Bohemia in 1805) about 10 km south of Deutschbrod on the road to Iglau.

An Austrian victory over the Bavarians.

(last action - Wonau, 2 December. This was the last action in the Danube Valley campaign.)

Bavarian Forces Gl v Wrede commanding the 3rd and 5th Bavarian Brigades 7th and 8th IRs (2 bns each); 2nd LtI Bn (1 bn) ChLR Nr 4 (4 sqns).

Bavarian totals 5 bns, 4 sqns, 12 guns, ca 4,000 men.

Bavarian losses ca 200 killed and wounded, 600 captured.

Austrian Forces FML Prince Schwarzenberg commanding

IR Reuss-Plauen Nr 17 (6th Bn); IR Reuss-Greitz Nr 18 (4th and 6th Bns); IR Gemmingen Nr 21 (4 bns); IR Froon Nr 54 (6th Bn); KürR Eh Franz Nr 2 (8 sqns); DragR Hohenlohe Nr 2 (4 sqns); ChLR Rosenberg Nr 6 (6 sqns); UlR Merveldt Nr 1 (6 sqns).

Austrian totals 8 bns, 24 sqns, 12 guns, ca 7,000 men.

Austrian losses Not known, slight.

Comment The Bavarians withdrew south to Mährisch-Budwitz, 35 km south of Iglau.

Sources Wrede, Leyh, Schulz, Bezzel.

IN Lippa, 6 December 1805, skirmish

A village in present-day Croatia, nowadays known as Studena, about 16 km north of Rijeka (Fiume in 1805) in the mountains.

A French victory over the Austrians.

(Last action – Castelfranco Veneto, 24 November; next action – St Mathia, 9 December.)

French Forces GdB Gilly and GdB Guillet of Serra's 5th Division. No details known.

French losses Not known, slight.

Austrian Forces Obst Boxich commanding 5th Bn GzIR Ottocaner Nr 2 (4 coys).

Austrian losses Not known, slight.

Comment Most Grenz-Infanterie-Regimenter had hurriedly raised 5th Bns as danger approached; they were badly armed and equipped and consisted of boys, semi-invalides and veterans. Boxich fell back south to his reserve.

Sources von Angeli, Wrede, Martinien.

IN St Mathia, 9 December 1805, skirmish

A village in present-day Croatia; nowadays known as Marcelji, about 8 km north of Rijeka (Fiume in 1805) in the mountains.

A French victory over the Austrians.

(Last action – Lippa, 6 December. This was the last action in the campaign.)

French Forces GdB Gilly and GdB Guillet of Serra's 5th Division. No details known.

French losses Not known, slight.

Austrian Forces Obst Boxich commanding: GzIR Ottocaner Nr 2 (6 coys).

Austrian losses 600 captured.

Comment News of the armistice concluded by Napoleon and Emperor Franz II put an end to fighting in this theatre.

Sources von Angeli, Wrede, Martinien.

1806

1806 THE ACTIONS

IS Campo Tenese, 9 March 1806, battle

A plateau in southern Italy just south of Lauria which is about 25 km from the west coast Gulf of Policastro, 180 km south of Naples.

A French victory over the Sicilians.

(This was the opening action of the war here; next action – Maida, 4 July.)

French Forces GdD Reynier commanding: 1er RILé (2 bns); 42e RILé (1 bn); 23e RILé; 1st IR Polish-Italian Legion (2 bns each); 1st Swiss (4e Bn); 9e ChàCh (4 sqns.)

French total 6,000 men.

French losses Not known exactly but light.

Sicilian Forces LG Count Dumas commanding. Exact details not known.

Sicilian total ca 10,000 men.

Sicilian losses 3,000 mostly captured; all artillery and baggage.

Comment This action broke the back of the Kingdom of the Two Sicilies. The south of the Italian mainland became the French satellite Kingdom of Naples; the island of Sicily remained the rump, Bourbon-ruled state under British naval protection.

Sources: Bodart, Oman.

XX Bazardjik, 3 June 1806, battle

A town in eastern Bulgaria, about 40 km north of the Black Sea port of Varna. Now called Dobric, at the junction of Routes 21, 27 and 29.

(A drawn match between the Russians and the Turks.)

This was the only action of note in this area in 1806.

Exact details not known; Gen Kamenskoi commanded the Russians who suffered about 800 killed and wounded.

IS Maida (Santa Eufemia), 4 July 1806, battle

A village near the west coast of the toe of Italy, on Route 18, about 20 km west of Catanzaro.

An allied victory over the French.

(Last action – Campo Tenese, 9 March 1806; next action – Monteleone, 6 July.)

French Forces GdD Reynier commanding: GdB Compère: 1er RILé (2 bns), 42e RIdLi (1 bn). GdB Digonnet: 23e RILé (2 bns); 1er IR Polish-Italian Legion (2 bns). GdB Peyri: 1er RISuisse (4e Bn); 9e ChàCh (4 sqns). Artillery HAB; 112 men, 4 guns. Pioniers and train – 311 men.

French totals 7 bns, 4 sqns, 4 guns, ca 6,440 men.

French losses 490 killed, 870 wounded 722 captured, 4 guns.

Allied Forces MG Sir John Stuart commanding:.

Advanced Guard Col Kempt: Combined Lt Bn (light companies of the 20th, 1st/27th, 1st/35th, 1st/58th, 1st/61st, 1st/81st and de Watteville's Foot plus the flankers of the 1st/35th; Corsican Rangers (2 coys); Sicilian Volunteers (1 coy). Total 966 men. **1st Brigade** Col Cole: 1st/27th (1 bn); Combined Grenadiers (20th, 1st/27th, 1st/35th, 1st/58th, 1st/81st and de Watteville's – 1 bn). **Total** 1,266 men. **2nd Brigade** Col Acland: 2nd/78th (1 bn); 1st/81st (1 bn). **Total** 1,341 men.

3rd Brigade Col Oswald: 20th (1 bn); 1st/58th (1 bn); de Watteville's (½ bn). **Total** 1,487 men. Artillery: HAB 136 men, 3 guns.

Allied losses 45 killed, 282 wounded.

Comment This convincing tactical victory momentarily scattered French forces in Calabria. The victory was totally squandered as no pursuit or follow up was made. Reynier was given time to regroup and reassert control over the area.

Sources Oman, Fortescue, Martinien.

IS Monteleone, 6 July 1806, surrender

A small village in the mountainous toe of Italy, near Route 18, north of Mileto towards the coast of the Gulf of St Eufemia.

A British victory over the French.

(Last action – Maida, 4 July; next action – Tropea, 7 July.)

Franco-Italian Garrison: Polish-Italian Legion (½ bn).

Franco-Italian losses All captured.

British Forces MG Sir John Stuart's force as for Maida on 4 July.

British total ca 4,500 men.

British losses None.

Comment The Poles surrendered without firing a shot.

Sources Fortescue, Oman.

IS Tropea, 7 July 1806, surrender

A coastal fortress on the west coast of the toe of Italy, on Route 522, 30 km west of the port of Pizzo.

A British victory over the Franco-Italians.

(Last action – Monteleone, 6 July; next action – Reggio, 9 July.)

Franco-Italian Garrison 1st Bn Polish-Italian Legion (3 coys).

Franco-Italian losses 370 captured.

British Forces Captain Fellowes commanding HMS *Apollo*.

British losses None.

Comment British naval power allowed them to raid at will along any coastline.

Source: Fortescue, Oman.

IS Reggio, 9 July 1806, surrender

A port on the toe of Italy, on the Straits of Messina.

A British-Neapolitan victory over the French.

(Last action - Tropea, 7 July; next action - Gaëta, 18 July.)

French garrison Parts of 1er RILé and 42 RidLi.

French total 632 men.

French losses ca 600 captured.

British Forces BG Broderick with 1,200 British and Neapolitan troops from Sicily on HMS *Amphion* (Captain Hoste).

British losses Not known exactly, insignificant.

Sources Fortescue, Oman.

IS Gaëta, 26 Feb – 18 July 1806, siege and surrender

A formidable fortress on the western coast of Italy, between Rome and Naples on Route 213.

A Franco-Neapolitan victory over the forces of the Kingdom of the Two Sicilies.

(Last action - Reggio, 9 July; next action - Scilla, 24 July.)

Franco-Neapolitan Forces M Massena commanding. 1st Division GdD Partounneaux: 1st Bde GdB Lucotte: 22e RILé (1er and 2e Bns); 29e RIdLi (1er and 2e Bns); 2nd Bde GdB Lanchantin: 52e and 101e RIdLi (1er and 2e Bns each). 2nd Division GdD Gardanne: 3rd Bde GdB Camus: 62e RIdLi (4 bns); 102e RIdLi (1er and 2e Bns); 4th Bde GdB Valentin: 20e RIdLi (3 bns); 32e RILé (1er Bn); R Corse (Elite Bn). Light Cav Div GdD Espagne: 5th Bde GdB Montbrun: 4e ChàCh (3 sqns); 6th Bde: GdB Merlin: 14e and 25e ChàCh (4 sqns each). Dragoon Division GdD Mermet: 7th Bde (vacant): 23e DragR (4 sqns); 8th Bde GdB Debelle: 29e and 30e DragRs (4 sqns each). 1 x FAB, 1 x HAB. By 25 April 1806 the 32e RILé and the R Corse had left and were replaced by the 10e RIdLi (3 bns). The 4th Sqn, 4e ChàCh joined the Light Cav Div.

Franco-Neapolitan final total ca 12,000 men.

Franco-Neapolitan losses ca 1,000 killed and wounded.

Sicilian Garrison General Prince von Hesses-Philippsthal commanding IRs 'Reali Presidi', 'Real Principi', 'Real Carolina', 'Valdemone', 'Valdinoto' (1 bn each). 'Valdimazzara' (2 bns). Artillery.

Sicilian total From an initial 4,000 the garrison rose to 7,000.

Sicilian losses ca 1,000 killed and wounded, 171 guns taken. The garrison was released on condition that they would not fight against France or her allies for one year.

Comment Following the British victory at Maida on 4 July, Sir Sidney Smith was supposed to have sailed north to relieve this vital point. He wasted time playing politics and the fortress surrendered.

Sources Crociani, Fortescue, Oman.

IS Scilla, 24 July 1806, surrender

A minor coastal fortress on the Italian coast at the northern end of the Straits of Messina.

A British victory over the French.

(Last action - Gaëta, 18 July; next action - Cotrone, 28 July.)

French Garrison 23e RIdLi (281 men).

French losses All captured.

British Forces Col Oswald commanding: 10th and 21st Foot (1 bn each); Chasseurs Britannique (1 bn).

British total ca 2,600 men.

British losses not known exactly but insignificant.

Comment Instead of properly exploiting his victory at Maida on 4 July, MG Sir John Stuart squandered his advantages in such trivial raids.

Source Fortescue, Oman.

IS Cotrone, 28 July 1806, surrender

An Italian port on the east coast of the toe of Italy, just east of Route 106/E90.

A British victory over the Franco-Italians.

(Last action, Scilla, 24 July; this was the last action of note in southern Italy.)

Franco-Italian Garrison Polish-Italian Legion (3rd Bn); Total 500 men.

Franco-Italian losses ca 500 captured.

British Forces Col Macleod and the 78th Foot (1 bn) on HMS *Amphion* (Captain Hoste).

Comment By now the French had recovered from

their defeat at Maida and begun to secure their hold on southern Italy.

Source Fortescue, Oman

OP Schleiz, 9 October 1806, clash

A small town in eastern Germany, in the Vogtland area, at the junction of Routes B2, B94 and B282/E49, on the River Wisenta (Wiesenthal in 1806) and just east of the Autobahn A9.

A French victory over the Prussians and Saxons.

(This was the opening action of the campaign; next action – Saalfeld, 10 October.)

French Forces M Bernadotte commanding: GdD d'Erlon: GdB Maison: 27e RILé, 94e and 95e RIdLi (6 bns). GdB Tilly's Lt Cav Bde 4e HusR, 5e ChàCh (8 sqns). Artillery 12 guns.

French totals 6 bns, 8 sqns, 12 guns, ca 4,000 men.

French losses Not exactly known; light.

Prussian-Saxon Forces GM Bila II of Tauentzien's Corps: Schützen (1 bn); Füs Bn Rosen Nr 7 (1 bn); HusR von Bila Nr 11 (5 sqns); Jägers (2 coys) and the Saxon regiments IR Pz Max (2 bns); ChLR Pz Johann (2 sqns) 1 x FAB (8guns). About 2,600 men and 8 guns.

Prussian-Saxon losses 12 officers and 554 men killed, wounded, captured and missing and 1 gun (abandoned in a dyke during the retreat).

Comment The Allied cavalry blundered into an ambush by Tilly's light cavalry brigade and were badly cut up. This triggered their withdrawal.

Sources Höpfner, Lettow-Vorbeck, Martinien.

OP Saalfeld, 10 October 1806, clash

A small town in eastern Germany, on the River Saale and at the junctions of Routes B85 and B281.

(Last action – Schleiz, 9 October; next action – Jena, 14 October.)

A French victory over the Prussians and Saxons.

French Forces M Lannes' V Corps; GdD Suchet: GdB Claparède: 17e RILé, 34e and 40e RIdLi (10 bns). GdB Wedel: 64e and 88e RIdLi (6 bns). GdB Treilhard: 9e and 10e HusR (6 sqns). Artillery 2 x FAB, 1 x HAB 14 guns.

French totals 16 bns, 6 sqns, 14 guns, ca 12,800 men.

French losses ca 200 men killed and wounded.

Prussian-Saxon Forces GL Pz Louis Ferdinand of Prussia commanding: GM Pelet: Füs Bns Rabenau, Nr 13, Rühle Nr 15; Pelet Nr 14 (1 bn each); IR von Müffling Nr 49 (2 bns); Jäger coys Valentin and Masars (2 coys); Schimmelpfennig HusR Nr 6 (5 sqns); 1 x 6 pdr FAB, ½ HAB. GM von Bevilaqua* IR Pz Xaver* (2 bns); IR Kurfürst* (2 bns); IR Pz Clemens* (2 bns); HusR* (5 sqns); 1 x 4 pdr FAB*.

Prussian-Saxon totals 11 bns, 9 sqns, 2½ bties, ca 8,300 men.

Prussian losses Prince Louis and 4 other officers killed or fatally wounded, 24 officers wounded, 1,700–1,800 men killed, wounded or captured, the colours of IR von Müffling Nr 49 (1st Bn); IR Kurfürst (2nd Bn) and IR Pz Clemens (1st Bn), 15 Prussian and 18 Saxon guns with ammunition waggons and most of the baggage. Prince Louis was killed by a maréchal-de-logis of the 10e Hussars.

* = Saxon regiments.

Comment Prince Louis Ferdinand was a competent commander but had little practical experience and he completely underestimated the French threat.

Only Suchet's division and the cavalry of Lannes' corps took part in the action. The death of Prince Louis Ferdinand and the defeat of his Avantgarde much depressed the Allied army.

Sources Höpfner, Lettow-Vorbeck, Martinien, Fiebig.

OP Jena, 14 October 1806, battle

A town on the River Saale in eastern Germany, at the junction of Routes B7 and B88, 7 km north of the Autobahn A4/E40 and 20 km south of Auerstedt.

A French victory over the Allies.

(Last action – Saalfeld, 10 October; next action – Auerstedt, 14 October.)

French Forces Emperor Napoleon I commanding:.

The Imperial Guard M Bessières: Dismounted DragR (1er and 2e Regts); Gendarmes d'Élite (1 sqn).

IV Corps M Soult: 1st Division GdD St Hilaire: 10e RILé (2 bns); 36e, 43e and 55e RIdLi (6 bns). 2nd Division GdD Leval: 26e RILé (2 bns); 4e, 28e, 46e and 57e RIdLi (10 bns).

3rd Division GdD Legrand: 75e RIdLi (2 bns); Tirailleurs Corse (1 bn); Tirailleurs du Po (1 bn). Light Cavalry GdB Margaron: 8e HusR; 11e and 16e ChàCh (9 sqns). Artillery 8 x FAB, 2 x HAB.

IV Corps totals 29 bns, 9 sqns, 52 guns, ca 32,000 men.

V Corps M Lannes: 1st Division GdD Suchet: 17e RILé, 34e, 40e, 64e and 88e RIdLi (16 bns). 2nd Division GdD Gazan: 21e RILé, 100e and 103e RIdLi (9 bns).

Light Cavalry GdB Treilhard: 9e and 10e HusR, 21e ChàCh (9 sqns). Artillery: 3 x FAB, 2 x HAB.

V Corps totals 25 bns, 9 sqns, 38 guns, ca 18,500 men.

VI Corps M Ney: 1st Division GdD Marchand: 6e RILé, 39e and 69e RIdLi (6 bns). 2nd Division GdD Marcognet: 25e RILé, 27e, 50e and 59e RIdLi (8 bns). Light Cavalry GdB Colbert: 3e HusR, 10e ChàCh (8 sqns). Artillery: 4 x FAB, 2 x HAB.

VI Corps totals 14 bns, 8 sqns, 48 guns, ca 21,500 men.

VII Corps M Augereau: 1st Division GdD Desjardins: 16e RILé; 14e, 44e and 105e RIdLi (8 bns), 7e RILé, 24e and 63e RIdLi (8 bns); Hessen-Darmstadt Garde- and 1st Leib-Füs Bns (2 bns), Light Cavalry GdB Durosnel: 7e and 20e ChàCh (7 sqns). Artillery 3 x FAB, 3 x HAB.

VII Corps totals 18 bns, 7 sqns, 36 guns, ca 9,000 men.

Reserve Cavalry Corps Joachim Murat, Grand Duke of Berg: 2nd Cuirassier Division GdD d'Hautpoul 1er CuirR (4 sqns). 1st Dragoon Division GdD Klein: 1er, 2e, 14e, 20e and 26e DragR (20 sqns). 3rd Dragoon Division GdD Beaumont: 9e DragR (4 sqns).

Reserve Cavalry Corps total 28 sqns, 6 guns, ca 3,000 men.

French totals 87 bns, 58 sqns, 180 guns ca 54,000 men out of the total 96,000.

French losses 6 generals, 39 field officers, 288 officers and at least 5,700 men killed and wounded. Other sources give French killed and wounded as high as 6,794.

Allied Forces GdI Prince Hohenlohe-Ingelfingen commanding. Regiments marked '*' are Saxon:

Avantgarde GM von Schimmelpfennig (under command of GL von Grawert).

GM von Pelet: Füs Bns Pelet Nr 14; Rabenau Nr 13 and Rühle Nr 15 (3 bns); Jäger coys Masars and Valentin (2 coys); 1 x FAB (6 guns). GM von Schimmelpfennig: HusR Schimmelpfennig Nr 6 (10 sqns); 1 x HAB (6 guns). GM von Trützschler:* Saxon HusR* (8 sqns). GM von Bevilaqua*: IR von Müffling Nr 49 (2 bns); IR Pz Clemens* (2 bns); IR Kurfürst* (2 bns); 1 x 6 pdr FAB* (6 guns).

The Left Wing GdK von Zeschwitz*, GL von Niesemeuschel*, GM von Burgsdorff:* IR von Thümmel and Pz Xavier* (2 bns each), 2 x 8 pdr FABs* (16 guns); IR Pz Friedrich August* (2 bns). GM von Dyherrn:* IR von Low* and von Niesemeuschel* (2 bns each); IR von Bevilaqua* (2nd Bn); 1 x 12 pdr FAB* (10 guns). GL von Kochtitsky:* Carabiniers* and Kür R Kochtitsky* (4 sqns each); ChLR Pz Albert* (4 sqns); 1 x HAB* (10 guns). GL von Polenz* Füs Bn Boguslawsky Nr 22 (1 bn); ChLR von Polenz* (4 sqns), ½ x HAB (5 guns).

Left Wing totals 10 bns, 8,200 infantry, 16 sqns, 1,250 cavalry, 41 guns, 300 gunners.

Left Flank Guard GM von Tauentzien, GM von Zweiffel: Gren Bn Herwarth (1 bn); IR Zweiffel Nr 45 (2 bns). GM von Schöneberg*: Gren Bn a.d. Winkel (1 bn); IR von Rechten* and Pz Maximilian* (2 bns each); 1 x howitzer bty (6 pieces). GM von Bila: Jäger coys Werner and Kronheim (2 coys); Füs Bn Rosen (1 bn); ChLR Pz Clemens* (4 sqns); HusR Bila Nr 11 (5 sqns).

Left Flank Guard totals 9 bns, 4,500 infantry, 9 sqns, 1,800 cavalry, 6 guns, 70 gunners.

The Right Wing GL von Grawert, GM von Müffling: Gren Bn Hahn (1 bn); IR von Hohenlohe Nr 32 and von Sanitz Nr 50 (2 bns each); 1 x 12 pdr FAB (6 guns). Obst von Schimonsky: Gren Bn Sack (1 bn); IR von Zastrow Nr 39 and von Grawert Nr 47. 1 x 12 pdr FAB (6 guns). GL von Holtzendorff: GM von Henkel: KürR Henkel Nr 1 and Holtzendorff Nr 9, DragR Krafft Nr 11 (5 sqns each); 1 x HAB (6 x 6 pdrs). Obst von Erichsen: Füs Bn Erichsen Nr 10 (1 bn); HusR Gettkandt Nr 1 (10 sqns) ½ x HAB (4 x 4 pdrs).

Right Wing totals 17 bns, 7,500 infantry, 33 sqns, 1,900 cavalry, 22 guns, 230 gunners.

The Reserve GL von Prittwitz GM von Sanitz: Gren Bns von Losthin, Dohna, Borcke and Kollin (3½ bns) 1 x 12 pdr FAB (8 guns). GM von Cerrini:* Gren Bns Thiollaz*, Le Coq*, Lichtenhayn*, Hundt* and Metsch* (5 bns); 1 x FAB (8 guns). GM von Krafft: DragR Prittwitz Nr 2 (5 sqns); ChLR Pz Johann* (4 sqns); 1 x HAB (7 guns).

Reserve totals 8½ x bns, 6,900 infantry, 9 sqns, 1,000 cavalry, 23 guns, 190 gunners.

GL von Rüchel's Corps Avantgarde: GL von Winning: Füs Bns von Kayserlingk Nr 1 and von Bila Nr 2 (1 bn each); Jägers (2 coys); HusR von Pletz Nr 3 and von Köhler Nr 7 (5 sqns each); 1 x 6 pdr FAB and 1 x HAB (16guns). GM von Wobeser: Füs Bn Ernest Nr 19 (1 bn); Jägers (1 coy); DragR von Wobeser Nr 14 (5 sqns); ½ x HAB (4 x 4 pdrs).

Corps de Bataille Duke of Sachsen-Weimar: IR von Schenck Nr 9 and von Winning Nr 23 (2 bns each); Gren Bn von Borstell (1 bn). IR von Treuenfels Nr 29 and von Strachwitz Nr 43 (2 bns each); Gren Bn von Hellmann (1 bn). IR von Wedell Nr 10 and von Tschepe Nr 37 (2 bns each); Füs Bn von Sobbe Nr 18 (1 bn). KürR von Bailliodz Nr 5 (5 sqns); DragR von Katte Nr 4 (5 sqns); 2 x FAB (16guns); ½ x HAB 4 guns.

Rüchel's Corps totals 20 bns, 2 coys, 25 sqns, 40 guns, ca 15,000 men.

Allied total on the day of the battle was about 45-50,000 men with 175 guns.

Prussian-Saxon losses Due to the fact that the allied army disintegrated it is impossible to give accurate estimates of casualties. Of the Prussian officers 30 were killed or mortally wounded as were 19 Saxons. 168 Prussian officers were wounded, 95 Saxon officers were wounded.

The Prussians lost 24 guns from the artillery as well as battalion pieces. Most of the Saxon artillery (59 pieces) was also lost, only 17 cannon and 6 battalion pieces being saved.

The following colours and standards were also lost: Prussians: IR Alt-Larisch Nr 26 – 1; IR von Hohenlohe Nr 32 – 2; Saxon: IR von Thümmel – 2, IR Pz Friedrich – 2; IR von Low – 2; IR von Niesemeuschel – 2; KürR Kochtitsky – 1. Almost all the artillery train and baggage were also lost.

Comment The action started in thick fog. The French advance caught the Allies by surprise and the Allied formations were drawn – or thrown – into the struggle one by one and destroyed in turn by the French superiority of numbers and clarity of command.

Sources Höpfner, Lettow-Vorbeck, Martinien, Fiebig.

OP Auerstedt, 14 October 1806, battle

A village in Thuringia in eastern Germany, about 3 km northwest of Bad Sulza on the River Ilm and 20 km north of Jena, at the northern end of the rhombus formed by Routes B87, B88 and B7.

A French victory over the Allies.

(Last action – Jena, 14 October; next action – Erfurt, 16 October.)

French Forces M Davout commanding III Corps: **1st Division** GdD Morand: GdB Debilly, Bronard and d'Honières: 13e RILé (2 bns); 17e and 30e RIdLi (4 bns); 51e RIdLi (3 bns); 61e RIdLi (3 bns). Artillery: 2 x FAB, 13 guns. **2nd Division** GdD Friant, GdB Kister, Lochet and Grandeau: 33e, 48e, 108 and 111e RIdLi (2 bns each). Artillery 1 x FAB, 1 x HAB 8 guns. **3rd Division** GdD Gudin; GdB Petit and Gautier: 12e RIdLi (2 bns); 21e RIdLi (3 bns); 25e, 85e RIdLi (2 bns each). Artillery 1 x FAB 1 x HAB 8 guns. **Cavalry:** GdB Viallanes* 1er, 2e, and 12e ChàCh (9 sqns). Corps Artillery Reserve GdB Hannicque: 3 x FAB 17 guns.

French totals 29 bns, 9 sqns, 46 guns, ca 26,660 infantry, 1,622 cavalry and 1,681 artillery, engineers and train.

French losses Six generals, 27 field and 225 junior officers killed and wounded. French losses were never established but have been estimated at ca 7,000 killed, wounded and missing according to Davout.

* = Not present at the battle.

Prussian Forces King Friedrich Wilhelm III; FM Duke Karl Wilhelm Ferdinand of Brunswick.

Avantgarde GM von Blücher, GM von Oswald: Füs Bn Sachsen-Weimar, Kloch Nr 18, Oswald, Nr 16, Greiffenberg Nr 4 (4 bns and 6 guns). GM von Blücher: HusR von Blücher Nr 8; HusR Württemberg Nr 4 (10 sqns each); DragR Irwing Nr 3 (5 sqns). 1 x HAB 8 guns.

Avantgarde totals 4 bns, 2,350 infantry, 25 sqns, 3,500 cavalry, 1 x HAB, 150 gunners, 14 guns.

The Left Wing Gen von Schmettau; Obst von Scharnhorst, GM von Alvensleben: IR Pz Heinrich Nr 35 (2 bns); IR von Alvensleben Nr 33 (2 bns). Gren Bn von Schack (1 bn); 1 x FAB (6 guns). GM von Schimonsky: IR Malschitsky Nr 28 (2 bns); IR von Schimonsky Nr 40 (2 bns); Gren Bn Krafft (1 bn); 1 x FAB (6 guns). GM von Irwing: DragR Königin Nr 5 (10 sqns). GM von Bünting: KürR von Bünting Nr 12, KürR von Heising Nr 8 (5 sqns each).

Artillery – 1 x HAB (6 guns).

Left Wing totals 10 bns, 8,600 infantry, 20 sqns, 2,700 cavalry, 18 guns, 200 gunners.

The Centre GL von Wartensleben GM von Wedel: Gren Bn Hanstein (1 bn); IR von Kleist Nr 5 and von Renouard Nr 3 (2 bns each); 1 x FAB (6guns). GM von Renouard: Gren Bn Alt Braun (1 bn); IR Braunschweig Nr 21 and Pz Louis Nr 20 (2 bns each), 1 x FAB (6 guns). GM von Quitzow: KürR von Quitzow Nr 6 and von Reitzenstein Nr 7 (5 sqns each). 1 x HAB (6 guns).

Centre totals 10 bns, 8,300 infantry, 10 sqns, 1,800 cavalry, 18 guns, 200 gunners.

The Right Wing 1st Division GL Wilhelm, Prince of Orange: Obst-Pz Heinrich von Preussen Gren Bn Rheinbaben (1 bn); IR Pz Ferdinand Nr 34, IR von Puttkammer Nr 36 (2 bns each); 1 x FAB (6 guns). Obst von Lützow: Gren Bn Knebel (1 bn); IR von Möllendorf Nr 25, IR von Wartensleben Nr 59 (2 bns each); 1 x FAB (6 guns). Obstlt Wilhelm Pz von Preussen; KürR Leibkarabiniers Nr 12; Garde du Corps Nr 13 (5 sqns each); 1 X HAB (6 guns).

1st Division totals 10 bns, 7,300 infantry, 10 sqns, 1,700 cavalry, 18 guns, 200 gunners.

The Reserve GL Count von Kalkreuth 1st Division GL von Kühnheim, Obst von Pletz: Gren Bns Rabiel and Pz August (2 bns); IR König Nr 18 (2 bns); 1 x howitzer bty (6 pieces). GM von Hirschfeld: Gren-Garde Nr 6 (1 bn); IR Garde Nr 15 (2 bns); ½ x FAB (3 guns); KürR Gendarmes Nr 10 (5 sqns); KürR von Beeren Nr 2 (5 sqns); 1 x HAB (6 guns).

2nd Division GL von Arnim GM von Malschitsky: Gren Bns Schlieffen and Hülsen (2 bns); IR von Zenge Nr 24 (2 bns); 1 x FAB (8guns).

Reserve totals 18 bns, 13,000 infantry, 15 sqns, 2,550 cavalry, guns, 200 gunners.

Prussian totals 39,550 infantry, 12,250 cavalry, 163 guns.

Prussian losses The Duke of Brunswick, GL Count von Schmettau, GM von Quitzow and von Greiffenberg, 7 field officers and 36 junior officers were killed or died of their wounds. FM von Möllendorf, 5 generals, 34 field officers and 181 junior officers were wounded. Without counting battalion pieces, 57 guns were taken. The following colours were also lost: IR von Puttkammer Nr 36 -2, Bodart quotes French figures for Allied casualties as 10,000 dead and wounded and 3,000 captured.

Comment This battle also opened in thick fog, as did that at Jena this day.

Davout had no idea that he was taking on the main body of the Prussian army. French skirmishers proved to be most effective and the Prussians found no real answer to this threat.

There was no effective pursuit, as Davout's III Corps was too exhausted to follow them.

This was truly a remarkable achievement on the part of the French commanders and soldiers and contrasted vividly with the appalling performance of the Prussian general staff and officer corps.

Sources Höpfner, Lettow-Vorbeck, Martinien, Fiebig.

OP Erfurt, 16 October 1806, capitulation

A fortified city in Thuringia in eastern Germany; on the River Gera and at the junction of Routes B4 and B7, 40 km west of Jena.

A French victory over the Prussians.

(Last actions - Jena and Auerstedt, 14 October; next action - Halle, 17 October.)

French Forces M Murat's cavalry corps.

French totals ca 16,000 men.

French losses None.

Prussian Forces GL Prince of Orange commanding about 10,000 men of various corps and regiments, mostly refugees from the battle of Jena.

Prussian losses About 12,000 captured (some cavalry units escaped), 65 guns.

The following colours and standards were taken:.

IR Gren Garde Nr 6 - 2; IR von Schenck Nr 9 - 4; IR von Wedel Nr 10 - 4; IR von Arnim Nr 13 (2nd Bn) - 1; IR von Braunschweig Nr 21 (2nd Bn) - 1; IR von Winning Nr 23 - 4; IR von Zenge Nr 24 - 1; IR Alt-Larisch Nr 26 - 1; IR von Hohenlohe Nr 32 (2nd Bn) - 2; IR Pz Ferdinand Nr 34 - 2; IR Pz Heinrich Nr 35 (1st Bn) - 2; IR von Zweiffel Nr 45 (1st Bn) - 1: IR Hessen Nr 48 - 4; IR von Wartensleben Nr 59 (1st Bn) - 2. DragR von Irwing Nr 3 - 4.

Comment There was no combat. No French infantry were involved. A column of 9,000 Prussian prisoners from Erfurt, under escort by one battalion were freed two or three days later by a squadron of Prussian hussars.

Sources Höpfner, Martinien, Lettow-Vorbeck.

OP Halle, 17 October 1806, clash

A town in the eastern German state of Saxony, on the River Saale, at the junction of Autobahns B80 and B100, 30 km northwest of Leipzig and 65 km north of Jena.

A French victory over the Prussians.

(Last actions - Erfurt, 16 October; next action - Spandau, 25 October.)

French Forces M Bernadotte's I Corps: GdD Dupont GdB Rouyèrer: 9e RILé (3 bns), GdB d'Harvesse: 32e and 96e RIdLi (2 bns each). Artillery: 2 x FAB, 12 guns. GdD Drouet GdB Frère: 27e RILé (2 bns), GdB Werle: 94e RIdLi (2 bns); 95e RIdLi (3 bns). Artillery:

1 x FAB, 1 x HAB, 16 guns. GdD Tilly: 2e Hus, 4e Hus, 5e ChàCh (12 sqns). Corps Artillery Reserve: GdD Eblé 1 x FAB, 1 x HAB 12 guns.

French totals 16,000 men and 8 bties, 36 guns.

French losses Bernadotte reported less than 800 killed and wounded.

Prussian Forces Duke Eugene von Württemberg's Reserve Corps.

Avantgarde GM von Hinrichs: Füs Bns Hinrichs Nr 17, Borell Nr 9, Knorr Nr 12 (3 bns); HusR Usedom Nr 10 (2 sqns); DragR Hertzberg Nr 9 (1 sqn); DragR Heyking Nr 10 (1 sqn); 2 x HA guns. Main Body 1st Division: GM von Natzmer: Gren Bns Schmeling and Crety (2 bns); IRs Natzmer Nr 54, Kauffberg Nr 51 and Treskow Nr 17 (2 bns each). Artillery 1½ x FAB (12 guns). 2nd Division GM von Jung-Larisch: Gren Bn Vieregg (1 bn); IRs von Jung-Larisch Nr 53, von Kalkreuth Nr 4 and von Manstein Nr 55 (2 bns each). Artillery 1½ FAB (12 guns). Reserve Cavalry: DragR Hertzberg Nr 9 (4 sqns); DragR Heyking Nr 10 (4 sqns); HusR Usedom Nr 10 (8 sqns); 1 x HAB (6 guns).

Prussian totals 18 bns, 20 sqns, 32 guns, ca 11,000 men.

Prussian losses 13 officers killed, 26 wounded and 74 captured; ca 5,000 men killed wounded and missing/captured: 11 guns (and many battalion pieces) and four colours of IR von Treskow Nr 17. General Hinrichs was captured.

Comment The Duke of Württemberg dallied far too long in Halle after having had confirmed the Prussian defeats at Jena and Auerstedt. As it was, he posted his Avantgarde with the defile of the Saale bridge at its back and paid a heavy price for this classic error.

Sources Höpfner, Lettow-Vorbeck, Martinien.

OP Spandau, 25 October 1806, capitulation

A citadel in the lake of the River Havel in the western suburbs of modern Berlin, Germany.

A French victory over the Prussians.

(Last action – Halle, 17 October; next action – Zehdenick, 26 October.)

French Forces 17e RILé (3 bns) of Suchet's division of Lannes' V Corps.

French total ca 2000 men.

French losses None.

Prussian Garrison Maj Benekendorf commanding: IR König Nr 18 (3rd Bn); Invalides (3 coys).

Prussian totals 65 gunners, 71 guns, ca 920 men.

Prussian losses The garrison were released on condition that they not fight against France again in this campaign.

Comment The Prussian commandant was negotiating a capitulation of the run-down fortress when the French rushed the gate guard and forced their way in. Maj Benekendorf was court-martialled in 1808 and sentenced to be shot but the King commuted this to life imprisonment.

Sources Höpfner, Lettow-Vorbeck, Martinien.

OP Zehdenick, 26 October 1806, skirmish

A village in Mark Brandenburg in north eastern Germany, on the River Havel about 50 km north of Berlin.

A French victory over the Prussians.

(Last action – Spandau, 25 October; next action – Prenzlau, 28 October.)

French Forces GdD Lasalle's Light Cavalry Division of Murat's Reserve Cavalry: 5e and 7e HusR (6 sqns).

French totals ca 700 men.

French losses Not known, very light.

Prussian Forces GM von Schimmelpfennig commanding: DragR Königin Nr 5 (4 sqns); HusR Schimmelpfennig Nr 6 (8 sqns); Füsiliers (1 bn).

Prussian totals 1 bn, 12 sqns, (by now very weak), ca 1300 men.

Prussians losses 14 officers and 250 men killed, wounded and captured, 1 standard of DragR Königin Nr 5 (1st Bn) was lost.

Sources Höpfner, Fiebig, Lettow-Vorbeck, Martinien.

OP Prenzlau, 28 October 1806, capitulation

A small, walled town in northern Prussia (today Mark Brandenburg), on the River Uecker, at the junctions of Routes B109 and B198, about 45 km west of Szczecin (Stettin) on the River Oder, 92 km north of Berlin.

A French victory over the Prussians.

(Last action – Zehdenick, 26 October; next action – Pasewalk, 29 October.)

French Forces Joachim Murat, Grand Duke of Berg commanding the Reserve Cavalry. GdD Lasalle's Light Cavalry Division: 5e and 7e HusR, 1er Hus and 13e ChàCh (16 sqns). GdD Grouchy's 2nd Dragoon Division: 3e, 4e, 10e, 11e, 13e and 22e DragR (24 sqns). GdD Beaumont's 3rd Dragoon Division: 5e, 8e,

12e, 16e, 19e and 21e DragR (24 sqns). Artillery: 3 x HAB.

French totals ca 12,000 men and 12 guns.

French losses Not exactly known; slight. Martinien shows officer casualties here for the 6e, 10e, 13e, 16e and 21e Dragoons and for the 7e Hussars.

Prussian Forces Gen Prince Friedrich von Hohenlohe-Ingelfingen commanding.

The remnants of some of the troops who had fought at Jena (details may be taken from the listing of the colours and standards captured here in Prenzlau) ca 10,000 men and 64 guns.

Prussian losses Almost the entire force captured with the 64 guns and 1,800 horse.

The following colours and standards were taken:.

IR von Arnim Nr 13 (1st Bn) - 2; IR Garde Nr 15 (1st Bn) - 1; IR König Nr 18 - 4; IR Braunschweig Nr 21 - at least 1, possibly 3; IR von Möllendorf Nr 25 - 3; IR von Grawert Nr 47 - 1; KürR Nr 3, Leib-KürR - 5; DragR von Prittwitz Nr 2 - 5; DragR von Krafft Nr 11 - 5; DragR von Wobeser Nr 14 - 4. The remnants of the Gren. Bns Rabiel, Schack, Dohna, Osten, Borcke, Losthin and Hahn were captured here as were 1 x HAB and 2 x 12 pdr FABs.

Comment Murat bluffed that the Prussians were surrounded by 100,000 men (which was not true); Prince Hohenlohe and many of his staff were morally at an end and threw in the towel without attempting a break-out.

Sources Höpfner, Lettow-Vorbeck, Martinien.

OP Pasewalk, 29 October 1806, capitulation

A small town in northern Germany near the Baltic coast and 43 km west of Szczecin (Stettin in modern-day Poland) and about 110 km north of Berlin.

A French victory over the Prussians.

(Last action - Prenzlau, 28 October; next action - Stettin (Szczecin), 29 October.)

French Forces GdB Milhaud commanding 13e ChàCh, 1er HusR (700 men) of Lasalle's Light Cavalry Division of Murat's Cavalry Reserve.

French losses None.

Prussian Forces Obst von Hagen commanding the remnants of various corps whose identities can be seen by the colours and standards taken; a total of 4,200 men, 2,100 horses, 8 guns in one infantry brigade (Hagen's) and a cavalry brigade (Podewil's).

Prussian losses All captured; the officers released on their word of honour not to fight against France again in this campaign. The trophies included the colours and standards of IR von Pirch Nr 22 -3; IR von Zenge Nr 24 -3; IR von Treuenfels Nr 29 -4; IR Pz Ferdinand Nr 34 -2; KürR von Henkel Nr 1 -5; KürR von Heising Nr 8 -5; KürR von Holtzendorff Nr 9 -5; KürR Leib-Karabiniers Nr 11 -5; KürR von Bünting Nr 12 -5;. The horses and the 8 guns and 1 ammunition waggon were also taken.

Comment The balance of forces here illustrates just how low the morale of the Prussian army now was; this force capitulated without even being confronted by Milhaud's force.

Sources Höpfner, Lettow-Vorbeck, Martinien, Fiebig.

OP Stettin (Szczecin), 29 October 1806, capitulation

A fortified city on the River Oder, close to its estuary in the Baltic Sea, nowadays in Poland and 120 km north northeast of Berlin on Autobahn A6/E28/E65.

A French victory over the Prussians.

(Last action - Pasewalk, 29 October; next action - Boldekow, 30 October.)

French Forces GdB Lasalle's Light Cavalry Brigade of Murat's Cavalry Reserve Corps:.

5e and 7e HusR, ca 800 men and 2 guns.

French losses None.

Prussian Forces GL von Romberg commanding the remnants of various regiments and the 3rd Battalions of IRs von Kunheim Nr 1, von Arnim Nr 13, von Möllendorf Nr 25, Larisch Nr 26, von Winning Nr 23, Braunschweig Nr 21 and Pirch Nr 22.

Prussian totals ca 5,300 men, 281 guns.

Prussian losses 100 officers released on swearing not to fight against France again in this campaign. 5,200 men were captured. No colours or standards were lost.

Comment The commandant of Stettin (which was in a reasonable state of defence) was 81 years old. Not only did he fail to increase his garrison from the many regiments and corps flooding back from the defeats of Jena and Auerstedt, he actually refused General Bila I's corps passage through the fortress and thus caused the loss of these troops at the capitulation of Anklam on 1 November.

OP Boldekow, 30 October 1806, capitulation

A village in northern Germany, 14 km south of Anklam, on Route B197 to Friedland.

A French victory over the Prussians.

(Last action – Stettin (Szczecin), 29 October; next action – Anklam, 1 November.)

French Forces M Lannes' V Corps.

French losses None.

Prussian Forces Maj von Höpfner commanding Gen Blücher's Reserve Artillery Park and Parkkolonne Nr 5.

Prussian totals ca 600 men, 25 guns.

Prussian losses All captured, 25 guns, 48 ammunition waggons, 800 horses.

Comment Once again, the demoralised Prussians surrendered to an enemy that they had to seek out to be able to do it! No one even thought of destroying or even spiking the guns or of throwing the ammunition into the nearby rivers. They did not even make off with the horses. They gave everything intact to the enemy.

Sources Höpfner, Lettow-Vorbeck, Martinien, Fiebig.

OP Anklam, 1 November 1806, capitulation

A small, walled town in north Germany, on the River Peene, just opposite the island of Usedom in the Baltic Sea, at the junction of Routes B109, B110, B197 and B199, about 60 km north of Prenzlau.

A French victory over the Prussians.

(Last action – Boldekow, 30 October; next action – Küstrin, 1 November.)

French Forces GdB Becker's Dragoon Brigade of Sahuc's 4th Division of Murat's Reserve Cavalry.

French losses None.

Prussian Forces Gen von Bila I commanding the remnants of various regiments as shown by the colours and standards taken, ca 1,100 infantry and 1,073 cavalry, including the Gren Bn Sack and 1 squadron of KürR von Bailliodz.

Prussian losses All captured; colours and standards taken: IR von Grävenitz Nr 57 (1st Bn) – 2; KürR von Quitzow Nr 6 – 3; KürR Gendarmes Nr 10 – 1.

Comment Gen von Bila had been denied entry into Stettin a few days earlier and this caused the capture of his corps here this day. There was no combat.

Sources Höpfner, Lettow-Vorbeck, Martinien, Fiebig.

OP Küstrin, 1 November 1806, capitulation

A small town in present-day western Poland on the north bank of the River Warta, about 3 km east of its confluence with the River Oder on Route 22 and 25 km north of Frankfurt on the Oder.

A French victory over the Prussians.

(Last action – Anklam, 1 November; next action – Waren, 1 November.)

French Forces GdB Gauthier commanding the 25e and 85e RIdLi (4 bns) of Gudin's 3rd Division of Davout's III Corps: ca 1500 men.

French losses None.

Prussian Forces Obst von Ingersleben commanding 2,400 garrison troops and stragglers including the 3rd Musketier Bns of IRs Oranien Nr 19, von Zenge Nr 24 and Pz Heinrich Nr 35 and 75 Hussars of HusR von Usedom Nr 10.

Prussian losses All captured; together with 92 guns.

Comment There was no fight left in the commandant who could not wait to sign the fortress over to the enemy. The place was in a good state of defence and well stocked with ammunition and supplies. Von Ingersleben was court-martialled for cowardice and sentenced to be shot but the King commuted this to a life sentence.

Sources Höpfner, Lettow-Vorbeck, Martinien, Fiebig.

OP Waren and Nossentin, 1 November 1806, skirmish

Two villages in the Mecklenburg lake district in northern Germany on the northern edge of Lake Müritz, at the junction of Routes B108 and B192; 70 km southeast of Rostock on the Baltic coast.

A Prussian victory over the French.

(Last action – Küstrin, 1 November; next action – Granzin, 2 November.)

French Forces GdB Guyot and the 22e ChàCh of M Soult's IV Corps cavalry.

French totals ca 400 men.

French losses Several officers and 40 men as well as many horses captured, 6 officers killed and wounded; losses of men killed and wounded not known.

Prussian Forces GM von Pletz commanding the rearguard of GL von Blücher's corps: HusR von Köhler Nr 7 (10 sqns); ca 850 men.

Prussian losses 1 man killed, 3 officers and 12 men wounded, 10 men missing.

Comment Prussian Maj Schmude's detachment of 170 dragoons of the regiments Königin Nr 5 and others had just capitulated to the 22e ChàCh and were thus released. The 22e ChàCh were badly mauled in this action which was a pin-prick of light in the black, Prussian night of this campaign. The Prussians withdrew westwards hotly followed by Dupont's 1st Division of Bernadotte's I Corps. Later this day the 9e RILé lost 3 officers and many men just north of Malchow to the Prussian Jägers as did the 32e RIdLi.

Sources Höpfner, Lettow-Vorbeck, Martinien.

OP Granzin, 2 November 1806, skirmish

A hamlet in the north German state of Mecklenburg, 17 km west of Lake Plauen and 55 km south of Rostock.

A French victory over the Prussians.

(Last action – Waren and Nossentin, 1 November; next action – Wolgast, 2 and 3 November.)

French Forces Part of GdD Drouet's 3rd Division of Bernadotte's I Corps 27e RILé, 94e and 95e RIdLi (7 bns), ca 5,000 men.

French losses Not known, very light.

Prussian Forces Maj Puttkammer commanding 2nd Bn IR von Tschammer Nr 27, ca 500 men.

Prussian losses Maj Puttkammer and four officers captured, 52 men dead, wounded and captured, 1 battalion gun.

Comment This was a very successful raid on an isolated battalion by the French who were chasing Blücher's corps westwards towards Lübeck.

Sources Höpfner, Lettow-Vorbeck, Martinien.

OP Wolgast, 2 and 3 November 1806, capitulation

A small walled port on the German Baltic coast, opposite the island of Usedom in the Baltic Sea, on Route B111 and 20 km north of Anklam.

A French victory over the Prussians.

(Last action – Waren and Nossentin, 1 November; next action – Criwitz, 3 November.)

French Forces Col Daru commanding the 22e DragR of GdB Boussard's brigade of Grouchy's 2nd Dragoon Division.

French losses None.

Prussian Forces Obstlt von Prittwitz commanding Prince Hohenlohe's baggage train ca 2,500 men (mostly train personnel) and Parkkolonne Nr 8.

Prussian losses All captured together with 500 waggons and teams and the war chest.

Comment The countryside was now filled with isolated, uncoordinated columns of Prussian troops trying to escape capture. They were all demoralised, tired, hungry and leaderless. It seems there was no attempt on the part of the Prussian high command to gather up these forces, or to feed or motivate them. 'Prussian high command' had become a vacuum. The Prussians capitulated without putting up even a token resistance. Lieutenant Count Bronikowski of the Henkel Kürassiers rode into Wolgast and arranged the capitulation on his own initiative.

Sources Höpfner, Lettow-Vorbeck, Martinien, Fiebig.

OP Criwitz, 3 November 1806, clash

A village in the northern German state of Mecklenburg, on Route B321 about 70 km south of Rostock on the Baltic coast.

A Prussian victory over the French.

(Last action – Wolgast, 2 and 3 November; next action – Wismar, 5 November.)

French Forces GdB Pacthod's and GdB Maison's brigades of Rivaud's 2nd Division and GdD Tilly's Light cavalry Brigade of Bernadotte's I Corps. 8e RILé, 45e and 54e RIdLi (6 bns); 2e and 4e HusR and 5e ChàCh (12 sqns); 1 x FAB and 1 x HAB.

French totals ca 6,500 men and 12 guns.

French losses Not known.

Prussian Forces GM von Oswald's rearguard of Blücher's corps: Füs Bns Oswald Nr 16, Greiffenberg Nr 4 and the remnants of Füs Bn Knorr Nr 12; Gren Bns Schmeling and Vieregg; DragR von Hertzberg Nr 9 (5 sqns); HusR von Rudorff Nr 2 (2nd Bn, 5 sqns); 1 x HAB.

Prussian totals 4¼ bns, 10 sqns, 6 guns.

Prussian losses Not known; lighter than the French.

Comment The Prussian rearguard made a determined stand and gave the pursuing French a nasty surprise. That night the 1st Bn IR von Arnim Nr 13 of Blücher's corps was caught and destroyed by the French near Pinnow village, just west of Schwerin.

Sources Höpfner, Lettow-Vorbeck, Martinien.

OP Wismar, 5 November 1806, capitulation

A fortified port on the north German Baltic coast, on the bay of Lübeck at the junction of Routes B105 and B106.

A French victory over the Prussians.

(Last action – Wolgast, 2 and 3 November; next action – Lübeck, 6 November.)

French Forces Part of GdD Dupont's 1st Division of M Bernadotte's I Corps. GdB Savary's brigade.

French totals Not known.

French losses None.

Prussian Forces GM Usedom with his HusR Nr 10 (367 men) a part of Gen von Blücher's baggage train under Maj Panwitz.

Prussian losses All captured.

Comment These troops were just some of the wretched, beaten regiments and corps, all in isolation, all trying to escape the French and none having any clear idea of what their own headquarters were trying to achieve.

Sources Höpfner, Lettow-Vorbeck.

OP Lübeck, 6 November 1806, storming of

An old Hanseatic seaport on the north German Baltic Coast, about 50 km northeast of Hamburg on Autobahn A1/E47.

A French victory over the Prussians.

(Last action – Wismar, 5 November; next action – Schwartau, 6 November.)

French Forces M Bernadotte commanding the I Corps. 1st Division GdD Dupont (in reserve this day). **2nd Division** GdD Rivaud: 8e RILé, 45e and 54 e RIdLi (6 bns). **3rd Division** GdD Drouet: 27e RILé, 94e and 95e RIdLi (7 bns). **Light Cavalry** GdD Tilly: 2e and 4e HusR, 5e ChàCh (12 sqns); 3 x FAB, 4 x HAB. **M Soult commanding IV Corps. 1st Division** GdD St Hilaire: 10e RILé; 35e, 45e and 55e RIdLi (8 bns). **2nd Division** GdD Leval: 24e RILé, 4e, 28e, 46e and 57e RIdLi (10 bns). **3rd Division** GdD Legrand: 26e RILé, 18e and 75e RIdLi, Tirailleurs Corses, Tirailleurs du Po (9 bns). **Light Cavalry** GdBs Margaron and Guyot: 8e HusR, 11e, 16e and 22e ChàCh (16 sqns); 8 x FAB, 2 x HAB.

French totals ca 30,000 men and 90 guns.

Prussian Forces GL von Blücher commanding. 1st Division GM von Natzmer, IR von Natzmer Nr 54 (2 bns); IR von Manstein Nr 55 (2 bns); IR von Kauffberg Nr 51 (2 bns); DragR von Hertzberg Nr 9 (5 sqns); 1 x FAB, ½ HAB. IR von Tschammer Nr 27 (2 bns). **2nd Division** GM von Larisch: IR Jung-Larisch Nr 53 (2 bns); IR von Kalkreuth Nr 4 (2 bns); DragR von Heyking Nr 10 (5 sqns); 1 x HAB. IR von Owstein Nr 7 (2 bns); IR Braunschweig Nr 21 (2nd Bn). Light Troops: GM von Usedom: HusR von Usedom Nr 10 (10 sqns); GM von Oswald: HusR Blücher Nr 8 (10 sqns); remnants of some Füs Bns and of Gren Bns Schmeling and Vieregg; ½ HAB.

Prussian totals 17 bns, 30 sqns, 12 guns, ca 15,000 men (all regiments were by now very low in strength).

Prussian losses About 2,000 killed and wounded, 4,000 captured. The following colours and 22 guns (including battalion pieces) were also lost: IR von Owstein Nr 7 – 4; IR von Braunschweig Nr 21 (2nd Bn) – 2; IR von Tschammer Nr 27 (2 bns); IR Jung-Larisch Nr 53 (2nd Bn) – 2; IR von Natzmer Nr 54 – 4.

Comment Blücher bullied his way into this neutral city and tried to requisition money, food and drink. The weary Prussians put up a hard fight against heavy odds; infantry regiments Nrs 27, 53 and 54 were destroyed here. In other skirmishes around the city this day KürR von Bailliodz Nr 5 was captured and lost a standard at Steckenitz. At Krempelsdorf Maj Ende with 1 sqn DragR König von Bayern Nr 1 and the 2nd Bn HusR von Köhler Nr (5 sqns) and ½ HAB (4 guns) – 360 men in all – were forced to capitulate to Tilly's light cavalry brigade.

Two more standards of the DragR König von Bayern were also lost: one in the capitulation near Ratzeburg, together with ½ HAB on 5 November; the other, together with General Pelet and a sqn of the Usedom HusR Nr 10 at Boitzenburg on 12 November.

Blücher now rallied his few remaining forces and tried to fight his way back into Lübeck but was beaten off. The French looted the town. Blücher's aim was now to fight his way north to Travemünde to make a last stand, hoping to join up with 1,800 Swedish troops there.

Sources Höpfner, Lettow-Vorbeck, Martinien, Fiebig.

OP Schwartau, 6 November 1806, clash

A village on the north western edge of the present-day German city of Lübeck on the Baltic Coast.

A French victory over the Prussians.

(Last action – Lübeck, 6 November; next action – Ratkau, 7 November.)

French Forces M Bernadotte's I Corps.

French totals ca 8,000 men.

French losses Not known, light.

Prussian Forces Oberst Löben commanding the remnants of Füs Bn Bila Nr 2; IR von Kunheim Nr 1

(2 bns); IRs Jung-Larisch Nr 53 (1st Bn); von Manstein Nr 55 (2 bns); DragR von Osten Nr 12 (5 sqns).

Prussian totals ca 1,500 men.

Prussian losses The entire force taken. Killed and wounded not known, light. The following colours and standards were lost: IR Jung-Larisch Nr 53 (1st Bn) - 2; IR von Manstein Nr 55 - 3; DragR von Osten Nr 12 - 5.

Comment The Prussians put up a stiff fight; the regiments whose colours were taken were destroyed.

Sources Höpfner, Lettow-Vorbeck, Martinien, Fiebig.

OP Ratkau, 7 November 1806, capitulation

A village on the north western edge of the present-day city of Lübeck on the German Baltic Coast. Nowadays called 'Ratekow'.

(Last action - Lübeck, 6 November; next action - Magdeburg, 11 November.)

French Forces M Bernadotte's I and M Soult's IV Corps and Murat's Reserve Cavalry.

French totals ca 40,000 men.

French losses None.

Prussian Forces GL von Blücher with the remnants of his force as shown by the colours and standards taken.

Prussian totals 4,050 infantry, 3,760 cavalry, ca 7,800 men.

Prussian losses All captured: all the battalion pieces plus 16 guns. The following colours and standards were also lost: IR von Kunheim Nr 1 - 4; IR von Kalkreuth Nr 4 - 4; IR Alt-Larisch Nr 26 - 2; IR von Borcke Nr 30 - 4; IR von Kauffberg Nr 51 - 4; KürR von Beeren Nr 2 - 5; DragR von Katte Nr 4 - 2; DragR Königin Nr 5 - 1; DragR von Hertzberg Nr 9 - 5; DragR Heyking Nr 10 - 5; DragR von Wobeser Nr 14 - 1.

Comment Blücher's corps was finally cornered by three French corps up against the Danish border and with no room to deploy. He was forced to capitulate but annotated the document: 'I capitulate because I have no bread and no ammunition. Blücher'.

Thus within one month of the battles of Jena and Auerstedt, the Prussian-Saxon field army had ceased to exist.

Sources Höpfner, Lettow-Vorbeck, Martinien, Fiebig.

OP Magdeburg, 22 October - 11 November 1806, blockade and capitulation

A fortified city in north Germany, on the west bank of the River Elbe, 125 km north of Jena and 125 km west-southwest of Berlin just below the Autobahn A2/E30.

A French victory over the Prussians.

(Last action - Ratkau, 7 November; next action - Boizenburg, 12 November.)

French Forces M Ney's Corps ca 25,000 men.

French losses Not known, very slight.

Prussian Garrison GdI von Kleist commanding 24,118 men of the wrecks of many regiments from the battles of Jena and Auerstedt, 577 guns, plentiful ammunition, rations and forage. The regiments may be identified from the trophies taken.

Prussian Losses Captured were 20 generals, 800 officers, 22,000 men, 700 guns and the following colours and standards: IRs von Renouard Nr 3 - 4; von Kleist Nr 5 - 4; von Arnim Nr 3 (2n Bn) - 1; Garde Nr 15 - 3; Pz Louis Nr 20 - 4; von Malschitski Nr 28 - 4; von Alvensleben Nr 33 - 4; Pz Heinrich Nr 35 (2nd Bn) - 2; von Puttkammer Nr 36 - 2; von Tschepe Nr 37 - 4; von Zastrow Nr 39 - 4; von Strachwitz Nr 43 - 4; von Zweiffel Nr 45 - 3; von Grawert Nr 47 - 3; von Müffling Nr 49 - 3; von Sanitz Nr 50 - 4; von Tauentzien Nr 56 - 4; von Wartensleben Nr 59 (2nd Bn) - 2; KürR von Reitzenstein Nr 7 - 5.

Comment The commandant of this major fortress was 73 years old. His closest confidant was General Count von Wartensleben who was very willing to surrender the place despite his commander's determination to hold out. On 23rd October Wartensleben said to a French parliamentary: 'Just throw a few shells into the place and the governor will soon change his mind.' With Magdeburg in French hands the whole western half of the Prussian kingdom was secured by them.

Sources Höpfner, Lettow-Vorbeck, Martinien, Fiebig.

OP Boizenburg, 12 November 1806, capitulation

A village in northern Germany, on the north bank of the River Elbe, about 20 km southeast of Hamburg, at the junction of Routes B5 and B195.

A French victory over the Prussians.

(Last action - Magdeburg, 11 November; next action - Hameln, 22 November.)

French Forces A staff officer of GdD Drouet's division, Bernadotte's I Corps with a copy of the Capitulation of Ratkau.

Prussian Forces Gen Pelet with DragR König von Bayern Nr 1 (4 sqns); HusR Köhler Nr 7 (1 sqn); ½ x HAB.

Prussian total ca 420 men.

Prussian losses All captured.

Comment These were part of Blücher's corps who had become cut off. Four standards of the DragR König von Bayern were taken. The Prussians were cut off and surrounded.

Sources Höpfner, Lettow-Vorbeck, Fiebig.

OP Hameln, 22 November 1806, capitulation

A fortified town on the eastern bank of the River Weser in northern Germany at the junction of Routes B1, B83 and B217, about 36 km southwest of Hanover.

A French and Allied victory over the Prussians.

(Last action – Boizenburg, 12 November; next action – Plassenburg, 25 November.)

Allied Forces Mortier's VIII Corps (with King Louis of Holland) GdD Loison (as of 19 November GdD Savåry). **The Dutch Division** GdD Dumonceau: GdB Crass; 1st Bde; 2nd and 3rd Jagers (1st Bn). 2nd Bde GdB von Heldring: 2nd and 3rd LIR (2 bns each); 4th LIR (1st Bn). 3rd Bde GdB von Hasselt; 7th LIR (2 bns); 8th LIR (1st Bn). 4th Bde GdB Mascheck: 3rd HusR (4 sqns), 2 x HAB.

Allied totals ca 6,000 men and 12 guns.

Allied losses Not known, light.

Prussian Forces GM Schöler: IR Pz Oranien Nr 19 (2 bns); and the 3rd Musketier bns of IRs Hessen Nr 48, von Hagken Nr 44, Tschammer Nr 27 and Schenck Nr 9. **Total** 3,058 men and 175 guns. The place was well-stocked with ammunition and supplies. The Invalide Companies of IRs Tschammer, Schenck, Hessen and Hagken, 181 gunners and 40 hussars of the regiments von Köhler Nr 7 and von Pletz Nr 3 also joined in September, as did recruit drafts for IRs Treuenfels and Strachwitz and 1000 refugees from the battles, making a total of ca 10,000 men with Gen Lecoq's corps.

Prussian losses 600 soldiers captured.

Comment The Dutch corps had been in the area since 7 November but was in no condition to seriously threaten Hameln. Continued psychological pressure on the commandant by Mortier, and later Savåry, wore him down so much however that he capitulated. When the garrison heard this shameful news there was a mutiny and over 9,000 soldiers escaped. GM Schöler was 75 years old and in no way up to the task given to him.

Sources Höpfner, Lettow-Vorbeck, Martinien, Fiebig.

OP Plassenburg, 11 October – 25 November 1806, blockade and capitulation

A fortress just north of the town of Kulmbach on the River Weisser Main in central Germany at the junction of Routes B289, B85 and about 25 km north of Bayreuth.

A Bavarian victory over the Prussians.

(Last action – Hameln, 22 November; next action – Nienburg, 26 November.)

Bavarian Forces Gen Mezzanelli commanding the 2nd Division of which the 13e LIR was left to blockade the place. On 24th November the 6th Bavarian LIR took over.

Bavarian losses None.

Prussian Garrison GM Uttenhofen and 629 invalides and Füsiliers.

Prussian losses All captured.

Comment The Plassenburg was by nature impregnable. The 64-year-old commandant capitulated after hearing the news of the fall of Magdeburg, which he received on 20 November. The place was well stocked with ammunition, rations and other supplies, but the garrison did run out of tobacco. Not a shot had been fired at the place. Napoleon had the fortifications slighted.

Sources Höpfner, Lettow-Vorbeck, Leyh.

OP Nienburg, 26 November 1806, capitulation

A small, walled town in northern Germany, on the eastern bank of the River Weser, 45 km northwest of Hanover, at the junction of Routes B6, B214 and B215.

An Allied victory over the Prussians.

(Last action – Plassenburg, 25 November; next action – Glogau 2 December.)

Allied Forces GdD Savåry commanding the Dutch division of VIII Corps.

Organization as at Hameln.

Allied totals ca 6,000 men and 12 guns.

Allied losses None.

Prussian Garrison GM Strachwitz commanding the

3rd Musketier bns of IRs Pz Ferdinand Nr 34, von Lettow Nr 41, and von Wedell Nr 10, one company IR von Grävenitz Nr 57, three invalide companies, 168 gunners and 54 hussars, in all 2,911 men.

Prussian losses The officers were released on parole, the sergeants, corporals and married men sent home, all Westfalian-born soldiers sent to Minden and released; the few remaining men were sent to France as prisoners of war.

Comment Not a shot had been fired since the enemy arrived at Nienburg on 24 November.

Sources Höpfner, Lettow-Vorbeck.

OP Glogau, 2 December 1806, capitulation

A fortress in the Prussian province of Silesia, nowadays Poland, on the River Oder (Odra) and called 'Glogow'. On Route 34 , 120 km east of Cottbus.

An Allied victory over the Prussians.

(Last action - Nienburg, 26 November; next action - Czarnowo, 23 December.)

Allied Forces 1st Bavarian Division GL von Deroy, GdB Siebein: 1st and 10th LIR (2 bns each); 6th LtI Bn (1 bn); 1st ChLR (4 sqns); 1 x FAB. GdB Raglovich: 4th and 5th LIR (2 bns each); Fuss-Jägers (2 coys); 1st DragR (4 sqns); 1 x FAB. On 25 November the Bavarians left to become right flank guard of the French Army's advance into Russian-Poland and the Württemberg division replaced them: GL Baron von Seckendorff: 1st Bde GM von Lilienberg: I Bns Kronprinz, von Seckendorff, von Lilienberg (3 bns); 2nd Bde GM von Schröder: I Bns Herzog Wilhelm, von Schröder. Light Bde: Obst von Neubronn: Jägers (2 bns); LtI Bns von Neubronn and von Brüsselle (2 bns); 2 x FAB (20 guns).

Allied losses Bavarians - 1 officer and 24 men in a raid on 18 November, Württembergers - 1 dead and 4 wounded.

Prussian Garrison GL von Reinhard.

Prussian total 3,200 men and 124 guns.

Prussian losses The officers released on parole, the other ranks became prisoners of war.

Sources Höpfner, Leyh, Martinien.

OP Czarnowo, 23 December 1806, clash

A village on the northern bank of the River Bug in Poland, about 30 km northwest of Warsaw; not identifiable on some modern maps but on the road between the then fortresses of Modlin on the River Vistula (Wisla) and Sierok (Serock), also on the River Bug.

A French victory over the Russians.

(Last action - Glogau, 2 December; next action - Biezun, 23 December.)

French Forces Emperor Napoleon I commanding: M Davout's III Corps. 1st Division GdD Morand: 13e RILé; 17e, 30e, RIdLi (6 bns) and two combined Voltigeur Bns (8 coys). 2nd Division GdD Friant: 33e, 48e and 108e RIdLi (6 bns); 4 x FAB.

French totals 14 bns, 20 guns, ca 8,500 men.

French losses Admitted to be 16 officers and 830 men killed, wounded and missing.

Russian Forces GL Count Ostermann's 2nd Division: GM Mazovskoi: Pavlovski GrenR, Rostov MuskR (6 bns). GM Sukin II: Petersburg GrenR; Jeletzski MuskR (6 bns). GM Count Lieven: 1st and 20th Jägers (6 bns). Artillery: 2 x 12 pdr and 2 x 6 pdr FAB, 48 guns.

Russian totals 18 bns, 48 guns, ca 15,000 men.

Russian losses 3 generals, 38 officers and 1,360 men were killed, wounded and missing including 500 prisoners, 5 guns.

Comment This was a night attack so no cavalry was involved in this river crossing. The assault was very well planned and executed and local French superiority was achieved against the extended Russian line.

Sources Höpfner, Martinien.

OP Biezun, 23 December 1806, clash

A village in East Prussia (now Poland) on the River Wkra, 114 km northwest of Warsaw, about 20 km northeast of Sierpc.

A French victory over the Prussians.

(Last action - Czarnowo, 23 December; next action - Soldau, 25 December.)

French Forces M Bessières and GdD Grouchy's Dragoon Division.

French totals Not known; Martinien shows no losses for this action.

French losses Not known, light.

Prussian Forces Maj La Roche-Aymon of Gen l'Estocq's Corps. Gren Bn von Schlieffen (1 bn); Towarczys (1 bn); 1 x HAB.

Prussian totals ca 1,000 men and 6 guns.

Prussian losses Killed and wounded unknown; 500 prisoners, 5 guns and 2 standards of the Towarczys (these were not 'official' standards). This battalion was effectively destroyed.

Comment The Prussians made an armed reconnaissance against Biezun to establish enemy strength there and to restore communication with the Russians if possible. The French were far too strong however, the Prussian infantry were caught up against a swampy wood and captured together with the guns. The Prussians withdrew to Soldau to the northeast.

Sources Höpfner, Lettow-Vorbeck, Martinien, Fiebig.

OP Soldau (now Dzialdowo), 25 December 1806, clash

A small walled town in East Prussia (now Poland) on a stream of the same name, approximately 134 km northwest of Warsaw, and 35 km northeast of Biezun.

A French victory over the Prussians.

(Last action - Biezun, 23 December; next action - Pultusk, 26 December.)

French Forces One division of Ney's VI Corps: 27e, 39e, 69e and 76e RIdLi (8 bns) under GdB von der Weidt. 2 x FAB 12 guns.

French totals ca 6,000 men and 12 guns.

French losses GdB von der Weidt killed; 220 others killed and wounded.

Prussian Forces GM Diericke of Gen l'Estocq's Corps. IR von Rüchel Nr 2 (Sharpshooters); 1 x FAB (8 x 12 pdrs).

Prussian totals 4 bns, ca 3,000 men and 8 guns.

Prussian losses No Prussian returns exist; M Ney reported them as 800 killed, wounded, taken and deserted, one colour of IR von Schöning Nr 11, 2 x 12 pdr guns.

Comment M Ney aimed to cut the communications between the Prussians and Russians and advanced on Soldau eastwards from Lautenburg (Lidzbark). The Prussians withdrew to Neidenburg (now Nidzica) 23 km to the northeast; contact with the Russians (now at Pultusk) was lost.

Sources Höpfner, Lettow-Vorbeck, Martinien, Fiebig.

OP Pultusk, 26 December 1806, battle

A town in central Poland, about 50 km north of Warsaw on Route 61, on the western side of the River Narew.

Both the French and Russians claimed victory.

(Last action - Soldau, 25 December; next action - Golymin, 26 December.)

French Forces M Lannes' V Corps 1st Division GdD Suchet: 17e RILé, 34e, 40e, 64e and 88e RIdLi (16 bns). 2nd Division GdD Gazan: 21e RILé, 100e and 103e RIdLi (11 bns). Light Cavalry GdB Treilhard: 9e and 10e HusR; 21e ChàCh (12 sqns). Artillery 4 x FAB; 2 x HAB.

M Davout's III Corps 3rd Division GdD Gudin: 12e, 21e, 25e 85e RIdLi (9 bns) **Artillery** 1 x FAB; 1 x HAB. 2nd Dragoon Division GdD Becker: 3e, 4e, 10e 11e 13e and 22e DragR (24 sqns); 1 x HAB. 4th Dragoon Division GdD Sahuc, GdB Laplanche:15e and 25e DragR (8 sqns). GdB Chabanais' Light Cavalry Bde of VI Corps 9e and 10e HusR (8 sqns) and the 5e and 21e ChàCh (8 sqns).

French totals 36 bns, 43 sqns, 55 guns, ca 26,000 men.

French losses 5 generals, 140 officers dead and wounded, 3,200 men dead and wounded; 700 captured; M Lannes, Generals Claparède, Wedell and Bonnard were wounded.

Russian Forces GdC Bennigsen. **2nd Division** GL Count Ostermann: GM Koschin: Leib-KürR; DragR Kargopol; HusR Isum (20 sqns); GM Mazowski: Pavlovski GrenR; Rostow MuskR (6 bns); GM Suskin II Petersburg GrenR; Jeletz MuskR (6 bns). GM Count Liewen: 1st and 20th Jägers (6 bns); Cossack Rs Jlowaiski IX and Jefremov III. Artillery: 4 x FAB, 1 x HAB, 60 guns. **6th Division** GL Sedmoratsky: KürR Ekaterinoslav, DragR Kiev, HusR Alexandrov (20 sqns); Tartar R, Cossack R Popov V. GM Rachmanov: Musk Rs Wilna and Nizov (6 bns). GM Bikov: Musk Rs Reval and Wolhynia (6 bns). GM Baggowut: MuskR Starokolski, 4th Jägers (6 bns). 5 x FAB, 1 x HAB (72 guns).

Russian totals 66 bns, 55 sqns, 7 x FAB, 2½ x HAB*, 120 guns, ca 40,600 men. Some battalions of the 4th Infantry Division were also present.

Russian losses 3,500 killed, and wounded (of the latter, the French captured 1,500); 12 guns.

Comment This action was fought in a snowstorm. Only 29 Russian battalions came under fire. During the subsequent withdrawal through this desolate, thinly-populated area, the Russian army dissolved into a mob.

* = obviously not all the divisional artillery was present at the battle.

Sources Höpfner, Lettow-Vorbeck, Martinien, Fiebig.

OP Golymin, 26 December 1806, clash

A village in central Poland, 19 km northwest of Pultusk and about 53 km north of Warsaw.

A French victory over the Russians.

(Last action – Pultusk, 26 December. This was the last action in the 1806 campaign; first action in 1807 – Mohrungen, 25 January 1807.)

French Forces M Augereau's VII Corps 1st Division GdD Desjardins: 16e RILi (4 bns); 14e RIdLi (2e Bn); 44e and 105e RIdLi (3 bns each); 1 x FAB, 1 x HAB. 2nd Division GdD Heudelet: 7e RILé (3 bns); 24e RIdLi (3 bns); 63e RIdLi (2 bns); 1 x Fab, 1 x HAB. Light Cavalry GdB Durosnel: 7e and 20e ChàCh, 1 x HAB (8 guns). Artillery Reserve: 1 x FAB.

Murat's Reserve Cavalry: GdD Lasalle: 5e and 7e HusR (8 sqns); Dragoon Div: GdD Klein, GdB Fenerolz: 1er and 2e DragR (8 sqns). GdB Maraluz' Light Cavalry Bde 13e ChàCh (4 sqns).

I Corps M Davout 1st Division GdD Morand GdB d'Honières: 13e RILé (3 bns).

French totals 22 bns, 20 sqns, 12 guns *, ca 16,000 men.

French losses 'Equal to those of the Russians' was reported. General Rapp was wounded leading a cavalry charge.

* = French artillery could not keep up with the leading elements.

Russian Forces Prince Galitzin V commanding: GL Baron Sacken I's 3rd Division.

GM Baron Korf: KürR St George; DragR Pskov, Polish CavR (20 sqns),Cossack Rs Grekov IX and Grekov XVIII. Sum HusR (2 sqns). GM Uschakov: Tauride GrenR; Lithuanian MuskR (6 bns); GM Netting: Tschernigov and Dnieprovsk MuskRs (6 bns); DragR Moscow (5 sqns)*.

Russian totals 27 sqns and 2 sotnias; 12 bns, 38 guns** ca 9,000 men.

* = from Dochtorov's 7th Division.

** = some had been abandoned on the retreat.

Russian losses 8 officers and 80 men dead; 16 officers and 473 men wounded; 203 men missing.

Comment Despite being heavily outnumbered, the Russians held on until dark and then withdrew from the trap which was to have crushed them on three sides. They then withdrew east out of the inhospitable desert in which they had been fighting and went into winter quarters around Bialystock. Napoleon's army gave up the chase and did the same.

Sources Höpfner, Martinien.

1807

1807 THE ACTIONS

PS Breslau (Wroclaw), 6 December 1806 - 6 January 1807, siege and capture of

A fortified town (the capital of Silesia) on the River Oder (Odra) in southwestern Poland (Silesia in 1807) at the junction of routes 5 and 8/E67, just north of the motorway A4/E40.

An Allied victory over the Prussians.

(Last action - this was the opening action in Silesia; next action - Brieg, 17 January.)

Allied Forces Prince Jerome Bonaparte commanding the IX Corps*. **Württemberg Division** GdD Vandamme, GL von Seckendorff: 1st Brigade GM von Lilienberg: IBns Kronprinz, von Seckendorff and von Lilienberg (3 bns). 2nd Brigade GM von Schröder: IBns Herzog Wilhelm and von Schröder (2 bns). 3rd Brigade Obst von Neubronn: Jäger Bns von Hügel and Scharffenstein; LtIBns von Neubronn and von Brüsselle (4 bns). Artillery: 1 x HAB (4 x 6 pdr guns and 2 x 7 pdr how); 1 x FAB (8 x 6 pdr guns and 2 how). **Total Württembergers** ca 8,642 men. **1st (Bavarian) Cavalry Brigade** GM Count Mezzanelli: 1st DragR Minucci, 1st ChLR Kronprinz; 2nd ChLR König. 2nd (Württemberg) Cavalry Brigade: GdB Count Montbrun: Leib-ChLR; vacant ChLR; vacant JzPfR. **3rd (Bavarian) Cavalry Brigade** GdB Lefebvre-Desnouettes: 2nd DragR Taxis; 3rd ChLR Leiningen. **Total** 36 sqns. **1st Bavarian Division** GL Deroy (arrived on 18 December 1806). 1st Brigade GM von Siebein: 1st LIR 'Leib-R' (2 bns); 10th LIR 'Junker' (2 bns); 6th LtIBn 'Taxis' (1 bn); Jägers (2 coys), 1 x 6 pdr FAB. 2nd Brigade GM Raglovich: 4th LIR (2 bns); 5th LIR 'Preysing' (2 bns), 1 x 6 pdr FABs. **2nd Bavarian Division** GL von Wrede 1st Brigade GM Mezzanelli; 2nd LIR 'Kronprinz' (2 bns); 13th LIR (2 bns); 3rd LtIBn 'Preysing' (1 bn); 1 x 6 pdr FAB. 2nd Brigade GM Graf Minucci: 3rd LIR 'Herzog Karl', 7th LIR 'Löwenstein' (2 bns each); 4th LtIBn 'Zoller' (1 bn); 1 x 6 pdr FAB, 1 x 12 pdr FAB. **Total Bavarians** ca 14,000 men.

Allied totals 28 bns, 36 sqns, 52 field guns, ca 22,642 men.

Allied losses Bavarians: 259 killed and wounded; Württembergers: 32 killed, 111 wounded, 50 captured.

Prussian Forces GL von Thiele: IR von Thiele Nr 46 (3rd Bn) and various ad hoc and volunteer units including: 3rd Musk Bn IR von Hohenlohe Nr 32 and von Treuenfels Nr 29, the depot of Füs-Bn von Greiffenberg Nr 4, various cavalry depots and 714 gunners. **Prussian totals** 6,000 men with 268 guns, really the place needed 10,000 men.

Prussian losses 13 dead and 24 wounded, 568 sick. The 135 officers were released on parole; the garrison (5,300 men) marched out with honours of war, laid down their weapons and went into captivity.

* = The title 'IX Corps' was bestowed on 5 January 1807.

Sources: Höpfner, Leyh, Kraft.

PS Brieg (Brzeg), 17 January 1807, capitulation of

A fortress on the west bank of the River Oder (Odra) in Silesia (south western Poland today) just north of the motorway A4/E40.

A Bavarian victory over the Prussians.

(Last action - Breslau, 6 January; next action - Schweidnitz, 16 February.)

Bavarian Forces GL von Deroy commanding: MG Raglovich: Jägers (2 coys); 4th and 5th LIRs (4 bns). GM Mezzanelli: 3rd LIBn, 2nd and 13th LIR (5 bns); GM von Siebein: 1st and 10th LIR (4 bns), 4 x 6 pdr and 1 x 12 pdr FAB; GM Count Mezzanelli: 1st DragR Minucci, 1st ChLR Kronprinz, 2nd ChLR König (14 sqns).

Bavarian totals: 13½bns, 14 sqns, 30 field guns and 8 siege guns from Breslau as of 13 January, ca 13,000 men.

Bavarian losses 4 killed, 14 wounded.

Prussian Garrison 3rd Musk Bn IR von Malschitsky Nr 28 (1 bn); stragglers and volunteers, 600 men, 200 gunners and invalides, the depot of HusR Pletz (50 men), 50 Jägers.

Prussian totals Approximately 22 officers and 1,451 men, 48 guns.

Prussian losses 1,450 men captured, 1 killed and several wounded.

Sources Höpfner, Leyh.

OP Mohrungen (Morag), 25 January 1807, clash

A village in East Prussia (nowadays Poland), 40 km southeast of Elbing (now Elblag).

A French victory over the Russians.

(Last action - Golymin, 26 December 1806; next action - Bergfried, 3 February.)

French Forces Part of M Bernadotte's I Corps. 1st Division GdD Dupont: 9e RILé, 32e and 96e RIdLi (7 bns); 3rd Division GdD Drouet: 27e RILé 94e and 95e RIdLi (7 bns). GdD Rivaud's 2nd Division: GdB Pacthod: 9e RILé (3 bns); 8e RIdLi (3 bns). Light Cavalry GdD Tilley: 2e and 4e HusR; 5e ChàCh (12 sqns). 4th Dragoon Division of Murat's Reserve Cavalry GdD Sahuc: 17e, 27e, 18e and 19e DragR (16 sqns). Artillery: 4 x FAB, 2 x HAB.

French totals 20 bns, 28 sqns, 36 guns, ca 12,000 men.

French losses 26 officers and 670 men killed and wounded, 400 captured.

Russian Forces Gen Markov: Jekaterinoslav GrenR; Pskov MuskR, 5th, 7th and 25th Jäger R. (3 bns each); Elisabethgrad HusR (6 sqns); 4 x FAB, 1 x HAB.

Russian totals 15 bns, 19 sqns, ca 9,000 men.

Russian losses 1,100 killed and wounded, 300 captured, GM Anrepp killed.

Sources Höpfner, Lettow-Vorbeck, Martinien.

OP Bergfried, 3 February 1807, clash

A village in East Prussia (now Poland); a crossing point on the River Alle (now the Lyna), unidentifiable on a modern map.

A French victory over the Russians.

(Last action – Mohrungen, 25 January; next action – Waltersdorf, 5 February.)

French Forces GdD Leval's Division of Soult's IV Corps: GdBs Schinner, Ferrey and Viviès: 24e RILé 4e and 28e RIdLi; 46e and 57e RIdLi (10 bns); 2 x FAB; 16e and 22e DragR (6 sqns).

French totals 10 bns, 6 sqns, 12 guns, ca 8,000 men.

French losses Reported as '26 officers and 280 men killed, wounded and missing'.

Russian Forces: Part of LG Kaminskoi's 14th Infantry Division and Major Huguenin's Prussian FAB: GM Gersdorf and 4 bns including Musk R Uglitzki of which only 1 bn came into combat.

Russian totals 1 bn, ca 600 men and 6 guns.

Russian losses There are no Russian returns; the French claim that the Russians lost 1,100 men and 6 guns.

Sources Höpfner, Lettow-Vorbeck, Martinien.

OP Waltersdorf (now Wilzkowo), 5 February 1807, clash

A village in East Prussia (now Poland); about 15 km north east of Mohrungen (now Morag). Towards Dobre Miasto on Route 51 and on the River Lyna.

A French victory over the Prussians.

(Last action – Bergfried, 3 February; next action – Hof, 6 February.)

French Forces M Ney's VI Corps. 1st Division GdD Marchand: GdB Villatte and Roguet 6e RILé, 39e, 69e and 76e RIdLi (2 bns each). 2nd Division GdD Gardanne: GdB Marcognet, Delabassée: 25e RILé, 27e, 50e and 59e RIdLi (2 bns each). Cavalry: GdB de Chabanais: 9e HusR, 10e ChàCh (4 sqns each); Artillery: 4 x FAB, 2 x HAB. Light Cavalry Division: GdD Lasalle: 1er, 5e and 7e HusR, 13e ChàCh (3 sqns each); 9e and 20e DragR (7 sqns).

French totals 16 bns, 27 sqns, 36 guns, ca 10,000 men.

French losses Not known.

Prussian Forces: GM von Klüchzner commanding, GM Maltzahn, GM von Bülow, Füs Bns Wackenitz Nr 3; von Bülow Nr 24. Schachtmeyer Nr 23 and von Bergen Nr 11, IR von Besser Nr 14 (1stBn); HusR von Prittwitz Nr 5 (2nd Bn); Towarczys (1 bn), 1 x HAB.

Prussian totals 5 bns, 10 sqns, 6 guns, ca 4,500 men.

Prussian losses 1,100 men killed and wounded, 900 captured, 10 guns.

Sources Höpfner, Lettow-Vorbeck, Martinien.

OP Hof (Gorowo Haweckie), 6 February 1807, clash

A village in East Prussia (now Poland); 17 km south west of Preussisch-Eylau (now Bagrationovsk).

A French victory over the Russians.

(Last action – Waltersdorf, 5 February; next action – Preussisch-Eylau, 7 and 8 February.)

French Forces: M Murat commanding the Reserve Cavalry: **2nd Cuirassier Division** GdD d'Hautpoul: GdB Verdière and GdB Saint-Sulpice 1er, 5e and 10e CuirRs (4 sqns each); ½ x HAB. **1st Dragoon Division** GdD Klein; GdB Fenerolz, GdB La Motte: 1er, 2e, 4e, 14e, 21e and 26e DragR (20 sqns); ½ x HAB. The following infantry regiments are shown by Martinien to have suffered officer casualties in this action this day; 13e and 25e RILé and 75e RIdLi. As they came from the III, IV and VI Corps (as reported for Jena and Auerstedt in 1806) there must have been considerable regrouping in the French army by this time. 1 x FAB.

French totals 6 bns, 5,000 infantry, 32 sqns, 12 guns, 5,000 cavalry.

French losses 99 officers killed and wounded; ca

1,400 men killed, wounded and missing.

Russian Forces GM Barclay de Tolly commanding the Rearguard: Kostroma MuskR (3 bns), 1st, 3rd and 20th Jägers (3 bns each); Isum and Olviopol HusRs (10 sqns); the Polish CavR (5 sqns); 2 Cossack sotnias, 2 x HAB.

Russian totals 12 bns, 15 sqns, 2 sotnias, 12 guns, ca 7,000 men.

Russian losses 2,000 killed wounded and missing, 5 guns, 2 colours of the Kostroma MuskR.

Sources Höpfner, Lettow-Vorbeck, Martinien.

IS Amantea, 18 December 1806–6 February 1807, siege and capture of

A fortified port on the west coast of the toe of Italy (Calabria); about 23 km southwest of Cosenza and on Route 18.

A French victory over the Neapolitans.

(This was the only action of any note in this theatre this year.)

French Forces GdD Reynier commanding: 1er RIdLi (2 bns); 42e RIdLi (1 bn); 23e RILé (2 bns); 1er IR Swiss (4 bns); 9e ChàCh (3 sqns); 1 x FAB.

French totals 6 bns, 3 sqns, 6 guns, ca 4,700 men.

French losses 20 officers and 480 men killed and wounded.

Neapolitan Forces Col Mirabelli commanding 1,300 infantry, artillery and militia.

Neapolitan losses ca 400 killed, wounded and deserted; the rest marched out with honours of war and were sent to Sicily after agreeing not to fight against France for one year.

Sources Bodart, Martinien.

OP Preussisch-Eylau (now Bagrationovsk), 7 and 8 February 1807, battle

A town in East Prussia (now the Russian enclave around Kaliningrad – once Königsberg); about 33 km south of Königsberg.

Both the Russo-Prussians and French claimed a victory, but the Russo-Prussians withdrew.

(Last action – Hof, 6 February; next action – Ostrolenka, 16 February.)

French Forces Emperor Napoleon I commanding:

Imperial Guard Infantry M Lefebvre GdB Hulin: 1er Grenadiers à P (2 bns); GdB Soules: 1er ChàP (2 bns); 2e ChàP (2 bns). **Cavalry M Bessières** GdD Walther: GrenàCh (4 sqns); Col Dahlmann ChàCh (4 sqns); Mamelukes (1 sqn). Artillery à Cheval. **Imperial Guard totals** 6 bns, 9 sqns, 12 guns.

III Corps M Davout* **1st Division** GdD Morand GdB Debilly, GdB Brouard, GdB d'Honières: 13e RILé (2 bns); 17e and 30e RIdLi (2 bns each); 51e and 61e RIdLi (3 bns each). 2 x FAB (13 guns). **2nd Division** GdD Friant: GdB Kister; GdB Lochet, GdB Grandeau: 33e, 48e, 108e and 111e RIdLi (8 bns), 1 x FAB (8 guns). **3rd Division** GdD Gudin: GdB Petit and GdB Gauthier, 12e, 25e, and 85e RIdLi (2 bns each); 21e RIdLi (3 bns), 1 x FAB (8 guns). Light Cavalry: GdB Viallanes 1er and 12e ChàCh (6 sqns). Artillery Reserve: 3 x FAB, 1 x HAB (17 guns). **III Corps totals** 29 bns, 6 sqns, 46 guns.

* = III Corps arrived on the battle field at midday on the Russian left flank. The battle had been raging since about 0900 hrs.

IV Corps M Soult 1st Division GdD Saint-Hilaire: GdB Candras, GdB Waré: 10e RILé; 35e, 43e, 55e RIdLi (8 bns); 2 x FAB (12guns). **2nd Division** GdD Leval: GdB Schimmer, GdB Ferey, GdB Viviès: 24e RILé, 4e, 28e, 46e, 57e RIdLi (10 bns), 2 x FAB (12 guns). **3rd Division** GdD Legrand: GdB des Essarts, GdB Lavasseur: 26e RILé, 18e, 75e RIdLi (2 bns each); Tirailleurs Corses and Tirailleurs du Po (1 bn each), 2 x FAB (12 guns). Artillery Reserve: 1 x FAB (6 guns). **IV Corps totals** 26 bns, 36 guns.

VI Corps M Ney** **1st Division** GdD Marchand: GdB Villatte, GdB Roguet: 6e RILé; 39e, 69e and 76e RIdLi (8 bns). **2nd Division** GdD Gardanne: 25e RILé, 27e, 50e and 59e RIdLi (8 bns). Light Cavalry GdB Colbert: 10e ChàCh; 9e Hus (3 sqns each). Artillery: 4 x FAB, 2 HAB (24 guns). **VI Corps totals** 16 bns, 6 sqns, 24 guns.

** = Ney's corps did not arrive on the battlefield until 1915 hrs.

VII Corps M Augereau 1st Division GdD Desjardins: GdB Lapisse, GdB Lefranc: 16e RILé (4 bns); 14eRIdLi (2nd Bn); 44e and 105e RIdLi (3 bns each); 1 x FAB, 1 x HAB (8 guns). 2nd Division GdD de Bierre: GdB Amey, GdB Sarrut, GdB Anon. 7e RILé, 24e RIdLi (3 bns each); 63e RIdLi (2 bns), 1 x FAB, 1 x HAB (8 guns). Light Cavalry: GdB Durosnel: 20e ChàCh (3 sqns), 1 x HAB (4 guns). Artillery Reserve: 2 x FAB (16 guns). **VII Corps totals** 19 bns, 3 sqns, 36 guns.

The Reserve Cavalry M Prince Murat 1st Cuirassier Division GdD Nansouty: GdD La Houssaye, 9e and 11e CuirR (8 sqns); ½ x HAB (3guns). **2nd Cuirassier**

Division GdD d'Hautpoul: GdB Verdière, GdB Saint-Sulpice: 1er, 5e and 10e CuirR (4 sqns each); ½ x HAB (3guns). **1st Dragoon Division:** GdD Klein GdB Fenerolz, GdB la Motte, GdB Picard: 1er and 2e DragR (3 sqns each); 4e and 14e DragR (4 sqns each); 20e and 26e DragR (3 sqns each), ½ x HAB (3 guns). **2nd Dragoon Division** GdD Grouchy: GdB Roget, GdB Milet, GdB Boussard: 3e, 4e, 6e, 10e, 11e DragR (3 sqns each) ½ x HAB (3 guns). **3rd Dragoon Division** GdD Beaumont GdB Boyé, GdB Marizy, GdB Latour-Maubourg: 5e, 8e, 12e, 16e, 19e and 21e DragR (4 sqns each), ½ x HAB (3 guns). **4th Dragoon Division** GdD Sahuc, GdB Margaron, GdB Laplanche, GdB Anon: 17e, 18e, 19e and 27e DragR (3 sqns each), ½ x HAB (3 guns). **Light Cavalry Division** GdD Lasalle GdB Milhaud: 1er, 3e and 5e HusR, 13e ChàCh (3 sqns each). Light Cavalry Brigade: GdB Wathier: 11e ChàCh, Bavarian 1st ChLR Kronprinz (4 sqns each). Artillery Reserve: 1 x HAB (8guns). **Cavalry Corps total** 98 sqns, 26 guns.

French totals 96 bns, 123 sqns, 200 guns, ca 75,000 men.

French losses According to their bulletins there were 1,900 killed and 5,700 wounded. Other French sources say 2,000 killed and 15-16,000 wounded.

Eleven days after the battle l'Estocq's Prussians reported burying about 10,000 corpses on the battlefield over half of which were French. Bodart lists 23 generals and 924 other French officers as killed and wounded with about 21,000 other ranks killed and wounded. The following French generals were killed GdDs Desjardins and Hautpoul-Salette; GdBs Binot, d'Hommières, Corbineau, Dahlmann, Lochet and Varé.

In view of the very fierce nature of the combat, it is highly likely that the real French losses were heavier than officially reported. They also lost 6 eagles or colours and standards (1st Bn 10e Légère (eagle), 1st Bn, 18e de Ligne (eagle and colour); 2nd Bn 24e de Ligne (eagle and colour); 1st Bn 44e de Ligne (eagle); 51e de Ligne (eagle); and one other.

Prussian and Russian Forces GdC Baron von Bennigsen 2nd Division GL Count Ostermann (Russians). GM Koschin; Leib-KürR; Kargopol DragR (5 sqns each); Isum HusR (10 sqns); Cossack R Ilowaiski IX, Cossack R Jefremov III. GM Mazovskoi: Pavlovski GrenR, Rostov MuskR (6 bns); GM Sukin II, Petersburg GrenR; Jeletz MuskR (6 bns); GM Count Lieven: 1st and 20th Jägers (6 bns). Artillery: 2 x 12 pdr, 2 x 6 pdr and 1 x HAB (60 guns). **3rd Division** GL Baron Sacken I (Russians), GM Count Pahlen Little Russian KürR, Kurland DragR (5 sqns each); Sum HusR (10 sqns); Cossack R Ilowaiski X, Cossack R Papuzin. GM Uschakov: Tauride Grenadier R; Lithuanian MuskR (6 bns); GM Titov II: Kaporski and Muromsk MuskR (6 bns); GM Netting: Tschernigov and Dnieprov MuskR (6 bns). Artillery: 2 x 12 pdr, 3 x 6 pdr and 1 x HAB (72 guns). **4th Division** GL Somov (Russians) GM Baron Korff: KürR St George, Pskov DragR (5 sqns each); Polish CavR (10 sqns); Cossack R Grekov IX, Cossack R Grekov XVIII; GM Somov: Tula and Tengisk MuskRs (3 bns each); GM Arseniev: Tobolsk MuskR (3 bns). GM Barclay de Tolly: Polotzk and Kostroma MuskRs (3 bns each); 3rd Jägers (3 bns). Artillery: 2 x 12 pdr, 3 x 6 pdr and 1 x HAB (72 guns). **5th Division** GL Tutschkov I (Russians), GM Sacken: Riga DragR; Kasan DragR, Elisabethgrad HusR (20 sqns); Lithuanian CavR (5 sqns); Cossack R Gordejov. Sievsk, Kaluga, Perm and Mohilev MuskRs (12 bns); 24th and 25th Jägers (6 bns). Artillery: 2 x 12 pdr, 2 x 6 pdr and 1x HAB (60 guns). **7th Division** GL Dochtorov (Russians); GM Tschaplitz: Moscow DragR, Ingermannland DragR (10 sqns); Pavlograd HusR (10 sqns); Cossack Rs Malachov and Andronov. Ekaterinoslav GrenR (3 bns); Moscow, Vladimir, Voronesch, Pskov and Azov Musk Rs (15 bns); 5th Jägers (3 bns). Artillery: 2 x 12 pdr, 3 x 6 pdr FAB and 1 x HAB (72 guns). **8th Division** GL Essen III Obst Count Pahlen (Russians): Petersburg DragR; Livland DragR (10 sqns); Olviopol HusR (10 sqns); Cossack Rs Kieselev and Sysojev, Moscow GrenR (3 bns); Schlüsselburg, Alt-Ingermannland, Podolsk and Archangelgorod Musk Rs (12 bns); 7th Jägers (3 bns). Artillery: 4 x 12 pdr and 1 x HAB (60 guns).

Russian totals 126 bns, 145 sqns, 15 Cossack sotnias 336 guns, ca 58,000 men.

The following Russian generals were wounded: GL Dochtorov, GMs Barclay de Tolly, Count Lieven III, Sukin II, Korff, Mitzki, Arseniev, Gersdorf and Titov II.

Russian losses 18,000 killed and wounded, 3,000 captured, 24 guns and 16 colours.

Prussian Corps Gen l'Estocq commanding (arrived on the battlefield at 1320 hrs).

Avantgarde Auer DragR Nr 6 (10 sqns); Towarczys (½ sqn); 1 x HAB. **1st Division** Gen Diericke: GrenBn Fabecky (1 bn); IR Rüchel Nr 2 (2 bns); DragR Baczko Nr 7 (5 sqns); KürR Wagenfeld Nr 4 (4 sqns); ½ HAB. **2nd Division** Gen Rembow: IR vac Schöning Nr 11 (2 bns); GrenBn vac. Schlieffen (1 bn). **3rd Division** Gen Auer: Towarczys (9½ sqns); Russian IR Wyburg (3 bns); ½ HAB, 2 Füs coys; 21st Russian Jägers (3 bns).

Prussian totals 12½ bns, 29 sqns, 2 x HAB (9 guns), ca 5,584 men.

Prussian losses Not exactly known; ca 800 killed, wounded and missing.

Comment Höpfner (Vol III, page 289) states that 'Napoleon was displeased with M Augereau's conduct this day' (his corps suffered very heavy casualties). M Augereau left the army and his VII Corps was broken up and distributed among the others'. Bennigsen evacuated Eylau at 1830 hrs that night – against the advice of most of his staff – and the 4th French Division later occupied the town without a fight.

Sources Höpfner, Lettow-Vorbeck, Martinien.

OP Ostrolenka (now Ostroleka), 16 February 1807, clash

A small town in Russian-Poland, on the River Narew, about 100 km north of Warsaw (Warszawa).

A French victory over the Russians.

(Last action – Preussisch-Eylau, 7 and 8 February; next action – Dirschau, 23 February.)

French Forces GdD Saváry commanding. From M Davout's III Corps: 1st Division GdD Morand: 51e RIdLi (3 bns); 3rd Division. GdD Gudin: 21e RILé (3 bns), 2 x FAB. From M Soult's IV Corps: 2nd Division GdD Leval: 57e RIdLi (2 bns), 2 x FAB. From M Ney's VI Corps: 44e RIdLi (1 bn); 9e HusR (3 sqns), 1 x FAB, 1 x HAB. The following regiments were also present: Légère: 12e, 17e and 28e; Ligne: 8e, 45e, 54e, 94e, 100e and 103e. 1er Carabiniers, 7e ChàCh and 15e, 22e and 25e DragRs.

French totals ca 20,000 men.

French losses GdB Campaux killed, 1 general wounded, 71 other officers killed or wounded, 1,100 men killed, wounded and missing.

Russian forces GL Essen III commanding. 8th Division Obst Count Pahlen: Petersburg DragR; Livland DragR; Olviopol HusR; Cossack Rs Kieselev and Sysojev. Moscow GrenR, Schlüsselburg, Alt-Ingermannland, Podolsk and Archangelgorod Musk Rs. 7th Jägers. 20 sqns, 18 bns, 60 guns.

Russian totals ca 18,000 men.

Russian losses GM Count Suvorov killed, other losses not known exactly; reported as 2,500 killed, wounded and captured; 7 guns, 2 colours.

Sources Höpfner, Lettow-Vorbeck, Martinien.

PS Schweidnitz, (now Swidnica), 10 January–16 February 1807, siege and capture of

A fortress in Prussian Silesia (now Poland), on the River Weistritz 48 km south west of Breslau (Wroclaw) on Route 5/E261.

An Allied victory over the Prussians.

(Last action – Brieg, 17 January; next action – Kanth, 14 May.)

Allied Forces GdD Vandamme commanding the Württemberg Division: GL von Seckendorff: 1st Brigade GM von Lilienberg: I bns Kronprinz, von Seckendorff and von Lilienberg. 2nd Brigade GM von Schröder: I bns Herzog Wilhelm and von Schröder; 3rd Brigade Obst von Neubronn: Jäger Bns von Hügel and Scharffenstein; LtBns von Neubronn and von Brüsselle. Cavalry Brigade GdB Count Montbrun: LeibChLR; vacant ChLR, vacant JzPfR. Artillery: 1 x 8 pdr FAB (8guns, 2 how); 1 x HAB (4 x 6 pdr, 2 x 7 pdr how). 1 Bavarian FAB (6 guns).

Allied totals 9 bns, 12 sqns, 22 field guns, ca 8,000 men.

Allied losses 7 killed, 33 wounded, 54 captured.

Prussian Garrison Obstlt von Haacke commanding: 3rd MuskBns of IR von Schimonski Nr 40 and von Strachwitz Nr 43, the depot of the Niederschlesischen FüsBn (600men); stragglers, invalides and volunteers (1,100); gunners and miners (400); dismounted cavalry (250); Jägers (110). In early January the following troops came in: IR von Kropff Nr 31 (1 bn); 1 x HAB, depot of Heysing KürR Nr 8 (256).

Prussian totals 6,164 men and 242 guns. The fortress was designed for a garrison of 9,000 men and many of the gun carriages were rotten.

Prussian losses 1,466 men deserted during the siege; the garrison marched out with honours of war, laid down their weapons and went into captivity 4,000 strong. The 97 officers were released on parole.

Sources Höpfner, Lettow-Vorbeck, Martinien.

OP Dirschau, (now Tczew), 23 February 1807, clash

A fortified small town on the west bank of the River Vistula in East Prussia (nowadays Poland) about 25 km south of Danzig (Gdansk) on Route 1/E75.

An Allied victory over the Prussians.

(Last action – Ostrolenka, 16 February; next action – Braunsberg 26 February.)

Allied Forces GdD Ménard commanding part of M Lefebvre's X Corps:

Polish troops 1ère Légion du Nord; Gen Dabrowski commanding: 9th, 10th, 11th, 12th LIR (1 bn each); 5th and 6th CavRs (4 sqns) ca 3,000 men.

Polish losses GdD Ménard and Gen Dabrowski wounded; 9 officers killed, 19 men killed; 234 wounded.

Baden Troops GL von Clossmann: IR Grossherzog, IR Erbgrossherzog, IR Markgraf Ludwig, IR von Harrant, (8 bns); HusR (4 sqns); 2 x FAB (16 guns).

Baden losses 64 men killed and wounded.

Prussian Forces Part of the Danzig garrison; Maj Both commanding: parts of IR Hamburger Nr 52, Courbière Nr 58 and the 3rd Bns of IRs von Kalkreuth Nr 4, Besser Nr 14 and Kauffberg Nr 51 (9 officers and 497 men in all); 64 Schützen, 31 Jägers, 31 Hussars and 2 guns.

Prussian total 632 men.

Prussian losses 150 killed, 6 officers and 74 men wounded, Maj Both and 150 men captured; both guns disabled. 270 men returned to Danzig in small groups.

Comment This was a fierce, 6-hour long combat and was the baptism of fire for Dabrowski's Légion. French reports put the Prussian garrison as being 1,500 strong. The French were closing up to Danzig.

Sources Höpfner, Lettow-Vorbeck, KuKKA, 3 Folge, IV Band.

OP Braunsberg (now Braniewo), 26 February 1807, clash

A fortified small town in East Prussia (nowadays Poland) on the lower River Passarge (Pasleka), about 5 km from the Baltic coast, on Route 504 about midway between Königsberg (Kaliningrad) and Elbing (Elblag).

A French victory over the Russo-Prussians.

(Last action – Dirschau, 23 February; next action – Danzig, 24 May.)

French Forces GdD Dupont's 1st Division of M Bernadotte's I Corps: GdB Rouyère; GdB d'Harvesse: 9e RILé, 32e and 96e RIdLi (7 bns), 2 x FAB, 1 x HAB. Light Cavalry GdB Lahoussaye: 2e and 4e HusR, 5e ChàCh (12 sqns). A Dragoon brigade which did not come into action.

French totals 7 bns, 12 sqns, 12 guns.

French losses Not known, light.

Russo-Prussian Forces Gen Plötz commanding part of Gen l'Estocq's corps: IR Rüts Nr 8 (2 bns); IR Plötz Nr 42 (1 bn); IR Besser Nr 14 (1stBn); GrenBn Braun (1 bn); Füsiliers (½ bn); Russian MuskR Kaluga (3 bns); DragR von Esebeck Nr 8 (5 sqns); Kür R von Wagenfeld Nr 4 (5 sqns); HusR Prittwitz Nr 5, 1 x Prussian HAB (8guns); 1 x Russian FAB (12 guns).

Russo-Prussian totals 8½ bns, 15 sqns, 20 guns.

Russo-Prussian losses 100 killed and wounded, 700 captured (mostly Russians), 3 Prussian and 3 Russian guns.

Comment The Allies had expected the French army to continue its withdrawal on the Vistula after the Battle of Preussisch-Eylau and were caught by surprise when they bumped into serious opposition.

Sources Höpfner, Lettow-Vorbeck, Martinien.

PS Kanth, (now Katy Wroclawskie), 14 May 1807, clash

A village in Prussian Silesia (now Poland) about 17 km southwest of Breslau (now Wroclaw) on the River Weistritz, just north of the motorway A4/E40.

A Prussian victory over the Bavarians and Saxons.

(Last action – Schweidnitz, 16 February; next action – Neisse, 16 June.)

Allied Forces GdB Lefebvre-Desnouettes commanding the following Bavarian Troops: 1st LIR (2e Bn); 10 LIR (1 coy); 1st DragR (1 sqn); 2 ChLR (1 sqn); 2 guns. Saxon Troops: IR von Niesemeuschel (1 bn).

Allied totals 2 bns, 1 coy, 2 sqns, 2 guns, ca 2,000 men.

Allied losses Saxons: 270 captured; the killed and wounded are unknown. Bavarians: 22 dead, 59 wounded, 126 missing, 1 colour (2 Bn/1st LIR); 2 guns.

Prussian Forces Maj von Losthin commanding: Schützen Coys* Rekowski, Stengel, Freyburg, Blacha, Frankenburg, Sell, Clausewitz and Ingenheim, cavalry squadrons Stössel (110 men), Kleist (75); Ulanen (55); 2 x 3 pdr guns.

* = average strength of each company 170 men.

Prussian totals 8 coys, 3 sqns, 2 guns, ca 1,600 men.

Prussian losses 12 officers wounded (one mortally), 460 men killed, wounded and missing.

Comment General Lefebvre only escaped by swimming the River Weistritz and nearly drowned in the process.

Sources Höpfner, Lettow-Vorbeck, Leyh.

OP Danzig, (now Gdansk), 10 March – 24 May 1807, blockade, siege and capture

A fortified port just west of the mouth of the River Vistula (Wisla) on the Baltic coast of West Prussia (now Poland).

An Allied victory over the Prussians and Russians.

(Last action – Braunsberg, 26 February; next action – Spanden, 4 and 5 June.)

Allied Forces (as at 1 April 1807) M Lefebvre commanding the X Corps: **1st Division** GdD Michaud: 12e RILé (3 bns); 1ère (Polish) Légion du Nord (2,148 men); Saxons Composite Gren Bn (432 men); IR Pz Anton 1st Bn (416 men); IR von Sänger (2 bns, 937 men); IR von Bevilaqua (1st Bn, 415 men). **1st Division totals** 10 bns, 6,328 men. **2nd Division** Erbprinz von Baden: 19e RIdLi (2 bns, 1,352 men). **Baden Troops** Leib-R (2 bns, 769 men); IR Erbprinz (2 bns, 660 men); IR Markgraf Ludwig (2 bns, 695 men); IR von Harrant (2 bns, 570 men); Jägers (60 men). **2nd Division total** 4,133 men. **3rd Division** GdD Gielgud: 2e RILé (1er Bn, 1,010 men); 44e RIdLi (2 bns, 950 men); GdN Paris (2 bns, 967 men); 2nd Polish LIR (1 bn, 374 men); 3rd Polish LIR (2 bns, 946 men). **3rd Division totals** 8 bns, 4,247 men. **4th Division** GdD Gardanne: 2e RILé (2nd Bn, 774 men). **Saxons** Composite Gren Bn (774 men); IR Pz Max (1st Bn, 449 men); IR Pz Anton (2nd Bn, 482 men). Poles: 2nd LIR (1 bn, 646 men) 4th LIR (2 bns, 1,275 men). **4th Division totals** 7 bns, 3,974 men. **Total infantry** 35 bns, 18,682 men. **Cavalry Division** GL von Polenz. **French** 19e and 23e ChàCh (8 sqns, 815 men). **Baden** HusR (1 sqn, 136 men), DragR (2 sqns, 288 men). **Saxons** KürR (3 sqns, 588 men); ChLR (1 sqn, 156 men). **Poles** 1st CavR (80 men); 2nd CavR (3 sqns, 215 men); Noble Cav (2 sqns, 121 men). **Total cavalry** 20 sqns, 2,506 men. **Artillery** 2,917 men and 100 guns.

Allied Grand Total 24,105 men.

In May 1807 the following troops of M Lannes' Reserve Corps also joined **Oudinot's Élite Division** 8 regiments of 2 bns – 11,444 men; 3 sqns (659 men). Artillery (3 batteries – 619 men) **Total Oudinot's Élite Division** 12,722 men and **Dupas' Division** of M Mortier's VIII Corps: 4e RILé, 15e and 55e RIdLi, 1st IR of Berg and Würzburg IR (2 bns each). **Total Dupas' Division** 10 bns, 8,095 men. The **besiegers' total strength** thus rose to about 45,000 men and 100 heavy guns.

Allied losses 28 officers killed, 1 general and 104 officers wounded, about 6,000 men killed, wounded and died of sickness.

Prussian Garrison GdK Count Kalckreuth commanding: GrenBn Schmeling (1 bn); GrenBn Brauchitsch (1 bn); IR Hamberger Nr 52 (2 bns); IR Courbière Nr 58 (2 bns); IR Diericke Nr 16 (2 bns); the 3rd Musketier Bns of IRs Courbière Nr 58, Diericke Nr 16, Kalkreuth Nr 4; Besser Nr 14; Treskow Nr 17, Kauffberg Nr 51 and Kropff Nr 33. Remnants of Füs Bns Pelet Nr 14 and Rühle Nr 15; Füs Bn Rembow Nr 6 (1 bn); Jäger coy Werner. Depots of Füs Bns von Rembow, von Wackenitz Nr 3, von Bergen Nr 11, von Stutterheim Nr 21, von Bülow Nr 24, von Schachtmeyer Nr 23 and von Greiffenberg Nr 4. **Total infantry** 12,273 men and 296 officers. **Cavalry** Remnants of DragR Königin Nr 5 (1stBn); DragR Roquette Nr 13, DragR König von Bayern Nr 1; Depots of KürRs Bailliodz Nr 5 and Reitzenstein Nr 7, Reserve Sqns and fragments of various regiment, JzPf von Krockow (1 sqn). **Total cavalry** 40 officers and 1,613 men. Artillery: – 432 men, fortress artillery – 109 men; provisional gunners – 572 men; assistants from Füs Depots von Hinrichs, Knorr, Borell, Oswald and Kloch – 267 men. **Total field artillery** 1,380 men.

Engineers: 11 officers and 21 men.

Prussian Grand Total 370 officers, 15,287 men. This was far below the optimum garrison level of about 40,000 men.

Prussian losses 35 officers, 3,000 men killed, wounded or died of sickness.

Sources Höpfner, Lettow-Vorbeck, Leyh.

OP Spanden (now Spedy), 4 and 5 June 1807, clash

A small town in East Prussia (now Poland) just west of the River Passarge (now Pasleka) about midway between Elbing (Elblag) and Heilsberg (now Lidzbark Warminski).

A French victory over the Allies.

(Last action - Danzig, 24 May; next action - Lomitten, 5 June.)

French Forces GdB Frère of Villatte's Division of M Bernadotte's I Corps: 27e RILé (2 bns); 63e RIdLi (2 bns); 17e DragR, 19e DragR (3 sqns each). 2 x FAB.

French totals 4 bns, 6 sqns, 12 guns.

French losses Not known, the infantry lost 3 officers.

Allied Forces GM von Rembow of GL l'Estocq's Corps; Russian IRs Sievsk and Perm (3 bns each); Prussian DragR von Ziethen Nr 6 (10 sqns) and DragR von Baczko Nr 7 (5 sqns). Prussian Artillery: 1 x FAB, 1 x HAB, 29 cannon and 2 howitzers (including battalion pieces).

Allied totals 6 bns, 15 sqns, 2 batteries, ca 6,000 men.

Allied losses 500 killed and wounded, all from the Russian infantry.

Comment This was a totally stupid assault on a very well fortified bridgehead on the east bank of the Passarge and was undertaken on orders from GL l'Estocq who was persuaded by his Adjutant (Major St Paul) to do more than just demonstrate as had originally been agreed.

Sources Höpfner, Lettow-Vorbeck, Martinien.

OP Lomitten, 5 June 1807, clash

A village in East Prussia (now Poland) on the River Passarge (Pasleka) 7 km northeast of Liebstadt and about 8 km upstream from Spanden (Spedy).

The action took place around the bridgehead.

A Russian victory over the French.

(Last action - Spanden, 4 and 5 June ; next action - Guttstadt and Deppen, 5 and 6 June.)

French Forces M Soult commanding the IV Corps: GdD Carra St Cyr. GdB Ferey: 24e RILé (2 bns); 57e RIdLi (2 bns); 46e RIdLi (2 bns) 15e ChàCh (3 sqns) 4 x 6 pdrs, 12 x 12 pdrs.

French totals 16 guns, ca 6,000 men.

French losses 4 officers and 102 men killed; 54 officers and 1,025 men wounded.

Russian Forces GL Dochtorov commanding the 7th Division: GM Lvov: KürR Ekaterinoslav, DragR Kiev, HusR Alexandrov (20 sqns), Tartars (5 sqns). GM Rachmanov: Wilna and Nizov MuskRs (6 bns); GM Bikov: Reval and Volhynian MuskRs (6 bns), GM Baggowut; Starokol MuskR and 4th Jägers (6 bns), 2 x 12 pdr FABs, 3 x 6 pdr FABs, 1 x HAB. Later GM Chitrow brought up 3 bns, 5 sqns and 4 guns.

Russian totals 18 bns, 25 sqns, 72 guns; later 21 bns, 30 sqns and 76 guns, ca 12,000 men.

Russian losses French reports give them as 800 killed and 2,000 wounded.

Comment The Russian forced the French out of the bridgehead but did not cross the river. This action and that at Spanden were part of Bennigsen's preemptive strike to disrupt Napoleon's plans.

Sources Höpfner, Lettow-Vorbeck, Martinien.

OP Guttstadt and Deppen (now Dobre Miasto and Mostkowa), 5 and 6 June 1807, clash

Villages in East Prussia (now Poland) 21 km and 36 km respectively southwest of Heilsberg (now Lidzbark Warminski) on Route 51.

A Russian victory over the French.

(Last action - Lomitten, 5 June; next action - Heilsberg 10 June.)

French Forces M Ney's VI Corps; GdD Marchand: 6e RILé (2 bns), 39e, 69e and 76e RIdLi (2 bns each). GdD Bisson: 25e RILé, 27e, 50e and 59e RIdLi (2 bns each). Light Cavalry: 12e DragR (4 sqns), 3e, 5e, 7e, 8e HusR (12 sqns) 14e, 24e ChàCh (6 sqns).

French totals 16 bns, 20 sqns, 4 x FAB, 4 x HAB, ca 17,000 men.

French losses 400 killed or wounded, 1 general (Roget), 73 officers and 1,568 men captured along with 2 guns and all his baggage.

Russian Forces GdC Baron Bennigsen commanding: **GL Baron Sacken I's 3rd Division** GM Count Pahlen: Little Russia KürR; Kurland DragR, Sum HusR (20 sqns), Cossack Rs Ilowaiski X and Papuzin; GM Ushakov: Tauride GrenR, Lithuanian MuskR (6 bns), GM Titov II: Kaporski and Muromsk MuskRs (6 bns), GM Netting: Tschernigov and Dnieprov MuskRs (6 bns), 21st Jägers (3 bns); 2 x 12 pdr FAB, 3 x 6 pdr FAB, 1 x HAB. **3rd Division totals** 21 bns, 20 sqns, 2 cossack sotnias, 72 guns, ca 19,000 men. **2nd Division** GL Count Ostermann: GM Koschin: Leib-KürR, Kargopol DragR, Isum HusR (20 sqns); Cossack Rs Ilowaiski IX and Jefremov III. GM Mazovskoi: Pavlov GrenR, Rostov MuskR (6 bns); GM Sukin II. Petersburg GrenR, Jeletz MuskR (6 bns); GM Count Lieven: 1st and 20th Jägers (6 bns). 2 x 12 pdr FAB, 2 x 6 pdr FAB; 1 x HAB. **2nd Division totals** 18 bns, 20 sqns, 2 cossack sotnias, 60 guns. **14th Division** GL Anrepp: Finland DragR, Mittau DragR, Grodno HusR (20 sqns), Bielosersk, Riasan, Uglitsch, Sophia MuskRs, 23rd and 26th Jägers (18 bns). 1 x 12 pdr

FAB, 2 x 6 pdr FAB. **14th Division totals** 36 bns, 20 sqns, 36 guns. Together the 2nd and 14th Divisions had 9,615 men in the field this day. The regiments must have been very weak. Prince Galitzin commanded these divisions.

Russian totals 63,000 men.

Russian losses 3 generals wounded (including Ostermann and Somov), 2,500 killed, wounded and missing.

Comment Bennigsen planned to attack Ney's corps which was in an isolated position east of the River Passarge. Bennigsen alleged that Sacken refused to come into action despite repeated orders to do so and the French slipped away.

Sources Höpfner, Lettow-Vorbeck, Martinien.

OP Heilsberg (now Lidzbark Warminski) 10 June 1807, battle

A town in East Prussia (now Poland) on the River Alle (now Lyna) on Route 51, about 67 km south of Königsberg (now Kaliningrad in Russia).

A Russo-Prussian victory over the French.

(Last action – Guttstadt and Deppen, 5 and 6 June; next action – Königsberg and Friedland, 14 June.)

French Forces Emperor Napoleon I commanding

Reserve Cavalry M Murat Cuirassier Division GdD Nansouty GdB Defrance, la Houssaye and Saint-Germain: 1er* and 2e CarabinierR, 12e CuirR (4 sqns each). 1st Dragoon Division GdD Klein, GdB Fenerolz, la Motte, Picard: 1er and 2e, 4e and 14e, 20e and 26e DragR (20 sqns); 27e DragR (3 sqns). Light Cavalry GdD Lasalle: 5e and 7e HusR, 1er HusR* and 13e ChàCh (12 sqns); Württemberg Leib-ChLR (4 sqns). Light Cavalry GdB Watier: 11e ChàCh*, Bavarian 1st ChLR Kronprinz (4 sqns each). Cuirassier Division GdD ? 4e, 6e, 7e, 8e and 11e CuirRs (20 sqns). Light Cavalry of the III Corps: 12e ChàCh (3 sqns). Light Cavalry of the VI Corps: 9e HusR (4 sqns). Light Cavalry of the VII Corps: 7e and 20e ChàCh (7 sqns); The 3e HusR was also present (4 sqns). Artillery: 26 guns.

IV Corps M Soult: 1st Division GdD Saint-Hilaire, GdB de Candras, Waré. 10e RILé* and 35 RIdLi*; 43e and 55e RIdLi (2 bns each). 2nd Division GdD Carra, Saint-Cyr, GdB Schinner, Ferrey and Viviès. 24e RILé; 4e, 28e, 46e and 57e RIdLi (2 bns each). 3rd Division GdD Legrand GdB Ledru des Essarts, Lavasseur, 26e RILé; 18e and 75e RIdLi (2 bns each); Tirailleurs du Po (1 bn), Tirailleurs Corses (2 bns). Light Cavalry GdB Maragon and Guyot. 8e HusR and 22e ChàCh*; (3 sqns each). Artillery: 8 x FAB, 1 x HAB (52 guns).

V Corps M Lannes (arrived on the battlefield in the evening). 2nd Division GdD Gazan, GdB Graindorge and Campana. 21e RILe* (3 bns); 28e RIdLi (2 bns). Artillery: 5 x FAB, 1 x HAB (38 guns).

Imperial Guard GdD Savǻry Füsilier-GrenR (2 bns); Fusilier-ChasseursR (2 bns); ChàCh (4 sqns); Artillerie à Cheval. Martinien also shows considerable officer casualties for the following infantry regiments this day: 2e 10e and 12 RILé; 3e, 14e, 17e, 22e, 36e and 63 RIdLi and 4e Swiss.

* = Martinien shows no officer casualties for regiments marked '*' at Heilsberg.

French totals 36 bns, 87 sqns, 106 guns, 53,500 infantry and 11,500 cavalry.

French losses According to their casualty return the French lost 1,398 killed, 10,059 wounded and 864 captured. Soult's IV Corps alone lost 8,286 men. General Roussel (Chief of Staff of the Guard) was killed, Generals du Viviès, Ferey and Espagne were wounded – Lannes' corps lost 2,284 killed and wounded. Three eagles were lost; one of the 55e RIdLi and two others (unidentified).

Russo-Prussian Forces GdC Count Bennigsen commanding.

The main fighting was carried out by the 6th and 8th Divisions who were joined gradually by the 3rd, 7th and 14th Divisions. The 1st and 2nd Divisions, the Reserve and most of the cavalry were not engaged. The 4th and 5th Divisions under General Kaminskoi were on the left wing of the 6th and 8th Division.

Avantgarde Gen Prince Bagration commanding 9 Jäger regiments, 5 Musketier regiments, 2 Hussar regiments, 2,115 Cossacks. Exact details not known. **6th Division** GM Sedmoratzki GM Rachmanov: Musk Rs Wilna and Nizov (6 bns). GM Bikov: Musk Rs Reval and Wolhynian (6 bns). GM Baggowut: Starokol MuskR and 4th Jägers (6 bns). GM Lvov: KürR Ekaterinoslav (5 sqns); DragR Kiev (5 sqns); HusR Alexandrov (10 sqns). Artillery: 2 x 12 pdr FAB, 3 x 6 pdr FAB, 1 x HAB (72 guns). **8th Division** GL Essen III, GM ?: Moscow GrenR, (3 bns). GM ?: Musk Rs Schlüsselburg and Alt-Ingermannland (6 bns). GM ?: Musk R Podolien, (3 bns); 7th Jägers (3 bns). Oberst Count Pahlen: Drag Rs Petersburg and Livland (5 sqns each); HusR Olviopol (10 sqns). Artillery: 4 x 12 pdr FAB, 1 x HAB (60 guns). **3rd Division** GL Baron Sacken I, GM Uschakov: Tauride GrenR and Lithuanian MuskR (6 bns). GM Titov II: Musk Rs Kaporski and Muromsk (6 bns). GM Netting: Musk Rs Tschernigov and Dnieprov (6 bns). GM Count Pahlen: Little Russia Kür R, DragR Kurland (5 sqns each); Sum HusR (10 sqns); Cossack sotnias of Ilowaiski X and Papuzin. Artillery: 2 x 12 pdr FAB, 3 x 6 pdr FAB, 1 x HAB (72 guns). **7th Division** GL Dochtorov, GM ?: GrenR Ekaterinoslav, MuskR Moscow (6 bns). GM ?: Musk Rs Vladimir and Woronesch (6 bns). GM ?: Musk Rs Pskov, 5th Jägers (6 bns). GM Tschaplitz: DragRs Moscow and Ingermannland (5 sqns each); HusR Pavlograd (10 sqns). Artillery: 2 x 12 pdr FAB, 3 x 6 pdr FAB, 1 x HAB (72 guns). **14th Division GL Anrepp,** GM ?: MuskRs Bielosersk and Rijasan (6 bns). GM ?: Musk Rs Uglitsch and Sophia (6 bns). GM ?: 23rd and 26th Jägers (6 bns). GM ?: DragRs Finland and Mittau (5 sqns each); HusR Grodno (10 sqns). Artillery: 1 x 12 pdr FAB, 2 x 6 pdr FAB, (36 guns).

Cavalry of the Right Wing GM Kamenskoi: Leib-KürR, Kargopol DragR (5 sqns each); Isum HusR (10 sqns); cossack sotnias of Ilowaiski X and Jefremov III. GM von Prittwitz*: DragRs von Ziethen Nr 6* (10 sqns) and von Baczko Nr 7* (5 sqns), HusR von Prittwitz Nr 5* (2 sqns), 1 x HAB*. GM Kall: HusR Towarczys Nr 9* (15 sqns).

Prussian Forces GL l'Estocq. **Avantgarde** GM von Stutterheim*: HusR von Pletz Nr 3* (4 sqns); HusR von Prittwitz Nr 5* (8 sqns); HusR von Köhler Nr 7* (1 sqn); HusR Württemberg Nr 4* (4 sqns); FüsBn von Wackenitz Nr 3* (1 bn); FüsBn von Bergen Nr 11* (1 bn); FüsBn von Stutterheim Nr 21* (1 bn); Drag Bde von Wedell* (4 sqns); 1 x HAB*. **Main Body** 1st Division: GM von Diericke*: GrenBn Fabecky* (1 bn); GrenBn von Schlieffen* (1 bn); IR von Rüchel Nr 2* Pz Heinrich Nr 35* and von Plötz Nr 42* (2 bns each); KürR von Wagenfeld Nr 4* (6 sqns); KürR von Stülpnagel Nr 6* (4 sqns); KürR Garde du Corps Nr 13* (4 sqns); DragR von Esebeck Nr 8* (5 sqns). Artillery: 1 x 6 pdr FAB*, 2 x 12 pdr FAB*, 1 x HAB*. 2nd Division GM von Rembow*: MuskRs Sievsk, Perm and Kaluga (3 bns each). 1 x 6 pdr FAB.

Allied totals 175 bns, 318 sqns of which the 1st and 2nd Divisions, the Reserve and most of the cavalry ie 35 bns and 100 sqns did not come into action. The forces involved were 116 bns, 170 sqns and about 150 guns, ca 53,000 men.

Allied losses Generals Koschin, Warneck and Pahlen were killed, Generals Dochtorov, Werdrevski, Fock, Olsufiev, Duka, Laptiev, Passeck and Prince Karl von Mecklenburg were wounded. Total losses were 2-300 dead and 5-6,000 wounded and 2 guns.

Comment This was a successful Russo-Prussian rear-guard action. Napoleon did not realise that he was facing the whole Allied army at Heilsberg. Ney attacked prematurely. Although the Russians had built extensive fortifications on the right (eastern) bank of the River Alle, and only a few minor redoubts on the left bank they advance over the river to give battle thus squandering this advantage and incurring avoidable casualties.

Bennigsen was sick this day but remained in command even though he fell off his horse several times unconscious.

* = Prussian Regiments.

Sources Höpfner, Lettow-Vorbeck, Martinien, Charrié.

OP Königsberg (now Kaliningrad), 14 June 1807, clash

A fortified city-port in East Prussia (now Russia) at the mouth of the River Pregel (now Pregola) on the Baltic coast.

A 'drawn match'; the Allies held out in the city until 15 June.

(Last action – Heilsberg, 10 June; this was the last action of the war for l'Estocq's corps); next action – Friedland, 14 June.

French Forces M Murat commanding: **2nd Cuirassier Division** GdD d'Hautpoul: 1er CuirR (4 sqns) no other regiments were engaged. **3rd Dragoon Division** GdD Milhaud: 5e, 12e, 16e and 21e DragR (4 sqns each). **Light Cavalry** GdD Lasalle: 3e ChàCh, 5e HusR (4 sqns each). Artillery: 3 x HAB (18 guns).

IV Corps M Soult*: **2nd Division** GdD Carra St Cyr: 26e RILé, 28e, 46e and 47e RIdLi (2 bns each). **3rd Division** GdD Legrand: 15e RILé, Tirailleurs Corses, Tirailleurs du Po (1 bn), 75e RIdLi (2 bns). Artillery: 3 x FAB (36 guns).

* = The 1st Division of GdD Saint-Hilaire and the III Corps of M Davout did not come into action.

French totals 18 bns, 28 sqns, 54 guns, ca 20,000 men.

French losses Not exactly known, light.

Russo-Prussian Forces GL l'Estocq commanding: 1st

Outpost Brigade Obst Wiersbitzki: HusR von Prittwitz Nr 5 (2nd Bn); HusR von Köhler Nr 7 (1 sqn); Füs-Bn von Bergen Nr 11 (1 bn); ½ x HAB. **2nd Outpost Brigade** Maj von Ziethen: HusR Württemberg Nr 4 (4 sqns); Füs-Bn von Wackenitz Nr 3 (1 bn); ½ x HAB. Detachment of Maj Pfahl: HusR von Prittwitz Nr 5 (1st Bn). **3rd Outpost Brigade** Maj Prinz von Anhalt-Schaumburg (see below). Outpost Support GM von Stutterheim: Füs-Bn von Stutterheim Nr 21 (1 bn); IR Wyburg* (2½ bns); Drag-Bde von Wedell (4 sqns); 1 x HAB. Main Body 1st Division GM von Dierické: GrenBn Fabecky (1 bn); GrenBn von Schlieffen (1 bn); IR von Rüchel Nr 2 (2 bns); IR Pz Heinrich Nr 35 (2 bns); IR von Plötz Nr 42 (2 bns); DragR von Esebeck Nr 8 (5 sqns); KürR von Stülpnagel Nr (4 sqns); Garde du Corps Nr 13 (4 sqns); KürR von Wagenfeld Nr 4 (6 sqns). Artillery: 1 x 6 pdr FAB, 2 x 12 pdr FAB, 1 x HAB. 2nd Division GM von Rembow: GM von Warneck; IRs Azov*, Sievsk*. Perm* and Kaluga* (3 bns each); 1 x 6 pdr FAB. GM von Prittwitz: DragR von Ziethen Nr 6 (10 sqns); DragR von Baczko Nr 7 (5 sqns). **Reserve Division** GM Kaminskoi*: IRs Archangelgorod*, Nowaginski*, Mohilev* and 21st Jägers* (3 bns each), 1 cossack pulk*, ½ x 6 pdr FAB*. GM Kall: R Towarczys (3 bns).

Allied totals 10,500 infantry, 6,500 cavalry, 78 guns.

Allied losses Not known exactly; about 200 killed, wounded and captured.

NB: 3rd Outpost Brigade of Maj Pz von Anhalt-Schaumburg (HusR von Pless (4 sqns); IR Wyburg* (3 coys); ½ x HAB had become separated from l'Estocq on 12/13 June. They came up behind the French and tried to break through but were overwhelmed and capitulated. Maj von Arnim's polyglot company of this force was captured by 8e HusR.

Comment After the clash at Heilsberg on 10 June, l'Estocq's corps had withdrawn north to Königsberg; Bennigsen and the Russian main body to the north east on Friedland. Napoleon had lost sight of both parties and did not know where his enemy's main body was. The Prussian tactical conduct in this action was appalling.

* = Russian Regiments.

Sources Höpfner, Lettow-Vorbeck, Martinien.

OP Friedland (Pravdinsk), 14 June 1807, battle

A town in East Prussia (now Russia), on the west bank of the River Alle (now Lava), 43 km southeast of Königsberg (now Kaliningrad).

A French victory over the Russians.

(Last action – Königsberg, 14 June. This was the last action of the war in this theatre; the next siege to end was Colberg, 2 July.)

French Forces Emperor Napoleon I commanding.

I Corps M Victor. **1st Division** GdD Dupont: GdB Labuyère, GdB Barrois: 9e RILé (2 bns), 24e, 32e and 96e RIdLi (2 bns each). **2nd Division** GdD Lapisse: GdB Pacthod, GdB Darricau: 16e RILé (2 bns), 8e, 45e and 54e RIdLi (2 bns each). **3rd Division** GdD Villatte: GdB Frere, GdB Gerard: 27e RILé (2 bns), 63e, 94e and 95e RIdLi 2 bns each). **Light Cavalry** GdB Beaumont: 2e and 4e HusR, 5e ChàCh (9 sqns). Artillery 4 x FAB, 2½ x HAB. **I Corps totals** 24 bns, 23,547 infantry, 9 sqns, 1,487 cavalry.

VI Corps M Ney. **1st Division** GdD Marchand; GdB Maucune, GdB Marcognet, GdB Brun: 6e RILé (2 bns); 31e RILé, 39e, 69e and 76e RIdLi (2 bns each). **Light Cavalry** GdB Colbert: 3e HusR, 10e and 1e ChàCh (3 sqns each). Artillery 4 x FAB, 1½ x HAB. **VI Corps totals** 18 bns, 14,715 * infantry, 9 sqns, 1,117 cavalry. * = 3,339 men of the 2nd Division were detached to Guttstadt and Deppen.

VIII Corps M Mortier. **1st Division** GdD Dupas; GdB Veaux, GdB Gency, GdB Grandjean: 4e RILé (2 bns); 15e and 58e RIdLi (2 bns each); Garde Municipale de Paris 1er and 2e Regts. (1er Bns in each case). **2nd Division** GdD Dabrowski: 10th, 11th and 12th Polish LIR* (2 bns each). **Light Cavalry** GdB Fresia: 2nd Dutch CuirR (3 sqns); 2nd Dutch HusR (3 sqns). GdB Turno: 5th and 6th Polish CavR**(3 sqns each). Artillery 6 x*** FAB (of these, 3 Polish); 1 x Dutch HAB. **VIII Corps totals** 14 bns, 8,465 infantry, 12 sqns, 1,200 cavalry.

* = Until 4 June 1807 these regiments were the 2nd, 3rd and 4th Polish LIRs.

** = Until 4 June 1807 these regiments were the 1st and 2nd Polish CavRs.

*** = some may have been in Danzig.

Reserve Corps M Lannes. **Division d'Élite** GdD Oudinot: GdB Ruffin, GdB Conroux, GdB Coehron, GdB Albert. 1er R, 1er Bn (Carabinier coys of the 3e Bns of 6e, 9e, 25e and 27e RILé and 4e Bn 7e RILé); 2e Bn (Voltigeur coys as above); 2eR 3e Bn (Gren coys of 3e Bns of 30e, 33e, 51e, 95e and 96e RIdLi); 4e Bn (Voltigeur coys as above); 3eR 5e Bn (Carabinier coys of the 3e Bns of 10e, 17e, 21e, 24e, 26e and 28e RILé); 6e Bn (Voltigeur coys as above); 4e R, 7e Bn (Grenadier coys of the 3e Bns of 18e, 40e, 64e and 88e RIdLi and the 4e Bn, 34e RIdLi); 8e Bn (Voltigeur coys as above); 5eR 9e Bn (Gren coys of 3e Bns of 27e, 39e, 45e, 59e, 69e and 76e RIdLi); 10e Bn (Voltigeur coys as above); 6eR, 11e Bn (Grenadier coys of the 3e Bns of 44e, 54e, 63e, 94e and 105e RIdLi and the 4e Bn, 24e RIdLi); 12e Bn (Voltigeur coys as above); 7eR, 13e Bn (Grenadier coys of the 3e Bns of 21e, 22e, 32e 57e and 65e RIdLi and the Carabiniers, 4e Bn, 25e RILé); 14e Bn (Voltigeur coys as above); 8eR 15e Bn (Grenadier coys of 3e Bns of 12e, 14e, 61e, 85e and 111e RIdLi and 4e Bn, 3e RIdLi); 16e Bn (Voltigeur coys as above).

GdD Verdier's Division GdB Vedel, Harispe, Schramm: 2e and 12e RILé and 72e RIdLi (2 bns each); 3e RIdLi (3 bns each). **Saxon Division** GL von Polenz*: GrenBn von Süssmilch*, GrenBn von Larisch*; IR von Bevilaqua* (1stBn). **Light Cavalry** Gen von Besser*: 9e HusR (3 sqns); KürR König* (4 sqns); combined ChLR of the Saxon ChLRs von Polenz* and Pz Johann* (1 sqn). Artillery 4 x FAB, 2 x HAB.

* = Saxon troops. **Reserve Corps totals** 28 bns, 13,700 infantry, 5 sqns, 1,200 cavalry. This corps suffered 2,887 casualties at Heilsberg on 10 June.

The Imperial Guard M Bessières. **Infantry** GdD Hulin: Gren à P, ChàP, 1er and 2e Füs. **Cavalry** GdD Walther: Gren à Ch, ChàCh, Gendarmerie d'Élite, Dragons de l'Imperatrice, Gendarmes d'Ordonnance. Artillery: 6 x FAB, 9 x HAB. **Imperial Guard totals** 12 bns, infantry, 16 sqns.

Reserve Cavalry M Grouchy (M Murat was at Königsberg). **1st Cuir Division** GdD Nansouty; GdB Defrance, GdB Doumerc, GdD st. Germain: 1er and 2e Carabiniers R; 2e, 3e, 9e and 12e CuirR (4 sqns each), 4,282 men. **3rd Cuir Division** GdD Espagne, GdB Reynaud, GdB Fouler: 4e, 6e, 7e and 8e CuirR (4 sqns each); **3rd Division total** Unknown. **1st Dragoon Division** GdD Latour-Maubourg; GdB Perreimond, GdB d'Oullembourg, GdD Digeon: 1er, 2e, 4e, 14e, 20e and 26e DragR (3 sqns each). **1st Dragoon Division total** 18 sqns, 2,987 men. **2nd Dragoon Division** GdD Grouchy; GdB Bron, GdB Carrie: 3e, 6e, 10e and 11e DragR (3 sqns each). **2nd Dragoon Division total** 12 sqns, 1,859 men. **4th Dragoon Division** GdD Lahoussaye; GdB Margaron, GdB Laplanche: 17e, 18e, 19e and 27e DragR (3 sqns each). **4th Dragoon Division total** 12 sqns, 2,260 men. **Light Cavalry Brigade** GdB Durosnel (of Lasalle's Light Cavalry Division): 7e, 20e and 22e ChàCh (3 sqns each). **Light Cavalry total** 9 sqns. Artillery 1 x FAB, 3½ x HAB.

Grand total present at the battle 83,321 men.

French losses Reported as 11 generals wounded, 113 officers killed, 413 officers wounded, about 11,500 men killed, wounded and missing, 1 eagle, that of the 1er Bn, 15e RIdLi was taken by the Russian IR Schlüsselburg.

Russian Forces GdC Baron von Bennigsen commanding. From right to left; the **Right Wing**, Prince Gortschakov: **3rd Division** GL Baron Sacken I, GM Uschakov: Tauride GrenR and Lithuanian MuskR (6 bns). GM Titov II: Musk Rs Kaporski and Muromsk (6 bns) GM Netting: Musk Rs Tschernigov and Dnieprov (6 bns). GM Count Pahlen: Little Russia Kür R, DragR Kurland (5 sqns each); Sum HusR (10 sqns); Cossack sotnias of Ilowaiski X and Papuzin. Artillery: 2 x 12 pdr FAB, 3 x 6 pdr FAB, 1 x HAB (72 guns). **6th Division** GM Sedmoratzki, GM Rachmanov: Musk Rs Wilna and Nizov (6 bns). GM Bikov: Musk Rs Reval and Wolhynian (6 bns). GM Baggowut: Starokol MuskR and 4th Jägers (6 bns). GM Lvov: KürR Ekaterinoslav (5 sqns); DragR Kiev (5 sqns); HusR Alexandrov (10 sqns). Artillery: 2 x 12 pdr FAB, 3 x 6 pdr FAB, 1 x HAB (72 guns). **7th Division** GL Dochtorov GM ?: GrenR Ekaterinoslav, MuskR Moscow (6 bns). GM ?: Musk Rs Vladimir and Woronesch (6 bns). GM ?: Musk Rs Pskov, 5th Jägers (6 bns). GM Tschaplitz: DragRs Moscow and Ingermannland (5 sqns each); HusR Pavlograd (10 sqns). Artillery: 2 x 12 pdr FAB, 3 x 6 pdr FAB, 1 x HAB (72 guns). **8th Division** GL Essen III, GM ?: Moscow GrenR, (3 bns). GM ?: Musk Rs Schlüsselburg and Alt-Ingermannland (6 bns). GM ?: Musk R Podolien, (3 bns); 7th Jägers (3 bns). Oberst Count Pahlen: Drag Rs Petersburg and Liefland (5 sqns each); HusR Olviopol (10 sqns). Artillery: 4 x 12 pdr FAB, 1 x HAB (60 guns). **Cavalry** Gen Kvarov and Prince Gallitzin. **The Left Wing** Prince Bagration: **1st Division** Exact details not known. **2nd Division** GL Count Ostermann, GM Makovskoi: GrenR Pavlovski; MuskR Rostov (6 bns). GM Sukin II: Gren R Petersburg; Musk R Jeletz (6 bns). GM Count Lieven: 1st and 20th Jägers (6 bns). Musk Rs Pskov; 5th Jägers (6 bns). GM Koschin: Leib-KürR; DragR Kargopol (5 sqns each); cossack sotnias of Ilowaiski IX and Jefremov III.

Artillery: 2 x 12 pdr FAB, 2 x 6 pdr FAB, 1 x HAB (60 guns)*. **Avantgarde** Exact details not known. Cavalry GM Kollogribov: Exact details not known.

* = most of the artillery was held back on the right bank of the River Alle together with the 14th Division, 20 cavalry sqns and Hetmann Platov's flying column.

Cavalry GM Kollogribov. Exact details not known.

Russian totals 46,000 men were on the left bank of the River Alle.

Russian losses Estimates vary. The French 79th Bulletin says – 'between 15–18,000'; Jomini '20,000', others 25,000 and 80 guns. Ney, whose corps stayed on the battlefield, reported only 20 guns taken but found 6,000 Russians dead. Russian reports gave casualties as 8,000 killed, wounded and captured, 10 battalion pieces and 6 'position guns' (12 pounders).

Generals Masovskoi and Sukin I had been killed; Generals Essen I, Steinheil, Sukin II and Markov I wounded.

Comment This was Bennigsen's most stupid battle of a poor campaign. He completely underestimated the enemy's strength and made the classical 'beginner's error' of accepting battle with a defile – the River Alle – at his immediate back with the three bridges behind his extreme left flank. Napoleon's total victory was assured by the absolutely criminal conduct of the commander of the Russian right wing, Prince Gortschakov, who refused to obey repeated orders from Bennigsen to withdraw over the river on the grounds that he would rather fight a vastly superior enemy (the odds were about 2:1 in favour of the French) than turn his back on him! (Höpfner, Vol III, page 663). Lannes' Corps de Reserve was, for some considerable time, the only French formation on the field and fought extremely well until their comrades came up. The commander of the I (French) Corps artillery (Gen Sénarmont) must be credited with contributing most to their victory here this day.

Sources Höpfner, Lettow-Vorbeck, Martinien.

PS Neisse (now Nysa) , 23 February – 16 June 1807, siege and capture

A fortress in Prussian Silesia (now Poland) on the River Glatze Neisse (now Nysa Klodzka) 46 km southwest of Oppeln (Opole).

An Allied victory over the Prussians.

(Last action – Kanth, 14 May; next action – Glatz, 24 June.)

Allied Forces GdD Vandamme commanding the Württemberg division. Württemberg Regiments GL von Seckendorff*: GM von Lilienberg: I Bns Kronprinz, von Seckendorff and von Lilienberg (3 bns). GM von Schröder; I Bns Herzog Wilhelm and von Schröder (2 bns); Obst von Neubronn; Jäger Bns von Hügel and Scharffenstein; Lt I Bns von Neubronn and von Brüsselle (4 bns). Cavalry: GdB Count Montbrun: Leib ChLR; vacant ChLR; vacant JzPfR (12 sqns). Artillery: 1 x HAB, 1 x FAB – 16 guns and 1 x Bavarian FAB.

Allied totals 9 bns, 12 sqns, 24 guns, ca 6,000 men.

Allied losses 30 killed and 170 wounded.

Prussian Garrison GL von Steensen (71 years old) commanding: IR von Pelchrzim Nr 38; 3rd Musk Bn of IR von Müffling Nr 49 (1 bn), gunners, miners and invalides (700), stragglers and volunteers (2,600), HusR von Schimmelpfennig Nr 6 (50); Jägers (100).

Prussian totals ca 6,124 men, 267 cannon, 29 howitzers and 48 mortars. The fortress garrison should have been 12,000 strong, many of the defensive works were abandoned.

Prussian losses About 2,000 had died of sickness or been killed during the siege. The garrison (133 officers, 4,000 men) marched out with honours of war and laid down their weapons. The officers were released on parole (10 were permitted to rejoin the Prussian army at once as a mark of respect for the spirited defence of the place), the men became prisoners of war. Four colours were taken (IR Pelchrzim).

Sources Höpfner, Lettow-Vorbeck, Kraft.

* = On 3 May Seckendorff, who had been waging his own war with Vandamme, was replaced by GL von Camrer.

PS Glatz (now Klodzko), 20–24 June 1807, storming and capitulation of

A fortified town in Prussian Silesia (now southwest Poland) 82 km south of Breslau (now Wroclaw) on Route 8/E67.

An Allied victory over the Prussians.

(Last action – Neisse, 16 June; next action – Silberberg, 29 June).

Allied Forces GdD Vandamme commanding: **Bavarian Troops** GL von Deroy: 1st, 6th and 10th LIR (1 bn each); 1st DragR (4 sqns) 2 x FAB and the Württemberg I Bn von Scharffenstein (1 bn). **Bavarian losses** 26 killed, 95 wounded, 24 missing. French Troops 7e ChàCh (4 sqns). **Württemberg Troops** GL von Camrer, GM von Lilienberg; 1 Bns Kronprinz, von Seckendorf and von Lilienberg; GM von Schröder: I Bns Herzog Wilhelm and von Schröder. Obst von Neubronn; Jäger Bn von Hügel; LtIBn von Brüsselle (7 bns). Cavalry (under Vandamme's direct command): vacant ChLR, vacant JzPfR (8 sqns). Artillery 1 x HAB, 1 x FAB. **Württemberg losses** 14 killed, 164 wounded, 19 missing.

Allied grand totals 11 bns, 12 sqns, ca 5,000 men.

Total Allied losses 17 officers and 333 men killed wounded and missing.

Prussian Garrison Obstlt Count von Götzen: IR von Kropff Nr 31 (1,290), 3rd Musk Bn IR von Grawert Nr 47 (1,000), gunners, miners and invalides (700), stragglers and volunteers (1,000), Jägers (80), 8 x Schützen coys (600 en), 6 cavalry squadrons (850 men).

Prussian totals ca 6,570 men.

Prussian losses 18 officers, and 821 men, 34 guns.

Sources Höpfner, Lettow-Vorbeck, Leyh.

PS Silberberg (now Srebrna Gora), 28 and 29 June 1807, bombardment of

A fortress in Prussian Silesia (now Poland), midway between Glatz (Klodzko) in the south of Schweidnitz (Swidnica) in the north.

A Prussian victory over the Bavarians.

(Last action – Glatz, 24 June; next action – Kosel 14 July.)

Bavarian Forces GL von Deroy commanding: LIRs Nrs 1, 6 and 10 (2 bns each). 1st DragR and 2nd ChLR (4 sqns each), 2 x FAB.

Bavarian totals ca 6,500 men.

Bavarian losses None.

Prussian Garrison Line infantry (1,200), 3 x Schützen coys (450); 3 x sqns (215), gunners (400), stragglers, etc.

Prussian totals 2,225 men and 215 horses.

Prussian losses Not known, light.

Comment Silberberg was the only Prussian fortress in Silesia which did not capitulate.

Sources Höpfner, Lettow-Vorbeck, Leyh.

OP Colberg (now Kolobrzeg), 20 March – 2 July 1807, blockade and siege of

A fortified harbour in Prussian Pommerania (now Poland) at the mouth of the River Persante (now Parseta) on the Baltic coast.

A Prussian victory over the French and their allies.

(Last action – Friedland and Königsberg, 14 June; next action – Stralsund, 20 August.)

French and Allied Forces M Mortier commanding the VIII Corps: GdD Loison. **French Regiments** Füsilier Grenadiers and Füsilier Chasseurs of the Imperial Guard (Gen Saváry): 3e RILé (1st Bn); 19e, 72e and 93e RIdLi (5 bns); 3e and 15e ChàCh (8 sqns); DragR (1 sqn); Gendarmes d'Ordonnance (2 coys). **Dutch Regiments** Gen Grandjean: 2nd and 7th LIR (2 bns each); 4th and 8th LIR (2 bns each); 1st and 2nd LtIRs (2 bns each); 1st and 2nd HusRs (4 sqns). **Italian Regiments** Gen Teulie: 1st and 2nd LtIRs (1 bn each); 1st and 4th LIRs (2 bns each). Dragoni Regina, Dragoni Napoleone, Cacciatori Reali Italiani. **Polish Regiments** 1st LIR (2 bns). **Confederation of the Rhine Regiments** 4th IR of the Confederation (Ducal Saxon) (2 bns); IR Nassau (2nd, 3rd and 4th Bns); Württemberg LIBns von Seckendorf and von Romig.

Allied totals ca 14,000 men and 41 guns.

Allied losses GdD Teulie killed; 1 general wounded, 102 officers and 5,000 men killed and wounded or died of sickness.

Prussian Forces Initially Obst von Loucadou, as of May under Maj von Gneisenau: GrenBn von Waldenfels (4 coys); FüsBn Möller (1 bn); 2nd Pommeranian ResIBn; 3rd Neumark ResIBn, LtIBn von Schill (1 bn); IR von Owstein Nr 7 (3rd Bn); IR vac von Borke Nr 30 (3rd Bn); CavR von Schill (5 sqns).

Prussian totals ca 6,000 men and 230 guns.

Prussian losses 55 officers and 3,000 men killed, wounded and died of sickness.

Comment The Prussian garrison carried out an energetic and aggressive defence, thus forming one of the few bright spots of this campaign for this vanquished army.

Sources Höpfner, Lettow-Vorbeck, Martinien.

PS Kosel (now Kedzierzyn-Kozle), 24 January – 2 July 1807, blockade and siege of

A fortress in Prussian Silesia (now Poland) on the River Oder (now Odra) 40 km southeast of Oppeln (now Opole) on Route 49.

A Prussian victory over the Bavarians.

(Last action – Silberberg, 29 June; next action – this was the last action in Silesia in 1807.)

Bavarian Forces Initially GL von Deroy and finally GM von Raglovich commanding the 1st Division: GM Raglovich: 4th and 5th LIR (2 bns each); Jägers (2 coys), 1 x 6 pdr FAB. GM von Siebein: 1st and 10th LIR (2 bns each); 6th LtIBn (1 bn); 1 x 6 pdr FAB.

Bavarian totals 5½ bns, 2 x FAB, ca 6,000 men.

Bavarian losses 36 dead and wounded.

Prussian Garrison Initially Obst von Neumann (67 years old) commanding; after his death (on 16 April) Obst von Puttkammer: 3rd Musk, Bns of IR von Sanitz Nr 50 and von Pelchrzim Nr 38 (ca 2,000 men), stragglers and volunteers (1,480); invalides (107); gunners and miners (294); the depots of DragR von Osten Nr 12 (75) and KürR von Bünting Nr 12 (162); Jägers (60).

Prussian totals ca 4,300 men and 229 guns, many of the gun carriages were rotten. The fortress was designed for a garrison of 6,000 men.

Prussian losses ca 3,200 men killed, wounded and died of sickness.

Comment The fortress held out until arrival of news of the Peace of Tilsit when the Bavarians withdrew.

Sources Höpfner, Lettow-Vorbeck, Leyh.

OP Stralsund, 15 January – 20 August 1807, blockade siege and capitulation of

A Swedish fortress port on the Pommeranian coast of the Baltic Sea, opposite the island of Rügen and at the junction of Route B105/E22, B194 and B96A/E251.

A French victory over the Swedes.

(Last action – Colberg, 2 July; next action – Dänholm 25 August.)

French Forces M Brune commanding: GdD Boudet: 3eRILé and 93eRIdLi (7 bns, 7,773 infantry, 200 artillery). GdD Molitor: 2e, 16e and 67e RidLi (8 bns, 8,712 infantry, 205 artillery). GdD Dumonceau (**Dutch troops**): 3rd JgR, 3rd, 4th, 6th and 9th LIRs (11 bns, 9,924 infantry, 570 artillery). GdD Gratien (Dutch troops): 2nd, 7th and 5th LIRs (6 bns, 3,932 infantry, 159 artillery). GdD Carteret: 3rd Dutch HusR, Belgian ChLR Ahremberg, Gendarmerie (5 sqns, 1,112 cavalry). **Spanish Divisions*** of Gen Marqués de la Romana and Gen O'Farill: LIRs Asturias, Guadalajara, Princesa and Zamora (3 bns each), LtI Bns: 1st Barcelona and 1st Catalonia (1 bn each); CavRs: 1st Reg, 4th Infante, 9th Algarve. Light Cavalry (Cazadores): 3rd Alamanza, 5th Villaviciosa, 4 x FAB, engineers (1 coy). **Spanish totals** 14 bns, 9,763 infantry, 12 sqns, 2,340 cavalry, 324 artillery, 104 engineers.

Baden Troops* IRs Grossherzog, Erbgrossherzog, Markgraf Ludwig (2 bns each), HusR (1 sqn), 1 x FAB, **Würzburg IR*** (2 bns), **1st Berg** IR* (2 bns), **Nassau IR*** (2nd, 3rd, 4th Bns). GdD Pino's **Italians***: 1st and 4th LIRs, 1st and 2nd LtIRs (2 bns each). DragRs de la Reine and Napoleone (4 sqns each), 2 x FAB, 1 x HAB.

Allied total ca 40,000 men at the end of the action.

Allied losses 38 officers and 960 men killed, wounded missing and died of sickness.

Swedish Forces GL Essen commanding: GL Armfelt, GM Vegesack; GM Peyron: Leib-R der Königin; IR von Engelbrechten (1 bn each); Pommeranian Landwehr garrison troops and artillery; three Finnish battalions.

Swedish totals 15,000 men and 500 guns.

Swedish losses Not known exactly.

Comment When the Swedish king saw that his defence (alone against Napoleon) was hopeless, the Swedes spiked the guns left in the fortress, destroyed the gun-carriages and evacuated the powder and ammunition to Rügen before leaving.

Sources Höpfner, Lettow-Vorbeck, Martinien, Oman.

*Arrived early July 1807 from Colberg.

OP Dänholm, 25 August 1807, clash

A small fortified island (now joined to the Island of Rügen) in the Strelasund between Stralsund and Rügen in the Baltic Sea. It acts as a causeway for the Route B96/E22/E251 onto the latter island.

A French victory over the Swedes.

(Last action – Stralsund, 20 August; next action – Graudenz, 12 December.)

French Forces French Naval Captain Montcabrié and GdB Fririon commanding: 30e RILé (1 bn); an artillery detachment, mineurs and pontonniers (1 coy each); sapeurs (3 coys) and a detachment of sailors of the Imperial Guard.

French totals ca 1,200 men and 2 guns.

French losses 15 dead and 26 wounded.

Swedish Forces ca 800 men, mainly garrison troops and artillery. Several gun boats.

Swedish totals ca 900 men and 14 guns.

Swedish losses 50 killed, 75 wounded, 17 officers and 500 men captured, 6 field guns and 8 fortress guns.

Sources Höpfner, Lettow-Vorbeck, Martinien.

DK Kiøge, 29 August 1807, clash

A village on the eastern coast of the Danish island of Sjaelland (Zealand), about 32 km southwest of Copenhagen.

A British victory over the Danes.

(Last action – this was the first real clash of the campaign; next action – bombardment of Copenhagen, 2–5 September 1807.)

Danish Forces LG von Castenschiold commanding: GM P L Oxholm; Nordre Sjaelandske Landevaernsregiment (5th, 6th and 7th Bns); Sondre Sjaelandske Landevaernsregiment (1st, 2nd, 4th, 5th, 7th, 8th, 9th and 10th Bns); Sjaelandske Rytterregiment (70 men); Landryttern (80 men), 9 guns.

Danish totals 11 bns, ca 7,000 infantry, 2 sqns, 150 cavalry, 9 guns, ca 120 artillery, ca 7,270 men.

Danish losses 2 officers and 150 men dead, 4 officers and 200 men wounded; GM Oxholm 9 majors, 19 captains, 28 lieutenants and over 1,700 men captured; 9 guns, 1 battalion colour and 68 waggons with ammunition, weapons and equipment.

British Forces MG Sir Arthur Wellesley commanding: Col von Linsingen (KGL) 43rd Foot (1st Bn); 52nd Foot (2nd Bn); 92nd Foot (1stBn); 95th Foot (5 coys each of 1st and 2nd Bns); 6th Bn KGL (1 bn); 1st, 2nd and 3rd HusR KGL (3 sqns each); 1 x British HAB (Newhouse's); ½ x HAB (Sympher's, KGL).

British totals 5 bns, 6,000 infantry, 9 sqns, 1,620 cavalry, 350 artillery, 8 x 6 pdr cannon and 2 x 5½ inch howitzers.

British losses (from 16 to 31 August) 2 officers and 27 men dead, 6 officers and 116 men wounded, 21 men missing.

Comment The unfortunate Danes were no match for the experienced British and KGL. This action broke the back of the Danish field forces and ensured that the siege of Copenhagen would not be disturbed. This action forced Denmark to become an ally of France.

Sources Fortescue, Schwertfeger, Hedegaard (E.O.A. 'Krijgen pa Sjaelland 1807', Helsingor 1970).

DK Copenhagen, 2–5 September 1807, bombardment and capitulation of

The capital city of Denmark (and a major port) on the eastern coast of the island of Sjaelland, on the Öre-Sund opposite Malmö in southern Sweden and commanding the major entry into the Baltic Sea from the North Sea.

A British victory over the Danes.

(Last action – Kioge, 29 August; this was the end of the Danish adventure.)

Danish Forces GM von Peymann commanding Copenhagen garrison. The Danish fleet was not ready for sea and was concentrated in the city's harbour: 20 ships of the line, 17 frigates, 12 brigs, 24 sloops and 24 other vessels. Three more ships of the line were nearing completion in the dockyard.

Danish totals Approximately 5,000 soldiers and militia.

Danish losses Army: 135 dead, 300 wounded. Navy: 53 dead, 53 wounded. Civilians in Copenhagen: 1,600 dead, over 1,000 wounded. 16 ships of the line, 10 frigates, 8 brigs and 30 other vessels were taken by the British. 25 of these vessels were lost in a storm at sea en route for England; only 4 of the ships of the line were taken into British service.

Eight Danish ships of the line were destroyed in the dockyard as were 3 blockships and 3 gun prams. The new Congreve rockets were used to great effect.

British Forces Admiral Gambier commanding the fleet: 29 ships of the line, 43 frigates, 10 brigs. LG Lord Cathcart commanding the army contingent: 1st/Coldstream Gds, 1st/3rd Gds. Line Infantry; 1st/4th, 1st/7th, 1st/8th, 1st/28th, 1st/32nd, 1st/43rd, 1st/50th, 2nd/52nd, 1st/79th, 1st/82nd, 1st/92nd, 1st/95th, 2nd/95th.

British total 15 bns, 6 x FAB.

King's German Legion: 1st and 2nd LtIBns, 1st–8th LiBns, 1st and 2nd LtDrag.

King's German Legion total 10 bns, 8 sqns, 2 x HAB, 2 x FAB.

British losses 42 killed, 145 wounded, 24 missing.

Comment This operation had been kept a secret and surprised Europe. The British had assembled the expedition originally to operate together with the Swedes on Napoleon's northern flank but the French victory at Friedland nullified this plan.

Determined to prevent the Danish fleet from falling into French hands, this raid was mounted – a forerunner of the destruction by the British of the French fleet in Oran on 3 July 1940. The British fleet did not get heavily involved.

Sources Fortescue, Beamish.

OP Graudenz (now Grudziadz), 22 January - 12 December 1807 blockade and siege of

A fortified city on the eastern bank fo the River Vistula (Wisla), about 90 km south of Danzig (now Gdansk) in Poland on Route 16.

A Prussian victory over the Allies.

(Last action - Dänholm, 25 August; this was the last action of the campaign.)

Allied Forces Initially GdD Rouyer; after the fall of Danzig (24 May) GdD Victor.

Hessen-Darmstadt contingent: Leibgarde-Brigade (3 bns); Leib-Brigade (3 bns); ChLR (1 sqn); 1 x FAB (8 guns). **1st LIR of Berg; IR Würzburg** (2 bns each). **Polish Troops** GdD Zuyaczek: the Légion du Nord (6 bns, 8 sqns, 6 guns).

Allied totals 11 bns, ca 7,000 men.

Allied losses Not known, light.

Prussian Forces GdI l'Homme de Courbière (73 years old) commanding: IR vac von Besser Nr 14 (2nd Bn); the 3rd Bns of IRs von Manstein Nr 55, von Natzmer Nr 54, Jung-Larisch Nr 53, von Hamberger Nr 52, FüsBn Borell Nr 9 (1 bn); FüsBn von Knorr Nr 12 (depot); Jägers (1 coy); HusR von Blücher Nr 8 (a remount commando); the invalide companies of IR Jung-Larisch and von Manstein.

Prussian totals ca 4,500 men and 152 guns.

Prussian losses Not known.

Comment As many of the regiments of the garrison were recruited from the ex-Polish areas, desertion among them was high. In early September, 472 Poles, now subjects of the Grand Duchy of Warsaw, were released from the fortress. Despite the end of the war in July; the blockade of this place continued and lasted almost a year, but the garrison held out until the besiegers gave up and moved away.

Sources Höpfner, Lettow-Vorbeck, Martinien.

1808

1808 THE ACTIONS

XX Sveaborg, 6 April 1808, capitulation

An island fortress 6 km southeast of Helsinki (capital of Finland) in the Gulf of Finland.

A Russian victory over the Swedes.

(This was the opening action of the campaign; next action – Sandöström, 2 August.)

Swedish Garrison Vice Admiral Baron Cronstedt commanding 7,000 men.

Swedish losses 150 killed and wounded, the rest captured together with large stocks of war materials of all sorts and the entire Swedish inshore fleet.

Russian Forces 3,000 men.

Russian losses Not known but very light.

Comment The fall of this fortress, 'the Gibraltar of the North', in such a shameful way dealt a crushing blow to Swedish morale and let to the abandonment of Finland to Russia.

EN El Bruch Pass, 4 June 1808, skirmish

A mountain pass in southern Catalonia (north eastern Spain), on Route II, between Barcelona and Igualada.

A Spanish victory over the French.

(This was the opening action of the campaign here; next action – El Bruch, 15 June.)

French Forces GdB Schwartz commanding part of GdD Duhesme's Corps of Observation of the Eastern Pyrenees: 2nd Swiss IR (3e Bn); 1st Neapolitan LIR (2 bns); 1st Italian Vélites (1st Bn); 3e Pv Cuir R (1 sqn).

French total 3,247 men and 4 guns.

French losses Not exactly known but light; 1 gun was abandoned at the Abrera river.

Spanish Forces Initially only the 'Somatenes' (Home Guard) of Manresa (3–400 men) who were then joined by those of San Pedor and other villages of the Upper Llobregat area.

Spanish total Not known; probably several hundred.

Spanish losses Not known but extremely light.

Comment This tiny success raised Spanish spirits and caused similar resistance to break out against the French in surrounding areas of Catalonia.

Source Oman.

ES Alcolea, 7 June 1808, clash

A village on the north bank of the Rio Guadalquivir in the southern Spanish province of Andalusia, on Route IV/E5, 10 km northeast of the city of Cordoba.

A French victory over the Spanish.

(This was the first action of note in this region; next action – Bailén, 19–22 July.)

French Forces GdD Dupont commanding: Sailors of the Imperial Guard (1 bn); Légions de Reserve (6 bns); GdN de Paris (2 bns); 4th Swiss (2nd Bn); Swiss Regiments of Reding the Elder and Preux (4 bns taken over from the Spanish service); Prov Drag (4 rgts); 12 guns.

French total ca 13,000 men.

French losses 30 killed, 80 wounded.

Spanish Forces Col Don Pedro de Echávarri commanding: LtIR Campo Mayor (½ bn); Swiss IR Reding the Younger (2 coys); Granaderos Provinciales (2 bns); Dragones de la Reina (1 sqn) and 8 guns, ca 1,400 soldiers plus 5,000 armed citizens.

Spanish losses About 200 men killed, wounded and captured, 8 guns.

Comment Dupont's task was to subdue Andalusia and to seize the Spanish naval arsenal at Cartagena in Murcia on the eastern coast. After winning this action, Dupont took Cordoba, looted it and left nine days later with 500 carts filled with his plunder. This caused the entire area to rise in revolt; Dupont withdrew to Andujar, 80 km eastwards towards Bailén with his loot and waited for General Vedel's division to come south from Madrid to reinforce him. His communications with the capital were continuously being cut.

Sources Oman, Napier, Martinien.

EE Rio Cabriel, 14 June 1808, skirmish

Nowadays 'Puento de contreras' in the eastern Spanish province of Valencia where Route III/E901 crosses the Rio Cabriel between Motilla del Palancar (in the west) and Requena.

A French victory over the Spanish.

(This was the first action of note in this region; next action – Valencia, 28 June.)

French Forces M Moncey commanding 'The Corps of Observation of the Ocean Coast'.

Only the Advanced Guard was closely engaged; exact details not known.

French losses Not exactly known; very light.

Spanish Forces Traxler's Swiss IR (1st Bn); 500 armed peasants, 4 guns, ca 1,100 men.

Spanish losses Killed and wounded unknown, light. Half Traxler's Swiss were captured and taken into

King Joseph's service only to desert at the first opportunity. 4 guns.

Comment The Spanish had not expected a French advance along this difficult route and were taken by surprise. The French forded the river at unwatched places each side of the bridge and the Spanish peasants panicked and fled. The Spanish commander at Requena, Don Pedro Adorno, abandoned the reserve blocking position there and fell back south to join the main army at Almansa thus leaving the way clear for the French to advance to Valencia, brushing aside resistance in the Bavrilla mountains on 24 June.

Sources Oman, Napier, Martinien.

EN El Bruch Pass, 15 June 1808, clash

A mountain pass in southern Catalonia (northeastern Spain), on Route II, between Barcelona and Igualada.

A Spanish victory over the French and their Allies.

(Last action – El Bruch, 4 June; next action – Zaragoza, 15 June.)

French and Allied Forces GdD Chabran of GdD Duhesme's Corps of Observation of the East Pyrenees: GdB Goulas: 7e RIdLi (1er and 2e Bns); 16e RIdLi (3e Bn). GdB Schwartz: 2nd Swiss IR (3e Bn); 1st Italian Vélites (1st Bn); 1 x FAB.

French and Allied total ca 3,600 men.

French and Allied losses ca 400 killed, wounded and missing.

Spanish Forces Somatenes of the Upper Llobregat region and 400 regular troops from Lleida.

Spanish total Some thousands.

Spanish losses Not exactly known but very light.

Comment Chabran had occupied Tarragona before being recalled to Barcelona by Duhesme on 9 June. The coastal Somatenes tried to emulate their mountain brethren but foolishly came out into the open trying to stop Chabran's withdrawal; were easily beaten and scattered. The French then sacked every village along their route to Barcelona with great brutality.

Source Oman.

EN Zaragoza, 15 June 1808, clash

A city with medieval fortifications on the south bank of the Rio Ebro in Aragon, northern Spain, at the junction of Routes 330/E7, II/E90 and A2/E804. The capital of Aragon.

A Spanish victory over the French and their allies.

(Last action – El Bruch Pass, 15 June; next action – Mataro, 17 June.)

French and Allied Forces GdD Lefebvre-Desnouettes (of Bessières Corps of Observation of the Pyrenees) commanding: 15e, 47e and 70e RIdLi (1 bn each); 2e Supplementary R of the Légion de Réserve (2 bns); Lancers of the Vistula Legion (4 sqns); Escuadrón de Marche (1 sqn); 1st IR, Vistula Legion (2 bns); 6e bn de Marche (1 bn); 2 x FAB.

French totals 8 bns, 5 sqns, 12 guns, ca 6,000 men.

French losses 700 killed and wounded, 4 guns.

Spanish Forces BG José Palafox commanding: Voluntarios de Aragon (1 bn); 500 deserters from various infantry regiments; DragR 'Rey' (300 men); the citizens of Zaragoza, 24 guns.

Spanish losses 300 killed and wounded.

Comment Having pushed the Marquis of Lazan's* weak forces aside at Tudela on 8 June and Alagon on 12 June, Lefebvre-Desnouettes swaggered up to Zaragoza this day expecting to have the place handed to him on a plate. He received a bloody surprise. Palafox had himself proclaimed 'Captain General'.

The first siege of Zaragoza began.

Sources Oman, Napier, Gembarzewski, Martinien.

* = Lazan was Palafox's elder brother.

EN Mataro, 17 June 1808, storm

A coastal town in northeastern Spain, 13 km along Route II/A19 northeast of Barcelona.

A French and Allied victory over the Spanish.

(Last action – Zaragoza, 15 June; next action – Girona, 20 June.)

French and Allied Forces GdD Duhesme's Corps of Observation of the East Pyrenees: GdB Milosewitz: 2nd Italian Line (2nd Bn); 4th Italian Line (3rd Bn); 5th Italian Line (2nd Bn). (2,133 men). GdB Schwartz: 1st Neapolitan LIR (1st and 2nd Bns); 1st Italian Vélites (1st Bn). (2,163 men). Cavalry: 3e Pv CuirR (409 men); 3e Pv ChàCh (416 men); Italian ChàCh (504 men); 2nd Neapolitan ChàCh (388 men). (1,517 sabres).

French total ca 5,963 men, 8 guns.

French losses Not exactly known but minimal.

Spanish Forces About 10,000 Somatenes, 3–4 guns.

Spanish losses Not exactly known.

Comment Duhesme, alarmed at the flare-up of

Spanish hostility now marched north from Barcelona on Girona to re-open communications with France. The Somatenes were easily scattered; Mataro tried to defend itself against the invaders and the town was sacked for a period of 24 hours.

Source Oman.

EN Girona, 20 June 1808, failed storm

A fortified medieval town in northeastern Spain, on Route II, just east of the motorway A7/E15, midway between the French border and Barcelona.

A Spanish victory over the French and their Allies.

(Last action – Mataro, 17 June; next action – Épila, 23/24 June.)

French and Allied Forces GdD Duhesme's Corps of Observation of the East Pyrenees as for Mataro, 17 June.

French total ca 5,900 men, 8 guns.

French losses 700 killed, wounded and missing.

Spanish Forces LtCols O'Donovan and O'Daly commanding two battalions of the Irish IR Ultonia (350 men); some artillerymen, 1,600 armed citizens.

Spanish total ca 2,000 men.

Spanish losses Not known exactly but very light.

Comment Duhesme tried force and cunning to break into the town on three or four occasions; all failed. He returned to Barcelona.

Source Oman.

EN Épila, 23/24 June 1808, clash

A village in the northern Spanish province of Aragon, about 50 km southwest of Zaragoza, about 2 km east of the Rio Jalon and 35 km south of the Rio Ebro.

A French and Allied victory over the Spanish.

(Last action – Girona, 20 June; next action – Rosas, 11 July.)

French and Allied Forces Col Chlopiski commanding: 1st IR Vistula Legion (2 bns); 2e Supplementary R of the Légion de Réserve (1 bn); Lancers of the Vistula Legion (1 sqn); 4 guns, ca 2,500 men.

French losses Not known, very light.

Spanish Forces Capt Gen Joseph Palafox commanding: IR Ferdinand VII, 2nd of Aragon; 550 regular deserters from captured/disbanded regiments, DragR 'Rey' (350 men); 80 armed Capuchin monks, a gang of mounted smugglers and over 1,000 volunteers (mainly unarmed).

Spanish total ca 2,200 men.

Spanish losses Several hundred men.

Comment Palafox was advancing with his band of enthusiasts to threaten French communications northwestwards to Logroño and Vittoria. The French commander learned of his presence and mounted this pre-emptive strike. Palafox learned his lesson and avoided pitched battles in future.

Sources Oman, Napier, Gembarzewski, Martinien.

EE Valencia, 28 June 1808, clash

A fortified city, capital of the eastern Spanish province of the same name, at the mouth of the Rio Turia and at the junction of Routes III/E901, A7/E15 and 340.

A Spanish victory over the French.

(Last action – Rio Cabriel, 14 June; next action – Mougat, 31 July.)

French Forces M Moncey commanding the 'Corps of the Observation of the Ocean Coast'. **1st Division** GdD Musnier; GdBs Brun and Isenburg: 1er, 2e, 3e and 4e Prov. IRs (4 bns each); Westphalien Bn (1 bn). **Totals** 17 bns, ca 9,600 men. **2nd Division** GdD Gobert; GdBs Lefranc and Dufour: 5e, 6e, 7e and 8e Prov. IRs (4 bns each); Irish Legion (1 bn). **Total** 17 bns, 8,300 men. **3rd Division** GdD Morlot; GdBs Bujet and Lefebvre: 9e, 10e and 11e Prov. IRs (4 bns each); R Preusse (1 bn). **Total** 13 bns, 7,000 men. **Cavalry** GdD Grouchy; GdB Privé and Wathier: 1er and 2e Prov DragR; 1er and 2e Prov HusR (12 sqns).**Total cavalry** 2,850 men. **Artillery** 6 x FAB, 2 x HAB, (1,250 men).

French totals 47 bns, 24,900 infantry, 12 sqns, 2,850 cavalry, 48 guns, 1,250 gunners.

French losses 1,200 men killed and wounded.

Spanish Forces Admiral Don José Caro commanding: 1,500 regulars. 6,500 new levies. 12,000 armed citizens.

Spanish totals 20,000 men.

Spanish losses Not known, very light.

Comment The morale of the new French conscripts in the Provisional infantry regiments was not good. Two assaults on the town were beaten off and the whole countryside began to rise against the French. Moncey pulled out on the morning of 29 June, taking the longer but easier route back to Madrid, southwards via Almansa and Albacete thus, unknowingly, avoiding a large Spanish blocking force under General Llamas on the route by which he had come, at the defile of the Cabrillas River.

Sources Oman, Napier.

EN Rosas, 11 July 1808, failed storm

A fortified port in northeastern Spain, about 15 km south of the border with France.

A Spanish victory over the French.

(Last action – Épila, 23/24 June; next action – Zaragoza, 14 August.)

French Forces GdD Reille commanding: 113e RIdLi (2 bns); 2e Swiss (2 coys); GdN Pyrénées Orientales (560 men); Gendarmie and Departmental Reserves (ca 700 men) and some other March units and reinforcement drafts.

French total 4,000 men, 2 guns.

French losses 200 killed and captured.

Spanish Forces Miqueletes* (400), 5 guns in the town; Captain Don Juan Claros with 5,000 Somatenes in the French rear.

Spanish total ca 5,400 men, 5 guns.

Spanish losses Not known exactly but light.

Comment Rosas blocked the coast road from France to Barcelona. Napoleon had ordered Reille to clear the road and re-open communications with Barcelona. The Spanish were aided by the appearance of HMS *Montague* (74 guns) which landed marines in the harbour.

Source Oman.

* = Miqueletes – a levy en masse of the population, raised and paid at a provincial (not a central government) level. Named after Miquelot de Prats, a Catalan condottiere (mercenary commander) who served under Caesar Borgia in the War of the Spanish Succession, 1701-1714.

EW Valladolid (Cabezon), 12 July 1808, clash

A village in the valley of the Rio Arlanzón, northeast of Valladolid (not to be found on some modern maps), along the Route 620/E80 towards Palencia in Castilla Leon in north western Spain.

A French victory over the Spanish.

(This was the first action in this region; next action – Medina del Rioseco, 14 July.)

French Forces (of M Bessières Corps of Observation of the Pyrenees).

GdD Merle GdB Darmagnac, Gaulois: 47e RIdLi (1er Bn); 86e RIdLi (2 coys); 3e Swiss (2nd Bn); 1er R de Marche (2 bns); 1st Supplementary Légion de Réserve (2 bns). **Total** 6 bns, 2 coys, ca 52,600 men. 2 x FAB. **GdD Lasalle** 10e and 22e ChàCh (3 sqns each); Escadron de Marche (1 sqn of Cuirassiers). **Total** 7 sqns, 1 x HAB and 4 bns.

French totals 10 bns, 2 coys, 7 sqns, 18 guns.

French losses 12 killed, 30 wounded.

Spanish Forces Gen Cuesta commanding the Army of Castile. 4–5,000 Volunteers of the Valladolid area and about 400 cavalry, 4 guns.

Spanish losses Several hundred men and 4 guns.

Comment Cuesta's infantry had only been under arms for four weeks but clamoured for him to lead them into battle. Incredibly, Cuesta formed his infantry up in one line with the major obstacle of the river behind him with only one bridge available for retreat. The action was over briefly, the Spanish scattered and the French occupied Valladolid that night. Bessières' right flank was now secured for his further advance on Medina del Rioseco.

Sources Oman, Napier.

EW Medina del Rioseco, 14 July 1808, battle

A small town in the northwestern Spanish province of Castilla-Leon, 40 km northwest of Valladolid on Route 601 towards Leon. It lies on the north bank of the Rio Sequillo.

A French victory over the Spanish.

(Last action – Cabezon, 12 July; this was the last action of note in this region in 1808.)

French Forces M Bessières commanding: 1er Fusiliers of the Imperial Guard (3 bns); 1er ChLR of the Imperial Guard (3 sqns). GdB Ducos: 13e Prov IR (4 bns); 14e Prov IR (1 bn). GdB Sabathier: 17e and 18e Prov IRs (4 bns each). GdB d'Armagnac: 47e RIdLi (1 bn); 3e Swiss (1 bn). GdD Mouton, GdB Reynaud: 4e RILé (3 bns); 15e RIdLi (2 bns). GdB Lasalle; 10e and 22e ChàCh (3 sqns each).

French totals 13,700 men, 30 guns.

French losses About 1,100 killed and wounded were initially claimed but this figure seems now to be too high.

Spanish Forces Captain General Don G de la Cuesta commanding the Army of Castile. Six battalions of new Castilian Levies, IR Covadonga (2 bns) from Asturia. 350 cavalry.

The 'Army of Galicia' General Blake: **Vanguard** BG Mendizabal: 2nd Catalonian* LtIR (1 bn); Voluntarios de Navarra* (1 bn); combined grenadiers* (2 bns); Zaragoza* (1 bn); sappers* (1 coy). **Total** 2,187 men. **1st Division** Gen Cagigal: Rey* (2 bns); Majorca*, Hibernica*, combined light companies* (1 bn); Mondonedo, 'Batallon Literario' (1 bn each). **Total** 6,470 men. **4th Division** Gen Marquis Portago: Barbastro Lt*I (1 bn); Principe*; Toledo*; combined grenadiers* (2 bns each); Aragon*, Lugo, Santiago (1 bn each). **Total** 5,818 men. **Artillery** 20 guns.

Spanish totals ca 21,000 infantry, 350 cavalry, 20 guns.

Spanish losses 1,050 killed and wounded, 1,200 captured, 1,000 missing, 10 guns, 10 colours.

* = regiments of the old army; all other units were new levies, or old provincial militia.

Comment Cuesta's battlefield dispositions were so faulty as to be classified as criminally inept. Despite the poor quality of much of his infantry, his almost total lack of cavalry and his weak artillery, he divided his force by over 1.6 km in open terrain so that mutual support, and even visual contact, was impossible. Blake, with his Vanguard and 1st Galician Division were placed to the right front on a slight hill with their left flank wide open. Cuesta, the Army of Castile and the 4th Galician Division were in rear with the defile of the deep, steep-sided bed of the Rio Sequillo and the town of Medina del Rioseco, and only one available bridge, directly behind them.

Bessières saw these blindingly obvious errors; held Cuesta in check with part of Mouton's division and crushed Blake in isolation. The Spanish centre (4th Galician Division) tried to advance to support him but Cuesta's Army of Castile lost only 155 killed and wounded. The French did not pursue past the town, settling down to their usual session of rape, pillage, murder and drunkenness. Blake, totally enraged, withdrew westwards into Galicia again. Cuesta fell back north into Leon and Asturias. The threat to French communications between Bayonne and Madrid had been removed; King Joseph entered Madrid in triumph, the Army of Galicia and that of Castile were out of action for several weeks and the prospects for any effective cooperation between the armies of the Supreme Junta had received a severe setback.

Sources Oman, Napier, Martinien, Kausler, Bodart.

ES Bailén, 19–22 July 1808, battle and capitulation

A town in the southern Spanish province of Andalusia, about 10 km north of the Rio Guadalquivir at the crossing of Routes IV/E5, 322 and 323.

A Spanish victory over the French.

(Last action – Alcolea 7 June; next action – this was the last action of note in this region in 1808.)

French Forces GdD Dupont commanding the 2nd Corps of Observation of the Gironde:

1st Division GdD Barbou; GdB Chabert: 4e Légion de Réserve (3 bns); 3e Légion de Réserve (2 bns). GdN Paris (2 bns); 4e Swiss (2nd Bn); Sailors of the Imperial Guard (1 bn). **Total** 9 bns, ca 6,800 men. GdB Schramm: Reding the Elders' Swiss* (2 bns); Preux's Swiss* (2 bns); (ca 2,000 men). **Light Cavalry** GdD Fresia: GdB Privé: 1er and 2e Prov CuirRs (1,459 men); 6e Prov DragR (623 men); GdB Dupré: 1er and 2e ChàCh (1,179 men) **Total cavalry** 3,261. **2nd Division** GdD Vedel; GdB Poinsot: 5e Légion de Réserve (3 bns); 3e Swiss (1er Bn). GdB Cassagne: 1ère Légion de Réserve (3 bns). GdD Gobert: 6e, 7e and 8e Prov IRs (12 bns); 2e Prov CuirR (3 sqns). **Artillery** 36 guns.

French totals ca 22,000 men and 36 guns.

* = these regiments were mercenaries in Spanish service who had been 'co-opted' into French service. During the battle they threw up the butts of their muskets (a signal that they would not fire) and marched over to rejoin the Spanish.

French losses About 3,000 killed and wounded including GdD Gobert mortally wounded at Menjibar, GdB Dupré killed, GdD Dupont and GdB Schramm wounded in actions of 19th; 18,000 captured on 22 July together with 36 guns and all their colours. The Swiss lost their colours.

Spanish Forces LG Condé Francisco Xavier Castaños commanding: **1st Division** Gen Teodoro Reding: Walloon Gds* (3rd Bn); Reyna*; Corona*; Jaén* (1 bn each); Irlanda* (3 bns); Reding the Younger or 3rd Swiss* (1 bn); Barbastro* (½ bn); Jaén; 1st de Granada, Tejas and Cazadores de Antequera (1 bn each). **Total** 8,453 men. **Attached Cavalry** Montesa*, Farnesio*, Dragones de la Reina* and Numancia, Cazadores de Olivencia*; Lanceros de Utrera, Lanceros de Jerez. **Total** 900 men. **Artillery** 1 x FAB* (4 guns); 1 x HAB* (6 guns). Sappers* (2 coys) – 200 men. **1st Division total** 9,719 men. **2nd Division** MG Marquis Coupigny: Ceuta* (2 bns); Ordenes Militares* (3 bns); Granada (1 bn); Truxillo (½ bn); Voluntarios de Catalonia (1 bn each). **Total** 7,229 men. **Attached Cavalry** Borbon*; Espana* **Total** 521 men. **Artillery** 1 x HAB* (6 guns). Sappers (1 coy) - 200 men. **2nd Division total** 7,950 men.

Spanish totals 15,682 infantry, 1,421 cavalry, 420 artillery, 260 sappers and 16 guns.

* = units so marked were old regiments of the regular army; all others were militia or new levies.

Spanish losses About 1,000 killed and wounded, 1,000 captured, 2 guns and 2 colours (Irlanda 1st Bn and Militia of Jaén). All captured trophies and prisoners were returned as a result of the capitulation as were the 500 carts of loot from Cordoba.

Comment The actual battle was fought on 19 July. General Vedel was some miles north of Dupont, marching down from La Carolina, when the capitulation was signed and Dupont ordered him (secretly) to make good his escape to Madrid with his division. When the Spanish learned of this they threatened to massacre Dupont's men unless Vedel returned, which he then did.

The effects of this unprecedented defeat and capture of an entire French corps by the Spanish were far-reaching:

1. King Joseph evacuated Madrid on 1 August with 23,000 men and fled north 140 km to Aranda de Duero; by 9 August they were at Burgos, 245 km to the north of Madrid.
2. The siege of Girona was raised and French control of Catalonia was disrupted.
3. The siege of Zaragoza was raised and Verdier withdrew up the Ebro to the confluence with the Rio Aragon, north west of Tudela; Aragon was freed.
4. M Bessières withdrew east from Benavente on the Rio Esla (near the Portuguese border) to the area of Burgos on the Rio Arlanzón.
5. Strong French and Allied forces were diverted from central Europe to Spain.
6. Napoleon, all his theoretical plans for the subjugation of the Iberian Peninsula brought to nought by the bungling of his incompetent juniors, stormed into Spain to set matters aright again.

Under the terms of capitulation the French were to have been repatriated by sea to Rochefort and they were marched to the coast for this purpose but very few Spanish ships were available to move them and Lord Collingwood (commanding the Royal Navy squadron off Cadiz) refused to let any ships with Frenchmen aboard leave harbour. Eventually, Dupont, his staff and generals were sent home; most of the men died in captivity on the desolate Balearic island of Cabrera, starved to death.

Sources Oman, Napier, Bodart, Charrié.

PM Evora, 29 July 1808, clash

A town in central Portugal, west of the Rio Xarrama, at the junction of Routes 18, 114 and 256, about 115 km east of Lisboa (Lisbon).

A French victory over the Portuguese and Spanish.

(This was the first action note of the Portuguese uprising against Junot's army of occupation; next action - Roleia, 17 August.)

French Forces GdD Loison commanding: Grenadiers (2 bns); 12e and 15e RILé and 58e RIdLi (3rd Bns in each case); 86e RIdLi (1st and 2nd Bns); Légion Hannovrienne (1er Bn); 4e and 5e Provisional DragR; 8 guns.

French totals 8 bns, 8 sqns, ca 8,800 men.

French losses 90 killed and 200 wounded.

Spanish-Portuguese Forces Gen Leite commanding: 1½ bns of newly raised Portuguese infantry and 1 sqn of cavalry plus Spanish Col Moretti with 1½ bns and the HusR Maria Luisa and 7 guns.

Spanish-Portuguese totals ca 2,900 men and 7 guns.

Spanish-Portuguese losses Estimates vary between 2,000 to 8,000 killed and wounded and include many citizens of Evora who tried to defend their town with its medieval walls.

Comment Loison was marching east from Lisbon to reopen communications with the French armies in Spain which had been cut since that country rose in revolt against the French on 29 May.

Sources Oman, Napier.

EE Mougat, 31 July 1808, clash

A castle on the coast road between Barcelona and Mataró on the Catalan coast in northeastern Spain, about 10 km from Barcelona.

An Allied victory over the Franco-Neapolitans.

(Last action - Valencia, 28 June; next action - Girona, 16 August.)

Franco-Neapolitan Garrison 1st Neapolitan LIR (150 men) and 7 guns.

Franco-Neapolitan losses All captured.

Allied Forces The Spanish Guerrilla leader Francisco Barcelo and 800 miqueletes and HM Frigate *Impérieuse* under Lord Cochrane.

Allied losses Not known; slight.

Comment The Neapolitans surrendered to the British as they knew that the miqueletes would massacre them. Cochrane blew up the castle and the coast road to either side of it thus making it impassable for cavalry, artillery and transport. The bitter war against the French and their allies raged on throughout Catalonia.

Sources Oman, Napier.

XX Sandöström, 2 August 1808, clash

An estuary in southwestern Finland, at the southern end of the Gulf of Bothnia, 40 km north of Hangö, about halfway to Turku (Abo).

A Russian victory over the Swedes.

(Last action – Sveaborg, 6 April; next action – Grönvikssund, 30 August.)

Swedish Forces Rear Admiral Hjelmstjerna commanding 6 galleys, 9 gunboats, 22 sloops of the Coastal Fleet and 2,000 Landwehr infantry.

Swedish losses 393 men killed, wounded and missing, 2 sloops, 6 field guns.

Russian Forces Gen Count Buxhowden commanding 90 sloops and gunboats.

Russian losses 350 men killed, wounded and missing, 20 ships sunk or taken.

Comment The action was fought to prevent Buxhowden's force joining up with 70 more vessels coming north from Hangö.

Sources Stunsail, Anderson.

EN Zaragoza, 15 June – 14 August 1808, 1st siege

The capital city of the northern Spanish province of Aragon, on the south bank of the Rio Ebro, at the junction of Routes 330/E7, II/E90 and A2/E804.

A Spanish victory over the French and their allies.

(Last action – Rosas, 11 July; next action – Lerin, 25/26 October.)

French Forces GdD Verdier commanding the **2nd Division** (of Bessières Corps of Observation of the Pyrenees): 14e Provisional IR (3 bns); 4e and 7e bn de Marche (2 bns); 3rd IR Vistula Legion (2 bns); 5th IR Légion Portugaises (2 bns); GdN Hautes Pyrénées (1 bn); GdN Bas Pyrénées (1 bn); 1 French bn (unidentified); 3e, 5e, 6e, 8e and 9e Escadrons de Marche (5 sqns) **Totals** 12 bns, 5 sqns, 36 guns. **GdD Lefebvre-Desnouettes** 15e, 47e and 70e RIdLi (1 bn each); 1st and 2nd Supplementary R of the Légion de Réserve (4 bns); Lancers of the Vistula Legion (4 sqns); 1st IR Vistula Legion (2 bns); 6e Bn de Marche (1 bn); Légion Portugaises (Caçadores) (½ bn); 14e and 44e RIdLi (2 bns each); 11e Escadron de March (1 sqn); **Totals** 14½ bns, 5 sqns, 24 guns.

French and Allied totals 26½ bns, 10 sqns, 60 guns, 13,500 infantry, 1,500 cavalry, 500 artillery.

French losses 3,500 men killed, wounded and died of sickness, 54 guns, (many of them damaged) were abandoned.

Spanish Forces Capt Gen Joseph Palafox commanding: Voluntarios de Aragon (1 bn); Drag Rey (300 men).

Spanish totals 6,000 recruits, 7,000 armed citizens, 13,000 men and women.

Spanish losses About 3,000 killed and wounded.

Comment The entire city took part wholeheartedly in this defence. The French could never cut off access into Zaragoza from the bridgehead north of the river and reinforcements and supplies were brought in repeatedly. There was vicious house-to-house fighting almost continuously. News of the capitulation of Dupont's French Corps at Bailén (22 July) on 5 August caused the French to lift the siege and to withdraw 160 km northwest up the Ebro to Tudela. Aragon was now largely clear of the enemy.

Sources Oman, Napier, Gembarzewski, Martinien.

EE Girona, 24 July – 16 August 1808, failed siege

A fortified city in Catalonia, northeastern Spain, on the south bank of the Rio Ter where Route II crosses the river.

A Spanish victory over the Italo-Neapolitans.

(Last action – Mougat, 31 July; next action – Rosas, 5 December.)

Italo-Neapolitan Forces GdD Duhesme's Corps of Observation of the Eastern Pyrenees.

GdB Milosewitz (Italians): 2nd LIR (2nd Bn); 4th LIR (3rd Bn); 5th LIR (2nd Bn). GdB ? Italian Vélites (1st Bn); 1st Neapolitan LIR (2 bns-). **Cavalry** GdB Bessières, GdB Schwartz: 3e Provisional CuirR; 3e Provisional ChàCh (3 sqns each); Italian ChàCh (4 sqns); 2nd Neapolitan ChàCh (3 sqns). Artillery: 8 guns. **Totals** 6 bns; ca 4,000 infantry, 13 sqns, ca 1,500 cavalry and 8 guns.

Italo-Neapolitan losses Not exactly known but light.

GdD Reille's Provisional Division 113e RIdLi (2 bns); GdN Pyrénées Orientales (1 bn); 1er and 2e Provisional bns of Perpignan (2 bns); Composite Bn (16e and 32e RIdLi and 2e Swiss); Composite Bn (7e and 93e RIdLi); 5e Légion de Réserve de Grenoble (1 bn); Valais Bn (1 bn); Tuscan DragR (2 sqns); Escadrons de Marche (2 sqns); 2 x FAB. **Totals** 9 bns, 4 sqns, 12 guns, ca 8,300 men plus 9 coys of Gendarmerie and Departmental Reserve Troops. GdB Chabran: 7e RIdLi (1er and 2e bns); 16e RIdLi (3e Bn).

French Grand totals ca 13,000 men.

French losses 75 killed, 196 wounded.

Spanish Forces Col O'Donovan commanding: IR Ultonia (350 men); some gunners and local volunteers – 2,000 men in all in the city plus Conde de Caldagues with 1,000 regular infantry and artillery and 400 miqueletes and 5 guns from without the siege lines.

Spanish losses Not exactly known; light.

Comment Both sides had just received news of the French defeat at Bailén (22 July) and the Spanish were encouraged to mount a 'pincer' attack on the slack allied siege of the place.

It was a complete success; Duhesme's courage melted away and, despite having suffered only light casualties, he ordered Reille to abandon his position and return to Figueras while he buried his siege gun barrels, destroyed his stores and set off for Barcelona, 32 km away, harassed all the way by Milan's somatenes (irregular levies). When he reached the coast at Malgrat his situation become ever worse because Lord Cochrane and the frigate HMS *Impérieuse* blasted him whenever the coast road came into range.

Cochrane had already organized the local guerrillas to blow away the road at vulnerable points and Duhesme soon realized that he had no option but to throw his 8 field guns into the sea, abandon his baggage and to fight his way to Barcelona through the mountains; the survivors of his force staggered into the city on 20 August.

Sources Oman, Napier.

PM Roleia, 17 August 1808, clash

A village near the Portuguese Atlantic coast (not shown on modern maps, possibly 'Amoreira') about 5 km south of Obidos on Route 8 and 14 km east of Peniche.

A British victory over the French.

(This was the first action of any note in Wellesley's Portuguese campaign; last action – Mougat, 31 July; next action – Vimiero, 21 August.)

French Forces GdD Delaborde commanding the 1st Division of General Junot's 1st Corps of Observation of the Gironde (Army of Portugal). 2e and 4e RILé (1 bn each); 70e RIdLi (2 bns); 26e ChàCh (3 sqns) 1 x FAB 6 guns.

French totals 4 bns, 2 sqns, 6 guns, ca 4,765 men.

French losses 600 killed, wounded and captured, 3 guns.

British Forces Gen Sir Arthur Wellesley commanding: 1st/5th, 1st/9th, 1st/29th, 1st/82nd, 5th/60th (1 bn each); 2nd/95th (4 coys).

British totals 4,897 men.

British losses 441 killed, wounded and captured; of these 190 fell in the 1st/29th.

Comment Colonel Lake, commanding the 1st/29th took the bit between his teeth and, instead of skirmishing lightly with the French centre while Wellesley's outflanking columns took them in a pincer grip, he led a determined charge up the ridge into their position during which he was killed; the 1st/9th extracted the rash 1st/29th from a severe situation. The British advance south on Lisbon continued.

Sources Oman, Napier, Robinson, Martinien.

PM Vimiero, 21 August 1808, battle

A village in the coastal hills of central Portugal about 20 km south of Peniche and 19 km northwest of Torres Vedras.

An Anglo-Portuguese victory over the French.

(Last action – Roleia, 17 August; this was the last action of Wellesley's campaign this year.)

French Forces GdD Junot commanding the 'Army of Portugal'. **1st Division** GdD Delaborde; GdB Brennier: 2e RILé (3e Bn); 4e RILé (3e Bn); 70e RIdLi (1er and 2e bns); GdB Thomière: 86e RIdLi (1er and 2e bns); 4e Swiss (2 coys). **Total** 6,722 men.

2nd Division GdD Loison; GdB Solignac: 12e and 15e RILé (3e Bns each); 58e RIdLi (3e Bn); GdB Charlot: 32e and 82e RIdLi (3e Bns each). **Total** ca 5,000 men. **The Grenadier Reserve** GdD Kellermann; Col St Clair, Col Maransin 4 composite battalions. **Total** 2,100 men. **Cavalry** GdB Margeron GdB Maurin; 26e ChàCh (2 sqns); 3e, 4e and 5e Prov DragR. **Total** 2,100 men. **Artillery** 23 guns, 700 gunners. Sappers and train.

French totals About 16,622 men and 23 guns.

French losses 1,500 killed and wounded, 300 captured, 12 guns. French generals Charlot, Delaborde, Brennier and Solignac, Colonels Foy and Prost were wounded.

Anglo-Portuguese Forces Gen Sir Arthur Wellesley commanding: (all regiments of 1 bn each except where noted). **1st Brigade** Gen Hill: 1st/5th, 1st/9th and 1st/38th Foot. **Total** 2,698 men. **2nd Brigade** Gen Ferguson: 1st/36th, 1st/40th, 1st/71st Foot **Total** 2,449 men. **3rd Brigade** Gen Nightingale: 1st/29th and 1st/82nd Foot. **Total** 1,502 men. **4th Brigade** Bowes: 1st/6th and 1st/32nd Foot. **Total** 1,813 men. **5th Brigade** C Crawford: 1st/45th and 1st/91st Foot. **Total** 1,832 men. **6th Brigade** Fane: 1st/50th, 5th/60th and 2nd/95th Foot (4 coys). **Total** 2,005 men. **Anstruther's Brigade** 2nd/9th, 2nd/43rd, 2nd/57th, 1st/97th Foot. **Total** 2,703 men. **Acland's Brigade** 1st/2nd, 1st/20th, 1st/95th (2 coys) Foot . **Total** 1,332 men. **Cavalry** 20th LD. **Artillery** 2 x 6 pdr FAB, 1 x 9 pdr FAB; 18 guns; 2 troops, Irish Waggon Train. **Portuguese Brigade** Col Trant: 12th, 21st and 24th LIR (1,514 men), 6th Caçadores (562 men), 6th, 11th and 12th CavRs (258 men); Lisbon Police Guard (41 men). **Total** 2,375 men.

Anglo-Portuguese totals 24 bns, 6 coys, 5 sqns, 18 guns, ca 18,669 men.

Anglo-Portuguese losses 134 killed, 534 wounded, 51 missing.

Comment This battle was another classic of 'column versus line' with the inevitable outcome when the line was of British infantry.

Junot achieved surprise when he attacked. Wellesley expected an assault from the south, down the course of the Rio Maceira but Junot came in from the east (the Torres Vedras road) and Wellesley had to transfer his right wing across to extend his left. After the initial French assaults had been firmly repulsed, Junot committed his last reserve, Col Maransin's 1st Composite Grenadier Regiment but this column was taken in both flanks by the 2nd/43rd, 1st/2nd, 1st/20th and 1st/95th. Following a fierce and bloody hand-to-hand combat, this column too was broken and thrown back. The Allied force had practically no cavalry so the beaten French escaped destruction. General Sir Harry Burrard (Wellesley's senior) now came up (having just disembarked) and forbade any pursuit. Next morning General Sir Hew Dalrymple also landed and assumed command himself. Junot sued for peace; there followed the notorious Convention of Cintra by which the French, their weapons, artillery and baggage and some of their plunder, were returned to France on British ships. The British public were furious; all generals were court-martialled. Wellesley was cleared of any wrong-doing. Portugal was free of the French.

Sources Oman, Napier, Robinson, Martinien.

XX Grönvikssund, 30 August 1808, naval clash

A waterway in the Aaland islands at the southern end of the Gulf of Bothnia between Finland and Sweden, west of Turku (Abo).

A Swedish victory over the Russians.

(Last action - Sandöström, 2 August; next action - Orawais, 15 September.)

Swedish Forces Rear Admiral Hjelmstjerna commanding 29 sloops.

Swedish losses 242 men killed, wounded and missing, 2 sloops sunk.

Russian Forces Exact details not known.

Russian losses Casualties unknown; 9 sloops destroyed.

Sources Anderson, Stenzel.

XX Orawais, 15 September 1808, battle

A village on the Finnish coast of the Gulf of Bothnia, in the province of Wasa (nowadays Vaasa); midway between Vaasa and Jakobstad.

A Russian victory over the Swedes.

(Last action - Grönvikssund, 30 August; next action - Palva Sound, 18 September.)

Swedish Forces FM Count Klingspor commanding 7,000 men.

Swedish losses ca 1,000 killed and wounded.

Russian Forces LG Count Kaminskoi commanding 7,000 men.

Russian losses ca 1,000 killed and wounded.

Sources Bodart.

XX Palva Sound, 18 September 1808, naval clash

A waterway in the Aaland islands at the southern end of the Gulf of Bothnia, between Finland and Sweden; between the islands of Palva, Welkuannia,

Rajulolo, Munnima and Salavais, about 45 km north of Hangö port.

A Russian victory over the Swedes.

(Last action – Orawais, 15 September; this was the last action in the campaign.)

Swedish Forces Admiral Rajalin commanding 34 sloops and gunboats.

Swedish losses 100 killed or missing, 50 wounded, 1 sloop blown up, 2 badly damaged.

Russian Forces Rear Admiral Mäsojedoff commanding 7 'large vessels', 28 gunsloops. 52 yawls.

Russian losses 200 killed, wounded and missing, 3 sloops.

Comment The Swedes fell back westwards to Grönvikssund.

Sources Anderson, Stenzel.

IS Capri, 5 – 16 October 1808, invasion and surrender

An island at the southern end of the bay of Naples on the west coast of southern Italy.

A Franco-Neapolitan victory over the British.

(This was the only action of note here in 1808.)

Franco-Neapolitan Forces GdD Lamarque commanding: GdB Pignatelli, GdB Strongoli, GdB Cataneo. 52e RIdLi (élite coys only); Légion Corse (1 bn); IR Isenburg (1 coy), 23e and 62e RIdLi (élite coys only). Neapolitan troops: 1st and 2nd LIR (3 bns). Sailors of the Neapolitan Guard; sappers (1 coy). Italian troops: 3rd LIR (2 bns). The naval force under Capt Correale: frigate *Cerere*, corvette *Renomée*, 26 gunboats and 10 transports.

Franco-Neapolitan losses Not known exactly but light.

British Forces BG Hudson Lowe commanding Maltese R (9 coys); Corsican Rangers (6 coys).

British total ca 1,500 men.

British losses Maltese: 25 killed and wounded, 680 captured. Corsicans: 15 killed and wounded, 20 missing.

Comment Murat planned this action and it was well executed. The British frigate *Ambuscade* (44) was in the area but sailed off to get help; she returned on 8 October with the frigate *Mercury* but adverse weather hampered their operations. Hudson Lowe capitulated on 16 October and his troops were evacuated to Sicily. This gave a tremendous boost to French prestige in the area.

Sources Fortescue, JSAHR, Vol XXII.

EN Lerin, 25 and 26 October 1808, clashes

A small town in Navarra province in northern Spain in the valley of a tributary of the Rio Ebro, 40 km east of Logroño and 40 km south of Pamplona.

A French victory over the Spanish.

(Last action – Zaragoza, 14 August; next action – Zornoza, 30 October.)

French Forces M Moncey commanding the III Corps. **1st Division** GdD Mathieu: 14e RIdLi (4 bns); 44e (3 bns); 70e (1 bn); 2nd and 3rd IRs Vistula Legion (2 bns each). **Total** 12 bns. **3rd Division** GdD Morlot: 116e and 117e RIdLi (4 bns each); Irish Legion and Régt de Preusse (1 bn each). **Total** 10 bns. **Light Cavalry** GdB Wathier: 13e CuirR; 1er Prov HusR, 2e Prov LtCavR (9 sqns). **Artillery** 48 x FAB, 1 x HAB, 30 guns.

French totals 22 bns, 9 sqns, 30 guns, ca 20,000 men.

French losses Not known exactly, light.

Spanish Forces Gen Grimarest commanding: **2nd Andalusian Division** of the Army of the Centre: IRs Ceuta* (2 bns); Ordenes Militares* (3 bns); Truxillo, Bujalance, Cuenca, Ciudad Real, Tiradores de España, Voluntarios de Catalonia, Tiradores de Cadiz, Carmona (1 bn each) **Total** 13 bns. Cavalry: about 400 men:, artillery: 2 FAB 6 guns.

Spanish totals 13 bns, 400 cavalry, 6 guns, 10,000 men.

Spanish losses Not known exactly, moderate.

Comment There was no overall military supremo on the Spanish side; their moves were totally random and uncoordinated, inviting, and suffering, repeated disasters. Grimarest's vanguard (commanded by Col Cruz Murgeon) was 'forgotten' by the divisional commander and had to surrender after suffering losses of over 60% killed and wounded. Moncey seized the Ebro bridge at Lodosa following this action. Spanish General Castaños concentrated his Army of Andalusia around Tudela.

Sources Oman, Napier, Martinien.

EN Zornoza (now Amorebieta), 30 October 1808, clash

A village in the northern Spanish mountains about 12 km east of the fortified Biscayan port of Bilbao, at the junction of Routes 634 and 6315.

A Franco-Allied victory over the Spanish.

(Last action – Lerin, 25 and 26 October; next action – Valmaseda, 5 November.)

French and Allied Forces M Lefebvre-Desnouettes commanding the IV Corps. **1st Division** GdD Sebastiani: 28e RIdLi (3 bns); 32e and 58e (2 bns each); 75e (3 bns).

2nd Division GdD Leval: 2nd IR Nassau; 4th IR Baden; Hessen-Darmstadt IR Gross- und Erbprinz; IR Holland (2 bns each); IR Frankfurt (1 bn); GdN Paris (1 bn). 3rd Division GdD Villatte: 27e, 63e, 94e and 95e RIdLi (3 bns each).

French and Allied totals 32 bns, 21,324 infantry, 6 x FAB, 36 guns.

French and Allied losses Reported as 300 killed and wounded. IR Nassau lost 41 killed and wounded.

Spanish Forces LG Blake commanding The Army of Galicia. **Vanguard Brigade** Gen Mendizabal: Catalonian LtI*, Voluntarios de Navarra*, Zaragoza* (1 bn each); combined grenadiers* (2 bns each); Sappers* (1 coy). **Total** 2,884 men. **1st Division** Gen Figueroa: Rey* (2 bns); Majorca*, Hibernia*, combined light companies*, Mondonedo, Literario (1 bn each), sappers* (1 coy). **Total** 4,018 men. **3rd Division** Gen Riquelme: Seville* (2 bns), Girona LtI*, Santiago de Compostella (1 bn each), Marines* (3 bns), Sappers (1 coy). **Total** 4,789 men. **4th Division** Gen Carbajal: Principe*, Toledo*, combined grenadiers* (2 bns each); Barbastro LtI*, Aragon*, Lugo, Santiago (1 bn each). **Total** 3,531 men. **Reserve Brigade** Gen Mahy: Voluntarios de la Corona*, combined grenadiers* (1 bn each); militia grenadiers (2 bns); Batallon del General (1 bn). **Total** 3,025 men. **Artillery** 1 x FAB, 6 guns.

Spanish totals 18,247 men and 6 guns.

Spanish losses 300 killed and wounded, 300 captured.

* = regular regiments of the old army.

Comment Blake had been dithering about south of Bilbao since capturing the place in a surprise raid on 11 October. He thus wasted all the advantages which this unexpected strike gave him.

When the French advanced against him, he lost his nerve. Prior to the action he sent all artillery but one battery to the rear and then pulled this one out as well. Sebastiani's division broke his centre. Blake withdrew westwards to Valmaseda.

Sources Oman, Napier, Martinien.

EN Valmaseda, 5 November 1808, 1st clash

A small town in the Cantabrian mountains along the northern Spanish coast, 28 km west of Bilbao.

A Spanish victory over the French.

(Last action – Zornoza, 30 October; next action – Espinosa, 10 November.)

French Forces GdD Villatte's 3rd Division of M Lefebvre-Desnouettes's IV Corps: 27e RILé; 63e, 94e and 95e RIdLi (3 bns each) 2 x FAB, ca 12,000 men.

French losses About 200 killed and wounded, 300 captured, 1 gun, 'many' baggage waggons.

Spanish Forces LG Blake commanding The Army of Galicia. As for the clash at Zornoza on 30 October plus: **2nd Division** Gen Martinengo: Navarra*, Napoles* (2 bns each); Segovia, Pontevedra, Voluntarios de Victoria (1 bn each); Sappers* (1 coy). **Total** 5,066 men. **Cavalry** Reyna* (2 sqns), Montesa (1 sqn), detachments of various other regiments. **Total** 302 men. **5th Division** Gen Marqués de la Romana (from Denmark): Zamora*, Princesa* (3 bns each), Barcelona LtI* (1st Bn), Catalonian LtI* (1st Bn), sappers* (1 coy). **Total** 5,294 men. **Artillery** 38 guns, 1,038 men. * = old regiments of the regular army.

Spanish totals ca 24,000 men and 38 guns.

Spanish losses Not exactly known, light.

Comment Spanish Gen Acevedo's Asturian Division had become separated from Blake's army prior to Zornoza on 30 October, having been sent off on flank protection duties. Blake mounted this raid to rescue him from Victor's I Corps which had detected him. Blake drove Villatte out of Valmaseda and Acevedo bumped into his retreating column and cut off the baggage.

Blake slipped back into the mountains; the rearguard he left in Valmaseda was thrown out of the town on 8 November with a loss of 150 killed and wounded and 600 missing. Victor took up the chase.

Sources Oman, Napier, Martinien.

EM Gamonal, 10 November 1808, clash

A village 5 km east of the ancient city of Burgos in northern Spain, on the Rio Arlanzón and at the junction of Routes I /E5, 620/E80, and 623.

A French victory over the Spanish.

(Last action – this was the opening action of Napoleon's drive on Madrid; next action – Somosierra, 30 November.)

French Forces M Soult commanding the II Corps (ex Bessières): 1st Division GdD Mouton: 2e RILé, 4e, 15e and 36e RIdLi (3 bns each); GdN Paris (1 bn). **Light Cavalry** GdD Lasalle: 9e DragR, 10e and 22e

ChàCh (3 sqns each). **Dragoon Division** GdD Milhaud: 12e, 16e and 21e DragRs (9 sqns). **Artillery** 2 x FAB, 2 x HAB.

French totals 13 bns, 18 sqns, 24 guns, ca 14,000 men.

French losses About 200 killed and wounded.

Spanish Forces LG Conde de Belveder commanding part of the Army of Extremadura: **1st Division** MG de Alos: Spanish Guards* (4th Bn), Majorca* (2 bns), Granaderos Provinciales de Extremadura (1 bn), 2nd of Catalonia (1 bn), Tiradores (1 coy). **Total** 5 bns, 1 coy, ca 4,160 men. **2nd Division** MG Henestrosa: Walloon Guards* (4th Bn); Voluntarios de Badajoz (2 bns); 2nd DragR 'Lusitania'*; 2nd ChàCh 'Voluntarios de Espana*; 1st HusR 'Extremadura'* (1,100 men together); Tuy Militia and Benavente (1 bn each). **Artillery** 250 men*, 2½ FAB (16 guns), sappers* (1 bn).

Spanish totals 10 bns, 4 sqns, 16 guns, ca 11,000 men. (* = regular units of the old standing army).

Spanish losses About 1,500 killed, wounded and captured, 16 guns, 12 colours.

Comment The Spanish commander was young, rash and totally incapable of using his troops well. He adopted a position, easily outflanked, with its front obscured by a large wood through which the French made a concealed approach. Milhaud's dragoons rolled up the Spanish line; only the 4th Bn Walloon Guards was able to form square in time. This was the opening action in Napoleon's drive on Madrid and was aimed to secure his right flank. Burgos was sacked and partially burned.

Sources Oman, Napier, Martinien.

EN Espinosa de los Monteros, 10/11 November 1808, clash

A medieval town in the Cantabrian mountains of northern Spain 45 km southeast of Santander and 55 km southwest of Bilbao, on the east bank of the Rio Trueba.

A French victory over the Spanish.

(Last action – Valmaseda, 5 and 8 November; next action – Tudela, 23 November.)

French Forces M Victor commanding the I Corps: 1st Division GdD Ruffin: 9e RILé (3 bns); 24e RIdLi (3 bns); 96e RIdLi (4 bns). 2nd Division GdD Lapisse: 16e RILé, 8e, 45e and 54e RIdLi (3 bns each). GdD Villatte's 1st Division of IV Corps: 27e RILé; 63e, 94e and 95e RIdLi (3 bns each). Artillery 6 x FAB,. 36 guns.

French totals 34 bns, 21,000 men and 36 guns.

French losses About 1,100 killed and wounded.

Spanish Forces Capt Gen Blake with the Army of Galicia (as for Valmaseda, 5th November but with only 6 guns).

Spanish losses About 3,000 killed, wounded and captured, 6 guns, all the baggage.

Comment Blake turned at bay here to extract his rearguard (La Romana's 5th Division) from Victor's attacks. On the first day his troops stood fast and fought well but on 11 November a determined French thrust at the 1st Spanish Division caused the new levies in it to break and the entire line was swept away. Blake fell back west to Reinosa where he still commanded 12,000 half-starved scarecrows.

EN Tudela, 23 November 1808, battle

A town in the Spanish province of Navarra on the west bank of the Rio Ebro, on Route 232, 86 km upstream from Zaragoza.

A French victory over the Spanish.

(Last action – Espinosa, 10/11 November; next action – Rosas, 7 November – 5 December.)

French Forces M Lannes commanding: **III Corps** M Moncey (2nd and 4th Divisions were not engaged). 1st Division GdD Mathieu: 14e (4 bns); 44e (3 bns); 70e RIdLi (1 bn); 2nd and 3rd IRs Vistula Legion (2 bns each). 3rd Division GdD Morlot: 16e (2 bns) and 117e RIdLi (4 bns). Light Cavalry GdB Wathier 13e CuirR, 1er Prov HusR; 2e Prov Lt CavR (12 sqns). **VI Corps** (M Lannes): 2nd Division GdD Lagrange: 25e RILé (4 bns); 27e and 59e RIdLi (3 bns each); 50e RIdLi (4 bns). Dragoon Brigade GdB Digeon: 2e and 26e DragR (8 sqns). Artillery 6 x FAB, 2 x HAB.

French totals 32 bns, 20 sqns, 48 guns, ca 31,000 men.

French losses III Corps – 44 killed, 513 wounded (the 117e lost 303 killed and wounded assaulting the Cerro de Santa Barbara). VI Corps – about 100 killed and wounded.

Spanish Forces Capt Gen Conde de Castaños commanding: **The Army of Aragon** Gen José Palafox. **Gen O'Neille's 1st Division:** Spanish Guards*; Extremadura* and 1st Voluntarios de Aragon*; 1st LtI of Zaragoza; 4th Tercio of Aragon: 2nd of Valencia; 1st and 2nd Voluntarios de

Murcia; Huesca; Cazadores de Fernando VII; Suizos de Aragon (1 bn each); Escopeteros de Navarra and DragR del Rey* (2 sqns each); artillery (1 coy); sappers (½ coy). **Total** ca 10,000 men **Gen St March's 2nd Division** Voluntarios de Castile*; Turia and Alicante (3 bns each); Soria; Voluntarios de Borbon; Chelva; Cazadores de Fernando VII; Segorbe (1 bn each); DragR Numancia* (4 sqns); sappers (1 coy). **Total** ca 9,000 men. **Gen Roca's 5th (Murcian-Valencian) Division of Castaños Army of the Centre** Savoya* (2 bns); Valencia* and America* (3 bns each); Murcia, Avila Liria (1 bn each); Cazadores de Valencia (3 bns); Orihuela (2 bns); Tiradores de Xativa and Cartagena (2 coys); Peñas de San Pedro (1 bn). **Total** ca 8,000 men. **Gen La Peña's 4th Division of the Army of the Centre** Africa* and Burgos* (2 bns each); Zaragoza* (1 bn); Murcia* (2 bns); Granaderos Provinciales de Andalusia (2 bns); Siguenza; Navas de Tolosa; Bailén, 5th de Sevilla (1 bn each). **Total** ca 7,500 men.

Spanish totals 17,000 infantry, 2,000 cavalry, 36 guns.

Spanish losses The Army of the Centre - 200 killed and wounded; The Army of Aragon - 3,000 killed and wounded, 1,000 captured, 26 guns.

Comment Castaños' men were clothed mainly in summer uniforms and half starved.

Prior to the battle the Army of Aragon was east of the Rio Ebro, that of the Centre ('Andalusia') was about 16 km away to the west, over the river. This was the sort of crass mismanagement upon which the French generals thrived. Lannes concentrated on crushing Palafox's three divisions as they came over the river and deployed west of Tudela along the Rio Queiles, leaving Legrange's division and Digeon's dragoons to hold La Peña's division at arms' length about 5 km to the west at Cascante. Palafox's conduct bordered on sabotage in this action.

La Peña's conduct was so timid as to be cowardly; he sat and watched his compatriots being cut to pieces without moving to help them. He was to betray a British force in similar circumstances at Barossa on 5 March, 1811.

Napoleon was displeased with the result of this battle as Lannes had sprung the trap too soon and too many Spaniards had escaped.

Sources Oman, Napier, Martinien.

EM Somosierra, 30 November 1808, clash

A village and mountain pass in the Montes Carpetanos mountain range in central Spain 72 km north of Madrid on Route I/E5.

A French and Allied victory over the Spanish.

(Last action - Gamonal, 23 November; this was the last action in Napoleon's drive on Madrid.)

French and Allied Forces Emperor Napoleon I commanding. GdD Ruffin's 1st Division of M Victor's I Corps: 9e RILé, 24e RIdLi (3 bns each); 96e RIdLi (4 bns). Imperial Guard: 1st Polish ChLR (4 sqns); ChàCh (4 sqns).

French and Allied totals 10 bns, 8 sqns, 12 guns, ca 11,000 men.

French and Allied losses The Polish ChLR lost 4 officers and 40 men killed; 4 officers and 12 men wounded; total French and Allied loss was about 300.

Spanish Forces LG Benito de San-Juan commanding: IRs Reina*, Corona*, Cordova* (2 bns each); Militia of Alcazar and Toledo (1 bn each); 1st and 2nd Voluntarios de Madrid (2 bns each); Voluntarios de Sevilla (1 bn); CavRs Principe*, Voluntarios de Madrid* (2 sqns each). 3 x FAB.

Spanish totals 13 bns, 4 sqns, 16 guns, ca 7,800 men.

Spanish losses About 200 killed and captured, 16 guns.

* = old regiments of the regular army.

Comment San-Juan had detached 5 bns and 2 sqns with 6 guns to Sepulveda, ahead of the Somosierra pass, as an Advanced Guard; a total waste of valuable veteran troops. His own 16 guns were drawn up across the pass behind a low rampart. Napoleon ordered the Polish Chevau-Legers to charge straight into the battery. The first charge failed in the face of heavy fire and Napoleon sent his Aide-de-Camp, Philippe de Ségur, to harry them on. Despite this, they did not charge home and Ségur was wounded. A second charge, after the 9e, 24e and 96e RIdLi had arrived and attacked the front and flanks of the Spanish position was made by the Polish ChL and the ChàCh of the Guard and succeeded. Madrid capitulated to Napoleon on 4 December 1808 after an ineffective uprising by the populace.

Sources Oman, Napier, Martinien, Gembarzewski.

EN Rosas, 7 November - 5 December 1808, siege and capture of

A fortified harbour on the Catalonia coast in north-eastern Spain, 43 km northeast of Girona.

A French and Allied victory over the Spanish.

(Last action – Tudela, 23 November; next action Cardedeu, 16 December.)

French and Allied Forces GdD Gouvion St Cyr commanding the VII Corps. 3rd Division GdD Reille: 32e RILé, 16e, 56e and 113e RIdLi (1 bn each); Prov Regt of Perpignan (4 bns); 5e Légion de Réserve; Ch des Montagnes and Valais Bn (1 bn each). 2 x FAB. 5th Division GdD Pino's Italian Division: 1st and 2nd LtIRs (3 bns each); 4th LIR (2 bns); 5th LIR (1 bn); 6th LIR (3 bns); 7th LIR (1 bn). 2 x FAB.

French and Allied totals: 24 bns, 4 x FAB, ca 12,000 men.

French and Allied losses About 1,000 killed, wounded and died of sickness.

Spanish Forces Col O'Daly commanding: IR Ultonia* (150 men); Wimpffen's Swiss* (1 coy); 2nd LtIR of Barcelona* (½ bn); 120 gunners* as well as Miquelete Tercios of Lerida, Igualada, Berga and Figueras ca 3,500 men and 58 guns.

Spanish losses ca 1,500 killed, wounded and died of sickness.

Comment In the harbour throughout the siege were (successively) the Royal Naval ships of the line *Excellent* (74); *Fame* (74) and *Impérieuse* (74) and two bomb ships *Meteor* and *Lucifer*. These supported and supplied the Spaniards and their crews took part in action ashore. On 29 November a weak battalion of IR Borbon* was added to the garrison. Due to heavy French artillery fire, the Royal Navy could only evacuate the garrison of the detached Fort Trinity but not those in the town itself.

* = old regiments of the regular army.

Sources Oman, Napier, Martinien.

EG Rueda, 12 December 1808, ambush

A village in western Spain on Route VI, 11 km south of Tordesilla on the River Duero.

A British victory over the French.

(This was the opening action of Sir John Moore's advance into Spain; next action – Sahagun, 21 December.)

French Forces 22e ChàCh (½ sqn) of GdD Franceschi's cavalry division at Valladolid.

French losses 18 killed, 35 wounded and captured. 1 or 2 escaped to raise the alarm.

British Forces 18th LDR of General Charles Stewart's cavalry brigade of Moore's advanced guard (4 sqns).

British total ca 500 men.

British losses None.

Comment The French were completely surprised to be attacked by the British as their high command thought that General Moore was retreating on Lisbon. News of the action alerted Napoleon to the real situation; he rapidly regrouped to crush the British as they advanced north on Sahagun to strike at Soult's isolated II Corps.

Source Oman.

EN Cardedeu, 16 December 1808, battle

A village in the northeastern Spanish province of Catalonia, 17 km northeast of Barcelona.

A French and Allied victory over the Spanish.

(Last action – Rosas, 5 December; next action Molins del Rey, 21 December.)

French and Allied Forces GdD Gouvion St Cyr commanding the VII Corps. 4th Division GdD Souham: 1er, RILé (3 bns), 3e RILé (1 bn); 7e RIdLi (2 bns); 42e (3 bns) and 67e (1 bn). 5th Division GdD Pino's Italian Division 1st and 2nd LtIRs (3 bns each); 4th LIR (2 bns); 5th LIR (1 bn); 6th LIR (3 bns); 7th LIR (1 bn). 2 x FAB. Light Cavalry GdB Fontane's Italians: Royal ChàCh; 7th DragR (4 sqns each).

French and Allied totals 23 bns, 8 sqns, 5 batteries, 30 guns, ca 15,000 men.

French losses St Cyr reported 600 killed, and wounded.

Spanish Forces Capt Gen Conde de Vives commanding part of the Army of Catalonia and part of the Army of Granada. **Gen Reding's 1st Division, Army of Granada** 1st of Granada, Baza and Almeira (2 bns each). **Gen Vive's Catalans** (new levies) 12 bns, 4 sqns. **Totals** ca 4,000 men including 600 cavalry, 7 guns.

Spanish total ca 5,000 men.

Spanish losses 1,000 killed and wounded, 1,500 captured, 5 guns, 2 colours.

Comment St Cyr, finished at Rosas, took all available troops to dash through the mountains to break the Spanish blockade of Barcelona. He burst through the Spanish line in a massive column. The Spanish lifted the blockade of Barcelona and withdrew to Molins del Rey.

Sources Oman, Napier, Martinien.

EN Molins del Rey, 21 December 1808, battle

A village in the northeastern Spanish province of Catalonia, on the Rio Llobregat, 15 km west of Barcelona.

A French and Allied victory over the Spanish.

(Last action – Cardedeu, 16 December; next action Igualada, 18 February, 1809.)

French and Allied Forces GdD Gouvion St Cyr commanding the **VII Corps**. **1st Division** GdD Chabran: 2e RIdLi (1 bn); 7e RIdLi (2 bns); 10e, 37e, 56e and 93e RIdLi and 2e Swiss (1 bn each). **4th Division** GdD Souham: 1er RILé (3 bns), 3e RILé (1 bn); 7e RIdLi (2 bns); 42e (3 bns) and 67e (1 bn). **5th Division** GdD Pino's Italian Division 1st and 2nd LtIRs (3 bns each); 4th LIR (2 bns); 5th LIR (1 bn); 6th LIR (3 bns); 7th LIR (1 bn). 2 x FAB. 6th Division GdD Chabot: 2nd Neapolitan LIR (2 bns); Ch de la Pyrénées Orientales (1 bn). 1 x FAB. Light Cavalry GdB Fontane's Italians: Royal ChàCh; 7th DragR (8 sqns each). 1 x HAB.

French and Allied totals 29 bns, 8 sqns, 48 guns, ca 18,000 men.

French and Allied losses Reported as 400 killed and wounded.

Spanish Forces LG Conde de Caldagues commanding: 1st of Granada, Baza and Almeira (2 bns each). **Total** ca 4,600 men. **Gen Vive's Catalans** 12 bns, 4 sqns, ca 3,000 men including 400 cavalry.

Spanish losses 1,000 killed and wounded, 1,200 captured, 25 guns, 1 colour.

Comment Although the Spanish used the Rio Llobregat as a defensive obstacle on this occasion, they let themselves be outflanked and rolled up on both wings. Catalonia was now under French control for some time.

Sources Oman, Napier, Martinien.

EG Sahagun, 21 December 1808, skirmish

A small town in the northern Spanish province of Leon, at the junction of minor Routes 120 and 611, in the hills between Rio Cea and Rio Valderaduey.

A British victory over the French.

(Last action – Rueda, 12 December; next action – Benavente, 29 December.)

French Forces GdB Debelle commanding a brigade of light cavalry of Franceschi's division of the Cavalry Reserve: 8e DragR; 1er Prov, ChàCh (8 sqns).

French total ca 800 men.

French losses 20 killed and wounded, 13 officers and over 300 men captured.

British Forces Gen Lord Paget's 10th and 15th HusRs (8 sqns), ca 400 men.

British losses 4 died of wounds, 21 wounded, 4 horses killed, 4 wounded, 10 missing.

Comment This was a brilliant cavalry action in which the 1er Prov ChàCh was destroyed. Of the British cavalry, only the 15th Hussars was actually involved. These two regiments were Sir John Moore's point, advancing north from Salamanca to attack Soult's isolated II Corps at Saldanha. Although Moore knew of the Spanish defeat at Tudela (23 November), he still aimed to strike at Soult on 24 December together with the Spanish General la Romana, not knowing that Napoleon (with Ney's VI Corps, Lefebvre's IV Corps and the Imperial Guard) was rushing up northwards from Madrid to destroy him. Moore received the news of these dramatic changes in the strategic situation on 23 December; abandoned his planned offensive action and set off at once on the retreat to La Coruña and Vigo which was to save his army. A minor stand-off took place at Castro Gonzalon on 29 December. Despite having to withdraw, Moore had achieved his aim: to disrupt Napoleon's conquest of Spain; he also gave the Spaniards two months' breathing space to reorganize.

Sources Oman, Napier, Martinien, Robinson, Gordon.

EG Benavente, 29 December 1808, skirmish

A fortified town in the northern Spanish province of Leon, at the junction of Routes VI, 620 and 630, between the Rio Esla and Rio Orbigo, 60 km southeast of Astorga and 64 km north of Zamora.

A British victory over the French.

(Last action – Sahagun, 21 December; next action – Mansilla, 30 December.)

French Force Gen Lefebvre-Desnouettes commanding the ChàCh of the Imperial Guard.

French total ca 550 men.

French losses Gen Lefebvre-Desnouettes, 2 captains and 70 men captured, 55 killed or wounded.

British Forces Col Otway commanding 130 men (mainly of 18th LD), 1 troop of 3rd D. KGL and 10th HusR.

British total About 600 men in all.

British losses 50 killed, wounded and missing.

Comment Sir John Moore's withdrawal on La Coruña was now being executed at top speed, admirably screened by his cavalry who consistently bested their French opponents in many minor actions. Lefebvre was captured by Trooper Grisdale of 10 Hussars.

Sources Oman, Napier, Martinien, Robinson.

EG Mansilla de las Mulas, 30 December 1808, clash

A village in the northern Spanish province of Leon, on the east bank of the Rio Esla on Route 601, 17 km southeast of Leon city.

A French victory over the Spanish.

(Last action – Benavente, 29 December; next action – Fonce Badon, 2 January 1809.)

French Forces GdD Franceschi commanding the Light Cavalry Division of the Reserve Cavalry: 8e DragR, 22e ChàCh; Ch Hanovrienne; 1er Prov. ChàCh ca 2,200 men.

French losses Not exactly known, very light.

Spanish Forces The 2nd Division of La Romana's Army of Galicia General Martinengo. Navarra*, Naples* (2 bns each); Pontevedra +, Segovia +, Volunteers of Victory ** (1 bn each); Cavalry: Reina* (2 sqns), Montesa* (1 sqn), sappers (1 coy).

* = veteran units; + = provincial militia; ** = newly raised corps.

Spanish totals ca 3,000 men and 2 guns.

Spanish losses Some hundreds killed and wounded, 1,500 captured, 2 guns, 2 colours.

Comment The task of the 2nd Division was to defend the river crossing here to win time for the withdrawal of La Romana's and Sir John Moore's forces westwards into Galicia. The rash Spanish commander stood for battle with the bridge and river *behind* him. Franceschi just charged and destroyed them. La Romana then abandoned Leon and fled into the hills to Astorga and Soult's II Corps took Leon on 31 December together with 2,000 Spanish sick and wounded.

Sources Oman, Napier, Martinien.

1809

1809 THE ACTIONS

EG Fonce Badon, 2 January 1809, skirmish

A mountain pass in Galicia (north western Spain) on a by-road between Villafranca and Lugo which both lie on Route VI leading up to La Coruña.

A French victory over the Spanish.

(Last action – Mansilla, 30 December; next action – Cacabellos, 3 January.)

French Forces GdD Franceschi commanding: 1er HusR, 8e DragR, 22e ChàCh (4 sqns each); Ch Hanovrienne (3 sqns); ca 650 men.

French losses Not known, very light.

Spanish Forces G La Romana's rearguard under MG Rengel ca 2,000 infantry; exact details unknown.

Spanish losses About 200 killed and wounded, 1,500 men and 2 colours captured.

Comment This was an accidental clash; the starving Spanish were just looking for a place to hide and reorganize after their recent defeats. La Romana's artillery was with Sir John Moore on the high road to Lugo.

Sources Oman, Beamish, Schwertfeger, Martinien, Fortescue.

EG Cacabellos (Prieros), 3 January 1809, clash

A village in Galicia (north western Spain) on a by-road to the north of Route VI, between Villafranca and Ponferrada. In 1808 this by-road was the main road.

A British victory over the French.

(Last action – Fonce Badon, 2 January; next action – Lugo, 7 January.)

French Forces GdB Auguste de Colbert's brigade of Ney's Corps: 3e HusR, 15e ChàCh (8 sqns); ca 600 men. GdD Lahoussaye: 17e, 18e, 19e and 27e DragRs (16 sqns); ca 1,000 men. GdD Merle's 1st Division: 2e RILé (3 bns); 4e RILé (4 bns); 15e and 36e RIdLi (3 bns each); ca 4,500 men.

French losses 60–80 killed and wounded. GdB Colbert and his ADC (Latour-Maubourg) killed; Lahoussaye and Merle lost a further 120 later in the day.

British Forces Gen Sir Edward Paget commanding Sir John Moore's rearguard (4th or Reserve Division) 1st/28th, 1st/52nd, 1st/95th, 1st/20th and 1st/91st (5 bns). 1 x HAB, ca 3,000 men.

British losses ca 48 captured, 120 killed and wounded.

Comment Colbert was killed by Rifleman Tom Plunket of the 95th. Subsequent French attempts to cross the river here (Lahoussaye's dragoons and Merle's Division of Soult's II Corps) later in the day were also repelled with loss. That night Paget withdrew unmolested to Nogales.

Sources Oman, Beamish, Schwertfeger, Martinien, Fortescue.

EG Lugo, 7 January 1809, clash

A town in Galicia (north western Spain) at the junction of Routes VI, 547 and 630, 54 km southeast of La Coruña and 124 km from Cacabellos.

A British victory over the French.

(Last action – Cacabellos (Prieros), 3 January; next action – La Coruña, 16 January.)

French Forces M Soult commanding the II Corps. 1st Division GdD Merle: GdB Reynaud, GdB Sarrut, GdB Thomières. 2e RILé (3 bns); 4e RILé (4 bns); 15e and 36e RIdLi (3 bns each); ca 4,000 men.

French losses ca 300 men killed and wounded, mostly from the 2e RILé and 36e RIdLi.

LG British Forces Sir John Moore commanding. MG Hope's Division – BG Leith:

1st/51st, 2nd/59th, 1st/76th, ca 2,400 men.

British losses ca 50 killed and wounded.

Comment This was a rearguard action on the British retreat on La Coruña. They occupied a very strong position; Soult rested his men for a day before probing at it. A bayonet charge by Leith's brigade swept the French assault force away. The British then fell back on La Coruña.

Sources Oman, Beamish, Schwertfeger, Martinien, Fortescue.

EM Uclés, 13 January 1809, battle

A town in central Spain, about 80 km southeast of Madrid, in the hills at the end of a side road off Route III/E901 towards Valencia.

A French and Allied victory over the Spanish.

(Last action – Madrid, 4 December 1808; next action – Almonacid, 11 August.)

French and Allied Forces M Victor's I Corps 1st Division GdD Ruffin: 9e RILé, 24e and 96e RIdLi (3 bns each); 2 x FAB. 3rd Division GdD Villatte: 27e RILé 63e, 94e and 95e RIdLi (3 bns each); 2 x FAB. Light Cavalry GdB Beaumont: 2e HusR, 5e ChàCh, Westfalian ChLR (12 sqns); 2 x HAB. GdD Latour-

Maubourg; GdBs Oldenbourg, Perreymond, Digeon: 1er, 2e, 4e, 14e, 20e and 26e DragRs (24 sqns).

French and Allied totals 21 bns, 36 sqns, ca 12,000 infantry, 3,500 cavalry, 48 guns. **French losses** 200 killed and wounded.

Spanish Forces LG Venegas commanding the Advanced Guard of the Duke of Infantado's 'Army of Andalusia'. **Vanguard Division** MG Duke of Albuquerque: Murcia (1 bn); Cantabria (1st Bn); Provincial of Jaén, Provincial of Chinchilla, Voluntarios Catalanes, Cazadores de Barbastro, Campo Mayor (1 bn each); **Total** 7 bns, ca 2,800 men. **1st Division** LG Marquis de Coupigny: Africa (1st and 3rd Bns); Burgos (1st and 3rd Bns); Seville (3rd Bn); Provincial of Cuenca; Navas de Tolosa and Tiradores de Cadiz (1 bn each). **Total** 8 bns, 3,382 men. **2nd Division** MG Conde de Orgaz: Ordenes Militares (1st, 2nd and 3rd bns); Seville (4th Bn); Provincial de Toro; Bailén, Voluntarios de Carmona (1 bn each). **Total** 7 bns, 2,265 men. **Reserve** LG La Peña: Walloon Guards (1st Bn); Granaderos Provinciales de Andalusia and Irlanda (1st Bn); **Total** 3 bns, 1,324 men. **Cavalry** Reyna, Principe, Borbon, España, Santiago, Tejas, Pavia, Lusitania. **Total** 8 regiments, 1,814 men. **Artillery** 386 gunners, 383 sappers, 5 guns.

Spanish totals 25 bns, 9,771 infantry, 1,814 cavalry, 769 artillery and sappers, 5 guns.

Spanish losses About 1,000 killed and wounded, 4 generals, 323 officers and over 6,000 men captured, 5 guns, 20 colours.

Comment Venegas had been static at Tarancón, about 14 km nearer to Madrid than Uclés from 26 December 1808 until 11 January when he heard that Victor was finally moving against him. He pulled back into the trap of Uclés; stood to fight, and was badly beaten.

Sources Oman.

EG Coruña (La) 16 January 1809, battle

A fortified port in Galicia (north western Spain) on the south side of the Rio de Betanzos at the end of Route E1/A9.

A British victory over the French.

(Last action – Lugo, 7 January; next action – Ferrol, 26 January.)

French Forces M Soult commanding II Corps 1st Division GdD Merle; GdB Reynaud, GdB Sarvut, GdB Thomières: 2e RILé (3 bns); 4e RILé (4 bns); 15e and 36e RIdLi (3 bns each). **2nd Division** GdD Mermet; GdB Gaulois, GdB Jardon, GdB Lefebvre: 31e RILé, 41e and 122e RIdLi (4 bns each); 2e Swiss (2 bns); 3e Swiss (1 bn). **3rd Division** GdD Delaborde; GdB Foy, GdB Arnaud: 17e RILé (3 bns); 70e RIdLi (4 bns); 86e RIdLi (3 bns); 1er Swiss (1 bn). **Cavalry Division** GdD Lahoussaye; GdB Marissy, GdB Caulaincourt 17e, 18e, 19e and 27e DragRs (4 sqns each). **Cavalry Division** GdD Lorge: GdB Viallannes, GdB Fournier: 13e, 15e, 22e and 25e DragRs (4 sqns each). **Light Cavalry** GdD Franceschi; GdB Debelle, GdB Girardin: 1er HusR; 8e DragR; 22e ChàCh (3 sqns each); Ch Hanovrienne (3 sqns). Artillery: 6 batteries, 600 men.

French totals 39 bns, 41 sqns, 15,500 infantry, 4,500 cavalry. About 36 guns.

French losses 1,400 killed and wounded, 163 captured.

British Forces LG Sir John Moore commanding: **1st Division** Sir David Baird Warde's Bde: 1st Footguards (1st and 2nd Bns). Bentinck's Bde:1st/4th, 1st/42nd, 1st/50th (3 bns). Manningham's Bde: 3rd/1st, 1st/26th, 1st/81st (3 bns). **2nd Division** Sir John Hope Leith's Bde: 1st/51st, 2nd/59th, 1st/76th (3 bns). Hill's Bde:1st/2nd, 1st/5th, 2nd/14th, 1st/32nd (4 bns). Catlin Crawfurd's Bde:1st/36th, 1st/71st, 1/92nd (3 bns). **Reserve Division** MG E Paget: Anstruther's Bde: 1st/20th, 1st/52nd, 1st/95th (3 bns). Disney's Bde: 1st/28th, 1st/91st (2 bns). 9 guns.

The cavalry had all been embarked in La Coruña at this point and Fraser's 3rd Division was not engaged.

British totals 23 bns, ca 14,900 men.

British losses 137 killed, 497 wounded.

Comment The British army was drawn up on a line of hills south of La Coruña with an apparently open right flank; the inevitable French thrust into this inviting hole by Mermet's division was smartly stopped by Paget's division. Soult drew back.

After Sir John Moore's death during the battle, General Hope took over. The British army embarked unmolested during 16 and 17 January. One transport ship was lost in the late stages of the evacuation.

Sources Oman, Fortescue.

EG Ferrol, 26 January 1809, surrender of

A fortified port in Galicia, north western Spain, on the northern side of the estuary of the Rio de Betanzos, opposite La Coruña and on Route VI.

A French victory over the Spanish.

(Last action – Coruña, 16 January; next action – La Trepa, 6 March (PN).)

French Forces M Soult's II Corps ca 24,000 men.

French losses None.

Spanish Garrison Admiral Melgarejo commanding about 6,500 men of the depot companies of La Romana's division, marines and sailors.

Spanish losses None.

Comment The governor of Ferrol turned out to be pro-French and opened the gates to the French to the disgust of the inhabitants and his own garrison. Given to the French were thus eight ships of the line and three frigates (mostly dismasted and not ready for sea), 20,000 new British muskets; 1,500 naval guns, immense quantities of cordage and naval stores.

Sources Oman, Fortescue.

EE Capellades, 17 February 1809, clash

A village on the River Anoia in the north eastern Spanish province of Catalonia, about 40 km west of Barcelona.

A French victory over the Spanish.

(Last action – Molins del Rey, 21 December 1808; next action – Igualada, 18 February.)

French Forces GdD Chabran's 2nd Division of Gouvion St Cyr's VII Corps. 2e, 10e, 37e, 56e and 93e RIdLi and 2nd Swiss (1 bn each); ca 4,000 men and 12 guns.

French losses Not known exactly; very light, no officer casualties.

Spanish Forces LG Castro's 2nd Division of Reding's Army: IRs Santa Fé, Loxa (2 bns each); Antequera (1 bn); HusR de Granada; 6 guns.

Spanish losses Not known exactly, light.

Comment Both sides were moving forward to attack one another. Castro's many spies told him that Chabran was isolated so he seized the chance and assaulted him. Chabran fell back eastwards from Barcelona that evening. Castro then withdrew north-west towards Igualada.

Sources Oman, Martinien.

EE Igualada, 18 February 1809, clash.

A town on the River Anoia in north eastern Spain, in Catalonia, about 47 km west of Barcelona.

A Franco-Italian victory over the Spanish.

(Last action – Capellades, 17 February; next action – San Magin, 19 February.)

Franco-Italian Forces GdD Chabran's 2nd Division, Gouvion St Cyr's VII Corps. 2e, 10e, 37e, 56e and 93e RIdLi and 2nd Swiss (1 bn each); ca 4,000 men and 12 guns. GdD Pino's 5th (Italian) Division: 1st and 2nd LtIRs, 4th and 6th LIRs (3 bns each); 7th LIR (1 bn). ca 7,500 men and 12 guns.

Franco-Italian totals 19 bns and 24 guns, ca 10,300 men.

Franco-Italian losses Not exactly known.

Spanish Forces LG Castro's 2nd Division of Reding's Army: IRs Santa Fé, Loxa (2 bns each); Antequera (1 bn); HusR de Granada (4 sqns); 6 guns. Total 5 bns, 4 sqns, 6 guns, ca 3,800 men.

Spanish losses Not known exactly, light, 6 guns.

Comment Pino outflanked Castro's rearguard before it could cross the Rio Anoia; they had to abandon their artillery and escape over the mountains to Manresa.

Sources Oman, Napier.

EE San Magin, 19 February 1809, clash.

A village on the River Gaia in Catalonia (northeastern Spain), not marked on some modern maps, about 70 km west of Barcelona and 10 km east of Valls.

A Franco-Italian victory over the Spanish.

(Last action – Igualada, 18 February; next action – Valls, 25 February.)

Franco-Italian Forces M Gouvion St Cyr's VII Corps. GdD Pino's 5th (Italian) Division GdB Mazzuchelli: 1st and 2nd LtIRs, 4th and 6th LIRs (3 bns each); 7th LIR (1 bn). ca 7,200 men and 12 guns.

Franco-Italian losses Not exactly known, very light.

Spanish Forces MG Ivanzo and 2 bns, ca 1,200 men.

Spanish losses Not known, light.

Comment The Spanish had withdrawn down the River Gaia into the fortified abbey of Santes Creus. St Cyr arrived here next day to find it impregnable without siege guns. After blockading the place for 2 days, he abandoned it to join up with Souham's 1st Division at Valls to destroy Reding's Spanish army.

Sources Oman, Napier, Martinien.

EN Zaragoza, 19 December 1808 – 20 February 1809, 2nd Siege

The capital city of the northern Spanish province of Aragon, on the south bank of the Rio Ebro, at the junction of Routes 330/E7, II/E90 and A2/E804.

A French and Allied victory over the Spanish.

(Last action – Espinosa de los Montanes, 10/11 November 1808; next action – Pomar, 16 May.)

French Forces M Lannes commanding*; **III Corps** M Moncey (Junot as of February).

1st Division GdD Grandjean: 14e and 44e RIdLi (3 bns each); 2nd and 3rd IRs of the Vistula Legion (2 bns each). **Total** 5,866. **2nd Division** GdD Musnier: 114e and 115e RIdLi (3 bns each); 1st IR of the Vistula Legion (2 bns); 2nd Légion de Réserve**. **Total** 3,544. **3rd Division** GdD Morlot: 5e RILé (1 bn); 116e, 117e and 121e*** RIdLi (4 bns each). **Total** 2,637. **Cavalry** GdD Wathier: 13e CuirR, 4e HusR, Polish Lancers of the Vistula Legion: two PvCavRs **Total** 1,652. **Engineers and Sappers** 2,336 men. 40 guns. **Corps total** 16,071. **V Corps** M Mortier: 1st Division GdD Suchet: 17e RILé, 40e, 64e, 88e RIdLi (3 bns each); 34e RIdLi (4 bns). **Total** 8,477. **2nd Division** GdD Gazan: 21e, 28e, 100e, 103e RIdLi (4 bns). **Total** 7,110. **Cavalry** GdD Delaage: 10e HusR, 21e ChàCh. **Total** 926. **Artillery** 1,420 men, 30 guns. **Corps Total** 17,959. **French grand total** 24,030 men.

French losses Not known exactly; estimated at 10,000 killed, died of sickness and wounded. Gen Lacoste (chief engineer) shot dead.

* = totals present and fit for duty as on 1 February 1809.

** = detached to Alagon as garrison.

*** = detached to Tudela as garrison.

Spanish Garrison as at 1 January: Captain General Don José Palafox commanding.

1st Division BG Butron: Walloon Guards (1 bn). IR Extremadura (1 bn), Granaderos de Palafox (1 bn); Fusileros del Reyno (3 bns); Don Carlos, Batallon del Carmen, Batallon del Portillo, Batallon de Torrero, Batallon de Calatayud. 1st and 2nd Ligero de Zaragoza. 1st Cazadores Catalanes, 2nd Voluntarios de Aragon (1 bn each). **Total** 8,657 men. **2nd Division** BG Fiballer: Spanish Guards, 2nd of Valencia; 1st Voluntarios de Aragon, Cazadores de Fernando VII, (1 bn each). **Total** 2,717. **3rd Division** BG José Manso: Peñas de San Pedro (1 bn); 1st of Huesca (2 bns); Florida Blanca (½ bn); 1st Tiradores de Murcia, 1st, 2nd and 3rd Murcia (2 bns each); Suizos de Aragon (1 bn). **Total** 3,693. **4th Division** MG St March. Voluntarios de Borbon, Voluntarios de Castilla, Voluntarios de Chelva, Voluntarios de Turia, Cazadores de Fernando VII, Segorbe, Soria Militia, 1st of Alicante, 5th of Murcia (1 bn each); 2nd Tiradores de Murcia (1 coy). **Total** 3,077. **Gen Roca's Division** of the Army of the Centre: 1st of Savoia, Orihuela, 1st Cazadores de Valencia, Militia of Murcia (1 bn each); Militia of Avila (3 coys). **Total** 1,564 men. **Remnants of the 1st, 2nd, 3rd and 4th Divisions of the Army of the Centre's left wing,** destroyed at the Battle of Tudela (23 November 1808). Numbers vary from 200 to 10 men each: IRs Carmona Voluntarios de Madrid, Ordenes Militares, Africa, Navas de Tolosa, Bailén, 5th of Sevilla, Campo Mayor, Cadiz, Cuenca, Tiradores de Cartagena, 1st of Valencia and the Militia Regiments Guadix, Toro and Burgos. **Total** ca 1,200 men. **Cavalry** CavRs Rey, Numancia, Fuensanta, Husares de Palafox, Cazadores de Fernando VII, Husares de Aragon. **The remnants** of the following regiments of the Army of the Centre (ex-Tudela): Borbon, Lusitania, Olivenza, Pavia, Reyna, Santiago, Tejas. **Total** ca 2,000. **Artillery** 1,800 men. **Engineers** Zapadores de Aragon, Zapadores de Valencia, Zapadores de Calatayud.

Grand total of the regular garrison present and fit for duty: 24,808, 150 guns. A further 12,000 were sick. Thousands of the city's populace also fought with the regulars during the siege.

Garrison losses 18,000 killed or died of sickness, 4,000 captured during the siege, 8,000 surrendered. 34,000 civilians (60% of the city's population) died during the siege, the vast majority from sicknesses such as typhus. Col San Genis (chief engineer and designer of the defences) was killed on 13 January and the defence lost in effectiveness from this time.

Comment Palafox, together with the priests and clerics of the city, was the fiery soul of a resistance so bitter that every house in the place taken by the French was a miniature battle. The perimeter defences of Zaragoza had been extensively strengthened and improved after the end of the 1st siege (14 August, 1808) but the vital hill, Monte Torro – which dominates the southwest of the place – had been only lightly defended and soon fell into French hands. Palafox made two other major errors: 1. He concentrated far too many troops within the city and failed to provide an effective field force with which to harry the rear of the besiegers. 2. All his sorties were 'penny-packet' affairs which squandered the soldiers' lives to no great effect.

He lacked a strategic sense for warfare. The city was one great mess of unburied dead at the end of the siege and took many years to recover. Palafox was imprisoned in France.

Sources: Oman, Martinien.

EE Valls, 25 February 1809, battle

A town in Catalonia in north eastern Spain, about 20 km north of Tarragona on Route 240.

A Franco-Italian victory over the Spanish.

(Last action – San Magin, 19 February; next action – Alcañiz, 23 May.)

Franco-Italian Forces M Gouvion St Cyr's VII Corps. **GdD Souham's 1st Division** 1er RILé (3 bns); 3e RILé (1st Bn); 7e RIdLi (2 bns); 42e RIdLi (3 bns); 67e RIdLi (1 bn). **Total** ca 5,500 men, 12 guns. **GdD Pino's 5th (Italian) Division** 1st and 2nd LtIRs, 4th and 6th LIRs (3 bns each); 7th LIR (1 bn). **Total** ca 6,500 men. Italian Cavalry Brigade: Dragone Napoleone, Cacciatori Reale (4 sqns each). French Cavalry Brigade: 24e DragR, 3e Provisional CuirR, 3e Provisional ChàCh (4 sqns each).

Franco-Italian total ca 13,000.

Franco-Italian losses About 1,000 killed and wounded.

Spanish Forces LG Reding Granadan Division Reding's Swiss IR (1 bn); 1st Granada IR (2 bns); Santa Fé IR (2 bns); 1st Antequera IR (1 bn); **Total** 5,760 men. **Catalan Division** Guards (Spanish and Walloon) (430 men); Soria IR (1 bn); 2nd Savoia IR (1 bn); Provincial Grenadiers of Old and New Castile (2 bns); Wimpffen's Swiss IR (2 bns); Palma Militia (350 men). **Total** 5,020 men. **Cavalry** Hus de Granada (4 sqns); Hus Espanoles (2 sqns); **Total** 700 men.

Spanish totals 13 bns, 12,780 infantry, 700 cavalry, 8 guns.

Spanish losses 1,400 killed and wounded, 1,600 captured, 8 guns, several colours and all the baggage. General Reding was killed.

Comment The Spanish crossed the River Francoli and forced Souham's isolated division back up against Valls then, instead of either finishing Souham off or getting into Tarragona, Reding called a halt to the fighting to give his men a rest after their night march.

In this lull, St Cyr came up with the Italian cavalry and Pino's division. Reding panicked and withdrew over the bridge; amazingly enough, the Franco-Italians did not attack him during this extremely vulnerable manoeuvre. The Spanish formed line of battle on the adjacent hills and remained static for three hours. St Cyr ordered an assault. The Spanish let them close to about 100 metres, gave one volley and fled. Reding charged the 24e Dragons with his staff but was beaten off and fatally wounded. The Spanish fell back into Tarragona which St Cyr promptly blockaded.

Sources Oman, Napier, Martinien.

PN La Trepa, 6 March 1809, clash

A village near Puebla de Sanabria in the north western Spanish province of Zamora.

A French victory over the Spanish.

(Last action – Ferrol, 26 January (EG); next action – Povoa de Lanhoso, 20 March.)

French Forces GdD Franceschi with Soult's II Corps Light Cavalry: 1er HusR, 8e and 22e ChàCh, Ch Hanovrienne (4 sqns each).

French losses Not known, light.

Spanish Forces MG Mahy commanding: IRs Segovia, Zamora, Barcelona, Majorca, Orense, Betanzos and Aragon; all very weak, about 1,200 men in all.

Spanish losses 300 killed, 400 captured and three colours, one each from Orense, Betanzos and Aragon.

Comment Soult started out on 30 January along the coast road south from La Coruña to invade Portugal. The Spanish-held fortresses of Vigo and Tuy surrendered to him at once but his attempt to cross the border by boats at the village of Camposancos on the north bank of the Minho estuary on 16 February was beaten off by Portuguese militia with a loss of some drowned and 40 captured. On 17 February he had brushed aside Spanish guerrillas at Mourentan and Francelos and reached Orense to find the bridge intact and undefended. After resting his men Soult pushed south via Alariz, Ginzo, Monterey and Chaves.

Mahy's brigade of La Romana's army, was destroyed. Soult crossed the frontier into Portugal, between Monterey and Chaves on 9 March 1809.

Sources Oman, Napier, Martinien.

EG Villafranca, 17 March 1809, surrender of

A small town in the northern Spanish province of Leon, on Route VI, about 20 km northwest of Ponferrada.

A Spanish victory over the French.

(Last action – Ferrol, 26 January; next action – Gallegos, 19 May.)

French Garrison 6e RILé (1 bn) plus several hundred sick and wounded, ca 1,200 men.

French losses 700 killed and wounded, 574 unwounded prisoners.

Spanish Forces General La Romana. IR La Princesa (2 bns); Asturias (2 bns) 1 x FAB.

Spanish totals 3,800 men and 6 guns.

Spanish losses Not known exactly, very light.

Comment The Spaniards took the town against little opposition. This type of raid in French rear areas was to become all too frequent in future.

Sources Oman, Napier, Martinien.

EW Mesa de Ibor, 17 March 1809, clash.

A small town in the mountains of the Sierra de Altamira in western Spain; south of the River Tagus (Tajo), east of Deleitosa and of the River Ibor. Apparently now known as 'Castanar de Ibor'.

A Franco-Allied victory over the Spanish.

(This was the first action in this campaign; next action – Miajadas, 21 March.)

Allied Forces GdD Leval's 2nd Division of Sebastiani's IV Corps: IR Holland, Hessen-Darmstadt, (IR 'Gross-und Erbprinz'), 2nd Nassau LIR; Baden (2 bns each) and Frankfurt (1 bn).

Allied totals 9 bns, ca 3,000 men.

Allied losses 17 officers, 60 NCOs and 421 killed and wounded.

Spanish Forces LG Del Parque's Division: IRs Murcia*, Cantabria*, Provincial of Jaén, Provincial of Chinchilla, Voluntarios Catalanes*, Cazadores de Barbastro*, Campo Mayor*, Principe*, Zaragoza*.

* = regiments of the old regular army; the others were new levies or militia.

Spanish totals ca 5,000 men and 6 guns.

Spanish losses According to the French about 800 killed and wounded, 1,000 captured and all the baggage. The 6 guns they threw over a cliff. German sources give the Spanish casualties as much lighter.

Comment The Spaniards withdrew south and as a result of this action the Spanish division of General Henestrosa abandoned the Tagus bridge at Almáraz thus giving the French access into the area along a road fit for artillery. Although the bridge had been broken by the Spanish, the French ferried their guns over and this led directly to the battle of Medellin.

Sources Oman, Martinien, Isenbart, Bernays.

PN Povoa de Lanhoso (Cavalho d'Este or Braga), 20 March 1809, clash

A village in northern Portugal, 10 km east of Braga, just south of Route 103 from Chaves.

A French victory over the Portuguese.

(Last action – La Trepa, 6 March; next action – Vigo, 27 March.)

French Forces M Soult commanding II Corps:

4th Division GdD Heudelet: 15e and 32e RILé (1 bn each); 26e and 66e RIdLi (2 bns each); 82e RIdLi, Légion du Midi, Garde de Paris and Légion Hanovrienne (1 bn each). **Total** 10 bns, ca 3,000 men. **3rd Division** GdD Delaborde: 17e RILé, 17e, 70e and 86e RIdLi (3 bns each). **Total** 12 bns ca 5,800 men. **2nd Division** GdD Mermet: 31e RILé; 47e and 122e RIdLi (4 bns each); 2nd, 3rd and 4th Swiss (1 bn each). **Total** 15 bns, ca 5,400 men. **3rd Dragoon Division** GdD Lahoussaye: 17e, 18e, 19e and 27e DragR (4 sqns each). **Total** ca 1,200 men. **II Corps Light Cavalry** GdD Franceschi: 1er HusR, 8e DragR; 22e ChàCh; Ch Hanovrienne (4 sqns each). **Total** ca 1,250 men.

French totals 37 bns, 32 sqns, 12 guns, ca 16,650 men.

French losses Not known exactly, ca 600 killed and wounded.

Portuguese Forces General Baron von Eben commanding 2nd Bn Loyal Lusitanian Legion. 9th (Viana) Portuguese LIR, ca 22,000 Ordenenza and peasants only about half of whom were armed. 18 guns.

Portuguese losses 4,000 killed, 400 captured, 17 guns, 5 colours, all baggage.

Comment Soult, correctly assessing the low quality of his opposition, mounted a direct frontal assault which was totally successful. The Portuguese peasants were butchered.

Sources Oman, Martinien, Mayne.

EW Miajadas, 21 March 1809, ambush

A village in the western Spanish province of Extremadura, south of the Sierra de Guadalupe and on Route V/E90 between Trujillo in the north and Merida.

A Spanish victory over the French.

(Last action – Mesa de Ibor, 17 March; next action Ciudad Real, 27 March.)

French Forces GdD Lasalle's Light Cavalry Division of the Reserve Cavalry, spearheading M Victor's thrust south to find and destroy Cuesta's army. 10e ChàCh 4 sqns, ca 420 men under Col Subervie.

French losses 1 officer and 62 men killed, 70 wounded. Martinien gives no officer casualties for this day.

Spanish Forces LG Henestrosa: Infante and Almanza CavRs 8 sqns, ca 1,200 men.

Spanish losses None.

Comment This was a well-laid Spanish trap, baited with one cavalry squadron north of the village, the rest of the cavalry and the infantry concealed on either side of the road. The French rode straight into it.

After the action the Spanish withdrew south at the approach of Victor's main body.

Sources Oman, Martinien.

EW Ciudad Real, 27 March 1809, clash

A town in the central Spanish province of La Mancha, about 160 km south of Madrid at the junction of Routes 401, 415, 420 and 430.

A French victory over the Spanish.

(Last action – Miajadas, 21 March; next action – Medellin, 9 March.)

French Forces GdD Sebastiani commanding IV Corps. GdD Milhaud's 2nd Dragoon Division of the Reserve Cavalry: 1er, 2e, 4e, 9e, 14e and 26e DragRs (24 sqns); ca 2,500 men. IV Corps Cavalry: 3rd Dutch HusR; Polish Lancers of the Vistula Legion (4 sqns), ca 1,000 men.

French totals 32 sqns, ca 3,500 men.

French losses About 100 killed and wounded.

Spanish Forces LG Cartaojal commanding. Exact details not known; ca 10,000 infantry, 2,500 cavalry.

Spanish losses Killed and wounded not known (probably very light), 6 officers and over 2,000 men captured. 5 guns, 3 colours.

Comment The opposing forces had been sparring with each other around Ciudad Real for some days when Sebastiani saw his chance, caught Cartaojal in the open, charged the Spanish cavalry with his own and scattered them.

Sources Oman, Martinien, Malibran and Chelminski, Gembarzewski.

PN Vigo, 27 March 1809, capture of

A fortified port on the south side of the estuary of the Rio de Vigo, on the Atlantic coast of Galicia in north western Spain on Route A51/E1.

An Allied victory over the French.

(Last action – Povoa de Lanhoso, 20 March; next action – Oporto, 29 March.)

French Forces Col Chalot commanding one infantry battalion and several hundred sick, wounded, non-combatants and camp followers.

French losses All captured; 60 waggons, 339 horses and Soult's military chest of over 6,000 pounds sterling.

Spanish Forces Local guerrillas supplied with weapons from two British frigates HMS *Lively* and *Venus*.

Spanish losses Not known, very slight.

Comment Col Chalot surrendered on condition that he and his men be handed over to the British. This was done and 23 officers and over 800 men passed into captivity. Soult's isolation in Portugal deepened.

Sources Oman.

EW Medellin, 29 March 1809, battle

A town in the Spanish province of Extremadura, just south of the Rio Zújar, about 40 km east of Merida and 104 km east of Badajoz.

A Franco-Allied victory over the Spanish.

(Last action – Miajadas, 21 March; next action – Ciudad Real 27 March.)

Franco-Allied Forces M Victor commanding GdD Leval's (German) 2nd Division of Sebastiani's IV Corps: IR Baden; 2nd Nassau IR, Hessen-Darmstadt, IR 'Gross-und Erbprinz' (1 x Voltigeur Coy); 4 bns and 1 coy: 1 x FAB. GdD Lasalle's Light Cavalry Division 10e and 26e ChàCh; 8e DragR (4 sqns each); 1 x HAB. GdD Latour-Maubourg's 1st Dragoon Division 2e, 4e, 9e, 14e and 26e DragR (4 sqns each); 1 x HAB. GdD Villatte's 3rd Division of I Corps 27e RILé, 63e, 94e and 95e RIdLi (3 bns each); 2 x FAB. GdD Ruffin's 1st Division of I Corps was in reserve and not engaged.

Franco-Allied totals 16 bns, 1 coy, 32 sqns, 30 guns, ca 17,000 men.

Franco-Allied losses Victor reported '300 killed and wounded'; the 2nd Nassau LIR gives I Corps' loss as '700' with its own loss as '149 killed and wounded'.

Spanish Forces General Cuesta commanding the divisions of LGs Henestrosa (left flank); Del Parque, Trias, Portago and Albuquerque (right flank). **Infantry** Spanish Guards* (4th Bn); Walloon Guards* (2nd and 4th Bn); Majorca* (2nd Bn); Catalonia* (2ndLt); Badajoz (2 bns); Provinciales de Badajoz; Provincial Grenadiers, Merida, La Serena (1 bn each); Jaén* and Irlanda* (2 bns each); Provincial of Toledo, Provincial of Burgos; Sevilla* (3rd Bn); Volunteers of Madrid (2nd Bn); Albuquerque's Division (ex Army of the Centre); Campo Mayor*, Provincial of Guadix, Provincial of Cordoba, Osuna (2 bns); Granaderos del General and Tiradores de Cadiz. **Total** 27 bns, ca 20,000 men. **Cavalry** 1st Hus of Extremadura* (formerly 'Maria Luisa'); 4th HusR* (Voluntarios d'Espagne); CavR del Rey Nr 1* and Infante Nr 4*; DragR Almanza Nr 3*, de la Reyna Nr 2*, Cazadores de Llerena, Imperial de Toledo and Carabineros Reales.

All nine regiments very weak, about 3,000 men in all. **Artillery** 30 guns.

Spanish totals ca 24,000 men.

Spanish losses Estimates vary. Bodart gives 8,000 killed and wounded and 2,000 captured. Oman states: 8,150 killed and wounded, 1,850 captured. Isenbart shows 10,000 killed and 6,000 (mostly wounded) prisoners.

The number of cannon taken varies from 20 (Oman) to 16 (Bodart). Captured colours are variously put at 9 (Oman) to 12 (Bodart) to 'many' (Isenbart).

* = regiments of the old regular army.

Comment This battle won Victor the province of Extremadura and utterly destroyed Cuesta's army. It was many days before he could gather a battalion together. By the end of April Cuesta had gathered another 20,000 infantry and 3,000 cavalry.

Sources Oman, Isenbart, Martinien, Keim.

PN Oporto, 29 March 1809, 1st battle

A fortified city port on the north bank of the estuary of the River Douro in north western Portugal.

A French victory over the Portuguese.

(Last action – Vigo, 27 March; next action – Amarante, 18 April – 3 May.)

French Forces M Soult commanding the II Corps. **1st Division** GdD Merle: 2e and 4e RILé, 15e RIdLi (4 bns each); 36e RIdLi (3 bns). **2nd Division** GdD Mermet: 31e RILé; 47e and 122e RIdLi (4 bns each); 2nd, 3rd and 4th Swiss (1 bn each). **3rd Division** GdD Heudelet: 26e and 66e RIdLi (2 bns each); 15e and 32e RILé ; 82e RIdLi, Légion du Midi, Garde de Paris and Légion Hanovrienne (1 bn each). **II Corps Light Cavalry** GdD Franceschi: 1er HusR, 8e DragR; 22e ChàCh; Ch Hanovrienne (4 sqns each). **3rd Dragoon Division** GdD Lahoussaye:17e, 18e, 19e and 27e DragR (4 sqns each). From Lorge's 4th Drag Division: 13e and 22e DragR (4 sqns each).

French totals 40 bns, 24 sqns, 25 guns, ca 13,500 infantry and 3,500 cavalry.

French losses GdB Foy captured; 72 officers and 2,000 men killed and wounded.

Portuguese Forces A de Castro, Bishop of Oporto commanding. Gen Lima and Gen Pareiras: 6th, 18th and 21st Portuguese LIR (2 bns each); 9th LIR (1 bn); two other line infantry battalions, 2nd Bn Loyal Lusitanian Legion (remnants); 12th CavR (about 1½ sqns). **Total** regular troops – ca 4,500. Ordenanza – 10,000; armed citizens of Oporto – 9,000.

Portuguese totals ca 24,000 men and 197 guns.

Portuguese losses About 8,000 killed, some wounded, 225 captured, 197 guns, 20 colours.

Comment The vast, untrained mob of the Portuguese broke into fragments when the French charged. All Portuguese regiments involved were annihilated. There was massive loss of civilian life when they tried to escape south across the river. Soult took the city with large stocks of English military and civilian stores, a squadron of Spanish naval vessels and thirty merchantmen laden with wine.

Sources Oman, Napier, Martinien, Bodart, Kausler, Mayne, Ferreira.

DV Hirschau, 11 April 1809, skirmish

A village in north eastern Bavaria on the Ehenbach stream 14 km north northeast of Amberg, on Route B14.

A French victory over the Austrians.

(Last action – this was the first action of the campaign; next action Amberg, 13 April.)

French Forces GdB Grandeau's 3rd Bde of Friant's 2nd Division of Davout's III Corps. 111e RIdLi (1 bn); 1er ChàCh (part); 1 battery.

French totals ca 1,200 men.

French losses 2 officers and 20 men dead, wounded and missing.

Austrian Forces Oberst Steffanini commanding: 7e Jäger bn (1 bn); UlR Merveldt Nr 1 (2 sqns) of the II Corps' (Kollowrath) vanguard.

Austrian totals ca 950 men.

Austrian losses 6 men and 1 horse dead, 5 officers, 43 men and 4 horses wounded, 3 men missing.

Comment The Austrians were trying to catch Davout's isolated III Corps before the Emperor Napoleon could save it. Most Austrian casualties were caused by French artillery fire.

Sources Krauss, Martinien.

IN Venzone, 11 April 1809, 1st clash

A village in north eastern Italy on Route 13, up the valley of the River Tagliamento, about 13 km north of Udine.

An Austrian victory over the French.

(This was the opening action of the war in northern Italy this year; next action – Pordenone, 15 April.)

French Forces GdB Dessaix (of GdD Broussier's division) commanding: 9e, 84e and 92e RIdLi (4 bns each); 24e DragR (4 sqns); 1 x FAB (8 guns).

French totals 12 bns (of which only 6 came into action), 4 sqns, 8 guns, ca 6,000 men.

French losses Not known, light, GdB Dessaix wounded. Broussier reported 30 killed, 250 wounded, a dozen captured.

Austrian Forces Obstlt Volkmann commanding: IR J Jellačič Nr 53 (3rd bn); IR Eh Franz Nr 52 (1st Bn); GzIR 2nd Banal Nr 11 (1st Bn); HusR Ott Nr 5 (2 sqns).

Austrian totals 3 bns, 2 sqns, 4 guns, ca 3,500 men.

Austrian losses 17 dead, 143 wounded, 63 captured.

Comment Volkmann earned the Maria Theresia order for his conduct. Broussier fell back south to Dignano and Spilimbergo, crossing the Tagliamento and leaving a garrison of four companies of 92e RIdLi in Osoppo Fortress. The Austrians stayed in Venzone.

Sources Wrede, Hoehn-Veltze, Martinien.

TY Sterzing (Vipitino), 11 April 1809, clash

A town in the (now Italian) province of South Tyrol on the River Eisack (Isarco), at the junction of the Pfitscher Tal (Val de Vizzel) and the Passeier Tal (Val Passiria) on the old Route 12. The major motorway the E6/A22 now runs just west of the town.

A Tyrolean victory over the Bavarians.

(This was one of the opening actions in this campaign; next action – Innsbruck Pass, 11–13 April.)

Bavarian Forces Obstlt Baron Donnersberg commanding:

4th Lt I BN Donnersberg: 3 coys and 1 gun ca 420 men.

Bavarian losses All captured.

Tyrolean Forces Andreas Hofer [the 'Sandwirt' (Innkeeper) from Passeier] commanding: ca 5,000 local armed peasants.

Comment The rural population of the Tyrol, chafing under the Bavarian yoke since 1805, rose in revolt and overwhelmed the isolated Bavarian garrisons.

Sources Leyh, HGM 20, Charrié, Martinien.

TY Innsbruck, 11–13 April 1809, clashes

Centred around the Tyrolean capital of Innsbruck in the valley of the River Inn in Austria.

A Tyrolean victory over the Franco-Bavarians.

(This was one of three simultaneous openings in this theatre; next action – Lueg Pass, 1 May.)

Bavarians GL Baron Kinkel commanding: In Innsbruck: IR Nr 11 (2 bns); DragR Nr 1 (2 sqns); 3 guns. In Brixen: Obstlt Wrede commanding: 2nd Lt I Bn (1 bn); 4th Lt I bn (1 coy); DragR Nr 1 (1 sqn); 2 guns. Along the Inn valley from Hall to Wörgl Obstlt Bernclau: 3rd LtI Bn (1 bn).

Bavarian total 4 bns, 1 coy, 2 sqns, 5 guns, ca 4,030 men.

Bavarian losses 500 dead and wounded, 3,000 captured, 5 guns, 2 colours.

French Forces GdB Bisson commanding: 3,500 men (new conscript drafts) marching into Innsbruck from the Brenner Pass.

French losses 3,500 captured.

Tyrolean Forces Several thousand peasants without a centralized command structure.

Tyrolean losses Not known, very slight.

Comment The Franco-Bavarians were totally surprised by this popular uprising. The victorious peasants expected support from the Austrian army (Jellačič's division and Chasteler's brigade were in the area) but the events of Aspern, Wagram, Raab and Znaim dictated that these regular units were withdrawn eastwards and the rebellious peasants were left to their fate.

Sources HGM 20, Bessel, Wrede.

DV Amberg, 13 April 1809, skirmish

A town in north eastern Bavaria, on the River Vils, ca 50 km north of Regensburg, at the crossing of Routes B85 and B299, just north of the Autobahn A6/E50.

An Austrian victory over the French.

(Last action - Hirschau, 11 April; next action - Ursensollen, 14 April.)

French Forces GdB Grandeau's 3rd Brigade of Friant's 2nd Division, Davout's III Corps. 111e RIdLi (1 bn); 1er ChàCh (4 sqns); ca 1,050 men.

French losses 1 killed, 5 officers, 24 men and 15 horses wounded, 14 men and 8 horses captured.

Austrian Forces Obst Steffanini commanding: 7th and 8th Jägers (2 bns); UlR Merveldt Nr 1 (4 sqns); ca 1,750 men.

Austrian losses 3 killed, 37 men wounded, 7 men missing.

Comment Davout's rearguard gave a good account of itself in this action.

Sources Krauss, Martinien.

DV Ursensollen, 14 April 1809, skirmish

A small town in north eastern Bavaria (Germany), 6 km southwest of Amberg, on Route B299, ,just south of the Autobahn A6/E50.

An Austrian victory over the French.

(Last action - Amberg, 13 April; next action - Landshut, 16 April.)

French Forces 15e RILé (2 bns); 1er ChàCh (4 sqns); 1 x HAB, ca 1,600 men and 6 guns.

French losses Not known exactly; about 150 killed and wounded.

Austrian Forces GM Baron von Wintzingerode commanding: IR EH Johann Nr 35 (3rd bn); 3rd Jägers (1 bn); HusR Blankenstein Nr 6 (2 sqns); ca 1,400 men.

Austrian losses 40 men and 5 horses killed; 3 officers, 115 men and 12 horses wounded, 41 men missing.

Comment The Austrians were part of Bellegarde's I Corps' advanced guard. Their lack of artillery was a considerable disadvantage.

Sources Krauss, Martinien.

IN Pordenone, 15 April 1809, clash

A town in the north eastern Italian province of Friaul, on Route 13 from Udine (50 km to the east) to Vittorio Veneto (34 km to the west) and at the northern end of the Autobahn A28.

An Austrian victory over the French.

(Last action - Venzone, 11 April; next action - Sacile (Fontana Fredda), 16 April).

French Forces GdD Sahuc commanding: 35e RIdLi (3 bns); 8 HusR (4 sqns); 6e ChàCh (4 sqns); 1 x FAB.

French totals 3 bns, 8 sqns, 6 guns, ca 4,800 men.

French losses 500 killed and wounded, 2,000 captured, 4 guns; the eagle and two battalion flags of the 35e were taken by the 1st bn, 1st Banal GzIR Nr 10.

Austrian Forces FML Frimont commanding: the Avantgarde of VIII Corps: 1st Banal GzIR Nr 10 (2 bns); IR F Jellačič Nr 62 (1st bn); IR EH Franz Nr 52 (3rd Bn); ChL Hohenzollern Nr 2 (2 sqns); HusR Ott Nr 5 (6 sqns); HusR Frimont Nr 9 (4 sqns); 2½ x HAB.

Austrian totals 4 bns, 12 sqns, 15 guns, ca 5,900 men.

Austrian losses 221 killed and wounded, 32 captured.

Comment The rapid Austrian advance despite dreadful weather conditions, caught Viceroy Prince Eugène's forces by surprise. Before he could concentrate, Sahuc's isolated division was badly mauled at the hamlet of Rorai Grande (now a suburb of Pordenone). The 35e was practically destroyed.

Sources Wrede, Hoehn-Veltze, Martinien.

IN Sacile (Fontana Fredda), 16 April 1809, battle

A small town in the northeastern Italian province of Friaul, on Route 13 about 10 km west of Pordenone and 14 km east of Vittorio Veneto.

An Austrian victory over the French.

(Last action - Pordenone, 15 April; next action - Malghera, 23 April.)

French Forces Prince Eugène de Beauharnais, Viceroy of Italy commanding: GdD Seras; GdB Garreau: 35e RIdLi (½ bn); 53e and 106e RIdLi (8 bns); 6e ChàCh (4 sqns); 12 guns. GdD Severoli (Italians); 1st and 7th LIR (8 bns); 12 guns; Dragone Napoleone (4 sqns). GdD Grenier; GdB Teste 11e RIdLi (4th Bn); 52e RIdLi (4 bns); 102e RIdLi (2 bns); 1er RIdLi (4 bns); 1 sqn, 10 guns. GdD Sahuc; 6e HusR, 8e ChàCh (5 sqns). GdD Broussier: 9e and 84e RIdLi (8 bns); 92e RIdLi (3 bns); 25e ChàCh (4 sqns); 12 guns. GdD Barbou *: 8e and 18e RILé, 5e and 23e RIdLi (2 bns each); 60e, 79e and 81e RIdLi (6 bns); 8 guns.

* = this division was not engaged.

French totals 49 bns, 35,000 infantry, 16 sqns, 2050 cavalry, 54 guns.

French losses GdB Teste wounded, GdB Pages wounded and captured; 3,000 killed and wounded,

3,500 captured, (another 3,000 next day), 19 guns; 23 ammunition waggons, 2 colours (unidentified) were also taken.

Austrian Forces GdK Archduke John commanding:

VIII Corps FML Albert Gyulai; GM Colloredo: IR Strassoldo Nr 27 and St Julien Nr 61 (3 bns each); GM Gajoli: IR F Jellačič Nr 62 (3 bns); GzIR 1st Banal Nr 10 (2 bns). GM Kálnássy: GzIR Oguliner Nr 3 (2 bns); IRs Reisky Nr 13, Simbschen Nr 43 and J Jellačič Nr 53 (3 bns each). Artillery: 2 x FAB, 1½ x HAB, 1 x 12 pdr FAB*.

IX Corps FML Ignaz Gyulai; GM Kleinmayern: Grenadiers (4 bns); GzIR Szluin Nr 4 (2 bns); GM Marziani: IRs EH Franz Nr 52 and Allvintzy Nr 19 (3 bns each). GM Gavassini: GzIR Ottocaner Nr 2 (2 bns); GM Sebottendorf: LWIR Graz (3 bns). Artillery: 1½ FAB, 2 x HAB, 1 x 12 pdr FAB*.

Cavalry FML Wolfskeel, GM Hager, DragRs Savoy Nr 5 and Hohenlohe Nr 2 (6 sqns each); GM Splényi, HusR Ott Nr 5 and EH Josef Nr 2 (8 sqns each); HusR Frimont Nr 9 (6 sqns). **Total** 34 sqns.

Austrian totals 35 bns, 35,000 infantry, 34 sqns, 4,000 cavalry and 55-61 guns.

Austrian losses 2,617 killed and wounded, 532 captured, 697 missing.

* = it is not certain if either or both of these batteries were in action.

Comment Prince Eugène hoped to snatch a quick victory to 'paper over' his defeat at Pordenone but did not wait for Lamarque's infantry, Pully's dragoons and part of the Italian Guard (8,000 men and 10 guns) to join him. The IX Austrian corps drove into his left flank while his centre and right wing were heavily involved with VIII Corps around Porcia. Eugène was thrown back over the Livenza and onto his reserves; the Austrians rested for a day.

Sources Wrede, Hoehn-Veltze, Martinien.

DV Landshut, 16 April 1809, clash

A town in south eastern Bavaria on the River Isar about 60 km northeast of München (Munich), on Routes B11, B15 and motorway A92/E53.

An Austrian victory over the Bavarians.

(Last action - Ursensollen, 14 April; next action - Geisling 17 April.)

Bavarian Forces GdD von Deroy commanding (3rd Division): 5th LtI Bn Buttlar (1 bn); 7th LtI Bn Günther (1 bn); 5th LIR Preysing (2 bns); 10th LIR Juncker (2 bns); DragR Taxis Nr 2 (4 sqns). Artillery: 6 guns.

Bavarian totals ca 4,200 men.

Bavarian losses 1 officer, 12 men and 7 horses dead, 100 men and 22 horses wounded, 3 men captured, 1 officer and 51 men missing.

Austrian Forces GM Radetzky commanding: Gradiskaner GzIR Nr 8 (1st and 2nd Bns); HusR Kienmayer Nr 8 (4 sqns). Artillery: 6 guns of the Advanced Guard of the V Corps.

Austrian totals ca 930 men.

Austrian Losses 1 officer, 16 men and 8 horses dead, 1 officer, 77 men and 46 horses wounded, 1 man and 8 horses missing.

Comment The Austrians here forced the crossing of the River Isar; the 51 missing Bavarians were mostly deserters from the newly-raised Tyrolean 7th Lt I Bn.

Sources Krauss, Bezzel, Martinien, Leyh.

DV Geisling, 17 April 1809, skirmish

A village in the southern German state of Württemberg, 24 km north of Ulm.

An Austrian victory over the French.

(Last action - Landshut, 16 April; next action - Siegenburg, 18 April.)

French Forces 11e ChàCH (4 sqns).

French totals ca 450 men.

French losses 16 men and horses captured.

Austrian Forces Ch LR Klenau Nr 5 (2 sqns).

Austrian totals ca 250 men.

Austrian losses 4 horses.

Comment This was an Austrian 'Streifkorps' or raiding party disrupting the French lines of communication.

Sources Krauss, Martinien.

DV Siegenburg, 18 April 1809, skirmish

A village in eastern Bavaria (Germany), about 30 km east of Ingolstadt, just south of the crossing of Routes B299 and B301, just north of the motorway A93.

A Bavarian victory over the Austrians.

(Last action - Geisling, 17 April; next action - Hausn and Teugn (Thann), 19 April.)

Bavarian Forces GM Preysing commanding: ChLR König Nr 2 (4 sqns); ChLR Leiningen Nr 3 (4 sqns); ca 600 men.

Bavarian losses 10 killed, 14 wounded, 8 missing.

Austrian Forces GM Radetzky commanding the Advanced Guard of the V Corps: GzIR Gradiskaner Nr 8 (2 bns); UlR Eh Karl Nr 3 (4 sqns); ca 800 men.

Austrian losses 7 men and 2 horses killed, 11 men wounded, 7 men captured, 23 men missing.

Comment This was a minor brush as the opposing forces closed for the impending battle of Abensberg on 20 April.

Sources Krauss, Leyh.

DV Hausen and Teugn (Thann), 19 April 1809, clash

Two villages in eastern Bavaria (Germany), about 30 km south of Regensburg (Ratisbon) on the Danube, between Routes B16 and motorway A93.

A French victory over the Austrians.

(Last action – Siegenburg, 18 April; next action – Schneidhart, Dünzling and Regensburg, 19 April.)

French Forces M Davout (III Corps) commanding. III Corps also fought this day at Schneidhart and Dünzling and the losses shown here are for both actions: GdD Morand (1st Division): 13e RILé (3 bns); 17e RIdLi (3 bns) and 12 guns. GdD Friant: (2e Division) 15e RILé (3 bns); 33e RIdLi (3 bns); 48e RIdLi (3 bns); 12 guns. GdD Gudin (3e Division): 7e RILé (3 bns). GdD St Hilaire (4th Division): 10e RILé (4 bns); 3e, 57e, 72e and 105e RIdLi (16 bns) and 12 guns. GdD Montbrun (Light Cavalry Division): 7e HusR (4 sqns).

French totals 38 bns, 4 sqns, 36 guns, ca 28,000 men.

French losses ca 4,000 dead and wounded.

Austrian Forces Archduke Charles commanding the III Corps and the I Reserve Corps:

III Corps FZM Prinz Hohenzollern commanding. IR Schröder Nr 7 (3 bns); IR Manfredini Nr 12 (3 bns); IR Kaunitz Nr20 (3 bns); IR Würzburg Nr 23 (2 bns); IR Württemberg Nr 38 (2 bns); IR Wenzel Colloredo Nr 56 (3 bns); GzIR Peterwardeiner Nr 9 (2nd Bn); Legion EH Carl (1st Bn); HusR EH Ferdinand Nr 3 (8 sqns). Artillery: 8 batteries; engineers (3rd Division). **Totals** 18 bns, 8 sqns, 50 guns, ca 22,000 men.

I Reserve Corps Grenadier Division FML Lindenau commanding: Gren bns Stark, Leiningen, Georgy, Pecadue, Cappy, Hohenlohe, Hahn, Nissel, Portner, Legrand. **Totals** 10 bns, ca 6,000 men.

Austrian totals 28 bns, 8 sqns, 50 guns, ca 28,000 men.

Austrian losses III Corps – 4 generals wounded, 15 officers, ca 519 men and ca 20 horses killed, 76 officers, ca 2,386 men and ca 28 horses wounded, 4 officers, ca 162 men captured; 5 officers and ca 680 men and 3 horses missing. **Total** 3,862 men.

Wounded Generals: FML Lusignan, GM Alois Liechtenstein, GM Bieber, GM Moriz Liechtenstein. The casualty returns for the artillery are missing.

Comment Davout was moving from Regensburg back southwest (on Napoleon's orders) to concentrate with the main body of the Grande Armée between Geisenfeld and Pfaffenhofen.

At the same time, Archduke Charles was advancing west with the III, IV, and I Reserve Corps to destroy Davout whom he still believed to be in Regensburg.

Davout won the day and he made his junction with Napoleon in safety. The Austrians withdrew east to consolidate: Napoleon took up the chase in earnest.

Sources Krauss, Bezzel, Martinien, Leyh, Krausler.

DV Regensburg and Stadtamhof, 19–20 April 1809, clash and the capitulation

A suburb of present day Regensburg (Ratisbon) on the River Danube in south eastern Germany, at the crossing of motorways A3/E56 and A93.

An Austrian victory over the French.

(Last action – Hausen and Teugn (Thann), 19 April; next action – Schneidhart and Dünzling, 19 April.)

French Forces Col Baron Coutard commanding: 65e RIdLi (3 bns). Part of Gen Lagrange's 3rd Division of Junot's Reserve Corps.

French totals ca 2,300 men.

French losses 11 officers and ca 200 men dead, wounded and captured.

Austrian Forces Part of the II Army Corps FZM Count Kollowrath commanding: IR Froon Nr 54 (3 bns); IR Zedtwitz Nr 25 (3 bns); Jägers bns Nr 7 and Nr 8 (2 bns).

Austrian totals 8 bns, ca 5,600 men.

Austrian losses 4 officers and 69 men dead; 1 officer and at least 219 men wounded; 2 officers and 73 men captured; at least 85 men missing. **Total** at least 453 men.

The figures for the wounded, captured and missing for the Jäger bn Nr 8 are not known. IR Froon lost a colour.

Comment The 65e RIdLi were the garrison of Regensburg and capitulated next day with 55 officers and

1,933 men. The Austrian prisoners taken from II Corps on 19 April were released.

Sources Krauss, Martinien, Leyh.

DV Schneidhart and Dünzling (Thann), 19 April 1809, clashes

Two hamlets about 12 km south of Regensburg (Ratisbon) on the River Danube east of the motorway A93.

A French victory over the Austrians.

(Last action – Hausen and Teugn (Thann), 19 April: next action – Abensberg , 20 April.)

French Forces GdD Montbrun (4th Cavalry Division) and GdB Leclerc (1st Brigade, 3rd Division, III Corps) commanding: 7e RILé (3 bns); 5e and 7e HusR (4 sqns).

French totals 3 bns, 8 sqns, 6 guns, ca 4,000 men.

French losses ca 18 officers and 215 men killed, wounded and captured.

Austrian Forces FM Rosenberg commanding the IV Corps. IR EH Ludwig Nr 8 (3 bns); IR Czartoryski Nr 9 (3 bns); IR Coburg Nr 22 (3 bns); IR Bellegarde Nr 44 (3 bns); IR Reuss-Greitz Nr 55 (2 bns); GzIR Deutsch-Banater Nr 12 (2 bns); ChLR Vincent Nr 4 (6 sqns); HusR Stipsicz Nr 10 (8 sqns).

Austrian totals 6 bns, 14 sqns, 36 guns, ca 12,300 men.

Austrian losses 116 men and 20 horses dead, 17 officers, 435 men and 53 horses wounded; 5 officers, 352 men and 1 horse captured; 1 officer, 158 men and 3 horses missing. **Total** 1,084 men and 77 horses.

Comment These clashes were the run-up to the battle of Abensberg.

Sources Krauss, Martinien, Leyh.

DV Arnhofen, 19 April 1809, clash

A hamlet in south eastern Bavaria, just south of the River Danube, about 30 km east of Ingolstadt.

A French (Bavarian) victory over the Austrians.

(Last action – Schneidhart and Dünzling, 19 April; next action – Offenstetten, Biburg-Siegenburg, Rohr and Rothenburg , 20 April).

Bavarian Forces Part of VII Corps, Marshal Lefebvre, Duke of Danzig commanding: 1st Bavarian Division: LIR Nr 2 Kronprinz (2 bns); ChLR Kronprinz Nr 1 (4 sqns); DragR Minucci Nr 1 (4 sqns). 2nd Bavarian Division: LIR Nr 6 Herzog Wilhelm (2 bns); LIR Nr 3 Pz Karl (2 bns). Artillery: 1 x FAB.

Bavarian totals 6 bns, 8 sqns, 6 guns, ca 7,600 men.

Bavarian losses 13 killed, 201 wounded, 13 captured.

Austrian Forces GM Thierry's Brigade of the III Corps. IR Kaiser Nr 1 (2 bns); IR Lindenau Nr 29 (1st Bn); DragR Levenehr Nr 4 (4 sqns).

Austrian totals 3 bns, 4 sqns, 6 guns, ca 5,000 men.

Austrian losses Not exactly known but Lefebvre claimed 400 prisoners and 1 gun.

Comment Thierry's brigade's casualty returns give totals only for this day and 20 April at Abensberg; they are shown there. Thierry's brigade was the link between the III and V Corps and was quite isolated when it mistakenly attacked the VII Corps here. They withdrew southeast to Offenstetten in a very shaken state.

Sources Krauss, Leyh.

WW Raszyn (now Pruszkow), 19 April 1809, clash

A village on the River Utrata, about 9 km southwest of Warsaw, capital of Poland, just south of Route 2/E30.

An Austrian victory over the French Allies.

(Last action – This was the first action in this theatre; next action – Radzymin, 26 April.)

Allied Forces Prince Josef Poniatowski commanding:

Polish Troops Gen Sokolnicki: IR Nr 1, 6 and 8 (1st Bns), 6 guns. Gen Bieganski: IR Nr 3 (2 bns); 1st ChàCh (4 sqns); UlR Nr 2 (4 sqns); UlR Nr 3 (2 sqns). Gen Kaminskoi: IR Nr 1 (2nd Bn); IR Nr 6 (2nd Bn), 6 guns.

Saxon Troops Gen von Polenz: GM Dyherrn: Gren bn von Einsiedel (1 bn).

IR Oebschelwitz Nr9 (1 bn); IR von Rechten Nr 12 (2 bns); HusR (2 sqns); IR Nr 2* (2 bns); 12 guns.

Allied totals 11½ bns, 12 sqns, 28 guns, ca 14,000 men.

Allied losses 450 dead, 900 wounded and missing.

* = Attached Polish regiment.

Austrian Forces Archduke Ferdinand commanding. Avantgarde: FML Mondet, GM Mohr: GzIR Siebenburgen Nr 2 (1 bn); IR Vukassovich Nr 48 (3 bns); HusR Kaiser Nr 1 (2 sqns); HusR Palatin Nr 12 (7 sqns). GM Civallart: RI de Ligne Nr 40 (2 bns). FML Schauroth: IR Strauch Nr 24 (3 bns); IR Davidovich Nr 34 (3 bns); IR Weidenfeld Nr 37 (3 bns). GM Trautenberg: KürR Lothringen Nr 7 (6 sqns). GM Speth: KürR Sommariva Nr 5 (6 sqns).

Austrian totals 15 bns, 21 sqns, 24 guns, ca 19,500 men.

Austrian losses ca 450 dead and wounded.

Comment Shock action by the more numerous, battle-hardened Austrian cavalry rapidly decided this action. The Poles withdrew in good order into Warsaw; the Saxons marched off to Saxony to join the IX French Corps.

Poniatowski negotiated a cease-fire with Archduke Ferdinand and evacuated the main part of the city of Warsaw, maintaining Praga on the right bank.

Sources Wrede, Malibran and Chelminski, Gembarzewski.

DV Abensberg, 20 April 1809, Battle or clashes of Offenstetten, Biburg-Siegenburg, Rohr and Rothenburg, 20 April 1809

A series of hamlets south of the River Danube in south eastern Bavaria, about 34 km east of Ingolstadt, straddling the motorway A93.

An French and Allied victory over the Austrians.

(Last action – Arnhofen 19 April; next action – Landshut, 21 April.)

French and Allied Forces The Emperor Napoleon commanding:

VII Corps Marshal Lefebvre, Duke of Danzig commanding. **1st Bavarian Division** GL Crown Prince Ludwig of Bavaria commanding: Lt I Bn Habermann Nr 1(1 bn); 1st LIR Leibregiment (2 bns); 2nd LIR Kronprinz (2 bns); 4th LIR vac Salern (2 bns); 8th LIR Herzog Pius (2 bns); DragR Minucci Nr 1 (4 sqns); Chev LR Kronprinz Nr 1 (4 sqns). Artillery: 3 x foot and 1 HAB, **Totals** 9 bns, 8 sqns, 24 guns, ca 8,500 men. **2nd Bavarian Division** GL von Wrede commanding: Lt I bn Laroche Nr 1 (1 bn); 3rd LIR Prinz Karl (2 bns); 13th LIR vacant (2 bns); 6th LIR Herzog Wilhelm (2 bns); 7th LIR Löwenstein (2 bns). Artillery: 2 x FAB. **Totals** 9 bns, 12 guns, ca 7,000 men.

Bavarian totals 18 bns, 8 sqns, 6 bties, 36 guns, ca 15,500 men*.

*= the 3rd Bavarian Division did not come into action.

VIII (Württemberg) Corps GL Vandamme commanding: GL von Woelwarth second in command. LIR von Phull (1 Bn); Jäger- Bn König (1 bn); Jäger- Bn von Neuffer (1 bn); Lt I Bn von Brüsselle; Lt I Bn von Wolff (1 bn each); Chev LR Herzog Heinrich (4 sqns); JzPf R König (4 sqns); JzPf R Herzog Louis (3 sqns); Artillery 2 x HAB. **Totals** 5 bns, 11 sqns, 12 guns, ca 5,000 men.

Allied totals 23 bns, 19 sqns, 48 guns, ca 20,500 men.

Allied losses 1 officer and 33 men dead, 15 officers and 423 men wounded, 7 men missing, total 16 officers and 463 men.

NB Lannes' II Corps missed the main action but took part in the pursuit.

Austrian Forces FML Baron von Hiller commanding.

From III Corps (GM Thierry's brigade): IR Kaiser Nr 1 (2 bns); IR Lindenau Nr 29 (1st Bn); DragR Levenehr Nr 4 (4 sqns); 7 guns (1 had been lost at Arnhofen on 19 April).

From V Corps FML Prince von Hohenlohe commanding: GM Radetzky, IR Duka Nr 39 (3 bns). IR Gyulai Nr 60 (3 bns); IR Beaulieu Nr 58 (3 bns); GzIR Broder Nr 7 (2 bns); GzIR Gradiskaner Nr 8 (2 bns); UlR EH Carl Nr 3 (8 sqns); HusR Kienmayer Nr 8 (8 sqns). From VI Corps FML Baron von Hiller commanding: IR Deutschmeister Nr 4 (3 bns); ChLR Rosenberg Nr 6 (8 sqns).

Austrian totals 19 bns, 28 sqns, 46 guns, ca 22,000 men.

Austrian losses* At least 2 officers, 269 men and 114 horses killed; 8 officers, 621 men and 25 horses wounded; 5 officers, 467 men and 3 horses captured. 1 officer and 1,049 men missing (the 2nd Bn GzIR Broder Nr 7 was destroyed, losing 18 officers and 1,040 men).

* = to these figures must be added the following losses of Thierry's brigade for 19 and 20 April: 78 officers, 3,324 men, 491 horses.

Thus *approximate* total Austrian losses = at least 112 officers, 6,760 men, 38 guns, between 3,000 and 4,000 men were captured.

Comment By driving his German Allies very hard, Napoleon smashed through the Austrian army destroying Thierry's brigade and cutting off Hiller's army group from the main body under Archduke Charles. Both opposing commanders were now clear as to the positions of their opponent's main bodies.

Sources Wrede, Krauss, Martinien.

DV Landshut, 21 April 1809, clash

A town in south eastern Bavaria, 65 km northeast of Munich on the River Isar, at the junction of Routes B11, B15, B299 and motorway A92/E53.

A French and Allied victory over the Austrians.

(Last action – Abensberg, 20 April; next action – Eggmühl, 22 April.)

French and Allied Forces Emperor Napoleon I commanding:

Cavalry of the 1st Bavarian Division GM Baron von Zandt commanding: ChLR Kronprinz Nr 1 (4 sqns); **2nd Bavarian Division** GL von Wrede commanding: LIR vacant Nr 13 (2 bns); ChLR König Nr 2 * (? sqns); ChLR Leiningen Nr 3 (4 sqns*).

* = Both regiments lost only 1 man each this day. Two regimental histories of the ChLR König Nr 2 state that the regiment was not at Landshut this day. **Bavarian totals** 2 bns, 4 sqns*, 6 guns, ca 2,300 men. **Bavarian losses** Zandt's cavalry brigade: GM Baron von Zandt, 2 officers, 1 man and 4 horses killed; 1 officer, 10 men and 7 horses wounded, 1 man and 2 horses missing. **2nd Division** 6 men dead, 1 officer and 32 men wounded.

VIII (Württemberg) Corps GL Vandamme commanding: Jäger-Bn von Neuffer (1 bn); Lt I Bn von Brüsselle Nr 2 (1 bn); Leib Chev LR (4 sqns); Jäger JzPf König (4 sqns), 6 guns. **Württemberg totals** 2 bns, 8 sqns, 6 guns, ca 2,500 men. **Württemberg losses** 2 horses killed, 2 officers and 17 men wounded; 3 men captured.

French Troops (from Davout's III Corps) GdD Morand commanding: 13e RILé (3 bns); 61e RIdLi (3 bns); 1er Carabiniers R (4 sqns). Artillery 18 guns.

French totals 6 bns, 4 sqns, 18 guns, ca 6,000 men.

French losses ca 1,500 dead, wounded, captured and missing.

Austrian Forces FML Baron von Hiller commanding.

V Corps FML Prince von Hohenlohe commanding: IR Duka Nr 39 (3 bns); IR Stain Nr 50 (3rd Bn); IR Beaulieu Nr 58 (3 bns); IR Gyulai Nr 60 (3 bns); GzIR Broder Nr 7 (1st Bn); GzIR Gradiskaner Nr 8 (2 bns); Wiener Freiwilligen (1st, 2nd and 3rd bns); HusR Kienmayer Nr 8 (8 sqns). UlR EH Carl Nr 3 (8 sqns). Artillery: 8 guns. Engineers (5th Division). **V Corps Totals** 16 bns, 16 sqns, 8 guns. **V Corps Losses** 38 men and 42 horses killed; 1 officer, 138 men and 17 horses wounded, 5 officers, 115 men and 6 horses captured, 4 officers, 907 men and 82 horses missing.

VI Corps FML Baron von Hiller commanding: IR Deutschmeister Nr 4 (3 bns); IR Klebeck Nr 14 (3 bns); IR Benjowsky Nr 31 (3 bns); IR Kerpen Nr 49 (3 bns); IR Splényi Nr 51 (3 bns); IR Jordis Nr 59 (3 bns); GzIR Warasdin-St Georger Nr 6 (2 bns); HusR Liechtenstein Nr 7 (6 sqns); ChLR Rosenberg Nr 6 (8 sqns). Artillery 3 x FAB. Engineers (6th Division). **VI Corps totals** 20 bns, 14 sqns, 24 guns, ca 46,000 men. **VI Corps losses** 3 officers, 709 men and 6 horses killed; 21 officers, 1,081 men and 27 horses wounded, 37 officers, 3,155 men and 34 horses captured, 1,382 men and 127 horses missing.

II Reserve Corps Grenadiers (1 bn); DragR Levenehr Nr 4 (8 sqns); DragR Knesevich Nr 3 (8 sqns). **II Reserve Corps totals** 1 bn, 16 sqns, 6 guns. ca 2,000 men. **II Reserve Corps losses** 1 officer and 14 men dead, 35 men and 24 horses wounded, 152 men missing. IR Lindenau Nr 29 (remnant of Thierry's brigade) (1st Bn); ca 600 men. IR Lindenau losses 208 men missing.

Total Austrian losses 72 officers, 4,934 men, 365 horses, 11 guns and 226 waggons and 1 pontoon train (56 pontoons).

Comment The extremely high proportion of men missing indicates that Hiller's isolated army group was close to disintegration. He also underestimated the Allied strength and ignored his chance to escape. Napoleon had struck at Landshut thinking to find Archduke Charles' main body there. As Massena had already crossed the Isar at Mossburg, upstream from Landshut, the Austrians did not try to hold at the latter place, merely to gain time for an orderly retreat.

Sources Krauss, Leyh, Kraft, Martinien, Krausler.

DV Eggmühl, 22 April 1809, battle

A village in south eastern Germany, on the north bank of the River Laaber, about 25 km south of Regensburg on Route B15 towards Landshut.

A French and Allied victory over the Austrians.

(Last action – Landshut, 21 April; next action – Regensburg, 23 April.)

French and Allied Forces Emperor Napoleon I commanding:

French Forces M Lannes' II Corps: **3rd Division** GdD St Hilaire, GdB Marion 10e RILé (3 bns); 105e RIdLi (3 bns); GdB Lorencez 3e and 57e RIdLi (3 bns each); GdB Brun 72e RIdLi (3 bns).

III Corps M Davout 1st Division GdD Lacour: 17e and 30e RIdLi (3 bns each).

2nd Division GdD Friant: GdB Barbanègre: 48e RIdLi (3 bns); GdB Grandeau 108e and 111e RIdLi (3 bns each); 2 x FAB. **3rd Division** GdD Gudin: GdB Boyer: 12e RIdLi (3 bns): GdB Dupellin: 25e and 88e RIdLi (3 bns each); 2 x FAB. **Light Cavalry** GdB Pajol: 5e HusR (3 sqns); 1 x HAB.

III Corps totals 24 bns, 3 sqns, 5 batteries, ca 20,000 men and 30 guns. **Reserve Cavalry M Bessières 1st Division** GdD Nansouty: GdB Doumerc: 9e CuirR (4 sqns). GdB St Germain; 3e and 12e CuirR (4 sqns each). **2nd Division GdD St Sulpice** GdB Fiteau 1er and 5e CuirR (4 sqns each). GdB Guitton: 10e CuirR (4 sqns). **Reserve Cavalry totals** 24 sqns, 2 x HAB, ca 2,000 men. **IV Corps M Massena 1st Division GdD Legrand:** 26e RIdLi (3 bns). **Light Cavalry** GdB Maraluz: Baden Lt DragR (4 sqns). **1st Division totals** 4 sqns, ca 410 men.

Bavarian Forces M Lefebvre commanding:

VII Corps 1st Division Kronprinz Ludwig: 1st Brigade GM Baron Rechberg: 1st LIR 'Leib' and 2nd LIR Kronprinz (2 bns each); 1st LtI Bn (1 bn) 2nd Brigade GM Stengel: 4th LIR 'vacant Salern' and 8th LIR Herzog Pius (2 bns each); 3rd LtI Bn (1 bn). Light Cavalry GM Baron Zandt: 1st DragR vacant Minucci; 1st ChLR Kronprinz (4 sqns each). Artillery 2 x FAB, 1 x HAB. 3rd Division GL von Deroy: 1st Brigade GM von Vincenti: 9th LIR 'Ysenburg' and 10th LIR 'Junker' (2 bns each); 5th LtI Bn (1 bn). 2nd Brigade GM von Siebein: 5th LIR 'Preysing' and 14th LIR (2 bns each). Light Cavalry GM Graf Seydewitz: 2nd DragR 'Thurn and Taxis'; 4th ChLR Bubenhofen (4 sqns each). Artillery: 2 x FAB, 1 x HAB. **VII Corps totals** 20 bns, 16 sqns, 6 batteries, ca 21,000 men and 36 guns.

VIII Corps (Württembergers) GdD Vandamme, GL von Neubronn; GM von Hügel: 1st Jg Bn 'König', 2nd Jg Bn 'von Neuffer', LtI Bns 'von Wolff and von Brüsselle' (4 bns). GM von Röder: ChLR 'Herzog Heinrich', JzPfR 'Herzog Louis', JzPfR 'König' (4 sqns each); 2 x HAB, 1 x FAB, (22 guns). **VIII Corps totals** 4 bns, 12 sqns, 3 batteries, ca 5,000 men and 22 guns.

Allied totals 48 bns, 59 sqns, 16 batteries, ca 53,000 men and 96 guns.

Allied losses French: 19 officers and ca 3,000 men killed and wounded. Bavarians: 7 officers, 126 men and 20 horses killed; 12 officers, 340 men and 27 horses wounded, 77 men captured. Württembergers: 2 officers, 13 men and 38 horses killed; GM Schneller, 5 officers, 93 men and 8 horses wounded, 2 men captured. Badeners: 1 officer wounded.

Austrian Forces

III Corps FML Prinz Hohenzollern-Hechingen FML Sommariva's Division:.

GM Radivojevich: GzIR Peterwardeiner Nr 9 (2 bns); HusR EH Ferdinand Nr 3 (5 sqns).

FML Vukassovich's Division: Obst Giffing: IR W Colloredo Nr 56, IR K Schröder Nr 7 (3 bns each). FML St Julien's Division: GM Pfanzelter: IR Manfredini Nr 12 (3 bns); IR Würzburg Nr 3 (2 bns). GM Bieber: IR Kaunitz Nr 20 (3 bns); IR Württemberg Nr 38 (2 bns). **III Corps totals** 18 bns, 5 sqns, 9 FAB, ca 17,000 men and 54 guns.

IV Corps FML Rosenberg, FML Klenau: GzIR Deutsch-Banater Nr 10; HusR Stipsicz Nr 10 (8 sqns). FML Dedovich: IR EH Ludwig Nr 8; IR Coburg Nr 22 (3 bns each) IR Czartoryski Nr 9 (3 bns); IR Reuss-Greitz Nr 55 (2 bns) IR Chasteler Nr 46 (3 bns); IR Bellegarde Nr 44 (3 bns) ChLR Vincent Nr 4 (8 sqns). Artillery: 2 x HAB, 3 x FAB (30 guns). **IV Corps totals** 19 bns, 16 sqns, 5 batteries, ca 19,000 men and 30 guns.

I Reserve Corps Prinz von Liechtenstein commanding. KürR EH Franz Nr 2; KürR Hz Albert Nr 3; KürR Kronprinz Nr 4, KürR Liechtenstein Nr 6, KürR Hohenzollern Nr 8, DragR Riesch Nr 8 (36 sqns). Gren bns Hohenlohe, Hahn, Nissel, Georgy, Stark, Portner, Legrand, Leiningen, Pecadue, Cappy. **I Reserve Corps totals** 36 sqns, 10 bns, 6 batteries, ca 37,000 men and 36 guns.

Austrian totals 49 battalions, 57 sqns, 20 batteries, ca 54,000 men and 120 guns.

Austrian losses Kollowrath's II Corps and GM Vécsey's brigade had negligible losses. Hohenzollern's III Corps was badly mauled losing at least 463 killed, 447 wounded, 420 captured and 1,827 missing as well as 13 guns. Rosenberg's IV Corps lost 534 killed, 637 wounded, 773 captured, 865 missing and 26 guns. Their total manpower loss was 4,149. The I Reserve Corps' 10 grenadier battalions lost about 1,300 men.

Comment Archduke Charles delayed his intended thrust at what he thought was a minor part of the Allied army in order to allow Kollowrath's II Corps to come in from Regensburg. The unexpected bonus of five hours was fully exploited by Napoleon who rushed up the corps of Lannes and Massena from Landshut. Bavarian and Württemberg cavalry forced Vukassovich's division back onto the heights behind Eggmühl. The Austrians fell back north to escape across the River Danube to Regensburg.

Davout's III Corps was initially alone and outnumbered but held on until Napoleon came to deliver the decisive blow. For this feat Davout was created 'Prince d'Eckmühl'.

Sources Wrede, Kraft, Leyh, Martinien, Krausler, Zech/Porbeck.

DV Regensburg (Ratisbon), 23 April 1809, clash

A town in south eastern Germany, at the confluence of the Regen and Danube Rivers.

A French victory over the Austrians.

(Last action – Eggmühl, 22 April; next action – Neumarkt-St Vieth, 24 April.)

French Forces Emperor Napoleon commanding:.

III Corps M Davout; 1st Division GdD Morand: 13e RiLé (3 bns); 30e RIdLi (3 bns). 2nd Division GdD Friant: 33e RIdLi (3 bns); 48e RIdLi (3 bns). 3rd Division GdD Gudin: 7e RILé (1 bn); 12e RIdLi (3 bns); 21e RIdLi (3 bns); 25e RIdLi (3 bns); 85e RIdLi (3 bns).

Reserve Cavalry M Bessières; Nansouty's Division: 1er and 2e Carabiniers (4 sqns each); 2e and 9e Cuirassier R (4 sqns each). St Sulpice's Division: 11e Cuirassiers (4 sqns). **French totals** 25 bns, 20 sqns, 36 guns, ca 37,000 men.

French losses Not exactly known, approximately three generals (including Gen Cervoni, Lannes' Chief of Staff), 75 officers and 1,500–2,000 men. Napoleon was grazed by a musket ball.

Austrian Forces Archduke Charles commanding.

II Corps FZM Kollowrath commanding: IR Zach Nr 15 (3 bns); IR Stuart Nr 18 (3 bns); IR Zedtwitz Nr 25 (3 bns); IR Frelich Nr 28 (3 bns); IR Froon Nr 54 (3 bns); IR Josef Colloredo Nr 57 (2 bns); Jäger-Bn Nr 7 (1 bn); UlR Merveldt Nr 1 (8 sqns); DragR EH Johann Nr 1 (6 sqns); DragR Riesch Nr 6 (6 sqns). Brigade GM Vécsey: Jäger-Bns Nr 5 and 6 (2 bns); IR Rohan Nr 21 (3 bns); ChLR Klenau Nr 5 (8 sqns). Artillery 2 x HAB, 7½ x FAB.

Austrian totals 23 bns, 28 sqns, 54 guns, ca 26,000 men.

Austrian losses Information is fragmentary; the II Corps lost 61 officers, 5,045 men, 197 horses and 8 guns; Vécsey's brigade lost 14 officers, 698 men, 50 horses and 17 waggons. The IR Zach and IR Zedtwitz were practically destroyed and lost 6 colours between them.

Comment The I, III and IV Corps were only very lightly engaged. It was Archduke Charles' only aim now to save as much of his army as possible by a rapid withdrawal out of French and Allied clutches.

Sources Krauss, Leyh, Martinien.

IN Malghera, 23 April 1809, raid on

A newly-constructed bridgehead on the north bank of the River Dese, in the area where Route 13 now comes north from Venice to Mogliano Veneto.

A Franco-Italian victory over the Austrians.

(Last action – Sacile, 16 April; next action – San Bonifacio and Villanova, 27 April.)

Franco-Italian Forces GdD Count Caffarelli du Falga commanding: 7th Italian LIR (3 bns); 1st Italian ChàCh (1 sqn); 7e, 16e and 67e RIdLi (8 bns*), 12 guns.

Franco-Italian total 11 bns, 1 sqn, 12 guns.

Franco-Italian losses 20 killed and wounded.

* = only part of this force.

Austrian Forces Obst Gyurkovics with GzIR Ottočaner Nr (9 coys): IR EH Franz Nr 52 (1st and 3rd bns) and 1 x 12 pdr FAB (6 guns).

Austrian total ca 2,000 men.

Austrian losses No Austrian account can be found; the French reported 600 killed and wounded.

Comment Archduke John wished to advance west over the Piave River to neutralise the French garrison of Venice, which could have cut his lines of communication; he wished to take this bridgehead.

After this sharp defeat, Gyurkovics maintained a respectful distance and observed the enemy.

Sources Wrede, Hoehn-Veltze.

DV Neumarkt-St Vieth, 24 April 1809, clash

A village on the River Rott in south eastern Germany (Bavaria), on Route B299, about 32 km southeast of Landshut.

An Austrian victory over the Bavarians.

(Last action – Regensburg, 23 April; next action – Schärding, 26 April.)

Bavarian Forces GL von Wrede commanding the 2nd Bavarian Division: LIR Prinz Karl Nr 3 (2 bns); LIR vacant Nr 13 (2 bns); Lt I bn La Roche Nr 6 (1 bn); LIR Herzog Wilhelm Nr 6 (2 bns); LIR Löwenstein Nr 7 (2 bns); 2 x FAB, 1 x HAB. ChLR Leiningen Nr 3 (4 sqns).

Bavarian totals 9 bns, 4 sqns, 18 guns, ca 10,000 men.

Bavarian losses 42 officers and 1,650 men killed and wounded, 910 men missing or captured.

Austrian Forces FML Hiller's army group. From FML Reuss' IV Corps: Obst Hammer; IR Beaulieu Nr 58 (3 bns); IR Lindenau Nr 29 (3 bns), 1 x FAB. From EH Ludwig's V Corps: IR Duka Nr 39 (3 bns); IR Gyulai Nr 60 (3 bns); IR Stain Nr 50 (3 bns); GzIR Broder Nr 7 and Gradiskaner Nr 8 (2 bns each); 2 x FAB. From Hillers' VI Corps: IR Deutschmeister Nr 4 (3 bns); IR Klebeck Nr 14 (2nd Bn); IR Splényi Nr 51 (3 bns); IR Jordis Nr 59 (3 bns); ChLR Rosenberg Nr 6 (6 sqns); UlR EH Carl Nr 3 (6 sqns); GzIR Warasdiner St Georger Nr 6 (2 bns), 2 x FAB. From Kienmayers' II Reserve Corps: DragR Knesevich Nr 3 (6 sqns).

Austrian totals 31 bns, 18 sqns, 5 batteries of which only 24 bns, 10 sqns and 50 guns actually came into action.

Austrian losses Estimated at about 800 killed, wounded and missing.

Comment Hiller had already crossed to the east bank of the River Inn but, not knowing of Archduke Charles' defeat at Eggmühl on 22 April, he decided to return to the west bank to support his commander. Marshal Bessières came up with Molitor's division but, in view of Hiller's superiority, he ordered a withdrawal on Vilsbiburg.

Hiller followed to Eggelkofen. Next day however, he learned of the defeat of the Austrian main body and withdrew rapidly eastwards to Schärding crossing the River Inn again here.

Sources Leyh, Wrede, Martinien, HGM 9.

DV Schärding, 26 April 1809, clash

A village on the east bank of the River Inn on the Austro-German border, in the Austrian Province of Oberösterreich, about 45 km southwest of the confluence of the Inn and the Danube at Passau. At the junction of Routes B12, 129 and 136.

A French and Allied victory over the Austrians.

(Last action - Neumarkt-St Vieth, 24 April; next action - Schönberg, 30 April.)

French and Allied Forces GdD Legrand commanding (1st Division of Massena's IV Corps). 26e RILé (3 coys); 18e RIdLi (3 coys); Baden Jäger-Bn von Lingg (1 bn). Artillery 2 x FAB, 2 x HAB.

Allied totals 2 bns and 4 bties (24 guns); ca 1,700 men.

Allied losses Very slight.

Austrian Forces FML Dedovich's division of FZM Baron von Hiller's Army Group. IR Schröder Nr 7 (2 coys); IR Chasteler Nr 64 (3rd Bn); IR Mittrowsky Nr 40 (3rd Bn); IR Württemberg Nr 38 (3rd Bn); GzIR Gradiskaner Nr 8 (2 bns). Artillery: 3 guns.

Austrian totals 5 bns, 2 coys, 3 guns.

Austrian losses Not exactly known, light.

Comment Hiller had just managed to pull his forces back over the River Inn after his bold, but dangerous thrust at Neumarkt on 24 April and Dedovich was his rearguard. FZM Hiller was shattered to hear that the enemy was on the undefended road to Vienna. Luckily Marshal Massena ordered a three-day rest and Hiller was just able to concentrate to his rear and save his scattered forces.

Sources Leyh, Wrede, Martinien.

WW Radzymin (Grochow), 26 April 1809, clash

A suburb of Warsaw, capital of Poland, on the right bank of the River Vistula.

A Polish victory over the Austrians.

(Last action - Raszyn, 19 April; next action - Ostrowiek, 2/3 May.)

Polish Forces GdB Sokolnicki commanding: 6th IR (2 bns); 1st ChàCh (4 sqns); 2nd UlR (4 sqns); 3rd UlR (2 sqns).

Polish totals 2 bns, 10 sqns, 6 guns, ca 4,000 men.

Polish losses Not known, slight.

Austrian Forces GM Mohr commanding: IR de Linge Nr 30 (3 bns); IR Kottulinsky Nr 41 (2 bns); IR Vukassovich Nr 48 (3 bns); HusR Kaiser Nr 1 (2 sqns).

Austrian totals 8 bns, 2 sqns, 3 guns, ca 5,000 men.

Austrian losses 200 dead and wounded, 600 captured.

Comment The Austrians tried to rush the fortified bridgehead of Praga but were badly cut up by the defenders in the villages of Radzymin and Grochow.

Sources Wrede, Malibran and Chelminski.

IN San Bonifacio and Villanova, 27 April 1809, skirmish

Two hamlets in north eastern Italy about 20 km east of Verona, just south of the Autostrada A4/E70 and north of the River Adige (Etsch), on the eastern bank of the River Alpone.

An Austrian victory over the French and their Allies.

(Last action - Malghera, 23 April; next action - Soave, 29 April).

Franco-Italian Forces GdD Seras commanding: 106e RIdLi (3 bns); 1 sqn, 4 guns.

Franco-Italian total ca 3,000 men.

French losses Not known, very light.

Austrian Forces Obstlt Volkmann's Avantgarde: Obst Csivich and GzIR Oguliner Nr 3 (5 coys) against Villanova; Volkmann with IR J Jellačič Nr 53 (8 coys) against Bonifacio.

Austrian totals ca 1,800 men.

Austrian losses Not known, light.

Comment The assault on Villanova was beaten back. Volkmann took Bonifacio village but could not seize the bridge over the River Alpone. Darkness and pouring rain ended the fighting.

Sources Wrede, Hoehn-Veltze, Martinien.

IN Soave, 29 April 1809, clash

A wine growing village in northern Italy 20 km east of Verona, just north of the Autostrada A4/E70 and on the River Tramigna.

A victorious Austrian defence against the Franco-Italian assault.

(Last action – San Bonifacio and Villanova, 27 April; next action – Castelcerino, 30 April.)

Franco-Italian Forces Prince Eugène, Viceroy of Italy commanding:

Right Wing GdD Macdonald: GdD Broussier: 9e, 84e, 92e (5 bns)*; 30e DragR (2 sqns); 2 guns. GdD Lamarque: 29e RIdLi (4 bns); 30e DragR (2 sqns); 4 guns. **Centre** GdD Grenier: 53e RIdLi (4 bns) of GdD Serras' div, 8e HusR (2 sqns); 2 guns. GdD Abbé: 8e RILé (2 bns); 102e RIdLi (2 bns). **Left Wing** GdD Sorbier: GdB Bonfanti: 1st Italian LIR (3 bns); 2nd Italian LIR (1 bn); Italian Guard (3 bns); 20e DragR (4 sqns).

Franco-Italian totals 24 bns, 10 sqns, 8 guns, ca 23,000 men.

* = this brigade was not engaged.

Franco-Italian losses Not exactly known, ca 1,000.

Austrian Forces Archduke John commanding:

VIII Corps FML Albert Gyulai: GM Colloredo: IR Strassoldo Nr 27 (3 bns); IR St Julien Nr 61 (3 bns). GM Gajoli: IR F Jellačič Nr 62 (3 bns); GzIR 1st Banal Nr 10 (2 bns). GM Kálnássy: GzIR Oguliner Nr 3 (2 bns); IR Reisky Nr 13 (3 bns); IR Simbschen Nr 43 (3 bns); IR J Jellačič Nr 53 (3 bns).

Austrian totals 21 bns, 4 x FAB, ca 18,000 men and 24 guns.

Austrian losses 400 killed and wounded, ca 300 captured.

Comment The French assaults against Soave, Villanova and San Bonifacio were all beaten off but Sorbier's left hook through the mountains made good headway and he took Monte Bastiglia and Castelcerino. Archduke John was now forced to withdraw.

Sources Wrede, Hoehn-Veltze, Martinien.

IN Castelcerino, 30 April 1809, clash

A ruined castle on a ridge about 4 km north of Soave and about 20 km east of Verona; just north of the Autostrada A4/E70.

An Austrian victory over the Franco-Italians.

(Last action – Soave, 29 April; next action – Montebello, Tavernelle and Olmo, 2 May.)

Franco-Italian Forces GdD Sorbier commanding: GdB Bonfanti: Italian Guard (3 bns); 1st Italian LIR (3 bns); 2nd Italian LIR (1 bn).

Italian totals 7 bns, ca 5,000 men.

Italian losses GdD Sorbier killed, The Guard: 4 officers killed, 13 wounded, 392 men killed and wounded.

Austrian Forces FML Albert Gyulai commanding: GzIR 2nd Banal Nr 11 (2 bns): IR J Jellačič Nr 53 (3 bns); IR F Jellačič Nr 62 (3 bns).

Austrian totals 8 bns, ca 6,000 men.

Austrian losses 300 killed and wounded, 572 missing.

Comment Eugène was concerned that Sorbier's division might be defeated in isolation but instead of reinforcing it to make a real thrust at Archduke John's open flank, he called Sorbier back thus helping the Austrians. Eugène sent no effective help to the Italians this day and made no frontal demonstration to distract the Austrians. Archduke John's withdrawal began this afternoon.

Sources Wrede, Hoehn-Veltze, Martinien.

YU Zermanja River 26–30 April 1809, clashes

The river crossings at Ervenik, Zegar, Obrovac, Vagic and Kravibrod (now Kravli Most) about 45 km east of Zara (Zadar) on the Dalmatian Adriatic coast (ex Yugoslavia).

Austrian victories over the French.

(Last action – these were the opening actions in this theatre; next action – Stara Straza, 15 May).

French Forces XI Corps M Marmont commanding: 1st Division GdD Montrichard: GdB Soyez 18e RILé; 5e RIdLi (2 bns each); GdB Launay 79e and 81e RIdLi (2 bns each). 2nd Division GdD Clausel: GdB Delzons 8e RILé and 33e RIdLi (2 bns each); GdB Deveau 11e RIdLi (3 bns). 3e and 24e ChàCh (2 sqns); Dalmatian Legion (4 bns); 24 guns.

French totals 19 bns, 2 sqns, 24 guns, ca 14,000 men.

French losses ca 1,000 dead, wounded and 200 captured.

Austrian Forces GM Andreas Stojčevié commanding: GzIR Liccaner Nr 1 (2 field bns). GzIR Oguliner Nr 3 (1 Res Bn); GzIR Szluin Nr 4 (1Res Bn). GzIR Otto-caner Nr 2 (1 Res Bn); GzIR Liccaner Nr 1 (1 Res Bn); Serezaner (1 sqn); ChLR Hohenzollern Nr 2 (1 sqn); 1 Position bty (6 guns); 1 Brigade bty (12 x 3 pdrs).

Austrian totals 6 bns, 2 sqns, 18 guns, ca 8,000 men.

Austrian losses ca 250 dead and wounded.

Comment In this pre-emptive strike the Austrians seized the river crossing and thus the initiative in this theatre.

Sources Woinovich, Wrede.

DV Schönberg, 30 April 1809, skirmish

A hamlet in eastern Germany (Saxony) on Route B92 in the Elstergebirge mountains between Adorf and the Czech town of Cheb to the south.

A Saxon victory over Austrians.

(Last action – Schärding, 26 April; next action – Kallham, 1 May.)

Saxon Forces part of IX Corps' Advanced Guard, French Lt Col Steck commanding: Saxon Hus R. Total 50 men.

Saxon Losses Lt Col Steck and 9 others wounded, 2 captured.

Austrian Forces part of GM Am Ende's detached brigade: UlR Schawrzenberg No 2. Total 30 men.

Austrian Losses 1 killed, 12 wounded, 2 captured.

Comment This skirmish caused Am Ende to withdraw out of the way of IX Corps as the Saxons advanced south to join Napoleon's army (the VIII Corps) at Linz on the Danube.

Sources Süssmilch, Werde.

DV Kallham (or Riedau), 1 May 1809, clash

A village in the Austrian Province of Oberösterreich about 42 km southeast of Passau and between the Rivers Inn and Danube; on Route 137/E5.

A French and Allied victory over the Austrians.

(Last action – Schönberg, 30 April; next action – Räffelding 2 May.)

French and Allied Troops (part of Legrand's division of Massena's IV Corps) 26e RILé (2 coys); 4e RIdLi (2 coys); Baden DragR (4 sqns); Württemberg Leib ChLR (4 sqns).

Allied totals ca 1,400 men.

Allied losses 3 men dead, 10 wounded, many horses dead and wounded.

Austrian Forces of FML Schustekh's rearguard of Hiller's army group. IR Jordis Nr 59 (3rd Bn); HusR Kienmayer Nr 8 (2 sqns).

Austrian totals ca 850 men.

Austrian losses 16 officers and 690 men of IR Jordis captured by the Baden Dragoner-Regiment. The battalion colour was also taken, 10 hussars killed, 50 wounded and 23 captured. French Lt Col St Croix, an adjutant of M Massena, took this colour from the Baden trumpeter who originally found it and repre-sented to Massena that he had captured it himself. He was promoted colonel before the truth was established.

Comment Although the Austrian infantry were in square, the dragoons charged after the infantry had fired a volley and broke in. The Austrians only surrendered after their commander, Oberstleutnant Beck, had been cut down and wounded several times.

Sources Zech and Porbeck, Wrede, Obser.

TY Lueg Pass (and Golling), 1 May 1809, 1st clash

A pass on Route 311 in the Austrian Province of Salzburg, along the Salzach stream, about 40 km south of Salzburg.

An Austrian victory over the Bavarians.

(Last action – Innsbruck, 13 April; next action – 2nd Lueg, 5 May.)

Bavarian Forces GM Stengel commanding the 2nd Brigade of the Division Kronprinz of Lefebvre's VII Corps: IR Nr 4 vac Salern (1st Bn); IR Nr 8 Herzog Pius (2 bns); ChLR Kronprinz Nr 1 (1 sqn); 3 guns.

Bavarian totals 3 bns, 1 sqn, 3 guns, ca 1,850 men.

Bavarian losses ca 200 dead, wounded and captured.

Austrian Forces Capt Sessich commanding: GzIR Warasdiner-Kreutzer Nr 5 (3 coys).

Austrian totals ca 420 men.

Austrian losses ca 30 dead, wounded and captured.

Comment This was the first, half-hearted, attempt by the Bavarians to break into the rebellious Tyrol again; it failed hopelessly in the face of the fierce resistance of the Austrian Grenzer.

Sources HGM 41, Wrede, Bezzel, Vol VI.

DV Räffelding, 2 May 1809, clash

A hamlet in the Austrian Province of Oberösterreich about 4 km south of the River Danube and 20 km west of Linz; on Route 129.

A French and Allied victory over the Austrians.

(Last action – Kallham or Riedau, 1 May; next action – Ebelsberg, 3 May.)

French and Allied Forces GdD Carra St Cyr commanding the 2nd division of Massena's IV Corps 14 ChàCh (3 sqns); Baden DragR (2 sqns); Württemberg Leib ChLR (4 sqns).

Allied totals 9 sqns, 800 men.

Allied losses The Badeners lost 1 officer, 13 men and 20 horses killed or wounded.

Austrian Forces GM Bianchi commanding; part of Hiller's rearguard. IR Gyulai Nr 60 (3 bns); Oberst Baron Steigentesch: Wiener Freiwilligen (1st, 2nd and 3rd bns); HusR Kienmayer Nr 8 (2 sqns); 1 x FAB.

Austrian totals 6 bns, 2 sqns, 1 x FAB, ca 5,000 men.

Austrian losses Not known; IR Gyulai suffered 'heavy losses'.

Comment GM Bianchi's orders were to withdraw after winning time for the main body of Hiller's corps to move off and he did this. St Cyr halted west of Alkoven at Strass.

Sources Leyh, von Angeli, Wrede, Martinien, Starklof (Württ).

IN Montebello, Tavernelle and Olmo, 2 May 1809, clashes

Hamlets in between the Rivers Guia and Alpone in north eastern Italy, midway between San Bonifacio in the west and Vicenza in the east.

A Franco-Italian victory over the Austrians.

(Last action – Castelcerino, 30 April; next action – Treviso, 5 May.)

Franco-Italian Forces Avantgarde GdB Broc: 52e and 92e RIdLi (1 bn each); Voltigeurs (1 composite bn); 6e and 8e ChàCh, 30e DragR (1 sqn each); 4 guns. GdD Broussier: 9e RIdLi (1 bn); 84e RIdLi (2 bns); 30e DragR (3 sqns); Italian Drag Regina (4 sqns); 1 gun. GdB Quétard: 9e RIdLi (3 bns). GdD Grenier, GdB Abbé: 1er, 15e, 17e RIdLi (4 bns each); 42 e RIdLi (3 bns); 6 guns.

Franco-Italian totals 24 bns, 10 sqns, 11 guns, ca 20,000 men.

Franco-Italian losses GdB Broc wounded; 400 killed and wounded.

Austrian Forces FML Frimont commanding. **At Montebello** Maj Szentivany; IR Allvintzy Nr 19 (2nd Bn*) **At Olmo** FML Frimont: GzIR Ogulin Nr 3 (1 bn); IR Allvintzy Nr 19 (1st and 2nd bn); HusR EH Josef Nr 2 (4 sqns); ½ HAB. At Tavernelle: GM Splényi: GzIR Ogulin Nr 3 (1 bn); IR Allvintzy Nr 19 (1½ coys); HusR EH Josef Nr 2 (2 sqns); 3 guns. **At Montecchio Maggiore** GM Marziani: IR Allvintzy Nr 19 (1 bn); GzIRs Ogulin Nr 3 (1 bn) and 1st Banal Nr 10 (1 bn); HusR Frimont Nr 9 (1 sqn); HusR EH Josef Nr 2 (2 sqns); ½ HAB.

Austrian totals 7 bns, 9 sqns, 1½ x HAB.

Austrian losses 200 killed and wounded, 850 captured, including many sick and stragglers.

Comment This was a very hard fought but successful Austrian rearguard action in which their main body effected its withdrawal over two river lines and was well placed to continue moving eastwards over the River Brenta. The bridges over the rivers were broken by the Austrians as they passed.

Sources Wrede, Martinien, Hoen-Veltze.

* = withdrew into the Olmo position.

WW Ostrowiek (Gora Kalwaria) 2/3 May 1809, clash

A village on the right bank of the River Vistula in Poland, about 35 km southeast of Warsaw on Route 723 at the junction with Route 717.

A Polish victory over the Austrians.

(Last action – Radzymin (Grochow), 26 April; next action – Thorn, 14 May.)

Polish Forces GdB Sokolnicki: IR Nr 6 (3 bns); IR Nr 12 (2 bns); 1st and 5th ChàCh (2 sqns each); 7th UlR (2 sqns); 12 guns.

Polish totals 5 bns, 6 sqns, 12 guns, ca 6,000 men.

Polish losses About 400 dead and wounded.

Austrian Forces GM Trautenberg commanding. IR Baillet Nr 55 (2½ bns).

Austrian totals 2,000 men, 3 guns.

Austrian losses 38 officers, 1,800 men and 3 guns captured.

Comment This was a very successful raid on the Austrian bridgehead here. The next night the

Austrians burnt the bridge themselves.

Sources Wrede, Malibran and Chelminski, Gembarzewski.

DV Ebelsberg, 3 May 1809, clash

A village on the east bank of the River Traun, about 4km southeast of its confluence with the Danube and 4 km southeast of Linz in the Austrian province of Oberösterreich. Now a suburb of Linz; on Route A/7E14.

An Allied victory over the Austrians.

(Last action – Räffelding, 2 May; next action – Linz-Urfahr, 5 May.)

Allied Forces Marshal Massena commanding the IV Corps GdD Legrand; GdB Ledru: 26e RILé and 18e RIdLi (3 bns each). GdB Kister; GM von Harrant (The Baden contingent): 1st LIR 'Grossherzog' and 2nd LIR 'Erbgrossherzog' (2 bns each); Jäger-Bn von Lingg (1 bn); 24 guns. GdD Claparède; GdB Coehorn: 2e DBdeLé (4th bns of 17e, 21e and 28e RILé-3 bns), 4e DbdeLé (4e Bn), 26e RILé, Tirailleurs du Po and Tirailleurs Corses, 1 bn each). GdB Lesuire: 5e DBdeLi (4e bns of 27e and 39e RIdLi, 2 bns); 6e DBdeLi (4e Bns of 59e, 69e and 76e RIdLi-3 bns); GdB Ficatier: 7e DBdeLi (4e Bns 40e and 88e RIdLi, 2 bns); 8e DBdeLi (4e Bns 64e, 100e and 103e RIdLi, 3 bns); 18 guns. Light Cavalry GdB Maraluz: GdB Stettner: Baden LtDragR (4 sqns); Hessen-Darmstadt-Garde ChLR (3 sqns); Württemberg Leib-ChLR (4 sqns); 6 guns. 3e ChàCh (2 sqns); 14e, 19e and 23e ChàCh (3 sqns each).

Allied totals 28 bns, 22 sqns, 8 batteries, ca 22,000 men and 48 guns.

Allied losses Claparède's division had lost 850 killed, 1,200 wounded and 800 captured. Legrand's division had 150 killed and 550 wounded. The Baden infantry and artillery lost 3 officers and 40 men killed and wounded. The Württemberg Leib-ChLR lost 1 officer wounded and 11 horses killed.

Austrian Forces FML Hiller commanding. **FML Schustekh's Raiding Column** GM Hohenfeld: IR Klebek Nr 14, IR Jordis Nr 59 (3 bns each); HusR Kienmayer Nr 8 (8 sqns); 1 x HAB. GM Radetzky's Rearguard (of V Corps): GzIR Gradiskaner Nr 8 (2 bns); UlR Merveldt Nr 1, UlR EH Carl Nr 3 (8 sqns each); ½ x HAB.

FM EH Ludwig's V Corps FML Reuss: Obst Hammer: IR Beaulieu Nr 58 and IR Lindenau Nr 29 (3 bns each); IR Würzburg Nr 23 (3rd Bn); 1 X FAB. FML Reinwald: IR J Mittrowsky Nr 40 (3 bns). Reserve Artillery: 3 x FAB.

VI Corps FML Hiller; FML Kottulinsky; GM Weissenwolff: IR Deutschmeister Nr 4 and IR Kerpen Nr 49 (3 bns each); IR Czartoryski Nr 9 (3rd Bn); Wiener Freiwilliger (4th, 5th and 6th bns); 2 x FAB. IR Stuart Nr 18 (3rd Bn); IR C Schröder Nr 7 (2 coys); 1 x FAB.

Austrian totals 29 bns, 2 coys, 8½ batteries, ca 2,600 men and 52 guns.

Austrian losses 19 officers killed, 80 wounded (of these 45 were captured) 40 unwounded officers captured; 1,000 men killed, 1,000 wounded and captured, 1,000 wounded, ca 4,200 captured or missing. The 2nd bn IR Kerpen Nr 14 of Schustekh's corps was captured together with its colour. The Wiener Freiwilligen fought very well and lost 5 officers and 237 men. 4 guns were also lost.

Comment This was another 'accidental' action. Hiller's isolated army group was waiting behind the line of the River Traun for FML Schustekh's raiding column to come back in before burning the bridge and withdrawing. Massena was looking for a fight at all costs because he had achieved nothing so far in the campaign. Schustekh just managed to get over the river but lost one battalion in doing so and frustrated Hiller's attempt to burn the bridge. There was bitter fighting in Ebelsberg and about 1,000 wounded burned to death in the ensuing fire.

Austrian intelligence gathering and reporting had broken down completely.

Archduke Charles sent a sharp order to Hiller to cross to the north bank of the Danube and join up with him as quickly as possible.

Sources Wrede, HGM 9, Martinien, Zech/Porbeck.

PN Amarante, 18 April – 3 May 1809, 1st clash

A small town in northern Portugal on the River Tamega, just west of the new Route 15 from Vila Real to Porto (Oporto).

A French victory over the Portuguese.

(Last action – Oporto, 29 March; next action – Grijon, 11 May.)

French Forces GdD Loison commanding the following troops of Soult's Army of Portugal (II Corps). 3rd Division GdD Delaborde: 17e RILé, 70e and 86e RIdLi (3 bns each). 4th Dragoon Division GdD Lorge: 13e, 15e, 22e and 25e DragR (4 sqns each).

French totals 9 bns, 16 sqns, 18 guns, ca 5,600 men.

French losses Not known, light. On 3 May they lost 2 killed and 7 wounded.

Portuguese Forces Gen Silviera commanding: 12th LIR (2 bns) plus Ordenanza and Militia; about 10,000 men in all.

Portuguese losses ca 1,600 killed, wounded and captured, 10 guns, 5 colours.

Comment For twelve days Silviera's force blocked all French attempts to push eastwards from Oporto over the river. By so doing he kept French attention from Wellesley's advance north on Oporto. Finally in the early hours of 3 May, French engineers disarmed the mine on the Amarante bridge and Delaborde's infantry rushed it.

Sources Oman, Ferreira, Napier, Martinien.

TY Lueg Pass (and Abtenau), 4/5 May 1809, 2nd clash

A pass on the old Route 311 in the Austrian Province of Salzburg, along the Salzach stream, about 40 km south of Salzburg city and a village about 21 km east of the pass (along Route 162) in the valley of the Lammer stream.

Austrian victories over the Bavarians.

(Last action – 1st Lueg Pass, 1 May; next action – Kufstein, 11 April – 11 May.)

Bavarian Forces GM Stengel commanding the 2nd Brigade of the 1st Bavarian Division of Lefebvre's VII Corps: IR Nr 4 vac Salern (1st Bn); IR Nr 8 Herzog Pius (2 bns); ChLR Kronprinz Nr 1 (1 sqn); ½ FAB plus GM Raglovich with Leib IR Nr 1 (2 bns); IR Kronprinz Nr 2 (2nd Bn) and ½ FAB.

Bavarian totals 6 bns, 1 sqn, 6 guns, ca 1,000 men.

Bavarian losses Not known, moderate.

Austrian Forces FML Baron von Jellačič commanding: At Lueg Pass: Capt Sessich: GzIR Warasdiner-Kreutzer Nr 5 (3 coys), ca 380 men. At Abtenau: IR Esterházy Nr 32 (2 coys), ca 300 men.

Austrian totals ca 680 men.

Austrian losses ca 35 dead and wounded, 70 captured.

Sources HGM 41, Wrede, Bezzel, Vol VI.

GN Magdeburg, 5 May 1809, clash

A fortified town in north Germany's Brandenburg Province on the west bank of the River Elbe where the motorway A2/E30 crosses the river.

A victory of the Prussian Rebel Major Ferdinand von Schill over the Allies.

(Last action – this was the opening action of Schill's raid; next action – Dammgarten, 23 May.)

Allied Forces French Col Vautier commanding: 22e RIdLi (2 coys); 1st Westfalian LIR (4 coys); 7e French Artillery R – 3 x 6 pounders.

Allied totals ca 1,000 men and 3 guns.

Allied losses 140 dead and wounded, 6 officers and 160 men captured, Col Vautier killed, 3 ammunition waggons captured.

Schill's Forces 2nd Brandenburg HusR (400 men), 60 infantry.

Schill's losses 12 officers and 70 men killed, wounded and missing.

Sources Bartsch, Martinien, Lünsmann.

IN Treviso 5 May 1809, skirmish

A fortified town in north eastern Italy, on the River Sile, 25 km north of Venice, at the junction of Routes 13, 53 and 348.

An Austrian victory over the French.

(Last action – Montebello, Tavernelle and Olmo, 2 May; next action – Piave, 8 May.)

French Forces GdD Durutte: 18e, 22e and 23e RIdLi (6 bns).

French losses Not known.

Austrian Forces Obstlt Collenbach commanding: IR EH Franz Nr 52 (10 coys); GzIR Ottocaner Nr 2 and 1st Banal Nr 10 (2 plts each); LWIR Graz (10 coys); HusR Frimont Nr 9 (4 sqns); 1 x 3 pdr FAB.

Austrian totals 21 coys, 4 sqns, 1 x FAB.

Austrian losses 25 killed, 66 wounded, 97 captured and missing.

Sources Wrede, Hoen-Veltze, Martinien.

DV Linz-Urfahr, 5 May 1809, 1st skirmish

Two villages astride the River Danube in the Austrian province of Oberösterreich next to the confluence of the Danube with the River Traun, on Route 127.

A French and Allied victory over the Austrians.

(Last action – Ebelsberg, 3 May; next action – Blindenmarkt, 6 May.)

Württemberg Forces GdD Vandamme commanding: Fussjäger Bn von Neuffer Nr 2 (3 coys) GM von Hügel's brigade.

Württemberg totals ca 290 men of whom only 1 company (ca 80 men) was engaged.

Württemberg losses 1 man wounded.

Austrian Troops GM Richter commanding (part of FML Hiller's VI Corps). IR Deutschmeister Nr 4 (1 bn); IR Jordis Nr 59 (1 bn); Landwehr (1 bn).

Austrian totals ca 1,500 men.

Austrian losses GM Richter, 14 officers and 165 men captured.

Sources Nübling, von Angeli, Kraft.

DV Blindenmarkt, 6 May 1809, skirmish

A village in the Austrian province of Oberösterreich on the River Ybbs, about 7 km south of the motorway A1/E5.

A French victory over the Austrians.

(Last action – Linz-Urfahr, 5 May; next action – Linz-Urfahr, 17 May.)

French ForcesM Bessières commanding: Light Cavalry GdB Piré: 8e HusR and 16e ChàCh (3 sqns each). GdB Jacquinot: 1er and 2e ChàCh (3 sqns each): GdB Bruyère: 13e ChàCh (3 sqns); 24e ChàCh (2 sqns).

French totals 17 sqns. It is not clear which regiments were involved; none have officer losses recorded by Martinien.

French losses Not known, very light.

Austrian Forces GM Radetzky commanding the rearguard of Hiller's Corps. UlR EH Carl Nr 3 (8 sqns).

Austrian losses 146 men and 60 horses killed, wounded and captured.

Sources von Angeli, Leyh, Bezzel.

IN Piave River (Ponte della Priula), 7 and 8 May 1809, battle

A hamlet in north eastern Italy, on the River Piave, about 10 km south of Conegliano and 4 km west of the Autostrada A27.

A Franco-Italian victory over the Austrians.

(Last action – Treviso, 5 May; next action – San Daniele, 11 May.)

Franco-Italian Forces Prince Eugène de Beauharnais, Viceroy of Italy commanding. **Avantgarde** GdB Desaix: Voltigeurs (6 bns); 9e ChàCh (4 sqns); 4 guns. **Division of GdD Broussier** 9e RIdLi (4 bns); 84e RIdLi (4 bns); 92e RIdLi (4 bns); 24e DragR (1 sqn); 12 guns. **Division of GdD Durutte** 22e RILé (4 bns); 23e RILé (4 bns); 62e RIdLi (4 bns); 10 guns. **Division of GdD Lamarque** 13e RIdLi; 29e RIdLi, 42e RIdLi, 112e RIdLi (12 bns). **Division of GdD Pacthod (GdB Abbé)** 1e RILé; 1e RIdLi, 52e RIdLi, 102e RIdLi (14 bns). DragR 'Napoleone' (Italian) 1 sqn; 12 guns. **Division of GdD Seras** 35e RIdLi; 53e RIdLi, 106e RIdLi (10 bns); 12 guns. **Division of GdD Fontanelli (Italian)** 1e RILé; 2e RILé, 3e RIdLi, 4e RIdLi, Istrian bn (1 bn); Jg Regt Principe Real (2 sqns); 14 bns, 6 guns. Royal Italian Guard GdB Lecci: Grenadiers, Chasseurs and Vélites (1 bn each). DragR (2 sqns); Gardes d'Honneur (1 sqn); 6 guns. **Cavalry Light Cavalry Division of GdD Sahuc** (French): 6e HusR; 6e, 8e, 25e ChàCh (16 sqns); 4 guns. **Dragoon Division of GdD Pully** (French) 23e, 28e, 29e DragR (12 sqns); 4 guns. **Dragoon Division of Grouchy** 7e, 30e DragR (French); DragRegina (Italian) (12 sqns); 4 guns.

Franco-Italian totals 83 bns, 51 sqns, 84 guns, (39,000 inf, 5,800 cav) 84 guns.

Franco-Italian losses Officially '100 killed and 600 wounded'; more probably 2,000 killed and wounded.

Austrian Forces GdC EH Johann commanding.

VIII Corps FML Albert Gyulai: Bde of GM Colloredo: LIR Strassoldo Nr 27 (3 bns); LIR St Julien Nr 61 (3 bns). Bde of GM Gajoli: LIR Jellačič Nr 62 (3 bns); GzIR 1st Banal Nr 10 (2 bns). Brig GM Kálnássy: GzIR Oguliner Nr 3 (1 bn); LIR Reisky Nr 13 (3 bns); LIR Simbschen Nr 43 (3 bns).

IX Corps FML Ignaz Gyulai: Brig GM Kleinmayern: Gren Regt (4 bns); GzIR Szluiner Nr 4 (2 bns). Brig GM Marziani: LIR Franz-Karl Nr 52 (1 bn); LIR Allvintzy Nr 19 (3 bns). Brig GM Gavassini: GzIR Ottočaner Nr 2 (2 bns). LWBrig GM Sebottendorf LWGraz (3 bns). Freibataillon Dumontet (1 bn).

Cavalry FML Wolfskeel Brig GM Hager: DragR Hohenlohe Nr 2 (6 sqns); DragR Savoy Nr 5 (6 sqns). Brig GM Splényi: HusR Ott Nr 5 (8 sqns); HusR Frimont Nr 9 (6 sqns); HusR EH Josef Nr 2 (8 sqns).

Artillery GM Reisner: 10 batteries (3 pdr, brigader and cavalry each of 8 guns; positions battery (each of 6 guns), 6 and 12 pdrs).

Austrian totals 34 bns, 34 sqns, 70 guns, 18,000 infantry, 2,750 cavalry.

Austrian losses Killed: 5 officers, 393 men, 111 horses. Wounded: 26 officers, 671 men, 69 horses. Captured: 17 officers and 1,664 men, 26 horses. Missing: 4 officers, 1,116 men and 92 horses, 15 guns, 30 ammunition waggons.

Sources Wrede, Hoen-Veltze, Martinien.

PN Grijon, 11 May 1809, clash

A small village in north western Portugal; just to the north east of Ovar on Route 109 along the Atlantic coast. Not shown on modern maps. About 20 km south of Oporto.

An Allied victory over the French.

(Last action – Amarante, 18 April – 3 May; next action – Oporto, 12 May.)

French Forces GdD Mermet commanding the 2nd Division of Soult's II Corps: 31e RILé; 47e and 122e RIdLi (4 bns each); 2nd, 3rd and 4th Swiss (1 bn each). GdD Franceschi's Light Cavalry Division: 1er HusR, 8e DragR, 22e ChàCh, Ch Hanovrienne (4 sqns each).

French totals 15 bns, 16 sqns, ca 4,200 infantry, 1,200 cavalry and 12 guns.

French losses ca 250 killed, wounded and captured.

Allied Forces LG Sir Arthur Wellesley commanding: 1st Brigade BG Hill: 1st/3rd, 2nd/48th, 2nd/66th, (1 bn each); 5th/60th (1 coy). KGL Brigade BG Murray: 1st, 2nd, 5th and 7th Line bns (1 bn each). Stewart's Brigade: 1st/29th, 1st bn of Detachments, 1st/16th Portuguese LIR (1 bn each). Guards' Brigade BG H Campbell: Coldstream (2nd) Gds, 3rd Gds (1 bn each); 5th/60th (1 coy). Campbell's Brigade: 2nd/7th, 2nd/53rd (1 bn each); 5th/60th (1 coy). Sonntag's Brigade: 1st/97th, 2nd bn of Detachments, 2nd/16th Portuguese LIR (1 bn each). Cameron's Brigade: 2nd/9th, 2nd/83rd, 2nd/10th Portuguese LIR (1 bn each), 5th/60th (1 coy). Cavalry: Gen Stapleton Cotton: 14th (3 sqns) and 16th LD (4 sqns); 20th LD (2 sqns); 3rd LD KGL (1 sqn). Artillery: 5 batteries.

Allied totals 21 bns, 10 sqns, 30 guns, 7,000 infantry and 1,500 cavalry.

Allied losses 2 officers and 19 men killed, 6 officers and 63 men wounded, 16 men missing.

Sources Oman, Robinson, Martinien.

IN San Daniele del Friuli, 11 May 1809, clash

A village in northeastern Italy, about 20 km northwest of Udine and about 8 km east of the River Tagliamento and on Route 463.

An Allied victory over the Austrians.

(Last action – Piave River, 7/8 May; next action – Venzone, 12 May.)

Allied Forces Prince Eugène commanding. GdB Dessaix's Avantgarde: Voltigeurs (6 bns); 9e ChàCh (4 sqns). GdB Abbé: 1er RILé, 52e RIdLi (2 bns each); 23e DragR (of Pully's Dragoon Division) 12 guns.

Allied totals 10 bns, 8 sqns, 12 guns, ca 9,000 men.

Allied losses About 200 killed and wounded.

Austrian Forces GdC Archduke John commanding GM Gajoli (of VIII Corps): IR F Jellačič Nr 62 (3 bns); GzIR 2nd Banal Nr 11 (2 bns); IR Reisky Nr 13 (2 bns); GzIR Oguliner Nr 3 (10 coys); 6 guns. FML Frimont: HusR EH Josef Nr 2, Ott Nr 5 and Frimont Nr 9 (15 sqns).

Austrian totals 8 + bns, 15 sqns, 6 guns, ca 7,000 men.

Austrian losses 260 killed, 630 wounded, 1,000 captured, 1 colour (IR Reisky Nr 13).

Sources Wrede, Hoen-Veltze, Martinien.

TY Kufstein, 11 May 1809, defence of

A fortress of great natural strength just south of the Austrian border with Bavaria (Germany) on the Autobahn A93/E45/E60 on the right bank of the River Inn.

A Bavarian victory over the Austrians and Tyroleans.

(Last action – Lueg Pass, 5 May; next action – Lofer, 11 May.)

Bavarian Garrison Major d'Aicher commanding: one combined battalion of 1 company each of the 1st, 2nd, 5th and 6th Lt I Bns.

Bavarian totals 576 men and 64 guns.

Bavarian losses Very slight.

Austrian and Tyrolean Forces Commander unknown: 1 infantry bn and the armed 'Aufgebot' (Landwehr) of the counties of Kufstein, Kitzbühl and Rattenberg.

Austrian totals ca 3,000 men, 3 guns.

Austrian losses Very slight.

Sources Leyh.

TY Lofer, 11 May 1809, clash

A village in the Austrian province of Salzburg, at the junction of Routes 311 and 312, on the left bank of the River Saalach, about 3 km southwest of Salzburg.

A Bavarian victory over the Tyroleans.

(Last action – Lueg Pass, 5 May; next action – Waidring, 12 May.)

Bavarian Forces GL Baron Wrede commanding part of the 2nd Bavarian Division: 1st Brigade: GM Count Minucci IR Prinz Karl Nr 3 (2 bns); IR Nr 13 (2 bns);

IR Nr 14* (1 bn); LtI Bn Nr 6 (1 bn); 1 x FAB, 6 guns.
* = attached from the 3rd Division.

Bavarian totals 6 bns, 6 guns, ca 5,000 men.

Bavarian losses 22 dead, 44 wounded.

Tyrolean Forces Various local Schützenkompanien and Landsturm.

Tyrolean total ca 600 men.

Tyrolean losses 70 dead and wounded.

Sources Wrede, Bezzel, Leyh.

PN Oporto, 12 May 1809, 2nd battle

A fortified city port on the north bank of the estuary of the River Douro into the Atlantic.

An Allied victory over the French.

(Last action - Grijon, 11 May; next action - this was the final action in Soult's abortive invasion of Portugal.)

French Forces M Soult commanding. 1st Division GdD Merle: 2e and 4e RILé (4 bns each); 36e RIdLi (3 bns). 3rd Division GdD Delaborde: 17e RILé, 70e and 86e RIdLi (3 bns each), 47e RIdLi (2 bns); 31e RILé (3 bns). Light Cavalry GdD Franceschi: 1er HusR; 8e DragR, 22e ChàCh, Ch Hanovrienne (4 sqns each).

French totals ca 10,000 infantry, 1,200 cavalry, Mermet's division was already marching east with the baggage and artillery parks.

French losses Estimates vary widely; Bodart gives: 3 generals, 36 officers and about 600 men killed, wounded and captured. Oman states 300 killed and wounded, 1,800 captured.

Allied Forces Sir Arthur Wellesley commanding.

All regiments as for the clash at Grijon on 11th May, less Murray's brigade which had been sent up river to cross at Barca d'Avintas 5 km away and cut off Soult's withdrawal with 1st and 2nd bns KGL, 14th LD (2 sqns) and 2 guns.

Allied totals 17 bns, 8 sqns, 28 guns, ca 24,000 men.

Allied losses 23 killed, 18 wounded, 6 missing.

Sources Oman, Napier, Robinson, Martinien.

IN Venzone, 12 May 1809, 2nd clash

A village in north eastern Italy, on Route 13, up the valley of the River Tagliamento, about 30 km north of Udine and 25 km north of San Daniele del Fruili.

A French victory over the Austrians.

(Last action - San Daniele del Friuli, 11 May; next action - Tarvisio, 16 and 17 May.)

French Forces GdB Dessaix's Avantgarde: Voltigeurs (6 bns), 3 guns.

French losses Eugène reported 2 killed and 45 wounded.

Austrian Forces GM Colloredo: IR Strassoldo Nr 27 and IR St Julien Nr 61 (3 bns each).

Austrian losses GM Colloredo wounded, Obstlt Rétsey of IR St Julien killed, over 100 killed and wounded, about 90 captured.

Sources Wrede, Hoen-Veltze, Martinien.

TY Waidring, 12 May 1809, clash

A village in the east of the Austrian province of Tyrol on Route 312, 15 km east of St Johann in Tyrol.

A Bavarian victory over the Tyroleans.

(Last action - Lofer, 11 May; next actions - Söll, Wörgl and Rattenberg, 13 May.)

Bavarian Forces GL Baron Wrede's 2nd Bavarian Division. 1st Brigade GM Count Minucci: IR Prinz Karl Nr 3 (2 bns); IR Nr 13 (2 bns); Lt I Bn Nr 6 (1 bn); IR Nr 14 (1 bn); 1 x FAB. 2nd Brigade GM Count Beckers: IR Herzog Wilhelm Nr 6 (2 bns); IR Löwenstein Nr 7 (2 bns); 1 x FAB. Cavalry Brigade GM Count Preysing: ChLR König Nr 2 (4 sqns); ChLR Leiningen Nr 3 (4 sqns); 1 x HAB.

Bavarian totals 10 bns, 8 sqns, 18 guns, ca 7,500 men.

Bavarian losses 40 dead and wounded.

Austrian and Tyrolean Forces GM Fenner commanding: Jg bn Nr 9 (1 bn); ChLR Hohenzollern Nr 2 (3 sqns), ca 1,000 armed peasants including many women.

Austrian totals ca 4,500 men, 6 guns.

Austrian losses ca 100 dead, wounded and captured.

Sources Wrede, Leyh, Bezzel.

EW Alcántara, 14 May 1809, clash

A small town in the western Spanish province of Extremadura, on the south bank of the Rio Tajo (Tagus) on Route 523 just east of the Portuguese frontier.

A French victory over the Portuguese.

(Last action - Medellin, 29 March; next action - Talavera, 27/28 July.)

French Forces M Victor and GdD Lapisse's 2nd Division of I Corps: 16e RILé, 8e, 45e and 54e RIdLi (3 bns each); 12 guns. 'A brigade of dragoons'.

French totals 12 bns, 8 sqns, 9,500 men, 12 guns. (Villatte's 3rd Division was in reserve).

French losses Not known, light.

Portuguese Forces Col Mayne commanding the 1st Bn and 1 sqn Loyal Lusitanian Legion and 1 bn of the Idanha Militia, 2 guns, ca 1,850 men.

Portuguese losses About 250 killed, wounded and captured, 1 gun.

Sources Oman, Mayne, Bernays.

TY Söll, Wörgl and Rattenberg, 13 May 1809, clash

Three villages in the Austrian province of the Tyrol on Routes 312, 171 and 172 respectively, leading up the valley of the River Inn towards Innsbruck.

Bavarian victory over the Austrians.

(Last action – Waidring, 12 May; next actions – Schwaz and Strass, 14/15 May.)

Bavarian Forces M Lefebvre commanding: 2nd Bavarian Division GL Count Wrede. 1st Brigade GM Count Minucci: IR Prinz Karl Nr 3 (2 bns); IR Nr 13 (2 bns); Lt I Bn Nr 6 (1 bn). 2nd Brigade GM Count Beckers: IR Herzog Wilhelm Nr 6 (2 bns); IR Löwenstein Nr 7 (2 bns). Cavalry Brigade GM Count Preysing: ChLR König Nr 2 (4 sqns); ChLR Leiningen Nr 3 (4 sqns). Artillery: Major Baron Karl Zoller: 2FAB and 1HAB.

Bavarian totals 9 bns, 8,000 infantry; 8 sqns, 1,450 cavalry, 3 btys, 18 guns.

Bavarian losses 33 dead, 158 wounded.

Austrian Forces FML Marquis Chasteler commanding: GM Fenner, GM Marchal: Jg Bn Nr 9 (1 bn); LIR Hohenlohe-Bartenstein Nr 26 (3 bns); LIR Lusignan Nr 16 (3 bns); LWIR Bruck (2 bns); LWIR Judenburg (2 bns); ChLR Hohenzollern Nr 2 (3 sqns); 2 x FAB. Plus a detachment from FML Jellačič division: LIR de Vaux Nr 45 (4 coys); ChLR O'Reilly Nr 3 (½ sqn).

Austrian totals 11½ bns, 3½ sqns, 17 guns, ca 5,000 men.

Austrian losses Over 3,000 dead, wounded and captured, 9 guns, 27 ammunition waggons and 3 colours. Chasteler's division was effectively destroyed.

Sources Wrede, Leyh, Bezzel.

TY Strass and Schwaz, 14/15 May 1809, clashes

Two villages in the Austrian province of the Tyrol on Route 171 (nowadays the motorway A12/E17 also runs here) in the valley of the River Inn, 30 km and 20 km respectively east of Innsbruck.

Bavarian victories over the Austrians.

(Last action – Söll, Wörgl and Rattenberg, 13 May; next actions – Berg Isel, 25 May.)

Bavarian Forces 2nd Bavarian Division GL Count Wrede commanding: as at Wörgl etc on 13 May.

Bavarian totals 9 bns, 8 sqns, 18 guns, ca 9,250 men.

Bavarian losses 31 dead, 131 wounded.

Austrian Forces Speckbacker commanding some battalions of Landwehr and ca 1,200 armed peasants.

Austrian totals ca 3,000 men.

Austrian losses ca 90 dead and wounded, 3 officers and 182 men captured.

Sources Bezzel, Leyh, Heilmann.

WW Thorn (Torun), 14 May 1809, raid on

A fortified town on the right bank of the River Vistula in Poland, about 180 km west northwest of Warsaw, at the junction of Routes 1/E75, 10 and 52.

A 'drawn match' between the Austrians and Poles.

(Last action – Ostrowiec (Gora Kalwaria), 3 May; next action – Sandomierz, 18 May.)

Polish Forces Col Mielzynski commanding in the bridgehead on the left bank of the Vistula, about 1,000 new recruits and militia.

Polish losses Not known, light.

Austrian Forces GM Mohr commanding: IR Vukassovich Nr 48 (3 bns); ChLR Kaiser Nr 1 (5 sqns); HusR Kaiser Nr 1 (2 sqns); and Palatin Nr 12 (7 sqns); 12 guns.

Austrian totals 3 bns, 14 sqns, 12 guns.

Austrian losses Not known.

Sources Wrede, Malibran and Chelminski, Welden.

YU Stara Straza, 15 May 1809, clash

A village in Dalmatia, about 6 km northwest of Knin and about 60 km east of Zara (Zadar) on the Adriatic coast (ex-Yugoslavia). Not to be found on modern maps.

An Austrian victory over the French.

(Last action – Kravibrod, 30 April; next action – Mount Kita, 16 May.)

French Forces GdB Delzons commanding: 8e RILé and 33e RIdLi (2 bns each).

French totals 4 bns, ca 3,000 men.

French losses Not exactly known, ca 100 dead, 200 captured, 700 sheep, 34 oxen.

Austrian Forces Hauptmann Hrabovszky commanding: GzIR Szluin Nr 4 (1 coy); Dalmatian Freikorps (1 coy).

Austrian totals 2 coys, ca 150 men.
Austrian losses Not exactly known, slight.
Comment This was a very successful night raid, carried out with the help of the locals.
Sources Woinovich.

EN Pomar, 16 May 1809, skirmish

A town in northeastern Spain, 50 km north of the River Ebro in the valley of the River Cinca (one of its tributaries), 20 km south of Barbastro.
A Spanish victory over the French.
(Last action – Zaragoza, 20 February; next action – Monzon, 19 May.)
French Forces 1st Division, GdB Habert of Junot's III Corps: 14e RIdLi and 44e RIdLi (3 bns each); 116e RIdLi (4 bns); 2nd and 3rd IR of the Vistula Legion (2 bns each); 13e CuirR (2 sqns); 12 guns.
French totals 14 bns, 4 sqns, 12 guns, ca 9,000 men.
French losses Not known but 14e RIdLi (3 x Voltigeur coys) and 116e RIdLi (Grenadier and Voltigeur coys) cut off on the far side of the Cinca river and forced to surrender on 19 May.
Spanish Forces Col Perena with Catalan miqueletes and armed peasants, ca 10,000 men.
Spanish losses Not known, light.
Sources Oman, Napier, Gembarzewski, Martinien.

YU Mount Kita (now Golubio Jezero), 16 May 1809, battle

A mountain about 186 km north of Knin and 60 km east of Zara (Zadar) on the Adriatic coast of Dalmatia (ex-Yugoslavia, now Croatia).
A French victory over the Austrians.
(Last action – Stara Straza, 15 May; next action – Gračac (Grab), 17 May.)
French Forces XI Corps M Marmont commanding: Montrichard's and Clausel's divisions as at the Zermanja River 26 – 30 April.
French totals 19 bns, 2 sqns, 24 guns, ca 13,000 men.
French losses Not exactly known, slight.
Austrian Forces GM Stoičević commanding: As for the Zermanja River 26–30 April plus GzIR 1st Banal Nr 10 (2 bns) which he had 'borrowed' from Archduke John's Army of Italy.
Austrian totals 8 bns, 2 sqns, 18 guns, ca 9,000 men.
Austrian losses GM Stoičević captured, 200 dead, 500 wounded, 300 captured.
Sources Woinovich.

XX Braila, 18 April–17 May 1809, failed siege

A town in northeastern Romania, on the west bank of the River Danube, 15 km upstream from Galatz.
A Turkish victory over the Russians.
(This was the opening action of the campaign; next action – Constanta, 9 September.)
Turkish Garrison 10,000 men.
Turkish losses Not known.
Russian Forces FM Prince Prosorowskoi commanding: 39 bns, 20 sqns, 48 guns.
Russian total 24,000 men.
Russian losses Not known.
Source Bodart.

IN Tarvis (Saifnitz), 16 and 17 May 1809, clash

A town in north eastern Italy, on Route 13, just south of the Austrian border and east of the deep, narrow valley of the River Schlitza.
A Franco-Italian victory over the Austrians.
(Last action – Venzone, 12 May; next action – Malborghetto, 14–17 May.)
Franco-Italian Forces Prince Eugène de Beauharnais commanding. GdB Dessaix's Avantgarde: Vélites (6 bns). GdD Fontanelli: Italian 3rd LIR (3 bns); 60e RIdLi (2 bns); 112e RIdLi (3 bns). GdB Bonfanti (Italians): 1st and 2nd LIR (1 bn each); Dalmatian IR (2 bns). GdB Abbé and GdB Valentin were in close reserve but not engaged (12 bns).
Franco-Italian totals 18 bns engaged ca 10,000 men, no cavalry or artillery.
Franco-Italian losses Reported by Eugène as '80 killed and 300 wounded'.
Austrian Forces FML A Gyulai commanding. GzIR Ogulin Nr 3 (2 bns); GzIR Szluin Nr 4 (1 bn); IR F Jellačič Nr 53 (1 bn); IR Strassoldo Nr 27 (3 bns); IR Reisky Nr 13 (2 bns); LWIR Marburg (2 bns); HusR Ott Nr 5 (4 sqns); 6 guns.
Austrian totals 11 bns, 4 sqns, 6 guns, ca 3,500 men.
Austrian losses 6 officers, 211 men and 3 horses killed, 10 officers, 261 men wounded, 28 officers, 1,273 men and 27 horses captured; 170 men missing, 6 guns.
Sources Wrede, Martinien, Hoen-Veltze, HGM Nr 51.

IN Malborghetto Blockhouse, 14–17 May 1809, storming of

A fortified spur almost blocking the valley of the Fella River at the village of Malborghetto in northeastern

Italy, about 12 km west of Tarvisio, just south of the Austro-Italian border on Route 13.

A French victory over the Austrians.

(Last action – Tarvisio, 16/17 May; next action – Predil, 18 May.)

French Forces GdD Grenier commanding. GdB Abbé: 8e RILé (2 bns); 1er and 52e RIdLi (4 bns each). GdB Valentin: 22e RILé (1 bn); 23e RILé (4 bns). GdB Bruch: 60e RIdLi (2 bns); 62e RIdLi (3 bns); 102e RIdLi (3 bns).

French totals 23 bns, ca 15,000 men.

French losses '80 men dead and wounded' according to Grenier; totally unbelievable figures in the light of the heavy fighting.

Austrian Forces Hauptmann Hensel commanding: GzIR Ogulin Nr 3 (2 coys); 24 artillery men, 11 guns.

Austrian totals ca 390 men and 11 guns.

Austrian losses 5 officers and 345 men dead, 6 officers and 44 men (mostly wounded) captured.

Sources Wrede, Martinien, Hoen-Veltze, Hauptmann Caesar's report on the defence of the blockhouse.

YU Gračac (Grab), 17 May 1809, clash

A town in the province of Lika (in Croatia) about 45 km east northeast of Zadar (Zara) in ex-Yugoslavia. At the junction of Routes 6 and 13.

(Last action – Mount Kita, 16 May; next action – Gospić, 21 and 22 May.)

French Forces XI Corps M Marmont commanding: The divisions of Montrichard and Clausel as for the Zermanja River 30 April.

French totals 19 bns, 2 sqns, 24 guns, ca 12,700 men.

French losses Declared as '300 dead' by Marmont; locals claimed to have buried many more.

Austrian Forces Oberst Rebrović commanding – as for Mount Kita, 16 May.

Austrian totals 8 bns, 2 sqns, 18 guns, ca 8,000 men.

Austrian losses 300 dead and wounded.

Comment The outnumbered Austrians fell back northwest to Gospić after a hard fight.

Sources Woinovich.

DV Linz-Urfahr, 17 May 1809, clash

Two villages astride the River Danube in the Austrian province of Oberösterreich next to the confluence of the Danube with the River Traun on Route 127.

A French and Allied victory over the Austrians.

(Last action – Blindenmarkt, 6 May; next action – Aspern-Essling, 21–22 May.)

French and Allied Forces M Bernadotte commanding VIII (Württemberg) Corps GdD Vandamme: Infantry GL von Neubronn: 1st Brigade GM von Franquemont: LIRs Kronprinz and Herzog Wilhelm (2 bns each); Füs R von Neubronn (1st Bn). 2nd Brigade GM von Scharffenstein: LIRS von Phull and von Cammerer (2 bns each), FüsR von Neubronn (2nd Bn). 3rd Brigade GM von Hügel: 1st FussJgBn 'König', 2nd FussJgBn von Neuffer, 1st LtBn von Wolff, 2nd LtBn von Brüsselle (1 bn each), 1 x FAB (10 guns). **Cavalry Division GL von Woellworth** 1st Brigade GM von Röder 'Leib ChLR', ChLR 'Herzog Heinrich' (4 sqns each). 2nd Brigade GM von Stettner; JgzPfRs 'König' and 'Herzog Louis' (4 sqns each); 2 x HABs (12 guns).

Würtemberg totals 12,000 men, 22 guns.

Würtemberg losses 35 killed, 228 wounded, 40 missing.

IX (Saxon) Corps (M Bernadotte) 1st Division GL von Zeschwitz: 1st Brigade GM von Hartitsch: Lieb Gren Garde (1 bn), Gren Bn 'von Bose', Gren Bn 'von Hake' (1 bn each), LIR 'Konig' (2 bns), LIR 'von Dyherrn' (1st Bn) 2nd Brigade GM von Boxberg: LIRs Prinz Maximilian and Prinz Friederich August (2 bns each). Cavalry Brigade GM Baron von Gutschmid: ChLR Prinz Albrecht (1 sqn); HusR (3 sqns). Only these Saxon troops were engaged, the others arrived only when the combat was over.

Saxon totals ca 6,000 men.

Saxon losses 7 killed, 74 wounded, 7 captured.

Austrian Forces FZM Count Kollowrat commanding Right-hand column FML Sommariva: GzlR Peterwardeiner Nr 9 (1 bn), 5th JgBn, IR W Colloredo Nr 56 (3 bns), LWIR Pilsen (3 bns), UIR Merveldt Nr 1 (2 sqns), 2 x FAB (12 guns). Centre column FML Vukassovich: GzlR Peterwardeiner Nr 9 (1 bn), 6th JgBn (1bn), IRs Manfredini Nr 12 and Schröder Nr 7 (3 bns each), IR Wurzburg Nr 23 (2 Bns), UIR Merveldt Nr 1 (4 sqns). HusR Hessen-Homburg Nr 4 (4 sqns), 4 x FAB (24 guns). Left-hand column FML St Julien (only the cavalry came into action) HusR Hessen-Homburg Nr 4 (2 sqns).

Austria totals ca 15,000 men, 36 guns.

Austrian losses 49 killed, 263 wounded, 455 captured, 124 missing, 6 guns, 2 ammunition wagons.

Comment The Austrian assault was timid and badly coordinated. The Württembergers held a bridgehead over the Danube here to guard against just such an

Austrian thrust south out of Bohemia against Napoleon's lines of communications stretching east to Vienna. As a joint Würtemberg-Saxon cavalry charge took the Austrian battery on the Pfennigberg, the JgzPfR Herzog Louis recieved 4 of the guns and the Saxon HusR the other 2 as prizes.

Sources Welden, Wrede, Kraft Süssmilch.

IN Predil Blockhouse, 15–18 May 1809, storming of

A fortified position in the valley of the River Isonzo on Route 54 in northeastern Italy about 10 km south of Tarvisio just south of the border with Austria.

A French victory over the Austrians.

(Last action – Malborghetto, 14 to 17 May; next action – Klagenfurt, 8 June.)

French Forces GdD Serras commanding the 1st Division: GdB Moreau: 1er RILé (1 bn); 35e RIdLi (4 bns); 53e RIdLi (1 bn). GdB Roussel: 42e RIdLi (1 bn); 106e RIdLi (4 bns).

French totals 11 bns, 12 guns, ca 8,500 men.

French losses ca 450 dead and wounded.

Austrian Forces Hauptmann Hermann commanding the 1st Bn GzIR Szluiner Nr 4 (2 coys).

Austrian totals ca 250 men and 8 guns.

Austrian losses 250 dead.

Comment A heroic defence to the last man.

Sources Wrede, Hoehn-Veltze, Martinien.

WW Sandomierz 18 May 1809, capture of

A fortified town on the left bank of the River Vistula in Poland, about 160 km southeast of Warsaw, at the junction of Routes 723, 759, 777 and 859.

A Polish victory over the Austrians.

(Last action – Thorn, 14 May; next action – Zamosc, 20 May.)

Polish Forces General Sokolnicki commanding: IR Nr 6 (2 bns); IR Nr 8 (2 bns); IR Nr 12 (2 bns); 2nd UlR (3 sqns); 5th ChàCh (2 sqns); 6th UlR (1 sqn).

Polish totals 6 bns, 6 sqns, 12 guns, ca 6,500 men.

Austrian Forces GM Egermann commanding: 4,000 mostly new infantry recruits and 42 guns.

Austrian losses 1,000 killed or captured, 800 deserted to join the Poles.

Sources Malibran and Chelminski.

EN Monzon, 19 May 1809, failed raid

A small town in northeastern Spain, north of the River Ebro, in the valley of the River Cinca, 50 km northwest of Lleida on Route 240 towards Barbastro.

A Spanish victory over the French.

(Last action – Pomar, 16 May; this was the last action of note here in 1809.)

French Forces Part of GdB Habert's brigade, of GdD Junot's III Corps: 14e RIdLi (3 x Voltigeur coys); 2nd IR Vistula Legion (2 x Voltigeur coys); 116e RIdLi (1 x Grenadier and 2 x Voltigeur coys); 13e CuirR (½ sqn).

French total ca 1,100 men.

French losses 1,000 captured, only the Cuirassiers escaped.

Spanish Forces A force of armed peasants and some Catalan miqueletes under Colonel Perena.

Spanish totals and losses Unknown.

Comment Many French troops were withdrawn to fight against Austria early in 1809, greatly reducing the garrisons in Spain. On 6 May Spanish Colonel Perena descended on Monzon. The French garrison abandoned the place and withdrew to Barbastro, GdB Habert's brigade headquarters. In an attempt to retake Monzon, Habert's advanced guard got cut off over the River Cinca on 16 May and had to surrender on 19 May when their ammunition ran out and Habert's attempt to force the bridge at Monzon failed.

EG Gallegos, 19 May 1809, clash

A small town in the northern Spanish province of Asturias, on the River Narcea, 16 km west of Oviedo on Route 634. Not shown on modern maps.

A French victory over the Spanish.

(Last action – Villafranca, 17 March; next action – Pajares, 19 May.)

French Forces M Ney of the VI Corps. 1st Division GdD Marchand: 6e, 39e, 69e and 76e RIdLi (3 bns each). GdB Lorcet: 3e HusR; 15e ChàCh (3 sqns each), 2 x FAB.

French total 12 bns, 6 sqns, 8 guns, ca 7,800 men.

French losses Not known, very light.

Spanish Forces Gen Marqués de La Romana IRs La Princesa and Asturias (1 bn each), ca 1,500 men.

Spanish losses 'Heavy'; not exactly known.

Comment The Spanish forces dispersed into the mountains, the Junta of Asturias and La Romana embarked on a Spanish warship at Grijon and escaped.

Sources Oman, Napier, Martinien.

EG Pajares, 19 May 1809, clash

A mountain pass on the borders of the northern Spanish province of Asturias and Leon, on Route 630 between Oviedo and Leon.

A French victory over the Spanish.

(Last action - Gallegos, 19 May; next action - Santiago, 22 May.)

French Forces M Kellermann commanding a composite task force. GdD Girard (1st Division, V Corps): 17e RILé, 40e, 64e, 88e RIdLi (3 bns each); 34e RIdLi (4 bns); 1 Polish bn; 1 Prov IR (1 bn); 2 DragRs, 12 guns.

French total ca 12,500 men, 12 guns.

French losses Not known, very light.

Spanish Forces Col Quixanos' Asturian Brigade. No details known.

Spanish total 3,000 men and 2 guns.

Spanish losses Not known, light.

Sources Oman, Napier, Martinien.

WW Zamosc, 20 May 1809, capture of

A town in south eastern Poland, 88 km southeast of Lublin, 60 km south of Chelm and on Route 17.

A Polish victory over the Austrians.

(Last action - Sandomierz, 18 May; next action - Sandomierz, 26 May.)

Polish Forces GdB Pelletier commanding: IR Nr 2 (2 bns); IR Nr 6 (2 bns); 3rd UlR (4 sqns); 6th UlR (4 sqn).

Polish totals 4 bns, 8 sqns, 8 guns, ca 3,500 men.

Polish losses Not known, slight.

Austrian Forces Obst Pulski commanding various depot troops, recruits and train soldiers.

Austrian totals 2,500 men and 46 guns.

Austrian losses ca 450 dead and wounded, all survivors captured.

Comment The fall of Zamosc (and Sandomierz) left Archduke Ferdinand's lines of communication south from Warsaw to Krakau open to attack. The populace in the area flocked to the Polish colours.

Sources Malibran and Chelminski, Wrede, Welden.

YU Gospiċ, 21 and 22 May 1809, clash

A town in Croatia about 66 km north of Zadar (Zara) on the Adriatic coast in ex-Yugoslavia, near the River Lika, on Route 6.

An Austrian victory over the French.

(Last action - Gračac, 17 May; next action - Scardona, 20 July).

French Forces M Marmont commanding: 1st Division GdD Montrichard: 18e RILé; 5e, 79e and 81e RIdLi (2 bns each). 2nd Division GdD Clausel: 33e RIdLi (2 bns); 11e RIdLi (3 bns).

French totals 13 bns, 24 guns, ca 11,000 men.

French losses Gens Soyez and Launay wounded, 134 dead, 600 wounded, 270 captured.

Austrian Forces Oberst Rebroviċ commanding: GzIR Ottŏcaner Nr 2 (6 coys); GzIR Liccaner Nr 1 (1 bn); Dalmatian Freikorps (1 bn); LWI Bn (3 coys); ChLR Hohenzollern Nr 2 (1tp); 12 guns.

Austrian totals 2 bns, 9 coys, 1 troop, 12 guns, ca 3,000 men.

Austrian losses 64 dead, 500 wounded, 200 captured, 2 guns, 22 May.

Sources Woinovich, Martinien.

DV Aspern-Essling, 21 and 22 May 1809, battle

Two villages on the northeast side of the River Danube about 36 km east of Vienna.

An Austrian victory over the French and their allies.

(Last action - Linz-Urfahr, 17 May; next action - Pressburg and Engerau, 3 June.)

French Forces Emperor Napoleon I commanding: **2nd Light Cavalry Division:** GdB Piré: 8e HusR (3 sqns); 16e CháCh (3 sqns). GdB Bruyère: 13e (3 sqns) and 24e ChàCh (2 sqns).

IV Corps M Massena commanding: **1st Light Cavalry Division** GdD Maraluz commanding: 3e (2 sqns); 14e, 19e and 23e ChàCh (3 sqns each); Baden L DragR (4 sqns); Hessian Leib ChLR (3 sqns. **Total** 18 sqns. **3rd Division** GdD Molitor commanding: GdB Viviez: 37e RIdLi (3 bns); 67e RIdLi (2 bns). GdB Leguay: 2e RIdLi (2 bns); 16e RIdLi (3 bns). **Total** 10 bns and 12 guns. **4th Division** GdD Boudet commanding: GdB Fririon: 3e RILé (2 bns). GdB Valory: 56e RIdLi (3 bns); 93e RIdLi (2 bns). **Total** 7 bns and 12 guns. **1st Division** GdD Legrand commanding GdB Ledru: 26e RILé (3 bns); 18e RIdLi (3 bns); 3rd Baden LIR (2 bns). **Total** 8 bns and 20 guns.

2nd Division GdD Carra St Cyr commanding: GdB Cosson: 24e RILé (3 bns). GdB Dalesme: 4e RIdLi (3 bns); 46e RIdLi (3 bns). GdB Schinner Hessians = LeibgardeR (2 bns); LeibR (3 bns). **Total** 13 bns and 8 guns. Heavy Cavalry Reserve Marshal Bessières commanding. **3rd Division** GdD d'Espagne commanding: GdB Raynaud: 4e and 6e CuirR *. GdB

Fouler: 7e and 8e CuirR * **Total** 16 sqns and 6 guns. **2nd Division** GdD St Sulpice commanding: GdB L de Lagrange: 1er and 5e CuirR * GdB Guiton: 10e and 11e CuirR *. **Total** 16 sqns. **1st Division** GdD Nansouty commanding: GdB De France 1er and 2e Carabiniers *. GdB St Germain: 3e and 12e CuirR * **Total** 16 sqns and 4 guns.

* = 4 sqns each.

II Corps Marshal Lannes commanding (including Oudinot's Grenadier Corps).

1st Division GdD Tharreau commanding (these are all the 4e Bns of the regiments shown). GdB Conroux: 1ère DBdeLé: 6e, 24e and 25e RILé **. 3e DBdeLé: 9e, 16e and 27e RILé ** GdB Albert: 1ère DBdeLi: 8e, 24e and 45e RIdLi **. 2e DBdeLi: 94e, 95e and 96e RIdLi **GdB Jarry: 3e DBdeLi: 54e and 63e RIdLi **. 4e DBdeLi: 4e and 18e RIdLi **. **Total** 16 bns. **2nd Division** GdD Claparède commanding. GdB Coehorn: 2e DBdeLé: 17e, 21e and 28e RIe **. 4e DBdeLé: 26e RILé, Tirailleurs Corse and Tirailleurs du Po **. GdB Lesuire: 5e DBdeLi: 27e and 39e RIdLi ** 6e DBdeLi: 59e, 69e, 76e RIdLi ** GdB Ficatier: 7e DBdeLi: 40e and 88e RIdLi **.

8e DBdeLi: 64e, 100e and 103e RIdLi **. **Total** 16 bns. **3rd Division** GdD Demont commanding (present on 22 May only). 7e RILé; 12e, 17e, 21e, 30e, 33e, 61e, 65e, 85e, 111e RIdLi ** **Total** 10 bns, 15 guns. GdD St Hilaire (on 22 May only). GdB Lorencez: 10e RILé; 3e and 57e RIdLi (3 bns each). GdB Destabenrath: 72e and 105e RIdLi (3 bns each). GdD Oudinot (on 22 May only): Grenadiers and Voltigeurs. **Totals** bns, 36 guns.

** = 1 bn each.

The Imperial Guard The Old Guard GdD Dorsenne: Grenadiers (2 bns); Chasseurs (2 bns). GdD Curial (Mouton): GdB Gros Fusilier-Grenadiers (2 bns); Fusilier-Chasseurs (2 bns). GdB Rouget: 1er Tirailleur-Grenadiers (2 bns); 1er Tirailleur-Chasseurs (2 bns). ChLR (2 sqns); Gendarmerie d'Elite (1 sqn). **Totals** 12 bns, 3 sqns.

Allied grand totals 107 bns, 78 sqns.

Allied Officer Losses

French Army Officer Losses for Aspern-Essling

	Dead	Wounded	Captured	Total
Generals	4	14	2	20
General Staff	2	14	-	16
Adjutants	5	32	1	38
Imperial Guard (10 bns, 3 sqns)				
Infantry and Cavalry	10	48	1	59
Guard Artillery	1	1	-	2
Grenadier Corps	2	4	-	6
Cavalry Division				
Lasalle (11 sqns)	10	24	5	39
Maraluz (18 sqns)	15	30	1	46
Espagne (16 sqns)	16	39	7	62
St Sulpice (16 sqns)	18	45	3	66
Nansouty (10 sqns)	6	12	-	18
Württemberg ChLR Herzog Heinrich (4 sqns)	1	2	-	3
Infantry Divisions				
Molitor (10 bns)	11	47	1	59
Boudet (7 bns)	9	46	1	56
Legrand (8 bns)	13	53	4	70
Carra St Cyr (13 bns)	22	64	3	89
St Hilaire (15 bns)	18	111	1	130
Tharreau (16 bns)	25	81	-	106
Claparède (16 bns)	13	56	-	69
Demont (10 bns)	11	15	1	27

Foot artillery	3	8	1	12
Horse artillery	1	7	-	8
Train	-	3	-	3
TOTALS	216	756	32	1,004

These losses included 24 generals.

Total Allied losses were estimated at between 20–23,000 dead and wounded and 3,000 captured as well as 3 guns. The dead generals were Marshal Lannes, Generals d'Espagne, St Hilaire and Pouzet.

Austrian Forces Archduke Charles commanding.

1st Column (VI Corps) FML Hiller. **Avantgarde** GM Nordmann: HusR Liechtenstein Nr 7 (7 sqns); GzIR St Georger Nr 6 (1 bn); GzIR Broder Nr 7 (3 coys); Wiener Jägerfreikorps Schlegenberg (2 coys); Wiener Freiwilligen (1st and 2nd bns); IR Gyulai Nr 60 (2 bns) 2 bns. FML Kottulinsky: DragR EH Johann Nr 1 (6 sqns).

GM Hohenfeld: IR Klebek Nr 14 (2 bns); IR Jordis Nr 59 (bns); Wiener Freiwilligen (4th Bn). FML Vincent: Oberst Splényi: IR Splényi Nr 51 (2 bns); IR Benjowsky Nr 31 (3 bns); Moravian Freibataillon (3rd Bn). GM Bianchi: IR Duka Nr 39 (2 bns); Wiener Freiwilligen (3rd Bn). GM Mesko: HusR Kienmayer Nr 8 (7 sqns). **1st Column totals:** 19 bns, 5 coys, 20 sqns, 10,360 infantry, 1,774 cavalry, 3½ foot, 2 HA and 2 heavy batteries or 52 guns.

2nd Column (I Corps) GdK Bellegarde, FML Fresnel, GM Vécsey: ChLR Vincent Nr 4 (8 sqns); ChLR Klenau Nr 5 (8 sqns). GM Wintzingerode: Jäger bn Nr 2 (1 bn); IR Anton Mittrowsky Nr 10 (2 bns). FML Vogelsang; GM Henneberg: IR Reuss-Plauen Nr 17 (3 bns); IR Kolowrat Nr 36 (3 bns). FM Ulm; GM Wacquant: IR EH Rainer Nr 11 (3 bns); IR Vogelsang Nr 47 (3 bns). FML Nostitz; Oberst Schaeffer: IR Argenteau Nr 35 (3 bns); IR Erbach Nr 42 (2 bns). **2nd Column totals** 20 bns, 16 sqns, 21,742 infantry, 1,526 cavalry, 4 foot, 2 HA, 4 heavy batteries or 68 guns.

3rd Column (II Corps) FML Hohenzollern-Hechingen. **Avantgarde:** GM Provenchères: ChLR O'Reilly Nr 3 (5 sqns). GM Mayer: Jäger bns Nr 7 and 8 (2 bns); Legion EH Carl (2nd Bn), IR Stain Nr 50 (2 bns). FML Brady, GM Buresch: IR Zach Nr 15 (2 bns); IR Josef Colloredo Nr 57 (2 bns). GM Koller: IR (vacant) Zedtwitz Nr 25 (3 bns); IR Froon Nr 54 (1 ⅔ bns). FML Weber, GM Wied-Runkel: IR (vacant) Stuart Nr 18 (3 bns); IR Rohan Nr 21 (2 ⅔ bns); IR Frelich Nr 28 (3 bns). **3rd Column totals** 22⅓ bns, 5 sqns, 19,628 infantry, 665 cavalry, 4 foot, 2 HA, 3 heavy batteries or 62 guns.

4th Column (IV Corps) FML Rosenberg, FML Dedovich, Oberst Gratze: GzIR Wallachisch-Illyrisch Nr 13 (1 bn); Moravian Freibataillon (2nd Bn). GM Grill: IR EH Ludwig Nr 18 (3 bns); IR Coburg Nr 22 (3 bns). GM Neustädter: IR Czartoyski Nr 9 (3 bns); IR Reuss-Greitz Nr 55 (2 bns). Oberst Ignaz Hardegg: UlR Schwarzenberg Nr 2 (7 sqns); Jäger bn Nr 11 (1 bn); ChLR Rosenberg Nr 6 (4 sqns). **4th Column totals** 14 bns, 11 sqns, 9,953 infantry, 1,367 cavalry, 2 foot, 1 HA and 2 heavy batteries or 34 guns.

5th Column (IV Corps) FML Rosenberg, FML Hohenlohe, Oberst Frelich: HusR Stipsicz Nr 10 (8 sqns); IR EH Carl Nr 3 (3 bns). GM Carneville: Carneville Freikorps (2 coys and 1 sqn); GzIR Wallachisch-Illyrisch Nr 13 (1 bn). FML Hohenlohe: GM Riese: IR Chasteler Nr 46 (2 bns); IR Bellegarde Nr 44 (3 bns). GM Reinhard: IR Hiller Nr 2 (3 bns); IR Sztáray Nr 33 (3 bns). FML Rohan: GM Stutterheim: HusR EH Ferdinand Nr 3 (8 sqns); ChLR Rosenberg Nr 6 (8 sqns). **5th Column totals** 16⅓ bns, 2 coys, 25 sqns, 10,968 infantry, 2,247 cavalry, 2 foot, 1 HA and 2 heavy batteries or 34 guns.

I Reserve Corps GdK Prince Liechtenstein. **The Cavalry Reserve** FML Hessen-Homburg, GM Siegenthal: KürR Herzog Albert Nr 3 (6 sqns); KürR EH Franz Nr 2 (6 sqns). GM Lederer: KürR Kronprinz Ferdinand Nr 4 (6 sqns); KürR Hohenzollern Nr 8 (6 sqns). FML Kienmayer: GM Kroyher: KürR Kaiser Nr 1 (4 sqns); KürR Liechtenstein Nr 6 (6 sqns). GM Rottermund: DragR Riesch Nr 6 (6 sqns). GM Clary: DragR Knesevich Nr 3 (6 sqns). GM Kerekes: HusR Primatial (6 sqns); HusR Neutraer (4 sqns). GM Wartensleben: HusR Blankenstein Nr 6 (8 sqns). **Cavalry Reserve totals** 64 sqns, 6,674 men and 3 HA batteries or 18 guns.

The Grenadier Reserve FML Lindeman: GM Murray: Gren bns Leiningen, Portner, Georgy, Wieniawsky, Demontant, Legrand, Hohenlohe, Hahn. FML d'Aspre, Oberstleutnant Scovaud: Gren bns Brzeginski, Puteany, Scovaud, Scharlach, Mayblümel, Oklopsia, Bissingen, Kirchenbetter. **Grenadier Reserve totals** 16 bns, 11,423 men and 3 foot batteries or 24 guns.

Lackenau). Both sides now reorganized and prepared for the second attempt to cross the river. As usual, French casualty returns are fragmentary and unreliable for other ranks.

On 21 May 37,000 Austrian fought 30,000

Summary of Austrian Forces

	Battalions	Squadrons	Infantry	Cavalry	Guns
1st Column	19	20	10,360	1,774	52
2nd Column	20	16	21,742	1,526	68
3rd Column	22⅓	5	19,628	665	62
4th Column	14	11	9,935	1,367	34
5th Column	16⅓	25	10,908	2,247	34
Cav Reserve	—	64	—	6,674	18
Gren Reserve	16	—	11,423	—	24
Totals	107⅔	141	83,996	14,253	292

Austrian Losses at Aspern-Essling

		Killed			Wounded			Captured		
Columns	(Corps)	Officers	Men	Horses	Officers	Men	Horses	Officers	Men	Horses
1st	(VI)	8	507	87	70	1,548	71	—	53	1
2nd	(I)	26	878	212	148	4,076	197	—	180	8
3rd	(II)	18	720	146	108	2,931	84	—	15	—
4**	(IV)									
5**	(IV)	19	1321	137	197	3,021	176	11	415	—
Reserve										
Cavalry*		4	192	470	46	439	300	—	7	4
Grenadiers		11	306	—	80	2335	—	—	—	—
Totals		86	3,924	1,052	649	14,350	828	11	670	13

* = The losses of the Primatial and Neutraer Hussars are not known.

** = Including general staff casualties.

These casualties included 13 generals: FML Weber (II Corps) was killed GdK Johann Fürst Liechtenstein, FML Franz Fürst zu Hohenzollern-Hechingen, FML Ludwig Fürst Hohenlohe-Waldenburg, Bartenstein, FML Josef von Dedovich, FML Viktor Rohan, FML Karl Graf Fresnel, FML Johann Graf Nostitz, GM Freiherr von Winzingerode, GM von Siegenthal, GM Otto Graf Hohenfeld, GM Josef von Grill, GM Johann von Neustädter, GM Wenzel von Greifenbach, GM Josef Graf Colloredo, GM Johann von Delmotte, GM Ferdinand von Reinhard and GM Josef von Mayer were wounded.

Comment The Austrians prevented Napoleon from crossing the Danube in force (there had been an abortive attempted crossing on 13 May at Schwarze Frenchmen; on 22 May 85,000 Austrians fought 50,000 Frenchmen.

This was at least Napoleon's fourth defeat in battle. His first was at Bassano on 6 November 1796 against the Austrians under FZM Baron Allvintzy; the second was in the Battle of Caldiero on 12 November 1796, once more at the hands of Allvintzy, and the third was at the siege of Acre (17 March–21 May 1799).

Sources Martinien, Leyh, Hoehn-Veltze, HGM 11, Obser.

EG Santiago de Compostela, 22 May 1809, clash

A town in the north western Spanish province of Galicia, 45 km south of La Coruña on Route A9/E1.

A Spanish victory over the French.

(Last action - Pajares, 19 May; next action - Santander, 10 June.)

French Garrison Gd Maucune 4 bns, ? ChàCh 6 guns.

French total ca 3,600 men.

French losses 600 men and 2 guns.

Spanish Forces Gen Martin La Carrera commanding ca 2,000 men and 9 guns and Morillo's guerrillas 10,000 (only 7,000 were armed).

Spanish total 12,000 men and 9 guns.

Spanish losses Not known, light.

Sources Oman, Napier.

GN Dammgarten, 23 May 1809 clash

A small town on the German Baltic coast, on the estuary of the Rechnitz River on Route B105 halfway between Rostock and Stralsund.

An insurgent victory over the Mecklenburgers.

(Last action - Magdeburg, 5 May; next action - Stralsund, 31 May.)

Mecklenburg Forces Gen Candras and Gen Pressenthin commanding: Mecklenburg IR (2 bns); Polish UlR (100 men); HusR 60 men, 2 x 6 pounder guns.

Mecklenburg totals 900 infantry, 140 cavalry, 2 guns.

Mecklenburg losses Not known exactly; Gen Pressenthin, 30 officers, 300 men, 2 guns and 4 colours captured.

Prussian Rebel Major von Schill's Forces HusR (3 sqns); JzPf (1 sqn); 400 infantry, 3 guns.

Prussian Rebel Major von Schill's totals 450 cavalry, 400 infantry, 3 guns.

Prussian Rebel losses Not exactly known, very slight.

Comment Gen Candras and his remnants fled east past Stralsund abandoning over 100 guns and tons of powder and shot, Napoleon's gift to Denmark for supporting his cause. There were also about 50 French gunners there.

When Schill entered Stralsund on 25 May these gunners blasted his force with canister; as a result 40 of the Frenchmen were killed and the rest wounded.

Sources Bartsch.

EE Alcañiz, 23 May 1809, battle

A fortified town in north eastern Spain, on the Rio Guadalope, about 30 km south of the River Ebro on Routes 232 and 420, 88 km south east of Zaragoza.

A Spanish victory over the French.

(Last action - Valls, 25 February; next action - Maria de Huerve, 15/16 June.)

French Forces Suchet's III Corps. 2nd Division GdD Musnier: 114e and 115e RIdLi (3 bns each); 1st IR Vistula Legion (2 bns); 121e RIdLi (1 bn); Suchet's Escort (of 40e and 61e RIdLi 450 men). 1st Division GdD Laval: 14e RIdLi and 3rd IR Vistula Legion (2 bns each); 4e HusR (4 sqns); 13e CuirR (2 sqns). Artillery 3 x FAB.

French totals 14 bns, 7,292 infantry, 6 sqns, 526 cavalry, 18 guns.

French losses About 800 men killed and wounded.

Spanish Forces Lieutenant General Blake commanding: **Left Wing** Gen Areizaga: LIRs Daroca, Volunteers of Aragon, Tiradores de Doyle, Reserve of Aragon, 1st Tiradores de Murcia (1 bn each); Tiradores de Cartagena (1 coy). **The Centre** Gen Marquis de Lazan: Volunteers of Valencia, Ferdinando VII, (1 bn each); America (3rd Bn); Traxler's Swiss (½ bn). **Right Wing** Gen Roca: IRs Savoia (3rd Bn); America (2nd Bn); 1st of Valencia (3 bns); 2nd Cazadores of Valencia, 1st Volunteers of Zaragoza (1 bn each). **Cavalry** Detachments of the regiments Santiago, Olivencia and Husares Españoles. (445 men in all). Artillery: 19 guns.

Spanish totals 15⅚ bns, 8,101 infantry, 3 sqns, 445 cavalry, 19 guns.

Spanish losses About 300 killed and wounded.

Comment Blake's victory caused Suchet to abandon most of Aragon and recruits poured in to join the Spanish army. Within three weeks he had 25,000 men but could not arm, equip or train most of them.

Sources Oman, Napier, Martinien.

TY Berg-Isel, 25 May 1809, 1st clash

A wooded hill about 2 km south of Innsbruck, capital city of the Austrian province of the Tyrol.

A Bavarian victory over the Austrians.

(Last actions - Strass and Schwaz, 14/15 May; next action - St Michael-Leoben, 25 May.)

Bavarian Forces GL Deroy's 3rd Division. 1st Brigade: GM von Vicenti: IR Ysenburg Nr 9 (2 bns); IR Junker Nr 10 (2 bns); LtI Bn Nr 5 Buttler. 2nd Brigade: IR Preysing Nr 5 (2 bns); IR vac Nr 14 (2 bns); LtI Bn Nr 7 (1 bn). Cavalry Brigade: GM Count Seydewitz: DragR Thurn und Taxis Nr 2 (4 sqns); ChLR Bubenhofen Nr 4 (4 sqns). Artillery: Maj Lancy: 1 foot and 1 HA batteries - 12 guns.

Bavarian totals 10 bns, 8 sqns, 12 guns, ca 4,000 men.

Bavarian losses from 20 to 70 dead and from 100 to 150 wounded.

Austrian and Tyrolean Forces Andreas Hofer commanding.

Austrian Troops Obstlt Ertel IR Lusignan Nr 16 (1 bn); JgB Nr 9 (2 coys); ChLR O'Reilly Nr 3 (60 men); 5 guns, Salzburg Jägers (2 coys); IR de Vaux Nr 45 (3rd Bn); ca 900 men.

Tyrolean Forces led by Josef Eisenstecken, Josef Speckbacker and Martin Teimer.

The Schützenkompanien of the Eisack and Etsch, Lower and Upper Inn valleys.

Tyrolean totals 2 bns, 4 coys, ½sqn, 5 guns, (Austrians) and the following Schützenkompanien:

South Tyrol Passeier (3); Lana (4); Meran (9); Ritten (1); Jenesien and Karneid (5); Sarnthein (1); Kastelruth (5); Klausen (10); Schlanders (6); Sterziag (1); Mühlbach (1); Bruneck (2).

Total 48 companies, ca 5,000 men. **North Tyrol** 14 companies, ca 1,400 men. Villanderer, Rodenecker, Sarntaler, Michelsburg, Wilten, Sonnenburg, Rettenburg (Landsturm), Burggräfler, Vintschgau, Latzfons, ca 3,000 men.

Austrian and Tyrolean losses ca 50 dead and 30 wounded.

Comment The action ended in a draw but the insurgents, very disappointed that the population of the upper Inn valley had not risen to join them, withdrew south to Matrei.

Sources HGM 20, Leyh, Bezzel.

TY St Michael-Leoben, 25 May 1809, clash

A village in the Austrian province of Steyermark, on the River Mur, 6 km southwest of Leoben.

A French victory over the Austrians.

(Last action – Berg-Isel 25 May; next action – Berg-Isel, 29 May).

French Forces GdD Grenier commanding. GdB Valentin: 22e RILé (2 bns); 23e RILé (4 bns). GdB Desaix: 62e RIdLi (4 bns); 102e RIdLi (3 bns); 6e ChàCh (4 sqns); 2 guns. GdB Roussel: 1er RILé, 35e and 42e RIdLi (the 4th Bns of each regiment); 53e RIdLi (4 bns); 106e RIdLi (4 bns); 9e ChàCh (4 sqns); 10 guns.

French totals 24 bns, 8 sqns, 12 guns, ca 12,000 men.

French losses Reported as 200 dead, 400 wounded and 70 captured.

Austrian Forces FML Franz Baron von Jellačič commanding. MG von Ettinghausen: IR Esterházy Nr 32 (3 bns); IR de Vaux Nr 45 (2 bns). MG von Legisfeld: GzIR Warasdiner-Kreutzer Nr 5 (2 bns); Salzburger LW (1 bn); ChLR O'Reilly Nr 3 (¾ sqn); 1 x 3 pdr bty – 4 guns; IR Reuss-Greitz Nr 55 (3rd Bn); IR EH Carl Nr 3 (½ bn).

Austrian totals 92½ bns, ¾ sqns, 4 guns, ca 9,000 men.

Austrian losses 423 dead, 1,137 wounded, 4,963 captured, 50 missing.

Comment Jellačič's division lingered in Salzburg from 29 April until 19 May and was intercepted by part of Prince Eugène's Army of Italy as he sought to join Archduke John's army in Graz. Jellačič had detached his cavalry and 6 pounder artillery battery as being no use in the mountains and lacked scouting and patrol capability as well as artillery support.

Sources Wrede, HGM Nr 51.

WW Sandomierz, 26 May 1809, clash

A fortified town on the left bank of the River Vistula in Poland, about 160 km southeast of Warsaw, at the junction of Routes 723, 759, 777 and 859.

A Polish victory over the Austrians.

(Last action – Zamosc, 20 May; next action – Jedlinsko, 11 June.)

Polish Forces GdB Sokolnicki commanding: IR Nr 3 (2 bns); IR Nr 6 (2 bns); IR Nr 12 (2 bns); 1st ChàCh (1 sqn); 6th UlR (1 sqn) and 42 guns.

Polish totals 6 bns, 2 sqns, 46 guns, ca 5,000 men.

Polish losses Not known, slight.

Austrian Forces FML Schauroth commanding. GM Branowatzky: ChLR Kaiser Nr 1 (6 sqns); HusR Kaiser Nr 1 (6 sqns); HusR Palatin Nr 12 (1 sqn). **GM Trautenberg** IR Strauch Nr 24 (3 bns); IR Boullet Nr 55 (1 bn); KürR Lothringen Nr 7 (6 sqns). **Austrian totals** 4 bns, 14 sqns, 12 guns, ca 7,500 men.

Austrian losses Not known, slight.

Comment This was Archduke Ferdinand's attempt to resecure his communications southwards to Krakau and the main Austrian army in Bohemia. It failed and he evacuated Warsaw on 30 May.

Sources Malibran and Chelminski, Wrede, Welden.

TY Berg-Isel, 29 May 1809, 2nd clash

A wooded hill about 2 km south of Innsbruck, capital city of the Austrian province of the Tyrol on the River Inn. An impressive ski-jump tower and a museum now crown this hill.

A Bavarian victory over the Austrians.

(Last actions – Berg-Isel 25 May; next action – 3rd Lueg pass, 24 July.)

Bavarian Forces GL Deroy's 3rd Division (see 1st Berg-Isel, 25 May) plus the IR Junker Nr 10 (2 bns) and 1 foot artillery battery – 1,200 men and 6 guns.

Bavarian totals 12 bns, 8 sqns, 18 guns, ca 5,240 men.

Bavarian losses 87 dead, 156 wounded, 53 missing. (HGM 20 states 130 dead and 500 wounded).

Austrian and Tyrolean Forces see 1st Berg-Isel, 25 May.

Austrian and Tyrolean totals ca 1,200 line troops and 13,600 Schützen and Landsturm in 61 South Tyrolean and 35 North Tyrolean companies and 6 guns.

Austrian and Tyrolean losses 90 dead and 160 wounded.

Comment In a declaration signed at Wolkersdorf on 29 May, Emperor Franz I assured the inhabitants of the Tyrol and Voralberg that, as a result of Archduke Charles' victory over Napoleon at Aspern-Essling (21/24 May 1809), they would never again be separated from the Austrian state. Fate – in the shape of the Austrian defeat at Wagram (5/6 July 1809) – was to make these bold words soon ring very hollow indeed.

Sources HGM 20, Leyh, Bezzel.

GN Stralsund, 31 May 1809, storm of

A fortified city port on the German Baltic coast opposite the Island of Rügen (in 1809 this was Swedish Pommerania) 70 km east of Rostock.

An Allied victory over the Prussian rebel, Major Ferdinand von Schill.

(Last actions – Dammgarten, 23 May; next action – this was the last action of the campaign in this theatre.)

Allied Forces Dutch Contingent LG P G Gratien commanding: 6th and 9th LIR's (4 bns); 2nd KürR (3 sqns); 10 x 6 pounder guns, 2 howitzers. **Totals** ca 5,000 men and 12 guns. **Danish Contingent** MG Ewald: IR Oldenburg and IR Holstein (3 bns and 2 sharpshooter coys); HusR (2 sqns); Light Horse (1 tp). **Totals** 2,100 infantry, 215 cavalry, 140 gunners and 10 x 3 pounder guns.

Allied totals 7 bns, 5,500 infantry, 5¼ sqns, 500 cavalry and 22 guns.

Allied losses Not known exactly; Dutch GdB Carteret killed.

Schill's Forces 4 coys of infantry (300 men) ½bn Swedish Rügen LWI (300 men); 2nd (Brandenburg) HusR (400 men); 1UlR (200 men); 200 Swedish soldiers manning 15 guns.

Schill's totals 1,400 men and 15 guns.

Schill's losses 380 killed, 557 captured.

Comment The Allies stormed the town and Schill, seeing that all was lost, sought death in the ensuing mêlée and was shot by a Dutch soldier behind the St Johannis Church. His head was pickled and kept in Leyden Dutch army museum until 1839. Twenty-five of his men were later shot as 'highwaymen'. Many survivors were taken back into Prussian service by General Blücher; some joined the Black Brunswickers and some joined Andreas Hofer's Tyrolean rebels.

Sources Bartsch.

DV Pressburg (Bratislava) and Engerau, 1–4 June 1809, clashes

A fortified city on the east bank of the River Danube in the Slovak Republic, on the border with Austria, at the junction of Routes 61 and 2/D-2/E15. Engerau is a small village on the west bank, just outside the bridgehead.

An Austrian victory over the Allies.

(Last actions – Aspern, 21–22 May; next action – Weidensee, 29 June.)

Allied Forces GdD Lasalle and GdB Petit: 12e RIdLi (2 bns); Hessen-Darmstadt Füsiliers (2 bns) and Schützen (1 bn); 16e ChàCh (3 sqns); 1 x FAB.

Allied totals 5 bns, 3 sqns, 6 guns, ca 4,500 men.

Allied losses French losses not known; the Hessians lost 144 killed, wounded and missing.

Austrian Forces GM Hofmeister: IR Strassoldo Nr 27 (3 bns); IR Esterházy Nr 32 (1 bn); IR Duka Nr 39 (1 bn); IR Beaulieu Nr 58 (2 bns); IR Gyulai Nr 60 (2nd Bn); IR St Julien Nr 61 (3 bns); IR F Jellačič Nr 62 (1 bn); ChLR O'Reilly Nr 3 and Neutraer HusR (2 sqns each). Many of these units were very weak having suffered heavy casualties already in the campaign; they were not all present at these actions.

Austrian totals 12 bns, 4 sqns, ca 30 guns.

Austrian losses Not exactly known; one battalion of IR Beaulieu was captured losing 8 officers and 400 men as prisoners.

Comment In order to prevent the junction of Archduke John's corps with the main Austrian army at Wagram, Napoleon sent this ad hoc corps to seize the Danube crossing here.

Although the Allies took Engerau, they could make no impression on the bridgehead.

Sources Wrede, Martinien, Beck, Bigge, Keim.

IN Klagenfurt, 8 June 1809, clash

A fortified town in the Austrian province of Carinthia; at the eastern end of Lake Wörther and at the junction of Routes 70, 83, 91 and A2/E7.

An Italian victory over the Austrians.

(Last action – Predil, 15–18 May; next action – Papa, 12 June.)

Italian Forces GdD Rusca commanding: GdB Bertoletti: 4th Italian LIR, 1st and 3rd Italian LtIRs, Istrian bn (8 bns); 2nd Italian ChàCh (2 sqns); 2 x FAB.

Italian totals 8 bns, 2 sqns, 12 guns.

Italian losses Not known, light.

Austrian Forces FML Chasteler commanding: GM Marchal: IR Lusignan Nr 16, IR Hohenlohe-Bartenstein Nr 26 (3 bns each). GM Schmidt: IR J Jellačič Nr 53 (3 bns); GzIR 2nd Banal Nr 11 (2 bns). GM Fenner: 9th Jägers (1 bn); ChLR Hohenzollern Nr 2 (7 sqns). Artillery: 2 x FAB.

Austrian totals 12 bns, 7 sqns, 2 x FAB, ca 5,000 men.

Austrian losses IR Nr 26 lost 3 companies captured.

Sources Wrede, Martinien, Hoehn-Veltze, Hoen.

EG Santander, 10 June 1809, capture of

A fortified port on the Spanish coast of the Bay of Biscay, midway between Bilbao in the east and Oviedo in the west, at the junction of Routes 634/E70 and 623 from Burgos.

A Spanish victory over the French.

(Last action – Santiago de Compostella, 22 May; next action – this was the last action of note here in 1809.)

French garrison GdB Noirot and 1,600 men.

GdD Bonnet's division consisted of the 119e and 120e RidLi (4 bns each).

French total ca 6,500 men.

French losses 600 (including 400 sick) captured; all GdD Bonnet's stores and ammunition captured as well as £10,000 cash.

Three French corvettes and two luggers tried to escape but were captured by the British frigates *Amelia* and *Statira*. Initially the garrison captured on 10 June but all released again on 12 June.

Spanish Forces MG Francisco Ballasteros commanding IRs Luano, Castropol, Navia, Luarca, Villaviciosa, Lianes, Cangas de Oñor, Cangas de Tiner, Don Carlos.

Spanish total ca 5,000 men.

Spanish losses (on 12 June) 3,000 captured, the rest scattered. Ballasteros escaped by ship.

Comment Ballasteros' initial raid was a great success but he decided to stay and defend the place instead of withdrawing into the hills again. Bonnet heard of the capture and retook Santander on 12 June.

Sources Oman, Napier.

WW Jedlinsko (Jedlinsk), 11 June 1809, clash

A village in central Poland on the River Radomka about 80 km south of Warsaw on Route 7/E77, 10 km north of Radom.

An Austrian rearguard victory over the Poles.

(Last action – Sandomierz, 26 May; next action – Sandomierz, 15 June.)

Polish Forces GdD Zajonczek commanding: IR Nr 12; IR Nr 8, IR Nr 14 (2 bns each); 1st ChàCh (2 sqns); 8 UlR (2 sqns); 10th HusR (2 sqns).

Polish totals 6 bns, 6 sqns, 6 guns, ca 5,000 men.

Polish losses 600 dead and wounded, 400 captured.

Austrian Forces FML Mondet commanding: GM Mohr: HusR Kaiser Nr 1 (2 sqns); ChLR Kaiser Nr 1 (5 sqns); Palatin HusR Nr 12 (5 sqns); IR Vukassovich. GM Civallart: IR de Ligne Nr 30 (3 bns); IR Kottulinsky Nr 41 (2 bns).

Austrian totals 8 bns, 12 sqns, 12 guns, ca 9,000 men.

Austrian losses Not known.

Comment Archduke Ferdinand had now realized the hopelessness of achieving anything in Poland and was withdrawing south after hearing of the Austrian victory at Aspern-Essling on 21 and 22 May.

Sources Wrede, Malibran and Chelminski, Welden.

IN Papa, 12 June 1809, skirmish

A small town in the western Hungary about 24 km south of Raab (now Györ).

An Allied victory over the Austrians.

(Last action – Klagenfurt, 8 June; next action – Raab, 14 June).

Allied Forces Prince Eugène de Beauharnais commanding: GdB Bertoletti: 8e RILé (2 bns); 1er and 52 RIdLi (4 bns each); 9e and 29e RIdLi (4 bns); 1 x FAB. GdD Grouchy: 20e ChàCh, 9e HusR (8 sqns). GdD Lauriston: GM von Harrant: 1st Baden LIR 'Grossherzog' (1 bn); 2nd Baden LIR 'Erbgrossherzog' (2 bns); Jägers (1 bn); 1 FAB.

Allied totals 18 bns, 8 sqns, 12 guns, ca 16,000 men.

Allied losses Not exactly known, very light; the Baden brigade lost 2 killed and 9 wounded.

Austrian Forces FML Frimont; GM Andrássy: IR Allvintzy Nr 19 (2 bns); GzIR 1st Banal Nr 10 (2 bns); HusR EH Josef Nr 2 (2 sqns); 1 x HAB and 24 sqns Hungarian Insurrektions-Cavalry including the Pressburg, Neograd, Bars and Pest Regiments.

Austrian totals 8 bns, 26 sqns, 6 guns ca 800 men.

Austrian losses Not exactly known, light.

Comment Prince Eugène had been ordered by Napoleon to seek out and destroy Archduke John's remnants of his VIII and IX Corps. The Insurrektion troops were newly raised, scarcely organized and drilled and could not yet use their weapons or horses properly. Their combat value was thus very low.

The Austrians fell back north to Raab.

Sources Wrede, Martinien, Hoen-Veltze, Hoen, Zech/Porbeck.

IN Raab (Györ), 14 June 1809, battle

A fortified town in Hungary at the confluence of the Rivers Raab, Raabnitz and Little Danube on Route 85/E60.

An Allied victory over the Austrians.

(Last action – Papa, 12 June; next action – Raab, 15 – 22 June).

Allied Forces Prince Eugène de Beauharnais commanding. **Right Wing** GdB Jacquinot: 1er ChàCh (4 sqns); 2e ChàCh (3 sqns); 7e HusR (3 sqns); 1 x HAB. GdB Colbert: 7e ChàCh (4 sqns); 20e ChàCh (3 sqns); 9e HusR (4 sqns). GdB Guerin: 30e DragR (4 sqns); Drag Regina * (4 sqns); 1 x HAB. **Right Wing totals** 29 sqns, 2 x HAB. **The Centre** GdD Grenier **1st Division GdD** Serras: GdB Moreau: 1e RILé (1 bn); 35e and 53e RIdLi (4 bns each). GdB Roussel: 42e and 106e RIdLi (4 bns each); 9e ChàCh (4 sqns); 1 x FAB. **2nd Division** GdD Durutte: GdB Valentin: 22e RILé (1 bn); 23e RILé (2 bns); 60e RIdLi (2 bns). GdB Bruch: 62e and 102e RIdLi (3 bns each); 6e ChàCh (4 sqns); 1 x FAB. **1st Italian Division** GdD Rusca, GdB Bertoletti: 4th LIR*; Istrian bn*; 1st* and 3rd* LtIRs (8 bns); ChàCh* (2 sqns); 1 X FAB. **2nd Italian Division** GdD Severoli: GdB Bonfanti: 1st LIR* (3 bns); 2nd LIR* (1 bn); 3rd LIR* (4 bns); 7th LIR* (1 bn); Dalmatian IR* (1 bn); 112e RIdLi (3 bns); Drag Napoleone* (1 sqn); 1 x FAB. Italian Royal Guard* GdB Lecci; GdB Viani: Grenadiers*, Chasseurs*, Vélites* (1 bn each); Gardes d'Honneur*, Dragoni* (3 sqns); 1 x FAB*. GdD Lauriston: GM von Harrant's Baden Brigade: 1st LIR 'Grossherzog' (1 bn); 2nd LIR 'Erbgrossherzog' (2 bns); Jägers (1 bn); 1 x FAB. GdD Pacthod: 8e RILé (2 bns); 1er and 52e RIdLi (4 bns each); 1 x FAB, 9e and 29e RIdLi (4 bns). GdD Pully: 23e, 28e and 29e DragR (12 sqns); 1 x HAB. GdD Grouchy; GdD Montbrun, GdB Guerin: 3e, 7e and 24e DragR (12 sqns); Italian Drag Regina* (4 sqns); 1st Italian ChàCh* (1 sqn); 1 x HAB*. GdD Sahuc: 6e, 8e and 9e ChàCh (4 sqns each).

Allied totals 70 bns, 86 sqns, 10 bts, ca 35,000 men.

Allied losses 3 generals, 218 officers and ca 3,800 killed and wounded.

* = Italian troops.

Austrian Forces GdC Archduke John commanding; Archduke Josef, Palatine of Hungary:

The Right Wing FML Frimont: Sümegher HusR (6 sqns); DragR Hohenlohe Nr 2 (6 sqns); Szala HusR (6 sqns); ChLR Hohenzollern Nr 2, ChLR O'Reilly Nr 3, DragR Savoy Nr 5 (1 sqn each); HusR Blankenstein Nr 6 (2 sqns); 9th Jägers (½ coy); 4 guns.

The Centre FML Jellačič; GM Sebottendorf: GzIR 1st Banal Nr 10 (2 bns); LIR de Vaux Nr 45, Salzburg LWIR, IR Reuss-Greitz Nr 55 (1 composite bn); Judenburg LWIR (½ bn). Obst Eckhardt: IR Esterházy Nr 32 (3 bns); Veszprim Insurrektions-Bn Nr 9 and Pest Insurrektions-Bn Nr 2, Eisenburg Insurrektions-Bn Nr 5 (1 bn each). GM Legisfeld: Bruck LWIR (4 coys); Manhardsberg LWIR and Oberwienerwald LWIR (1 bn each). FML Colloredo; GM Lutz: IR Strassoldo Nr 27 (2½ bns); IR St Julien Nr 61 (2½ bns); 1st Innerösterreich Frei- Bn (2 coys). GM Marziani: IR F Jellačič Nr 62 (2 bns); Comorn Insurrektions-Bn Nr 7, Szala Insurrektions-Bn Nr 8 (1 bn each); Traunviertel LWI Bn, Mühlviertel LWI Bn; 4th Innerösterreich Frei-Bn (3 coys each). Defending the Kis-Megyer dairy: 2nd Graz LWI Bn (1 bn); IR Strassoldo Nr 27 (3 coys); IR St Julien Nr 61 (2 coys). Artillery of the centre 12 guns.

The Left Wing FML Mecséry; GM Andrássy: Eisenburg and Veszprim Insurrektions-CavRs (9 sqns); HusR Palatin Nr 12 (8 sqns); Oedenburg Insurrektions-CavR (2 sqns). Obst Gosztonyi: Insurrektions-CavRs Barser and Pest, (10 sqns); HusR Ott Nr 5 (6 sqns); Neograd Insurrektions-CavR (3 sqns). Reserve on Mount Szabad: GM Gajoli: IR Lusignan Nr 16 and GzIR Ogulin Nr 3 (2 bns each): LWI bns Cillier, 4th and 5th Graz (1 bn each). GM Kleinmayr: IR Allvintzy Nr 19 (3 bns); Grenadiers (4 bns: Salamon, Janusch, Chimani and Mühlen). **Total 14 bns.**

Reserve behind the Left Flank FML Graf Hadik: Heves and Zemplin Insurrektions-CavR (6 sqns). The fortified camp (north of the Raab River) GM Meskó: Insurrektions-Bns Pressburg Nr 1, Neutra Nr 3, Neograd Nr 4, 2nd Eisenburg Nr 6 (1 bn each); Insurrektions-CavRs Pressburg and Neograd (9 sqns); 10 guns.

Austrian totals 39 bns, 67 sqns, 18 guns, 23,329 infantry, 8,650 cavalry*.

Austrian losses Officers - 16 killed, 67 wounded, 24 captured, 7 missing. Men - 731 killed, 1,691 wounded, 2,384 captured, 1,315 missing. Horses - 255 killed, 135 wounded, 167 captured, 14 missing; 2 guns and 2 colours.

* = About half of these troops were Landwehr or Insurrektion.

Comment Archduke John now reaped the dubious fruits of his incredibly ill-advised policy of breaking up his army after the Battle of Piave River. This defeat foiled any hopes that Archduke John would be able to bring any significant forces to help in the epic struggle against Napoleon at Wagram on 5 and 6 July.

Sources Wrede, Martinien, Bodnár István, Zach/Porbeck.

EE Maria de Huerve, 15 and 16 June 1809, battle

A small town in Aragon northeastern Spain on Route 330, 21 km southeast of Zaragoza and on the west of the River Huerva.

A French victory over the Spanish.

(Last action - Alcañiz, 23 May; next action - Belchite, 18 June.)

French Forces Suchet's III Corps: GdD Musnier's **2nd Division** 114e and 115e RIdLi (3 bns each) 1st IR Vistula Legion (2 bns); 2nd Legion de Réserve (1 bn). GdB Habert (of Laval's **1st Division**): 14e RIdLi (3 bns), 2nd IR Vistula Legion (2 bns). **Reserve:** 5e RILé, 64e RILi (1 bn each). **Cavalry:** 4e HusR (4 sqns), 13e CuirR (2 sqns), Lancers of the Vistula Legion (4 sqns) and a Provisional Cavalry R. **Artillery:** 12 guns.

French totals 16 bns, 10,000 infantry, 6 sqns, 800 cavalry, 12 guns.

French losses '7–800 killed and wounded'.

Spanish Forces Capt Gen Blake commanding. Vanguard Brigade Colonel J Creagh: Almeria (2 bns); Cazadores de Valencia (1 bn). **1st Division** Major-General P Roca: 1st of Savoia (3 bns), Granada (1 bn), Avila Militia (1 bn), Tiradores de Cartagena (1 bn), Tercio Tortosa (1 bn). **2nd Division** Lieut-General Marquis of Lazan: 1st Volunteers of Zaragoza (1 bn), 3rd Cazadores de Valencia (1 bn), 1st of Valencia (3 bns), America (2 bns). Cavalry Brigade, Colonel J O'Donnell: Olivenza (4 sqns), Santiago (1 sqn). Artillery: 17 guns. Sappers 3 coys. **3rd Division** Lieut-General Areizaga (absent at Botorrita): Fernando 7th (1 bn), Grenadiers (4 coys), 1st and 2nd Volunteers of Aragon (1 bn each), Volunteers of Valencia (1 bn) Cazadores de Palafox (1 bn), Daroca (1 bn), Tiradores de Doyle (1 bn), Tiradores de Murcia (1 bn). **Cavalry:** Husares Españoles, Santiago (1 sqn each). **Artillery:** 8 guns. Gen Ariezaga's division had been left up the right bank of the River Huerva to Bototitta and was 10 km to Blake's rear during the battle.

Spanish totals ca 14,000 infantry, 1,000 cavalry, 18 guns.

Spanish losses 1,000 killed, 3,000–4,000 wounded, some hundreds captured, 20 guns, 3 colours.

Comment Suchet held Ariezaga's division in check on the right bank with GdD Laval and the 14e RIdLi (3 bns) and the 2nd IR Vistula Legion (2 bns) and 6 guns. Blake withdrew on Areizaga's division which he had left, isolated and inactive, at Botoritta and thence, that night to Belchite to the southeast. Thousands of his new recruits deserted. Ariezaga's inactivity (even though he could clearly hear the battle going on) was the major factor in Blake's defeat.

Sources Oman, Napier, Martinien.

EE Belchite, 18 June 1809, clash

A small fortified town in Aragon (north eastern Spain) on the north bank of the Rio Aguas, about 40 km southeast of Zaragoza, at the junction of Routes 221 and 222.

A French victory over the Spanish.

(Last action – Maria de Huerve, 15 and 16 June; next action – Girona, 6 June – 10 December.)

French Forces Suchet's III Corps: GdD Laval's 1st Division. GdD Musnier's 2nd Division; cavalry and artillery as for Maria del Huerve plus 44e RidLi (3 bns) and 3rd IR Vistula Legion (2 bns).

French totals 12,000 infantry, 1,000 cavalry, 12 guns.

French losses '200 killed and wounded'.

Spanish Forces Capt Gen Blake commanding. As for Alcañiz and Maria del Huerve (including Areizaga's division).

Spanish totals 11,000 infantry, 870 cavalry, 9 guns.

Spanish losses About 2,000 killed, wounded and captured, 9 guns, 1 colour, 20 ammunition waggons and all the food and military stores in Belchite.

Comment The battle was going fairly evenly when a French shell exploded a Spanish caisson in the rear right wing. The fire engulfed several other ammunition waggons which all went up with a terrific explosion which threw the Spanish into a panic, whole battalions throwing down their weapons and fleeing into the town. Control of the Ebro plain passed into French hands but guerrilla activity continued undiminished in the foothills.

Sources Oman, Napier, Martinien.

WW Sandomierz, 15–18 June 1809, assault and capture

A fortified town on the left bank of the River Vistula in Poland, about 160 km southeast of Warsaw, at the junction of Routes 723, 759, 777 and 859.

An Austrian victory over the Poles.

(Last action – Jedlinsko, 11 June; next action – Krakau, 14 July.)

Polish Forces GdB Sokolnicki commanding: IR Nr 3 (2 bns); IR Nr 6 (2 bns); IR Nr 12 (2 bns); 1st ChàCh (1 sqn); 6th UlR (1 sqn); 42 guns.

Polish totals 6 bns, 2 sqns, 42 guns, ca 5,000 men.

Polish Garrison About 1,000 dead and wounded; the rest captured and released on condition that they would not fight against Austria for the rest of the campaign.

Austrian Forces Archduke Ferdinand commanding. GM Geringer: HusR Szekler (8 sqns); Galician Frei-Bataillon Nr 2 (1 bn). GM Speth: KürR Sommariva Nr 5 (6 sqns). GM Pflacher: IR Davidovich Nr 34 (3 bns); IR Weidenfeld Nr 37 (3 bns); IR Kottulinsky Nr 41 (1 bn). FML Schauroth: GM Branowatzky: HusR Palatin Nr 12 (1 sqn); ChLR Kaiser Nr 1 (1 sqn); HusR Kaiser Nr 1 (6 sqns). GM Trautenberg: IR Strauch Nr 24 (3 bns); IR Baillet Nr 55 (4 coys); KürR Lothringen Nr 7 (6 sqns).

Austrian totals 11 bns, 4 coys, 28 sqns, 30 guns, ca 13,000 men.

Austrian losses 689 dead, 986 wounded.

Comment Archduke Ferdinand evacuated all military stores to Krakau and destroyed the fortifications. He then joined Archduke Charles at Wagram.

Sources Malibran and Chelminski, Wrede, Welden.

IN Raab (Györ), 15–22 June 1809, siege and capitulation

A fortified town at the confluence of the Little Danube and Raab Rivers, on Route 85/E60.

A Franco-Italian victory over the Austrians.

(Last action – Raab, 14 June; next action – Graz, 24 June.)

Allied Forces GdD Lauriston commanding: Baden Brigade GM von Harrant. 1st LIR 'Grossherzog' (1 bn); 2 LIR 'Erbgrossherzog' (2 bns); Jägers (1 bn); 1 x FAB. GdD Lasalle: GdB Piré; 8e HusR, 16e ChàCh (6 sqns); GdB Bruyère: 13e and 24e ChàCh (6 sqns). 1 x HAB.

Hessen-Darmstadt Garde-Füs-Bn and Leib-Füs-Bn (2 bns).

Italians GdD Severoli: GdB Bonfanti: 1st LIR (3 bns); 2nd LIR (1 bn); 3rd LIR (4 bns); 7th LIR (1 bn); Dalmatian IR (2 bns); 1 x FAB.

Allied totals 15 bns, 12 sqns, 3 batteries, ca 15,000 men.

Allied losses Not known, very light.

Austrian Garrison Obst Bechy commanding: 2,500 mainly Landwehr and Insurrektion, but including 2 companies each of IRs EH Franz Nr 52 and J Jellačič Nr 53. The fortress had 18 guns.

Austrian losses Not known, light. The garrison were allowed to go home on condition that they would not fight against France or her allies again in 1809.

Comment Siege artillery came up from Pressburg (now Bratislava) on 18 June, the bombardment of 20

June caused many fires. According to a French officer sent in to negotiate the capitulation, most of the garrison was drunk. The Italians provided the garrison after the Austrians left.

Sources Wrede, Hoen-Veltze, Zech/Porbeck, Martinien, Keim.

IN Graz (Karlsdorf), 24 June 1809, clash

A village in the Austrian province of Steyermark, about 5 km south of the city of Graz on the River Mur, at the junction of Routes A2 and A9/E93.

A French victory over the Austrians.

(Last action – Raab (Györ), 15–22 June; next action – Graz St Leonhard, 25/26 June.)

French Forces GdB Broussier commanding: 9e RIdLi (1 bn); 84e RIdLi (4 bns).

French totals 5 bns, 6 guns, ca 5,000 men.

French losses Not known, mostly in the 9e which was driven back by the Frimont Hussars.

Austrian Forces GM Splényi commanding FML Baron Ignaz Gyulai's Avantgarde: HusR Frimont Nr 9 (4 sqns); Massal I Bn Nr 4 (1 bn); GzIR Ottočaner Nr 2 (2 coys); IR Franz Carl Nr 52 (1 bn); ½ HAB.

Austrian totals 2 bns, 2 coys, 4 sqns, ½ HAB, ca 2,000 men.

Austrian losses Not known, slight; 400 prisoners taken this day were released in the combat of the next day.

Comment The raw Austrian Insurrektions infantry (4th Massal) fled when the French approached. The French decided to attack Gyulai's corps next day.

Sources HGM 58, Wrede.

IN Graz (St Leonhard), 25/26 June 1809, clash

A suburb of the capital city of the Austrian province of Steyermark, on the River Mur, about 150 km southwest of Vienna; at the junction of Routes A2 and A9/E93.

A French victory over the Austrians.

(Last action – Graz (Karlsdorf), 24 June. This was the last action in this theatre.)

French Forces GdB Broussier commanding: 9e RIdLi (1 bn); 84e RIdLi (4 bns); 92e RIdLi (2 bns).

French totals 7 bns,10 guns, ca 6,000 men.

French losses '32 dead, 231 wounded, captured and missing', 3 guns. Other sources say 400 dead and wounded, 500 captured.

Austrian Forces FML Count I Gyulai commanding: 2nd GzIR Banal Nr 11 (LW Bn); Banderial Insurrektion (2 bns); Personal-Bn (2 bns); IR EH Franz Carl Nr 52 (1 bn); IR Simbschen Nr 43 (½ bn); IR St Julien Nr 61 (2 coys); GzIR Ottočaner Nr 2 (Res Bn); GzIR Szluiner Nr 4 (Res Bn); HusR Frimont Nr 9 (2 sqns); Banderial HusR (2 sqns).

Austrian totals 10½ bns, 2 coys, 4 sqns, ca 10,000 men.

Austrian losses 164 dead, 816 wounded, captured, missing. 2 colours.

Comment The French, particularly the 84e, fought extremely well; as a result Napoleon had the base of the regiment's eagle engraved with 'Un Contra Dix' (One Against Ten).

The Austrian Insurrektions and Personal infantry, raw and partially trained, were worthless and fled the field, the Personal battalions abandoned their colours.

Sources HGM 58, Wrede.

DV Weidensee, 29 June 1809, clash

A village in north eastern Bavaria near Neumarkt-St Viet on the River Rott, on Route B299 (not located on many modern maps).

An Austrian victory over the Allies.

(Last action – Pressburg and Engerau, 3 June; next action – Wagram, 5 and 6 June.)

Allied Forces French General La Roche commanding: Provisional DragR (4 sqns); Bavarian HA (1 bty).

Allied totals ca 650 men, 6 guns.

Allied losses Not exactly known, the detachment was scattered.

Austrian Forces GM Radivojevich commanding: GzIR Peterwardeiner Nr 9 (2 bns); Deutsch-Banater Nr 12 (2 bns); Legion EH Carl (½ Jg Bn).

Austrian totals ca 4,000 men.

Austrian losses Not known, slight.

Comment This was a pin-prick Austrian raid with no strategic significance; symptomatic of the way the Austrian high command squandered scarce resources in penny-packets instead of concentrating them into significant bodies.

Sources Leyh, Wrede.

DV Wagram, 5 and 6 July 1809, battle

A village on the 'Marchfeld' about 10 km east of Vienna (Austria), on the east bank of the River Danube.

An Allied victory over the Austrians.

(Last action – Weidensee, 29 June; next action – Korneuburg, 7 July.)

French Forces Emperor Napoleon I commanding:

Imperial Guard Old Guard GdD Curial; GdB Michel: Grenadiers (2 bns); GdB Gros: Chasseurs (2 bns). **Young Guard** GdD Reille; GdB Dumoustier: Fusilier-Grenadiers (2 bns); Fusilier-Chasseurs (2 bns). GdB Roguet 1er Tirailleurs-Grenadiers (2 bns); 1er Tirailleurs-Chasseurs (2 bns). **Cavalry of the Guard** GdD Walter; GdB Lepic: GrenàCh (4 sqns); ChàCh (4 sqns). GdB Guyot DragR (4 sqns); Polish ChLR (4 sqns); Gendarmerie (2 sqns). **Imperial Guard totals** 12 bns, 18 sqns, 60 guns.

II Corps GdD Oudinot: 1st Division GdD Tharreau; GdB Conroux: 1ère DBdeLi (2 bns); 3e DBdeLé (2 bns). GdB Albert: 1ère DBdeLi (2 bns); 2e DBdeLi (2 bns). GdB Jarry: 3e DBdeLi (2 bns); 4e DBdeLi (2 bns). **2nd Division** GdD Frère; GdB Coehorn: 2e DBdeLé (3 bns); 4e DBdeLé (3 bns). GdB Razout: 5e DBdeLi (2 bns); 6e DBdeLi (3 bns). GdB Ficatier: 7e DBdeLi (2 bns); 8e DBdeLi (3 bns). **3rd Division** GdD Grandjean. GdB Marion: 10e RILé (3 bns). GdB Lorencez: 3e RIdLi (3 bns); 57e RIdLi (3 bns). GdB Brun: 72e RIdLi (3 bns); 105e RIdLi (3 bns). GdB Carcomelego: Portuguese Legion and 13e DBde (3 bns and 2 sqns). **Light Cavalry Brigade** GdB Colbert 9e HusR (3 sqns); 7e ChàCh (3 sqns); 20e ChàCh (3 sqns). **II Corps totals** 46 bns, 11 sqns, 48 artillery guns and 34 regimental pieces.

III Corps M Davout 1st Division GdD Morand; GdB Lacour: 13e RILé (3 bns); 17e RIdLi (3 bns). GdB L'Huillier: 30e and 61e RIdLi (3 bns each). **2nd Division** GdD Friant; GdB Gilly: 15e RILé (3 bns); 33e RIdLi (3 bns). GdB Barbanègre: 48e RIdLi (3 bns). GdB Grandeau: 108e and 111e RIdLi (3 bns each). **3rd Division** GdD Gudin; GdB Boyer: 12e and 21e RIdLi (3 bns each). GdB Duppelin: 25e and 85e RIdLi (3 bns each). GdB Leclerc: 7e RILé (4 bns). **4th Division** GdD Puthod; GdB Girard-Vieux: The 4th bns of the 17e, 30e, 61e and 65e RIdLi (4 bns). GdB Dessailly: the 4th bns of the 12e, 21e, 33e, 85e and 111e RIdLi (5 bns). **Light Cavalry Division** GdD Montbrun; GdB Pajol: 5e and 7e HusR and 11e ChàCh (3 sqns each). GdB Jacquinot: 1er, 2e and 12e ChàCh (3 sqns each). **Dragoon Division** GdD Pully; GdB Poincot: 23e , 28e and 29e DragR (4 sqns each). **Dragoon Division** GdD Grouchy; GdB Guérin: 7e and 30e DragR, Italian Drag Regina (4 sqns each) and 1er Italian ChàCh (1 sqn). **III Corps totals** 52 bns, 43 sqns, 60 foot artillery, 8 HA guns and 30 regimental pieces.

IV Corps M Massena 1st Division GdD Legrand; GdB Ledru: 26e RILé and 18e RIdLi (4 bns each). Oberst Neuenstein Baden Bde: LeibR (2 bns); IR Erbgrossherzog (2 bns); IR Hochberg (2 bns); Jäger bn (1 bn); 1 FAB. **2nd Division** GdD Carra-St Cyr; GdB Cosson: 24e RILé (4 bns). Hessian Bde GdB Schinner: Leibgarde (3 bns); Leibbrigade (3 bns). GdB Stabenrath: 4e RIdLi (4 bns); 46e RIdLi (3 bns). **3rd Division** GdD Molitor; GdB Leguay: 2e RIdLi (2 bns); 16e RIdLi (3 bns). GdB Viviez: 37e RIdLi (3 bns); 67e RIdLi (2 bns). **Light Cavalry Division** GdD Lasalle; GdD Bruyère: 13e and 24e ChàCh (3 sqns each). GdB Piré: 8e HusR and 16e ChàCh (3 sqns each). GdB Maraluz: 3e, 14e, 19e and 23e ChàCh (3 sqns each); Baden LDragR (4 sqns); Hessen-Darmstadt Garde ChLR (3 sqns). **IV Corps totals** 49 bns, 31 sqns, 66 artillery guns (including 18 German guns) and 24 regimental pieces, a total of 90 guns.

IX Corps M Bernadotte The Saxons: 1st Division GL von Zezschwitz; GM Gutschmidt: Gardes du Corps (2 sqns); Carabiniers (2 sqns); Prinz Klemens ChLR (4 sqns); HusR (3 sqns); Herzog Albert ChLR (1 sqn). GM von Hartitzsch: Leibgrenadiergarde (1 bn); Gren Bn Radoloff; Gren Bn Bose; Gren Bn Winkelmann and Gren Bn Hacke (1 bn each). GM von Zeschau: IR König; IR Niesemeuschel; combined IR von Öbschelwitz and von Dyherrn (1 bn each). **2nd Division** GL von Polenz; GM von Feilitzsch: LeibkürR and Prinz Johann ChLR (4 sqns each). GM Lecoq: IR Prinz Klemens; IR von Löw; IR von Cerrini (1 bn each). Oberst von Steindel: IR Prinz Anton; IR Prinz Maximilian; IR Prinz Friedrich August: Schützen-Bn Egidy and Schützen-Bn Metzsch (1 bn each). Artillery: 26 guns. **French Division** GdD Dupas; GdB Gency: 5e RILé (2 bns). GdB Veaux 19e RIdLi (3 bns). Artillery: 16 guns.

The Army of Italy Viceroy Prince Eugène 1st Division GdD Broussier; GdB Quétard: 9e and 84e RIdLi (3 bns each). GdB Dessaix: 92e RIdLi (4 bns); 18 guns. **2nd Division** GdD Lamarcque; GdB Almeyras: 18e RILé and 13e RIdLi (3 bns each). GdB Huart: 23e RIdLi (2 bns) and 29e RIdLi (4 bns); 18 guns. **The Centre** GdD Grenier: **1st Division** GdD Serras; GdB Moreau: 35e RIdLi (1 bn); 53e RIdLi (4 bns). GdB Roussel: 42e RIdLi (1 bn);106e RIdLi (3 bns); 18 guns. **2nd Division** GdD Durutte; GdB Valentin: 23e RILé (4 bns);

60e RIdLi (2 bns). GdB Bruch: 62e and 102e RIdLi (3 bns each). **The Reserve** GdD Pachtod: 8e RILé (2 bns); 1er and 52e RIdLi (4 bns each); 112e RIdLi (3 bns); 20 guns. **Cavalry** GdD Sahuc: GdB 6e, 8e and 9e ChàCh (4 sqns each); 4 guns. **The Italian Guard** GdD Fontanelli; GdB Lecchi: Grenadiers (1 bn); Carabiniers (1 bn); Vélites (1 bn). GdB Viani: Gardes d'Honneur (1 sqn); Garde DragR (2 sqns); 6 guns. **Army of Italy totals** 58 bns, 15 sqns, 100 guns.

XI Corps 'Army of Dalmatia' GdD Marmont 1st Division GdD Claparède; GdB Bertrand: 18e RILé, 5e, RIdLi (2 bns each). GdB Delzons: 79e and 81e RIdLi (2 bns each). **2nd Division** GdD Clausel; GdB Soyez: 8e RILé (2 bns); 23e RIdLi (2 bns). GdB Bachelu: 11e RIdLi (3 bns). **XI Corps totals** 15 bns, 12 guns.

VII (Bavarian) Corps GL Count Wrede 2nd Bavarian Division 1st Bde GM Minucci: LtI Bn Laroche Nr 6 (1 bn); LIR Prinz Karl Nr 3 and LIR Nr 13 (2 bns each). 2nd Bde GM Beckers: LIR Herzog Wilhelm Nr 5 and LIR Löwenstein Nr 7 (2 bns each). **Cavalry Bde** GM Preysing: ChLR König Nr 2 and ChLR Leiningen Nr 3 (4 sqns each). Artillery: 36 guns (including 2 batteries of the 1st Bavarian Division). **VII (Bavarian) Corps totals** 9 bns, 8 sqns, 36 guns. **Cavalry Reserve** M Bessières **Heavy Cavalry Division** GdD Nansouty; GdB Defrance: 1er and 2e Carabiniers (4 sqns each). GdB Doumerc: 2e and 9e CuirR (4 sqns each). GdB Berckheim: 3e and 12e CuirR (4 sqns each), 12 guns. **Avantgarde Heavy Cavalry Division** GdD St Germain; GdB Fiteau: 1er and 5e CuirR (4 sqns each) GdB Guiton: 10e and 11e CuirR (4 sqns each). 6 guns. Heavy Cavalry Division GdD Arrighi; GdB Brady, GdB Reynaud: 4e and 6e CuirR (4 sqns each) GDB Bordesoult: 7e and 8e CuirR (4 sqns each). 6 guns. **Cavalry Reserve totals** 56 sqns, 24 guns.

French and Allied Losses at Wagram

30,000 dead and wounded including GdD Lasalle, GdB Duprat, GdB Gauthier, GdB Guiot de La Cour and the Saxon GM von Hartitsch killed; 426 officers killed (including 186 who died of their wounds); 37 generals and 1,336 officers wounded. 4,000 were captured. Trophies lost included 11 guns and 12 eagles and colours. French officer losses were: Dead – 5 generals, 9 colonels, 41 field and 376 junior officers, and 6,858 men. Wounded: 37 generals, 48 colonels, 176 field and 1,112 junior officers. The Saxon contingent lost 590 dead, 2,289 wounded and 1,356 missing. The Baden contingent lost 1 officer and 70 men killed, 6 and 192 wounded and 1 and 25 missing. The Hessen-Darmstadt contingent lost over 100 killed, 467 wounded and 234 missing or captured and also a colour of 2nd Bn, Leib-Regiment in the bitter struggle for the village of Aderklaa. French eagles taken were: 4e RIdLi (3e Bn); 24e RILé, 106e RIdLi.

The Austrian Army at Wagram Archduke Charles commanding.

Avantgarde FML Nordmann GM Peter Vécsey: Primatial HusR (6 sqns); IR Beaulieu Nr 58 (2 bns); U Manharts-Berg LWR (3rd Bn); Jägers (1st Bn) 14 guns. **GM Frelich** Stipsicz HusR Nr 10 (8 sqns); GzIR Wallachesch-Illyrisch Nr 13 (2 bns); Jägers (7th Bn); 6 guns. **GM Riese** IR Bellegarde Nr 4 (3 bns); LWR Untere-Wiener-Wald (2e Bn); IR Chasteler Nr 46 (3 bns); LWI Bn Untere Wiener Wald (1st Bn). 8 guns. **GM Mayer** IR Deutschmeister Nr 4 (3 bns); LWI Bn Untere Wiener Wald (6th Bn); IR Kerpen Nr 49 (3 bns); LWR Untere Wiener Wald (5th Bn). 8 guns. **GM Schneller** HusR Hessen-Homburg Nr 4 (8 sqns). 6 guns. Artillery

Summary of Allied Forces

	Battalions/Men	Squadrons/Men	Guns
Imperial Guard	12/7,300	18/3,700	60
II Corps, Oudinot	46/18,000	11/1,200	82
III Corps, Davout	52/30,000	43/4,800	98
IV Corps, Massena	49/24,000	31/3,200	90
IX Corps Saxons	21/15,700	20/2,200	42
Army of Italy, Prince Eugène	58/22,000	15/1,200	100
Army of Dalmatia; Marmont	15/9,000	—	12
Bavarian Division	9/4,800	8/1,000	36
Cavalry Reserve	—	56/6,000	24
Totals	262/130,800	202/23,300	544

Reserve 1 Position Bty. **Avantgarde totals** 23 bns, 22 sqns, 48 guns.

I Corps GdK Count Bellegarde GM Henneberg: IR Reuss-Plauen Nr 17 and IR Kolowrat Nr 36 (3 bns each). 8 guns. **GM Wacquant** IR EH Rainer Nr 11 and IR Vogelsang Nr 47 (3 bns each). 8 guns. **FML Fresnel; GM Clary** IR Anton Mittrowsky Nr 10 (2 bns); LWR Hradischer (1st Bn); IR Erbach Nr 42 (2 bns). 8 guns. **GM Motzen** IR Argenteau Nr 35 (3 bns); Legion EH Carl (4th Bn). 8 guns. GM Stutterheim: ChLR Klenau Nr 5 (8 sqns); Jägers (2e Bn). 6 guns. Artillery Reserve: 4 Position and 1 HAB (30 guns). **I Corps totals** 2 bns, 8 sqns, 68 guns.

II Corps FML Prince Hohenzollern GM Hardegg ChLR Vincent Nr 4 (6 sqns); Jägers (8th Bn); Legion EH Carl (2nd Bn). 6 guns. **FML Brady; GM Paar** IR Froon Nr 54 (3 bns); LWR Hradischer (3rd Bn); IR Zedtwitz Nr 25 (3 bns); LWR Znaim (2nd Bn). 8 guns. **GM Buresch** IR Josef Colloredo Nr 57 (3 bns); LWR Brünn (1st Bn); IR Zach Nr 15 (2 bns); LWR Brünn (3rd Bn). 8 guns. **FML Siegenthal; GM Altstern** IR Rohan Nr 21 (3 bns). 8 guns. **GM Wied-Runkel** IR d'Aspre (ex Stuart) Nr 18 and IR Frelich Nr 28 (3 bns each). 8 guns. Artillery Reserve: 4 Postions and 1 HAB. **II Corps totals** 26 bns, 6 sqns, 68 guns.

III Corps FZM Kollowrath, Oberst Schmuttermayer: UlR Schwarzenberg Nr 2 (6 sqns); Lobkowitz Jägers (1 bn). 6 guns. **FML St Julien; GM Lilienberg** IR Würzburg Nr 23 (2 bns); IR Kaiser Nr 1 (2 bns); IR Manfredini Nr 12 (3 bns). 8 guns. **GM Bieber** IR Kaunitz Nr 20 (3 bns); IR Württemberg Nr 38 (2 bns). 8 guns. **FML Vukassovich; GM Grill** IR Wenzel Coloredo Nr 56 and IR Carl Schröder Nr 7 (3 bns each). 8 guns. **Oberst Wratislaw** LWR Prague (1st and 2nd coys); LWR Beraun (1st and 2nd Bns). 4 guns. Artillery: Reserve 4 Position batteries 24 guns. **III Corps totals** 22 bns, 6 sqns, 58 guns.

IV Corps FML Rosenberg; FML Radetsky; GM Provenchères HusR EH Ferdinand Nr 3 (8 sqns); Watrich-Jägers (1 bn); Moravian Freikorps (2nd Bn); Carneville Freikorps (⅓ bn and ½ sqn). 6 guns. **GM Weiss** IR Stain Nr 50 (3 bns); LWR Unterer Wiener Wald (4th Bn); IR EH Carl Nr 3 (3 bns); LWR Obere Manharts-Berg (4th Bn). 8 guns. **FML Hohenlohe Bartenstein; GM Hessen-Homburg** IR Hiller Nr 2 (3 bns); IR Sztáray Nr 33 (2 bns); 8 guns. **FML Rohan; GM Swinburn** IR EH Ludwig Nr 8 (3 bns); LWR Iglau (1st Bn); IR Coburg Nr 22 (3 bns); LWR Znaim (1st Bn). 8 guns. Artillery Reserve 4 Position and 1 HAB. 30 guns. **IV Corps totals** 24⅓ bns, 8½ sqns, 60 guns.

VI Corps FML Klenau FML Vincent; GM Wallmoden: HusR Kienmayer Nr 8 (8 sqns); HusR Liechtenstein Nr 7 (8 sqns). 8 guns. **GM Mariássy** Wiener-Freiwilligen (1st and 2nd Bns); LWR Untere Manharts-Berg (4th Bn). **GM August Vécsey** GzIR St Georger Nr 6 (1 bn); GzIR Broder Nr 7 (⅓ bn). **FML Hohenfeld; GM Adler** Legion EH Carl (3e Bn); IR Klebek Nr 14 (2 bns); LWR Obere Wiener Wald (1st Bn); IR Jordis Nr 59 (2 bns); LWR Oberösterreich (1 bn). 8 guns. **GM Hoffmeister** IR Gyulai Nr 60, IR Duka Nr 39 (3 bns each). 8 guns. **FML Kottulinsky; GM Splényi** Wiener Freiwilligen (3rd and 4th bns); IR Splényi Nr 51 (3 bns); IR Benjowsky Nr 31 (2 bns); Moravian Freikorps (3rd Bn). 8 guns. Artillery Reserve: 4½ Position batteries. **VI Corps totals** 25⅓ bns, 16 sqns, 64 guns.

The Reserve Corps GdK Prince Liechtenstein Grenadier Reserve FML d'Aspre; GM Merville Gren bns Scharlach, Scovaud, Jambline, Brzeczinski (4 bns) 8 guns. **GM Hammer** Gren bns Kirchenbetter, Bissingen, Oklopsia, Locher, LWR Ober Manharts-Berg (1st Bn), (5 bns), 8 guns. **FML Prochaska; GM Murray** Gren bns Frisch, Georgy, Portner, Leiningen (4 bns). GM Steyrer: Gren bns Hahn, Hromada, Legrand, Demontant and Berger (5 bns) 8 guns. **Cavalry Reserve FML Hessen-Homburg; GM Roussel** KürR Herzog Albert Nr 3 and KürR EH Franz Nr 2 (6 sqns each). **GM Lederer** KürR Kronprinz Ferdinand Nr 4 and KürR Hohenzollern Nr 8 (6 sqns each). **GM Kroyher** KürR Kaiser Nr 1 (4 sqns); KürR Moriz Liechtenstein Nr 6 (6 sqns each). 6 guns. **FML Schwarzenberg; GM Teimern** ChLR Rosenberg Nr 6 (8 sqns); DragR Knesevich Nr 3 (6 sqns) 6 guns. **GM Kerékes**: HusR Neutraer (6 sqns). **FML Nostitz; GM Rothkirch** DragR EH Johann Nr 1 (6 sqns); DragR Riesch Nr 6 (6 sqns), 6 guns. **GM Wartensleben:** HusR Blankenstein Nr 6 (10 sqns); ChLR O'Reilly Nr 3 (8 sqns). 6 guns. **Reserve Corps totals** 18 bns, 84 sqns, 48 guns.

Summary of Austrian Forces

	Battalions/ Men	Squadrons/ Men	Guns
Avantgarde	23/11,837	22/2,528	48
I Corps	22/20,892	8/801	68
II Corps	26/25,434	6/517	68
III Corps	22/15,929	6/667	58

	Battalions/ Men	Squadrons/ Men	Guns
IV Corps	24⅓/17,395	8 /792	60
VI Corps	25⅓/12,465	16/1,275	64
Reserve Corps	18/9,882	84/8,054	48
Totals	160⅔/113,834	150/14,634	414

Austrian Losses at Wagram
4 generals killed (FML Baron d'Aspre, FML Baron von Nordmann, FML Baron von Vukassovich and GM Baron von Vécsey), 120 officers and 5,507 men killed on the field. 13 generals and 616 officers and 17,490 wounded, 18,000 all ranks captured.
Trophies lost included 9 guns and 1 colour.
Comment The Austrian Army's open left (eastern) flank was rolled up by Davout's corps after Archduke Charles had successfully repelled Macdonald's famous, 20,000-strong 'Column of Wagram'. This open flank was where the prodigal Archduke John's army should have been, but he had successfully sabotaged all the efforts of his brother and all the sacrifices of the Austrian armies in this epic struggle by remaining out of touch. Archduke Charles' army withdrew northwards on Znaim and Charles resigned command of the army.
Sources Wrede, Martinien, HGM 36, Schuster and Franke, Beck, Bigge, Keim.

DV Korneuburg, 7 July 1809, clash
A fortified village near the east bank of the River Danube, about 19 km north of Vienna in Austria, on Route 6 towards Stockerau.
A rearguard clash; an Allied victory over the Austrians.
(Last action – Wagram 5 and 6 July; next action – Stockerau, 8 July.)
Allied Forces 1st Division of Massena's IV Corps GdD Legrand commanding. GdB Ledru: 26e RILé and 18e RIdLi (4 bns each). Baden Bde Oberst Neuenstein: LeibR (2 bns); IR Erbgrossherzog (2 bns); Jäger bn (1 bn); 1 FAB, Baden LtDr (½ sqn). GdD St Sulpice: 1er and 5e, 10e and 11e CuirRs (16 sqns). GdB Maraluz: 3e, 14e, 19e and 23e ChàCh (3 sqns each); Hessen-Darmstadt Garde ChLR (3 sqns).
Allied totals 13 bns, 31½ sqns, 24 guns, ca 13,000 men.
Allied losses Not known exactly, estimated at about 350 killed and wounded.
Austrian Forces VI Corps FMK Klenau commanding. FML Vincent; GM Wallmoden: HusR Kienmayer Nr 8 and Liechtenstein Nr 7 (8 sqns each), 12 guns. GM Mariássy: Wiener-Freiwilligen (1st and 2nd bns); LWR Untere Manharts-Berg (4th bn). GM August Vécsey: GzIR St Georger Nr 6 (1 bn); GzIR Broder Nr 7 (⅓ bn). FML Hohenfeld; GM Adler: Legion EH Carl (3rd Bn); IR Klebek Nr 14 (2 bns); LWR Obere Wiener Wald (1st Bn); IR Jordis Nr 59 (2 bns); LWR Oberösterreich (1 bn). 8 guns. GM Hoffmeister: IR Gyulai Nr 60, IR Duka Nr 39 (3 bns each). 8 guns. FML Kottulinsky; GM Splényi: Wiener Freiwilligen (3rd and 4th bns); IR Splényi Nr 51 (3 bns); IR Benjowsky Nr 31 (2 bns); Moravian Freikorps (3rd Bn). 8 guns. Artillery Reserve: 4½ Position batteries.
VI Corps Totals 25⅓ bns, 16 sqns, 64 guns, ca 18,000 men of whom about 3,000 came into action.
Austrian losses Killed and wounded, unknown; over 300 captured.
Comment The Badeners stormed the town and lost 2 officers and 18 men killed and wounded. Pelet attributes this victory to the French 26e RILé. The Austrian army continued to withdraw northwards.
Sources Pelet vol 4, p254, von Barsewisch, Zech/Porbeck, Obser.

DV Gefrees, 8 July 1809, clash
A village in northern Bavaria on Route B2 between Kulmbach, Hof and Bayreuth.
An Austrian victory over the Allies.
(Last action – Korneuburg, 7 July; next action – Stockerau, 8 July.)
Allied Forces GdD Junot commanding GdD Rivaud, GdB Lameth: 4e bns of the 19e, 25e and 28e RIdLi (2 bns). GdB Taupin: 4e bns of the 36e, 50e and 75e RIdLi (3 bns). Artillery: 2 btys, 12 guns. 1 Provision DragR (4 sqns); Bavarian Depot bn (1 bn).
Allied totals 7 bns, 4 sqns, 12 guns, ca 5,600 men.
Allied losses Not known, light.
Austrian Forces FML von Kienmayer commanding II Corps GM Radivojevich: GzIR Peterwardeiner Nr 9 (2 bns); GzIR Deutsch-Banater Nr 12 (2 bns); Legion EH Carl Jägers (½ bn).
Austrian totals ca 12,000 men.
Austrian losses Not known, light.
Comment A minor, insignificant Austrian raid.
Sources Leyh, Wrede.

DV Stockerau, 8 July 1809, skirmish

A fortified village on the north bank of the River Danube, about 30 km north of Vienna, in Austria, on Route 14/53/E84.

An Austrian victory over the Allies.

(Last action - Korneuburg, 7 July; next action - Hollabrunn, 9 July.)

Allied Forces M Massena commanding the IV Corps. GdG Maraluz 14e and 23e ChàCh (3 sqns each); Baden LtDragR (4 sqns); Hessen-Darmstadt Garde ChLR (3 sqns); Baden Jäger-Bn von Lingg (1 bn).

Allied totals 13 sqns, 1 bn.

Allied losses Not known exactly, light.

Austrian Forces FML Klenau's VI Corps: HusR Kienmayer Nr 8 (4 sqns); HusR Liechtenstein Nr 7 (8 sqns).

Austrian totals 12 sqn.

Austrian losses Not known, light.

Comment Massena was following up the beaten, but unbroken, Austrian army after the battle of Wagram on 5 and 6 July. His cavalry received a sharp check here. The Austrians held on all day and then withdrew northwards on Hollabrunn and Schöngraben.

Sources Wrede, Martinien, Zech/Porbeck.

DV Hollabrunn, 9 July 1809, clash

A village near the east bank of the Göllers stream, about 43 km north of Vienna, in Austria, on Route 2/E84.

A 'drawn match' between the Allies and the Austrians on the retreat from Wagram to Znaim.

(Last action - Stockerau, 8 July; next action - Schöngraben, 10 July.)

Allied Forces Massena's IV Corps as for Korneuburg (7 July); Stockerau (8 July) and Schöngraben (10 July).

Allied totals 13 bns, 31½ sqns, 24 guns.

Allied losses The Baden brigade lost 8 officers and 93 men killed and wounded, 44 men missing. French losses are not known, the Hessen-Darmstadt brigade was not engaged. The 1er Cuirassiers lost three officers.

Austrian Forces VI Corps of FML Klenau as at Korneuburg (7 July) and at Stockerau (8 July), see Korneuburg for details.

Austrian totals 25⅓ bns, 16 sqn, 64 guns, ca 17,000 men.

Austrian losses Not known exactly.

Comment Despite having fought and marched for the last five days, the Austrian rearguard was still a cohesive force capable of stiff resistance.

Massena's Corps was similary robust; this was another hard-fought action.

For his excellent defence here FML Klenau was awarded the Commander's Cross of the Order of Maria-Theresia.

Sources Wrede, Martinien, Zech/Porbeck, Beck.

DV Schöngraben, 10 July 1809, clash

A village near the north bank of the River Danube, about 30 km north of Vienna, in Austria.

A drawn match between the French and the Austrians.

(Last action - Hollabrunn, 9 July; next action - Znaim, 10 - 11 July.)

Allied Forces 1st Division of Massena's IV Corps GdD Legrand commanding. As for Korneuburg (7 July); Stockerau (8 July) and Hollabrunn 9 July.

Allied totals ca 11,000 men and 24 guns.

Allied losses Not known exactly.

Austrian Forces V Corps FZM Reuss GM Weissenwolf: IR Deutschmeister Nr 4 and IR Kerpen Nr 49 (3 bns each); Jägers (3rd Bn); Wiener Freiwilliger (5th Bn); LWR Manharts-Berg (1 bn); HusR Kienmayer Nr 8 (1 sqn). FML Radetsky: Jägers (4th bn); GzIR Gradiskaner Nr 8 (1 bn); UlR EH Carl Nr 3 (8 sqns). FML Schustekh: IR Lindenau Nr 29 (3 bns); IR Josef Mittrowsky Nr 40 (3 bns); IR Stain Nr 50 (3rd Bn); GzIR Gradiskaner Nr 8 (1 bn); Legion EH Carl (5th and 6th bns); Moravian Freikorps (1st Bn); LWR Oberösterreich (1 bn); DragR Levenehr Nr 4 (3 sqns). GM Hoffmeiser: IR Beaulieu Nr 58 (2 bns); ChLR O'Reilly Nr 3 (2 sqns); HusR Neutraer (2 sqns).

V Corps totals 25 bns, 16 sqns, 32 guns, ca 27,000 men. **V Corps losses** Not known exactly, moderate.

Comment The Austrian defence was laid out in depth and made full use of all terrain features.

DV Znaim (now Znojmo), 10 and 11 July 1809, battle

A town in Moravia (nowadays the Slovak Republic), on the River Thaya, about 75 km north north west of Vienna, at the junction of Routes 38/E84 and 54.

A drawn match between the French and their Allies and the Austrians.

(Last action - Schöngraben, 10 July; next action -

apart from a minor skirmish at Stampfen on the River March in Hungary, this was the last action in the Danube Valley campaign.)

Allied Forces (on 10 July)

M Marmont commanding the XI Corps 1st Division GdD Claparède; GdB Bertrand; 18e RILé, 5e, 79e and 81e RIdLi (2 bns each). GdB Delzons 79e and 81e RIdLi (2 bns each). **2nd Division** GdD Clausel; GdB Soyez: 8e RILé and 23e RIdLi (2 bns each). Artillery 12 guns. **2nd Bavarian Division** GL Count Wrede: 1st Bde GM Minucci: 3rd LIR 'PzKarl' and 13th LIR (2 bns each);6th LtI Bn 'la Roche' (1 bn). 2nd Bde GM Beckers: 5th LIR 'Herzog Wilhelm' and 7th LIR 'Löwenstein' (2 bns each). Light Cavalry GM Preysing: 2nd ChLR 'König' and ChLR 'Leiningen' (4 sqns each). **Artillery** 36 guns. **Light Cavalry Division** GdD Montbrun; GdB Pajol: 5e and 7e HusR, 11e ChàCh (3 sqns each). GdB Jacquinot: 1er, 2e and 12e ChàCh (3 sqns each). **Artillery** 6 guns.

Allied totals on 10 July 29 bns, 26 sqns, 54 guns, ca 30,000 men.

On 11 July at about 4000 hrs **Massena's IV Corps** arrived **1st Division** GdB Ledru des Essarts: 1st Brigade, GdB Friedrich: 26e RILé and 18e RIdLi (4 bns each); 19e RIdLi (3 bns); 2nd Brigade GM von Harrant: Baden: 1st and 2nd LIR (2 bns each); Jäger-Bn von Lingg (1 bn). Artillery: 3 x FAB. **2nd Division** GdD Dessaix: 1st Brigade GdB Casson: 24e RILé (4 bns); 4e RIdLi (4 bns); 46e RIdLi (3 bns. Artillery: 1½ FAB. GM von Nagel (Hessen-Darmstadt): Leibgarde-Brigade and Leib-Brigade (3 bns each); 1 x FAB. **3rd Division** GdD Molitor: 1st Brigade GdB Leguay: 2e RILé (2 bns); 37e RIdLi (3 bns). 2nd Brigade GdB Viviez: 16e RILé (3 bns); 67e RIdLi (2 bns). Artillery: 1½ x FAB. **4th Division** GdD Puthod: 1st Brigade GdB Grillot: 3e RILé and 93e RIdLi (2 bns each). 2nd Brigade GdB Valory: 5e RILé (3 bns); 56e RIdLi (3 bns). Artillery: 1½ x FAB. **Light Cavalry** GdD Quesnel: 1st Brigade GdB Bruyère: 13e and 24e ChàCh (3 sqns each); 2nd Brigade GdB Piré: 8e HusR and 16e ChàCh (3 sqns each); 3rd Brigade GdB Bordesoulle: 3e and 23e ChàCh, (3 sqns each); Baden: Lt DragR (4 sqns); 2 x HAB. GdB Jacquinot; 1er and 2e ChàCh, 7e HusR (3 sqns each). **Cuirassier Division** GdD St Germain; GdB Fiteau: 1er and 5e CuirRs (4 sqns each). GdB Guiton: 10e and 11e CuirRs (4 sqns each) 1 x HAB (6guns). **Corps totals** 53 bns, 44 sqns, 11½ batteries (72 guns), ca 43,000 men.

Allied totals on 11 July 82 bns, 64 sqns, 126 guns, ca 73,000 men.

Allied losses As usual, French figures are scarce and contradictory. Bodart shows 4,000 killed and wounded including four generals and 160 officers.

Kausler gives no figures but says that losses on both sides were about equal in which case they were about 6,000 men according to Wisnar.

Austrians Forces Archduke Charles commanding.

The Reserve Corps GdK Prince Liechtenstein Grenadiers FML d'Aspre GM Merville: Gren bns Scharlach, Scovaud, Jambline and Brzeczinski and 8 guns. GM Hammer: Gren bns Kirchenbetter, Bissingen, Oklopsia and Locher and 8 guns. **FML Prochaska** GM Murray: Gren bns Frisch, Georgy, Portner and Leiningen. GM Steyrer: Gren bns Hahn, Hromada, Legrand, Berger and Demontant and 8 guns. **Total** 17 bns and 24 guns.

I Corps GdK Bellegarde FML Dedovich; GM Henneberg: IRs Reuss-Plauen Nr 17 and Kollowrath Nr 36 (3 bns each); 8 guns. GM Wacquant IR EH Rainer Nr 11 and Vogelsang Nr 47 (3 bns each): 8 guns. **FML Fresnel** GM Clary IRs Mittrowsky Nr 10 (2 bns); 1st Hradischer LWI Bn (1 bn); IR Erbach Nr 42 (2 bns); 8 guns. GM Motzen IR Argentau Nr 35 (3 bns); 4th Bn Legion EH Carl (1 bn); 8 guns. GM Stutterheim: ChLR Klenau Nr 5 (8 sqns); 2nd Jägers (1 bn). Reserve Artillery: 4 x 12 pdr FAB, 1 x HAB. **I Corps totals** 22 bns, 8 sqns, 68 guns.

III Corps FML Kollowrath Avantgarde Obst Schmuttermayer: UlR Schwarzenberg Nr 2 (6 sqns); Lobkowitz Jägers (1 bn). **FML St Julien** GM Lilienberg: IRs Würzburg Nr 23 and Kaiser Nr 1 (2 bns each); IR Manfredini Nr 12 (3 bns): 8 guns. GM Bieber: IR Kaunitz Nr 20 (3 bns); IR Württemberg Nr 38 (2 bns); 8 guns. **FML Vukassovich** GM Grill IRs W Colloredo Nr 56 and C Schröder Nr 7 (3 bns each); Obst Wratislaw: 1st and 2nd LWI Bns Prag (1 bn); 1st and 2nd LWI Bns Berauner (2 bns); 4 guns. Reserve Artillery: 4 x 12 pdr FAB. **III Corps totals** 22 bns, 6 sqns, 58 guns.

Austrian totals on 10 July 61 bns, 14 sqns, 150 guns, ca 46,000 men.

On 11 July also present were the **II, V and VI Corps** of which the V came into action

V Corps EH Ludwig FZM Prince Reuss; GM Weissenwolff: IRs Deutschmeister Nr 4 and Kerpen Nr 49 (3 bns each); Jägers (3rd Bn); Wiener Freiwilligen (5th Bn); 4th u.d. Manharts-Berg LWI Bn (1 bn); HusR Kienmayer Nr 8 (1 sqn); GM Radetzky: Jägers (4th Bn); GzIR Gradiskaner Nr 8 (1 bn). FML Schustekh: IR Lindenau Nr 29 (3 bns); IR J Mittrowsky Nr 40 (3 bns); IR Stain Nr 50 (3rd Bn); GzIR Gradiskaner Nr 8 (1 bn); Legion EH Carl (5th and 6th bns); Moravian Frei-Bn (1 bn); Oberösterreichisches LWR (1combined bn); DragR Levenehr Nr 4 (3 sqns). GM Hoffmeister: IR Beaulieu Nr 58 (2 bns); ChLR O'Reilly Nr 3 (2 sqns); Neutraer HusR (2 sqns). **V Corps totals** 25 bns, 16 sqns, 6 batteries ca 15,000 men.

Austrian totals on 11 July 86 bns, 30 sqns, 180 guns, ca 61,000 men.

Austrian losses No exact figures known; estimated at about 6,000 in all.

Comment Already on 10 July Archduke Charles had proposed a cease-fire to Marmont in order to end useless bloodshed as peace negotiations were in preparation but Marmont stupidly refused to consider the offer. Next day, Napoleon agreed to it. The Archduke resigned command of the Austrian army.

Sources Wrede, Martinien, Bodart, Krausler, Wisnar, Obser.

DV Stampfen (Stupava), 13 July 1809, clash

A village near the River March (Morava) in Hungary, about 45 km east of Vienna and 15 km north of Pressburg (now Bratislava) on Route 2.

A Saxon victory over the Austrians.

(Last action – Znaim, 10/11 July; this was the last action in the Danube Valley campaign.)

Allied Forces GM von Gutschmidt of the Saxon IX Corps commanding: Leibkür-Garde (4 sqns); ChLR Pz Johann (4 sqns); 2nd Schützen-Bn 'von Egidy' (4 coys); ½ x HAB (2 guns. ca 1,600 men).

Allied losses Not known exactly; light.

Austrian Forces Oberst Trautenberg commanding: IR Beaulieu Nr 58 (2nd Bn); HusR Stipsicz Nr 10 (1 sqn); ca 700 men.

Austrian losses Killed and wounded unknown; 12 officers, 340 men, 2 guns and 1 colour captured.

Comment The Austrians had not received official news of the cease fire of Znaim and attacked the dismounted squadron of the Prinz Johann Chevaulegers. Gutschmidt counter-attacked, freed the Saxons and broke the barely-formed Austrian square.

Sources Wrede, Schuster and Franke.

WW Krakau, 14 July 1809, clash

A fortified city in southwest Poland, on the River Vistula, 250 km south of Warsaw, at the junction of Routes 7/E77, 4/E40, A4 and 96/E462.

A Polish victory over the Austrians.

(Last action – Sandomierz, 15/18 June; this was the last action of this campaign.)

Polish Forces Prince Poniatowski commanding 1st (Warsaw) Legion: 1st, 2nd, 3rd and 4th IRs (2 bns each); 1st and 2nd CavR (6 sqns).

Polish totals 8 bns, 6 sqns, 12 guns, ca 8,000 men.

Polish losses Not known.

Austrian Forces The rearguard under GM Mohr: ChLR Kaiser Nr 1 (5 sqns); HusR Kaiser Nr 1 (2 sqns); HusR Palatin Nr 12 (7 sqns); IR Vukassovich Nr 48 (3 bns). **Austrian Totals** 3 bns, 14 sqns, 40 guns, ca 4,000 men. **Austrian losses** 1,000 dead and wounded, 500 captured.

Comment GM Mohr capitulated and evacuated Krakau. As Napoleon had won the battle of Wagram on 5 and 6 July and an armistice had been signed after the battle of Znaim on 11 July, this was the end of the campaign.

YU Scardona, 20 July 1809, skirmish

A village on the River Kerka, about 7 km north of Sebenico (now Sibenik on the Dalmatian coast (ex-Yugoslavia) on Route 29.

An Austrian victory over the French.

(Last action – Gospic, 21/22 May; next action – Sebenico (Sibenik) 21 June.)

French Garrison and totals ca 2,000 men of the Dalmatian Legion.

French losses Not known; slight, a 2-gun felucca was captured at Sebenico.

Austrian Forces Liccaner LW (1 bn) and local inhabitants.

Austrian totals Not known.

Austrian losses Not known, slight.

Comment Austrian High Command had decided to invade Dalmatia after Marmont's departure for Austria.

Sources Woinovich.

YU Sebenico (Sibenik), 21 July 1809, clash

A port town on the mouth of the River Kerka, on the Dalmatian Adriatic coast, about 100 km southeast of Zara (Zadar) in ex-Yugoslavia (now Croatia), on Route 2/E65.

An Austrian victory over the French.

(Last action – Scardona, 20 July; next action – Zara (Zadar), 25 July.)

French Garrison ca 2,000 men under GdB Deviaux.

French losses Not known; slight.

Austrian Forces GM Peter Baron von Kneževič commanding: IR Reisky Nr 13 (2 weak bns); Liccaner Res Bn (1 bn); Dalmatian Freikorps (2 coys); Liccaner LW (3 coys); ChLR Hohenzollern Nr 2 (1 sqn); Serezaner (1 sqn); ½ Positions battery (3 guns); 1 Brigade battery (6 x 3pdrs).

Austrian totals 3 bns, 5 coys, 2 sqns, 9 guns, ca 3,000 men.

Austrian losses Not known, slight.

Comment The French garrison escaped in 2 gunboats and some other small ships to Fort San Nicolo, abandoning the town.

Sources Woinovich.

TY Lueg Pass, 24 July 1809, 3rd clash

A pass on the old Route 311 in the Austrian Province of Salzburg, along the Salzach stream, about 40 km south of Salzburg city.

A Bavarian victory over the Austrians.

(Last action – 2nd Berg Isel, 29 May; next action – Oberau, 4/5 August.)

Bavarian Forces GdD Deroy commanding: IR Isenburg Nr 9 (2nd Bn); ca 1,000 men.

Bavarian losses Not known.

Austrian Forces Captain Kettner commanding: Salzburger Schützenkompanien: St Johann (50 men); Werfen (65 men); Gastein, Goldegg and St Johann (90 men) and the Tyrolean Schützenkompanie of Captain Harasser (40 men); some Pinzgauer Schützen and some Landsturm.

Austrian totals ca 300 men.

Austrian losses Not known, slight.

Comment Andreas Hofer's call for another revolt against the Bavarians led to the reoccupation of the pass. Arrival of the news of the Armistice of Znaim (12 July) caused the fighting here to stop.

Sources HGM 41, Wrede, Bezzel, Vol VI.

EW Talavera (de la Reina), 27 and 28 July 1809, battle

A town in western Spain, on the north bank of the Rio Tajo, at the junction of Routes V/E90 and 503 about 110 km southwest of Madrid.

An Allied victory over the French.

(Last action – Alcántara, 14 May; next action – Arzobispo (El Puente), 8 August.)

French Forces King Joseph commanding.

I Corps M Victor 1st Division GdD Ruffin: 9e RILé, 24e and 96e RIdLi (3 bns each). **2nd Division** GdD Lapisse: 16e RILé, 8e, 45e and 54e RIdLi (3 bns each). **3rd Division** GdD Villatte: 27e RILé, 63e, 94e and 95e RIdLi (3 bns each). **Light Cavalry** GdB Beaumont: 2e HusR, 5e ChàCh (4 sqns each).

IV Corps GdD Sebastiani 1st Division GdD Sebastiani: 28e, 32e, 58e and 75e RIdLi (3 bns each). **2nd Division** GdD Valence: 4th Polish LIR (2 bns). **3rd Division** GdD Leval: 2nd Nassau IR, IR Baden, Hessen-Darmstadt IR 'Gross-und Erbprinz', IR Holland (2 bns each), IR Frankfurt (1 bn). **Light Cavalry** GdD Merlin: 10e and 26e ChàCh, Vistula Lancers, Westfalian ChLR (4 sqns each). **Reserve Cavalry** 1st Dragoon Division GdD Latour-Maubourg: 1er, 2e, 4e, 9e, 14e and 26e DragR (24 sqns) **2nd Dragoon Division** GdD Milhaud: 5e, 12e, 16e, 20e and 21e DragR, 3e Dutch HusR (24 sqns).

From King Joseph's Reserve at Madrid One brigade of Dessolles's Division: 12e RILé, 51e RIdLi (3 bns each). **Royal Guards**: Grenadiers (2 bns). Royal Guard Cavalry (2 sqns). 27e ChàCh (2 sqns).

French and Allied totals 64 bns, 76 sqns, 38,335 infantry and artillery, 8,400 cavalry, 80 guns.

French and Allied Losses: I Corps 26 officers and 410 men killed; 120 officers and 3,280 men wounded, 1 officer and 67 men captured, **total** 3,904. **IV Corps** 19 officers and 287 men killed; 91 officers and 2,692 men wounded; 138 men captured, **total** 3,227 men. **The Cavalry Reserve** (1st and 2nd Dragoon Divisions and Merlin's division): 19 men killed, 9 officers and 109 men wounded: **Total** 137 men.

Grand Total French and Allied losses* 7,268 and 17 guns (of Leval's division).

* = this figure does not include the wounded who were captured on 28 July but released again on 9th August.

GdD Lapisse and the Baden GM von Porbeck were killed.

British Forces Lieutenant-General Sir Arthur Wellesley commanding.

Cavalry Division LG Payne MG Fane's Brigade: 3rd DG, 4th Drag (4 sqns each). MG Cotton's Brigade: 14th and 16th LD (4 sqns each). MG Anson's Brigade: 23rd LD, 1st LD (KGL) (4 sqns each), **total** 2,969. **The Infantry 1st Division** LG Sherbrooke: H Campbell's Brigade: 2nd (Coldstream) Gds (1st Bn), 3rd Gds (1st Bn). 5th/60th (1 coy). Langwerth's Brigade: 1st and 2nd Line bns KGL (2 bns), Lt Coys KGL (1 coy). Cameron's Brigade: 1st/61st, 2nd/83rd (2 bns), 5th/60th (1 coy). Low's Brigade: 5th and 7th Line bns KGL (2 bns), **total** 5,964. **2nd Division** LG Hill: Tilson's Brigade: 1st/3rd, 2nd/48th, 2nd/66th (3 bns), 5th/60th (1 coy). R Stewart's Brigade: 1st/29th, 1st/48th, 1st bn of Detachments (3 bns). **3rd Division** LG Mackenzie: Mackenzie's Brigade: 2nd/24th, 2nd/31st, 1st/45th (3 bns). Donkin's Brigade: 2nd/87th, 1st/88th, 5th/60th (5 coys). **4th Division** LG Campbell A Campbell's Brigade: 2nd/7th, 2nd/53rd, (2 bns), 5th/60th (1 coy). Kemmis' Brigade: 1st/40th, 1st/97th, 2nd bn of Detachments (1 bn each), 5th/60th (1 coy). **Artillery** 3 British and 2 KGL batteries.

British totals 17,600 infantry and artillery, 2,969 cavalry, 30 guns.

British losses In the preliminary combat of Casa de Salinas 14th LG, 1st LD KGL and the 3rd Division lost 4 officers and 66 men killed, 19 officers and 265 men wounded, 93 men missing. In the main battle on 27 and 28 July:

British losses	Killed		Wounded		Missing	
	Officers	Men	Officers	Men	Officers	Men
1st Division	19	344	73	1,749	0	318
2nd Division	1	128	41	741	3	37
3rd Division	1	102	27	641	1	55
4th Division	1	32	6	171	1	25
Arty, Eng, Staff	6	10	7	53	0	1
Totals	28	616	154	3,355	5	436

The seriously wounded had to be left in Talavera and were well cared for by the French.

Spanish Forces Lieutenant-General Gregorio de la Cuesta.

Infantry Vanguard BG José Zayas: 2nd Voluntarios de Catalonia; Cazadores de Barbastro (2nd Bn), Cazadores de Campo-Mayor; Cazadores de Valencia y Albuquerque; Cazadores Voluntarios de Valencia (2nd Bn), **total** 5 bns. **1st Division** MG Marques de Zayas: IRs Cantabria (3 bns), Granaderos Provinciales, Canarias, Provincial de Truxillo, **total** 6 bns. **2nd Division** MG Vicente Iglesias: IRs 2nd of Majorca; Velez-Malaga (3 bns); Osuna (2 bns); Voluntarios Estrangeros; Provincial de Burgos, **total** 8 bns. **3rd Division** MG Marques de Portago: IRs Badajoz (2 bns); 2nd of Antequera, Imperial de Toledo, Provincial de Badajoz, Provincial de Guadix, **total** 6 bns. **4th Division** MG R Manglano: IRs Irlanda (2 bns); Jaén (2 bns); Leales de Fernando VII (1st Bn); 2nd Voluntarios de Madrid; Voluntarios de la Corona, **total** 7 bns. **5th Division** MG L A Bassecourt: Real Marina (1st Regt), Africa (3rd Bn); Murcia (2 bns); Reyna (1st Bn); Provincial de Sigüenza, **total** 7 bns.

Cavalry 1st Division LG I de Henestrosa: Rey, Calatrava, Voluntarios de Espana, Imperial de Toledo, Cazadores de Sevilla, Reyna, Villaviciosa, Cazadores de Madrid.

2nd Division LG Duque de Albuquerque: Carabineros Reales (1 sqn); Infante, Alcántara, Pavia, Almanza, 1st and 2nd Hus of Extremadura. No individual cavalry totals known.

Spanish totals About 28,000 infantry, 6,000 cavalry and 800 artillery with 30 guns.

Four battalions were detached; Merida and 3rd Seville with Sir Robert Wilson's raid on Madrid; two others (Seville and Merida) under General del Reino at the pass of Puerto de Baños, supposedly guarding Wellesley's left flank. Another, unidentified, battalion was guarding the Tagus bridge at Almáraz.

Spanish losses Cuesta stated '1,201' but never made a proper return; as only one cavalry regiment (Rey) five or six battalions (of Bassecourt's 5th Division) and three batteries had actually been engaged – and none of these heavily - this figure must represent killed, wounded and missing.

Comment Sir Arthur Wellesley was created Viscount Wellington for his victory; he had also learned never to trust any Spanish promises again. Wellesley had agreed to advance against Madrid in cooperation with Cuesta based on the assurances that supplies and transport would be provided and that his flanks would be protected. None of this happened.

The fighting was extremely hard; the French had had enough on 28 July even though King Joseph's Reserve of about 12,000 men had scarcely been engaged.*

Line had, once again, triumphed convincingly over much-vaunted French assault columns; the French would treat the British infantry with more respect in future.

The Spanish armies were not competent to operate alone and survive. Disunity among the French commanders played into Allied hands. Soult had been given command of the corps of Ney and Mortier by Napoleon and told to advance south via Plasencia and take Wellington in the rear. Wellington had to withdraw rapidly on Portugal.

Sources Oman, Napier, Robinson, Martinien, Bernays, Isenbart, Mayne, Gembarzewski.

* = Napoleon said: 'To be repulsed when one has 12,000 men in reserve who have not fired a shot, is to put up with an insult'.

YU Zara (Zadar), 25/29 July 1809, clash and blockade

A port town on the Dalmatian Adriatic coast in ex-Yugoslavia (now Croatia), on Route 2/E65.

A drawn match between the French and the Austrians.

(Last action - Sebenico (Sibenik), 21 July; this was the last action in the campaign.)

French Forces GdD Baron Maureillan commanding: ca 3,500 troops of various units. **French losses** Not known; moderate.

Austrian Garrison GM Peter Baron von Knežević commanding: IR Reisky Nr 13 (2 bns); Liccaner Res Bn (1 bn); ChLR Hohenzollern Nr 2 (1 sqn); Serezaner (½ sqn); 7 guns. **Austrian totals** ca 2,000 men and 7 guns.

Austrian losses Not known, slight.

Comment Two sorties by the garrison were repulsed with loss. News of the Armistice of Znaim stopped hostilities.

Sources Woinovich.

GN Halberstadt, 29 July 1809, clash

A fortified town in northern Germany, on the Hotemme stream, at the junction of Routes B79 and B81, 55 km southwest of Magdeburg on the River Elbe.

A Brunswick victory over the Westfalians.

(Last action - this was the first action of the Duke of Brunswick's race to the coast; next action - Oelpe, 1 August.)

Westfalian Forces Obst Graf Wellingerode commanding the 5th LIR (2 bns, 1,800 men).

Westfalian losses 600 men killed, wounded, 900 captured, 2 colours.

Brunswick Forces Frederick (dispossessed) Duke of Brunswick commanding: infantry (2½ bns); Scharfschützen (1 coy); HusR (4 sqns); UlR (1 sqn); 4 guns.

Brunswick totals 2,110 men.

Brunswick losses 400 killed and wounded, 300 Westfalians joined the force.

Comment The Duke had raised a Freikorps under Austrian protection but refused to acknowledge the armistice between Archduke Charles and Napoleon reached at Znaim.

Sources Pivka, von, Lünsmann.

GN Oelpe, 1 August 1809, clash

A village in northern Germany, nowadays a suburb in the northwest of Braunschweig, then a fortified town. At the junction of Autobahns A2/E30, A39 and A395.

A Brunswick victory over the Westfalians.

(Last action - Halberstadt, 29 July; next action - this was the last action for the Brunswick corps.

Westfalian Forces GdB Rewbell commanding: 1st and 6th LIR (2 bns each); 1st KürR (4 sqns); 3rd Berg IR (2 bns); 10 guns, ca 6,500 men.

Westfalian losses Not known exactly, light. Many men deserted.

Brunswick Forces The (dispossessed) Duke Frederick Wilhelm commanding: Jägers (2 bns); Scharfschützen (1 coy); Freiwillige Jäger (1 coy); HusR (4 sqns); UlR (2 sqns); 4 guns, ca 2,010 men.

Brunswick losses 24 killed, 62 wounded.

Comment Rewbell's force was in no condition to

pursue the Duke, whose men spent the night in Braunschweig. The Duke then led his force northwards to Elsfleth on the west bank of the River Weser, above Bremen, where on 6/7 August, they embarked on British ships and went into British service in the Peninsula until 1814.

Sources Lünsmann, Ernstberger, Schirmer.

NL Veere, 31 July – 1 August 1809, capture of

A small fortified town on the north of the island of Walcheren in the estuary of the River Schelde.

A British victory over the Franco-Dutch forces.

(This was the opening action of the Walcheren campaign; next action – Flushing, 16 August).

Franco-Dutch Garrison ca 400 men and 12 guns.

Franco-Dutch losses 200 captured.

British Forces LG Mackenzie Fraser: MG Picton 1st/71st, 1st/36th, 2nd/63rd, 77th, 2nd/95th (1 coy) 6 gunboats, ca 3,200 men and 1 x FAB.

British losses 2 gunboats sunk, 35 men killed.

Comment Veere had been bombarded into submission by the gunboats throughout the night; about 200 of the garrison escaped by boat to the island of North Beveland (Schouwen Duiveland) to the north.

Sources Fortescue.

TY Oberau (Franzensfeste), 4/5 August 1809, clash

A village on the left bank of the River Eisack (Isarco) on the old Route 12 in the (now Italian) South Tyrol, about 10 km upstream (to the north) of Brixen (Bressanone). The new motorway E6/A22 now passes through this very narrow valley. The Franzensfeste is a huge fortress which blocks the valley here.

A Tyrolean victory over Napoleon's allies (Ducal Saxons and Bavarians).

(Last action – Lueg Pass, 24 July; next action – Sterzing, 8/9 August.)

Allied Forces GdD Rouyer commanding: 4th IR Confederation of the Rhine (Ducal Saxon IR; 2 bns); 5th IR Confederation of the Rhine (Anhalt and Lippe; 2 bns); 6th IR Confederation of the Rhine (Waldeck and Reuss; 1 bn); 4th Bavarian ChLR 'Bubenhofen' (2 sqns). Bavarian artillery – 2 guns and 1 howitzer – less 2 coys in Sterzing.

Allied totals ca. 3,600 men.

Bavarian losses ca 100 killed, wounded and missing; 2 guns.

Ducal Saxon losses 40 officers and 948 men, including 500 dead and wounded and both colours. General Rouyer abandoned the Saxons 'to get help' and did not show his face again!

Tyrolean Forces The monk Haspinger commanding: Speckbacker and armed Schützen and Landsturm.

Tyrolean totals ca 5,000.

Tyrolean losses Not known but very slight.

Comment This was an excellent example of insurgents operating 'in their own backyard' against conventional forces incapable of adapting to the skirmishing tactics so vital in this very mountainous terrain. The valley at Oberau is now known as the 'Sachsen klemme' (the Trap of the Saxons) and the place where the Saxon dead were buried (at the Pleiser bridge) is known as the 'Sächsischen Totenacker' (the Saxon Burial Field). The allied rearguard (the Ducal Saxons) were cut off and destroyed.

Lefebvre came up afterwards with the 1st Bavarian Division to force his way through this defile but was repelled with loss.

Sources Leyh, Pfannenberg.

EW Arzobispo (El Puente), 8 August 1809, clash

A fortified town on the north bank on the Rio Tajo (Tagus) in western Spain, on a minor road south from Oropesa (on Route V/E90) and 25 km southwest of Talavera.

A French victory over the Spanish.

(Last action – Talavera (de la Reina), 27/28 July; next action – Puerto de Baños, 12 August.)

French Forces M Soult commanding: 1st Division (of Mortier's V Corps) GdD Girard: 40e and 88e RIdLi (3 bns each); GdB Caulaincourt's Dragoon Brigade: 17e, 18e and 19e DragR (4 sqns each) of Lahoussaye's 3rd Dragoon Division; 1 x FAB.

French totals 6 bns, 12 sqns, 6 guns, ca 4,000 men.

French losses Soult reported: 28 killed and 83 wounded dragoons, a few infantry drowned crossing the Tagus and 4 gunners wounded.

Spanish Forces The Duke of Albuquerque commanding: MG L A Bassecourt's 5th Division: 2 or 3 battalions (not exactly identified) from IRs Real Marina* (1 Regt); Africa* (3rd Bn); Murcia* (2 bns); Reyna* (1er Bn) and Provincial de Sugüenza(3 bns). Cavalry: 1st and 2nd Husares de Extremadura* (6 sqns). Artillery: 16 guns.

Spanish totals 3 bns, 6 sqns, 16 guns, ca 2,500 men.

Spanish losses The cavalry lost 600 men and 400 horses captured and over 800 killed and wounded. The 1st Hussars lost a standard. 16 guns.

Comment This was a brilliant raid. The French recovered the 17 guns lost at Talavera and returned them to Leval who subsequently denied ever having lost them.

Sources Oman, Napier, Martinien.

* = regiments of the old regular army.

TY Sterzing (Vipitino), 8/9 August 1809, 2nd clash

A town in the northern Italian Province of South Tyrol in the valley of the River Eisack (Isarco) on the old Route 12, 34 km upstream (north) of Brixen (Bressanone). The new motorway E6/A22 now runs just west of the town.

A Tyrolean victory over the Bavarians.

(Last action – Oberau 4/5 August; next action – Prutz, 8/9 August.)

Bavarian Forces M Lefebvre commanding: part of the 1st Bavarian Division GM von Raglovich: IR vac Salern Nr 4 (2 bns); IR Herzog Pius Nr 8 (2 bns).

Bavarian totals 4 bns, ca 3,500 men.

Bavarian losses Some dead and wounded, 50 captured.

Tyrolean Forces ca 2,000 armed peasants.

Tyrolean losses Not known exactly, slight.

Comment Lefebvre proposed a cease fire and about 500 peasants then mingled with the Bavarians then suddenly started the fight again and made off with the 50 prisoners.

Sources HGM 20, Leyh, Bezzel.

TY Prutz or the Pontlatzer Bridge, 8/9 August 1809, clash

A bridge on the upper River Inn in the Austrian Province of the Tyrol (on Route 315) 8 km southeast of Landeck.

A Tyrolean victory over the Bavarians.

(Last action – Sterzing 8/9 August, next action – Berg-Isel, 13 August.)

Bavarian Forces Obst Burscheidt commanding (of Deroy's division, Lefebvre's corps). IR Nr 10 (2 bns); DragR Nr 2 (2 sqns); 2 guns.

Bavarian totals ca 2,000 men and 2 guns.

Bavarian losses 200 dead and wounded, 700 captured, 140 horses, 2 guns. 500 more were killed or captured before the survivors (200) reached Zirl.

Tyrolean Forces The Schützenkompanien and individuals of the area: Kaunertal, Prutz, Tösens, Fendels under Hauptmann Roman Burger from Ried, Johann Anton Praxmarer of Kauns and Johann Schlapp.

Tyrolean totals 920 men.

Tyrolean losses 7 dead.

Comment This was a spontaneous uprising against the Bavarians; the women and children broke the bridge at Prütz and bombarded the enemy with rocks from the steep hillsides. The original Bavarian aim was to help their main thrust south through the Brenner Pass.

Sources HGM 48, Leyh, Bezzel, Wrede.

EM Almonacid (de Toledo), 11 August 1809, battle

A small town in central Spain, about 65 km south of Madrid and 20 km southeast of Toledo on Route 400 and on the south bank of the Rio Guazalette.

A French and Allied victory over the Spanish.

(Last action – Uclés, 13 January; next action – Ocaña, 18–19 November.)

French and Allied Forces King Joseph and GdD Sebastiani commanding the **IV Corps* 1st Division** (Sebastiani): 28e, 32e, 58e and 75e RIdLi (3 bns each). **2nd Division** GdD Leval: IRs Holland, 2nd Nassau, Baden, Hessen-Darmstadt IR 'Gross-und Erbprinz' (2 bns each), Frankfurt (1 bn). **3rd Division** GdD Valence: 4th, 7th and 9th Polish IRs (2 bns each). **Cavalry** 3rd Dutch HusR; Polish Lancers of the Vistula (4 sqns each). **Artillery:** 30 guns. **GdD Dessolles' Division** (of King Joseph's Reserve): 12e RILé, 43e, 51e and 55e RIdLi (3 bns each). 12 guns. **1st Dragoon Division** GdD Latour-Maubourg: 1er, 2e, 4e, 9e, 14e and 26e DragR (4 sqns each). **2nd Dragoon Division** GdD Milhaud: 12e, 16e, 20e and 21e DragR (4 sqns each).

French and Allied totals 39 bns, 16,000 infantry, 40 sqns, 2,200 cavalry, 48 guns.

French and Allied losses 2,400 killed and wounded.

* = King Joseph's Royal Guard (2,299) and the 27e ChàCh were also present but not engaged.

Spanish Forces General Venegas commanding. **Infantry: 1st Division** BG T Lacy: IRs Burgos (2 bns); Cuenca, 1st of Loxa, Alcala, 1st of España (1 bn each), **total** 8 bns. **2nd Division** BG Gaspar Vigodet: IRs Corona and Ordenes Militares (2 bns each), Ronda, Alcazar, Ciudad Real and 1st of Guadix (1 bn each), **total** 8 bns. **3rd Division** BG Pedro Giron: IRs 2nd of Jaén, Ecija, 2nd of Cordova and Bailén (2 bns each); Walloon Guards (1st Bn); Alpujarras and Velez-Malaga (1 bn each), **total** 11 bns. **4th Division** BG Franciso Casteljon: IRs 5th Seville, 1st of Malaga, Spanish Guards (2nd Bn); Jerez, 2nd of Loxa, Bujalance and 3rd Cordova, **total** 7 bns. **5th Division** MG T Zerain: 2nd España (2 bns); 1st Cordova (3 bns), Provincial of Seville (1 bn), **total** 6 bns. **Cavalry** Regiments Montesa, Reina, Granada, España, Farnesio, Santiago, Alcántara, Principe, Granaderos de Fernando VII, Drag de la Reina, Cazadores de Cordova, **total** about 3,300 sabres. **Artillery** 1,100 gunners and sappers, 40 guns.

Spanish totals 38 bns, 32 sqns, 40 guns, ca 23,000 men.

Spanish losses 800 killed, 2,500 wounded, 2,000 captured, 21 guns.

Comment Despite being beaten, the Spaniards had fought stubbornly and did not disintegrate on the withdrawal south through Mora to Madridejos 48 km away.

King Joseph returned to Madrid, content with having banished the immediate danger. The IV Corps went into cantonments around Toledo and Aranjuez.

Sources Oman, Napier, Bernays, Martinien.

EC Puerto de Baños, 12 August 1809, clash

A mountain pass on Route 630/E803 in western Spain about 50 km northeast of Plasencia, on the road from Salamanca.

A French victory over the Allies.

(Last action – Arzobispo (El Puente) 8 August; next action – Tamames, 18 October.)

French Forces

M Ney's VI Corps Advanced Guard: 50e RIdLi of GdD Mathieu's 2nd Division and 15e ChàCh of the Corps Light Cavalry; 1 x HAB.

French totals 3 bns, 4 sqns, 6 guns, ca 2,400 men.

French losses Ney admitted 5 officers and 30 men killed, 10 officers and 140 men wounded. It is likely that the real figures were larger.

Allied Forces General Sir Robert Wilson commanding the Loyal Lusitanian Legion (2 bns, 2 sqns); 5th Portuguese Caçadores (1 bn); Spanish IRs Seville and Merida (1 bn each)*.

Allied Totals 5 bns, 2 sqns, no artillery, ca 4,000 men.

Allied Losses Less than 400 killed, wounded and missing (Ney claimed to have killed 1,200 alone.)

Comment Despite the criticality of the situation, Sir Robert Wilson could not resist holding the Puerto de Baños against Ney and there followed a 9-hour running fight in three positions before the French artillery forced the dispersal of the Allied force.

They fell back west through the hills to Perales del Puerto and rejoined the Portuguese army at Castello Branco.

Sources Oman, Napier, Mayne, Martinien.

* = from Cuesta's army.

TY Berg-Isel, 13 August 1809, 3rd clash

A wooded hill about 2 km south of Innsbruck, capital city of the Austrian province of the Tyrol, on the River Inn.

A Tyrolean victory over the Bavarians.

(Last actions – Prutz, 8/9 August, next action – Pass Lueg and Mellek, Unken, Lofer and Luftenstein, 25 September, 4th clash.)

Bavarian Forces GL von Deroy commanding the 3rd Infantry Division. 2nd Brigade GM von Siebein: IR Preysing: Nr 5 (2 bns); IR Nr 14 (2 bns).

Bavarian totals 4 bns, ca 3,000 men.

Bavarian losses 200 dead, 250 wounded.

Tyrolean Forces Andreas Hofer commanding: ca 70 Landesschützenkompanien from North and South Tyrol. ca 18,000 men.

Tyrolean losses 100 dead, 220 wounded.

Comment Lefebvre and his Bavarians hurriedly evacuated Innsbruck yet again, taking prominent hostages with them. By 18 August the Tyrol was clear of the enemy. Andreas Hofer, the Tyrolean leader, was betrayed to the French on 20 January 1810 and shot in Mantua on the 20 February.

Sources HGM 20, Leyh, Bezzel.

NL Flushing (Vlissingen), 30 July – 16 August 1809, capitulation of

A fortified port on the south coast of the island of Walcheren in the estuary of the River Schelde in Holland.

A British victory over the Franco-Dutch.

(Last action – Veere, 1 August; next action – this was the last action of the campaign.)

Franco-Dutch Garrison GdD Monnet including battalions of the 48e, 65e and 72 RIdLi the R Irlandais, 'Chasseurs of Flushing', R de Prusse and the 1er Colonial Bn.

Franco-Dutch totals 6,000 men (the garrison was continually reinforced over the river during the action).

Franco-Dutch losses About 900 men killed and wounded, 5,803 captured; about 1,800 had deserted during the action and 1,000 sick and wounded had been evacuated.

British Forces LG The Earl of Chatham commanding: 3rd/1st Guards; 1st/5th, 2nd/23rd; 1st/26th, 1st/36th, 2nd/63rd, 1st/68th, 1st/71st, 77th, 1st/81st, 1st/85th, 2nd/95th. 4 x FAB, (24 guns). Certain ships of the fleet aided the bombardment.

British totals 13 bns, 24 guns, ca 14,000 men.

British losses 738 killed, wounded and missing.

Comment The British force was far too small to achieve anything and the Franco-Dutch fleet had already escaped up-river to Antwerp. The low-lying country was flooded and miasmic fever broke out among the British troops. Total battle deaths in this sorry affair were 106; by 1 February 1810 4,000 had died of 'Walcheren Fever'!

Sources Fortescue.

XX Ratan, 20 August 1809, clash

A village in northeastern Sweden, at the mouth of the River Umea about 28 km south of the port of Umea on the Gulf of Bothnia.

A Russian victory over the Swedes.

(This was the only action of note in the campaign.)

Swedish Forces Admiral Baron von Puke commanding 3 ships of the line, 5 frigates, 6 fully-decked and 36 open sloops, 6 galleys, 4 mortar boats and 11,000 troops under General Count Wachtmeister.

Swedish losses Not known exactly.

Russian Forces Gen Kaminskoi commanding 9,000 men.

Russian losses Not known exactly.

Comment Wachtmeister was totally incompetent, acted passively and was bottled up in a peninsula. Only the Swedish fleet's presence saved him.

Sources Anderson, Stenzel.

XX Constanta (Kostenje), 9 September 1809, capitulation

A Romanian Black Sea port, at the junction of Routes 2A/E60/E87, 3 and 38.

A Russian victory over the Turks.

(Last action – Braila, 17 May; next action – Rasova, 15 September.)

Turkish Garrison 1,800 men.

Turkish losses Not known.

Russian Forces GM Markoff commanding 8 bns, 10 sqns.

Russian total 6,000 men.

Russian losses Not known.

Comment The garrison were released on condition that they would not fight against Russia for the rest of the war.

Sources Bodart.

XX Rasova (Rassewat), 15 September 1809, clash

A town on the eastern bank of the River Danube in eastern Romania, 55 km northeast of Silistria. Now called Rasnova.

A Russian victory over the Turks.

(Last action – Constanta, 9 September; next action – Tataritza, 21 October.)

Turkish Forces Seraskier Chosrev Pasha commanding.

Turkish total 12,000 men.

Turkish losses 1,000 killed and wounded, 700 captured, 11 guns.

Russian Forces GdI Prince Bagration commanding 23 bns, 58 sqns.

Russian total 18,000 men.

Russian losses ca 500 men.

Sources Bodart.

TY Mellek, Unken, Lofer and Luftenstein, 25 September 1809, clashes

Villages in the west of the Austrian province of Salzburg on Route 312 running north into the German town of Bad Reichenhall along the valley of the Saalach River.

Tyrolean victories over the Bavarians.

(Last action – 3rd Berg-Isel, 13 August; next action – Hallein, 3 October.)

Bavarian Forces Leib IR Nr 1 (2 companies in each village).

Bavarian total ca 700 men.

Bavarian losses 50 dead and wounded, 300 captured, 100 missing.

Tyrolean Forces Speckbacker commanding about 2,000 armed peasants of the Landesschützenkompanien and the Landsturm.

Tyrolean losses Not known, slight.

Comment The fighting spirit of the Tyroleans was still not broken! Only the Bavarian detachment in Mellek managed to fight its way out north to Bad Reichenhall.

Sources Leyh.

TY Lueg Pass (and Golling), 25 September 1809, 4th clash

A pass on the old Route 311 in the Austrian Province of Salzburg, along the Salzach stream, about 40 km south of Salzburg city.

An Austrian (Tyrolean) victory over the Bavarians.

(Last action – 3rd Berg-Isel, 13 August; next action – Hallein, 3 October.)

Bavarian Forces GM Stengel commanding: IR Herzog Pius Nr 8 (2 bns); IR vac Salern Nr 4 (2 bns); ChLR Kronprinz Nr 1 (4 sqn); 3 guns.

Bavarian totals 4 bns, 4 sqn, 3 guns, ca 3,500 men.

Bavarian losses 27 dead and wounded, 10 missing.

Austrian Forces Peter Joachim Haspinger commanding: Tyrolean Schützenkompanien; Innsbruck, Hötting, Rattenburg, Sarntal, 6th Passeier, Martersteig, Strub and Sieber; one company each. Salzburg Schützenkompanien: 1st and 2nd Pongau. Goldegg and Taxenbach, Radstadt, one company each; Oberpongauer Landsturm – 600 men.

Austrian totals ca 2,400 men and 6 guns.

Austrian losses 4 dead, 6 wounded.

Comment Lefebvre had ordered the fortifications in Lueg and Strub passes destroyed before this action. Three times already the Salzburgers and Tyroleans had successfully defended this pass against the Bavarians and now they took it from them. GM von Stengel withdrew through Hallein to Salzburg.

Sources HGM 41, Wrede, Bezzel Vol VI.

TY Hallein, 3 October 1809, clash

A town on the River Salzach in the Austrian Province of Salzburg, about 23 km south of the city of Salzburg.

An Bavarian victory over the Tyroleans.

(Last action – Pass Lueg and Mellek, Unken, Lofer and Luftenstein, 25 September; next action – Bodenbichl, 17 October.)

Bavarian Forces M Lefebvre commanding: GM von Stengel IR vac Salern Nr 4 (2 Bn); GdB Montmarie IR Nr 14 (2 bns).

Bavarian totals 3 bns, ca 2,000 men, 4 guns.

Bavarian losses Very slight.

Tyrolean Forces Peter Joachim Haspinger commanding: ca 2,400 men and 6 guns.

Tyrolean losses Not known, slight, all 6 guns were taken.

Comment The Bavarians retook Hallein and chased the insurgents back to the Lueg Pass. There followed the third invasion of the Tyrol – Lefebvre was removed from command of the Bavarians and replaced by Count Drouet d'Erlon.

Sources HGM 20, HGM 41, Leyh, Bezzel.

TY Bodenbichl, 17 October 1809, clash

A pass between southern Germany and the Austrian Tyrol, on Route B21 between Bad Reichenhall and Lofer.

A Bavarian victory over the Tyroleans.

(Last action – Hallein, 3 October; next action – Berg-Isel (4th clash), 1 November.)

Bavarian Forces 1st Bavarian Division: GM Baron von Rechberg commanding: 1st Brigade: GM Baron von Rechberg: Leib IR Nr 1 (1 bn); IR Kronprinz Nr 2 (2 bns); LtI Bn Nr 1 Habermann (1 bn). Artillery: 1x FAB.

Bavarian totals 4 bns, ca 3,000 men, 6 guns.

Bavarian losses 9 wounded.

Tyrolean Forces Speckbacker commanding: about 2,000 Landesschützen and Landsturm.

Tyrolean losses 300 dead, 400 captured.

Comment The Tyroleans had not put out adequate outposts and patrols and were totally surprised and crushed. GM von Rechberg was rewarded with the Order of Max-Joseph. The three Bavarians divisions reoccupied North Tyrol and Innsbruck without much further trouble.

Sources HGM 20, Leyh.

EW Tamames, 18 October 1809, battle

A small town in western Spain on Route 525, 56 km southwest of Salamanca.

A Spanish victory over the French.

(Last action – Puerto de Baños, 12 August; next action – Alba de Tormes, 26 November.)

French Forces GdD Marchand commanding the **VI Corps** in Ney's absence in Paris: **1st Division** (Marchand): 6e RILé, 39e, 69e and 76e RIdLi (3 bns each). **2nd Division** GdD Mathieu: 25e RILé, 27e and 59e RIdLi (3 bns each), 50e (1 bn only). **Cavalry** GdB Lorcet: 3e HusR, 15e ChàCh 15e and 25e DragR (4 sqns each). Artillery: 30 guns. **French totals** 22 bns, 16 sqns, 30 guns, ca 11,000 men.

French losses GdB Lorcet and 54 other officers wounded, 23 officers killed; 1,300 men killed, wounded and missing, 1 gun.

Spanish Forces LG Duke del Parque. **Vanguard** MG Martin de la Carrera: IRs Principe and Zaragoza (3 bns each); 1st and 2nd of Catalonia, Girona, Barbastro, Escolares de Leon; Vittoria; Monforte de Lemos, Voluntarios de la Muerte (1 bn each); **total** 14 bns, 1 x FAB. **1st Division** MG Francisco Xavier Losada: Granaderos Provinciales de Galicia; Leon (2 bns each); 1st and 2nd of Aragon, Voluntarios del la Corona, Betanzos (2 bns each); Regimento del General; 1st and 2nd de La Union; Orense, Campana de Guardias Nacionales, **total** 15 bns, 1 x FAB. **2nd Division** MG Conde de Belveder: Rey (1st and 2nd bns); Zamora (1st and 2nd bns); Sevilla (1st and 2nd bns); Toledo (1st and 2nd bns); Hibernia (2 bns); Voluntarios de Navarra; Santiago; Lovera (2 bns), **total** 14 bns, 1 x FAB. **3rd (Asturian) Division** MG Francisco Ballasteros: Navarra (3 bns); Princesa (2 bns); Oviedo; Covadonga; Villaviciosa; Candas y Luanco; Castropol; Pravia; Cangas de Tines; Grado; Infiesto; Lena; **total** 15 bns, 1 x FAB. **5th (Leon) Division** MG Marques de Castrofuerte: Tiradores de Ciudad Rodrigo; Ciudad Rodrigo (2nd Bn); Voluntarios de Fernando VII; Leon; Logroño; Toro; Valladolid, **total** 7 bns, 1 x FAB. **Cavalry** General the Prince of Anglona: Borbon; Sagunto, Granaderos de Llerena - 1,000 men and 868 horses. Reyna, Provisional Regt*, Cazadores de Ciudad Rodrigo - 500 men in all. 1 x FAB.

Spanish totals About 20,000 infantry and 1,400 cavalry, 5 batteries, 30 guns.

Spanish losses 713 killed and wounded, mostly in Carrera's Vanguard, 1 gun.

* = this regiment became '2nd of Algarve' in December 1809.

Comment The contempt which all French commanders had for their Spanish foes led Marchand into this sharp and humiliating defeat.

Del Parque now appealed to Wellington to join him in an offensive to take control of all of Leon and Old Castile but Wellington, still smarting from his experiences with Cuesta at Talavera, forbade any British or Portuguese participation.

Sources Oman, Napier, Martinien.

XX Tataritza, 21 October 1809, battle

A village in northern Bulgaria, 6 km west of Silistria on the south bank of the River Danube. Not shown on modern maps.

A Turkish victory over the Russians.

(Last action - Rasova, 15 September; next action - Ismail, 25 October.)

Turkish Forces Seraskier Pechlivan Khan commanding:

Turkish total 30,000 men.

Turkish losses 2,000 killed and wounded.

Russian Forces GdI Prince Bagration commanding: 17 bns, 55 sqns; total ca 15,000 men.

Russian losses ca 1,000 killed and wounded.

Source Bodart.

XX Ismail, 18 August - 25 October 1809, siege and capture

A town in southern Ukraine, on the Danube delta (also known as Tuchkoy) on Route 26, about 80 km from the Black Sea.

A Russian victory over the Turks.

(Last action - Tataritza, 21 October; next action - Silistria, 26 October.)

Turkish Garrison - 4,500 men.

Turkish losses Not known. The garrison surrendered and were allowed to go free.

Russian Forces GM Zass commanding: 8 bns, 12 sqns; total 6,000 men.

Russian losses Not known.

Source Bodart.

XX Silistria, 22 September - 26 October 1809, failed siege

A town in northern Bulgaria on the south bank of the River Danube about 115 km from the Black Sea, at the junction of Routes 3, 7 and 21.

A Turkish victory over the Russians.

(Last action - Ismail, 25 October; next action - Poti, 13 November.)

Turkish Garrison Chosrev Pasha commanding.

Turkish total 15,000 men.

Turkish losses Not known.

Russian Forces GdI Prince Bagration commanding 32 bns, 86 sqns, total 26,000 men.

Russian losses Not known.

Comment Following his victory at Tataritza on 21

October, Seraskier Pechlivan Khan advanced and forced the Russians to lift the siege.

Source Bodart.

XX Poti, 13 November 1809, clash

A Georgian Black Sea port, just south of the mouth of the River Rioni and 50 km north of the port of Batumi.

A Russian victory over the Turks.

(Last action – Silistria, 26 October; next action – Braila, 4 December.)

Turkish Forces Seraskier Sheriff, the Pasha of Trapezunt commanding: 9,000 men.

Turkish losses 1,500 killed and wounded, 300 captured, 1 gun.

Russian Forces GM Prince Orbeljanov commanding 7,000 men.

Russian losses 500 killed and wounded.

Source Bodart.

EM Ocaña, 18/19 November 1809, battle

A small town in central Spain, 11 km southwest of Aranjuez, just off Route VI/E5 and 62 km south of Madrid.

A French and Allied victory over the Spanish.

(Last action – Almonacid, 11 August; this was the last action here in 1809.)

French Forces King Joseph commanding:

IV Corps M Jourdan GdD Sebastiani: **2nd Division** GdD Leval: IRs Holland, 2nd Nassau, Baden, Hessen-Darmstadt 'Gross- und Erbprinz' (2 bns each); Frankfurt (1 bn); 2 x FAB. **3rd Division** GdD Werle: 4th, 7th and 9th Polish IRs (2 bns each); 2 x FAB. **Corps Light Cavalry** 3rd Dutch Hus R; Lancers of the Vistula Legion (4 sqns each); 1 x HAB.

V Corps M Mortier 1st Division GdD Suchet: 17e RILé, 40e, 64e and 88e RIdLi (3 bns each); 34e RIdLi (4 bns); 2 x FAB. **2nd Division** GdD Gazan: 21e and 28e RILé, 100e and 103e RIdLi (3 bns each) 2 x FAB. **Corps Light Cavalry** 10e HusR; 21e ChàCh (4 sqns each); 1 x HAB. **Dessolles' Division** 12e RILé; 43e, 51e and 55 RIdLi (3 bns each), 2 x FAB. Milhaud's **2nd Dragoon Division** 12e, 16e, 20e and 21e DragR (4 sqns each); 2 x HAB. GdB Paris' Cavalry (later Perreymond): 10e and 27e ChàCH. Beauregard's Cavalry: 5e, 8e and 26e DragR, 10e and 26e ChàCh. **Spanish Royal Guard:** Grenadiers (2 bns); ChLR (2 sqns); 1st Spanish ChàCh (4 sqns).

French totals 24,000 infantry, 5,000 cavalry, 50 guns.

French losses About 90 officers and 1,900 killed and wounded, GdB Paris killed; GdB Girard wounded.

Spanish Forces: 'The Army of La Mancha' Gen Areizaga commanding. **Infantry Vanguard Division** Gen José Zayas: Voluntarios de Valencia; 2nd of Majorca, Provincial de Plasencia, Voluntarios de España, Granaderos Provinciales, Cantabria, **total infantry** 7 bns, ca 5,768 men. **1st Division** Gen L Lacy: Burgos, 1st of España, Provincial de Cordova, 1st of Loxa, Alcala, 1st of Seville, Provincial de Chinchilla, **total** 9 bns, 7,400 men. **2nd Division** Gen Gaspar Vigodet: Corona, Ordenes Militares, Ronda, Alcazar, Ciudad Real and 1st of Guadix (1 bn each), **total** 9 bns, 6,800 men. **3rd Division** Gen P Giron: Spanish Guards (1st and 2nd Bns); Cordova (2nd Bn); Bailén, Provincial de Jaén, Provincial de Toledo, **total** 8 bns, ca 5,000 men. **4th Division** Gen F Castejon: 1st of Malaga, 5th of Seville, 2nd of Loxa, Bujalance, Cazadores de Velez' Malaga, Xeres, 3rd of Cordova, **total** 8 bns, ca 6,100 men. **5th Division** Gen N Zerain: Cazadores de Barbastro; 2nd España; 2nd of Seville, 2nd of Madrid, Walloon Guards (3rd Bn), Provincial de Granada, **total** 7 bns, 5,677 men. **6th Division** Gen N Jacomé: Badajoz, Jaén, 4th of Seville, Alpujarras, Tiradores de Extremadura, Provincial de Ecija, **total** 9 bns, ca 7,325 men. **7th Division** BG F Copons: Murcia, Africa, Reyna, Real Marina, **total** 6 bns, ca 5,000 men. Troops not in divisional organizations: Granaderos del General, Compana de Buen Orden, Companas Sueltas ca 780 men. **Cavalry** Gen Manuel Freire: **1st Division** BG Juan Bernuy: Rey, Infante, Almanza, Voluntarios de Madrid, Carabineros y Lanceros de Extremadura. **2nd Division** BG José Rivas: Pavia, Cazadores de Toledo, 1st and 2nd Hussars of Extremadura. **3rd Division** BG Miguel March: Reyna, Montesa, Principe, Santiago, Alcántara, Cordova. **4th Division** Col V Osorio: Espana, Lusitania, Farnesio, Granaderos de Fernando VII, Cazadores de Granada. **Cavalry total** ca 5,700 men (probably only 5,000 at the battle). **Artillery** ca 1,500 men and 60 guns, sappers – 600.

Spanish totals 59 bns, 49,939 infantry, ? sqns, 5,000 cavalry, 1,500 artillery and 60 guns.

Spanish losses 4,000 killed and wounded, 14,000 captured, 50 guns, 30 colours, the entire baggage train and 43,000 horses.

Comment This was a crushing and well-deserved defeat. After making a semi-lunge at Madrid on 8 November, Areizaga had been dithering about along the upper Tajo between Toledo and Aranjuez, achieving absolutely nothing whilst his enemies, now alerted to his presence, concentrated to bring about his destruction. Only Zaya's vanguard remained intact to cover the withdrawal. The Spanish survivors fled south into the Sierra Morena. Astoundingly enough, the Supreme Junta retained Areizaga in his command position.

Sources Oman, Napier, Bernays, Isenbart, Martinien.

TY Berg-Isel, 1 November 1809, 4th clash

A wooded hill about 2 km south of Innsbruck, capital city of the Austrian province of the Tyrol.

A Bavarian victory over the Tyroleans.

(Last actions – Bodenbichl, 17 October; this was the last action of note in the Tyrol.)

Bavarian Forces GL Baron Wrede commanding the 2nd Division. 1st Brigade GM Count Minucci: IR Nr 13 (2 bns); LtI Bn Nr 6 La Roche (1 bn). 2nd Brigade GM Count Beckers: IR Herzog Wilhelm Nr 6 (2 bns); IR Löwenstein Nr 7 (2 bns). Artillery: 2 batteries 12 guns.

Bavarian totals 7 bns, 12 guns, ca 6,000 men.

Bavarian losses 1 dead and 40 wounded.

Tyrolean Forces Andreas Hofer and Peter Haspinger commanding about 70 Schützenkompanien and Landsturm.

Tyrolean totals 8,535 men.

Tyrolean losses 350 dead, wounded and captured, 5 guns, 1 flag.

Comment This action, coming after the defeat of Bodenbichl, broke the resistance of the Tyroleans. The rebellion had been finally crushed.

Sources HGM 20, Leyh, Bezzel.

EW Alba de Tormes, 26 November 1809, clash

A small fortified town in western Spain on the eastern bank of the Rio Tormes, on Route 510 about 21 km southeast of Salamanca.

A French victory over the Spanish.

(Last action – Tamames, 18 October; next action – this was the last action here in 1809.)

French Forces GdG Count Kellermann commanding: 3e, 10e, 15e and 25e DragR (4 sqns each). Light Cavalry GdB Lorcet: 3e HusR, 15e ChàCh (4 sqns each). GdD Marchand commanding M Ney's VI Corps came up at the end of the action but was not engaged.

French totals 3,000 cavalry and 12 guns.

French losses GdB Carrié wounded; 29 officers and between 300 and 600 men killed and wounded.

Spanish Forces LG Duke Del Parque commanding (most regiments newly-formed and only partially trained). **Vanguard Division** MG Martin de la Carrera: IRs Principe and Zaragoza (3 bns each); 1st and 2nd of Catalonia, Girona, Barbastro, Vittoria, Monforte de Lemos, Escolares de Leon, Voluntarios de la Muerte, **totals** 14 bns, ca 7,000 men and 1 x FAB. **1st Division** M G Francisco Xavier Losada: Leon, Aragon La Union, Voluntarios de la Corona, Betanzos and Granaderos Provinciales de Galicia (2 bns each); Orense, Compana de Guardias Nacionales, **totals** 13 bns and 1 coy – ca 8,000 men and 1 x FAB. **2nd Division** MG Conde de Belvedere: Rey, Zamora, Seville, Toledo, Hibernia and Lovera (2 bns each); Santiago, Voluntarios de Navarra, **totals** 14 bns, ca 6,300 men and 1 x FAB. **Cavalry** MG Prince of Anglona: Borbon, Sagunto, Granaderos de Llerena, Reyna, Cazadores de Ciudad Rodrigo, a Provisional Regiment, **total** 1,500 sabres.

Spanish totals 41 bns, 21,300 infantry, ?? sqns, 1,500 cavalry, 18 guns.

Spanish losses About 2,000 killed and wounded, 1,000 captured, 9 guns, 5 colours and most of the baggage.

Comment Del Parque occupied Salamanca on 20 November (still ignorant of Areizaga's crushing defeat at Ocaña the previous day) and proceeded to dally while the French concentrated to destroy him. He heard the news of Ocaña on 24 November, panicked, and set off via Alba de Tormes to hide in the mountains again. Del Parque had put out no rearguard and he was taken by surprise, also his army was split by the Rio Tormes. This battle, coupled with Areizaga's defeat at Ocaña on 18 and 19 November, gave the French temporary control of most Spanish cities and allowed them to turn their eyes to the reconquest of Portugal.

Sources Oman, Napier, Martinien.

XX Braila, 13 November – 4 December 1809, blockade and capture

A town in northeastern Romania, on the west bank of

the River Danube, 15 km upstream from Galatz.

A Russian victory over the Turks.

(Last action - Poti, 13 November; this was the last action in this theatre in 1809.)

Turkish Garrison: 8,000 men survived. Losses - not known, the survivors were captured.

Russian Forces GM Count Essen commanding 10,000 men.

Russian losses Not known.

Comment The blockade was supported by a covering force of 30,000 men under GdI Prince Bagration.

Source Bodart.

EE Girona, 6 June - 10 December 1809, siege and capture

A fortified town in north eastern Spain, about 80 km northeast of Barcelona on Route 11 and 40 km from the coast and on the right bank of the River Ter.

A French and Allied victory over the Spanish.

(Last action - Belchite, 18 June; next action - Granollers, 21 January 1810.)

French Forces

The Siege Corps GdD Reille of VII Corps Gouvion St Cyr 4th Division GdD Verdier; GdB Jouba : 32e RILé, 2e, 16e and 56e RIdLi (1 bn each). GdB Amey: IR Würzburg, 1st and 2nd Berg IRs (2 bns each). **German Division** GdD Morio: GdB Boerner; GM von Hadeln (Westfalians) 2nd, 3rd and 4th LIRs (2 bns each) and 4th LtI Bn (1 bn). **6th Division** GdD Lecchi (Italians): Vélites of the Guard (1 bn); 5th LIR (2 bns). Neapolitans: 1st and 2nd LIR (2 bns each). **Totals** 24 bns, 38 guns.

The Covering Corps, VII Corps Gouvion St Cyr 1st Division GdD Souham: GdB Bessières: 1er RILé (3 bns); 3e RILé (1 bn); 24e DragR (3 sqns). GdB Espert: 42e RIdLi (3 bns); 67e RIdLi (1 bn). **5th Division** GdD Pino (Italians): GdB Mazzuchelli: 1st LtIR, 4th LIR (3 bns each). GdB Fontane: 2nd LtIR, 6th LIR (3 bns each); 7th LIR (1 bn). GdB Palombini; ChàCh DragR (3 sqns each). **3rd Division** GdD Chabot: 7e RIdLi (2 bns); 93e RIdLi (1 bn); 3e Provisional ChàCh (4 sqns).

French and Allied totals 16,000 in the Covering Corps, 18,000 in the siege corps **French and Allied losses** 15,000 fatalities, over half due to sickness. Westfalian GM von Hadeln and French GdB Jouba died of malaria.

Spanish Garrison LG don Mariano Alvarez commanding. **Original force** LIRs Ultonia and Borbon (3 bns each), Miqueletes de Girona (1st and 2nd bns), Miqueletes de Vich (1st Bn); Voluntarios de Barcelona (2nd Bn); cavalry of San Narciso (1 sqn); sailors (1 coy), sappers (22 men), artillery (3 coys). **Total** 5,723. **Reinforcements received on 17 August** Miqueletes de Cervera (1 bn); draft for 1st Vich (3 coys); draft for 2nd Girona (1 coy). **Reinforcements received on 1 September** LIR Baza (2 bns); Miqueletes de Talarn (1st and 2nd Bns); Miqueletes de Vich (2nd Bn); Volunteers of LIRs Santa Fé, Hibernia and Voluntarios de Tarragona (2 coys). **Total Reinforcements** 3,684. The 'Crusade' (local volunteers) 1,100.

Spanish grand total 9,371 men, 168 guns. There was also a battalion of women 'The 5th Barbe company' who carried out ammunition resupply.

Spanish losses 5,122 killed or died of sickness, 4,248 captured.

Sources Oman, Napier, Lünsmann, Martinien, Grosch.

1810

1810 THE ACTIONS

EE Granollers, Mollet and Sta Perpetua, 21 January 1810, clashes

Three villages northeast of Barcelona, a fortified Catalonian port city in northeastern Spain.

Spanish victories over the French.

(Last action – Girona, 10 December; next action – Vic, 20 February.)

French Forces Col Guétry commanding: 7e RIdLi (2 bns); 112e RIdLi (1 bn); 5th Italian LIR (2 bns); 3e Prov CuirR (250 men), ca 4,300 men, 6 guns.

French losses 400 killed and wounded, 600 captured, 2 guns. Guétry was captured.

Spanish Forces MG Henry O'Donnell commanding the main body of the Army of Catalonia. Exact details not known.

Spanish totals ca 7,000 men.

Spanish losses Not known, light.

Sources Oman, Napier, Martinien.

EE Vic, 20 February 1810, clash

A fortified town in Catalonia, northeastern Spain, on Route 152, 60 km north of Barcelona.

A French victory over the Spanish.

(Last action – Granollers, 21 January; next action – Manresa, 5 April.)

French Forces GdD Souham's 1st Division, VII Corps: 1er RILé (3 bns); 3e RILé (1 bn); 7e RIdLi (2 bns); 42e (3 bns); 93e (1 bn); 3e ChàCh (? sqns); 24e DragR. Italian Drag Napoleone (2 sqns) 2 x FAB.

French totals 10 bns, 4,000 infantry, 1,500 cavalry, 12 guns.

French losses Souham wounded; 600 killed and wounded.

Spanish Forces MG Henry O'Donnell's Army of Catalonia Swiss IRs Kayser and Traxler. Rovera's and Milans' Somatenes: 3–4,000 men.

Spanish totals 10–11,000 men including 500 cavalry.

Spanish losses 800 killed and wounded, 1,000 captured.

Sources Oman, Napier, Martinien.

EE Manresa, 21 March – 5 April 1810, clashes

A fortified town in Catalonia, (northeastern Spain), on Route 1141/E9, on the left bank of the Rio Cardener, about 40 km northwest of Barcelona.

A Spanish victory over the Germans.

(Last action – Vic, 20 February; next action – Margalef, 23 April.)

German Forces GdB Schwarz commanding: 3rd Confederation of the Rhine (1st Nassau) 2 bns; 4th Confederation of the Rhine (Ducal Saxon) 2 bns; ca 3,000 men.

German losses GdD Rouyer's division VII Corps. 1st Nassau: 42 killed, 203 wounded, 75 captured, 164 missing. Total 484 men. Ducal Saxons: 6 officers and 162 men killed, wounded and missing. 200 wounded were abandoned in Manresa.

Spanish Forces MG Henry O'Donnell commanding: Col Roviera's Miqueletes ca 3,000 men; local somatenes ca 2,300 men; MG Juan Caro's* division including the Swiss Regiment Kayser and DragR Numancia ca 2,000 men.

Spanish total About 7,300 men.

* = wounded on 2 April; Gen Campo Verde took command.

Spanish losses Not known, fairly light.

Sources Müller, Pfannenberg, Oman.

AD Santa Maura (Leucadia), 22 March – 16 April 1810, capture of

A Greek Island in the Ionian group, 80 km southeast of Corfu, in the southern Adriatic.

An Anglo-Allied victory over the Franco-Italians.

(Last action – Zante (Zakynthos) and Cephalonia, October 1809; next action – Corfu, 15 June.)

Franco-Italian Forces GdB Camus commanding the Bn Septinsulaire (1 bn) and the 2nd Italian LIR (1 bn) and 600 irregular locals.

Franco-Italian total 1,600 men, 4 guns.

French Losses Killed and wounded not known; 800 captured, 4 guns.

British Forces BG Oswald commanding: Greek LtI bn (1 bn); De Roll's Swiss (2 coys); Royal Corsican Rangers (2 coys); Royal Marines (2 coys); 1st/35th Foot (1 coy), supported by the Royal Naval Frigate HMS *Leonidas*.

British losses 44 killed and wounded.

Sources Fortescue, Martinien.

EN Astorga, 21 March – 22 April 1810, siege and surrender of

A fortified town in northern Spain (Leon) in the mountains at the junction of Routes VI and 120, 48 km west of Leon.

A French victory over the Spaniards.

(This was the only action of note in this region in 1810.)

French Forces GdD Junot commanding the **VIII Corps: 1st Division** GdD Clausel: 22e RIdLi (4 bns); 14e, 19e, 25e, 28e, 34e, 36e, 50e and 75e RIdLi (1 bn each). 2 x FAB. **3rd Division** GdD Solignac:15e, 47e, 70e and 86e RIdLi; R. Irlandais; R de Prusse (2 bns each). 2 x FAB. Siege artillery: 4 x 24 pdrs, 1 x 16 pdr, 4 x 12 pdrs; 8 x 16" howitzers, 1 x 6" mortar.

French totals 24 bns, ca 19,000 men, 1,000 artillery.

French losses 160 killed, 400 wounded; 80% of these in the unsuccessful storming of 21 April. The storm was led by 47e and R Irlandais.

Spanish Garrison Col Santocildes commanding five battalions: 2,700 men with 13 guns. **Spanish losses** 2 officers and 49 men killed; 10 officers and 99 men wounded, 2,500 surrendered.

Sources Oman, Napier, Martinien.

EE Margalef, 23 April 1810, clash

A ruined village in Catalonia (northeastern Spain), 10 km southeast of Lleida, on Route 240 leading to Tarragona.

A French victory over the Spaniards.

(Last action - Manresa, 5 April; next action - Hostalrich, 12 May.)

French Forces GdD Suchet's **III Corps:** GdD Musnier's **2nd Division** 114e and 115e RIdLi (3 bns each); 1st IR Vistula Legion (2 bns); 2 x FAB; 13e CuirR (500 men); 4e HusR.

French totals 8 bns, 5,500 infantry, 500 cavalry.

French losses Reported as '100 killed and wounded' all from the 13e Cuirassiers. The infantry were not engaged.

Spanish Forces MG Henry O'Donnell commanding the Army of Catalonia. MG Ibarrola's Division. No details known.

Spanish totals 7,000 infantry, 300 cavalry, 6 guns.

Spanish losses 500 killed and wounded, 2,000 captured, 3 guns, 4 colours.

Sources Oman, Napier, Martinien.

EE Hostalrich, 16 January - 12 May 1810, siege of

A small fortified town in the mountains of the northeastern Spanish province of Catalonia, about 55 km northeast of Barcelona. Not shown on many modern maps.

An Italian victory over the Spanish.

(Last action - Margalef, 23 April; next action - Lleida, 13 May.)

Italian Forces GdB Mazzuchelli's brigade of GdD Severoli's 2nd Division, VII Corps:.

1st and 2nd LtIRs; 4th, 5th and 6th LIR (2 bns each). 6 guns.

Italian losses Not known exactly.

Spanish Garrison Col Julio Estrada commanding 1st of Granada (1 bn) and a tercio of Gironese levies ca 1,200 men.

Spanish losses Col Estrada, 10 officers and 300 men captured.

Sources Oman, Napier.

EE Lleida, 29 April - 13 May 1810, siege and capture of

A fortified town in Catalonia (northeastern Spain) on the west bank of the Rio Segre and at the junction of Routes II, 250 and 1313, about 135 km west of Barcelona.

A French victory over the Spanish.

(Last action - Hostalrich, 12 May; next action - Mequinenza, 15 June.)

French Forces GdD Suchet's III Corps: 2nd Division GdD Musnier: 114e, 115e and 121e RIdLi (3 bns each); 1st IR Legion of the Vistula; (2 bns). 2 x FAB. 3rd Division GdD Habert: 5e RILé and 116e RIdLi (2 bns each); 117e (3 bns); 2 x FAB. Light Cavalry: GdB Boussard: 4e HusR; 13e CuirR (8 sqns); 1 x HAB.

French Totals 18 bns, 8 sqns, 30 guns, ca 13,000 men.

French losses About 1,000 killed and wounded.

Spanish Forces MG Garcia Conde.

Spanish totals ca 8,000 men (including 350 gunners) and 105 guns.

Spanish losses 1,700 killed and wounded, 6 generals, 307 officers, 7,000 men captured, 105 guns, 10 colours.

Sources Oman, Napier, Martinien.

XX Bazardjik, 3 June 1810, storm

A town in eastern Bulgaria about 40 km north of the Black Sea port of Varna, at the junction of Routes 21, 27 and 29. Now called Dobric.

A Russian victory over the Turks.

(This was the opening action in this theatre; next action - Silistria, 11 June.)

Turkish Garrison Seraskier Pechlivan Khan commanding 5,000 men.

Turkish losses 3,000 killed and wounded, 2,000 captured, 68 'colours', 17 guns.

Russian Forces LG Count Sergei Kamenskoi commanding 23,000 men.

Russian losses ca 1,000 killed and wounded.

Source Bodart.

EE Mequinenza, 15 May – 5 June 1810, siege and capture of

A medieval fortified town in northeastern Spain, at the confluence of the Rio Ebro and the Rio Segre.

A French victory over the Spanish.

(Last action – Lleida, 13 May; next action – Palamos, St Feliu, La Bisbal, 14 September.)

French Forces GdD Suchet commanding the III Corps: 2nd Division GdD Musnier: 114e, 115e and 121e RIdLi (3 bns each); 1st IR Vistula Legion (2 bns). 2 x FAB. 3rd Division GdD Habert: 5e RILé and 116e RIdLi (2 bns each); 117e (3 bns); 2 x FAB.

French totals 18 bns, 24 guns, ca 16,000 men.

French losses Not known very light.

Spanish Garrison Col Carbon commanding ca 1,000 men.

Spanish losses Killed and wounded unknown, the entire garrison captured.

Sources Oman, Napier.

XX Silistria, 3 – 11 June 1810, siege and capture

A town in northeastern Bulgaria, on the south bank of the River Danube, 93 km southeast of Bucharest in Romania, at the junction of Routes 3, 7 and 21.

A Russian victory over the Turks.

(Last action – Bazardjik, 3 June; next action – Razgrad, 12 June.)

Turkish Garrison Ilik Oglu Pasha commanding 7,000 men.

Turkish losses They were allowed to go free but without any baggage. Apart from large stocks of warlike material the Russians took 196 guns and 42 'colours'.

Russian Forces LG Count Nikolai Kamenskoi commanding 30,000 infantry and 10,000 cavalry.

Russian losses Not known exactly but very light.

Source Bodart.

XX Razgrad, 12 June 1810, capitulation

A town in northeastern Bulgaria, on the River Beli Lom, 60 km southeast of Ruse on the River Danube and on Route 2/E70 towards Schumen.

A Russian victory over the Turks.

(Last action – Silistria, 11 June; next action – Schumla, 23/24 June.)

Turkish Garrison 3,000 men.

Turkish losses All captured.

Russian Forces GM Sabaniev commanding 6,000 men.

Russian losses Not known but very light.

Source Bodart.

AD Corfu, 15 June 1810, raid

An island of the Ionian group in the southern Adriatic just of the coast of Albania and Greece.

(Last action – Santa Maura, 16 April; this was the last action here in 1810.)

French Forces IR Albanaise (1 bn).

French losses Not known; part of the regiment was captured.

Russian Forces Exact details and losses not known.

Sources Fortescue, Martinien.

XX Schumla (now Schumen), 23/24 June 1810, battle

A fortress in eastern Bulgaria, in the hills, 110 km west of the Black Sea port of Varna. At the junction of Routes 2, 7 and 73.

A Turkish victory over the Russians.

(Last action – Razgrad, 12 June; next action – Taschlimechle, 2 August.)

Turkish Forces Seraskier Kuschanz Ali commanding 30,000 men.

Turkish losses 1,600 killed and wounded.

Russian Forces GdI Count Kamenskoi commanding 20,000 men.

Russian losses 1,800 killed and wounded.

Source Bodart.

EW Ciudad Rodrigo, 26 April – 9 July 1810, siege and surrender of

A fortified city in western Spain, 27 km from the border of Portugal, on Route 620/E80 and on the eastern bank of the Rio Agueda; 91 km southwest of Salamanca.

A French victory over the Spanish.

(Last action – Almonacid, 11 August 1809; next action – Coa River, 24 July.)

French Forces M Ney's **VI Corps 1st Division** GdD

Marchand: 6e RILé (2 bns); 39e, 69e and 76e RIdLi (3 bns each); 2 x FAB. **2nd Division** GdD Mermet: 25e RILé (2 bns); 27e and 59e RIdLi (3 bns each); 50e (2 bns). 2 x FAB. **3rd Division** GdD Loison: 28e and 82e RIdLi (4 bns each); 66e (3 bns); Légion du Midi and Légion Hanovrienne (2 bns each); 15e and 32e RILé (1 bn each); 2 x Prov bns; 2 x FAB. **Dragoon Division** GdD Montbrun: 3e, 6e, 10e, 11e DragRs - 20 sqns 2 x HAB. **Light Cavalry** GdD Lorges: GdB Lamotte: 3e HusR; 15e ChàCh GdB Gardanne: 15e and 25e DragR - 14 sqns. 2 x HAB.

French totals 40 bns, 34 sqns, 60 guns, ca 42,000 men.

French losses 180 killed, over 1,000 wounded.

Spanish Garrison MdC Don A de Herrasti commanding: IRs Avila, Segovia, 1st Majorca (1 bn each), Voluntarios de Ciudad Rodrigo (3 bns); Urban Guard (1 bn); artillery (375 men); sappers (60 men) Total 5,500 men, 118 guns.

Spanish losses 461 killed, 994 wounded, 4,000 captured.

Comment Ownership of this fortress brought with it control of the northern invasion route between Spain and Portugal.

Sources Oman, Napier.

PM Coa River, 24 July 1810, clash

A section of the River Coa just to the southwest of the fortress of Almeida which lies just west of the Spanish-Portuguese border, about 17 km north of (Portuguese) Route 16/E80, leading to the fortress of Ciudad Rodrigo in Spain.

An Anglo-Portuguese victory over the French.

(Last action - Ciudad Rodrigo, 9 July; next action - Almeida, 27 August.)

French Forces M Ney commanding the **VI Corps 1st Division** GdD Marchand: (Not engaged; in reserve). GdB Maucune: 6e RILé (2 bns); 69e RIdLi (3 bns), 1 x FAB. GdB Marcoguet: 39e and 76e RIdLi (3 bns each), 1 x FAB. **2nd Division** GdD Mermet; GdB Bardet: 25e RILé (2 bns); 27e RIdLi (3 bns) 1 x FAB. GdB Labassée: 50e and 59e RIdLi (3 bns each), 1 x FAB. **3rd Division** GdD Loison; GdB Simon: 26e RIdLi (3 bns); Légion Hanovrienne (2 bns); Légion du Midi (1 bn), 1 x FAB. GdB Ferey: 32e RILé (1 bn); 66e RIdLi (3 bns); 82e RIdLi (2 bns), 1 x FAB. **Cavalry** GdD Lorges; GdB Lamotte: 3e HusR; 15e ChàCh (8 sqns), 1 x HAB. GdB Gardanne: 15e and 25e DragRs (8 sqns), 1 x HAB.

French totals (excluding Marchand's 1st Division) 23 bns, 24 sqns, 6 batteries, (36 guns).

French losses: 7 officers killed and 17 wounded, 110 men killed and 397 wounded.

Anglo-Portuguese Forces BG R Craufurd commanding the Light Division:.

Col Beckwith's Brigade 1st/43rd (1 bn); 1st/95th (4 coys); 3rd Caçadores (1 bn). Barclay's Brigade: 1st/52nd (1 bn); 1st/95th (4 coys); 1st Caçadores (1 bn). Cavalry 16th LD; 1st Hus KGL, 1 x HAB.

Anglo-Portuguese totals 5 bns, 8 sqns, 6 guns.

Anglo-Portuguese losses 36 killed, 189 wounded, 83 missing.

Comment This was a successful rearguard action which nearly went wrong because Craufurd delayed his withdrawal too long.

Sources Oman, Napier, Fortescue, Martinien.

XX Taschlimechle, 2 August 1810, clash

A village in eastern Bulgaria 16 km north of the hill fortress of Schumen, Not shown on modern maps.

A Russian victory over the Turks.

(Last action - Schumla, 23/24 June; next action - Batin, 7 September.)

Turkish Forces Seraskier Kuschanz Ali commanding 30,000 men.

Turkish losses 3,000 killed, wounded and captured, 38 'colours'.

Russian Forces LG Count Sergei Kamenskoi commanding 19,000 men.

Russian losses 1,400 killed, wounded and missing.

Source Bodart.

ES Villagarcia, 11 August 1810, clash

A small town in the southwestern Spanish province of Extremadura, on Route 432, 85 km southeast of Badajoz and 90 km north of Seville.

A French victory over the Spanish.

(This was the first action in southern Spain in 1810; next action - Fuengirola, 13 October.)

French Forces GdD Girard's 1st Division of M Mortier's V Corps: 34e, 40e, 64e and 88e RIdLi (3 bns each) 2 x FAB. Light Cavalry GdD Marisy: 10e HusR; 21 ChàCh, 1 x HAB.

French totals 12 bns, 7,000 infantry, 8 sqns, 1,200 cavalry, 30 guns.

French losses About 200 killed and wounded.

Spanish Forces Conde de la Romana commanding:

Gen La Carrera's division and Gen Ballasteros' division. Exact composition not known.

Spanish totals ca 10,000 infantry, 1,000 cavalry, 18 guns.

Spanish losses About 600 killed, wounded and captured.

Sources Oman, Napier, Martinien.

PM Almeida, 25 July – 27 August 1810, siege and surrender of

A fortress in eastern central Portugal, on Route 332, about 35 km northwest of Ciudad Rodrigo and 35 km northeast of Guarda.

A French victory over the Portuguese.

(Last action – Coa River, 24 July; next action – Bussaco, 27 September.)

French Forces M Massena and M Ney commanding the VI Corps: 1st, 2nd and 3rd Divisions as at Ciudad Rodrigo except that the one battalion of Marchand's 1st Division was now the garrison of Ciudad Rodrigo. Light Cavalry GdD Lorges: GdB Lamotte: 3e HusR; 15e ChàCh. GdB Gardanne 15e and 25e DragR.

French totals 14,000 infantry, 1,000 cavalry, 1,000 gunners, 100 guns (50 of them siege artillery). Gd Junot's VIII Corps formed the Covering Force.

French losses 58 killed, 320 wounded.

Portuguese Garrison BG William Cox commanding: 24th LIR (2 bns); Arangil, Trancoso and Viseu Militia (1 bn each); 11th CavR (1 sqn); 400 gunners, 100 guns.

Portuguese totals ca 5,000 men and 100 guns.

Portuguese losses 600 killed, 300 wounded, 4,000 captured.

Comment The main ammunition magazine of the fortress was in the medieval castle in the centre of the town; on 26 August the French siege guns began their bombardment and a lucky shell exploded this magazine. The resultant explosion gutted the town and caused most of the casualties.

Sources Oman, Napier.

XX Batin, 7 September 1810, battle

A village in northern Bulgaria on the south bank of the River Danube, 30 km southwest of Ruse.

A Russian victory over the Turks.

(Last action – Taschlimechle, 2 August; next action – Rustchuk, 26 September.)

Turkish Forces Seraskier Kuschanz Ali commanding 25,000 infantry, 10,000 cavalry and 14 guns.

Turkish losses 5,000 killed and wounded, 5,000 captured, 14 guns, 178 colours and the entire Turkish Danube flotilla. Kuschanz Ali and Galim Pasha were killed.

Russian Forces GdI Count Nikolai Kamenskoi commanding 17,000 infantry, 5,000 cavalry and 100 guns.

Russian losses 2,000 killed and wounded GM Illowaiski killed.

Source Bodart.

EE Palamos, St Feliu, La Bisbal, 14 September 1810, clashes

Three villages in the northeastern Spanish province of Catalonia, southeast of Girona.

Palamos and St Felin are coastal ports, La Bisbal about 15 km southeast of Girona.

Allied victories over the Franco-Germans.

(Last action – Mequinenza, 5 June; next action – Tortosa, 2 January 1811.)

Franco-German Forces GdB Schwartz commanding the 5th Confederation of the Rhine (Anhalt-Lippe) and 6th Confederation of the Rhine (Schwarzburg-Reuss-Waldeck) 2 bns each ca 1,700 men, 18 guns of M Macdonald's VII Corps.

Franco-German losses 400 killed and wounded, 1,242 captured, 17 guns. GdB Schwartz also captured.

Allied Forces Spanish Capt Gen Henry O'Donnell with part of the Army of Catalonia including the Swiss IR Kayser, the DragR Numancia, Somatenes and Miqueletes, ca 6,600 men; supported by two Royal Naval frigates under Captain Fane of HMS *Cambrian.*

Allied losses Not known; light. O'Donnell was wounded and Gen Campo Verde took over command.

Comment This was a highly successful allied amphibious operation. Macdonald (in Barcelona) was so isolated that he did not hear of this disaster for over two weeks and the news reached him via France and Zaragoza.

Sources Oman, Napier, von Hagen, von Dalwigk.

IS Sicily, 17 September 1810, invasion of

An island in the central Mediterranean, separated from the toe of Italy by the Straits of Messina.

A British victory over the Neapolitans.

(This was the only action of note in this theatre this year.)

Neapolitan Forces GdD Cavaignac commanding IR 'Royal Corse' (2 bns) and 4th LIR 'Royal Abruzzes' (2 bns); 1st LtIR (1 bn), ca 3,000 men.

Neapolitan losses ca 1,200 men including 41 officers and 900 men of the Royal Corse (Murat's favourite regiment) who were cut off and surrendered and 200 captured of the other regiments; 1 colour.

British Forces Col Adam commanding 1st/21st Foot, 3rd Line bn KGL (1 bn each); 2 guns, ca 1,800 men.

British losses Three wounded.

Comment Now King of Naples, Murat mounted his attempted invasion against Napoleon's advice and received a sharp check. Not one Sicilian soldier took part in this action to defend their homeland. Napoleon was suitably enraged. The Royal Naval squadron now came up and took or destroyed 60 transports and 2 gunboats.

Sources Fortescue, Martinien.

XX Rustchuk (now Ruse), 20 July – 26 September 1810, siege and capture

A fortified town in northern Bulgaria on the south bank of the River Danube, near the confluence with Beli Lom at the junction of Routes 2/E70, 5/E85 and 21.

A Russian victory over the Turks.

(Last action – Batin, 7 September; this was the last action here in 1810.)

Turkish Garrison Bosniak Aga commanding 15,000 men.

Turkish losses 6,000 killed and wounded. The rest were allowed to go free.

Russian Forces GdI Count Nikolai Kamenskoi commanding 25,000 men.

Russian losses 3,000 killed including GM Sievers, 5,000 wounded.

Comment Most casualties were lost in a failed storm attempt on 3 August.

Source Bodart.

PM Bussaco, 27 September 1810, battle

A fortified convent and village in central Portugal, just south of Route 234 between Mealhada in the west and Sta Comba Dao in the east. The ridge on which the battle was fought runs south to the village of Penacova on the north bank of the River Mondego.

An Anglo-Portuguese victory over the French.

(Last action – Almeida, 27 August; This was the opening action of Massena's invasion of Portugal; next action – Pombal, 5 October.)

French Forces M Massena commanding:.

II Corps GdD Reynier: **1st Division** GdD Merle; GdB Sarrut: 2e RILé, 36e RIdLi (4 bns each). GdB Graindorge: 4e RILé (4 bns). **1st Division totals** 6,589 men. **2nd Division** GdD Heudelet; GdB Foy: 17e RILé (3 bns); 70e RIdLi (4 bns). GdB Arnauld: 31e RILé, 47e RIdLi (4 bns each), **2nd Division totals** 8,078 men. **Cavalry Brigade** GdB P Soult: 1er HusR; 8e DragR; 22e ChàCh, Ch Hanovrienne (4 sqns each). **Total Cavalry** 1,397 men. **Artillery, train, engineers:** 1,579 men. **I Corps totals** 27 bns, 17,718 infantry, 16 sqns, 1,397 men, 1,579 artillery.

VI Corps M Ney **1st Division** GdD Marchand; GdB Maucune: 6e RILé (2 bns); 69e RIdLi (3 bns). GdB Marcognet: 39e and 76e RIdLi (3 bns each). **2nd Division** GdD Mermet; GdB Bardet: 25e RILé (2 bns); 27e RIdLi (3 bns). GdB Labassée: 50e and 59e RIdLi (3 bns each). **3rd Division** GdD Loison; GdB Simon: 26e RIdLi (3 bns); Légion du Midi (1 bn); Légion Hanovrienne (2 bns). GdB Ferey: 32e RILé (1 bn); 66e RIdLi (3 bns); 82e RIdLi (2 bns). **Cavalry** GdB Lamotte: 3e HusR; 15e ChàCh (4 sqns each). **Artillery, engineers and train** 1,431 men. **VI Corps totals** 34 bns, 20,895 men, 8 sqns, 1,680 men; 1,431 artillery, etc.

VIII Corps GdD Junot (held in reserve; no casualties to speak of). **1st Division** GdD Clausel; GdB Ménard:19e, 25e, 28e and 34e RIdLi (the 4e bn of each). GdB Taupin: 15e RIdLi, 46e and 75e RIdLi (the 4e bn of each). GdB Godard: 22e RIdLi (4 bns). **2nd Division** GdD Solignac; GdB Gratien: 15e and 86e RIdLi (3 bns each). GdB Thomières: 65e RIdLi (4 bns); R Irlandais and R de Prusse (1 bn each). Cavalry GdD Ste Croix: 1er, 2e, 4e, 9e, 14e and 26e DragR (2 sqns each). Artillery, engineers train: 981 men. **VIII Corps** totals 23 bns, 14,020 infantry, 12 sqns, 1,763 cavalry, 981 artillery, etc.

The Reserve Cavalry GdD Montbrun. GdB Lorcet: 3e DragR (3 sqns); 6e DragR (4 sqns). GdB Cavrois: 11e DragR (4 sqns). GdB Ornano: 15e and 25e DragR (4 sqns each). Horse Artillery: 2 x HAB. **Reserve Cavalry totals** 19 sqns, 3,479 cavalry, 12 guns.

French totals It is likely that actual strength on the

day of the battle was 45,774 (including staff officers, gendarmerie, engineers, etc, but excluding Junot's VIII Corps.)

French losses (Killed, wounded and missing).

II Corps Merle's Division 1,041 GdB Graindorge killed. Heudelet's Division 978; Corps Troops 4, **Total** 2,023.

VI Corps Marchand's Division 1,173 Mermet's Division 24 (all in Bardet's brigade) Loison's Division 1,252 (GdB Simon captured). Corps Troops 7. **Total** 2,456.

Total French losses 4,479.

Anglo-Portuguese Forces Viscount Wellington commanding.

1st Division G Brent Spencer; **E Stopford's Brigade** 1st/Coldstream Gds; 1st/3rd Gds (1 bn each); 5th/60th (1 coy). **Total** 1,684 men. **Lord Blantyre's Brigade** 2nd/24th, 2nd/42nd, 1st/61st, (1 bn each); 5th/60th (1 coy). **Total** 1,516 men. **S von Löwe's Brigade (KGL)** 1st, 2nd, 5th and 7th Line bns (4 bns); Lt Bn (1 coy). **Total** 2,061 men. **E Pakenham's Brigade** 1st/7th, 1st/79th (1 bn each). **Total** 1,792 men.

2nd Division G Rowland Hill: **W Stewart's Brigade** 1st/3rd, 2nd/31st, 2nd/48th, 2nd/66th (1 bn each); 5th/60th (1 coy). **Total** 2,247 men. **W Ingles' Brigade** 1st/29th, 1st/48th, 1st/57th (1 bn each); 5th/60th (1 coy) **Total** 1,818 men. **C Craufurd's Brigade** 2nd/28th, 2nd/34th, 2nd/39th (1 bn each); 5th/60th (1 coy) **Total** 1,672 men.

MG John Hamilton's Portuguese Division (attached to the 2nd Division). **A Campbell's Brigade** 4th and 10th LIRs (2 bns each) **Total** 2,250 men. **Fonseca's Brigade** 2nd and 14th LIRs (2 bns each). **Total** 2,690 men.

3rd Division MG T Picton **BG H Mackinnon's Brigade** 1st/45th, 1st/74th, 1st/88th. **Total** 1,808 men. **S Lightburne's Brigade** 2nd/5th, 2nd/83rd (1 bn each); 5th/60th (3 coys) **Total** 1,160 men. **C Champlemond's Portuguese Brigade** 9th LIR (2 bns); 21st LIR (1 bn) **Total** 1,175 men.

4th Division MG L Cole **BG A Campbell's Brigade** 2nd/7th, 1st/11th, 2nd/53rd (1 bn each); 5th/60th (1 coy) **Total** 2,109 men. **J Kemmis' Brigade** 3rd/27th, 1st/40th, 1st/97th (1 bn each); 5th/60th (1 coy) **Total** 2,448 men. **Collin's Portuguese Brigade** 11th and 23rd LIR (2 bns each) **Total** 2,834 men.

5th Division MG J Leith **Barnes' Brigade** 3rd/1st, 1st/9th, 2nd/38th (1 bn each) **Total** 1,879 men **Spry's Portuguese Brigade** 3rd and 15th LIR (2 bns each); Tomar Militia bn (1 bn) **Total** 2,619 men. **Baron Eben's Portuguese Brigade** Loyal Lusitanian Legion (3 bns); 8th LIR (2 bns) **Total** 2,807 men.

The Light Division BG R Craufurd. **Col S Beckwith's Brigade** 1st/43rd, 3rd Caçadores (1 bn each); 1st/95th (4 coys) **Total** 1,896 men. **Col R Barclay's Brigade** 1st/52nd, 1st Caçadores (1 bn each); 1st/95th (4 coys) **Total** 1,891 men.

Independent Portuguese Brigades D Pack 1st and 16th LIR (2 bns each); 4th Caçadores (1 bn) **Total** 2,769 men. **A Campbell** 6th and 18th LIR (2 bns each); 6th Caçadores (1 bn) **Total** 3,249 men. **Colemann** 7th and 19th LIR (2 bns each); 2nd Caçadores (1 bn) **Total** 2,345 men. **Cavalry** 4th DragR (2 sqns).

Anglo-Portuguese totals 50 bns, 33,325 infantry, 2 sqns, 210 cavalry, 60 guns, 2,230 artillery, excluding the 2nd and 4th Divisions which were not engaged.

Anglo-Portuguese losses (killed, wounded and missing).

1st Division (Spencer) 141. **2nd Division** (Hill) not engaged; no losses. **3rd Division** (Picton) 473. **4th Division** (Cole) not engaged; no losses. **5th Division** (Leith) 191. **Light Division** (Craufurd) 177. **Pack's Portuguese** 138. **Coleman's Portuguese** 83. **A Campbell's** Portuguese 23. Artillery British 8, Portuguese 8, KGL 3, General Staff 6. **Grand Total** 1,252 of whom 626 Anglo-German and 626 Portuguese.

Comment This well-prepared trap gave the French a very bloody nose and stopped their third invasion of Portugal temporarily in its tracks. Wellington used all his cunning, well chosen defensive ground, concealment, surprise, husbanding of forces and economy of effort. The five French assaults all fell upon the northern third of the ridge and all were defeated in the classic 'column versus line' style. The Portuguese regiments fought very well. Allied skirmishers held their own easily against the French at almost all points. After a day's pause for thought, Massena abandoned the hope of breaking through this barrier and went off north to outflank it. He abandoned 400 badly wounded men on the battlefield; Wellington put them into Bussaco convent.

Sources Oman, Napier, Fortescue, Martinien.

PM Pombal, 5 October 1810, skirmish

A small town in central Portugal, at the junction of Routes 1 and 237, 44 km southwest of Coimbra.

A French victory over the British.

(Last action – Bussaco, 27 September; next action – Coimbra, 6 October.)

French Forces GdB Lamotte's Light Cavalry Brigade of Ney's VI Corps: 3e HusR; 15e ChàCh (3 sqns each) ca 1,580 men.

French losses: 8 killed, 17 wounded, 20 captured.

British Forces Anson's brigade: 16th LD; 1st HusR KGL. ca 902 men.

British losses 50 killed, wounded and captured.

Sources Oman, Napier, Martinien.

PM Coimbra, 6 October 1810, skirmish

A town in central Portugal, at the junction of Routes 17 and E3/E80/1, on the northern side of the Rio Mondego.

A Portuguese victory over the French.

(Last action – Pombal, 5 October; next action – Sobral, 14 October.)

French forces 44e Equipage de la Marine (156 men) and about 300 stragglers from various regiments guarding 400 British and Portuguese and 3,000 French wounded from the battle of Bussaco.

French losses 400 able-bodied soldiers, 3,507 French sick and wounded and some hundreds of hospital and commissariat staff (ca 4,500 in all) captured; 8 killed.

Portuguese Forces Col Trant commanding the Militia battalions Porto, Penafiel, Coimbra, Aviero, Maia and a battalion of combined light companies and 1 squadron of Dragoons.

Portuguese total ca 4,000 men.

Portuguese losses 3 killed, 26 wounded.

Comment Trant heard from locals that Massena had left Coimbra to chase Wellington southwards and struck at once.

Sources Oman, Napier, Martinien.

ES Fuengirola, 13 October 1810, clash

A small fortified port on the southeastern Spanish coast, on Route E15, about 30 km southwest of Malaga and 90 km northeast of Gibraltar.

A French victory over the Anglo-Spanish.

(Last action – Villagarcia, 11 August; next action – Baza, 4 November.)

French Forces GdD Sebastiani's 1st Division, IV Corps: 58e RIdLi (3 bns); 2 x FAB ca 3,000 men.

French Losses Not known; very light.

Anglo-Spanish Forces Gen Lord Blayney commanding 1st/82nd and 1st/89th Foot (1 bn each); Spanish IR Imperial de Toledo, ca 2,200 men and 6 guns.

Anglo-Spanish losses Lord Blayney and 200 British captured; 40 British killed. Spanish losses – very light.

Comment Blaney's original plan was to raid Fuengirola (with its garrison of 150 Poles) from Gibraltar by sea to lure the French out of Malaga (30 km to the northeast) so that another Allied amphibious force could seize Malaga in their absence. Unfortunately, Blayney got carried away, developed a serious assault on Fuengirola and was surprised by Sebastiani who rolled his brigade into the sea. Blayney, short-sighted and without his glasses, rode into the arms of the French.

Sources Oman, Napier.

PM Sobral, 14 October 1810, skirmish

A village in the hills of central Portugal, 13 km southeast of Torres Vedras and 16 km northwest of Vila Franca de Xira on the north bank of the Rio Tejo.

A British victory over the French.

(Last action – Coimbra, 6 October; next action – Pombal, 11 March 1811.)

French Forces 19e RIdLi (4e Bn); ca 600 men of Ménard's brigade, Clausel's division of Junot's VIII Corps.

French losses 120 men killed, wounded and captured.

British Forces 1st/71st Foot of Erskine's brigade, Spencer's 1st Division.

British losses 38 killed and wounded; other units in 1st Division lost 29 men between them.

Sources Oman, Napier, Martinien.

ES Baza, 4 November 1810, clash

A small town in Andalusia (southern Spain) on Route 342, north of the Sierra de Baza and about 80 km north of Almeria.

A French victory over the Spanish.

(Last action – Fuengirola, 13 October; next action – Barrosa (Chiclana), 5 March 1811.)

French Forces GdB Rey with 32e (1 bn) and 58e (3

bns) RIdLi of Sebastiani's 1st Division, IV Corps. 1 x FAB GdD Milhaud with 5e, 12e, 16e, 20e and 21e DragR and the Polish Lancers of the Vistula Legion; 2 x HAB.

French totals 1,300 cavalry.

French losses About 200 men killed and wounded, all in the cavalry; no infantry involved.

Spanish Forces Capt Gen Blake commanding the 1st and 2nd Division of the Centre; exact composition not known.

Spanish totals 8,000 infantry, 1,000 cavalry, 12 guns.

Spanish losses 500 killed and wounded; 1,000 captured; 12 guns and some colours.

Sources Oman, Napier, Martinien.

1811

1811 THE ACTIONS

EE Tortosa, 16 December 1810 – 2 January 1811, siege and capture

A fortified town on the north bank of the lower Rio Ebro in northeastern Spain, 14 km west of Motorway A7/E15 and 80 km southwest of the port of Tarragona.

A French victory over the Spanish.

(Last action – La Bisbal, 14 September 1810; next action – L'Illa, 15 January.)

French Forces GdD Suchet's **IV Corps** ('Army of Aragon'). GdD Musnier: 1er RILé, 114e & 121e RIdLi (3 bns each); 1st IR Vistula Legion (2 bns). GdD Frère: 14e & 42e RIdLi (3 bns each), 115e (4 bns); 2nd IR Vistula Legion (2 bns). GdD Harispe: 7e RIdLi (4 bns); 116e (3 bns); 44e RIdLi & 3rd IR Vistula Legion (2 bns each). GdD Habert: 5e RILé (2 bns); 16e & 117e RIdLi (3 bns each). GdD Peyri's Italian Division: 1st & 2nd LtIRs, 4th, 5th & 6th LIRs (2 bns each); ChàCh 'Royal'; 2nd DragR 'Napoleone' (2 sqns each). GdB Compère's Neapolitan Brigade*: 1st LtIR, 1st & 2nd LIRs (1 bn each); ChàCh (2 sqns). GdB Boussard's Cavalry: 13e CuirR, 4eHusR, 24e DragR.

French total 12,000 men.

French losses Not known exactly; estimated as about 400 killed and wounded.

* = from Macdonald's Army of Catalonia.

Spanish Garrison MdC Conde de Alacha commanding 7,179 men including 600 gunners and 1 bn Urban Guards; 182 guns.

Spanish losses 1,400 killed and wounded, 3,974 captured (the rest had deserted); 182 guns, 9 colours. Exact details of the regiments involved are not known.

Comment de Alacha was old and demoralized; the defence very weak. Suchet acted with such speed that no relief attempt could be made.

Sources Oman, Malibran and Chelminski, Gembarzewski.

EE L'Illa, 15 January 1811, clash

A village in the mountains of northeastern Spain, 8 km north of Valls on Route 240 and 40 km north of Tarragona.

A Spanish victory over the Italians.

(Last action – Tortosa, 2 January; next action – Figueras, 10 April.)

Italian Forces GdD Pino commanding*. 1st & 2nd LtIRs, 2nd, 4th, 5th LIRs (2 bns each); 8th LIR (1 bn). ChàCh Royal (30 men).

Italian total ca 6,000 men.

Italian losses ca 600 killed, wounded and captured; GdB Eugenio mortally wounded.

* = of Macdonald's Army of Catalonia.

Spanish Forces Gen Sarsfield with 3,000 infantry, 800 horse from Tarragona; exact details not known.

Spanish losses ca 160 killed and wounded.

Comment The two Italian brigades were defeated in detail.

Sources Oman, Gazalas.

PM Olivenza, 11–23 January 1811, siege and capture of

A fortress in the western Spanish province of Extremadura, 25 km southwest of Badajoz on Route 436, 15 km from the Portuguese border.

A French victory over the Spanish.

(Last action – Ciudad Rodrigo, 9 July 1810; next action – Rio Gebora, 19 February.)

French Forces M Soult commanding the Army of Andalusia. GdD Girard (of d'Erlon's V Corps): 34e, 40e & 63e RIdLi (2 bns each); 64e & 88e (3 bns each) 2 x FAB. ca 6,000 men, 12 guns (siege artillery arrived from 19–22 Jan).

French losses 15 killed, 40 wounded.

Spanish Garrison Gen Don Manuel Herck commanding: Voluntarios de Navarra, Mérida, Truxillo, Barbastro and Monforte (1 bn each), ca 4,361 men.

Spanish losses ca 200 killed and wounded; 4,161 captured, 18 guns.

Comment Olivenza had been stormed in 1801 and was still a neglected, unrepaired ruin which should never have been defended. The governor was an old man and just not up to the job, remaining passive throughout and making no effort to disrupt the siege or even to cut his way out.

Sources Oman, Bodart, Martinien.

XX Lovca, 11 February 1811, storm

A town in Bulgaria, 32 km south of Pleven.

A Russian victory over the Turks.

(This was the first action here this year; next action – Rustchuk, 4 July).

Russian Forces GM Count Saint-Priest with 6,000 infantry and 2,000 cavalry.

Russian losses 1,000 killed and wounded.

Turkish Garrison 10,000 men.

Turkish losses 4,000 killed and wounded, 1,400 captured.

Source Bodart.

PM Rio Gebora, 19 February 1811, battle

A tributary of the Rio Guadiana, joining it just northeast of Badajoz in Spain.

A French victory over the Spanish.

(Last action – Olivenza, 23 January; next action – Badajoz, 11 March).

French Forces M Mortier commanding the V Corps. **1st Division** GdD Girard: 34e, 88e, 100e RIdLi (3 bns each); 2 x FAB. Cavalry GdB Briche: 10e HusR, 21e ChàCh (3 sqns each); GdD Latour-Maubourg: 4e, 14e, 26e DragR, 2e HusR, 27e ChàCh, 4th Spanish Juramentados (13 sqns).

French total 4,500 infantry, 2,500 cavalry, 12 guns. Losses 403 killed and wounded, mostly in the cavalry.

Allied Forces LG Mendizabal's Army of Extremadura. **Vanguard Division** BG Carlos de España: IRs Principe (3 bns); 1st & 2nd Catalonia, Girona, Vitoria (1 bn each). **1st Division** MG Garcia: IRs Leon, del General, (3 bns each), La Union (2 bns), 1st of Barcelona, Voluntarios Catalanes, Osuna, Zafra, Valladolid and La Serena (1 bn each). **2nd Division** MG Virues: IRs Rey, Princesa, Toledo, Zamora and Hibernia (2 bns each); Lobera (3 bns); Tiradores de Castilla, Voluntarios de Navarra and 1st of Sevilla (1 bn each). **Cavalry** MG Butron: Carabineros Reales, Reina, Infanta, Borbon, Algarve, Sagunto, Lusitania, Hus de Extremadura, Perseguidores de Albuquerque. All regiments very weak, only 2,600 sabres in all. 4 x FAB (500 men). Attached Portuguese cavalry: BG Madden: 3rd, 5th & 8th Regiments (950 men).

Allied totals 12,480 infantry, 3,550 cavalry, 17 guns. Losses 850 killed and wounded, 4,000 captured, 17 guns, 6 colours.

Comment Mendizabal's conduct of this battle bordered on the criminal (not unusual for Spanish generals of this era) and his cavalry fled the field leaving the infantry line's flank exposed to be rolled up by the French cavalry. 2,000 men fled into Badajoz; 2,500 escaped to Portugal. This disgraceful and unnecessary defeat squandered the last available Spanish field army and sealed the fate of Badajoz.

Sources Oman, Martinien.

ES Barrosa (Chiclana), 5 March 1811, battle

A hill on the southwestern Spanish coast about 4 km south of Cadiz.

An Allied victory over the French.

(Last action – Baza, 4 November 1810; next action – Zujar, 9 August).

French Forces M Victor commanding the **I Corps** of M Soult's Army of the South. **1st Division** GdD Ruffin: 9e RILé (2e bn), 24e RIdLi (1er & 2e bns), 96e (1er bn); Combined grenadiers (2 bns). **2nd Division** GdD Laval: 81e RIdLi (1er & 2e bns); 45e (1er bn), 54e (1er & 2e bns); Combined grenadiers (1 bn). **3rd Division** GdD Villatte: 27e RILé, 94e & 95e RIdLi (5 bns). **Cavalry** 1er & 2e DragRs (3 sqns each); 4 x FAB.

French total ca 10,700 men, 24 guns.

French losses 244 killed, 1,684 wounded, 134 missing (plus Villatte's 377 killed & wounded skirmishing with Lardizabal), 5 guns, 1 eagle (1er Bn, 8e Ligne) 500 captured. GdD Ruffin and GdB Chaudron-Rousseau killed.

Allied Forces Sir Thomas Graham commanding: Dilke's Brigade: 2/1st Footguards (1 bn); 2/2nd Footguards (2 coys); 2/3rd Footguards (3 coys); 2/95th (2 coys). Wheatley's Brigade: 1/28th (8 coys); 2/67th, 2/87th (1 bn each). Browne's Flank Bn, 1/9th, 1/28th, 2/82nd (2 coys each). Barnard's Flank Bn, 3/95th (4 coys); 2/47th (2 coys); 20th Portuguese LIR (4 coys). **Gen Lardizabal's Spanish Division** IRs Campo Mayor, Carmona, Canarias (1 bn each); Murcia (2 bns). BG Whittingham: 2nd HusR KGL (2 sqns); artillery (362 men); sappers and staff (96 men).

Allied total 8,217 men (including 3,000 Spanish troops), 10 guns.

Allied losses 201 killed, 1,037 wounded British and Portuguese, 390 Spaniards of Lardizabal's division skirmishing with Villatte.

Comment This battle was yet another convincing demonstration of the steadiness of the British infantry and the superiority of their linear tactics over the French column. Spanish Gen La Peña (initially commander of the Allied troops) fled into

Cadiz at sight of the French. The eagle of the 8e Ligne was taken by the 87th Foot, now the Royal Irish Fusiliers.

Sources Oman, Martinien, Charrié.

PM Badajoz, 26 January – 11 March 1811, siege and capture

A fortified city in western Spain, on the left bank of the Rio Guadiana, at the junction of Routes V/E90, 432, 436 & 523, about 6 km from the Portuguese border and 25 km northeast of Olivenza.

A French victory over the Spanish.

(Last action – Rio Gebora, 19 February; next action – Pombal, 11 March).

French Forces M Soult commanding the Army of Andalusia.

V Corps M Mortier. **1st Division** GdD Girard: 40e & 64e RIdLi (2 bns each); 34e & 88e (3 bns), 2 x FAB. **2nd Division** GdD Gazan: 21e, 28e, 100e & 103e RIdLi (3 bns each), 2 x FAB. **Corps Cavalry** GdB Briche: 10e HusR, 21e ChàCh (3 sqns each), 1xHAB. Attached from IV Corps: 27e ChàCh (4 sqns); 4th Spanish Juramentados (2 sqns), 1 x HAB. Artillery and engineers – 698 men. Attached from I Corps: GdD Latour-Maubourg: 63e RIdLi (3 bns); 4e, 14e & 26e DragRs (4 sqns each); 2e HusR (3 sqns), 1 x FAB, 2 x HAB.

French total 24 bns, 13,000 infantry, 27 sqns, 3,900 cavalry, 54 guns.

French losses 1,900 killed & wounded.

Spanish Garrison Gen Rafael Menacho commanding. 2nd de Sevilla (2 bns); 2nd de Majorca (2 bns), 1st de Badajoz, Provincial de Truxillo, Provincial de Plasencia (1 bn each); dismounted cavalry (800 men), artillery – 1,024 men, sappers – 173 men.

Spanish total ca 4,340 men, 150 guns. After the failed Spanish relief attempt on 19 February (Rio Gabora), the following regiments joined the garrison: Valladolid, Osuna, Zafra & La Serena (2,000 men in all).

Spanish losses 1,851 killed & wounded, 7,880 captured plus 1,100 sick. The losses of Rio Gabora (850 killed & wounded & 4,000 captured) are included.

Comment Gen Menacho, the resolute and active Spanish commander, was unfortunately killed in action on 3 March and was replaced by the defeatist Gen José Imaz who was summoned to surrender on 9 March and obliged. Soult left as garrison M Mortier with 16 bns & 5 cavalry regiments [including 100e (3 bns) 28e Lé (1 bn) & 103e (3e Bn)] and hastened back to Sevilla on 14 March.

Sources Oman, Napier, Martinien.

PM Pombal, 11 March 1811, skirmish

A small town in central Portugal, on the eastern bank of the Rio Soure (a tributary of the Rio Mondego), at the junction of Routes 1 and 237, 36 km south of Coimbra.

A drawn match between the French and the Anglo-Portuguese.

(Last action – Badajoz, 11 March; next action – Redinha, 12 March).

French Forces M Ney's VI Corps' rearguard: GdB Maucune's brigade of GdD Marchand's 1st Division: 6e RILé, 69e RIdLi (4 bns) ca 900 men.

French losses 4 officers & 59 men killed, wounded & missing.

Anglo-Portuguese Forces LtCol Elder commanding. 3rd Caçadores (1 bn), 1/95th Foot (2 coys).

Anglo-Portuguese losses 11 killed, 26 wounded.

Comment Massena's Army of Portugal had starved in front of the Lines of Torres Vedras since 14 October 1810 and was finally forced to start to withdraw (northwards) on 8 March in two main columns. Wellington chose to follow Ney's column. Massena had destroyed most of his artillery prior to moving off because he had no draught animals to move it.

Sources Oman, Martinien.

PM Redinha, 12 March 1811, skirmish

A hamlet in central Portugal, on the Rio Ancos, 10 km north of Venda Nova (Venda Cruz in 1811) and between Route 1/E3/E80 and the new motorway A1.

A drawn match between the French and the Anglo-Portuguese.

(Last action – Pombal, 11 March; next action – Casal Novo, 14 March).

French Forces M Ney's **VI Corps** GdD Marchand's **1st Division** 6e RILé (1er & 2e bns); 69e RIdLi (1er, 2e & 3e bns); 39e & 76e RIdLi (3 bns each). GdD Mermet's **2nd Division** 25 RILé (1er & 2e bns); 27e, 50e & 59e RIdLi (3 bns each). GdB Lamotte: 3e HusR, 15 ChàCh (3 sqns each); 6 guns.

French total 8,500 infantry, 840 cavalry.

French losses 14 officers & 213 men killed &

wounded, mostly in Mermet's division.

Anglo-Portuguese Forces Viscount Wellington commanding. **Light Division** MG Craufurd: 1/43rd, 1/52nd & 1/95th Foot (1 bn each). **3rd Division** MG Picton: 2/5th, 1/45th, 5/60th, 2/83rd, 1/88th & 1/94th Foot (1 bn each). **4th Division** MG Cole: 2/27th, 1/40th, 1/97th Foot (1 bn each). BG **Pack's Portuguese** 1st, 3rd, 4th & 6th Caçadores (1 bn each). **Cavalry** 1st Royal DragR, 4th DragR, 1 x FAB.

Anglo-Portuguese total ca 16,000 men & 6 guns.

Anglo-Portuguese losses 12 officers & 193 men killed & wounded, mostly in the Light & 3rd Divisions.

Comment Ney conducted a skilful rearguard action and withdrew north to Condeixa, south of Coimbra.

Sources Oman, Martinien.

ZZ Lissa (nowadays Vis), 13 March 1811, naval clash

An Austrian island in Dalmatia, 50 km south of Split (Spalato).

A British victory over the French.

(This was the only naval action of note this year).

French Forces Captain Dubourdieu commanding: 6 frigates; *Flore, Danae, Favorite* & *Corona* (44 guns each) and *Bellona and Carolina* (32). Also the brig *Mercure*, two schooners, a xebec and a gunboat. 276 guns, 2,500 men.

French losses 600 killed & wounded, 800 captured; *Favorite* destroyed, *Corona* & *Bellona* taken. Captain Dubourdieu killed.

British Forces Captain W Hoste: Frigates *Amphion, Active, Cerberus* & *Volage*, 124 guns, 1,000 men.

British losses ca 200 killed & wounded.

Source Bodart.

PM Casal Novo, 14 March 1811, clash

A hamlet in the hills in central Portugal, about 3 km west of Villa Seca and 14 km south of Coimbra.

A French victory over the Anglo-Portuguese.

(Last action – Redinha, 12 March; next action – Foz do Arouce, 15 March).

French Forces GdD Marchand's 1st Division, M Ney's VI Corps: as for Redinha, ca 4,600 men & 6 guns.

French losses reported as 55 killed & wounded.

Anglo-Portuguese Forces MG Sir William Erskine's Light Division (vice Gen Craufurd): as for Redinha, ca 7,000 men & 6 guns.

Anglo-Portuguese losses British: 11 officers, 119 men killed & wounded. Portuguese: 25 men killed & wounded.

Comment The British advanced along a valley road in thick fog in close order. The fog cleared and they found themselves directly under the guns of the French who were deployed in line. Wellington was very displeased with these heavy casualties. Martinien's accounts of the French casualties are dubious and are attributed to 'Condeixa', 7 km northwest of this site where there was no combat.

Sources Oman, Martinien.

PM Foz do Arouce, 15 March 1811, skirmish

A hamlet in the hills of central Portugal, 10 km northeast of Miranda do Corvo, 8 km south of Coimbra and on the south bank of the Rio Ceira.

An Anglo-Portuguese victory over the French.

(Last action – Casal Novo, 14 March; next action – Albuquerque, 15 March).

French Forces M Ney's VI Corps as for Redinha on 12 March.

French total 7,000 men actually engaged.

French losses 250 killed wounded and captured, the eagle and the commanding officer of the 39e RIdLi captured.

Anglo-Portuguese Forces Viscount Wellington commanding. The Light Division (Sir William Erskine) and Gen Picton's 3rd Division as for Redinha on 12 March. The 1st Division, Gen Sir Brent Spencer: 2/24th, 2/42nd & 1/79th Foot (1 bn each; ca 1,850 men).

Anglo-Portuguese total 8,000 men, 12 guns.

Anglo-Portuguese losses 2 officers & 7 men killed, 2 officers & 60 men wounded (including 2 Portuguese).

Comment The 39e RIdLi was the last French unit south of the river; when charged by parts of Picton's 3rd Division they panicked and in the crush to get over the river lost their eagle which the Portuguese peasants recovered. After this combat Ney turned east into the mountains – exactly as Wellington wished him to do.

Sources Oman, Martinien, Charrié.

PM Albuquerque, 15 March 1811, capture

A small, fortified town in western Spain, on Route 530 about 44 km north of Badajoz and 10 km from the border with Portugal.

A French victory over the Spanish.

(Last action – Foz do Arouce, 15 March; next action – Campo Major, 21 March).

French Forces GdD Latour-Maubourg of Soult's Army of the South: 2 dragoon regiments (which is not clear; he commanded the 1er, 2e, 4e, 9e & 26e Regiments.

French losses Nil.

Spanish Garrison MG José Cagigal commanding. IR Fernando VII (2 bns) ca 800 men, 17 guns.

Spanish losses All captured.

Comment No real defence was attempted; Cagigal surrendered when summoned.

Source Oman.

PM Campo Mayor, 15 – 21 March 1811, siege and capture

A small, fortified town in eastern Portugal, at the junction of Routes 371 & 373 and about 18 km northwest of Badajoz in Spain.

A French victory over the Portuguese.

(Last action – Albuquerque, 15 March; next action – Campo Mayor, 25 March).

French Forces M Mortier with GdD Gazan's 2nd Division, V Corps: 28e, 100e & 103e RIdLi (3 bns each). Gen Latour-Maubourg's cavalry: 26e DragR, 2e & 10e HusRs.

French total 4,500 men.

French losses Not known but light.

Portuguese Garrison Maj José Talaya commanding. Portalegre Militia bn (300 men), artillery (1 coy); Ordenança (300 men).

Portuguese total 800 men.

Portuguese losses 100 captured, 50 guns (mostly old and worn out).

Comment Talaya, an old officer of engineers, put up an excellent defence within this run-down medieval fort.

PM Campo Mayor, 25 March 1811, skirmish

A small, fortified town in eastern Portugal, at the junction of Routes 371 & 373 and about 18 km northwest of Badajoz in Spain.

An Anglo-Portuguese victory over the French.

(Last action – Campo Mayor, 21 March; next action – Sabugal, 3 April).

French Forces Gen Latour-Maubourg commanding. 100e RIdLi (3 bns); 26e DragR, 2e & 10e HusRs (2 sqns each); ½ x HAB.

French total ca 2,400 men.

French losses 200 in all including 108 in the 26e Drag.

Anglo-Portuguese Forces BG Long commanding*. 13th LDR; Portuguese 1st & 7th CavRs.

Anglo-Portuguese total 7½ sqns, 1 x FAB (KGL). ca 700 men.

Anglo-Portuguese losses British: (All in 13th LDR) 10 killed, 27 wounded, 22 captured. 1st & 7th Portuguese CavRs: 14 killed, 40 wounded, 55 prisoners.

Comment Gen Long's 13th LDR charged and overthrew the 26e DragR and then embarked on a wild chase of over 11 km after their beaten enemy almost to Badajoz, cutting down the drivers of a convoy of siege guns being taken from Campo Mayor into that fortress. Instead of securing these valuable prizes, the British (followed by 2 sqns 7th Portuguese) careered on after the 26e. The French came out of Badajoz in force and recovered all the guns except 1. No wonder Wellington complained that the ordinary British cavalry regiment was 'good for nothing but galloping'. Beresford recovered the fortress of Campo Mayor intact.

Sources Oman, Martinien.

* Part of M Beresford's force of 2nd & 4th Divisions and Hamilton's Portuguese.

PM Sabugal, 3 April 1811, clash

A small, walled town in central Portugal, on the eastern bank of the Rio Coa, on Route 233, 39 km southeast of Guarda and 35 km from the Spanish border by Ciudad Rodrigo.

An Anglo-Portuguese victory over the French.

(Last action – Campo Mayor, 25 March; next action – Fuentes de Oñoro, 5 May).

French Forces GdD Merle's 1st Division of Reynier's II Corps: 2e & 4e RILé, 36e RIdLi (3 weak bns each). GdD Heudelet's 2nd Division: 17e RILé (4 bns), 70e RIdLi (3 bns), 31e & 47e RIdLi (4 bns each); 1e HusR, 22e ChàCh, Chasseurs Hanovriens (1 sqn each), 6 guns.

French total 12,000 men.

French losses 72 killed, 502 wounded, 186 captured, 1 howitzer.

Anglo-Portuguese Forces The Light Division MG Erskine* commanding. BG Beckwith: 1/43rd (1 bn); 1/95th (4 coys); 3rd Caçadores (½ bn). BG Drummond: 1 & 2/52nd (2 bns); 2/95th (4 coys); 3rd Caçadores (½ bn). **MG Picton's 3rd Division** 2/5th, 1/45th (1 bn each); 5/60th 2/83rd, 1 & 2/88th 1/94th (1 bn each). 16LD, 1st HusR KGL (1 sqn each). 1 x HAB.

Anglo-Portuguese total ca 8,000 men. 6 guns.

Anglo-Portuguese losses 17 killed, 139 wounded, 6 missing (Bodart's casualty figures for both sides are wildly exaggerated).

Comment*: Erskine was well out of the firing line; the only orders he gave were tactically wrong. 90% of the fighting was done by 1/43rd who opposed almost the entire French corps, took half the total British casualties and captured a howitzer. Wellington said that this clash 'was one of the most glorious that British troops were ever engaged in'. The 3rd Division was only engaged for a few minutes and lost only 3 killed, 31 wounded and 2 missing.

Sources Oman, Martinien, Bodart.

EE Figueras, 10 April 1811, capture

A fortress in northern Catalonia (Spain) on Route 11 and just east of the Motorway A7/E15, 120 km northeast of Barcelona.

A Spanish victory over the Italians.

(Last action – L'Illa, 15 January; next action – Figueras, 3 May).

Italian Garrison BG Guillot commanding: 1 Italian march battalion ca 900 men.

Italian losses 35 killed & wounded, hundreds of guns, 16,000 muskets, large stocks of shoes & clothing, rations for 2,000 men for 4 months & 400,000 francs.

Spanish Forces Miquelete Chief Rovira and 2,000 men.

Spanish losses ca 25 killed & wounded.

Comment The governor was lax and Spanish patriots, posing as French collaborators, made copies of the keys to a postern gate. BG Martinez and a Spanish garrison of 3,000 men was quickly sent in. This bold stroke caused much consternation in French quarters and an enraged Napoleon ordered the concentration of 14,000 men to retake the place.

Source Oman.

EE Figueras, 3 May 1811, clash

A fortress in Catalonia (northeastern Spain) on Route 11 and just east of the Motorway A7/E15, 120 km northeast of Barcelona.

A French victory over the Spanish.

(Last action – Figueras, 10 April; next action – Tarragona, 29 June).

French Forces GdD Baraguay d'Hilliers commanding part of VII Corps (Army of Catalonia). GdD Quesnel 23e RILé (2 bns), 79e RIdLi (3 bns); 93e (1 bn); 29e ChàCh (3 sqns). GdD Plauzonne 3e RILé (4 bns), 11e RIdLi (3 bns); 67e RIdLi (4 bns) 79e RIdLi (3 bns), 16e RILé (1 bn).

French total ca 20,000 men.

French losses ca 400 killed & wounded.

Spanish Forces Gen Campoverde commanding: Sarsfield's division: IRs Santa Fé, Hibernia, Zaragoza, Girona, 1st & 2nd of Savoia, Grenadiers, Cazadores de Valencia and some other troops plus Rovira's Miqueletes.

Spanish total 6,000 infantry, 800 horse, ca 2,000 Miqueletes and Gen Baron Erole's with his division of 2,000 men. Losses over 1,000 killed, wounded & captured.

Comment This tardy and languid Spanish attempt to relieve the Spanish-held key fortress deservedly failed but at least Sarsfield managed to throw some gunners into the place to man the abundant artillery.

Sources Oman, Martinien.

PM Fuentes de Oñoro, 3 – 5 May 1811, battle

A village in western Spain, in the valley of the Rio de Dos Casas, 27 km west of the fortress of Ciudad Rodrigo on Route 620/E80 and about 2 km from the Portuguese border.

An Anglo-Portuguese victory over the French.

(Last action – Sabugal, 3 April; next action – Badajoz, 12 May).

French Forces.

M Massena commanding the Army of Portugal

II Corps Reynier: **GdD Merle's Division** 2e & 4e RILé, 36e RIdLi (3 bns each). **GdD Heudelet's Division** 17e & 31e RILé, 47e & 70e RIdLi (3 bns each). **Cavalry** 1er HusR (1 sqn); 22e ChàCh (3 sqns); 8e DragR (2 sqns).

VI Corps Loison. **GdD Marchand's Division** 6e RILé, 39e, 69e & 76e RIdLi (1er, 2e & 4e bns each). **GdD Mermet's Division** 25e RILé, 27e, 50e & 59e RIdLi (1er, 2e & 4e bns each). **GdD Ferey's Division** 26e, 66e & 82e RIdLi (4e, 5e & 6e bns each); Légion du Midi & Légion Hanovrienne (1 bn each). **GdB**

Lamotte's Light Cavalry 3e HusR, 15e ChàCh (1 sqn each).

VIII Corps M Junot: **GdD Solignac's Division** 15e, 65e & 86e RIdLi (3 bns each); R Irlandais (1 bn).

IX Corps GdD Drouet: **GdD Claparède's Division** 21e & 28e RILé, 40e, 54e, 63e, 64e, 88e, 100e & 103e RIdLi (1 bn each). **GdD Conroux's Division** 9e & 16e RILé, 8e, 24e, 27e, 45e, 94e, 95e & 96e RIdLi (1 bn each). **GdB Fournier's Cavalry** 7e, 13e & 20e ChàCh (2 sqns each). **GdD Montbrun's Reserve Cavalry** GdB Cavrois: 3e, 10e & 15e DragRs (4 sqns). GdB Ornano: 6e, 11e & 25e DragRs (6 sqns). Artillery: 5 x FAB. 1 bn Engineers, 1 bn Train. **Total Army of Portugal** 1,795 officers, 44,919 men, 30 guns.

M Bessières' Army of the North Gen Lepic's Brigade, Cavalry of the Imperial Guard: Lancers (3 sqns); ChàCh (2 sqns), Mamelukes (1 sqn); GrenàCh (2 sqns). GdB Wathier's Light Cavalry: 11e, 12e & 24e ChàCh, 5e HusR (6 sqns). 1 x HAB. **Total Army of the North** 102 officers, 1,636 men.

French grand total 1,897 officers, 46,555 men, 36 guns.

Brigade: 5th, 83rd & 88th Foot (2nd bns each); 1/94th (1 bn). Power's Portuguese Brigade: 9th & 21st LIR (2 bns each). **3rd Division total** 204 officers, 5,276 men. **5th Division** MG Sir W Erskine: Hay's Brigade: 3/1st, 1/9th & 2/38th Foot (1 bn each), Brunswick Oels (1 coy). Dunlop's Brigade: 1/4th, 2/30th, 3/44th Foot (1 bn each); Brunswick Oels (1 coy); Spry's Portuguese Brigade: 3rd & 15th LIR (2 bns each); 8th Caçadores (1 bn). **5th Division total** 178 officers, 4,980 men. **6th Division** MG A Campbell: Hulse's Brigade: 1/11th, 2/53rd, 1/61st Foot (1 bn each); 5/60th (1 coy). Burne's Brigade: 1/36th Foot (1 bn). Madden's Portuguese Brigade: 8th & 12th LIR (2 bns each). **6th Division total** 135 officers, 4,557 men. **7th Division** MG Houson: Sontag's Brigade: 2/51st & 1/85th Foot, Chasseurs Britanniques (1 bn each); Brunswick Oels (8 coys). Doyle's Portuguese Brigade: 7th & 19th LIR (2 bns each), 2 Caçadores (1 bn). **7th Division total** 124 officers, 4,466 men. **Light Division** MG R Craufurd: Beckwith's Brigade 1/43rd (1 bn); 1/95th (4 coys); 2/95th (1 coy). Drummond's Brigade 1/52nd, 2/52nd (1 bn each), 4/95th (4 coys). Portuguese: 1st & 3rd Caçadores (1 bn each). **Light Division total** 122 officers, 3,693 men. **Ashworth's Independent Portuguese Brigade** 6th & 18th LIR (2 bns each): 6th Caçadores (1 bn), **total** 2,539 all ranks. **Cavalry** Slade's Brigade: 1st DragR, 14th LDR (3 sqns each); Arentschildt's Brigade: 16th LDR, 1st HusR KGL (3 sqns each). Portuguese Brigade: 4th & 10th CavRs (1 & 2 sqns respectively). **Total Cavalry** 109 officers*, 1,745 men. Artillery: 2 x HAB, 6 x FAB. 987 all ranks. Engineers - 40 men; Train - 226 men.

Allied grand total 36,946 all ranks.

French losses VI Corps on 3 May (Ferey's & Marchand's Divisions):

	Killed		Wounded		Missing		Total
	officers	men	officers	men	officers	men	
5 May	7	69	17	392	3	164	652
II Corps (all in 31e Lé)	—	3	3	46	—	—	52
VI Corps (all divisions)	12	95	47	757	—	33	944
VII Corps	—	2	—	—	—	—	
IX Corps (both divisions)	15	103	48	669	—	—	835
Montbrun's cavalry	1	36	25	283	1	13	359
French Total Losses	35	308	140	2,147	4	210	2,844

Anglo-Portuguese Forces Viscount Wellington commanding. **1st Division** LG Sir Brent Spencer: Stopford's Brigade: 2nd & 3rd Footguards (1st bns each); 5/60th (1 coy). Nightingale's Brigade: 2/24th, 2/42nd, 1/79th, 5/60th (1 coy). Howard's Brigade: 50th, 71st & 92nd Foot (1st bns each), 3/95th (1 coy). Löwe's Brigade: 1st, 2nd, 5th & 7th Line bns KGL (1 bn each); light coys (2 coys). **1st Division total** 388 officers, 7,177 men. **3rd Division** MG T Picton: Mackinnon's Brigade: 1/45th, 1/74th, 2/88th (1 bn each); 5/60th (3 coys); Colville's

Allied losses 3 May

	killed		wounded		missing		Total
	officers	men	officers	men	officers	men	
1st Division							
Nightingale's Brigade	1	5	3	26	—	1	36
Howard's Brigade	1	7	9	54	—	6	77
Löwe's Brigade	—	3	—	23	—	—	26
1st Division Total	*2*	*15*	*12*	*103*	—	*7*	*139*
3rd Division							
Mackinnon's Brigade	—	4	2	23	—	10	39
Colville's Brigade	—	—	—	22	—	3	25
3rd Division Total	—	*4*	*2*	*45*	—	*13*	*64*
Cavalry							
Slade	—	1	—	1	—	1	3
Arentschildt	—	—	1	4	—	—	5
Cavalry Total	—	*1*	*1*	*5*	—	*1*	*8*
Total British	2	20	15	153	—	21	211
Portuguese (nearly all in 6th Caçadores)	—	14	6	27	—	1	48
Total Allied Loss 3 May	***2***	***34***	***21***	***180***	—	***22***	***259***

Allied Losses 5 May

	killed		wounded		missing		Total
	officers	men	officers	men	officers	men	
1st Division							
Stopford's Brigade	1	9	3	101	2	19	135
Nightingale's Brigade	1	36	9	189	1	98	334
Howard's Brigade	3	19	5	107	2	39	175
Löwe's Brigade	—	3	3	29	—	10	45
1st Division Total	*5*	*67*	*20*	*426*	*5*	*166*	*689*
3rd Division							
Mackinnon's Brigade	2	6	5	115	1	1	130
Colville's Brigade	1	5	2	35	—	—	43
3rd Division Total	*3*	*11*	*7*	*150*	*1*	*1*	*173*
5th Division							
Hay's Brigade	—	—	—	13	—	—	13
Dunlop's Brigade	—	—	—	8	—	—	8
5th Division Total	—	—	—	*21*	—	—	*21*

The 6th Division suffered no losses.

	killed		wounded		missing		Total
7th Division							
Sontag's Brigade	1	43	8	64	—	61	177

	killed		wounded		missing		Total
	officers	men	officers	men	officers	men	
7th Division Total	*1*	*43*	*8*	*64*	—	*61*	*177*
Light Division							
Beckwith's Brigade	—	—	—	16	—	—	16
Drummond's Brigade	—	3	—	24	—	—	27
Light Division Total	—	*3*	—	*40*	—	—	*43*
Cavalry							
Slade's Brigade	—	7	6	63	—	3	79
Arentschildt's Brigade	—	9	4	55	1	1	70
Cavalry Total	—	*16*	*10*	*118*	*1*	*4*	*149*
Artillery & General Staff	—	6	5	19	—	—	30
British Total	***9***	***146***	***50***	***838***	***7***	***232***	***1,282***
Portuguese (mainly in 6th & 21st Line, 2e & 3rd Caçadores)	—	50	7	151	—	51	259
Total Allied Loss 5 May	***9***	***196***	***57***	***989***	***7***	***283***	***1,541***
Total Allied Loss on both days	***11***	***230***	***78***	***1,169***	***7***	***305***	***1,800***

Comment Massena's starving Army of Portugal had left that country on 8 April and Wellington had judged its condition to be so bad that it would not trouble him again until the autumn. Massena had to make one more effort to save his reputation however, and his men were remarkably resilient. By energetic reorganization he soon cobbled together a new strike force, sweeping together all formations and units he could command or borrow. In a few weeks he took the offensive again albeit very weak in cavalry and artillery due to lack of horses. His immediate target was the relief of Almeida. Wellington was prepared and had selected the ground on which to fight. The French thrust on 3 May was decisively stopped; on 4 May they looked for ways around the obstacle, found one and Massena tried to turn Wellington's southern (right) flank on 5 May via the village of Pozo Bello. All the exertions of his men were in vain however; Massena acknowledged defeat and withdrew. On 12 May Marmont replaced him, by command of Napoleon signed on 20 April.

The garrison of Almeida (1 bn 82e RIdLi and a provisional bn, total 1,300 men) under GdB Brennier escaped on 10 May late at night and reached Ciudad Rodrigo safely, largely due to General Erskine's neglect of Wellington's instructions. Brennier had mined Almeida and it was destroyed.

Sources Oman, Martinien.

PM Badajoz, 22 April – 12 May 1811, 1st failed blockade and siege

A fortified city in western Spain, on the left bank of the Rio Guadiana, at the junction of Routes V/E90, 432, 436 and 523 about 6 km from the Portuguese border and 25 km northeast of Olivenza.

A French victory over the Anglo-Portuguese.

(Last action – Fuentes de Oñoro, 5 May; next action – Albuera, 16 May).

French Garrison GdB Phillipon commanding 1e/34e, 3e/40e, 1er/88e, 3e/100e RIdLi & 1er/12e RILé.

French total ca 4,000 men.

French losses Not known but light.

Anglo-Portuguese Forces M Beresford commanding. **MG William Stewart's 2nd Division**: 1/3rd, 2/31st, 2/48th, 2/66th, 1/29th, 1/48th, 1/57th, 2/28th, 2/34th & 2/39th Foot (1 bn each); 5/60th (3 coys). **4th Division** MG L Cole: 1/7th, 2/7th, 1/23rd. Kemmis' Bde detachments of 2/27th, 1/40th, 1/97th Foot. Alten's Independent Bde: 1st & 2nd Lt Bns KGL. MG Lumley's cavalry: 3rdDG, 4DragR, 13th LDR. 4 x FAB. **Portuguese Division** 11th & 23rd IRs (2 bns each); Loyal Lusitanian Legion (1 bn). **Hamilton's Division** 2nd, 4th, 10th & 14th LIR (2 bns each). Collins' Bde: 5th LIR (2 bns); 5th Caçadores (1 bn). Otway's cavalry: 1st, 5th, 7th & 8th CavRs. 2 x FAB.

Anglo-Portuguese totals British: ca 10,500 men. Portuguese ca 10,200 men.

Anglo-Portuguese losses British: 533 (all but 7 in Kemmis' Bde, 4th Division); Portuguese: 200.

Comment Beresford had to lift the siege at the approach of M Soult's Army of the South from Sevilla.

Sources Oman, Martinien.

PM Albuera, 16 May 1811, battle

A village in southwestern Spain, 24 km southwest of Badajoz on Route 432.

An Allied victory over the French.

(Last action - Badajoz, 12 May; next action - Usagre, 25 May).

French Forces M Soult's Army of the South:.

V Corps GdD Girard's **1st Division** 34e, 40e & 88e RIdLi (2 bns each); 64e (3 bns). GdD Gazan's **2nd Division** 21e RILé & 100e RIdLi (2 bns each); 28e RILé & 103e RIdLi (3 bns each). GdB Werle's Brigade: 12e RILé, 55e & 58e RIdLi (3 bns each); GdB Godinot's Brigade: 16e RILé & 51e RIdLi (3 bns each). Combined grenadiers of 45e, 63e, 95e RIdLi (of I Corps) & 4th Polish IR (of IV Corps) - 11 coys. GdD Latour-Maubourg's **Cavalry** GdB Briche's Brigade: 2e & 10e HusR & 21e ChàCh (2 sqns each). GdB Bon's Brigade: 4e, 20e & 26e DragRs (3 sqns each); GdB Bouvier des Éclat's Brigade: 14e, 17e & 27e DragRs (3 sqns each). Unattached cavalry: 27e ChàCh (4 sqns), 4th Spanish ChàCh (2 sqns); 1st Lancers, Vistula Legion (4 sqns). Artillery 1,200 men.

Total V Corps ca 19,000 infantry, 4,000 cavalry, 40 guns.

French losses Godinot's Brigade - 384, combined grenadiers - 372. Cavalry - 496, Artillery & Train V Corps 95 (no other data available); general staff 13. Total Loss 5,936 men,* GdBs Werle & Pepin killed.

* patently too low. French historians agree that 7,000 is much more likely.

Anglo-Portuguese Forces M Beresford commanding. British Troops: **2nd Division** MG W Stewart; Colborne's Brigade: 1/3rd, 2/31st, 2/48th, 2/66th Foot (1 bn each). Hoghton's Brigade: 1/29th, 1/48th, 1/57th Foot (1 bn each). Abercrombie's Brigade: 2/28th, 2/34th, 2/39th Foot (1 bn each). Divisional light troops: 5/60th (3 coys). **2nd Division total** 288 officers, 5,172 men. **4th Division** MG L Cole; Myers' Brigade: 1/7th, 2/7th, 1/23rd Fusiliers (1 bn each). Kemmis' Brigade: 2/27th, 1/40th, 1/97th Foot (1 coy each). **4th Division total** 104 officers, 2,076 men. **Alten's Independent Brigade** 1st & 2nd Lt Bns KGL (1 bn each), **total** 42 officers, 1,056 men. **Cavalry** MG Lumley BG de Grey's Brigade: 3DG, 4 DragR, 13th LDR. **Total Cavalry** 76 officers, 1,088 men. Artillery: 2 x British & 2 x KGL FABs. **Grand Total British Troops** 529 officers, 9,920 men. **Portuguese Troops** Harvey's Brigade (attached to 4th Division): 11th & 23rd LIRs (2 bns each); Loyal Lusitanian Legion (1st bn). MG Hamilton's Division: 2nd, 14th, 4th & 10th LIRs (2 bns each). Collins' Brigade: 5th LIR (2 bns); 5th Caçadores (1 bn). Cavalry (Otway's): 1st & 7th CavRs (4 sqns each), 5th & 8th CavRs (1 sqn each). 2 x FAB. **Total Portuguese** 10,201 officers & men. **Spanish Troops** Capt Gen Blake commanding: **Vanguard Division** (Lardizabal): IRs Murcia (2 bns); Canarias, 2nd of Leon & Campo Mayor (1 bn each), **total** 107 officers, 2,291 men. **3rd Division** (Ballasteros). IRs 1st of Catalonia, Barbastro, Pravia, Lena, Castropol, Cangas de Tineo, Infiesto (1 bn each), **total** 154 officers, 3,371 men. **4th Division** (Zaya): Spanish Guards (2nd & 4th bns),Walloon Guards (4th bn), IRs Irlanda, Patria, Toledo, Legion Estranjera, Ciudad Real, **totals** 197 officers, 4,685 men. **Cavalry** (Loy): CavRs Santiago, Granaderos, Escuadron de Instruction; HusR de Castilla, **total** 93 officers, 1,072 men. Artillery: 1 x FAB. **Total Blake's Troops** 558 officers, 11,515 men. **Castaños' Army Infantry** (Carlos de Espana): IRs Rey, Zamora, Voluntarios de Navarra (1 bn each); sappers (1 coy), **total** 57 officers, 1,721 men. **Cavalry** (Penne Villemur): 1 composite regiment (7 sqns, 87 officers, 634 men). Artillery: 1 x FAB. **Total Castaños' Troops** 148 officers, 2,413 men. **Grand Total Spanish Troops** 706 officers, 13,928 men.

Allied Grand Totals 35,284 men.

Allied Losses

	killed		wounded		missing		Total
	officers	men	officers	men	officers	men	
British Troops							
2nd Division	25	636	104	1,605	11	484	2,865
4th Division	5	191	39	824	—	6	1,065
Alten's Brigade	1	7	5	90	—	3	106
Cavalry	1	12	2	28	2	3	48
Artillery & Staff	1	3	9	27	1	31	72
British Total	33	849	159	2,574	14	527	4,156
Portuguese Troops							
Harvey's Brigade	1	71	9	97	—	15	193*
Hamilton's Division	—	12	1	68	—	10	91
Collins' Brigade	—	15	4	61	—	11	91
Otways' Cavalry	—	—	—	2	—	—	2
Artillery & Staff	1	2	1	8	—	—	12
Portuguese Total	*2*	*100*	*15*	*236*	—	*36*	*389*
Spanish Troops							
Blake's Army							
Vanguard Division	4	59	13	215	?	?	291
3rd Division	3	64	15	193	?	?	275
4th Division	—	106	26	549	?	?	681**
Cavalry	—	7	2	31	?	?	40
Artillery & Staff	2	?	9	?	?	?	11
Total Blake's Army	*9*	*236*	*65*	*988*	*?*	*?*	*1,298*
Castaños' Army							
Infantry	—	—	4	29	?	?	33
Cavalry	—	11	3	14	?	?	28
*Total Castaños' Army****	—	*11*	*7*	*43*	*?*	*?*	*61*
Spanish Grand Total	***9***	***247***	***72***	***1,031***	***?***	***?***	***1,359***
Allied Grand Total	***44***	***1,196***	***246***	***3,841***	***14***	***563***	***5,904***

*: of these 203, 171 were in the Loyal Lusitanian Legion
**: of these 681 no less than 98 killed & 517 wounded were in the Spanish Guards & IR Irlanda which fought for so long against Girard's division
***: the artillery & staff suffered no losses
The French took 1 howitzer and the following five colours: 3rd Foot—1, 48th and 66th Foot — 2 each.

Comment There are, as usual, mysteries concerning the casualties reported by the French. Soult reported 262 officer losses, Martinien recorded 362!.

Soult had advanced from Sevilla to help his comrades besieged in Badajoz and had succeeded in forcing Beresford to raise the siege and to give battle. Once again, it was a case of French column versus British line at the close of the battle and the V (French) Corps suffered terribly as it was enveloped and hammered by the British from three sides. Apart from Harvey's Portuguese Brigade of the 4th Division, all Spanish and Portuguese troops were in the second line at this point. At one point, when Colborne's Brigade was about to destroy Girard's Division with well aimed volleys in flank at close range (the British were deployed in their usual 2-deep line and their right flank was open) Latour-Maubourg seized his chance and sent in the 2e Hussars and the 1st Lancers of the Vistula Legion who practically wiped out the British brigade. Blame for this disaster seems to lie with MG Stewart who ordered the formation and the advance. Zaya's 4th Spanish Division fought extremely well as did Harvey's Portuguese.

Soult's infantry was very badly shaken; he withdrew unmolested, at dawn on 18 May; his superior cavalry kept the Allies at bay. The British lost five colours here (Colborne's Brigade). This was the bloodiest battle of the Peninsular campaign.

Sources Oman, Martinien.

PM Usagre, 25 May 1811, clash

A village in western Spain, just to the north of Route 432 between Zafra and Llerena and 104 km south-east of Badajoz.

An Allied victory over the French.

(Last action – Albuera, 16 May; next action – Badajoz, 10 June).

French Forces GdD Latour-Maubourg of Soult's Army of the South's rearguard commanding. GdB Bron: 4e, 20e, 26e DragRs (2 sqns each) 1 x HAB.

French total ca 920 men.

French losses 250 killed & wounded, 6 officers & 72 men captured.

Allied Forces BG Lumley commanding 3rd DG, 4th DragR, 13th LDRs, (ca 1,000 men); 1 x HAB.

Allied total 1,100 men.

Allied losses ca 20 killed & wounded.

Comment Lumley sprang a trap as the French crossed the bridge over a deep stream. After allowing the 4e & 20e to cross, he charged from behind the crest of a hill and practically destroyed both regiments.

Sources Oman, Martinien.

PM Badajoz, 18 May – 10 June 1811, 2nd failed siege

A fortified city in western Spain, on the left bank of the Rio Guadiana, at the junction of Routes V/E90, 432, 436 & 523, about 6 km from the Portuguese border and 25 km north of Olivenza.

A French victory over the Anglo-Portuguese.

(Last action – Usagre, 25 May; next action – Elvas, 22 June).

French Garrison GdB Phillipon commanding: 1e/34e, 3e/40e, 1er/88e & 3e/100e RIdLi, 1er/12e RILé (1 bn each).

French total ca 3,600 men.

French losses Not exactly known but light.

Anglo-Portuguese Forces Viscount Wellington commanding: 3rd Division MG T Picton Mackinnon's Brigade: 4th, 74th & 88th Foot (1st bns each); 5/60th (3 coys) Colville's Brigade: 5th, 83rd & 88th Foot (2nd bns each); 1/94th (1 bn). 7th Division MG Houston: Sontag's Brigade: 51st & 85th Foot (2nd bns each); Chasseurs Britanniques (1 bn). Brunswick Oels (8 coys). Doyle's Portuguese Brigade: 7th & 19th LIR (2 bns each); 2nd Caçadores (1 bn). Hamilton's Portuguese Division: 2nd, 4th, 10th & 14th LIR (2 bns each). Collins' Portuguese Brigade: 5th LIR (2 bns); 5th Caçadores (1 bn). Artillery 700 British & Portuguese gunners.

Anglo-Portuguese total ca 14,000 men*.

Anglo-Portuguese losses 54 killed, 81 wounded. 4 missing all from the 51st & 85th Foot, Chasseurs Britannique, 17th Portuguese & the Brunswick Oels in the failed storm attempt of 9 June.

Comment Wellington's siege artillery was so old and ineffective that it was practically useless and his engineering support was totally inadequate.

* = The 17th Portuguese LIR and the Militia of Lagos & Tavira joined on 25 May.

PM Elvas, 22 June 1811, skirmish

A spot on the Rio Guadiana almost in front of Elvas, between that place and the French-held fortress of Badajoz.

A French victory over the British.

(Last action – Badajoz, 10 June; next action – Carpio, 25 September).

French Forces Latour-Maubourg's Cavalry of Soult's Army of the South. 1er, 2e, 4e, 9e DragRs.

French total 14 sqns ca 800 men.

French losses Not exactly known, light.

British Forces Gen Long commanding 11th LDR, 2nd HusR KGL.

British total ca 600 men.

British losses 10 killed, 24 wounded, 56 captured.

Comment The British regiments had just arrived in

Spain and were completely unaccustomed to outpost duty.
Sources Oman, Schwertfeger.

EN Cogorderos, 23 June 1811, clash*
A village in northern Spain, on the Rio Orbigo between Astorga and Leon.
A Spanish victory over the French.
(Last action – Astorga, 22 April 1810; this was the only action of note in northern Spain in 1811).
French Forces GdB Valletaux of Bonnet's Division, Army of the North: 119e & 122e RIdLi (3 bns each) ca 1,500 men.
French losses ca 450 killed, wounded & captured. Valletaux was killed.
Spanish Forces Gen Santocildes with part of the 6th Army of Galicia. Exact details not known.
Spanish total 2,000 men.
Spanish losses Not exactly known but light.
Comment This defeat caused panic among the French in northern Spain and stopped them sending troops south to fight Wellington.
Sources Oman, Martinien.
* = the French call this action Quintanilla de Valle.

EE Tarragona, 5 May – 29 June 1811, siege and storm
A fortified Spanish Mediterranean harbour in eastern Spain, on Route 340 about 75 km southwest of Barcelona.
A Franco-Polish-Italian victory over the Spanish.
(Last action – Figueras, 3 May; next action – Figueras, 19 August).
French Forces GdD Suchet's Army of Aragon: GdD Frère: 1er RILé & 42e RIdLi (3 bns each); 14e RIdLi (1 bn); 1st IR Vistula Legion (2 bns). GdD Harispe: 7e & 16e RIdLi (3 bns each); Italians: 2nd LtIR, 4th, 5th & 6th LIRs (2 bns each). GdD Habert: 5e RILé, 116e & 117e RIdLi (2 bns each). GdB Abbé*: 114e, 115e & 121e RIdLi (2 bns each). **Total infantry** 18,127. GdD Boussard's Cavalry: 13e CuirR, 24e DragR (3 sqns each); 4e HusR, Italian Dragone Napoleone (2 sqns each). **Total cavalry** 1,447. Artillery & train 1,352; engineers – 708.
French total 21,634.
French losses 4,300 killed & wounded; GdB Salme killed.
* = arrived on about the 20th June.
Spanish Garrison** GL Senen de Contreras commanding: Courten's Division: IRs America, Almanza, Almeria, Granada. Part of Sarsfield's Division: IRs Santa Fé, Hibernia, Zaragoza, Girona, 1st & 2nd Savoia, Grenadiers, Cazadores de Valencia; cavalry, 166 men. **Total divisions** ca 5,000 men. **Sedentary Garrison** Catalan Sections, Tarragona, Artillery & Engineers. **Total garrison** ca 3,020.
Spanish grand total ca 8,000 men.
Spanish losses 14–15,000 in all throughout the siege, killed, wounded & captured including 8,000 captured.
** Full details not known, the records were destroyed in the siege.
Comment Suchet's Marshal's baton 'lay within Tarragona' as Napoleon had told him. So he pressed the siege with all vigour, hence his considerable losses. On 21 June he stormed and took the lower city. Commodore Codrington's small Royal Navy squadron (2 x 74s & 2 frigates) could not compete with the French 24 pdr siege guns and had to stand off. Campoverde danced around the besiegers ineffectively and command in the city was divided. A small British force under Colonel Skerrett arrived in the harbour on 26 June but, after inspecting the defences together with Contreras, Skerrett decided that it was a hopeless situation and left again. The morale of the remaining defenders plummeted. On 28 June Suchet stormed the upper town and over 4,000 Spaniards – half of them civilians including 450 women and children – were massacred. Almost two thirds of the Spanish Army of Catalonia had been destroyed and the last major base of Allied operations in eastern Spain was gone. Suchet grasped eagerly for this marshal's baton with a bloody hand.
Sources Oman, Martinien.

XX Rustchuk (now Ruse), 4 July 1811, battle
A fortified town in Bulgaria, on the right bank of the Danube, near its confluence with the River Lom.
A Russian victory over the Turks.
(Last action – Lovca, 11 February; next action – Giurgevo, 9 September).
Russian Force GdI Count Kutusov with 27 bns, 60 sqns.
Russian total 20,000 men.
Russian losses 800 killed & wounded, 1 gun.

Turkish Forces Grand Vizier Achmet Pasha with 60,000 men.

Turkish losses 1,500 killed & wounded, 2,000 captured.

Source Bodart.

ES Zujar, 9 August 1811, clash

A village in southeastern Spain, 7 km south of the Rio de Baza on Route 323, 13 km northwest of Baza.

A French victory over the Spanish.

(Last action - Barrosa (Chiclana), 5 March; next action - Arroyo dos Molinos, 28 October).

French Forces GdD Godinot (of Soult's Army of the South): 16e RILé (3 bns); 8e RIdLi (4 bns); 54e RIdLi (3 bns).

French total ca 8,000 men.

French losses Not known but light.

Spanish Forces Gen O'Donnell's division of the Army of Murcia. Exact details not known.

Spanish losses 423 killed & wounded, 1,000 missing & prisoners.

Comment This action - and another next day at Las Vertientes, 16 km from Baza where Pierre Soult's cavalry broke the Spanish rearguard - led to the scattering of the Army of Murcia.

Source Oman.

EE Figueras, 4 April – 19 August 1811, blockade and capitulation

A fortress in northeastern Spain (Catalonia), on Route 11 and just east of the Motorway A7/E15, 120 km northeast of Barcelona.

A French victory over the Spanish.

(Last action - Tarragona, 29 June; next action - this was the last action of note in eastern Spain in 1811).

French Forces M Macdonald commanding the Army of Catalonia: GdD M Mathieu: 5e RIdLi (3 bns); 18e RILé, 23e & 56e Li (1 bn each); 1st IR Nassau (2 bns). GdD Quesnel 23e RILé (2 bns); 79e RIdLi (3 bns); 93e (1 bn); 29e ChàCh (3 sqns). GdD Plauzonne: 3e RILé (4 bns); 32e RILé (1 bn); 11e RIdLi (3 bns); GdB Petit: 67e RIdLi (4 bns); 16e & 81e RIdLi (1 bn each); GdB Lefebvre: 8e RILé, 37e & 60e RIdLi (1 bn each); IR de Westphalie (1 bn); provisional bns (3 bns); IR Würzburg & 2nd Swiss (1 bn each).

French total ca 15,000 men.

French losses 4,000 killed or died of disease.

Spanish Garrison BG Martinez with five weak regular battalions Ultonia (1); Antequera (2) & 1st & 2nd bns Voluntarios de Valencia & 3,000 Miqueletes.

Spanish total 7,000 men.

Spanish losses 1,500 killed, the rest captured.

Comment The Spanish put up a most creditable defence and held out for months longer than expected even though they knew that there was no hope of relief. A last-minute break-out attempt failed. This was the last Spanish outpost in Catalonia - the guerrilla and supply base on Montserrat had been overrun by Suchet on 25 July - but General Lacy reorganized the wreck of the Spanish Army of Catalonia and, with the help of the Royal Navy, captured the Island of Medas in the mouth of the Rio Ter and conducted guerrilla raids which made the French abandon their outposts again to concentrate against him. On 28 October M Macdonald was sacked and recalled to France; GdD Decaen took over in Catalonia.

Sources Oman, Martinien.

XX Giurgevo, 9 September 1811, clash

A town in Rumania, on the left bank of the Danube, 60 km south of Bucharest and opposite Ruse in Bulgaria.

A Turkish victory over the Russians.

(Last action - Rustchuk, 4 July; next action - Giurgevo, 8 December).

Russian Forces GM Bulatov & 6,000 men.

Russian losses 2,100 killed and wounded, 1 gun.

Turkish Forces Grand Vizier Achmet Pasha with 6,000 Janissaries & 6 guns.

Turkish losses 1,000 killed & wounded.

PM Carpio, 25 September 1811, skirmish

A village in western Spain, 10 km west of Ciudad Rodrigo on Route 620/E80 towards the Portuguese border on the lower Rio Azava.

A British victory over the Franco-Germans.

(Last action - Elvas, 22 June; next action - El Bodon, 25 September).

French Forces GdD Wathier of the Army of Portugal commanding: 26e ChàCh, Lancers of Berg (4 sqns each).

French total ca 450 men.

French losses 11 killed, 37 captured (mostly wounded).

British Forces BG Anson commanding: 14 & 16th LDRs (3 sqns each) & 11th, 61st & 53rd Foot (light coys only) of Graham's 6th Division.

British total ca 800 men.

British losses 11 wounded, 1 missing.

Comment This was a probe by M Marmont to clear the way for him to break the Allied blockade of Ciudad Rodrigo.

Sources Oman, Martinien.

PM El Bodon, 25 September 1811, clash

A village in western Spain on Route 526, 13 km southwest of Ciudad Rodrigo and about 30 km from the Portuguese border.

A drawn match between the French and the Anglo-Portuguese.

(Last action – Carpio, 25 September; next action – Aldea de Ponte, 28 September).

French Forces GdD Montbrun commanding: GdB Lamotte 1er & 3e HusR. GdB Fournier: 7e, 13e & 20e ChàCh. GdB Cavrois: 3e, 10e & 15e DragRs. GdB Ornano: 6e, 11e & 25e DragRs, 1 x HAB.

French total ca 2,500 men.

French losses Not reported; probably about 200 killed & wounded.

Anglo-Portuguese Forces Part of the 3rd Division MG T Picton commanding. Wallace's Brigade: 1/45th, 1/88th Foot (1 bn each); Colville's Brigade: 2/5th, 1/77th, 2/83rd & 1/94th Foot (1 bn each). Alten's Light Cavalry Brigade 11th LDR, 1st HusR KGL (5 sqns in all).

Anglo-Portuguese total 1,000 infantry, 500 cavalry, 2 x Portuguese FAB.

Comment The 3rd Division was caught by surprise in extended encampments but rallied well and withdrew over 10 km southwards towards the main lines in excellent order with the French cavalry swarming around them but not daring to charge home. The 1st Hussars KGL was awarded the battle honour 'El Bodon' which was worn by its descendant regiment until 1918. The superior French cavalry alone could not seriously damage the inferior Allied force of all arms.

Sources Oman, Martinien, Schwertfeger, Beamish.

PM Aldea de Ponte (nowadays Aldeia), 28 September 1811, skirmish

A hamlet in eastern Portugal, near the source of the Rio Aguedo, 3 km from the Spanish border and ca 40 km southwest of Ciudad Rodrigo.

A French victory over the Allies.

(Last action – El Bodon, 25 September. This was the last action of note in this theatre in 1811).

French Forces GdD Thiebault's Division of the Army of Portugal: 34e RILé (3 bns), IR Neufchâtel (1 bn); 4th IR Legion of the Vistula (2 bns). GdD Wathier's Light Cavalry: 11e & 24e ChàCh, 5e HusR; GdD Souham's Division of the Army of the North: 23e RILé (2 bns); 1er, 62e & 101e RIdLi (4 bns each) 1 x FAB. Total ca 12,000 men. Losses 30

El Bodon	killed		wounded		missing		Total
	officers	men	officers	men	officers	men	
Anglo-Portuguese losses:							
1/45th	—	—	—	—	—	1	1
1/88th	—	—	—	—	—	5	5
2/5th	—	5	1	13	—	—	19
1/77th	—	4	—	14	—	5	23
2/83rd	—	5	—	14	—	5	24
1/94th	—	—	—	—	—	1	1
11th LDR	—	8	2	14	—	—	24
1st Hus KGL	—	5	2	32	—	5	44
Total Anglo-Portuguese losses	—	*27*	*5*	*87*	—	*22*	*141*
Portuguese	—	1	—	5	—	2	8
Grand Total	—	28	5	92	—	24	149

killed, 120 wounded.

Allied Forces BG Pakenham's Fusilier Brigade of MG L Cole's 4th Division: 1/7th, 1/23rd & 1/48th Foot (1 bn each); Brunswick Oels (1 coy), 5/60th (1 coy). BG Slade's cavalry: 1st Royal DragR; 12th LDR (3 sqns each); 1 x HAB; 1 unidentified Portuguese regiment (11th or 23rd LIR or 7th Caçadores).

Allied total 3,300 men.

Aldea de Ponte	**killed**		**wounded**		**missing**		**Total**
Allied losses:	officers	men	officers	men	officers	men	
1/7th	—	9	4	29	—	—	42
1/23rd	1	2	2	13	—	1	19
1/48th	—	—	1	7	—	2	10
5/60th	—	—	1	—	—	—	1
Brunswick Oels	—	1	—	3	—	—	4
1st Royal DragR	—	—	—	3	—	1	4
12th LDR	—	—	—	2	—	4	6
HAB	—	—	1	—	—	—	1
Total	*1*	*12*	*9*	*57*	—	*8*	*87*
Portuguese	—	1	—	11	—	1	13
Grand Total	1	13	9	68	—	9	100

Comment The village was not essential to Wellington's defensive plan so he did not press the engagement. The French Armies of Portugal and of the North were now concentrated against him and he lifted the blockade of Ciudad Rodrigo. The French withdrew, being unable to feed themselves in this region.

Sources Oman, Martinien.

ES Arroyo dos Molinos, 28 October 1811, clash

A village in southwestern Spain near Route 630/E803 and between Casas de Don Antonio and Alcuescar.

An Allied victory over the French.

(Last action – Zujar, 9 August; next action – Bornos, 5 November).

French Forces GdD Girard's Division of V Corps (M Soult). GdB Dombrowski: 34e & 40e RIdLi (3 bns each). 27e ChàCh & one other regiment. 3 guns.

French total 4,000 men.

French losses Killed & wounded unknown, 1,300 captured, 3 guns. GdB Bron captured & 5,000 dollars which he had levied in Caceres a few days before.

Allied Forces Gen Hill commanding the 2nd Division: BG Howard's Brigade: 1/71st, 1/92nd (1 bn each). BG Wilson's Brigade: 1/28th, 1/34th, 1/39th (1 bn each). BG Long's Cavalry 9th LDR, 2nd HusR KGL. Portuguese infantry. 3 unidentified bns* & the 5th & 8th CavRs. 1 x Portuguese FAB. Spanish troops: Gen Penne Villemur's cavalry brigade – exact details not known.

Allied total ca 10,000 men.

Allied losses British & Portuguese: 7 killed, 7 officers & 57 men wounded. Spanish: 30 killed & wounded.

Comment Hill had learned that Girard's isolated division was around Caceres and moving slowly south back to his base at Mérida. After a wild chase through the mountains in appalling weather, Hill caught his unsuspecting prey and inflicted a crushing defeat on him.

Napoleon recalled Girard in disgrace; the remnants of his division were given to Barrois.

Sources Oman, Martinien.

* could have been Ashworth's Brigade: 6th & 18th LIR's (2 bns each) & 6th Caçadores.

ES Bornos, 5 November 1811, clash

A village in southern Spain just south of Route 342 and north of the Rio Guadalete, 40 km northeast of Jerez de la Frontera.

A French victory over the Spaniards.

(Last action – Arroyo dos Molinos, 28 October; this was the last action in southern Spain in 1811).

French Forces GdB Sémele & the 16e RILé (1,500 men), Spanish Juramentados* (1 bn).

French total ca 2,300 men.

French losses 100 killed, wounded & captured; the Juramentados went over to their Spanish compatriots en masse, during the action.

Spanish Forces General Ballasteros with a mixed force of regulars & guerrillas; exact details & losses not known.

* = Juramentados – literally 'sworn men' ie, deputies.

Sources Oman, Martinien.

XX Giurgevo, 8 December 1811, capitulation

A town in Rumania, on the left bank of the Danube, 60 km south of Bucharest and opposite Ruse in Bulgaria.

A Russian victory over the Turks.

(Last action – Giurgevo, 9 September; this was the last action here in 1811).

Russian Forces GdI Kutusov commanding 40,000 men.

Russian losses Not known.

Turkish Garrison. Tschappan Oglu & 8,000 men.

Turkish losses The garrison was allowed to leave without their weapons. The Russians took 56 guns & 22 ammunition waggons.

Comment Kutusov had blockaded Grand Vizier Achmet Pasha in this entrenched camp near Giurgevo since 10 September.

Source Bodart.

1812

For better understanding of the Russian campaign we have split the actions into four sectors with the following alpha codes.

RM: the main body of the Grande Armée which marched on Moscow.

RS: the southern flank guard of the Austrians and Saxons (VII Corps) under Schwarzenberg.

RN: the north flank guard, the II Corps and the Bavarians' VI Corps at Polotsk.

RL: Macdonald's X Corps up in Latvia, blockading Riga.

Please note that all Prussian units involved were combined regiments, each drawn from several corps.

1812 THE ACTIONS

EW Fuente del Maestre, 3 January 1812, clash

A village in the southwestern Spanish province of Extremadura, about 50 km south of Mérida and between Routes 432 and 630.

An Allied victory over the French.

(This was the opening action in western Spain this year; next action – Ciudad Rodrigo, 20 January.)

French Forces The rearguard of Gen Dombrowski's 5th Division, Army of the South: 26e DragR (3 sqns).

French total ca 400 men.

French losses 6 killed, many wounded, 37 captured.

Allied Forces MG Abercrombie commanding 1/50th Foot (1 bn); 2nd HusR KGL, 10th Portuguese CavR (2 sqns each), 3 guns.

Allied total ca 1,200 men.

Allied losses 2nd HusR KGL 1 killed, 14 wounded. 10th Portuguese cavalry: 6 wounded.

Comment Abercromby was part of Gen Hill's corps conducting a diversionary raid into Extremadura to cover the siege of Ciudad Rodrigo.

Sources Oman, Martinien.

ES Tarifa, 19 Dec 1811 – 5 Jan 1812, failed siege

A medieval fortified port in the southern Spanish province of Andalusia, 65 km southeast of Cadiz, on Route 340/E5 on the southernmost tip of Spain.

An Anglo-Spanish victory over the French.

(Last action – this was the opening action in southern Spain in 1794; next action – Alhourin, 14 April.)

French Forces GdD Leval commanding: 27e RILé (1 bn); 16e RILé (3 bns); 8e RIdLi (1 bn); 43e, 51e, 54e, 63e, 94e and 95e RIdLi, 7th and 9th Polish IRs (2 bns each), 16e and 21e DragRs (4 sqns each); 16 siege guns.

French total 15,000 men.

French losses ca 500 killed or died of exposure, 180 wounded, 30 captured, 14 guns.

Anglo-Spanish Garrison General Copons commanding: Col Skerrett's bde: 2/47th, 2/87th (1 bn each); 95th (1 coy); 2nd HusR KGL (1/2 sqn), 1x FAB; 1/82nd (1 bn), 2/11th (flank coys only). Spanish bde: IRs Irlanda and Cantabria (1 bn each), Cazadores (1 coy), gunners (120); cavalry (25 men).

Anglo-Spanish total ca 3,000 men and 26 guns.

Anglo-Spanish losses British: 9 killed, 58 wounded. Spanish: 1 killed and wounded.

Sources Oman, Martinien.

EE Valencia, 3 November 1811 – 9 January 1812, siege and capture

A fortified port city in the eastern Spanish province of the same name near the estuary of the Rio Turia, on Routes III/E901 and A7/E15.

A French victory over the Spanish.

(Last action – this was the first action in eastern Spain this Year; next action – Alicante, 16 January.)

French Forces M Suchet commanding: Army of Aragon: **1st Division** GdD Musnier: 114e and 121e RIdLi (3 bns each); 1st and 2nd IRs Vistula Legion (2 bns each). **2nd Division** GdD Harispe: 7eRIdLi (4 bns), 44e RIdLi (2 bns); 116e RIdLi (3 bns); 3rd IR Vistula Legion (2 bns). 3rd Division GdD Habert: 15e RIdLi (2 bns); 16e and 117e RIdLi (3 bns each). **Palombini's Italian Division** 2nd LtIR, 4th and 6th LIR (3 bns each), 5th LIR (2 bns). GdD Compère's Neapolitan Division: 1stLt, 1st and 2nd LIRs (1 bn each). **Cavalry** GdB Boussard: 4eHusR, 13e CuirR (4 sqns each); 24e DragR (2 sqns) Italian Drag Napoleone (4 sqns); Neapolitan ChàCh (1 sqn).

French total 20,595 men.

French losses ca 2,000 killed and wounded. Gen Boussard killed.

Spanish Forces Capt Gen Don Blake commanding:

The Expeditionary Corps Lardizabal's Division IRs Africa, Murcia, 2nd of Badajoz (2 bns each); Campo Mayor and Tiradores de Cuenca (1 bn each). **Zaya's Division** 2nd and 4th Spanish Guards, 1st Walloon Guards, Voluntarios de la Patria, IRs Toledo, Ciudad

Rodrigo, Legion Estangera (1 bn each). Cazadores (2 coys). **Loy's Cavalry** Granaderos (2 sqns), Rey (1 sqn); Hus de Castilla (1 sqn); 2 x HAB. **Total** 6,041 men.

The 2nd Army (Valencian Troops) Miranda's 1st Division IRs Valencia (3 bns): Voluntarios de Castilla (2 bns); 1st of Avila, 2nd Cazadores de Valencia (1 bn). **Obispo's Division** IRs Carinena (2 bns); 2nd of Avila and 1st Voluntarios de Aragon, Dacora and Tiradores de Doyle (1 bn each). **Villacampa's Division** IRs Princesa, Soria (2 bns each); 2nd Voluntarios de Aragon, 1st Cazadores de Valencia, Molina (1 bn each). **The Reserve** Gen Valesco: IRs Voluntarios de Castilla, Don Carlos, Avila, Cazadores de Valencia, Voluntarios de Orihucla (3rd bns each). **Cavalry** Gen San Juan: Cuenca, Dragones del Rey, Reina, Numancia, Husares de Aragon, Cazadores de Valencia, Alcántara, Husares Españoles, Husares de Granada (1 or 2 sqns each), 2 x FAB, 1 x HAB. **Total** 16,468 men.

The 3rd Army (Murcian Troops) Gen Creagh's Bde: IRs Corona, Alcazar, Tiradores de Cadiz (1 bn each); Gen Montijo's Bde: 1st of Badajoz, 1st of Cuenca, Voluntarios de Burgos, Sappers (1 bn each). Cavalry: Reina, Pavia, Granada (2 sqns each); Madrid, Husares de Fernando VII (1 sqn each); 1 x HAB. **Total:** 5,535.

Spanish total 28,044 men.

Spanish losses 4,011 killed or died of sickness. 7,071 of the army escaped and rallied at Alicante by 14 January. 16,270 surrendered with 21 colours and 374 guns.

Comment Blake conducted a very sloppy defence and after his defeat at the Rio Xucar on 26 December by Harispe he withdrew into himself and took no further active part in matters. The Valencians hated him. After the surrender Blake was held in the castle of Vincennes, near Paris until 1814. Creagh's brigade, the divisions of Obispo and Villacampa and all the cavalry escaped to Alicante.

Sources Martinien, Oman.

EE Alicante, 16 January 1812, clash

A fortified port on the Spanish Mediterranean coast, south of Valencia and at the junction of Routes A7/E15, 330, 332 and 340.

A Spanish victory over the French.

(Last action – Valencia, 9 January; next action – Peniscola, 20 January.)

French Forces GdD Montbrun commanding: GdD Sarrut: 2e and 4e RILé, 36e RIdLi (3 bns each); 1er, 3e and 5e Hus; 7e, 15e, 17e, 22e and 24e ChàCh.

French total 4,000 infantry, 1,500 horse, 6 guns.

French losses Not known exactly but light.

Spanish Garrison Gen Mahy commanding: Creagh's Bde: IRs Corona, Alcazar, Tiradores de Cadiz (1 bn each). **Villacampa's Division** IRs Princesa and Soria (2 bns each), 2nd Voluntarios de Aragon, 1st Cazadores de Valencia, Molina (1 bn each); **Obispo's Division** IRs Carinena (2 bns), 2nd of Avila, 1st Voluntarios de Aragon (1 bn each); **Bassecourt's Division** (no details known) **Freire's Division** IRs Canarias, Burgos and Ligero de Aragon (1 bn each). Murcian Cavalry: Reina, Pavia and Granada (2 sqns each), Madrid (1 sqn), Hus de Fernando VII (1 sqn). Valencian Cavalry: Cuenca, Drag del Rey, Reina, Numancia, Hus de Aragon, Cazadores de Valencia, Alcántara, Hus Españoles, Hus de Granada (1 or 2 sqns each) 2 x HAB.

Spanish total ca 6,300 men.

Spanish losses Not known, but very light.

Comment Montbrun was detached from Marmont's Army of Portugal to help Suchet subdue Valencia but Suchet had been successful so quickly that his help was not needed. On his own initiative Montbrun raided Alicante but was beaten off. During his absence from his proper place, Wellington captured Ciudad Rodrigo.

Sources Oman, Martinien.

EE Col de Balaguer, 18 January 1812, skirmish

A mountain pass between the eastern Spanish coastal town of Tarragona and the town of Reus, about 11 km to the west of Tarragona.

A Spanish victory over the French.

(Last action – Peniscola, 20 January; next action – Altafalla, 24 January.)

French Forces Gen Lafosse (Governor of Tortosa): 121e RIdLi (1 bn), dragoons (1tp).

French total ca 850 men.

French losses The 121e was captured, Lafosse and 22 dragoons escaped back to Tarragona.

Spanish Forces Gen Baron Eroles' division ca 4,000 men and 2 guns, 250 cavalry; exact details not known.

Spanish losses Not known but light.

Sources Oman, Martinien.

EW Ciudad Rodrigo, 7–20 January 1812, siege and capture

A fortified city in the western Spanish province of Salamanca, 83 km south west of that city, 21 km from the Portuguese border on Route 620/E80.

An Anglo-Portuguese victory over the French.

(Last action – Fuente del Maestre, 3 January; next action – Badajoz, 6 April.)

French Garrison GdB Baron Barrie commanding: 34e RILé and 113e RIdLi (1 bn each); gunners (2 coys); sappers (½ coy).

French total 2,000 men, 142 siege guns.

French losses 29 officers and 500 men killed and wounded; 60 officers and 1,300 men captured. The entire siege train of the Army of Portugal was lost.

Anglo-Portuguese Forces Viscount Wellington commanding: **The Light Division** MG R Craufurd: 1/43rd, 1/52nd, 2/52nd (1 bn each); 95th (9 coys) 1st and 3rd Caçadores (1 bn each). **3rd Division** Maj Gen T Picton: 1/45th, 1/74th, 1/88th (1 bn each); 5/60th (3 coys); 2/5th, 1/77th, 2/83rd, 1/94th, 9th and 21st Portuguese LIRs (1 bn each). **BG Pack's Portuguese** 1st and 16th LIR (2 bns each); 4th Caçadores (1 bn). 36 siege guns.

Anglo-Portuguese total ca 10,700 men.

Anglo-Portuguese losses 9 officers killed, 70 wounded; 186 men killed, 846 wounded. 59 officers and 503 men were killed and wounded in the storming of the place. Gen Craufurd and Gen MacKinnon killed.

Comment Wellington distracted French forces away from this key fortress by a series of raids in Extremadura. He attacked the place in exactly the same way that Ney had done in 1810 but achieved in 12 days siegework what it took Ney to do in 24. The French garrison was far too weak to man the defences adequately. Despite the efforts of their officers, the British soldiers sacked the town. Wellington now controlled one of the two main entrances into Spain and the French high command in Madrid were panic-stricken.

Sources Bodart, Oman, Napier, Martinien.

EE Altafalla, 24 January 1812, clash

A village in the eastern Spanish province of Tarragona, on the Mediterranean coast, 10 km southwest of Tarragona on Route 340.

A French victory over the Spanish.

(Last action – Col de Balaguer, 18 January; next action – Peniscola, 2 February.)

French Forces GdD M Mathieu commanding: 3e RILé (3 bns); 18e RILé, 23e and 115e RIdLi (1 bn each), 1st Nassau IR (2 bns) Partisans (2 coys).

French total ca 8,000 men.

French losses Not exactly known but light.

Spanish Forces Gen Baron Eroles' division: ca 4,000 men and 2 guns, 250 cavalry; exact details not known.

Spanish losses 2,000 killed, wounded and missing, 2 guns.

Comment The action started in heavy fog and Eroles thought he was fighting only a battalion.

Sources Oman, Martinien, Roessler.

EE Peniscola, 20 January – 2 February 1812, siege and capture

A fortified coastal port in the eastern Spanish province of Tarragona, 50 km south of Tortosa just east of Route A7/E15.

A French victory over the Spanish.

(Last action – Altafalla, 24 January; next action – Roda, 5 March.)

French Forces GdD Severoli of Suchet's Army of Valencia: 2 Italian and 2 French battalions (exact details not known).

French total ca 3,000 men, 6 guns.

French losses None.

Spanish Garrison Gen Garcia Navarro and 1,000 men.

Spanish losses All captured.

Comment Due to its impregnable nature, Peniscola was known as 'Little Gibraltar' and Severoli's force was no threat to it. Navarro however, was pro-French and at once accepted his extremely generous terms. A very useful harbour was this lost to the Allied fleet.

Sources Oman, Martinien.

EE Roda, 5 March 1812, clash

A village in Aragon in northern Spain ca 72 km north of Lleida, in the mountains between the two rivers Esera and Noguera Ribagorcana.

A Spanish victory over the Franco-Italians.

(Last action – Peniscola, 2 February; next action – Castalla, 21 July.)

Franco-Italian Forces Gen Bourke with 61e RIdLi /1 bn) and 7th Italian LIR (3 bns.)

Franco-Italian total ca 3,000 men.

Franco-Italian losses 600 killed and wounded.

Spanish Forces Gen Baron Eroles' division ca 3,000 men (exact details not known).

Spanish losses Not known but light.

Comment Eroles' pin-prick raids had paralysed French operations, absorbed almost half of Reille's 'Army of the Ebro' for two critical months and had also enraged Napoleon.

Sources Oman, Martinien.

EW Badajoz, 17 March – 6 April 1812, siege and storm

A fortified city in western Spain, on the left bank of the Rio Guadiana, on Route V/E90, 6 km from the Portuguese border.

An Anglo-Portuguese victory over the Franco-Germans.

(Last action – Ciudad Rodrigo, 20 January; next action – Villagarcia, 11 April.)

Franco-German Garrison GdD Baron Philippon commanding. Hessen-Darmstadt IR Gross-und-Erbprinz (2 bns); 9e RILé, 58e, 64e, 88e, 103e RIdLi (1 bn each); 'New Spaniards' (2 coy) gunners (250 men) sappers (1 coy).

Franco-German total 5,000 men.

Franco-German losses 1,300 killed and wounded, 3,700 captured, 2 colours (IR Gross-und-Erbprinz).

Anglo-Portuguese Forces The Duke of Wellington commanding: **3rd Division** Gen Sir T Picton: 1/45th, 1/74th, 1/88th, 9th and 21st Portuguese LIRs (1 bn each); 3/60th (3 coys); 2/5th, 1/77th, 2/83rd, 1/94th Foot. **4th Division** MG Lowry Cole: 3/28th, 1/40th, 1/7th, 1/23rd, 1/48th (1 bn each); 5/60th and Brunswick Oels (1 coy each), 11th and 23rd Portuguese LIRs, 7th Caçadores (1 bn each). **5th Division** BG Walker's Bde: 1/4th, 2/30th, 2/44th (1 bn each); Brunswick Oels (1 coy). **The Light Division** 1/43rd, 1/52nd, 1/95th (8 coys); 2/95th (1 coy); 3/95th (3 coys). 1st and 3rd Portuguese Caçadores. Gunners 300 british, 560 Portuguese, engineers 115 men. 92 guns including 52 siege guns of which 20 were Russian naval 18 pdrs taken from Admiral Seniavin's squadron captured in the Tagus in 1808.

Anglo-Portuguese total ca 17,100 men.

Anglo-Portuguese losses ca 2,900 killed and wounded in the storm, a further 1,200 during the rest of the siege.

Comment Wellingtons sieges were always bloody affairs, in contrast to his economy with his men's lives in field operations. The garrison put up an excellent and spirited defence. Badajoz was sacked. Wellington now controlled both major entrances from Portugal into Spain. The French were surprised by the speed of the capture of the place.

Sources Oman, Martinien, Keim.

EN Puerto de Arlaban, 9 April 1812, ambush

A mountain pass on Route I/E5 between Vitoria Gasteiz and Mandragon in northern Spain, also known as the Pass of Salinas.

A Spanish victory over the Franco-Poles.

(Last action – this was the only action of note in northern Spain in 1812.)

Franco-Polish Forces A large convoy of convalescents, civilians, baggage and food supplies escorted by the 7th Polish IR (2 bns).

Franco-Polish total (escort): 2,000.

Franco-Polish losses 500 killed, 150 captured.

Spanish Forces Mina's guerrillas 3-4,000 men.

Spanish losses Not known but light.

Comment Mina liberated 450 Spanish prisoners and took a chest of several hundred thousand francs. At this time no less than 30,000 French troops were engaged in trying to hunt Mina down and were not available for operations against Wellington.

Sources Oman, Martinien, Gembarzewski, Malibran and Chelminski.

EW Villagarcia, 11 April 1812, clash

A village in the southwestern Spanish province of Extremadura, on Route 432, 12 km northwest of Llerena on the road to Badajoz.

A British victory over the French.

(Last action – Badajoz, 6 April; next action – Guarda, 14 April.)

French Forces GdB Perreymond: 2e Hus, 5e ChàCh (3 sqns each), 17e and 27e DragRs (3 sqns each).

French total ca 1,100 men.

French losses 53 killed and wounded, 4 officers and 132 men captured.

British Forces Gen Sir Stapleton Cotton's Cav Div: BG Ponsonby 12th, 14th and 16th LDs BG Le Marchant: 5th DG.

British total ca 1,400 men.

British losses 14 killed, 37 wounded.

Sources Oman, Martinien.

British Losses at the storming of Badajoz, 6 April 1812

	killed		wounded		Total	(including these
	officers	men	officers	men		missing men)
General Staff, artillery engineers	4	6	23	14	47	
3rd Division						
1/45	6	19	8	64	97	
3/60	1	4	4	26	35	
1/74	—	12	7	33	54	(2)
1/88	3	28	7	106	144	
2/5	1	11	3	28	43	
1/77	—	—	3	11	14	
2/83	1	22	7	39	69	
1/94	1	12	1	51	65	
Total	13	108	40	358	519	(2)
4th Division						
3/27	4	37	12	132	185	
1/40	2	51	13	170	236	
1/7	5	44	12	119	180	
1/23	3	22	14	92	131	(20)
1/48	3	32	16	122	173	
Total	17	186	67	635	905	(20)
5th Division (the 3/1st and 1/9th had no losses)						
2/38	1	12	3	26	42	
1/4	2	40	15	173	230	
2/30	—	38	6	86	130	
2/44	2	37	7	88	134	
Total	5	127	31	373	536	
Light Division						
1/43	3	74	15	249	341	
1/52	5	58	14	248	325	
1/95	8	27	10	154	199	
3/95	4	9	4	47	64	
Total	20	168	43	698	929	
Total British losses	59	595	204	2,079	2,936	(22)

These include the Brunswick Oels (7 men killed, 2 officers and 26 men wounded).

Portuguese losses	8	147	45	500	700	(30)
Grand Totals	67	742	249	2,578	3,636	(52)

EW Guarda, 14 April 1812, clash

A town in eastern Portugal, on Route 16, 47 km from the Spanish frontier and 74 km west of the fortress of Ciudad Rodrigo.

A French victory over the Portuguese.

(Last action – Villagarcia, 11 April; next action – Almáraz, 18 May.)

French Forces 13e ChàCh of M Marmont's Army of Portugal (3 sqns).

French total ca 400 men.

French losses Not known but negligible.

Portuguese Forces Gen Trant commanding: Militia IRs Aveiro, Olivenca and Penafiel and some dragoons.

Portuguese total ca 2,000 men.

Portuguese losses 1,500 captured, 5 of the 6 colours.

Comment The French (3 divisions) were on a spoiling raid, looking for food and Trant was foolhardy enough to try to stop them. Most of the prisoners were let go by the French.

Sources Oman, Martinien.

ES Alhourin, 14 April 1812, clash

A village in southern Spain, in the mountains about 30 km west of Malaga on the Mediterranean coast.

A Spanish victory over the French.

(Last action – Tarifa, 5 January; next action – Cadiz, 1 June.)

French Forces G Rey commanding: 43e and 58e RIdLi (3 bns); 21e DragR (3 sqns), 2 guns of Sebastiani's IV Corps.

French total ca 3,000 men.

French losses Over 200 killed, wounded and captured, 2 guns.

Spanish Forces Gen Ballasteros and a mixed force of regulars and guerrillas; exact details and losses not known.

Sources Oman, Martinien.

EW Almáraz, 18 May 1812, clash

A town in western Spain on Route V/E90 between Talavera and Trujillo, about 5 km north of the Rio Tajo (Tagus). A vital bridge over this river.

An Allied victory over the French.

(Last action – Guarda, 14 April; next action – Salamanca, 27 June.)

French Garrison: GdB Aubert commanding: 4e R Étranger (R de Prusse) (1 bn, 366 men); 39e RIdLi (1 bn); 6e RILé (2 coys), gunners (1 coy), sappers (1 coy), 18 guns.

French total ca 1,000 men.

French losses Killed and wounded unknown; 17 officers and 262 men captured, 18 guns, 1 colour (4e R Étranger), 1 pontoon train, bridging stores, much ammunition. The battalion of the 4e R Étranger was destroyed.

Allied Forces Gen Rowland Hill commanding: BG Howard: 1/50th, 1/71st, 1/92nd (1 bn each); 6th Portuguese LIR (2 bns), 20 gunners, 6th Caçadores.

Allied total ca 4,600 men.

Allied losses 1/50th – 27 killed, 100 wounded; 1/71st – 5 killed, 52 wounded; 1/92nd – 2 wounded; 6th Caçadores – 2 wounded. Total 189.

Comment Wellington was now ready to invade northern Spain through Ciudad Rodrigo. To insulate his southern flank from French interference he sent Hill to take and destroy the French-held fortified bridge over the Tagus at Almáraz. The raid was a brilliant success and the bridge was destroyed.

Sources Oman, Martinien.

ES Cadiz, 1 June 1812, clash

A fortified port city in southwestern Spain at the junction of Routes IV/E5 and 340.

A French victory over the Spanish.

(Last action – Alhourin, 14 April; next action–Maguilla, 11 June.)

French Forces Gen Conroux commanding the 9e RILé and 96e RIdLi (2 bns each); 16 RILé (1 bn); 5e ChàCh.

French total 4,500 men.

French losses Not known; moderate.

Spanish Forces Gen Ballasteros and 8,500 men exact details not known.

Spanish losses ca 1,500 men, 4 guns.

Sources Oman, Martinien.

ES Maguilla, 11 June 1812, clash

A village in the southwestern Spanish province of Extremadura, on a side road about 17 km northeast of Llerena.

A French victory over the British.

(Last action – Cadiz, 1 June; next action – Sevilla, 28 August.)

French Forces GdB Lallemand commanding: 17e and 27e DragRs.

French total ca 700 sabres.

French losses 51 killed and wounded, 100 captured (most escaped subsequently).
British Forces BG Slade commanding 1st DragR (Royals); 3rd Drag Guards.
British total ca 700 men.
British losses 22 killed, 2 wounded, 118 captured.
Comment In true British cavalry tradition, Slade's initial success went completely out of control and the French reserve squadron took them in flank and caused mayhem.
Sources Oman, Martinien.

EW Salamanca, 17–27 June 1812, siege and capture
A city in western Spain, on Routes 620/E80, 630/E803 and 501, 178 km north west of Madrid.
An Allied victory over the French.
(Last action – Almáraz, 18 May; next action – Salamanca, 22 July.)
French Forces Maj Duchemin commanding: 15e, 65e, 82e and 86e RIdLi, 17e RILé (parts of); 1 artillery coy.
French total 800 men, 36 guns.
French losses 3 officers and 40 men killed, 11 officers and 140 men wounded, 590 unwounded captured.
British Forces The Earl of Wellington commanding: 37,000 Anglo-Portuguese infantry, 3,500 Anglo-Portuguese cavalry, 3,000 Spaniards. Of these, the 6th Portuguese Caçadores and the light companies of the 6th Division carried out the abortive storm on 23 June and the final storm on 27th: 1/11th, 2/53rd, 1/61st, 1/2nd, 1/32nd, 1/36th Foot.
British losses 5 officers and 94 men killed; 29 officers and 302 men wounded. Gen Bowes killed.
Comment M Marmont's Army of Portugal (ca 40,000 men) was circling around Salamanca but made no serious attempt to save the garrison. Wellington missed a good opportunity to destroy Marmont on 20 June. Once again, siege work proved to be Wellington's weak point and cost far too many casualties.
Sources Oman, Martinien.

RM Korelitchi, 9 July 1812, clash
A village on the Minsk-Wolkowysk road, near Mir, in Belarus.
A Russian victory over the Allies (Poles).
(This was the opening action of Napoleon's thrust at Moscow; next action – Mir, 10 July.)
Polish Forces GdB Turno's 2nd Bde of GdD Rozniecki's 4th Lt Cav Div of the IV Cavalry Corps: 3rd, 15th and 16th Lancers (3 sqns each).
Polish total ca 900 men.
Polish losses 356 killed, wounded and captured.
Russian Forces Hetman Platov's Don Cossacks of the 1st Army of the West, Pulks of Grekov VIII, Ilovaiski V, Ilovaiski IX, Ilovaiski XI, Ilovaiski XII, Karpov II, Sysojev III and 1 x HAB.
Russian total ca 4,500 men.
Russian losses Not exactly known, very light.
Sources Vaudoncourt, Malibran and Chelminski, Bogdanovich.

RM Mir, 10 July 1812, clash
A small town in Belarus, on the road from Minsk to Wolkowysk; about 180 km southwest of Minsk and 11 km north to Route 1.
A Russian victory over the Poles.
(Last action – Korelitchi, 9 July; next action – Romanovo, 15 July.)
Polish Forces GdD Rozniecki commanding the 4th Lt Cav Div of Latour-Maubourg's IV Cav Corps: 2nd, 3rd, 9th, 11th, 15th and 16th Lancers (3 sqns each).
Polish total ca 1,600 men.
Polish losses Not exactly known, moderate.
Russian Forces Hetman Platov's Don Cossacks of the 1st Army of the West (3 Pulks of Ilovaisky's); HusR Achtyrsk, DragR Kiev, 1x HAB, MG Kuteinikov's infantry brigade (3 bns).
Russian total ca 5,000 men.
Russian losses ca 180 men killed and wounded.
Comment Despite this tactical success the Russians knew that they were too weak to fight the enemy main body; the withdrawal continued.
Sources Vaudoncourt, Malibran and Chelminski, Bogdanovich.

RM Romanovo, 15 July 1812, clash
A village in the Republic of Belarus, on the road from Minsk to Wolkowysk.
A Russian victory over the Poles.
(Last action – Mir, 10 July; next action – Saltanovka, 23 July.)
Polish Forces Gen Dziewanovski's Lt Cav Bde of the 17th Division V (Polish) Corps.
Polish total ca 700 men.
Polish losses 279 killed, wounded and captured.

Russian Forces Hetman Platov's rearguard of the 1st Army of the West: Cossack Pulks of Ilovaiski (2 Pulks); Karpov (2 Pulks); Kuteinikov (3 Pulks) and Atamanski (1 Pulk); HusR Achtyrsk; DragR Kiev and the Litowski UlR; 5th Jägers (2 bns); 1 x HAB.

Russian total ca 12,000 men.

Russian losses Not known, light.

Sources Vaudoncourt, Malibran and Chelminski, Bogdanovich.

RL Eckau, 19 July 1812, 1st clash

A village in Latvia about 12 km east of Mitau (now Jelgava), about 40 km south of Riga, on the river of the same name.

A Prussian victory over the Russians.

(This was the opening action of the campaign in the north; next action - Schlock, 5 August.)

Prussian Forces GdI von Grawert commanding: IRs 3 and 4 (2 bns each); 2nd and 6th Füs Bns; Ostpreussisches Jg bn; DragRs 1 and 2 (2 sqns each); HusR 3 (2 sqns); 2½ HAB, 1½ FAB.

Prussian total ca 6,585 men.

Prussian losses 10 killed, 68 wounded, 15 missing, 116 horses.

Russian Forces Part of Gen Lewis' corps, mainly depot troops and militia.

Russian total 8 bns (4,200 infantry); 8 sqns(1,200 men); 1 cossack Pulk (500 men), 12 guns.

Russian losses Killed and wounded not known; 319 captured; 1 colour, 3 ammunition waggons.

Comment The Prussian units were combined regiments drawn from the whole army in order to spread the experience of active operations as widely as possible.

Sources KGE 24, Bogdanovich.

EE Castalla, 21 July 1812, clash

A small town in the eastern Spanish province of Alicante, 32 km northwest of Alicante on a minor road between Routes 330 and 340 south of the Rio Seco.

A French victory over the Spanish.

(Last action Roda, 5 March; this was the last action of note in eastern Spain in 1812.)

French Forces GdD Harispe commanding: 1er RILé (3 bns); 7e, 116e RIdLi (2 bns each), 44e RIdLi (1 bn) GdB Delort's Cavalry: 13e CuirR, 24e DragR.

French total 4,000 men.

French losses ca 200 killed and wounded.

Spanish Forces LG J O'Donnell (exact details not known) MG Roche's Division: BG Montijo; IR Cuenca; BG Mijares: 3 bns; BG Michelana's Bde: 2 sqns of cavalry, 2 guns. BG Santesteban's cavalry (800 horse). **Total** ca 10,000 infantry, 1,000 cavalry; 2 guns. **Losses** ca 1,000 killed and wounded, 2,135 unwounded prisoners, 2 guns, 3 colours.

Sources Oman, Martinien.

EW Salamanca (Arapiles), 22 July 1812, battle

A city in the Spanish province of the same name, 178 km northwest of Madrid on the Rio Tormes and at the junction of Routes 620/E80, 630/E803 and 501.

An Allied victory over the French.

(Last action - Salamanca, 27 June; next action - Garcia Hernandez, 23 July.)

French Forces M Marmont commanding: **The Army of Portugal** GdD Foy's **1st Division** 6 RILé, 39e, 69e, 76e RIdLi (2 bns each). GdD Clausel's **2nd Division** 25e RILé (3 bns); 27e RIdLi (2 bns); 50e RIdLi (3 bns); 59e RIdLi (2 bns); GdD Ferey's **3rd Division** 31e RILé, 26e and 70e RIdLi (2 bns each), 47e RIdLi (3 bns). GdD Sarrut's **4th Division** 2e and 4e RILé, 36e RIdLi (3 bns each). GdD Maucune's **5th Division** 15 RIdLi (3 bns); 66e, 82e and 86e RIdLi (2 bns each). GdD Brennier's **6th Division** 17e RILé (2 bns); 22e and 65e RIdLi (3 bns each); Regiment de Prusse (88 men). GdD Thomières' **7th Division** 1er RIdLi (1er and 3e bns); 62e RIdLi (2 bns). GdD Bonnet's **8th Division** 118e, 119e, 120e and 122e RIdLi (3 bns each). GdD Curto's **Lt Cav Division** 3e HusR (3 sqns); 22e and 26e ChàCh (2 sqns each); 28e ChàCh (1 sqn); 13e ChàCh (5 sqns); 14e ChàCh (4 sqns); 1x Escadron de marche. GdD Boyer's **Dragoon Division** 6e, 11e, 15e and 25e DragRs (2 sqns each).

French total 43,266 infantry, 3,575 cavalry, 2,811 artillery, engineers and train, 78 guns.

French losses ca 10,000 killed and wounded, 4,000 captured, 10,000 stragglers. Generals Ferey, Thomières and Berthelot killed, M Marmont, GdDs Clausel and Bonnet wounded, 20 guns, 2 eagles (22e and 101e RIdLi) and 6 colours (66e, 82e and 26e RIdLi).

Allied Forces The Earl of Wellington commanding:

British Troops Cavalry Gen Stapleton Cotton: Le Marchant's Brigade: 3rd, 4th and 5th DragRs. G Anson's Brigade: 11th, 12th and 16th LDRs. Von Alten's Brigade: 14th LDR, 1st HusR KGL; von Bock's

Brigade: 1st and 2nd DragRs KGL. **Infantry** H Campbell's **1st Division** 1/2nd Guards, 1/3rd Guards, (1 bn each), 5/60th Foot (1 coy). 2/24th, 1/42nd, 2/58th, 1/79th Foot (1 bn each); 5/60th Foot (1 coy). Löwe's Brigade 1st, 2nd and 5th bns KGL (1 bn each). **3rd Division** (Pakenham): 1/45th, 1/74th, 1/88th Foot (1 bn each); 5/60th Foot (3 coys). 1/5th, 2/5th, Caçadores (1 bn each); 1 x FAB. **Portuguese total** 18,017 men, 6 guns.

Spanish Troops Gen Carlos de Espana commanding: IRs Princesa (2nd bn); 2nd of Jaén (1 bn); 1st Seville (3rd bn), Cazadores de Castilla and Tiradores de Castilla (1 bn each); Lanceros de Castilla (2 sqns). **Spanish Total**: 3,360 men.

Allied Losses at Salamanca

	killed		wounded		missing		Total
	officers	men	officers	men	officers	men	
British	28	360	176	2,491	—	74	3,129
Portuguese	22	484	50	976	—	86	1,627
Spanish	—	2	—	4	—	—	6
Total	50	846	235	3,471	—	160	4,762

Gen Le Marchant killed.

2/83rd, 1/94th Foot (1 bn each). **4th Division** (Lowry Cole): 3/27th, 1/40th Foot (1 bn each); 5/60th Foot (1 coy). 1/7th, 1/23rd, 1/48th Foot (1 bn each); Brunswick Oels (1 coy). **5th Division** (Leith): 3/1st, 1/9th, 1/38th, 2/38th (1 bn each), Brunswick Oels (1 coy) 1/4th, 2/4th, 2/30th, 2/44th Foot (1 bn each); Brunswick Oels (1 coy). **6th Division** (Clinton): 1/11th, 2/53rd, 1/61st Foot (1 bn each); 5/60th Foot (1 coy) 1/2nd, 1/32nd, 1/36th Foot (1 bn each). **7th Division** (Hope): 1st, 2nd LtI Bns KGL, Brunswick Oels (9 coys). 1/51st, 1/68th Foot, Chasseurs Britanniques (1 bn each). **Light Division** (C. Alten); 1/43rd (1 bn); detachments of 2/95th and 3/95th (1 bn). 1/52nd Foot (1 bn); 1/95th (8 coys). 3 x HAB 6 x FAB. **British Total:** 30,562 men, 54 guns.

Portuguese Troops d'Urban's Cavalry Brigade: 1st and 11th DragRs (3 sqns each). Power's Brigade (with the 3rd Division): 9th and 21st LIR (2 bns each); 12th Caçadores (1 bn). Stubbs' Brigade (with the 4th Division): 11th and 23rd LIR (2 bns each); 7th Caçadores (1 bn). Spry's Brigade (with the 5th Division): 3rd and 15th LIR (2 bns each); 8th Caçadores (1 bn). Rezende's Brigade (with the 6th Division): 8th and 12th LIR (2 bns each); 9th Caçadores (1 bn). Collins' Brigade (with the 7th Division): 7th and 19th LIR (2 bns each); 2nd Caçadores (1 bn). Pack's Independent Brigade: 1st and 16th LIR (2 bns each); 4th Caçadores (1 bn). Bradford's Independent Brigade: 14th and 18th LIR (2 bns each); 5th Caçadores (1 bn). Attached to the Light Division: 1st and 3rd

Comment This brilliant and crushing victory came after some weeks of cautious manoeuvring about the area by both commanders. Wellington's excellent use of ground to conceal his troops this day led Marmont to overextend his army in the face of the enemy and for this he paid a high price. This battle is commemorated in the phrase '40,000 men defeated in 40 minutes'.

The Army of Portugal was totally incapable of coherent operations for days afterwards but, inexplicably, Wellington did not pursue with any real energy even though his 7th Division had hardly been engaged. Even over the next few days Wellington allowed the beaten enemy time to regroup and thus lost the chance to destroy Marmont completely.

Sources Oman, Martinien.

EW Garcia Hernandez, 23 July 1812, clash

A village in western Spain about 20 km southeast of Salamanca and on the minor road from Alba de Tormes (on the Rio Tormes) eastwards to Penaranda.

An Allied victory over the French.

(Last action - Salamanca, 22 July; next action - Las Rozas, 11 August.)

French Forces GdD Foy commanding the 1st Division, Army of Portugal: 6e RILé, 76e RIdLi, 39e and 69e RIdLi (2 bns each), 1x FAB and some of Curto's ChàCh who fled before the action began.

French total 4,000 men.

French losses ca 1,100 killed, wounded and captured.

One battalion of 76e was destroyed; the 6eLé was also badly mauled.

Allied Forces BG von Bock commanding: 1st and 2nd DragRs KGL (2 sqns each).

Allied total ca 770 men.

Allied losses 1st DragR: 2 officers and 28 men killed, 2 officers and 37 men wounded. 2nd DragR: 1 officer and 21 men killed, 1 officer and 29 men wounded, 6 men missing.

Comment This was a classically successful cavalry charge against infantry in battalion squares whose morale was deeply shaken by the shattering defeat of Salamanca the previous day. Anson's 11th and 16th LDRs followed up the retreating French.

Sources Oman, Martinien.

RM Saltanovka (Mohilev), 23 July 1812, clash

A village 10 km west of the town of Mohilev on the road to Minsk in Belarus, about 2 kms west of the River Dniepr.

A French victory over the Russians.

(Last action – Romanovo, 15 July; next action – Ostrovno, 25–27 July.)

French Forces M Davout commanding the I Corps: GdD Desaix's 4th Div: 85e RIdLi (1er–4e bns); GdD Compans' 6th Div: 61e RIdLi (1er–4e bns); 108e RIdLi (1er–4e and 6e bns). GdB Bourdesoulle's 2nd Lt Cav Bde: 3e ChàCh (4 sqns), GdD Valence's 5th Cuir Div of I Cavalry Corps (present but not engaged); 2 x FAB.

French total ca 28,000 men and 12 guns.

French losses 4,134 killed, wounded and missing.

Russian Forces LG Raievsky commanding the VII Corps of the 2nd Army of the West. MG Kolubakin's 12th Inf Div*: IRs Smolensk, Narva, Alexopol and New Ingermannland, 6th and 41st Jägers (2 bns each). MG Paskievich's 26th Inf Div: IRs Ladoga, Poltava, Nishegorod and Orel; 5th and 42nd Jägers (2 bns each). Gen Count Sievers' IV Cavalry Corps*, 20 guns.

Russian total ca 20,000 men.

Russian losses 2,548 killed, wounded and missing.

* = seem not to have been engaged.

Comment The 2nd Russian Army had failed to break through to join up with the 1st at Mir on 10 July. This was a re-run; a tactical victory but the drive north had to be abandoned again. The two armies eventually united at Smolensk on 1 August.

Sources Vaudoncourt, Martinien, Foord, Stein, Bogdanovich.

RM Ostrovno, 25–27 July 1812, clash

A village on the left bank of the River Dwina, 20 km west of Witebsk in the Republic of Belarus.

A French victory over the Russians.

(Last action – Saltanovka, 23 July; next action – Jakubovo, 28 July.)

French Forces M Murat commanding. GdD Nansouty's I Cavalry Corps; GdD Bruyère's 1st Lt Cav Div; GdB Jacquinot's 3rd Lt Cav Bde: 7e HusR (4 sqns); GdB Piré's 4th Lt Cav Bde: 8e HusR, 16e ChàCh (4 sqns each); GdB Nienwiewski's 15th Lt Cav Bde: 6th and 8th Polish Lancers (4 sqns each); 2nd Prussian HusR (4 sqns). GdD Delzons' 13th Inf Div (IV Corps): 8e RILé (1st and 2nd bns); 84e, 92e and 106e RIdLi (4 bns each); 1st Croatian IR (2 bns). 2 x HAB; 2 x FAB.

French total ca 22,000 men.

French losses 3,000 killed and wounded, 300 captured.

Russian Forces LG Count Ostermann-Tolstoi's IV Corps, 1st Army of the West: 11th Inf Div MG Choglokov: IRs Kexholm, Pernau, Polotsk and Jeletz, 1st and 33rd Jägers (2 bns each). 23rd Inf Div MG Bakhmetiev: IRs Ryisk, Yekaterinburg, Zelenginsk, 18th Jägers (2 bns each). Cavalry: Life Guard HusR, Sumy HusR; DragRs Ingermannland and Kargopol (5 sqns each); 4 x FAB, 1 x HAB.

Russian total 14,000 men, 66 guns.

Russian losses 2,500 killed and wounded, 6 guns.

Sources Vaudoncourt, Foord, Stein, Martinien Bogdanovich.

RS Kobryn, 27 July 1812, 1st clash

A village in Grodno province 47 km east of Brest-Litowsk, in the southwestern corner of the Republic of Belarus, on Route E30.

A victory of the Russians over the Saxons.

(This was the first action of note on the southern flank; next action – Rudnia, 8 August.)

Saxon Forces GM von Klengel commanding: IRs König (2 bns) and vacant von Niesemeuschel (1½ bns); UlR Prinz Clemens (3 sqns), 8 guns.

Saxon total ca 3,500 men.

Saxon losses 108 killed, 178 wounded, the rest captured; 4 colours.

Russian Forces GdC Count Tormasov's Third Army of the West: 18th Inf Div MG Cherbatov: IRs Vladimir, Tambov, Kostroma and Dnieprov, 28th and 32nd Jägers (3 bns each); DragR Tver, Taganrog, Starodub (5 sqns each).

Russian total 12,000 men, 22 guns.

Russian losses Not known, light.

Sources Stein, Schuster and Franke, Vaudoncourt, Foord, Bogdanovich.

RM Jakubovo, 28 July 1812, clash

A village near the River Dwina, about 10 km west of the town of Witebsk in the Republic of Belarus.

A Franco-Polish victory over the Russians.

(Last action - Ostrovno, 26/27 July; next action - Krasnoi, 14 August.)

Franco-Polish Forces M Murat commanding: GdB Niemojewski's Polish Lt Cav Bde: 6th and 8th Lancers (4 sqns each); GdB Axamitowski's Polish Lt Cav Bde: 10th Hussars (4 sqns). M Oudinot's II Corps: GdD Legrand's 6th Inf Div: 56e RIdLi (4 bns); 128e RIdLi (2 bns). GdD Verdier's 8th Inf Div: 37e RIdLi (4 bns); GdB Castex's 5th Lt Cav Bde: 23e ChàCh (2 sqns). Also the 8e DragR (4 sqns).

Franco-Polish total ca 11,000 men.

Franco-Polish losses Not known, light.

Russian Forces LG Count Ostermann-Tolstoi's IV Corps, 1st Army of the West (see details for Ostrovno, 26/27 July).

Russian total ca 11,000 men, 12 guns.

Russian losses ca 1,000, mostly captured.

Comment The 8th Polish Lancers overran a Russian infantry battalion square.

Sources Vaudoncourt, Martinien, Malibran and Chelminski, Bogdanovich.

RN Kliastitzy, 28 July 1812, 1st skirmish

A village in the north of the Belarussian province of Witebsk, 35 km north of Polotsk, close to the River Drissa and on the River Swolna.

A Russian victory over the Franco-Poles.

(Last action - this was the opening action on the Northern Central Flank; next action - Kliastitzy, 30 July - 1 August.)

Franco-Polish Forces GdB Corbineau's 6th Lt Cav Bde: 7e and 20e ChàCh (2 sqns each), 8th Polish Lancers (4 sqns).

Franco-Polish total ca 650 men.

Franco-Polish losses 167 men captured.

Russian Forces MG Kulniev of Wittgenstein's I Corps, 1st Army of the West. Life Guard HusR (4 sqns); HusR Grodno (8 sqns), Don Cossack Pulk of Platov IV.

Russian total ca 2,000 men.

Russian losses Not known, very light.

Sources Martinien, Vaudoncourt, Bogdanovich, Malibran and Chelminski, Gembarzewski.

RN Kliastitzy, Oboarszina 30/31 July/1 August 1812, 2nd skirmish

A village in the north of the Belarussian province of Witebsk, 35 km north of Polotsk, close to the River Drissa and on the River Swolna.

A Russian victory over the French.

(Last action - Kliastitzy, 28 July; next action - Golovchtchitzy, 2 August.)

French Forces M Oudinot commanding the II Corps: 6th Division GdD Legrand: 26e RILé, 19e and 56e RIdLi (4 bns each) 2 x FAB. GdB Castex's 5th Lt Cav Bde: 23e ChàCh (3 sqns).

French total ca 10,000 men.

French losses Not known exactly; moderate to heavy.

Russian Forces LG Count Wittgenstein's I Corps, 1st Army of the West: Advanced Guard MG Kulniev: 5th Cavalry Brigade HusR Grodno (8 sqns): Don Cossack Pulk of Platov IV, 25th and 26th Jägers (2 bns each), 1 x HAB. 23rd and 24th Jägers. 5th Division MG Berg: IRs Kiev, Kaluga, Perm, Mohilev, 14th Division MG Sasanov: IRs Tula, Navaginsk, Tenginsk, Estonia; GrenR Pavlov (2nd bn). 3rd Cav Bde: DragRs Riga and Yamburg (4 sqns each) 6 x FAB.

Russian total ca 26,000 men.

Russian losses Not known; moderate.

Comment Oudinot broke off his probe to the north and withdrew south to Polotsk.

Sources Vaudoncourt, Martinien, Bogdanovich.

RN Golovchtchitzy, 2 August 1812, clash

A village in the north of the Republic of Belarus, north of Polotsk, close to the River Drissa.

A Russian victory over the French.

(Last action - Kliastitzy, 30/31 July, next action - Swolna, 11 August.)

French Forces GdD Verdier's 8th Division, II Corps: 11e RILé (4 bns) 6th Division GdD Legrand: 26e RILé,

56e RIdLi (4 bns each). 9th Division GdD Merle: 3rd Swiss IR (3 bns).

French total ca 9,000 men.

French losses Not known, moderate.

Russian Forces MG Berg's 5th Division of LG Count Wittgenstein's I Corps, 1st Army of the West: IRs Perm, Mohilev, 23rd and 24th Jägers (2 bns each), MG Kazatchkowski's Brigade. IRs Kaluga, Sievsk, 25th and 26th Jägers (2 bns each); Rostov GrenR (Depot bn).

Russian total ca 13,000 men.

Russian losses Not known; light.

Comment This was a successful Russian ambush; the French withdrew to Polotsk.

Sources Martinien, Bogdanovich, Vaudoncourt.

RL Schlock, 5 August 1812, 1st skirmish

A village in Latvia about 18 km west of Riga, on the Baltic coast.

An Anglo-Russian victory over the Prussians.

(Last action - Eckau, 19 July; next action - Wolgund, 7 August.)

Prussian Forces Majors von Crammon and von Thümen commanding: 1st Füs Bn (1 bn); Ostpreussisches Jg Bn (30 men); HusR Nr 3 (2 sqns).

Prussian total ca 620 men.

Prussian losses ca 10 killed and wounded, 50 captured.

Russian Forces Gen Lewis with several battalions, some cavalry and 13 British gunboats.

Russian total Not known.

Russian losses Not known.

Comment The gunboats sailed up the River Aa and bombarded the Prussians who fled into a swamp where they hid all night. The gunboats also carried a battalion of Russian infantry with them.

Sources KGE 24.

RL Wolgund, 7 August 1812, clash

A small village near Riga, capital of Latvia, 10 km downstream from Mitau towards Riga on the River Aa.

A Prussian victory over the Russians.

(Last action - Schlock, 5 August; next action - Dahlenkirchen, 22 August.)

Prussian Forces GM von Kleist commanding: IR Nr 3 (1st and 2nd bns); IR Nr 6 (3 coys); Füs Bn Nr 1, HusR Nr 3 (2 sqns); DragR Nr 2 (2 sqns), 5 guns.

Prussian total ca 2,700 men.

Prussian losses 65 killed and wounded.

Russian Forces Gen Lewis with 8 bns of Militia and Depot Grenadiers, 200 cavalry, 6 guns and 6 gunboats.

Russian losses ca 140 killed and wounded.

Sources KGE 24.

RS Rudnia, 8 August, 1812, clash

The location of this village in the Republic of Belarus is not known but it was somewhere east of Kobryn.

The outcome of the action was a set back for the Russians.

(Last action - Kobryn, 27 July; next action - Gorodeczna, 12 August.)

Austrian Forces FML Bianchi commanding the 1st Div: IR Hiller Nr 2 (2 bns); IR Davidovich Nr 34 (2nd bn). From FML Trautenberg's 3rd Div: 5th Jägers (1 bn); HusR Kienmayer Nr 8 (6 sqns); From FML Frimont's Res Div: ChLR Hohenzollern Nr 2 (6 sqns).

Austrian total ca 4,200 men.

Austrian losses Not known.

French Forces 24 RILé (4 bns) (of 10th Division); 11e and 12e ChàCh (3 sqns each) of 7th Lt Cav Bde, II Cav Corps.

French total ca 2,300 men.

French losses Not known.

Russian Forces Exact details not known; part of GdC Tormasov's Third Army of the West (see Gorodeczna, 12 August).

Russian losses Not known.

Comment Another action involving Schwarzenberg's Austrians took place at Pruszany on 10 August but further details are unknown.

Sources Wrede, Martinien, Bogdanovich.

RN Swolna, 11 August 1812, clash

A village in the southeastern corner of the Baltic Republic of Latvia, on the River Swolna, 90 km east of Dünaburg (nowadays Dugavpils).

A Russian victory over the French.

(Last action - Golovchtchitzy, 2 August; next action - Polotsk, 16-18 August.)

French Forces M Oudinot commanding II Corps. 8th Division GdD Verdier: 11e RILé, 2e and 37e RIdLi (4 bns each); 124e RIdLi (3 bns). 3rd Cuirassier Div GdD Doumerc: 4e and 7e CuirRs (4 sqns each).

French total ca 9,000 men.

French losses 1,200 killed and wounded, 300 captured.

Russian Forces GM d'Auvray commanding. d'Auvray was standing in for Count Wittgenstein (commander, I Detached Corps, 1st Army of the West) who had been wounded at Golovchtschitzy. Avantgarde MG Kazatchowski: 23rd JgR (2 bns); DragR Jamburg (2 sqns); 1st HAB (9 guns). Main Body, First Rank MG Berg's 5th Division: Combined KürR (4 sqns); IRs Perm, Mohilev, Sievsk and Kaluga (2 bns each); 5th and 28th PosBs (24 guns). Second Rank MG Sasanov's 14th Division: IRs Tula, Navaginsk, Tenginsk, Estonia (2 bns each); 14th PosB, 27th FAB. The Reserve MG Kachowski: Combined Grenadiers of 14th Division (2 bns); Depot Grenadier bns (6 bns) DragR Jamburg (2 sqns) 27th PosB (6 guns), 3rd HAB (12 guns). MG Helfreich: 24th, 25th and 26th JgRs (2 bns each); HusR Grodno (8 sqns), 2 Cossack Pulks, 1 x HAB, 1 x FAB.

Russian total 32 bns, 14 sqns, 2 Cossack Pulks, 75 guns. ca 20,000 men.

Russian losses 800 killed, wounded and missing.

Sources Bodart, Vaudoncourt, Martinien, Bogdanovich.

EW Las Rozas, 11 August 1812, clash

A village in central Spain, 17 km northwest of Madrid on the road to El Escorial.

A drawn match between the Allies and the French.

(Last action – Garcia Hernandez, 23 July; next action – Retiro, 13 August.)

French Forces Treilhard's Cavalry Division: 19e and 22e DragR (3 sqns each); Italian Drag de Napoleone, Westfalian ChLL, 13e and 18e DragRs.

French total ca 2,000 men.

French losses Not known exactly, probably about 200 in all.

Allied Force Gen d'Urban commanding: 1st, 11th and 12th Portuguese DragRs, 1st and 2nd DragRs KGL, 4 guns. Later in the action the 1st KGL LtI Bn joined in.

Allied total ca 2,300 men.

Allied losses KGL cavalry: 1 officer and 13 men killed, 5 officers and 35 men wounded, 1 officer and 6 men captured. Portuguese: 3 officers and 30 men killed, 3 officers and 49 men wounded, 1 officer and 22 men captured. KGL LtI Bn – 7 wounded.

Comment Treilhard had been sent by King Joseph to find out if Wellington's advance on Madrid from Salamanca was a serious threat. He caught the Allied cavalry by surprise and took 3 guns but these were later recovered when the Allies rallied and counter-attacked. On the basis of Treilhard's subsequent report, Joseph hastily abandoned Madrid and fled south to Aranjuez.

Sources Oman, Martinien.

RS Gorodeczna (Podobna), 12 August 1812, battle

A village in the Republic of Belarus, in the province of Grodno, 53 km northeast of Brest-Litowsk, towards Slonim.

An Austro-Saxon victory over the Russians.

(Last action – Rudnia, 8 August; next action – Neswitsch, 20 September.)

Austro-Saxon Forces GdK Prince Schwarzenberg commanding.

Austrian Troops 1st Division FML Bianchi: IRs Simbschen Nr 48, Allvintzy Nr 19, Colloredo Nr 32, Hiller Nr 2, Esterházy Nr 32 (2 bns each): Gren Bn Brzeczinski (1 bn). **2nd Division** FML Siegenthal: IR Kottulinsky Nr 41 (2 bns); GzIR Warasdiner-Kreutzer Nr 5 (1 bn). **3rd Division** FML Trautenberg: IRs Duka Nr 39 and Beaulieu Nr 58 (2 bns each); Jägers (5th bn); GzIR St Georger (1 bn). Reserve Division FML Frimont: HusR Kaiser Nr 1, ChLRs O'Reilly Nr 3 and Hohenzollern Nr 2 (6 sqns each), DragR Levenehr Nr 4 (4 sqns).

Saxon Troops (GL Reynier) VII Corps. **21st Division** GL von Lecoq: 1st Bde GM von Steindel: Gren Bn von Liebenau (1 bn); IRs Prinz Friedrich and Prinz Clemens (2 bns each): 2nd Bde GM von Nostitz: IR Prinz Anton, 1st LtIR (2 bns each). Cavalry Bde GM von Gablenz: UlR Prinz Clemens, ChLR vacant von Polenz (4 sqns each). **22nd Division** GL von Funck: 2nd Bde GM von Sahr: Gren bns von Anger and von Spiegel (1 bn each); 2nd LtIR (2 bns) Artillery 18 guns.

Allied total ca 18,000 men, 48 guns.

Allied losses Austrians: 1,300 killed, wounded and missing. Saxons: 175 killed, 687 wounded, 68 captured.

Russian Forces GdC Count Tormasov's **Third Army of the West** LG Markov. **9th Inf Division** IRs Nascheburg, Riashsk and 10th Jägers (2 bns each). 15th Inf Div MG Nazimov: IRs Koslov and Kura, 14th Jägers (2 bns each). 18th Inf Div LG Count Kamenskoi: IRs Kostroma and Dnieprovsk, 28th

Jägers (2 bns each); IRs Vladimir and Witebsk, (2 bns each). Cavalry (5th Div) MG Count Lambert: 15th Cav Bde: DragRs Tver and Starodub (5 sqns each). 17th Cav Bde: HusR Alexandria; Tartar UlanR, 14th Cav Bde: Pavlograd HusR; Taganrog DragR; Don Cossack Pulk.

Russian total ca 38,000 men and 42 guns.

Russian losses ca 3,000 killed, wounded and missing.

Comment The Russians withdrew south to Lutzk and were joined by Langeron's division.

Sources Vaudoncourt, Wrede, Schuster and Franke, Stein, Bogdanovich.

EW Retiro (Madrid), 13 August 1812, surrender of

A fortified place on the western side of Madrid, capital of Spain.

An Allied victory over the French.

(Last action - Las Rozas, 11 August; next action - Burgos, 21 October.)

French Garrison Gen Lafon Blaniac commanding: 12e RILé (3e bn); 27e RILé (2 coys); 45e RIdLi (3e bn), detachments of 50e and 51e RIdLi and some reinforcement drafts.

French total 2,046 men.

French losses All captured.

Allied Forces The Earl of Wellington commanding: 600 men of the 3rd and 7th Divisions including 300 from the 51st and 68th Foot.

Allied losses 10 killed and wounded.

Comment Apart from large stocks of shoes, clothing and equipment, the eagles of the 13e DragR and 51e RIdLi (which were stored there) were also taken. Wellington occupied Madrid for some weeks.

Sources Oman, Martinien, Charrié.

RM Krasnoi, 14 August 1812, 1st clash

A village in the western Russian province of Smolensk, 40 km southwest of Smolensk city, near the border with the Republic of Belarus.

A French victory over the Russians.

(Last action - Jakubovo, 28 July; next action - Smolensk, 17/18 August.)

French Forces M Ney commanding the III Corps. GdD Ledru's 10th Inf Div: (was in reserve, not engaged); 9th Lt Cav Bde Mouriez: 6eChLL (3 sqns); 4th Württemberg; JzPf (4 sqns). 1st Cuir Div GdD Defrance: 1er CuirR (4 sqns): 14th Lt Cav Bde GdB Beuermann: 1st and 2nd Württemberg ChLRs (4 sqns each); 2e and 3e (French) ChàCh. (3 sqns). 9th Polish Lancers (4 sqns); 6e ChLL (4 sqns).

French total 15,000 cavalry, 30 guns.

French losses ca 500 men.

Russian Forces MG Neverovski commanding the 27th Inf Div, VIII Corps, 2nd Army of the West: IRs Wilna, Zimbirsk, Poltava, 41st, 49th and 50th Jägers (2 bns each); DragR Charkov (4 sqns); Cossack Pulks of Olienin and Leslie.

Russian total 7,200 men, 14 guns.

Russian losses 640 killed, wounded and missing, 7 guns.

Comment During this action the 9th Polish Lancers overran a battery of 8 Russian guns but were unable to bring them off.

Sources Vaudoncourt, Martinien, Malibran and Chelminski, Bogdanovich.

RN Polotsk, 16–18 August 1812, 1st battle

A town in the north of the Belarussian province of Witebsk, on the right bank of the River Dwina, 95 km northwest of Witebsk town.

A 'drawn match' between the Franco-Bavarians and the Russians.

(Last action - Swolna, 11 August; next action - Polotsk, 18–20 October.)

Franco-Bavarian Forces M Oudinot commanding: **II Corps** M Oudinot: 6th Div GdD Legrand: 26e RILé, 19e, 56e RIdLi (4 bns each). 8th Div GdD Verdier: 11e RILé (4 bns); 2e RIdLi (5 bns). 9th Div GdD Merle: 3rd Croatian IR (2 bns). 1st, 2nd, 3rd Swiss IRs (8 bns). 3rd Cuir Div GdD Doumerc: 4e and 7e CuirR (4 sqns each). 5th Lt Cav Bde GdB Castex: 24e ChàCh (3 sqns). 6th Lt Cav Bde GdB Corbineau: 20e ChàCh (2 sqns). 7 x FAB, 4 x HAB.

VI (Bavarian) Corps M Gouvion St Cyr: 19th Div GL Count Deroy: 1st LtI Bn (1 bn), 1st and 9th LIRs (2 bns each); 3rd LtI Bn (1 bn); 4th and 10th LIRs (2 bns each); 6th LtI Bn (1 bn), 8th LIR (2 bns). 20th Div LG von Wrede: 2nd and 6th LIRs (2 bns each), 4th LtI Bn (1 bn); 3rd and 7th LIR (2 bns each); 5th LtI Bn (1 bn), 5th and 11th LIRs (2 bns each). 9 x FAB.

Franco-Bavarian total ca 18,000 men, 120 guns.

Franco-Bavarian losses ca 6,000 killed, wounded and missing. M Oudinot wounded. Bavarian GL Count Deroy and GM von Siebein killed. 2 guns were lost. Generals von Vincenti, Valentin and Raglowitsch were wounded.

Russian Forces LG Count Wittgenstein commanding the **I Detached Corps, 1st Army of the West:** First Rank, Right Wing: 23rd, 25th and 26th JgRs (6 bns); PosB Nr 28 (6 guns); HAB Nr 1 (9 guns). Centre: IRs Tula, Estonia (2 bns each) 18th JgR (Depot Bn); IR Navaginsk (1 bn); PosBs Nr 5 and 27 (6 guns each). Left Wing: IR Perm, Mohilev, Kaluga, 1st Combined IR (2 bns each); Combined Gren Bns of the 5th Division (2 bns); PosB Nr 5 (6 guns); FAB Nr 26 (12 guns); HAB Nr 3 (6 guns). Second Rank, Right Wing: Life DragR (Depot Sqn); PosB Nr 28 (6 guns). Centre: IR Sievsk (2 bns); Combined IRs (6 bns); Life HusR (Depot Sqn); HAB Nr 1, PosB Nr 5, FAB Nr 9 (33 guns). Left Wing: PosB Nr 28 (6 guns); FAB Nr 26 (12 guns). Gen Wlastov's Advanced Guard: 24th JgR (2 bns); HusR Grodno (4 sqns); Life UlR (Depot Sqn); IR Tenginsk (2 bns), 11th JgR (Depot Bn); PosB Nr 14, PosB Nr 28, FAB Nr 10, HAB Nr 3 (33 guns). Reserve: Combined Depot and Grenadier bns (9 bns); DragRs Jamburg and Riga.

Russian total ca 22,000 men, 135 guns.

Russian losses ca 5,500 killed, wounded and missing including Generals Berg, Hamen and Kazatchkowski wounded.

Comment At about 1800 hrs, 17 August, the Russians were reinforced by 1 bn Pawlow GrenR and 1 combined grenadier bn. The Russian left wing was scarcely engaged. At one point on 18 August the DragR Riga and HusR Grodno captured a battery of 15 guns but could only bring off 2 of them. All officers of the Grodno Hussars were casualties this day.

Sources Vaudoncourt, Martinien, Preysing-Moos, Leyh, Bogdanovich, Holzhausen.

RM Smolensk, 17/18 August 1812, battle

A fortified city in western Russia, capital of the province Smolensk, on both banks of the River Dniepr, about 70 km from the border with Belarus.

A 'drawn match' between the Allies and the Russians.

(Last action – Krasnoi, 14 August; next action – Valutina Gora 19 August.)

Allied Forces Emperor Napoleon I commanding.

M Ney's III Corps GdD Ledru's 10th Inf Div: 24e RILé 46e and 72th RIdLi (4 bns each), 1st Portuguese IR (2 bns) GdD Razout's 11th Inf Div: 4e RIdLi (4 bns). GL Scheeler's 25th Inf Div (Württembergers): 1st LtI Bn, 1st and 2nd Jäger bns (1 bn each); 1st, 2nd, 4th and 6th LIRs (2 bns each); 9th Lt Cav Bde GdB Mouriez: 11e HusR (4 sqns); 14th Lt Cav Bde GdB Beuermann: 28e ChàCh (1 sqn+); 1st and 2nd Württemberg ChLRs (4 sqns each). Also the 8e ChàCh and the 7e HusR (4 sqns each). 6 x FAB, 3 x HAB.

V Corps LG Prince Poniatowski commanding 16th Inf Div GdD Zayonchek: 3rd, 13th, 15th and 16th IRs (3 bns each); 4th ChàCh (4 sqns). 18th Inf Div GdD Kamienicki: 2nd, 8th and 12th IRs (3 bns each). 20th Lt Cav Bde: 5th ChàCh, 12th Lancers (4 sqns each); 4 x FAB, 1 x HAB.

Allied totals ca 50,000 men, 84 guns.

Allied losses The Poles lost 2,064, the III Corps ca 6,500 killed, wounded and missing. Imperial Guard: 4e Tirailleurs (1 bn); 1er Voltigeurs (2 bns), were also involved.

Russian Forces GdI Barclay de Tolly commanding:.

The 1st Army of the West VI Corps GdI Dochtorov: 7th Inf Div MG Kapsevich: IRs Pskov, Moscow, Libau and Sophia, 11th and 36th Jägers (2 bns each). 24th Inf Div MG Lichatschev: IRs Ufa, Shirvan, Butyrsk, Tomsk, 19th and 40th Jägers (2 bns each).

The 2nd Army of the West GdI Prince Bagration: **VII Corps** LG Raievsky: 12th Inf Div: MG Kolubakin: IR Smolensk, Narva, Alexopol and New Ingermannland, 6th and 41st Jägers (2 bns each), 3 x FAB, 1 x HAB. 26th Inf Div MG Paskievich: IRs Ladoga, Poltava, Nishegorod, Orel, 5th and 42nd Jägers (2 bns each). **VIII Corps** LG Borosdin I: 2nd Grenadier Div MG Prince Karl of Mecklenburg: GrenRs Kiev, Astrakhan, Moscow, Phanagoria, Siberia and Little Russia (2 bns each), 3 x FAB, Combined Grenadier bns. MG Count Woronzov: 2 bns each from 2nd, 12th and 26th Divisions. 27th Inf Div MG Neverovski: IRs Odessa, Zhitomir, Wilna, Zimbirsk, 49th and 50th Jägers (2 bns each). **IV Cavalry Corps** MG Count Sievers I: DragRs Charkov, Tschernigov, Kiev, New Russia (4 sqns each), HusR Achtyrsk, Lithuanian Ulans (8 sqns each) 1 x HAB. 2nd Cuirassier Div MG Knorring: CuirRs Yekaterinoslav, Military Order, Gluchov, Novgorod and Little Russia (4 sqns each). Cossacks MG Ilovaiski V: 9 cossack Pulks, 1 x HAB.

Russian total 30,000 men, 108 guns.

Russian losses ca 6,000 killed, wounded and captured.

Comment It was here that the Russians united their 1st and 2nd Armies of the West and thus frustrated Napoleon's plans to catch them in isolation and destroy them individually. The campaign had now been decided but the Russians continued their withdrawal to lure the enemy even further eastwards.

Sources Martinien, Vaudoncourt, Malibran and Chelminski, Lünsmann, Bogdanovich.

RM Valutina-Gora (Lubino), 19 August 1812, battle

A village in the western Russian province of Smolensk, 8 km northeast of Smolensk city.

A drawn match between the French and the Russians.

(Last action – Smolensk, 17/18 August; next action – Schewardino, 5 September.)

French Forces M Ney commanding.

III Corps 10th Inf Div GdD Ledru: 24e RILé, 46e, 72e, RIdLi (4 bns each); 1st IR Portuguese Legion (2 bns) 11th Inf Div GdD Razout: 4e, 18e and 93e RIdLi (4 bns each). 25th Inf Div (Württembergers) LG Scheeler: 1st and 2nd Jäger bns, 1st and 2nd LtI Bns (1 bn each); LIRs Nrs 1,2 4 and 6 (2 bns each). 14th Lt Cav Bde GdB Beuermann 4e ChàCh (4 sqns); 28e ChàCh (1 sqn+); 1st and 2nd Württemberg ChLRs (4 sqns each); 9th Lt Cav Bde GdB Mouriez: 11e HusR (4 sqns).

I Corps M Davout commanding: 3rd Inf Div GdD Gudin: 7e RILé, 12e and 21e RIdLi (5 bns each); 127e RIdLi (2 bns). Also the 7e and 11e HusRs (4 sqns each).

VIII Corps (Westfalians) GdD Junot commanding: 24th Inf Div GL von Ochs: Ch Carabinier bn, 1st Light bn (1 bn each); Lt Cav Bde GM von Hammerstein: 1st and 2nd HusR (4 sqns each).

French total ca 41,000 men.

French losses 9,000 killed, wounded and missing. GdD Gudin killed.

Russian Forces LG Tutschkov I commanding.

III Corps 3rd Inf Div LG Konovnitzin: IRs Murom, Reval, Tschernigov, Kaporie, 20th and 21st Jägers (2 bns each), 3 x FAB. 1st Gren Div GM Count Stroganov: LeibGrenR, GrenRs Arakchejev, Pavlovsk, Yekaterinoslav, St Petersburg and Tauride (2 bns each) 3 x FAB. Life Guard CossackR (4 sqns); Teptjärsk Cossacks (5 sqns). 1 x HAB.

IV Corps LG Count Ostermann-Tolstoi: 11th Inf Div GM Bakhmetiev II: IRs Kexholm, Pernau, Polotsk, Jeletz, 1st and 33rd Jägers (2 bns each); 3 x FAB. 23rd Inf Div GM Bakhmetiev I: IRs Rilsk, Yekaterinburg, Selenginsk, 18th Jägers (2 bns each) Combined Grenadiers of 11th and 23rd Divisions (3 bns). Cavalry: HusRs Elisabethgrad, Isum, Sumy and Maripol (4 sqns each).

LG Baggowut's **II Corps** LG Baron Korff: 7th Jägers (2 bns) 3 Cossack Pulks, 1 x HAB.

Russian total 22,000 men.

Russian losses 5,000 killed and wounded.

Comment Junot so mishandled his VIII Corps that the Russians slipped out of Napoleon's clutches once again.

Sources Vaudoncourt, Martinien, Foord, Bogdanovich, Lünsmann, von Millers, Holzhausen.

RL Dahlenkirchen (Olai, Schlock), 22 August 1812, clash

A village in the western Russian province of Coeurland (nowadays the Baltic Republic of Latvia), on the left bank of the River Düna (nowadays the Daugava), 14 km southeast of Riga.

A Russian victory over the Prussians.

(Last action – Wolgund, 7 August; next action – Olai, 22 August.)

Prussian Forces Obst von Horn commanding: Füs Bns Nrs 2,3 and 6 (Nrs 3 and 6 less 2 coys each); Ostpreussisches Jg Bn (2 coys); HusR Nr 3 (2 sqns); 1 x HAB.

Prussian total ca 1,450 men.

Prussian losses 801 men and 56 horses killed, wounded and captured.

Russian Forces Rear Admiral Möller with a flotilla of gunboats, Col von Clemens with part of the 25th Infantry Division: 31st and 44th JgRs, IRs Voronesch, 1st Marine IR (2 bns each).

Russian total ca 3,000 men.

Russian losses 17 killed, 23 captured (KGE 24); 600 killed and wounded (Bogdanovich).

Comment York certainly did not intend a serious defence of the line of the Düna to be attempted by von Horn's small, overextended force. Von Horn however, was thirsting for action and bit off more than he could chew. The Russians took Dahlenkirchen, but abandoned it again on 26 August when the Prussians launched a counter attack.

Sources KGE 24, Bogdanovich.

RL Olai, 22 August 1812, skirmish

A small village in Latvia, southwest of Riga, midway towards Mitau.

A Prussian victory over the Russians.

(Last action – Dahlenkirchen, 22 August; next action – Schlock 22 August.)

Prussian Forces Majors von Clausewitz and von Rudolphi commanding: Füs Bn Nr 5 (3 coys); Füs Bn Nr 7 (2 coys); IR Nr 6 (1st bn); Ostpreussisches Jg Bn (2 coys); DragR Nr 1 (2 sqns).

Prussian total ca 900 men

Prussian losses Not exactly known, light.

Russian Forces Gen Wiljeminov with several battalions including the Finland Jägers (2 bns).

Russian total ca 3,300 men.

Russian losses 100 killed and wounded, 250 captured.

Sources KGE 24.

RL Schlock, 22 August 1812, 2nd skirmish

A village in Latvia about 18 km west of Riga, on the Baltic coast.

A Prussian victory over the Anglo-Russians.

(Last action – Olai, 22 August; next action – Eckau, 27 September.)

Prussian Forces Obst von Jeanneret commanding: IR Nr 6 (2 coys); Füs Bn Nr 1 (1 bn); HusR Nr 3 (2 sqns).

Prussian total ca 1,300 men.

Prussian losses Not exactly known, light (KGE 24); 350 killed and wounded (Bogdanovich).

Anglo-Russian Forces Rear Admiral Möller with a flotilla of gunboats and about 1,000 infantry under Col von Clemens.

Russian Troops losses 17 killed, 23 captured.

Comment The sources vary considerably as to numbers involved and casualties.

Sources KGE 24, Bogdanovich.

ES Sevilla, 28 August 1812, capture of

A fortified city in southwestern Spain on the Rio Guadalquivir and at the junction of Routes 630/E803, A49/E1, A4/E5 and 334.

An Allied victory over the French.

(Last action – Maguilla, 11 June; next action – Cadiz, 25 August.)

French Forces M Soult's rearguard: 63e RIdLi (2 bns).

French losses Unknown killed and wounded, 200 captured, 2 guns.

Allied Forces Spanish Gen Cruz Murgeon with 4,000 men including Col Downie's Legion de Extremadura (1 bn); British Col Skerrett with the Footguards (6 coys); 2/87th (½ bn); 2/95th (2 coys); 20th Portuguese LIR (1 bn-); 2nd HusR KGL (1 sqn).

Allied total ca 6,000 men.

Allied losses Not known exactly but very light.

Comment As a consequence of Wellington's victory at Salamanca on 22 July, Soult was forced to evacuate Andalusia; this Allied force harried his retreat and captured a huge convoy of French plunder in the city.

Sources Oman, Martinien.

ES Cadiz, 5 February 1810 – 25 August 1812, siege

A fortified seaport on the southern Spanish Atlantic coast 85 km northwest of Gibraltar on Route A4/E5 and 340.

An Allied victory over the French.

(Last action – Sevilla, 28 August; next action – this was the last action of note in Southern Spain in 1812.)

French Forces M Victor commanding the I Corps, Army of the South: GdD Conroux: 9e RILé (4 bns); 24e and 96e RIdLi (3 bns each). GdD Godinot: 8e RIdLi (4 bns); 16e RIdLi, 45e and 54e RIdLi (3 bns each). GdD Villatte: 27e RILé, 63e, 94e, 95e RIdLi (3 bns each). GdB Perreymond's Light Cavalry: 2e HusR, 5e ChàCh. GdD Latour-Maubourg's Dragoons: 1er, 2e, 4e, 9e, 14e and 26e DragRs, Artillery and engineers (1,985 men). Sailors of the Cadiz Lines flotilla (1,456 men).

French total (July 15, 1811) 27,201 present and fit for duty. Sick and detached: 8,739.

Grand total 35,940.

French losses Including Barrosa (3,000) ca 5,000 killed, wounded and died of sickness.

Allied Garrison Gen Manuel La Peña commanding: MG Lardizabal: IRs Campomayor, Carmona, Murcia (2 bns); Canarias. MG Anglona: IRs Africa (2 bns), Siguenza, Cantabria (2 bns); Voluntarios de Valencia. Gen Zaya: Ordenes Militares and other regiments, exact details not known: **Allied Garrison total** ca 15,000 men. **Anglo-Portuguese Division** LG Graham: Footguards (2 composite bns); 2/47th, 2/67th, 2/87th (1 bn each); 2/95th (½ bn); 20th Portuguese LIR (2 bns); Provisional German bn (1 bn); 2nd HusR KGL (2 sqns); 2 x FAB.

Allied total ca 5,600 men.

Comment Wellington's victory at Salamanca (22 July 1812) caused – among other dramatic events – the 2½ year siege to be abruptly lifted. The Allied garrison had been well supported by the Royal Navy during the siege and Cadiz was almost impregnable. The French fired off all their siege ammunition and destroyed their guns before leaving.

Sources Oman, Martinien.

RM Schewardino, 5 September 1812, clash

A village and redoubt in Russia, about 110 km west of Moscow and 3 km southwest of the village of Borodino.

A French and Allied victory over the Russians.

(Last action – Valutina Gora, 19 August; next action – Borodino, 7 September.)

French Forces Emperor Napoleon I commanding M Davout's **I Corps** GdD Morand's 1st Division: 17e RIdLi (5 bns). GdD Compans' 5th Division: 25e, 57e, 61e and 111e RIdLi (5 bns each). GdD Razout's 11th Division of Ney's III Corps: 2nd IR Portuguese Legion (2 bns). 9th Lt Cav Bde: 11e HusR (4 sqns). GdD Delzons' 34th Division of Prince Eugène's IV (Italian) Corps: 84e RIdLi (4 bns). GdD Prince Poniatowski's V (Polish) Corps: MG Rybinski and the combined Voltigeurs (14 coys). GdD Bruyère's 1st Lt Cav Div (I Cav Corps): 3rd and 8th Polish Lancers, Prussian Hussars (4 sqns each).

French total ca 30,000 men, 80 guns.

French losses ca 4,000 killed and wounded.

Russian Forces GdI Prince Bagration commanding:.

GL Borosdin I's **VIII Infantry Corps** (2nd Army of the West): GM Prince Karl von Mecklenburg's 2nd Gren Div, GrenR's Kiev, Astrakhan, Moscow, Phanagoria, Siberia and Little Russia (2 bns each) 2 x FAB. GM Neverovski's 27th Inf Div: IRs Wilna, Simbirsk, Odessa, Tarnopol, 49th and 50th Jägers (2 bns each), 2 x FAB. GM Duka's 2nd Cuirassier Div: CuirRs Military Order, Gluchov, Little Russia, Novgorod and Yekaterinoslav (4 sqns each).

GM Count Sievers I's **IV Cavalry Corps** DragRs Charkov, Tschernigov, Kiev and New Russia (4 sqns each); HusR Achtyrsk (8 sqns). 1 x HAB. GM Count Woronzov's Combined Gren Div: 6 bns from the 2nd, 12th and 26th Divs.

Russian total ca 20,000 men.

Russian losses 6,000 killed, wounded and captured, 3 guns.

Comment The tiny Schewardino redoubt could not be supported from the main Russian position. It was small and built on a hillock with weak defences. Its tactical value was nil. The 61e RIdLi was almost destroyed in this rather pointless struggle.

Sources Vaudoncourt, Martinien, Ditfurth, Malibran and Chelminski, Millers.

RM Borodino (La Moskwa), 7 September 1812, battle

A village in western Russia about 105 km west of Moscow, just southwest of the River Moskwa.

A French and Allied victory over the Russians.

(Last action – Schewardino, 5 September; next action – Moshaisk, 10 September.)

French and Allied Forces Emperor Napoleon I commanding. Light cavalry of the Imperial Guard. GdD Walther: DragR (5 sqns); 2e ChLL (4 sqns), 1 x HAB.

I Corps M Davout: 1st Div GdD Morand: 17e, 30e RIdLi, 13e RILé (5 bns each), 2nd Div GdD Friant: 15e RILé, 33e and 48e RIdLi (5 bns each); IR Joseph Napoleon (2nd and 3rd bns); 3rd Div GdD Gérard: 7e RILé, 12e, 21e RIdLi (5 bns each); Mecklenburg-Strelitz I Bn (1 bn); 4th Div GdD Desaix: 85e, 108e RIdLi (5 bns each); Hessen-Darmstadt LeibIR (2nd bn). 5th Div GdD Compans: 25e, 57e, 61e RIdLi (5 bns each) 1st Lt Cav Bde: 2e ChàCh, 9th Polish Lancers (4 sqns each). 2nd Lt Cav Bde: 1er and 3e ChàCh (4 sqns each).

III Corps M Ney: 10th Div GdD Ledru: 24e RILé, (2 bns) 46e, 76e RIdLi (4 bns each) 1st Portuguese IR (1 bn). 11th Div GdD Razout: 4e, 18e, 93e RIdLi (4 bns each); 2nd IR Portuguese Legion (2 bns). 25th Div GL Scheeler (Württembergers): 1st, 2nd and 3rd Provisional I Bns (3 bns). 9th Lt Cav Bde: 11e Hus, 6e ChLL, 4th Württemberg JzPf (4 sqns each). 14th Lt Cav Bde: 4e and 28e ChàCh, 1st and 2nd Württemberg ChLRs (4 sqns each).

IV Corps Prince Eugène commanding: 13th Div. GdD Delzons: 8e RILé (2bns), 92e, 106e RIdLi (4 bns each) 1st Croatian IR (2bns). 14th Div GdD Broussière: 18e RILé (1 bn); 9e, 35e and 53e RIdLi (4 bns each) IR Joseph Napoleon (1st and 4th bns). 15th Italian Div GdD Pino (arrived only at 2100hrs, not engaged): GdB Ornano, 12th Lt Cav Bde: 9e ChàCh, 19e ChàCh (3 sqns each). 13th Italian Lt Cav Bde: 2nd and 3rd ChàCh (4 sqns each). GdB Triaire, Italian Guard Cav Bde: Drag R Regina, Guard Drag R (4 sqns each). 21st Light cav Bde, Gen Count Seydewitz: 3rd and 6th Bavarian ChLR (4 sqns each). 22e Lt Cav Bde, Gen Preysing: 4th and 5th Bavarian ChLRs (4 sqns each).

V (Polish) Corps Prince Poniatowski commanding. 16th Div Gen Zayonchek: 3rd, 15th, 16th IRs (3 bns each); 4th ChàCh (4 sqns). 18th Div GdD Kamienicki: 2nd, 8th, 12th IRs (3 bns each) 19th Lt Cav Bde: 1st

ChàCh (1 sqns), 12th Lancers (4 sqns). 20th Lt Cav Bde: 5th ChàCh, 13th HusR (4 sqns each).

VIII (Westfalian) Corps GdD Junot: 23rd Div GL Tharreau: 3rd LtI Bn (1 bn); 2nd LIR (4 bns). 3rd and 6th LIR (2 bns each), 7th LIR (3 bns). 24th Div GL von Ochs: Chass Carabiniers and Garde Jägers (1 bn each) 1st LtI Bn (1 bn) 5th LIR (2 bns); 1st and 2nd HusRs (4 sqns each).

I Cav Corps GdD Nansouty: 1st Lt CavDiv GdD Bruyère: 9e ChLL, 7e HusR (4 sqns each), 8th HusR, 16e ChàCh (4 sqns each); 6th and 8th Polish Lancers, 2nd Prussian HusR (4 sqns each). 1st Cuirassier Div GdD St Germain: 2e, 3e, 9e CuirRs (4 sqns each) 1er ChLLR, 5th Cuirassier Div GdD Valence: 6e, 11e and 12e CuirRs (4 sqns each), 5e ChLL (4 sqns).

II Cav Corps GdD Montbrun: 2nd Lt Cav Div GdD Sebastiani: 5e and 9e HusRs (4 sqns each); 11e and 12e ChàCh (4 sqns each); 1st Prussian UlR, 3rd Württemberger JzPf, 10th Polish HusR (4 sqns each). 2nd Cuirassier Div GdD Wathier: 5e, 8e and 10e CuirRs (4 sqns each). 4th Cuir Div GdD Defrance: 1er, 2e Carabiniers, 1er CuirR, 4e ChLLR (4 sqns each).

III Cav Corps GdD Grouchy: 3rd Lt Cav Div GdD Chastel: 6e and 25e ChàCh, 6e and 8e HusRs, 1st and 2nd Bavarian ChLRs, Saxon ChLR 'Prinz Albrecht' (4 sqns each). 6th Cav Div GdD Lahoussaye: 7e and 23e DragRs (3 sqns each). 28e and 30e DragRs (3 sqns each).

IV Cav Corps GdD Latour-Maubourg: 4th (Polish) Lt Cav Div GdD Rozniecki: 3rd, 11th and 16th LancerRs (4 sqns each); 7th Hy Cav Div GdD Lorge: Saxon Garde du Corps and Saxon KürR vac von Zastrow (4 sqns each); 14th Polish KürR, 1st and 2nd Westfalian KürRs (4 sqns each).

French and Allied total ca 103,000 men, 587 guns.

French and Allied losses ca 6,600 killed and 21,400 wounded. The following generals were killed: GdDs Caulaincourt, Montbrun and Tharreau; GdBs Compère, Huard, Lanabère, Marion, Plauzonne, Romeuf, von Breuning, Damas and von Lepel. The national breakdown of officer losses was as follows (killed and wounded): French - 1,232; Poles - 205; Westfalians - 160; Württembergers - 50; Bavarians - 47; Saxons - 40; Portuguese - 36; Prussians - 11; Italians - 5; Spanish - 5; Swiss - 1; total 1,792.

Russian Forces GdI Prince Kutusov commanding.

GdI Barclay de Tolly: **The Right Wing** GdI Miloradovitch:

II Corps LG Baggowut: 4th Inf Div GM Duke Eugen von Württemberg: IRs Tobolsk, Wolhynien, Krementchug, Minsk, 4th and 34th Jägers (2 bns each) 1 x FAB. 17th Inf Div LG Olsufiev: IRs Riasan, Bielosersk, Brest, Willmannstrandt, 30th and 48th Jägers (2 bns each); 1 x FAB.

IV Corps LG Count Ostermann-Tolstoi: 11th Inf Div GM Bakhmetiev II: IRs Kexholm, Pernau, Polotsk, Yeletz, 1st and 33rd Jägers, Combined Grenadiers (2 bns each) 1 x FAB.

I Cav Corps Gen Adjutant Uvarov: Life Guard DragR, Life Guard HusR, Life Guard UlR, Life Guard CossackR, DragR Nieschin (4 sqns each); HusR Yelizavetgrad (8 sqns) 1 x HAB.

II Cav Corps Gen Adjutant Baron Korff: MG Kreuz: DragRs Pskov, Moscow, Kargopol, Ingermannland (4 sqns each); Polish UlR, Isum HusR (8 sqns each), 1 x HAB.

The Centre GdI Bennigsen.

VI Corps GdI Dochtorov: 7th Div LG Kapsevich: IRs Moscow, Pskov, Sophia, Libau, 11th and 36th Jägers; Combined Grenadiers (2 bns each), 1 x FAB. 24th Div GM Lichatschev: IRs Ufa, Schirwan, Butirsk, Tomsk. 19th and 40th Jägers; Combined Grenadiers (2 bns each), 1 x FAB.

III Cav Corps Gen Adjutant Baron Korff: GM Kreuz: DragRs Kurland, Orenburg, Siberia, Irkutsk (4 sqns each); HusRs Sum and Mariupol (8 sqns each), 1 x HAB.

The Reserve of the Right Wing and the Centre.

V Corps GL Lavrof: Life Guard Regiments Preobraschenski, Semenov, Ismailov, Lithuania, Finland and Jägers (3 bns each); Guard Marine Equipage (1 bn). Combined Grenadiers of the 1st, 3rd, 4th and 17th Divisions (2 bns each). 1st CuirDiv GM Borosdin II: Chevalier Guards, Horse Life Guards, CuirRs Tsar, Tsarina, Astrakhan (4 sqns each). Reserve Artillery GM Count Kutaisov, GM Löwenstern: 21 x FAB, 5 x HAB (300 guns); 1 x Pionier coy; 2 x Pontonnier coys.

The Left Wing GdI Prince Bagration, GL Prince Gortschakov II and GL Prince Golitzin.

VII Corps GL Raievsky: 26th Div GM Paskievich: IRs Ladoga, Poltava, Nishegorod, Orel, 5th and 42nd Jägers (2 bns each); 2 x FAB. 12th Div GM Wasiltschikov: IRs Narva, Smolensk, New Ingermannland, Alexopol, 6th and 41st Jägers (2 bns each).

VIII Corps GL Borosdin I: 2nd Grenadier Div GM Prince Karl von Mecklenburg: GrenRs Kiev, Astrakhan, Moscow, Phanagoria, Siberia, Little Russia (2 bns each) 2 x FAB. 27th Div GM Neverovski: IRs Wilna, Simbirsk, Odessa, Tarnopol, 49th and 50th Jägers (2 bns each).

IV Cav Corps GM Count Sievers I: DragRs Charkov, Tschernigov, Kiev, New Russia (4 sqns each); HusR Achtyrsk, UlR Lithuania (8 sqns each); 1 x HAB.

The Reserve of the Left Flank GM Count Woronzov: Combined Grenadiers of 12th, 26th and 27th Divs (2 bns each). The combined grenadiers of the 7th and 24th Divs were deployed in support of the Jägers skirmishing in advance of the Russian line. 2nd CuirDiv GM Duka: CuirRs Yekaterinoslav, Military Order, Gluchov, Little Russia, Novgorod (4 sqns each). Reserve Artillery of the Left Wing: 7 x FAB, 1 pionier and 1 pontonier coy.

On the old Smolensk road (the extreme south of the Russian line):

III Corps GL Tutschkov I: 1st Grenadier Div GM Strogonov: Life GrenR, GrenRs, Arakcheyev, Pavlovski, St Petersburg, Yekaterinoslav, Tauride (2 bns each); 3 x FAB. 3rd Div GL Konovnizin: IRs Murom, Reval, Tschernigov, Kaporie, 20th and 21st Jägers (2 bns each); 3 x FAB. GM Karpov's Detachment: 6 cossack Pulks (1,500 men).

The Moscow Militia GL Count Markov: Smolensk Militia GL Lebedev – 10,000 men.

Russian total 180 bns, 164 sqns, 55 batteries, 2 pionier and 3 pontonier coys; 103,800 men, 640* guns plus 7,000 cossacks and 10,000 Militia.

Russian losses Not known; estimates vary widely and have never been confirmed. Generally accepted as being *about* 43,000 killed and wounded and 1,000 captured, 20 guns. The following generals were killed: GdI Prince Bagration (died of wounds), GL Tutschkov I, GM Tutschkov IV, GM Kutaisov.

* of these, 300 were concentrated in a reserve under MG Count Kutaisov who was killed early in the battle; GM Löwenstern took over but the great majority of these guns were not employed at all.

Comment This was an extremely bloody battle but the Russian army withdrew in good order despite their very heavy losses. Napoleon was again cheated of the victory he so desperately needed and his army was very badly knocked about. The Russians withdrew through Moscow and abandoned their capital, much to Napoleon's amazement.

Sources Vaudoncourt, Martinien, Ditfurth, Schuster and Franke, Bogdanovich, Holzhausen.

RM Moshaisk, 10 September 1812, clash

A town in western Russia, 95 km west of Moscow and 13 km east of Borodino.

A French victory over the Russians.

(Last action – Borodino, 7 September; next action – Winkowo, 18 October.)

French Forces M Murat commanding the **Avant-garde**. 2nd Div (of I Corps) GdD Friant: 15e RILé, 33e and 48 RIdLi (5 bns each); IR Joseph Napoleon (2nd and 3rd bns). 9th Lt Cav Bde: 11e HusR (4 sqns); 6e ChàCh (3 sqns); 4th Württemberg JzPf (4 sqns); 1st Lt Cav Div (of I Cav Corps). GdD Bruyère: 7e and 8e HusR (4 sqns each). 2nd Lt Cav Div (of II Cav Corps) GdD Sebastiani: 5e HusR (4 sqns); 10th Lt Cav Bde (of III Cav Corps). 3rd Lt Cav Div GdD Chastel: 8e and 25e ChàCh (3 sqns each). 25th Inf Div GL Scheeler (Württembergers): 1st, 2nd and 3rd Provisional I Bns (3 bns).

French total 24 weak bns, 29 weak sqns ca 10,000 men 3 x FAB, 2 x HAB.

French losses ca 2,000 killed and wounded.

Russian Forces GL Miloradovitch commanding. **II Corps** GL Baggowut: 4th Div GM Duke Eugen von Württemberg: IRs Tobolsk, Wolhynia, Krementschug, Minsk, 3rd and 34th Jägers (2 bns each). 17th Div GL Olsufiev: IRs Riasan, Bielosersk, Brest, Willmannstrandt, 30th and 48th Jägers (2 bns each) 2 x FAB. HusRs Isum and Sum (8 sqns each).

Russian total ca 8,600 men, 24 guns.

Russian losses 2,000 killed and wounded. The wounded from the Battle of Borodino (10,000 men) were also captured in the town.

Sources Vaudoncourt, Bodart, Bogdanovich.

RS Neswitsch, 20 September 1812, raid

A village on the western bank of the upper River Styr in northwestern Ukraine; a tributary of the Pripet, near the town of Lutzk.

A Russian victory over Austro-Saxon-Polish cavalry.

(Last action – Gorodeczna – 12 August; next action – Luboml, 29 September.)

Austro-Saxon-Polish Forces MG Zechmeister commanding: Austrian ChLR O'Reilly Nr 3 (6 sqns); Saxon ChLR von Polenz and HusR (1 sqn each);

Polish UlR (3 sqns); Warsaw Militia CavR (3 sqns).

Austro-Saxon-Polish total 14 sqns.

Austro-Saxon-Polish losses 9 officers and 141 men captured (others claim 15 officers and 295 men captured); 3 standards of the ChLR O'Reilly.

Russian Forces MG Count Lambert commanding: HusR Alexandria, Tatar UlR (3 sqns each); DragR Arsamas (3 sqns); Cossack Pulks of Wlasov and Tschikilef.

Russian total ca 1,000 men.

Russian losses 2 killed, 3 hussars wounded.

Comment Tsar Alexander I had the three captured standards returned to Emperor Francis I. This raid signalled the start of a new offensive by the united armies of Tormasov and Tchichagov.

Sources Bogdanovich.

RL Eckau, 27 September 1812, 2nd Clash

A village in Latvia about 12 km east of Mitau (now Jelgava) and about 40 km south of Riga.

A Russian victory over the Prussians.

(Last action – Schlock, 22 August; next action – Mesoten, 29 September.)

Prussian Forces GL von Massenbach commanding: HusR Nr 3 (2 sqns). DragR Nr 1 (4 sqns); DragR Nr 2 (3 sqns); 2 x HAB.

Prussian total ca 850 men.

Prussian losses 13 killed, 97 wounded, 93 captured. 34 horses.

Russian Forces LG Count Steinheil and Gen Lewis with 18,000 infantry, 1,300 cavalry and 23 guns. Main Russian Column LG Count Steinheil's Finnish Corps' Avant Garde: 3rd JgR (1 bn); 4th, 20th and 21st JgRs (Depot Bns); Finland DragR (3 sqns); Seliwan Cossack Pulk (200 men); Loschtschilin's Cossack Pulk (300 men), 11th FAB (6 guns).

Russian total ca 3,000 men.

Russian losses Not known, light.

Comment The Russian advance was so cautious that the Prussians slipped away.

Sources KGE 24, Bogdanovich.

RS Luboml, 29 September 1812, clash

A village on the River Bug (the border between Poland and Belarus) about 60 km south of Brest on Route M1/E30.

A Russian victory over the Austrians.

(Last action – Neswitsch, 20 September; next action – River Muchaviec, 11 October.)

Austrian Forces From FML Bianchi's 1st Div: IRs Colloredo Nr 33 and Esterházy Nr 32 (2 bns each). From FML Frimont's Res Div: DragR Riesch Nr 6 (4 sqns); HusR Blankenstein Nr 6 (6 sqns).

Austrian total ca 3,600 men.

Austrian losses Not known, moderate.

Russian Forces GdI Count Langeron's Corps of Admiral Tchichagov's Army of the Danube. Exact details and losses not known.

Sources Wrede, Martinien, Schuster and Franke.

RL Mesoten, 29 September 1812, skirmish

A village in the Russian province of Courland (nowadays the Baltic Republic of Latvia), on the River Aa, 30 km southeast of Mitau (nowadays Jelgava).

A Prussian victory over the Russians.

(Last action – Eckau, 27 September; next action – Gräfenthal, 29 September.)

Prussian Forces GL York commanding. Füs Bns Nrs 2, 4, 5, 6 and 7 (1 bn each), HusR Nr 3 (4 sqns), DragR Nr 2 (1 sqn); 1 x HAB.

Prussian total ca 5,400 men.

Prussian losses Not known, very light.

Russian Forces LG Count Steinheil with part of his Finnish Corps: 21st Division MG Alexejew: IRs Newa, Petrowsk, Lithuania, Podolia, 2nd JgR (2 bns each), DragR Finland (2 sqns), 21st PosB (6 guns); 11th FAB (6 guns).

Russian total 9,000 infantry, 200 cavalry, 12 guns.

Russian losses Not known – light.

Comment In the open countryside, the Prussian superiority of cavalry won the day. The Russians withdrew to Riga.

Sources KGE 24, Preysing-Moos, Bogdanovich.

RL Gräfenthal, 29 September 1812, clash

A small village in Latvia, southwest of Riga.

A Prussian victory over the Russians.

(Last action – Mesoten, 29 September; next action – Lautschkruge, 30 September.)

Prussian Forces GL York commanding: IRs Nrs 3, 5 and 6 (2 bns each) Füs Bns Nrs 1 and 3 (1 bn each); DragR Nr 1 (2 sqns); 1 x HAB, ½ x FAB.

Prussian total ca 7,000 men.

Prussian losses 32 killed, 205 wounded 26 missing; 14 horses.

Russian Forces MG Count Bellegarde with IRs Asov and Nisov (2 bns each), 11th FAB (6 guns.)

Russian losses Killed and wounded not known, 303 men captured.

Sources KGE 24, Bogdanovich.

RL Lautschkruge, 30 September 1812, clash

A small village in Latvia, south of Riga.

A Prussian victory over the Russians.

(Last action – Gräfenthal, 29 September; next action – Garosse River, 1 October.)

Prussian Forces GL York commanding: IRs Nrs 1, 2, 4, 5 and 6 (2 bns each); Füs Bns Nrs 3, 4, 5 and 6 (1 bn each); HusR Nr 3 (4 sqns); DragR Nr 1 (2 sqns); DragR Nr 2 (1 sqn); 3 x HAB, 2½ x FAB.

Prussian total ca 12,000 men.

Prussian losses Not known, very light.

Russian Forces Part of LG Count Steinheil's Finnish Corps under MG Fok exact details not known. Grenadier Depot Bns (3 bns); Combined Gren Bns (3 bns); 3rd JgR (2 bns); 21st PosB, 6 battalions of infantry, 12 guns.

Russian losses Killed and wounded unknown, 608 captured.

Comment The Prussian cavalry caught the 3rd JgR (2 bns) of Russian infantry in the open, in act of forming square and forced them to surrender.

Sources KGE 24, Bogdanovich.

RL Garosse River, 1 October 1812, skirmish

A minor Latvian river, south of Riga.

A Prussian victory over the Russians.

(Last action – Lautschkruge, 30 September; next action – Dahlenkirchen, 15 November.)

Prussian Forces GL York commanding: Füs Bns Nrs 4, 5, 6 and 7 (1 bn each); Ostpreussisches Jg Bn (1 bn); HusR Nr 1 (1 sqn); HusR Nr 3 (2 sqns); DragR Nr 2 (2 sqns); ½ x HAB.

Prussian total ca 3,600 men.

Polish Forces LtCol Kaminski: IR Nr 5 (1 bn);.

Polish total ca 500 men.

Prusso-Polish losses Not known, very light.

Russian Forces Exact details not known.

Russian losses Not known, very light. Gen Essen I was already in the act of withdrawing into Riga after the defeats at Gräfenthal and Lautschkruge.

Comment In the period 26 September – 1 October the Russians lost 1,900 killed and missing, 578 wounded. They had captured 403 Prussians.

Sources KGE 24, Bogdanovich.

RS River Muchaviec (Tryczine Hof), 11 October 1812, clash

A river crossing in the western Republic of Belarus, on Route M1/E30 between Kobryn and Brest on the Polish border.

An Allied victory over the Russians.

(Last action – Luboml, 28 September; next action – Biala Podlaska, 13 October.)

Austrian Troops FM Schwarzenberg commanding: FML Bianchi's 1st Div: IRs Simbschen Nr 48, Hiller Nr 2, Esterházy Nr 32, Davidovich Nr 34 (2 bns each) Gren Bn Brzeczinski (1 bn). FML Siegerthal's 2nd Div: IR Kottulinsky Nr 41 (2 bns). FML Trautenberg's 3rd Div: HusR Kienmayer Nr 8 (6 sqns).

Austrian total ca 11,300 men, 12 guns.

Austrian losses Not known, light.

Saxon Troops GdD Reynier commanding the VII (Saxon) Corps: Gren Bns von Anger, von Ryssel, von Spiegel (1 bn each); IRs Prinz Anton, Prinz Clemens, Prinz Friedrich and von Niesemeuschel, 1st and 2nd LtIRs (2 bns each); HusR, UlR Prinz Clemens (4 sqns each).

Saxon total ca 9,000 men.

Saxon losses 12 killed, 78 wounded.

Allied totals ca 24,000 men.

Allied losses Not known, light.

Russian Forces Part of Admiral Tchichagov's Army of the Danube under LG Osten-Sacken.

LG Essen III IRs Schlüsselburg, Old Ingermannland, Archangelgorod, Ukraine (2 bns each); Olonez (3 bns); 37th JgR (3 bns); DragR Serpuchov (4 sqns); DragR Wladimir (3 sqns); DragR Twer (1 sqn); HusR Lubno (8 sqns) 2nd BaschkirR; 1st KalmuckR; 4th Ural Cossack Pulk. Cossack Pulk of Tschikilev; 8th PosB, 14th and 15th FABs, 15th HAB. pioniers (½ coy). **MG Bulatov** IRs Wiatka (3 bns); Wyborg; Starokolsk; Ochotsk, Mingrelien, Galicia (2 bns each); Kamtchatka (1 bn); 45th JgR (1 bn); 29th JgR (2 bns); DragRs Perejeslavl, Smolensk (4 sqns each); Tschugujef UlR (8 sqns); 2nd KalmuckR, 22nd PosB, 41st FAB; pioniers (coy). **The Reserve MG Count Lieven** IRs Jaroslavl (2 bns); Crimea; Bialystok (3 bns each); 8th JgR (3 bns); 39th JgR (2 bns); DragRs Wladimir (1 sqn); Twer (3 sqns); 10th PosB, 18th FAB.

Russian total ca 24,000 men.

Russian losses Not known exactly but heavier than those of the Allies.

Sources Wrede, Martinien, Schuster and Franke, Bogdanovich.

RS Biala Podlaska, 13 October 1812, clash

A village in eastern present-day Poland, on Route 2/E30, 39 km west of Brest on the Russo-Polish border.

A successful Austrian rearguard action against the Russians.

(Last action – River Muchaviec, 11 October; next action – Wolkowisk, 14–16 November.)

Austrian Forces FML Bianchi commanding the 1st Division: IRs Allvintzy Nr 19, Hiller Nr 2, Esterházy Nr 32 (2 bns each); Gren Bns Kirchenbetter and Brzeczinski (1 bn each).

Austrian total ca 7,300 men, 12 guns.

Austrian losses Not known.

Russian Forces Exact details not known, part of Admiral Tchichagov's Third Army of the West. Avantgarde MG Count Lambert commanding: 7th JgR (3 bns); 14th JgR (2 bns); 38th JgR (2 bns); Tartar UlR (8 sqns); HusR Alexandria (8 sqns); DragRs Starodub, Arsamas and Schitomir (4 sqns each); Cossack Pulks of Grekov VIII, Grekov XI, Melnikov V and Babarantschikof IX, TatarR Evpatoria, 11th and 12th HABs.

Russian total 7 bns, 28 sqns, 5 Cossack Pulks, 24 guns.

Russian losses Not known exactly but light.

Sources Wrede, Martinien, Bogdanovich.

RM Winkowo (Tarutino, Tschernischna), 18 October 1812, battle

A village in the western Russian province of Kaluga, 67 km southwest of Moscow, north of the River Proma, near the present-day town of Visokinichi.

A Russian victory over the French.

(Last action – Moshaisk, 10 September; next action – Slonim, 20 October.)

French Forces M Murat commanding.

I Cav Corps GdD Nansouty, 1st Cav Div: GdD Bruyère: 9e ChLR, 7e HusR; 8e HusR (4 sqns each).

II Cav Corps GdD Montbrun: 2nd Lt Cav Div GdD Sebastiani: 5e and 9e HusR (4 sqns each).

III Cav Corps GdD Grouchy: 3rd Lt Cav Div: 6e ChàCh, 6e HusR (4 sqns each). 6th Cav Div GdD Lahoussaye: 23rd DragR (4 sqns). Württemberg 3rd JzPf (4 sqns).

V (Polish Corps) GdD Prince Poniatowski commanding: 16th Inf Div GdD Zayonchek: 3rd, 13th, 15th and 16th IRs (2 bns each); 4th ChàCh (4 sqns). 18th Inf Div GdD Kamienicki: 2nd, 8th and 12th IRs (2 bns each). 19th Lt Cav Bde 1st ChàCh, 12th Lancers (4 sqns each); 20th Lt Cav Bde 5th ChàCh, 13th HusR (4 sqns each). Also the 1er, 2e, 4e and 5e ChLR and the 1st and 2nd Bavarian ChLRs (4 sqns each).

French total ca 18,000 men.

French losses 2,000 killed and wounded, 1,500 captured, 36 guns.

Russian Forces FM Prince Kutusov commanding GdI Miloradovitch.

II Corps GL Baggowut: 4th Inf Div GM Duke von Württemberg: IRs Tobolsk, Wolhynien, Krementschug, Minsk, 4th and 34th Jägers; 1 x FAB. 17th Inf Div GL Olsufiev: IRs Riasan, Bielosersk, Brest, Wilmannstrandt, 30th and 48th Jägers (2 bns each), 1 x FAB.

IV Cavalry Corps GM Count Sievers I: Drag Rs Charkov, Tschernigov, Kiev, New Russia (4 sqns each); HusR Achtyrsk, Lithuanian UlR (8 sqns each); 1 x HAB.

III Corps LG Tutschkov I: 1st Gren Div GM Count Stroganov: Life GrenR, GrenRs Arakchejev, Pavlovsk, Yekaterinoslav, St Petersburg and Tauride (2 bns each); 3 x FAB. 3rd Div GM Tustchkov IV: IRs Murom, Reval, Tschernigov, Kaporie, 20th and 21st Jägers (2 bns each); 3 x FAB. Lifeguard CossackR (4 sqns); Teptjärsk CossackR (5 sqns).

IV Corps GL Count Schuwalov: 11th Div: IRs Kexholm, Pernau, Polotsk, Yelez, 1st and 33rd Jägers (2 bns each). 3 x FAB. 23rd Div GM Bakhmetiev I IRs Rilsk, Katherinburg, Selenginsk, 18th Jägers; combined grenadiers of 11th and 23rd Divs. (2 bns each), 3 x FAB, HusR Isum (8 sqns).

I Cav Corps Lifeguard HusR, Lifeguard UlR, Lifeguard DragR, DragRs Nieschin and Kasan (4 sqns each); 1 x HAB. DragRs Pskov, Moscow, Kargopol, Ingermannland (4 sqns each); Polish UlR (8 sqns) 1 x HAB. 6 x cossack Pulks.

Russian total 36,000 men.

Russian losses 800 killed and wounded, 700 captured. GL Baggowut killed.

Comment This was a very successful surprise attack by the Russians after they had lulled Murat into a false sense of security for some weeks. Despite the terrible battering they had received at Borodino, the

Russians had reorganized and now proved their combat-readiness. This marked the start of Napoleon's retreat from Moscow. The remnants of 1st and 2nd Bavarian ChLRs were destroyed here. Murat fought his way through to Moscow.

Sources Vaudoncourt, Martinien, Preysing-Moos, Leyh, Malibran and Chelminski.

RN Polotsk, 18–20 October 1812, 2nd Battle

A town in the western Russian province of Witebsk (nowadays the Republic of Belarus), on the right bank of the River Dwina, 95 km northwest of Witebsk city.

A drawn match between the Russians and the Franco-Bavarians.

(Last action – Polotsk 16-18 August; next action – Tschaschniki, 31 October.)

Franco-Bavarian Forces M Oudinot **(II Corps)** commanding. 6th Division GdD Legrand: 26 RILé, 19e, 56e RIdLi (4 bns each); 128e RIdLi (2 bns); Portuguese Legion 3rd IR (2 bns). 8th Division GdD Verdier: 11e RILé (4 bns); 2e RIdLi (5 bns); 37e RIdLi (4 bns). 9th Division GdD Merle: 1st-4th Swiss IRs (3 bns each except the 1st which had 2); 3rd Croatian IR (2 bns); 128e RIdLi (3 bns). 3rd Cuir Div GdD Doumerc: 4e, 7e and 13e CuirRs (4 sqns each); 5th Lt Cav Bde GdB Castex: 24e ChàCh (3 sqns); 6th Lt Cav Bde GdB Corbineau 20e ChàCh (2 sqns).

VI (Bavarian) Corps M Gouvion St Cyr: 19th Division GM Vincenti: 1st LtI Bn (1 bn); 1st and 9th LIRs (2 bns each); 3rd LtI Bn (1 bn); 4th and 10th LIRs (2 bns each) 6th LtI Bn (1 bn), 8th LIR (2 bns) 20th Division LG von Wrede: 2nd and 6th LIR (2 bns each). 4th LtI Bn (1 bn), 3rd and 7th LIRs (2 bns each), 5th LtI Bn (1 bn), 5th and 11th LIR (2 bns each).

Franco-Bavarian total ca 23,000 men.

Franco-Bavarian losses 6-7,000 killed and wounded, 2,000 captured.

Russian Forces LG Count Wittgenstein's **I Detached Corps**, 1st Army of the West Right Hand Column:.

LG Prince Jaschwil commanding the **I Corps Advanced Guard** MG Wlastov: 23rd and 24th JgRs (4 bns); 1st and 9th St Petersburg Militia bns; HusR Grodno (4 sqns); Cossack Pulk of Platov IV, 1st HAB (6 guns). **Main Body** LG Sasanov: 14th Infantry Division: IRs Tula, Navaginsk, Tenginsk, Estonia (2 bns each); 2nd, 3rd, 7th and 8th St Petersburg Militia bns; IR Mohilev (2 bns). Combined DragR (3 sqns); PosB Nr 27 (6 guns), PosB Nr 28 (11 guns); PosB Nr 50; FABs Nr 26 and 27, FAB Nr 9 (6 guns), 1st HAB (3 guns). **Totals** 14 bns, 7 sqns, 6 Militia bns, 68 guns – 11,000 men.

Centre Column LG Berg Advanced Guard MG Balk: JgRs Nr 25 and 26 (4 bns); IR Kexholm (Depot Bn); Grodno HusR (4 sqns), Cossack Pulk of Rodionov II, 3rd HAB (6 guns). Main Body: 5th Infantry Division: IRs Perm, Sievsk, Kaluga (6 bns); Combined Guards CavR (3 sqns); Polish UlR (2 sqns) DragR Riga (4 sqns); PosB Nr 5, 27th FAB, 3rd HAB (6 guns). **Reserve** MG Kachowski: 1st, 2nd and 3rd Grenadier Depot bns, Guards Depot bns (2 bns); Combined KürR (4 sqns); 14th PosB, 23rd HAB (8 guns). **Totals** 18 bns, 16 sqns, 50 guns – 12,000 men.

Left Hand Column MG Begitschef: Advance Guard MG Baron Diebitsch: 4 x Combined Grenadier bns of the 5th and 14th Divisions; Combined Jg Bns (3 bns); DragR Jamburg (2 sqns); DragR Riga (1 sqn); DragR Ingermannland (1 sqn); Cossacks (1 sotnia – about 100 men); 49th FAB (6 guns). **Main Body** IR Polotsk (Depot bn); 4th, 5th, 6th, 10th, 11th and 12th St Petersburg Militia bns; 35th FAB. Reserve: 13th and 14th St Petersburg Militia bns. **Totals** 16 bns, 4 sqns, 18 guns.

Russian totals ca 40,000 men (including 9,000 militia) and 136 guns.

Russian losses ca 8,000 killed and wounded.

Comment The Franco-Bavarians were now so weak that they had to abandon Polotsk and withdraw southwestwards.

Sources Bogdanovich, Leyh, Martinien, Preysing-Moos, Vaudoncourt.

RM Slonim, 20 October 1812, clash

A town in southwestern Belarus, about 90 km east of the Polish border and 190 km northeast of Brest-Litowsk.

A Russian victory over the French.

(Last action – Winkowo 18 October; next action – Malojaroslawetz, 24 October.)

French Forces 3e (Lithuanian) ChLL of the Imperial Guard (4 sqns).

French total 600 men.

French losses 480 killed, wounded and captured. The regiment was destroyed.

Russian Forces Gen Chaplitz Pavlograd HusR (8 sqns), 1 Cossack Pulk

Russian total ca 900 men.
Russian losses Not known exactly but light.
Sources Martinien, Vaudoncourt, Foord, Bogdanovich.

EW Burgos, 19 September – 21 October 1812, failed siege

A fortified city in the Spanish province of the same name, 210 km north of Madrid at the junction of Routes 620/E80, 623, I/E5 and A1.
A French victory over the Anglo-Portuguese.
(Last action – Retiro 13 August; next action – Venta del Pozo, 23 October.)
French Garrison GdB Dubreton commanding: 34e RIdLi (2 bns); 130e RIdLi (1 bn), artillery (1 coy), engineers (1 coy).
French total ca 2,000 men, 9 heavy guns, 11 field guns, 6 mortars.
French losses 304 killed, 323 wounded.
Anglo-Portuguese Forces The Marquess of Wellington commanding: 1st, 3rd, 4th, 5th, 6th, 7th, Light Divisions with their attached Portuguese troops and Espana's Spanish Division (see OOB for Salamanca, 22 July for full details).
Anglo-Portuguese total 32,000 men. Of these, the following units came into action: Pack's Portuguese Brigade; 1/42nd and the flank companies of the 1/42nd, 1/24th and 1/79th Foot who assaulted and took the San Miguel hornwork on 19 September with a loss of 421 killed and wounded. The French garrison (1 bn, 34e RIdLi) lost 198 including 60 captured and 7 guns. Another assault on 23rd September failed as did a third on 29 September. Wellington had brought no siege train with him* and Dubreton's defence was so aggressive and effective that Wellington was just wasting time and men. News of the approach of Marmont's reorganized and reinforced Army of Portugal (now under Souham and with 38,000 men), forced Wellington to lift the siege.
Anglo-Portuguese losses 550 killed, 1,550 wounded, 3 guns.
* = he also ignored Admiral Sir Home Popham's offer to send heavy naval guns south from Santander until 2 October when he asked for 2 x 24 pdrs but these only got to Reynosa (80 km from Burgos) before Wellington raised the siege.
Comment This whole operation was a badly-managed waste of time and resources. Wellington withdrew over the Rio Duero at Tordesillas.
Sources Oman, Martinien.

EW Venta del Pozo, 23 October 1812, clash

A hamlet in northern Spain about 34 km southwest of Burgos on Route 620/E80, just north of the Rio Arlanzón and on the Hormaza stream.
A drawn match between the British and Germans on the one hand and the French and Germans on the other.
(Last action – Burgos 21 October; next action – Tordesillas, 28 October.)
French Forces Gen Curto's Light Cavalry: 3e HusR, 22e and 26e ChàCh (2 sqns each) 28e ChàCh (1 sqn); 13e ChàCh (5 sqns); 14e ChàCh (4 sqns). GdB Faverot: 15e ChàCh, 1st Berg ChLL, Gendarmes, Gen Boyer's Dragoons: 6e, 11e, 15e and 25e DragRs.
French total ca 3,200 men.
French losses ca 200 in all.
Allied Forces Gen Anson, Gen von Bock: 11th and 12th LDRs, 1st and 2nd DragRs KGL; 1st and 2nd LtI Bns KGL.
Allied total ca 2,800 men.
Allied losses 165 killed and wounded, 65 captured.
Comment This rearguard action was one of the most furious cavalry mêlées of the entire war. The steady conduct of the 1st and 2nd LtI Bns KGL decided the end of the contest and they were awarded the battle honour 'Venta del Pozo' which their descendant regiments wore until 1918.
Sources Oman, Martinien, Schwertfeger, Beamish.

RM Malojaroslawetz, 24 October 1812, battle

A town in the western Russian province of Kaluga, on the River Luscha, 103 km southwest of Moscow.
A Russian victory over the French and Allies.
(Last action – Slonim, 20 October; next action – Wiasma, 3 November.)
French and Allied Force Emperor Napoleon commanding:.
IV Corps (Italians) Prince Eugène: 13th Div GdD Delzons: 8e RILé (2 bns); 84e, 92e, 106e RIdLi (4 bns each), 1st Croatian IR (2 bns). 14th Div GdD Broussière: 18e RILé (2 bns); 9e, 35e, 53e RIdLi (4 bns each). 15th (Italian) Div GdD Pino: 1st LtIR (4th Bn); 3rd LtIR (4 bns); 2nd IR, 3rd IR (4 bns each), Dalmatian IR (3 bns). Italian Guard Div GdD Lecchi: Gardes

d'Honneur (5 coys); Vélites (2 bns), Grenadiers (2 bns), Conscripts (2 bns); Chasseurs (1 bn). Guards Cav Bde GdB Villata: Dragoons of the Guard (2 sqns); Dragoni Regina 2nd and 3rd ChàCh (4 sqns each). 12th French Lt Cav Bde GdB Ornano: 9e and 19e ChàCh (3 sqns each); 7th Polish Lancers (4 sqns).

I Corps M Davout: 3rd Div GdD Gérard: 7eRILé; 12e, 21e RIdLi (5 bns each). 4th Div GdD Desaix: 85e RIdLi (5 bns). 5th Inf Div GdD Compans: 25e, 57e and 111e RIdLi (5 bns each). The 23rd DragR (4 sqns). Also the ChàCh and the artillery of the Imperial Guard.

French total ca 24,000 men.

French losses ca 6,000 killed, wounded and missing. GdD Delzons and Italian GdB Levie were killed.

Russian Forces FM Prince Kutusov commanding.

VI Corps GdI Dochtorov: 7th Inf Div GL Kapsevich: IRs Moscow, Pskov, Sophia, Libau, 11th and 36th Jägers (2 bns each) 1 x FAB. 24th Inf Div GM Lichatschev: IRs Ufa, Schirwan, Butirsk, Tomsk, 19th and 40th Jägers (2 bns each), 1 x FAB. 17th Inf Div GL Olsufiev: IRs Riasan, Brest, Bielosersk, Wilmannstrandt, 30th and 48th Jägers (2 bns each), 3 x FAB; HusRs Elisabethgrad and Isum (8 sqns each); 4 cossack Pulks.

Russian total ca 24,000 men.

Russian losses ca 8,000 killed, wounded and missing. GM Dorochov killed.

Sources Vaudoncourt, Martinien, Bogdanovich, Preysing-Moos.

EW Tordesillas, 28 October 1812, raid

A town in northern Spain on the north bank of the Rio Duero and at the junction of Routes 620/E80, 122/E82 and VI.

A French victory over the Allies.

(Last action – Venta del Pozo, 23 October; next action – Tajuna 30 October.)

French Forces Captain Guingret and 54 men of the 6e RILé.

French losses None.

Allied Forces Brunswick Oels Jägers (1/2 coy).

Allied losses 9 captured.

Comment This action occurred during Wellington's retreat from Burgos after his failed siege. The French party swam the Duero naked with their weapons on a raft to take in rear the Brunswickers in the tower in the centre of the bridge here. The Brunswick commander was surprised, panicked and abandoned his post. With this bold stroke GdD Souham was able to turn the line of the Duero and Wellington was forced to continue his withdrawal.

Source Oman.

EW Tajuna, 30 October 1812, skirmish

A village on a river of the same name in central Spain; the river joins the Tajo just west of Aranjuez; Tajuna lies between Aranjuez and Fuenteduena de Tajo.

An Allied victory over the French.

(Last action – Tordesillas, 28 October; next action – Alba de Tormes, 10 November.)

French Forces M Soult commanding the Advanced Guard of his Army of the South: 12RILé (1 bn).

French losses ca 105 killed and wounded.

Allied Forces Col Skerrett with 2/47th and 2/87th Foot (1 bn each), 95th (2 coys). 3 Portuguese guns; the rearguard of Gen Hill's corps.

Allied losses 3 officers and 40 men killed and wounded.

Comment Skerrett held the northern end of an extremely long stone bridge over an unfordable river. The 12 Lé tried twice to charge over the obstacle but accurate fire from the defenders drove them back with heavy loss. After dark, Skerrett set up dummy sentries and slipped away to Madrid, having gained valuable time for Hill's corps to withdraw in good order from Madrid to join Wellington near Salamanca.

Source Oman.

RN Tschaschniki, 31 October 1812, clash

A village in the western Russian province of Witebsk (nowadays in the Republic of Belarus), 70 km southwest of that city and on the River Ula.

A Russian victory over the French.

(Last action – Polotsk, 18–20 October; next action – Witebsk, 7 November.)

French Forces M Victor commanding IX Corps: 26th Inf Div GdD Daendels: Baden Bde Gen Count Hochberg: 1st and 3rd LIRs, (2 bns each); 1st Jägers (1 bn). From M Oudinot's II Corps: 9th Inf Div GdD Merle: 3rd Croatian IR (2 bns); 1st (2 bns), 2nd, 3rd & 4th Swiss IRs (3 bns each); 8th Inf Div GdD Verdier: 37e RIdLi (4 bns); 124e, 123e RIdLi (3 bns), 4 x FAB, 2 x HAB.

French total ca 18,000 men.

French losses 400 killed and wounded, 23 officers, 800 men captured.

Russian Forces MG Prince Jaschwil's Avantgarde of Wittgenstein's I Corps: 2nd, 3rd and 25th JgRs (2 bns each); 23rd JgR (1 bn); St Petersburg Militia (3 bns); HusR Grodno (8 sqns); Combined HusR (3 sqns); Combined DragR (4 sqns); Cossack Pulks of Rodionof II and Platov IV, 1st HAB (10 guns); 26th FAB (12 guns); 14th PosB (6 guns). These forces were joined in the evening by: 26th JgR (1 bn); IR Lithuania (2 bns); Combined Gren Bn of the 5th Division (1 bn); St Petersburg Militia (1 bn); DragR Riga (1 sqn); DragR Mitau (2 sqns); 5th and 6th PosBs (24 guns).

Russian total ca 11,000 men.

Russian losses 400 killed, wounded and missing including Col Silin of the Grodno Hussars who was wounded.

Sources Vaudoncourt, Martinien, Bodart, Bogdanovich.

RM Wiasma, 3 November 1812, clash

A town in the western Russian province of Smolensk, on the River Dniepr, 150 km northeast of Smolensk city.

A Russian victory over the French and Allies.

(Last action – Malojaroslawetz, 24 October; next action – Liachowo, 9 November.)

French and Allied Forces Viceroy Prince Eugène commanding.

I Corps M Davout: 1st Inf Div GdD Morand; 13e RILé, 17e and 30e RIdLi (5 bns each); 2nd Baden LIR (2 bns) 2nd Inf Div GdD Friant: 48e RIdLi (5 bns); IR Joseph Napoleon (2 bns). 3rd Inf Div GdD Gérard: 12e, 21e RIdLi (5 bns each), 127e RIdLi (2 bns), Mecklenburg-Strelitz I Bn (1 bn). 4th Inf Div: GdD Desaix: 85e, 108e RIdLi (5 bns each). 5th Inf Div GdD Compans: 25e, 57e, 61e, 111e RIdLi (5 bns each). 1er ChàCh (4 sqns).

II Corps (parts of): 8e ChàCh (4 sqns).

III Corps (parts of): 10th Inf Div GdD Ledru: 24e RILé, 72 RIdLi (4 bns each). 14th Lt Cav Bde: 28e ChàCh (2 sqns).

IV Corps (parts of): 13th Inf Div GdD Delzons: 92e and 106e RIdLi (4 bns each). 14th Inf Div: GdD Broussière: 18e RILé (2 bns); 53e RIdLi (4 bns); IR Joseph Napoleon (2 bns). 13th Lt Cav Bde 2nd and 3rd Italian ChàCh (4 sqns each). 12th Lt Cav Bde 9e ChàCh (4 sqns).

V Corps Prince Poniatowski: 16th Inf Div GdD Zayonchek: 3rd, 13th, 15th and 16th IRs (2 bns each). 18th Inf Div GdD Kamienicki: 2nd, 8th and 12th IRs (2 bns each); 20th Lt Cav Bde: 5th ChàCh, 13th HusR (4 sqns each).

IX Corps M Victor: 12th Inf Div GdD Partouneaux: 36e RILé (4th bn); 26th Inf Div GdD Daendels 1st, 2nd, 3rd and 4th Berg IRs (2 bns each).

I Cav Corps GdD Nansouty: 5th Div GdD Valence: 6e and 11e CuirRs (4 sqns each).

III Cav Corps 6th Cav Div GdD Lahoussaye: 7e and 30e DragRs (4 sqns each). Also the 5th Bavarian ChLR, 28e ChàCh, 1er and 6e ChLL (4 sqns each) and 48e RIdLi (3 bns).

French total ca 25,000 men.

French losses 4,000 killed and wounded, 3,000 captured, 3 guns. Prince Poniatowski was wounded.

Russian Forces GdI Miloradovitch commanding.

II Corps GL Duke Eugen von Württemberg. 4th Division: IRs Tobolsk, Wolhynien, Krementschug, Minsk, 4th and 34th Jägers (2 bns each). 17th Inf Div IRs Riasan, Brest, Bielosersk, Wilmannstrandt, 30th and 48th Jägers (2 bns each) 6 x FAB. HusR Elisabethgrad (8 sqns), 1 x HAB.

II Cav Corps Gen Adjutant Baron Korff : DragRs Pskov, Moscow, Kargopol, Ingermannland (4 sqns each); Polish UlR (8 sqns).

IV Cav Corps GM Count Sievers: DragRs Charkov, Tschernigov, Kiev, New-Russia (4 sqns each); Lithuanian UlR, HusR Achtyrsk (8 sqns each) 1 x HAB. GM Ilovaisky V: 9 Cossack Pulks 1 x HAB. 27th Inf Div GL Neverowski: IRs Wilna, Simbirsk, Odessa, Tarnopol, 49th and 50th Jägers (2 bns each).

IV Corps GL Count Ostermann-Tolstoi: 11th Division GM Bachmetjef II: GM Tschoglokof: IRs Kexholm, Pernau. GM Filisof: IRs Polozk, Jelez. Col Bistrom I: JgRs Nrs 1 and 33 (all 2 bns each). 11th PosB, 3rd and 4th FABs (12 guns each). 23rd Division GM Bachmetjef I; GM Okunef: IRs Rilsk, Katherinburg. GM Alexopol: IR Selenginsk; JgR Nr 18 (all 2 bns each); Combined Grenadier bns of 11th and 33rd Divisions (3 bns). HusR Isum (8 sqns); 23rd PosB, 43rd and 44th FABs (12 guns each). GdC Ataman Platov's Cossacks: 14 Pulks and 1 x HAB.

Russian total ca 24,500 men.

Russian losses ca 1,800 killed and wounded.

Comment Even at this stage in the retreat, many regiments of the Grande Armée had ceased to exist or had been reduced to company strength.

The French totals include thousands of unarmed stragglers.

Sources Vaudoncourt, Martinien, Preysing-Moos, Malibran and Chelminski, Lünsmann, Bogdanovich.

RN Witebsk, 7 November 1812, capture

A town in northeastern Belarus, on the River Dwina, at the junction of Routes 20 and 24, about 130 km northwest of Smolensk.

A Russian victory over the French.

(Last action – Tschaschniki, 31 October; next action – Axenzi, 13 November.)

French Garrison GdB Ponget (?) commanding: exact strength and details not known.

French losses Killed and wounded not known; GdB Ponget, 10 officers and 400 men captured, 2 guns.

Russian Forces MG Harpe commanding part of GdC Count Wittgenstein's I Corps: IR Nawaginsk (2 bns); DragR Riga (1 sqn); Polish UlR (1 sqn); 7th St Petersburg Militia bn (1 bn); 1st HAB (2 guns). These were later joined by 26th JgR (2 bns); DragR Jamburg (2 sqns); 4 guns, Cossacks (1 sqn); Kalmucks (a detachment).

Russian total ca 2,400 men, 6 guns.

Russian losses 40 killed and wounded.

Comment From French officers captured here, Harpe learned of the evacuation of Moscow and reported it to Wittgenstein.

Source Bogdanovich.

RM Liachowo, 9 November 1812, clash

A village in the western Russian province of Smolensk, 40 km southeast of that city.

A Russian victory over the French.

(Last action – Wiasma, 3 November; next action – Novo Swerschen, 13 November.)

French Forces GdB Augereau commanding: 30e and 85e RIdLi, 7e and 24e RILé; 5e CuirR, 9e ChàCh, 3rd Italian ChàCh.

French total ca 2,000 men.

French losses Not known exactly; moderate.

Russian Forces Part of Admiral Tchichagov's Army of the Danube, exact details and losses not known.

Sources Malibran and Chelminski, Martinien.

EW Alba de Tormes, 10 and 11 November 1812, clash

A town in northern Spain, on the east bank of the Rio Tormes, 21 km down a side road southeast of Salamanca.

An Allied victory over the French.

(Last action – Tajuna, 30 October; next action – Matilla, 16 November.)

French Forces M Soult commanding the Advanced Guard of the Army of the South: 12 Voltigeur coys and 45e RIdLi of the 5th Division, 3 x FAB.

French losses 2 officers killed, 6 wounded; 150 men killed and wounded.

Allied Forces BG Howard's brigade, 2nd Division of Wellington's army: 1/50th, 1/71st and 1/92nd Foot (1 bn each). On the night 10/11 November these were joined by 2nd and 14th Portuguese LIR (1 bn each).

Allied losses British: 13 killed, 56 wounded; Portuguese: 8 killed, 36 wounded.

Comment Not daring to force a river crossing with their 90,000 men if it were defended by Wellington's much smaller force, King Joseph and Soult now marched south up the Rio Tormes to cross at various fords and thus turn the Allied defence line.

Sources Oman, Martinien.

RM Novo Swerschen, 13 November 1812, clash

A village in the western Russian province of Minsk (nowadays the Republic of Belarus), on the upper River Niemen, 70 km southwest of Minsk city.

A Russian victory over the Poles.

(Last action – Ljachowo, 9 November; next action – Mir, 13 November.)

Polish Forces GdB Kosezky commanding the newly raised 18th, 19th, 20th and 22nd Lithuanian IRs (1 bn each), 1 combined CavR, 1 gun.

Polish total ca 3,200 infantry, 300 cavalry.

Polish losses 1,000 killed and wounded, 1 gun; captured – unknown.

Russian Forces Gen Count Lambert with the 10th and 14th JgRs (4 bns). Exact total not known.

Russian losses Not exactly known but very light.

Comment The strategic bridge over the Niemen was captured intact.

Sources Vaudoncourt, Malibran and Chelminski, Martinien, Bogdanovich.

RN Axenzi, 13 November 1812, clash

A village in northern Belarus about 40 km east of Tschaschniki, west of Senno and about 60 km southwest of Witebsk.

A Franco-German victory over the Russians.

(Last action – Witebsk, 7 November; next action – Smoljäntzi, 14 November.)

French Forces GdD Partouneaux commanding 12th Division, IX Corps (M Victor): 10e RIdLi (4e Bn); 29e RIdLi (4 bns); PvIR (3 bns); 44e RIdLi (3e and 4e bns); 126e RIdLi (4 bns); 3 x FAB. 30th Light Cavalry Brigade GdB Fournier: 2nd ChLL of Berg (4 sqns); Hessen-Darmstadt Garde ChLR (4 sqns). 31st Light Cavalry Brigade GdB Delaitre: Saxon ChLR Prinz Johann; Baden HusR (4 sqns each).

French total 14 bns, 16 sqns, 18 guns, ca 6,000 men.

French losses Killed and wounded unknown, 300 captured.

Russian Forces MG Alexejev's Avantgarde of Wittgenstein's I Detached Corps: 25th JgR, IRs Podolien, Tenginsk, Neva and Woronesch (2 bns each), 2 x FAB.

Russian total 10 bns, 24 guns, ca 5,600 men.

Russian losses ca 500 killed, wounded and missing.

Sources Bogdanovich, Vaudoncourt, Martinien.

RM Mir, 13 November 1812, capture

A small town in western Belarus, 11 km north of Route 1 (the main road between the capital, Minsk, and Brest on the border with Poland) about 120 km southwest of Minsk.

A Russian victory over the French.

(Last action – Novo Swerschen, 13 November; next action – Kaidanowo, 15 November.)

French Garrison Details unknown; total ca 500 men.

French losses Killed and wounded unknown; 400 captured.

Russian Forces GM Orurk commanding Gen Count Lambert's Advanced Guard (of Admiral Tchichagov's Army): Jägers (2 coys); Tatar UlR (2 sqns).

Russian total ca 130 men.

Russian losses Total Russian losses for Novo Swerschen and Mir this day were 7 killed and 37 wounded.

Source Bogdanovich.

RN Smoljäntzi, 14 November 1812, clash

A village in northeastern Belarus, 70 km southwest of Witebsk.

A Russian victory over the French and their allies.

(Last action – Axenzi, 13 November; next action – the IX Corps now moved south; next action – Minsk, 17 November see RM).

French Forces M Victor commanding IX Corps. **12th Division** GdD Partouneaux: 10e RILé (4e Bn); 29e RILé (1er–4e bns); 36e, 51e and 55e RIdLi (4e Bns each); 125e RIdLi (1er, 2e, 3e bns); 126e RIdLi (4 bns); 3 x FAB. **26th Division** GdD Daendels: 1st, 3rd, 4th LIRs of Berg (2 bns each); 1st and 3rd Baden LIRs (2 bns each); Baden Jägers (1 bn); 2 x FAB, 2 x HAB. **28th (Polish) Division** GdD Girard: 4th, 7th, 9th IRs, Grand Duchy of Warsaw (2 bns each) 1 x FAB. **30th Light Cavalry Brigade** GdB Fournier: 2nd Lancers of Berg, Hessen-Darmstadt Garde-ChLR (4 sqns each).

French total 41 bns, sqns, 48 guns.

French losses 2,200 killed and wounded, 800 captured.

Russian Forces GdI Count Wittgenstein's I Detached Corps: **14th Division** IRs Tula, Nawaginsk, Tenginsk, Estonia (2 bns each); IR Newa (2 bns); 14th PosB (2 guns); 1 x FAB (6 guns); 6th PosB (12 guns); 11th FAB (6 guns); IR Woronesch (2 bns). **5th Division** GM Berg: IRs Sievsk, Kaluga (2 bns each). GM Prince Sibirsk: IRs Perm, Mohilev; JgRs 23 and 24 (2 bns each); Combined Grenadiers (2 bns) 5th PosB, 9th and 10th FABs (36 guns); IR Lithuania (2 bns). **Advanced Guard** Gen Prince Jaschwil: IRs Mohilev, Podolien, 2nd , 3rd and 25th JgRs (2 bns each); HusR Grodno, Combined HusR, Combined DragR (15 sqns); Cossack Pulks of Rodion II and Platov IV St Petersburg Militia (3 bns); 1st PosB (10 guns); 26th FAB (12 guns); 14th PosB (6 guns). LG Count Steingel: IRs Neva, Petrowsk, Asov, 26th JgR (8 bns). St Petersburg Militia (3 bns); 5th PosB, 27th FAB (24 guns). **Reserve** MG Fok: IR Nisov, 1st Marine IR (2 bns each); Depot Grenadiers (3 bns); Combined Grenadier bns of 5th and 14th Divisions (4 bns); Combined KürR (4 sqns); St Petersburg Militia (4 bns); 21st PosB, 3rd HAB (12 guns each); 14th PosB (6 guns); 23rd HAB (4 guns).

Russian totals 20,000 regular infantry, 7,000 Militia, 3,500 cavalry, 114 guns.

Russian losses ca 3,000 killed, wounded and missing.

Comment Victor withdrew south to Tschereja on 15 November and stayed there until 22 November. Wittgenstein did not pursue.

Sources Bogdanovich, Martinien, Vaudoncourt, Gerdes.

RM Kaidanowo, 15 November 1812, clash

A village in the western Russian province of Minsk (nowadays the Republic of Belarus), 30 km southwest of that city.

A Russian victory over the Franco-Poles.

(Last action – Mir, 13 November; next action – Minsk, 17 November.)

Franco-Polish Forces GdB Kosezky commanding the 18th, 19th, 20th and 22nd Lithuanian IRs (1 bn each); 46e RIdLi (1 bn); combined Württemberg infantry (150 men); 300 French cavalry, 2 guns.

Franco-Polish total ca 1,300 men.

Franco-Polish losses All captured except the cavalry.

Russian Forces MG Count Lambert of Tchichagov's Army of the Danube. HusR Alexandria (4 sqns); Cossack Pulks of Grekov VIII and Grekov XI, DragR Starodub, Tatar UlR, Don Cossack Pulk of Babaranchtschikov, TatarR Evpatoria, DragR Schitomir; 10th and 14th JgRs (2 bns each); 2 x HAB, 1 x FAB.

Russian total ca 3,800 men.

Russian losses 'Insignificant'.

Comment In the period 13–15 November, Lambert took 65 officers and 3,870 men prisoner, captured 2 guns, 10 ammunition waggons and 2 colours.

Sources Martinien, Vaudoncourt, Foord, Bogdanovich.

RL Dahlenkirchen, 15 November 1812, skirmishes

A village in Latvia (Coeurland), on the left bank of the River Düna (now Daugava), 14 km southeast of Riga.

(Last action – Garosse River, 1 October; next action – Piktupönen, 26 December.)

Prussian Forces Obst von Horn commanding IR Nr 2 (skirmishers only); IR Nr 5 (1st bn); Füs Bn Nrs 4 and 7 (1 bn each); HusR Nr 1 (2 tps); DragR Nr 1 (2 ¼ sqns); 1 x HAB; ⅓ x FAB.

Prussian total ca 3,000 men.

Prussian losses Not known, light.

Russian Forces Exact details not known; Part of LG Count Steinheil's Army of Finland, probably the 25th Division: IRs Voronesch, 1st, 2nd and 3rd Marines, 31st and 47th Jägers (2 bns each).

Russian losses Killed and wounded not known, about 1,000 captured.

Comment French General Bachelu was placed, at Napoleon's insistence, in command of the united Allied effort this day. Other units involved (at different locations) were the 1st Westfalian and 13th Bavarian IRs (2 bns each); 3 Polish battalions and ½ x Polish FAB.

Sources KGE 24, Preysing-Moos, Bogdanovich.

RS Wolkowysk (Izabelin), 14 – -16 November 1812, clash

A town in the southwest corner of the Republic of Belarus, on the river of Wolkowysk, 70 km southeast of Grodno.

An Allied victory over the Russians.

(Last action – Biala Podlaska, 13 October. This was the last action of note on the southern flank.)

Allied Forces GdD Reynier commanding the **VII (Saxon) Corps** IRs Prinz Anton, Prinz Clemens, Prinz Friedrich, von Niesemeuschel, 1st and 2nd LtIRs (2 bns each); HusR, UlR Prinz Clemens (4 sqns each) Gren Bns von Anger, von Ryssel, von Spiegel. GdD Durutte's 32nd Division, XI Corps: 131e, 132e RIdLi, IR Belle-Isle, IR Würzburg (3 bns each); 35e RIdLi (2 bns); 133e RIdLi (1 bn). **Austrian Troops** GdK Prince Schwarzenberg commanding (attacked Russian flank and rear on 16 November): FML Trautenberg: GM Pflacher: IRs Beaulieu Nr 58, Duka Nr 39 (2 bns each). FML Bianchi: GM Lilienberg: IRs Simbschen Nr 48 and Allvintzy Nr 19 (2 bns each); GM Prince Philipp von Hessen-Homburg: IRs Hiller Nr 2 and Colloredo Nr 33 (2 bns each), GM Prince Alois Liechtenstein: IRs Esterházy Nr 32, Davidovich Nr 34 (2 bns each); Gren Bns Kirchenbetter and Przeszinsky (1 bn each). FML Frimont: GM Fröhlich: ChLRs O'Reilly Nr 3 and Hohenzollern Nr 2 (6 sqns each); GM Wrede: DragR Levenehr Nr 4 (4 sqns); HusR Liechtenstein Nr 7 (6 sqns). Artillery: 2 x 3pdr and 4 x 6pdr FABs each of 8 guns; 1 x 6pdr PosB, 1 x 12pdr PosB each of 4 guns and 2 x 7pdr howitzers, 2 x HAB each of 6 guns and 2 howitzers.

Allied totals ca 28,000 men.

Allied losses 1,300 killed and wounded, 500 captured. The Saxons lost over 500 men.

Russian Forces LG Baron von Sacken's corps of Admiral Tchichagov's 3rd Army of the West. **LG Essen III** IRs Schlüsselburg, Old Ingermannland, Archangelgorod, Ukrain (2 bns each); Olonez (3 bns); 37th JgR (3 bns); DragRs Serpuchov (4 sqns), Vladimir (3 sqns); Twer (1 sqn), HusR Lubno (8 sqns); 2nd BaschkirR; 1st KalmuckR, Cossack Pulk of Tschikelef. 4th Ural Cossack Pulk; 8th PosB, 14th and 15th FABs, 15th HAB. **Total** 14 bns, 6 sqns, 4 Pulks, 48 guns, ca 9,000 men. **MG Bulatov** IRs Wiatka (3 bns); Wyborg (2 bns); Starokolsk (3 bns); Ochotsk (2 bns); Mingrelia, Galizia (2 bns each); Kamchatka (1 bn); 45th JgR (1 bn); 29th JgR (2 bns). DragRs Perejaslawl and Smolensk (4 sqns each); UlR Tschugujef (8 sqns); Cossack Pulk of Wlastov, 2nd KalmuckR; 22nd PosB, 41st FAB. **Total** 18 bns, 16 sqns, 2 Pulks, 24 guns. **MG Count Lieven's Reserve** IRs Jaroslawl (2 bns); Crimea and Bialystok (3 bns each); 8th JgR (3 bns); 39th JgR (2 bns); DragRs Vladimir (1 sqn), Twer (3 sqns); 10th PosB, 18th FAB. **Total** 13 bns, 4 sqns, 24 guns.

Total of Sacken's Corps 45 bns, 36 sqns, 6 Pulks, 92 guns, ca 27,000 men.

Russian losses 1,500 killed and wounded, 2,500 captured on the battlefield.

Comment Schwarzenberg's Austrians penetrated the Russian rear and took most of their baggage. The Russians withdrew to Swislotsch and by 25 November had fallen back south to Kobryn and occupied the line of the River Bug both sides of Brest. The Saxons captured 4,700 men between Wolkowysk and Brest, took the Russian military chest and many waggons including 19 with ammunition. Austrian cavalry charged the IR Ukraine and took 10 officers and 400 men prisoner.

Sources Wrede, Martinien, Grosch/Hagen/Schenk, Schuster and Franke, Bogdanovich.

EW Matilla, 16 November 1812, skirmish

A village and brook of the same name in northern Spain about 40 km southwest of Salamanca on Route 620/E80.

An Allied victory over the French.

(Last action – Alba de Tormes, 10 November; this was the last action of any note.)

French Forces Part of Soult's Army of the South: 7e ChLL, 2e HusR, 5e and 27e ChàCh ca 2,000 men.

French losses 50 men, mostly wounded and captured.

Allied Forces BG Von Alten's LtCav Bde: 14th LDR, 1st and 2nd Hus KGL; 1/28th Foot (light coy); 2 guns.

Allied total ca 1,300 men.

Allied losses 34 killed, wounded and missing.

Comment This little action demonstrates how much more effective a force of all arms (cavalry, infantry and artillery) can be than one arm operating alone. Apart from a minor clash at San Munoz on the Huebra river on 17 November, this was the last action in Wellington's retreat from Burgos to Ciudad Rodrigo and the last in the campaign of 1812 in Spain.

Sources Oman, Martinien.

RM Minsk, 17 November 1812, capture of

The capital of the Republic of Belarus, on the River Svislotch and at the junction of Routes 1 and 26.

A Russian victory over the Poles.

(Last action – Kaidanowo, 15 November; next action – Krasnoi, 14–18 November.)

Polish Garrison GdB Bronikowski commanding: 22nd Lithuanian IR (2 bns); a French March Battalion.

Polish total ca 2,000 men.

Polish losses The Lithuanians were captured, Bronikowski and the French escaped.

Russian Forces MG Count Lambert commanding the Avantgarde Army of the Danube: 10th and 14th JgRs (2 bns each); DragRs Starodub and Schitomir, HusR Alexandria (4 sqns); Cossack Pulks of Grekov VIII, Grekov XI and Babaranchtschikov, Tatar UlR, and Tatars of Evpatoria. 2 x HAB, 1 x FAB.

Russian total ca 3,600 men.

Russian losses 'Extremely light'.

Comment Apart from the garrison, in Minsk were 2,000 sick and wounded and a huge magazine of two million rations all of which fell into Russian hands thus hastening the destruction of the Grande Armée. 110 Russian prisoners were released. On 17 November Tchichagov reached Minsk with part of his main body and the reserve. Col Paradowski (of MG Orurk's Avantgarde) with DragR Livland and Kirejev's Cossack Pulk took 2,000 prisoners on the Wilna road at Rakov.

Sources Bogdanovich, Vaudoncourt, Gembarzewski, Malibran and Chelminski.

RM Krasnoi, 14–18 November 1812, 2nd clash

A village in the western Russian province of Smolensk, 40 km southwest of that city.

Russian victories over the Allies.

(Last action – Minsk, 17 November; next action – Borisov, 21 November.)

Allied Forces Emperor Napoleon I commanding. NB it is no longer meaningful to quote numbers of battalions and squadrons; many regiments had already ceased to exist, others were mere handfuls. Imperial

Guard: 1er, 2e and 3e Grenadiers, Fus, Grenadiers, 1er, 4e, 5e and 6e Tirailleurs, 1er ChàP, FusChas, 1er, 4e and 6e Voltigeurs. Flanqueurs Chas. ChàCh, Foot and Horse Artillery, Train. The following RIdLi: 9e, 17e, 25e, 35e, 36e, 53e, 57e, 61e, 72e, 85e, 92e, 93e, 106e, 108e, 111e, 127e, 129e. The following RILé: 7e, 8e, 18e, 24e, 33e. The Neufchâtel bn, Regt Illyrie, Vistula Legion (3rd IR); IR Joseph Napoleon, Portuguese Legion (2nd IR), 1st Croatian IR, Cuirassiers: 1er, 12e Rs. Dragoons: 7e, 23e and 30e. ChLL: 3e. ChàCh: 9e, 16e, 19e, 28e. Hussars: 11e. Westfalians: ChLL of the Guard.

Allied totals In these five days all 50,000 survivors of the Grande Armée passed through Krasnoi

IRs Libau, Sophia. GM Balla: JgRs Nrs 11 and 36 (all 2 bns each). 7th PosB, 12th and 13th FABs (12 guns each). 24th Division GM Lichatschev: GM Zibulsky: IRs Ufa, Schirwan. Col Denisjef: IRs Butirsk, Tomsk. Col Wuitsch: JgRs Nrs 19 and 40 (all 2 bns each); HusR Ssum (8 sqns). 24th PosB, 45th and 46th FABs, 7th HAB (12 guns each). 2nd Kür Div. GM Duka: KürRs Military Order and Jekaterinoslav.

VII Corps GL Raievsky: 26th Division GM Paskewitsch: Col Libardt: IRs Ladoga and Poltava. Col Savoini: IRs Nischegorod and Orel. Col Gogel I : JgRs Nrs 5 and 42 (all 2 bns each). 26th PosB, 47th and 48th FABs. 12th Division GM Kolubakin: Col Rilejef IRs Narva and Smolensk. Col Panzerbieter: IRs New

Allied losses

			—— Captured ——					Eagles &
		Killed	Generals	Officers	Men	Guns	Limbers	Colours
I Corps	14 Nov	400	3	24	1,220	—	—	—
IV Corps	15 Nov	800	1	20	1,100	12	20	—
IV Corps	16 Nov	1,800	1	53	2,700	24	30	5
The Guard	17 Nov	4,000	2	58	9,160	60	30	6
III Corps	18 Nov	6,000	—	100	12,000	27	18	4
Totals		13,000	7	255	26,180	123	98	15

These casualty figures include stragglers of all Corps. 112 other guns had been abandoned en route from Smolensk.

Russian Forces GDI Miloradovitch commanding (Kutusov was on the scene as well). Gen Tormasov with the V, VI and VIII Infantry Corps.

V Corps GL Lawrof: GM Baron Rosen: LifeGuardRs Preobraschenski and Semenow (3 bns each). Col Udom: LifeGuardRs Ismailof and Lithuania (3 bns each). Col Bistrom III: LifeGuard JgR, Finland JgR (3 bns each); Guards Marine Equipage. 2 x PosBs, 2 x FABs, 2 x HABs (12 guns each) plus 2 guns with the Marine Equipage. 1st Combined Grenadier Division: Combined Gren Bns of the 1st Grenadier, 3rd, 4th and 17th Divisions (7 bns); 1x pionier coy. 1st Kürassier Division GL de Preradowitsch: GM Schewitsch: Chevalier Guards, Horse Guards. GM Borosdin II: KürRs His Majesty and Her Majesty, KürR Astrakhan (4 sqns each).

III Corps General Adjutant Count Stroganof. 3rd Division Gen. Prince Schachowskoi: IRs Murom, Reval.

VI Corps GdI Dochtorov: 7th Division GL Kapsevich; Col Ljäpunof: IRs Moscow, Pskov. GM Count Balman: Ingermannland and Alexopol. GM Palizin: JgRs Nrs 6 and 41 (all 2 bns each). HusR Achtyrsk (8 sqns). 12th PosB, 22nd and 23rd FABs, 8th HAB (12 guns each).

VIII Corps GL Borosdin I: 2nd Grenadier Division GM Prince Karl von Mecklenburg: Col Schatilof: GrenadierRs Kiev and Moscow. Col Buxhowden: GrenadierRs Astrakhan and Phanagoria. Col Hesse: GrenadierRs Simbirsk, Little Russia (all 2 bns each). 2nd PosB, 20th and 21st FABs. Combined Grenadier Division: GM Count Woronzov: the combined grenadier bns of the 7th and 24th Divisions (4 bns) and of the 2nd, 12th and 26th Divisions (6 bns); 31st and 32nd PosBs (12 guns each).

Comment Kutusov, fearing to become heavily involved if Napoleon was in command, held back Tormasov's force south of the battle for three hours and eventually only General Rosen's advanced guard of this force came into action at Little Dobroje when most of the Grande Armée had slipped out of the trap. The square of the 1er Voltigeurs of the Imperial Guard was broken by canister then cut down by KürRs Military Order and Jekaterinoslav and the tail end unit of the French (33e RILé) was also destroyed.

The day's entry on 17 November in the Russian Army Journal read: 'Captured - 2 generals, 57 officers, 6,170 men, 45 guns, 2 colours, 4 standards, 1 marshal's baton' (Davout's). Kutusov then reported to the Tsar: 'Captured - 2 generals, 134 officers, 9,170 men, 70 guns, 2 colours and standards and 1 baton' (M Davout's). He reported Russian losses at '700 killed and wounded,' Despite having let Napoleon's army slip out of the trap, Kutusov received the title 'Smolenski' for this action, Miloradovitch received the Order of St George, II Class and Platov was created a count.

Sources Martinien, Bogdanovich, Vaudoncourt, Bodart, Malibran and Chelminski.

RM Borisov, 21 November 1812, 1st clash

A town in the western Russian province of Minsk (nowadays the Republic of Belarus), on the left bank of the River Beresina, 58 km northeast of Minsk city.

A Russian victory over the Franco-Poles.

(Last action - Krasnoi, 14-18 November; next action - Borisov, 23 November.)

Franco-Polish Forces GdD Dombrowski. 17th Inf Div of the V (Polish) Corps: IRs Nr 1 (3 bns), 6, 14 and 17 (2 bns each); 2nd and 7th Lancers. Also: RIllyrien; 4e, 72e and 108e RIdLi and the ChàCh of the Guard.

Franco-Polish total ca 5,000 men and 20 guns.

Franco-Polish losses Most killed, wounded or captured, 8 guns, 1 eagle, 2 colours. Gen Dziewanovski fatally wounded. The 1st Polish Infantry Regiment escaped.

Russian Forces MG Count Lambert's newly reformed Avantgarde of Admiral Tchichagov's Army of the Danube: IR Witebsk, 7th, 13th, 14th and 18th JgRs (10 bns or 3,200 men); DragR Arsamas; HusR Alexandria (4 sqns each); PosB Nr 34, 11th and 112th HABs.

Russian total 4,500 men, 36 guns.

Russian losses 2,000 killed and wounded.

Comment Despite heavy loss, Lambert had seized the bridge over the River Beresina, so vital for the withdrawal of the Grande Armée. On 22 November Tchichagov's army concentrated around Borisov.

Sources Bogdanovich, Vaudoncourt, Martinien, Malibran and Chelminski.

RM Borisov, 23 November 1812, 2nd clash

A town in northern Belarus, on the left bank of the River Beresina, 58 km northeast of Minsk and on Route 1 between Minsk and Orscha.

A French victory over the Russians.

(Last action - Borisov, 21 November; next action - Cholopenitsche, 23 November.)

French Forces GdB Castex commanding a mixed force of Oudinot's II Corps: 5th Light Cavalry Brigade: 23e ChàCh (2 sqns); 24e ChàCh (3 sqns), a Polish lancer regiment (4 sqns); 2,500 infantry.

French total 1,100 cavalry, 2,500 infantry, 3 x FAB.

French losses ca 1,000 killed, wounded and missing.

Russian Forces MG Count Pahlen commanding the Avantgarde of Admiral Tchichagov's Army of the Danube: DragRs Irkutsk, Siberia, Orenburg and Kurland (4 sqns each); HusR Mariupol (8 sqns); 9th HAB; JgRs 7, 14, 38 (2 bns each).

Russian total 24 sqns, 6 bns, 12 guns, ca 3,000 men.

Russian losses 1,000 killed, wounded and missing, much of the 3rd Army's baggage train, many sick and wounded. The French claimed 2,000 Russian casualties.

Comment Pahlen had captured 2 prisoners on 22 November who told him that Napoleon and the remnants of the Grande Armée were only a day's march away and making for Borisov to cross the Beresina. Tchichagov, in Borisov, refused to believe the report. When Pahlen's force was pushed back to the town Tchichagov ordered a withdrawal but did not organise it. Chaos resulted; particularly as most Russian cavalry regiments had dispersed to forage. The Russians were forced over the river but held the bridgehead on the western bank.

Sources Bogdanovich, Vaudoncourt, Martinien.

RM Cholopenitsche, 23 November 1812, clash

A village near Borisov in Belarus.

A Russian victory over the Franco-Germans.

(Last action - Borisov, 23 November; next action - Baturi, 24 November.)

Franco-German Forces Part of Victor's IX Corps: 126e RIdLi (remnants) of Partouneaux's 12th Division and 2nd Berg ChLR (4 sqns) of Fournier's 30th Light Cavalry Brigade.

Franco-German totals Not known.

Franco-German losses The Russians claimed to have broken in 126e's square, killed 200 and taken 27 officers and over 300 men prisoner.

Russian Forces Colonel Gerngross commanding the Combined HusR (4 sqns) and the Cossack Pulks of

Loschtschilin and Panteljejef of Wittgenstein's I Corps.

Russian totals and losses Not known.

Sources Bogdanovich, Martinien.

RM Baturi, 24 November 1812, clash

A village near Borisov in Belarus.

A Russian victory over the French (Germans).

(Last action – Cholopenitsche, 23 November; next action – Beresina Crossing, 26–28 November.)

French (German) Forces GdD Daendel's 26th Division of Victor's IX Corps: 1st–4th Berg LIRs (2 bns each); 1st and 3rd Baden LIRs (2 bns each), Baden Jägers (1 bn).

German total Not known.

German losses 'Some hundreds'.

Russian Forces MG Harpe with Wittgenstein's Avantgarde: IRs Nawaginsk, Petrowsk (2 bns each); Combined Grenadiers (4 bns); HusR Grodno (8 sqns); Combined DragR (4 sqns); Cossack Pulks of Platov IV; 1 x HAB, 1 x FAB.

Russian total ca 4,000 men, 18 guns.

Russian losses Not known.

Source Bogdanovich.

RM Beresina Crossing, 26–28 November 1812, battle

A group of towns and villages in Belarus, along the upper reaches of the River Beresina between Minsk in the west, and Mohilev in the east. The main actions are dealt with below. (Brili, Staroi-Borisov, Studianka, Brili).

A French victory over the Russians.

(Last action – Baturi, 24 November; next action – Brili, 26 November.)

RM Brili, 26 November 1812, 1st clash

A village on the south bank of the River Beresina. Between Brili and Studianka (on the north bank) the two bridges for the crossing of the Grande Armée were built.

French Forces M Oudinot commanding **II Corps** (remnants): **6th Division** GdD Legrand: 26e RILé, 19e and 56e RIdLi (4 bns each); 128e RIdLi (2 bns); 3rd IR Portuguese Legion (2 bns); 1 x HAB, 1 x FAB. **8th Division** GdD Verdier: 11e RILé (4 bns); 2e RIdLi (5 bns); 37e RIdLi (4 bns); 124e RIdLi (3 bns). 1 x FAB, 1 x HAB. **9th Division** GdD Merle: 3rd Croatian IR (2 bns); 1st Swiss IR (2 bns); 2nd, 3rd and 4th Swiss IRs (3 bns each); 123e RIdLi (3 bns); 1 x HAB, 1 x FAB. GdD Doumerc's **3rd Cuirassier Division** 4e, 7e, 14e CuirRs (4 sqns each); 2 x HAB.

French total 5,600 infantry, 1,400 cavalry and 2 guns (the rest of the artillery joined a battery of 40–56 guns on the heights east of Studianka village which commanded the ground in front of II Corps).

Russian Forces MG Tschaplitz commanding Admiral Tchichagov's Avantgarde: 32nd JgR (2 bns); HusR Pavlograd (8 sqns); DragR Twer (4 sqns); KalmuckR, Baschkirs (detachment); 13th HAB. 8guns.

Russian total ca 5,000 men.

Russian losses Not known.

Comment Tschaplitz had advanced west from Bolshoi Stachov where Tchichagov's main body now was but was too late to prevent the French crossing the ramshackle but now completed bridges and his artillery could not be brought to bear on the bridges. The escape route of the Grande Armée to Wilna was now open. Tchichagov was informed of the event by Tschaplitz and sent an officer to Kutusov (advancing west from Mohilev) to give him the news but Kutusov only received it after the Grande Armée had crossed the Beresina. There was no combat at Brili on 27 November; the opposing forces just watched each other. Oudinot was joined by Ney's III Corps; the Imperial Guard formed a reserve behind them.

RM Staroi-Borisov, 27 November 1812, clash (part of the Beresina action)

A village and dairy on the north bank of the River Beresina about 4 km west of Borisov.

French Forces GdD Partouneaux's 12th Division of Victor's IX Corps: 10e RILé (4e Bn); 29e RILé (4 bns); PvIR (3 bns); 125e RIdLi (3 bns); 44e RIdLi (3e and 4e bns): 126e RIdLi (4 bns); 1 x FAB. Saxon ChLR Prinz Johann (4 sqns).

French total 17 bns, 4 sqns, ca 12,000 men and 6 guns.

French losses See Comment below.

Russian Forces MG Wlastov's Avantgarde of GdI Wittgenstein's I Detached Corps: IR Nawaginsk (2 bns); DragR Riga, Polish UlR (1 sqn each); St Petersburg Militia (7th Bn); 26th JgR (2 bns); DragR Jamburg (2 sqns); Cossacks (1 sqn); Kalmucks (a detachment), 9th FAB, 27th PosB.

LG Count Steingel's Corps (arrived towards the end of the action): IRs Tenginsk, Tula, Estonia, Woronesch, Neva, Petrowsk, Lithuania 26th JgR (16 bns); DragR Mitau (4 sqns); DragR Riga (3 sqns); St Petersburg Militia (3 bns); 6th PosB (12 guns); 28th PosB (4 guns); 11th FAB (12 guns).

LG Berg's Corps: IRs Perm, Sievsk, Kaluga, Asov, Combined JgR (11 bns), Combined Guards CavR (2 sqns), DragR Jamburg (2 sqns), 5th PosB (12 guns); 27th FAB (12 guns). From LG Steingel's Corps: Novgorod Militia (2 bns).

Russian total 37 bns, 17 sqns, 76 guns, ca 12,000 men.

Comment Partouneaux set out from Borisov to march to Studianka but was cut off and overwhelmed by the Russians. On the morning of 28 November he and most of his division surrendered. The Saxon ChLR Prinz Johann, last element of the rearguard, got lost and capitulated 260 strong. Generals Partouneaux, Billard, Blamont, Delaitre, 240 officers, 7,800 men, 2 colours and 3 guns were taken. Only one battalion (4e/55e RIdLi, part of the Provisional IR) fought its way out with 4 guns. It was in Borisov on 28 November that Admiral Tchichagov finally met up with Count Wittgenstein.

RM Studianka, 28 November 1812, clash

A village on the north bank of the River Beresina, about 15 km west of Borisov.

Part of the Beresina Crossing action.

French and Allied Forces GdI Girard commanding 28th (Polish) Infantry Division, IX Corps: 4th, 7th and 9th Polish LIRs (2 bns each). 1 x FAB (6 guns). Baden Brigade Gen Count Hochberg: 1st and 3rd LIRs (2 bns each); Jägers (1 bn). 30th Light Cavalry Brigade GdB Fournier: 2nd Berg ChLR; Hessen-Darmstadt Garde-ChLR; Baden HusR (4 sqns each).

French total 11 bns (5,000 men), 12 sqns (300 men), 14 guns.

French losses The Baden Brigade infantry alone lost 28 officers and 1,100 men. The Baden Hussars were destroyed, only 50 surviving. The Hessian Garde ChLR was also destroyed. Only 2–300 Poles survived and the Berg Brigade consisted at the end of the day of a colonel and 60 men.

Russian Forces GdI Count Wittgenstein's Avantgarde under MG Wlastov (see Staroi Borisov, 27 November above) plus MG Fok commanding LG Berg's corps: IRs Perm, Sievsk, Kaluga, Asov, Combined JgR (11 bns), Combined Guards CavR (3 sqns), DragR Jamburg (4 sqns), St Petersburg Militia (3 bns); 5th PosB; 27th FAB (24 guns).

Russian total 8,000 men.

RM Brili, 28 November 1812, 2nd clash

A French victory over the Russians.

French Forces M Oudinot commanding the II and III Corps (M Ney) with the Imperial Guard in reserve as for 1st Brili on 26 November.

French losses M Oudinot, Generals Legrand, Zayonchek, Claparède, Dombrowski and Kniashewitz wounded. 5,000 officers and men killed, wounded and captured.

Russian Forces MG Tschaplitz commanding Admiral Tchichagov's Avantgarde as for 1st Brili on 26 November, plus the following forces. 9th Division: IRs Nascheburg, Jakutsk, Apscheron, Riashsk. 18th Division: IRs Wladimir, Tambov, Kostroma, Dnieprovsk; 12th, 22nd, 27th, 7th 14th, 28th and 32nd JgRs.

Russian total ca 12,000 men; 6 x artillery batteries.

Russian losses 2,000 killed and wounded; Tschaplitz wounded, three artillery batteries destroyed, 600 Jägers captured.

Comment As can be imagined, it is impossible to expect clear and accurate accounts to have come from these three days of desperate struggle. Estimates of Russian losses on 27 and 28 November are about 4,000 killed, wounded and captured. French losses on these two days (including Partouneaux's division) are about 13,000 killed, wounded and captured, 4 guns, 2 colours. General Candras was killed, Fournier, Girard and Damas wounded. Three-quarters of Napoleon's troops who fought here were non-French. On 29 November the Russians took a further 5,000 prisoners, 12 guns, many ammunition waggons and other vehicles. Despite suffering heavy losses, Napoleon had outwitted his superior enemies and escaped. Admiral Tchichagov was blamed for allowing the Grande Armée to escape across the Beresina. Almost all Russian commanders were extremely cautious in attacking the French as they could not believe that their enemy's strength had fallen to only 60-70,000 men. Kutusov – who did know the true state of the Grande Armée – must also be criticized for not pursuing them more vigorously.

This was the last major action of the Russian campaign's central sector.

Sources Bogdanovich, Martinien, Vaudoncourt, Lünsmann, Gembarzewski.

RL Riga, 24 July – 18 December 1812, blockade

A fortified city-port on the Baltic Sea, capital of the Russian province of Courland (nowadays the Baltic Republic of Latvia), on the estuary of the River Düna (now the Daugava).

A Russian victory over the Allies.

(Last action – Eckau, 19 July; next action – Piktupönen, 26 December.)

Allied Forces

M Macdonald commanding the X Corps 7th Division GdD Grandjean: GdB Ricard: Bavarian IR Nr 13 (2 bns); Polish IR Nr 5 (4 bns). GdB Prince Radziwill: Polish IR Nr 10 (4 bns). GdB Bachelu: Westfalian IR Nr 1 (2 bns); Polish IR Nr 11 (4 bns); Prussian HusR Nr 1 (4 sqns), 2x Polish HABs. **Total** ca 11,000 men.

Prussian Corps GL York commanding: Obst von Horn's Bde: IRs Nrs 2, 3 and 4 (2 bns each); 1½ x FAB. Obst von Raumer's Bde: IRs Nrs 5 and 6 (2 bns each); Füs Bn Nr 6 (1 bn); 2 x FAB. **Avantgarde** BG Jeanneret: Füs Bns Nrs 1, 2, 4 and 5 (1 bn each); Ostpreussisches Jg Bn (1 bn); DragR Nr 2 and HusR Nr 3 (4 sqns each); 2 x HAB. **The Reserve** DragR Nr 1 (4 sqns); 1 x HAB. Coastal Detachment. Obst von Below: IR Nr 1 (2 bns); Füs Bn Nr 7 (1 bn); 1 x FAB. Other detachments: Füs Bn Nr 3 (1 bn); HusR Nr 1 (to Grandjean's 7th Div,), HusR Nr 2 and UlR (4 sqns each) – in Montbrun's II Cavalry Corps with the main body of the Grand Armée. **Total Prussians** ca 20,000 men.

Total X Corps 31,000 men, 130 siege guns.

Prussian losses not known exactly; see actions coded 'RL'.

Russian Garrison of Riga LG Essen I commanding. **25th Division** IR Woronesch, 1st, 2nd, 3rd Naval (Marine) Rs; 31st and 47th JgRs. Cavalry Chevalier Guard, Life Guards; KürR Pskov; DragR Lithuania (4 sqns each). Artillery: 1xPosB, 1 x FAB, 1 x HAB. **Total** 13,000 men, 36 field guns plus the fortress artillery (1 coy). **MG Lewis' Corps** 4th, 20th, 21st JgRs (Depot Bns); Seliwanov's Cossack Pulk 1 x FAB. **Total** ca 2,000 men.

On 23 September **LG Count Steinheil's Finnish Corps** entered the city: 6th Division*: MG Rachmanov: IRs Asov, Nisov, Uglitsch; 3rd JgR; 35th JgR (2 bns each). 21st Division**: MG Alexejev: IRs Neva, Petrowsk, Lithuania, Podolia, 2nd JgR. Cavalry: DragR Finland (3 sqns); Cossack Pulk Loschtschilin. Artillery: 21st PosB (6 guns); 11th FAB (12 guns). **Total** ca 10,000 men.

* = IR Briansk remained on Aland.

** = 44th JgR remained on Aland.

Comment From an initial 13,000 men the garrison grew to 27,000 by 1 October. Although LG Essen I was senior to LG Count Steinheil, the latter received command of the joint force. Subsequent friction between the two men bedevilled and paralysed Russian operations here. Local militia regiments augmented the regiments shown above. The Russians had a flotilla of 21 gunboats and were supported by a British squadron with 18 vessels in all including gunboats. For actions in this theatre of operations track entries coded 'RL' starting with Eckau, 19 July.

Sources KGE 24, Preysing-Moos, Bogdanovich.

RL Piktupönen, 26 December 1812, skirmish

A small village in Lithuania (not marked on modern maps) midway between Tauroggen (now Taurage) and Tilsit (now Sowietsk) on the River Memel.

(Last action – Dahlenkirchen, 15 November; this was the last action in the campaign here.)

Prussian Forces Obstlt von Tresckow commanding: DragR Nr 1 (3 sqns); HusR Nr 1 (1 sqn).

Prussian total 300 men.

Prussian losses Not known, very light.

Russian Forces Col Wlastov's cossacks, 2 infantry bns, 2 guns.

Russian losses 1 bn captured, 1 gun.

Comment For some weeks the Russians had been trying to get York to defect from the French cause and the X Corps was withdrawing from Courland. York informed his king and asked for instructions; a verbal answer came back: 'act according to circumstances'! When informed of the total destruction of the Grande Armée, York signed the 'Convention of Tauroggen' on 30 December with German-born Russian General Diebitsch. Prussia had now joined the Allies against France.

Sources KGE 24.

1813

1813 THE ACTIONS

SX Königsberg, 1 and 5 January 1813, skirmishes

A Baltic port (now Kaliningrad in Russia) near the mouth of the River Pregel (now Pregolja) in the Russian enclave between Poland and Lithuania.

Russian victories over the French.

(Last action - Piktupönen, 26 December 1812; next action - Kalisz, 13 February.)

French Forces 1 January: 93e RIdLi, 15e RILé. 5 January: 29e RIdLi, 28e ChàCh, 6e HusR.

French total and losses Unknown.

Russian Forces Part of LG Count Steinheil's Army of Finland: 6th Inf Div: IRs Briansk, Nizov, Uglitsch, Azov, 3rd and 35th Jägers. 21st Inf Div: IRs Petrowsk, Podolsk, Neva, Lithuania, 2nd and 44th Jägers. 25th Inf Div: IRs Voronesch, 1st, 2nd, 3rd Marines, 31st and 47th Jägers. Each division with 3 x FAB. Cavalry: Chevalier Guard, Life Guards, KürR Pskov, DragR Lithuania (4 sqns each). Exact units involved and losses incurred not known.

Russian losses Unknown.

Comment The French units came from a variety of Corps as shown: I Corps, 2nd Division - 15e Lé; III Corps, 11th Division - 93e Li; III Corps, 14th Light Cavalry Brigade - 28e ChàCh. XI Corps, 34th Division - 29e Li; III Cavalry Corps - 6e Hus. This typified the confusion of the remnants of the Grande Armée at this time.

Sources KGE 24, Preysing-Moos, Bogdanovich.

EN Tiebas, 8 February 1813, clash

A small town in northern Spain, 18 km south of Pamplona on Route 121 and on the Rio Leoz.

A Spanish victory over the French.

(Last action - this was the opening action in northern Spain in 1813; next action - Béjar, 20 February.)

French Forces GdD Abbé of Caffarelli's Army of the North: 10e RILé, 3e, 52e and 105e RIdLi (2 bns each), 150 ChàCh.

French total 3,150 men.

French losses Not known exactly, moderate.

Spanish Forces Mina and 4 bns of guerrillas.

Spanish total ca 2,800 men.

Spanish losses Not exactly known but light.

Comment Abbé had been trying to break through to relieve the trapped garrison in Tafalla (16 km to the south). When this garrison heard of his defeat on 11 February they surrendered (11 officers, 317 men) and French communications to Madrid and Zaragoza were cut.

Sources Oman, Martinien.

SX Kalisz, 13 February 1813, clash

Two identified villages in western Poland, 10 km north of the town of Kalisz and on Route 25.

A drawn match between the Russians and the French, Germans, Poles and Saxons.

(Last action - Königsberg, 5 January; next action - Wrietzen, 17 February.)

Polish-Saxon Forces GL von Le Coq of VII Corps' 24th Division commanding: GM von Nostitz: IRs Prinz Anton and Prinz Clemens (1 bn each); ChLR von Polenz (200 men); 1 Polish UlR (150 men); 1 x FAB. Gren Bn von Liebenau (1 bn). **Polish-Saxon total** ca 1,200 men. **Polish-Saxon losses** GM von Nostitz, 19 officers, 300 men, 2 x 4 pdr guns and 2 colours (IR Prinz Anton) captured. Killed and wounded unknown. **German and French Forces** GdD Baron Durutte's 32nd Division: 35e RILé (1er Bn); 36e RILé (4e Bn); 131e, 132e and 133e RIdLi (3e and 4e bns each); IR Würzburg (3rd and 4th bns).

Allied total ca 4,000 men.

Allied losses Not known.

Russian Forces GL Winzingerode commanding:

Avantgarde GM Lanskoi: 39th Jägers (1 bn); Alexandria and White Russia HusR (3 sqns each); Lithuanian MtdRR (3 sqns); 1 x HAB. Don Cossack Pulks of Grekov III, Grekov IX and Grekov XXI; Ural Cossack Pulk, Cossack Pulks of Kutainikov and Sutcherinov.

II Corps GL Prince Eugen von Württemberg: 1st Brigade (of 3rd Division) GM Count Schachafskoi: IRs Murmansk, Reval and Tchernigov, Schlüsselburg, Ukraine, 7th Jägers (1 bn each); 1 x FAB. 2nd Brigade (of 4th Division) GM Pischnitzky: IRs Tobolsk, Volhynien, Riask, Archangelsk, Yaroslav, 4th and 8th Jägers (1 bn each), 1 x FAB.

The Corps of GM Bachmetiev 1st Brigade GM Tallisin: IRs Witebsk, Kourin, Kolyvan, Koslov, Narva, 4th and 5th Jägers (1xRes Bn each): 2nd Brigade GM Zapolsky: IRs Dniepr, Kostroma, Tambov, Vladimir, 13th and 14th Jägers (1xRes Bn each). Marines (1 bn). Cavalry: GM Count Trubetzskoi; 1st Brigade: GM Count Witte: 1st and 3rd Ukrainian Cossack Pulks (3 sqns each); 2nd Brigade GM Allenine: DragRs Kiev, Karkov, Tchernigov, New

Russian, Moscow, Orenburg, Siberia (1 x Res Sqn each); 3rd Brigade GM Knorring: Sum HusR Lithuanian UlR, Tartar UlR (2,2 and 3 sqns resp); 1 x HAB. Streifkorps of Obst Davidov: Achtyrsk HusR (½ sqn); 1st Bug Cossack R, Cossack Pulk of Popov XIII, 1 combined sqn.

Russian total ca 5,000 men.

Russian losses ca 450 killed and wounded. Gen Zapolsky fatally wounded.

Sources Hauthal, Holleben, Martinien, Plotho.

SX Wrietzen, 17 February 1813, ambush

A small town in eastern Germany about 50 km northeast of Berlin, at the junction of Routes B167 and B158, 10 km west of the River Oder.

A Russian victory over the Westfalians.

(Last action – Kalisz, 13 February; next action – Lüneburg, 2 April.)

Westfalian Forces Obst von Seyboldsdorff commanding a battalion of reinforcements (600 men).

Westfalian losses All captured.

Russian Forces LtCol von Benkendorf and 500 Cossacks.

Russian losses None.

Comment The Russians and Prussians were to make much use in 1813 of such 'Streifkorps' (small, highly mobile raiding parties) to disrupt French rear areas. Napoleon was outraged by their successes.

Sources Lünsmann, Sporschil.

EN Béjar, 20 February 1813, skirmish

A small, walled town in western Spain, 74 km south of Salamanca on Route 630/E803 and 75 km southwest of Ciudad Rodrigo.

An Anglo-Portuguese victory over the French.

(Last action – Tiebas, 8 February; next action – San Pelayo, 24 March.)

French Forces GdD Foy's 1st Division of Souham's Army of Portugal. 6e RILé (2 bns); 76e RIdLi (1 bn). 60 cavalry.

French total 1,500 men.

French losses Not known exactly but quite heavy.

Anglo-Portuguese Forces Col Harrison and 1/50th Foot and 6th Caçadores (1 bn each).

Anglo-Portuguese total ca 1,200 men.

Anglo-Portuguese losses Not known exactly, very light.

Comment Foy had been wrongly told that Harrison was a very negligent commander; he mounted a dawn raid, received a very hot reception and fled back to Piedrahita.

Sources Oman, Martinien.

EN San Pelayo, 24 March 1813, clash

A village in the mountains of northern Spain, south of the fortified Biscayan harbour of Castro Urdiales.

A drawn match between the Spanish and the Italians.

(Last action – Béjar, 20 February; next action – Lerin, 31 March.)

Italian Forces Gen Palombini's Division of the Army of the Centre: 2nd LtIR (3 bns); 4th and 6th LIRs (2 bns each), Dragoni Napoleone (3 sqns). 2 x FAB.

Italian total ca 3,000 men.

Italian losses Reported as '110' but must be more like 350.

Spanish Forces Gen Mendizabal. Exact details and losses not known.

Sources Oman, Martinien.

EN Lerin, 31 March 1813, clash

A village in northern Spain between Logroño and Tafalla 45 km southwest of Pamplona.

A Spanish victory over the French.

(Last action – San Pelayo, 24 March; next action – Castro Urdiales, 12 May.)

French Forces Col Gaudin with 25e RILé and 27e RIdLi (1 bn each) of Barbot's 2nd Division, Souham's Army of Portugal.

French total ca 1,500 men.

French losses 8 officers killed, 23 wounded, 28 officers and 635 men captured. Only Gaudin and a few mounted officers escaped.

Spanish Forces The guerrilla leader Mina with 2 bns and 200 Navarese Lancers.

Spanish total ca 2,100 men.

Spanish losses Not exactly known but light.

Comment The French were part of a punitive expedition sent to reopen communications after the fall of Tafalla. Whilst busy sacking Lerin they were annihilated by Mina. Gen Barbot was at this point only 3 km away from Lerin with 6 bns but did nothing to help his comrades.

Sources Oman, Martinien.

SX Lüneburg, 2 April 1813, clash

A fortified town in northern Germany (Hannover) 103 km northeast of Hannover city and about 30 km southeast of Hamburg on Routes B4, B209 and B216.

A Russo-Prussian victory over the Franco-Saxons.

(Last action – Wrietzen, 17 February; next action – Möckern, 5 April.)

Franco-Saxon Forces GdD Morand commanding: 152e RIdLi (4e Bn); 2 x FAB, Douaniers (272 men) Gendarmes (45 men) **Saxon** 3rd LIR Prince Max (2 bns) 1 x Saxon FAB.

Franco-Saxon total ca 2,600 men, 10 guns.

Franco-Saxon losses GdD Morand killed.

500 killed and wounded, both regiments were captured, 10 guns. The three colours of the Saxon and French regiments were also taken.

Russian Forces Gen Wittgenstein's Advanced Guard: Gen von Dörnberg: 2nd Jägers (1 bn); Grodno HusR (4 sqns); Baschkirs (1 regiment); Cossacks (2 Pulks); ½ x HAB (2 guns).

Prussian Forces 1st Pommeranian IR (Füs Bn); 350 Berlin Volunteers, ½ x HAB.

Russo-Prussian total ca 4,000 men, 6 guns.

Russo-Prussian losses 9 officers, 300 men killed and wounded.

Comment Holleben refers to the 152e RIdLi as the '54e Cohort'.

Sources Sporschil, Sichart, Cazalas, Holleben.

SX Möckern, 5 April 1813, clashes

The actual combats took place in northeastern Germany about 25 km east of Magdeburg on the River Elbe.

Russo-Prussian victories over the French and their allies.

(Last action – Lüneburg, 2 April; next action – Schwarzhausen, 13 April.)

The individual combats:

1. **Dannigkow** – a village on Route B184 ca 20 km east of Magdeburg.

French Forces 154 RIdLi (1 bn-) of 18th Division, V Corps, a composite CavR of 3rd Light Cavalry Division, I Cavalry Corps (ca 100 men).

Prussian Forces GM von Hünerbein's 1st Brigade, 1st Division of York's Corps: 1st Ostpr IR (1st, 2nd and Füs Bns); 1st LeibHusR (2 sqns); ½ x HAB (4guns).

2. **Vehlitz** – a village about 20 km east of Magdeburg on Route B246a.

French Forces A composite CavR of 3rd Light Cavalry Division, I Cavalry Corps (2 sqns), 2 guns.

Russo-Prussian Forces MG von Borstell's detachment of York's Corps: 1st PommIR (2nd Bn); 4th OstprIR (Füs Bn); Pomm Gren Bn (1 bn); DragR Königin Nr 1 (4 sqns); ½ x HAB (4 guns); 1 x FAB. MG Roth*: 26th JgR (1 bn); Militia (1 bn); Grodno HusR (4 sqns); Cossack Pulk of Illowaisky IV.**.

* = Russian troops.

3. **Zeddenick** – a village ca 22 km east of Magdeburg and 4 km west of Möckern, between Route B246 and the railway to the north.

Franco-Italian Forces 2nd Italian LtIR (2 bns) of 35th Division, XI Corps; 1 x composite CavR of 1st Light Cavalry Division; I Cavalry Corps, 1 x HAB.

Russo-Prussian Forces Combined LeibHusR, Combined DragR (4 sqns each) Cossack Pulk of Illowaisky IV**; 1 x HAB.

Franco-Italian losses Prince Eugène reported them as: Generals Grenier and Gründler wounded; 5 officers and 230 men killed, 14 officers and 450 men wounded; 2 officers and 58 men captured; 1 gun. On this day and in these locations however, the Russo-Prussians reported capturing 28 officers and 953 men.

Prussian losses 413 killed and wounded.

Prussian losses Not known.

Comment The main bodies of the French V and XI Corps were deployed to the west, before Magdeburg but only the elements shown above came into action.** Illowaisky IV's Cossacks took part in both actions at Zeddenick and Vehlau which are only about 3 km apart.

Sources Sporschil, Plotho, Bredow-Wedel, Voigt, Holleben.

EE Yecla, 11 April 1813, clash

A town in the southeastern Spanish province of Murcia, 65 km north of Murcia city, on the Rio Jumilla at the crossing of Routes 3223 and 3314.

A French victory over the Spaniards.

(Last action – this was the first action this year; next action – Biar, 12 April.)

French Forces GdD Count Harispe commanding: 4e HusR, 24e DragR (2 sqns each).

French total ca 500 men.

French losses 18 killed, 61 wounded.

Spanish Forces Gen Mijares commanding the Murcian Division: IRs Jaén, Cuenca, Cadiz and 1st of Burgos.

Spanish total ca 3,000 men.

Spanish losses IRs Cadiz and 1st of Burgos destroyed; 400 killed, 1,000 captured.

Comment Harispe was part of Suchet's 'Army of Aragon and Valencia' which struck a very effective surprise blow at the Allied left wing in eastern Spain. The French infantry did not really come into action at all.

Sources Oman, Martinien.

EE Biar, 12 April 1813, skirmish

A mountain village and pass in the southeastern Spanish province of Valencia, on a minor road between Villena (on Route 330) and Castalla.

An Allied victory over the French.

(Last action – Yecla, 11 April; next action – Castalla, 13 April.)

French Forces M Suchet commanding the 'Army of Aragon and Valencia': 1er and 3e RILé, 14e, 114e and 121e RIdLi from GdD Musnier's and Habert's Divisions (11 bns) ca 8,000 men; 13e CuirR (1 sqn), ca 90 men.

French losses ca 300 killed and wounded.

Allied Forces Col Adam's 'Light Brigade': 2/27th Foot (1 bn); 3rd and 8th Line bns KGL (light coys only); 1st Italian Levy and Calabrian Free Corps (1 bn each); 20th LD, Spanish CavR Olivenca (2 sqns each); Foreign HusR (1tp).

Allied total 2,200 men and 4 mountain guns.

Allied losses ca 260 killed and wounded, 41 missing, 2 guns (carriages collapsed).

Comment Col Adam was Gen Murray's rearguard and his defensive tactics were well thought out; the French walking into repeated ambushes (particularly the 13e CuirR). The previous day Suchet had cowed the Spanish garrison of Villena (1 bn IR Velez Malaga) into surrender. Adam fell back into the Castalla position.

Sources Oman, Martinien.

EE Castalla, 13 April 1813, battle

A town in southeastern Spain, 30 km northwest of Alicante in the hills just south of Rio Seco.

An Anglo-Spanish victory over the French.

(Last action – Biar, 12 April; next action – Tarragona, 11 June.)

French Forces M Suchet commanding the Army of Aragon and Valencia: 1st Division GdD Robert: 1er and 3e RILé, 114e and 121e RIdLi (1 bns each). 3rd Division GdD Habert: 14e RIdLi (2 bns); 16e and 117e RIdLi (1er Bns each). GdD Boussard: 13e CuirR, 24e DragR (1 sqn). 12 guns.

French total 8,000 infantry, 1,600 cavalry.

French losses Suchet reported only 800 killed, wounded and captured for the three combats of Yecla, Biar and Castalla but, as Martinien shows 65 officers killed and wounded over this period, his real loss must have been about 1,300 men killed and wounded. Murray claimed to have buried 800 French dead at Castalla and to have caused 2,500 casualties in all.

Anglo-Spanish Forces LG Sir J Murray commanding: Light Brigade, Col Adam: 2/27th Foot (1 bn); 3rd and 8th Line bns KGL (light coys only); 1st Italian Levy and Calabrian Free Corps (1 bn each); 20th LD, Spanish CavR Olivenca (2 sqns each); Foreign HusR (1 tp) J. Mackenzie's Division: 1/27th Foot, 4th and 6th Line bns KGL (1 bn each), Sicilian IR 'Estero' (2 bns). Clinton's Division: 1/10th, 1/58th, 1/81st Foot, De Roll's and Dillon's*, 2nd Italian Levy (1 bn each). Whittingham's Spanish Division: IRs Cordoba, Mallorca, Guadalajara, 2nd Burgos, 2nd Murcia and 5th Granaderos (1 bn each). Roche's Spanish Division: Voluntarios de Aragon, IRs Alicante, Chinchilla, Canarias, Voluntarios de Portuguese and 1 x Sicilian FAB.

Anglo-Spanish total 18,200 men.

Anglo-Spanish losses Mackenzie's Division – 47, Clinton's – 20, Adam's – 70, Whittingham's – 233, Cavalry and artillery 10.

Anglo-Spanish total 400 killed and wounded.

Comment The 121e suffered 19 officers and 350 men killed and wounded in the usual column versus line combat in 5 minutes with the 2/27th Foot. The French were stunned at the high combat quality of Whittingham's Spaniards. Suchet was allowed to escape without further loss by a very cautious Murray, who continued his withdrawal to his ships.

Sources Oman, Martinien.

* = Émigrés.

SX Schwarzhausen, 13 April 1813, skirmish

A small town in the Thüringian hills in eastern Germany, 10 km southeast of Eisenach and south of the A4/E40 Autobahn.

A Prussian victory over the Ducal Saxons.

(Last action – Möckern, 5 April; next action – Thorn, 16 April.)

Ducal Saxon-Weimar Forces Major von Linker's infantry battalion; 11 officers and 400 men.
Losses All captured.
Prussian Forces Lt Count Pinto with 1 squadron 1st Silesian HusR and some volunteer Jäger zu Pferde.
Prussian total 50 men.
Prussian losses None.
Comment The Saxons had no ammunition and no stomach for a fight against their German brethren. They were taken into Prussian service and sent to the blockade of Glogau.
Sources Specht, Sporschil.

SX Thorn, 16 February – 16 April 1813, siege and capture

A fortified town in West Prussia on the right bank of the River Vistula, 145 km south of Danzig and at the junction of Routes 1/E75, 10 and 52.
A Russian victory over the French and Allies.
(Last action – Schwarzhausen, 13 April; next action – Langensalza, 16/17 April.)
French and Allied Garrison GdB de Morelhon commanding: Bavarians: GM Voller; 2nd, 3rd, 5th, 6th, 7th and 11th LIRs*, 2nd, 4th and 5th LtI Bns* (total ca 4,000 men). GdB Poitevan's French troops: 85e and 108e RIdLi (total ca 350 men); 1er ChàCh (9men). Artillery (French and Polish), ca 250 men.
French total ca 4,500 men.
French losses Killed and wounded not known. The French and Polish troops went into captivity, the 2,100 surviving Bavarians were released on condition that they did not fight against the Allies again during 1813.
Russian Forces Gen Barclay de Tolly's Army of the West:
Langeron's Corps: **9th Division** GM Udom II: IRs Nascheburg, Apscheron, Jakutsk, Rjäsk, Jägers Nr 10 and 38 (8 bns); **15th Division** GM Rudsevitch: IRs Witebsk, Koslowsk, Kursk, Kolivan, Jägers Nr 12 and 22 (7 bns); 3 x FAB.
Woinov's Corps: Exact details unknown.
Russian totals and losses Not known.
* = remnants of.
Sources Martinien, Leyh, Plotho, Sporschil.

SX Langensalza, 16/17 April 1813, clash

A town in the Thüringian hills in eastern Germany on the River Unstrut and at the junction of Routes B84, B176 and B247.
A Prussian victory over the Bavarians.
(Last action – Thorn, 16 April; next action – Wanfried, 18 April.)
Bavarian Forces GM Count von Rechberg commanding the 1st Infantry Brigade: Obst von Treuberg: 1st Lt I Bn (101 men); 3rd Lt I Bn (138 men); 6th Lt I Bn (475 men); 2nd Combined LIR (481 men); 3rd Combined LIR (220 men); Artillery (55 men); 6 guns.
Bavarian total 1,551 men, 6 guns.
Bavarian losses 45 killed and wounded, 12 captured, 5 guns, 3 ammunition waggons.
Prussian Forces Maj von Hellwig's Streifkorps: 150 hussars.
Prussian losses Very light.
Comment This was another very successful hit and run raid.
Sources Specht, Leyh, Plotho, Sporschil.

SX Wanfried, 18 April 1813, ambush

A town in the central German province of Hessen, on the River Werra at the junction of Routes B249 and B250.
A Prussian victory over the Westfalians.
(Last action – Langensalza, 16/17 April; next action – Bleicherode, 19 April.)
Westfalian Forces Obstlt von Göcking: One company of infantry, one squadron of hussars.
Westfalian total ca 132 men.
Westfalian losses 2 officers, 50 infantry, 80 hussars and 100 horses captured.
Prussian Forces Maj von Hellwig's Streifkorps: 150 hussars.
Prussian losses Nil.
Comment The Westfalian army was disintegrating; these men put up no resistance, indeed, several joined Hellwig's Streifkorps. Obstlt Göcking entered Prussian service.
Sources Lünsmann, Specht.

SX Bleicherode, 19 April 1813, skirmish

A village in the Thüringian hills in eastern Germany, 30 km northeast of Kassel, north of Route B80.
A Russian victory over the Westfalians.
(Last action – Wanfried, 18 April; next action – Nordhausen, 19 April.)
Westfalian Forces Maj von Göcking with the ChLGardeR (2 sqns).

Westfalian total 150 men.

Westfalian losses 3 officers and 103 men and horses captured.

Russian Forces A Cossack Pulk; exact strength not known.

Russian losses None.

Comment The Westfalians had no advanced or flank guards and blundered into an ambush. That the Russians could already operate with impunity so far west is indicative of the lax state of the German states' defences.

Sources Lünsmann, Sporschil.

SX Nordhausen, 19 April 1813, skirmish

A small town in eastern Germany, at the junction of Routes B4 and B80, midway between Halle and Göttingen.

A Russian victory over the Westfalians.

(Last action – Bleicherode, 19 April; next action – Spandau, 21 April.)

Westfalian Forces A squadron of hussars.

Westfalian losses 3 officers, 103 men and horses captured.

Russian Forces GM Landskoi and a Cossack Pulk.

Russian losses None.

Comment Once again, the Westfalians surrendered almost without a fight.

Sources Specht, Lünsmann, Sporschil.

SX Spandau 1–21 April 1813, siege and capture

A citadel in the Prussian province of Brandenburg, 9 km west of Berlin.

A Russo-Prussian victory over the French.

(Last action – Nordhausen, 19 April; next action – Halle, 2 May.)

French Garrison GdB Bruny commanding: 24e RILé; 22e Lithuanian CavR, Artillery and other detachments*.

French total 3,200 men, 115 guns.

French losses Not known exactly; the surviving garrison was allowed free passage to France on condition that they did not fight against the Allies again for six months.

* = 129e RIdLi (3e Bn); 4e Li (1 coy); 18e Li (2 coys); 46e Li (1 coy); 72e Li, 93e Li, 24e Lé (2 coys each); Vistula Legion 1st, 2nd, 3rd, 4th IRs (1 coy each); 5th Italian LIR (1 coy).

Russo-Prussian Forces GM von Thümen commanding the 4th Brigade of Bülow's III Corps: 4th Ostpr IR (3 bns); 5th Res IR (4 bns); Ostpr Jäger bn (2 coys); Elb IR (2 bns); Pomm NKR (4 sqns); 1 x 6 pdr HAB.

Russo-Prussian total ca 9,000 men.

Russo-Prussian losses Not exactly known but very light.

Sources Plotho, Sporschil, Martinien.

SX Halle, 2 May 1813, clash

A town in northern Germany (Saxony), on the River Saale, 32 km northwest of Leipzig on Route B6/E49 and B80.

A Prussian victory over the French.

(Last action – Spandau, 21 April; next action – Lützen (Gross-Görschen), 2 May.)

French Forces GdB Lacroix commanding: 135e and 153e RidLi.

French total 2,600 men, 6 guns.

French losses 300 killed, 450 wounded and captured, 50 unwounded captured, 3 guns.

Prussian Forces GL von Bülow: 3rd Ostpr IR (3 bns, 2 x Füs coys); 2nd Ostpr Gren Bn (1 bn); Ostpr Jägers (½coy); DragR Königin (4 sqns); 2nd Westpr DragR (2 sqns); 1st Leib HusR (3 sqns); 2 x FAB, 1 x HAB.

Prussian total 3,300 infantry, 1,500 cavalry, 24 guns.

Prussian losses Not exactly known but light.

Sources Plotho, Sporschil, Martinien.

SX Lützen (Gross-Görschen), 2 May 1813, battle

A village in Saxony, 20 km southeast of Merseburg and 20 km southwest of Leipzig.

A French victory over the Russo-Prussians.

(Last action – Halle, 2 May; next action – Königswartha, 19 May.)

French and Allied Forces Emperor Napoleon I commanding:

Imperial Guard M Mortier. **Old Guard** GdD Roguet: 1er GrenàP, 1er, 2e, 3e, 6e and 7e Tirailleurs. Young Guard GdD Dumoustier: 2e ChàP, 1er, 2e, 3e, 4e Voltigeurs; Vélites de Florence, Vélites de Turin, Gendarmes d'Élite. Foot Artillery of the Old and **Young Guard** 6 x 12 pdrs, 12 x 6 pdrs, 6 x howitzers. **Guard Cavalry** M. Bessières: GdD Walther, GdB Ornano: 2e ChLL (4 sqns); ChàCh (4 sqns); Gendarmes d'Élite (2 sqns); 2nd ChLL of Berg (4 sqns). GdB Letort: 1er ChLL, DragR, GrenàCh (4 sqns each).

III Corps M Ney. 8th Division GdD Souham: 1st

Brigade GdB Chasseraux: 6e PvLé (2e Bn/6eLé, 3e Bn/25eLé - 2 bns); 10e PvLé (3e Bn/16eLé, 1er/28e Lé - 2 bns); 14e PvLi (3e Bn/34e Li; 3e Bn/40e Li - 2 bns); 19e PvLi (6e/32e Li; 3e/58e Li - 2 bns). 2nd Brigade GdB Chemineau: 21e PvLi (3e Bn/59e Li, 4e Bn/69e Li - 2 bns); 24e PvLi (3e Bn/88eLi, 3e Bn/103e Li - 2 bns); 22e RIdLi (1er, 3e, 4e and 6e bns); 2 x FAB, Spanish Sappers (1 coy). **9th Division** GdD Brennier: 1st Brigade GdB Anthing: 2e PvLé (3e bns of 2e and 4e Lé - 2 bns); 29e RILé (2 bns); 136e RIdLi (4 bns). 2nd Brigade GdB Grillot: 138e RIdLi (4 bns); 145e RIdLi (4 bns); 2 x FAB, Spanish Sappers (1 coy). **10th Division** GdD Girard; GdB Goris: 4e PvLé (4e Bns of 5e and 12e RILé - 2 bns). GdB van Dedem: 140e RIdLi (4 bns); 141e RIdLi (4 bns); 2 x FAB; Spanish Sappers (1 coy). **11th Division** GdD Ricard: GdB Tarayre: 9e RILé (3e and 4e bns); 17e PvLi (4e Bn/43e RIdLi, 3e Bn/75e RIdLi); 18e PvLi (3e Bn/50e RIdLi, 4e Bn/65e RIdLi). GdB Dumoulin: 142e RIdLi (4 bns); 144e RIdLi (4 bns); 2 x FAB; Spanish Sappers (1 coy). **39th Division** GdD Marchand: Baden Brigade GM von Stockhorn: 1st LIR (2nd Bn); 3rd LIR (2 bns). Hessen-Darmstadt Brigade GM Prinz Emil von Hessen-Darmstadt: Leib-Garde (2 bns); 2nd LIR (2 bns); FüsR (2 bns); IR Frankfurt (1 bn). Light Cavalry Brigade GdB Laboissière; 10e HusR (4 sqns); Baden LDR (3 sqns); 1 x Hessian FAB, 1 x Baden FAB.

VI Corps M Marmont. **20th Division** GdD Compans: GdB Calcault: 1er and 3e Naval Artillery Rs (4 bns each); GdB Joubert: 25e PvLi (3e Bn/47e RIdLi, 3e Bn/86e RIdLi - 2 bns). 20e PvLi (5e Bn/66e RIdLi, 3e Bn/122e RIdLi - 2 bns). 2 x FAB. **21st Division** GdD Bonnet; GdB Buquet: 2e Naval Artillery R (6 bns); 4e Naval Artillery R (3 bns). GdB Jamin: 37e RILé (4 bns); IR Joseph Napoleon (1er Bn); 2 x FAB, Sappers (1 coy).

IV Corps GdD Bertrand. **12th Division** GdD Morand; GdB Bellair: 13e RIdLi. 29th Light Cavalry Brigade GdB Beaumont: Hessen-Darmstadt Garde ChLR (4 sqns). **22nd Division** GdD Friedrichs; GdB Ficatier: 23e RILé (3e and 4e bns); 13e and 16e RIdLi (4 bns); GdB Nagel: Pv Croatian IR (2nd Bn/3rd and 1st Bn/4thRs); 23e RIdLi (1er, 2e, 4e and 6e bns). **15th Division** GdD Peyri: 4th Italian LtIR (2 bns); Regiment d'Élite (elite coys of 4th, 6th and 7th Italian LIRs). 2 x Italian FAB.

XII Corps M Oudinot. **13th Division** GdD Pacthod, GdB Pourailly: 1er RILé (4e Bn); 12e PvLi (4e Bn/10e RIdLi). **14th Division** GdD Lorencz, GdB d'Henin: 5e PvLé (14e RILé - 7e Bn).

V Corps GdD Lauriston. **17th Division** GdD Puthod, GdB Gachod; 147e RIdLi (4 bns).

XI Corps M Macdonald. **31st Division** GdD Fressinet: 11e PvDBde (4e Bn/27e RILé, 4e Bn/50e RIdLi); 13e PvDBde (4e Bn/5e RIdLi, 4e Bn/11e RIdLi, 4e Bn/79e RIdLi); Neapolitan ÉliteR (1 bn). 1 x FAB. **36th Division** GdD Charpentier, GdB Simmer: 14e RILé (3e and 4e bns); 22e RILé (4 bns); GdB Meunier: 14e PvDBde (3e Bn/67e RIdLi, 6e Bn/10e RIdLi, 6e Bn/20e RIdLi). The following regiments also took part in the battle: 22e, 39e, 57e, 59e, 69e and 132e RIdLi but their allocation to corps, divisions and brigades is uncertain.

Cavalry I Cavalry Corps GdD Latour-Maubourg, **1st Light Cavalry Division** GdD Bruyère, 2nd Brigade GdB Cambraceres: 8e ChLL (3 sqns). **3rd Light Cavalry Division** GdD Chastel; 2nd Brigade GdB Richter 1er ChàCh (3 sqns). **1st Cuirassier Division** GdD Bourdesoulle; 1st Brigade GdB Berkheim: 2e CuirR (3 sqns); 2nd Brigade GdB Quinette: 11e CuirR (3 sqns). **3rd Cuirassier Division** GdD Doumerc, 2nd Brigade GdB Reizet: 30e DragR (3 sqns). The Italian Dragone Napoleone R (3 sqns) was also present at the battle.

French and Allied totals Of the 144,000 troops available, only the 78,000 shown above actually came into action.

French and Allied losses M Ney estimated French and Allied losses as 2,757 killed, 16,898 wounded. GdB's Gouré and Grillot had been killed; 5 guns were lost.

Russo-Prussian Forces Russian GdC Count Wittgenstein commanding:

Avantgarde GM Karpov II: Don Cossack Pulks of Karpov II, Grekov II, Jagodin II, Zikelef (2 sqns each), Bug Cossack R (2 sqns). GM Illowaisky IV: Don Cossack Rs of Grekov III and Grekov IX, Semenschenkov Cossack R (2 sqns each). GM Illowaisky X: Gorin I; 5th Baschkir R (2 sqns each). 2nd Bug Cossack Pulk, Stavropol Kalmuck R, Streifkorps of Colonel Davidov and Mandatov.

First Line GdC von Blücher: Right Wing (Oberschlesische Brigade): GM von Ziethen: Cavalry: Maj Laroche von Starkenfeld: Maj von Blücher: 1st Schl HusR (2nd and 4th sqns); 2nd Schl HusR (3rd and 4th sqns). Maj von Schmiedburg: Schl UlR (1st and

2nd sqns). 1 x HAB. Infantry: Obst von Pirch I: Maj von Carnall: Schl Gren Bn (1 bn). 1st Schl. IR (2 bns). 1 x Russian heavy FAB, 1 x Prussian 6 pdr FAB. Obst von Losthin: 2nd Schl IR (2 bns); 1st Schl IR (Füs Bn); Schl Schützen (1 bn). 1 x 6 pdr FAB, ½ x 12 pdr FAB.

Left Wing (Niederschlesische Brigade): Obst von Klüx: Cavalry: Obst von Mutius: Neumark DragR (4 sqns); 1st Westpr DragR (2nd and 4th sqns); 1 x Prussian HAB. Infantry: Maj von Jagow: Westpr Gren Bn (1 bn); 1st Westpr IR (2nd and 3rd bns). Maj von Anhalt: 2nd Westpr IR (2nd and 3rd bns). 1 x Prussian 6 pdr FAB, 1 x heavy Russian FAB. 1st Westpr IR (Füs Bn). **Reserve of the First Line** (or Brandenburg Brigade) GM von Röder: Obstlt Katzler: Westpr UlR (4 sqns); Brand HusR (1st and 2nd sqns); 1 x Prussian HAB. Obstlt von Tippelskirch: Maj von Alvensleben: Garde Jg Bn (1 bn); Garde IR (1st and 2nd Füs Bns); Normal I bn (1 bn); Garde 6 pdr FAB, 1 x 6 pdr FAB. Maj von Natzmer: Leib Gren Bn (1 bn); 1st Ostpr Gren Bn (1 bn); Leib IR (3rd bn); Garde Freiwillige Jg bn (1 bn).

Second Line GL York. **Right Wing** GM Berg (Russians): GM Alexejev: Mitau DragR, 1 x heavy FAB. 5th Division GM Lukov: GM Mesenzov: IRs Perm, Sievsk (1 bn each); Grand Princess Katharina Bn (1bn). GM Sibirsky: IRs Kaluga, Mohilev (1 bn each); **14th Division** GM Lalin, GM Helfreich, IRs Tenginsk, Estonia (1 bn each); 1 x light FAB. **Left Wing (Prussians)** GM von Hünerbein: 1st Combined IR: 1st Ostpr IR (2nd and Füs bns); 2nd Ostpr IR (1st Bn); Leib IR (Füs bn); Lithuanian DragR (4 sqns); 1½x 6 pdr FAB. Obst Horn: 5th Combined IR: 1st Westpr IR (1st bn); 2nd Westpr IR (2nd and Füs bn). 6th Combined IR: 1st Schl IR (2nd bn); 2nd Schl IR (2nd and Füs bn); 2nd Combined DragR: Westpr DragR (1st and 2nd sqns); Brand DragR (1st and 3rd sqns); 1 x pdr FAB; ½ x 12 pdr FAB. **Reserve of the Right Wing (Russians)** GM Kasatschkosky: Ataman Cossack Pulk. Don Cossack HAB. Col Brischinsky: Combined Grenadiers of 5th and 14th Divisions (2 bns each); Res Gren Bns, 1st Division (5 bns). **Reserve of the Left Wing (Prussians)** Obstlt von Steinmetz: 2nd Leib HusR (4 sqns); 1 x 6 pdr HAB; Colberg IR (1st, 2nd and Füs bns), 1 x 3 pdr FAB.

1st Reserve Army GL Baron von Winzingerode.

Prussian Res Cavalry Brigade: Obst von Dolffs: Obstlt von Werner: Garde du Corps (5 sqns); Garde Light Cavalry R (6 sqns); Garde HAB. Obst von Jürgass: Ostpr KürR, Schl KürR, Brand KürR (4 sqns each); 2 x HAB. **Russian Res Cavalry** GM Count Trubetzkoi; Hussar Division GM Lanskoi; GM Paradovsky Hus Rs Alexandria, Ssum and White Russia; Lithuanian MtdRR (3 sqns each except Ssum Hus with 2). GM Knorring: Lithuanian UlR (2 sqns); Tartar UlR (4 sqns); Combined DragR (2 sqns); 5 x HAB. GM Illowaisky XII: Don Cossack Rs of Illowaisky XII, Kutainikov IV, Grekov III, Grekov XXI and Sementschenkov.

II Corps GL Prince Eugen von Württemberg:

Avantgarde: 1st Ukrainian Cossack Pulk, 1 x HAB. **3rd Division** GM Count Schachafskoi: Col Schilvinsky: IRs Murmansk, Reval, Tchernigov (1 bn each). Col Kapustin: 20th and 21st JgRs (1 bn each); 1 x FAB. **4th Division** GM St Priest: Col Treffurt: IRs Tobolsk, Volhynien, Krementchug (1 bn each). Col Ivanov: 4th and 34th JägerRs (1 bn each). 3rd Ukrainian Cossack Pulk, 1 x FAB.

Reserve Army GdC Tormasov:

1st Line GL Konovnizin: Guard Light Cavalry Division GM Schävitch: GM Tschailkov: Guard UlR, Guard HusR (4 sqns each). 1 x HAB. GM Tichischerin. Guard DragR, Guard Cossack R, Guard Black Sea Cossack Sotnia. **1st Grenadier Division** GM Sulima: Col Count Kniaschnin II: Gren Rs Arakcheyev, Ekaterinoslav (2 bns each). Col Acht: Gren Rs St Petersburg, Tauride (2 bns each); 2 x FAB. **2nd Grenadier Division** GM Zwielniev: Col Pissareff: Gren Rs Kiev and Moscow (2 bns each). Col Golowin: Gren Rs Astrakhan and Phanagoria (2 bns each). Col Hesse: Gren Rs Little Russia and Siberia (2 bns each); 1 x FAB.

2nd Line GL Prince Galitzin V: 1st Kürassier Division GM Depreradovich; GM Arsenief: Chevalier Guards; Horse Guards. GM Rosen: Life Guard KürR; Tsarina KürR (3 sqns each). GM Kretov: KürRs Astrakhan and Ekaterinoslav (3 sqns each); 1 x HAB. **1st Guards Division** GM Baron Rosen. GM Potemkin: Preobrazhenski Guards R, Semenovsky Guards R (2 bns each); GM Krapovitsky: Ismailovski Guards R, Guards Jäger R (2 bns each); 2 x FAB. **2nd Guards Division** GM Udom II; Col Krischanovsky: Lithuanian and Finland Guards Rs (2 bns each). GM Scheltuchin II: Pavlov and Life Grenadier Rs (2 bns each); 2 x FAB. **2nd Kürassier Division** GM Duka: GM Leontiev: KürRs Gluchov and Pskov. GM Gudowitsch: KürRs Military Order and Starodub. Col Massalov: KürRs

Little Russia and Novgorod (all regiments 3 sqns each). 1 x HAB.

Artillery Reserve GM Euler: 2 x heavy and 4 x light FABs.

Russo-Prussian total 37,000 Prussians, 56,000 Russians (including 8,000 Cossacks) 553 guns. Of these, 34,000 Prussians and 36,000 Russians came into action.

Russo-Prussian losses 8,500 Prussians, 3,500 Russians killed, wounded and missing. Russian GL Konovnizin was killed; Prussian GL von Scharnhorst was mortally wounded.

Comment The Allies failed to exploit their great superiority in cavalry. After the battle they withdrew eastwards in good order.

Sources Plotho, Sporschil, Martinien, Bigge, Nübling.

EN Castro Urdiales, 4–12 May 1813, siege and capture

A Spanish Biscayan port on Route 634/E70 between Santander and Bilbao.

A Franco-Italian victory over the Spanish.

(Last action – Lerin, 31 March; next action – Morales, 2 June.)

Franco-Italian Forces GdD Foy commanding: 1st Division, Army of Portugal: 6e RILé (1 bn); 39e, 69e, 76e RIdLi (2 bns each); GdD Sarrut's 4th Division: 2e and 4e RILé, 36e RIdLi (2 bns each. GdD Palombini's Italian Division, Army of the Centre: 2nd LtIR, 4th and 6th LIRs (7 bns); Dragoni Napoleone (3 sqns); 2 x FAB and the siege artillery (18 guns).

Franco-Italian total ca 10,000 men.

Franco-Italian losses ca 150 killed and wounded.

Spanish Garrison Col Pedro Alvarez commanding: IR Iberia and a corps of gunners.

Spanish total 1,000 men.

Spanish losses ca 160 killed and wounded.

Comment Just before the final storm, the Spanish garrison was taken off by British ships having thrown the guns into the sea and blown up the magazines. This minor port had occupied three French divisions for 16 vital days.

Sources Oman, Martinien.

SX Königswartha, 19 May 1813, clash

A village in Saxony, 15 km north of Bautzen on Route B96 towards Hoyerswerda.

A Russian victory over the Italians.

(Last action – Lützen (Gross-Görschen), 2 May; next action – Weissig, 19 May.)

Italian Forces GdD Peyri commanding the 15th Italian Division of IV Corps: 1st and 2nd LtIRs (2 bns each); 1st LIR (3rd and 4th bns); 4th LIR (4 bns); 6th LIR (3rd and 4th bns); 7th LIR (4 bns); Milan Municipal Guards (1 bn); 1st ChLL (2 sqns); 3 x FAB.

Italian total 8,300 infantry, 200 cavalry, 20 guns

Italian losses 2,100 killed and wounded, 800 captured, 2 guns. GdB Martel and Balathier mortally wounded.

Russian Forces GdI Barclay de Tolly commanding: Advanced Guard of the 3rd Army of the West: GL Tschaplitz. GM Rudsevitch: 12th and 22nd Jäger Rs (1 bn each). 18th Division GM Scherbatov (of Langeron's Corps): GM Umanetz; Kinburn DragR, Sievsk MtdRR (2 sqns each). GM Bernodossov: IRs Vladimir and Dniepr (1 bn each). Col Heidenreich: IRs Kostroma and Tambov (1 bn each). GM Karnielov 28th and 32nd Jägers (1 bn each). Col Koslovsky: Olviopol HusR, Zhitomir UlR (2 sqns each). GM Grekov VIII. Don Cossack Pulks of Grekov VIII, Kutainikov and Isaeva II. 4 x FAB, 2 x HAB.

Russian total 16,000 infantry, 4,000 cavalry, 72 guns.

Russian losses ca 1,100 killed and wounded.

Comment The Italians neglected to mount adequate security patrols and were quickly overwhelmed by the Russians.

Sources Plotho, Sporschil, Martinien.

SX Weissig (Eichberg), 19 May 1813, clash

A village in Saxony, 16 km north of Bautzen (not marked on modern maps).

A French victory over the Russo-Prussians.

(Last action – Königswartha, 19 May; next action – Bautzen and Wurschen, 20/21 May.)

French Forces GdD Count Lauriston commanding: **V Corps: 16th Division** GdD Maison: GdB Avril: 151e RIdLi (4 bns); 153e RIdLi (4 bns); 2 x FAB. 18th Division GdD Lagrange GdB Charrière: 134e RIdLi (2 bns); 154e RIdLi (4 bns); GdB Suden: 155e RIdLi (4 bns); 2 x FAB. **19th Division** GdD Rochambeau: 135e RIdLi (4 bns). The 3e RILé also took casualties here this day.

French total 13,400 men.

French losses 1,800 killed and wounded.

Russo-Prussian Forces GL York commanding: Avantgarde: 3rd HusR (3 sqns); Combined Füsiliers (of

Leib IR and 1st Ostpreussisches IR, Leib IR and 1st Ostpreussisches IR) (2 bns each); 1st Westpreussisches DragR (2 sqns); 1 x HAB. Later joined by: Combined Füsiliers of 5th and 6th LIRs; Brigade of Obst Horn. 1st Russian Gren Div GM Sulima: Gren Rs Ekaterinoslav, Arakcheyev, St Petersburg, Lithuanian DragR, Silesian HusR, 1 x 12 pdr FAB.

Russo-Prussian total 5,600 Prussians, 2,000 Russians, 18 guns.

Prussian losses 13 officers, 246 men killed, 62 officers, 1,411 men wounded, 2 officers, 119 men missing.

Russian losses Not exactly known; light.

Sources Plotho, Sporschil, Martinien.

SX Bautzen and Wurschen, 20/21 May 1813, battle

Bautzen: a town in Saxony (northern Germany) on the River Spree, 52 km northeast of Dresden. Wurschen: a village 10 km east of Bautzen.

A French victory over the Russo-Prussians.

(Last action – Weissig, 19 May; next action – Reichenbach, 22 May.)

French and Allied Forces Emperor Napoleon I commanding.

Imperial Guard Old Guard 1er, 2e and 7e Tirailleurs. **Young Guard** 3e Voltigeurs, Foot Artillery.

The Right Wing M Ney commanding:

IV Corps GdD Count Bertrand: 12 Division GdD Morand: 23e RIdLi (1er, 2e, 4e and 6e bns); 2 x FAB. **38th (Württemberg) Division** GL Franquemont: 1st, 2nd and 7th LIRs (2 bns each); 9th and 10th LIRs (1st Bns each); 1 x FAB, 1 x HAB. **24th (Württemberg) Light Cavalry Brigade** GM Jett: 1st ChLR 'Prinz Adam' and 3rd ChàCh R 'Herzog Louis' (4 sqns each); 1 x HAB. **V Corps** GdD Lauriston: **16th Division** GdD Maison: 151e RIdLi (4 bns); 2 x FAB. 17th Division GdD Puthod: GdB Pastol; 148e RIdLi (4 bns). **18th Division** GdD Lagrange, GdB Charrière: 134e RIdLi (2 bns); GdB Suden: 155e RIdLi (4 bns 2 x FAB.

VI Corps M Marmont: **20th Division** GdD Compans: GdB Cacault; 1st Naval Artillery R (4 bns); 3rd Naval Artillery R (3 bns). GdB Joubert: 25e PvLi (3e Bn/47 RIdLi); 20e PvLi (5e Bn/66e RIdLi, 3e Bn/122e RIdLi) 2 x FAB. **21st Division** GdB Bonnet; GdB Buquet: 2e Naval Artillery R (6 bns); 4th Naval Artillery R (2 bns). GdB Jamin: 37e RILé (3 bns); IR Joseph Napoleon (1 bn). **22nd Division** GdD Friedrichs GdBs Ficatier, Coehorn: 23e RILé (3e and 4e bns); 13e PvLi (3e Bn/14e RIdLi); 16e PvLi (6e Bn/26e RIdLi; 6e Bn/82e RIdLi); 15e, 70e and 121e RIdLi (3e and 4e bns each). 2 x FAB.

VII Corps GdD Reynier: **32nd Division** GdD Durutte, GdB Devaux: 35e RILé (2e and 4e bns). Saxons GdK Zeschau: **1st Division** Obst von Brause: 1st LtIR von Lecoq (1 bn); Garde-GrenR (1 bn); Jägers (1 coy); **2nd Division** GL von Sahr: Gren Bn von Anger (1 bn); 2 x FAB.

XI Corps M Macdonald: **31st Division** GdD Ledru: 11e PvDBde (4e Bn/27e RILé, 4e Bn/50e RIdLi); 13e PvDBde (4e Bn/5e RIdLi). GdB Bardet; Neapolitan Élite IR (2 bns), 1 x FAB, 1 x Neapolitan HAB. **35th Division** GdD Gérard, GdB Senecal: 6e RIdLi (3e and 4e bns); 112e RIdLi (4 bns). GdB Zucchi: 2nd Italian LtIR (2 bns); 5th Italian LIR (4 bns); 4th Italian ChàCh (2 sqns). 2 x FAB. **36th Division** GdD Charpentier; GdB Simmer: 14e RILé (3e and 4e bns); 22e RILé (4 bns); 14e PvDBde (6e bns of 10e and 20e RIdLi, 3e Bn/67e RIdLi); 15e PvDBde (4e Bns 3e RILé and 102e RIdLi), 2 x FAB.

XII Corps M Oudinot: **13th Division** GdD Pacthod; GdB Pourailly: 1er RILé (4e Bn); 7e RIdLi (3e and 4e bns); 12e PvLi (4e Bns of 10e and 42e RIdLi). GdB Gruger: 1st Neapolitan LtIR (2 bns); 101e RIdLi (2e, 3e, 4e bns). **14th Division** GdD Lorencz; GdB Leclerc: 52e RIdLi (3e and 4e bns); 137e RIdLi (4 bns). GdB d'Henin: 156e RIdLi (4 bns); 2 x FAB. **29th (Bavarian) Division** GL Raglovich: 1st Brigade: GM Beckers: 1st Combined LtI Bn (3rd and 4th LtI Bns); 3rd LIR Prinz Karl (2nd Bn); 13th LIR (Res Bn); 4th LIR Isenburg (2nd Bn); 8th LIR Herzog Pius (2nd Bn). 2nd Brigade Obst Maillot de la Treille: 2nd Combined LtI Bn (5th and 6th LtI Bns); 5th LIR Preysing (2nd Bn); 7th LIR (2nd Bn); 9th LIR (2nd Bn); 10th LIR Junker (2nd Bn). Combined ChLR (3 sqns); 3 x FAB.

III Corps M Ney. **8th Division** GdD Souham; GdB Chasseraux: 10e PvLé (3e Bn/16e RILé, 1e Bn 28e RILé); 14e PvLi (4e Bn/34e RIdLi, 3e Bn/40e RIdLi); 19e PvLi(6e Bn/32e and 3e BN/58e RIdLi); 21e PvLi (3e/59e and 4e/69e RIdLi); 24e PvLi (3e Bns 88e and 103e RIdLi); 22e RIdLi (1er, 3e, 4e and 6e bns). 2 x FAB. **9th Division** GdD Delmas; GdB Anthing: 2e PvLé (3e Bns 2e and 4e RILé); 29e RILé (1er Bn); 138e and 145e RIdLi (4 bns each). 2 x FAB. **10th Division** GdD Albert; GdB Goris: 4e PvLé (4e Bns 5e and 12e RILé); 139e RIdLi (4 bns). GdB Van Dedem: 140e and

141e RIdLi (4 bns each); 2 x FAB. **11th Division** GdD Ricard; GdB Tarayre: 9e RILé (3e and 4e bns); 17e PvLi (4e Bn/43e RIdLi, 3e Bn/75e RIdLi). GdB Dumoulin: 142e and 144e RIdLi (4 bns each). 2 x FAB. The 52e and 57e RIdLi and the 23e, 24e, 32e, 35e RILé and the 2nd Croats also took casualties here this day but which divisions they belonged to is not clear.

Cavalry. 5e and 10e HusR (3 sqns each). Baden LDR (4 sqns).

I Cavalry Corps GdD Latour-Maubourg. **1st Light Cavalry Division** GdB Bessières: 9e ChLL (½ sqn); 16e ChàCh (1 sqn). GdB Cambraceres: 8e ChLL (2 sqns). 1st Cuirassier Division GdD Bourdesoulle: 3e CuirR (2 sqns). 3rd Cuirassier Division GdD Doumerc; GdB Reizet: 30e DragR (2 sqns); Italian Dragone Napoleone (4 sqns). 2 x HAB. The 31e ChàCh was also engaged this day.

French totals 167,000 men.

French losses GdBs Garnier-Laboissière and Sicard killed. 21,200 killed and wounded, 800 captured.

Russo-Prussian Forces GdC Count Wittgenstein commanding.

Advanced Guard of the Right Wing GM Lanskoi; GM Paradovsky: HusRs Alexandria and White Russia (3 sqns each); Lithuanian MtdRR (3 sqns), 1 x HAB. GM Illowaisky XII: Don Cossack Pulks of Illowaisky XII, Platov IV, Lotschilin I, Gorin I and Koschkin; 5th Baschkir R (2 sqns each); Streifkorps Prendel (4 sqns).

Advanced Guard of the 3rd Army of the West GL Tschaplitz; Col Koslovsky: Olviopol HusR, Zhitomir UlR (2 sqns each). GM Rudsevitch: 12th and 22nd Jägers (2 bns each); GM Grekov VIII; Don Cossack Pulks of Grekov VIII, Isaeva II and Kutainikov I (2 sqns each); 1 x light FAB.

Prussian Advanced Guard GL von Kleist: GM Rüdiger (Russians): Grodno HusR (4 sqns). GM Vlastov (Russians: 23rd and 24th Jägers (1 bn each). GM Roth (Russians): 25th and 26th Jägers (1 bn each); 1 x Russian HAB. Obstlt von Steinmetz (Prussians): Colberg IR (1st, 2nd and Füs bns); Maj von Thümen; 1st Schl HusR (1st and 3rd sqns); 2nd Schl HusR (1st and 2nd sqns); 1 x Prussian HAB. GM Radionov II (Russians): Don Cossack Pulks of Radionov II, Illowaisky IV and Selwanov II (2 sqns each).

Advanced Guard of the Left Wing GdI Count Miloradovitch:

II Corps GL Prinz Eugen von Württemberg (Russians): GM Knorring: Ssum HusR (2 sqns); Tartar UlR (4 sqns); Combined DragR (2 sqns). **3rd Division** GM Count Schachafskoi; Col Schilvinsky: IRs Murmansk, Reval and Tchernigov (1 bn each). Col Kapustin: 20th and 21st Jägers (1 bn each). 1 x heavy, 1 x light FAB, 1 x HAB. **4th Division** GM Pischnitzky; Col Treffurt: IRs Krementchug, Volhynien and Riask (1 bn each). Col Ivanov: 4th and 34th Jägers (1 bn each). GM Pantschulid: Tchernigov MtdRR (3 sqns); New Russia DragR (2 sqns); Lithuanian UlR (2 sqns). GM Emmanuel: GM Millesimo; DragRs Kiev and Kharkov (3 sqns each); 1 x HAB. GM Rebrikov III: Cossack Pulk of Rebrikov III; Stavropol Kalmuck R (2 sqns each); Streifkorps Orlov-Denissov (4 sqns).

3rd (Russian) Army of the West GdI Barclay de Tolly:

Right Wing (18th Division) GM Count Scherbatov: GM Umaretz: Kinburn DragR, Sievsk MtdRR (2 sqns each) 1 x light FAB. GM Bernodossov: IRs Vladimir, Dniepr (1 bn each). Col Heidenreich: IRs Kostroma, Tambov (1 bn each). GM Karnielov: 28th and 32nd Jägers (1 bn each). **Left Wing (9th Division)** GM Isonov; GM Poltaratzky: IRs Nacheburg and Yakutsk (1 bn each). GM Udom I: 10th and 38th Jägers (1 bn each). 1 x light FAB. GM Pahlen II: DragRs Tver and Dorpat (2 sqns each).

Prussian Army GdC von Blücher Oberschlesische Brigade GM von Ziethen; Cavalry; Maj Laroche von Starkenfeld; Maj von Blücher: 1st Schl HusR (2nd and 4th sqns); 2nd Schl HusR (3rd and 4th sqns). Maj von Schmiedburg: Schl UlR (1st and 2nd sqns). 1 x HAB. Infantry Obst von Pirch. Maj von Carnall: Schl Gren Bn (1 bn); 1st Schl IR (1st, 3rd and Füs bns); 1 x 6 pdr FAB. Obst von Losthin: 2nd Schl IR (1st and 3rd Bns); Schl Schützen Bn (1 bn); Leib IR (3rd and 5th Res bns). 1 x 6 pdr FAB. 2 x Russian heavy FABs. Niederschlesische Brigade Obst von Klüx: Cavalry Obst von Mutius: Neumark DragR (4 sqns); 1st Westpr DragR (2 sqns); 1 x HAB. Infantry: Maj von Jagow; Maj von Anhalt: Westpr Gren Bn (1 bn); Westpr IR (2nd, 3rd and Füs bn); Leib IR (2nd and 3rd Res bn); 2nd Westpr IR (2nd Bn); 3rd Westpr IR (3rd bn); 1 x 6 pdr FAB.

The Prussian Corps GL York.

Right Wing GM Corswandt: Obstlt von Wuthernov: 1st Westpr DragR (1st and 3rd sqns). 1 x 6 pdr HAB. Obst Zielinsky: 2nd Ostpr IR (Füs bn); 1st Ostpr IR

(1st and 2nd bns); Leib IR (1st and 2nd bns); Combined Füs bn (of 1st Ostpr and Leib IRs); 2 x pdr FABs. Obst von Horn: 1st Westpr IR (1st bn); 2nd Westpr IR (2nd bn); 1st Schl IR (2nd bn); 2nd Schl IR (2nd bn); Combined Füs Bn (of 5th and 6th Combined IRs); 2nd Westpr IR (Füs bn); 2nd Schl IR (Füs bn); 1 x 3 pdr FAB, 1 x 6 pdr HAB. Lithuanian DragR (4 sqns); Brand DragR (2 sqns).

2nd Line of Battle (Russians) GL Gortschakov II; GL Berg; Cavalry Col Uvarov: DragRs Mitau, Moscow, HusR Lubny (2 sqns each); 1 x HAB. GM Lissanevitch: Achtyrsk HusR; Tchuguchev UlR, Kargopol Drag (2 sqns each). **5th Division** GM Lukov; GM Prince Sibirsky: IRs Perm, Mohilev (1 bn each); 1 x FAB. GM Kasatschkovsky: IRs Kaluga, Sievsk, Grand Princess Katharina's bn (1 bn each). **14th Division** GM Helfreich: IRs Tenginsk, Estonia (1 bn each). GL St Priest **7th Division** GM Tallisin III: IRs Sophia, Pskov, 11th Jägers (1 bn each). 8th Division GM Engelhardt I: Col Schindschin: IRs Archangel, Schlüsselburg, Old Ingermannland (1 bn each). Col Stegeman: IR Kaporzsch, 37th Jägers (1 bn each). 1 x heavy FAB.

Reserve of the 3rd Army of the West GL Baron Sass. Artillery GM Wassilizky. 2 x heavy FAB. Col Tern: IRs Witebsk, Koslov (1 bn each). Col Suthov: IRs Kurin, Kolyvan, 7th Jägers (1 bn each). 1 x heavy FAB, 1 x light FAB, 1 x pionier coy. Arsamas UlR (1 sqn); Kirov Cossack R (2 sqns).

Prussian Reserve GM von Röder: Obstlt Katzler: Westpr UlR (4 sqns). Obstlt von Tippelskirch: Maj von Alvensleben: Garde IR (1st, 2nd and Füs bns); Garde Jägers (1 bn); Normal I bn (1 bn); Garde FAB. Maj von Natzmer: Leib Gren Bn (1 bn); 1st Ostpr Gren Bn (1 bn); Leib IR (3rd and 1st Res Bns); Garde-Freiwillige-Jägers (1 bn). Maj Hobe: Brand-HusR (1st and 2nd sqns); 2nd Leib-HusR (4 sqns); **Reserve Cavalry Division** Obstlt von Dolffs; Obstlt von Werder: Garde du Corps (5 sqns); Garde-Light Cavalry R (6 sqns); Garde HAB. Obst von Jürgass: Ostpr KürR; Schl KürR; Brand KürR (4 sqns each); 1 x HAB. Russian 2nd Line: GL Markov: GM Karpenkov: 1st and 33rd Jägers (1 bn each); 1 x light FAB. GM Bistram: IRs Podolsk, Jeletz (1 bn each). Col Schertov: IRs Riasan, Brest (1 bn each). 22nd Division GM Turtschaninov: IRs Olonetz, Staroskol (1 bn each). Col Kern: IR Bielosersk, 45th Jägers (1 bn each), 1 x light FAB.

Main Russian Reserve Grand Duke Constantine. 1st Line GL Raievsky: Guard Light Cavalry Division GM Schävitch: GM Tschailkov: Guard DragR, Guard HusR, Guard UlR (4 sqns each). 1st Grenadier Division: GM Sulima; Col Kniaschnin II: Gren Rs Arakcheyev, Ekaterinoslav (2 bns each). Col Acht: Gren Rs Tauride, St Petersburg (2 bns each). GM Tschoglikov: IRs Pernau, Kexholm (2 bns each). Col Brischinsky: Combined Grenadiers of the 5th Division and of the 14th Division (2 bns each). Artillery: 1 x heavy and 2 x light FABs. **2nd Grenadier Division** GM Zwielniev; Col Pissareff: Grenadier Rs Kiev, Moscow (2 bns each). Col Golowin: Grenadier Rs Astrakhan, Phanagoria (2 bns each). Col Hesse: Grenadier Rs Siberia, Little Russia (2 bns each); 1 x heavy FAB. 2nd Kürassier Division GM Duka (all regiments 3 sqns each): GM Leontiev: KürRs Gluchov, Pskov. GM Gudowitsch: KürRs Military Order, Starodub. Col Massalov: KürRs Novgorod, Little Russia.

2nd Line GL Prince Galitzin V. The Guard GL Lavrov: 1st Kür Division (all regiments 3 sqns each): GM Araniev: Chevalier Guard, Horse Guards, Life KürR, Guards HAB. GM Rosen: KürRs Tsarina, Astrakhan, Ekaterinoslav; Guard HAB. 1st Guards Division GM Baron Rosen; GM Potemkin: Preobrazhenski and Semenovsky Guard IRs (2 bns each). 1 x Guard heavy FAB. GM Krapovitsky: Guard Jägers, Ismailovski Guard IR (2 bns each). 2 x Guard light FABs. 2nd Guards Division GM Yermelov; Col Krischanovsky: Lithuanian and Finland Guard IRs (2 bns each). GM Scheltuchin: Pavlov Gren and Leib GrenRs (2 bns each). 1 x Guard heavy FAB. **Artillery Reserve** GL Prince Jachvill; GM Enter: 4 x heavy and 1 x light FABs. GM Merlin: 4 x HAB. GM ? 4 x light FABs.

Allied totals 66,000 Russians (including 7,000 Cossacks); 31,000 Prussians.

Allied losses 7,300 Russians, 3,700 Prussians killed, wounded and missing, 9 guns.

Comment Once again, the Allies failed to exploit their superiority in cavalry. Souham's division suffered very heavy losses as did the Württembergers. Ney's failure to follow Napoleon's orders reduced his success. Tsar Alexander I meddled in the Allied conduct of the battle and nearly caused a disaster. Napoleon's lack of cavalry meant that the Allied withdrawal was not seriously disturbed.

Sources Plotho, Sporschil, Martinien.

SX Reichenbach (Markersdorf), 22 May 1813, clash

A small town in Saxony (northeastern Germany) on the Polish border, on Route B6, 12 km west of Görlitz.

A French victory over the Russians.

(Last action – Bautzen, 20/21 May; next action – Haynau, 26 May.)

French Forces Emperor Napoleon I commanding:

The Imperial Guard Cavalry GdD Lefebvre-Desnouettes: 2nd Berg ChLL (4 sqns); 1er and 2e ChLRs (4 sqns each); ChàCh (3 sqns); Mamelukes (1 sqn).

VII Corps GdD Reynier: 32nd Division GdD Durutte: 35e RILé (3e and 4e bns); 36e RILé (4e Bn); 131e and 132e RIdLi (4e Bns each). 133e RIdLi (3e and 4e bns): IR Würzburg (2nd and 3rd bns). 1st (Saxon) Division, GdC Zeschau: 1st LtIR (1 bn); Gren-Garde-R (1 bn); IR Prinz Friedrich (1 bn); IR Steindel (1 bn); Jägers (1 coy); 2nd (Saxon) Division, GL von Sahr: Gren Bn von Anger (1 bn); IR Prinz Anton and IR von Löw (1 bn each); 2 x FAB, 1 x HAB. 2 x French FABs.

I Cavalry Corps GdD Latour-Maubourg: 1st Light Cavalry Division GdD Bruyère: GdB Cambraceres: 1er ChàCh (1 sqn). GdB Jacquet: Saxon HusR and Saxon UlR (4 sqns each). 2 x French HAB, 1 x Italian and 1 x Saxon HAB.

The French and Italian cavalry regiments of I Cavalry Corps reported no casualties.

French totals ca 14,000 men.

French losses 1,400 killed and wounded. GdD Count Bruyère and Duroc (Duke of Frioul) mortally wounded, GdD de Planta killed, ca 500 captured.

Russian Forces GL Prince Eugen von Württemberg commanding. GM Knorring: Ssum HusR (2 sqns), Tartar UlR (4 sqns); combined DragR (2 sqns). 3rd Division GM Count Schachafskoi: GM Baron Wolff: IRs Murmansk, Reval, Tchernigov (1 bn each). Col Treffurt: IRs Riask, Tobolsk, Volhynien (1 bn each). Col Ivanov: 4th and 34th Jägers (1 bn each). GM Pantschulid I: Tchernigov MtdRR (3 sqns); New Russia DragR, Lithuanian UlR (2 sqns each). **The Reserve (5th Division)** GM Lukov. GM Prince Sibirsky: IRs Perm, Mohilev (1 bn each). GM Kasatschkovsky: IRs Kaluga, Sievsk, Grand Duchess Katharina bn (1 bn each). **2nd Kürassier Division** GM Duka: GM Leontiev: All regiments with 3 sqns: KürRs Gluchov, Pskov. GM Gudowitsch: KürRs Military Order and Starodub. Col Massalov: KürRs Little Russia, Novgorod. 1 x HAB.

Reinforcements which arrived during the battle: General Prince Trubetzkoi with Prince Obolensky's Ukranian Brigade and some other units: Avantgarde: 3rd Ukranian Cossack Pulk (4 sqns) under GM Count Obolensky; GM Pahlen II: DragRs Tver and Dorpat (2 sqns each). Col Uvarov Lubny HusR (2 sqns), 1 x HAB. GM Gengross: DragRs Mitau and Moscow (2 sqns each). GM Millesimo: DragRs Kiev and Kharkov (3 sqns each), 1 x HAB. Artillery Reserve: ½ x 12 pdr FAB, 1 x 6 pdr FAB. There was also some unidentified infantry under General Mellentin. Artillery GM Nikitin: 1 x heavy FAB, 1 x light FAB, 1 x HAB.

Russian total ca 16,000 men.

Russian losses 1,100 killed and wounded.

Comment This successful rearguard action by the Russians ended when they evacuated the village of Nieder-Markersdorf and burned the bridge over the River Neisse. It was not until noon on 23 May that the French crossed the river over a pontoon bridge built by the Saxons.

Sources Plotho, Sporschil, Martinien.

SX Haynau (now Chojnow), 26 May 1813 ambush

A town in the Prussian province of Silesia (now Poland), 17 km northwest of Liegnitz (now Legnica) towards Bunzlau (now Boleslawiec).

A Prussian victory over the French.

(Last action – Reichenbach, 22 May; next action – Hoyerswerda, 28 May.)

French Forces GdD Count Maison (of Lauriston's V Corps) commanding: 16th Division GdB Avril: 151e RIdLi (4 bns); 153e RIdLi (3 bns); 2 x FAB.

French total ca 3,700 infantry, 18 guns.

French losses 1,400 killed, wounded and captured, 11 guns.

Prussian Forces GdC von Blücher: GM von Ziethen's Reserve Cavalry Oberst von Dolff: Garde du Corps (5 sqns); Guard Light Cavalry, R (6 sqns). Obst von Jürgass: Ostpr KürR; Schles KürR, Brand KürR (4 sqns each). 3 x HAB. Obst von Mutius: Maj von Bork: Neumark DragR (3 sqns). Infantry: Obst von Pirch: 1st Schles IR (3 bns); 2nd Schles IR (3 bns); Schles Gren Bn (1 bn); Schles Schützen (2 coys); 2 x FAB.

Prussian total 8,000 infantry, 6,400 cavalry, 40 guns.

Prussian losses 86 killed and wounded.

Comment Maison was extremely lax and neglected to put out security patrols. The two cavalry regiments under his command fled and abandoned the infantry who were cut down. The Prussian infantry scarcely came into action. 15 guns were taken but only 11 could be taken off.

Sources Plotho, Sporschil, Martinien.

SX Hoyerswerda, 28 May 1813, clash

A small town in northeastern Germany, about 30 km west of the Polish border (the River Neisse), 34 km south of Cottbus, 33 km northwest of Bautzen on Routes B96 and B97.

A Franco-German victory over the Prussians.

(Last action – Haynau, 26 May; next action – Halberstadt, 30 May.)

Franco-German Forces M Oudinot commanding the XII Corps. 29th Division GL Raglovich's Bavarians: 2nd Brigade Obst Maillot: 2nd LtI Bn; LIR Nr 5 'Preysing', LIR Nr 7, LIR Nr 9, LIR Nr 10 'Junker' (2nd Bns each). 29th Light Cavalry Brigade GM Wolff: Westfalian ChLR (2 sqns); Hessen-Darmstadt Garde ChLR (3 sqns). 14th Division GdD Lorencz: GdB Leclerc: 137e RIdLi (4 bns) 2 x FAB.

Franco-German total ca 12,000 men (of whom only those shown above came into action).

Franco-German losses 130 killed, some hundreds wounded.

Russo-Prussian Forces GL von Bülow commanding; GM von Borstell: Pomm Gren Bn (1 bn); Pomm IR (1st and 2nd bns); 4th Ostpr IR (Füs Bn); Königin DragR (3 sqns); ½ x HAB. GM Oppen: 3rd Ostpr IR (Füs Bn); Lithuanian Füs (1st and 3rd Bns); 1st Leib-HusR; Russian Col Krafft: 2 x Cossack Pulks.

Russo-Prussian total ca 6,000 men.

Russo-Prussian losses Not known exactly but light.

Sources Plotho, Sporschil, Martinien, Leyh.

SX Halberstadt, 30 May 1813, clash

A walled town in northern central Germany, 90 km northwest of Halle in Saxony, at the junction of Routes B6, B27 and B81.

A Russian victory over the Westfalians.

(Last action – Haynau, 26 May; next action – Luckau, 4 June.)

Westfalian Forces GdD von Ochs commanding: 1,200 men (recruits, invalides, veterans and gendarmerie) 14 guns.

Westfalian losses 33 killed, 40 wounded; Gen von Ochs, 8 officers and over 1,000 men captured; 12 x 12 pdr and 2 x 4 pdr guns, 80 ammunition waggons, 1 field smithy and several supply waggons.

Russian Forces Gen Tschernitcheff with the Riga DragR, Isum HusR (2 sqns each); 4 x Cossack Pulks and 2 x 6 pdr guns.

Russian total 1,200 men.

Russian losses 43 killed and wounded.

Sources Specht, Lünsmann.

EN Morales, 2 June 1813, skirmish

A village in northern Spain on Route 122/E82, between Zamora and Tordesillas, 7 km east of Toro and near a tributary of the Rio Duero.

A British victory over the French.

(Last action – Castro Urdiales, 12 May; next action – Osma, 18 June.)

French Forces 16e and 21e DragRs of Pierre Soult's Dragoon Division, M Soult's Army of the South, ca 800 men.

French losses (apparently all in 16e Regiment). 2 officers and 308 men captured (of these 100 wounded). The 16e was effectively destroyed.

British Forces BG Grant and the 10th Hussars ca 600 men.

British losses 16 killed and wounded.

Comment This was the first action of Wellington's advance on Vittoria. Most of the French horses were in dreadfully poor condition with 'horrible sore backs'. With this action Wellington had turned the line of the Duero and the French abandoned it to fall back eastwards. By similar, oblique outflanking movements, Wellington forced the French (nominally commanded by King Joseph) to abandon the lines of the Rivers Hormazan, Arlanzón and Urbel and to give up Burgos without a fight.

Sources Oman, Martinien.

SX Luckau, 4 June 1813, clash

A town in northern Germany, 70 km southeast of Berlin, at the junction of Routes B87, B96 and B102; 65 km northwest of Hoyerswerda.

A Russo-Prussian victory over the French and their allies.

(Last action – Halberstadt, 30 May; next action – Pirna, 27 August.)

Franco-Allied Forces M Oudinot commanding the XII Corps: 13th Division GdD Pacthod: GdB Pourailly: 6e RIdLi (7e Bn); 7e RIdLi (3e and 4e Bns); 1er RILé (4e Bn); 10e RIdLi (4e Bn). GdB Gruger: 101e RIdLi (2e,

3e, 4e bns); 1st Neapolitan LtIR (1st and 2nd bns). 2 x FAB. Combined Bavarian ChLR (2 sqns); Hessen-Darmstadt Garde ChLR (2 sqns).

Franco-Allied total ca 20,000 men.

Franco-Allied losses 1,500 killed and wounded, 700 captured, 1 gun, 2 ammunition waggons.

Russo-Prussian Forces GL von Bülow commanding: Russian GM Harppe: Polish UlR (2 sqns); Niejinsk MtdRR (2 sqns); Cossack Pulk of Grekov IX, Tver Militia Cossack Pulk; IR Novaginsk (1 bn); 2 x heavy FAB. GM von Thümen: 4th Ostpr IR (2 bns); 2 x 6 pdr FAB. Prinz Ludwig von Hessen-Homburg: 2nd Ostpr Gren Bn (1 bn); 2nd Ostpr IR (3 bns); Westpr DragR (2 sqns); ½ x 12 pdr FAB, 1 x 6 pdr FAB, 1 x HAB. Leib IR (4th Res Bn); Jägers (3 coys); 1st Leib-HusR (4 sqns); 3rd Ostpr IR (3 bns); 4 guns; Cossack Pulk of Beschenzov.

Russo-Prussian total 16½ bns, 10 sqns, 1 Pulk, 58 guns. 15,800 men.

Russo-Prussian losses ca 800 killed and wounded.

Comment The brigades of General Borstell and Obst Boyen did not arrive until the combat was over. Oudinot withdrew 40 km southwest to Übigau. The armistice of Poischwitz, signed on 4 June, ended the fighting until 10 August.

Sources Plotho, Sporschil, Martinien, Leyh.

EE Tarragona, 3–11 June 1813, failed siege

A fortified Spanish Mediterranean port (in ruins since Suchet's siege) about 75 km southwest of Barcelona.

A French victory over the Allies.

(Last action – Castalla, 13 April; next action – Ordal, 13 September.)

French Garrison GdB Bertoletti commanding: 20e RIdLi (1 bn), 7th Italian LIR (1 bn); Spanish Juramentados (1 coy), artillery (2 coys) some armed sailors.

French total 1,600 men.

French losses 13 killed, 85 wounded.

Allied Forces Gen Sir John Murray commanding: Calabrian Free Corps, 1st Anglo-Italian Levy (1 bn each). 1st Division Gen W Clinton: 1/58th, 2/67th, 4th Line bn KGL (1 bn each); Sicilian IR 'Estero' (2 bns). 2nd Division Gen J Mackenzie: 1/10th, 1/27th, 1/81st, De Roll-Dillon, 2nd Italian Levy (1 bn each). Gen Whittingham's Spanish infantry: IRs Guadalajara, Cordoba, 2nd of Murcia, Mallorca, 5th Grenadiers (1 bn each). Cavalry: 20th LDR, Brunswick HusR (2 sqns each); Foreign HusR (1tp), 2 x British and 1 x Portuguese FABs. Gen Copons' 1st Spanish Army: 2nd Division – 7 bns, 2 sqns (exact details not known) ca 5,500 men.

Allied grand total ca 15,000 men and a siege train of 18 guns.

Allied losses at Tarragona

	Killed	Wounded	Missing	Total
British, German, Calabrian, Italians	14	60	5	79
Sicilians	—	15	—	15
Whittingham's Spaniards	1	7	—	8
Totals	*15*	*82*	*5*	*102*
				and 18 guns

Comment Murray badly mishandled this action. Having achieved a surprise landing, he started a formal siege instead of just storming the place. Hearing of the approach of Suchet's relief force (which was only 7,000 strong) he panicked, spiked his siege train and fled, leaving Gen Copons behind in a potentially very dangerous situation. On 18 June he was relieved of his command and Gen Lord William Bentinck took over.

Sources Oman, Martinien.

EN Osma, 18 June 1813, skirmish

A village in northern Spain, on Route 625, 45 km south of Bilbao and 40 km west of Vittoria.

A drawn match between the French and British.

(Last action – Morales, 2 June; next action – San Millan, 18 June.)

French Forces GdD Sarrut's 4th Division, Army of Portugal: 2e and 4e RILé, 36e RIdLi (2 bns each) ca 3,800 men.

French losses 120 killed and wounded.

British Forces BG Halkett's Brigade of MG Howard's 1st Division: 1st and 2nd LtI Bns KGL ca 1,200 men.

British losses 50–60 killed and wounded.

Comment By this time, Wellington's surprise advance

through the mountains of northern Spain had succeeded in forcing the French to evacuate most of the country south of the Ebro. GdD Reille and three division were hurrying north to protect Bilbao when they bumped into Gen Graham's main column (1st and 5th Divisions, Ansons's Light Dragoons and Bradford's Portuguese) marching for Orduna to attack the Vittoria position. Reille withdrew south to rejoin King Joseph at Miranda de Ebro.

EN San Millan, 18 June 1813, clash

A village in the mountains of northern Spain, about 35 km west of Vittoria.

An Anglo-Portuguese victory over the French.

(Last action – Osma, 18 June; next action – Vittoria, 21 June.)

French Forces GdD Maucune's 5th Division, Army of Portugal: 15e, 66e, 82e and 86e RIdLi (2 bns each.)

French total ca 4,800 men.

French losses Killed and wounded unknown, 300 captured as well as the entire divisional baggage.

Anglo-Portuguese Forces MG Charles Alten's Light Division: 1/43rd, 1, 2 and 3/95th, 1/52nd, 2/95th, 3rd Caçadores (1 bn each).

Anglo-Portuguese total ca 4,000 men.

Anglo-Portuguese losses ca 100 killed and wounded.

Comment Half of Maucune's division escaped over the mountains, throwing away their packs. He regathered his division in Miranda de Ebro.

Sources Oman, Martinien.

EN Vittoria (Gasteiz), 21 June 1813, battle

A fortified city in northern Spain, 50 km southeast of Bilbao on Route I/E5.

An Allied victory over the French.

(Last action – San Millan, 18 June; next action – Tolosa, 25 June.)

French Forces King Joseph commanding.

Army of the South 1st Division GdD Leval: 9e RILé, 24e, 88e and 96e RIdLi, 1 x FAB. **Total** 4,800 men. **3rd Division** GdD Villatte: 27e RILé, 63e, 94e and 95e RIdLi, 1 x FAB. **Total** ca 5,800 men. **4th Division** GdD Conroux: 32e, 43e, 55e and 58e RIdLi; 1 x FAB. **Total** ca 6,500 men. **5th Division** GdB Maransin's Bde: 12e RILé, 45e RIdLi **Total** 2,900 men. **6th Division** GdD Daricau: 21e and 28e RILé. 100e and 103e RIdLi, 1 x FAB. **Total** ca 5,900 men. **Total infantry** ca 26,000 men. **Cavalry GdD Pierre Soult** 2e HusR, 5e, 10e and 21e ChàCh, 1 x HAB **Total** 1,670 men. **GdD Tilly** 2e, 4e, 14e, 17e, 26e and 27e DragRs. **Total** ca 1,900 men. GdD Digeon: 5e, 12e, 16e, 24e DragRs. Artillery Park: 2 x artillery coys, 1 x pontonnier coy, 1 x artificer coy, 1 x train coy, 2 coys sappers, 2 coys miners.

Total Army of the South ca 34,600 men.

Army of the Centre 1st Division GdD Darmagnac: 28e and 75e RIdLi, 2nd Nassau IR, 4th Baden IR, Frankfurt bn. **Total** 4,400 men. **2nd Division** GdD Cassagne: 16e RILé, 8e, 51e and 54e RIdLi. **Total** 9,680 men. GdB Avy's Light Cavalry Brigade: 27e ChàCh, Nassau ChàCh ca 470 men. GdD Treilhard: 13e, 18e, 19e, 22e DragR ca 1,000 men. 3 x FAB.

King Joseph's Spanish Army Royal Guard GdD Guy: Grenadiers, Voltigeurs and Tirailleurs ca 2,380 men. Hussars and Lancers: 425 men. The Line; IRs Castile, Toledo and Royal Étranger – 2,070 men. Cavalry: 1st and 2nd ChàCh, HusR Guadalajara; 1 x FAB. **Total Spanish Army** ca 5,600 men.

Army of Portugal 4th Division GdD Sarrut: 2e and 4e RILé, 36e, 65e RIdLi, 1 x FAB. **Total** 4,800 men. **6th Division** GdD Lamartinière: 118e, 119e, 120e and 122e RIdLi, 1 x FAB. **Total** ca 6,700 men. **Cavalry** GdD Mermet: 13e and 22e ChàCh, 3e HusR, 14e and 26e ChàCh. GdD Boyer: 6e, 11e, 15e and 25e DragR. **Total** ca 3,400 cavalry. Reserve Artillery 1 x HAB, 4 x FAB. Pontonniers, artificers and train 1 coy each; 2 coys sappers. **Total Army of Portugal** ca 17,000 men on 1 May. At Vittoria this total had probably reduced to about 14,000 men.

Total French Army at Vittoria 46,000 infantry, 9,000 cavalry, 2,300 gunners and sappers.

Losses

Army of the South

	Killed		Wounded		Prisoners		Missing		Total
	Officers	Men	Officers	Men	Officers	Men	Officers	Men	
Leval's Division	4	98	17	395	4	133	—	108	759
Villatte's Division	—	43	2	212	—	22	—	—	279
Conroux's Division	5	74	27	712	4	265	—	—	1,087

	Killed		Wounded		Prisoners		Missing		Total
	Officers	Men	Officers	Men	Officers	Men	Officers	Men	
Maransin's Division	3	80	21	510	4	63	—	—	681
Daricau's Division	3	89	20	389	1	49	—	280	831
Pierre Soult's Cavalry	—	—	3	—	—	—	—	3	6
Digeon's Dragoons	—	18	11	69	1	3	—	—	102
Tilly's Dragoons	—	2	—	19	1	3	—	—	25
Artillery	2	20	—	366	—	100	—	—	488
Engineers, &c.	1	2	—	2	—	23	—	—	28
Army of the South Total	*18*	*426*	*101*	*2,674*	*15*	*661*	—	*391*	*4,286*

Army of the Centre

	Killed		Wounded		Prisoners		Missing		Total
	Officers	Men	Officers	Men	Officers	Men	Officers	Men	
Darmagnac's Division	9	96	33	414	3	791	—	—	1,346
Cassagne's Division	—	9	6	70	—	178	—	—	263
Treilhard's Dragoons	—	6	1	17	—	56	—	—	80
Avy's Chasseurs	—	2	1	3	—	51	—	—	57
Artillery: no Returns	?	?	?	?	?	?	—	—	?
Engineers	—	—	—	—	—	4	—	—	4
Casapalacios' Spaniards	5	20	12	21	—	300	—	—	358
Army of the Centre Total	*14*	*133*	*53*	*525*	*3*	*1,380*	—	—	*2,108*

Army of Portugal

	Killed		Wounded		Prisoners		Missing		Total
	Officers	Men	Officers	Men	Officers	Men	Officers	Men	
Sarrut's	2	51	26	505	4	224	—	—	812
Lamartinière's Division	7	70	30	362	1	116	—	—	586
Mermet's Light Cavalry	—	18	8	42	—	29	—	—	97
Boyer's Dragoons	1	16	8	80	—	—	—	—	105
Artillery, Engineers, &c	?	?	?	?	?	?	—	—	?
Army of Portugal Total	*10*	*155*	*72*	*989*	*5*	*369*	—	—	*1,600*
Grand Total Losses of the three armies	***42***	***714***	***226***	***4,188***	***23***	***2,801***		***391***	***8,008***

No return from King Joseph's Royal Guards.

In addition 151 guns, 415 ammunition waggons, thousands of carts of loot, Marshal Jourdan's baton, 25 million francs; one colour, that of the disbanded 100e RIdLi.

Allied Forces The Marquess of Wellington commanding.

1st Division MG Howard: 1/2nd Guards, 1/3rd Guards (1 bn each); 5/60th (1 coy); 1st, 2nd and 5th Line bns KGL, 1st and 2nd LtI Bns KGL (1 bn each). **Total** 4,800 men. **2nd Division** MG Sir William Stewart: 1/50th, 1/71st, 1/92nd (1 bn each); 5/60th (1 coy); 1/3rd, 1/57th (1 bn each); 1st Provisional Bn (2/31st and 2/66th) (1 bn); 1/28th, 2/34th, 1/39th (1 bn each); 5/60th (1 coy). Ashworth's Portuguese: 6th and 18th LIR (2 bns each); 6th Caçadores (1 bn). **Total** 10,800 men. **3rd Division** MG Thomas Picton: 1/45th, 1/74th, 1/88th (1 bn each); 5/60th (3 coys); 1/5th, 2/83rd, 2/87th, 1/94th (1 bn each). Power's Portuguese: 9th and 21st LIR (2 bns each), 11th Caçadores (1 bn). **Total** 7,400 men. **4th Division** MG Sir Lowry Cole: 3/27th, 1/40th, 1/48th, 2nd Provisional Bn (2and 3/53rd) (1 bn each); 5/60th (1 coy); Brunswick Oels (1 coy). 1/7th, 1/20th, 1/23rd

Stubbs' Portuguese: 11th and 23rd LIR (2 bns each); 7th Caçadores (1 bn). **Total** 6,700 men. **5th Division** MG Oswald: 3/1st, 1/9th, 1/38th (1 bn each), Brunswick Oels (1 coy). 1/4th, 2/47th, 2/59th (1 bn each), Brunswick Oels (1 coy). Spry's Portuguese: 3rd and 15th LIR (2 bns each); 8th Caçadores (1 bn). **Total** 6,725 men. **7th Division** MG Lord Dalhousie: 1/6th, 3rd Provisional Bn (2/24th, 2/58th) (1 bn each); Brunswick Oels (9 coys); 1/51st, 1/68th, 1/82nd, Chasseurs Britanniques (1 bn each); Lecor's Portuguese 7th and 19th LIR (2 bns each); 2nd Caçadores (1 bn). **Total** 7,200 men. **Light Division** MG Charles Alten: 1/43rd, 1/95th, 3/95th, 1/52nd, 2/95th (1 bn each). 17th Portuguese LIR (2 bns); 1st and 3rd Caçadores (1 bn each). **Total** 5,400 men. **MG Silveira's Portuguese Division** 2nd and 14th LIR, 4th and 10th LIR (2 bns each); 10th Caçadores (1 bn). Pack's Portuguese Brigade: 1st and 16th LIR (2 bns each); 4th Caçadores. Bradford's Portuguese Brigade: 13th and 24th LIR (2 bns each), 5th Caçadores. **Total Portuguese** ca 9,800 men. **Cavalry** Hill's Brigade: 1st and 2nd Life Guards, Horse Guards - 870 men. Ponsonby's Brigade 5th DG, 3rd and 4th DragRs - 1,200 men. G Anson's Brigade: 12th and 16th LD - 800 men. Long's Brigade: 13th LD - 390 men. V Alten's Brigade: 14th LD, 1st HusR KGL - 630 men. Bock's Brigade - 1st and 2nd DragR KGL - 630 men. Fane's Brigade: 3rd DG, 1st DragR - 840 men. Grant's Brigade: 10th, 15th and 18th HusRs - 1,620 men. d'Urban's Portuguese Brigade: 1st, 11th and 12th CavRs - 685 men. Campbell's Portuguese Brigade: 6th CavR - 208 men. **Total Cavalry** ca 8,300 men. Foot artillery, Train, etc - 2,800 men. Horse Artillery - 800 men. KGL Artillery - 350 men. Portuguese Artillery - 330 men. Engineers and Sappers - 340 men. Staff Corps - 147 men. Wagon Train - 200 men. **Anglo-Portuguese grand total** 81,276.

Spanish Troops General Giron's 4th Army. Morillo's 1st Division: 1st Brigade: IRs León, Unión, Legion Extremena. 2nd Brigade: Tiradores de Doyle; IRs Victoria, 2 de Jaén. 1 x FAB. 6th Spanish Division Gen Longa: LtIR Iberia (4 bns light infantry). 2e de Alava (1 bn); HusR de Alava (1 sqn).

Spanish total ca 7,000 men.

Allied Grand Total 88,276 men and 90 guns.

Losses

British Losses

	Killed		Wounded		Prisoners		
	Officers	Men	Officers	Men	Officers	Men	Total
1st Division, Gen Howard							
Stopford's Brigade 1st Coldstream Guards							
1/3rd Guards			No casualties				
Halkett's Brigade 1st, 2nd and							
5th Line KGL	—	1	—	1	—	—	2
1st Light KGL	—	1	1	7	—	—	9
2nd Light KGL	—	4	—	39	—	—	43
1st Division Total	—	*6*	*1*	*47*	—	—	*54*
2nd Div Gen Sir W Stewart							
Cadogan's Brigade							
1/50th Foot	—	27	7	70	—	—	104
1/71st Foot	3	41	12	260	—	—	316
1/92nd Foot	—	4	—	16	—	—	20
Byng's Brigade							
1/3rd Foot	—	8	7	96	—	—	110
1/57th Foot	—	5	2	21	—	—	28
1st Provisional Batt.	—	3	2	35	—	—	40
O'Callaghan's Brigade							
1/28th Foot	—	12	17	171	—	—	200

	Killed		Wounded		Prisoners		
	Officers	Men	Officers	Men	Officers	Men	Total
2/34th Foot	—	10	8	63	—	—	76
1/39th Foot	—	26	3	181	—	—	215
2nd Division Total	*3*	*136*	*58*	*913*	—	—	*1,110*
3rd Division, Gen Sir Thomas Picton							
Brisbane's Brigade							
1/45th Foot	—	4	4	66	—	—	74
74th Foot	—	13	4	66	—	—	83
1/88th Foot	—	23	5	187	—	—	215
5/60th Foot (8 comp)	—	2	2	47	—	—	51
Colville's Brigade							
1/5th Foot	2	22	6	133	—	—	163
2/83rd Foot	2	18	4	50	—	—	74
2/87th Foot	1	54	12	177	—	—	244
94th Foot	—	5	6	56	—	—	67
3rd Division Total	*5*	*141*	*43*	*782*	—	—	*971*
4th Div Gen Sir Lowry Cole							
W Anson's Brigade							
3/27th Foot	—	7	3	32	—	—	42
1/40th Foot	—	5	3	34	—	—	42
1/48th Foot	—	1	—	18	—	—	19
2nd Provisional	—	4	—	6	—	—	10
Skerrett's Brigade							
1/7th Foot	—	2	—	2	—	—	4
20th Foot	—	3	—	1	—	—	4
1/23rd Foot	—	1	—	3	—	—	4
4th Division Total	—	*23*	*6*	*96*	—	—	*125*
5th Div General Oswald							
Hay's Brigade							
3/1st Foot	—	8	7	96	—	—	111
1/9th Foot	1	9	—	15	—	—	25
1/38th Foot	—	—	1	7	—	—	8
Robinson's Brigade							
1/4th Foot	1	12	6	72	—	—	91
2/47th Foot	2	18	4	88	—	—	112
2/59th Foot	—	11	8	130	—	—	149
5th Division Total	*4*	*58*	*26*	*408*	—	—	*496*
7th Div Gen Lord Dalhousie							
Barnes's Brigade	No casualties						
Grant's Brigade							
1/51st Foot	1	10	—	21	—	—	32
1/68th Foot	2	23	9	91	—	—	125
1/82nd Foot	1	5	3	22	—	—	31

	Killed		Wounded		Prisoners		
	Officers	Men	Officers	Men	Officers	Men	Total
Chasseurs Britanniques	—	29	2	109	—	—	140
Light Comp Brunswick Oels	1	—	—	5	—	—	6
7th Division Total	*5*	*67*	*14*	*248*	—	—	*334*
Light Div Gen Charles Alten							
Kempt's Brigade							
1/43rd Foot	—	2	2	27	—	—	31
1/95th Rifles	—	4	4	37	—	—	45
3/95th Rifles	1	7	—	16	—	—	24
Vandeleur's Brigade							
1/52nd Foot	1	3	1	18	—	—	23
2/95th Rifles	—	—	1	8	—	—	9
Light Division Total	*2*	*16*	*8*	*106*	—	—	*132*
Cavalry							
R Hill's Brigade (Household Cavalry)	No casualties						
Ponsonby's Brigade	—	—	—	2	—	—	2
G Anson's Brigade							
12th Light Dragoons	1	3	—	8	—	—	12
16th Light Dragoons	—	7	1	13	—	—	21
Long's Brigade	—	—	—	1	—	—	1
V Alten's Brigade			No casualties				
Bock's Brigade	—	1	—	—	—	—	1
Fane's Brigade							
3rd Dragoon Guards	—	3	1	4	—	—	8
1st Royal Dragoons	—	—	—	1	—	—	1
Grant's Brigade							
10th Hussars	—	6	—	10	—	—	16
15th Hussars	—	10	2	47	—	—	59
18th Hussars	1	10	2	21	—	—	34
Cavalry Total	*2*	*40*	*6*	*107*	—	—	*155*
Royal Horse Artillery	—	4	1	35	—	—	40
Field Artillery	—	5	—	18	—	—	23
KGL Artillery	—	2	—	5	—	—	7
Royal Engineers	—	—	1	—	—	—	1
General Staff	—	—	8	—	—	—	8
Total British Losses	***21***	***498***	***172***	***2,765***	—	—	***3,456***
Portuguese Losses							
Ashworth's Brigade (2nd Division)							
6th Line	—	1	—	10	—	1	12
18th Line	—	—	—	1	—	—	1
6th Caçadores	1	1	—	7	—	—	9
Power's Brigade (3rd Division)							
9th Line	3	43	9	157	—	—	212

	Killed		Wounded		Prisoners		
	Officers	Men	Officers	Men	Officers	Men	Total
21st Line	3	55	8	115	—	6	187
11th Caçadores	—	3	2	7	—	—	12
Stubbs' Brigade (4th Division)							
11th Line	1	36	6	109	—	1	153
23rd Line	—	20	3	35	—	—	58
7th Caçadores	—	9	4	21	—	—	35
Spry's Brigade (5th Division)							
3rd Line	—	2	3	8	—	—	13
15th Line	—	6	3	19	—	—	28
8th Caçadores	—	13	2	25	—	—	40
Lecor's Brigade (7th Division)							
7th Line	—	—	—	—	—	6	6
Light Division							
1st Caçadores	—	2	—	2	—	—	4
3rd Caçadores	—	—	—	1	—	—	1
17th Line	—	7	1	20	—	—	28
Silveira's Division							
Da Costa's Brigade		No casualties					
A Campbell's Brigade	—	2	—	1	—	7	10
Pack's Brigade							
1st Line	—	3	—	—	—	—	3
16th Line	1	10	2	24	—	—	37
4th Caçadores	—	16	1	18	—	—	35
Bradford's Brigade							
13th Line	—	—	—	1	—	16	17
24th Line	—	—	—	3	—	3	6
5th Caçadores	—	4	—	5	—	2	11
Cavalry: in 6th Regiment	—	—	—	2	—	—	2
Artillery		No casualties					
Total Portuguese Losses	*9*	*233*	*44*	*591*	—	*42*	*919*
Spanish Losses							
All in Morillo's and Longa's Divisions	4	85	10	453	—	—	552
Total Allied Losses							
British	21	498	172	2,765	—	—	3,456
Portuguese	9	233	44	591	—	42	919
Spanish	4	85	10	453	—	—	552
Total	*34*	*816*	*226*	*3,809*	—	*42*	*4,927*

Comment Although a victory of major proportions, over 55,000 French soldiers escaped due to the lack of speed of Dalhousie and Graham in closing the road to Bayonne. The loss of the artillery was quickly made good from the arsenals in southern France and the French army was soon in the field again.

Sources Oman, Martinien.

EN Tolosa, 25 June 1813, clash

A walled town in northern Spain, in the valley of the Rio Orio on Route I/E5/E80, 20 km south of San Sebastián.

An Allied victory over the French.

(Last action – Vittoria, 21 June; next action – Roncesvalles, 25 July.)

French Forces GdD Foy commanding 1st Division, Army of Portugal: 6e RILé (1 bn); 39e, 69e, 76e RIdLi (2 bns each). GdB St Paul's Italian Brigade: 2nd LtIR, 4th and 6th LIRs (2 bns each). GdD Maucune's 5th Division: 15e, 66e, 82e and 86e RIdLi (2 bns each). GdB de Couchy's Brigade (Army of the North): 1er RILé (2 coys); 22e RIdLi (1 bn); 34e (4 coys); 64e (2 bns).

French total ca 16,000 men.

French losses Foy admitted 400 killed and wounded; this seemed to be too low.

Allied Forces Gen Graham commanding: BG Halkett's Brigade: 1st, 2nd and 5th Line bns KGL; 1st and 2nd Light bns KGL (5 bns). BG Anson's Cavalry: 12th and 16th LDRs. ca 750 men. BG Pack's Portuguese Brigade: 1st and 16th LIRs (2 bns each), 4th Caçadores (1 bn). Stopford's Brigade: 1/2nd Guards, 1/3rd Guards, 5/60th (1 coy). BG Bradford's Portuguese Brigade: 13th and 24th LIRs (2 bns each); 5th Caçadores (1 bn). Spanish Gen Longa's 6th Division: LtIR Iberia (4 bns light infantry); 2 de Alava (1 bn); HusR de Alava (1 sqn). Gen Porlier's Asturian Division (3 bns). The Spanish divisions of Generals Longa and Lardizabal (exact details and totals not known; they came up in the rear of the French position partway through the contest). 3 x FAB.

Allied total ca 16,000 men.

Allied losses 58 killed, 316 wounded, 45 missing.

Comment Graham could have much reduced his casualties by using artillery against the town's gates and walls much earlier than he did. Foy withdrew to the Franco-Spanish border and on 1 July left Spain via the bridge at Hendaye on the River Bidassoa.

Sources Oman, Martinien.

EN Roncesvalles (Roncevaux), 25 July 1813, clash

A village in northern Spain, in the Pyrenees, on a side road leading from Pamplona north over the French border to St-Jean-Pied-de-Port. Just south of the Puerto de Ibaneta pass.

An Allied victory over the French.

(Last action – Tolosa, 25 June; next action – Maya, 25 July.)

French Forces GdD Reille commanding the **'Right Wing'**: GdD Foy's 1st Division: 6e RILé, 76e RIdLi (1 bn each); 69e, RIdLi (2 bns). **Total** ca 3,000 men. GdD Clausel's **'Left Wing'** GdD Vandermaesen's 5th Division: 1er RIdLi, 25e RILé; 27e RIdLi, 130e RIdLi. **French Total** ca 2,200 men, 6 mountain guns. Of 17,000 men, only these came into action.

French losses '160 killed and wounded'; in fact it was about 530.

Allied Forces BG Byng (of Hill's 2nd Division): 1/3rd, 1/57th, 1st Provisional Bn (2/31st and 2/66th) (1 bn each), 5/60th (1 coy). 20th Portuguese LIR (2 bns). MG Morillo's Spanish Division: IRs Vittoria, Tiradores de Doyle, La Union, Legion Extremena, Leon.

Allied total 2,000 British and 3000 Spanish troops.

Allied losses 350 killed and wounded, over half of them Spanish.

Comment Due to the very difficult mountain terrain over which they advanced, the two French columns could neither deploy their total 17,000 men nor outflank the Allies on the Leicar Atheca and Altobiscar peaks. Heavy fog ended the action after 11 hours. A French diversionary probe by Col Loverdo with 1 bn 59e RIdLi and the local National Guard against the Spanish IR Leon at the iron foundry of Orbaiceta on the right flank failed.

Sources Oman, Martinien.

EN Maya, 25 July 1813, clash

A Spanish Pyrenean mountain village and pass, near the Biscayan coast on Route 121 from Pamplona to Bayonne.

A British victory over the French.

(Last action – Roncesvalles, 25 July; next action – San Sebastián, 25 July.)

French Forces GdD d'Erlon's 'Centre Group': GdD Darmagnac's 2nd Division: 16e RILé, 8e and 25e RIdLi, 51e, 54e and 75e RIdLi. **Total** 6,900 men. **Losses**: 1,400 killed and wounded.

GdD Maransin's 6th Division: 21e RILé, 24e and 96e RIdLi; 28e RILé, 101e and 103e RIdLi. **Total** 6,000 men. **Losses** 600 killed and wounded. Abbé's 3rd Division was in reserve but did not come into action until late: 27e RILé, 63e and 64e RIdLi, 5e RILé, 94e and 95e RIdLi. **Total** 8,000 men. **Losses** 100 killed and wounded.

French Grand Total 20,900 men.

Total French Losses 2,100.

British Forces MG Sir Rowland Hill's* 2nd Division): 1/50th, 1/71st, 1/92nd (1 bn each). 5/60th (1 coy). 1/28th, 2/34th, 1/39th (1 bn each); 5/60th (1 coy). 7th Division (BG Barnes): 1/6th Foot (1 bn); Brunswick Oels (1 coy). 1 x Portuguese FAB.

British total ca 6,000 men.

British losses 2nd Division. 1,330 killed and wounded, 140 captured. 7th Division 140 killed and wounded. 4 guns.

Comment This was an extremely bloody action ending in d'Erlon's withdrawal. On the British side the absence of General Hill – and his deputy Stewart until the latter stages – meant that in the opening phase the decisions were being taken at regimental (battalion) level.

Superior British musketry contributed to this hard won victory. The British abandoned both Roncesvalles and Maya. There was no pursuit.

* = Hill was absent during this action; General Pringle (just arrived from England) was in command.

Sources Oman, Martinien.

EN San Sebastián (Donostia), 7–25 July 1813, failed siege

A fortified Spanish Biscayan port, 15 km west of Irun and on Autoroute A1/E5/E70/E80 and Route I.

A French victory over the Allies.

(Last action – Maya, 25 June; next action – Sorauren, 25 July.)

French Garrison Forces GdB Rey commanding: 1er RILé (2 coys); 22e RIdLi (1 bn); 34e (4 coys), 64e (2 bns). Sappers and pioniers (1 coy each); artillery (2 coys).

French total ca 3,000 men.

French losses: 58 killed, 258 wounded.

Allied Forces Gen Graham commanding. 1st Division MG Howard: 1/2nd and 1/3rd Footguards (1 bn each); 5/60th (1 coy); 1st, 2nd and 5th Line bns KGL; 1st and 2nd Light bns KGL. BG Pack's Portuguese: 1st and 16th LIRs (2 bns each); 4th Caçadores (1 bn). 5th Division MG Leith: 3/1st, 1/9th, 1/38th (1 bn each); Brunswick Oels (1 coy); 1/4th, 2/47th, 2/59th (1 bn each), Brunswick Oels (1 coy). Spry's Portuguese: 3rd and 15th LIR (2 bns each); 8th Caçadores (1 bn). Bradford's Portuguese: 13th and 24th LIR ((2 bns each); 5th Caçadores (1 bn). The siege train: 40 heavy guns.

Allied total ca 11,000 men.

Allied losses Killed and wounded: 3/1st Foot – 330; 1/9th – 105, 1/38th – 53; 8th Caçadores – 205. Nine officers, 316 men captured.

Comment This was the usual amateurish British siege against a place of immense natural strength. French advances into Spain caused the fiasco to be ended.

Sources Oman, Martinien.

EN Sorauren, 28–30 July 1813, battle

A hamlet in the foothills of the western Spanish Pyrenees, on Route 121 leading north out of Pamplona along the valley of the Rio Ulzama.

An Allied victory over the French.

(Last action – San Sebastián, 25 July; next action – Yanzi, 1 August.)

French Forces M Soult commanding (all regiments of 1 battalion unless otherwise shown).

GdD Reille's 'Right Wing' 1st Division GdD Foy: 6e RILé, 69e RIdLi (2 bns); 76e RIdLi, 36e and 65e RIdLi (2 bns each); 39e RIdLi. **7th Division** GdD Maucune: 17e and 34e RILé; 15e RIdLi (2 bns); 66e, 82e and 86e RIdLi. **9th Division** GdD Lamartinière: 2e RILé, 118e, 119e, 122e (2 bns each); 120e (3 bns).

GdD d'Erlon's Centre 2nd Division GdD Darmagnac: 16e RILé; 8e, 51e RIdLi; 28e and 75e RIdLi (2 bns each). **3rd Division** GdD Abbé: 5e RILé, 64e and 94e RIdLi (2 bns each); 27e RILé, 63e and 95e RIdLi. **6th Division** GdD Maransin: 101e RIdLi (2 bns); 21e and 28e RILé, 24e, 96e and 101e RidLi.

GdD Clausel's 'Left Wing'. 4th Division GdD Conroux: 12e RILé, 32e and 43e RIdLi (2 bns each); 45e, 55e and 58e RIdLi. **5th Division** GdD Vandermaesen: 130e RIdLi (2 bns); 25e RILé; 1er, 27e, 50e and 59e RIdLi. **8th Division** GdD Taupin: 9e RILé, 47e and 70e RIdLi (2 bns each); 26e and 88e RIdLi, 31e RILé. French cavalry was present in the rear of the columns in the valleys but did not come into action.

French total ca 60,000 men.

French losses: see overleaf.

No figures for artillery, engineers, train, or other auxiliary services , or for general staff. Martinien lists supply 4 casualties of generals (Conroux, Schwitter, Rignoux, Meunier), and 12 of staff officers.

French losses (these apparently include the losses incurred at Maya and Roncesvalles):

	Killed		Wounded		Prisoners		
	Officers	Men	Officers	Men	Officers	Men	Total
Reille's Wing							
1st Division (Foy)	6	78	9	303	—	69	465
7th Division (Maucune)	14	189	27	500	25	1,102	1,857
9th Division (Lamartinière)	10	79	16	657	3	216	981
Total Reille's Wing	30	346	52	1460	28	1,387	3,303
d'Erlon's 'Centre'							
2nd Division (Darmagnac)	13	191	65	1,952	1	30	2,252
3rd Division (Abbé)	9	130	21	560	1	30	750
6th Division (Maransin)	11	105	34	783	—	126	1,059
Total d'Erlon's 'Centre'	33	426	120	3,295	2	185	4,062
Clausel's Wing							
4th Division (Conroux)	16	145	85	1,432	12	747	2,437
5th Division (Vandermaesen)	16	158	80	978	2	301	1,535
8th Division (Taupin)	6	125	38	1,007	—	26	1,202
Total Clausel's Wing	38	428	203	3,417	14	1,074	5,174
Cavalry	—	12	2	33	1	10	58
General Total of Army	*101*	*1,212*	*377*	*8,205*	*45*	*2,657*	*12,501*

Allied Forces The Marquess of Wellington commanding.

On 28 July the 3rd Division and the 7th Division were not engaged. **2nd Division** MG Sir Rowland Hill: 1/3rd, 1/57th, 1st Provisional Bn (1 bn each). **3rd Division** MG Sir Thomas Picton: 1/45th, 1/74th, 1/88th (1 bn each); 5/60th (4 coys). **4th Division** MG Sir G Lowry Cole: 3/27th, 1/40th, 1/48th; 2nd Provisional Bn (1 bn each). **Ross' Brigade***: 1/7th, 1/20th, 1/23rd (1 bn each); Brunswick Oel's (1 coy); **6th Division** MG Pack; Lambert's Brigade 1/11th, 1/32nd, 1/36th and 1/61st Foot. **Total on 28 July** ca 13,800 men. **Total on 30 July** ca 16,500 men.

Portuguese Troops present on 28 and 30 July A Campbell's Brigade: 4th and 10th LIR (2 bns each); 10th Caçadores (1 bn). Madden's Brigade: 8th and 12th LIR (2 bns each); 9th Caçadores (1 bn). Stubbs' Brigade: 11th and 23rd LIR (2 bns each); 7th Caçadores (1 bn). **Portuguese Troops present only on 30 July** Lecor's Brigade: 7th and 19th LIR (2 bns each); 2nd Caçadores (1 bn). Power's Brigade: 9th and 21st LIR (2 bns each); 11th Caçadores (1 bn). Present only at Buenza, 30 July: Da Costa's Brigade: 2nd and 14th LIR (2 bns each); Ashworth's Brigade: 6th and 18th LIR (2 bns each); 6th Caçadores (1 bn). Cavalry: BG d'Urban's Brigade: 1st, 11th and 12th CavRs ca 600 men. **Total on 28 July** ca 7,200 men. **Total on 30 July** ca 11,200.

Spanish Forces The Spanish divisions of O'Donnell and Morillo were present at the battle. IRs Principe and Pavia were heavily engaged and lost 190 killed and wounded. The Allies employed 36 guns in the battle.

* = engaged only on 28 July, NOT on 30 July.

French Forces at Beunza: GdD Abbé's Division: 5e RILé, 64e and 94e RIdLi (2 bns each); 27e RILé, 63e and 95e RIdLi (1 bn each).

French total at Buenza: 8,000 men.

French losses at Buenza: 750 killed and wounded.

British Forces engaged in the clash at Beunza (on the Allied left wing) 30 July 1813: 2nd Division MG Sir R Hill commanding: 1/50th, 1/71st, 1/92nd, 1/28th, 2/34th, 1/39th (1 bn each). MG V Alten's Lt Cav Bde: 14th LDR, 1st HusR KGL. **Total** ca 3,000 men.

Portuguese Forces at Beunza: Da Costa's Brigade: 2nd and 14th LIR (2 bns each).

Ashworth's Brigade: 6th and 18th LIR (2 bns each); 6th Caçadores (1 bn). **Total** ca 3,600 men.

Allied losses at Buenza British: 156 killed and

British Losses at Sorauren 28 July

	Killed		Wounded		Prisoners		
	Officers	Men	Officers	Men	Officers	Men	Total
2nd Division:							
Byng's Brigade1/3rd Foot	—	—	—	2	—	—	2
1/57th Foot	—	2	2	59	—	—	63
1st Provisional Batt.	—	—	1	4	—	—	5
(2/31st & 2/66th)							
2nd Division Total	—	*2*	*3*	*65*	—	—	*70*
3rd Division: no losses							
4th Division (Cole):							
Anson's Brigade							
3/27th Foot	2	41	9	195	—	7	254
1/40th Foot	1	19	4	105	—	—	129
1/48th Foot	2	10	8	104	—	11	135
2nd Provisional Batt							
2nd & 2/53rd	—	1	1	18	—	—	20
Ross's Brigade							
1/7th Foot	1	46	10	159	1	—	217
1/20th Foot	1	23	5	79	—	—	108
1/23rd Foot	2	16	4	59	—	—	81
1 company Brunswick Oels	—	1	—	3	—	1	5
4th Division Total	*9*	*157*	*41*	*722*	*1*	*19*	*949*
6th Division (Pack):							
Stirling's Brigade							
1/42nd Foot	—	3	—	19	—	—	22
1/79th Foot	—	4	1	30	—	—	35
1/91st Foot	—	12	6	92	—	2	112
1 company 5/60th	—	1	—	4	—	—	5
Lambert's Brigade							
1/11th Foot	—	5	4	42	—	—	51
1/32nd Foot	—	—	1	23	—	—	24
1/36th Foot	—	—	2	16	—	—	18
1/61st Foot	—	2	2	58	—	—	62
6th Division Total	—	*27*	*16*	*284*	—	*2*	*329*
Artillery	—	—	—	6	—	—	6
General Staff	2	—	2	—	—	—	4
Total British	11	184	59	1,012	1	21	1,288
Total Portuguese	3	160	45	850	—	44	1,102
General Total	14	344	104	1,862	1	65	2,390

British losses at second Sorauren 30 July

	Killed		Wounded		Prisoners		
	Officers	Men	Officers	Men	Officers	Men	Total
2nd Division:							
Byng's Brigade1/3rd Foot	1	3	1	25	—	—	30
1/57th Foot	—	2	2	33	—	—	37
1st Provisional Batt.							
2/31st & 2/66th	1	5	6	52	—	—	64
2nd Division Total	*2*	*10*	*9*	*110*	—	—	*131*
3rd Division (Picton):							
Brisbane's Brigade							
1/45th Foot	—	—	1	7	—	—	8
5/60th (4 companies)	—	2	1	28	—	—	31
1/74th Foot	1	6	4	38	—	—	49
1/88th Foot	—	—	—	1	—	—	1
3rd Division Total	*1*	*8*	*6*	*74*	—	—	*89*
Colville's Brigade: no casualties.							
4th Division (Cole):							
Anson's Brigade							
3/27th Foot	—	—	—	—	—	—	—
1/40th Foot	—	—	1	6	—	—	7
1/48th Foot	—	—	—	—	—	—	—
2nd Provisional Batt							
2nd & 2/53rd	—	—	—	6	—	—	6
Brigade Total	—	—	*1*	*12*	—	—	*13*
Ross's Brigade: no casualties.							
6th Division (Pakenham):							
Stirling's Brigade							
1/42nd Foot	—	1	—	7	—	—	8
1/79th Foot	—	1	—	17	—	—	18
1/91st Foot	—	1	1	7	—	—	9
Lambert's Brigade							
1/11th Foot	—	2	—	20	—	1	23
1/32nd Foot	—	3	2	28	—	—	33
1/36th Foot	—	6	1	19	—	—	26
1/61st Foot	—	1	2	10	—	—	13
4th Division Total	—	*15*	*6*	*108*	—	*1*	*130*
7th Division (Dalhousie):							
Barnes's Brigade							
1/6th Foot	—	—	1	5	—	1	7
3rdProvisional Batt.							
2/24th & 2/58th	—	1	—	2	—	—	3

	Killed		Wounded		Prisoners		
	Officers	Men	Officers	Men	Officers	Men	Total
Brunswick Oels							
(9 companies)	—	2	—	1	—	14	17
Inglis's Brigade							
51st Foot	—	2	—	22	—	—	24
68th Foot	1	3	3	16	—	—	23
1/82nd Foot	—	9	7	76	—	—	92
Chasseurs Britanniques	1	12	9	19	—	4	45
7th Division Totals	*2*	*29*	*20*	*141*	—	*19*	*211*
Artillery	—	1	—	8	—	—	9
General British Total	5	63	42	453	—	20	583

Combat of Beunza. 30 July

	Killed		Wounded		Prisoners		
	Officers	Men	Officers	Men	Officers	Men	Total
Fitzgerald's (late Cameron's) Brigade:							
1/50th	—	3	2	14	2	9	30
1/71st	—	8	1	28	—	13	50
1/92nd	—	9	1	26	—	1	37
Pringle's Brigade:							
1/28th	—	—	—	—	—	—	—
2/34th	1	5	1	15	—	9	31
1/39th	—	—	—	3	—	—	3
General Staff	—	—	1	—	—	—	1
Cavalry (14th Light Dragoons and 1st Hussars KGL)	—	—	1	2	—	2	5
Total	*1*	*25*	*7*	*88*	*2*	*34*	*157*

Portuguese losses in the battles of the Pyrenees

	Killed		Wounded		Prisoners		
	Officers	Men	Officers	Men	Officers	Men	Total
Da Costa's Brigade							
2nd Line	3	85	9	81	—	21	200
14th Line	1	23	5	36	—	19	84
All at Beunza, July 30							
Brigade Total	*4*	*108*	*14*	*117*	—	*40*	*283*
A Campbell's Brigade							
4th Line	2	24	7	78	—	3	114
10th Line	2	75	7	116	—	13	213
10th Caçadores	—	3	3	12	—	10	28
Almost all at two battles of Sorauren.							
Brigade Total	*4*	*102*	*17*	*206*	—	*26*	*355*

	Killed		Wounded		Prisoners		
	Officers	Men	Officers	Men	Officers	Men	Total
Ashworth's Brigade (2nd Division)							
6th Line	—	29	5	63	—	8	105
18th Line	1	51	4	82	—	12	150
6th Caçadores	1	13	1	37	—	10	62
All at Beunza, July 30							
Brigade Total	*2*	*93*	*10*	*182*	—	*30*	*317*
Lecor's Brigade (7th Division):							
7th Line	—	—	—	—	—	4	4
19th Line	—	—	2	—	—	—	2
2nd Caçadores	1	12	1	44	—	—	58
Almost all at 2nd Sorauren, July 30.							
Brigade Total	*1*	*12*	*3*	*44*	—	*4*	*64*
Madden's Brigade (6th Division):							
8th Line	—	—	—	3	—	—	3
12th Line	2	58	2	208	—	4	274
9th Caçadores	—	15	3	86	—	—	104
At the two battles of Sorauren.							
Brigade Total	*2*	*73*	*5*	*297*	—	*4*	*381*
Power's Brigade (3rd Division):							
9th Line	—	—	—	—	—	2	2
21st Line	—	5	—	9	—	—	14
11th Caçadores	—	1	—	5	—	—	6
All at 2nd Sorauren.							
Brigade Total	—	*6*	—	*14*	—	*2*	*22*
Stubbs' Brigade (4th Division):							
11th Line	1	34	1	105	—	1	142
23rd Line	1	17	6	26	—	—	50
7th Caçadores	2	47	5	67	—	—	121
At the two battles of Sorauren.							
Brigade Total	*4*	*98*	*12*	*198*	—	*1*	*313*
Total	17	492	61	1,058	—	107	1,735

wounded. Portuguese: 730 killed and wounded, 170 captured.

No artillery losses save those at the combat of Maya, which were about 15. No cavalry losses at all, though d'Urban's brigade was in the field at Sorauren.

Comment Soult's aggressive conduct was mainly induced by a wish to show Napoleon how much more effective a commander he was than his predecessors. In these actions his aim was to relieve Pamplona and to defeat the Allies. Happily, under Wellington's firm and careful management, he was defeated and fell back north into France again. The mountainous nature of the country here meant that cavalry involvement in these actions was negligible. Due to Soult's thoughtlessness, his artillery and cavalry were locked into a narrow mountain valley at the rear of his column and most of it could not be brought forward into action.

Wellington's artillery wrought havoc among the dense French assault columns as did the musketry of the Allied infantry deployed in two-deep line.

Sources Oman, Martinien.

EN Yanzi*, 1 August 1813, clash

A village and bridge in the western Spanish Pyrenees on a minor road along a river valley between Hendaye (in the north) to Sumbilla.

* nowadays Ventas de Yanci.

(Last action – Sorauren, 28 – 30 July; next action – Echalar, 2 August.)

French Forces The wreck of GdD Reille's 'Right Wing' retreating back into France after their defeat at Sorauren: 120e RIdLi (1er Bn). GdD Treilhard's Dragoons: 4e, 14e, 16e, 17e, 21e and 26e DragRs ca 2,300 cavalry. Lamartinière's Division (5 bns only); the wounded of the recent battle; the baggage train, the remnants of Maucune's 7th Division; GdD P Soult's cavalry: 5e, 10e and 21e ChàCh; Nassau ChàCh, ca 1,600 cavalry. d'Erlon's Corps of the Centre plus another baggage train, Clausel's 'Left Wing'.

French totals Impossible to state accurately, maybe 25,000. It was not an army but a mob of refugees.

French losses Killed and wounded unknown (possibly 500), over 1,000, mostly wounded from the last battle, were abandoned and captured.

Allied Forces Two Spanish bns (1 of Longa's division, 1 of Barsena's division). IR Asturias (1 bn). Later in the day, part of Alten's Light Division joined in the fight: 1 and 3/95th, 1/43rd, 1st Caçadores (1 bn each) and part of the 4th Division.

Allied totals ca 4,000 men.

Allied losses Spanish: Not known but light. Light Division: 1 officer, 15 men; 4th Division: 3 officers and 45 men killed and wounded.

Comment The retreating French were subject to severe harrying musketry from the far side of the valley as they fled northwards. In the utter chaos many regiments dissolved into mobs: it was every man for himself. Wellington had not expected this bad road to be used by Soult and neglected to block it effectively or to break the bridge. Treilhard's dragoons panicked and fled back south, crashing into Reille and his staff. It was weeks before the chaos of this action in the French army was fully sorted out.

Sources Oman, Martinien.

EN Echalar, 2 August 1813, clash

A hamlet in the Spanish west Pyrenean mountains, on a minor road close up to the French border, about 6 km east of Yanzi.

(Last action – Yanzi, 1 August; next action – San Sebastián, 31 August.)

French Forces The disorganized wrecks of Soult's beaten army. Conroux's 4th Division: 12e RILé, 32e, 43e, 45e, 55e and 58e RIdLi; GdD Lamartinière's 9th Division 2e RILé, 118e, 119e, 120e and 122e RidLi.

French total Impossible to say; probably only about 30% of their start-out strength of 14,200 men.

French losses ca 300 men.

Allied Forces The Marquess of Wellington commanding: 4th Division Gen Cole: Ross's Brigade: 1/7th, 1/20th, 1/23rd. 7th Division Gen Dalhousie: 1/6th, 3rd Provisional Bn (2/24th and 2/58th) 1 bn each; Brunswick Oels (9 coys). Light Division Gen Alten: 95th (5 coys).

Allied total ca 6,000 men.

Allied losses at Echalar

	Killed		Wounded		Prisoners		
	Officers	Men	Officers	Men	Officers	Men	Total
General Staff	—	—	1	—	—	—	1
4th Division:							
Ross's Brigade							
1/7th Foot	—	—	—	4	—	—	4
1/20th Foot	1	—	3	26	—	—	30
1/23rd Foot	—	—	—	3	—	—	3
7th Division:							
Barnes's Brigade							
1/6th Foot	1	12	3	119	—	8	143

3rd Provisional Batt.	—	15	9	115	—	2	141
Brunswick Oels	—	1	4	7	—	2	14
Light Division:							
1/43rd	—	—	—	1	—	—	1
1/95th	—	1	1	10	—	—	12
3/95th	—	1	—	18	—	—	19
Total	2	30	21	303	—	7	368

Sources Oman, Martinien

SX Pirna, 22 August 1813, clash

A village in the northeastern German state of Saxony, on the right bank of the River Elbe, about 8 km southeast of Dresden.

A Russian victory over the French.

(Last action - Luckau, 4 June; next action - Gross-Beeren, 23 August.)

French Forces.

M Gouvion St Cyr commanding the **XIV Corps** 42nd Division GdD Dupas: 9e, 10e, 11e and 12e RILé (1 bn each). 43rd Division GdD Claparède: 27e, 45e, 65e, 95e, 100e and 103e RidLi.

I Cavalry Corps GdD Latour-Maubourg: 1st Light Cavalry Division GdD Bourcier: 3e ChLL. 3rd Light Cavalry Division GdD Chastel: 2e ChàCh.

III Cavalry Corps GdD Arrighi, Duke of Padua: 4th Division GdD Defrance: 15e, 18e, 19e DragRs. 1st Division GdD Fournier: 26e ChàCh.

IV Cavalry Corps GdD Kellermann: 3rd Division GM Normann: 1st and 2nd Württemberg JzPfRs. The following units also show officer casualties for this action: 21e and 24e RILé; 33e, 59e RidLi.

French total ca 28,000 men.

French losses Not exactly known, light.

Russian Forces GdK Count Wittgenstein:

II Corps GL Prince Eugen von Württemberg: 3rd Division GM Prince Schachafskoi: IRs Murom, Reval, Tchernigov, Selenginsk, 20th Jägers (2 bns each); 21st Jägers (1 bn). 4th Division GM Pischnitzky: IRs Tobolsk, Volhynien, Krementchug, 4th Jägers (2 bns each); 34th Jägers (1 bn). 1 x light and 1 x heavy FAB.

Cavalry GM Millesinov: GM Illowaisky XII: Cossack Pulks of Illowaisky XII, Radionov II, Ataman. 1st Hussar Division GL Count Pahlen III: Grodno HusR (6 sqns); Ssum HusR (7 sqns); Olviopol HusR (2 sqns); Lubny HusR (4 sqns).

Russian total ca 30,000 men.

Russian losses Not known but light.

Comment The French were pushed back to Dresden; the Russians did not follow up too closely.

Sources Plotho, Sporschil, Martinien.

SX Gross-Beeren, 23 August 1813, clash

A village in northeastern Germany, 17 km south of Berlin on Route B101, north of the Autobahn A10/E30/E55.

A Prusso-Russian victory over the French and their Allies.

(Last action - Pirna, 22 August; next action - Katzbach, 26 August.)

Franco-Allied Forces M Oudinot commanding:

IV Corps GdD Bertrand commanding: 15th Division (Italians) GdD Count Fontanelli: 4th LIR (3 bns), 1 x FAB.

VII Corps GdD Count Reynier: 24th Division (Saxons) GL von Lecoq: Leib Gren Garde (1 bn); Combined IR (Prinz Maximilian(1st Bn); von Rechten (2 Bn); LtIR von Lecoq (2 bns); Gren Bn von Spiegel (1 bn); IR Prinz Friedrich August (2 bns); IR Steindel (2 bns). 2 x FAB. 25th Division (Saxons) GL von Sahr: Gren Bn von Anger (1 bn); Combined IR (IR König(1st Bn); IR von Niesemeuschel (2nd Bn); LtIR von Sahr (2 bns); IRs Prinz Anton and von Low (2 bns each). 2 x FAB. 32nd Division GdD Durutte: 35e RILé (1er Bn); 131e and 132e RIdLi (3e and 4e bns each); 36e RILé (4e Bn); 133e RIdLi (3e and 4e Bns); IR Würzburg (2nd and 3rd Bns). 2 x FAB. 26th Light Cavalry Brigade (Saxons) GM von Gablenz: HusR (8 sqns); UlR Prinz Clemens (5 sqns). 1 x HAB.

Franco-Allied totals 32 bns, 13 sqns, 8 batteries, ca 22,000 men, 48 guns.

Franco-Allied losses 1,700 killed and wounded, 1,500 captured, 14 guns, 58 ammunitions waggons. The Saxons lost 2,100 killed, wounded and missing.

Prussian Forces III Corps GL von Bülow commanding (part of the Army of the North); complete with losses for all actions from 21 to 23 August (Mölln, Nussdorf, Willmersdorf, Wittstock (now Wietstock) and Gross Beeren.

	Killed Officers	Wounded Men	Missing Horses
3rd Brigade			
GM Prince Ludwig von Hessen-Homburg			
2nd Ostpr. Gren Bn (1 bn)	2	80	—
3rd Ostpr IR (2 bns)	6	211	—
4th Res IR (3 bns)	3	102	—
3rd Ostpr LWIR (4 bns)	—	52	—
1st Leib HusR (4 sqns)	—	49	53
4th Brigade			
GM von Thümen			
4th Ostpr IR (3 bns)	3	59	—
5th Res IR (3 bns)	5	238	—
Elb-IR (2nd Bn)	—	54	—
Ostpr Jägers (2 coys)	—	5	—
Pomm NKR (4 sqns)	2	18	—
5th Brigade GM von Borstell			
1st Pomm IR (Füs bn)	—	7	—
Pomm HusR (4 sqns)	1	4	23
6th Brigade Obst von Krafft			
Colberg IR (3 bns)	2	59	—
9th Res IR (3 bns)	1	13	—
1st Neumark LWIR (2nd and 4th bns)	8	375	—
1st Pomm LWKR (3 sqns)	—	13	13
Cavalry Reserve GM von Oppen			
Brand DragR (4 sqns)	1	56	87
DragR Königin (4 sqns)	5	31	43
Westpr UlR (4 sqns)	—	17	18
2nd Pomm LWKR (4 sqns)	—	2	3
4th Kurmark LWKR (4 sqns)	—	8	13
2nd Kurmark LWKR (4 sqns)	7	25	56
Prussian Artillery			
2 x 12 pdr, 4 x 6 pdr FABs, 3 x 6 pdr HABs, pioniers (2 coys)	1	49	47
Russian Artillery 2 x heavy FABs	1	24	27
TOTALS	48	1,551	383

Also the Don Cossack Pulks of Bychalov II and Illowaisky V.

III Corps totals 30 bns, 4 coys, 39 sqns, 11 batteries, 2 Pulks.

The Swedish Corps FM Count Stedingk commanding: **1st Division** GM von Posse; GM Schulzenheim: Svea Life Guards, 2nd Life Guards, Gren Life Guards (1 bn each). GM Lagebring: IRs Upland, Södermannland (2 bns each); Nord Schonen (1 bn); Pomm Legion (1 coy). Life Guard DragR (5 sqns); Pomm Legion (1 sqn). 2 x 6 pdr FABs.

2nd Division GL Sandels: GM Reuterskjöld: IRs Westgotha, Westmannland, Nerike (2 bns each). GM Boije: IRs Skaraborg, Elfsborg (2 bns each), Kronoberg, Calmar (1 bn each), Wermland Feldjägers (1 bn). 2 x 6 pdr FAB. GL Skjöldebrand: Life-KürR (4 sqns); Schonen HusR (6 sqns); Mörner HusR (5 sqns); Smöland DragR (6 sqns). 1 x HAB. Artillery Reserve: 1 x 12 pdr and 1 x 6 pdr FAB. **Total** 23 bns, 1 coy, 27 sqns, 7 batteries, ca 16,650 men, 46 guns. Attached Don Cossack Pulk of Rebrejev (360 men).

IV (Prussian Corps) GL Count von Tauentzien: GM Count Lindenau: 3rd ResIR (4 bns); 1st Kurmark LWIR (3 bns); 2nd Neumark LWIR, 5th Kurmark LWIR, 2nd Schl LWIR (4 bns each), 1st Schl LWIR (1 bn). Cossack Pulk of GM Mowaisky III; 2nd Neumark LWKR (2 sqns); 3rd Neumark, 2nd and 3rd Ostpr LWKRs (4 sqns each); 1st and 7th Kurmark LWKR and 3rd Pomm LWKRs (4 sqns each). ½ x 6 pdr British FAB, 1 x 6 pdr British HAB, 1 x heavy 6 pdr FAB; ½ x light 6 pdr FAB, ½ x 8 pdr FAB. Losses - not known exactly but light.

Comment The battle was fought by the allied Prussians and Swedes in defence of Berlin. It took place in two locations about 5 km apart: Gross-Beeren - the Swedes and the III Prussian Corps against the Saxons of the VII Corps and, at Blankenfelde to the east, the IV Prussian Corps against Bertrand's IV French Corps. There was very little action at Blankenfelde. Oudinot's XII Corps came up from the west to aid the Saxons but were too late to intervene.

Sources Plotho, Sporschil, Martinien, Grosch/Hagen/Schenk.

IN Villach, 24 August 1813, clash

A town in southeastern Austria, on the River Drau (then in French-occupied Illyria) close to the borders of Italy and Slovenia (ex-Yugoslavia) and at the junction of Routes 100/E14, 83, 93 and A2/E7.

An Austrian victory over the Franco-Italians.

(This was the opening action of the campaign in northern Italy; next action - Villach, 28/29 August.)

Franco-Italian Forces GdB Piat (of 3rd Division) commanding: 35e RILé (2 bns); 36e RILé (1 bn).

Franco-Italian total ca 3,000 men.

Franco-Italian losses 189 dead, 320 wounded, 95 captured (98 badly wounded were also abandoned).

Austrian Forces GM Vlasitch (of FML Frimont's division) commanding: GzIR Peterwardeiner Nr 9 (3 coys). 4 guns. Stipsic HusR Nr 10 (1 sqn).

Austrian total ca 500 men.

Austrian losses 18 killed, 63 wounded, 170 missing.

Comment The bridge over the River Drau in Villach was a key point in this campaign and originally held by the French under Col Duché. For unknown reasons he abandoned the town. In trying to recover the bridge, the French suffered very badly from canister from the Austrian artillery as they rushed it in column.

Sources Wrede, Vaudoncourt, Martinien, HGM 56.

SX Katzbach River (now The Kaczawa), 26 August 1813, battle

A tributary of the River Oder in Prussian Silesia (now Poland) between Liegnitz and Goldberg (now Legnica and Jelenia Gora).

A Prusso-Russian victory over the French and their Allies.

(Last action - Gross-Beeren, 23 August; next action - Dresden, 26/27 August.)

French and Allied Forces M Macdonald commanding 'The Army of the Bober'.

XI Corps 21st Division GdD Gérard: Westfalians BG Hannstein: 4th LIR (4 bns); 8th LIR (2 bns); 2nd LtI Bn (1 bn). 36th Division GdD Charpentier: 3e, 14e and 22e RILé, 10e RIdLi. 35th Division (Italians) GdD Fressinet: 2nd and 5th LIRs, 6th and 112e French RIdLi.

V Corps GdD Count Lauriston: 16th Division GdD Maison: 152e, 153e, 154e RIdLi. 19th Division GdD Rochambeau: 149e, 150e, 155e RIdLi. From M Ney's III Corps: 8th Division GdD Souham 22e RIdLi, 14e PvLi (34e and 40e RIdLi); 19e PvLi (32e and 58e); 21e PvLi (59e and 69e); 24e PvLi (88e, 103e). The 138e RIdLi of Delmas' 9th Division was also present.

II Cavalry Corps GdD Sebastiani: 2nd Light Cavalry Division GdD Roussel d'Hurbal: 5e and 9e HusRs, 11e and 12e ChàCh, 2e and 4e ChLL. 4th Light Cavalry Division GdD Exelmans: 11e HusR, 6e ChLL, 4e, 20e, 23e and 24e ChàCh. The 10e HusR also reported officer casualties here this day. Total ca 35,000 men, 170 guns.

French and Allied losses 12,000 killed and wounded, 18,000 captured, 105 guns, 300 ammunition waggons, 2 eagles, possibly of the 59e Li but details are not clear.

Russo-Prussian Forces GdK von Blücher commanding the Army of Silesia.

I (Prussian) Corps GL York: 1st Brigade, Obst von Steinmetz: Grenadiers (3 bns); Ostpr Jägers (2 coys); 5th and 13th Schl LWIRs (4 and 2 bns resp); 2nd Leib-HusR (4 sqns), 1 x 6 pdr FAB. 2nd Brigade GM Prinz Carl von Mecklenburg-Strelitz: 1st and 2nd Ostpr IRs (3 bns each); 6th Schl LWIR (3 bns); Mecklenburg-Strelitz HusR (4 sqns); 1 x 6 pdr FAB. 7th Brigade GM von Horn: Leib-IR (3 bns); Thüringians (1 bn); Garde-Jägers (2 coys); 15th Schl LWIR (4 bns); Brand HusR (2 sqns); 3rd Schl LWKR (2 sqns); 1 x 6 pdr FAB. 8th Brigade GM von Hünerbein: Brand IR; 12th Res IR (3 bns each); 14th Schl LWIR (4 bns); Brand HusR (2 sqns); 3rd Schl LWKR (2 sqns); 1 x 6 pdr FAB. Reserve Cavalry: GM von Jürgass: 1st Westpr DragR, Lith DragR, Brand UlR, Ostpr NKR, 1st Neumark LWKR, 5th and 10th Schl LWKRs (all 4 sqns each). 2 x HAB. Reserve Artillery: 2 x 12 pdr FAB, 2 x 6 pdr FAB, 1 x 3 pdr FAB, 2 x HAB.

The XI (Russian) Corps GL Baron Sacken: 10th Division GM Count Liewen III: IRs Jaroslav, Bialystock, 8th and 39th Jägers (2 bns each); IRs Kursk and Crimea (1 bn each). 16th Division GM Reppinsky: IRs Ochotsk and Kamchatka (2 bns each). 27th Division Obst Stavitski: IRs Odessa, Wilna, 49th and 50th Jägers (2 bns each), IRs Teraspol and Simbirsk (1 bn each). 2 x heavy, 2 x light FABs. **Cavalry Corps** GL Baron Vassilitschkov: From the 3rd Dragoon Division GM Pantschulidsev: DragRs Kurland and Smolensk (2 sqns each). 2nd Hussar Division GM Landskoi: HusRs Achtyrsk, Mariupol, Alexandria and White Russia (4 sqns each), 1 x HAB. Light Cavalry GM Karpov II: Cossack Pulks of 4th Ukraine, Karpov II, Lukovkin, Tscharnusubov V, Kutainikov IV, Sementschenkov, Grekov VIII and St Petersburg Volunteers.

GdI Count Langeron's VI Corps GM Prince Scherbatov: 7th Division GM Tallisin I: IRs Pskov,

Moscow, Libau, 11th Jägers (2 bns each); IR Sophia, 36th Jägers (1 bn each). 18th Division GM Bernodossov: IRs Vladimir, Dnieprov, Tambov, Kostroma, 28th and 32nd Jägers (1 bn each); 1 x heavy FAB, 2 x light FABs.

IX Corps GL Alsufiev 9th Division GM Udom II: IRs Nascheburg, Yakutsk, 10th and 38th Jägers (1 bn each); IRs Apscheron and Riask (2 bns each). 15th Division GM Rudsevitch: IRs Witebsk, Klasovsk, Kolivan, 22nd Jägers (1 bn each); IRs Kurinsk and 12 th Jägers (2 bns each); 1 x heavy FAB, 2 x light FABs.

X Corps GL Kapzewitsch 8th Division GM Prince Urusov: IRs Archangel, Old Ingermannland, 37th Jägers (2 bns each); Schlüsselburg and 7th Jägers (1 bn each). 22nd Division GM Turtschaninov: IRs Viatka, Staroskol, 29th Jägers (2 bns each); IR Olonetz, 45th Jägers (1 bn each); 1 x heavy FAB, 2 x light FABs.

I Cavalry Corps GL Baron Korff: From the 3rd Dragoon Division: GM Berdäev: DragRs Tver and Kinburn (2 sqns each). 1st Mounted Rifle Division GM Pantschulidsev I: Tchernigov MtdRR (3 sqns); Sievsk MtdRR (2 sqns); Arsamas MtdRR (1 sqn). From the 2nd Mounted Rifle Division GM Count Pahlen II: Lifland and Dorpat MtdRRs (2 sqns each); 2 x HAB. Light Cavalry GM Grekov VIII: GM Count Witte: 1st, 2nd and 3rd Ukrainian Cossack Pulks (3 sqns each); Cossack Pulks of Kutainikov VIII, Selwanov II, Isaef II, Zikelef I, the Teptar Cossack Pulk. Reserve Artillery: 1 x heavy FAB, 1 x light FAB, pontonniers (2 coys), pioniers (1 coy); 75th Marine or ship coy.

GL Count St Priest's VIII Corps 11th Division GM Prince Gurgalov: IRs Jeletz, Polotsk, Ekaterinburg, Rijlsk, 1st and 3rd Jägers (2 bns each). 17th Division GM Pillar: IRs Riasan, Bielosersk (2 bns each); Brest, Wilmannstrand, 30th and 48th Jägers (1 bn each), 1 x heavy FAB, 2 x light FABs. 1st Dragoon Division GM Barasdin: Kargopol DragR (4 sqns), Mitau DragR (5 sqns), Moscow Dragoons (3 sqns), New Russia DragR (4 sqns). From the 4th DragR GM Emanuel: DragRs Kharkov and Kiev (5 sqns each). Cossack Pulks of Grekov XXI, Grekov III, Stavropol Kalmuck R, 3rd Black Sea Cossack R.

Allied total ca 86,000 men (39,000 were Prussians).

Allied losses The Prussians lost 1,000 killed and wounded, the Russians about 3,000 killed and wounded.

Comment Blücher saw a chance to inflict a defeat on the French when Macdonald's columns became too scattered and seized it with both hands. The French broke and fled off the plateau and tried to cross the raging River Neisse where hundreds of them drowned and much artillery was abandoned. The pouring rain made musketry on both sides ineffective. This was mainly a cavalry combat. The flooded rivers caused the destruction of GdD Puthod's 17th Division at Plagwitz on 29 August.

Sources Plotho, Sporschil, Martinien, von Kausler.

SX Dresden, 26 and 27 August 1813, battle

Capital city of the kingdom of Saxony, on the left bank of the River Elbe and at the junction of Routes B6, B97, B170/E55 and B173.

A French and Allied victory over the Allies (Prussians, Russians and Austrians).

(Last action – Katzbach, 26 August; next action – Hagelberg, 27 August.)

French Forces Emperor Napoleon I commanding.

1st Division of the Old Guard GdD Count Friant: GdB Christiani: 2e ChàP (2 bns). GdB Baron Michel: 1er and 2e Gren à P (2 bns each), 1 x FAB. **2nd Division of the Old Guard** GdD Baron Curial: GdB Rousseau: Fus Gren (2 bns), 1 x FAB.

I Corps of the Young Guard M Oudinot Duke of Reggio: 1st Division GdD Dumoustier: GdB Lacoste 1er, 2e, 3e, 6e Voltigeurs (2 bns each). GdB Couloumy: 7e and 11e Voltigeurs (2 bns each). 3rd Division GdD Decouz: GdB Boyer de Rebeval: 4e, 5e, 8e Voltigeurs (2 bns each). GdB Pelet: 9e and 10e Voltigeurs (2 bns each), 3 x FAB.

II Corps of the Young Guard M Mortier Duke of Treviso. 2nd Division GdD Barrois: GdB Poret de Morvan: 1er, 2e, 3e Tirailleurs (2 bns each). GdB Dulong: 6e Tirailleurs (2 bns), 3 x FAB. 4th Division GdD Roguet: GdB Flamand: Flanqueur Grenadiers, Flanqueur-Chasseurs, 5e Tirailleurs (2 bns each). GdB Marquet: 8e, 9e, 10e Tirailleurs (2 bns each), 3 x FAB.

Cavalry of the Guard GdD Count Nansouty: 1st Division GdD Count Walter, GdB Baron Lyon: 1er ChLL (3 sqns).

II Corps M Victor, Duke of Belluno. 4th Division GdD Dubreton: GdB Ferrière: 24e RILé. 19e RIdLi (3 bns each). GdB Brun: 37e, 56e RIdLi (3 bns each), 2 x FAB. 6th Division GdD Vial; GdB Valory: 11e RILé, 93e

RIdLi (3 bns each). GdB Bronikowski: 4e RIdLi (3 bns), 2 x FAB. 8th Division GdD Baron Brayer; 10e PvLé (16e and 25e RILé - 1 bn each); 14e PvLi (34e and 40e RIdLi - 1 bn each). 19e PvLi (32e and 58e RIdLi - 1 bn each). GdB Charrière: 21e PvLi (59e and 69e RIdLi - 1 bn each), 24e PvLi (88e and 103e RIdLi - 1 bn each), 2 x FAB. 9th Division GdD Delmas: GdB d'Anthing: 2e PvLé (2e and 4e RILé - 3e Bns each). 29e RILé (2 bns). 11th Division GdD Baron Ricard; GdB Van der Gelder: 17e PvLi (43e and 75e RIdLi - 1 bn each); 50e RIdLi (2 bns), 65e RIdLi (1 bn). 1 x FAB.

VI Corps M Marmont, Duke of Ragusa: 20th Division GdD Count Compans; GdB Pelleport: 32e RILé (2e and 3e Bns); 1er Naval IR (5 bns). 21st Division GdD Count Lagrange: GdB Baron Jamin: 37e RILé (4 bns); 4e Naval IR (3 bns). 1 x FAB.

XIV Corps M St Cyr: 42nd Division GdD Dupas: 40e RIdLi. 43rd Division GdD Claparède: 27e RILé; 45e, 95e, 100e RIdLi. 44th Division GdD Serrurier: 18e RILé (1 bn); 24e, 51e, 95e RIdLi (1 bn each). 45th Division: 11e, 60e RIdLi. The following regiments also show officer casualties for Dresden: 13e, 15e and 26e Le; 17e, 21e, 25e, 33e, 51e, 57e and 94e Li but it is not clear with which divisions they fought.

I Cavalry Corps GdD Count Latour-Maubourg: 1st Light Cavalry Division GdD Corbineau: 1st Brigade GdB Baron Piré: 6e HusR (2 sqns). 2nd Brigade GdB Count Montmarie: 1er and 8e ChLL (2 sqns each), 2 x HAB. 1st Heavy Cavalry Division GdD Count Bordesoulle: 1st Brigade GdB Sopranski: 2e and 3e CuirRs (2 sqns each); 9e CuirR (2 sqns). 2nd Brigade GdB Bessières: 11e and 12e CuirRs (3 and 2 sqns resp). 2 x HAB. 3rd Heavy Cavalry Division GdD Baron Doumerc, GdB Baron d'Audenarde: 4e and 7e CuirRs (3 sqns each). GdB Baron Reizet: 7e DragR (2 sqns); 23e DragR (3 sqns); 28e and 30e DragRs (2 sqns each), 2 x HAB.

V Cavalry Corps GdD Pajol: 9th Light Cavalry Division GdD Subervie: GdB Klicky: 27e ChàCh (4 sqns). GdB Vial: 26e ChàCh (3 sqns). 6th Heavy Cavalry Division GdD Milhaud: 19e DragR (2 sqns).

II Cavalry Corps GdD Count Sebastiani: 2nd Heavy Cavalry Division GdD St Germain; GdB Baron Davrauge: 1er and 2e Carabiniers (2 sqns each). The following cavalry regiments also reported officer casualties for this action: 7e ChLL, 3e, 6e and 7e ChàCh, 14e HusR; Italian Dragone Napoleone, 1st and 2nd Italian ChàCh and the Neapolitan 2nd ChàCh.

French totals ca 155,000 men.

French losses Sources vary widely; generally agreed to be at least 10,000 men. GdB Combelle was killed.

Austro-Prussian Austrian FM Prinz Schwarzenberg commanding:

Austrians 1st Light Division FML Prince Moritz Liechtenstein: GM Count Hardegg: Jägers Nr 1 and 2 (1 bn each); ChLR Kaiser Nr 1 (6 sqns), 1 x 6 pdr HAB. GM Baron Scheither: Jäger Nr 7 (1 bn); GzIR Broder Nr 7 (1 bn); ChLR Vincent Nr 4 (6 sqns), 1 x 6 pdr HAB.

The Right Wing Prince of Hessen-Homburg: FML Count Civalart: GM Baron Quosdanovich: IRs Gyulai Nr 21 (2 bns); Reuss-Plauen Nr 17 (1 bn); 1 x 6 pdr FAB. GM von Giffing: IRs Strauch Nr 24 and Bellegarde Nr 44 (2 bns each), 1 x 6 pdr FAB. GM Baron Reichlin-Meldegg: IR Weidenfeld Nr 37 (2 bns), 1 x 6 pdr FAB. FML Count Colloredo: GM Chiese: IRs de Vaux Nr 25 and Froon Nr 54 (2 bns each), 1 x 6 pdr FAB. GM Drechsel: IRs Erbach Nr 42, Argenteau Nr 35 (2 bns each), 1 x 6 pdr FAB. GM Andrásy: IRs Czartoryski Nr 9 and de Ligne Nr 30 (2 and 3 bns resp).

Reserve Division FML Baron Bianchi: GM Prince Philipp von Hessen-Homburg: IRs Hiller Nr 2, Colloredo Nr 33 (2 bns each), 1 x 6 pdr FAB. GM Mariassy: IRs Simbschen Nr 48, Hessen-Homburg Nr 19 (2 bns each). Reserve Grenadier Division FML Marquis Chasteler: GM Freiherr Koller: Gren Bns Obermayer, Czarnotzky, Berger, Oklopsia. GM Count Murray: Gren Bns Habinay, Portner, Fischer, Rüber; 1 x 6 pdr FAB. GM von Qualenberg: IRs Esterházy Nr 32, Davidovich Nr 34 (2 bns each), 1 x 6 pdr FAB. Reserve Division of FML Count Crenneville: GM von Greth: GzIRs Warasdiner-Creuzer Nr 5, Warasdiner-St Georger Nr 6, Gradiskaner Nr 8, Deutsch-Banater Nr 12, Wallachisch-Illyrisch Nr 13 (1 bn each), 1 x 6 pdr FAB. GM von Paumgarten: ChLRs Klenau Nr 5 and Rosenberg Nr 6 (6 sqns each). Cavalry Division of FML Count Nostitz: GM Baron Rothkirch: KürRs EH Franz Nr 2, Ferdinand Nr 4 (4 sqns each). GM Kroyher: KürR Hohenzollern Nr 8 (4 sqns). Division of FML von Schneller; GM von Zechmeister: ChLRs O'Reilly Nr 3 (4 sqns); Hohenzollern Nr 2 (5 sqns). GM Prince Gustav von Hessen-Homburg: HusRs Hessen-Homburg Nr 4, Kienmayer Nr 8 (6 sqns each). Pioniers (8 coys), pontonniers (1 coy).

Left Wing FZM Count Ignaz Gyulai: FML Prince Aloys

Liechtenstein: GM von Seethal: IR Kaunitz Nr 20 (2 bns), 1 x 6 pdr FAB. GM Baron von Mecsery: IRs Reuss-Greitz Nr 18, Vogelsang Nr 47 (2 bns each), 1 x 6 pdr FAB. FML Count Weissenwolf: GM Baron Czollich: IRs Kaiser Nr 1, Kottulinsky Nr 41 (3 bns each), 1 x 6 pdr FAB. GM Grimmer: IRs Fröhlich Nr 28, Kollowrath Nr 36 (1 and 2 bns resp), 1 x 6 pdr FAB. GM Baron Herzogenberg: IRs Würzburg Nr 7 (2nd Bn), EH Ludwig Nr 8 (2 bns), 1 x 6 pdr FAB.

Cavalry Division of FML Baron Lederer: Obst Count Desfours: KürR Kaiser Nr 1 (4 sqns). GM Count Raigecourt: DragRs Levenehr Nr 4 (4 sqns); Riesch Nr 6 (6 sqns), Pioniers (8 coys).

Corps of GdK Count Klenau Light Division: GM Baumgarten: GzIRs Deutsch-Banater Nr 12, Wallachisch-Illyrisch Nr 13 (1 bn each); HusR Palatinal Nr 12 (6 sqns); 1 x 3 pdr FAB. GM Szeckzen: HusR EH Franz Nr 3 (6 sqns). Division of FML Metzko: GM von Muhlheim: IRs EH Rainer Nr 11, Lusignan Nr 16 (2 bns each); IR Beaulieu Nr 58 (2 bns). 1 x 6 pdr FAB. Division of FML Prince Hohenlohe-Bartenstein: GM von Schäffer: IRs Zach Nr 15, J Colloredo Nr 57 (2 bns each), 1 x 6 pdr FAB. GM Baron von Splényi: IRs Lindenau Nr 29, Württemberg Nr 38 (2 bns each), 1 x 6 pdr FAB. GM Czerwenka: IRs Kerpen Nr 49, St Julien Nr 61 (2 bns each), 1 x 6 pdr FAB. Cavalry of GM von Ehrengreiff: KürR Lothringen Nr 7 (4 sqns). Artillery Reserve - 18 batteries, 108 guns.

Austrian total ca 100,000 men.

II (Prussian) Corps of GL von Kleist: 9th Brigade GM von Klüx: 1st Westpr IR (3 bns); 6th Res IR (3 bns); Schl Schützen (2 coys); 7th Schl LWIR (4 bns); Neumark DragR (4 sqns); 1 x 6 pdr FAB. 10th Brigade GM Pirch I: 2nd Westpr IR (3 bns); 7th Res IR (3 bns); 9th Schl LWIR (4 bns); Schl LWKR (4 sqns); 1 x 6 pdr FAB. 11th Brigade GM von Ziethen: 1st Schl IR (3 bns); 10th Res IR (3 bns); Schl Schützen (2 coys); 8th Schl LWIR (4 bns); 1st Schl HusR (4 sqns); 1 x 6 pdr FAB. 12th Brigade: GL Prinz August von Preussen: 2nd Schl IR (3 bns); 11th Res IR (3 bns); 10th Schl LWIR (4 bns); 1st Schl LWKR (4 sqns); 1 x 6 pdr FAB. Reserve Cavalry GM von Röder: Ostpr KürR, Schl KürR, Brand KürR (4 sqns each). Schl UlR (4 sqns); Schl NKR (2 sqns); 2nd Schl HusR (2 sqns); 7th and 8th Schl LWKRs (4 sqns each); 2 x HAB. Reserve Artillery Obstlt von Braun: 2 x 12 pdr FABs, 3 x 6 pdr FABs, 1 x 7 pdr howitzer FAB, 2 x HAB.

Russian Corps of GdK Count Wittgenstein I Corps GL Prince Gortschakov: 5th Division GM Mesenzov: IRs Perm, Kaluga, 23rd and 24th Jägers (2 bns each); IRs Mohilev, Sievsk and the Grand Princess Catharina (1 bn each). 14th Division GM Helfreich: IRs Tenginsk, Estonia, 25th and 26th Jägers (2 bns each); 1 x heavy and 1 x light FAB.

II Corps Prince Eugen von Württemberg: 3rd Division GM Prince Schachafskoi: IRs Murom, Reval, Selenginsk, Tchernigov, 21st Jägers (2 bns each); 20th Jägers (1 bn). 4th Division: GM Pischnitzky: IRs Tobolsk, Wolhynien, Krementchug, 4th Jägers (2 bns each). IR Minsk, 34th Jägers (1 bn each), 1 x heavy and 1 x light FABs.

Cavalry Corps GL Count Pahlen III: GM Illowaisky XII: Cossack Pulks of Illowaisky XII, Radionov II, Ataman. 1st Hussar Division GM Count Pahlen III: Grodno HusR (6 sqns); Ssum HusR (7 sqns); Olviopol HusR (2 sqns); Lubny HusR (4 sqns). GM Lissanevitch: Tartar UlR (4 sqns); Tchuguchev UlR (6 sqns); Serpuchov UlR (4 sqns). 1st Grenadier Division. GM Sulima: Gren Rs Ekaterinoslav, Arakcheyev, Tauride, Pernau and Rexholm (2 bns each). 2nd Guards Division GM Udom I: Lithuanian and Finland Life Guards (3 bns each); Life Guard GrenR, Pavlovsky GrenR (2 bns each), 1 x heavy and 2 x light Guards FABs.

Allied totals ca 200,000 men.

Allied losses There is great unclarity about the losses in this battle. The Austrians lost about 13,000 men captured when General Metzko's division of 5 infantry regiments was surrounded and captured by Murat's cavalry. About 10,000 Allied troops were killed and wounded. Russian generals Moreau, Luckow and Millesinov and Austrian General von Andrásy were killed. The French took 40 guns and 15 colours. (Metzko's division).

Comment Napoleon was defending the city of Dresden and was able to make best use of the defences and the interior lines at his disposal.

Sources Plotho, Sporschil, Wrede, Martinien.

SX Hagelberg, 27 August 1813, clash

A village in northeastern Germany, 50 km southwest of Potsdam, just north of Route B246 and 5 km west of Belzig. Known to the French as 'Lübnitz', a hamlet 5 km north of Hagelberg.

A Prussian victory over the French.

(Last action - Dresden, 26/27 August; next action - Pirna, 27/28 August.)

French Forces GdD Baron Girard commanding: 18e, 56e and 72e RIdLi; 1st Croatian IR, 1er Carabiniers, 13e HusR (4 sqns); 4 x march sqns.

French total ca 10,000 men, 22 guns.

French losses 2,000 killed and wounded; (GdB Baville killed); 140 officers, 2,000 men surrendered to the Prussians with 5 guns and 2 howitzers, a further 1,700 with 1 gun and 3 ammunition waggons were taken by Tschernitcheff's Cossacks. The division was effectively destroyed.

Prussian Forces The Corps of Magdeburg and the Lower Elbe of the Army of the North. GM von Puttlitz, GM von Hirschfeldt: 1st Res IR (3 bns); 3rd Kurmark LWIR (2 bns); 4th Kurmark LWIR (3 bns); 6th Kurmark LWIR (4 bns); 7th Kurmark LWIR (2 bns); Elb IR (4th Bn). Cavalry Obst von Bismark: 3rd, 5th and 6th Kurmark LWKRs (4 sqns each); 10 x Russian, 1 x Prussian guns.

Prussian total ca 16,000 men.

Prussian losses 39 officers, 67 NCOs, 913 men killed and wounded.

Tschernitcheff's Cossacks Lt Col Prince Lapuchin: Pulks of Illowaisky IV and Diätschkin. GM Illowaisky IV; Pulks of Vlassov III, Balabin II and Rebrikov II, Col Melnikov V; Pulks of Melnikov IV and Melnikov V; Col Benkendorf; Pulks of Sissojev III, Giroff and Grekov XVIII. GM Count Narischkin; Pulks of Andrejanov II and Lotschilin I.

Cossack total ca 4,000 men.

Cossack losses Not known exactly but very light.

Sources Plotho, Sporschil, Martinien.

SX Pirna, 27/28 August 1813, clash

A town in northeastern Germany (Saxony) on the right bank of the River Elbe, 18 km southeast of Dresden.

A French victory over the Russians.

(Last action - Hagelberg, 27 August; next action - Retschow, 28 August.)

French Forces GdD Count Vandamme commanding: I Corps and the Young Guard: 5e Voltigeurs (2 bns). I Corps, 2nd Division GdD Philippon: 13e RILé, 25e, 51e and 57e RIdLi. The 9e, 18e and 37e Lé also show casualties for this action as do the 26e ChàCh. **Totals and losses** Not exactly known.

Russian Forces GL Prince Eugen von Württemberg commanding the II (Russian) Corps. 3rd Division GM Prince Schachafskoi: IRs Murom, Reval, Tchernigov, Selenginsk, 20th Jägers (2 bns each); 21st Jägers (1 bn). 4th Division GM Pischnitzky: IRs Tobolsk, Volhynien, Krementchug, 4th Jägers (2 bns each); IR Minsk, 34th Jägers (1 bn each); 1 x heavy and 1 x light FAB.

Russian total ca 21,000 men.

Russian losses Not exactly known but fairly light.

Sources Plotho, Sporschil, Martinien.

SX Retschow, 28 August 1813, clash

A hamlet in the northern German state of Mecklenburg, about 20 km southwest of the Baltic port of Rostock.

An Allied victory over the French.

(Last action - Pirna, 27/28 August; next action - Plagwitz, 29 August.)

French Forces GdD Loison's 3rd Division of M Davout's XIII Corps: 15e RILé 44e, 48e, 108e RidLi.

French total ca 6,000 men.

French losses Not known exactly, light.

Allied Forces Part of the Army of the North, GL Count Wallmoden commanding. 4th Swedish Division GL von Vegesack: Mecklenburg-Schwerin Brigade GM von Fallois: Gren Garde (1 bn); LIR (2 bns); Freiwillige Jäger (1 bn); Freiwillige Jäger CavR (4 sqns), 4 guns. Swedish troops Obst von Bergenstrohla's 6th Brigade: IRs Smaland, Nord Schonischen, Engelbrechten, Königin Leib-R (1 bn each); Schonischen Carabiniers (4 sqns), 1 x FAB. Attached: Schill's Prussian HusR (2 sqns).

Allied total ca 10,000 men.

Allied losses Not exactly known light.

Sources Plotho, Sporschil, Martinien.

SX Plagwitz, 29 August 1813, clash

Known to the French as 'River Bober': a village in western Poland, on the River Bober (Bóbr), between Liegnitz (Legnica) and Görlitz on the border with Germany.

A Russian victory over the French.

(Last action - Retschow, 28 August; next action - Kulm, 29/30 August.)

French Forces GdD Puthod's 17th Division of Lauriston's V Corps: 134e, 146e, 147e, 148e RIdLi; 3e Etranger IR; 16 guns.

French total ca 7,500 men.

French losses Gen Puthod, 100 officers and 3,000 men captured; all regiments suffered very heavy casualties and were destroyed. The 28th Russian Jägers took 3 eagles. 1 each of the 134e*, 146e and 148e all with their colours attached. 16 guns were captured and the French burnt 70 ammunition waggons when they realised that they were trapped up against the flooded River Bober.
* = found in the river after the action.
Russian Forces Part of the Army of Silesia:
VI Corps GM Prince Scherbatov: 7th Division GM Tassisin I: IRs Pskov, Moscow, Libau, 11th Jägers (2 bns each); IR Sophia, 36th Jägers (1 bn each). 18th Division GM Bernodossov: IRs Vladimir, Dnieprov, Tambov, Kostroma, 28th and 32nd Jägers (1 bn each), 1 x heavy FAB, 1 x light FAB. From IX Corps: 15th Division GM Rudsevitch: IRs Witebsk, Klasovsk, Kolivan, 22nd Jägers (1 bn each); IRs Kurinsk and 12th Jägers (2 bns each).
I Cavalry Corps GL Baron Korff: GM Berdäev: DragRs Tver and Kinburn (2 sqns each). 1st Mounted Rifle Division GM Pantschulidsev I; MtdRRs Tchernigov (3 sqns); Sievsk (2 sqns) and Arsamas (1 sqn). 2nd Mounted Rifle Division GM Count Pahlen II; Lifland and Dorpat MtdRRs (2 sqns each); 2 x HAB. Light Cavalry GM Grekov VIII; GM Count Witte: 1st, 2nd and 3rd Ukrainian Cossack Pulks (3 sqns each); Cossack Pulks of Kutainikov VIII, Selwanov II, Isaef II, Zikelef I, the Teptar Cossack Pulk.
Russian total ca 25,000 men.
Russian losses Not exactly known light.
Sources Plotho, Sporschil, Martinien.

IN Villach, 28/29 August 1813, clash

A town in southeastern Austria, on the River Drau (then in French-occupied Illyria) close to the borders of Italy and Slovenia (ex-Yugoslavia) and at the junction of Routes 100/E14, 83, 93 and A2/E7.
A Franco-Italian victory over the Austrians.
(Last action – Villach, 24 August; next action – Novacco, 4 September.)
Franco-Italian Forces GdD Gratien's 3rd Division: GdB Piat: 35e RILé, 36e RILé; 42e and 102e RIdLi (2 bns each); 31e DBde Pv (3 bns); 8 guns.
Franco-Italian total ca 10,000 men.
Franco-Italian losses 12 killed, 100 wounded.
Austrian Forces IR Duka Nr 39 (1 bn); 4 guns.
Austrian total 600 men.
Austrian losses 26 killed, 141 wounded.
Comment With this action, Prince Eugène regained the key town and Drau crossing that he had just lost. About 80% of the town was burned down as were three arches of the vital bridge. The Drau was in flood and impassable.
Sources Wrede, Vaudoncourt, Martinien, HGM 56.

SX Kulm (now Chlumec), 29/30 August 1813, battle

A hamlet in Bohemia (today the Czech republic), 12 km northeast of Teplitz and 9 km northwest of Aussig on the River Elbe (now Usti N Lab).
An Allied victory over the French.
(Last action – Plagwitz, 29 August; next action Dennewitz, 6 September.)
French Forces GdD Count Vandamme commanding (+ = suffered extremely heavy casualties).
I Corps 1st Division GdD Dumonceau: 7e RILé (+), 12e (+), 17e (+) and 36e RIdLi. 2nd Division GdD Philippon: 13e RILé (+), 25e and 51e RIdLi. 23rd Division GdD Dufour: 33e, 55e, 85e RIdLi. GdB Gobrecht: 16e ChàCh, 9e ChLL (+).
XIV Corps M Count St Cyr: 42nd Division GdD Dupas: 12e RILé, 40e, 43e, 63e and 96e RIdLi. 43rd Division GdD Claparède: 27e RIdLi. From M Victor's II Corps, 5th Division GdD Corbineau: 46e (+), 72e RIdLi. The 4e, 9e and 28e RILé and the 76e RIdLi were also involved in the fighting and took casualties.
I Cavalry Corps GdD Latour-Maubourg: 1st Light Cavalry Division GdD Chastel: 1er ChàCh. The 3e HusR was also present. About 80 guns were used.
French total ca 37,000.
French losses 5,000 killed and wounded, 10,000 captured, including Vandamme and Generals Haxo, Guyot and Heimbrot, 21 guns, 200 ammunition waggons, all baggage, 2 eagles (33e Li and 4e Lé)and three colours – details very obscure.
Allied Forces GdI Barclay de Tolly commanding the Army of Bohemia:
Austrian Troops FZM Count Hieronimus Colloredo commanding: 1st Division, FML Schneller; GM Prince Gustav of Hessen-Homburg: HusR Hessen-Homburg Nr 4 (6 sqns), DragR Riesch Nr 6 (6 sqns); 1 x 6 pdr HAB. 2nd Division FML Count Wimpfen; GM Torry: IR de Vaux Nr 25, Erbach Nr 42 (2 bns each). GM Czerwenka: IR Argenteau Nr 35 (2 bns), 2 x 6 pdr FABs. 3rd Division FML Greth; GM Mumb: IR De Ligne Nr 30 and Czartoryski Nr 9 (2 bns each), 1 x 6

pdr FAB. From the II Corps of GdK Count Meerfeldt: 1st Division FML Ignaz Lederer, GM Sorbenberg: DragR EH Johann Nr 1 (6 sqns). From the Reserve Army of GdK Crownprince of Hessen-Homburg: Grenadier Division of FML Count Weissenwolf: GM Gabelkowen: Gren Bn Rüber. Division of FML Bianchi; GM Prince Philipp of Hessen-Homburg: IR Hiller Nr 2 and H Colloredo Nr 33 (2 bns each); GM Quallenberg: IR Davidovich Nr 34 (2 bns).

Prussian Troops GL von Kleist's **II (Prussian) Corps:** 10th Brigade GM Pirch I; 2nd Westpr IR, 7th Res IR, 9th Schl LWIR (2 bns each). 9th Brigade, GM von Klüx: 1st Westpr IR (3 bns); 6th Res IR (1st and 3rd bns). 12th Brigade GL Prince August von Preussen: 2nd Schl IR (3 bns); 11th Res IR (2 bns); 10th Schl LWIR (4 bns). From the Reserve Cavalry of GM von Röder: 7th Schl LWKR (4 sqns).

Russian Troops Grand Duke Constantine commanding: Guards Light Cavalry Division GM Schävitch: Life Guard HusR; Life Guard UlR, Life Guard Dragoon R (6 sqns each). 2 x HAB. 2nd Guards Division GM Udom I: Lithuanian and Finland Life Guards (3 bns each); Life Grenadiers, Pavlovsky Grenadiers (2 bns each). 1 x heavy, 2 x light FABs. 2nd Kür Division GM Kretov: KürRs Ekaterinoslav and Astrakhan (3 sqns each); KürR Gluchov (5 sqns); KürR Pleskowschett (4 sqns). 3rd Kür Division GM Duka: KürRs St Georger, Starodub, Novgorod and Little Russia (4 sqns each). 2 x HAB. 1st Guards Division GM Baron Rosen: Preobrazhenski, Semienovski and Ismailovski Life Guards (3 bns each); Life Guards (2 bns); Marine Equipage (½ bn).

I Corps GL Prince Gortschakov II: 5th Division GM Mesenzov IRs Perm, Kaluga, 23rd and 24th Jägers (2 bns each), 1 x heavy, 1 x light FAB.

II Corps GL Prince Eugen von Württemberg (now very weak): 3rd Division GM Prince Schachafskoi: IRs Murom, Reval, Tchernigov, Selenginsk, 20th Jägers (2 bns each); 21st Jägers (1 bn). 4th Division GM Pischnitzky: IRs Tobolsk, Volhynien, Krementchug, 4th Jägers (2 bns each); IRs Minsk, 34th Jägers (1 bn each). Cossacks of Illowaisky XII: Pulks of Illowaisky XII, Radionov II, Ataman. 1st Hussar Division GL Count Pahlen III: Grodno HusR (6 sqns); Ssum HusR (7 sqns); Olviopol HusR (2 sqns); Lubny HusR (4 sqns); Tartar UlR (4 sqns); Tchuguchev UlR (6 sqns); Serpuchov UlR (4 sqns). Reserve Artillery GM Hüne 3 x heavy FAB, 3 x HAB.

Allied total ca 70,000 men, 100 guns.

Allied overall losses 11,319 killed and wounded, 1,000 prisoners, of these the Austrians lost 1 general, 816 others; the Russians lost 2 generals, 9,000 others and the Prussians lost about 1,500 officers and men.

Comment Sources vary as to how many French guns were used and captured in this hard-fought battle which put a bloody stop to Napoleon's pursuit of the Allies after Dresden. Von Kausler states 'all guns lost', others give '21'. Austrian IR Froon Nr 54 took the eagle of the 33e Li.

Sources Plotho, Sporschil, Martinien, Wrede, von Kausler, Bodart.

EN San Sebastián, 25 July – 31 August 1813, siege and storm

A fortified Spanish Biscayan port about 16 km west of the French border and at the junction of Routes A1/E5/E70/E80 and Route I.

An Anglo-Portuguese victory over the French.

(Last action – Echalar, 2 August; next action – Bidassoa, 1 September.)

French Garrison GdB Rey commanding: 1er, 22e, 34e, 62e and 119e RIdLi (1 bn each); Chasseurs de Montagnes (½ bn); Artillery (2 coys) engineers and sappers (2 coys); detachments of Sailors, Spanish troops, etc (330 men).

French total ca 3,600 men, 97 guns.

French losses 1,900 killed and wounded, 1,200 captured (the garrison was reinforced by sea during the siege).

Anglo-Portuguese Forces The Marquess of Wellington commanding: **1st Division** MG Howard: 1/2nd and 1/3rd Footguards (1 bn each); 5/60th (1 coy). 1st, 2nd, 5th LI Bns KGL and 2nd LtI Bn KGL (1 bn each). **4th Division** MG Sir G Lowry Cole: 3/27th, 1/40th, 1/48th, 2nd Provisional Bn (1 bn each); 5/60th (1 coy); 1/7th, 1/20th, 1/23rd (1 bn each). Brunswick Oels (1 coy). Stubbs' Portuguese Brigade: 11th and 23rd LIRs (2 bns each); 7th Caçadores (1 bn). **5th Division** MG Leith: 3/1st, 1/9th, 1/38th (1 bn each); Brunswick Oels (1 coy); 1/4th, 2/47th, 2/59th (1 bn each); Brunswick Oels (1 coy). **Light Division** MG C Alten: 1/43rd, 1/95th, 3/95th, 1/52nd, 2/95th (1 bn each); Vandeleur's Portuguese: 17th LIR (2 bns); 1st and 3rd Caçadores (1 bn each). Spry's Portuguese (with the 5th Division): 3rd and

15th LIR (2 bns each); 8th Caçadores (1 bn). Bradford's Portuguese: 13th and 24th LIR (2 bns each); 5th Caçadores. Artillery and engineers.

Anglo-Portuguese total ca 18,000 men. Losses – 1,200 killed, 3,800 wounded, 300 missing. Of these, the casualties in the storm were 856 killed, 1,216 wounded and 44 missing.

Comment Another of Wellington's needlessly bloody sieges. San Sebastián was of immense strength and the garrison very active. After the storm there was a disgraceful period of rape and pillage by the British which completed the destruction of the town.

Sources Bodart, Oman, Martinien.

EN Bidassoa (Vera), 31 August – 1 September 1813, battle

A town in northern Spain, on the north bank of the River Bidassoa, close up against the border with France and about 20 km from the Bay of Biscay.

An Allied victory over the French.

(Last action – San Sebastián, 31 August; next action – Bidassoa, 7–9 October.)

French Forces M Soult commanding.

1. At San Marcial (by Irun and Behobie) GdD Reille's Corps.

9th Division GdD Lamartinière: 2e RILé (1 bn); 118e, 119e, RIdLi (2 bns each); 120e RIdLi (3 bns); 122e RIdLi (2 bns). GdD Villatte's Reserve (all 1 bn each); 4e, 10e, 31e RILé: 3e, 34e, 40e, 101e, 105e, 114e, 115e, 116e, 117e, 118e, 119e RIdLi; 2nd Nassau IR (2 bns). 4th Baden IR and IR Frankfurt (1 bn each). King Joseph's Guards (3 bns); Spanish IRs Royal Étranger Castile, Toledo. GdD Maucune's 7th Division: (all 1 bn except 15e RIdLi which had 2); 17e RILé, 34e, 66e, 82e, 86e RIdLi. **Total** ca 12,000 men, 48 guns. **Losses** 308 killed, 1,894 wounded, 221 missing.

2. At Salain de Lesaca and Vera (12 km upstream from San Marcial).

8th Division GdD Taupin: 9e RILé, 47e, 70e RIdLi (2 bns each); 31e RILé, 26e, 88e RIdLi (1 bn each). GdD Darmagnac's 2nd Division: 16e RILé, 8e, 51e, 54e RIdLi (1 bn each); 28e, 75e RIdLi (2 bns each). GdD Vandermaesen's 5th Division: 25e RILé, 1er, 27e, 50e, 59e RIdLi (1 bn each); 130e (2 bns). **Total** ca 11,500 men, 12 guns. **Losses** 109 killed, 809 wounded, 135 missing.

3. At Sare and St Barbara (7 km east of Vera).

4th Division GdD Conroux: 12e RILé, 32e, 43e RIdLi (2 bns each); 45e, 55e, 58e RIdLi (1 bn each). **Total** ca 5,000 men. **Losses** Not known, very light.

4. At Ainhoa (12 km east of St Barbara).

3rd Division GdD Abbé: 27e RILé and 63e RIdLi (1 bn each); 5e RILé, 64e, 94e, 95e RIdLi (2 bns each). **Total** 5,600 men. **Losses** 50 killed, 274 wounded, 1 missing.

French Losses 467 killed, 2,977 wounded, 357 missing, GdD Vandermaesen killed, GdBs Menné, Rémond and Guy wounded.

Allied Forces The Marquess of Wellington commanding.

1. At San Marcial.

The Spanish Divisions of Porlier, Losada and Del Barco (exact details not known). **Total** 10,000 men. **Losses** 261 killed, 1,347 wounded, 71 missing. The 1st British Division was present in reserve but not engaged.

2. Salain and Vera.

Salain: 4th Division: 3/27th, 1/40th and 2nd Provisional Bn (1 bn each); Miller's Portuguese: 11th and 23rd LIR (2 bns each), 7th Caçadores (1 bn). 4th Division: 51st, 68th, 1/82nd (1 bn each), Chasseurs Britanniques (1 bn). **Total** ca 8,600 men. **Losses** 73 killed, 356 wounded, 44 missing.

3. Sare and St Barbara.

Part of Gen Giron's Spanish Division (exact details not known). Losses – none reported.

4. Ainhoa.

Madden's Portuguese Brigade 8th and 12th LIRs (2 bns each); 9th Caçadores. Le Cor's Portuguese Brigade: 7th and 19th LIRs (2 bns each); 2nd Caçadores. **Total** ca 3,800 men. **Losses** 85 killed, 157 wounded, 12 missing.

Comment Soult was stung into mounting another assault against the Allies by Clarke (French Minister for war). All three of his thrusts south over the river were defeated. Vandermaesen's Division was cut off by the rising river south of it and could have been destroyed if Skerrett (of the Light Division) had moved to support a picquet of the 95th which was blocking his escape route over the bridge at Vera but, for inexplicable reasons, he did nothing and Vandermaesen's Division got away even though he himself was killed.

Sources Oman, Martinien.

IN Novacco, 4 September 1813, clash

A hamlet in the centre of the Istrian peninsula in Slovenia (ex-Yugoslavia), northeast of Pazin (then Pisino or Mitterburg). Not shown on many modern maps.

An Austrian victory over the Franco-Italians.

(Last action – Villach, 29 August; next action – Feistritz, 6 September.)

Franco-Italian Forces Chef de Bataillon Spring commanding: 4th Italian LtI Bn (1 bn); Otočaner (ex Austrian GzIR; 2 coys); French gunners and Douaniers (80 men).

Franco-Italian total 1,200 men, 3 guns.

Franco-Italian losses 40 killed and wounded, 26 officers, 900 men, 3 guns captured.

Austrian Forces Capt Lazarich commanding: Warasdiner-Kreutzer GzIR Nr 5 (40 men); HusR Radetzky Nr 5 (12 men); 2,400 peasants, mostly armed with flails, axes and scythes.

Austrian total 2,452 men.

Austrian losses 7 wounded.

Comment The Italians were new recruits, scarcely trained; the Otočaners (in French service only since 1809) went over to the Austrians and Spring, cut off in a valley and surrounded, surrendered. On 10 September Lazarich occupied the strategic road junction at Pinguente (now Lupoglav) and next day he took part of Capodistria (now Koper) just south of Trieste where two British men of war joined him and cooperated in the future liberation of Istria.

Sources vom Holtz, Wrede.

SX Dennewitz (Jüterbog), 6 September 1813, battle

A village in northeastern Germany (Brandenburg province), 60 km southwest of Berlin and 4 km southwest of Jüterbog which is at the junction of Routes B101, B102 and B115 and 25 km northeast of Wittenberg on the River Elbe.

An Allied victory over the Franco-Allies.

(Last action – Kulm, 29/30 August; next action Pirna, 8 September.)

Franco-Allied Forces M Ney commanding.

IV Corps GdD Bertrand: 12th Division GdD Count Morand; GdB de Belair: 8e RILé (4 bns); 13e RIdLi (4 bns); 23e RIdLi (1er, 2e, 4e bns); 137e RIdLi (3 bns). 2 x FAB. 15th Division (Italians) GdD Count Fontanelli: GdB St André: 1st LtIR (2 bns). Milan Guards (1 bn). GdB Moroni: 1st, 4th, 6th, 7th LIRs (1 bn each). 1 x FAB. 38th Division GM von Stockmayer (Württembergers): 1st, 2nd, 3rd Combined IRs (1 bn each). 24th Light Cavalry Brigade GM von Jett: ChLR Nr 1 Prinz Adam, JzPfR Nr 3 Herzog Louis (1 sqn each), 1 x HAB. 29th Light Cavalry Brigade: GM Wolff: Westfalian Garde-ChLR, Hessen-Darmstadt Garde ChLR (1 sqn each).

XII Corps M Oudinot: Division GdD Count Guilleminot; GdB Gruyer: 1er RILé (4e Bn); 18e RILé (2 bns); 7e RIdLi (3e Bn); 156e RIdLi (2 bns). GdB Lejeune: Illyrien IR (2nd Bn); 52e RIdLi (3e Bn); 67e RIdLi (3e Bn); 101e RIdLi (2e and 3e bns), 1 x FAB. GM Raglovich (Bavarians): IRs König Nr 1, Preysing Nr 5, Herzog Pius Nr 8 (1 bn each); IR Prinz Carl Nr 3 (2 bns); IRs Isenburg Nr 4 and Nr 9 (1 bn each); IRs Junker Nr 10 and Nr 13 (2 bns each). BG Pappenheim: ChLRs Taxis Nr 2 and Bubenhofen Nr 6 (4 sqns each), 1 x HAB.

VII Corps GdD Count Reynier: 24th Division GL von Zeschau; Obst von Brause: LtIR von Lecoq; Gren Bn von Spiegel; IR von Rechten; IR Prinz Friedrich August; IR von Steindel (1 bn each). 32nd Division GdD Durutte; GdB Devaux: 35e RILé (1er Bn); 131e, 132e RIdLi (3e Bns each). GdB Baron Jarry: 36e RILé (4e Bn); 133e RIdLi (3e Bn), IR Würzburg (2nd Bn).

III Cavalry Corps GdD Arrighi, Duke of Padua: 5th Light Cavalry Division GdD Lorge: 12th Light Cavalry Brigade GdB Baron Jacquinot: 5e, 13e ChàCh (2 sqns each). 13th Light Cavalry Brigade; GdB Baron Merlin: 21e ChàCh (1 sqn); 22e ChàCh (2 sqns). 6th Light Cavalry Division GdD Baron Fournier: 14th Light Cavalry Brigade GdB Baron Mouriez: 1er HusR, 29e ChàCh (1 sqn each). 4th Heavy Cavalry Division GdD Count Defrance: 1st Brigade, GdB Baron Avice: 12e and 24e DragRs (1 sqn each); 2nd Brigade GdB Baron Quinette de Cernay: 21e and 26e DragR (1 sqn each). 8th Light Cavalry Division GdB Kruckowiecki (Poles): 2nd UlR (4 sqns); 4th ChàCh (4 sqns). The Bavarian 9th LIR (2nd Bn) was also engaged.

Franco-Allied total 46 bns, 25 sqns, ca 45,000 men.

Franco-Allied losses 6,500 killed and wounded, 13,500 captured, 54 guns, 300 waggons, 4 colours (2nd bn 9th Bavarian LIR, 2nd and 7th Württemberg LIR) and the standard of the Italian Gardes d'Honneur. GdB Cacault was killed. The Saxons lost 12 officers and 2,200 men captured as well as 7 x 6 pdrs, 2 x 12 pdrs and 3 x 8 pdr guns and 40 ammunition waggons. The IR Würzburg lost 55 killed and wounded and 370 captured as it covered the withdrawal of the disintegrating VII Corps. The Württembergers lost 2,155 killed, wounded and captured.

The III Prussian Corps of GL von Bülow and its losses at Dennewitz, 6 September 1813.

Killed, wounded and missing.

	Officers	Men	Horses
3rd Brigade			
GM Prinz Ludwig von Hessen-Homburg			
2nd Ostpr Gren Bn (1 bn)	3	164	—
3rd Ostpr IR (2 bns)	9	391	—
4th Res IR (3 bns)	9	401	—
3rd Ostpr LWIR (4 bns)	21	463	—
1st Leib HusR (4 sqns)	2	35	45
4th Brigade			
GM von Thümen			
4th Ostpr IR (3 bns)	12	568	—
5th Res IR (3 bns)	18	562	—
Elb-IR (2nd bn)	1	20	—
Ostpr Jägers (coys)	7	325	—
Pomm NKR (4 sqns)	—	6	10
5th Brigade			
GM von Borstell			
1st Pomm IR (Füs bn)	8	212	—
Pomm Gren Bn (1 bn)	7	150	—
2nd Res IR (3 bns)	4	275	—
2nd Märk LWIR (3 bns)	7	151	—
Pomm HusR (4 sqns)	4	54	91
6th Brigade			
Obst von Krafft			
Colberg IR (3 bns)	26	763	—
9th Res IR (3 bns)	10	572	—
1st Märk LWIR (2nd & 4th bns)	34	551	—
1st Pomm LWKR (3 sqns)	—	—	2
Cavalry Reserve			
GM von Oppen			

Killed, wounded and missing.

	Officers	Men	Horses
Brand DragR (4 sqns)	8	107	184
DragR Königin (4 sqns)	4	39	45
Westpr UlR (4 sqns)	—	3	6
2nd Pomm LWKR (4 sqns)	—	—	13
4th Kurmark LWKR (4 sqns)	—	44	67
2nd Kurmark LWKR (4 sqns)	1	8	27
2nd Westpr DragR (4 sqns)	3	26	44
Prussian Artillery 2 x 12 pdr, 4 x 6 pdr FABs, 3 x 6 pdr HABs, Pioniers (2 coys)	2	67	83
Russian Artillery 2 x heavy FABs	1	11	16
Don Cossack Pulks of Bychalov II and Illowaisky V: losses unknown			
Totals	201	5,968	633

Tauentzien's IV (Prussian) Corps 1st Brigade GM von Dobschütz: 3rd Res IR (4 bns); 1st Kurmark LWIR (3 bns); 2nd and 3rd Neumark LWKR; 2nd and 3rd Ostpr LWKR (4 sqns each). 2nd Brigade GM Count von Lindenau: 2nd and 5th Neumark LWIR (4 bns each); 1st Schl LWIR (1 bn); 2nd Schl LWIR (4 bns); Berlin LWKR, 7th Kurmark LWKR (2 sqns each); 1st Kurmark and 3rd Pomm LWKRs (4 sqns each). 1½ x 6 pdr FAB. Artillery Reserve 1 x FAB, 1 x HAB.

IV Corps total ca 2,200 men.

IV Corps losses Most of the fighting was done by Bülow's I Corps, the IV Corps had only light losses.

IN Feistritz/Rosenthal, 6 September 1813, clash

A village in the southern Austrian province of Carinthia, just south of the lake Feistritz on the River Drau, ca 30 km southwest of Klagenfurt.

A Franco-Italian victory over the Austrians.

(Last action - Novacco, 4 September; next action - Lippa, 7 September.)

French Forces Prince Eugène de Beauharnais commanding: **1st Division** GdD Baron Quesnel: 84e and 92e RIdLi and 30e DBde Prov (4 bns each); Chasseurs of the Italian Guard (2 bns), 28 guns. **Total** 7,700 men. **2nd Division** GdD Count Rouyer: 9e and35e RIdLi (4 bns each). 28e DBde Prov (3 bns); 18 guns. **Total** 7,486 men.

French grand total 15,186 men.

French losses 60 killed, 300 wounded. As Martinien lists 12 officer casualties for the 84e alone, the French casualty figures seem suspect.

Austrian Forces FZM Baron Hiller commanding. GM Vécsey: IRs Reisky Nr 10 and Chasteler Nr 27 (2 bns each); UlR Merveldt Nr 1 (4 sqns); Gren Bn Chimani (6 coys), 4 guns; Jäger bn Nr 9 (4 coys).

Austrian total ca 3,300 men.

Austrian losses '300 killed, 500 captured' (Vaudoncourt)*.

* HGM 56 gives the Austrian losses as 67 killed, 384 wounded, 390 captured.

Comment This position was strongly fortified in front but the Austrians were too weak to cover the flanks and it was outflanked through the Bärental. This victory gave Eugène secure communications to his southern wing in Slovenia.

Sources Wrede, Vaudoncourt, Martinien HGM 56, vom Holtz.

IN Lippa*, 7 September 1813, clash

(*= nowadays Lipa). A village in northwestern Croatia (ex Yugoslavia) about 24 km northwest of Rijeka (once Fiume) at the head of the Gulf of Rijeka.

An Austrian victory over the Italians.

(Last action – Feistritz, 6 September; next action – Tersain, 8 September.)

Franco-Italian Forces GdB Ruggieri of GdD Palombini's 5th Division (Italian troops): 2nd LtIR, 1st LIR (1 bn each); Dalmatian IR (2 bns), 4 guns.

Franco-Italian total 2,563 men.

Franco-Italian losses 104 killed, 200 captured. Not all units were engaged.

Austrian Forces GM Nugent commanding: GM Csivich: HusR Radetzky Nr 5 (1½ sqns), 6 guns. GzIR Warasdiner-Kreutzer Nr 5 (2nd Bn); IR EH Franz Carl Nr 52 (1 bn); 2 x 3pdr guns.

Austrian total ca 2,100 men.

Austrian losses Not known, but very light. The Italians fell back to Trieste.

Sources Wrede, Vaudoncourt, Martinien, vom Holtz.

IN Tersain (Trzin), 8 September 1813, ambush

A village in the mountains of northwestern Slovenia (ex Yugoslavia) in the centre of a triangle based on Ljubljana (Laibach), Kranz (Krainburg) and Kamnik (Stein), on Route 10/E57.

An Austrian victory over the Franco-Italians.

(Last action – Lippa, 7 September; next action – Mühlbacher Klause, 8 September.)

Franco-Italian Forces GdB Belotti commanding: 3rd and 4th Italian LtIR (2 bns each); ChàCh (1 sqn).

Franco-Italian total ca 3,600, 2 guns.

Franco-Italian losses 255 killed and wounded, 650 captured, 2 guns, 2 colours. Belotti wounded and captured.

Austrian Forces GM Fölseis commanding: GzIR Broder Nr 7 (2nd Bn); IR Lusignan Nr 16 (2 bns); IR Chasteler Nr 27 (1 bn); HusR Radetzky Nr 5 (2 sqns) UlR Merveldt Nr 1 (1 sqn), ½ 3pdr FAB.

Austrian total ca 2,000 men, 3 guns.

Austrian losses 1 killed, 14 wounded.

Comment Belotti was marching without proper security in hostile country and paid the price; his brigade was almost destroyed. This action caused Prince Eugène to concentrate his forces on his southern flank.

Sources Wrede, Vaudoncourt, Martinien HGM 56, vom Holtz.

SX Dohna and Pirna, 8 September 1813, clash

Villages in the northeastern German state of Saxony on opposite banks of the River Elbe, about 8 km southeast of Dresden.

A French victory over the Allies.

(Last action – Dennewitz, 6 September; next action – Göhrde, 16 September.)

French Forces.

At Pirna: M St Cyr's **XIV Corps** (later Emperor Napoleon I in person). 44th Division GdD Serrurier; 8e RILé (2 bns); 18e RILé (1 bn); 24e, 39e, 50e, 54e, 75e, 94e RIdLi (1 bn each); 64e RIdLi (2 bns); 2 x FAB.

At Dohna: **XI Corps** M Macdonald: 31st Division GdD Gérard: 27e RILé, 5e, 11e, 102e RIdLi. 35th Division (Italians) GdD Fressinet: 2nd LtIR, 5th LIR; 6e, 112e French RIdLi. The 14e HusR was also engaged.

French total ca 20,000 men.

French losses Not exactly known but light.

Allied Forces The Army of Bohemia FM Prince Schwarzenberg commanding:

At Pirna: **The Right Wing** GdK Count Wittgenstein: I Corps GL Prince Gortschakow. 5th Division GM Mesenzov: IRs Perm, Kaluga, 23rd and 24th Jägers (2 bns each); IRs Mohilev, Sievsk and Grand Princess Katharina (1 bn each). 14th Division GM Helfreich, IRs Tenginsk, Estonia, 25th and 26th Jägers (2 bns each), 1 x heavy and 1 x light FABs. **Cavalry** GL Count Pahlen III: GM Illowaisky XII: Cossack Pulks of Illowaisky XII, Radionov II and Ataman. 1st Hussar Division: Grodno HusR (6 sqns); Ssum HusR (7 sqns); Olviopol HusR (2 sqns); Lubny HusR (4 sqns).

Austrian Troops 2nd Light Division FML Count

Bubna: GzIR Peterwardeiner Nr 9 (1st Bn), Jägers (6th Bn); IR Vogelsang Nr 47; HusRs Blankenstein Nr 6 and Liechtenstein Nr 7 (6 sqns each).

At Dohna: **The Left Wing** GL Count von Kleist's II (Prussian) Corps. GM von Ziethen's 11th Brigade: 1st SchlIR and 10th Res IR (3 bns each); Schl Schützen bn (2 coys), 8th Schl LWIR (4 bns); 1st Schl HusR (4 sqns), 1 x 6 pdr FAB. The 10th and 12th Brigades of this corps were in reserve.

Allied total ca 30,000 men.

Allied losses Not known exactly but light.

Comment The news that Napoleon was coming up to take personal command with reinforcements caused Schwarzenberg to break off this reconnaissance in force.

Sources Plotho, Sporschil, Martinien.

IN Mühlbacher-Klause, 11 September 1813, 1st raid

A village in the valley of the River Rienz (a tributary of the Eisack/Isarco) in northern Italy's South Tirol province, about 10 km north of Brixen (Bressanone).

An Austrian victory over the Franco-Italians.

(Last action – Tersain, 8 September; next action – Pola, 11 September.)

Franco-Italian Forces Part of GdD Bonfanti's newly forming Reserve Division of Prince Eugène's army – 1 company ca 110 men.

Franco-Italian losses 100 captured.

Austrian (Tyrolean) Forces Part of FML Fenner's Avantgarde and Volunteer Tyrolean Landesschützen (local militia or home guard).

Austrian total ca 150 men.

Austrian losses Not known exactly but very light.

Comment The Italian battalion in Brixen withdrew south to Trient to Bonfanti's headquarters. Bonfanti, in turn, abandoned Trient and fell back to Verona just east of the southern end of Lake Garda. Eugène sacked Bonfanti and replaced him with General Giflenga. Thus a tiny raid resulted in an entire division abandoning over 144 km of easily defendable terrain.

Source vom Holtz.

IN Pola, 11 September 1813, surrender

A port at the southern tip of the Istrian peninsula in Slovenia (ex-Yugoslavia, now 'Pula' on Route 2) in the northern Adriatic.

An Austrian victory over the French.

(Last action – Mühlbacher Klause, 11 September; next action – St Marein, 13 September.)

French Garrison The local National Guard; exact details unknown.

French losses None.

Austrian Forces Lt Deusz commanding GzIR Warasdiner-Kreutzer Nr 5 (20 men); Landsturm (1 coy).

Austrian total ca 130 men.

Austrian losses None.

Comment The appearance of a British naval brig in the harbour caused the garrison to surrender the place together with 57 guns. The seizure of Istria secured the rear of the local Austrian commander, GM Count Nugent, and opened up access to the Adriatic and thus to the Royal Naval squadron of three ships of the line and a brig under Admiral Freemantle.

IN St Marein, 13 September 1813, clash

A village in western Slovenia (ex-Yugoslavia) about 12 km southeast of Ljubljana, on the road to Weichselburg (now Visnija Gora).

An Austrian victory over the Italians.

(Last action – Pola, 11 September; next action – Jelšane, 14 September.)

French Forces Viceroy Eugène commanding: Italian Guard (4 bns), DragR Regina (2 sqns), 1 x HAB.

French total ca 3,300 men, 6 guns.

French losses ca 300 killed and wounded, 97 captured.

Austrian Forces Obst Eugène Milutinovich commanding: GzIR Gradiskaner Nr 8 (1 bn); GzIR Warasdiner-Kreutzer Nr 5 (2 coys), HusR Radetzky Nr 5 (2 sqns), 2 guns.

Austrian total ca 1,000 men, 2 guns.

Austrian losses 47 killed and wounded, 28 captured.

Comment Vaudoncourt does not mention Eugène's presence in this action (a successful defence of a very strong position); the Italians fell back to Ljubljana.

Sources: Vaudoncourt, Wrede, vom Holtz, Martinien.

EE Ordal, 13 September 1813, clash

A village in the northeastern Spanish province of Catalonia, 23 km west of Barcelona.

A French victory over the Anglo-Spanish.

(Last action – Tarragona, 11 June; next action – Villafranca, 13 September).

French Forces M Suchet commanding: GdD Harispe's 2nd Division: 7e, 44e, 116e RIdLi (2 bns each); GdD Habert's 3rd Division: 14e, 16e, 117e RIdLi (2 bns each); 4e HusR (3 sqns).

French total ca 12,000 men.

French losses Not exactly known, probably about 300 killed and wounded.

British Forces LG Lord William Bentinck commanding: BG Adam's Advanced Guard: 2/27th (1 bn); De RollÉ's and 4th LI Bn KGL (1 rifle coy each); Calabrian Free Corps (1 bn).

British total 1,508 men.

British losses 75 killed, 109 wounded, 333 missing (mostly captured), 4 guns.

Spanish Troops Col Torres commanding: IRs Badajoz, Tiradores de Cadiz, Voluntarios de Aragon.

Spanish total 2,300.

Spanish losses 87 killed, 239 wounded, 132 missing.

Comment Bentinck was incredibly lax and put out no patrols. Suchet's night attack caught the Allies completely unawares. The Spanish troops fought extremely well.

Sources Oman, Martinien.

EE Villafranca, 13 September 1813, skirmish

A town in northeastern Spain, on Route 340, about 35 km west of Barcelona.

A French victory over the Allies.

(Last action – Ordal, 13 September; this was the last action of note in eastern Spain.)

French Forces GdD Boussard commanding: GdB Meyers 4e HusR, 13e CuirR (4 sqns each), 24e DragR (3 sqns); Westfalian ChLR (4 sqns).

French total ca 1,750 men.

French losses 7 officers and 100 men killed and wounded.

Allied Forces 20th LDR, Brunswick HusR; Sicilian CavR (2 sqns each); Foreign HusR (1 tp).

Allied total ca 770 men.

Allied losses 25 killed, 69 wounded, 40 missing.

Comment Although outnumbered, the Allied cavalry succeeded in protecting their retreating infantry from being charged and cut down.

Following this action and the Ordal fiasco, Lord William Bentinck handed over his command of the British forces in eastern Spain to General William Clinton.

Sources Oman, Martinien.

IN Jelšane, 14 September 1813, clash

A hamlet in western Croatia (ex-Yugoslavia) ca 18 km north of Rjeka (Fiume), a port on the Adriatic Kvarna Gulf. Not shown on some modern maps.

A Franco-Italian victory over the Austrians.

(Last action – St Marein, 13 September; next action – Weichselburg, 16 September.)

Franco-Italian Forces LG Count Pino commanding: GdD Palombini's 5th Division: 1st and 2nd Italian LtIRs (1 bn each); 2nd and 3rd Italian LIRs (4 bns each); Dalmatian IR (2 bns); ChàCh (4 sqns); 2 x FAB.

Franco-Italian total ca 9,000 men, 12 guns.

Franco-Italian losses Count Pino wounded, 420 killed, wounded and missing.

Austrian Forces GM Nugent commanding: IR EH Franz Carl Nr 52 (1st bn); GzIR Warasdiner-Kreutzer Nr 5 (4 coys); HusR Radetzky Nr 5 (3 troops); 4 x 3pdr guns.

Austrian total 2,000 men, 4 guns.

Austrian losses 24 killed, 88 wounded, 3 guns damaged. Vaudoncourt's very brief account of this successful Austrian rearguard action gives Austrian losses as: 'about 300 men killed or wounded, 200 captured and 1 gun'.

Comment Pino decided to destroy Nugent's annoying force but, by skilful use of the terrain, Nugent held his ground until dark then slipped away to Castua and Mitterburg southwards in the Istrian peninsula. Pino now resigned his command but was reactivated in October to command a newly-formed reserve division.

Sources vom Holtz, Vaudoncourt, Wrede, Martinien.

IN Weichselburg, 16 September 1813, clash

A village in northwestern Slovenia (ex Yugoslavia), about 28 km southeast of Ljubljana (Laibach). Nowadays known as Visnija Gora.

An Austrian victory over the Franco-Italians.

(Last action – Jelšane, 14 September; next action – St Hermagor, 18 September.)

Franco-Italian Forces GdB Baron Lecchi: Italian Royal Guard (4 bns); DragR Regina (2 sqns); 1 x HAB.

Franco-Italian total ca 2,900 men, 5 guns.

Franco-Italian losses 910 men captured (killed and wounded not known), 2 guns, 1 colour, 2 standards. Vaudoncourt shows only '200 casualties and 2 guns,'.

Austrian Forces GM Rebrovich commanding. IR EH Franz Carl Nr 52 (1st bn); GzIR Gradiskaner Nr 8 (2nd Bn); GzIR Broder Nr 7 (2nd Bn); GzIR St Georger Nr 6 (4 coys), HusR Radetzky Nr 5 (2 sqns); ½ x FAB.

Austrian total ca 3,200 men.

Austrian losses 16 killed, 68 wounded, 27 captured.

Comment This was the same Italian force that was defeated under Viceroy Eugène at St Marein on 13 September. One entire battalion threw down their arms and surrendered to the Radetzky Hussars. This defeat caused Viceroy Eugène to postpone his current plan for an offensive.

Sources Vaudoncourt, vom Holtz, Wrede, Martinien.

SX Göhrde (Forest), 16 September 1813, clash

A village in a large, wooded area in northern Germany, on the left bank of the River Elbe, 25 km southeast of Lüneburg on Route B216.

A Prusso-Russian victory over the French.

(Last action – Dohna and Pirna, 8 September; next action – Teplitz, 17 September.)

French Forces GdD Mécheux (50th Division of Davout's Corps) commanding: 105e RIdli.

French total 6 bns, 1 sqn, 6 guns, ca 4,500 men.

French losses ca 400 killed, 1,900 (including 7–800 wounded) captured, 6 guns.

Allied Forces Russian LG Count Ludwig von Wallmoden-Gimborn commanding: **Avantgarde** GM von Tettenborn: 4 Cossack Pulks, Lützow's Freikorps (3 bns, 5 sqns, 8guns), Jäger bn von Reiche. **Anglo-German Division** MG Lyon: Light Brigade: Lt Col Martin: LtI Bns Lüneburg, Bremen-Verden, Dessau (1 bn each). Line Brigade; Lt Col Hugh Halkett: KGL (½ composite bn); LI Bns Bennigsen, von Langrehr and Lauenburg (1 bn each); 1/73rd Foot, von Kielmansegge's Jägers (2 coys); Russian-German Jägers (1 coy), 1 x FAB. **Russian-German Division** GM von Arentschildt: 6 bns. Cavalry GM von Dörnberg: 1st and 2nd HusRs Russian-German Legion (4 sqns each); 3rd HusR KGL (5 sqns); Lüneburg HusR (3 sqns); Bremen-Verden HusR (1 sqn); 1st and 2nd HAB KGL, (12 guns), 1st and 2nd HAB Russian-German Legion (16 guns); ½ rocket battery (British).

Allied total ca 12,000 men.

Allied losses 530 men killed and wounded, 250 horses (mostly from 3rd HusR KGL).

Comment Pécheau had been sent out from Hamburg to find and destroy Allied raiding parties. Through a captured despatch Wallmoden learned of this and ambushed him.

Sources Sichart, Sporschil, Beamish, Schwertfeger.

SX Teplitz, 17 September 1813, clash

A town in the Erzgebirge mountains in the northwest of the Czech Republic, near the border with Germany and at the junction of Routes 27/E55 and 30. Now called Teplice.

An Allied victory over the French.

(Last action – Göhrde, 16 September; next action – Braunschweig, 25 September.)

French Forces Emperor Napoleon I commanding:

Imperial Guard Cavalry GdD Walther: Dragoons, Grenadiers à Ch, 1st (Polish) and 2nd (Dutch) ChLLs.

I Corps 1st Division GdD Dumonceau: 7e RILé, 17e RIdLi. 23rd Division GdD Dufour: 33e RIdLi; 9 ChLL.

III Corps M Ney: 9th Division GdD Delmas: 29e RILé. 11th Division GdD Ricard: 9e RILé.

IV Corps GdD Count Bertrand: 12th Division GdD Count Morand: 8e RILé.

French totals ca 25,000 men.

French losses Not known exactly; moderate, 3 guns, 1 eagle (apparently the 33e Li).

Allied Forces Part of the Army of Bohemia:

II Prussian Corps GL von Kleist: 11th Brigade GM von Ziethen: 1st Schl IR and 10th Res IR (3 bns each); Schl Schützen (2 coys); 8th Schl LWIR (4 bns); 1st Schl HusR (4 sqns); 1 x 6 pdr FAB. 12th Brigade GL Prince August von Preussen: 2nd Schl IR and 11th Res IR (3 bns each); 10th Schl LWIR (4 bns); 1st Schl LWKR (4 sqns), 1 x 6 pdr FAB.

Russian II Corps GL Prince Eugen von Württemberg: 3rd Division Prince Schachafskoi: IRs Murom. Tchernigov, Selenginsk, Reval, 20 Jägers (2 bns each); 21st Jägers (1 bn). 4th Division GM Pischnitzky: IRs Tobolsk, Volhynien, Krementchug, 4th Jägers (2 bns each), 34th Jägers (1 bn); 1 x heavy FAB, 1 x light FAB.

Cavalry GL Count Pahlen III: GM Illowaisky XII: Cossack Pulks of Illowaisky XII, Radionov II, Ataman. 1st Hussar Division LG Count Pahlen III: Grodno HusR (6 sqns); Ssum HusR (7 sqns); Olviopol HusR (2 sqns); Lubny HusR (4 sqns). GM Lissanevitch: Tartar UlR (4 sqns); Tchuguchev UlR (6 sqns); Serpuchov UlR (4 sqns). 1 x HAB.

Allied total ca 35,000 men.

Allied losses Not exactly known, light. Gyulai's III Austrian Corps was in close support.

Sources Plotho, Sporschil, Wrede, Martinien.

IN St Hermagor, 18 September 1813, clash

A village in the southeastern Austrian province of Carinthia, on Route 111 in the valley of the River Gail at the junction with Route 87, just north of the Italian border.

An Austrian victory over the Franco-Italians.

(Last action – Weichselburg, 16 September; next action – Tchernütz, 19 September.)

Franco-Italian Forces GdB Piat's brigade of GdD Gratien's 3rd Division of GdD Grenier's Left Wing: 35e RILé (2 bns), 31e PvDBde (1 bn).

Franco-Italian total ca 2,600 men.

Franco-Italian losses ca 200 killed and wounded, 242 captured, 800 muskets and 3 colours.

Austrian Forces Obstlt Mumb commanding: Jäger bn Nr 8 (1 coy); 2nd GzIR Szeckler Nr 15 (2 coys); HusR Frimont Nr 9 (1 sqn), IR Jellačič Nr 53 (2 bns).

Austrian total ca 2,700 men.

Austrian losses Not exactly known but light.

Comment The French initially withdrew in good order but were then taken in flank and fled in a panic back eastwards to Arnoldstein.

Vaudoncourt does not mention the panic or the loss of the colours and muskets. This defeat left a large hole in the Franco-Italian line. An Austrian counter offensive was started on 19 September with GM Vécsey's brigade of Frimont's division to retake the Loibl pass, between present day Austria and Slovenia. This action succeeded that day.

Sources Wrede, Vaudoncourt, Martinien HGM 56, vom Holtz.

IN Tchernütz (Zirknitz) (now Cerknica, ex Yugoslavia), 19 September 1813, clash

A village in western Slovenia about 4 km north of the outskirts of Ljubljana (once Laibach) and a bridgehead over the River Save.

A Franco-Italian victory over the Austrians.

(Last action – St Hermagor, 18 September; next action – Gross-Laschitz, 25 September.)

Franco-Italian Garrison: 84e RIdLi (1 bn), 3rd Italian LIR (1 bn); ChàP of the Italian Guard (100 men). Total 12,000 men, 4 guns. Losses not known.

Austrian Forces GM Fölseis commanding: GzIR Broder Nr 7 (2nd Bn); IR Lusignan Nr 16 (2 bns), HusR Radetzky Nr 5 (2 sqns), ½ x 3 pdr FAB.

Austrian total ca 2,800 men.

Austrian losses '400 killed and wounded, 200 captured' (Vaudoncourt).

Comment Martinien lists 5 officer casualties for the 84e; 10 for the 3rd (It) LIR. Prince Eugène was now withdrawing westwards to the line of the River Isonzo and Tchernütz would very soon be evacuated.

Sources Wrede, Vaudoncourt, Martinien, HGM 56, vom Holtz.

IN Gross-Laschitz, 25 September 1813, raid

A village in Croatia (ex-Yugoslavia) about 20 km southeast of Ljubljana (Laibach) not shown on some modern maps.

An Austrian victory over the Franco-Italians.

(Last action – Tchernütz, 19 September; next action – Zirknitz, 27 September.)

Franco-Italian Forces GdB Perreymond with two battalions and one squadron.

Franco-Italian total ca 2,000 men.

Franco-Italian losses 8 officers and 300 men captured (Vaudoncourt says '200').

Austrian Forces Obst Count Starhemberg commanding GzIR Gradiskaner Nr (1 bn); GzIR Georger Nr 6 (1 bn); HusR Radetzky Nr 5 (1 sqn).

Austrian total ca 1,500 men.

Austrian losses 1 wounded.

Comment This was a most successful Austrian raid.

Sources vom Holtz, Vaudoncourt.

SX Braunschweig, 25 September 1813, capture

A walled town in central northern Germany, on the River Oker, 42 km east of Hannover at the junction of Autobahn A2, A39 and A395.

A Prussian victory over the Westfalians.

(Last action – Teplitz, 17 September; next action – Altenburg, 28 September.)

Westfalian Forces GM von Klösterlein commanding: Veterans (1 coy); Prefectoral Guard (40 men); Westfalian Gendarmes (40 men); a reinforcement draft of 260 unarmed recruits for the Lippe and Waldeck IR; Depots of 1st LIR (146 men), 2nd LIR (156 men); Jäger-Carabiniers of the Guard.

Westfalian totals 981 men.

Westfalian losses 26 officers and 350 men captured (none killed or wounded).

Prussian Forces Obstlt von der Marwitz's 3rd Neumark LWKR (400 men) from the besieging force at Magdeburg.

Prussian losses None.

Comment The garrison melted away and fled to Wolfsburg. Those prisoners who agreed to join the Prussians were formed into a Volunteer-Jäger squadron.

Sources Specht, Sporschil.

IN Tchernütz (Zirknitz) (now Cerknica, ex Yugoslavia), 27 September 1813, clash

A village in western Slovenia in a mountain valley, about 12 km east of Postonja Route 10/E70 (once Adelsberg and site of the huge caves), 30km south of Ljubljana.

An Austrian victory over the Franco-Italians.

(Last action – Tchernütz, 19 September; next action – Bruneck, 28 September.)

Franco-Italian Forces GdD Palombini commanding the 5th Italian Division: 2nd LtIR (1 bn); 1st LIR (1 bn); 2nd and 3rd LIR (4 and 3 bns resp). Dalmatian IR (2 bns); 7 guns.

Franco-Italian total 5,000 men.

Franco-Italian losses Killed and wounded unknown; 300 captured. The 2nd LtIR was destroyed.

Austrian Forces FML Radivojevich commanding: GM Csivich: GzIR Warasdiner-Kreutzer Nr 5 (2nd Bn); IR EH Franz Carl Nr 52 (1st bn); GzIR St Georger Nr 6 (2nd Bn). GM Rebrovich: GzIR Gradiskaner Nr 8 (2nd Bn); GM Nugent: HusR Radetzky Nr 5 (4 sqns), ½ x 3 pdr FAB.

Austrian total ca 4,000 men, 9 guns.

Austrian losses Not known.

Comment Palombini's 5th Division was already at 50% of its start-out strength before the action began. He fell back westwards to Postonja. Martinien lists no officer casualties for the Italians this day. The Viceroy (Prince Eugène) fell back west over the Isonzo River.

Sources Wrede, Vaudoncourt, Martinien.

IN Bruneck, 28 September 1813, skirmish

A small town in northeastern Italy's South Tyrol province, in the Puster valley on Route 49, on the River Rienz, between Brixen and Toblach.

A Franco-Italian victory over the Austrians.

(Last action – Zirknitz, 27 September; next action – Tarvis (Saifnitz), 7 October.)

Franco-Italian Forces GdD Giflenga commanding the newly formed Reserve Division of Prince Eugène's army: 3 bns.

Franco-Italian total ca 3,000 men.

Franco-Italian losses Not exactly known but very light.

Austrian Forces FML Fenner's Avantgarde: Jg Bn Nr 4 (1 bn); 400 men mostly local Tyrolean Volunteer Landesschützen (militia or homeguard).

Austrian losses Not exactly known but light.

Comment This was Eugène's answer to the embarrassing débâcle of the Mühlbacher Klause on 11 September. Fenner withdrew east to Toblach (Dobbiaco) without further loss. Eugène had by now decided to withdraw southwestwards so this minor victory was not exploited.

Sources vom Holtz, von Welden.

SX Altenburg, 28 September 1813, clash

A town in northeastern Germany, 40 km south of Leipzig, just west of the River Pleisse and at the junction of Routes B7, B93 and B180.

An Allied victory over the French.

(Last action – Braunschweig, 25 September; next action – Kassel, 30 September.)

French Forces GdD Lefebvre-Desnouettes commanding the cavalry of the Imperial Guard: GrenàCh (4 sqns); ChàCh (6 sqns); 2e ChLL (10 sqns), Mamelukes (1 sqn). From I Cavalry Corps GdB Piré: 6e, 7e, 8e HusRs (8 sqns); 8e ChLLR (2 sqns). From III Cavalry Corps: 5e ChàCh (1 sqn). From V Cavalry Corps: 14e ChàCh (3 sqns); 6e and 19e DragRs (3 sqns). Baden IR Graf Hochberg Nr 2 (4 cos).

French total 6,500 men, 12 guns.

French losses 600 killed and wounded, 1,500 captured, 5 guns, 3 standards (possibly 8e Hus, 8e ChàCh, 19e Drag).

Allied Forces The Streifkorps of GL von Thielemann: Austrians – Obstlt Baron von Gasser: ChLR Hohenzollern Nr 2 (2 sqns); ChLR Klenau Nr 5 (1 sqn); HusR Kienmayer Nr 8 (1 sqn). Prussians – GM Prince Biron von Kurland: 2nd Silesian HusR (2 sqns); 2nd Silesian NKR (2½ sqns); DragR Neumark (1 sqn). Russians: GM Count Orlov-Denissov: Don Cossack Pulks of Gorin II and Jagondin II (600 men). 2 x Austrian cavalry howitzers, 2 Russian Unicorns.

Allied total ca 1,500 men.

Allied losses 200 killed and wounded.

Comment This was a very successful ambush. The

Streifkorps of Platow and Mensdorff were also engaged. The 8e HusR was overthrown by the Allied cavalry and fled the field, riding down their own infantry in the process. The Baden IR Nr 2 (the French rearguard) was abandoned at the bridge over the Gersta stream and destroyed losing 8 officers and 408 men.

Sources Wrede, Martinien, MKuKKA 3rd Folge Vol IV, Charrié, Obser.

SX Kassel, 30 September 1813, clash and capitulation

A city in the German province of Hessen (in 1813 the capital of the Napoleonic state of the Kingdom of Westfalia) on the River Fulda, at the junction of the Autobahns A7(E45), A49 and A44 (E331).

A Russian victory over the Westfalians.

(Last action – Altenburg, 28 September; next action – Wartenburg, 30 October.)

Westfalian Forces Gen Allix commanding: Jäger Garde (1 bn, 840 men); Chass Carabiniers (160 men); Füs Garde Depot (160 men); 2nd LIR Depot (150 men); 5th LIR Depot (150 men); 7th LIR (2nd Bn, 150 men); 8th LIR Depot (150 men); 4th Lt Bn Depot (300 men); ChLL Garde Depot (140 men); Gendarmes (30 men); Garde Arty Bty (209 men); Arty Depot (24 men); Ouvrier coy (103 men).

Westfalian total 2,060 infantry, 170 cavalry, 34 guns, 336 artillery.

Westfalian losses A few wounded.

Russian Forces G Czernicheff commanding: Combined HusR (3 sqns); Isum HusR (3 sqns); Finland DragR (2 sqns); 5 Cossack Pulks; four 6 pounder guns and two 'Unicorns'.

Russian total ca 2,300 men.

Russian losses Very light.

Comment This raid on King Jerome's capital city spread panic throughout the Francophile administration and lifted the spirits of the increasingly patriotic German populace. The Westfalian army melted away or were allowed to go home without their weapons. King Jerome had fled; he returned when the Russians left on 16 October and finally left again on 26 October.

Sources Specht, Sporschil, Lünsmann.

SX Wartenburg, 3 October 1813, clash

A village in Saxony (northeastern Germany) 12 km southeast of Wittenberg and west of the confluence of the River Schwarze Elster with the Elbe.

A Prussian victory over the French.

(Last action – Kassel, 30 September; next action – Bremen, 14/15 October.)

French Forces GdD Count Bertrand commanding the IV Corps: 12th Division GdD Count Morand: 8e RILé (2 bns); 13e RIdLi (5 bns); 23e RIdLi (4 bns). 38th Division GL Count Franquemont's Württembergers: 1st Combined LtI Bn, 1st, 2nd and 3rd Combined LI Bns (1 bn each). 29th Light Cavalry Brigade GdD Beaumont: Westfalian ChLGarde (4 sqns); Hessen-Darmstadt ChLGarde (3 sqns). 15th Division (Italians) GdD Fontanelli: 1st LIR (2 bns); 4th LIR (3 bns); 1st LtIR (3 bns); 6th LIR (2 bns); 7th LIR (3 bns); Milan bn (1 bn).

French total ca 14,000 men, 24 guns.

French losses 900 killed and wounded, 1,000 captured, 13 guns, 80 ammunition waggons. GdD Beaumont killed.

Prussian Forces GL York commanding the I Corps: Avantgarde: Obst von Katzler: Brandenburg HusR (5 sqns); 2nd Leib-HusR (2 sqns); Brandenburg UlR (4 sqns); Ostpreussisches NKR (5 sqns); 5th Silesian LWKR (4 sqns); 1 x HAB (8guns). Leib-Gren-Bn, Westpreussisches Gren-Bn (1 bn each); 12th ResIR (2nd Bn); Brandenburg IR (1st Bn); 2nd Ostpreussisches IR (Füs Bn); LWIRs Rekowsky, Thiele and Wedell (1 bn each); Jägers (3 coys). Brigade of Obst von Steinmetz: 1st Ostpreussisches Gren Bn; 2nd Ostpreussisches IR (1st Bn); LWI bns Fischer, Mumm, Seidlitz, Walter, von Cronegk, Larisch and Martitz (1 bn each); 1 x FAB. Brigade of GM Prince Karl von Mecklenburg: Silesian Gren Bn; 1st Ostpreussischen IR (3 bns); 2nd Ostpreussischen IR (2nd Bn); LWI Bn Kosecky (1 bn); Mecklenburg-Strelitz HusR (4 sqns); 2nd Leib-HusR (3 sqns); 2 x FAB (13 guns). Brigade of GM von Horn: Leib-IR (3 bns); Thüringian bn (1 bn); LWI Bns Sommerfeld, Pettingkofer, Reichenbach and Knorr-Kottulinsky (1 bn each); ½ x FAB (3 guns). Brigade of GM von Hünerbein: Brandenburg IR (2nd and Füs bns); 12th ResIR (1st and Füs Bn); LWI Bn Kempky, 1 x FAB (8 guns). Reserve Cavalry Obst Baron von Wahlen-Jürgass: Lithuanian DragR (5 sqns); Westpreussisches DragR, 10th Silesian LWKR, 1st Neumark LWKR (4 sqns each), 2 x HAB (16 guns).

Prussian total 16,000 men, 64 guns.

Prussian losses 1,900 killed and wounded, 200 missing.

Comment York received the title 'von Wartenburg' for this highly successful action, heralding Blücher's new offensive.
Sources Plotho, Martinien, Friedrich.

IN Tarvis (Saifnitz), 7 October 1813, clash
A village in northeastern Italy, in the valley of the River Fella, close to the borders of Austrian and Slovenia, on Route 13.
An Austrian victory over the Franco-Italians.
(Last action - Bruneck, 28 September; next action - Mühlbacher Klause, 7 October.)
Franco-Italian Forces 42e, 102e and 131e RIdLi (1 bn each) of GdD Baron Gratien's 3rd Division of GdD Grenier's 'Corps de Gauche'.
Franco-Italian losses ca 100 killed, wounded and missing. The 42e lost 2 officers, the 102e - 3 and the 131e - 2.
Austrian Forces GdK Frimont; FML Marschall: IR Reisky Nr 10 (1 bn); IR Hohenlohe-Bartenstein Nr 26 (6 coys); Jg Bn Nr 9 (4 coys); IR Chasteler Nr 27 (4 x LW coys); GzIR Peterwardeiner Nr 9 (1 bn); 2 x FAB.
Austrian total ca 2,600 men, 12 guns.
Austrian losses '600 killed and wounded, 100 captured'. (Vaudoncourt).
Comment The French withdrew west to Pontebba to concentrate with Prince Eugène who had fallen back westwards out of Croatia. Vaudoncourt's casualties for the Austrians are highly exaggerated.
Sources Wrede, Martinien, Vaudoncourt, vom Holtz.

IN Mühlbacher Klause, 7 October 1813, 2nd raid
A village in the valley of the River Rienz (a tributary of the Eisack/Isarco) in northern Italy's South Tyrol province, about 10 km north of Brixen (Bressanone).
An Austrian victory over the Franco-Italians.
(Last action - Tarvis (Saifnitz), 7 October; next action - San Marco and Volano, 26/27 October.)
Franco-Italian Forces One battalion.
Franco-Italian losses Killed unknown; none escaped, 7 officers and 450 men were captured.
Austrian Forces FML Fenner commanding: 8th Jg Bn (2 coys); GzIR Szeckler Nr 2 (2 coys); Tyrolean Landesschützen (3 coys).
Austrian total ca 700 men.
Austrian losses Not known exactly but light. Several men were killed in climbing accidents.
Comment This successful raid opened the way for the Austrians to push south on Brixen and Bozen.
Sources Vaudoncourt, vom Holtz, Wrede.

EN Bidassoa and Rhune, 7–9 October 1813, clash
Including Croix-des-Bouquets, San Marcial, Bayonette and Sainte-Barbe.
A series of French fortifications on the north side of the River Bidassoa which marks the western border between France and Spain, about 15 km northwest of Vera.
Allied victories over the French.
(Last action - Bidassoa, 1 September; next action - Ste Barbe, 12 October.)
French Forces M Soult commanding: GdD Reille: 7th Division GdD Maucune: 17e RILé, 3e, 15e, 101e RIdLi (1 bn each). Plus 10e RILé and 105e RIdLi (2 bns each) from Villatte's Reserve.
French total ca 6,500 men, 8 guns.
French losses 390 killed and wounded, 60 captured, 8 guns.
Allied Forces The Marquess of Wellington commanding: 1st Division MG Howard: 1/2nd and 1/3rd Footguards; 1st, 2nd, 5th LI Bns KGL; 1st and 2nd Lt Bns KGL (1 bn each). 5th Division MG Leith: 3/1st, 1/9th, 1/38th, 1/4th, 2/47th and 2/59th Foot (1 bn each). Light Division MG C Alten: 1/43rd, 1/52nd, 1/95th, 2/95th, 3/95th (1 bn each). Brunswick Oels (2 coys); 5/60th (2 coys). Portuguese Troops: with the Light Division: 17th LIR (2 bns); 1st and 3rd Caçadores (1 bn); Madden's Brigade (with 6th Division) 8th and 12th LIRs (2 bns each); 9th Caçadores (1 bn); Wilson's Brigade (with 5th Division): 1st and 16th LIRs (2 bns each); 4th Caçadores (1 bn).
Spanish Troops Del Barco's Division and Bargena's Division. Exact details and losses not known.
Allied totals 24,000 men.
Allied losses British - 82 killed, 486 wounded, 5 missing. Portuguese - 48 killed, 186 wounded, 8 missing.
Comment This was one of Wellington's cleverest, and most economical, victories. He fooled Soult into believing that he would attack in the east and centre of the river line: Soult obligingly concentrated 35,000 men in that sector and denuded his western wing, believing the Bidassoa estuary to be unfordable. Wellington knew better; in a perfectly timed and executed operation the Allies turned a major

obstacle line at astoundingly small cost. On the inland (eastern) sector of the line, Wellington ordered feint assaults by the Light Division (turning east after crossing the Bidassoa at Vera) and 4 Spanish bns under Giron (including IR Ordenes Militares which distinguished itself) on the Rhune mountains.

The French were Taupin's 8th Division: 9e RILé, 47e and 70e RIdLi (2 bns each), 31e RILé, 26e and 88e RIdLi (1 bn each) plus 12e RILé, 32e and 34e RIdLi of Conroux's 4th Division and the 4e Lé and 40e Li. Despite occupying positions of great natural and artificial strength, the demoralised French would not fight and just ran off. Allied losses include those suffered in this sector. French losses here were over 1,200 including 22 officers and 576 men captured, and 9 guns. Soult withdrew north.

Sources Oman, Martinien.

EN Ste Barbe Redoubt, 12 October 1813, raid and capture

A redoubt in southwest France, in the mountains between Ainhoa and the Grande Rhune mountain, about 15 km inland from the Biscayan Port of St Jean-de-Luz.

A French victory over the Spanish.

(Last action – Bidassoa and Rhune, 7–9 October; next action – Pamplona, 31 October.)

French Forces GdD Conroux's 4th Division: 32e, 43e, 55e, 58e RIdLi (2, 2, 1 and 1 bns resp).

French total ca 2,000 actually involved.

French losses Not exactly known; possible 300 in all.

Spanish Forces The garrison, ½ bn of La Torre's Division; later a counter-attack was made by 5 bns but failed.

Spanish losses The garrison (200) captured; 300 killed and wounded.

Comment Wellington ordered no further attempts to be made to retake the place.

Sources Oman, Martinien.

SX Liebertwolkwitz, 13/14 October 1813, clash

A village in Saxony (northeastern Germany), 15 km southeast of Leipzig, just west of the railway to Chemnitz.

A drawn match.

(Last action – Wartenburg, 3 October; next action – Bremen, 14/15 October).

French Forces Joachim Murat, King of Naples, commanding:

IV Corps GdD Count Lauriston: 16th Division GdD Count Maison: 152e, 153e, 154e RIdLi. 19th Division GdD Rochambeau: 135e, 150e, 155e RIdLi. Cavalry of the Imperial Guard: Grenadiers à Ch.

I Cavalry Corps GdD Latour-Maubourg: 1st Light Cavalry Division GdD Bourcier: 1er and 3e ChLLs. 3rd Light Cavalry Division GdD Chastel: 25e ChàCh.

III Cavalry Corps GdD Arrighi: 1st Division GdD Fournier: 5e, 14e, 26e ChàCh. 2nd Division GdD Lorge: 3e HusR, 27e ChàCh. 3rd Division 2e, 12e, 19e, 20e DragRs. 4th Division GdD Defrance: 15e, 18e, 22e, 25e DragRs. The 25e ChàCh also show officer casualties for this action.

French total ca 11,000 infantry, 7,000 cavalry.

French losses GdB Bertrand wounded; 1,500 killed and wounded, 1,000 captured.

Allied Forces The Army of Bohemia. FM Prince Carl von Schwarzenberg commanding. **Russian troops** GdK Count Wittgenstein: Cavalry GL Count Pahlen III; GM Illowaisky XII: Cossack Pulks of Illowaisky XII, Radionov II, Ataman. 1st Hussar Division: Grodno HusR (6 sqns); Ssum HusR (7 sqns); Olviopol HusR (2 sqns); Lubny HusR (4 sqns); GM Lissanevitch: Tartar UlR (4 sqns); Tchuguchev UlR (6 sqns); Serpuchov HusR (4 sqns).

II (Prussian) Corps GL von Kleist: 9th Brigade GM von Klüx; 1st Westpr IR; 6th Res IR (3 bns each); Schl Schützen (2 coys); 7th Schl LWIR (4 bns); Neumark DragR (4 sqns); 1 x 6 pdr FAB. 10th Brigade GM Pirch I: 2nd Westpr IR, 7th Res IR (3 bns each); 9th Schl LWIR (4 bns); 2nd Schl LWKR (4 sqns). 11th Brigade GM von Ziethen: 1st Schl IR and 10th Res IR (3 bns each); Schl Schützen (2 coys); 8th Schl LWIR (4 bns); 1st Schl HusR (4 sqns), 1 x 6 pdr FAB. Reserve Cavalry GM von Röder: Ostpr KürRR, Schl KürR, Brand-KürR (4 sqns each); Schl UlR (4 sqns); Schl NKR (2 sqns); 2nd Schl HusR (2 sqns); 7th and 8th Schl LWKRs (4 sqns each), 2 x HAB.

IV (Austrian) Corps GdK Count Klenau: 1st Division FML Baron Mohr: GzIR Wallachisch-Illyrisch Nr 13 (1 bn); ChLR Hohenzollern Nr 2 (6 sqns); HusR EH Ferdinand Nr 3 (6 sqns), 1 x 6 pdr HAB.

Further details of Austrian participation are unclear.

Allied total 6,000 cavalry, 20,000 infantry.

Allied losses Russian GL Dochtorov killed, 2,500

killed and wounded, 500 captured.

Sources Plotho, Sporschil, Martinien, Wrede.

SX Bremen, 14/15 October 1813, capture

A fortified city port in northwestern Germany, on the right bank of the River Weser, about 60 km from the mouth of that river.

A Prusso-Russian victory over the French.

(Last action – Liebertwolkwitz, 13/14 October; next action – Leipzig, 16, 18 and 19 October.)

French Garrison Col Devallant commanding. 1st Swiss IR (1 bn); some French detachments, 14 guns.

French total 1,100 men.

French losses Killed and wounded not known but very light; the garrison was allowed to go but the 14 guns were taken. Col Thuillier killed.

Allied Forces GM Baron von Tettenborn of the Army of the North with 800 cossacks and Lützow's Freikorps (1st Bn).

Allied total 1,600 men, 4 guns.

Allied losses Very light.

Sources Plotho, Sporschil, Martinien.

SX Leipzig, 16, 18 and 19 October 1813, battle

A town in eastern Germany, on the eastern bank of the River Weisse Elster, at the junction of Routes B6, B2 and B87 and about 120 km west of Dresden in Saxony.

An Allied victory over the French.

(Last action – Liebertwolkwitz, 13/14 October; next action – Lützen, 20 October.)

French Forces Emperor Napoleon I commanding.

The Old Guard 1st Division GdD Count Friant: GdB Baron Michel: 1er and 2e Grenadiers (2 bns each). GdB Christiani: 1er and 2e Chasseurs (2 bns each), 1 x FAB. 2nd Division GdD Curial: GdB Rousseau Fusilier Grenadiers (2 bns); Fusilier Chasseurs (2 bns); Vélites de Florence and Vélites de Turin (1 bn each). GdB Rothembourg: Saxon Leibgrenadier-Garde, Westfalian Garde-Grenadier-Bn*, Polish Guards (1 bn each), 1 x FAB. **Old Guard totals** 10,919 men, 14 guns.

* = Garde-Füs-R plus elite coys 2nd and 3rd LIRs.

I Corps of the Young Guard M Oudinot Duke of Reggio: **1st Division** GdD Pacthod: GdB Lacoste: 1er, 2e, 3e, 6e Voltigeurs (2 bns each). GdB Couloumy: 7e, 11e, Voltigeurs (1 bns each). **Total** 6,000 men. **3rd Division** GdD Decouz: GdB Boyer: 4e, 5e, 8e Voltigeurs (2 bns each). GdB Pelet 9e, 10e, 12e Voltigeurs (2 bns each), 3 x FAB. **Totals** 4,731 men, 24 guns. **I Corps Young Guard total** 10,775 men, 24 guns.

II Corps of the Young Guard M Mortier, Duke of Treviso: **2nd Division** GdD Barrois: GdB Poret de Morvan: 1er, 2e, 3e Tirailleurs (2 bns each). GdB Dulong: 6e, 7e Tirailleurs (2 bns each), 3 x FAB. **Total** 5,470 men, 24 guns. **4th Division** GdD Roguet: GdB Flamand: Flanqueur Chasseurs, Flanqueur Grenadiers, 4e, 5e Tirailleurs (2 bns each). GdB Marquet: 8e, 9e, 10e Tirailleurs (2 bns each), Sailors of the Guard (1 bn), 3 x FAB. **Total** 5,521 men, 24 guns. **Young Guard total** 19,500 men 72 guns.

Cavalry of the Guard GdD Nansouty: **1st Division** GdD Count Ornano: GdB Colbert: 2nd Lancers of Berg (6 sqns); 2e (Dutch) ChLL (4 sqns); DragR (Young Guard) 1 x HAB. **Total** 1,861 men, 6 guns. **2nd Division** GdD Lefebvre-Desnouettes; GdB Krasinski: 1er ChLL (4 sqns); ChàCh(4 sqns). GdB Castex GrenàCh (2 sqns), 1 x HAB. **Total** 1,585 men, 6 guns. **3rd Division** GdD Walther: GdB Baron Lyon: 1st (Polish) ChLL (Old Guard) 3 sqns; 1er, 4e Gardes d'Honneur (4 sqns each); ChàCh (Old Guard) and Mamelukes (6 sqns). GdB Lefort: DragR (Old Guard), 3e Gardes d'Honneur (4 sqns each). GdB Laferrière: GrenàCh (Old Guard); 2e Gardes d'Honneur (4 sqns each), 1 x HAB. **Total** 4,457 men, 6 guns. **Cavalry of the Imperial Guard totals** 7,903 men. 18 guns. **Guard Artillery Reserve** GdD Dulang: 10 batteries, 2 coys sappers, 12 Gendarmerie coys (74 guns, 2,750 men).

II Corps M Victor, Duke of Belluno: **4th Division** GdD Dubreton: GdB Ferrière 24e RILé, 19e RIdLi (3 bns each). GdB Brun; 37e, 56e RIdLi (3 bns each), 2 x FAB. **Total** 5,618 men. **5th Division** GdD Dufour: GdB d'Etzko: 26e, 39e RIdLi (3 bns each); 46e, 72e RIdLi (1 bn each); 1 x FAB. **Total 4,235** men. **6th Division** GdD Vial: GdB Valory: 11e RILé, 93e RIdLi (3 bns each). GdB Bronikowski: 4e, 18e RIdLi (3 bns each), 2 x FAB. **Total 6,235** men. **II Corps totals** 17,292 men, 40 guns.

V Corps GdD Count Lauriston: **10th Division** GdD Albert; GdB Bachelet: 4e PvLé (5e, 12e RILé) 2 bns; 139e RIdLi (3 bns). GdB Bertrand 140e, 141e RIdLi (3 bns each). 2 x FAB. **Total** 3,250 men. **16th Division** GdD Maison; GdB Montevalle: 152e RIdLi (3 bns). GdB Count Montesquieu: 153e, 154e RIdLi (3 bns each). 2 x FAB. **Total** 3,656 men. **6th Light Cavalry Brigade** GdB Dermoncourt: 2, 3e, 6e ChàCh (2, 2 and 3 sqns resp). **Total** 761 men. Reserve Artillery 2 x FAB, 1 x HAB. **V Corps totals** 13,332 men, 53 guns.

VIII (Polish) Corps M Prince Josef Poniatowski, 26th Division GdD Krasinski, GdB Grabowski; 12th and 14th LIR (2 bns each); 1½ x FAB. 27th Cavalry Brigade GdB Uminski: 14th KürR (2 sqns); Krakus (4 sqns). Reserve Artillery 2 x FAB. **VIII Corps totals** 5,000 men, 42 guns.

IX Corps M Augereau Duke of Castiglione: 51st Division GdB Lagarde: 32e PvLé (25e and 32e RILé) 2 bns; 63e RIdLi (1 bn). GdB Aymard: 34e PvLé (10e and 21e RILé), 35e PvLi (32e and 58e RIdLi) 2 bns each. **Total** 4,350 men. **52nd Division** GdD Sémélé: GdB Bagneries: 37e PvLé (17e and 29e RILé) 2 bns, 39e RIdLi (2e Bn). GdB Godard: 86e RIdLi (2e Bn); 121e RIdLi (6e Bn), 122e RIdLi (6e Bn). **Total** 4,297 men. Artillery: 2 x FAB. **IX Corps totals** 9,186 men, 12 guns.

XI Corps M Macdonald Duke of Tarentum. **31st Division** GdD Ledru-des-Essarts: GdB Fressinet: 11e PvLi (27e RILé, 20e RIdLi (6e Bn); 102e RIdLi (4e Bn) 3 bns; 13e PvLi (5e, 11e, 79e RIdLi) 3 bns. GdB Baron O'Henin: 4th Westfalian LtI Bn (1 bn); 8th Westfalian LIR (2 bns). GdB Macdonald: 4th Neapolitan LtIR (2 bns); Neapolitan Élite IR (elite coys, 5th, 6th, 7th LIRs). Artillery 1 x French FAB, 2 x Westfalian FABs. **Total** 5,023 men, 20 guns. **35th Division** GdD Baron Gérard: GdB Le Senecal: 6e RIdLi (3 bns); 112e RIdLi (4 bns). GdB Zucchi 2nd Italian LtIR (3rd, 4th bns); 5th Italian LIR (4 bns), 1 x Italian FAB, 1 x Italian HAB. **Total** 3,551 men, 14 guns. **36th Division** GdD Count Charpentier: GdB Simmer: 22e RILé (4 bns); 10e RIdLi (4e and 6e Bns); GdB Meunier: 3e RILé (3e,4e Bns), 14e RILé (3e, 4e, 7e Bns). 2 x FABs. **Total** 4,299 men, 16 guns. **39th Division** GdD Count Marchand. GM von Stockhorn's Baden Brigade: 1st IR von Stockhorn (2 bns); 3rd IR Grossherzog (2 bns). GM Prinz Emil von Hessen-Darmstadt's Brigade: Füs-Garde-R, Leib-Garde-R, 2nd IR (2 bns each). 1 x Baden and 1 x Hessen-Darmstadt FAB. **Total** 4,602 men, 7 guns. 28th Light Cavalry Brigade GdB Montbrun: 4th Italian ChàCh (2 sqns); 2nd Neapolitan ChàCh (4 sqns); Würzburg ChLR (1 sqn). Total 446 men. **39th Division total** 4,602 men, 7 guns. Reserve Artillery: 1 x French HAB, 2 x French FABs. **XI Corps totals** 20,533 men, 79 guns.

I Cavalry Corps GdD Count Latour-Maubourg: **1st Light Cavalry Division** GdD Corbineau: 1st Light Cavalry Brigade GdB Baron Piré: 6e, 7e, 8e HusR (2, 3 and 3 sqns resp); ½ x HAB. GdD Baron Berckheim; GdB Count Montmarie's 2nd Light Cavalry Brigade: 16e ChàCh, 1er and 3e ChLLs (2 sqns each). GdB Baron Piquet's 3rd Light Cavalry Brigade: 5e, 8e ChLLs (2 sqns each). 1½ x HAB. **Total** 1,850 men, 9 guns. **3rd Light Cavalry Division** GdD Baron Castel: 4th Light Cavalry Brigade; GdB Baron Vallin: 8e, 9e ChàCh (2 sqns each). 5th Light Cavalry Brigade: GdB Vial (or Merlin); 1er, 19e, 25e ChàCh (3, 4 and 2 sqns resp). **Total** ca 3,200 men, 1 x HAB (6 guns). **1st Heavy Cavalry Division** Count Bordesoulle: 1st Brigade GdB Sopranski: 2e, 3e, 6e, 9e CuirRs (2, 2, 3 and 3 sqns resp). 2nd Brigade GdB Bessières: 11e, 12e CuirRs (3 and 2 sqns resp). 3rd Brigade (Saxons) GM Lessing: Leibkürassiergarde, Kür-R von Zastrow (4 sqns each). 1 x French HAB. **Total** ? men, 6 guns. **3rd Heavy Cavalry Division** GdD Baron Doumerc: 1st Brigade GdB Baron de Lalaing: 4e, 7e, 14e CuirRs (3, 3 and 2 sqns resp); Italian DragR Napoleone (4 sqns). 2nd Brigade GdB Baron Reizet: 7e, 23e, 28e, 30e DragRs (2, 3, 2, and 2 sqns resp); 7e, 23e, 28e, 30e DragRs (2, 3, 2, and 2 sqns resp). 1 x Italian HAB **Total** ca 3,300 men, 6 guns. **I Cavalry Corps totals** 6,480 men, 27 guns.

II Cavalry Corps GdD Count Sebastiani: **2nd Light Cavalry Division** GdD Baron Roussel d'Hurbal. 7th Light Cavalry Brigade: GdB Gérard: 2e ChLL, 11e, 12e ChàCh (3 sqns each). 8th Light Cavalry Brigade 4e ChLL, 5e HusR (3 sqns each). 9e HusR (4 sqns). ½ x HAB (3 guns). **4th Light Cavalry Division** GdD Baron Exelmans: 9th Light Cavalry Brigade GdB Baron Maurin: 6th ChLL, 4e ChàCh (2 sqns each); 7e ChàCh (3 sqns); 20e ChàCh (4 sqns); 10th Light Cavalry Brigade GdB Wathier: 23e ChàCh (4 sqns); 24e ChàCh (3 sqns); 11e HusR (2 sqns); ½ x HAB (3 guns). **2nd Heavy Cavalry Division** GdD Baron St Germain 1st Brigade: GdB Baron d'Haugranville 1er and 2e Carabiniers (2 sqns each). 2nd Brigade GdB Thiry 1er, 8e and 10e CuirRs (2 sqns each); 5e CuirR (3 sqns); 1 x HAB (6 guns). **II Cavalry Corps totals** 5,680 men, 12 guns.

III Cavalry Corps GdD Arrighi, Duke of Padua: **5th Light Cavalry Division** GdD Baron Lorge: 12th Light Cavalry Brigade GdB Baron Jacquinot: 5e, 10e, 13e* ChàCh (2 sqns each). 13th Light Cavalry Brigade GdB

Baron Merlin: 15e, 21e, 22e* ChàCh (1, 1 and 2 sqns resp); ½ x HAB. **6th Light Cavalry Division** GdD Baron Fournier: 14th Light Cavalry Brigade GdB Baron Mouriez: 29e, 31e ChàCh, 1er HusR (1 sqn each), 15th Light Cavalry Brigade GdB Baron Amiel: 2e, 4e, 12e HusRs (1sqn each), ½ x HAB **4th Heavy Cavalry Division** GdD Comte Defrance 1st Brigade, GdB Baron Avice: 4e, 5e, 12e, 14e DragRs (1 sqn each) 2nd Brigade, GdB Baron Quinette de Cernay: 16e, 17e, 21e, 26e, 27e DragRs; 13e CuirR (1sqn each); ½ x HAB. **III Cavalry Corps totals** 4,000 men.

IV Cavalry Corps M Kellermann. **7th (Polish) Cavalry Division** GdB Tolinski: 1st ChàCh, 3rd UlR (4 sqns each), 1 x HAB. **8th (Polish) Light Cavalry Division** GdD Prince Sulkowski: GdB Krustowski: 6th and 8th UlRs (4 sqns each), 1 x HAB. **IV Cavalry Corps totals** 3,000 men, 8 guns.

V Cavalry Corps GdD Pajol: **9th Light Cavalry Division** GdD Subervie; GdB Klicky: 3e HusR, 27e ChàCh (3 and 4 sqns resp). GdB Vial: 14e, 26e ChàCh, 13e HusR (3, 3 and 4 sqns resp). **Total** 1,700 men. **5th Heavy Cavalry Division** GdD l'Heritier: GdB Quennot: 2e and 6e DragRs (3 and 4 sqns resp). GdB Collard: 11e, 13e, 15e DragRs (4, 2 and 3 sqns resp). ½ x HAB. Total 1,700 men 3 guns. **6th Heavy Cavalry Division** GdD Milhaud: GdB Lamotte: 18e, 19e, 20e DragRs (2, 2 and 3 sqns resp). GdB Monte Legier: 22e, 25e DragRs (3and 4 sqns resp). Total 1,600 men. **V Cavalry Corps total** 5,000 men, 11 guns.

III Corps GdD Count Souham commanding: **8th Division** GdD Baron Brayer: GdB Bony 6e PvLé (6e, 25e RILé), 10e PvLé (16e, 28e RILé), 14PvLi (34e, 40e RIdLi), 19e PvLi (32e, 58e RIdli), 2 bns each. GdB Baron Charrière: 21 PvLi (59e, 69e RIdLi), 24e PvLi (88e, 103e RIdLi) 2 bns each. 2 x FAB. **Total** 4,442 men, 12 guns. **9th Division** GdD Delmas: GdB Anthing 2e PvLé (2e, 4e, RILé), 29e RILé (2 bns each), 136e RIdLi (3 bns). GdB Vergez de Brareaux: 138e, 145e RIdLi (3 bns each). 2 x FAB. **Total** 4,235 men, 13 guns. **11th Division** GdD Baron Ricard: GdB Vandedem van der Gelder: 9e RILé, 17e PvLi (43e, 75e RIdLi), 50e RIdLi (2 bns each), 65e RIdLi (1 bn). GdB Dumoulin: 142, 144e RIdLi (3 bns each), 2 x FAB. **Total** 4,357 men, 12 guns. 23rd Light Cavalry Brigade GdB Baron Beurmann, 10e HusR (6 sqns), Baden Light DragR (5 sqns), 1 x HAB (6 guns). Reserve Artillery 2 x 12 pdr FAB (16 guns) **III Corps totals** 17,168 men, 59 guns.

IV Corps GdD Count Bertrand. **12th Division** GdD Count Morand: GdB de Belair: 8e RILé (4 bns). GdB Toussaint: 13e RIdLi (4 bns). GdB Hulot: 23e, 137e RIdLi (3 bns each). 2 x FAB. **Total** 5,705 men, 12 guns. **15th (Italian Division)** GdD Count Fontanelle: GdB St Andrea: 1st LtIR (2 bns), Milan Municipal Guards (1 bn). GdB Moroni*: 1st, 4th, 6th, 7th LIRs (1 bn each). 1 x FAB. **Total** 1,859 men, 6 guns. **38th (Württemberg) Division*** GL Count Franquemont: GM von Stockmayer: 1st (1st); 2nd (4th); 3rd (6th) Combined IRs (1 bn each). **Total** 1,043 men. **24th Light Cavalry Brigade*** (Württemberg) GM von Jett: ChLR Prinz Adam Nr 1, JzPfR Herzog Louis Nr 3 (1 sqn each), 1 x HAB. **Totals** 125 men, 6 guns. **29th Light Cavalry Brigade** BG von Wolff: Westfalian ChL Garde R; Hessen-Darmstadt ChL Garde R (1 sqn each). **Total** 221 men. Reserve Artillery 8 x 12 pdr guns. **IV Corps totals** 9,824 men, 26 guns.

VI Corps M Marmont Duke of Ragusa: **20th Division** GdD Count Compans. GdB Baron Pelleport: 32e RILé (2 bns), 1er Naval R (5 bns). GdB Baron Joubert: 3e Naval R (3 bns); 20e PvLi (66e, 122e RIdLi); 25e PvLi (47e, 86e RIdLi) 2 bns each. 2 x FAB. **Totals** 5,079 men, 16 guns. **21st Division** GdD Count Lagrange; GdB Baron Jamin: 37e RILé (4 bns); 4e Naval R (3 bns); IR Joseph Napoleon (1 bn). GdB Baron Buquet: 2e Naval R (6 bns); 2 x FAB (16 guns). **Total** 5,543 men. **22nd Division** GdD Baron Friedrichs: GdB Baron von Coehorn; 23e RILé, 11e PvLi (1er, 62e RIdLi); 13e PvLi (14e, 16e RIdLi); 15e RIdLi (2 bns each). GdB Choisy: 16e PvLi (26e, 82e RIdLi); 70e, 121e RIdLi (2 bns each), 2 x FAB. **Total** 4,720 men, 16 guns. **25th (Württemberg) Light Cavalry Brigade**** GM Count Normann: Leib ChLR Nr 2, JzPfR König Nr 4 (4 sqns each). 1 x HAB. **Total** 935 men, 6 guns. Reserve Artillery 16 x 12 pdrs, 12 x 6 pdrs.

VI Corps total 19,304 men. (According to Bleibtreu, 3 bns of Sailors were detached at this time and did not take part in the battle. The total thus fell to 17,700 men). 82 guns.

* = no officer casualties, probably not engaged.

** = casualties not known. This brigade went over to the Allies on 18 October.

VII Corps GdD Count Reynier. **13th Division** GdD Count Guilleminot: GdB Gruyer: 1er RILé (4e Bn); 18e RILé (1er and 2e Bn); 7e RIdLi (3e Bn); 156e RIdLi (1er and 2e Bn). GdB Baron Lejeune: IR Illyrien (2e Bn); 52e, 67e RIdLi (3e Bns each); 101e RIdLi (2e and 3e

Bn); 1 x FAB (6 guns). **24th Division (Saxons)** GL von Zeschau: 1st Brigade Obst von Brause LtIR von Lecoq, 1st Gren Bn von Spiegel, IR von Rechten, IR Prince Friedrich August, IR Steindel (1 bn each). 2nd Brigade GM von Ryssel: LtIR von Sahr; 2nd Gren Bn Anger, IR Prince Anton, IR Niesemeuschel (1 bn each); Feldjäger (1 coy). 2 x FAB (16 guns). 32nd Division GdD Baron Durutte: GdB Devaux: 35e RILé (1er bn); 131e RIdLi (3e Bn); 132e RIdLi (3e Bn). GdB Jarry: 36e RILé (4e Bn); 133e RIdLi (3e Bn); IR Würzburg (3rd Bn). 1 x FAB (6 guns), 1 x HAB (6 guns). 27th Light Cavalry Brigade (Saxons): Obst von Lindenau: HusR (8 sqns); UlR Prince Clemens (5 sqns), 1 x HAB (4 guns). Reserve Artillery: Saxon: 1 x 12 pdr FAB (6 guns); 1 x HAB (4 guns). French: 1 x 12 pdr FAB (6 guns).

VII Corps totals 12,837 men, 48 guns. On 18 October the Saxon troops went over to the Allies.

Dombrowski's 27th Division (Poles) GdB Zoltowski 2nd and 4th LIRs (2 bns each); GdB Kruckowiecki 2nd UlR and 4th ChàCh (4 sqns each). 1 x FAB, 1 x HAB (4 guns each). **Total** 2,850 men, 8 guns.

The Provisional Division GdD Lefol 1st Brigade: 54e RIdLi (2e Bn); 1½ Provisional bns (formed of parts of 29e RILé and 25e, 33e RIdLi), 1 x FAB (6 guns).

The Garrison of Leipzig GdD Margaron commanding: GdB Morio d'Isle: Combined LtI Bn (35e, 36e RILé, 1 combined bn); 96e RIdLi (2e Bn); 103e RIdLi (2e Bn); 132e RIdLi (4e Bn). The Baden Brigade GM Count Hochberg: 2nd LIR (1 bn); LtI Bn von Lingg (1 bn). ½ x FAB (4 guns). 2 x French HAB (12 guns).

Totals of the Grande Armée at Leipzig 16–19 October

	Battalions	Companies	Squadrons	Batteries	Men	Guns
Imperial Guard	66	16	61	27	44,499	202
II Corps	32	3	—	8	17,292	40
III Corps	38	4	11	9	17,168	59
IV Corps	24	3	4	5	9,824	26
V Corps	29	3	7	9	13,332	53
VI Corps	42	4	8	11	19,304	82
VII Corps	24	2	13	8	12,837	48
VIII Corps	14	1	6	6½	5,000	42
IX Corps	13	1	—	2	9,186	12
XI Corps	46	3	7	12	20,533	79
Dombrowski's Division	4	1	8	2	2,850	8
Margaron's Division	—	—	—	2½	4,820	16
Lefol's Division	4	—	—	1	2,229	6
I Cavalry Corps	—	—	75	4	6,480	27
II Cavalry Corps	—	—	52	2	5,679	12
III Cavalry Corps	—	—	27	1½	4,000	12
IV Cavalry Corps	—	—	16	2	3,000	11
V Cavalry Corps	—	—	47	½	5,000	3
Grand Totals	*336*	*41*	*342*	*113½*	*203,133*	*738*

French Officer Losses 16—19 October

The Imperial Guard	Killed	Wounded
1st Division Old Guard	—	9
2nd Division Old Guard	2	37
1st Div Young Guard	3	40
2nd Div Young Guard	3	36
3rd Div Young Guard	4	19
4th Div Young Guard	2	23
1st Cavalry Division	6	15
2nd Cavalry Division	—	—
3rd Cavalry Division	2	26
Artillery Reserve	7	26
Total Imperial Guard	*29*	*222*
II Corps		
4th Division	20	94
5th Division	17	60
6th Division	17	78
Total II Corps	54	232

	Killed	Wounded
III Corps		
8th Division	17	105
9th Division	18	58
11th Division	15	62
23rd Light Cav Bde	1	1
Total III Corps	*51*	*226*
IV Corps		
12th Division	7	38
15th Division (Italians)	—	3
38th Div (Württemberg)	—	—
24th Light Cav Bde (Württemberg)	?	?
29th Light Cav Bde (Hess & Württemb)	—	6
Total IV Corps	*7*	*47*
V Corps		
10th Division	13	76
16th Division	7	45
19th Division	7	64
6th Light Cav Bde	1	13
Total V Corps	*28*	*198*
VI Corps		
20th Division	42	146
21st Division	23	108
22nd Division	28	102
25th Light Cav Bde (Württemberg)	—	—
Total VI Corps	*93*	*356*
VII Corps		
13th Division	—	14
24th Division (Saxons)	—	9
32nd Division (Saxons)	4	32
27th Light Cav Bde (Saxons)	—	
Total VII Corps	*4*	*55*
VIII Corps (Poles)		
26th Division	1	71
27th Division	—	25
27th Cavalry Brigade	—	22
Total VIII Corps	*1*	*118*
IX Corps		
51st Division	4	45

	Killed	Wounded
52nd Division	3	31
Total IX Corps	*7**	*76**

* = losses of 25e Lé and 29e Lé shown in III Corps: of 17e and 32e Lé and 122e Li in VI corps.

	Killed	Wounded
XI Corps		
31st Div (Westfalians, Neapolitans)	6	51
35th Division	2	43
36th Division	11	75
39th Div (Baden, Hessians)	5	9
28th Light Cav Bde (Italians, Neapolitans, Würzburg)	—	4
XI Corps Total	*24*	*182*
Margaron's Division	—	8
March Division	1	16
Dombrowski's Division	—	44
I Cavalry Corps		
1st Light Cav Div	9	65
3rd Light Cav Div	3	22
1st Heavy Cav Div	8	71
3rd Heavy Cav Div	12	47
Total I Cavalry Corps	*32*	*205*
II Cavalry Corps		
2nd Light Cav Div	8	22
4th Light Cav Div	14	71
2nd Heavy Cav Div	4	25
Total II Cav Corps	*26*	*118*
III Cavalry Corps		
5th Light Cav Div	—	9
6th Light Cav Div	3	9
4th Heavy Cav Div	2	9
Total III Cavalry Corps	*5*	*27*
IV Cavalry Corps (Poles)		
7th Light Cav Div	—	13
8th Light Cav Div	—	9
Total IV Cavalry Corps	*—*	*22*
V Cavalry Corps		
9th Light Cav Div	4	21

	Killed	Wounded
5th Heavy Cav Div	4	35
6th heav Cav Div	2	12
Total V Cavalry Corps	*10*	*68*

Total Officer losses of the Grand Armée at Leipzig 16–19 October: 397 killed, 2,546 wounded. The following generals were casualties: killed – Marshal Prince Poniatowski; GdDs Count Aubry, Bachelet d'Amville, Boyer, Camus de Richemont, Baron Cochoru, Couloumy, Delmas, Estko, Ferrière, Friedrichs, Kwasniewsky, Pelletier de Montmarie, Count Rochambeau, Vial. In all, 66 generals and 2,546 officers were killed and wounded. Other ranks killed and wounded were estimated at 43,500 but the real figure will never be known. 8,000 wounded were captured on the battlefield and a further 15,000 sick and wounded were taken in Leipzig in the hospitals. 15,000 unwounded officers and men were captured, 325 guns, over 900 waggons, 28 eagles, colours and standards were taken, including the eagles of the 143e Li, the Sailors of the Imperial Guard, an unnumbered eagle and an Italian standard, the last three items taken at Möckern on 16 October. Possibly the Saxon and Württemberg colours were counted as trophies.

On the 18 October 5,400 Saxons, 700 Württembergers with 38 guns went over to the enemy.

The Allied Main Army Commander in Chief FM Prince Carl von Schwarzenberg.

The Austrian I Corps FZM Hieronymus Count Colloredo Mansfeld. **1st Light Division** FML Prince Moritz Liechtenstein: GM Prince von Hessen-Homburg: Jägers (1st and 2nd bns); ChLR Kaiser Nr 1 (6 sqns); 1 x HAB (6 guns). GM Baron von Scheither: GzIR Broder Nr 7 (1 bn); Jägers (7th bn); DragR Levenehr Nr 4 (4 sqns); ChLR Vincent Nr 4 (6 sqns); 1 x HAB (6 guns). **2nd Light Division** FML Ferdinand Count Bubna: GM Baron Zechmeister von Rheinau: GzIR Peterwardeiner Nr 9 (1 bn); Jägers (6th Bn); HusR Liechtenstein Nr 7 (6 sqns). 1 x HAB (6 guns). Obst Baron von Wieland: IR EH Rainer Nr 11 (3rd Bn); IR Würzburg Nr 7 (1st LW Bn); HusR Blankenstein Nr 6 (6 sqns), 1 x 3 pdr FAB (6 guns). **Division of FML Ignaz Count Hardegg** GM Count Neipperg: Jägers (5th bn); HusR Kaiser Nr 1 (6 sqns); 1 x HAB (6 guns). GM Count Raicourt: GzIR Deutsch-Banater Nr 12 (2 bns); HusR Hessen-Homburg Nr 4 (5 sqns); DragR Riesch Nr 6 (6 sqns). **Division of FML Baron von Wimpfen** GM von Giffing: IRs Froon Nr 54 and de Vaux Nr 25 (3 bns each). 1 x FAB (8 guns). GM Czerwenka: IR Argenteau Nr 35 (3 bns); IR Erbach Nr 42 (2 bns); 1 x FAB (8 guns). **Division of FML Karl von Greth** GM von Mumb: IR Czartoryski Nr 9 (2 bns); RIdLi Nr 30 (3 bns), 1 x FAB (8 guns). GM von Quosdanovich: IR Reuss-Plauen Nr 17 (3 bns), IR A Gyulai Nr 21 (2 bns), 1 x FAB (8 guns).

II Corps GdK Maximilian Count Merveldt: **Division of FML Ignaz Baron von Lederer** GM Count Sobenburg: GzIR Gradiskaner Nr 8 (1st Bn); HusR Kienmayer Nr 8 (5 sqns); DragR EH Johann Nr 1 (4 sqns); 1 x FAB (8 guns). GM von Longueville: IR Strauch Nr 24 (3 bns), IR Bellegarde Nr 44 (2 bns); 1 x FAB (8 guns). **Division of FML Prince Alois Liechtenstein** GM Baron von Ennsbruck: IRs Kaunitz Nr 20 and W Colloredo Nr 56 (3 bns each), 1 x FAB (8 guns). GM Baron von Mecsery: IR Reuss-Greitz Nr 18 (2 bns); IR EH Rainer Nr 21 (1 bn); IR Vogelsang NR 47 (3 bns); 1 x FAB (8 guns). Reserve Artillery 1 x 12 pdr and 1 x 6 pdr FABs (16 guns).

III Corps FZM Ignaz Count Gyulai: **Division of FML Karl Count Crenneville** GM von Haecht: GzIR Warasdiner-Kreutzer Nr 5 (1st Bn); GzIR Warasdiner St Georger Nr 6 (1st bn); ChLR Klenau Nr 5 (6 sqns); ChLR Rosenberg Nr 6 (6 sqns). **Division of FML Franz Count Murray de Melgum** GM Count Sallins: IR Würzburg Nr 7 and EH Ludwig Nr 8 (3 bns each); 1 x FAB (8 guns). GM von Wöwenwarth: IR Mariassy Nr 37 and I Gyulai Nr 60 (2 bns each); 1 x FAB (8 guns). **Division of FML Prince Philipp von Hessen-Homburg** GM von Csollich: IR Kaiser Nr 1 (2 bns); IR Kottulinsky Nr 41 (3 bns); 1 x FAB (8 guns). GM Grimmer von Riesenburg: IR Kollowrath Nr 4 (2 bns); IR Frehlich Nr 28 (3 bns), 1 x FAB (8 guns). Reserve Artillery 1 x 12 pdr and 2 x 6 pdr FABs (18 guns.

IV Corps GdK Johann Count Klenau: **Division of Josef Baron von Mohr** GM von Baumgarten: 1st GzIR Wallachia Nr 16 (1st Bn); GzIR Illyrier Nr 13 (2 bns); ChLR Hohenzollern Nr 2 (5 sqns); HusR Palatinal Nr 12 (6 sqns); HusR EH Ferdinand Nr 3 (5 sqns); 2 x HAB (10 guns). **Division of FML Prince Ludwig von Hohenlohe-Bartenstein** GM von Schäffer: IR Zach Nr 15 (3 bns); IR J Colloredo Nr 57 (2 bns); 1 x FAB (8 guns). GM Splényi: IRs Lindenau Nr 29 and Württemberg Nr 40 (3 bns each); 1 x FAB

(8 guns). **Division of FML Anton von Mayer Heldensfeld** GM Baron von Abele: IRs Liechtenstein Nr 12 and Koburg Nr 22 (2 bns each); 1 x FAB (8 guns). GM De Best: IRs EH Karl Nr 3 and Kerpen Nr 49 (2 bns each); 1 x FAB (8 guns). GM Count Desfours: KürR Kaiser Nr 1 and ChLR O'Reilly Nr 3 (6 sqns each). Artillery Reserve: 1 x 3 pdr and 1 x 12 pdr FABs (14 guns).

The Army Reserve GdK Prince Friedrich von Hessen-Homburg: **Grenadier Division of FML Count Nicolaus Weissenwolf** GM Baron von Fürstenwärther: Gren Bns Berger, Czarnotzky, Obermayer and Oklopsia (4 bns); GM ? Gren Bns Call, Fischer, Habinay, Portner (4 bns), 2 x 6 pdr FAB (16 guns). **Division of FML Friedrich von Bianchi** GM von Beck: IRs Hiller Nr 2 and H Colloredo Nr 33 (2 bns each), 1 x FAB (8 guns). GM Count Haugwitz: IRs Hessen-Homburg Nr 19 and Simbschen Nr 48 (2 bns each). 1 x FAB (8 guns). GM von Quallenberg: IRs Esterházy Nr 32 and Davidovich Nr 34 (2 bns each); 1 x FAB (8 guns). **Division of FML Johann Count Nostitz** GM Baron von Rothkirch KürRs EH Franz Nr 2 and Kronprinz Ferdinand Nr 4 (4 sqns each). **Division of GM Count Klebelsberg** GM Count Auersperg: KürRs Sommariva Nr 5 and Hohenzollern Nr 8 (6 sqns each). **Division of FML Count Ciartart** GM von Ehrengreiff: KürRs Albert Nr 3 and Lothringen Nr 7 (4 sqns each). Artillery Reserve of FML Anton von Reisner: 2 x 3 pdr, 2 x 6 pdr, 6 x 12 pdr, 2 x 18 pdr FABs, 4 x HABs (112 guns); 20 x artillery coys, 21 x artillery assistant coys; 3½ x pionier coys, 1 x medical bn, 1 x staff inf bn, 2 x staff drag- sqns, 1 sqn LW Staff dragoons. GHQ Commando FML Johan von Prochaska: IRs de Vaux Nr 25 (1 coy) and Froon Nr 54 (1 x LW Bn).

The Mobile Column of GM Baron von Herzogenberg: IR Erbach Nr 42 (1x LW Bn); 2nd Silesian LWKR* (2 sqns).

* = from Kleist's Prussian corps.

Total Austrian Forces 120 bns, 44½ coys, 132 sqns, 57 batteries, 121,599 men, 15,645 horses, 388 guns.

The Russian Army of GdI Count Barclay de Tolly

The Cavalry of GdK Count Wittgenstein: **GL Pahlen's Division** GM Rüdiger: Ssum HusR (6 sqns); Grodno HusR (8 sqns). GM Lissanevitch: Lubno HusR (4 sqns); UlR Tschugujev (8 sqns): GM Illowaisky's Cossacks: Pulks of Grekov VIII, Illowaisky XIII and Radionov II; Eupatoria Tartars. (2,600 men).

I Corps GL Prince Gortschakov: **5th Division** GM Mesenzov: IRs Perm, Sievsk, Mohilev, Kaluga, JägerRs 23 and 24 (2 bns each); IR Grand Princess Katharina (1 bn). 14th Division: GM Helfreich: IRs Tenginsk, Estonia, Tulsk, Novaginsk, 25th and 26th Jägers (2 bns each); 1 x heavy and 2 x light FABs (36 guns).

II Corps Prince Eugen von Württemberg: **3rd Division** GM Schachafskoi: IRs Murom, Reval, Selenginsk, Tchernigov, 20th and 21st Jägers (2 bns each). 4th Division GM Pischnitzky: IRs Tobolsk, Wolhynien, Krementchug, IR Minsk, Jägers 4th and 34th (2 bns each). 1 x heavy and 2 x light FABs, 2 x HABs (60 guns).

IX Corps GL Olsufiev: **15th Division** GM Kornilov: IRs Witebsk, Koselsk and Kolyvan (1 bn each), IR Kura (2 bns). Jägers 13 and 22 (2 bns each).

X Corps GL Olsufiev: **8th Division** GM Urusov: IRs Archangelogorod and Old Ingermannland (2 bns each); IR Schlüsselburg and 37th Jägers (1 bn each); 7th Jägers (2 bns). 22nd Division GM Turtchenikov: IRs Wiatka and Stari Oskol (2 bns each); IR Olonetz (1 bn); Jägers29 and 45 (2 bns each). Artillery Reserve 4 x heavy, 3 x light FABs, 1 x Don Cossack HAB, (86 guns). Pioniers and pontonniers (2 coys each), Marines (1 coy). Attached from I Cavalry Corps' 1st MtdR Division Seversk and Arsamas MtdRRs (2 sqns each).

VIII Corps GL St Priest: **11th Division** GM Gurialov: IRs Jeletz, Polotsk and Rylsk (1 bn each). IR Yekaterinburg and 33rd Jägers (2 bns each); 3rd Jägers (1 bn); 17th Division GM ? IRs Riasan, Bielosersk, Brest, Wilmannstrand, Jägers 30 and 48 (2 bns each).

Grand Prince Constantine of Russia's Reserve Corps

The Grenadier Corps GL Raievsky: **1st Division** GM Pisarrev: GrenRs Arakcheyev, Yekaterinoslav, Tauride, St Petersburg, Kexholm and Bernau (2 bns each). **2nd Division** GrenRs Moscow, Kiev (2 bns each); Astrakhan, Fanagoria (1 bn each); Siberia and Little Russia (2 bns each); 1 x heavy and 2 x light FABs (36 guns).

The Footguards GL Yermelov: GL Rosen's Division: Preobrazhenski and Siemenowski Lifeguards Rs (3 bns each): Ismailovski Lifeguards and Guards Jägers R (1 bns each). **GM Udom II's Division** Lithuanian Lifeguards and Guards GrenR (2 bns each); Finland

and Pavalovsk Lifeguard Rs (2 bns each); 1 x heavy and 2 x light FABs (36 guns). **1st Kür Division** GL Depreradovich: Horse Guards R, Chevalier Guards R (6 sqns each); Life KürR of the Tsar, Life KürR of the Tsarina (4 sqns each). **2nd Kür Division** GM Kretov: KürRs Pskov, Gluchov (5 sqns each); Yekaterinoslav and Astrakhan (4 sqns each). 3rd Kür Div GL Duka: KürRs Starodub, Novgorod, Order of St George and Little Russia (4 sqns each). **Light Cavalry Division** GL Schevisch: Hussars, Dragoons and Ulans of the Guard (6 sqns each); 3 x HAB (36 guns).

Prussian Footguards Obstlt von Alvensleben: 1st and 2nd Garde-Regiment (6 bns); Garde-Jäger-Bn (1 bn). Prussian Horse Guards Obstlt Laroche von Starkenfeld; Regiment Gardes du Corps (4 sqns); Garde DragR (4 sqns); Garde-Leichte-Kavallerie-Regiment (4 sqns).

Prussian Guard Artillery 2 x FAB (16 guns).

The Cossack Corps Obst Bergemann: The Pulks of Kostine and Black Sea and the Don Cossack Pulks of Schaltroka, Elmurusin, Ataman, Tschlikev, Tschernotukov V, Greckov V, Platov V and Wlassov V (3,800 men). 7½ HAB (94 guns), pioneers (3 coys).

Russian total 95 bns, 3 coys, 107 sqns, 14 Pulks, 26½ batteries 48,650 men, 314 guns.

The II Prussian Corps GL von Kleist: 9th Brigade GM von Klüx: Silesian Sharpshooters (½ bn); 1st West Prussian IR (3 bns); 6th ResIR (3 bns); 7th Silesian LWIR (2 bns); 1st Silesian LWKR (2 sqns); 1 x HAB (8 guns). 10th Brigade GM von Pirch I: 2nd West Prussian IR (3 bns); 7th ResIR (2 bns); 9th Silesian LWIR (2 bns); 1st Silesian LWKR (1 sqn); 1 x FAB (8 guns). 11th Brigade GM von Ziethen: Silesian Sharpshooters (½ bn); 1st Silesian IR (3 bns); 10th ResIR (2 bns); 8th Silesian LWIR (2 bns); Neumark DragR (6 sqns); 2nd Silesian LWKR (1 sqn); 1 x FAB (8 guns). 12th Brigade GM Prince August von Preussen: 2nd Silesian IR (3 bns); 11th ResIR (3 bns); 10th Silesian LWIR (2 bns); Silesian UlR (4 sqns); 2nd Silesian LWKR (1 sqn); 1 x FAB (8 guns). Heavy Cavalry Brigade GM von Röder: East Prussian KürR, Brandenburg KürR and Silesian KürR (4 sqns each); 2 x HAB (16 guns). Landwehr Cavalry Brigade Obst von Mutius: 7th and 8th Silesian LWKRs (5 sqns). Artillery Reserve: 1 x 12 pdr and 2 x 6 pdr FABs, 1 x HAB (32 guns), pioniers (2 coys). **Prussian Corps totals** 31 bns, 2 coys, 32 sqns, 10 batteries, 80 guns.

The Streifkorps of GL von Thielemann Austrians Obstlt Baron von Gasser: ChLR Hohenzollern Nr 2 (2 sqns); ChLR Klenau Nr 5 and HusR Kienmayer Nr 8 (1 sqn each). Prussians: GM Prinz Biron von Kurland: 2nd Silesian HusR (2½ sqns); Silesian NKR (2 sqns). **Russians** Obst Orlov-Denissov: Don Cossack Pulks of Count Gorin II and Count Jagodin II. Artillery: 2 x Austrian HA howitzers, 2 x Cossack HA guns. **Totals** 8½ sqns, 2 Pulks, 4 guns, 1,500 men.

The Austro-Russian Streifkorps of Obst Count Mensdorff-Pouilly HusR EH Ferdinand Nr 3 (2 sqns); HusR Hessen-Homburg Nr 4 (1 sqn); Don Cossack Pulks of Gorin I and Illowaisky X. **Totals** 3 sqns, 2 Pulks, 790 men.

Grand Total of the Main Allied Army 246 bns, 49½ coys, 282½ sqns, 18 Pulks, 93¼ batteries, 196,790 men, 786 guns.

The Army of Silesia GdK Leberecht von Blücher commanding

I Prussian Corps GL York: Avantgarde Brigade: Obst von Katzler: Leibgren-Bn, West Prussian Gren Bn (1 bn each); East Prussian Rifles (½ bn); Gardejäger (1 coy); East Prussian IR, Brandenburg IR, 12th ResIR, 13th, 14th, 15th Silesian LWIRs (1 bn each); 2nd Leib-HusR (1 sqn); Brandenburg HusR (2 sqns); Brandenburg UlR, East Prussian NKR and 5th Silesian LWKR (4 sqns each); 1 x 6 pdr FAB, 1 x HAB (16 guns). 1st Brigade Obst von Steinmetz: 1st East Prussian Gren Bn, Silesian Gren Bn (1 bn each); 5th and 13th Silesian LWIRs (3 bns each); 2nd Leib-HusR (3 sqns); 1 x 6 pdr FAB (8 guns). 2nd Brigade GM Prince Karl von Mecklenburg: 1st East Prussian IR (3 bns); 2nd East Prussian IR (1 bn); 6th Silesian LWIR (1 bn); Mecklenburg-Strelitz HusR (4 sqns); 1 x 6 pdr FAB (8 guns). 7th Brigade GM von Horn: Leib IR (3 bns); Thüringian bn (1 bn); 4th Silesian LWIR (2 bns); 15th Silesian LWIR (1 bn); 3rd Silesian LWKR (2 sqns); 10th Silesian LWKR (4 sqns); 1 x 6 pdr FAB (8 guns). 8th Brigade GM von Hünerbein: Brandenburg IR and 12th ResIR (2 bns each); 14th Silesian LWIR (1 bn); Brandenburg HusR (2 sqns); 1 x 6 pdr FAB (8 guns). Reserve Cavalry Obst von Jürgass: Lithuanian DragR, 1st Westprussian DragR and 1st Neumark LWKR (4 sqns each); 2 x HAB (16 guns). Artillery Reserve Maj von Fiebig 2 x 12 pdr, 1 x 6 pdr, 1 x 3 pdr FABs, 1 x HAB (40 guns). **I Prussian Corps totals** 33½ bns, 1 coy, 42 sqns, 13 batteries, 21,149 men and 104 guns. Following the heavy losses at

Möckern on 16 October this corps was partially reorganized.

The Russian Corps of GL Baron Osten-Sacken 10th Division GM Count Lieven III: IRs Crimea (1 bn); Yaroslav, Bialystock and 8th Jägers (2 bns each); 39th Jägers (1 bn). **16th Division** (part of) GM Reppinsky: IRs Ochotsk and Kamchatka (2 bns each). **27th Division** GL Neverovski: IRs Simbirsk, Tarnopol, Odessa, Wilna and 50th Jägers (1 bn each); 49th Jägers (2 bns). **3rd Dragoon Division** (part of) GM Pentchulichef: DragR Smolensk (2 sqns); DragR Kurland (5 sqns). **2nd Hussar Division** GM Lanskoi: HusRs Alexandria (5 sqns); Mariupol (6 sqns); White Russia (4 sqns); Achtyrska (6 sqns). **Cossack Corps of GM Karpov II:** 4th Ukrainian Pulk (3 sqns); St Petersburg Cossacks (4 sqns); the Don Cossack Pulks of Grekov I, Illowaisky IX, Karpov II, Kutainikov IV, Lukovkin II and Sementchikov IV; 2nd Baschkir R, 2nd Kalmuck R. Artillery Reserve: 1 x HAB, 2 x light and 2 x heavy FABs (60 guns); pioniers (1 coy).

GdI Count Langeron's Russian Corps Avantgarde: DragRs Kargopol and Kiev (4 sqns each); DragR Kinburn (2 sqns); MtdRRs Dorpat and Latvia (2 sqns each); 1st and 3rd Ukrainian Cossack Pulks (3 sqns each); Don Cossack Pulks of Kutainikov VIII and Selwanov II. **9th Division** GM Udom II: IRs Apscheron and Riask (2 bns each); Yakutsk and Nascheburg; 10th and 38th Jägers (1 bn each); 1 x HAB, 1 x FAB (24 guns). **Cossack Division of GL Borozdin:** Don Cossack Pulks of Grekov XXI and Jeschov II, Stavropol Kalmucks. 1 x heavy, 2 x light FABs (36 guns). **Total of Langeron's Corps** 53 bns, 6 coys, 36 sqns, 13 batteries, 28,914 men, 146 guns.

The Army of the North Carl Johann, Crown Prince of Sweden commanding.

III Prussian Army Corps GL Bülow commanding: **3rd Division** GM Prinz Ludwig von Hessen-Homburg commanding: 2nd East Prussian Gren Bn (1 bn); 3rd East Prussian IR (2 bns); 4th ResIR (3 bns); 4th East Prussian LWIR (4 bns); 1st Leib HusR (4 sqns); 1 x 6 pdr FAB (8 guns). **5th Division** GM von Borstell: Pommeranian Gren Bn (1 bn); Pommeranian IR (3 bns); 2nd ResIR (3 bns); 2nd Kurmark LWIR (4 bns); Pommeranian HusR and West Prussian UlR (4 sqns each); 1 x 6 pdr FAB (8 guns). **6th Division** Obst von Krafft: Colberg IR; 9th Res IR and Neumark LWIR (3 bns each); Pommeranian Nat KR (3 sqns); 1 x 6 pdr FAB (8 guns); East Prussian Rifles (2 coys); DragR Königin, DragR Brandenburg, 2nd West Prussian DragR (4 sqns each); 2 x HABs (16 guns). 2nd and 4th Kurmark LWKRs and 2nd Pommeranian LWKR (4 sqns each). **Artillery Reserve:** 2 x 12 pdr and 1 x 6 pdr FABs, 1 x HAB (32 guns); pioniers (2 coys).

III Prussian Corps totals 30 bns, 4 coys, 39 sqns, 9 batteries, 24,619 men, 72 guns.

Attached Russian Troops: Don Cossack Pulks of Bychalov II and Illowaisky V, 2 x FABs (22 guns).

The Russian Corps of GL Baron von Winzingerode Avantgarde GL Woronzov: HusR Pavlograd (6 sqns); UlR Wolhynien (3 sqns); Jatschkir Cossack Pulk; 1 x HAB (12 guns). Cossack Pulks of Melnikov IV, Melnikov V, 1st Bug Cossacks, 3rd Ural Cossacks; Cossack Pulk of Andrejanov II; 1st Baschkir R; 2nd, 13th and 14th Jägers (1, 2 and 2 bns each). **21st Division** GM Laptef: IRs Lithuania, Petrowska and Podolia (1 bn each); IR Neva (1 bn); 44th Jägers (2 bns); 1 x light and 1 x heavy FABs (24 guns). **24th Division** GM Wuitsch: IRs Schirwan, Ufa, Butyrsk and 19th Jägers (2 bns each); IR Tomsk and 40th Jägers (1 bn each), 1 x light FAB (12 guns). **Division of GM Harpe** IRs Tula and Nowagingsk (2 bns each); Grenadiers (3 bns); 2 x heavy FABs, 1 x HAB (36 guns). DragR St Petersburg (4 sqns); HusR Yelisawetgrad (6 sqns); St Petersburg Cossack Volunteers (2 sqns); ½ HAB (6 guns). DragR Riga (3 sqns); DragR Finland (2 sqns); Isum HusR (4 sqns); 2 x HAB (24 guns). Nieschin MtdRR (2 sqns); Polish UlR (6 sqns); Cossack Pulks of Illowaisky IV, Grekov IX, Barabantschikov II, Lotschilin I (1,748 men). **Winzingerode's Corps total** 20 bns, 30 sqns, 11 Pulks, 10 batteries, 24,951 men, 86 guns.

The Swedish Army Corps of FM Count Stedingk 1st Division GM von Posse; 1st Brigade GM Schulzenheim: Svea Leibgarde-R, 2nd Leibgarde-R, Grenadiers of the Leib-Brigade (1 bn each). 2nd Brigade GM Lagebring: IRs Upland and Södermannland (2 bns each); Nord Schonen IR (1 bn); Pommeranian Legion (1 coy). Leibgarde-DragR (5 sqns); Pommeranian Legion (1 sqn). 2 x 6 pdr FAB. **2nd Division** GL Baron Sandels: 3rd Brigade GM Reuterskjöld: IRs Westgotha, Westmannland and Nerike (2 bns each). 6th Brigade GM Boije: IRs Skaraborg and Elfsborg (2 bns each); IRs Calmar and Kronoberg and Warmland

Feldjäger (1 bn each); 2 x 6 pdr FAB. Cavalry: GL Skjöldebrand: Leib-KürR (4 sqns); HusR Schonen (6 sqns); HusR Mörner (5 sqns); Smaland DragR (6 sqns); 1 x 12 pdr FAB, 1 x 6 pdr FAB, 1 x 6 pdr HAB. **Swedish Corps totals** 23 bns, 1 coy, 27 sqns, 7 batteries, 16,652 men, 46 guns.

Attached Troops: Don Cossack Pulk of Rebrejev (362 men); 1 x British rocket battery (151 men).

The Reserve Army of Poland GdK von Bennigsen.

Avantgarde 6th and 41st Jägers (2 bns each); 1 x HAB, 1 x FAB (14 guns); Sappers (1 coy). Combined HusR and Combined UlR (5 sqns each); Don Cossack Pulks of Platov V, Andrejanov III and Vlassov III; 4th Ural Cossack Pulk, Baschkirs (2 Pulks). Simbirsk LW Cossack Pulk, Penza LW Cossack Pulk.

Dochtorov's Corps 12th Division GM Chowansky: IRs Smolensk, Narva, Alexopol, New Ingermannland (2 bns each), 1 x heavy and 1 x light FABs (24 guns). 26th Division GM Paskievich: IRs Ladoga, Poltava, Nishninovgorod, Orel, 5th and 42nd Jägers (2 bns each); 1 x heavy and 1 x light FABs (24 guns). GL Tschaplitz's Division: Combined DragR (5 sqns); 1st Combined MtdRR (4 sqns); 2nd Combined UlR (4 sqns); Taganrog UlR (4 sqns); Siberian UlR and Schitomir UlR (2 sqns each); 1 x HAB (12 guns). Tartar UlR (6 sqns); Radionov Don Cossack Pulk, Poltava LW Cossack Pulk; 14th Baschkir Pulk, 1 x HAB (12 guns). Miners (1 coy); pontonniers (2 coys). **Reserve Army of Poland totals** 34 bns, 4 coys, 41 sqns, 11 Pulks, 12 batteries, 33,875 men, 134 guns.

The British Rocket Battery list 1 officer killed.

5,000 Allied troops were missing.

The following generals were killed: Russians, GLs Neverovski, Schävitch; GMs Hüne, Prince Kudaschoff, Lindfors, Count Manteuffel, Reuven, Schmidt, Austrian GM Giffing.

Comment It is evident that the Russians bore the brunt of the fighting here and that the Swedes were very carefully husbanded.

Of his 175,000-men Grande Armée, Napoleon was able to bring only 80,000 back over the River Saale. French losses must thus have been in the area of 95,000 killed, wounded, missing and gone over to the Allies. Thousands were cut off by the premature destruction of the bridge over the River Elster. The French withdrew westwards to their depot and arsenal at Erfurt to re-equip; the Allies were too battered to be able to mount a rapid chase to complete Napoleon's destruction but the 1813 campaign had been won here at the 'Battle of the Nations'.

Sources Friedrich, Martinien, Wrede, von Stoen.

SX Lützen, 20 October 1813, skirmish

A town in Saxony (northeastern Germay), 16 km southeast of Merseburg and on Route B87, 6 km northwest of Grossgörschen.

A Russian victory over the French.

(Last action - Leipzig, 16 - 19 October; next action - Freiburg, 21 October).

French Forces 2,000 stragglers from the battle of Leipzig - all captured.

Allied Total	Bns	Coys	Sqns	Pulks	Batteries	Men	Guns
Main Army	246	49	282	18	93	196,790	786
Silesian Army	105	8	113	13	31	63,861	310
Army of the North	81	5	104	14	29	67,416	226
Reserve Army of Poland	34	4	41	11	12	33,875	134
Totals	*466*	*66*	*540*	*56*	*165*	*361,942*	*1,456*

Allied Losses at Leipzig (killed and wounded)

	Russians		Prussians		Austrians		Swedes		Total	
	Officers	Men	Officers	Men	Officers	Men	Officers	Men	Officers	Men
Main Army	512	11,411	244	7,882	420	14,538	—	—	1,176	33,831
Silesian Army	250	6,897	176	5,467	—	—	—	—	426	12,364
Army of the North	33	432	78	2,186	—	—	9	169	120	2,787
Army of Poland	70	3,000	—	—	—	—	—	—	70	3,000
Grand Totals	*865*	*21,740*	*498*	*15,535*	*420*	*14,538*	*9*	*169*	*1,792*	*51,982*

Allied Forces From the Army of Poland: GL Baron Vassilitschkoff's Combined Cavalry Corps: DragRs Kurland, Smolensk (2 sqns each); HusRs Achtyrsk, Mariupol, Alexandrowsk, White Russia (4 sqns each); 1 x HAB. Don Cossack Pulks of Karpov II, Lukovkin, Kutainikov V, Sejmentschikoff, Popov XIII, (ca 1,000 men); 2nd Kalmuck R (2 sqns). 4th Ukrain Cossack R (3 sqns); St Petersburg Volunteer Cossack R (3 sqns).

Allied totals ca 3,900 men, 12 guns.

Allied losses Not known exactly but light.

Sources Plotho, Friedrich, Martinien.

SX Freiburg (now Freyburg), 21 October 1813, clash

A town in Saxony on the River Unstrut, 22 km southwest of Merseburg and at the junction of Routes B180 and B176.

A Prussian victory over the French.

(Last action – Lützen, 20 October; next action – Kösel, 21 October.)

French Forces M Oudinot commanding the French rearguard: II Corps M Victor, Duke of Belluno: 5th Division GdD Dufour: 26 RILé, 13e RIdLi (4 bns); VII Corps: GdD Durette's 32nd Division: 35e, 36e RILé (4 bns); 132e RIdLi (2 bns). Also the 37e RILé, 23e, 128e RIdLi, 1er and 25e ChàCh; exact strengths not known.

French losses 800 killed and wounded, 1,200 men and 18 guns captured.

Prussian Forces GL York commanding the I Prussian Corps: Avantgarde: Obst Count Henckel von Donnersmark: Brandenburg HusR (5 sqns); 2nd Leib-HusR (2 sqns); Brandenburg UlR (4 sqns); Ostpreussisches NKR (5 sqns); 5th Silesian LWKR (4 sqns); Silesian Gren Bn, (1 bn); LeibIR (1st Bn); Thüringian bn (1 bn); Garde-Jägers (4th coy); 2nd Austrian Jäger bn (1 bn); Ostpreussisches Jäger bn (1 bn). 1½ x HAB, 1 x FAB. GM von Horn's Division: LeibIR (Füs Bn); 2nd Ostpreussisches IR (1 bn); 1st Ostpreussisches IR (Füs Bn); 1st Ostpreussisches and 2nd bn-LeibIR (1 combined bn); 2 x LWI Bns; 1st Westpreussisches DragR (4 sqns); Ostpreussisches NKR; 1 x FAB, ½ x HAB. Saxon UlR (2 sqns).

Prussian total ca 9,000 men.

Prussian losses ca 950 killed and wounded.

Comment York tried to block the retreat of Napoleon's army over the River Unstrut but came up too late to effect much damage. The 2nd Leib-HusR and the Saxon UlR released a convoy of 4,000 Allied prisoners of war. The Grande Armée was in a very disorganised state. The Saxon army had now abandoned Napoleon and joined the Allies.

Sources Plotho, Friedrich, Martinien, Sporschil.

SX Kösen, 21 October 1813, clash

A village in eastern central Germany, on the southern bank of the River Saale, on Route B87 about 6 km west of Naumburg on the Unstrut and 22 km north of Jena.

An Austro-Prussian victory over the French.

(Last action – Freiburg, 21 October; next action – Ekartsberga, 22 October.)

French Forces Imperial Guard: 1er ChLL (2 sqns); IV Corps GdD Bertrand: 12th Division GdD Morand: 13e and 23e RIdLi; Württembergers Gen Franquemont – 3 combined bns; VII Corps GdD Reynier: 14th Division GdD Guilleminot: 18e RILé, 52e, 156e RIdLi; R Illyrien: 1 combined IR formed of the remnants of GdD Pacthod's 13th Division; 20 guns.

French total ca 6,000 men.

French losses ca 1,000 killed and wounded, 649 captured including 460 French, 73 Bavarians, 14 Dutch, 14 Poles, 8 Italians, 1 Saxon and 1 Württemberger. 78 Poles of the 1er ChLL of the Guard deserted to the Allies.

Austro-Prussian Forces FZM Ignaz Gyulai commanding the III Austrian Corps: FML Moritz Liechtenstein's I (Light) Corps: 1st and 7th Jägers (1 bn each); GzIR Broder Nr 7 (1st Bn). FML Crenneville's Division (III Corps): ChLRs Klenau Nr (7 sqns) and Rosenberg Nr 6 (6 sqns), GzIR Warasdiner-Kreutzer Nr 5 (1 bn); FML Murray's Division: Nr 7 and EH Ludwig Nr 8 (3 bns each). Obst Mensdorff's Streifkorps: HusR EH Ferdinand Nr 3 (2 sqns); HusR Hessen-Homburg Nr 4 (1 sqn); Cossack Pulks of Gorin I and Illowaisky X.

Austro-Prussian total ca 5,500 men.

Austro-Prussian losses 154 killed, 679 wounded, 95 missing or captured.

Comment The Grand Armée was withdrawing westwards after Leipzig north of the River Saale; Napoleon sent Bertrand to destroy the bridge at Kösen to prevent any Allied interference from the southern bank. The Austrians saved the bridge.

Sources Plotho, Martinien, Friedrich, Wrede.

SX Eckartsberga, 22 October 1813, clash

A village in eastern central Germany, about 20 km north of Jena, at the junction of Routes B87 and B250.

A French victory over the Allies.

(Last action – Kösen, 21 October; next action – Würzburg, 24–26 October.)

French Forces Emperor Napoleon I commanding: 2nd Division Imperial Guard GdD Count Lefebvre-Desnouettes: ChàCh (4 sqns); II Cavalry Corps, 2nd heavy Cavalry Division GdD Count St Germain: 2e Carabiniers (2 sqns); 2nd Light Cavalry Division GdD Roussel d'Hurbal: 11e ChàCh (3 sqns); 2e ChLL (3 sqns); I Cavalry Corps GdD Milhaud; GdB Piré: HusR (3 sqns); V Cavalry Corps GdD Heretier 15e and 18e DragRs (5 sqns); 2 x HAB.

French total ca 2,300 men.

French losses Not known exactly; moderate.

Austrian Forces III Corps FZM Ignaz Gyulai: FML Crenneville's Division: IRs Gyulai Nr 60 and Kollowrath Nr 36 (2 bns each); IR Frelich Nr 28 (3 bns). FML Prince zu Hessen-Homburg's Division: GzIR Warasdiner-St Georger Nr 6 (1 bn). Cavalry: ChLRs Klenau Nr 5, Rosenberg Nr 6 (5 sqns each), ChLR Vincent Nr 4 (from Liechtenstein's 1st Light Division – 6 sqns).

Austrian total ca 8,000 men.

Austrian losses 35 killed, 169 wounded, 58 missing and captured.

Comment Once again the retreating Grand Armée managed to block off an Allied attempt to cut off their retreat to their major arsenal and depot at Erfurt with a thrust from the south.

Sources M KuKKA, 3rd Folge, IV Vol, Plotho, Martinien, Wrede.

SX Würzburg, 24–26 October 1813, bombardment

A fortress and fortified city in central Germany on the River Main at the Junction of Routes B8, B13, B19; just north of Autobahn A3/E41.

A French victory over the Allies.

Last action – Eckartsberga, 22 October; next action – Hörselberg, 26 October.

French Garrison GdD Turreau de Linière commanding: 127e RIdLi (1 bn); 128e RIdLi (1 bn); 113e RIdLi (2 bns). Würzburg IR (1 depot bn); 13e HusR (1sqn); French artillery (2 coys) and sappers (1 coy); ca 3,000 men.

French losses Not known but extremely light.

Allied Forces Wrede's Bavarian Corps as for the Battle of Hanau, 30 and 31 October.

Allied losses Not known but extremely light.

Sources Plotho, Sporschil, Müller.

Comment Würzburg was an extremely strong place, Wrede's field artillery pieces did not effect it at all. The French agreed to evacuate the city and to withdraw into the fortress (the Marienburg) where they were blockaded until 2 May 1814. Wrede wasted over half his ammunition in the useless exercise; this helped him to lose the Battle of Hanau on 30–31 October.

SX Hörselberg (Eisenach), 26 October 1813, clash

A ridge just east of the town of Eisenach in eastern Germany, 72 km west Weimar; on the River Hörsel and at the junction of Routes B7, B19, B84; just south of the River Neisse.

A drawn match between the Prussians and the French.

(Last action – Würzburg, 24–26 October; next action – Hanau, 30–31 October.)

French Forces Emperor Napoleon I commanding: M Mortier: Young Guard, 2nd Division GdD Decouz: 4e, 5e, 8e Voltigeurs, 9, 10, 12 Voltigeurs (12 bns); 3rd Division GdD Barrois: 1er, 2e, 3e, 6e and 7e Voltigeurs (10 bns); Flanqueur Grenadiers, Flanqueur Chasseurs (2 bns each).

French total ca 13,000 men.

French losses 600 killed and wounded, 2,000 captured (including many stragglers).

Prussian Forces GdK von Blücher commanding The Army of Silesia GL York's I Corps: 2nd Division GM von Hünerbein: 8th Brigade, Obst von Gilsa; Brandenburg IR (1combined bn); 12th ResIR (1 combined bn); Combined Füs Bn (Brandenburg and 12th ResIRs); 14th Silesian LWIR (1 combined bn); 3rd Silesian LWKR (2 sqns); 2 x FAB (16 guns). Ostpreussisches Jäger Bn (2 coys). Reserve Cavalry Obst von Jürgass: Obst Graf Henkel: 1st Westpreussisches DragR (5 sqns); Lithuanian DragR (4½ sqns). Obst von Katzler: Brandenburg UlR (4½ sqns); Ostpreussisches NKR (5 sqns); Maj von Bieberstein: 1st Neumark and 5th Silesian LWKR (4 sqns each); Cossack Pulk Grekov III (1 sqn); Baschkirs (1 regiment). 2 x HAB.

Prussian total ca 5,600 men.

Prussian losses 400 killed and wounded.

Comment The beaten Grand Armée was withdrawing westwards from their great depot at Erfurt where they had been refitted and re-equipped.

As they approached Eisenach along the present Route B7, the Prussians tried to cut them off from the north. Although achieving a limited tactical success, the Prussians were unable to stop the withdrawal as the French occupied the dominant heights of the Hörselberg in strength.

Sources M KuKKA, 3rd Folge, IV Vol, Plotho, Martinien.

IN San Marco and Volano, 26/27 October 1813, clash

A village in northern Italy, northeast of Lake Garda, on Route 12, 8 km north of Rovereto on Autostrada A22/E6.

An Austrian success over the Franco-Italians.

(Last action - Mühlbacher Klause, 7 October; next action - Trieste, 12–28 October.)

Franco-Italian Forces GdD Giflenga commanding the 6th Division (Italians) Vélites of the Guard (1 bn); ChàP (4 bns); IR of the Guard (1 bn); 3rd LtIR (4 bns); 4th LtIR (2 bns); 6 guns.

Franco-Italian total ca 7,000 men.

Franco-Italian losses ca 400 killed and wounded, 677 captured.

Austrian Forces FML Fenner; GM Vlasitch commanding: Jägers (8th bn); HusR Frimont Nr 9 (1 sqn); Tyroler Jäger (5 coys); ½ x 3 pdr HAB. Later reinforced by FML Sommariva with GM Mayer; IR Chasteler Nr 27 (2 bns); Jägers (9th Bn, 4 coys); UlR Merveldt Nr 1 (4 sqns), 1 x 6 pdr FAB, and other, unidentified units.

Austrian total Not known.

Austrian losses Not known exactly, but light.

Comment Following this defeat Giflenga withdrew south down the River Adige (Etsch) to Rivoli. On 31 October the citadel of Trient (Trento/Adige) surrendered to the Austrians. FML Fenner was wounded.

Sources Wrede, Martinien, Vaudoncourt, vom Holtz.

IN Trieste, 12–28 October 1813, siege and capitulation

A fortified port city in northeastern Italy, at the head of the Adriatic.

An Anglo-Austrian victory over the Franco-Italians.

(Last action - San Marco and Volano, 27 October; next action - Bassano, 30/31 October.)

Franco-Italian Garrison Col Rabie commanding 800 men.

Anglo-Austrian Forces GM Count Nugent commanding: IR EH Franz Carl Nr 52 (1st Bn); GzIR Warasdiner-Kreutzer Nr 5 (1 bn); HusR Radetzky Nr 5 (½ sqn); 1 x FAB. Admiral Freemantle's Royal Naval squadron; Royal Marines (1 bn); Calabrian Free Corps (1 bn).

Anglo-Austrian total ca 3,500 men.

Anglo-Austrian losses 63 killed and wounded.

Comment The garrison surrendered 641 strong and were escorted to the nearest French post and handed over.

Sources vom Holtz, Vaudoncourt.

IN Bassano, 30/31 October 1813, clash

A town in northern Italy, on the River Brenta and at the junction of Routes 47 and 248, 35 km northeast of Vicenza.

A Franco-Italian victory over the Austrians.

(Last action - Trieste, 12–28 October; next action - Caldiero, 15 November.)

Franco-Italian Forces GdD Grenier commanding: GdD Quesnel's Division 84e and 92e RIdLi (4 bns each); 30e DBde Prov. (3/1er and8/14e RILé; 8/6e and 3/10e RIdLi); 18 guns. From 3rd Division: 42e RIdLi (3e and 6e Bns).

Franco-Italian total ca 9,000 men.

Franco-Italian losses Not known.

Austrian Forces GM Eckhardt commanding: IRs Hohenlohe-Bartenstein Nr 26, Jellačič Nr 53, Bianchi Nr 63 (parts of), GzIR Szeckler (1 bn); Jägers (8th Bn, 4 coys); HusR Frimont Nr 9 (2 sqns); ½ x 3 pdr HAB.

Austrian total ca 3,000 men, 4 guns.

Austrian losses Vaudoncourt gives 500 killed (!), 700 wounded, 300 captured and 1 gun.

Comment Eckhardt's brigade headed an Austrian thrust south into Eugène's rear left flank. Eckhardt was repulsed but Vaudoncourt's figures for Austrian losses are incredibly high. Austrian sources do not record any such disaster. Eugène was able to withdraw westwards over the Brenta safely from 1-4 October to Verona and to put strong garrisons into Venice and Legnano.

Sources Wrede, Martinien, Vaudoncourt, vom Holtz.

SX Hanau, 30/31 October 1813, battle

A town in western central Germany at the confluence of the Rivers Main and Kinzig about 25 km east of Frankfurt/Main.

A French victory over the Allies.

(Last action – Hörselberg, 26 October; next action – Sachsenhausen, 31 October.)

French Forces Emperor Napoleon I commanding.

The Imperial Guard GdD Drouot: **Old Guard** GdD Friant: 1er GrenàP (2 bns); 2e ChàP (2 bns); GdD Curial Vélites de Turin (1 bn); 2 x FAB.

Young Guard M Oudinot Duke of Reggio: 3rd Division GdD Barrois: 7e Tirailleurs (1 bn). Cavalry: 3rd Division GdD Count Walther: GrenàCh (4 sqns); DragR (4 sqns); ChàCh (6 sqns); 1er ChLL (Poles) (3 sqns); 3e Gardes d'Honneur (5 sqns); 2 x HAB.

II Corps M Victor, Duke of Belluno: 4th Division GdD Dubreton: 10e and 56e RIdLi (4 bns each). 5th Division GdD Dufour: 43e RIdLi (3 bns); 72e RIdLi (4 bns). 6th Division GdD ?? 4e RIdLi (3 bns). 18e RIdLi (4 bns).

III Corps M Marmont Duke of Ragusa: 8th Division GdD Souham: 10e RILé (2 bns); 22e RIdLi (3 bns). 11th Division GdD Ricard: 50e RIdLi (2 bns); 23rd Light Cavalry Brigade GdB Beuermann: 10e HusR (6 sqns).

VI Corps (M Marmont): 21st Division GdD Lagrange: 37e RILé (4 bns); IR Joseph Napoleon (1 bn); 22nd Division 12e and 13e RIdLi (4 bns); 15e RIdLi (2 bns). 32nd Division GdD Durutte: 35e, 36e RILé (2 bns each).

IV Corps GdD Count Bertrand: 12th Division GdD Morand: 8e RILé (2 bns); 23e RIdLi (4 bns). 14th Division GdD Guilleminot: IR Illyrien (1 bn); 52e RIdLi (2 bns).

V Corps M Macdonald: 20th Division GdB Joubert: 20e RIdLi (1 bn). 19th Division GdD ??: 155e RIdLi (3 bns); 6th Light Cavalry Brigade GdB Dermoncourt: 2e, 3e ChàCh (2 sqns each).

XI Corps M Macdonald: 31st Division GdD Ledru Neapolitans: Regiment d'Élite, 4th LtIR (1 bn each). 35th Division GdD Gérard: 112e RIdLi (4 bns); 5th Italian LIR (4 bns). 36th Division: GdD Charpentier: 22e RILé (4 bns), 14e RILé (3 bns).

VIII Corps GdB Sierakowski: 1st Polish Combined LIR (2 bns). The division of GdB Count Margaron: 103e RIdLi (1 bn) and elements of the following regiments: 17e Lé, 20e, 46e, 58e, 66e, 101e, 102e, 103e Li.

I Cavalry Corps GdD Milhaud: 3rd Light Cavalry Division GdB Vallin: 1er and 8e ChàCh (5 sqns). 1st Light Cavalry Division GdD Count Berkheim: 16e ChàCh, 1er and 3e ChLL, 5e, 8e ChLL (2 sqns each), 1st Italian ChàCh (4 sqns). GdB Piré: 7e HusR (2 sqns); 3rd Heavy Cavalry Division GdD Doumerc: 23e DragR (2 sqns); Italian Dragone Napoleone (4 sqns).

II Cavalry Corps GdD Count Sebastiani: 2nd Light Cavalry Division: 11e ChàCh (3 sqns), 9e HusR (4 sqns); 2e ChLL (3 sqns). 4th Light Cavalry Division GdD Count Exelmans: 6e ChLL (2 sqns), 7e ChàCh (2 sqns), 24e ChàCh (3 sqns). 2nd Heavy Cavalry Division GdD Count St Germain: 1er and 2e Carabiniers, 1er CuirR (6 sqns); 5e, 8e, 10e CuirRs (7 sqns).

III Cavalry Corps GdD Arrighi Duke of Padua: 4th Heavy Cavalry Division: GdD Defrance: 5e DragR (1 sqn). And elements of the following regiments: 5e, 19e, 20e DragRs, 7e ChLL; 14e, 16e, 24e, 27e ChàCh, 11e HusR.

French totals ca 60,000 men, 100 guns.

French losses Impossible to establish accurately; generally given at about 6,000 killed and wounded, 4,000 captured, 5 guns.

Austro-Bavarian Forces GdK Count von Wrede (Bavarian) commanding:

Austrian Forces FML Fresnel commanding: Light Division (Fresnel); 1st Brigade: GM Count Hardegg: 1st GzIR Szeckler (2 bns); HusR EH Joseph Nr 2 (6 sqns). 2nd Brigade GM Baron von Volkmann: UlR Schwarzenberg Nr 2 (6 sqns); 1 x 6 pdr HAB (6 guns).

The Line Division GM Baron von Bach: IRs EH Rudolph Nr 14 and Jordis Nr 59 (4 bns each). The Reserve Division FML Baron von Trautenberg: 1st Brigade GM Klenau; Gren Bns De Best, Berger, Frisch and Putheany; 1 x 6 pdr FAB (8 guns). 2nd Brigade GM Baron von Diemar: Gren Bns Hromada, Kramer and Possmann 1 x 3 pdr FAB (8 guns). Cavalry Division FML Baron von Splényi: 1st Brigade GM Minutillo: HusR Szeckler Nr 11 (4 sqns), HusR Frimont Nr 9 (6 sqns). 2nd Brigade Obst von Flachenfeld: KürR Liechtenstein Nr 6 (4 sqns), DragR Knesevich Nr 3 (6 sqns), 1 x 6 pdr HAB (6 guns), pioniers (1 coy), LW Stabs-IR (2 coys), LW Stabs DragR (2 sqns), pontonniers, Tschaikisten (1 coy).

Austrian totals ca 13,000 men, 68 guns*.

Austrian losses 13 officers, 1,400 men killed, 48 officers, 1,961 men wounded.

Bavarian Forces 2nd Division GL Count Beckers: 1st Brigade GM Count Pappenheim: 4th LIR (2 bns); Nat Füs bns Regenkreis (1st Bn), Salzachkreis (2nd Bn); 4th LtI Bn (1 bn). 2nd Brigade GM Baron von Zoller:

6th LIR (2 bns); 1st LtI Bn (1 bn); Nat Füs bn Rezatkreis (1st Bn). 3rd Division GL De Lamotte; 1st Brigade GM von Habermann: 7th LIR (1st Bn), 11th LIR (2 bns); Nat Füs bns Unterdonaukreis and Illerkreis (1st bns each). 2nd Brigade GM von Deroy: 5th, 8th, 9th LIRs (1st bns each); Nat Füs bns Isarkreis (1st Bn); Illerkreis (2nd Bn). Cavalry: 1st Brigade GM von Vieregg: 1st, 2nd, 7th ChLRs (4 sqns each). 2nd Brigade GM von Elbracht: 3rd and 6th ChLR (4 sqns each). 3rd Brigade Obst Diez: 4th and 5th ChLRs (4 sqns each).

Bavarian totals 17,000 men, 4 x FAB, 3 x HAB (all 6 pdrs) and 4 x 12 pdr FABs = 66 guns*.

Bavarian losses 20 officers, 270 men and 244 horses killed; 2 generals, 74 officers. 1,109 men and 10 horses wounded, 10 officers, 1,406 men and 98 horses missing and captured.

* = of the 134 guns available only 58 were deployed as the rest had used up all their first line ammunition uselessly bombarding Würzburg on 25 October.

Comment On 29 October Sebastiani had seized the defile at Gelnhausen, 18 km to the east, and thus secured the Grande Armée's withdrawal route. Wrede's conduct in this operation was extremely amateurish. He wasted most of his Bavarian artillery's first line ammunition before the battle and his staff work was so bad that it could not be replenished as the artillery park had been 'forgotten' in Uffenheim (120 km southeast of Hanau) on 23 October. It was not rediscovered until 7 November.

His dispositions for the battle were almost criminally bad. Although he knew that he might be facing Napoleon, he set up his army facing a thick forest (which gave cover to the enemy), divided by an unfordable river (the Kinzig) - over which he had not thrown extra bridges - and his northern flank had this obstacle at their backs. Hundreds drowned when the French, having silenced the weaker Austrian artillery, pushed this flank back into the river. Napoleon claimed to have captured several trophies in this action: like so much of what he wrote, this was a lie. The Grand Armée continued its withdrawal westwards to Frankfurt and Mainz. Wrede was wounded; Austrian GM von Flachenfeld and Bavarian GM von Stockhausen were killed.

The Freiwillige Jäger sqn of the 3rd (Prussian) Neumark DragR (of Orloff-Denissov's Streifkorps) took part in the fighting on the extreme north flank.

Sources Wrede, Martinien, Leyh, Müller.

SX Sachsenhausen, 31 October 1813, skirmish

A suburb and bridgehead of the fortified city of Frankfurt, on the southern bank of the River Main, on Route B3.

A drawn match between the French and the Bavarians.

(Last action - Hanau, 30/31 October; next action - Schönebeck, 8 November.)

French Forces Part of the Imperial Guard under GdD Pacthod: 1er and 5e Tirailleurs, 3e Voltigeurs.

French total ca 2,000 men.

French losses Not known, light.

Bavarian Forces GM von Rechberg (of the 1st Division): 1st and 10th LIR (2 bns each), 4th LtI Bn (1 bn); 1 x FAB.

Bavarian total ca 3,300 men.

Bavarian losses 11 killed, 32 wounded.

Comment The French army was streaming back through Frankfurt after the battle of Hanau; they engaged in a fire-fight over the bridge with the Bavarians.

Sources Sporschil, Leyh.

EN Pamplona, 26 June - 31 October 1813, siege and capture

A fortified town in northern Spain, on the River Arda and at the junction of Routes 111 and 121, and on the west of Motorway A15.

A Spanish victory over the French.

(Last action - Ste Barbe Redoubt, 12 October; next action - Nivelle, 10 November.)

French Garrison GdB Baron Cassan commanding. Exact details not known.

French losses 500 killed, 800 wounded, 2,150 captured.

Spanish Forces Gen Prince Don Carlos de Borbon commanding:

Spanish total 10,000 men; exact details not known.

Spanish losses ca 2,000 killed and wounded.

Sources Oman, Martinien.

SX Schönebeck, 8 November 1813, clash

A small town in northeastern Germany, on the west bank of the River Elbe at the crossing of Route B246a, about 16 km southeast of Magdeburg.

A Russian victory over the French.

(Last action – Sachsenhausen, 31 October; next action – Hochheim, 9 November.)

French Forces Part of the garrison of Magdeburg. 135e, 136e, 137e, 138e, 139e, 140e, 142e, 144e, RIdLi, 4th Polish IR; 27e DragR, 8e HusR.

French total ca 8,000 men.

French losses ca 400 killed, wounded and captured, 4 guns.

Russian Forces GdK Count Bennigsen's 'Army of Poland': GL Count Tchaplitz's Cavalry Division: Combined DragR, 1st MtdRR (5 sqns each); 2nd MtdRR (4 sqns); 2nd UlR, Taganrog UlR (4 sqns each); Siberian UlR, Zhitomir UlR (2 sqns each); 1st HusR (5 sqns); 2 x HAB. GdI Dochtorov's Infantry: 12th Division GM Prince Chowansky: IRs Smolensk, Narva, Alexopol, New Ingermannland, 6th and 41st Jägers (2 bns each). 26th Division GM Paskievich: IRs Nishninovgorod, Ladoga, Poltava, Orel, 5th and 12th Jägers (2 bns each). 18th Division IRs Welikiluck, Halicz, Saratov, Pensa (2 bns each); 4 x FAB.

Russian totals and losses Not exactly known.

Comment The Russians hoped to cut off the French (who were on a foraging sortie from Magdeburg) but failed.

Sources Plotho, Schulz, Martinien.

SX Hochheim, 9 November 1813, clash

A village in western central Germany, on the north bank of the River Main, about 4 km from the confluence with the River Rhine and from the city of Mainz.

An Austrian victory over the French.

(Last action – Schönebeck, 8 November; next action – Dresden, 11 November.)

French Forces GdD Guilleminot's 14th Division VII Corps: 18e RILé, 52e and 156e RIdLi R Illyrien (8 bns); Combined IR (3 bns made up of Pacthod's disbanded 13th Division*). 2 x FAB. GdD Morand's 12th Division IV Corps: 8e RILé, 13e, 23e and 137e RIdLi (14 bns), 2 x FAB.

* = remnants of 1er Lé, 7e, 42e, 67e and 101e RIdLi.

French total ca 5,000men, 24 guns.

French losses Not known exactly; moderate.

Austrian Forces FZM Count Ignaz Gyulai commanding III Corps. FML Count Crenneville's Division: GzIRs Warasdiner Kreutzer Nr 5 and Warasdiner-St Georger Nr 6 (1 bn each); ChLRs Klenau Nr 5, Rosenberg Nr 6 (5 sqns each). FML Murray's Division: IRs EH Ludwig Nr 8, Würzburg Nr 7, Kottulinsky Nr 41 (3 bns each); IR Kaiser Nr 1 (2 bns), 2 x 6 pdr FAB (16 guns). FML Prince zu Hessen-Homburg's Division: IRs Mariassy Nr 37, Gyulai Nr 60 and Kollowrath Nr 36 (2 bns each); IR Frelich Nr 28 (3 bns), 2 x 6 pdr FAB (16 guns).

Austrian total ca 30,000 men.

Austrian losses Not known, light.

Comment These French Forces were the rearguard of the Grande Armée making their way westwards into the fortress of Mainz. The Austrians set up a battery on the south bank of the Main just east of Costheim and caused them considerable damage. Gyulai's III Corps assaulted Hochheim and bore the brunt of the action; the other forces (II Corps and Bubna's Division) were scarcely engaged.

Sources Plotho, M KuKKA, 3rd Folge, Vol IV, Martinien, Wrede.

EN Nivelle River, 10 November 1813, battle

A fortified river in the southwestern French Département of Pyrénées-Basses, joining the Bay of Biscay at St Jean-de-Luz.

An Allied victory over the French.

(Last action – Pamplona, 31 October; next action – Bayonne, 9–13 December.)

French Forces M Soult commanding: **1st Division** GdD Foy: 6e RILé, 36e, 39e, 65e, 69e RIdLi (2 bns each); 76e RIdLi (1 bn). **Total** ca 5,000 men; **losses** 28 killed, 192 wounded. **2nd Division** GdD Darmagnac: 16e RILé, 8e, 51e and 54e RIdLi (1 bn each); 28e and 75e RIdLi (2 bns each). **Total** ca 4,700 men; **losses** 35 killed, 340 wounded, 32 missing. **3rd Division** GdD Abbé: 5e and 27e RILé, 63e and 95e RIdLi (1 bn each); 64e and 94e RIdLi (2 bns each). **Total** ca 6,300 men; **losses** 6 killed, 156 wounded, 37 missing. **4th Division** GdD Conroux: 12e RILé, 32e and 43e RIdLi (2 bns each); 45e, 55e and 58e RIdLi (1 bn each). **Total** ca 5,350 men; **losses** 71 killed, 529 wounded, 397 missing. **5th Division** GdD Maransin: 4e RILé; 27e, 34e, 50e, 59eRIdLi (1 bn each); 40e, 130e RIdLi (2 bns each). **Total** ca 5,500 men; **losses** 157 killed, 600 wounded, 260 missing. **6th Division** GdD Daricau: 21e and 28e RILé, 24e, 96e, 100e, 103e RIdLi (1 bn each). **Total** ca 5,700 men; **losses** 18 killed, 80 wounded. **7th Division** GdD Leval: 16e RILé and 105 RIdLi (2 bns each); 17e RILé, 3e, 15e, 101e RIdLi (1 bn each). **Total** ca 4,500 men; **losses** 21 killed, 93 wounded. **8th Divi-**

sion GdD Taupin: 31e RILé (3 bns); 9e RILé and 47e RIdLi (2 bns each); 27e, 70e, 88e RIdLi (1 bn each). **Total** ca 4,800 men; **losses** 68 killed, 375 wounded, 498 missing. **9th Division** GdD Boyer: 2e RILé, 32e, 43e, 120e, 122e RIdLi (2 bns each). **Total** ca 6,500 men; **losses** 26 killed, 163 wounded. **Reserve** GdD Villatte: 34e RILé, 115e RIdLi (2 bns each), 66e, 82e RIdLi (1 bn each); **Spanish Troops:** IRs Castile, Toledo; Royal Étranger, Guard (1 bn each). **Italian Troops:** 2nd LtIR, 4th and 6th LIRs (1 bn each). **German Troops:** 2nd Nassau IR (2 bns); 4th Baden IR (1 bn), Frankfurt IR (1 bn). **Total** ca 8,300 men; **losses** 15 killed, 77 wounded. No cavalry and very little artillery involved. Reserve loss 4 killed, 26 wounded, 9 missing.

French grand total 56,650 men.

French overall losses 451 killed, 2,637 wounded, 2,033 missing = 4,321 men, 59 guns. GdD Conroux killed.

Allied Forces The Marquess of Wellington commanding:

British Troops 1st Division MG Howard: 1/1st and 3/1st Footguards, 1/2nd and 1/3rd Footguards; 1st, 2nd and 5th LI Bns KGL; 1st and 2nd LtI Bns KGL (1 bn each). **Total** 6,898 men; **losses** 29 killed, 159 wounded, 5 missing. **2nd Division** MG W Stewart: 1/50th, 1/71st, 1/92nd, 1/3rd, 1/57th, 1st Provisional Bn, 1/28th, 2/34th, 1/39th Foot (1 bn each). **Total** 5,767 men; **losses** 18 killed, 121 wounded, 1 missing. **3rd Division** MG Colville: 1/45th, 1/74th, 1/88th, 5/60, 1/5th, 2/83rd, 2/87th, 1/97th Foot (1 bn each). **Total** 5,031 men; **losses** 56 killed, 362 wounded, 8 missing. **4th Division** MG Cole: 3/27th, 1/40th, 1/48th, 2nd Provisional Bn, 1/7th, 1/20th and 1/23rd Foot (1 bn each). **Total** 4,166 men; **losses** 41 killed, 280 wounded, 4 missing. **5th Division** MG Hay: 3/1st, 1/9th, 1/38th, 1/4th, 2/47th, 2/59th Foot. **Total** 2,788 men; **losses** 4 killed, 15 wounded, 19 missing. **6th Division** MG Clinton: 1/42nd, 1/79th, 1(91st, 1/11th, 1/32nd, 1/39th, 1/61st Foot (1 bn each). **Total** 4,651 men; **losses** 21 killed, 138 wounded. **7th Division** MG Le Cor: 1/6th, 3rd Provisional Bn, Brunswick Oels, 1/51st, 1/68th, 1/82nd Foot; Chasseurs Britanniques (1 bn each). **Total** 3,742 men; **losses** 51 killed, 252 wounded, 34 missing. **BG Aylmer's Independent Bde** 1/76th, 2/84th, 1/85th Foot. **Total** 1,930 men; **losses** 3 killed, 19 wounded. **Light Division** MG C Alten: 1/43rd, 1(95th, 3/95th, 1/52nd, 2/95th Foot. **Total** 3,291 men; **losses** 44 killed, 364 wounded, 3 missing. Staff, artillery, engineers 7 killed, 41 wounded. 13th LDR 1 wounded.

British infantry overall total 38,264 men.

British overall losses 274 killed, 1,752 wounded, 74 missing.

Portuguese Troops (all LIR of 2 bns each; all Caçadores of 1 bn each). **With 2nd Division** Ashworth's Brigade: 6th and 18th LIR, 6th Caçadores. **Total** 2,713 men; **losses** 2 killed, 9 wounded. **With 3rd Division** Power's Brigade: 9th and 21st LIR, 11 Caçadores. **Total** 2,303 men; **losses** 25 killed, 59 wounded, 6 missing. **With 4th Division** Vasconecellos' Brigade: 11th and 23rd LIR, 7th Caçadores. **Total** 2,419 men; **losses** 6 killed, 17 wounded, 1 missing. **With 5th Division** De Regoa's Brigade: 3rd and 15th LIR, 8th Caçadores. **Total** 1,765 men; **losses** 9 killed, 10 wounded. **With 6th Division** Douglas' Brigade: 8th and 12th LIR, 9th Caçadores. **Total** 2,067 men; **losses** 17 killed, 42 wounded. **With 7th Division** Doyle's Brigade: 7th and 19th LIRs, 2nd Caçadores. **Total** 2,326 men; **losses** 7 killed, 17 wounded, 2 missing. **With Light Division** 17th LIR (1 bn only); 1st and 3rd Caçadores. **Total** 1,679 men; **losses** 10 killed, 26 wounded, 2 missing. **Independent Brigades** Wilson's 1st and 16th LIRs; 4th Caçadores. **Total** 2,185 men; **losses** 7 killed, 11 wounded. Bradford's 13th and 24th LIRs; 5th Caçadores. **Total** 1,614 men; no losses. **Hamilton's Portuguese Division** Da Costa's Brigade 4th and 10th LIR, 10th Caçadores. **Total** 2,558 men; **losses** 26 killed, 64 wounded. Buchan's Brigade 2nd and 14th LIRs. **Total** 2,391 men; **losses** 13 killed, 14 wounded, 6 missing Artillery (3 x FAB) 220 men.

Portuguese overall total 24,240. Total.

Portuguese losses 83 killed, 191 wounded, 9 missing.

Spanish Troops (exact details not known).

Army	Division	Officers	Men	Battalions	Losses
Giron	Virue	152	3,971	6	?
	La Torre	149	3,381	6	?
Freire's 4th	Morillo	205	4,924	6	?
	Longa	112	2,495	5	?

Army	Division	Officers	Men	Battalions	Losses
	Del Barco	226	5,604	8	?
	Barcena	138	4,016	6	?
	Total	*982*	*24,391*	*37*	*820*

Wellington's total force thus was about 88,000 men.

Comment Once again Wellington achieved a break through of an extremely strong defensive position by fooling Soult as to where and when the real blow would fall. He concentrated 60,000 men (3rd, 4th, 7th Light Divisions, Giron's, Barcena's and Del Barco's Spaniards) against Clausel's 15,000 men (the 4th, 5th and 8th Division) in the mountainous central sector of the front, from Ascain to the bridge of Amotz. In the western (coastal) sector and in the east, by Ainhoa, demonstrations were to be made simultaneously to the central thrust to prevent Soult from reinforcing the threatened sector. It worked beautifully; again the French soldiers put up only feeble resistance before abandoning their positions. Soult withdrew north again to just south of Bayonne. The 88e RIdLi was captured in entirety and Clausel's three divisions were shattered. Had Wellington pursued energetically, Soult's entire army must have been destroyed.

Sources Oman, Martinien.

SX Dresden, 13 October – 11 November, 1813, blockade and capture

Capital of the Kingdom of Saxony, on the left bank of the River Elbe, at the junction of Routes B6, B170/E55 and B173; 132 km east of Leipzig.

An Allied victory over the French.

(Last action – Hochheim, 9 November; next action – Stettin, 21 November.)

French Forces M Gouvion St Cyr commanding I and XIV Corps: Governor GdD Count Durosnel. From I Corps (GdD Count Vandamme): 1st Division GdD Dumonceau: 12e, 17e, 36e RIdLi. 2nd Division GdD Philippon: 13e RILé, 25e, 51e, 57e RIdLi, 23rd (M Count St Cyr). 42nd Division GdD Dupas: 9e, 10e, 11e, 12e RILé, 39e, 40e, 43e, 63e, 96e RIdLi. 43rd Division: 27e, 29e RILé, 27e, 45e, 65e, 95e, 100e, 103e RIdLi. 44th Division GdD Serrurier: 8e RILé (2 bns); 16e, 18e RILé (1 bn each); 24e, 39e, 50e, 54e, 64e, 75e, 95e RIdLi. 45th Division GdD Razout: 6e, 17e RILé; 5e, 8e, 11e, 28e, 32e, 60e RIdLi. The following regiments also show officer casualties for the defence of Dresden: 21e, 25e, 26e RILé, 34e, 37e, 58e, 76e, 79e, 81e RIdLi; 7e, 8e ChLL, 14e HusR. 2nd Italian ChàCh; 5th, 6th 7th Neapolitan LIRs: 13th Polish LIR, 16th Polish CavR.

French total originally 36,000 men.

French losses 4,000 killed and wounded. The garrison was to have marched out with honours of war to France on condition that they would not fight against the Allies for 6 months but the Allied supreme commander (Schwarzenberg) refused to ratify the capitulation and they marched into captivity in Austria. The Allies took 94 French field guns and 151 Saxon fortress guns.

Allied Forces GdK Count Klenau.

IV Austrian Corps of the Army of Bohemia: 1st Division FML Baron Mohr: Avantgarde: GM Baumgarten: GzIR Wallachisch-Illyrisch Nr 13 (1 bn); ChLR Hohenzollern Nr 2, HusR Palatin Nr 12 and HusR EH Ferdinand Nr 3 (6 sqns each), 1 x HAB. 2nd Division FML Prince Hohenlohe-Bartenstein: IRs J Colloredo Nr 57 (2 bns); IRs Zach Nr 15, Württemberg Nr 40 and Lindenau Nr 29 (3 bns each); 2 x 6 pdr FABs. 3rd Division FML Mayer: IRs Liechtenstein Nr 12, Coburg Nr 22, EH Carl Nr 3 (3 bns each); IR Kerpen Nr 49 (2 bns); 2 x 6 pdr FABs. Reserve Artillery 1 x 6 pdr, 2 x 12 pdr FABs. **Total** ca 24,000 men; **losses** – not known but light.

The Corps of GL Count Ostermann-Tolstoy 1st Militia Corps GM Muraviev: 1st–4th Nischegorod MIRs; 1st Kazan MIR (3 bns each); 1 x heavy FAB, 1 x pionier coy.

Militia Corps of GM Titov 1st, 2nd, 3rd Pensa MIRs, 1st Kostroma, Riasan MCRs (5 sqns each); Kazan MCR (2 sqn); 5th Ural Cossack Pulk and 3rd Orenburg Cossack Pulks (5 Sotnias each), 1 x HAB.

Allied total ca 17,000 men.

Allied losses Not known.

Sources Plotho, Sporschil, Wrede.

IN Caldiero, 15 November 1813, clash

A village in central northern Italy on Route 11 about 15 km east of Verona, just south of Autostrada A4/E70 and north of the River Adige (Etsch).

A Franco-Italian victory over the Austrians.

(Last action – Bassano, 30/31 October; next action – Ferrara, 18 November.)

Franco-Italian Forces Prince Eugène de Beauharnais commanding: 1st Division GdD Quesnel 92e RIdLi (3 bns); 30e DBde Prov (1er and 14e Lé; 10e Li, 1 bn each). 2nd Division GdD Rouyer: 9e RIdli (2 bns); 35e RIdLi (3 bns); 1er R Étranger (4 bns); 28e DBde Prov (7e, 52e, 61e Li 1 bn each). GdB Bonnemain: 31e ChàCh (3 sqns); 4th Italian ChàCh (2 sqns).

Franco-Italian total 18 bns, 5 sqns, 2 x FAB, 2 x HAB; ca 16,000 men.

Franco-Italian losses 500 killed, wounded and missing.

Austrian Forces FML Radivojevich commanding: FML Merville: GM Starhemberg: Jägers (9th Bn); IR Lusignan Nr 16; GzIR Gradiskaner Nr 8; GzIR Warasdiner-Kreutzer Nr 5 (1 bn each); HusR Radetzky Nr 5 (5½ sqns); UlR Merveldt Nr 1 (2 sqns); 1 x HAB. GM Eckhardt: IR Benjowsky Nr 31 (3 bns); Jägers (8th Bn); IR Jellačič Nr ; IR Bianchi Nr 63 (2 bns each); Gren Bn Chimani; HusR Frimont Nr 9 (3½ sqns); ½ x 3 pdr HAB. GM Vécsey: IR Chasteler Nr 46 (4 bns); UlR EH Carl Nr 2 (6 sqns); 1 x HAB.

Austrian total 10 bns, 11 sqns, 9 guns, ca 8,000 men.

Austrian losses 500 killed and wounded, 900 captured, 2 guns.

Sources Martinien, Vaudoncourt, HGM 56, Wrede, vom Holtz.

IN Ferrara, 18 November 1813, capture

A fortified town in northeastern Italy just south of the River Po, 47 km northeast of Modena and at the junction of Routes 16, 64 and 255.

An Austrian victory over the Franco-Italians.

(Last action – Caldiero, 15 November; next action – San Michele, 19 November.)

Franco-Italian Garrison Local militia; exact details, totals and losses not known.

Austrian Forces GM Nugent commanding: IR EH Franz Carl Nr 52 (1st Bn); GzIR Warasdiner-Kreutzer Nr 5; (Res Bn), Istrian Landwehr (1 bn each). HusR Radetzky Nr 5 (5½ sqn); 2 x 3 pdr guns.

Austrian total ca 2,800 men.

Austrian losses Nil.

Comment After the fall of Trieste (23 October) Nugent crossed the Adriatic in British ships, landed at Goro, south of the Po delta, and took Ferrara, spreading great concern among Eugène's generals for the safety of their southern flank. Joachim Murat, King of Naples, had now abandoned Napoleon and joined the Allies as had Bavaria. Eugène forced Nugent out of Ferrara again on 27 November.

Sources Martinien, Vaudoncourt, HGM 56, Wrede.

IN San Michele, 19 November 1813, clash

A village in northeastern Italy on the eastern outskirts of Verona, north of Route 11.

An Austrian victory over the Franco-Italians.

(Last action – Ferrara, 18 November; next action – Rovigo and Boara, 3 December.)

Franco-Italian Forces Viceroy Prince Eugène commanding: GdD Grenier: GdD Marcognet's 4th Division: GdB Jeannin: 53e RIdLi (3 bns); 102e and 106e RIdLi (2 bns each). GdB Deconchy: 29e PvDBde (20e and 101e RIdLi – 1 bn each); 31e PvDBde (131e and 132e RIdLi – 1 bn each). 2 x FAB.

Franco-Italian total ca 10,000 men, 12 guns.

Franco-Italian losses GdD Grenier wounded; ca 700 killed, wounded and missing.

Austrian Forces FZM Hiller commanding: FML Baron von Merville's division: GM Vécsey: IR Chasteler Nr 27 (4 bns). GM Count von Stutterheim: IR Benjowsky Nr 31 (3 bns). GM Gober: IR Deutschmeister Nr 4 (4 bns); UlR EH Carl Nr 3 (2 sqns); 3 x FAB.

Austrian total ca 11,000 men, 18 guns.

Austrian losses Not known exactly.

Comment Vaudoncourt states that only Jeannin's 4,000 men were engaged against the Austrians. This Austrian assault cancelled out Eugène's victory at Caldiero on 15 November. Hiller halted his advance to await clear news as to Murat's conduct (Murat was King of Naples).

Sources vom Holtz, Wrede, Martinien, Vaudoncourt.

SX Stettin (Szczecin), 18 March – 21 November 1813, blockade and capitulation

A fortified Baltic Sea port (nowadays in Poland) on the River Oder (now Odra) about 80 km from its mouth.

A Prusso-Russian victory over the French.

(Last action – Dresden, 11 November; next action – Danzig, 29 November.)

French Garrison GdD Grandjean commanding: 17e, 25e, 63e, 96e, 111e, 124e RIdLi; artillery and engineers.

French total 8,500 men.

French losses 900 killed or died of sickness, 7,600 captured, 351 guns.

Allied Forces Prussian GM von Plötz: Obst von Sydow: 8th ResIR (3 bns); 1st Pomm LWIR, 2nd Pomm LWIR, 3rd Pomm LWIR (4 bns each); 1st Pomm IR, Colberg IR (garrison and reinforcement battalions); 1st Ostpr LWKR (4 sqns); 2 x 6 pdr FABs, pioniers (1 coy).

Allied total 11,500 men.

Allied losses Not known exactly but light.

Sources Plotho, Sporschil, Martinien.

SX Danzig, (Gdansk), 16 January – 29 November 1813, siege and capture

A fortified Baltic Sea port (nowadays in Poland) on the estuary of the River Vistula (Vista).

A Prusso-Russian victory over the French.

(Last action – Stettin, 21 November; next action – Arnhem, 30 November.)

French and Allied Garrison GdD Count Rapp commanding: **GdD Grandjean's 7th Division** 1st Westfalian LIR, 13th Bavarian LIR (1 bn each); 5th, 10th, 11th Polish IRs (2 bns each). **30th Division** GdD Heudelet: the 4th bns of the following French regiments organized into Demi-Brigades as shown: 1ère DBde (2e, 4e,17e RILé); 6e DBde (16e, 21e, 28e RILé); 7th DBde (8e, 14e, 94e RIdLi); 8e DBde (24e, 45e, 59e RIdLi); 9e DBde (54e, 88e, 95e RIdLi); 17e DBde (6e, 25e RILé, 39e RIdLi). **33rd Division** GdD Destre's Neapolitans: Royal Guard (1 coy), 5th, 6th, 9th LIRs (2 bns each); Regiment d'Élite (1 bn formed of the élite coys of these regiments). **34th Division** GdD Franceschi (the old 'Division Princière'): 22e RILé (2 coys); 3e RIdLi (1 coy of 4e Bn); 29e RIdLi (1 bn); 105e RIdLi (1 coy); 113e RIdLi (2 coys); Regiment Frankfurt (2 coys); 4th IR Confederation of the Rhine (Ducal Saxon) (½ bn); 5th IR Confederation of the Rhine (Anhalt and Lippe) (1 bn); 6th IR Confederation of the Rhine (Schwarzburg, etc) (½ bn). **Cavalry:** Remnants of the following regiments: 3e, 6e, 8e CuirR; 2e, 4e, 5e, 11e, 12e, 13e, 14e, 15e, 19e, 20e, 28e DragRs; 3e, 7e, 11e, 19e, 23e, 24e, 25e ChàCh, 7e, 8e, HusR; 9th and 16th Polish Cav Rs.

French total 36,000 men, 1,300 guns.

French losses 6,000 killed and wounded, 6,000 sick, 8,000 deserted, 16,000 captured. GdB Breissand killed.

Allied Forces GdK Duke Alexander of Württemberg commanding:

Russian Troops IV Corps GL Prince Volkonsky: 6th Division GM Rachmanov: IRs Asov and Nisov, 3rd and 18th Jägers (2 bns each); IRs Briansk, Kaporzsch (1 bn each). 3rd Division: Res bns of IRs Reval, Kaporzsch, 20th and 21st Jägers. 4th Division: Res bns of IRs Volhynien, Tobolsk, Minsk, 4th and 34th Jägers.

II Corps GL Löwis: 25th Division: GM Kolubakin: IRs Woronesch, 31st and 47th Jägers, 1st and 2nd Marines (2 bns each). Res bns of 17th Division: IRs Riasan, Bielosersk, Brest, 30th Jägers. 25th Division: Res bns of 21st Jägers (21st Division), 31st and 47th Jägers.

III Corps GL Barasdin I: GM Mordvinov: St Petersburg Militia (16 bns); Novgorod 1st, 2nd and 3rd Militia Rs (3 bns each). 1 x heavy, 2 x light FABs. Cavalry: GM Czarnisch: Kazan DragR, Yamburg UlR (2 sqns each); Combined DragR (3 sqns)9th; St Petersburg Militia CavR (4 sqns). 1 x HAB. Cossacks GM Tscharnusubov IV: GM Illowaisky IX: Pulks of Illowaisky IX, Grekov V, Grekov XVII, Charitanoff VII, Tscharnusubov IV, Sutchilin II, Perekop Tartar R, Semphiropol Tartar R. Siege artillery: 47 Russian guns, 55 Prussian guns, 116 British guns. 2 x pontonnier coys, 4 x pionier coys, 2 x miner coys, the Anglo-Russian flotilla of Rear Admiral Greihs: 11 ships, 2,300 crew, 154 guns.

Prussian Troops Obst Count von Dohna: Ostpr LWIR (7th and 13th bns); 4th Ostpr LWIR (14th, 15th, 16th, 17th bns); 5th Ostpr LWIR (9th, 10th, 18th, 19th bns); 4th and 5th Ostpr LWKRs. 1 x 6 pdr FAB.

Allied total 40,000 men; losses – not known.

Sources Plotho, Martinien, Sporschil.

NL Arnhem, 30 November 1813, storm

A fortified town in the eastern Netherlands, on the right bank of the Rhine, just downstream from the confluence with the River Issel and at the junction of Autobahns A12, A48 and A52.

A Prussian victory over the French.

(Last action – Danzig, 29 November; next action – Boden, 4 December.)

French Garrison GdB Marie commanding: 22e RILé, 22e, 51e, 55e, 102e, 112e, 123e RIdLi. Total ca 4,000 men.

French losses 500 killed and wounded, 1,000 captured, 14 guns.

Allied Forces GL von Bülow's Prussian Corps. GM von Oppen: IR Colberg (2 bns and Füs bn); 5th Ostpr Res IR (2 bns); 9th Res IR (1st and 2nd bns); 3rd Neumark LWI Bn (2 bns); Ostpr Jägers (2 coys); Füs bn Zglinitzky (1 bn); Braunschweig LWI Bn (2 coys); DragR Königin (4 sqns); Brand DragR (4 sqns); Pomm NKR (4 sqns); Maj Colomb's Streifkorps (2 combined sqns); 2 x HAB. General von Thümen's division was in support.

Allied total 10,000 men.

Allied losses 600 killed and wounded.

Sources Plotho, Sporschil, Martinien.

IN Rovigo and Boara, 3 December 1813, skirmish

Rovigo is a small town in northeastern Italy at the junction of Routes 16 and 499, between the Rivers Po and Adige (Etsch) about 50 km from the Adriatic coast. Boara is a hamlet - and was a bridgehead - on the north bank of the Adige, 4 km north of Rovigo.

An Austrian victory over the Franco-Italians.

(Last action - San Michele, 19 November; next action - Zadar, 6 December.)

Franco-Italian Forces GdB Deconchy of Marcognet's 4th Division: 29e PvDBde, 31e PvDBde (2 bns each), 106e RIdLi (1 bn), ChàCh (2 sqns), 8 guns.

Franco-Italian total ca 5,600 men.

Franco-Italian losses 40 killed, 135 wounded.

Austrian Forces FML Marschall with IR Benjowsky Nr 31 (2 bns) of Gen Count Starhemberg's brigade.

Austrian total ca 1,800 men.

Austrian losses 1 company captured. Vaudoncourt claims: '400 killed and wounded, 900 captured'.

Comment Deconchy aimed to capture the bridge of boats at Boara to disrupt the Austrian blockade of Venice but he failed and returned to Villanova del Ghebbo, about 8 km to the west.

Sources Wrede, vom Holtz, Vaudoncourt.

SX Boden, 4 December 1813, clash

Now Gross-Boden; a village in northern Germany, halfway between the harbour cities of Hamburg and Lübeck, on a minor road about 11 km southeast of Bad Oldesloe.

A Danish victory over the Allies.

(Last action - Arnhem, 30 November; next action - Bornhöft, 7 December.)

Danish Forces MG Lasson commanding the 2nd Brigade: IRs Fynske and Slevsigske (2 bns each); IRs Dronningen (2nd Bn, rifle coy); Holsten (3rd Bn, rifle coy); Oldenburg (3rd Bn, rifle coy). Slevsigske Jäger Corps (3rd Coy); Fynske LDR (60 men); HusR (50 men).

Danish total ca 4,000 men.

Danish losses 5 killed, 17 wounded.

Allied Forces G Wallmoden-Gimborn commanding: Avantgarde: GM Dörnberg: 2nd Brigade: Russo-German Legion Obstlt Warburg: (3rd, 4th, 6th and 7th bns), 1 x FAB (8guns). Hanoverian Light Brigade Obst Klencke: Lüneburg, Bremen-Verden and Anhalt-Dessau bns; Kielmansegge's Jägers (3 coys); 1st, 2nd HusRs Russo-German Legion. KGL 3rd HusR.

Allied total ca 6,000 men.

Allied losses 100 killed and wounded.

Comment The action was the result of a reconnaissance in force by Wallmoden. It ended in thick fog with the battalions Bremen-Verden and Anhalt-Dessau being badly mauled and with the 3rd and 4th Bns, Russo-German Legion firing upon one another. The Danish corps began to withdraw into their fortress at Rendsburg.

Source Gottschalck.

IN Zadar (Zara), 22 November - 6 December 1813, blockade and capitulation

A fortified Adriatic port in Slovenia (ex-Yugoslavia), on Route 2/E65 opposite Ancona on the Italian coast.

An Austrian victory over the Franco-Italians.

(Last action - Rovigo and Boara, 3 December; next action - Boara, 8 December.)

Franco-Italian Garrison GdB Roize commanding: IR Liccaner (1 bn) and a battalion of French troops (600 men).

Franco-Italian total ca 1,200 men, 286 guns.

Franco-Italian losses 80 Liccaners were shot by the French; the rest were expelled from the fort on 3 December. The Liccaners revolted inside the fortress twice; both revolts were put down. The French garrison was transported to France on condition that they would not serve against Austria or her allies until exchanged.

Austrian Forces GM Baron von Tomassich commanding: GzIR Liccaner (1 bn); Banal (Hungarian) Insurrektions IR (2 coys); 1st Banal-GzIR Nr 10 (1 bn).

Austrian total ca 1,500 men. Captain Cadogan of the Royal Navy with his ship of the line supported the operation.

Austrian losses Not known but very light.

Comment During the latter part of 1813 Austrian troops and Royal Naval vessels under Captain Hoste cooperated to reclaim many ports and islands in the Adriatic and the Dalmatian border provinces lost to France in 1809. These included the port of Sibenik on 1 November, the island of Lesina (Losinj), including Forts Napoleone and Spagna, 10–14 November, Split (Spalato) on 24 December and Klissa, 26 December.

Sources Wrede, Vaudoncourt, vom Holtz, Clowes, James.

SX Bornhöft, 7 December 1813, skirmish

Nowadays Bornhöved. A village in northern Germany at the junction of Routes B404 and 430 in Schleswig-Holstein, 30 km south of Kiel, between Neumünster and Lake Plön.

A Danish victory over the Swedes.

(Last action – Boden, 4 December; next action – Sehestadt, 10 December.)

Danish Forces Prince Friedrich of Hessen-Kassel commanding: GdD Lallemand: IR Jutland (1 bn); Holstein Scharfschützen (2 bns); Schleswig Jägers (2 coys); Holstein CavR, 17th Lithuanian UlR (3 sqns each); Danish HusR (1 sqn); 6 guns.

Danish total ca 4,000 men.

Danish losses 80 killed, wounded and missing.

Swedish Forces LG Skjöldebrand commanding. Mörner HusR (4 sqns); Schonen HusR (1 sqn).

Swedish total ca 550* men.

Swedish losses Obst Baron Cederstrom and about 200 men killed and wounded.

* = the Prussian 1st Schl HusR ('Schill's') was in rear but not engaged.

Comment The Danes held a strong position in very close country in which the Swedish cavalry could not deploy, despite having a victorious encounter with the 17th Lithuanian Ulans and having broken the 2nd Bn Holstein Scharfschützen in the act of forming square. It was infantry country and the Swedes were a purely cavalry force. The Danes withdrew north on Sehestadt, aiming for Rendsburg fortress.

Source Schulz.

IN Boara, 8 December 1813, clash

A hamlet and fortified bridgehead on the lower River Adige (Etsch) in northeastern Italy just east of the Motorway A13 bridge.

An Austrian victory over the Franco-Italians.

(Last action – Zadar, 22 November – 6 December; next action – Cervia, 26 December.)

Franco-Italian Forces GdD Marcognet commanding the 4th Division: GdB Jeannin: 93e RIdLi (3 bns); 102e and 103e RIdLi (2 bns each). GdB Deconchy: 29e and 31e PvDBdes (2 bns each). GdB Schmitz (of Rouyer's 2nd Division): 9e RIdLi (2 bns); 28e PvDBde (3 bns).

Franco-Italian total ca 12,000 men and 18 guns. Of these only 5,000 came into action.

Franco-Italian losses 800 killed and wounded, 102 captured.

Austrian Forces GM Count Starhemberg commanding: 9th Jg Bn (1 bn); IRs Lusignan Nr 16 (1 bn); GzIR Gradiskaner Nr 8 (2nd Bn); GzIR Warasdiner-Kreutzer Nr 5 (2nd Bn); HusR Radetzky Nr 5 (5½ sqns); UlR Merveldt Nr 1 (1 sqn); 1 x FAB. IR Benjowsky Nr 31 (2 bns); IR EH Carl Nr 3 (LW bn).

Austrian total ca 6,000 men.

Austrian losses Not known exactly but less than those of the enemy.

Comment After initial success, Marcognet relaxed his guard. At 22.00 hrs that night Starhemberg led a counterattack which threw the Franco-Italians back south to Rovigo. Next day Marcognet withdrew east to Costa then to Lendinara.

Sources Wrede, vom Holtz, Vaudoncourt.

SX Sehestadt, 10 December 1813, clash

A village then in Denmark, now in Germany, 20 km west of Kiel, just to the north of the Kiel canal and 14 km northeast of Rendsburg.

A Danish victory over the Russo-Germans.

(Last action – Bornhöft, 7 December; next action – Zamosc, 22 December.)

Danish Forces Gen Prince Friedrich von Hessen-Kassel commanding: LIRs Königin (1st Bn); Holstein (3rd Bn); Oldenburg (4 bns); Fünen and 3rd Jutland (2 bns each). LDR Jutland (1st and 2nd sqns); HusR (2 sqns); CavR Holstein (4 sqns), Schleswig-Holstein LtIR (2 bns): Schleswig Jäger Corps (2nd Bn).

Danish total 9,500 men, 50 guns.

Danish losses ca 600 killed, wounded and captured.

Russo-German Forces GL Count Wallmoden-Gimborn commanding: Avantgarde: Gen von Dörnberg: Hanoverian Light Brigade: LtCol Martin: Kielmansegge's Jägers (2 coys); LtI Bns Bremen-Verden and Lüneburg (2 bns). 2nd Brigade: Russian-German Legion (2 bns); 1st HusR Russian-German Legion (4 sqns); 3rd HusR KGL (5 sqns); HusR Lüneburg (3 sqns); 2nd HAB Russian-German Legion. Russian-German Division: Gen von Arendtschildt: 5 bns and 1 x FAB. English-German Division Gen Lyon: Hanoverian Line Brigade: LtCol Halkett: LI Bns Bennigsen, Dessau, Langrehr, Lauenburg (1 bn each); KGL Bn Holtzermann (½ bn); 1 x FAB. Cavalry: 2nd HusR Russian-German Legion: HusR Bremen-Verden (4 sqns each); 1st and 2nd HAB KGL; 1st HAB. Russian-German Legion: Mecklenburg JzFuss (1 bn); Mecklenburg JzPf (2 sqns). The Reserve: Hanseatic Brigade Obst von Witzleben: 2 bns, 8 sqns, 8 guns.

Russo-German total ca 5,000 men.

Russo-German losses 620 killed and wounded, 600 captured, 2 guns.

Comment Wallmoden had tried to cut the Danes off from their target, the fortress of Rendsburg, but was just not strong enough.

Sources Sichart, Sporschil, Gottschalck.

EN Bayonne, 9–13 December 1813, battle

(Including the actions of the Nive, Arcangues, St-Pierre-d'Irube.)

A French Biscayan port, 6 km from the coast, at the confluence of the Rivers Nive and Adour and east of Biarritz, on Routes N117/E80 and N10/E5.

An Allied victory over the French.

(Last action – Nivelle, 10 November; next action – Motte de Garris, 15 February 1814.)

French Forces M Soult commanding: **1st Division** GdD Foy: 6e RILé, 36e, 39e, 65e, 69e RIdLi (2 bns each); 76e RIdLi (1 bn). **Total** 5,608 men. **2nd Division** GdD Darmagnac: 16e RILé, 8e, 51e, 54e RIdLi (1 bn each), 31e RILé (2 bns). **Total** 5,914 men. **3rd Division** GdD Abbé: 5e and 27e RILé, 63e and 95e RIdLi (1 bn each). **Total** 6,372 men. **4th Division** GdD Taupin: 12e RILé, 32e and 43e RIdLi (2 bns each); 45e, 55e and 58e RIdLi (1 bn each). **Total** 6,098. **5th Division** GdD Maransin: 4e RILé, 27e, 34e, 50e and 59e RIdLi (1 bn each); 40e and 130e RIdLi (2 bns each). **Total** 5,216. **6th Division** GdD Daricau: 21e and 28e RILé, 96e, 100e, 103e and 119e RIdLi (1 bn each). **Total** 5,519. **7th Division** GdD Leval: 16e RILé and 105e RIdLi (2 bns each); 17e RILé, 3e, 15e, 101e RIdLi (1 bn each). **Total** 4,704. **8th Division** dissolved after the Nivelle. **9th Division** GdD Boyer: 2e RILé, 24e, 120e and 122e RIdLi (2 bns each); 118e RIdLi (3 bns). **Total** 6,423. **The Reserve** GdD Villatte: 9e RILé (1 bn); 34e RIdLi, 66e and 82e RIdLi (2 bns each). **Spanish Troops** IRs Castile, Toledo; Royal Étranger, Guard (1 bn each). **German Troops** 2nd Nassau IR (2 bns); 4th Baden IR (1 bn); Frankfurt IR (1 bn). **Total** 5,397. **GdB Paris' Brigade** 10e, 81e and 115e RIdLi (2 bns each), 114e and 117e RIdLi (1 bn each). **Total** 3,881. Artillery. 2,000 men and 90 guns. Bayonne Garrison – 8,801.

French Total 65,933.

French losses (Killed, wounded and missing) 1st Division – 903; 2nd Division – 778; 3rd Division – 1,276; 4th Division – 197; 5th Division – 299; 6th Division – 869; 7th Division – 395; 9th Division – 1,149; Reserve – 48. Artillery – 33. **Total losses** 5,947. Soult reported 513 killed, 4,835 wounded, 290 captured, 276 missing. **Total** 5,914. 16 guns were lost.

Allied Forces Marquess of Wellington commanding.

As for the Nivelle, 10 November 1813 except that the only Spanish troops taken into France were Morillo's 4,500 who did not come into action here.

Allied totals 36,000 British and 23,000 Portuguese troops.

Allied losses 9 December

1. Hill's Corps at the crossing of the Nive. 2nd Division MG Stewart: 9 killed, 78 wounded. 6th Division MG Clinton: 23 killed, 174 wounded, 7 missing. 2. The Combats of Anglet and Bassussary (Hope's Corps and the Light Division): 1st Division: 10 killed, 93 wounded. 5th Division: 22 killed, 158 wounded, 6 missing. Light Division: 3 killed, 30 wounded, 1 missing. Brunswick Oels: 2 killed, 1 wounded, 1 missing. Artillery: 1 killed, 5 wounded. **Total losses 9 December** 73 killed, 542 wounded, 15 missing.

Allied losses 10 December.

1. Combat of Arcangues, Light Division: 25 killed, 126 wounded, 73 missing. 2. First combat of Barrouillet, Hope's Corps (5th Division plus Lord Aylmer's newly-landed brigade (2/62nd, 1/76th and 1/85th Foot), Brunswick Oels and artillery. **Total losses 10 December** 62 killed, 391 wounded, 97 missing.

Allied losses 11 December Second combats of Barrouillet and Arcangues (5th and Light Divisions and Brunswick Oels): 32 killed, 483 wounded, 13 missing. Portuguese Losses (10 and 11 December; brigades of De Regoa, A Campbell and Bradford): 153 killed, 457 wounded, 337 missing.

Allied losses 12 December Third combat of Barrouillet, cavalry clash at Hasparren: Guards' Brigade, 1st Division, 5/60th, 14 LDR and Artillery: 29 killed, 174 wounded, 4 missing.

Allied losses 13 December Combat of St-Pierre-d'Irube. 2nd Division (all three brigades) and 5/60th: 92 killed, 789 wounded, 23 missing. Portuguese (Le Cor's Division and Ashworth's Brigade, 9 Caçadores, Portuguese artillery): 269 killed, 603 wounded, 31 missing. General Staff and British Artillery 1 killed, 11 wounded. **Total losses 13 December** 362 killed, 1,368 wounded, 54 missing.

Allied overall losses 9–13 December 41 officers, 690 men killed; 212 officers, 3,125 men wounded, 18 officers, 575 men missing. Total overall 4,662. Wellington reported 5,047 in his Nive dispatch and figures from the Public Record Office were 4,650.

Comment Wellington deliberately refused to take many Spanish troops (rightfully keen to avenge over six years of rape, torture, pillage and destruction wrought on their compatriots by the French) into France. His policy, which was totally successful, was to win the hearts and minds of the French populace with good relations based on paying cash for anything he needed in the area under his command. By doing this he deprived himself of considerable numerical superiority but his commanders and men repaid his trust in their combat-worthiness.

Sources Oman, Martinien.

SX Zamosc, 10 February – 22 December 1813, blockade and capitulation

A fortified town in southeastern Poland, 110 km southeast of Lublin on Route 17 towards L'viv in the Ukraine.

A Russian victory over the Poles.

(Last action – Sehestadt, 10 December; next action – Modlin, 25 December.)

Polish Garrison GdB Haucke with 13th Polish IR (2 bns); 3rd Polish CavR.

Polish total 3,000 men, 130 guns.

Polish losses Not known exactly; the garrison was sent home.

Russian Forces LG von Radt with 21 bns of Little Russian militia mostly unarmed and half trained. GM Prince Schewachov: 1st, 2nd, 3rd Poltava Militia Rs, 1st and 2nd Tchernigov Militia Rs; 5th Nischegorod Militia R, 1st Simbirsk Militia R (3 bns each). Cavalry: GM Reppinsky: Perejeslav MtdRR (2 sqns); Teraspol MtdRR (3 sqns); 2nd Teptar Cossack Pulk; Orenburg Atamann Cossack Pulk; 7th Baschkir R. 2 x heavy and 1 x light FABs.

Russian total 7,000 men.

Russian losses Not known but light.

Sources Plotho, Sporschil.

SX Modlin, 23 February – 25 December 1813, blockade and capitulation

A town and fortress in Poland at the confluence of the Rivers Narev and Vistula (Visla), 28 km northwest of Warsaw and on Route 623.

A Russian victory over the Franco-Poles.

(Last action – Zamosc, 22 December; next action – Torgau, 26 December.)

Franco-Polish Garrison GdD Daendels commanding: IR Würzburg (4th bn); 18th Lithuanian IR (3,000 men); remnants of Saxon and French infantry regiments.

Franco-Polish total 5,200 infantry and gunners, 120 guns.

Franco-Polish losses ca 1,400 died of sickness, 1,600 deserted. The Lithuanians, Saxons and Würzburgers went home, the French were captured.

Russian Forces GM Kleinmichel commanding: Russian Militia formations. Exact total and losses not known.

Sources Plotho, Sporschil, Schulz.

SX Torgau, 18 October – 26 December 1813, siege and capture

A town and fortress in Saxony (north eastern Germany) on the left bank of the River Elbe; at the junction of Routes B87, B182 and B183.

A Prussian victory over the French.

(Last action – Modlin, 25 December; this was the last action of the campaign in Saxony.)

French Garrison GdD Count Narbonne commanding: 6e and 8e RILé, 8e, 10e, 52e, 65e RIdLi, DragR 28e and 10e HusR; Polish IR of the Vistula Legion, Saxon 1st LtIR; IR Würzburg (5th bn).

French total 13,000 men.

French losses 3,000 killed and died of sickness, all

the French were declared captured; the Saxons, Germans and Poles were sent home.

Allied Forces GL Count Tauentzien's Prussian Corps of the Army of the North: The Reserve GM Count von Lindenau: 3rd Res IR, 2nd Neumark IR; 5th Kurmark IR, 2nd Schl LWIR (4 bns each); 1st Kurmark LWIR (3 bns); 1st Schl LWIR (1 bn). GM Illowaisky III's Cossack Pulk; 2nd Neumark LWKR (2 sqns); 3rd Neumark LWKR, 2nd and 3rd Ostpr LWKRs (4 sqns each); Berlin LWKR (2 sqns). 1st and 7th Kurmark LWKRs, 3rd Pomm LWKR (4 sqns); ½ x British 6 pdr FAB, 1 x British 6 pdr HAB; ½ x Prussian 6 pdr FAB, ½ x Prussian 8 pdr FAB.

Allied total ca 23,000 men.

Allied losses Not known exactly but light.

Sources Martinien, Plotho, Sporschil, Grosch/Hagen/Schenk.

IN Cervia and Forli, 26 December 1813, clash

Cervia is a small Adriatic port on the northeastern Italian coast, about 30 km southeast of Ravenna, just off Route 16. Forli is a town on Route 9 about 20 km west of Cervia.

An Austrian victory over the Franco-Italians.

(Last action – Boara, 8 December; this was the last action of the campaign in 1813.)

Franco-Italian Garrisons in Cervia: Part of GdB d'Arnaud's Brigade of Rouyer's 2nd Division: 1er R Étranger (5e Bn – 300 men); 2 guns.

In Forli: 1er R Étranger (5e Bn – 300 men): 53e RIdLi (1 march bn), (800 new conscripts); 2 guns.

Franco-Italian total ca 1,500 men, 4 guns.

Franco-Italian losses 6 officers and 500 men captured, 4 guns. Killed and wounded unknown.

Austrian Forces GM Nugent commanding: At Cervia – GzIR Warasdiner-Kreutzer Nr 5 (1 coy under Capt Jankovich); HusR Radetzky Nr 5 (1tp).

At Forli: LtCol Gavenda: IR EH Franz Carl Nr 52 (1st Bn–3 coys); GzIR Warasdiner-Kreutzer Nr 5 (2 coys); Italian Volunteers (1 coy); HusR Radetzky Nr 5 (50 men).

Austrian total ca 900 men.

Austrian losses Not known exactly but very light.

Comment Vaudoncourt states that there were 5 Austrian companies at Cervia. The Franco-Italians either withdrew south into the fort at Cesenatico or were scattered into the hills.

Sources Wrede, Vaudoncourt, vom Holtz.

1814

1814 THE ACTIONS

In order to simplify comprehension of the multitude of actions which took place with high intensity over this brief campaign, they have been grouped geographically (and by army) in the following sections:.

FE - the Allied Army of Bohemia under Schwarzenberg.

FM - the Allied Army of Silesia under Blücher.

FP - Wellington's Anglo-Spanish-Portuguese army coming north over the Pyrenees.

FS - that part of Schwarzenberg's Army of Bohemia operating in the Rhône valley around Lyon in central, southern France.

IN - northern Italy.

NL - the British and the Allied Army of the North in Holland.

SX - the 'hangover' sieges from the Saxon campaign of 1813.

NL Hoogstraaten, 11 January 1814, clash

A village in the Belgian province of Antwerp, 30 km northeast of Antwerp city.

A Prussian victory over the French.

(This was the first action in the Netherlands in 1814; next action - Merxem, 13 January).

French Forces Part of GdD Roguet's 3rd Division of the Young Guard: 9e, 10e, 11e, 12e, 13e Tirailleurs and other units under GdB Aimar.

French total 6,500 men.

French losses 547 killed and wounded, 200 captured.

Prussian Forces GM von Borstel's 5th Brigade of GL von Bülow's III (Prussian) Corps of the Army of the North: Pomm Gren Bn (1 bn); Pomm IR (3 bns); 2nd ResIR (3 bns); 2nd Kürmärk LWIR (4 bns). Cavalry: GM von Oppen: Brand DragR (4 sqns); Königin DragR (4 sqns); 2nd Westpr DragR (4 sqns); 2 x FAB.

Prussian total ca 11,000 men.

Prussian losses 16 officers, 445 men killed and wounded. GM v Thümen's 4th Brigade (Part of), 5th ResIR (4 bns); Ostpr Jg bn (2 coys); Elb IR (2 bns). total 4th Brigade, ca 4,000 men; Losses 2 officers, 20 men killed and wounded.

Sources Sporschil, Martinien, Zelle.

SX Wittenberg, 14 September 1813 - 13 January 1814, siege and storm

A fortified town in eastern Germany, on the right bank of the River Elbe, 63 km northeast of Halle, at the junction of Routes B2, B100, B182 and B187.

A Prussian victory over the French.

(This was the opening action in Saxony in 1814; next action - Küstrin, 7 March).

French Garrison GdD Marquis de Lapoype commanding: 108e, 123e and 124e RIdLi, Polish Vistula Legion IR .

French total 5,000 men, 96 guns.

French losses 3,500 killed or died of sickness, 1,500 captured.

Prussian Forces GdI Count Tauentzien's IV (Prussian) Corps: 3rd ResIR, 2nd Neumark LWIR; 5th Kurmark LWIR; 2nd Schl LWIR (4 bns); 1st Kurmark LWIR (3 bns); 1st Schl LWIR (1 bn). Cossack Pulk of GM Illowaisky III; 2nd Neumark LWKR (2 sqns); 3rd Neumark LWKR; 2nd Ostpr LWKR, 3rd Ostpr LWKR (4 sqns each); Berlin LWKR (2 sqns); 1st Neumärk LWKR, 7th Kurmark LWKR, 3rd Pomm LWKR (4 sqns each); ½ x 6 pdr British FAB, 1 x 6 pdr British HAB; ½ x 6 pdr Prussian FAB; ½ x 8 pdr Prussian FAB.

Prussian total 20,000 men.

Prussian losses not known exactly but very light.

NL Merxem, 13 January 1814, clash

A hamlet in the Belgian province of Antwerp, 4 km east of that city, nowadays a suburb.

An Anglo-Prussian victory over the French.

(Last action - Hoogstraaten, 11 January; next action - Wyneghem, 13 January).

French Forces GdD Maison with GdD Ambert's I Corps: 1,000 infantry, 2 x FAB, GdD Castex's Cavalry Division (apparently not engaged). 3,600 new conscripts. In Merxem itself GdB Avis GdD Barrois with 5 bns including 4eLé.

French total ca 12,000.

French losses 246 killed and wounded, 600 captured. GdB Avis killed.

Anglo-Prussian Forces GL von Bülow's III (Prussian) Corps: GM von Thümen's 4th Brigade: 4th Ostpr IR (3 bns); 5th ResIR (4 bns) Ostpr Jäger Bn (2 coys); Elb IR (2 bns); GM von Oppen's Cavalry: Brand DragR, Königin DragR; 2nd Westpr DragR (4 sqns each).

Prussian total ca 9,500 men.

Prussian losses 5 officers, 222 men killed and wounded.

British Forces MG Gibbs commanding. 54th, 56th, 73rd (1 bn each) and 95th Foot (1 coy).

British total 3,500 men.
British losses Not known exactly but light.
Sources Sporschil, Martinien, Fortescue, Zelle.

NL Wyneghem, 13 January 1814, storm
A village in the Belgian province of Antwerp, on the outskirts of that city.
A Prussian victory over the French.
(Last action - Merxem, 13 January; next action - 's-Hertogenbosch, 26 January).
French Garrison 13e Tirailleur R of GdD Roguet's 3rd Tirailleur Division of the Young Guard.
French total ca 800 men.
French losses Not exactly known; moderate.
Prussian Forces GL von Bülow's III (Prussian) Corps: 3rd Ostpr IR, Colberg IR (3 bns each).
Prussian total ca 4,000 men.
Prussian losses 7 officers, 112 men killed, wounded and missing.
Sources Sporschil, Zelle.

FM Bar-sur-Aube, 24 January 1814, clash
Also known as Colombey-les-deux-Eglises; a town in the northeastern French Département of the Aube, 53 km east of Troyes, 24 km southeast of Brienne, on Route N19/E54 towards Chaumont.
A French victory over the Allies.
(This was the first action in this theatre in 1814; next action - St Dizier, 27 January).
French Forces M Mortier commanding: GdB Cambronne's 1er and 2e ChàP (2 bns each) of Friant's Division of the Old Guard. Fusilier Chasseurs, Fusilier Grenadiers (2 bns each). GdD Laferrière: DragR, ChàCh of the Young Guard.
French total 5,885 infantry, 2,567 cavalry, 50 guns.
French losses 500 killed and wounded, 200 captured: Gen Cambronne wounded.
Allied Forces FZM Count Ignaz Gyulai's III Corps of the Army of Bohemia: 3rd Division FML Prince Philipp von Hessen-Homburg. GM Trenk: IRs Ignaz Gyulai Nr 60 (2 bns); Mariassy Nr 37 (2 bns). GM Czollich: IRs Kaiser Nr 1 (1st, 3rd bns); Kottulinsky Nr 41 (3 bns); ChLR Klenau Nr 5 (6 sqns); DragR Knesevich Nr 3 (4 sqns); Gren Bn Puteani, GzIR Warasdiner St Georger Nr 6 (1st Bn); 2 x FABs. **Allied total** 12,500 men.
Allied losses 1,400 killed, wounded and missing.
Comment The French put up fierce resistance until the IV (Württemberg) Corps arrived on the scene. Then they withdrew on Troyes.
Sources Sporschil, Zelle.

NL 's-Hertogenbosch, 26 January 1814, capture
A city and fortress in central Holland, just south of the Rivers Maas and Waal, at the junction of Motorways A2/E25, A59 and N50; 35 km southwest of Nijmegen.
A Prussian victory over the French.
(Last action - Wyneghem, 13 January; next action - Gorkum, 7 February).
French Garrison Exact details and losses not known.
Prussian Forces GL von Bülow's III (Prussian) Corps (as for Merxem, 13 January).
Prussian losses Not exactly known but very slight if any.
Comment The citizens rose against the French garrison and helped the Prussians; there was no formal combat.
Sources Sporschil, Zelle.

FN St Dizier, 27 January 1814, clash
A town in northeastern France, on the north bank of the River Marne, at the junction of Routes N4/E17, N35 and N67, 205 km east of Paris.
A French victory over the Russians.
(Last action - Bar-sur-Aube, 24 January; next action - Brienne, 29 January).
French Forces GdD Milhaud's cavalry: DragRs 2e, 11e, 13e, 19e; ChLR 5e ChàCh 10e and 26e. GdD Duhesme's infantry was not engaged.
French total Cavalry ca 2,100 men.
French losses Not known.
Russian Forces GM Landskoi's 2nd Hussar Division of GL Baron Sacken's Corps of the Army of Silesia: HusRs Achtyrsk, Mariupol, Alexandria, White Russia (4 sqns each) 1 x HAB.
Russian total ca 1,500 men.
Russian losses Not known.
Comment The Russian cavalry was overthrown and withdrew south to Joinville up the River Marne.
Sources Sporschil, Zelle.

FN Brienne, 29 January 1814, battle
A town in the northeastern French Département of the Aube, 24 km northwest of Bar-sur-Aube and at the junction of Routes D396, D400 and D960.

A French victory over the Russo-Prussians.

(Last action – St Dizier, 27 January; next action – La Rothière, 1 February).

French Forces Emperor Napoleon I commanding:

M Ney (3 divisions of the Imperial Guard) 1er and 2e Tirailleurs; 7e and 8e Tirailleurs of the Old Guard; from the Young Guard Fusilier Chasseurs, 1er, 2e, 6e, 7e and 16e Voltigeurs; Flanqueur Chasseurs.

Guard Cavalry GrenàCh, ChàCh. GdD Forestier's 2nd Division: 18e and 46e RIdLi, 26e RILé. GdD Duhesme's 3rd Division (II Corps): only one brigade: 11e RILé, 2e RIdLi. The following regiments also show officer casualties for this action: 19e, 37e, 38e, 56e, 62e and 93e RIdLi. Grouchy's cavalry: Dragoon divisions of Briche and L'Heretier: 7e, 9e, 12e CuirRs; 15e, 18e, 19e, 20e, 22e DragRs.

French total 36,000 men, 128 guns.

French losses ca 3,500 men killed, wounded and missing. GdD Decouz, GdB Forestier, Rear Admiral Baste were killed, M Oudinot was wounded, 11 guns. The 26e RILé was reduced to 150 men.

Allied Forces FM von Blücher commanding part of the Army of Silesia:

IV (Prussian) Corps GL Count von Tauentzien commanding: GM Count Lindenau's Brigade: 3rd ResIR (3 bns); 3rd Neumark. LWIR (2 bns); 11th and 16th Schl LWIRs, 1st Kurmark LWIR (3 bns each). 1 x 6pdr FAB.

IX (Russian) Corps LG Olsufiev: 9th Division: MG Udom II: IRs Nascheburg, Apscheron, Yakutsk, Riask, 10th and 13th JgRs (2 bns each). 15th Division MG Karnielov: IRs Witebsk, Koslovsk, Kolivan, Kurinsk; 12th and 22nd JgRs (2 bns each). Cavalry of Gen Count Pahlen III: MG Scherbatov: 4 x Cossack Pulks, Tschugujev UlR (6 sqns). 4th and 34th JgRs (2 bns each) of 3rd Division (LG Prince von Schachoffskoi) of II (Russian) Corps.

Parts of GdI von Sacken's Russians:

VI Corps LG Prince Scherbatov 7th Division MG Tallisin II: IRs Pskov, Moscow, Sophia, Liebau, 11th and 36th Jägers (2 bns each); 18th Division MG Bernodossov: IRs Vladimir, Dnieprov, Tambov, Kostroma, 28th and 32nd Jägers (2 bns each).

XI Corps MG Count Lieven III: 10th Division: IRs Yaroslav, Krim, Bialystock, 8th and 39th Jägers (2 bns each); 16th Division: IRs Ochotsk, Kamtschatka. 27th Division, MG Stawitzky: IRs Odessa, Wilna, Teraspol, Simbirsk, 49th and 50th Jägers (2 bns each). Cavalry of LG Wassiltschikov: 2nd Hussar Division LG Lanskoi: HusRs Achtyrsk, Mariupol, White Russia, Alexandria. 3rd Dragoon Division MG Pantschulidschev: DragRs Kurland, Smolensk, Twer, Kinburn, 2 x HAB.

Allied total ca 28,000 men.

Allied losses 3,000 killed, wounded and missing.

Comment The action seemed to have ended in favour of the Allies as darkness fell but Napoleon had other ideas. Blücher, Sacken and their staff took over the castle in the town for the night but the 56e RIdLi overpowered the Prussian guards (8th coy; LeibR) and the Russo-Prussians were forced out of the castle at a rush. Despite violent counterattacks, the French retained the castle in their control and caused the Russians heavy losses as they repeatedly stormed against them.

Sources Bodart, Zelle.

FN La Rothière, 1 February 1814, battle

A village in the northeastern French Département of the Aube 20 km northwest of Bar-sur-Aube and on Route D396 towards Brienne.

An Allied victory over the French.

(Last action – Brienne, 29 January; next action – La Ferté-sous-Jouarre, 9 February).

French Forces Emperor Napoleon I commanding:

The Old Guard GdD Curial: Füsilier GrenR 1er, 4e, 5e, 6e, Tirailleurs (2 bns each): **The Young Guard:** 3e, 6e and 8e Voltigeurs (2 bns each). Guard Cavalry: 2e ChLLR (3 sqns); FABs and HABs of the Old and Young Guard.

II Corps M Victor, Duke of Belluno: 4th Division GdD Teste: 24e RILé, 56e RIdLi. 5th Division GdD Corbineau: 46e and 72e RIdLi. 6th Division GdD Count Mouton: 2e, 4e and 18e RIdLi, 3 x FAB. The following regiments: 6e, 15e, 29e and 37e RILé; 12e, 16e, 40e, 88e, 111e, 121e, 132e and 144e RIdLi. The cavalry under Grouchy: 2e, 3e, 4e and 7e CuirRs, 7e and 15e DragRs, 2e ChLLR, 27e ChàCh.

French totals 57 bns, 62 sqns, 128 guns, ca 45,000 men.

French losses 4,600 killed and wounded, 1,000 captured, 73 guns. Gen Forestier mortally wounded.

Allied Forces FM Count von Blücher commanding the Army of Silesia.

Russian Corps of GL Baron von Sacken:

XI Corps Count Liewen III: **10th division:** IRs Jaroslav,

Bialystock, 8th and 39th Jägers (2 bns each); IRs Kursk and Crimea (1 bn each). **27th Division:** IRs Odessa and Wilna, 49th and 50th Jägers (2 bns each); IRs Simbirsk and Tiraspol (1 bn each). 2 x heavy FAB, 2 x light FAB. **Total** 8,000 men.

VI Corps GL Prince Scherbatov: IRs Pleskov, Moscow, Liebau, 11th Jägers (2 bns each); IR Sophia, 36th Jägers (1 bn each). **18th Division:** IRs Vladimir, Dnieprov, Tambov, Kostroma, 28th and 32nd Jägers (1 bn each). 1x heavy FAB, 1x light FAB. **Total** 8,000 men.

IX Corps GL Olsufiev: **9th Division** IRs Nascheburg, Yakutsk, 10th and 38th Jägers (1 bn each); IRs Apscheron, Riask (2 bns each). **15th Division:** IRs Witebsk, Koslovsk, Kolivan, 22nd Jägers (1 bn each); IR Kurinsk, 12th Jägers (2 bns each). 1x heavy FAB, 2x light FAB. **Total** 5,000 men. Cavalry: Gen Wassiltschikov: **3rd Dragoon Division:** DragRs Twer and Kinburn (2 sqns each); **1st Mounted Rifle Division:** MtdRRs Tchernigov (3 sqns), Sieversk (2 sqns); Arsamas (1 sqn). **2nd Mounted Rifle Division:** MtdRRs Livland and Dorpat (2 sqns each). **Cossack Corps** of Gen Karpov: exact details not known. Prussian Light Cavalry Brigade: GM Prince Biron of Kurland: 2nd Schl HusR (4 sqns); Schl NatKR (2 sqns); Neumark DragR (3 sqns).

IV (Württemberg) Corps FZM Crownprince of Württemberg commanding: **Infantry Division: GL von Koch;** 1st Brigade GM von Stockmeyer: LIRs 7 and 9 (2 bns each); JgR König (1 bn). 2nd Brigade GM von Döring: IR Nr 2 Herzog Wilhelm, IR Nr 3 (2 bns each), 1 x 6 pdr FAB (6 guns). 3rd Brigade GM Prince Hohenlohe-Kirchberg: LIR Nr 4, LIR Nr 6 Kronprinz (2 bns each); 1 x 6 pdr FAB (6 guns). **Cavalry Division GL Prince Adam.** 1st Brigade GM von Walsleben JzPfR Nr 2 Herzog Louis (4 sqns); DragR Kronprinz Nr 3 (4 sqns); 1 x HAB (6 guns). 2nd Brigade GM von Jett: CavR Nr 4 Prinz Adam (4 sqns), 1 x HAB (6 guns). Reserve Artillery: 1x Austrian 12 pdr FAB.

V (Austro-Bavarian) Corps GdK Count von Wrede:

Austrian Corps GdK Baron von Frimont: **Light Division FML Count Frimont:** 1st Brigade GM Count Hardegg: GzIR Szeckler Nr 14 (2 bns); HusR EH Joseph Nr 2 (6 sqns). 2nd Brigade GM von Volkmann Jg Bn Nr 3 (1 bn); UlR Schwarzenberg Nr 2 (6 sqns); 1 x HAB (6 guns). **Line Division GM Baron von Bach:** IR EH Rudolf Nr 14 (4 bns); IR Jordis Nr 59 (4 bns); 2 x 6 pdr FAB (16 guns). **Reserve Division FML Baron von Trautenberg:** 1st Brigade GM Count Klenau: Gren Bns Frisch, De Best, Berger, Putheany, 1 x 6 pdr FAB (8 guns). 2nd Brigade GM von Diemar: Gren Bns Possmann, Hromada, Kramer; 1 x 3 pdr FAB (8 guns). **Reserve Cavalry:** FML Baron von Splényi: 1st Brigade Obst von Flachenfeld: DragR Knesevich Nr 3 (6 sqns); KürR Liechtenstein Nr 6 (4 sqns); 1 x HAB (6 guns). **Reserve Artillery** GM von Swrtnik: 1 x 6pdr FAB (6 guns); 3 x 12 pdr FAB (18 guns).

Bavarian Corps (Wrede) 1st Division GL Count Rechberg. 1st Brigade GM Prince Karl von Bayern. LIR Nr 1 (2 bns) Nr 3 (1 bn), 10th NatFd Bn (1st Oberdonaukreis) 1 bn; LtI Bn Nr 3 (1 bn). 2nd Brigade GM von Maillot: LIRs Nr 2 and Nr 10 (1 bn each), 11th NatFd Bn (2nd Oberdonaukreis) 1 bn, 15th NatFd Bn (1st Mainkreis) 1 bn; LtI Bn Nr 2 (1 bn). 1st Light Cavalry Brigade GM von Vieregg ChLRs Nr 1, 2 and 7 (4 sqns each). 1 x HAB (6 guns), 1 x FAB (8 guns). **2nd Division** GL Count Beckers: 1st Brigade GM Count Pappenheim: LIR Nr 4 (2 bns); NatFd Bn of the Salzachkreis (1 bn). 9th NatFd Bn (1st Regenkreis) 1 bn; LtI Bn Nr 4 (1 bn). 2nd Brigade GM Baron von Zoller: LIR Nr 6 (2 bns); 14th NatFd Bn (1st Rezatkreis) 1 bn; 13th NatFd Bn (1st Innkreis) 1 bn; LtI Bn Nr 1 (1 bn). 2nd Light Cavalry Brigade GM von Elbrecht: ChLRs Nr 3 and Nr 6 (4 sqns each); 1 x HAB (6 guns) 1 x 6pdr FAB (8 guns). **3rd Division** GM de Lamotte. 1st Brigade GM von der Stockl: LIR Nr 7 (1 bn); LIR Nr 11 (2 bns); NatFd Bn (1st Unterdonaukreis) 1 bn; 16th NatFd Bn (1st Illerkreis) 1 bn. 2nd Brigade GM von Deroy: LIRs Nrs 5, 8, 9 (1 bn each); 6th NatFd Bn (2nd Illerkreis) 1 bn; 5th NatFd Bn (1st Isarkreis) 1 bn. 3rd Light Cavalry Brigade Obst von Diez ChLRs Nrs 4 and 5 (4 sqns each) 1 x HAB (6 guns) 1 x FAB (8 guns) Reserve Artillery: 4 x 12pdr FABs (24 guns).

III (Austrian) Corps FZM Count Ignaz Gyulai: **1st Division** FML Crenneville: Avantgarde GM Hecht GzIR Warasdiner Creuzer Nr 5 (1 bn) GzIR Warasdiner St Georger Nr 6 (1 bn) ChLR Klenau Nr 5 (6 sqns); ChLR Rosenberg Nr 6 (5 sqns); 1 x 6 pdr HAB. 1st Division FML Murray: GM Salins: IR EH Ludwig Nr 8 (3 bns); IR Würzburg Nr 23 (2 bns), 1 x 6 pdr FAB. GM Weigel IRs Mariassy Nr 37 and Gyulai Nr 60 (2 bns each); 1 x 6 pdr FAB. **2nd Division** FML Prince Philipp von Hessen-Homburg: GM Czollich: IRs Kaiser Nr 1 and Kottulinsky Nr 41 (3 bns each), 1 x 6 pdr FAB. GM Grimmer: IRs Fröhlich Nr 28 and

Kollowrath Nr 36 (2 bns each); 1 x 6 pdr FAB. Reserve Artillery 1 x 6pdr and 2 x 12 pdr FABs.

Allied total ca 120,000 men. Of these, only 80,000 actually came into action.

Allied losses 6-7,000 killed, wounded and missing.

Comment This was a very significant Allied victory which destroyed the myth of Napoleon's invincibility in the eyes of his own army. The superior Allied cavalry and the very wet ground led to considerable loss of French artillery pieces; they admitted losing 54 but the total taken by the Allies was 73: Sacken's Corps took 25, the V (Austro-Bavarians) – 19, IV (Württemberg) – 14, III (Austrian) – 8 and Prince Biron's Prussian cavalry took 7.

NL Gorkum, 7 February 1814, capitulation

A fortified town in the Dutch Province of South Holland, 38 km southeast of Rotterdam.

A Prussian victory over the French.

(Last action – 's-Hertogenbosch, 26 January; next action – Bergen-op-Zoom, 8 March).

French Garrison GdD Count Rampon: 3,500 men, 176 guns including the GdN d'Anvers (1er and 2e bns).

French losses All captured.

Prussian Forces GM von Zielinsky's 3rd Brigade of GL von Bülow's III (Prussian) Corps: 2nd Ostpr Gren Bn; 3rd Ostpr IR (3 bns); 4th ResIR (3 bns); 3rd Ostpr LWIR (3 bns) 1 x 6pdr FAB; 1st Leib-Hus-R (1 sqn).

Prussian total 5,000 men.

Prussian losses Not exactly known but very light.

Sources Sporschil, Zelle, Damitz, Martinien.

IN Mincio River, 8 February 1814, battle

Also known as Roverbella, Vallegio, Monzambano: villages along the left hand tributary of the River Po in northeastern Italy, 10–15 km south of Peschiera at the southern end of Lake Garda, towards Mantua (Mantova).

A Franco-Italian victory over the Austrians.

(This was the opening action of the campaign in Italy; next action – Parma, 2 March).

Franco-Italian Forces Prince Eugène de Beauharnais commanding: **2nd Division** GdD Rouyer: GdB Schmitz: 9e RIdLi (3 bns); 28e PvDBde (1 bn each of 52e and 67e Li). GdB d'Arnaud: 35e RIdLi, 1er RÉtranger (3 bns each). 1 x FAB, 1 x HAB (12 guns). **4th Division** GdD Marcognet; GdB Jeannin: 29e PvDBde (1 bn each of 6e, 20e and 102e Li); 31e PvDBde (1 bn each of 131e and 132e Li). GdB Deconchi: 36e RILé (1 bn); 102e and 106e RIdLi (2 bns each). 2 x FAB (12 guns). **6th Division** GdB Zucchi (Italians); GdB St Paul: 1st and 2nd LtIR (2 bns each); 4th and 5th LIR (2 bns each); 1 x HAB (6 guns). **1st Division** GdD Quesnel GdB Campi: 92e RIdLi (3 bns); 30e PvDBde (1 bn each of the 1er and 14e Lé and 10e Li). GdB Forestier: 35e RILé (1 bn); 84e RIdLi (3 bns); 1 x FAB, 1 x HAB (12 guns). **Cavalry** GdD Mermet; GdB Perreymond: Drag de la Reine (3 sqns); Free HusR (2 sqns). GdB Bonnemain: 31e ChàCh (3 sqns); 4th Italian ChàCh (2 sqns); GdB Rambourg 19e ChàCh (2 sqns); 3rd Italian ChàCh (4 sqns); 1 x HAB 6 guns.

Franco-Italian total 34,000 men.

Franco-Italian losses 3,000 killed and wounded, 500 captured.

Austrian Forces FM Count Bellegarde commanding: LIRs Liechtenstein Nr 12, EH Carl Nr 3, Hoch-und-Deutschmeister Nr 4, Reisky Nr 10 (3 bns each), Chasteler Nr 27 (4 bns), Duka Nr 39 (2 bns), Kerpen Nr 49 (1 bn), Splényi Nr 51 (3 bns), Hiller Nr 53 (2 bns), Bianchi Nr 55 (3 bns), Beaulieu Nr 58 (2 bns); Jäger Bns 4, 9 and 10 (1 bn each); DragRs Hohenlohe Nr 2 (4 sqns), Savoy Nr 5 (4 sqns); HusR Frimont Nr 9 (2 sqns), Stipsics Nr 10 (4 sqns); UlR EH Carl Nr 3 (4 sqns); UlR Merveldt Nr 1 (6 sqns); GzIR Warasdiner-Creuzer Nr 5 (2nd Bn). GM Stutterheim: Grenadier bns De Best, Welsperg, Puteani, Purcell, Faber, Chimani.

Austrian total 32,000 men.

Austrian losses 2,800 killed and wounded, 1,200 captured.

Comment Bellegarde assumed that Eugène had abandoned the line of the Mincio and was surprised to be confronted with determined resistance when he tried to cross the river. Vaudoncourt's estimates of totals and losses favour the Franco-Italians a little too much. Austrian Jäger bn Nr 9 was almost destroyed here. The Grenadier Brigade of GM Stutterheim at Pozzolo lost 32 officers and 758 men and was reduced to 1,200 all ranks.

Sources Wrede, Martinien, Vaudoncourt, vom Holtz.

FN La-Ferté-sous-Jouarre, 9 February 1814, clash

A small town in northern France, on the River Marne, on Route N3 between Paris and Château-Thierry.

An Allied victory over the French.

(Last action – La Rothière, 1 February; next action – Champaubert, 10 February).

French Forces M Macdonald's XI Corps: GdD Molitor: 28e RILé (312 men); 46e (328 men), 70e (260 men), 139e (317 men), 149e (298 men) RIdLi. 1 x FAB. GdD Brayer: 19e RILé (272 men); 5e (283 men), 11e (304 men), 107e (268 men) RIdLi; Swiss Grenadiers (98 men). 1 x FAB. 16e ChàCh (2 sqns).

French total ca 3,450 men.

French losses Not exactly known but moderate; 3 guns.

Allied Forces GdI von Sacken's Russian Army (VI and XI Corps) of the Army of Silesia:

Cavalry of LG Wasiltschikov: 2nd Hussar Division LG Lanskoi: HusRs Achtyrsk, Mariupol, White Russia, Alexandria. 3rd Hussar Division MG Pantschulidschev: DragRs Kurland, Smolensk, Twer, Kinburn; 1 x HAB (10 guns).

Cossack Corps of MG Karpov II: Pulks of Karpov II, Sementschenko, Lukowkin, Kutainikov IV, Grekov; St Petersburg Volunteers, 4th Ukrainian Cossacks; 2nd KalmuckR, 2 x HAB (24 guns).

Allied total ca 5,800 men.

Allied losses Not exactly known but light.

Sources Zelle, Damitz, Martinien.

FE Nogent-sur-Seine, 10 February 1814, clash

A town in northern France, on the south bank of the River Seine, at the crossing of Route N19/E54, between Troyes and Paris, at the confluence of the rivers Seine and Ardusson.

A drawn match between the French and the Austro-Russians and Bavarians.

(This was the opening action in eastern France; next action – Sens, 11 February).

French Forces GdB Bourmont commanding: 11e and 29e RILé, 18e RIdLi.

French total ca 1,000 men.

French losses Not exactly known; moderate. Zelle claims 400 killed and wounded.

Austro-Russian Forces FM Prince Schwarzenberg commanding: The Army of Bohemia: Wrede's V Corps: FML Hardegg's Division: Austrian UlR Schwarzenberg Nr 2 (6 sqns); HusR EH Joseph Nr 2 (6 sqns). Gen Count Pahlen III's Russian Avantgarde: 25th and 4th JgR (1 bn each); Grodno and Olviupol HusRs 2x Cosssack Pulks 2 x HAB.

Austro-Russian total ca 4,000.

Austro-Russian losses Not exactly known. Zelle claims 1,000 killed!

Comment The 25th Russian Jägers also had heavy casualties. The 10th Bavarian LIR and the Ingolstadt NatFd Bn were also involved.

Sources Sporschil, Martinien, Zelle, Damitz.

FN Champaubert, 10 February 1814, clash

A village in the northeastern French Département of the Marne, 22 km southwest of Epernay and 85 km east of Paris on Route D33, at the junction with Route D51.

A French victory over the Russians.

(Last action – La-Ferté-sous-Jouarre, 9 February; next action – Montmirail, 11 February).

French Forces Emperor Napoleon I commanding GdD Doumerc's cavalry of Marmont's VI Corps and GdDs Ricard's and Lagrange's infantry: 1er, 4e, 15e, 37e RILé; 113e, 121e, 132e RIdLi; a naval bn. Cavalry: 1er PvHusR; 2e, 3e, 4e ChàCh (14 sqns); 2 x FAB, 1 x HAB.

French total ca 13,300 infantry, 1,700 cavalry.

French losses ca 600 killed, wounded and missing.

Russian Forces GM Olsufiev commanding the IX (Russian) Corps of GdI Count Langeron's Russian Contingent: 9th Division MG Udom II: IRs Nascheburg, Apscheron, Yakutsk, Riask; 10th and 38th Jägers (2 weak bns each).

Russian total ca 3,700 men, 2 x FAB (24 guns).

Russian losses 2,400 men killed, wounded and missing, 9 guns. Olsufiev and Poltaratzky were captured.

Comment The Russians had no cavalry and were very isolated; MG Poltaratzky's whole brigade* was captured. Gen Olsufiev was captured as the other brigade (Kornieloff's) fought its way back to Kapsevich's corps. Blücher's faulty dispositions caused this disaster.

* = IRs Nascheburg and Apscheron.

Sources Plotho, Sporschil, Martinien, Zelle.

FN Montmirail, 11 February 1814, battle

A town in the northeastern French Département of the Marne, 39 km southwest of Epernay and 18 km west of Champaubert on Route D33 towards Paris.

A French victory over the Russo-Prussians.

(Last action – Champauberg, 10 February; next action – Château-Thierry, 12 February).

French Forces Emperor Napoleon I commanding.

The Old Guard M Mortier: 1st Division GdD Friant: GdD Michel: 1er ChàP, 2e ChàP (2 bns each); GdD Cambronne 1er and 2e Gren à P (2 bns each); Sailors (3 coys); Sapeurs (3 coys). 2nd Division GdD ? Flanqueur-Chasseurs, Flanqueur-Grenadiers (2 bns each); Fus-Chasseurs, Fus-Grenadiers (2 bns each), Vélites de Florence, Vélites de Turin (1 bn each).

The Young Guard M Ney. 1st Voltigeur Division GdD Meunier: 1er, 2e, 3e, 4e Voltigeurs. 2nd Voltigeur Division GdD Decouz: 5e, 6e, 7e, 8e Voltigeurs. **The Guard Cavalry** GdD Nansouty: GdD Colbert: 1er ChLL (Poles); ChàCh; GrenàCh; Drag de l'Imperatrice; 2e EclaireurR; 1 x HAB. Artillery: 7 x FAB, 4 x HAB.

VI Corps 8th Division GdD Ricard: 2e RILé (2e Bn); 4e RILé (1er Bn); 6e RILé (2e Bn); 9e RILé, 16e RILé (1 bn each). 22e RIdLi (1 bn); 40e RIdLi (2e Bn); 50e RIdLi (2e Bn); 65e RIdLi (3e Bn); the 1er bns of the following: 136e, 138e, 142e, 144e, 145e RIdLi. Cavalry Division GdD Defrance: Gardes d'Honneur (1er, 2e, 3e Regts); 10e HusR Artillery 3 x FAB 1 x HAB. The 149e RIdLi, 1er and 2e Carabiniers, 8e CuirR and the 6e DragR also recorded casualties for this action.

French totals ca 25,000 men.

French losses 2,100 killed and wounded. Generals Michel and Boudin killed.

Allied Forces GdI York commanding part of the Army of Silesia:

I (Prussian) Corps 1st Brigade GM von Pirch II: Leib-Gren-Bn, Westpr-Gren-Bn (1 bn each); Ostpr Jägers (2 coys); Ostpr-Gren-Bn, Schl.-Gren-Bn (1 bn each); 5th Schl LWIR (4 bns); 13th Schl LWIR (4 bns); 2nd Leib-HusR (4 sqns); 1 x 6 pdr FAB. 7th Brigade. GM von Horn: LeibIR (3 bns); Thüringian Bn (1 bn); 4th Schl LWIR (4 bns); 15th Schl LWIR (3 bns); Brand HusR, 3rd Schl LWKR (2 sqns each); 1 x 6 pdr FAB.

XI Russian Corps GL Baron Osten-Sacken: 10th Division GM Count Liewen III: IRs Yaroslav, Bialystock, 8th, 39th Jägers (2 bns each), IRs Kursk and Crimea (1 bn each). 16th Division (part of): IRs Kamchatka and Ochotsk (2 bns each). 27th Division Obst Stawitsky: IRs Odessa, Wilna, 49th and 50th Jägers (2 bns each); IRs Teraspol and Simbirsk (1 bn each). 2 x light FABs.

VI (Russian) Corps GM Tallisin II. 18th Division MG Bernodossov: IRs Vladimir, Dniepr, Tambov, Kostroma, 28th and 32nd Jägers (1 bn each). 7th Division GM Prince Scherbatov: IRs Pskov, Moscow, Sophia, Libau, 11th and 36th Jägers (1 bn each). Cavalry: GL Wassiltschikov: 3rd Dragoon Division GM Pantschulidschev: Kurland and Smolensk DragRs (2 sqns each). 2nd Hussar Division GM Landskoi: HusRs Achtyrsk (6 sqns), Mariupol (5 sqns), Alexandria (5 sqns) and White Russian (4 sqns); 1 x HAB. Light Cavalry GM Karpov II: Cossack Pulks of Karpov II, Lubovkin, Tschernusubov V, Kutainikov IV, Siementschenkov, Grekov VIII, St Petersburg Volunteers, 4th Ukrainians, Popov XIII, 2nd Kalmucks.

Allied totals ca 32,000 men.

Allied losses Prussians: 33 officers, 854 men killed, wounded and missing. Russians: 1,500 killed and wounded, 1,000 captured, 17 guns of which 8 were abandoned in the deep mud during the retreat after the action. Six colours were lost.

Comment Once again, Napoleon had caught his foes separated. Sacken had ignored York's warning that Napoleon was in command here and paid heavily for his foolhardiness. At this point in the campaign, most Russian infantry regiments were so weak that they were reorganized into one battalion each.

Sources Plotho, Sporschil, Martinien, Damitz, Zelle.

FE Sens, 11 February 1814, storm

A small, walled town in eastern France, at the confluence of the Rivers Vanne and Yonne, at the point where Route N60 from Orléans to Troyes crosses the river; 67 km west of Troyes.

A Württemberg victory over the French.

(Last action – Nogent-sur-Seine, 10 February; next action – Nemours, 16 February).

French Garrison Gen Alix commanding. Exact details not known.

French total ca 2,500 men.

French losses 56 killed, 250 wounded and/or missing.

Württemberg Forces GL Baron von Koch commanding part of the IV (Württemberg) Corps of the Army of Bohemia: JgR Nr 9 (2 bns); LtIR Nr 10 (1 bn); 4th LIR (2 bns).

Württemberg total ca 4,000 men.

Württemberg losses 34 killed, 164 wounded.

Sources Stadlinger, Damitz.

FN Château-Thierry, 12 February 1814, clash

A town in the northeastern French Département of the Aisne, on the River Marne, 73 km southwest of Laon, at the junction of Routes N3 and D1 about 75 km northeast of Paris.

A French victory over the Russo-Prussians.

(Last action - Montmirail, 11 February; next action - Vauchamps, 14 February).

French Forces Emperor Napoleon I commanding: as for Montmirail on 11 February less Ricard's division.

French total ca 20,000 men.

French losses 400 killed and wounded (according to French sources).

Russo-Prussian Forces GdI York's I (Prussian) Corps and GL Baron Sacken's Russian Corps as for the battle of Montmirail, 11 February.

Russo-Prussian total ca 30,000 men.

Russo-Prussian losses 3,000 killed, wounded and missing. Of these casualties 1,300 were Prussians, 1,700 Russians; 6 Prussian and 8 Russian guns were lost.

Comment The Russian brigade of GM Freudenreich (IRs Tambov and Kostroma) was isolated on the extreme right of the Allied line, attacked and ridden down by French cavalry. GM Freudenreich was captured along with 3 guns. M Macdonald had been ordered by Napoleon to seize the Marne bridge at Château-Thierry which would have cut off the Allies' retreat. He failed to do this and they slipped out of the trap to fight another day.

Sources Plotho, Sporschil, Martinien, Zelle.

FN Vauchamps (Etoges), 14 February 1814, clash

A village in the northeastern French Département of the Marne, 33 km southwest of Epernay, on Route D33 between Montmirail and Champaubert, about 70 km east of Paris.

A French victory over the Russo-Prussians.

(Last action - Château-Thierry, 12 February; next action - Soissons, 14 February).

French Forces Emperor Napoleon I commanding:.

The Imperial Guard M Mortier: Old Guard 1st Division GdD Friant: 1er and 2e Gren à P, 1er and 2e Ch à P (2 bns each). Sapeurs (3 coys); marines (3 coys). 2nd Division GdD Michel: Flanqueur GrenR, Flanqueur ChassR, Fus GrenR, Fus ChassR (2 bns each); Vélites de Florence, Vélites de Turin (1 bn each).

Young Guard M Ney: 1st Division GdD Meunier: 1er, 2e, 3e, 4e VoltigeurRs; 2nd Division GdD Curial: 5e, 6e, 7e, 8e VoltigeurRs. **Guard Cavalry** GdD Lefebvre-Desnouettes: 1er ChLLR; ChàCh; DragR; GrenàCh; Gendarmes d'Élite.

VI Corps M Marmont: 3rd Division GdD Legrange: 1er, 15e, 16e, 62e, 70e, 121e RIdLi (1 bn each); 1er, 2e, 3e, 4e NavalRs (13 bns); 23e RIdLi (2e Bn); 37e RIdLi (1er and 3e bns). 8th Division GdD Ricard: 2e, 4e, 6e, 9e and 16e RILé (1 bn each); 22e RIdLi, 40e RIdLi (2 bns); 50e RIdLi (2 bns); 65e RIdLi (3 bns); 136e and 138e RIdLi (1 bn each); 142e, 144e, 145e RIdLi (1 bn each); 2 x FAB (13 x 6 pdrs); 2 x HAB (9 guns); 1 x heavy FAB (8 x 12 pdrs).

Cavalry: GdD Grouchy: **I Cavalry Corps** GdD Bordesolle: 1st Light Cavalry Division: GdD Merlin: 1st Brigade GdB Wathier: 6e, 7e, 8e HusRs; 1er, 3e, 5e, 7e, 8e ChLLRs. 2nd Brigade GdB Guyon: 1er, 2e, 3e, 6e, 8e, 9e, 16e, 25e ChàCh. 2nd Heavy Cavalry Division GdD Bordesolle: 1st Brigade GdB Thiry: 2e, 3e, 6e, 9e, 11e, 12e CuirRs. 2nd Brigade GdB Laville: 4e, 7e, 14e CuirRs; 7e, 23e, 28e, 30e DragRs; 1 x HAB.

II Cavalry Corps GdD St Germain. 2nd Light Cavalry Division GdD Berkheim; 3rd Brigade GdB Dommanget: 5e, 9e HusRs, 11e, 12e ChàCh. 2e, 4e ChLLRs. 4th Brigade GdB Jamin: 10e HusR; 6e ChLLR, 7e, 20e, 23e, 24e ChàCh. 2nd Heavy Cavalry Division GdD St Germain: 3rd Brigade GdB Blancarde: 1er and 2e Carabiniers, 1er CuirR. 4th Brigade GdB Sopranzy: 5e, 8e, 10e, 13e CuirRs. 2 x HAB. 7th Division GdD Leval (ex Spain): GdB Pinoteau: 10e RILé (1 bn); 3e, 45e RIdLi (1 bn each). GdB de Montfort: 17e RILé (1 bn); 101e, 105e RIdLi (2 bns each). 2 x FAB, 1 x HAB.

French total 11,000 men.

French losses ca 600 killed, wounded and missing.

Allied Forces FM Blücher commanding part of the Army of Silesia.

II (Prussian) Corps GM von Kleist: 10th Brigade GM von Pirch I: 2nd Westpr IR (3 bns); 7th ResIR (3 bns); 8th Schl LWKR (5 sqns); 1 x 6pdr FAB (8 guns). 11th Brigade GM von Ziethen: 1st Schl IR, 10th ResIR (3 bns each); Schl Scharfschützen (2 coys); 1st Schl HusR (4 sqns); 1 x 6pdr FAB (8 guns). 12th Brigade GM Prince August von Preussen: 2nd Schl IR (3 bns); 11th Res IR (2 bns); 7th Schl LWKR (4 sqns); 1 x 6 pdr FAB (8 guns). Cavalry Brigade: Obst von Hacke: Schl KürR, Schl UlR (4 sqns each) 1 x HAB (8 x 6 pdrs); Cavalry Brigade GM von Röder: Ostpr KürR, Brand KürR (4 sqns each). Artillery Reserve Obst Braun: 2 x 12 pdr FABs (16 guns); 2 x 6 pdr FABs (16 guns); 2 x HABs (16 x 6 pdrs); 1 x Howitzer Bty. **Total** 13,000 men.

X (Russian) Corps GM Kapsevich: 8th Division GM Urusov: Obst Schenschen: IRs Archangelsk, Schlüsselburg, Alt Ingermannland (2 bns each). Obst Suthof 7th Jägers (2 bns); 37th Jägers (1 bn). 22nd Division GM Turtschaninov: GM Schapskoi: IRs Olonetz, Staroskol (1 bn each); Viatka (2 bns). GM Vassiltschikov: 29th, 45th Jägers (1 bn each). 1 x heavy, 2 x light FABs (36 guns).

IX (Russian) Corps GM Olsufiev: 9th Division GM Udom II: This corps had been badly mauled on 9 February at La-Ferté-sous-Jouarre. The 1,500 survivors were organized into four combined battalions and 1 x FAB.

Russian totals ca 8,000 men.

Russian losses Estimates vary widely. The Prussians seem to have lost 1,251 (Zelle: 4,036!) killed, wounded and missing and 6 guns. The Russians lost 2,000 killed, wounded and missing and 9 guns. Prince Urusov was captured. The colour of 2nd Bn, 1st Schl IR was taken by the Grenadiers à Cheval.

Comment Napoleon demonstrated once more his amazing ability to exploit his enemies' errors and to motivate his own forces. The Prussian 1st Schl IR, 7th and 10th Res IRs suffered particularly heavy casualties. Blücher, however, was able to escape total destruction, largely due to Napoleon being distracted from him by the advance of Schwarzenberg's Army of Bohemia. Blücher went into a period of deep depression for almost a week after this defeat and Gneisenau (his chief of Staff) effectively commanded the army for him although this has been a closely guarded secret until now.

Sources Plotho, Sporschil, Martinien, Zelle, Schubert.

FN Soissons, 14 February 1814, storm

A town in the northern French Département of the Aisne, on the River Aisne, 35 km southwest of Laon at the junction of Routes N2 and N31, about 70 km northeast of Paris.

A Russian victory over the French.

(Last action – Vauchamps, 14 February; next action – Mèry-sur-Seine, 22 February).

French Garrison GdD Rusca commanding: Reserve troops and Garde-National of the Eure, Oise, Seine-Inférieure, Seine-et-Oise. A Naval infantry regiment.

French total 4,000 men, 13 guns.

French losses GdD Rusca killed, ca 800 others killed and wounded, 3,500 captured, 13 guns.

Russian Forces Gen Adj Prince Tchernichev with Winzingerode's Avantgarde (part of the Army of the North) 4,200 men, mostly Cossacks; 2 Jäger coys, 22 guns.

Russian losses ca 200 killed and wounded.

Comment For this bold raid, Tchernichev was promoted Generallieutnant. No garrison was put into the town and Mortier reoccupied it.

Sources Plotho, Sporschil, Martinien, Zelle.

FP Garris, 15 February 1814, clash

A village in southwestern France, in the foothills of the Pyrenees, about 4 km west of the River Bidouse, on Route 11, 75 km southeast of Bayonne.

An Allied victory over the French.

(Last action – this was the opening action in southern France; next action – Orthez, 27 February).

French Forces GdD Harispe commanding. GdB Paris: 9e, 25e, 34e RILé (2 bns each); 45e, 81e, 115e, 116e, 117e RIdLi (1 bn each).

French total ca 7,000 men.

French losses 300 killed and wounded, 200 captured.

Allied Forces The Marquess of Wellington commanding: MG W Stewart's 2nd Division: BG Pringle 1/28th, 1/39th (1 bn each). Le Cor's Portuguese: Da Costa's Brigade: 2nd and 14th LIR (2 bns each); Buchan's Brigade: 4th and 10th LIR (2 bns each); 10th Caçadores (1 bn).

Allied total ca 11,000 men.

Allied losses 170 killed and wounded; of these, about 40 were Portuguese. The 1/39th lost 1 officer and 42 men in close combat with the 81e Li.

Comment Harispe only just escaped being cut off and destroyed here. He fell back in haste, abandoning the Bidouse bridge at St Palais thus frustrating Soult's plan to hold the line of that river.

Sources Oman, Martinien.

FE Nemours, 16 February 1814, storm

A small town in northern France, on the River Loing and at the junction of Routes N7, Motorway 6/E15 and D403, 15 km south of Fontainebleau.

A Russian victory over the French.

(Last action – Sens, 11 February; next action – Nangis, 17 February).

French Garrison The depot battalion of the Imperial Guard.

French total 600 men.

French losses All captured.

Russian Forces GdC Hettmann Platov's Cossacks of the Army of Bohemia: MGs Kaisarov, Grekov VIII, Illowaisky X with 5x Pulks.

Russian total ca 2,100 men.

Russian losses Not exactly known but very light.

Sources Zelle, Damitz.

FE Nangis (Mormant and Valjouan), 17 February 1814, clash

A town in the north French Département of the Seine-et-Marne, 25 km west of Provins on Route N19 towards Paris and 40 km southeast of Paris.

A French victory over the Austro-Russians.

(Last action – Nemours, 16 February; next action – Montereau, 18 February).

French Forces Emperor Napoleon I commanding: M Victor's II Corps (Divisions of Chateau and Duhesme and the Paris Reserve); GdD Alix's division and Montbrun's cavalry; GdD Charpentier's division: the Duke of Valmy's VI Corps with the dragoon divisions of L'Heretier and Treilhard and Milhaud with Pire's Light Cavalry and Briche's Dragoon Division. In reserve were the VII and XI Corps and the Imperial Guard. The regiments which actually fought were: 5e RILé, 32e, 58e, 81e, 122e RIdLi; 4e, 6e, 14e, 16e and 25e DragR and 3e ChàCh.

French total Present 18–20,000.

French losses ca 600 killed and wounded.

Allied Forces Part of the Army of Bohemia: GL Count Wittgenstein's.

VI Corps Avantgarde. GL Count Pahlen III's: Grodno and Ssum HusRs (4 sqns); Tschugujev UlR (4 sqns), Cossack Pulks of Illowaisky and Rebrikoff.

II (Russian) Corps 3rd Division LG Prince Schachoffskoi: 20th and 21st Jägers, IRs Reval, Selenginsk, 12 guns. From the V (Austro-Bavarian) Corps (Wrede): FML Count Hardegg's UlR Schwarzenberg Nr 2 (4 sqns); HusR Palatin Nr 12 (6 sqns).

Allied total 2,500 infantry, 1,800 cavalry (550 of these Austrians).

Allied losses 3,114 killed, wounded and missing, 9 guns, 40 caissons.

Comment Although Pahlen was obviously being crushed by the French masses as he withdrew, Hardegg refused to become seriously involved in the fight and only sent the Schwarzenberg Ulans to help. The regiments Reval and Selenginsk were badly mauled and had to be sent back to the rear to reform. Zelle claims the Allies lost 'over 5,000 men'.

Sources Sporschil, Martinien, Wrede, Zelle, Damitz.

FE Montereau, 18 February 1814, battle

A town in the northern French Département of the Seine-et-Marne, at the confluence of the Rivers Yonne and Seine, 23 km east of Fontainebleau, ca 40 km southeast of Paris. Nowadays Montereau-faut-Yvonne.

A French victory over the Austro-Württembergers.

(Last action – Nangis, 17 February; next action – Bourg-en-Bresse, 19 February).

French Forces Emperor Napoleon I commanding: Victor's II Corps, the Paris Reserve (GdD Gérard); the divisions of Chateau and Duhesme; the Imperial Guard in reserve. Regiments which actually took part in the combat were: Imperial Guard Cavalry (ChàCh, 2e ChLL, the foot and horse artillery); 4e, 11e, 15e, 16e, 24e, 26e and 29e RILé; 4e, 18e, 19e, 20e, 32e, 46e, 58e, 72e and 134e RIdLi. 18e and 25e DragR; 7e and 9e ChLL; 9e and 22e ChàCh; 2e, 3e and 7e HusRs.

French totals 25,000 infantry, 5,000 cavalry, 70 guns.

French losses ca 2,000 killed, wounded and missing; General Chateau killed.

Austro-Württemberg Forces

IV (Württemberg) Corps, Army of Bohemia, Crown-prince of Württemberg commanding; Infantry: GL Baron von Koch: GM von Stockmeyer, JgR Nr 9 (2 bns); LtIR Nr 10 (1 bn). GM von Döring: IRs Nr 2, 3, 7 (2 bns each). GM Prince von Hohenlohe-Kirchberg: IRs 4 and 6 (2 bns each); 2 x 6pdr FAB. Cavalry: GL Prince Adam von Württemberg: GM von Walsleben: JzPfR Nr 2, DragR Nr 3 (4 sqns each), 1 x HAB. GM von Jett: JzPfR Nr 4 (4 sqns); 1 x HAB.

Austrian Troops GM Schäffer: IRs Zach Nr 15 (3 bns); Gyulai Nr 21 (2 bns); Esterházy Nr 32 (2 bns); J Colloredo Nr 57 (2 bns); HusR EH Ferdinand Nr 3 (6 sqns); 2 x FAB.

Austro-Württemberg total 11,000 Württembergers, 4,000 Austrians.

Austro-Württemberg losses 1,400 killed and wounded, 3,600 captured, 2 guns, 2 ammunition waggons. Of these casualties 7 officers, and 85 men dead, 26 officers and 688 men wounded were Württembergers, 2,000 Austrians. Prince Hohenlohe was killed; GM Schäffer was captured.

Comment The Allies were caught with the Seine at their backs and crushed by superior forces. There was only one bridge available for the retreat. Zelle quotes 4,895 Allied casualties and 15 guns.

Sources Sporschil, Martinien, Wrede, Zelle.

FS Bourg-en-Bresse, 19 February 1814, skirmish

A town in eastern France, at the junction of Routes N83, N79, D975, D979 and D996, 62 km northeast of Lyon.

An Austrian victory over the French.

(Last action – Montereau, 18 February; next action – St Julien, 1 March).

French Forces: 20e and 67e RIdLi (2 bns each).

French total ca 1,400 men.

French losses Not known exactly but light.

Austrian Forces FML Count von Bubna's 1st Light Division, Army of Bohemia: IRs Kaunitz Nr 20* (2 bns); Vogelsang Nr 47* (1st Bn); HusRs Hessen-Homburg Nr 4, Blankenstein Nr 6 (6 sqns each); 1 x FAB, 1 x HAB.

Austrian total ca 4,500 men.

Austrian losses Not exactly known but light.

* = temporarily attached to Bubna's division.

Sources Damitz, Zelle, Wrede, Sporschil, Martinien.

FE Chambéry, 19 February 1814, skirmish

A town in eastern France, between Geneva and Grenoble, at the junction of Routes A43/E70 and A41/E21 and N6.

An Austrian victory over the French.

(Last action – Bourg-en-Bresse, 19 February; next action – Troyes, 23/24 February).

French Forces Part of GdD Brayer's Division of M Macdonald's XI Corps: 11e and 23e RIdLi.

French total ca 760 men.

French losses Not known exactly but light.

Austrian Forces FML Count von Bubna's 1st Light Division, Army of Bohemia: IR Kaunitz Nr 20* (2 bns); GzIR Warasdiner-Creuzer Nr 5 (1st Bn); GzIR Peterwardeiner Nr 9 (1st Bn).

Austrian total ca 3,300 men.

Austrian losses Not known exactly but light.

* = temporarily attached to Bubna's division.

Sources Damitz, Zelle, Wrede, Sporschil, Martinien.

FN Mèry-sur-Seine, 22 February 1814, clash

A village in northern France, on the north bank of the River Seine, at the junction of Routes D373 and D441, about 28 km northwest of Troyes.

A Russo-Prussian victory over the French.

(Last action – Soissons, 14 February; next action – Gué-à-Tresmes, 28 February).

French Forces GdB Gruyère's Brigade of GdD Boyer's Division: 24e, 36e, 122e RIdLi; 2eRILé, 6e ChLLR.

French total ca 3,600 men.

French losses about 800 killed, wounded and missing. GdB Gruyère wounded.

Russian Forces LG Prince Scherbatov's VI (Russian) Corps of GdI von Sacken's Army (part of the Army of Silesia): 7th Division MG Tallisin II: IRs Pieskov, Moskow, Sophia, Liebau; 11th and 36th Jägers (2 bns each). 18th Division MG Bernodossov: IRs Wladimir, Dnieprov, Tambov, Kostroma; 28th and 32nd Jägers (2 bns each). **Total** ca 5,000 men.

GdI York's I (Prussian) Corps Avantgarde: GL Prinz Wilhelm von Preussen: 2nd HusR (4 sqns); Ostpr Jägers (2 coys); Brand IR (Füs Bn); 12th ResIR (1 bn); 14th LWIR (1 bn); Brand HusR (1 sqn); Mecklenburg HusR (1 sqn); Ostpr N at KR (1 sqn). **Total** ca 1,200 men.

Allied losses ca 800 men.

Comment The sudden appearance of Blücher's Army of Silesia on his left flank was a complete surprise to Napoleon; however, lack of Allied cooperation saw Schwarzenberg now withdraw the Army of Bohemia!

Sources Zelle, Damitz, Martinien.

FE Troyes, 23/24 February 1814, clash

Principal town of the northern French Département de l'Aube, on the River Seine, 167 km southeast of Paris and at the junction of Routes N19/E54, N60/E511, N77 and D960.

A French victory over the Allies.

(Last action – Chambéry, 19 February; next action – Bar-sur-Aube, 26/27 February).

French Forces GdB Amiel's 12th Light Cavalry Brigade of Kellermann's VI Cavalry Corps: 21e and 26e DragRs (4 sqns each).

French total ca 1,290 men.

French losses Not known.

Austrian Forces FML Prince Moritz von Liechtenstein's 2nd Light Division, Army of Bohemia: ChLRs Kaiser Nr 1, O'Reilly Nr 3, Klenau Nr 5, Rosenberg Nr

6 (6 sqns each); Jäger Bn Nr 1 (1 bn).

Austrian total ca 3,600 men.

Austrian losses Not exactly known; the cavalry lost at least 311 men; 3 companies of Jägers were captured.

Sources Wrede, Zelle, Damitz, Martinien.

FE Bar-sur-Aube, 26/27 February 1814, battle

A town on the River Aube in northern France, 53 km east of Troyes on Route N19 towards Chaumont.

An Allied victory over the French.

(Last action – Troyes, 23/24 February; next action – La Ferté-sur-Aube, 28 February).

French Forces M Oudinot commanding:

II Corps (M Victor) and VII Corps (Oudinot) GdD Duhesme: GdB Dornier*: 11e and 24e RILé, 2e, 19e, 27e and 56e RIdLi (1,400 men, 8 guns). GdB Montfort*: 17e RILé (1er Bn); 36e RIdLi (1er Bn); 101e and 105e RIdLi (1er Bns); 118e RIdLi (4e Bn). GdB Pinoteau*: 10e RILé (1er and 2e Bns); 3e, 15e, 130e RIdLi (1er Bns each). GdB Chassé*: 16e RILé (1er Bn); 8e RIdLi (1er Bn); 28e RIdLi (1er, 3e, 4e bns), 54e RIdLi (1er Bn).

XI Corps M Macdonald: GdD Molitor: 28e RILé, 46e, 70e, 138e and 149e RIdLi. GdD Brayer: 19e RILé, 5e, 11e, 107e RIdLi. The divisions of Rothenburg and Pacthod were present but not engaged. GdB Amiel's 9th Cavalry Brigade: 4e and 14e DragRs of Treilhard's 5th Division, VI Cavalry Corps. The following regiments were also engaged: 1er RIdLé; 4e, 18e, 93e and 122e RIdLi; 2e ChLLR; 5e, 10e, 13e, 26e and 27e ChàCh.

French total ca 30,000 men, 60 guns (of which only 8 were brought into action).

French losses 2,600 killed and wounded, 500 captured, 2 guns.

* = so-called 'Spanish Brigades' as they contained many veteran regiments recently withdrawn from Spain.

Allied Forces FM Prince Schwarzenberg and part of the Army of Bohemia.

GL von Wrede's V Corps Bavarian Troops: 1st Division GL Count von Rechberg: GM von Vieregg: 1st, 2nd and 7th ChLRs (4 sqns each). GM Prince Carl von Bayern: IRs König (2 bns); Prinz Carl (1 bn); NatFd Bn Augsburg (1 bn); 3rd LtI Bn (1 bn); 10th IR (1 bn); 10th NatFd Bn (1 bn). **Austrian Troops:** GdC Count Frimont: IRs EH Rudolf Nr 14; EH Ludwig Nr 8 (4 bns each); Mariassy Nr 37 (2 bns); Baden Nr 59 (3rd Bn). HusR EH Joseph Nr 2 (6 sqns); 2 x FAB. **Russian Troops** GdC Count von Wittgenstein's VI Corps: Cavalry Division of LG Count von Pahlen III: HusRs Grodno, Ssum (6 sqns each); HusRs Olviupol and Lubno (4 sqns each); UlR Tschugujev (6 sqns). MG Illowaisky XII (5 cossack Pulks). Of MG Mejenzov's 5th Infantry Division: 23rd and 24th Jägers (2 bns each).

Allied total ca 30,000 men, 70 guns.

Allied losses 250 Austrians, 400 Bavarians, 1,250 Russians killed, wounded and missing. FM Schwarzenberg was wounded.

Comment Oudinot accepted battle with his army divided by the River Aube; most of his artillery could not be brought into action. The 'Spanish brigades' bore the brunt of the fighting and were shattered by it. Generals Pinoteau and Chassé were wounded. This battle proved to be the turning point of the campaign after a long string of French successes.

Sources Bodart, Wrede, Zelle, Damitz, Martinien.

FP Orthez, 27 February 1814, battle

A town in the southeastern French Département of the Basses-Pyrénées, 40 km northwest of Pau along Motorway A64/E80 towards Bayonne and on the northeastern bank of the River Gave.

An Anglo-Portuguese victory over the French.

(Last action – Garris, 15 February; next action – Aire-sur-l'Adour, 2 March).

French Forces M Soult commanding.

Reille's Corps GdD Marinsin; GdB Barbot: 4e RILé, 50e RIdLi (1 bn each); 40e RIdLi (2 bns). GdB Rouget: 27e, 34e, 59e RIdLi (1 bn each). **Total** 3,717 men. **GdD Taupin**; GdB Rey: 12e RILé, 32e, 43e RIdLi (2 bns each); GdB Gasquet: 47e RIdLi (2 bns); 55e and 58e RIdLi (1 bn each). **Total** 5,455 men.

Clausel's Corps GdD Villatte GdB St Pol 21e RILé, 86e, 96e, 100e RIdLi (1 bn each). GdB Lamorandière: 103e RIdLi; 119e RIdLi (2 bns); 28e RILé (1 bn) **Total** 4,609 men. **GdD Harispe's Division** GdB Dauture 9e, 25e, 34e RILé (2 bns each). GdB Baurot: 10e RIdLi (2 bns); 45e, 81e, 115e, 116e, 117e RIdLi (1 bn each) **Total** 5,084 men*.

D'Erlon's Corps GdD Foy; GdB Fririon 6e RILé, 76e RIdLi (1 bn each); 69e RIdLi (2 bns) GdB Berlier: 36e and 65e RIdLi (2 bns each); 39e RIdLi (1 bn) **Total** 3,839 men. **GdD Darmagnac** GdB Lescur: 31e RILé,

75e RIdLi (2 bns each); 51e RIdLi (1 bn); GdB Menne: 118e and 120e RIdLi (3 bns each) **Total** 5,022 men. **Cavalry** GdD Paul Soult: 15e, 21e, 22e ChàCh (7 sqns). Reserve Division: GdD Travot: GdB's Pourailly and Vuillemont: new conscript levies. **Total** 7,267 men.

French total 34,993 men.

Portuguese – 2,358 men. 7th Division **Total** 5,643 men. **Light Division** MG Alten: 1/52nd, 2 and 3/95 – 1,777 men, Portuguese (9 bns) – 1,703 men. Light Division **Total** 3,480 men. **Le Cor's Portuguese Division** Da Costa's Brigade – 2,109 men; Buchan's Brigade – 2,356 men. **Cavalry** MG Stapleton Cotton; Fane's Brigade – 765 men; Vivian's Brigade – 989

French Losses

	Killed		Wounded		Prisoners		
	Officers	Men	Officers	Men	Officers	Men	Total
Reille's Corps							
Division Rouget	3	93	17	348	4	56	521
Division Taupin	8	69	19	444	5	46	591
Brigade Paris (of Harispe's division)	1	71	13	102	1	260	448
D'Erlon's Corps							
Division Darmagnac	2	46	33	369	—	116	566
Division Foy	4	40	20	272	—	13	349
Clausel's Corps							
Division Villatte	—	35	5	96	5	198	339
Division Harispe	2	95	5	129	4	599	834
Cavalry of P. Soult	2	58	5	150	1	50	266
Artillery	—	10	—	41	—	8	59
Engineers	—	—	—	4	—	—	4
État-Major Général	3	—	5	—	—	—	8
Totals	*25*	*517*	*122*	*1,955*	*20*	*1,346*	*3,985*

GdD Foy, GdB Barbot and Gruardet wounded; GdB Béchaud killed; 6 guns taken.
* = plus GdN Basses Pyrénées (1 bn).

Allied Forces The Marquess of Wellington commanding: **2nd Division** MG W Stewart: Barnes' Brigade – 2,013 men; Byng's Brigade – 1,805 men; O'Callaghan's Brigade – 1,664 men, Harding's Portuguese – 2,298 men. 2nd Division **Total** 7,780 men. **3rd Division** MG T Picton: Brisbane's Brigade – 2,491 men, Keane's Brigade – 2,006 men, Power's Portuguese – 2,129 men 3rd Division **Total** 6,626 men. **4th Division** MG Cole: Anson's Brigade – 1,814 men; Ross' Brigade – 1,735 men, Vasconcellos' Portuguese – 2,385 men. 4th Division **Total** 5,952 men. **6th Division** MG Clinton: Pack's Brigade – 1,415 men; Lambert's Brigade – 2,300 men; Douglas' Portuguese – 1,856 men. 6th Division **Total** 5,571 men. **7th Division** MG Walker: Gardiner's Brigade – 1,865 men; Inglis' Brigade – 1,420 men; Doyle's men; Somerset's Brigade – 1,619 men. **Total** cavalry 3,373 men. Artillery and train 6 x British, 1 x KGL and 1 x Portuguese batteries – 1,162 men, 54 guns. Staff corps, engineers and Wagon Train – 350. **Allied totals** 26,798 British and 17,604 Portuguese.

British losses See overleaf.

Comment After a hard fight the French right wing (Rouget's division, Paris' Brigade, parts of Darmagnac's division) crumbled and fled to the rear. Hill's Corps (2nd Division, Ashworth's and Da Costa's Portuguese) turned the weak French left and captured two of Harispe's battalions. The French fled to the rear in great confusion over the River Luy. Wellington was lightly wounded and did not press the pursuit.

Sources Oman, Martinien.

British Losses at Orthez

	Killed		Wounded		Prisoners		
	Officers	Men	Officers	Men	Officers	Men	Total
Cavalry							
Fane's Brigade							
13th LDR	—	2	1	6	—	—	9
14th LDR	—	—	—	2	—	—	2
Vivian's Brigade							
18th Hus and	—	—	—	—	—	—	—
1st Hus KGL	—	—	—	—	—	—	—
Somerset's Brigade							
7th HusR	—	4	3	9	—	—	16
10th HusR	—	—	—	1	—	—	1
15th HusR	—	—	—	9	—	—	9
Total Cavalry	—	6	4	27	—	—	37
2nd Division (W Stewart)							
Barnes' Brigade							
1/50th	—	1	1	12	—	—	14
1/71st	—	2	1	9	—	—	12
1/92nd	—	—	—	3	—	—	3
Byng's Brigade							
1/3rd	—	—	—	2	—	—	2
1/57th	—	—	—	—	—	—	—
2/31st	—	—	—	2	—	—	2
1/66th	—	—	—	—	—	—	—
O'Callaghan's Brigade had no Losses							
2nd Division Total	—	*3*	*2*	*28*	—	—	*33*
3rd Division (Picton)							
Brisbane's Brigade							
1/45th	1	14	9	106	—	2	132
5/60th	—	4	2	35	—	1	42
74th	—	8	5	21	—	—	34
1/88th	2	41	12	214	—	—	269
Keane's Brigade							
1/5th	1	5	—	31	—	3	40
2/83rd	—	5	6	47	—	—	58
2/87th	1	14	5	66	—	23	109
94th	—	1	1	12	—	1	15
3rd Division Total	*5*	*92*	*40*	*532*	—	*30*	*699*

	Killed		Wounded		Prisoners		
	Officers	Men	Officers	Men	Officers	Men	Total
4th Division (Cole)							
Anson's Brigade							
3/27th	—	1	1	4	—	—	6
1/40th	—	1	—	4	—	—	5
1/48th	—	1	—	13	—	—	14
Ross's Brigade							
1/7th	—	6	4	56	—	2	68
1/20th	2	16	6	97	1	1	123
1/23rd	—	16	3	69	—	—	88
4th Division Total	*2*	*41*	*14*	*243*	*1*	*3*	*304*
6th Division (Clinton)							
Pack's Brigade							
1/42nd	—	5	4	40	—	11	60
1/91st	—	—	4	8	—	—	12
Lambert's Brigade							
1/61st	—	—	—	7	—	—	7
Total	—	5	8	55	—	11	79
7th Division (Walker)							
Gardiner's Brigade							
1/6th	2	24	8	111	—	—	145
2/24th	—	1	3	31	—	—	35
2/56th	—	3	3	25	—	—	31
Brunswick-Oels	2	5	5	32	—	4	48
Inglis's Brigade							
68th	—	3	1	27	—	—	31
1/82nd	—	2	2	34	—	—	38
Chasseurs Britanniques	1	2	5	20	—	12	40
7th Division Total	*5*	*40*	*27*	*280*	—	*16*	*368*
Light Division (Alten)							
1/52nd	—	7	6	76	—	—	89
Artillery	**1**	**3**	**1**	**23**	—	—	**28**
Engineers and sappers	1	—	—	1	—	—	2
General Staff	—	—	6	—	—	—	6
General British Total	***14***	***197***	***108***	***1,265***	***1***	***60***	***1,645***

Portuguese Losses

	Killed		Wounded		Prisoners		
	Officers	Men	Officers	Men	Officers	Men	Total
3rd Division							
Power's Brigade							
9th Line	—	11	2	36	—	—	49
21st Line	1	13	1	22	—	—	37
11th Caçadores	3	5	1	14	—	—	23
4th Division							
Vasconcellos's Brigade							
11th Line	1	44	9	78	—	16	148
23rd Line	1	36	5	77	—	3	122
7th Caçadores	—	8	1	16	—	—	25
6th Division							
Douglas's Brigade							
8th Line	—	1	—	8	—	—	9
12th Line	—	—	1	4	—	—	5
9th Caçadores	—	3	—	7	—	—	10
7th Division							
Doyle's Brigade							
2nd Caçadores	—	—	—	3	—	—	3
Light Division							
1st Caçadores	—	11	3	33	—	—	47
3rd Caçadores	—	13	—	13	—	—	26
Le Cor's Division							
Da Costa's 2nd Line	—	2	—	1	—	—	3
Buchan's Brigade							
4th Line	—	—	—	1	—	—	1
10th Line	—	—	1	—	—	—	1
10th Caçadores	—	3	1	6	—	—	10
Total	6	150	25	329	—	19	529
General Total							
British and Portuguese	20	347	133	1,594	1	79	2,174

FE La Ferté-sur-Aube, 28 February 1814, clash

A village on the River Aube in northern France.

An Austrian victory over the French.

(Last action - Bar-sur-Aube, 26/27 February; next action - Laubressel, 3/4 March).

French Forces GdD Brayer of Macdonald's XI Corps: Swiss grenadiers, 1er R Étranger (1 coy); 19e RILé, 5e, 11e, 107e RIdLi, 2 x FAB.

French total ca 2,500 men.

French losses ca 600 men.

Austrian Forces FZM Count Ignaz Gyulai's III Corps*: 1st Division FML Count von Crenneville: ChLR Klenau Nr 5 (7 sqns); GzIR Warasdiner-St Georger Nr 5 (2 bns). ChLR Rosenberg Nr 6 (6 sqns); 1 x HAB. 2nd Division FML Prince Hohenlohe-Bartenstein: IR Mariassy Nr 37 and Ignaz Gyulai Nr 60 (2 bns each), 1 x FAB. IRs Kollowrath Nr 36 (4 bns), Frelich Nr 28 (3 bns); 1 x FAB. 3rd Division FML von Fresnell: IRs Würzburg Nr 23 (4 bns); 1 x FAB. IRs Kottulinsky Nr 41 (3 bns), Kaiser Nr 1 (1st and 3rd bns); 1 x FAB. 2nd Light Division FML Prince M Liechtenstein: ChLR O'Reilly Nr 3 (6 sqns); GzIR Wallachisch-Illyrisch Nr 13 (2 bns); Jäger Bn Nr 7 (1 bn); ChLR Kaiser Nr 1 (6 sqns); HusR Szeckler Nr 11 (4 sqns); Jäger Bns Nr 1 and 2 (2 bns) 2 x HAB.

Austrian total ca 23,000 men.

Austrian losses Not exactly known but light; Zelle gives '600' killed, wounded and missing.

* = only part of this force was engaged.

Sources Wrede, Zelle, Damitz, Martinien.

FN Gué-à-Tresmes, 28 February 1814, clash

A village in northern France, about 20 km northeast of Paris at the point where Route 405 from Soissons crosses the Thérouanne stream, a tributary of the River Marne.

A French victory over the Prussians.

(Last action – Mèry-sur-Seine, 22 February; next action – Soissons, 3 March).

French Forces M Marmont commanding the VI Corps: GdD Ricard: 2e, 4e, 6e, 9e, 16e RILé (790 men); 22e, 40e, 50e, 69e, 136e, 138e, 142e, 144e and 145e RIdLi (ca 2,000 men). GdD Lagrange: 1er, 15e, 16e, 70e, 121e, RIdLi, 1er and 3e Naval IRs; 3e and 62e RIdLi; 2e and 4e Naval IRs; 132e RIdLi; 4 x FAB. ca 5,000 men. 1st Cavalry Division GdD Doumerc: 1er R Gardes d'Honneur; 10e HusR; 1er PvHusR; 2e, 3e and 4e ChàCh; 3 x FAB, 1 x HAB; ca 3,000 men. 3rd Pv Guards Division: Nr 9 GdD Poret Morvan (3,600 men); Pv Guards Cavalry Division GdD Boulnier (900 men). The 29e RIdLi was also engaged. The Vélites of Turin and Florence distinguished themselves as did the Fusilier Chasseurs and the Flanqueur Grenadiers of the Imperial Guard.

French total ca 14,500 men.

French losses not known exactly but light (ca 250 killed, wounded and missing). Gen Pelleport wounded.

Prussian Forces Gen von Katzler of von Kleist's II Prussian Corps of the Army of Silesia. Brandenburg Füs Bn, 1st and 2nd Ostpreussische Füs Bns; Gren Bn Leslie* (1 bn each); Ostpr KürR; Schl UlR (4 sqns each); Schl KürR, Brand KürR (4 sqns each); 2nd Westpr IR (Füs Bn); 2nd Schl. IR (2 bns); 11th and 12th ResIRs (3 bns each).

Prussian totals ca 12,000 men.

Prussian losses 1,035 killed and wounded.

* = made up of the Ostpreussischen and Schlesischen Gren Bns.

Sources KGE Heft 12, Plotho, Sporschil, Zelle, Damitz, Martinien.

FS St Julien, 1 March 1814, clash

Also known as Landecy, Les Lusiettes; a town in the eastern French Département of Haute-Savoie, on the River Aire, 9 km southwest of Geneva on Route 201/E712.

An Austrian victory over the French.

(Last action – Bourg-en-Bresse, 19 February; next action – Mâcon, 11 March).

French Forces GdD Count Marchand commanding. Exact details not known, but including 1er, 5e, 11e and 24e RIdLi.

French total 11,000 men, 13 guns.

French losses 1,000 killed and wounded, 300 captured; 5 guns.

Austrian Forces FML Count Klebelsberg (of Liechtenstein's Southern Corps) commanding: IRs Reuss-Greitz Nr 18, Kaunitz Nr 20, W Colloredo Nr 56 (2 bns each); HusRs Kaiser Nr 1 (6 sqns); Liechtenstein Nr 7 (4 sqns) 1 x FAB, 1 x HAB.

Austrian total ca 6,000 men.

Austrian losses 650 killed, wounded and missing.

Sources Bodart, Wrede, Sporschil, Martinien.

FP Aire-sur-l'Adour, 2 March 1814, clash

A village in southwestern France, on the northern bank of the River Adour and at the junction of Routes N124 and N134, 105 km east of Bayonne.

An Allied victory over the French.

(Last action – Orthez, 27 February; next action – Vic-en-Bigorre, 19 March).

French Forces GdD Clausel commanding GdD Villatte: GdB Lamorandière's brigade had no loss and was not actively engaged; GdB St Pol: 21e RILé, 86e RIdLi (1 bn each). GdD Harispe GdB Dauture (not engaged);

GdB Baurot: 81e and 115e RIdLi (1 bn each). Reserve GdB Paris: 39e, 69e RIdLi (1 and 2 bns resp).

French total ca 8,000 men.

French losses 12 officers, 250 men killed and wounded, 100 captured.

Allied Forces MG Hill commanding: 2nd Division MG W Stewart: Barnes' Brigade: 1/50th, 1/71st, 1/92nd Foot; Byng's Brigade: 1/3rd, 1/57th, 2/31st, 1/66th Foot (1 bn each). Le Cor's Portuguese: Da Costa's Brigade: 2nd and 14th LIR (2 bns each).

Allied total ca 10,000 men.

Allied losses Barnes' Brigade ca 136 killed and wounded; Byng's Brigade ca 20 killed and wounded. Da Costa's Brigade 5 officers and over 100 men killed and wounded.

Comment Da Costa made a frontal attack against Dauture's Brigade in a very strong position and was repulsed. He did not try to rally his men and was sacked, being replaced by Col João de Almeida. French resistance was otherwise very weak and the demoralised battalions suffered much desertion in the next days. Soult withdrew southeast on Tarbes to be on Wellington's southern flank thus luring him away from Bordeaux and towards Toulouse.

Sources Oman, Martinien.

IN Parma, 2 March 1814, capture

A town in northeastern Italy, at the confluence of the Rivers Parma and Baganza and at the junction of Routes 9, 62 and 343, 28 km northwest of Reggio.

A Franco-Italian victory over the Austrians.

(Last action – Mincio River, 8 February; next action – Reggio, 7 March).

Franco-Italian Forces GdD Count Grenier commanding: 36e RILé, 9e, 35e, 106e, RIdLi; 28e PvDBdeLi; 2nd Italian LtIR (2 bns); 4th, 5th, 6th Italian LIRs (2bns each); 1st and 4th Italian ChàCh (6 sqns); 3 x FAB, 1 x HAB.

Franco-Italian total 12,000 men.

Franco-Italian losses 400 killed, wounded and missing.

Austrian Forces GM Count von Starhemberg commanding: IRs EH Carl Nr 3 (1 x LW coy), EH Franz Nr 52 [1st (part) and 3rd Bn]; JgBn Nr 8 (1 bn); HusR Radetzky Nr 5 (6 sqns).

Austrian total ca 4,500 men.

Austrian losses 600 killed and wounded, 1,700 captured, 2 guns, 7 caissons.

Comment Austrian IRs Benjowsky Nr 31 and Splényi Nr 51 (3 bns each) were also near Parma this day. It seems that the townspeople let the French into the place.

Sources Wrede, Sporschil, vom Holtz.

FM Soissons, 3 March 1814, clash

A fortified town in northern France, 80 km northwest of Paris on Route N2 towards Laon, on the south bank of the River Aisne.

An Allied victory over the French.

(Last action – Gué-à-Tresmes, 28 February; next action – Craonne, 7 March).

French Garrison GdB Moreau commanding: 2 x Polish IRs.

French total 1,000 men and 20 guns.

French losses 143 killed and wounded. The garrison marched off to rejoin the French army with 6 guns.

Allied Forces Gen von Bülow's III Corps and Gen Winzingerode of the Army of Silesia.

Allied total 45,000 men.

Allied losses Very light. The handover of the town was negotiated.

Comment With this spiritless conduct, Moreau gave the Allies a strategic crossing point on the Aisne, just before Napoleon advanced to secure it. Blücher now crossed the river to join up with Bülow and Winzingerode and Napoleon was deprived of the chance of a crushing victory.

Sources KGE Heft 12, Plotho, Sporschil, Zelle.

FE Laubressel, 3/4 March 1814, clash

(Also known as La Guillotière, Troyes). A town in the northeastern French Département of Champagne, 10 km east of Troyes, on the River Barse.

An Allied victory over the French.

(Last action – La Ferté-sur-Aube, 28 February; next action – Belfort, 12 April*).

French Forces M Macdonald commanding.

II Corps GdD Gérard: GdD Duhesme: 24e RILé, 19e, 37e, 56e RIdLi. GdD Rothembourg's 2nd Tirailleur Division of the Young Guard: 1er–8e Tirailleurs (2,700 men); Also the regiments 56e, 58e, 72e, 134e RIdLi.

II Cavalry Corps GdD Count St Germain: 2nd Heavy Cavalry Division: 1er, 5e, 8e, 10e and 13e CuirRs. 2nd Light Cavalry Division GdD Maurin: 2e, 3e, 4e ChLLRs; 9e, 11e, 23e ChàCh, 6e HusR (2,600 men).

VII Corps The 'Spanish' brigades of Leval (4,300), Chassé (2,500) and Pacthod (10 bns – 4,000 men).

French total ca 20,000 men.

French losses 1,000 killed and wounded, 2,000 captured, 11 guns.

Allied Forces FM Prince Schwarzenberg** commanding part of the Army of Bohemia:.

FM von Wrede's V Corps Bavarian Troops: 1st Division GL Count von Rechberg: GM Von Vieregg: 1st, 2nd and 7th ChLRs (4 sqns each). GM Prince Carl von Bayern: IRs König (2 bns), Prinz Carl (1 bn); NatFd Bn Augsburg (1 bn); 3rd LtI Bn (1 bn); 10th IR (1 bn); 10th NatFd Bn (1 bn); IR Kronprinz (1 bn); 2nd LtI Bn (1 bn); 11th and 15th NatFd Bns (1 bn each). 2nd Division GL Count von Beckers: 3rd and 6th ChLRs; 4th LtI Bn (1 bn) 4th LIR, 6th LIR (2 bns each); 1st LtI Bn; 13th and 14th NatFd Bns (1 bn each). 3rd Division GL de la Motte: 4th and 5th ChLRs; 7th LIR (1 bn); 11th LIR (2 bns); 5th LIR (2 bns); 8th and 9th LIRs (1 bn each); Mobile Legion (2 bns); NatFd Bns München and Lindau; 6 x 6pdr FABs, 2x12pdr FAB's.

Part of the VI (Russian) Corps GdC Count von Wittgenstein: Cavalry Division of LG Count von Pahlen III: HusRs Grodno, Ssum (6 sqns each); Olviupol and Lubny (4 sqns each); Tschugujev UlR (6 sqns).

Allied total ca 32,000 men.

Allied losses ca 1,000 killed, wounded and missing.

* = On 25 March the Armies of Bohemia and Silesia acted jointly against Marshals Marmont and Mortier at Fère-Champenoise (see code FN) and subsequently advanced on Paris.

** = only part of these forces came into action.

Sources Bodart, Zelle, Wrede, Martinien.

IN Reggio, 7 March 1814, skirmish

A town in northeastern Italy, on the River Crostolo and at the junction of Routes 9 and 63, 28 km southeast of Parma and 70 km south of Mantua.

A drawn match between the Franco-Italians and the Austrian-Neapolitans.

(Last action – Parma, 2 March; next action – Peschiera, 10 March).

Franco-Italian Forces GdB Severoli commanding: GdB Rambourg: 92e RIdLi (2 bns); 1st and 7th Italian LIR, 2nd Italian LtIR (2 bns each).

Franco-Italian total ca 4,000 men.

Franco-Italian losses Not known, but light. General Severoli's leg was smashed by a cannonball early in the action.

Austrian Forces GM Nugent commanding: IRs EH Carl Nr 3 (1st LW Bn), Benjowsky Nr 31 (1 bn), EH Franz Nr 52 (1 bn); HusR Radetzky Nr 5 (4 sqns).

Austrian total ca 2,800 men.

Austrian losses Not known but light.

Comment Nugent had the Franco-Italians bottled up in the old town and almost ready to surrender when Joachim Murat, King of Naples, arrived and allowed them to march off with all their weapons to rejoin General Gratien. Nugent was furious but could do nothing.

Sources Bodart, Wrede, Martinien, vom Holtz.

FN Craonne, 7 March 1814, battle

A town in the northern French Département of the Aisne, 25 km southeast of Laon and about 90 km northeast of Paris.

An Allied victory over the French.

(Last action – Soissons, 3 March; next action – Laon, 9 March).

French Forces Emperor Napoleon I commanding.

M Ney's Corps GdD Meunier, 1st Young Guard Division: 1er, 2e, 3e, 4e Voltigeurs. GdD Curial's 2nd Young Guard Division: 5e, 6e, 7e, 8e Voltigeurs; 2 x FAB. GdB P Boyer's 'Spanish' Brigade: 2e RILé (3 bns); 24e RIdLi (1er Bn); 122e RIdLi (1er and 2e bns).

M Victor's II Corps 7th Young Guard Division. GdD Boyer de Rebeval; 8th Young Guard Division GdD Charpentier: 1er, 2e, 4e, 10e, 13e, 14e Tirailleurs.

M Mortier's Old Guard 1er and 2e ChàP (2 and 1 bns resp); 1er and 2e Grenadiers (2 bns each); Flanqueur Chasseurs, Flanqueur Grenadiers, Vélites of Turin and Florence (1 bn each). Cavalry: GdD Colbert: Gren à Ch, ChàCh; 1er and 2e ChLLRs, 1er and 2e Éclaireurs; 3e Gardes d'Honneur. 7 x FAB, 4 x HAB. 9th Young Guard Division GdD Poret de Morvan, GdB Lecamus, GdB Leclerc: 15e and 16e Voltigeurs (2 bns each); 3e and 4e Tirailleurs (1er, 2e bns each); 11e Voltigeurs (2e and 3e bns); 7e and 8e Voltigeurs (3e Bns); 2e and 9e Voltigeurs (3e Bns) (3,600 men); GdD Roussel's 6th Heavy Cavalry Division: 5e, 12e, 21e and 26e DragRs (2,200 men). GdD Exelmans 2nd Cavalry Division: 1er PvHusR; 2e Pv ChàCh; 3e Pv ChLLR (1,360 men); 4e Pv Carabiniers, 5e Pv Cuirassiers; HusR Jerome Napoleon (1,000 men).

M Marmont's VI Corps GdD Ricard: 2e, 4e, 6e, 9e, 16e

RILé; 22e, 40e, 50e, 69e, 136e, 138e, 142e, 144e, 145e RIdLi (ca 2,700 men). GdD Lagrange: 1er, 15e, 16e, 70e, 121e RIdLi; 1er and 3e Naval IRs, 62e RIdLi; 2e and 4e Naval IRs, 132e RIdLi; 4 x FAB (ca 4,600 men). GdD Doumerc's 1st Cavalry Division: 1er Gardes d'Honneur, 10e HusR, 1er Pv HusR, 2e, 3e, 4e ChàCh. 4 x FAB, 2 x HAB. The 10e and 12e ChàCh and the 2e ChLLR were also engaged. Arrighi's Parisian Reserve Division (4,000 men) was present but not engaged.

French total Estimates vary widely; Marmont: '31-33,000 men'; Zelle: '28,000 infantry, 2,000 artillery, 9,000 cavalry:' Only 17,000 infantry and 6,000 cavalry were involved in the action, almost entirely Guards infantry and cavalry of both Guards and line.

French losses As unclear as the totals! Between 5,400 and 8,000 killed, wounded and missing. M Victor, GdD Marquis Grouchy, Generals Sparre, Lecamus, Cambronne, Lecapitaine, Count Laferrière-Lévêcque were wounded, Gen Rouzier was mortally wounded.

Allied Forces GdC Baron Winzingerode's II (Russian) Corps of the Army of Silesia and III (Russian) Infantry Corps GL Count Woronzov commanding: 21st Division MG Laptieff: IRs Nevski, Lithuania, Podolsk, Petrovsk; 2nd and 44th Jägers (2 bns each). 24th Division, MG Vuitsch: IRs Schirwan, Butirsk; 19th Jägers (2 bns each). 14th Division MG Harpe: IRs Tula, Novaginsk, 3 x combined grenadier bns of the 9th, 15th and 18th Divisions. LG Count Stroganoff's Corps (from the Army of Poland): 12th Division MG Prince Cherwanski: IRs Smolensk, Narva, Alexopol, New-Ingermannland; 6th and 41st Jägers (2 bns each). 13th Division MG Scheltuchin: IRs Pensa and Saratov.

I Cavalry Corps LG Count O'Rourke: 3rd Hussar Division MG Baron von Pahlen. HusRs Elisabethgrad, Pavlograd, Isum.

The Cavalry Corps of LG Wassiltschikov 2nd Hussar Division LG Lanskoi: HusRs Achtyrsk, Mariupol, White Russia, Alexandria.

Allied totals ca 19,000 infantry, 4,000 cavalry.

Allied losses ca 4,785 men killed, wounded and missing (Zelle claims 'over 6,000' but gives no substantiation for this figure). Gen Lanskoi killed, Gen Uschakoff mortally wounded, Gens Laptieff and Schwarskin wounded.

Comment This was one of the bloodiest battles of the campaign. Well-placed Russian artillery caused havoc in the advancing French. The rest of Blücher's army did not take part in this action although part of it came up at the end. Many of the French troops were raw recruits.

Sources Bodart, Zelle, Damitz, Martinien.

SX Küstrin (Kostrzyn), April 1813 – 7 March 1814, blockade and capture

A fortress at the confluence of the Rivers Wartha and Oder, just east of the present-day German-Polish border and 25 km north of Frankfurt-on-the-Oder on (Polish) Route 22.

A Prussian victory over the French.

(Last action – Wittenberg, 13 January; next action – Glogau, 10 April).

French Garrison GdB Fournier d'Albe commanding: 5,000 men; exact details not known.

French losses Not exactly known; the garrison marched out with honours of war and then went into captivity.

Prussian Forces GM von Hinrichs: 1st and 2nd Ostpr LWIR; 3rd Neumark LWIR (3 bns each); 2nd Neumark LWKR (2 sqns), 1 x 6 pdr FAB.

Prussian total 8,400 men.

Prussian losses Not exactly known; light.

Sources Plotho, Sporschil, Martinien.

NL Bergen-op-Zoom, 8 March 1814

A fortified town in southwest Holland, on the eastern bank of the Schelde estuary 35 km north of Antwerp; just off the Motorway A58/E312.

A French victory over the British.

(Last action – Gorkum, 7 February; next action – Courtray, 31 March).

French Garrison Governor: GdB Bizonet. GdB Ambert commanding: 12e RIdLi (1 bn); 17e RIdLi (½ bn); 21e RIdLi (½ bn); 51e RIdLi (1 bn). Veterans: 4e R (2e Bn); 6e R (2 bns); total Veterans 350 men. 4e Naval IR (detachment); artillery (26e coy, 6e Foot ArtilleryR – 79 men). Sappers (42 men); 400 sailors, 145 others.

French total 2,700 men.

French losses 500 killed and wounded, 100 captured.

British Forces LG Sir Thomas Graham commanding: MG Cooke, MG Skerrett: 2/1st Guards (3 coys); 2/2nd Guards (4 coys); 2/3rd Guards (4 coys). Flankers of 21st and 37th Foot: 2/44th and 4/1st Foot. BG Henry: 2/21st, 2/37th, 2/91st, 2/35th Foot.

1/33rd, 1/55th; 2/69th Foot (1 bn each).
British total ca 4,000 men.
British losses 2,100 killed, wounded and captured. MGs Skerrett and Goore killed.
Comment The British stormed into the town but a determined counterattack drove them out again. Trapped by the rising tide, the 4th bn, 1st Foot capitulated and was released next day after agreeing not to serve against France until exchanged. A futile assault on one of the best fortresses in Holland. The British lost four colours.
Sources Bodart, Zelle.

IN Peschiera, 10 March 1814, clash

A fortified town in northeastern Italy, at the southern end of Lake Garda, on the River Mincio.
An Austrian victory over the Italians.
(Last action – Reggio, 7 March; next action – Monzambano, 10 March).
Italian Forces GdeD Palombini with parts of GdB Ruggieri: 3rd Italian LtIR (2 bns); 2nd Italian LIR (4 bns). GdB Galimberti: 3rd Italian LIR (3 bns); 6th Italian LIR (2nd Bn); Milan Guards (1 bn). DragR Napoleone (5th Sqn). 1 x HAB.
Italian total 2,000 men.
Italian losses Not known exactly; light.
Austrian Forces IRs Hohenlohe-Bartenstein Nr 26 (1 bn), Lindenau Nr 29 (1 bn); GzIR Warasdiner-Kreutzer Nr 5 (1 bn); HusR Stipsics Nr 10 (1 sqn).
Austrian total ca 3,000 men.
Austrian losses Not known exactly but light.
Sources Wrede, vom Holtz, Vaudoncourt.

IN Monzambano bridgehead, 10 March 1814, clash

A village on the west bank of the River Mincio in northeastern Italy, about 10 km south of Peschiera on Lake Garda.
An Austrian victory over the French.
(Last action – Peschiera, 10 March; next action – Goito, 10 March).
French Forces GdD Fressinet's 3rd Division: GdB Montfalcon: 25e PvDBde (3 bns); 42e RIdLi (2 bns). GdB De Conchy: 7e RIdLi (3rd Bn); 53e RIdLi (3 bns); 1 x FAB.
French total ca 8,000 men, 6 guns.
French losses Not known exactly but heavy.
Austrian Forces GM Paumgartten's Brigade: 4th Jg Bn (1 bn); ChLR Hohenzollern Nr 2 (6 sqns). HusR Stipsics Nr 10 (3 sqns). GM Bogdan's Brigade: 11th Jg Bn (1 bn); IRs Deutschmeister Nr 4 (4 bns); Beaulieu Nr 58 (3 bns); HusR Frimont Nr 9 (8 sqns). 2 x FAB.
Austrian total ca 9,500 men, 12 guns.
Austrian losses Not known exactly but light.
Comment The French launched an assault eastwards out of their bridgehead but were taken in both flanks and repulsed with considerable loss.
Sources Wrede, vom Holtz, Martinien, Vaudoncourt.

IN Goito, 20 March 1814, clash

A village on the west bank of the River Mincio in northeastern Italy, midway between Lake Garda and Mantua, where Route 236 crosses the river.
An Austrian victory over the French.
(Last action – Monzambano, 10 March; next action – Mantua, 10 March).
French Forces GdB Jeannin's Brigade of Marcognet's 4th Division: 29e PvDBde (2 bns); 102 RIdLi (3rd and 6th bns); 1 x FAB.
French total ca 3,000 men, 6 guns.
French losses Not known exactly but moderate.
Austrian Forces GM Baron von Spiegel from the Mantua blockading force: IR Lusignan Nr 16 (3 bns); GzIR Ottočaner Nr 2 (1 bn); HusR Radetzky Nr 5 (4 sqns) 1 x FAB.
Austrian total ca 4,300 men, 6 guns.
Austrian losses Not known exactly but light.
Sources Wrede, vom Holtz, Martinien, Vaudoncourt.

IN Mantua, 10 March 1814, clash

A fortress in the River Mincio in north eastern Italy, at the junction of Routes 10, 62, 420; between Lake Garda and the River Po.
An Austrian victory over the French.
(Last action – Goito, 10 March; next action – Taro River, 13 April).
French Garrison GdB Zucchi commanding.
Totals and losses Not exactly known.
Austrian Forces GM Baron von Suden: IR Bianchi Nr 63 (3 bns); GzIR Gradiskaner Nr 8 (2nd Bn).
Austrian total ca 3,600 men.
Austrian losses Not known exactly but light.
Comment French casualties on 10 March amounted to over 2,000 killed, wounded and missing. Austrian casualties amounted to 300 killed and wounded, 100 captured.
Sources Wrede, vom Holtz, Vaudoncourt.

FN Laon, 9/10 March 1814, clash

A fortified town, the capital of the French Département de l'Aisne, 140 km northeast of Paris, at the junction of Routes N2 and N44.

An Allied victory over the French.

(Last action - Craonne, 7 March; next action - Reims, 13 March).

French Forces Emperor Napoleon I commanding. As for Craonne plus: 36e, 43e, 50e, 62e, 66e, 88e and 122e RIdLi; 11e, 17e DragRs, 11e CuirR, 1er and 5e ChLIR, 7e HusR. Marmont's corps came up only at the end of the action with the VI Corps and the I Cavalry Corps (9,500 men, 53 guns).

French totals 31,000 infantry, 8,000 cavalry, 260 guns.

French losses 4,000 killed and wounded, 2,500 captured, 45 guns, 130 vehicles and caissons. Generals Poret and Grouvelle wounded.

Allied Forces FM von Blücher commanding.

I Corps GdI York: 1st Division GM von Horn: 7th Brigade Obstlt von Zepelin: LeibIR (3 bns); LWIRs 4 and 15* (1 bn). 1st Brigade Obstlt von Hiller: LWIRs 5 and 13* (1 bn); Ostpr and Schl Gren Bns* (1 bn); Leib-Gren Bn and Westpr Gren Bn (1 bn); Ostpr Jägers (2 coys). 2nd Division GL Prinz Wilhelm von Preussen: 2nd Brigade Obst von Warburg: 1st Ostpr IR (3 bns); LWIR Nr 6* (1 bn); 2nd Ostpr IR (Füs and 1 bn*). 8th Brigade Obst von Borcke: Brandenburg IR (Füs Bn) and 12th ResIR* (1 bn); Brandenburg IR (1 bn*); 12th ResIR (1 bn*); LWIR Nr 14 (1 bn*). Ostpr National HusR (4 sqns); Mecklenburg HusR (4 sqns); 1st and 3rd 6pdr FABs. Reserve Cavalry GM von Jürgass: Obst Graf Henkel von Donnersmark: Westpr DragR; Lithuanisches DragR, 5th, 10th and 3rd Schl LWCR (5 sqns*); Brandenburg UlR, Brandenburg HusR, 2nd Leib-HusR. 2nd and 12th HABs. Reserve Artillery: 1st and 3rd HABs, 2nd and 15th 6pdr FABs, 1st and 2nd 12 pdr FABs; 4 x 7 pdr and 2 x 10 pdr howitzers, 2 engineer coys.

II Corps GL von Kleist: Infantry Division GL Prinz August von Preussen: 9th Brigade GM von Klüx: 1st Westpr IR (3 bns); 6th ResIR (2 bns); Schützen (2 coys); 10th Brigade GM von Pirch: 2nd Westpr IR (3 bns); 7th ResIR (1 bn*); 10th ResIR and 1st Schl IR (1 bn*); 2nd Schl IR and 11th ResIR (1 bn*); Combined Füs Bn of 11th ResIR and 1st and 2nd Schl IRs (1 bn); Schützen (2 coys). Schl National HusR (2 sqns); 7th Schl LWCR (1 sqn); 2nd Schl HusR (2 sqns); 8th Schl LWCR (1 sqn); 7th and 8th 6pdr FABs. Reserve Cavalry GL von Ziethen; GM von Röder: Ostpr KürR, Brandenburg KürR, Schl KürR, Schl UlR; Neumärkisches DragR, 1st Schl HusR; 7th and 8th HABs. Reserve Artillery: 9th and 10th HABs, 9th and 11th 6 pdr FABs, 3rd and 6th 12 pdr FABs, 1st 7 pdr howitzer battery. Average battery strength was 8 guns.

From GdC Baron Winzingerode's II (Russian) Corps**: **III Infantry Corps** LG Count Woronzov: 24th Division MG Wuitsch: IRs Schirwan, Butirsk, 19th Jägers (2 bns each).

Of LG Count Stroganoff's Polish Army Corps: 12th Division MG Prince Cherwanski: IRs Smolensk, Narva, Alexopol, New-Ingermannland, 6th and 41st Jägers (2 bns each).

Allied totals ca 75,000 infantry, 25,000 cavalry, 176 guns.

Allied losses ca 166 killed and 566 wounded, 12 men missing.

* = combined battalions.

** = engaged only on 10 March.

Comment Marmont arrived as darkness fell and went into bivouac without adequate security patrols. The Prussian corps of York and Kleist mounted a night raid and scattered his command which is where most French casualties occurred and guns and vehicles were taken. French cuirassiers threw off their armour so that they could flee faster; next day a whole Prussian regiment was equipped with their cuirasses. Napoleon renewed the assault on 10 March and so impressed the Allies that they did not dare to pursue him when he finally withdrew.

Sources Bodart, Zelle, Damitz.

FS Mâcon, 11 March 1814, clash

A town in the eastern French Département of the Saône-et-Loire, on the River Saône, 72 km north of Lyon, at the junction of Routes N62 and A15 and A21.

An Austrian victory over the French.

(Last action - St Julien, 1 March; next action - Limonest, 16-20 March).

French Forces GdD Count Musnier commanding: 32e RILé; 20e, 23e and 67e RIdLi, 13e CuirR, 12e HusR (of Arrighi's corps); GdN de Toulon (2eR, 2 bns).

French total ca 6,000 men.

French losses 800 killed and wounded, 500 captured; 2 guns.

Austrian Forces FML Baron von Bianchi commanding: IRs Hiller Nr 2, Reuss-Plauen Nr 17 (3 bns each); Hessen-Homburg Nr 19 (1st and 2nd Bns); De Ligne Nr 30 (3 bns); H Colloredo Nr 33, Argenteau Nr 34 (3 bns each); Vogelsang Nr 47 (1st Bn); GrenBn Oklopsia, Járossy and Storr; JgBn Nr 5 (1 bn); KürR Kronprnz Nr 4; ChLR Vincent Nr 4 (6 sqns); HusR Kaiser Nr 1 (6sqns).

Austrian total ca 8,000 men.

Austrian losses 450 killed and wounded, 450 captured/missing.

Sources Bodart, Zelle, Damitz, Martinien.

FN Reims, 12/13 March 1814, storm and recapture

A town in the northern French Département of the Marne, on the River Vesle, 160 km northeast of Paris on Route A4/E50.

A French victory over the Russo-Prussians.

(Last action – Laon, 9/10 March; next action – Berry-au-Bac, 14 March).

French Garrison GdB Dentzel: 2e Tirailleurs; 2e Éclaireurs, 1er and 3e Gardes d'Honneur; Guard Artillery. Parts of the following regiments: 15e, 43e, 50e, 66e and 138e RIdLi.

French total 1,206 infantry, 150 cavalry.

French losses Not known exactly, at least 100 killed; most captured with 11 guns. GdB Lacoste captured. The colours of the 95e, 96e and 97e Cohorts of the GdN were taken.

Russo-Prussian Forces LG Count St Priest (of GdI Count Langeron's Corps) commanding the VIII (Russian) Infantry Corps: 11th Division MG Prince Gurgalov: IRs Ekaterinburg, Rylsk, Geletz, Polotzk, 1st and 38th Jägers (2 bns each). 17th Division MG Pillar: IRs Bielosersk, Brest, Willmannstrand, Riasan, 30th and 48th Jägers (2 bns each). 1st Dragoon Division LG Barasdin II: DragRs Mitau, New-Russia, Moscow and Kargopol. 4th Dragoon Division: MG Emanuel: DragRs Charkov, Kiev.

Russian total ca 7,800 men.

Russian losses 1,400 men, 12 guns.

Prussian Troops GM von Jagow [of II (Prussian) Corps]: 1st and 3rd Pomm LWIRs (3 bns each); 1st Westpr and 7th Kurmark; LWCRs (4 sqns each).

Prussian total 5,600 men.

Prussian losses 1,300 men, 10 guns.

Comment Next morning, Napoleon retook the town with Marmont's corps. Friant's division, Rousseau's brigade, the Guard Cavalry and the I Cavalry Corps and inflicted losses of 1,400 men and 12 guns on the Russians, 1,300 men and 10 guns on the Prussians for the recorded loss of 8 French infantry officers and 25 cavalry officers (loss of men probably ca 900 men). General St Priest mortally wounded.

Sources Zelle, Damitz, Martinien.

FN Berry-au-Bac, 14 March 1814, clash

A village in northern France on the upper River Aisne, near Pontavert between Soissons and Reims.

A Prussian victory over the French.

(Last action – Reims, 12/13 March; next action – Arcis-sur-Aube, 21 March).

French Forces GdD Merlin's 1st Light Cavalry Division, I Cavalry Corps: 1st Brigade GdB Wathier: 6e, 7e, 8e HusR; 1er, 3e, 5e, 7e, 8e ChLL. 2nd Brigade GdB Guyon: 1er, 2e, 3e, 6e, 8e, 9e, 16, 25e, ChàCh. All units 1 sqn strong.

French total ca 1,600 men.

French losses Killed and wounded not known; 238 captured.

Prussian Forces From York's I (Prussians) Corps: 2nd Leib-HusR, Brand HusR (4 sqns each).

Prussian total ca 650 men.

Prussian losses 3 killed, a score wounded and missing.

Comment In Martinien, the only French cavalry regiment to record officer casualties here is the 6th ChàCh and those on a different date.

Sources Martinien, Zelle, Damitz.

FP Vic-en-Bigorre, 19 March 1814, clash

A hamlet in the valley of the River Adour in the foothills of the Pyrenees in southwestern France, on Route 935, 17 km north of Tarbes.

An Allied victory over the French.

(Last action – Aire-sur-l'Adour, 2 March; next action – Tarbes, 20 March).

French Forces GdD d'Erlon commanding: GdD Paris*: 3e, 6e, 12e, 31e, RILé; 36e and 118 RIdLi.

French total ca 8,000 men.

French losses ca 300 killed, wounded and missing.

* After his defeat at Orthez on 27 February, Soult had reshuffled his forces and Paris took over Foy's division (after Fririon had commanded it for some days); Daricau took over from Paris before the battle of Toulouse on 10 April.

Allied Forces The Marquess of Wellington commanding: MG T Picton's 3rd Division: Brisbane's Brigade: 1/45th, 5/60th, 1/74th, 1/88th (1 bn each); Keane's Brigade: 1/5th, 2/83rd, 2/87th, 1/94th (1 bn each); Power's Portuguese Brigade: 9th and 21st LIR (2 bns each); 11th Caçadores 1 bn. Von Bülow's KGL Cavalry Brigade 1st and 2nd LDRs (6 sqns).

Allied total ca 12,000 men.

Allied losses ca 250 killed and wounded.

Comment The French cavalry were present but did not suffer casualties. Soult withdrew south to Tarbes.

Sources Oman, Martinien.

FS Limonest*, 16–20 March 1814, clashes

Also known as Belleville, St Georges, Lyon; villages in the eastern French Département of the Rhône, 9 km northwest of Lyon.

* = including St Georges, 18 March.

Austrian victories over the French.

(Last action – Mâcon, 11 March; next action – Romans, 2 April).

French Forces M Augereau (Duke of Castiglione) commanding: GdD Pannetier: 1er RILé, 7e, 16e, 20e RIdLi, 13e CuirR, 4e and 12e HusRs (1,800 cavalry); 23e, 32e, 67e RIdLi; GdN de la Rhône.

French total ca 20,000 men, 36 guns.

French losses 800 killed and wounded, 1,200 captured.

Austrian Forces, FML Count von Bubna's 1st Light Division, Army of Bohemia: GM von Scheither; HusR Kaiser Nr 1 (6 sqns); ChLR Vincent Nr 4 (6 sqns); GzIR Warasdiner-Creuzer Nr 5 (1 bn). GM von Zechmeister: HusR Liechtenstein Nr 7 (4 sqns); Jg Bn Nr 6; GzIR Broder Nr 7 (1st Bn). GdC Prince von Hessen-Homburg's Corps (Army of Bohemia, part of); 1st Infantry Division FML von Bianchi: IRs Hessen-Homburg Nr 19, A Gyulai Nr 21 (2 bns each), De Vaux Nr 25 (2nd Bn), Erbach Nr 42 (1 bn), Froon Nr 54 (1 bn), I Gyulai Nr 60 (3rd Bn). 2nd Kürassier Division FML von Lederer: KürRs EH Franz Nr 2, Kronprinz Nr 4, Lothringen Nr 7 (5 sqns each). Also at St Georges (18 March) were IRs Czartoryski Nr 9, De Ligne Nr 30; Esterházy Nr 32 (2 bns each); H Colloredo Nr 33, Argenteau Nr 35 and Simbschen Nr 48 (2 bns each).

Austrian total ca 30,000 men.

Austrian losses ca 1,100 killed and wounded, 600 captured.

Sources Wrede, Zelle, Damitz.

FP Tarbes, 20 March 1814, clash

A small town in southwestern France, on the western bank of the River Adour, on Route N117, about midway between Bayonne and Toulouse.

An Allied victory over the French.

(Last action – Vic-en-Bigorre, 19 March; next action – Étauliers, 6 April).

French Forces M Soult commanding: GdD Harispe GdB Baurot: 45e, 86e, 116e RIdLi.

French total ca 2,300 men.

French losses ca 200 killed, wounded and missing.

Allied Forces The Marquess of Wellington commanding; MG Alten's Light Division: 95th Foot (3 bns).

Allied total ca 2,400 men.

Allied losses 11 officers, 80 men killed and wounded.

Comment Hill's 2nd Division, pushing east through Tarbes over the bridge (which had been left intact) had about a score of casualties in a long-range fire fight with Taupin's division but the French fell back east when Wellington turned their northern flank with the 6th Division and Somerset's cavalry.

Sources Oman, Martinien.

FN Arcis-sur-Aube, 20/21 March 1814, battle

A town in the northern French Département of the Aube, 28 km north of Troyes on Route N77.

An Allied victory over the French.

(Last action – Berry-au-Bac, 14 March; next action – Fère-Champenoise, 25 March).

French Forces, Emperor Napoleon I commanding. **The Corps of Ney, Sebastiani** Divisions of Exelmans, Colbert. At this stage of the campaign organizations were changing on a daily basis. Oudinot's troops were: GdB Montfort: 17e Lé, 36e, 101e, 105e, 118e Li (1 bn each). GdB Maulmont: 10e RILé; 3e and 15e RIdLi (4 bns); GdB Chassé: 16e RILé; 8e and 28e RIdLi (5 bns). Other regiments actually involved in the combat were: The Guard: 1er GrenR, 2e ChàPR. 9th PV Guards division: GdBs Lecamus, Leclerc: 7e and 8e Voltigeurs (3e Bn each); 11e Voltigeurs (2e and 3e bns); 15e and 16e Voltigeurs (2 bns each). 2e Tirailleurs (3e Bn); 3e and 4e Tirailleurs (1er and 2e bns each); 9e Tirailleurs (3e Bn). 10th Pv Guards Division GdD Henrions: 7e and 8e Voltigeurs (2e Bn each); 11e Voltigeurs (3e Bn); 15e Tirailleurs (3e Bn); 16e Tirailleurs (2e Bn); 8e Tirailleurs; Sailors. Guard Cavalry: DragR. 1er ChLLR, 1er, 2e, 3e Éclaireurs; Garde d'Honneur. Line Infantry Regiments: 12e, 15e,

34e, 104e, 121e, 122e, 136e. 2e Vistula IR. Cavalry Regiments: 4e, 14e, 16e, 17e, 27e. DragRs; 6e ChLLR; 5e ChàCh. Spanish Gendarmes (2 bns). GdN de Rochefort.

French total 23,000 infantry; 7,000 cavalry.

French losses Estimates vary widely. Bodart gives 3,400 killed and wounded, 800 captured, 3 guns. Zelle quotes 700 killed and wounded, 500 unwounded prisoners. As the regimental records for this period are far from complete, we can only guess at what the real figures were.

Allied Forces FM Prince von Schwarzenberg commanding. Although about 100,000 men of the Army of Bohemia were present, only a fraction of them were actually involved in the conflict.

V Corps GdC (now FM) Count von Wrede.

Austrian Troops GdC Baron von Frimont: 1st Division FML von Hardegg: HusR EH Joseph Nr 2 (6 sqns); UlR Schwarzenberg Nr 2 (6 sqns). 2nd Division FML von Splényi: HusR Szeckler Nr 11 (6 sqns); IRs EH Rudolph Nr 14 (3 bns), Jordis Nr 59 (3rd Bn); 2 x HAB, 2 x FAB. **Bavarian Troops** 1st Division LG Count von Rechberg: GM von Vieregg: 1st, 2nd, 7th ChLRs (4 sqns each). GM Prince Carl von Bayern: IRs König (2 bns), Prinz Carl (1 bn); NatFd Bn Augsburg (1 bn); 3rd LtI Bn (1 bn). GM von Maillot: IR Kronprinz (1 bn); LtI Bns (2 bns); NatFd Bns Bayreuth and Ingolstadt (1 bn each). 2 x 6pdr FAB. 2nd Division GL Count von Beckers: GM von Elbrecht: ChLRs Kronprinz and Bubenhofen (4 sqns each). GM von Pappenheim: 3rd LIR (1 bn); NatFd Bns Salzburg and Regensburg (1 bn each). GL von Zollern: IR Herzog Wilhelm (2 bns); LtI Bn (1 bn); NatFd Bns Innsbruck and Ansbach. 2 x 6pdr FAB.

Austrian Troops of FZM Count Hieronymus Colloredo's I (Austrian) Corps from 2nd Division, FML von Wimpfen: IR Erbach Nr 42 (1st Bn). From the III (Austrian) Corps of FZM Count Ignaz Gyulai: 1st Division FML Count von Crenneville: GM von Hecht: ChLR Kienmayer Nr 5 (6 sqns); GM von Trenck ChLR Rosenberg Nr 6 (6 sqns); 2nd Division FML Prince von Hohenlohe-Bartenstein. GM von Spleny: IRs Mariassy Nr 37, I Gyulai Nr 60 (2 bns each). GM von Grimmer: IRs Kollowrath Nr 36 (4 bns), Frelich Nr 28 (3 bns); 1 x HAB, 1 x FAB. 3rd Division FML von Fresnell: GM von Pflüger: IR EH Ludwig Nr 8 (3 bns); 1 x FAB. From the Austrian Reserve Corps of FML Count von Nostitz: 1st Kürassier Division FML Count von Klebelsberg: KürRs Liechtenstein Nr 6 and Constantin Nr 8 (5 sqns each). From FML Weissenwolf's 2nd Division, GM von Klenau's brigade: Gren Bns Putheany, Mösel and Frisch. DragR Knesevich Nr 3 and HusR EH Ferdinand Nr 3 (6 sqns each) were also engaged.

Russian Troops From GdC Rajewsky's Grenadier Corps 1st Grenadier Division LG Tschoglikov: MG von Jemelianoff GrenRs Perm, Kexholm (1 bn each). MG von Kniäschen: GrenRs Ekaterinoslav, Araktschejev (1 bn each). GM von Sulima: GrenRs St Petersburg, Tauride (1 bn each). It is not clear which other Russian units took part in this action apart from Kaisaroff's cavalry (Cossacks) and Wittgenstein's Corps.

From Wittgenstein's VI (Russian) Corps Cavalry Division of LG Count von Pahlen III: HusRs Grodno and Ssum (6 sqns each); HusRs Olviupol and Lubny (4 sqns each), Tschugujev UlR (6 sqns). GM Illowaisky XII: 5x Cossack Pulks; 1 x HAB.

Württemberg Troops FM the Crownprince of Württemberg commanding: Cavalry Division of GL Prince Adam: GM von Walsleben: DragR Nr 3, JzPfR Nr 2 (4 sqns each); 1 x HAB. GM von Jett: JzPf Nr 4 (4 sqns); 1 x HAB. The infantry division was not engaged.

Allied total ca 43,000 men.

Allied losses Not known exactly. The Bavarians and Württembergers each lost 'some hundreds'; the Russians considerably more. Bodart quotes '3,000'; Zelle agrees.

Comment Having repulsed all French assaults on 20 March, Schwarzenberg was far too cautious next day as they withdrew – practically unmolested – over the river again and missed an opportunity to inflict a significant defeat on Napoleon.

Sources Bodart, Martinien, Wrede, Zelle, Damitz.

FN Fère-Champenoise, 25 March 1814, battle

A town in the northern French Département of the Marne, 112 km east of Paris, just north of Route N4.

An Allied victory over the French.

(Last action – Arcis-sur-Aube, 20/21 March; next action – Bannes, 25 March).

French Forces M Mortier and Marmont commanding.

The Imperial Guard GdD Michel: Flanqueurs Chasseurs (2 bns); Flanqueurs Grenadiers (1 bn); Vélites de Florence (½ bn); Vélites de Turin (2 coys); Fusilier Chasseurs (2 bns); Fusilier Grenadiers (1 bn); 1er, 2e,

3e, 4e, 5e, 6e, 7e, 8e, 14e Voltigeurs; 1er, 5e, 6e, 7e, 8e, 14e Tirailleurs.

VI Corps (Marmont) GdD Ricard: 2e, 4e, 6e, 9e, 16e RILé (1 coy each); 22e, 40e, 50e, 69e, 136e, 138e, 142e, 144e, 145e RIdLi (1–4 coys each). GdD Christiani: 1er, 15e, 16e, 70e, 121e RIdLi (1–4 coys each); 1er, 2e, 3e, 4e Naval IR (1 bn each); 62e and 132e RIdLi (3 coys each). Also 28e, 43e, 48e, 54e, 65e, 70e, 112e, 149e RIdLi (1 bn each). GdN de Cherbourg (2e Bn), Rochefort, Eure-et-Loire (Élite-Bn), Indre-et-Loire (Élite-Bn), Seine (1er Élite-Bn), Seine-et-Marne (Élite-Bn). The cavalry of **GdD Count Bordesolle and GdD Belliard (I Cavalry Corps):** GdB Wathier: 6e, 7e, 8e HusR, 1er, 3e, 5e, 7e, 8e ChLLR. GdB Guyon: 1er, 2e, 3e, 6e, 8e, 9e, 16e, 25e ChàCh. GdB Thiery: 2e, 3e, 6e, 9e, 11e, 12e CuirRs. GdB Laville: 4e, 7e, 14e CuirRs, 7e, 23e, 28e, 30e DragRs. Average strength of these cavalry regiments was 2 sqns each. From the **V Cavalry Corps (GdD Count Milhaud)** 5e, 6e, 21e, 25e, 26e DragRs (2 sqns each). Also the 23e ChàCh. Various 'March Regiments'.

French total 17,000 infantry, 4,000 cavalry*, 84 guns.

French losses Sources vary widely: Bodart: '5,000 killed and wounded, 8,000 captured, 46 guns, 25 ammunition waggons,' Zelle: '3,000 killed and wounded, 3,000 captured, 30 guns have been claimed – this is far too high, should be 1,500 killed and wounded, at the most 3,000 captured – 2,000 deserted'.

* = Zelle (always over-Francophile) states: '19,000 including 5,000 cavalry and 60 guns'.

Allied Forces The Crown Prince of Württemberg commanding:

The IV (Württemberg) Corps Cavalry Division GL Prince Adam von Württemberg: GM von Walsleben: DragR Nr 3, JzPfR Nr 2 (4 sqns each), 1 x HAB. GM von Jett: JzPfR Nr 4, 1 x HAB. Infantry Division GL Baron von Koch; GM von Stockmeyer: JgR Nr 9 (2 bns); LtIR Nr 10 (1 bn). GM von Döring: IRs Nrs 2, 3, 7 (2 bns each), 1 x 6 pdr FAB. GM Prince von Hohenlohe-Kirchberg: IRs Nr 4 and 6 (2 bns each); 1 x 6pdrFAB. 1 x Austrian 12pdr FAB. **Prussian Troops:** from **LG von Kleist's II (Prussian) Corps, Army of Silesia:** 11th Brigade LG von Ziethen; 1st SchlHusR (4 sqns); 1st SchlIR; 10th ResIR (3 and 2 bns resp,); SchlSchützen Bn (2 coys). **Russian Troops: from the Imperial Cavalry Reserve of GL Prince Galitzin V:** GM Tschailikov: LifeGuard Dragoons, LifeGuard Hussars, LifeGuard Ulans (4 sqns each). LG Count Orlov-Denissov: Don LifeGuard CossackR (4 sqns); Black Sea Guard CossackR (4 sqns). 1st Kürassier Division: LG Depreradovitsch; GM Arsenief: Chevalier Guards, Horse Guards (4 sqns each). GM Rosen: Life Guard KürR, KürR Tsarina (4 sqns each).

Cossack Corps of GdC Count Hettmann Platov: Under GMs Kaisarov, Grekov VIII and Illowaisky X: 5 x Cossack Pulks, 1 x Don Cossack HAB (12 guns). GM von Seslavin: Ssum HusR (2 sqns); 4 x Cossack Pulks; 2 x HAB guns. **From the VI (Russian) Corps of GdC Count von Wittgenstein:** LG Count von Pahlen III's Cavalry Division: GM von Rhüdiger Grodno HusR (6 sqns); Ssum HusR (4 sqns). GM von Dochtorov: Olviupol and Lubny HusR (4 sqns each). GM von Lissanewitz: Tschugujev UlR (6 sqns); GM von Illowaisky XII: 5 x Cossack Pulks; 1 x HAB. **Austrian Troops: from GdC Erbprinz von Hessen-Homburg:** FML Count von Nostitz: 1st Kürassier Division FML Count von Klebelsberg: GM Count von Auersperg: KürRs Constantin Nr 8, Sommariva Nr 5 (4 sqns each). GM Count von Desfours: KürRs Kaiser Nr 1, Liechtenstein Nr 6 (4 sqns each). 2nd (Grenadier) Division FML von Weissenwolf: GM von Klenau: Gren Bns Frisch, Mösel, Putheany. GM von Luz: Gren Bns Rosmann, Lany, Hromada (1 bn each). **From III (Austrian) Corps of FZM Count Ignaz Gyulai;** GM von Trenck: ChLR Rosenberg Nr 6 (6 sqns); GzIR Warasdiner-St Georger Nr 6 (1 bn); 1 x HAB. Also HusR EH Ferdinand Nr 3 (6 sqns).

Allied total ca 28,000 men (mainly cavalry), 80 guns.

Allied losses ca 2,000 killed, wounded and missing.

Comment The square of the 14e Tirailleurs was broken by the Württemberg 4th JzPfR and the Austrian HusR EH Ferdinand Nr 3. A brigade of the Young Guard (5e, 6e and 7e Voltigeurs) under GdB Jamin was surrounded, cut down and captured by the Austrian HusRs Kaiser and EH Ferdinand and KürR Constantin.

Sources Bodart, Martinien, Zelle, Damitz.

FN Bannes, 25 March 1814, clash

A small village in northern France, ca 112 km east of Paris, between Routes N4 and N33, about 10 km northwest of Fère-Champenoise.

A Russian victory over the French.

(Last action – Fère-Champenoise, 25 March; next action – Claye-Souilly, 28 March).

French Forces GdD Pacthod commanding: GdBs Delort, Bonté, Loszinsky: 149e RIdLi (2 bns); 3rd Pv IR; GdN Indre-et-Loire (2 bns), Eure-et-Loire (2nd Bn), Seine-et-Marne, Somme (1 bn each). GdD Amey: 54e RIdLi (1 bn); GdN Cherbourg (2e Bn), Rochefort (1 bn). 13e HusR (100 men); 16 guns, 100 ammunition waggons, 125 waggons loaded with bread.

French total ca 3,800 men.

French losses 1,500 killed and wounded, 1,900 captured, all guns and vehicles taken. GdD Pacthod wounded and captured, GdB Delort, Bonté, Thévenet and Loscynski captured.

Russian Forces. Tsar Alexander of Russia commanding: Russian Troops. **From Langeron's Corps, Army of Silesia** GL Baron Korff: 1st Dragoon Division, GL Barasdin II; GM Gernegross: DragRs Mitau, New Russia, Moscow, Kargopol (4 sqns each). 4th Dragoon Division GM Emanuel: DragRs Charkov, Kiev (4 sqns each). 2nd Mounted Rifle Division GM Count Pahlen II: Livland and Dorpat MtdRRs (4 sqns each). 1st Mounted Rifle Division GM Denissiev: Tschernigov, Arsamas and Sewersk MtdRRs (4 sqns each); 2 x HAB. **From Sacken's Corps, Army of Silesia** GL Wassiltschikov: 2nd Hussar Division GL Lanskoi: HusRs Achtyrsk, Mariupol, White Russia, Alexandria (4 sqns each). 3rd Dragoon Division GM Pantschulidschev II: DragRs Kurland, Smolensk, Twer, Kinburn (4 sqns each); 1 x HAB. **From the Imperial Russian Guard Cavalry of Prince Galitzin V** 1st Kürassier Division GL Depreradovitsch; GM Arsenief: Chevalier Guard; Horse Guards (4 sqns each); GM von Rosen: LG KürR Tsarina (4 sqns each); 2 x HAB.

Russian totals 28,000 men, 64 guns.

Russian losses Not known.

Comment The National Guard troops, mostly without uniforms, fought and died like hardened veterans. The Allies switched their cavalry from Fère-Champenoise to destroy this convoy.

Sources Martinien, Bodart, Zelle, Damitz.

FN Claye-Souilly, 28 March 1814, ambush

A small town on the eastern side of Paris (in northern France), between that city and Meaux on the River Marne.

A French victory over the Prussians.

(Last action – Bannes, 25 March, next action – Paris, 30 March).

French Forces GdD Compans commanding: GdB Guye with 3 bns Young Guard. Col Digeon: 12e Pv CavR (400 Cuirassiers); Polish Krakus (1 sqn); 1 x FAB. GdD Ledru des Essarts: 25e RIdLi (6e Bn); 54e and 62e RIdLi (1er Bns each); 1 x FAB, 11e Pv CavR (400 men), GdN (3 bns).

French total 5,600 infantry, 1,650 cavalry.

French losses 200 killed and wounded, 150 captured.

Prussian Forces. LG York's I (Prussian) Corps, Army of Silesia: Avantgarde: 1st Westpr IR (1st and 2nd Bns); 1st Ostpr Füs Bn (1 bn); ResIR Nr 7 (Füs Bn); 2nd Leib-Hus-R (4 sqns).

Prussian total ca 4,500 men.

Prussian losses ca 600 men including 189 from the 1st Westpr IR. 145 of these were captured.

Comment The 1st Westpr IR was surprised and scattered by Digeon's Cuirassiers and the Polish Krakus; only a counter-charge by the 2nd Leib-Hus-R saved them from complete destruction.

Sources Zelle, Damitz, Martinien.

FN Paris, 30 March 1814, battle

Capital city of France, in the north of the country at the confluence of the Rivers Seine et Marne. The action took place on the northern edge of the city from Montmartre to Romanville.

An Allied victory over the French.

(Last action – Claye-Souilly, 28 March; this was the last action in northern France.).

French Forces King Joseph Napoleon commanding.

M Mortier's Corps – The Imperial Guard. GdD Michel: the combined Depots of the Guard infantry. GdB Secretant (2,000 men); GdB Robert (2,000 men); GdD Curial (1,820 men); GdD Christiani (1,630 men); GdD Charpentier (1,500 men).

M Marmont's VI Corps GdD Arrighi (1,250 men) GdD Ricard (726 men); GdD Lagrange (1,395 men).

GdD Compans' Pv Corps GdB Chabert (2,220 men); GdD Ledru; GdB Bongars (1,600 men); GdD Boyer de Rebeval 11e Voltigeurs (3 bns); Flanqueur Grenadiers (1 bn); ? Tirailleurs (1 bn); some men of the Guards Depots – 1,850 men; GdD Michel (3,600 men). GdD Roussel d'Hurbal's 6th Dragoon Division: 4e, 5e, 12e, 14e, 16e, 17e, 21e, 24e, 26e, 27e DragRs. GdD Ornano: 7e, 8e and 9e Pv CavRs, Guard Cavalry Depots (321 men). Marmont had 12,386 men; Mortier 10,800. Manning the defences of Paris were 6,000 GdN (VII and IX Légions).

The regiments which actually fought here this day were as follows: Old Guard: 1er and 2e Grenadiers. 1er, 3e, 4e, 5e, 9e, 10e, 11e, 12e, 14e Tirailleurs. Young Guard: Flanqueur Grenadiers; 1er and 2e ChàP; FüsCh; 1er, 3e, 5e, 7e, 8e, 9e, 10e, 12e, 13e, 15e, 16e Voltigeurs; Flanqueur Chasseurs; Vélites de Turin. Cavalry: ChàCh; 2e ChLLR; 1er, 2e, 3e Éclaireurs; 3e Gardes d'Honneur; Foot and Horse Artillery. From the RIdLi: 1er, 2e, 4e, 16e, 25e, 40e, 50e, 58e, 62e, 65e, 70e, 72e, 86e, 88e, 96e, 113e, 121e, 132e, 136e, 141e, 152e, 156e. From the RILé: 1er, 3e, 11e, 16e, 23e, 37e. From the GdN: Brest (1er Bn); Seine (1er Bn Mobile). 1er Corps Franc de la Seine; IR Neufchâtel. From the Cavalry: 1er Carabiniers; 1er, 6e, 8e, 10e CuirRs, 5e, 6e, 7e, 11e, 14e, 18e, 23e, 26e, 28e, 30e DragRs. 1er ChLLR. 2e, 8e, 10e ChàCh; Polish Krakus. Artillery: deployed with Mortier and Marmont were 78 guns; a further 76 were set up in the defences.

French total ca 41,000 men.

French losses 4,000 killed and wounded, 1,000 captured, 126 guns, 2 colours. GdD Ricard, Michel, Arrighi and GdB Pelleport, Cambronne, Fournier and Clavel were among the casualties.

Allied Forces FM Prince von Schwarzenberg commanding.

Prussian Troops – The Army of Silesia FM von Blücher. **I (Prussian) Corps** GdI York: 1st Brigade GM von Pirch II; 1st Ostpr Gren Bn, LeibGren Bn, Westpr Gren Bn, Schl Gren Bn (4 bns); Ostpr Jg Bn (2 coys); 13th Schl LWIR (3 bns); 1 x FAB. 2nd Brigade GL Prince Carl von Mecklenburg: 1st and 2nd Ostpr IRs, 6th Schl LWIR (3 bns each); 1 x FAB. 7th Brigade GM von Horn: LeibIR, 4th Schl LWIR, 15th Schl LWIR (3 bns each); Brand HusR (4 sqns); 1 x FAB. 8th Brigade: GL Prince Wilhelm von Preussen: Brand IR, 12th ResIR, 14th LWIR (3 bns each); 1st Leib-HusR (4 sqns); 1 x FAB. **From GL Kleist's II (Prussian) Corps:** 9th Brigade GM von Klüx: 1st Westpr IR; 6th ResIR (3 bns each); Schl Schützen Bn (2 coys) 12th Brigade GL Prince August von Preussen: 2nd Schl IR, 11th ResIR (3 bns each). **From the Reserve Corps, Army of Bohemia** Obst von Alvensleben: 1st and 2nd Garde zu Fuss (2 bns each); Garde-Jg Bn (1 bn); 1 x FAB. Attached Baden Troops: Garde I Bn (1 bn); 1 x HAB.

Prussian total ca 30,000.

Prussian losses ca 1,353 men.

Baden total ca 600 men.

Baden losses ca 60 men.

Württemberg troops IV Corps (FM Crownprince von Württemberg) of the Army of Bohemia (only the infantry were engaged): GL Baron von Koch; GM von Stockmeyer: Fuss-JgR Nr 9 (2 bns); LtIR Nr 10 (1 bn). GM von Döring: IRs Nr 2, 3, 7 (2 bns each). GM Prince von Hohenlohe-Kirchberg: IRs Nr 4 and 6 (2 bns each); 2 x 6pdr FABs, 1 x Austrian 12pdr FAB.

Württemberg total ca 6,500 men.

Württemberg losses 160 killed, wounded and missing.

Austrian troops of the Army of Bohemia III (Austrian) Corps FZM Count Ignaz Gyulai. Only the following regiments were engaged: IR EH Rudolf Nr 13 (3 bns); ChLLR Rosenberg Nr 6 (6 sqns). Of the Imperial Austrian Reserve of GdC Erbprinz von Hessen-Homburg: Cavalry: 1st Kürassier Division FML Count von Klebelsberg: KürR Kaiser Nr 1 (5 sqns). 2nd Infantry Division FML von Weissenwolf: GM von Luz: Gren Bns Hromada, Lányi.

Austrian total ca 5,000 men.

Austrian losses 82 killed, wounded and missing.

Russian Troops From GdC Count Wittgenstein's VI (Russian) Corps, Army of Bohemia I Infantry Corps GL Prince Gortschakoff II. 5th Division GM Mejenzov: IRs Perm, Mohilev, Sewersk, Kaluga, 23rd and 24th Jägers (2 bns each). 14th Division GM von Helfreich: IRs Tula, Navaginsk, Tenginsk, Estonia, 25th and 26th Jägers (2 bns each); 2 x FAB.

II Infantry Corps GL Prince Eugen von Württemberg: 3rd Division GL Prince Schachoffskoi: IRs Tschernigov, Muromsk, Reval (2 bns each), Selenginsk (1 bn); 20th and 21st Jägers (2 bns each). 4th Division GM von Puschnizky: IRs Tobolsk, Krementschug, Wolhynia (2 bns each); IR Minsk (1 bn); 4th Jägers (2 bns); 34th Jägers (1 bn); 2 x FAB. Cavalry of GL Count von Pahlen III: HusRs Grodno, and Ssum (6 sqns each); HusRs Olviupol and Lubny (4 sqns each); UlR Tschugujev (6 sqns); 5 x Cossack Pulks; 1 x HAB. **From the Imperial Reserve Grenadier Corps of GdC von Rajewsky** 1st Grenadier Division, GL von Tschoglikov: GrenRs Ekaterinoslav, Arakcheyev, Tauride, St Petersburg, Perm, Kexholm (1 bn each). 2nd Grenadier Division GL von Paskevitsch: GrenRs Kiev, Moscow, Astrakhan, Fanagoria, Siberia, Little Russia and Grand Princess Catharina (1 bn each); 3 x FAB. From the Reserve Cavalry, 2nd Kürassier

Division: GL von Kretov: KürRs Ekaterinoslav, Astrakhan, Gluchov, Pleskov (4 sqns each). Part of **Langeron's Corps (Army of Silesia)** was involved right at the end of the battle; mainly artillery: exact details not known.

Russian total 16,000 men.

Russian losses ca 5,050 killed, wounded and missing; of these, 650 were from Langeron's corps.

Comment Due to very poor management of their superior forces and badly coordinated timing, the Allied commanders allowed the Russian troops first engaged (Pahlen's cavalry, Kretov's Kürassiers, Gortschakoff's I and Württembergs's II Infantry Corps) to be very badly mauled, fighting alone for some hours before the Prussians, Württembergers and Austrians came up. As usual, the losses suffered by both sides are variously reported and contradictory. This was the end for Napoleon (temporarily at least); on 6 April he abdicated.

Sources Zelle, Wrede, Damitz, Martinien, Stadlinger.

NL Courtray, 31 March 1814, clash

A small town in western Belgium, between Bruges and Lille and on the River Leie, near the junction of Motorways A14/E17 and A17.

A French victory over the Saxons.

(Last action – Bergen-op-Zoom, 8 March; next action – Antwerp, 4 May).

French Forces GdD Maison commanding: GdDs Barrois, Solignac, Roguet and the Cavalry of the Imperial Guard; 2e (Dutch) ChLLR, ChàCh, 1er Gardes d'Honneur; 3e, 4e, 9e, 10e, 12e, 13e, Tirailleurs, 17e and 51e RIdLi, 27e RILé.

French total ca 7,500 infantry, 2,000 cavalry, 36 guns.

French losses Not known exactly; 24 officer casualties were reported; perhaps 800 men were killed, wounded and missing.

Saxon Troops [of the II (Federal German) Corps of GdC the Duke of Weimar and Eisenach]: GL Baron von Thielemann commanding: 1st, 2nd, 3rd and 4th Saxon LWIRs; 1 cavalry sqn. The Russian Cossack Pulks of Colonels Bihalof I and Robreef. 1 x FAB.

Saxon total ca 3,800 men, 6 guns.

Saxon losses 20 officers, 675 men killed and wounded; 19 officers, 1,194 men and 2 guns captured.

Sources Martinien, Zelle, Damitz.

FS Romans-sur-l'Isère 2 April 1814, capture

A small town in southern France on the River Isère (an eastern tributary of the Rhône), at the junction of Routes 532 and 538, 18 km northeast of Valence.

An Austrian victory over the French.

(Last action – Limonest, 16–20 March; next action – Voreppe, 2 April).

French Forces 1er and 23e RILé; 7e RIdLi.

French total ca 1,000 men.

French losses Not known exactly but very light.

Austrian Forces FML Baron Bianchi commanding: IRs Hiller Nr 2 (3 bns); Esterházy Nr 32 (3 bns); H Colloredo Nr 33 (2nd Bn); Davidovich Nr 34 (1st and 2nd bns); ChLR Vincent Nr 4 (6 sqns); 4 x FAB.

Austrian total ca 6,200 men.

Austrian losses Not known exactly but very light.

Comment 'Mopping up' operation.

Sources Wrede, Martinien.

FS Voreppe, 2 April 1814, capture

A village in southern France, just north of the River Isère, on Route N95 about 18 km northwest of Grenoble and 60 km upstream from Romans.

An Austrian victory over French.

(Last action – Romans, 2 April; next action – Besançon, 20 April).

French Forces 18e RILé; 62e and 156e RIdLi.

French total ca 1,300 men.

French losses Not known exactly but very light.

Austrian Forces IRs Hessen-Homburg Nr 19 (3 bns); Argenteau Nr 35 (3 bns); Erbach Nr 42 (1st Bn); Simbschen Nr 48 (1st Bn); Froon Nr 54 (3 bns); Ignaz Gyulai Nr 60 (3rd Bn).

Austrian total ca 10,000 men.

Austrian losses Not known exactly but very light.

Comment 'Mopping up' operation.

Sources Wrede, Martinien.

FP Étauliers, 6 April 1814, clash

A hamlet in western France, about 7 km east of the estuary of the River Gironde, 13 km northeast of Blaye on a minor road west of the motorway N137/E5. Not shown on modern maps.

An Allied victory over the French.

(Last action – Tarbes, 20 March; next action – Toulouse, 10 April).

French Forces GdB L'Huillier commanding: 27e, 105e, 120e RIdLi (4 bns); Pv CavR (3 sqns), 2 guns.

French total ca 2,000 men.

French losses 20 officers, 300 men captured, 2 guns; the rest mainly dispersed and went home.

Allied Forces. MG Dalhousie commanding: Gardiner's Brigade: 1/6th, 2/24th, 2/56th Foot (1 bn each); Brunswick Oels (2 coys). Doyle's Brigade: 7th Portuguese LIR (2 bns); 2nd Caçadores (1 bn); 12th LDR (1 sqn), 4 guns.

Allied total ca 2,500 men.

Allied losses ca 20 killed and wounded.

Sources Oman, Martinien.

SX Glogau, 1 September 1813 – 10 April 1814, siege and capitulation

A fortified town in the Prussian Province of Silesia, nowadays 'Glogow' in Poland, on Route 34, 120 km east of Cottbus at the crossing of the River Oder (Odra).

An Allied victory over the French.

(Last action – Küstrin, 7 March; next action – Würzburg, 2 May).

French Garrison GdD Laplane commanding: elements of: 138e, 151e RIdLi, 1st Croatian IR, 12e RILé, IR Joseph Napoleon, 2nd Baden LIR, IR Frankfurt.

French total ca 5,000 men.

French losses Not exactly known but light.

Russo-Prussian Forces Russian GL Baron Rosen commanding. **Russians:** Kostroma Militia Division GL Bardakov: 1st–4th Kostroma MIRs (3 bns each). Riasan Militia Division GM Ismailov: 1st, 2nd, 4th Riasan MIRs (3 bns each); Riasan Militia JgR (3 bns). Simbirsk Militia Division GM Vassilkichov: 2nd and 3rd Simbirsk MIRs (3 bns each). 1 x heavy FAB, 2 x light FABs. Light Cavalry: 2nd Metscherenski Cossack Pulk, 8th, 12th, 13th, 16th BaschkirRs. **Prussians:** GM von Heister: 3rd, 12th, 16th Schl LWIRs (3 bns each), 1st and 2nd Westpr and 1st Schl Garrison bns. Schl Landjägers (1 bn each); 4th Schl LWKR (4 sqns), 2 x 6pdr FABs. **Total** ca 8,400 men.

Russo-Prussian total ca 21,000 men.

Russo-Prussian losses Not exactly known but light.

Comment The German and Croatian troops were released and marched home; the remaining 2,400 French troops marched out with honours of war, laid down their arms and marched off to France on condition that they would not serve against the Allies for a year.

Sources Plotho, Sporschil, Martinien, Damitz.

FP Toulouse, 10 April 1814, battle

The capital city of the southeastern French Département of Haute-Garonne on the eastern bank of the River Garonne, between it and the Canal du Midi and at the junction of Routes N72 and N80.

An Anglo-Portuguese victory over the French.

(Last action – Étauliers, 6 April; next action – Bayonne, 14 April).

French Forces M Soult commanding: **GdD Daricau's 1st Division** GdB Fririon: 6e RILé, 76e RIdLi (1 bn each); 69e RIdLi (2 bns) – 1,840 men. GdB Berlier: 36e and 65e RIdLi (2 bns each); 39e RIdLi (1 bn) – 1,999 men. **GdD Darmagnac's 2nd Division** GdB Leseur: 31e RILé, 75 RIdLi (2 bns each); 51e RIdLi (1 bn) – 2,387 men. GdB Menne: 118e, 120e RIdLi (3 bns each) – 2,635 men. **GdD Taupin's 4th Division** GdB Rey: 12e RILé, 32e and 43e RIdLi – 3,039 men. GdB Gasquet: 47e RIdLi (2 bns); 55e and 58e RIdLi (1 bn each) – 2,416 men. **GdD Maransin's 5th Division** GdB Barbot: 40e RIdLi (2 bns); 4e RILé; 50e RIdLi (1 bn each) – 2,045 men. GdB Roguet: 27e, 34e, 59e RIdLi (1 bn each) – 1,672 men. **GdD Villatte's 6th Division** GdB St Pol: 21e RILé, 86e, 96e, 100e RIdLi (3 bns) – 2,658 men. GdB Lamorandière: 28e RILé, 103e RIdLi (1 bn each); 119e RIdLi (2 bns) – 1,951 men. **GdD Harispe's 8th Division** GdB Dauture: 9e, 25e and 34e RILé (2 bns each) – 2,198 men. GdB Baurot: 10e RILé (2 bns), 45e, 81e, 115e, 116e, 117e RIdLi (1 bn each) – 2,886 men. **GdD Travot's Reserve Division** GdBs Pourailly and Vuillemont: 8 bns conscripts of the new levy – 7,267 men. **Divisional total** 34,993 men. Cavalry GdD P Soult: GdB Berton: 2e HusR, 13e and 21e ChàCh – 1,339 men. GdB Vial: 5e, 10e, 15e, 22e ChàCh – 1,361 men. Artillery, train, pontonniers (2 coys) – 3,603 men. Engineers and sappers – 541 men. Gendarmerie – 206 men.

French total 42,043 men.

French losses 231 officers, 3,005 men killed, wounded and missing.

French officer losses at Toulouse

	Killed	Wounded	Total
Taupin's Division	5	23	28
Maransins's Division	1	11	12
Daricau's Division	5	18	23
Darmagnac's Division	9	32	41
Villatte's Division	1	20	21

	Killed	Wounded	Total
Harispe's Division	10	54	64
Travot's Conscripts	—	3	3
Cavalry	2	12	14
Artillery	—	6	6
Engineers and Train	—	3	3
État-Major	2	14	16
Total	35	196	231

These officer-casualties, 231 in all out of a total of 3,236 casualties of all ranks, are 1 to 15, when we have deducted the 16 État-Major casualties. The British proportion was 1 to 14.

Allied Forces The Marquess of Wellington commanding.

Infantry:	
2nd Division (W Stewart):	
British Brigades of Barnes, Byng and O'Callaghan	4,838
Harding's Portuguese	2,102
	6,940
3rd Division (Picton):	
British Brigades of Brisbane and Keane	3,157
Power's Portuguese	1,409
	4,566
4th Division (Cole):	
British Brigades of Ross and Anson	3,539
Vasconcellos's Portuguese	1,824
	5,363
6th Division (Clinton):	
British Brigades of Pack and Lambert	3,803*
Douglas's Portuguese	1,890
	5,693
Light Division:	
British	2,799
Portuguese	1,476
	4,275
Le Cor's Division:	
Brigades of Buchan and Almeida	3,952

Total	
Anglo-Portuguese Infantry	30,789
Of which	
British	18,136
Portuguese	12,653
Freire's Spaniards:	
Marcilla's Division	3,959
Espeleta's Division	3,576
Sappers, &c.	381
	7,916
Morillo's Spaniards	2,001
Total infantry, sappers etc	40,706

Cavalry:	
C Manners's Brigade	1,426
Bülow's Brigade	701
Fane's Brigade	816
Vivian's Brigade	939
Somerset's Brigade	1,717
Clifton's Brigade	891
Total Cavalry	6,490

* = The 1/32nd of Lambert's brigade was absent

Artillery:	
British	1,510
Portuguese	440
	1,950

NB It is impossible to give the numbers of engineers, train, &c, as the figures in the returns include all those present at the siege of Bayonne and at Bordeaux. The total must have been under 500:

Total	
Infantry	40,706
Cavalry	6,490
Artillery	1,950
	49,146

British losses

	killed		wounded		missing		Total
	officers	men	officers	men	officers	men	
2nd Division							
Byng's Brigade	no losses						
Barnes's Brigade:							
1/50th Foot	—	2	2	8	—	—	12
1/71st Foot	—	3	—	13	—	—	16
1/92nd Foot	—	—	—	—	—	—	—

	killed		wounded		missing		Total
	officers	men	officers	men	officers	men	
O'Callaghan's Brigade:							
1/28th Foot	—	3	3	25	—	—	31
2/34th Foot	—	2	1	11	—	—	14
1/39th Foot	—	—	1	4	—	—	5
2nd Division Total	—	*10*	*7*	*61*	—	—	*78*
3rd Division							
Brisbane's Brigade							
1/45th Foot	1	7	8	72	—	5	93
1/74th Foot	—	32	7	72	2	—	113
1/88th Foot	—	8	2	76	—	—	86
5/60th Foot	—	11	3	48	—	—	62
Keane's Brigade							
1/5th Foot	—	—	—	3	—	—	3
2/83rd	—	—	—	1	—	—	1
2/87th	1	7	2	17	—	—	27
94th Foot	—	1	—	5	—	—	6
3rd Division Total	*2*	*66*	*22*	*294*	*2*	*5*	*391*
4th Division							
Anson's Brigade							
3/27th Foot	2	23	5	76	—	—	106
1/40th Foot	—	7	8	71	—	—	86
1/48th Foot	—	5	4	39	—	—	48
2nd Provisional (2nd and 2/53rd Foot)	—	2	4	27	—	—	33
Ross's Brigade							
1/7th Foot	—	1	—	3	—	—	4
1/20th Foot	2	—	7	—	3	12	
1/23rd Foot	—	1	—	7	—	—	8
4th Division Total	*4*	*39*	*28*	*223*	*3*	*12*	*309*
6th Division							
Pack's Brigade							
1/42nd Foot	4	50	22	337	1	—	414
1/79th Foot	3	16	15	179	—	1	214
1/91st Foot	—	18	6	87	—	—	111
Lambert's Brigade							
1/11th Foot	1	14	6	121	—	—	142
1/36th Foot	1	38	9	100	—	4	152
1/61st Foot	1	16	18	136	—	—	171
6th Divisional Total	*10*	*152*	*76*	*960*	*1*	*5*	*1,204*
Light Division							
1/52nd Foot	—	—	—	5	—	—	5

	killed		wounded		missing		Total
	officers	men	officers	men	officers	men	
1/95th Foot	—	7	1	11	—	—	19
3/95th Foot	—	3	—	29	—	—	32
No Losses in 1/43rd and 2/95th	—	—	—	—	—	—	—
Light Division Total	—	*10*	*1*	*45*	—	—	*56*
Cavalry:							
No Losses in Fane's, Bülow's and Clifton's Brigades.							
C Manners's Brigade							
5th DG	—	1	1	2	—	—	4
3rd Dragoons	—	—	1	5	—	—	6
4th Dragoons	—	2	1	5	—	—	8
Somerset's Brigade							
7th Hussars	—	—	—	—	—	—	—
10th Hussars	1	4	1	6	—	—	12
15th Hussars	—	—	—	4	—	—	4
Vivian's Brigade							
1st Hussars KGL	—	1	1	14	—	—	16
18th Hussars	—	—	—	—	—	—	—
Cavalry Total	*1*	*8*	*5*	*36*	—	—	*50*
Artillery:							
Horse Artillery	—	1	—	7	—	—	8
Field Artillery	—	6	—	5	—	—	11
KGL Artillery	1	2	—	5	—	—	8
Artillery Total	*1*	*9*	—	*17*	—	—	*27*
Total British losses	***18***	***294***	***139***	***1,636***	***6***	***22***	***2,115***

Portuguese losses

No losses in Le Cor's divisions (brigades Almeida and Buchan) nor in Harding's brigade (2nd Division).

	killed		wounded		missing		Total
	officers	men	officers	men	officers	men	
3rd Division:							
Power's Brigade							
9th Line	—	—	—	—	—	—	—
21st Line	1	4	1	14	—	—	20
11th Caçadores	—	8	3	12	—	—	23
4th Division:							
Vasconcellos's Brigade							
11th Line	1	5	—	16	—	—	22
23rd Line	—	25	2	25	—	—	52
7th Caçadores	—	7	2	25	—	—	34

	killed		wounded		missing		Total
	officers	men	officers	men	officers	men	
6th Division:							
Douglas' Brigade							
8th Line	2	32	3	65	—	—	102
12th Line	1	30	3	139	—	—	173
9th Caçadores	—	7	2	32	—	—	41
Light Division:							
17th Line	—	—	—	5	—	—	5
1st Caçadores	—	7	—	28	—	—	35
3rd Caçadores	—	5	—	13	—	—	18
Artillery	—	3	1	4	—	—	8
Total Portuguese	5	133	17	378	—	—	533
Total Spaniards	12	193	86	1,631	—	—	1,922
Total British	16	296	132	1,643	3	13	2,103
General Allied Total	***33***	***622***	***235***	***3,652***	***3***	***13***	***4,558***

Comment Wellington's army had cracked a very tough nut, rich in natural and artificial obstacles, with surprising ease. Soult evacuated the city on the morning of 11 May after Beresford, Freire's Spaniards, the 6th Division, Douglas' and Vasconcellos's Portuguese captured the key Mont Rave after a heavy fight with the divisions of Villatte, Harispe and Taupin. The city was royalist and declared for the king, inviting Wellington to enter. Apart from General Thouvenot's spiteful, and totally needless sortie from Bayonne on 14 April, this was the last action of the war in southern France.

Sources Oman, Martinien.

FE Belfort, 24 December 1813 – 12 April 1814, blockade and capitulation

A fortress in eastern France, 75 km northeast of Besançon, at the junction of Routes N54 and N60, west of Bâsle.

An Austrian victory over the French.

(Last action – Laubressel, 3/4 March; next action – Hüningen, 15 April).

French Garrison Col Legrand commanding: exact details not known but including 5e, 11e, 93e, 154e RIdLi (parts of); GdN Jura (2e Élite Bn).

French total 3,000 men.

French losses 1,000 killed or died of wounds and sickness. After laying down their weapons the survivors went free. The fortress was armed with 71 guns.

Austrian Forces GM Drechsel commanding: IRs Kaiser Nr 1 (2nd Bn); Hiller Nr 2 (3 bns); Hessen-Homburg Nr 19 (2 bns); Esterházy Nr 32 (2 bns); Davidovich Nr 34 (2 bns); Vogelsang Nr 47 (3rd Bn); Simbschen Nr 48 (3 bns); J Colloredo Nr 57 (2 bns). NB not all these regiments were present at the same time; about 3,000 men was the total at any one time.

Austrian losses Not exactly known but light.

Sources Martinien, Wrede, Bodart.

IN River Taro, 13 April 1814, clash

A southern tributary of the River Po in northern Italy, 10 km west of Parma towards Piacenza on Route 9.

An Austro-Neapolitan victory over the Franco-Italians.

(Last action – Mantua, 10 March; this was the last action of note in the campaign).

Franco-Italian Forces GdD Maucune: GdB Vandeden. 1ère PvDBde (3 bns); 2e PvDBde (3 bns). GdB Rambourg: 1st Italian LIR (1 bn); 1er ChàCh (3 sqns); 1st and 3rd Italian ChàCh (4 sqns each); 2 x FAB.

Franco-Italian total ca 6,000 men, 12 guns.

Franco-Italian losses Not exactly known but considerable.

Austro-Neapolitan Forces Joachim Murat, King of Naples, commanding; Right hand column: IR Lusignan Nr 16 (1 bn). Centre column: MG Count Starhemberg: IRs Benjowsky Nr 31 (2 bns); GzIR Warasdiner-Kreutzer Nr 5 (2nd Bn); 8th Jg Bn (1 bn); Istrian LW (1 bn); Italian Freikorps (1 bn); HusR Radetzky Nr 5 (8 sqns). MG Eckhardt: IR Bianchi Nr 63 (3 bns); GzIR Gradiskaner Nr 8 (2nd Bn). Left hand column: MG Gober: IR Lusignan Nr 16 (1 bn); IR EH Franz Carl 52 (3 bns); IR EH Carl Nr 3 (1 x LW Bn). A Neapolitan contingent was also present; exact details not known.

Austro-Neapolitan total ca 16–20,000 men.

Austro-Neapolitan losses Not known exactly but light.

Comment Joachim Murat, King of Naples, had at last been spurred into taking action against his ex-allies, the French and Italians, by Napoleon's recent reverses in France. The Franco-Italians withdrew northwest over the River Nura onto Piacenza. A rearguard action took place here next day then hostilities ended as news of Napoleon's abdication became known.

The Blockades 1814 in Italy

The following Austrian forces were deployed at the fortresses shown, all of which held out until the end of hostilities.

Mantua GM von Vlasitz: IRs Württemberg Nr 40 (3 bns), Hohenlohe-Bartenstein Nr 26 (1 bn); GzIR 2nd Szeckler Nr 15 (2nd Bn); HusR Stipsics Nr 10 (2 sqns). FML Ritter von Grammont: GM von Ekhardt: IRs Bianchi Nr 63 (3 bns); GzIR Gradiskaner Nr 8 (2nd Bn); HusR Frimont Nr 9 (4 sqns). GM Baron von Spiegel: IR Lusignan Nr 16 (3 bns); GzIR Otočaner Nr 2 (2nd Bn); HusR Radetzky Nr 5 (4 sqns). FML von Marziani; GM Baron von Wattlet: IR Reisky Nr 10 (4 bns); 9th Jg Bn (1 bn); DragR Hohenlohe Nr 2 (2 sqns). GM von Winzian: IR Splényi Nr 51 (3 bns); IR Wacquant Nr 62 (1 bn). GM Quosdanovich (wounded in the battle of the River Mincio 8 February; replaced by GM Baron von Eberl): IR Coburg Nr 22 (3 bns); IR St Julien Nr 61 (2 bns).

Legnano GM Ritter von Fölseis: GzIR Broder Nr 7 (1 bn); GzIR Deutsch-Banater Nr 12 (2 bns); IR Liechtenstein Nr 12 (LW Bn); HusR Stipsics Nr 10 (2 sqns).

The Blockades: Allied losses	Killed		Wounded		Missing		Total
	officers	men	officers	men	officers	men	
General Staff	2	—	3	—	3	—	8
1st Division (Stopford's, Howard's, and Hinüber's Brigades):							
1/1st Footguards	—	1	—	6	—	—	7
3/1st Footguards	—	2	2	31	1	17	53
1/2nd Footguards	2	32	5	122	—	84	245
1/3rd Footguards	—	35	5	106	1	57	204
1st Lt Bn KGL	—	7	3	17	—	1	28
2nd Lt Bn KGL	—	20	2	39	1	28	90
1st LI Bn KGL	—	4	—	5	—	—	9
2nd LI Bn KGL	2	11	2	21	—	4	40
5th LI Bn KGL	2	7	2	11	—	—	22
5th Division (Hay's Brigade):							
3/1st Foot	—	8	1	12	—	21	42
1/9th Foot	—	2	—	8	—	—	10
1/35th Foot	—	2	2	5	—	—	9
2/47th Foot	—	3	2	11	—	10	26
5/60th Foot (1 coy)	—	—	1	4	—	5	10
Royal Artillery	—	—	2	2	—	—	4
Royal Engineers	—	—	2	—	—	—	2
Portuguese (5th Caçadores and 13th Line)	—	8	2	19	—	—	29
Total losses	8	142	36	419	6	227	838

Venice FML Ritter Marschall; GM Pulszky von Cséfalva: GzIR Oguliner Nr 3 (2nd Bn); IR Deutschmeister Nr 4 (LW Bn); IR Kerpen Nr 49 (1 bn); HusR Stipsics Nr 10 (2 sqns). GM Ritter von Mayer: IR Lindenau Nr 29 (1 bn); IR Württemberg Nr 40 (1 bn); GzIR St Georger Nr 6 (1 bn); GzIR Gradiskaner Nr 8 (1 bn); GzIR 2nd Banal Nr 11 (1 bn); HusR Stipsics Nr 10 (2 sqns).

Palmanuova and Osoppo GM Baron von Rohr: GzIR Szluiner Nr 4 (1 bn); GzIR Peterwardeiner Nr 9 (1 bn); IR Lusignan Nr 16 (1 bn); IR Hohenlohe-Bartenstein Nr 26 (LW Bn); IR Chasteler Nr 27 (LW Bn); Hungarian Insurrektions-HusR (3 sqns).

Baden and Russian troops were employed in the blockades of **Strasbourg**, **Landau**, **Bitche** and **Lichtenberg** on the upper Rhine. **Baden troops** 1st and 2ndDragRs (5 sqns each); Freiwilliges JgRzPf (3 sqns and 2 x 3pdr cannon); 1st Brigade IR Grossherzog Nr 3 (2 bns); LWI Bns Nr 2, 3, 4 (1 bn each). 2nd Brigade IR Graf von Hochberg Nr 2 (2 bns); LWI Bns Nr 1, 5, 6 (1 bn each). 3rd Brigade IR von Stockhorn Nr 1 (2 bns); LWI Bns Nr 7, 8 (1 bn each); 2 x FAB. **Russian troops** Lubenski HusR (3 sqns); Don Cossacks (1 sqn); 10 x 6pdrs, 10 x 12pdr cannon; Cossack Pulk Tschernuschkin; IRs Jaroslav and Libau (3 bns each); DragR Twer (½ sqn).

Sources Wrede, vom Holtz, Vaudoncourt.

FP Bayonne, 14 April 1814, sortie

A Biscayan port in the southwestern French Département of Basses-Pyrénées, on the Rivers Adour and Nive and at the junction of Routes N70 and N80.

An Allied victory over the French.

(Last action – Toulouse, 10 April; next action – Bayonne, 26 April).

French Forces GdD Thouvenot commanding: 66e, 82e, 94e, 119e RIdLi (1 bn each).

French total ca 6,000 men.

French losses total 905: 11 officers, 100 men killed, 42 officers, 736 men wounded, missing – 16 men.

Allied Forces LG Sir John Hope commanding: 1st and 5th Division (see losses for details).

Allied total ca 8,000 men.

Comment Thouvenot already knew that Napoleon had abdicated but mounted this pointless sortie in a fit of spite and frustration. He thus caused over 1,700 casualties to no end whatever. Sir John Hope was wounded and captured after galloping into a mêlée. MG Andrew Hay was killed.

Sources Oman, Martinien.

FE Hüningen, 21 December 1813 – 15 April 1814, failed blockade

A town in Alsace-Lorraine, on the left bank of the Rhine, 4 km north of Bâsle.

A French victory over the Allies.

(Last action – Belfort, 12 April; this was the last action of note in eastern France).

French Garrison GdD Pinaud commanding.

French total 4,000 men including: GdN Bas-Rhin (1er bn d'Élite).

French losses Not known, but light.

Allied Forces GM Baron von Zoller commanding: Austrian Troops. IR Czartoryski Nr 9 (3rd Bn); IR Kaiser Nr 1 (3 bns). Bavarian troops: 2,000 Landwehr and National Guard.

Allied total ca 4,000 men.

Allied losses Not known exactly but light.

FS Besançon, 8 January – 20 April 1814, failed siege

A fortified town in eastern central France, capital of the Département de Doubs on Routes N73, N83 and N57, 200 km west of Bâsle.

A French victory over the Austrians.

(Last action – Voreppe, 2 April; next action – this was the last action of note in southern France).

French Garrison GdD Maraluz commanding: 2e, 38e, 64e, 93e and 154e RIdLi, 3rd Swiss, 4th Swiss, 25e ChàCh and armed citizens of the place.

French total ca 9,000 men.

French losses Not known exactly; 15 officers were killed, 35 wounded; total losses all ranks possibly 1,000.

Austrian Forces FML Prince A Liechtenstein commanding a division of FZM Gyulai's Left Wing of the Army of Bohemia: 12th Jg Bn (1 bn); IRs EH Rainer Nr 11 (2 bns); Reuss-Plauen Nr 17 (LW Bn); Reuss-Greitz Nr 18 (2nd Bn); Strauch Nr 24 (2 bns); Bellegarde Nr 44 (3 bns); Nationales GzIR (1 bn), J Colloredo Nr 57 (3rd and Res Bns); KürR EH Franz Nr 2 (4 sqns); DragR Kaiser Nr 1 (4 sqns); ChLR Vincent Nr 4 (4 sqns); HusR Kienmayer Nr 8 (6 sqns); Gren Bns Haller, Hauenfeld, Moeser (1 bn each).

Austrian total ca 12,000 men.

Austrian losses Not known exactly but light.

Sources Martinien, Wrede, Zelle.

FP Bayonne, 23 February – 26 April 1814, failed blockade

A Biscayan port in the southwestern French Département of Basses-Pyrénées on the Rivers Adour and Nive and at the junction of Routes N70 and N80.

A French victory over the Allies.

(Last action – Bayonne, 14 April. This was the last action in the war in southern France).

French Forces GdD Thouvenot commanding: 5e, 27e RILé; 64e, 66e, 82e, 94e, 95e, 119e, 130e RIdLi. Artillery, engineers, pioniers.

French total ca 14,000 men, 280 guns. Losses* 1,600 killed and wounded, 400 captured.

* = including the 905 casualties of the sortie on 14 April.

Allied Forces LG Sir Hope commanding: **1st Division** Maitland's Brigade 1/1st and 3/1st Footguards. Stopford's Brigade: 1/2nd and 1/3rd Footguards. Hinüber's KGL Brigade: 1st and 2nd Lt Bns, 1st, 2nd and 5th Line Bns. **Total** ca 6,800 men. **5th Division** Hay's Brigade: 3/1st, 1/9th, 1/35th, 2/47th Foot (1 bn each), 5/60th (1 coy). **Total** ca 2,750 men. **Bradford's Portuguese** 13th and 24th LIRs (2 bns each), 5th Caçadores (1 bn). **Total** ca 1,600 men. **Campbell's Portuguese** 4th and 10th LIRs (2 bns each), 10th Caçadores (1 bn). **Total** ca 2,500 men. **Gen Lord Aylmer's Independent Brigade** 1/76th, 2/84th 1/85th Foot (1 bn each). **Total** ca 1,900 men. **Freire's Spaniards****: Divisions of Marcilla, Espeleta, Morillo. **Total Spaniards** ca 10,000 men. Carlos de España's Division – ca 4,000 men. **Allied total** ca 29,500 men.

Allied losses *** ca 1,700 killed and wounded, 300 captured.

** = later called away to join Wellington in time for the battle of Toulouse, 10 April.

*** = including the 838 casualties in the sortie of 14 April.

Sources Oman, Martinien.

SX Würzburg (Marienburg), 24 October 1813 – 2 May 1814, blockade and surrender.

A fortress in central Germany, on the west bank of the River Main at the junctions of Routes B8, B13, B19, just north of Autobahn A3/E41.

An Allied victory over the French.

(Last action – Glogau, 10 April; next action – Mainz, 4 May).

French Garrison GdD Turreau de Linière commanding: 113e RIdLi (2 bns); 127e RIdLi (1 bn); 13e Hus R (1 sqn); Würzburg IR (1 x depot bn); French artillery (2 coys) and sappers (1 coy).

French Total ca 3,000 men.

French losses not known exactly; the French elements (they were of Hanseatic and Italian extraction) marched off to France with 1,886 all ranks, 6 guns and 8 ammunition waggons.

Allied Forces MG Count Spreti commanding the following Baravian units: 2nd LIR (2nd Bn); 4th (2nd Bn); Mobile Legion of the Junkers (1st Bn); Würzburg IR (1 bn). **Total** 1,774 Bavarians, 502 Würzburgers, 1 x FAB. Other Würzburg troops came up later.

Allied losses Not known but very light.

Comment Würzburg's fortress, the Marienburg, is a massive work and easily held the blokading force at bay.

Sources Plotho, Sporschil.

NL Antwerp, 14 January – 4 May 1814, failed blockade

A fortified Belgian port city on the River Schelde.

A French victory over the Allies.

(Last action – Courtray, 31 March; this was the last action of note in Holland).

French Garrison GdD Count Carnot commanding most of I Corps and GdD Roguet's 3rd Division of the Young Guard (9e–13e TirailleurRs). GdD Boyer's 3rd Voltigeur Division (9e–13e VoltigeurRs); 2e ChLLR of the Guard. 13e and 15e RILé, 25e, 28e, 58e and 108e RIdLi, 3e RÉtranger.

French total ca 10,000 men.

French losses Not known exactly.

Allied Forces This force was subject to many changes during the blockade and saw no action other than has already been covered earlier in this work. It included British, Russian, Prussian, Saxon troops and contingents from several minor German states.

Comment Count Carnot (the famous organizer of the French army in the early Revolutionary years) came out of retirement to volunteer his sword for France.

Sources Martinien, Pfannenberg, Lettow-Vorbeck.

SX Mainz, 21 November 1813 – 4 May 1814, failed blockade

A fortress in western Germany, on the west bank of the River Rhine, opposite the confluence with the River Main.

A French victory over the Allies.

(Last action – Würzburg, 2 May; next action – Wesel, 10 May).

French Garrison GdD Count Morand commanding: 9e Tirailleurs and 2e G d'Honneur of the Young Guard; 5e, 10e and 24e RILé; 47e, 67e, 86e, 95e, 102e, 137e, 152e, 156e RIdLi, 2e ChLL GdN.

French total 17,000 men.

French losses Not known exactly.

Allied Forces Russian GdI Count Langeron commanding:

VI Corps GM Prince Scherbatov: 7th Division GM Tallisin. IRs Pskov, Moskow, Liebau, 11th Jägers (2 bns each); IR Sophia, 36th Jägers (1 bn each). 18th Division MG Bernodossov: IRs Vladimir, Dnieprov, Tambov, Kostroma, 28th and 32nd Jägers (1 bn each), 1 x heavy FAB, 2 x light FABs. IX Corps GL Olsufiev: 9th Division GM Udom II. IRs Nascheburg, Yakutsk, 10th and 38th Jägers (1 bn each); IRs Apscheron, Riask (2 bns each). 15th Division GM Rudsevitch: IRs Witebsk, Koslovsk, Kolivan, 22nd Jägers (1 bn each); IR Kurinsk, 12th Jägers (2 bns each). 1 x heavy FAB, 2 x light FABs.

X Corps GL Kapsevitch: 8th Division GM Prince Urusov: IRs Archangel, Old Ingermannland, 37th Jägers (2 bns each), IR Schlüsselburg, 7th Jägers (1 bn each); 22nd Division GM Turtschaninov. IRs Viatka, Staroskolski, 29th Jägers (2 bns each); IR Olonetz, 45th Jägers (1 bn each). 1 x heavy FAB, 2 x light FABs.

I Cavalry Corps GL Baron Korff. From 3rd Dragoon Division: DragRs Tver and Kinburn (2 sqns each). 1st Mounted Rifle Division GM Pantschulidschev: Tchernigov MtdRR (3 sqns); Arsamas MtdRR (1 sqn); Sieversk MtdRR (2 sqns). 2nd Mounted Rifle Division GM Count Pahlen II: Lifland and Dorpat MtdRR (2 sqns each). Light Cavalry GM Grekov VIII: GM Count Witte: 1st, 2nd and 3rd Ukrainian Cossack Pulks (3 sqns each) Cossack Pulks of Kutainikov VIII, Selivanov II, Jsaef II, Zikelef I; 1st Tieptär Cossack Pulk. Reserve Artillery: 1 x heavy FAB, 1 x light FAB, pioniers (2 coys), pontonniers (1 coy), Marines (1 coy).

Allied total ca 30,000 men.

Allied losses Not known exactly; light.

Sources Plotho, Sporschil, Martinien.

SX Wesel, 18 December 1813 – 10 May 1814, failed siege

A fortified town in western Germany, on the east bank of the River Rhine, just north of the confluence with the River Lippe and at the junction of Routes B8, B58 and B70.

A French victory over the Prussians.

(Last action – Mainz, 4 May; next action – Hamburg, 12 May).

French Garrison GdD Bourke commanding: 123e and 127e RIdLi and other units.

French total ca 8,000 men.

French losses Not known exactly.

Allied Forces Initially GM Borstell's 5th Brigade of von Bülow's II (Prussian) Corps until 14 January, then (until early February) the Russian cavalry corps of GL Count Orurk thence GM Putlitz's Prussian brigade of Tauentzien's IV Corps. Average strength ca 8,000 men.

Allied losses Not known exactly.

Sources Plotho, Sporschil, Martinien.

SX Hamburg, 24 December 1813 – 12 May 1814, failed blockade

A fortified port city in northern Germany, on the eastern bank of the River Elbe, 56 km southwest of Lübeck and at the junction of Autobahns A1, A7, A23 and A24.

A French victory over the Allies.

(Last action – Wesel, 10 May; next action – Magdeburg, 14 May).

French Garrison M Davout, Prince of Eckmühl commanding the XIII Corps. 3rd Division GdD Loison: 15e RILé; 44e, 48e, 108e RIdLi. 40th Division GdD Pecheux: 33e RILé, 30e, 61e, 111e RIdLi (2 bns each). The Division of GdD Thiebault: 24e RILé, 3e, 29e, 105e RIdLi (2 bns each); 28e ChàCh; 17e Lithuanian ChLL. The 26e RILé, 18e, 93e and 155e RIdLi, CuirR 4e, 8e and 15e Drag 13e, 20e, ChàCh 2e, 25e, 5e HusR also show officer casualties here.

French total Originally ca 40,000 men.

French losses Not exactly known.

Allied Forces Originally the Hanoverian-Hanseatic Corps of GL Count Wallmoden – Gimborn Hanoverians: I Bns Lüneburg, Bremen-Verden, Bennigsen, Osnabrück (1 bn each), Kielmansegge's Jägers (2 coys); I Bns Lauenburg, Langrehr, Grubenhagen (1 bn each); HusRs Lüneburg, Bremen-Verden (4 sqns each), 1 x FAB. Hanseatic Brigade: 2 bns, 6 sqns, 10 guns. As of 14 April GdK Count Bennigsen's Reserve Army of Poland: Avantgarde: 12th, 26th Divisions, GL Puschkin's Cavalry Division, GL Count Tolstoy's Militia Corps, GM Titov's Militia Corps; GL Tschaplitz's cavalry corps.

Allied total ca 52,000 men.

Allied losses Not exactly known; moderate.

Comment Davout conducted an aggressive defence and refused to recognize the armistice until the end of April. From 25–30 May the French troops marched off home in several columns.

Sources Plotho, Sporschil, Martinien, Sichart.

SX Magdeburg, 15 September 1813 – 14 May 1814, failed blockade

A fortified town in northern Germany, on the west bank of the River Elbe, at the junction of Routes B1, B71, B81 and Autobahn A2, 68 km west of Berlin.

A French victory over the Allies.

(Last action – Hamburg, 12 May; this was the last action in Saxony in 1814).

French Garrison GdD Count Lemarois: initially 20,000 men including elements of: 11e, 24e RILé; 2, 4e, 7e, 46e, 56e, 72e, 85e, 93e, 113e, 125e, 134e, 135e, 136e, 137e, 138e, 139e, 140e, 142e and 144e RIdLi; 4th Polish IR; 1er Carabiniers; 7e, 17e, 27e DragR, 6e ChLL, 2e, 25e, 31e ChàCh, 4e and 11e HusR plus artillery, engineers and reinforcement drafts.

French total ca 20,000 men.

French losses 1,200 killed and died of sickness.

Allied Forces. Prussian GM von Hirschfeldt: 1st ResIR, 6th and 7th Kurmark LWIRs (4 bns each); 5th and 6th Kurmark LWKRs (4 sqns each), 1½ x 6 pdr FABs.

Allied total ca 14,000 men.

Allied losses Not known exactly; moderate.

Comment The garrison strength varied somewhat throughout the blockade as the tide of battle ebbed and flowed.

Sources Plotho, Sporschil, Martinien.

1815

1815 THE ACTIONS

IC Modena, 4 April 1815, clash

A fortified city in northern central Italy, between Reggio and Bologna at the junction of Routes 9 and 12 and between the Rivers Seschia and Panaro.

A Neapolitan victory over the Austrians.

(This was the opening action in central Italy; next action – Occhiobello 7 April).

Neapolitan Forces Gen Filangieri, Gen Carascosa: 1st Infantry Division: GdB Pepe: 2nd LtIR, 1st LIR. GdB Genarro: 3rd and 5th LIR.

Neapolitan totals 8 bns, 12 guns, ca 7,000 men.

Neapolitan losses Gen Filangieri killed (other dead and wounded not known), 9 officers and 400 men captured.

Austrian Forces FML Bianchi commanding: 9th Jägers (1 bn); IR Hessen-Homburg Nr 19 (2 bns); IR Splényi Nr 51 (3 bns); HusR Prinz Regent Nr 5 (6 sqns); 1 FAB and 1 HAB.

Austrian totals 6 bns, 6 sqns, 12 guns, ca 6,600 men.

Austrian losses 79 dead, 316 wounded, 66 missing.

Comment Murat tried to rush the fortified bridge at Castelfranco and was repulsed; he tried again at Spilimbergo, got across but was then thrown back with heavy losses. He tried a third time at Castelfranco where, due to a misunderstanding, the Austrians had evacuated the bridge. The Neapolitans crossed the river and occupied Modena but their nerve was badly shaken. The 2nd Bn IR Hessen-Homburg Nr 19 was cut off and surrounded but fought its way to freedom under General Steffanini. The Austrians fell back via Buonporto to Carpi.

Sources Wrede, ÖMZ 1822 Heft 7.

IC Occhiobello, 7 April 1815, clash

A small town in northeastern central Italy, on the northern bank of the lower River Po, about 10 km north of Ferrara, just west of the Autostrada A13.

An Austrian victory over the Neapolitans.

(Last action – Modena, 4 April; next action – Carpi, 10 April).

Neapolitan Forces King Joachim Murat commanding: Exact details not known; some of the units shown below.

1st Division Gen Carascosa: GdB Pepe: 2nd LtIR, 1st LIR; GdB de Genarro: 3rd and 5th LIR (8 bns); 2 x FAB (12 guns). 2nd Division GdD d'Ambrosio: GdB d'Aquino: 3rd LtIR, 2nd LIR; GdB Medici: 6th and 9th LIR (8 bns); 2 x FAB (12 guns). 3rd Division GdD Lecchi: GdB de Majo: 1st LtIR; 4th LIR; GdB Caraffa: 7th and 8th LIR (8 bns); 2 x FAB (12 guns). 4th (Reserve) Division GdD Prince Pignatelli-Cerchiera: GdB Rossaroli: 7th LtIR; 10th LIR; GdB Roche: 11th and 12th LIR (8 bns); 2 x FAB (12 guns). Line Cavalry Division GdD Rosetti: GdB Fontaine: 1st and 3rd ChLRs; GdB Napoletani: 2nd and 4th ChLRs (16 sqns), 1 x HAB (10 guns).

Neapolitan totals and losses Not known.

Austrian Forces FML Mohr commanding: IR Chasteler Nr 27 (1st and 2nd bns); IR Davidovich Nr 34 (1 bn); IR Hiller Nr 53 (3rd bn).

Austrian losses 22 killed.

Comment Following his initial success at Modena on 4 April, Murat attempted to force the line of the River Po but was thrown back. With disunity among his commanders, desertions increasing daily and with the receipt of Britain's declaration of war against him of 5 April, Murat's resolve began to crumble and he decided to withdraw south again.

Sources Wrede, Revue Historique de l'Armée 1968 Nr 2.

IC Carpi, 10 April 1815, capture of

A small walled town in central Italy, about 18 km north of Modena, over the River Secchia.

An Austrian victory over the Neapolitans.

(Last action – Occhiobello, 7 April; next action – Casaglia, 12 April).

Neapolitan Forces GdB Pepe 2nd LtIR, 1st LIR (4 bns).

Neapolitan totals 5,000 men and 2 guns.

Neapolitan losses Killed and wounded not known, slight, 12 officers and 600 men captured.

Austrian Forces Gen Baron Frimont commanding: FML Baron Bianchi: 9th Jägers (1 bn-), IR Esterházy Nr 32 (1½ bns), HusR Frimont Nr 9 (5 sqns), ½ HAB.

Austrian totals 2 bns, 5 sqns, ½ HAB, ca 2,500 men.

Austrian losses 14 killed, 70 wounded, 32 missing.

Comment The assault was to have been made in two columns but that of Obst Gavenda got lost and did not take part (Jägers (1coy); LI (7coys); HusR (1½ sqns), ½ HAB); Bianchi decided to go in anyway. The Austrian artillery shot in the Novi gate of the town and Bianchi sent a column to take the town from the south side. Seeing the enemy behind them instead of the expected relief column from Modena, the Neapolitans fled.

Sources Wrede, ÖMZ 1822, Heft 7.

IC Casaglia, 12 April 1815, clash

A fortified village in eastern central Italy, 10 km northwest of Ferrara.

An Austrian victory over the Neapolitans.

(Last action – Carpi, 10 April; next action – Ronco, 21 April).

Neapolitan Forces Exact details not known.

Neapolitan losses Unknown killed and wounded, 1 gun.

Austrian Forces FML Mohr commanding: IR St Julien Nr 61 (2 bns); IR Wied-Runkel Nr 34 (3 bns).

Austrian totals 5 bns, ca 4,500 men.

Austrian losses 22 killed, 6 officers and 202 wounded (all from IR St Julien).

Comment GdK Baron Frimont ordered Mohr to raid the Neapolitan-held villages of Ravale and Casaglia out of the Austrian bridgehead at Occhiobello. Ravale was taken but the Neapolitans held on to Casaglia until nightfall when they abandoned it and Ponte-Lagoscurion and fell back into Ferarra.

Sources Wrede, ÖMZ 1823, Heft 7, Chapter VI.

IN Ronco, 21 April 1815, clash

A village in northeastern Italy 4 km southeast of Forli on Route 9 towards Cesena and ca 25 km south of Ravenna.

An Austrian victory over the Neapolitans.

(Last action – Casaglia, 12 April; next action – Cesenatico, 23 April).

Neapolitan Forces King Joachim Murat commanding: GdD Lecchi's 3rd Division: GdB de Majo: 1st LtIR; GdB Caraffa, 7th and 8th LIR (8 bns); 2 x FAB (12 guns); 1st and 3rd ChLRs (8 sqns).

Neapolitan total ca 8,000 men.

Neapolitan losses Not known exactly; moderate.

Austrian Forces FML Count Neipperg commanding: GM Geppert: 11th Jg Bn (1 bn); 1 x bn from Parma; Prince Regent HusR Nr 5 (2 sqns); Liechtenstein HusR Nr 7 (7 sqns); 1 x HAB, pioniers (1coy).

Austrian total ca 3,000 men, 6 guns.

Austrian losses Not known exactly but light.

Comment Lecchi withdrew through Cesena and over the River Savio.

Sources Wrede, Veltzé.

IC Cesenatico, 23 April 1815, clash

A small town on the eastern coast of central Italy, about 20 km northwest of Rimini on Route 16.

An Austrian victory over the Neapolitans.

(Last action – Ronco, 21 April; next action – Pesaro, 28 April).

Neapolitan Forces Gen Neapolitani commanding: exact details not known; probably part of the 3rd Division.

Neapolitan total ca 3,000 men.

Neapolitan losses Over 300 killed and wounded; Gen Neapolitani and 200 others captured. Neapolitani subsequently escaped.

Austrian Forces Major Pirquet commanding the Fenner Jägers (1 bn); 226 men DragR EH Toscana (38 men).

Austrian totals 1 bn, ½ sqn.

Austrian losses 1 officer killed, 2 wounded, 36 Jägers killed and wounded, 5 dragoons killed, 6 wounded.

Comment Major Pirquet gambled that the enemy – who knew how small his force was – would be off guard and rushed into the town and over the single, stone bridge, made his strike and left with his captives before the astonished enemy could gather their wits or their weapons.

Sources Wrede, ÖMZ 1823, Heft 7, Chapter VI.

IC Pesaro, 28 April 1815, raid

A small town on the eastern coast of central Italy, about 35 km southeast of Rimini and 59 km northwest of Ancona, at the mouth of the River Foglia.

An Austrian victory over the Neapolitans.

(Last action – Cesenatico, 23 April; next action – Scapezzano, 1 May).

Neapolitan Forces GdD Carascosa's 1st Division: GdB Pepe: 2nd LtIR, 1st LIR (4 bns); ? ChLR (4 sqns); 1 x FAB (6 guns).

Neapolitan total ca 3,000 men.

Neapolitan losses Killed and wounded not known but very light; 250 captured.

Austrian Forces GM Geppert's Avantgarde: 11th Jg Bn (3coys), HusR Liechtenstein Nr 7 (1 sqn).

Austrian totals ca 400 men.

Austrian losses Unknown but extremely light.

Comment A classical bold raid which really paid off well. It took Carascosa and Pepe some hours to regroup their scattered force. The then withdrew that night to Fano, down the coast.

Sources Wrede, Veltzé.

IN Scapezzano, 1 May 1815, clash

A village in the coastal foothills of northeastern Italy, midway between Ancona and Pesaro, about 4 km inland from Senigallia.

An Austrian victory over the Neapolitans.

(Last action – Pesaro, 28 April; next action – Tolentino, 2/3 May).

Neapolitan Forces LG Carascosa's 1st Division: GdB Pepe: 2nd LtIR, 1st LIR; GdB de Genarro: 3rd and 5th LIRs (8 bns); 2 x FAB (12 guns).

Neapolitan total ca 6,000 men*.

Neapolitan losses Not known

* = another brigade came up in support; exact details not known.

Austrian Forces FML Count Neipperg commanding: GM Geppert: 11th Jg Bn (1 bn); 1 bn of infantry from Parma; HusR Prinz-Regent Nr 5 (2 sqns); HusR Liechtenstein Nr 7 (7 sqns); 1 x HAB, pioniers (1 coy). GM Baron Lauer: IRs Splényi Nr 51, Hessen-Homburg Nr 19 (3 bns each); 1 x FAB. GM Count Haugwitz: IRs Wied-Runkel Nr 34, St Julien Nr 61 (3 bns each); 1 x FAB.

Austrian totals 14 bns, 9 sqns, 20 guns, ca 15,300 men.

Austrian losses Not known exactly but light.

Comment Neipperg wasted 29 April trying to outflank the enemy. His assault on 1 May was completely successful. Carascosa withdrew in good order southeast to behind the River Esino.

Sources Wrede, Veltzé.

IC Tolentino, 3 May 1815, battle

A small town in eastern central Italy on the northern bank of the River Chienti, on Route 77, ca 53 km southwest of Ancona.

An Austrian victory over the Neapolitans.

(Last action – Scapezzano, 1 May; next action – Pontecorvo, 13 May).

Neapolitan Forces King Joachim Murat commanding: **Guards Infantry Division** GdD Prince Pignatelli-Strongoli: Col Taillade: 1st Vélites (2 bns); Voltigeurs (1st and 2nd bns); Col Merliot: 2nd Vélites (2 bns); 2nd ArtilleryR*, EngineerR* (1 bn each). **Divisional total** 5,890 men, 12 guns. **Guards Cavalry Divisions** GdD Livron: GdB Campana: HusR, ChLR (2 sqns each). GdB Giuliani CuirR, ChLLR (2 sqns each); Gren à Ch (1 sqn). **Divisional total** 2,109 men, 8 guns. **1st Division** GdD Carascosa: GdB Pepe: 2nd LtIR, 1st LIR (2 bns each); GdB de Cennaro: 3rd and 5th LIR (2 bns each). **Divisional total** 9,684 men, 12 guns. **2nd Division** GdD d'Ambrosio: GdB d'Acquino 3rd LtIR, 2nd LIR (3 bns each); GdB Medici: 6th and 9th LIR (3 and 2 bns resp). **Divisional total** 8,968 men, 12 guns. **3rd Division** GdD Lecchi: BG de Majo: 1st LtIR, 4th LIR (3 bns each); GdB Caraffa: 7th and 8th LIRs (3 bns each). **Divisional total** 9,358 men, 12 guns. 2nd and 3rd ChLRs (3 sqns each).

Neapolitan total 36,009 men, 56 guns.

Neapolitan losses 1,700 killed and wounded, 2,400 captured, 1 gun, 6 caissons. Gen d'Ambrosio wounded.

* = serving as infantry.

Austrian Forces FML Baron von Bianchi commanding: **FML Baron Mohr Light Division** GM Count Starhemberg 9th Jg Bn (1 bn); Modena IR (1 bn); HusR Prinz-Regent Nr 5 (6 sqns); pioniers (1 coy); 1 x HAB (6 guns). GM Senitzer: IR Wacquant Nr 62 (1 bn); IR Simbschen Nr 48 (2 bns); IR Hiller Nr 2 (2 bns); 1 x FAB (8 guns). **Division of GM Baron von Eckhardt** IR Chasteler Nr 27 (2 bns); IR EH Carl Nr 3 (3 bns); IR Modena (1 bn); 1 x FAB (6 guns). GM Baron von Taxis: DragR Toscana Nr 4 (6 sqns). Reserve FAB (8 guns).

Austrian total ca 9,800 infantry, 933 cavalry, 28 guns.

Austrian losses 210 killed 457 wounded, 143 missing.

Comment The Neapolitan army was a 'one man band' and that man – Murat – could not be everywhere at once, nor could he make up for the deficiencies of his subordinate commanders. The Austrians acted with firm resolution and won the day. In their subsequent retreat eastwards to Macerata, the Neapolitans began to drift away from their colours. Murat's gamble was over and his army fell apart.

Sources Bodart, Wrede, Sporschil, Veltzé.

IN Pontecorvo, 13 May 1815 battle

A town in western central Italy on the River Liri at the crossing of Route 628, about 40 km northeast of the coastal fortress of Gaëta.

A drawn match between the Neapolitans and the Austrians.

(Last action – Tolentino, 2/3 May; next action – Castel di Sangro, 13 May).

Neapolitan Forces Gen Manhe's 'Armata dell Interiore': 11th and 12th LIRs, 9th and 10th PvLIRs, 4th ChLR; Depot troops, Gendarmerie.

Neapolitan total ca 8,000 men. Only the cavalry were engaged.

Neapolitan losses Not known exactly; very light.

Austrian Forces FML Count Nugent's Avantgarde: Obst Urmenyi, Major d'Aspre commanding: 8th Jg Bn (4 coys); IR Wacquant Nr 6 (2 bns); HusR Prinz-Regent Nr 5 (1½ sqns); HusR Liechtenstein Nr 7 (1 sqn); 4 guns.

Austrian total ca 2,400 men.

Austrian losses Not known exactly but very light.

Comment Since Tolentino the Neapolitan army had withdrawn south, its morale decaying daily and the men melting away in hundreds every day. There had been minor skirmishes at Popoli on 7 May and Navelli on 8 May but nothing of any significance. Ancona fortress capitulated on 30 May; Gaëta under Gen Begani, held out until 5 August.

Sources Wrede, Veltzé.

IN Castel di Sangro, 13 May 1815 skirmish

A mountain village in the Appenines of central Italy on the upper River Sangro just east of Route 17 and north of Routes 83 and 558.

An Austrian victory over the Neapolitans.

(Last action – Pontecorvo, 13 May; next action – Mignano, 17 May).

Neapolitan Forces GdB Neri of 4th (Reserve) Division commanding: 7th and 10th LIRs. **Neapolitan total** ca 2,000 men.

Neapolitan losses Killed and wounded unknown; 6 officers and 200 men captured.

Austrian Forces GM Starhemberg commanding: 9th Jg Bn (1 bn). Modena IR (1 bn); HusR Prinz-Regent Nr 5 (4 sqns).

Austrian total ca 2,000 men.

Austrian losses 'Some' killed, 15 wounded.

Comment The Austrian hussars broke the square of the 10th LIR and scattered it. The Neapolitans withdrew southwest towards Gaëta.

Sources Wrede, Veltzé.

IN Mignano, 17 May 1815, raid

A hamlet in the hills of central Italy on the River Volturno between the motorway E45 and Route 6, northeast of the coastal fortress of Gaëta.

An Austrian victory over the Neapolitans.

(Last action – Castel di Sangro, 13 May; next action – This was the last action of the campaign).

Neapolitan Forces M Macdonald, Neapolitan War Minister, commanding the 'Armata dell Interiore' see Pontecorvo for details.

Neapolitan total ca 6,000 men.

Neapolitan losses Killed and wounded very few; 1,000 men, all guns and baggage captured.

Austrian Forces FML Count Nugent commanding: Major d'Aspre's Avantgarde 8th Jg Bn (4 coys); IR Wacquant Nr 6 (2 bns); HusR Prinz-Regent Nr 5 (1½ sqns); HusR Liechtenstein Nr 7 (1 sqn); 4 guns.

Austrian total ca 2,200 men.

Austrian losses None.

Comment D'Aspre mounted a midnight raid and the entire enemy force fled. On 20 May peace negotiations began. Joachim Murat, once 'King of the Cossacks' as Napoleon scornfully dubbed him in 1812, sometime King of Naples, was arrested on 8 October 1815 in Pizzo, tried and shot on 13 October.

Sources Wrede, Veltzé.

IC Ancona 5–30 May, blockade and capitulation of

A fortified port on the eastern Italian coast, on Route 16 between Pesaro (in the north) and Civitanova Marche in the south.

An Allied victory over the Neapolitans.

(Last action – Mignano, 17 May; next action – Gaëta, 5 August).

Neapolitan Forces GM Baron Monte Majo commanding: Exact details not known; 1,500 men.

Neapolitan losses ca 1,000 men marched out with honours of war, laid down their weapons and were declared prisoners of war.

Allied Forces Austrians GM Geppert commanding: 11th JG Bn (1 bn); Parma IR (1 bn); HusR Prinz-Regent Nr 5 (2 sqns); HusR Liechtenstein Nr 7 (7 sqns).

* = An Anglo-Austrian Flotilla sealed off the fortress on the sea side.

Allied total ca 2,300 men.

Allied losses Not known exactly but very light.

NL Fleurus, Gilly and Gosselies, 15 June 1815, clashes

Villages in the southern Belgian province of Hainaut; 3 km to 8 km northeast of Charleroi on the River Sambre, close to the French border.

A victory of the French over the Prussians.

(This was the opening action of the campaign in the Netherlands; next action – Ligny, 16 June).

French Forces Emperor Napoleon I commanding:

Imperial Guard Cavalry: GdD Count Guyot;

Grenadiers à Ch and DragR (13 sqns). **3rd Cavalry Division (of Vandamme's III Corps)** GdD Baron Domon; 4e ChàCh (3 sqns). **Reserve Cavalry Division of IV Corps** GdD Jacquinot; 15e DragR (3 sqns); 63e DragR (4 sqns). **8th Division of III Corps** GdD Baron Lefol 15e RILé (3 bns).

French totals 3 bns, 24 sqns, 36 guns, ca 8,000 men.

French losses ca 600 killed (including Gen Letort) and wounded.

Prussian Forces LG von Ziethen's I Corps: **1st Brigade** MG von Steinmetz = 12th and 24th LIR, 1st Westfalian LWIR and Silesian Rifles (1st and 3rd coys); 9½ bns. **2nd Brigade** MG von Pirch II = 6th and 28th LIR and 2nd Westfalian LWIR; 9 bns. **3rd Brigade** MG von Jagow = 7th and 29th LIR, 3rd Westfalian LIWR and Silesian Rifles (2nd and 4 coy); 9½ bns. **Reserve Cavalry LG von Röder** 1st Brigade MG von Treskow = Brandenburg DragR; 1st Westprussian DragR Nr 2; Brandenburg UlR (12 sqns). 2nd Brigade Obstlt von Lützow = UlR Nr 6; 1st and 2nd Kurmark LWCR; 1st Silesian HusR; 1st Westfalian LWCR; (20 sqns). **Artillery** Obst von Lohmann. 12-pounder foot batteries Nrs 2, 6 and 9; 9-pounder foot batteries Nrs 1, 3, 7, 8 and 15; howitzer battery Nr 1; HA batteries Nrs 2, 7 and 10. 1,019 gunners. Totals 28 bns, 23,166 infantry, 32 sqns, 1925 cavalry, 12 batteries, 96 guns.

Prussian losses 1,200 men killed, wounded, captured and missing.

Comment Napoleon's initial strikes at the divided Allies with himself at Charleroi and Ney at Quatre-Bras were well thought through and had not been expected by Wellington.

Sources Siborne, Bredow-Wedel.

NL Ligny, 16 June, battle

A village in southern Belgium, 20 km northwest of Namur.

A French victory over the Prussians.

(Last actions – Fleurus, Gilly and Gosselies, 15 June; next action – Quatre Bras, 16 June).

French Forces Emperor Napoleon I commanding.

The Imperial Guard GdD Count Drouot. GdD Count Friant: 1er and 2e Grenadiers (4 bns). GdD Count Roguet: 3e and 4e Grenadiers (3 bns). GdD Count Barrois: 1er and 3e Voltigeurs (4 bns). GdD Count Guyot: DragR and GrenàCh (13 sqns); 2e ChàCh (4 sqns). Artillery: 9 x foot and 4 x HABs, Sailors (1 coy); Engrs (1 coy). **Imperial Guard totals** 11 bns, 6,040 infantry, 17 sqns, 1,900 cavalry, 13 batteries, 96 guns.

III Corps GdD Count Vandamme. 8th Division GdD Baron Lefol: 23e, 37e and 64e RIdLi, 15 RILé (11 bns). **10th Division** GdD Baron Habert: 22e, 34e, 70e and 88e RIdLi (12 bns). **11th Division** GdD Berthezène: 12e, 56e, 86e RIdLi (6 bns). **3rd Cavalry Division** GdD Baron Domon: 12e ChàCh (4 sqns). 5 artillery batteries – 38 guns. **III Corps totals** 29 bns, 4 sqns, 38 guns.

IV Corps GdD Count Gérard. 12th Division GdD Baron Pecheux: 30e, 63e and 96e RIdLi (10 bns). **13th Division** GdD Baron Vichery: 48e, 59e, 69e and 76e RIdLi (8 bns). **14th Division** GdD Hulot: 9e RILé, 44e, 50e and 111e RIdLi (8 bns). **Reserve Cavalry Division** GdD Baron Jacquinot: 6e and 16e DragR (8 sqns). 5 artillery batteries, 38 guns. **IV Corps totals** 26 bns, 8 sqns, 38 guns.

Reserve Cavalry Marshal Grouchy.

I Cavalry Corps GdD Count Pajol. **4th Cavalry Division** GdD Baron Soult: 4e, 5e HusR (8 sqns). **5th Cavalry Division** GdD Baron Subervie: 1er ChLL (4 sqns). 2 HAB.

II Cavalry Corps GdD Count Exelmans. **9th Cavalry Division** GdD Strolz: 5e DragR (4 sqns). **10th Cavalry Division** GdD Baron Chastel: 4e, 12e, 14e and 17e DragR (15 sqns). 2 x HAB.

III Cavalry Corps GdD Count Kellermann. **11th Cavalry Division** GdD Baron L'Heritier: 8e and 11e CuirR (5 sqns). 1 HAB.

Reserve Cavalry totals 36 sqns, 66 guns.

IV Cavalry Corps GdD Count Milhaud. **14th Cavalry Division** GdD Baron Delort: 6e, 9e and 10e CuirR (9 sqns).

VI Corps GdD Count Lobau. **20th Division** GdD Baron Jeannin 107e RIdLi (2 bns).

I Corps GdD Count d'Erlon **1st Division** GdD Guyot: 55e RIdLi (2 bns). **2nd Division** GdD Donzelot: 51e RIdLi (2 bns).

French totals 70 bns, 74 sqns, 244 guns.

French losses Not exactly known; estimated generally to have been about 12,000 killed, wounded and missing.

Officer losses were as follows: 3 generals, 3 colonels, 9 majors and 74 others dead. 11 generals, 7 colonels, 24 majors and 394 wounded.

Sources Siborne, Zelle, Martinien.

The Prussian Army at Ligny, 16 June 1815 FM Prince Blücher von Wahlstadt commanding.

I Corps GL von Ziethen. **1st Brigade** GM von Steinmetz: 2nd Brandenburg IR Nr 12 (3 bns); LIR Nr 24 (3 bns): 1st Westfalian LWIR (3 bns); Silesian Rifles (1st and 3rd coys). **Total** 9½ bns. **2nd Brigade** GM von Pirch II: 1st West Prussian IR Nr 6 (3 bns); 28th LIR (1 bn*); 2nd Westfalian LWIR (3 bns*). **Total** 7 bns*. **3rd Brigade** GM von Jagow: 2nd West Prussian IR Nr 7 (3 bns); 29th LIR (3 bns); 3rd Westfalian LWIR (3 bns); Silesian Rifles (2nd and 4th coys). **Total** 9½ bns. **4th Brigade** GM von Henkel: 19th LIR (3 bns); 4th Westfalian LWIR (3 bns). **Total** 6 bns. **Reserve Cavalry** GL von Röder **1st Brigade** GM von Treskow: 1st West Prussian DragR Nr 2, 5th DragR (Brandenburg) Brandenburg UlR Nr 3 (4 sqns each). **2nd Brigade** Obstlt von Lützow: 6th UlR; 1st and 2nd Kurmark LWCR; 1st Westfalian LWCR (4 sqns each); 1st Silesian HusR Nr 4 (4 sqns). **Reserve Artillery** Obst von Lehmann: 12-pounder foot batteries Nrs 2, 9, 6-pounder foot batteries Nrs 1, 3, 7, 8 and 15; howitzer battery Nr 1; HA batteries Nrs 2, 7 and 10. **I Corps totals** 32 bns, 26,000 infantry, 32 sqns, 1,925 cavalry, 12 batteries, 1,019 gunners and 96 guns.

* = The Füsilier bns of the 28th LIR and the 2nd Westfalian LWIR had lost so many men at Gosselies and Gilly on 15 June that they were combined into 1 weak battalion as were the two weak Musketier bns of 28th LIR.

II Corps LG von Pirch I: **5th Brigade** GM von Tippelskirchen: 1st Pommeranian LIR Nr 2; 25th LIR; 5th Westfalian LWIR (9 bns). **6th Brigade** GM von Krafft: Colberg LIR Nr 9; 26th LIR, 7th Elb LWIR (9 bns). **7th Brigade** GM von Brause: LIR Nr 14; 22nd LIR; 2nd Elb LWIR (9 bns). **8th Brigade** Obst von Langen: 21st and 23rd LIRs; 3rd Elb LWIR (9 bns). **Reserve Cavalry** LG von Jürgass. **1st Brigade** Obst von Thümen: Silesian UlR Nr 2; Neumark DragR Nr 6; HusR Nr 11 (12 sqns). **2nd Brigade** Obst Count von Schulenburg: DragR Königin Nr 1; 4th Kurmark LWCR (8 sqns). **3rd Brigade** Obstlt von Sohr: Brandenburg HusR Nr 3; Pommeranian HusR Nr 5; 5th Kurmark LWCR; Elb LWCR (16 sqns). **Reserve Artillery** Obst von Röhl. 12-pounder foot batteries Nrs 4 and 8; 6-pounder foot batteries Nrs 5, 10, 12, 34 and 37; HA batteries Nrs 5, 6 and 14. **II Corps totals** 36 bns, 25,836 infantry, 36 sqns, 4,468 cavalry, 10 batteries, 1,454 gunners and 80 guns.

III Corps LG Count von Thielmann. **9th Brigade** GM von Borcke: Leib IR Nr 8; 30th LIR; 1st Kurmark LWIR (9 bns). **10th Brigade** Obst von Kämpffen: 27th LIR; 2nd Kurmark LWIR (6 bns). **11th Brigade** Obst von Luck: 3rd and 4th Kurmark LWIR (6 bns). **12th Brigade** Obst von Stülpnagel: 31st LIR; 5th and 6th Kurmark LWIR (9 bns). **Reserve Cavalry** G von Hobe. **1st Brigade** Obst von der Marwitz: 7th UlR (3 sqns); 8th UlR (4 sqns); **2nd Brigade** Obst Count von Lottum: 5th UlR (3 sqns); 7th DragR Nr 4 (4 sqns); 3rd, 6th and 9th HusR (3 sqns). Kurmark LWCR (8 sqns). **Reserve Artillery** Obst von Mohnhaupt: 6-pounder foot batteries Nrs 18 and 35; 12-pounder foot battery Nr 7; HA batteries Nrs 18, 19 and 20. **III Corps Totals** 30 bns, 20,611 infantry, 24 sqns, 2,405 cavalry, 6 batteries, 964 gunners and 48 guns.

Prussian totals at Ligny 100 bns, 74,334 infantry, 92 sqns, 8,798 cavalry, 28 batteries, 3,437 gunners, 224 guns.

Prussian losses Different sources give widely varying figures. Bodart says 16,000 killed and wounded, 8,000 missing and 21 guns. Renouard gives 11-12,000 killed, wounded and missing and 16 guns. The 11th Brigade lost only 98 men.

Comment Due to the very cut-up terrain, the Prussian high command soon lost control of the battle and it passed down to company commander level.

Sources Siborne, Zell, Renouard, Martinien.

NL Quatre-Bras, 16 June 1815, battle

A village in southern Belgium, about 15 km south of Brussels, at the junction of the roads from Brussels to Charleroi and from Nivelles to Namur.

A drawn match.

(Last action – Charleroi (Gilly); 15 June; next action – Waterloo, 18 June).

French Forces M Ney, Prince of the Moskwa, commanding.

II Corps GdD Count Reille*. **5th Division** LG Baron Bachelu: 2e RILé; 61e, 72e and 108e RIdLi (11 bns). **6th Division** Prince Jerome Napoleon: 1er RILé; 1er, 2e and 3e RIdLi (11 bns). **9th Division** GdD Count Foy: 4e RILé; 92e, 93e and 100e RIdLi (10 bns). **2nd Light Cavalry Division** LG Baron Piré: 1er and 6e ChàCh (8 sqns); 5e and 6e Lanciers (7 sqns). Artillery 5 foot and 1 x HAB, 46 guns.

GdD Lefebvre-Desnouettes Lanciers and ChàCh of the Imperial Guard** (19 sqns, ca 1,900 men).

III Cavalry Corps***GdD Kellermann, Count de Valmy. **11th Heavy Cavalry Division** GdD Baron l'Heritier: 8e and 11e Cuir R (5 sqns); 1 x HAB, 6 guns.

French totals 32 bns, 19,750 infantry, 58 sqns, 6,945 cavalry, 8 artillery batteries, 58 guns.

French losses Not exactly known; estimated at 4,400 dead, wounded and missing.

* = the 7th Division (GdD Count Girard) was at Ligny.

** = left soon after the start of the battle.

*** = did not arrive until late afternoon; I Corps did not arrive until after the battle was over.

Allied Forces The Prince of Orange, (later the Duke of Wellington) commanding.

2nd Dutch-Belgian Division LG H G Baron de Perponcher. **1st Brigade** MG W F Count van Bylandt: 27th Jagers (1 bn); 7th and IR* (1 bn); 5th, 7th* and 8th Militia bns (1 bn each); 1 x HAB. **2nd Brigade** Col F W Goedecke: 2nd Nassau LIR (3 bns); 28th LIR 'Orange-Nassau' (2 bns); Volunteer jagers (1 coy); 1 x FAB. **2nd Dutch Light Cavalry Brigade** MG van Merlen: 5th LD; 6th HusR. 8 sqns. **Totals** 10 bns, 1 coy, 8 sqns, 1,802 cavalry, 16 guns. **Brunswick Brigade** Duke Frederic William of Brunswick commanding.

Avantgarde Gelernte Jäger (2 coys); LtI (2 coys). **Light Infantry Brigade** Leib-Bn (1 bn); 1st, 2nd and 3rd Leichte-Bataillone (1 bn each). **Line Infantry Brigade**: 1st, 2nd and 3rd LI Bns (1 bn each). **Cavalry**: HusR (4 sqns); Ul Sqn (1 sqn). **Artillery:** 1 foot and 1 HAB. **Totals** 7 bns, 4 coys, 5,730 infantry, 5 sqns, 973 cavalry, 16 guns, 415 gunners.

British Troops LG Sir Thomas Picton commanding the 5th Division. **1st Brigade**** MG Maitland: 2nd/1st Foot (1 bn); 3rd/1st Foot (1 bn). **2nd Brigade**** MG Sir John Byng: 2nd/Coldstream Gds; 2nd/3rd Foot (1 bn each). **5th British Brigade** MG Sir Colin Halkett: 30th Foot (2nd Bn); 33rd Foot (1st Bn); 69th Foot (2nd Bn); 73rd Foot (2nd Bn). **8th Brigade** MG Sir James Kempt: 1st/28th; 1st/32nd; 1st/79th and 1st/95th Foot (1 bn each). **9th Brigade** MG Sir Denis Pack: 3rd/1st; 1st/42nd; 2nd/44th and 1st/92nd Foot (1 bn each). **4th Hanoverian Brigade** Col Best: LWI Bns Verden, Lüneburg, Osterode, Münden (1 bn each). **Artillery** 1 British and 1 Hanoverian foot batteries. **Totals** 16 bns, ca 11,000 infantry and 12 guns. **1st Hanoverian Brigade** (arrived at 1700 hrs). MG Count von Kielmansegge. Feld bns Bremen, York, Grubenhagen (1 bn each); Feldjäger (2 coys).

* = did not take part in this action. ** = from the 1st British Division.

Allied Losses at the Battle of Quatre-Bras

(Hanoverian losses are included with those of Waterloo).

British Troops

	Dead	Wounded	Missing	Total
1st Division				
1st British Brigade				
1st Guards (2nd bn)	24	260	—	284
2nd British Brigade				
1st Guards (3rd bn)	21	241	—	262
2nd Guards (2nd bn)	—	—	—	—
3rd Guards (2nd bn)	—	7	—	7
3rd Division				
5th British Brigade				
30th Foot (2nd bn)	5	30	5	40
33th Foot (1st bn)	19	74	9	102
69th Foot (2nd bn)	38	114	—	152
73rd Foot (2nd bn)	4	48	—	52
5th Division				
8th British Brigade				
28th Foot (1st bn)	11	64	—	75
32nd Foot (1st bn)	24	172	—	196

	Dead	Wounded	Missing	Total
79th Foot (2nd bn)	29	274	1	304
95th Foot (1st bn)	9	55	—	64
9th British Brigade				
1st Foot (3rd bn)	26	192	—	218
42nd Foot (1st bn)	45	243	—	288
44th Foot (2nd bn)	12	109	17	138
92nd Foot (1st bn)	39	247	—	286
Royal Artillery	9 (19*)	19 (14*)	— (1*)	28 (34*)
General Staff	2	5	—	7
Totals	317 (19*)	2154 (14*)	32 (1*)	2,503 (34*)

Brunswick Troops

	Dead	Wounded	Horses
Husar-Regiment	17	29	(68)
Ulan Squadron	4	10	(8*)
Horse Battery	—	—	(2*)
Advanced Guard Battalion	9	47	
Leib-Bn	15	111	
1st Leichte-Bn	—	3	
2nd Leichte-Bn	18	52	
3rd Leichte-Bn	—	—	
1st Linien-Bn	17	88	
2nd Linien-Bn	25	166	
3rd Linien-Bn	4	20	
General Staff	1	—	
Totals	110	526	210**

NB: There were also 210 rank and file missing from all the units present here.

* = horses ** = overall total

Dutch-Belgian Losses (including those of the 15 June):

27th Jagers - 263; 7th LIR - 94; 5th Militia - 303; 8th Militia - 25; 2nd Nassau LIR - 143; 28 LIR 'Nassau-Oranien' - NIL; Volunteer Jagers - 17.

Comment Due to blunders on d'Erlon's and Ney's part, d'Erlon's I Corps was taken from Ney early on 16 June and spent the whole day marching and counter-marching between Quatre-Bras and Ligny without firing a shot. Had Ney been able to use d'Erlon's Corps he would almost certainly have won at Quatre-Bras. And had d'Erlon's Corps joined in against the Prussians at Ligny, their defeat may well have been disastrous.

Sources Siborne, Zelle, Martinien, Sporschil.

NL Waterloo (Belle-Alliance) 18 June 1815, battle

A village on the road south out of the Belgian capital of Brussels leading to Charleroi on the River Sambre, about midway between the two.

An Allied victory over the French.

(Last actions - Quatre-Bras and Ligny, 16 June; next action - Wavre 18/19 June).

French Forces Emperor Napoleon I commanding.

The Imperial Guard: The Old Guard 1st Division GdD Friant and Count Roguet: 1er, 2e, 3e and 4e Gren à P (8 bns). **2nd Division** GdD's Morand and Michel: 1er, 2e, 3e and 4e ChàP (8 bns). **Young Guard** The divisions of GdD's Chartron and Mellinet: 1er Tirailleurs and 1er Voltigeurs (4 bns). GdD Count Guye: 3e Tirailleurs and 3e Voltigeurs (4 bns).

Heavy Cavalry GdD Count Guyot: GrenàCh, DragR; Gendarmerie d'Élite (13 sqns). **Light Cavalry** GdD Lefebvre-Desnouettes: 1er ChàCh (5 sqns); ChLLR (7 sqns); Gendarmerie d'Élite (1 sqn); Sailors (1 coy). **Artillery** 96 guns (9 x FAB and 4 x HAB). **Imperial Guard totals** 22 bns, 32 sqns, 96 guns, ca 18,000 men.

I Corps GdD Count d'Erlon: **1st Division** GdD Quiot: 28e, 54e, 55e and 105e RIdLi (8 bns). **2nd Division** GdD Donzelot: 13e RILé, 17e, 19e and 51e RIdLi (8 bns). **3rd Division** GdD Marcognet: 21e, 25e, 45e, and 46e, RIdLi (8 bns). **4th Division** GdD Durutte: 8e, 29e, 85e and 95e RIdLi (8 bns). **1st Cavalry Division** GdC Jaquinot: 3e ChàCh, 3e and 4e ChLL, 7e HusR (11 sqns). **Artillery** 5 x FAB, 1 x HAB, 46 guns. **I Corps totals** 32 bns, 8 sqns, 6 bties, 46 guns, ca 18,000 men.

II Corps GdD Count Reille: **5th Division** GdD Baron Bachelu: 2e RILé, 61e, 72e, 108e RIdLi (11 bns). **6th Division** GdD Prince Jerome Napoleon: 1er RILé, 1er, 2e, 3e RIdLi (11 bns). **9th Division** GdD Count Foy: 4e RILé, 92e, 93e and 100e RIdLi (10 bns). **2nd Cavalry Division** GdD Baron Piré: 1er and 6e ChàCh (8 sqns); 5e and 6e ChLL (7 sqns). **Artillery** 5 x FAB 1 x HAB, 46 guns. **II Corps totals** 32 bns, 15 sqns, 6 batteries, 46 guns.

III Corps GdD Count Vandamme: **3rd Cavalry Division** GdD Domont: 4e, 9e and 12e ChàCh (9 sqns). **Artillery** 1 x HAB, 6 guns. **III Corps totals** 9 sqns, 1 bty, 6 guns, ca 900 men.

VI Corps GdD Count Lobau: **19th Division** GdD Baron Simmer: 5e, 11e, 27e and 84e RIdLi (8 bns). **20th Division** GdD Baron Jeannin: 5e RILé, 10e, 107e RIdLi (6 bns). Artillery 2 x FAB, 12 guns. **IV Corps totals** 14 bns, 12 guns, ca 6,500 men.

I Cavalry Corps GdD Count Pajol: **5th Cavalry Division** GdD Baron Subervie: 1er and 2e ChLL (8 sqns); 11e ChàCh (4 sqns). **Artillery** 1 x HAB. **I Cavalry Corps totals** 12 sqns, 6 guns, ca 1,400 men.

III Cavalry Corps GdD Count Kellermann: **11th Cavalry Division** GdD Baron L´Heritier: 2e and 7e DragR (7 sqns); 8e and 11e CuirR (5 sqns). **12th Cavalry Division** GdD d'Hurbal; 1er and 2e Carabiniers (6 sqns); 2e and 3e CuirR (6 sqns). **Artillery** 2 x HAB, 12 guns. **III Cavalry Corps totals** 24 sqns, 12 guns, ca 3,500 men.

IV Cavalry Corps GdD Count Milhaud: **13th Cavalry Division** GdD Wathier: 1er, 4e, 7e and 12e CuirR (11 sqns). **14th Cavalry Division** GdD Baron Delort; 5e, 6e, 9e and 10e CuirR (13 sqns). **Artillery** 2 x HAB, 12 guns. **IV Cavalry Corps totals** 22 sqns, 12 guns, ca 2,800 men.

French Army totals 100 bns, 122 sqns, 236 guns, ca 72,000 men.

French Army losses Not exactly known; estimated as 42,000 (25,000 killed and wounded, 7,000 captured and 10,000 missing).

All the artillery and baggage was taken as were two eagles (those of the 45e RIdLi - taken by Sgt Ewart of Scots Greys - and that of the 105e RIdLi by the 1st Royal Dragoons.

The following Generals were killed: GdDs Desvaux de St Maurice, Duhesme, Michel.

GdBs: Aulard, Bauduin, Donop and Jamin. Wounded were Prince Jerome and GdD Friant.

Count Lobau and Generals Compans and Cambronne were captured.

Allied Forces The Duke of Wellington commanding.

I Corps HRH The Prince of Orange. **1st Division** MG Cooke: 1st British Bde MG Maitland: 1st Guards (2nd and 3rd bns). 2nd British Bde MG Sir John Byng: Coldstream Guards (2nd bn); 3rd Guards (2nd bn). **Artillery** Lt Col Adye: 1 British and 1 KGL foot batteries, 12 guns. **Totals** 4,061 men, 12 guns. **3rd Division** LG Sir Charles Alten: 5th British Bde MG Sir Colin Halkett: 30th Foot (2nd bn); 33rd Foot (1st bn); 69th Foot (2nd bn); 73rd Foot (2nd bn). 2nd KGL Bde Col von Ompteda: 1st and 2nd Lt Bns; 5th and 8th Line bns. 1st Hanoverian Bde MG Count Kielmansegge: Field bns Bremen, Verden, York, Lüneburg, Grubenhagen, Jäger Corps. **Artillery** 1 British and 1 KGL Foot batteries, 12 guns. **Total** 6,970 men and 24 guns. **2nd Dutch-Belgian Division** LG Baron de Perponcher: 1st Brigade MG Count van Bylandt: 7th LIR (1 bn); 27th Jager bn (1 bn), 5th, 7th, 8th, Militia bns (3 bns). 2nd Brigade HSH The Prince Bernhard of Saxe-Weimar: 2nd Nassau IR (3 bns); Regt of Orange Nassau (1st and 3rd bns). **Artillery** Maj van Opstal: 1 Dutch-Belgian foot and 1 Dutch-Belgian horse batteries, 16 guns. **Totals** 7,553 men and 16 guns. **3rd Dutch-Belgian Division** LG Baron Chassé: 1st Brigade MG Ditmers: 2nd LIR (1 bn); 35th Jager bn (1 bn), 4th, 6th, 17th and 19th Militia bns (4 bns). 2nd Brigade MG d'Aubremé: 3rd, 12th and 13th LIRs (3 bns); 36th Jager bn, 3rd and 10th Militia bns (2 bns). **Artillery** Maj van der

Smissen: 1 Dutch-Belgian foot and 1 Dutch Belgian horse artillery batteries, 16 guns. **Totals** 6,669 men and 16 guns. **I Corps totals** 25,233 men and 56 guns.

II Corps LG Lord Hill. **2nd Division** LG Sir H Clinton: 3rd British Brigade MG Adam: 52nd Foot (1st Bn); 71st Foot (1st Bn); 95th Foot (2nd and 3rd Bns). 1st KGL Brigade Col du Plat: 1st, 2nd, 3rd and 4th Line bns (4 bns). 3rd Hanoverian Brigade Col Halkett: LWI bns Bremervörde, Osnabrück, Quackenbrück and Salzgitter (4 bns). **Artillery** LtCol Gold: 1 British foot and 1 KGL horse artillery batteries, 12 guns. **Totals** 6,833 men and 12 guns. **4th Division** LG Sir Charles Colville: 4th British Brigade Col Mitchell: 14th Foot (3rd Bn); 23rd Foot (1st Bn); 51st Foot (1st Bn). **Artillery** LtCol Hawker: 1 British and 1 Hanoverian foot batteries, 12 guns. **1st Dutch-Belgian Division** LG Stedmann: 2nd Brigade MG Eerens: 1st LIR (1 bn); 18th Jager bn (1 bn); 1st, 2nd and 18th Militia bns (2 bns). **Artillery** Capt Wynand: 1 foot battery, 8 guns. Detachments of 6th and 7th Line bns KGL and 2 orderlies – 16 men. **Total II Corps** 24,033 men and 40 guns.

The Reserve 5th Division LG Sir Thomas Picton: 8th British Brigade MG Sir James Kempt: 1st Bns of the 28th, 32nd, 79th and 95th Foot. 9th British Brigade MG Sir Denis Pack: 1st Foot (3rd Bn); 42nd Foot (1st Bn); 44th Foot (2nd Bn); 92nd Foot (1st Bn). 5th Hanoverian Brigade Col von Vincke: LWI Bns Hameln, Gifhorn, Hildesheim and Peine. Artillery: Maj Heisse: 1 British and 1 Hanoverian foot artillery batteries, 12 guns. **6th Division** LG the Hon Sir L Cole: 10th British Brigade MG Sir John Lambert: 1st bns of the 4th, 27th and 40th Foot (3 bns); 81st Foot (2nd Bn). 4th Hanoverian Brigade Col Best: LWI Bns Verden, Lüneburg, Osterode, Münden (4 bns). Artillery: LtCol Brückmann: 2 British foot batteries, 12 guns. British Reserve Artillery: Maj Drummond: 2 horse and 3 foot artillery batteries, 30 guns. **The Brunswick Corps** HSH The Duke of Brunswick. Adv Gd bn Maj von Rauschenplatt (1 bn). Light Brigade LtCol von Buttlar: Leib-Bn (1 bn); 1st, 2nd and 3rd Lt bns (3 bns) Hus R (4 sqns), UIR (1 sqn). Line Brigade LtCol von Specht: 1st, 2nd and 3rd Line bns (3 bns). Artillery Maj Mahn: 1 horse and 1 foot battery. **Brunswick totals** 5,376 men, 16 guns. **Hanoverian Reserve Corps** LG von der Decken:1st Brigade Lt Col von Bennigsen: Fd bn Hoya (1 bn); LWI Bns Mölln and Bremerlehe (2 bns). 2nd Brigade LtCol von Beaulieu: LWI Bns Nordheim, Ahlefeldt, Springe (3 bns). 3rd Brigade LtCol Bodecker: LWI Bns Otterndorf, Celle, Ratzeburg (3 bns). 4th Brigade LtCol Wissel: LWI Bns Hanover, Uelzen, Neustadt, Diepholz (4 bns). **Total** ca 9,000 men. **Nassau Contingent** Gen v Kruse: 1st Regt (3 bns), 2,880 men. **Reserve totals** ca 32,796 men and 64 guns.

Allied Cavalry.

British and KGL 1st Brigade MG Lord Somerset: 1st and 2nd Life Guards, Royal Horse Guards (the Blues); 1st DG (King's). 2nd Brigade MG Sir W Ponsonby: 1st (Royal) D; 2nd D (Scots Greys); 6th (Inniskilling) D. 3rd Brigade MG Sir W Dörnberg: 1st and 2nd LD, KGL; 23rd LD. 4th Brigade MG Sir J Vandeleur: 11th, 12th and 16th LD. 5th Brigade MG Sir Colquhoun Grant: 7th Hus and 15th Hus. 6th Brigade MG Sir H Vivian: 1st Hus KGL; 10th and 18th Hus. 7th Brigade Col Sir F von Arentschild: 3rd Hus KGL; 13th LD. British Horse Artillery: 1st (Bull's) Howitzers; 2nd Webber-Smith's; 3rd Gardiner's; 4th (Rocket) Whinyate's; 5th Mercer's; 6th Ramsay's. 1st Hanoverian Cavalry Brigade Col von Estorff: Cumberland HusR. Brunswick Cavalry HusR, Ul sqn. **Dutch-Belgian Cavalry Division** 1st Brigade MG Trip: 1st (Dutch) and 2nd and 3rd (Belgian) Carabiniers. 2nd Brigade MG de Ghigny: 4th (Dutch) LD; 8th (Belgian) HusR. 3rd Brigade MG van Merlen: 5th (Belgian) LD; 6th (Dutch) HusR. Artillery: Two half horse artillery batteries.

Total Allied Strengths 82,062 infantry, 14,482 cavalry, 8,166 artillery, 1,240 engineers, waggon train etc: 105,950 men and 204 guns.

Allied losses See opposite and subsequent pages.

The Prussian Army at Waterloo FM Prince Blücher von Wahlstadt commanding.

I Corps GL von Ziethen II. **1st Brigade** GM von Steinmetz: 12th LIR (3 bns); 24th LIR (3 bns): 1st Westfalian LWIR (3 bns); Silesian Rifles (1st and 3rd coys). **Total** 9½ bns. 8,647 men. **2nd Brigade** GM von Pirch II: 6th LIR (3 bns); 28th LIR (1 bn); 2nd Westfalian LWIR (3 bns). **Total** 9 bns, 7,666 men. **3rd Brigade** GM von Jagow: 7th LIR (3 bns); 29th LIR (3 bns); 3rd Westfalian LWIR (3 bns); Silesian Rifles (2nd and 4th coys). **Total** 9½ bns, 6,853 men. **4th Brigade** GM von Henkel: 19th LIR (3 bns); 4th Westfalian LWIR (3 bns). **Total** 6 bns, 4,721 men. **Reserve Cavalry** GL von Röder **1st Brigade** GM von Treskow: DragR Brandenburg Nr 5 (4

Allied losses at Waterloo

I Corps

	Killed	Wounded	Missing	Total
1st Division				
1st British Brigade				
1st Guards (2nd Bn)	51	101	—	152
1st Guards (3rd Bn)	84	251	—	335
2nd British Brigade				
2nd Guards (2nd Bn)	55	249	4	308
3rd Guards (2ndBn)	42	197	—	239
1st Division Totals	*232*	*798*	*4*	*1,034*
3rd Division				
5th British Brigade				
30th Foot (2nd Bn)	51	165	14	230
33rd Foot (1st Bn)	35	102	48	185
69th Foot (2nd Bn)	18	53	15	86
73rd Foot (2nd Bn)	52	187	41	280
2nd KGL Brigade				
1st Light Bn	41	91	13	145
2nd Light Bn	43	129	30	202
5th Line Bn	38	50	74	162
8th Line Bn	47	84	16	147
1st Hanoverian Brigade				
Fd Bn Bremen	12	124	35	171
Fd Bn Verden	63	101	53	217
Fd Bn York	24	72	45	141
Fd Bn Lüneburg	32	142	48	222
Fd Bn Grubenhagen	16	78	48	142
Jäger-Corps	12	41	19	72
3rd Division totals	*484*	*1,419*	*499*	*2,402*

2nd Dutch-Belgian Division (16, 17 and 18 June)

	Killed	Wounded	Missing	Total	
1st Brigade					
7th LIR	20	138	83	241	
27 Jäger Bn	16	178	158	352	
5th Militia Bn	73	139	109	321	
7th Militia Bn	20	64	201	285	
8th Militia Bn	17	107	70	194	
2nd Brigade					
1st/2nd Nassau	27	97	59	183	—
2nd/2nd Nassau	21	95	38	154	—
3rd/2nd Nassau	18	113	3	134	—
1st/Orange Nassau	5	36	20	61	—
3rd/Orange Nassau	6	46	52	104	—

	Killed	Wounded	Missing	Total	Horses
Artillery and Train	15	89	14	118	114
2nd Division Totals	*238*	*1,132*	*807*	*2,147*	*114*

3rd Dutch-Belgian Division	Killed	Wounded	Missing	Total	Horses
1st Brigade					
2nd LIR	6	28	57	91	—
35th Jäger Bn	8	63	—	71	—
4th Militia Bn	6	26	38	70	—
6th Militia Bn	5	15	22	42	—
17th Militia Bn	1	27	30	58	—
19th Militia Bn	1	28	50	79	—
2nd Brigade					
3rd LIR	1	24	56	81	—
12th LIR	2	13	9	24	—
13th LIR	6	20	34	60	—
36th Jäger Bn	3	10	41	54	—
3rd Militia Bn	5	26	2	33	—
10th Militia Bn	7	15	3	25	—
Horse Artillery	2	16	—	18	19
Foot Artillery	—	3	10	13	—
Artillery Train	3	2	12	17	28
3rd Division Totals	*56*	*316*	*364*	*736*	*47*
I CORPS TOTALS	1,012	3,656	1,674	6,319	161

II Corps

2nd Division	Killed	Wounded	Missing	Total
3rd British Brigade				
1st/51st	17	182	—	199
1st/71st	25	174	3	202
2nd/95	34	193	20	247
3rd/95	3	40	7	50
1st KGL Brigade				
1st Line Bn	23	75	17	115
2nd Line Bn	19	81	7	107
3rd Line Bn	18	98	31	147
4th Line Bn	14	84	14	112
3rd Hanoverian Brigade				
LWI Bn Bremervörde	18	22	9	49
LWI Bn Osnabrück	20	68	6	94
LWI Bn Quackenbrück	2	10	2	14
LWI Bn Salzgitter	20	62	1	83
2nd Division Totals	*273*	*1,251*	*135*	*1,659*

	Killed	Wounded	Missing	Total
4th Division				
4th British Brigade				
3rd/14th	7	22	—	29
1st/23rd	15	84	—	99
1st/51st	9	22	—	31
4th Division Totals	*31*	*128*	—	*159*
II Corps total	201	1007	48	1256
5th Division				
8th British Brigade				
1st/28th	19	158	—	177
1st/32nd	28	146	—	174
1st79th	31	143	1	175
1st/95th	21	135	—	156
5th Division Totals	*99*	*582*	*1*	*682*
9th British Brigade				
3rd/1st	15	129	—	144
1st/42nd	5	45	—	50
2nd/44th	4	60	—	64
1st/92nd	14	102	—	116
9th Brigade Totals	38	336	—	374
5th Hanoverian Brigade				
LWI Bn Hameln	9	64	7	80
LWI Bn Gifhorn	15	72	—	87
LWI Bn Hildesheim	3	21	—	24
LWI Bn Peine	8	42	6	56
5th Brigade Totals	35	199	13	247

6th Division	Killed	Wounded	Missing	Total
10th British Brigade				
1st/4th	12	112	—	124
1st/27th	105	373	—	478
1st/40th	32	169	18	219
2nd/81st	— No losses —		—	—
6th Division Totals	149	654	18	812
4th Hanoverian Brigade (including losses at Quatre Bras on 16 June & the retreat on 17 June)				
LWI Bn Verden	12	101	46	159
LWI Bn Lüneburg	10	42	—	52
LWI Bn Osterode	14	98	14	126
LWI Bn Münden	12	103	17	132
6th Brigade Totals	48	344	77	469
The Brunswick Corps				
Husar Regt	28	50	78	40
Ulan Sqn	—	15	15	15

	Killed	Wounded	Missing	Total	Horses
Avantgarde Bn	7	21	28	—	
Leib-Bn	14	37	51	—	
1st Light Bn	4	44	48	—	
2nd Light Bn	39	75	114	—	
3rd Light Bn	36	80	50	116	—
1st Line Bn	9	46	55	—	
2nd Line Bn	3	7	10	—	
3rd Line Bn	10	53	63	—	
Horse Battery	3	6	9	16	
Foot Battery	—	18	18	6	
General Staff	1	4	5	—	
BRUNSWICK CORPS TOTAL	154	456	544	193	77
Nassau Contingent					
1st LIR	254	389	—	643	—
Allied Cavalry					
1st Brigade					
1st Life Guards	18	43	4	65	85
2nd Life Guards	17	41	97	155	173
Royal Horse Guards (Blues)	17	60	21	98	103
1st Dragoon Guards	43	104	128	275	311
1st Brigade Totals	95	248	250	593	672
2nd Brigade					
1st Royal Dragoons	89	97	10	196	196
2nd (Scots Greys)	102	97	—	199	228
6th Dragoons (Inniskillings)	73	116	28	217	207
2nd Brigade Totals	264	310	38	612	631
3rd Brigade					
1st LD KGL	33	111	10	154	149
2nd LD KGL	20	55	2	77	68
23rd LD	14	28	32	74	79
3rd Brigade Totals	67	194	44	305	296
4th Brigade					
11th LD	12	28	23	63	73
12th LD	47	64	—	108	110
16thLD	10	20	—	30	55
4th Brigade Totals	69	112	23	201	238
5th Brigade					
7th Hussars	56	99	—	155	200
15th Hussars	23	51	5	79	105
5th Brigade Totals	79	150	5	234	305

	Killed	Wounded	Missing	Total	Horses
6th Brigade					
1st Hussars KGL	1	6	—	7	22
10th Hussars	22	46	26	94	116
18th Hussars	12	73	17	102	97
6th Brigade Totals	35	119	43	203	235
7th Brigade					
3rd Hussars KGL	44	86	—	130	102
13th Light Dragoons	12	78	18	108	113
7th Brigade Totals	56	164	18	238	215
1st Hanoverian Cavalry Brigade					
Cumberland Hussars	18	33	2	53	—
Dutch Belgian Cavalry Division (16th, 17th and 18th of June)					
1st Brigade					
1st (Dutch) Carabiniers	12	75	15	102	150
2nd (Belgian) Carabiniers	58	68	30	156	162
3rd (Belgian) Carabiniers	37	29	26	92	82
1st Brigade Totals	107	172	71	350	394
2nd Brigade					
4th Dutch Light Dragoons	54	143	52	239	304
8th Belgian Hussars	11	151	122	284	268
3rd Brigade					
5th Belgian Light Dragoons	10	76	71	157	123
6th Dutch Hussars	12	70	132	214	302
Horse Artillery	8	9	4	21	37
Train	1	10	4	15	39
Totals Netherlands cavalry, artillery train	203	631	456	1,280	1,467

sqns each); 1st West Prussian DragR Nr 2 (4 sqns); UlR Brandenburg (4 sqns). **2nd Brigade** Obstlt von Lützow: 1st and 2nd Kurmark LWCR; (4 sqns each); 1st Silesian HusR (4 sqns); 1st Westfalian LWCR (4 sqns each). **Reserve Artillery** Obst von Lehmann: 12-pounder foot batteries Nrs 2, 6, 9; 6-pounder foot batteries Nrs 1, 3, 7, 8 and 15; howitzer battery Nr 1; HA batteries Nrs 2, 7 and 10. **I Corps totals** 34 bns, 27,887 infantry, 32 sqns, 1,925 cavalry, 12 batteries, 1,019 gunners and 96 guns.

II Corps LG von Pirch I: **5th Brigade** GM von Tippelskirchen: 2nd LIR (3 bns); 25th LIR (3 bns); 5th Westfalian LWIR (3 bns); Feldjäger (1 coy). **Total** 9 bns, 1 coy, 6,851 men. **6th Brigade** GM von Krafft: 9th LIR (3 bns); 26th LIR (3 bns); 1st Elb LWIR (3 bns). **Total** 9 bns, 6,469 men. **7th Brigade** GM von Brause: 14th LIR (3 bns); 22nd LIR (3 bns); 2nd Elb LWIR (3 bns). **Total** 9 bns, 6,224 men. **8th Brigade** Obst von Langen: 21st LIR (3 bns); 23rd LIR (3 bns); 3rd Elb LWIR (3 bns). **Total** 9 bns, 6,292 men.

Reserve Cavalry GL von Jürgass **1st Brigade** Obst von Thümen: Silesian UlR (4 sqns); Neumärk DragR Nr 9 (4 sqns); DragR Nr 1 (4 sqns). **2nd Brigade** Obst von Sohr: 1st DragR Königin (4 sqns); HusR Nr 11 (4 sqns). **3rd Brigade** Obst Count Schulenberg: 4th Kurmark LWCR (4 sqns); HusR Pommern Nr 5 (4 sqns); 5th

Kurmark LWCR (4 sqns); Elb LWCR (4 sqns). **Reserve Artillery** Obst von Röhl: 12-pounder foot batteries Nr 4 and 8; 6-pounder foot batteries Nrs 5, 10, 12, 34 and 37; HA batteries Nrs 5, 6 and 14. **II Corps Totals** 36 bns, 25,836 infantry, 36 sqns, 4,468 cavalry, 10 batteries, 1,454 gunners and 80 guns.

IV Corps General Count Bülow von Dennewitz. **13th Brigade** GL von Hacke: 10th LIR (3 bns); 2nd and 3rd Neumark LWIR (3 bns each). **Total** 9 bns, 6,395 men. **14th Brigade** GM von Ryssel: 11th LIR (3 bns); 1st and 2nd Pommern LWIR (3 bns each). **Total** 9 bns, 6,953 men. **15th Brigade** GM von Losthin: 18th LIR (3 bns); 3rd and 4th Silesian LWIR (3 bns each). Total 9 bns, 5,881 men. **16th Brigade** Obst von Hiller: 15th LIR (3 bns); 1st and 2nd Silesian LWIR (3 bns each). **Total** 9 bns, 6,162 men. **Reserve Cavalry** Gen Prince William of Prussia. **1st Brigade** GM von Schwerin: UlR West Prussian Nr 1 (4 sqns); Silesian HusR Nr 2 (4 sqns); 10th HusR (3 sqns). **2nd Brigade** Obstlt von Watzdorff: 8th HusR (4 sqns). **3rd Brigade** GM von Sydow: 1st Silesian LWCR (4 sqns). 1st and 2nd Neumark LWCR; 1st and 2nd Pomm LWCR (4 sqns each). **Reserve Artillery** Obstlt von Bardeleben: 12-pounder foot batteries Nr 3, 5, 13; 6-pounder foot batteries Nr 2, 11, 13, 14 and 21; HA batteries Nr 1, 11 and 12. **IV Corps Totals** 36 bns, 25,381 infantry, 43 squadrons, 3,081 cavalry, 11 batteries, 1,866 gunners and 88 guns.

Prussian Losses at Waterloo

I Corps	Killed	Wounded	Missing	Total	Horses
1st Brigade	31	158	111	300	9
2nd Brigade	no losses				
3rd Brigade	no losses				
4th Brigade	no losses				
Cavalry	2	11	—	13	26
Artillery	1	4	—	5	6
I Corps Totals	*34*	*173*	*111*	*318*	*41*
II Corps					
5th Brigade					
25th LIR	—	8	—	8	—
5th Westfalian LWIR	2	8	7	17	—
7th Brigade					
2nd Elbe LWIR	1	4	—	5	—
8th Brigade					
21st LIR	—	15	4	19	—
23rd LIR	7	36	9	52	—
3rd Elbe LWIR	21	68	50	139	—
3rd Cavalry Brigade					
3rd HusR Brandenburg	—	1	8	9	13
5th HusR Pommern	1	3	1	5	9
Artillery					
6 pdr Foot Bty Nr 10	—	3	—	3	1
HA Bty	—	3	—	3	6
II Corps Totals	*32*	*149*	*79*	*260*	*29*
IV Corps					
13th Brigade					
1st SclIR	—	3	45	48	—
2nd Neumark LWIR	10	105	109	224	—
3rd Neumark LWIR	27	133	134	294	1

	Killed	Wounded	Missing	Total	Horses
14th Brigade					
2nd SclIR	44	314	52	410	—
1st Pommern LWIR	115	258	—	373	3
2nd Pommern LWIR	287	178	2	467	—
15th Brigade					
18th LIR	132	595	88	815	2
3rd Silesian LWIR	143	452	57	652	3
4th Silesian LWIR	38	217	101	356	—
16th Brigade					
15th LIR	63	569	25	657	9
1st Silesian LWIR	156	417	55	628	2
2nd Silesian LWIR	37	192	308	537	4
IV Corps Totals	*1,052*	*3,433*	*976*	*5,461*	*24*
Reserve Cavalry					
1st Brigade					
UlR West Prussian Nr 1	1	20	—	21	18
Silesian HusR Nr 2	7	146	45	198	139
8th HusR	8	58	2	68	44
2nd Brigade					
10th HusR	1	5	15	21	32
1st Neumärk LWCR	1	—	—	1	18
2nd Neumärk LWCR	7	105	10	122	249
1st Pommern LWCR	—	3	—	3	13
3rd Brigade					
1st Silesian LWCR	1	1	3	5	27
2nd Silesian LWCR	1	15	4	20	35
3rd Silesian LWCR	12	42	6	60	71
Reserve Cavalry Totals	*39*	*395*	*85*	*519*	*646*
Artillery					
12 pdr bties Nrs 3,5,13	5	28	3	36	31
6 pdr bties Nrs 2,11,13,14 and 21	5	17	7	29	32
HA bties Nrs 1,11, and 12	5	21	—	26	39
Artillery Totals	*15*	*66*	*10*	*91*	*102*
General Staff	2	1	—	3	—
Prussian Totals	1,125	4,387	1,386	6,998	742

Comment It is not the purpose of this book to recount the battle. Suffice it to say that Wellington only stood his ground, with his largely young and untried army because he had been assured by Blücher that he would be supported by at least one Prussian corps. Blücher was better than his word. Even so, the last, desperate assault by the Imperial Guard infantry was defeated on the Allied left after d'Erlon's I Corps and the French cavalry had been practically destroyed in successive attacks which were poorly coordinated and suffered accordingly.

A word to the losses; Bodart gives the Allied losses as shown below in totals of killed, wounded and missing all together, with officer casualties in brackets and shows the casualties as a percentage of those involved:

	Totals	Officers	
British	7000	460	29.9%
Prussians	7000	223	13.5%
Dutch—Belgians	4000	154	22.5%
Hanoverians	2000	84	17.7%
KGL	1600	104	27.6%
Brunswickers	700	33	11.7%
Nassauers	700	24	25.0%
Total	23,000	1,082	19.2% (average)

Sources Siborne, Zelle, Martinien, Plotho.

NL Wavre, 18/19 June 1815, clash

A village in Belgium, about 20 km southeast of Brussels, on the left bank of the River Dyle and to the north of the motorway A4/E411.

A French victory over the Prussians.

(Last action – Waterloo, 18 June; next action – Namur, 20 June).

French Forces M Grouchy commanding.

III Corps GdD Count Vandamme. 8th Division GdD Baron Lefol: 23e, 37e and 64e RIdLi (9 bns). **10th Division** GdD Baron Habert: 22e, 34e, 70e and 88e RIdLi and 2e Étranger (Swiss) IR (12 bns). **11th Division** GdD Barthezène: 56e (2 bns). **Artillery** 3 x FAB. **III Corps totals** 23 bns, 18 guns ca 13,000 men.

IV Corps GL Count Gérard. 13th Division: GdD Baron Vichery: 59e and 76e RIdLi (4 bns). **14th Division** GdD Baron Hulot: 50e and 111e RIdLi(4 bns). **6th Cavalry Division** GdD Maurin: 6e HusR, 8e ChàCh (6 sqns). **Artillery** 2 x FAB and 1 x HAB. **IV Corps totals** 6 bns, 6 sqns, 18 guns, ca 12,000 men.

VI Corps LG Count Lobau. 21st Division GdD Baron Teste: 8e RILé (2 bns). **Artillery** 1 x FAB. **VI Corps totals** 2 bns, 6 guns, ca 2,000 men.

II Cavalry Corps GdD Exelmans. 9th Cavalry Division GdD Strolz: 5e and 13e DragR (6 sqns). **Artillery** 1 x HAB. **II Cavalry Corps totals** 6 sqns, 6 guns, ca 1,000 men.

French Army totals 31 bns, 12 sqns, 48 guns, ca 28,000 men. This figure is very approximate as the losses of the 16–18 June are not known and no returns were preserved.

French losses Not known; estimated at, at least, 2,500.

Prussian Forces at Wavre 18/19 June

III Corps GdD Baron von Thielemann commanding. 9th Brigade MG von Borcke: Leib IR Nr 8 (3 bns); 30th LIR (3 bns); 1st Kurmark LWIR (3 bns). 10th Brigade Col von Kämpfen: 27th LIR (3 bns); 2nd Kurmark LWIR (3 bns). 11th Brigade Col von Luck: 3rd and 4th Kurmark LWIR (3 bns each). 12th Brigade Col von Stülpnagel: 31st LIR (3 bns); 5th and 6th Kurmark LWIR (3 bns each). **Reserve Cavalry** MG von Hobe. Col von der Marwitz: 7th UlR (2 sqns); 8th UlR (4 sqns); 12th HusR (3 sqns). Col Count von Lottum: 5th UlR (3 sqns); 7th DragR (4 sqns); 9th HusR (4 sqns). **Reserve Artillery Col von Mohnhaupt** 6-pounder foot batteries Nrs 18 and 35; 12-pounder foot battery Nr 7; HA batteries Nrs 18, 19, 20. Engineers - 5th coy. From Ziethen's I Corps LG von Stengel commanding: 19th LIR (3 bns); 6th UlR (4 sqns); 10th HusR (4 sqns).

Prussian totals 33 bns, 24 sqns, 6 batteries, 23,600 infantry, 2,400 cavalry, 964 gunners and 48 guns.

Prussian losses 2,467 killed, wounded and missing.

Comment This action was an exemplary defence of a river line in the face of considerable odds. Thielmann tied down one-third of Napoleon's army at a crucial point in the campaign and prevented Grouchy from participating in the Battle of Waterloo. Borcke's 9th Prussian Brigade was absent for much of the action.

Sources Siborne, Bredow-Wedel, Plotho.

NL Namur, 20 June 1815, clash

Capital city of the Belgian province of Namur, at the confluence of the Rivers Sambre and Meuse, just south of the junctions of the Routes E42 and E411.

A French victory over the Prussians.

(Last action – Wavre, 18/19 June; next action – Aisnes-sur-Helpe, 22 June).

French Forces M Grouchy commanding.

III Corps GdD Count Vandamme. **10th Division** GdD Baron Habert: 22e and 34e RIdLi (6 bns). **11th Division** GdD Barthezène: 12e, 33e, 56e and 86e RIdLi (12 bns).

IV Corps GdD Count Gérard **12th Division** GdD Baron Pecheux: 30e and 96e RIdLi (6 bns). **7th Cavalry Division** GdD Maurin: 6e HusR (3 sqns).

VI Corps GdD Count Lobau **21st Division** GdD Baron Teste: 8e RILé, 65e and 75e RIdLi (5 bns).

I Cavalry Corps GdD Count Pajol **4th Division** GdD Baron P Soult: 1er HusR (4 sqns).

II Cavalry Corps GdD Count Exelmans **9th Division** GdD Strolz: 20e DragR (4 sqns).

French totals 29 bns, 11 sqns. Exact manpower not known as the losses from Ligny and Wavre are not known.

French losses Not exactly known. estimated at 1,300 including 150 captured.

Prussian Forces (of LG Baron von Thielemann's III Corps).

Reserve Cavalry GM Hobe. Obst von der Marwitz: 7th UlR (3 sqns); 8th UlR (4 sqns); 9th HusR (3 sqns). Obst Count von Lottum: 5th UlR (3 sqns); 4th DragR (3 sqns). 2 x HAB. 3rd and 6th Kurmark LWCRs (8 sqns).

From GL von Pirch I's II Corps LG von Sohr: 3rd Brandenburg HusR (4 sqns); 5th Pommeranian HusR (4 sqns); 5th Kurmark LWCR (4 sqns); Elb LWCR (4 sqns). **6th Brigade** BG von Krafft: 9th and 26th LIR; 1st Elb LWIR (9 bns). **7th Brigade** BG von Brause: 14th and 22nd LIR; 2nd Elb LWIR (7 bns); 2 x FAB.

Prussian totals 16 bns, 36 sqns, 4 batteries, 32 guns.

Prussian losses ca 1,700 dead, wounded and missing.

Comment The Prussians tried to rush the fortified city of Namur but were bloodily repulsed, the 6th Brigade alone lost 44 officers and 1,274 men trying to get into the city with a quick charge.

Sources Siborne, Bredow-Wedel, Zelle, Martinien.

UR Anweiler, Gottramstein (Godramstein) and Offenbach on the River Queich, 20 June 1815, skirmish

Three villages in the west of Germany, about 12 km northwest of Karlsruhe on the River Rhine and just to the north of Landau.

A Bavarian victory over the French.

(Last action – this was the first action on the Upper Rhine; next action – Saarbrücken and Saargemünd, 23 June).

French Forces Gen Rapp's Corps. Exact regiments not known.

French losses No officer losses recorded.

Bavarian Forces GM Count Deroy commanding the 2nd Brigade, 1st Infantry Division: 11th National-Feld-Bn (Ingolstadt) (1 bn).

Bavarian totals ca 800 men.

Bavarian losses Not known, slight.

Comment The Bavarian 'National Guard' fought well here. This was the southernmost of the three-pronged Allied assault into eastern France and was 2–3 days' march behind the other two columns. Rapp had just received the news of Waterloo and withdrew on Strasbourg.

Sources Plotho, Sporschil, Leyh.

FJ Meillerie, 21 June 1815, clash

A village on the southern shore of Lac Leman (Lake Geneva) in France.

An Allied victory over the French.

(Last action – this was the opening action in this theatre; next action – Césanne, 21 June).

French Forces Gen Dessaix commanding the Armée des Alpes.

French totals ca 2,500 men, 12 guns. Exact details not known.

French losses Not known; light.

Allied Forces FML Count Crenneville's Light Division of FML Radivojevich's Corps: 7th Jäger bn (2 coys); GzIR Wallachisch-Illyrisch (2 coys); GM Bogdan: ChLR O'Reilly Nr 3 (4 sqns); ChLR Rosenberg Nr 6 (6 sqns).

Austrian totals 4 coys, 10 sqns, ca 1,800 men.

Austrian losses 73 killed and wounded.

Comment M Suchet had been ordered by Napoleon not to open hostilities before 14 June; he sent Gen Dessaix to seize St Moritz and the Mont Cenis passes but the Austrians acted first and threw Dessaix's force back to Carrouge, south of Geneva. This GM Bogdan achieved even without any artillery. The chase went on to Evian.

Sources Plotho, Sporschil, Wrede, Voss.

FJ Césanne (Cesana-Torinsese), 21 June 1815, skirmish

A village on the Italian side of the Col de Montgenèvre into France over the Alps on route 23 between Turin and Briançon.

An Austrian victory over the French.

(Last action – Meillerie, 21 June; next action – Aiguebelle, Conflans and Les Rousses Pass, 28 June).

French Forces 7e RIdLi (1 bn); ca 800 men.

French losses Not known; light.

Austrian Forces The Avantgarde of FML Count Bubna's Corps, Maj Pirquet commanding: Tyroler Fenner-Jäger Corps (6 coys) of Obst O'Brien's column.

Austrian totals ca 600 men.

Austrian losses Not known, light.

Comment The Austrians beat off a French attack in no uncertain manner to seize control of this Alpine pass to secure the southern flank of FML Bubna's thrust into the French Jura region.

Sources Plotho, Sporschil, Wrede.

NL Avesnes-sur-Helpe, 22 June 1815, capture of

A fortified town in northern France on Route N2, 80 km south of Waterloo and 184 km northeast of Paris.

A Prussian victory over the French.

(Last action – Namur, 20 June; next action – Guise, 24 June).

French Garrison 1,700 GdN and 200 line troops including the 108e RIdLi with 47 guns.

French losses Dead and wounded unknown; the GdN were sent home, the line troops sent to Köln as prisoners of war.

Allied Forces GL von Ziethen's I Prussian Corps. **Reserve Cavalry** GM v Röder: 1st Silesian HusR (4 sqns). **Reserve Artillery** Obst von Lehmann: 1 x 6-pounder FAB; Howitzer Bty Nr 1.

Allied totals 9½ bns, 4 sqns, 2 batteries, ca 8,000 men.

Allied losses Not exactly known; very slight.

Comment In the night of 21/22 June a Prussian shell hit the main magazine of the fort which exploded. The garrison surrendered next day.

Sources Sporschil, Plotho, Bredow-Wedel, Martinien.

UR Saarbrücken and Saargemünd, 23 June 1815, skirmishes

Two towns on the River Saar, the former in the western German state of Saarland at the junction of motorways A6/E50 and A8/E29, the latter now in eastern France ('Saarguemines') on Route N61 about 15 km apart.

Bavarian victories over the French. No exact details known; losses very light.

(Last action – Anweiler, Gottramsteiner and Offenbach, 20 June; next action – Rheinzabern, 23 June).

Saarbrücken

French Forces Part of Rapp's V Corps; GdB Mériage and about 300 dismounted cavalry and militia. **French Losses** 100 dead and wounded, 4 officers and 20 men captured.

Bavarian Forces GL Count Beckers commanding the 2nd Infantry Division: 5th LtI Bn (1 bn); 14th National-Feld-Bn 'Ansbach' (1 bn).

Bavarian totals ca 1,800 men.

Bavarian losses 19 dead and 41 wounded.

Saargemünd

French Forces Part of Rapp's V Corps; exact details not known, but mostly militia.

French losses Not known; light.

Bavarian Forces GL von Raglovich commanding the 1st Infantry Division: 4th LtI Bn (3 coys).

Bavarian totals ca 350 men.

Bavarian losses None.

Sources Leyh, Sporschil, Plotho, Voss.

UR Rheinzabern, 23 June 1815, skirmish

A village in southwest Germany, about 8 km west of the River Rhine, midway between Karlsruhe and Germersheim.

An Allied victory over the French.

(Last action – Saarbrücken and Saargemünd, 28 June; next action – Surburg and Selz, 26 June).

French Forces Part of Rapp's V Corps, exact details not known.

French losses Not known; light.

Allied Forces The Hessen-Darmstadt division under GL Prinz Emil; GM Folenius: Garde-Füs-R (2 bns); IR Gross-und Erbprinz (1st Bn).

Allied totals 3 bns, 6 guns, ca 2,000 men.

Allied losses About 15 men dead and wounded.

Sources Plotho, Sporschil, Voss.

NL Guise, 24 June 1815, surrender of

A fortified town in northern France, on the River Oise, at the junction of Routes N29/E44 and D960, D934 and D967; 105 km south southwest of Waterloo and 150 km northeast of Paris.

A Prussian victory over the French.

(Last action – Avesnes-sur-Helpe, 22 June; next action – Le Quesnoy, 23–26 June).

French Garrison 18 officers and 750 men of the GdN and 14 guns.

French losses The garrison was sent home.

Prussian Forces GL von Ziethen's I Corps: **2nd Brigade** GM v Pirch II: 1st West Prussian IR Nr 6 (3 bns); 28th LIR (2 bns) and 2nd West Prussian LWIR (2 bns).

Prussian losses Not known, very slight.

Comment The badly mauled 28th LIR and the 2nd

West Prussian LWIR were left in the citadel as garrison.

Sources Sporschil, Plotho, Bredow-Wedel.

NL Le Quesnoy, 23–26 June 1815, bombardment and surrender of

A small fortress in northern France on Route D934, 10 km southeast of Valenciennes.

An Allied victory over the French.

(Last action – Guise, 24 June; next action – Compiègne-sur-Oise, 27 June).

French Garrison Mainly Garde Nationale and refugees from the battle of Waterloo.

French losses Not known, very slight.

Allied Forces GdB Anthing: 5th LIR (2 bns); Flankers (1 bn); 10th and 11th Jägers (2 bns); 1 x FAB.

Allied totals 5 bns, 1 x FAB, ca 3,400 men.

Allied losses Not known, very slight.

Comment The 2nd Bn, 5th LIR of Anthing's brigade were left in le Quesnoy as garrison.

Sources Siborne, Lettow-Vorbeck, Martinien.

UR Surburg and Selz, 26 June 1815, clash

A village in eastern France, about 2 km west of the Rhine River, just east of Route D300 and between Haguenau (in France) and Rastatt in southern Germany.

Allied victories over the French.

(Last action – Rheinzabern, 23 June; next action – Dannemarie, 27 June).

French Forces GdD Rothembourg commanding the 15th Division of Rapp's V Corps: 18e, 36e, 39e, 40e and 103e RIdLi (2 bns each; 2e and 7e ChàCh (3 sqns each); 2 x FAB.

French totals ca 6,000 men and 12 guns.

French losses Not known. The French admitted 300 killed, wounded and captured.

Allied Forces FM the Crownprince of Württemberg commanding the III Corps: Austrian IR Reuss-Greitz Nr 18 (2 bns) and Vogelsang Nr 47 (2 bns); Württemberg JzPfR Prinz Adam Nr 4 (4 sqns); Hessen-Darmstadt Garde-ChLR (1 sqn). Frankfurt (1 bn); Reuss (1 bn).

Allied totals 6 bns, 4 sqns, ca 4,800 men.

Allied losses 95 dead, 372 wounded.

Comment General Rapp tried to hold off the Allies but was forced to withdraw into Strasbourg fortress.

Sources Plotho, Sporschil, Starklof.

NL Compiègne-sur-Oise, 27 June 1815, clash

A town in northern France on the River Oise and on Routes N31/E46 and D932A, about 70 km northeast of Paris.

An French victory over the Prussians.

(Last action – Le Quesnoy, 23–26 June; next action – Creil and Senlis, 27 June).

French Forces Part of d'Erlon's shattered I Corps; totals not known.

French Losses Not known, slight.

Allied Forces Part of GL von Ziethen's I Corps. 3rd Brigade GM von Jagow: 7th and 29th LIRs, 3rd Westfalian LWIR (3 bns each); Silesian Rifles (2nd and 4th coys); 1 x FAB. Cavalry Brigade GM von Treskow: 1st West Prussian DragR Nr 2, Brandenburg UlR (4 sqns each) 1 x HAB.

Allied totals 9½ bns, 8 sqns, 2 bties, ca 6,000 men.

Allied losses Not known, slight.

Comment The Prussians tried to block the retreat of d'Erlon's Corps but the French managed to slip around them and continue on towards Paris.

Sources Plotho, Sporschil, Bredow-Wedel, Martinien.

UR Dannemarie, 27 June 1815, clash

A village in eastern France on Route D419 about 20 km east of Belfort towards Basel.

An Austrian victory over the French.

(Last action – Surburg and Selz, 26 June; next action – Suffelweyersheim, 28 June).

French Forces GdD Lecourbe and GdD Abbé's 18th Division 6e, 52e, 62e and 102e RIdLi (2 bns each). 8th Light Cavalry Division GdB Meziau: 2e and 3e HusR (3 sqns each), 12 guns.

French totals 8 bns, 6 sqns, 12 guns, ca 4,000 men.

French losses Not known 'moderate'.

Austrian Forces GM Geramb's Avantgarde of FM Schwarzenberg's I Corps: Jägers (2nd Bn); HusR EH Ferdinand Nr 3 (4 sqns); GzIR Gradiskaner Nr 8 (1 bn).

Austrian totals 2 bns, 3 sqns, ca 3,000 men.

Austrian losses 7 officers and 182 men killed and wounded.

Sources Wrede, Lettow-Vorbeck, Martinien.

NL Creil and Senlis, 27 June 1815, clash

Two towns in northern France, Creil is on the River Oise, Senlis 11 km to the east; both are about 43 km north northeast of Paris.

A Prussian victory over the French.

(Last action – Compiègne, 27 June; next action – Villers-Cotterêts, 28 June).

French Forces The remnants of the following corps (exact details not known): d'Erlon's I Corps, Kellermann's III Cavalry Corps; Milhaud's IV Cavalry Corps.

French totals Unknown.

French losses Unknown.

Allied Forces GL von Bülow's IV Corps. **13th Brigade** GM von Hacke: 3rd Neumark LWIR (3 bns). **16th Brigade** Obst von Hiller: 1st Silesian LWIR (1 bn) **Cavalry Brigade** GM von Sydow: HusR Nr 8 (4 sqns). **Cavalry Brigade** Count von Schwerin: 1st Pommeranian LWCR (4 sqns). **Artillery** ½ x HAB Nr 12.

Allied totals 4 bns, 8 sqns, 4 guns, ca 3,000 men.

Allied losses Not known, slight.

Comment Having failed to cross the Oise at Compiègne early that day, the French pushed their way through Senlis and Kellermann's 1st Cuirassier Brigade (8e and 11e Cuirassiers) crossed the river at Creil.

Sources Plotho, Sporschil, Bredow-Wedel, Martinien.

NL Villers-Cotterêts, 28 June 1815, clash

A village in northern France about 72 km northeast of Paris on Route N2 to Soissons.

A Prussian victory over the French.

(Last action – Creil and Senlis, 27 June; next action – Nanteuil-le-Hauduin, 28 June).

French Forces Part of M Grouchy's Reserve Cavalry, about 9,000 men, including the 1er HusR and 50e RIdLi.

French losses 150 infantry captured, 14 HA guns and 20 ammunition waggons.

Prussian Forces The 2nd Brigade of GL von Ziethen's I Corps: 1st Westprussian LWIR (Füs Bn); Brandenburg DragR Nr 5(4 sqns); ca 1,100 men.

Prussian losses Not known; slight.

Comment The Prussian raid took place in the early hours; later Gen Count Vandamme and the remnants of his III Corps came up to support Grouchy and the Prussians withdrew. The French pressed on towards Paris.

Sources Plotho, Sporschil, Bredow-Wedel, Martinien.

UR Suffelweyersheim, 28 June 1815, clash

A town in eastern France (Alsace-Lorraine) at the junction of Routes N62 and N63 and D27, D263, D919, about 28 km north of Strasbourg and 15 km west of the River Rhine.

An Allied victory over the French.

(Last action – Dannemarie, 27 June, next action – Strasbourg, 28 June).

French Forces GdD Rothembourg's 15th division of Rapp's V Corps: 36e, 39e, 40e and 103e RIdLi (2 bns each); 2e and 7e ChàCh (3 sqns each); 2 x FAB 11e DragR (3 sqns).

French totals 6 bns, 9 sqns, 12 guns, ca 5,600 men.

French losses 700 killed and wounded, 6 guns and 2 colours.

Allied Forces GM Luxem's Austrian brigade: IR Reuss-Greitz Nr 18 (2 bns); Vogelsang Nr 47 (2 bns) and Württemberg JzPFR Herzog Louis Nr 2 (4 sqns) and IR Nr 2 (2 bns). Hessen-Darmstadt: Leibgarde (2nd Bn); Garde-Füs-R (1 bn).

Allied totals 8 bns, 4 sqns, ca 7,700 men.

Allied losses Not known, slight.

Comment The Württemberg cavalry regiment overthrew the 2e ChàCh and destroyed their élite company; the French withdrew through Hagenau and were driven out of Brumath (Brumpt) that night. They then withdrew into Strasbourg fortress.

Sources Plotho, Sporschil, Wrede, Starklof, Voss.

FJ Conflans (Hôpital), 28 June 1815, clash

A village in the eastern French Jura mountains in the valley of the River Isère, just east of Albertville on Route N212.

A French victory over the Austro-Sardinians.

(Last action – Césanne, 21 June, next action – Les Rousses Pass, 28 June).

French Forces GdB Bugeaud commanding: 14e RIdLi, 20e RIdLi (2 bns each). 10e ChàCh (4 sqns).

French total About 1,200 men.

French losses Light; the 14e lost 4 officers wounded, the 20e lost 5 and the 10e 1 officer killed.

Sardinian Forces Gen d'Audezene commanding: Cacciatori Italiani (2 bns).

Sardinian losses Not known.

Austrian Forces Obst O'Brien's column of FML Bubna's corps: Jägers (1 bn); IR Duka Nr 39, IR Kerpen Nr 49 (10 coys); HusR Frimont Nr 9 (1 sqn); 2 guns and 1 howitzer.

Allied totals ca 2,000 men.

Allied losses Not known; IR Duka lost 16 officers and 500 men.

Comment The French withdrew to Montmelian on the River Isère.

Sources Plotho, Sporschil, Wrede, Martinien, Voss.

FJ Les Rousses Pass, 28 June 1815, clash

A pass in the eastern French Jura mountains on Route N5, south of the village of Morez and about 26 km north of Geneva.

An Austrian victory over the French.

(Last action – Aiguebelle and Conflans, 28 June; next action – Nantua, 6 July).

French Forces GdB Bugeaud commanding: 14e and 20 e RIdLi (2 bns each); 10e ChàCh (4 sqns), 6 guns. Exact details not known; part of Dessaix's and Maransin's divisions.

French losses Not known.

Austrian Forces Gen Fölseis (of FML Radivojevich's Corps) commanding IR Beaulieu Nr 58 (2 bns) and IR Württemberg Nr 38 (2 bns); ChLR O'Reilly Nr 3 (4 sqns); ChLR Rosenberg Nr 6 (4 sqns); IR Gyulai Nr 60 (3 bns).

Austrian totals 7 bns, ca 3,000 men.

Austrian losses Not known, slight.

Comment The French force was mainly National Guard and held out well from the dawn assault until midday when they attempted a counter-attack and were taken in flank by the Austrian cavalry. This victory gave the Austrians control of the most vital passes into the French-held Saône valley.

Sources Plotho, Sporschil, Wrede, Martinien.

NL Nanteuil-le-Hauduin, 28 June 1815, skirmish

A village in northern France, about 46 km northeast of Paris on Route N100 to Soissons.

An Prussian victory over the French.

(Last action – Villers-Cotterêts, 28 June; next action – Versailles, 1 July).

French Forces Parts of Gen Count Reille's II Corps including the 5e ChLL.

French totals and losses Unknown; 'some prisoners and 2 guns'.

Prussian Forces Reserve Cavalry of GL von Ziethen's I Corps; GL von Röder: 1st Westprussian DragR Nr 2 (4 sqns); 1st Silesian Hussars (4 sqns); 1 x HAB.

Prussian losses Not known, slight.

Comment This slight defeat served to increase the disintegration of the French army.

Sources Plotho, Sporschil, Bredow-Wedel.

NL Versailles, 1 July 1815, clash

Nowadays a suburb of Paris in France, to the west of the city.

An French victory over the Prussians.

(Last action – Nanteuil, 28 June; next action – Issy, 2 and 3 July).

French Forces II Cavalry Corps of Gen Count Exelmans: 9th Cavalry Division GdD Strolz: 5e, 13e, 15e and 20e DragR (4 sqns each); GdD Piré 5e HusR and 6e HusR (6 sqns) 1er and 9e ChàCh (4 sqns each); 44e RIdLi (3 bns); GdN Sèvres (½ bn).

French totals ca 5,000 men.

French losses Not known, slight.

Prussian Forces Obstlt Sohr: Brandenburg HusR Nr 3; Pommeranian HusR Nr 5 (4 sqns each).

Prussian totals ca 750 men.

Prussian losses 10 officers and 500 men killed, wounded and captured. Obstlt Sohr was killed.

Brandenburg HusR loss = 1 officers, 15 men and 76 horses killed; 7 officers, 36 men and 35 horses wounded; 7 men and 178 horses captured.

Pommeranian HusR loss = 1 officer, 57 men and 56 horses killed; 4 officers, 77 men and 25 horses wounded; 8 officers, 227 men and 243 horses captured.

Comment The victory did much to lift the flagging spirits of the French, the two Prussian regiments were effectively destroyed.

Sources Plotho, Sporschil, Bredow-Wedel, Martinien, Voigt, Voss.

UR Marsal, 25 June – 1 July 1815, blockade

A small fortress in the hills of eastern France, just north of Route D955 and 30 km along the road from Nancy towards Dieuze in the east.

A French victory over the Bavarians.

(Last action – Saarbrücken and Saargemünd, 23 June; next action – Hausbergen, 9 July).

French Garrison 600 men and 15 guns.

French losses Unknown; slight.

Bavarian Forces 4th Lt Bn (1 bn) of GM Count Pocci's 1st Brigade of the 1st Infantry Division.

Bavarian Losses Not known, very light.

Comment After a fruitless bombardment of the fort by the artillery of the 1st Division in the night of 30 June/1 July, the Bavarians handed over the blockade to the Russians.

Sources Leyh, Sporschil, Plotho.

NL Issy, 2–3 July 1815, capture

Nowadays a suburb in the southwest of the city of Paris in France.

A Prussian victory over the French.

(Last action – Versailles, 1 July; next action – Maubeuge, 20 June – 12 July).

French Forces Gen Vandamme commanding the III Corps: 9e RILé, 59e, 69e, 72e, 76e and 108e RIdLi.

French totals and losses Not known exactly.

Prussian Forces Gen von Ziethen's I Corps: **1st Brigade** GM von Steinmetz: 12th and 24th LIRs (6 bns); **2nd Brigade** GM von Pirch II: 2nd Westfalian LWIR (3 bns); 4th Westfalian LWIR (1 bn), ½ x FAB.

Prussian totals ca 6,500 men.

Prussian losses 12th LIR – 5 officers and 71 men killed, wounded and missing. 24th LIR – 168 officers and men killed, wounded and missing; 2nd Westfalian LWIR – not known but the total Prussian loss was 30 officers and 1,216 men of all arms.

Comment Ziethen took Issy in the night 2/3 July and threw out its garrison of 15 bns, some cavalry and artillery. Vandamme's counter-attack on 3rd July was beaten off. This was the last action before the surrender of Paris.

Sources Plotho, Sporschil, Martinien, Bredow-Wedel, Voigt.

FJ Nantua, 6 July 1815, clash

A small town in the eastern French Jura mountains, on Route N84 about 45 km west of Geneva.

An Austrian victory over the French.

(Last action – Les Rousses Pass, 28 June; next action – Forts l'Ecluse and la Grotte, 5 – 7 July).

French Forces Part of GdD Dessaix's or Maransin's divisions 42e and 53e RIdLi.

French totals ca 3,000 infantry, 1 cavalry sqn, 5 guns.

French losses 6 officers and 400 men killed, wounded and captured.

Austrian Forces Part of FML Baron Merville's Reserve Corps: IR Kerpen Nr 49 (1st LW bn); IR Deutschmeister Nr 4 (1st and 2nd Bn); GzIR Wallachisch-Illyrisch (2 coys); IR EH Ludwig Nr 8 (1st LW bn); 1 x 6 pdr FA Bty.

Austrian totals 4 bns, 2 coys, 1 bty, ca 4,000 men and 6 guns.

Austrian losses 150 dead and wounded.

Sources Plotho, Sporschil, Wrede, Martinien, Voss.

FJ Fort L'Ecluse 5–7 July 1815, bombardment and surrender

A fortress cut into the rock in the gorge of the River Rhône about 20 km southeast of Geneva (in Switzerland) on the French Route N84.

An Austrian victory over the French.

(Last action – Nantua, 6 July; next action – Fort la Grotte, 5 – 7 July).

French Garrison GdN de Haute-Saône (2e Bn); Veterans (4 coys).

French losses Not known, all the garrison were captured with 4 guns and a colour.

Austrian Forces Parts of FML Count Bubna's Corps and GM Mumb's brigade of FML Baron Merville's Reserve Corps: IR Esterházy Nr (1st and 2nd bns); IR Deutschmeister Nr 4 (2 coys); 2 x FAB.

Austrian totals 2 bns, 2 coys, 12 guns.

Austrian losses Not known, slight.

Comment A lucky Austrian shell exploded the magazine of the fort and the garrison surrendered. In the redoubt the Austrians took 4 guns and a colour.

Sources Plotho, Sporschil, Wrede, Martinien.

FJ Fort la Grotte 5–7 July 1815, siege and surrender

A fortress in the valley of the River Durance in eastern France, on Route N94, ca 32 km east of Gap.

(Last action – Nantua, 6 July; next action – Belfort, 29 June – 8 July).

French Garrison Maj Spring, 4 officers, 2 drummers and 83 veterans.

French losses The garrison was captured and sent home on condition that they did not fight against the Allies again.

Austrian Forces Obst O'Brien's column of FML Bubna's Corps: Jägers (1 bn); IR Kerpen Nr 49 (1 bn and 3 coys).

Austrian totals 2 bns and 3 coys; ca 2,000 men.

Austrian losses Not known, slight.

Sources Plotho, Sporschil, Wrede, Martinien.

FJ Belfort, 29 June – 8 July 1815, blockade

A fortress in eastern France, just north of the Swiss border at the junction of Routes N19, N83 and D419 (to Basel).

(Last action – Fort de la Grotte, 5–7 July; next action – Grenoble, 9 July).

French Garrison GdD Boyer commanding: GdN Jura

(1er and 2e Bns); Doubs (1er, 2e and 3e Bns); Veterans (16 coys); GdN Sedentaire (1 bn and 1 arty coy); Militaire Retraités (2e Bn).

French totals ca 8,000 men.

French losses 70 officers and 1,430 men killed and wounded.

Austrian Forces GM von Scheither commanding: IR Kaiser Alexander Nr 2 (4th Bn); IR EH Rainer Nr 11 (3rd Bn); IR Reuss-Plauen Nr 17 (2 bns); IR Benjowsky Nr 31 (4th Bn); IR Württemberg Nr 40 (4th Bn); IR Kottulinsky Nr 41 (4 bns); IR Bellegarde Nr 44 (Res Bn); IR Froon Nr 54 (3 bns); IR W Colloredo Nr 56 (3 bns).

Austrian totals 17 bns, ca 14,000 men.

Austrian losses ca 2,000 men killed, wounded and died of sickness.

Sources Plotho, Sporschil, Wrede, Martinien, Voss.

FJ Grenoble, 9 July 1815, surrender

A town in the eastern French Jura mountains at the junction of Routes N75, N85 and A41/E4, about 100 km south east of Lyon.

An Allied victory over the French.

(Last action – Belfort, 29 June – 8 July; next action – Mâcon, 10 July).

French Forces GdD (8 bns); 54 guns, 8 mortars.

French totals ca 7,500 men.

French losses Very slight; the GdN were sent home when they surrendered the town.

Allied Forces Austrian GL Latour's Piemont Army Corps; Liechtenstein Vélites (2 coys); Jägers (2 bns) plus Austrian IRs Kerpen Nr 49 (1 bn) and HusR Frimont Nr 9 (6 sqns) and 1,300 Sardinian troops under Gen d'Antezaine: Reg della Guardie (2 bns); Cacciatori di Nizza (1 bn).

Allied totals ca 13,000 men.

Allied losses 180 men killed and wounded.

Sources Plotho, Sporschil, Wrede, Martinien.

UR Hausbergen, 9 July 1815, clash

A village in Alsace in eastern France just northwest of Strasbourg on a minor road between Routes N4 and N63.

An Allied victory over the French.

(Last action – Marsal, 25 June; next action – Strasbourg, 28 June – 30 July).

French Forces Count Rapp Commanding. GdD Albert: 10e RILé, 18e RIdLi (3 bns each); 32e RIdLi (2 bns);11e and 19e DragR (3 sqns each); 7e ChàCh (3 sqns).

French totals 9,500 infantry, 1,500 cavalry.

French losses 21 officers, 479 men killed and wounded, 32 officers and 1,700 men captured.

Allied Forces FM Kronprinz von Württemberg commanding the III Corps: FML Mazzuchelli: IR Erbach Nr 42 (2 bns); Baden Infantry Regiments Leib-Gren-Gd (1 bn); IR Grossherzog Nr 3 (2 bns); LWIR's Nrs 6, 7, 8: Jägers (1 bn); Baden Cavalry: GdC (2 sqns); 1st and 2nd DragRs (10 sqns).

Allied totals 12 bns, 12 sqns, 18 guns, ca 13,200 men.

Allied losses Austrians – 759 killed and wounded; Baden – 9 officers and 160 men dead and wounded.

Comment The French garrison made a sortie in strength and initially surprised the Austrians under cover of thick fog. They were then forced back into the fortress.

Sources Plotho, Sporschil, Wrede, Martinien, von Brasewisch, Voss.

FJ Mâcon, 10 July 1815, surrender of

A fortified town and bridgehead on the River Saône in eastern France on Route N6/E1 about 60 km north of Lyon.

An Austrian victory over the French.

(Last action – Grenoble, 9 July; next action – This was the last action in the Jura campaign).

French Forces GdN (1 bn).

French totals 800 men and 5 guns.

French losses Dead and wounded not known; 4 guns and 1 howitzer taken.

Austrian Forces Part of FML Radivojevich's I Corps: IR EH Ludwig Nr 8 (6 coys).

Austrian totals ca 1,000 men.

Allied losses 3 officers and 76 men killed and wounded.

Comment The French abandoned the bridgehead on the eastern bank of the river. Next day, M Suchet in Lyon signed an armistice with GdC Baron Frimont ending hostilities in this theatre.

Sources Plotho, Sporschil, Wrede, Martinien, Voss.

NL Maubeuge 20 June – 12 July 1815, siege and capitulation

A fortified town in northern France, on the River Sambre, at the crossing of route N2 and N49 about 55 km southwest of Waterloo.

A Prussian victory over the French.

(Last action – Issy, 2 and 3 July; next action – Landrecies, 14–21 July).

French Garrison GdB Baron Latour commanding: 3,000 GdN and veterans and 160 line troops.

French losses Unknown dead and wounded; the GdN and the veterans went home. GdB Latour, 150 line troops and 2 guns marched off to join the rump of Davout's army behind the River Loire.

Prussian Forces GL von Pirch I commanding.

II Prussian Corps 5th Brigade GM von Tippelskirchen: 2nd LIR, 25th LIR, 5th Westfalian LWIR (2 bns each). 7th Brigade GM von Brause: 14th LIR, 22nd LIR; 2nd Elb-LWIR (3 bns each).

Prussian totals ca 12,000 men, 24 field guns, 60 siege guns.

Prussian losses 16 dead, 67 wounded.

Sources Renouard, Zelle, Plotho, Sporschil, Martinien.

NL Landrecies, 14–21 July 1815, siege and capitulation

A fortified town on the River Sambre in northern France, on Route 959 about 85 km southwest of Waterloo and 170 km north northeast of Paris.

A Prussian victory over the French.

(Last action – Maubeuge, 20 June – 12 July; next action – Marienbourg, 24 June – 28 July).

French Garrison Col Plaige and 2,000 GdN and 150 line troops.

French losses Dead and wounded not known. The 4 battalions of GdN went home; Col Plaige and 150 line troops marched off to join the rump of Davout's army behind the River Loire.

Prussian Forces GM von Brause and the 7th Brigade; 14th and 22nd LIR; 2nd Elb-LWIR (3 bns each); 12 field guns.

Prussian totals ca 6,000 men and 12 field guns; on 16 July the 60 siege guns arrived from Maubeuge.

Prussian losses 3 dead, 4 wounded.

Sources Renouard, Zelle, Plotho, Sporschil, Martinien.

NL Marienbourg, 24 June – 28 July 1815, blockade and surrender

A fortified town in northern France, on the River Virvin, just to the east of Route N5, 70 km south of Waterloo and 210 km northeast of Paris.

A Prussian victory over the French.

(Last action – Landrecies 14-21 July; next action – Philippeville, 22 July – 9 August).

French Garrison 400 GdN and veterans.

French losses Not known, very slight; the garrison was released and went home.

Prussian Forces Obst von Langen commanding the 8th Prussian Brigade: 21st and 23rd LIR and 3rd Elb-LWIR (3 bns each).

Prussian total ca 6,000 men, 12 field guns.

Prussian losses 1 dead, 3 wounded.

Sources Renouard, Zelle, Plotho, Sporschil, Martinien.

UR Strasbourg, 28 June – 30 July 1815, clash and blockade

A fortified city in eastern France, just west of the Rhine River and at the junction of Routes N4, N63, A4/E42, A35.

An Allied victory over the French.

(Last action – Hausbergen, 9 July; next action – Neu-Briesach, 2 July – 10 August).

French Forces General Count Rapp commanding: 10e RILé, 32e, 36e and 40e RIdLi and several GdN bns; 11e and 19e DragR; 2e and 7e ChàCh, GdN (11 bns); Invalides (2 bns).

French totals 24 bns, 16 sqns, 36 guns, ca 21,000 men.

French losses ca 1,000 dead, wounded and captured, 6 guns, 2 colours.

Allied Forces FM Crownprince of Württemberg: FL Palombini's Austrian Division: Brigade of GM Luxem: IR Reuss-Greitz Nr 18 (2 bns); IR Vogelsang Nr 47 (2 bns); IR Württemberg Nr 40 (3 bns). HusR Kronprinz von Württemberg Nr 6 (2 sqns). FML Prince Philipp von Hessen-Homburg: Hessen-Darmstadt IR Leibgarde (3 bns); IR Gross- und Erbprinz (1st Bn); Lt I Bn (1 bn); Garde ChLR (1 tp); 1st and 2nd FAB; 12 guns.

Allied totals 12 bns, 2 sqns, and 1tp, 12 guns, ca 8,000 men.

Allied losses ca 2,000 killed, wounded and missing.

Sources Plotho, Sporschil, Wrede, Martinien, Voss.

IC Gaëta 28 May – 8 August 1815, siege and surrender

A fortress on the western Italian coast, on Route 7 between Naples and Rome on Route 213.

An Allied victory over the Neapolitans.

(Last action – Tolentino, 3 May; next action – this was the last action in Italy).

Neapolitan Forces Maresciallo di Campo Begani

commanding. 2,000 soldiers of various regiments. 31 x 12 pdrs, 42 x 24 pdrs, 7 x 8inch howitzers, 18 x 15inch mortars. A total of 244 guns, howitzers and mortars. At the end of the siege the garrison numbered 133 officers and 1,629 men. They were disarmed and sent either to Volturno or Trieste. Much ammunition, military stores and rations were found in the fortress.

Allied Forces GM Baron Lauer.

Austrian troops IR Splényi Nr 51 (2nd Bn); IR Wacquant Nr 62 (3rd Bn)*; 12 Pionier coy (1 coy), Artillery (1 coy), Total 1,441 men.

Tuscan Troops Jägers (1 bn).

Sicilian and Neapolitan Troops 2 LIR Estero (2 Bn); Sappers (½ coy) Artillery (1 coy); Total 654 men. British naval squadron under Captain Fahie including 41 British gun boats and 10 Neapolitan gun boats.

Allied losses Slight; about 27 officers and 250 men killed and wounded.

* = departed for Capua on 23 July and was replaced by 4th Sicilian LIR.

Comment Begani conducted a very tough, but ultimately pointless defence of this extremely strong fortress. His loyalty was to Murat alone.

Sources ÖMZ 1823, Heft 9, Chapter II, Plotho.

NL Philippeville, 22 July – 9 August 1815, blockade and surrender

A fortified town in northern France, at the junction of Routes N5, N40 and N97, 60 km from Waterloo and 215 km from Paris.

A Prussian victory over the French.

(Last action – Marienbourg, 24 June – 28 July; next action – Valenciennes and Condé, 30 June – 12 August).

French Garrison GdB Cassaigne and 1,700 line troops, GdN and veterans.

French losses Dead and wounded unknown; the GdN and the veterans went home, GdB Cassaigne, 150 line troops and 2 guns marched off to join the rump of Davout's army behind the River Loire.

Prussian Forces The 5th and 6th Prussian Brigades: 5th Brigade GM von Tippelskirchen: 2nd and 25th LIR; 5th Westfalian LWIR (3 bns each). 6th Brigade GM von Krafft: 9th and 26th LIR, 1st Elb-LWIR (3 bns each); Neumark DragR (2 sqns); Elb-LWCR (2 sqns); 24 guns.

Prussian totals 18 bns, 4 sqns, 24 guns.

Prussian losses Not known, very slight.

Sources Renouard, Zelle, Plotho, Sporschil, Martinien.

UR Neu-Briesach (Neuf-Brisach) 2 July – 10 August 1815, siege

A fortified town in eastern France, about 3 km west of the River Rhine on Route N415 coming out of Colmar.

(Last action – Strasbourg, 28 June – 30 July; next action Hüningen, 15 – 26 August).

French Garrison GdB Dremencourt and about 2,000 GdN.

French losses Not known; the garrison were discharged.

Allied Forces Initially: Hessen-Darmstadt IR Gross- und Erbprinz (2nd Bn). As of 10 July: GM Baron Volkmann and Baden LWI bns (1st, 5th and 8th bn); Austrian IR Bianchi Nr 63 (4th Bn); ChLR Kaiser Nr 1 (2 sqns); 2 x FAB.

Allied totals 5 bns, 2 sqns, 12 guns.

Allied losses Not known, slight.

Sources Plotho, Sporschil, Wrede, Martinien, Voss.

NL Valenciennes and Condé, 30 June – 12 August 1815, siege and capitulation

A fortress in northern France at the junction of Routes N49, A2/E19 and A23, about 30 km southeast of Lille.

An Allied victory over the French.

(Last action – Philippeville, 22 July – 9 August; next action – Soissons, 14 August).

French Garrison General Count Roy. Exact details and losses not known.

Allied Forces LG Stedman's 1st (Dutch-Belgian) Division: 1st Brigade: MG Hauw: 4th and 6th LIR (2 bns each); 16th Jagers (1 bn); 9th, 14th and 15th Militia bns (3 bns). 2nd Brigade: MG Eerens: 1st LIR (2 bns); 18th Jagers (1 bn); 1st, 2nd and 18th Militia (3 bns). Artillery 1 x FAB. Indian Brigade: LG Anthing: 5th LIR (1 bn); Flankers (1 bn); 10th and 11th Jagers (2 bns). 1 x FAB.

Allied totals 18 bns, 2 x FAB, ca 9,000 men.

Allied losses Not known, very slight.

Comment On 12 August Valenciennes – and Condé – capitulated; the garrisons were sent home. The Fortresses of Lille, Douai and Bouchain had already declared for Louis XVIII.

Sources Siborne, Lettow-Vorbeck, Martinien.

NL Soissons, 14 August 1815, surrender

A fortified city in northern France (Département de l'Aisne) on the River Aisne, about 90 km northeast of Paris.

An Allied victory over the French.

(Last action - Valenciennes and Condé, 30 June - 12 August; next action - Rocroy, 22 July - 16 August).

French Forces Gen Baron Choisy and GdN Marne (1 bn) and Meuse (1 bn).

French total 153 officers, 1,000 men and 30 guns.

French losses None.

Allied Forces GL von Engelhard, Hessen-Kassel Jäger-Bn (1 bn).

Allied totals ca 800 men.

Allied losses None.

Sources Renouard, Martinien, Plotho, Wrede, Sporschil.

NL Rocroy, 22 July - 16 August, blockade and surrender

A fortified town in northern France, on Route N51, up against the borders of Luxembourg, 95 km from Waterloo and 190 km from Paris.

A Prussian victory over the French.

(Last action - Soissons, 14 August; next action - Sedan, 25 June - 20 August).

French Garrison GdB Projean and 2,000 GdN and veterans and the 34e RIdLi.

French losses Dead and wounded not known; the garrison were released and sent home.

Prussian Forces GM von Brause's 7th Brigade: 14th and 22nd LIR; 2nd Elb-LWIR (3 bns each) and the 5th Westfalian LWIR (3 bns) of GM von Tippelskirchen's 5th Brigade.

Prussian totals 12 bns, 12 guns, ca 6,400 men.

Prussian losses 12 wounded.

Sources Renouard, Zelle, Plotho, Sporschil, Martinien.

NL Sedan, 25 June - 20 August, siege and surrender

A fortified town in north eastern France, near the border with Luxembourg, on the River Meuse and Route N43, 125 km south of Waterloo and 210 km east north east of Paris.

An Allied victory over the French.

(Last action - Rocroy, 22 July - 16 August; next action - Mézières and Charleville, 3 July - 2 September).

French Garrison GdB Baron Choisy: GdN Marne (1 bn); GdN Moselle (1 bn); GdN artillery det. Gendarmes and Douaniers and 29 heavy guns.

French totals ca 1,300 men.

French losses Not known; the garrison was released and sent home.

Allied Forces GL von Engelhard (Kurhessen): IR Kurprinz (2nd and Füs Bns); IR Kurfürst (1st and Füs Bns); IR Landgraf Karl (2nd and Füs Bns); IR Prinz Solms (2nd and Füs Bns); 2nd Gren. Bn von Lossberg (1 bn); Jäger bn (1 bn); 2 x FAB.

Allied losses Minor.

Sources Renouard, Plotho, Sporschil, Zelle, Martinien.

UR Hüningen (Huningue), 15–26 August, siege and capitulation

A fortress in eastern France, up against the borders with Germany and Switzerland and just north of the Swiss city of Basel and west of the River Rhine.

An Allied victory over the French.

(Last action - Neu-Briesach, 2 July - 10 August; next action - This was the last action of this theatre).

French Garrison GdB Baron Barbanègre commanding 3,000 GdN and the 52e RIdLi (1 bn).

French losses 1,100 men deserted during the siege; the rest marched out with honours of war and then disbanded and went home.

Allied Forces GdC Archduke John of Austria commanding: IR Kollowrath Nr 36 (2nd and 3rd bns); IR Kottulinsky Nr 41 (4th Bn); IR Bellegarde Nr 44 (1 bn); IR Reuss-Greitz Nr 18 (2 bns); IR Vogelsang Nr (2 bns); Hessen-Darmstadt IR Gross-und Erbprinz (2nd Bn); Leib-garde (2 bns); LeibIR (2 bns); IR Prinz Emil (2 bns); 5 artillery batteries.

Allied totals ca 15,000 men.

Allied losses Not known; slight.

Comment Gen Barbanègre threatened to bombard Basel but the Allies brought up heavy siege artillery and silenced his guns. Hüningen fortifications were slighted after the surrender.

Sources Plotho, Sporschil, Wrede, Martinien.

NL Mézières and Charleville, 3 July - 2 September, siege and capitulation

Twin fortresses and arsenals in northeastern France, on the River Meuse, near Luxembourg and at the junction of Routes N43 and N51, 110 km south of Waterloo and 195 km northeast of Paris.

An Allied victory over the French.

(Last action - Sedan, 25 June - 20 August; next action

- Longwy, 2 June - 18 September).

French Garrison of Charleville: GdB La Planche and 1,000 GdN and veterans. 11e ChàCh (5 sqns).

French losses Charleville was stormed on 29 June and an eagle of the GdN was taken. GdB La Planche, 18 officers and most of the garrison were captured; only a few escaped to Mézières.

French Garrison of Mézières GdD Lemoine; GdN Meuse (5th and 6th bns); Douaniers (350 men) and about 300 refugees from the battle of Waterloo.

French totals 2,500 men and 60 guns.

French losses ca 600 men killed, wounded and died of sickness.

Allied Forces Prussian GL von Hake commanding the North German Federal Corps:

Hessen-Kassel troops GL Engelhard: IR Kurprinz (1st and Füs Bns); IR Kurfürst (3 bns); IR Landgraf Karl (1st and Füs Bns); IR Prinz Solms (1st and Füs Bns); 2nd Gren Bn von Lossberg (1 bn); Jägers (1 bn); 2 FAB. **Mecklenburg Troops** GL Erbgrossherzog von Mecklenburg-Schwerin: Obst von Both: Garde-Gren (1 bn); Leib-Bn (1 bn); 2nd LIR (1 bn); 1st, 2nd and 3rd LWI Bns (3 bns). **Thüringian Brigade** GM von Egloffstein: Sachsen-Weimar - 1 line and 1 LWI Bns; Sachsen-Gotha - 1 line and 1 LWI Bns; Anhalt-Dessau - 1 line bn; Anhalt-Bernburg-Köthen - 1 line bn; Schwarzburg - 1 line bn; Waldeck - 1 line bn; Schaumburg-Lippe - 1 line bn; Lippe-Detmold - 1 line bn; Oldenburg - 1st and 2nd line bns. **Cavalry Brigade** GM von Warburg: Hessen-Kassel: Leib-DragR (4 sqns); HusR (4 sqns); Mecklenburg-Strelitz - HusR (4 sqns); ½ x FAB.

Allied totals 30 bns, 12 sqns, 2½ FAB, 15 guns, ca 25,000 men.

Allied losses A total of 9 officers, 23 NCOs and 205 men dead and wounded; in the storm of Charleville on 29 June. The Hessians lost 11 dead and 30 wounded.

Comment On 10 August the French surrendered the town and withdrew into Mézières citadel. The Hessian troops left on 15 August to join the blockade of Montmédy.

Sources Renouard, Zelle, Plotho, Sporschil, Martinien.

NL Longwy, 2 June - 18 September, siege and capitulation

A fortified town in northern France, just west of Luxembourg, on the River Chiers and on Route N5/E44 and N52.

An Allied victory over the French.

(Last action - Mézières and Charleville, 3 July - 2 September, next action - Montmédy, 18 July - 18 September).

French Garrison GdB Baron Ducos and about 423 GdN, 125 officers and 476 line troops and 65 guns.

French losses Dead and wounded unknown (at least 25 officers); all survivors declared prisoners of war and sent to Metz to the disposal of the French government.

Allied Forces Initially Prince Ludwig von Hessen-Homburg with 2,500 Austrian troops of Luxembourg garrison with 12 guns and 8 howitzers. As of 24 July these were reinforced by the Avantgarde of GL von Horn's VI Prussian Corps; Obst von Lange, 6th, 7th, 19th and 24th Grsn I bns, Obstlt von Kleist: 4th Elb-LWIR (3 bns) and the 1st bns of the 6th, 7th and 8th Westfalian LWIRs; Maj von Kaibel: 1st and 2nd Field Pionier coys, Mansfeld Pionier coy; Maj von Ludwig: 13th, 14th and 15th Provisional Arty coys and Obst von Marschall with the Kurhessian Leib-DragR (2 sqns). On 27 August 1,500 Prussian LWI recruits joined. The Mecklenburg brigade (Garde-Gren-Bn, 1st and 2nd Musketier-Bns) of 3,000 men came up and on 12 September the 23rd Prussian LIR (of the 8th Brigade) also joined.

Allied losses 48 dead and 219 wounded.

Comment The Allied losses were incurred by the 23rd Prussian LIR which stormed a lunette in the night of 13/14 September. There had been a cease-fire agreement with the garrison from 11 August to 8 September.

Sources Renouard, Plotho, Sporschil, Martinien.

NL Montmédy, 18 July - 18 September, blockade and siege

A fortified town on the River Chiers in north eastern France on Route N43, 150 km south-southeast of Waterloo and 228 km east of Paris.

An Allied victory over the French.

(Last action - Longwy, 2 June - 18 September; next action - Givet and Charlemont, 22 August - 24 September).

French Garrison GdD Laurent with ca 2,000 GdN, veterans and line troops and 53 guns.

French losses Dead and wounded unknown. General Laurent and the line troops with 2 guns marched off to join the rump of Davout's army on the River Loire.

Allied Forces GL von Hake. **18 July – 15 August** Obst von Marschall with IR Weimar (1 bn); IR Lippe (1 bn); Kurhessian Leib DragR (2 sqns); Kurhessian Jägers (1 bn).

15 August – 4 September Mecklenburg Brigade GL Erbgrossherzog von Mecklenburg-Schwerin: Garde-Gren-Bn (1 bn); 1st Musketier-Bn (1 bn); 2nd Musketier-Bn (1 bn); 1st, 2nd and 3rd LWI Bns. **4–14 September** GM von Warburg: 1st and 2nd IR Oldenburg; IR Lippe-Waldeck; Mecklenburg-Strelitz HusR (4 sqns). On 8 September the 21st Prussian LIR (3 bns) joined the blockading force.

Allied totals Initially 2,800 men, from 15 August, 8,500; from 4 September, 13,000 and from 8 September ca 16,000 men.

Allied losses Not exactly known; very slight.

Comment On 16 August a cease-fire was agreed with the garrison. In mid-September GL von Hake planned to storm the fortress of Medybas with GM von Warburg's brigade but this general refused due to the imminent prospect of peace. Von Hake thus sent this brigade to Thionville as a punishment and assaulted – and took – Medybas on the night 14/15 September with the 21st Prussian LIR, IR Lippe-Waldeck, IR Weimar and the Kurhessian Jägers with a loss of 10 killed and 108 wounded; the French lost 14 dead.

Sources Renouard, Plotho, Sporschil, Wrochem and Haevernick.

NL Givet and Charlemont, 22 August – 24 September 1815, siege

Twin fortresses astride the River Meuse in north eastern France, at the junction of Routes N51, N40 and N96, 70 km south of Waterloo and 230 km northeast of Paris.

An Allied victory over the French.

(Last action – Montmédy, 18 July – 18 September; next action – this was the last action in this theatre).

French Garrison GdD Count Bourke and 3,500 GdN and officer refugees from Waterloo and 34e RIdLi.

French losses Not known, slight.

Allied Forces.

II Prussian Corps Prince August of Prussia and GL von Pirch I:

6th Brigade GM von Krafft: Colberg LIR Nr 9, 26th LIR, 1st Elb-LWIR (3 bns each). 7th Brigade GM von Brause: LIRs Nr 14 and Nr 22, 2nd Elb-LWIR (3 bns each). Reserve Artillery: 12 pdr FAB Nr 4 and 8, 6 pdr FAB Nrs 5, 10, 12, 34 and 36;.

Totals 18 bns, 7 FAB, 56 guns.

Kurhessian Division GL von Engelhard (from Mézières and Charleville) 2nd Brigade GM von Müller: IR Kurfürst (3 bns); IR Kurprinz 1st and Füs Bns); Jägers (1 bn). Artillery: 2 x 6 pdr FAB.

Allied totals ca 14,000 men, 66 guns, 14 howitzers, 49 mortars.

Allied losses Not known, light.

Comment The fortresses comprising the defences of these places were: Petit Givet (10 guns); Grande Givet (10 guns); Fort des Vigres (12 guns); Mont d'Haurs (30 guns) and Charlemont (98 guns). Bourke raised the white, Bourbon flag and was thus spared the attentions of the English siege artillery train but would not open the fort to the Allies.

Sources Renouard, Plotho, Sporschil, Martinien.

BIBLIOGRAPHY

Over the last thirty years in general, and over the last three in particular, I have consulted hundreds of books in order to analyse and record the data which now constitutes this volume. This, of course, is only a tiny fraction of the thousands of books in many languages which have been and still are being published on the Napoleonic era.

I have necessarily been strictly selective in my use of source material and have concentrated on finding the best appropriate source for research on the specific issue of actual battle participation and the precise composition of armies present at a given action.

Most of the sources used are not in the English language. This is not to say that English language sources do not provide excellent material, but most of the older English language works concentrated on the British forces and their allies in the field in the years 1793–1795 or on the Iberian campaigns of 1808–1813. These allies included the Hanoverians, Hessen-Kassel, Hessen-Darmstadt, some Austrian, Prussian and United Provinces (Dutch) regiments, the Spanish and Portuguese armies and the King's German Legion.

In addition, of course, there are many fine works written by modern authors and published in recent years which I have not sought to include but are of considerable merit. These have fallen outside the very selective criteria I have set for this present work, as I have attempted to return to original sources as far as possible, but Napoleonic scholarship has benefited from such excellent works as David Chandler's *Campaigns of Napoleon* and his *Dictionary of the Napoleonic Wars*, John Elting's *Swords Around the Throne* and (with V. J. Esposito) *A Military History and Atlas of the Napoleonic Wars*, and works by modern contemporary authors such as Michael Glover, John Gill, George Nafziger and Charles Esdaile, all of which are much more acceptable to the modern reader than the rare works I cite here.

All the sources quoted are rated as being either 'excellent', 'very good', or 'good' as regards their provision of details as to who fought where, when and to casualties and losses suffered. Those works not specifically commented upon are classified 'good' for the particular themes they cover. The vast majority of those listed are very old, rare and difficult to locate. I have made a deliberate effort to consult nineteenth-century sources in order to return, as closely as possible, to original and primary sources and thereby avoid the risk of repeating errors in data that, upon repetition, become accepted as fact. It is an inevitable truth that the more times data is copied, the more errors occur. There is an opportunity for a modern researcher to write a study revealing how some classic errors were created and have been repeated from century to century.

Alt, George, 'Geschichte der königlichen Preussischen Kürassiere und Dragoner seit 1691 resp. 1631–1870', out of *Das königliche Preussische Stehende Heer*, Schropp, Berlin, 1870. Very good for Prussian Kürassier and Dragoon regiments.

Anderson, R. C., *Naval Wars in the Baltic 1522–1850*, Gilbert Wood, London, 1910, Edwards, London, 1969.

Angeli, Moritz Edlen von, *Erzherzog Karl als Feldherr, und Heeresorganisator*, Volumes 1–5: 1, 1796–1797; 2, 1799; 3, 1805; 4, 1809; 5, 1813. Wilhelm Braunmüller, Wien und Leipzig, 1896. Excellent for Austrian participation 1796, 1799, 1805, 1809 and 1813.

Anon, *Betrachtungen über den Feldzug welchen die Allierten Armeen im Jahre 1794 in den Niederlanden führen werden*, 1795.

Anon, *Denkwürdigkeiten des Mecklenburg-Strelitzschen Husaren-Regiment in den Jahren des Befreiungskampfes 1813–1815*, C. Brünslow, Neubrandenburg, 1854. Excellent but quite narrowly focused on this regiment.

Anon, *Freymüthige Beurteilungen der Operationen der österreichischen und französischen Armeen in dem vierten Feldzuge 1795 des österreichischen-französischen Krieges*, Germanien, 1796.

Anon, *Geschichtliche Landeskunde der Festung Mainz*, Volume III, Mainz, Universität.

Arndt, Ernst Moritz, *Schwedische Geschichten unter Gustav III, vorzüglich aber unter Gustav IV Adolf*, Leipzig, 1839.

Austrian General Staff *Krieg 1809*, Wien 1907-1909, L. W. Seidel und Sohn. An excellently detailed, multi-volume work, concentrating mainly on the Austrian army but with some details of the French.

Barsewisch, von, *Geschichte des Grossherzoglich Badischen Leib-Grenadier-Regiments*, Karlsruhe, 1906.

Bartsch, Oberleutnant, *Die Schill'chen Offiziere 1809*, C. W. Stern, Wien, 1909. One of the best works on Ferdinand Schill's march through north Germany in 1809.

Bas, Francois de, *Prins Frederik der Nederlanden en zyn tijd*, Schiedam, 1884-1914, Vol 1 of 4 Volumes. Very good for the organization and orders of battle of the army of the United Provinces (Holland); 1792-1795. Includes details of British, Hanoverian, Austrian and Hessian regiments.

Beamish, Major North Ludlow, *Geschichte der Königlich Deutschen Legion*, Hahn, Hannover, 1832-1837.

— *History of the King's German Legion*, Boone, London, 1832-1837 (and 1985). Highly detailed history of the King's German Legion.

Beck, Fritz and Hahn, Karl von, *Geschichte des Grossherzoglich Hessischen Feld-Artillerie-Regiments Nr 25*, E. S. Mittler und Sohn, Berlin 1899. Excellent for Hessen-Darmstadt.

Beck, Fritz, *Geschichte des 1 Grossherzoglich Hessischen Infanterie-(Leibgarde-) Regiments Nr 115, 1621-1899*, E. S. Mittler und Sohn, Berlin 1899.

Belhomme, Lieutenant Colonel, *Histoire de l'Infanterie en France*, Tome IV; Charles-Lavauzelle, Paris, Limoges, 1893-1902.

Bernays, Guillaume, *Schicksale des Grossherzogtum Frankfurt und seiner Truppen*, E. S. Mittler und Sohn, Berlin, 1882. Quite the best source for the Grand Duchy of Frankfurt.

Bezzel, Oskar, *Geschichte des Königlich-Bayerischen Heeres unter König Maximilien I Joseph von 1806-1825*, München, 1933. Excellent for Bavarian regimental participation, 1792-1800.

Bigge, Wilhelm, *Geschichte des Infanterie-Regiments Kaiser Wilhelm (2. Grossherz. Hess.) Nr 116*, E. S. Mittler und Sohn, Berlin 1903.

Bleibtreu, C., *Die Völkerschlacht bei Leipzig*, Leipzig, 1907. Excellent for the Battle of Leipzig, 1813.

Bodart, Gaston, *Militär-Historisches Kriegslexikon 1618-1905*, Wien und Leipzig, 1907.

Bogdanovich, M. Generalmajor, *Geschichte des Feldzuges im Jahre 1812*, C. W. Stern, Leipzig, 1863.

Bogdanovich, M., Generalmajor, *Geschichte des Feldzuges im Jahre 1813 in Deutschland*, Leipzig. Excellent for Russian participation in 1812, 1813.

Bosscha, J., *Nêerlands heldendaten te land, van de vroegste tijden af tot in onze dagen*, Leeuwarden, 1868-1875, Vol III/1.

Brancaccio, Nicola, *L'Esercito del Vecchio Piemonte (1560-1859)*, Rome, 1922. Very good for Piedmontese forces 1793-1798.

Bredow-Wedel, Claus von, Generalmajor, *Historische Rang- und Stammliste des deutschen Heeres*, Berlin, 1905, 3 volumes. Very good for all Prussian and associated German regiments if very brief.

Carl, Erzherzog von Österreich, *Der Feldzug von 1794-1795*, Wien, 1872.

— *Der Feldzug von 1796 in Deutschland; Behelfe zum Studium der Kriegsgeschichte*, Wien, 1876.

Cazalas, E., *De Stralsund à Lunebourg, Épisode de la Campagne de 1813*, Paris, 1911. Excellent for Stralsund and Lüneburg 1813.

Chodzko, Leonard, *Histoire des Légions Polonaises en Italie*, Barbezat Paris, 1829. Excellent for the Polish Legions in Italy in the 1790s.

Charrié, Pierre, *Drapeaux et Etendards de la Révolution et de l'Empire*, Copernic, Paris, 1982. Very good for French colours and standards throughout the period.

Christen, Hauptmann von, *Österreich im Kriege gegen die Französische Revolution*, Kriegsarchiv Wien, 1898-1900. Excellent for Revolutionary Wars; concentrating on Austrian participation.

Chuquet, Arthur, *Les Guerres de la Révolution*, Librarie Leopold Cerf, Paris, 1887-1892. Good for French participation and for that of the Austrians 1792-1798.

Clausewitz, Carl von, General, *The Campaign of 1812 in Russia*, John Murray, London, 1843; Greenhill, London, 1992.

Clausewitz, Carl von, General, *Hinterlassene Werke über Krieg und Kriegführung*, Berlin, 1832-1837, Ferdinand Dümmler.

Clowes, Sir W. L., *The Royal Navy*, London 1897-1903, Sampson Low, London, 1996-97. Excellent for the Royal Navy's participation.

Colin, Jean L., *La Campagne de 1793 en Alsace et dans le Palatinat*, Chapelot, Paris, 1902.

Crociani, Boeri, *L'Escercito Borbonico Dal 1789 al 1815*. Italian Army Historical Department, 1989.

Cunliffe, Marcus, *The Royal Irish Fusiliers*, 1793-1950, OUP, London, 1952.

Dalwigk, zu Lichtenfels, Freiherr von, *Geschichte der Waldeckischen und Kurhessischen Stammtruppen des Infanterie-Regiments von Wittich, (3. Kurhess.) Nr 83, 1681-1866*, Oldenburg, 1909. Excellent for Waldeck and Kurhessian participation.

Damitz, *Geschichte des Feldzuges von 1814 in dem östlichen und nördlichen Frankreich bis zur Einnahme von Paris*, E. S. Mittler und Sohn, Berlin, Posen, Bromberg 1842.

Darmstaedter, Paul, *Das Grossherzogtum Frankfurt*, Frankfurt/Main, 1901.

David, Charles, *History of the Campaigns of General Pichegru March 1794-27 February 1795*, London, 1796.

David, Pierre, *Histoire chronologique des Opérations de l'Armée du Nord et de celle Sambre-et-Meuse*, Guebart Paris and Hamburg, 1799. Very good detail on French activities 1795.

Dedon, l'aine, Citoyen, *Précis Historique des Campagnes de l'Armée de Rhin et Moselle, pendant l'an IV et l'an V*, Paris and Strassburg.

Ditfurth, Max von, *Die Hessen in den Feldzügen von 1793, 1794 und 1795*, Kassel, 1893.

— *Die Hessen in der Champagne, am Maine und Rheine während der Jahre 1792, 1793 und 1794*, Marburg, 1881. Excellent for Hessians 1792-1795.

Dohna, Albrecht von Reichs-Burggrafen zu, *Der Feldzug der Preussen gegen die Franzosen in den Niederlanden im Jahre 1793*, Stendal (Berlin) 1798. Excellent for Prussian, Austrian, German States and Britain 1793.

Dupuis, V., Commandant, *Les Opérations Militaires sur la Sambre en 1794*, Paris 1907.

Eck, Major, *Geschichte des 2. Westfälischen Husaren-Regiments Nr 11 und seiner Stammtruppen von 1807-1913*, August Bagel, Düsseldorf, 1913. Excellent for 2nd Westfalian Hussars (Grand Duchy of Berg), 1807-1815.

Elster, Otto, *Geschichte der Stehenden Truppen im Herzogtum Braunschweig-Wolfenbüttel von 1714-1806*, M. Heinsius, Leipzig, 1901. Excellent for Brunswick 1792-1806.

Ernstberger, Anton, *Die Deutschen Freikorps 1809 in Böhmen*, Prag. 1942; Volk- und Reich Verlag. Very good for the Brunswick and Hessen-Kassel Freikorps 1809.

Fabry, Capitaine G, *Mémoires sur la Campagne de 1794 en Italie*, Chapelot. Paris, 1904.

— *Campagne de l'Armée d'Italie 1796-1797*, Champion, Paris, 1900-1901.

— *Campagne de Russia 1812*, Chapelot, Paris, 1900-1903.

Fahrmbacher, Hans, *Der Kampf um die Rheinschanze bei Mannheim am 25 Januar 1798*,

Feller, Professor Doktor Richard, *Die Schweizer Halbbrigaden im Dienste Frankreichs 1798-1805*, Bern, 1934. Good for Swiss in French service 1798-1805.

Ferreira (see Martins).

Fervel, J. N., *Campagnes de la Révolution Française dans les Pyrénées Orientales*, Paris, 1861. Good for the campaigns in the east Pyrenees 1793-1795.

Fiebig, Ewald, *Unsterbliche Treue*, Andermann, Essen 1935. Excellent for tracking down the fate of the German colours and standards.

Fortescue, J. W., The Hon, *A History of the British Army*, Macmillan and Co, London 1899-1930. Excellent for the British army.

Freydorf, Rudolph von, *Geschichte der Badischen Truppen 1809 im Feldzug der französischen Hauptarmee gegen Österreich*, Heidelberg 1909. Excellent for the Baden army 1809.

Friedrich, Major, *Geschichte des Herbstfeldzuges 1813*, E. S. Mittler und Sohn, Berlin 1903.

Gebler, Wilhelm, Edler von, *Das K. K. Österreiches Auxiliarcorps im Russischen Feldzug 1812*, Braunmüller, Wien, 1863. Very good for the Austrian contingent in Russia in 1812.

Gembarzewski, Bronislaw, *Zolnierz Polski*, Ministry of Defence, Warsaw 1964. Very good for Poland/Grand Duchy of Warsaw.

— *Rodowody Pulkow Polskich i Oddzialów równorzednych od r. 1717 do r. 1831.*, Warsaw.

Gerdes, A, *Die Geschichte der Truppen Bergs und Westfalen 1812 in Russland*, Langendreer, 1914.

Gerhardt, O., *Die Württemberger in Russland 1812*, Steinkopf, Stuttgart, 1937.

Gottschalck, Maximilian, Generalmajor, *Geschichte*

des 1. Thüringischen Infanterie-Regiments Nr 31, E. S. Mittler und Sohn, Berlin, 1894.

Grosch, Fedor, Generalmajor z. D.; Hagen, Eduard; Schenk, Albert, *Geschichte des K. B. 12. Infanterie-Regiments Prinz Arnulf und seiner Stammabteilungen*, J. Landauer, München, 1914.

Günther, Reinhold, *Der Feldzug der Division Lecourbe im Schweizerischen Hochgebirge 1799*, J. Huber, Frauenfeld, 1896.

— *Geschichte des Feldzuges von 1800 in Ober-Deutschland, der Schweiz und Ober Italien*, J. Huber, Frauenfeld, 1893. Very good for the 1799 campaign in Switzerland and for the 1800 campaign.

Hagen, Benno von, *Das Reussische Militär in den Kriegsjahren 1806–1815*, Gera, Reuss, Lange, 1904. Very good for the principality of Reuss 1806–1815.

Hardy, *Le Siège de Maestricht l'armée de Sambre et Meuse pendant la Campagne d'automnes 1794*, Paris, 1878.

Has, Dr Wilhelm, *Geschichte des 1. Kurhessischen Feldartillerie-Regiments Nr 11 und seine Stammtruppen*, Marburg, 1913. Excellent for Hessen-Kassel.

Hedegaard, E. O. A., *Krigen pä Sjaelland 1807*, Forlag von Paul A. Andersen, Helsingör 1970. Very good for the Copenhagen affair 1807, particularly the Danish side.

HGM: Heeresgeschichtliches Museum, Vienna, Austria. A series of monographs numbered as shown below:

3: *Das Gefecht bei Dürnstein-Loiben 1805*, by Dr. R. Egger, 1965.

9: *Das Gefecht bei Ebelsberg am 3 Mai 1809* by R. W. Litschel, 1968.

11: *Die Schlacht von Aspern am 21 und 22 Mai 1809* by M. Rauchensteiner, 1982.

20: *Die Kämpfe am Bergisel 1809* by W. Köfler, 1972.

27: *Das Gefecht bei Hollabrunn und Schöngraben 1805* by Dr. R. Egger, 1974.

36: *Die Schlacht bei Deutsch Wagram am 5 und 6 Juli 1809* by M. Rauchensteiner, 1994.

41: *Die Kampfe am Pass Lueg im Jahre 1809* by W. Köfler, 1980.

48: *Die Gefechte an der Pontlatzer Brücke 1703 und 1809* by F. Kirchmair, 1983.

51: *Das Gefecht bei St. Michael-Leoben am 25 Mai 1809* by A. H. Wagner, 1984.

52: *Die Gefechte bei Feldkirch 1799 und der Kampf um Vorarlberg bis 1801* by E. Hillbrand, 1985.

56: *Die Kämpfe in Südkärnten 1813* by R. Jerábek, 1986.

58: *Die Kämpfe um den Grazer Schlossberg 1809* by C. Teppersberg, 1987.

59: *Kriegsschauplatz Bodensee 1799/1800 und 1809* by G. Wanner, 1987.

60: *Die Kämpfe um die Pässe Strub, Scharnitz und Leutasch 1805* by F. Bauer, 1987.

All these booklets are excellent for Austrian participation and frequently for French as well.

Herold J. Christopher, *Bonaparte in Egypt*, London, 1963. Very good for the French in Egypt.

Hoen, Maximilian, Ritter von, *Das Kriegsjahr 1809 in Einzeldarstellungen*, Wien und Leipzig, 1909. Excellent for Austrian participation in 1809.

Hoehn, Maximilian Ritter von; Veltzé Alois, *Kriege unter der Regierung des Kaisers Franz I*, Wien, 1908.

Holleben, von, General, *Geschichte des Frühjarsfeldzuges 1813 und seine Vorgeschichte*, E. S. Mittler und Sohn, Berlin 1904. Excellent for 1813.

Holtz, Georg Freiherr von, *Die Innerösterreichische Armee, 1813 and 1814.* Wien und Leipzig, 1912. Very good for events in northern Italy.

Holtzendorff, Albrecht, Graf von, *Geschichte der Königlich Sächsischen Leichten Infanterie von Ihrer Errichtung bis zum 1 Oktober 1859*, Leipzig, 1860.

Höpfner, Eduard von, *Der Krieg von 1806 und 1807*, Simon Schropp & Co, Berlin, 1851. Excellent for Prussia 1806 and 1807; very good for Russia 1807.

Horsetzky von Hornthall, Adolf, *Kriegsgeschichtliche Übersicht der Wichtigsten Feldzüge seit 1792*, L. W. Seidel und Sohn, Wien, 1905.

Hutter, Hermann, *Das Königliche 1. Chevaulégèrs-Regiment Kaiser Alexander von Russland 1682–1882*, R. Oldenburg, München, 1885.

Isenbart, Wilhelm, *Die Geschichte des 2. Nassauischen Infanterie-Regiments Nr 88, 1806–1866*, Eisenach, 1902. Excellent for Nassau regiments in Spain.

Istvaán, Bodnar, 'Agyöri csata I–II'. From the periodical *Hadtörténelmi Közlemények*, Budapest, 1897. Excellent for the Austrians at Raab, 1809.

Istvaán, R. Kiss, *Az utolsó nemesi felkelés 100 évfordulójának emlékére*, Budapest, 1909, idem.

James, William, *The Naval History of Great Britain from the Declaration of War by France in 1793 to the Accession of George IV*, Macmillan, London, 1860. Excellent for the Royal Navy.

Jany, Curt, *Geschichte der Preussischen Armee*, Biblioverlag, Osnabrück, 1967. Very good for Prussian participation 1792–1795 and 1806–1807.

Jomini, Henri, Baron de, *Militärische Bemerkungen über die Eroberung von Holland durch die Franzosen in den Jahren 1793, 1794, 1795*, Paris.

Kausler, Franz von, *Atlas der Merkwürdigsten Schlachten, Treffen und Belagerungen der Alten, Mittleren und Neuern Zeit*,

Kausler, Franz von and Woerl, Professor J. E., *Die Kriege von 1792–1815 in Europa und Aegypten mit besondere Rücksicht auf die Schlachten Napoleons und seiner Zeit*, Karlsruhe and Freiburg, 1842.

Keim, August, *Geschichte des Infanterie-Leibregiments (3. Grossherzoglich Hessisches) Nr 117*, Verlag A. Bath, Berlin, 1903. Excellent for Hessen-Darmstadt.

— *Geschichte des 4. Grossherzoglich Hessisches Infanterie-Regiments (Prinz Karl) Nr 118 1688–1878.* Berlin, 1879.

Kessler, J, *Die drei Feldzüge der Franzosen gegen die Spanier in den West-Pyrenäen in den Jahren 1793, 1794, 1795*, Johann Conrad Hinrichs, Leipzig, 1804. (A translation from the French original by Beaulac, 1801.) Good for the Franco-Spanish war 1793–1795.

KGE: Kriegsgeschichtliche Einzelschriften. Published by the Prussian Grand General Staff, Abteilung für Kriegsgeschichte. Berlin. E. S. Mittler und Sohn. Identified by year of publishing and serial number. Excellent for the various themes selected.

Kraft, Keinz, *Die Württemberger in den Napoleonischen Kriegen*, W. Kohlhammer, Stuttgart, 1865. Very good for Württemberg regiments 1805–1815.

Krauss, Alfred, Generalmajor, *Der Feldzug von Ulm 1805*, L. Seidel und Sohn, Wien 1912. Excellent for the Ulm campaign, 1805.

Krebs, L. und Moris, H., *Campagnes dans les Alpes Pendant la Révolution*, Paris, 1854.

Kriege, F. II, *Kriege unter der Regierung des Kaisers Franz. Krieg gegen die französische Revolution*, Vol II, Austrian General Staff, Vienna. Excellent for French and Austrian participation, 1792.

Kuhl, Hermann von, *Bonapartes Erster Feldzug 1796*, Berlin, 1902.

Kummer, E., *Mühsale der Schweizer-Regimenter auf Napoleon's Feldzug nach Russland im Jahre 1812*, 1972. Very good for the Swiss regiments in Russia 1812.

Langermann und Erlencamp, Freiherr von; and Voigts-Rhetz, Hauptmann, *Geschichte des Grossherzoglich Mecklenburgischen Grenadier-Regiments Nr 89*, J. Ritter, Schwerin, 1895. Excellent for Mecklenburg 1806–15.

Lantz, Georg, *Geschichte der Stammtruppen der 6. Thüringischen Infanterie-Regiments Nr 95*, Braunschweig, 1897. Excellent for the Thuringian contingents.

Lehmann, Gustav, *Die Trophäen der Preussischen Armee in der Hof- und Garnisonskirche zu Potsdam*, Berlin, 1898.

Lehnert, 'Geschichte der K. u. K. Kriegsmarine'. II Heil, I Band: *Die österreichische venetianische Marine 1797–1802.* Wien.

Lettow-Vorbeck, Oscar Oberst a. D. von, *Der Krieg von 1806 und 1807*, E. S. Mittler und Sohn, Berlin 1892–1893. Very good for 1806 and 1807.

Leyh, Max, Dr, *Die Feldzüge des Königlich Bayerischen Heeres unter Max I Joseph von 1805 bis 1815*, Verlag Max Schick, München 1935. Excellent for Bavarian regiments 1805–15.

Lossberg, von, *Briefe in die Heimat Geschrieben während des Feldzugs 1812 in Russland*, Leipzig, Georg Wigand.

Lufft, August, *Der Feldzug am Mittelrhein in den Monaten Mai, Juni und Juli 1794*, Karlsruhe, 1870.

Lünsmann, Fritz, *Die Westfälische Armee 1807–13*, E. S. Mittler und Sohn, Berlin 1935. Very good for the Westfalian army 1807–1813.

Maag, Dr A., *Die Schicksale der Schweizer-Regimenter in Napoleons I Feldzug nach Russland 1812*, Ernst Kuhn, Biel, 1890. Very good for the Swiss regiments in Russia, 1812.

Mahon, Patrice, *Études sur les Armées du Directoire*, Paris 1905.

Malibran H. and Chelminski, *L'Armée du Duché de Varsovie de 1807 à 1815*, Paris, 1913. Very good for the Grand Duchy of Warsaw 1807–15.

Marinelle-Fitzgerald, Alexander, *Die Feldzüge der Französischen Revolution; Der Feldzug 1794*, Wien, 1892.

Martinien, A, *Tableaux par Corps et par Batailles des Officiers Tués et Blessés Pendant les Guerres de l'Empire 1805–1815*, Lavauselle, Paris, 1890. Very good for officer casualties (listed by name; killed and wounded) of French and satellite armies 1805–1815. Contains many errors of location.

Martins, Ferreira, General, *Historia do Exercito Portugues*, Lisbon. Very good for the Portuguese army 1793-1814.

Marx, *Geschichte des Infanterie-Regiments Kaiser Friedrich, König von Preussen (7. Württembergisches) Nr 125*, Stuttgart.

Mayne, William, Lt Col and Lillie, Captain, *A Narrative of the Campaigns of the Loyal Lusitanian Legion*, London, 1812 and Cambridge 1986. Excellent for the Loyal Lusitanian Legion 1808-11 in Spain and Portugal.

Menge, August, *Die Schlacht von Aspern am 21 und 22 Mai 1809*, Berlin, 1900. Excellent for the battle of Aspern, 21 and 22 May 1809.

Microys, Wilhelm, Ritter von, *Die Schlacht von Magnano am 5 April 1799*, Eperjes, 1899.

Michaelovsky-Danielevski, Aleksander I. and Milyutin, Oberst, *Geschicht des Krieges Russlands mit Frankreich unter der Regierung Kaiser Paul I, 1799*, Lindauerschen Buchhandlung, München, 1856-1858. Excellent for Suvorov's Italian and Swiss campaign 1799.

Mitteilungen des K. u. K. Kriegsarchivs (MKuKKA), Dritte Folge, IV Band, *Ein Seekrieg in Schwaben, 1799 und 1800*, Wien, 1906. Excellent for actions on and around the Lake Constance (Bodensee).

Montagu, V. M., *Eugène de Beauharnais*, Long, London, 1913.

Müller, Herbert, *Geschichte des 4. Württembergischen Infanterie-Regiments Nr 122 Kaiser Franz Josef von Österreich, König von Ungarn, 1806-1906*, Heilbronn, 1906.

Müller, Hermann, *Die Schlacht bei Hanau am 30 und 31 Oktober 1813 und Ihre Vorgeschichte*, Müller, Hanau, 1913. Excellent for the battle of Hanau.

Münich, Friedrich, *Geschichte der Entwicklung der Bayerischen Armee seit zwei Jahrhunderten*, München, 1864.

Napier, William, F. P., *History of the War in the Peninsula and in the South of France 1807-1814*, London, 1828-1840. Reprinted London, 1995-1996.

Neff, W, *Geschichte des Infanterie-Regiments von Goeben (2. Rheinisches) Nr 28*, E. S. Mittler und Sohn, Berlin, 1890.

Nübling, *Geschichte des Grenadier-Regiments König Karl (5. Württembergisches) Nr 123*, Stuttgart.

Obpacher, Josef, *Das K. B. 2. Chevaulegers-Regiment Taxis*, Bayerischen Kriegsarchiv, München, 1926.

Obser, Karl, *Denkwürdigkeiten des Markgrafen Wilhelm van Baden*, Heidelberg, 1906.

Oman, Sir Charles, *A History of the Peninsular War*, Clarendon Press, Oxford, 1902-1930; Greenhill Books, London, 1995-1997. Excellent for the war in Spain, Portugal and southern France 1808-1814, using a very wide selection of sources from all participating nations.

— *Studies in the Napoleonic Wars*, Greenhill Books, 1989.

Ondorza, Oberleutnant, *Geschichte der Grossherzoglichen Mecklenburgischen Artillerie (Fuss-Artillerie-Regiment Nr 60)*, Miesenbach, Riffarth und Co, Leipzig und Dresden, 1913. Very good for Mecklenburg 1806-15.

ÖMZ: *Österreichische Militärische Zeitschrift* An Austrian periodical published by the Kriegsarchiv in Vienna, printed by L. W. Seidel und Sohn and identified by year of publishing and volume number. Usually very good to excellent on Austrian participation in the themes selected.

Otterstedt, F. von, *Kurze Geschichte des 7. Thüringer Infanterie-Regimentes Nr 96 und seiner Stämme*, Gera, 1885. Very good for the Thuringian contingents 1806-1815.

Pascal, Adrian, *Histoire de l'Armée et de tous les Regiments*, Paris, 1847-58.

Pépé, General Guglielmo, *Memoirs of General Pépé*, London, 1846.

Pfannenberg, *Geschichte des Infanterie-Regiments Grossherzog von Sachsen (5. Thüringisches) Nr 94 und seiner Stammtruppen*, Berlin, 1912. Excellent for the Thuringian contingents 1806-15.

Pfister, A., *König Friedrich von Württemberg*, Stuttgart, 1888.

Pflugk-Harttung, Dr Julius, *Belle-Alliance (Verbundetes Heer)*, R. Eisenschmidt, Berlin, 1914.

Phipps, Colonel Ramsay Weston, *The Armies of the First French Republic and the Rise of the Marshals of Napoleon I*, OUP, London, 1926-1939; Westport, Connecticut, 1980.

Picard, Ernst, *Hohenlinden*, Paris 1909. Excellent for the Hohenlinden campaign up through December 1800.

Plotho, Carl von, *Der Krieg in Deutschland und Frankreich in den Jahren 1813 und 1814*, Berlin, 1817. Very good for the 1813 and 1814 campaigns in Germany and France.

Porbeck, Heinrich P. von, *Kritische Geschichte der Operationen welche die English-Combinierte Armee zur Verteidigung von Holland in den Jahren 1794 und 1795 ausgeführt hat*, Braunschweig, 1802–1804.

Preussisches Militair-Wochenblatt, 1816–1859. E. S. Mittler und Sohn, Berlin, a periodical.

Preysing-Moos, Maximilian, Graf von, Generalmajor, 'Tagebuch 1812', in *Darstellungen aus der Bayerischen kriegs- und Heeresgeschichte*, München 1912. Excellent for Bavarian cavalry participation in Russia, 1812.

Rau, Ferdinand, *Geschichte des 1. Badischen Leib-Dragoner-Regiments Nr 20*, E. S. Mittler und Sohn, Berlin, 1878.

Reiche, Ludwig von, Bemerkungen zu Einigen Stellen des Buches: *Zur Geschichte des Feldzuges von 1815 bis nach der Schlacht von Belle Alliance von dem General von Hoffmann*, Berlin, 1849.

Renouard, C. Hauptmann a. D., *Das Norddeutsche Bundes-Corps im Feldzuge von 1815*, Carl Rümpler, Hannover, 1859.

Robinson, C. W. Major-General, *Wellington's Campaigns 1808–1815. Also Moore's Campaign of Corunna*, Hugh Rees, London, 1905.

Rocca, M. de, *Mémoires sur la Guerre des Françaises en Espagne*, Paris 1814. (Translated as 'In the Peninsula with a French Hussar'), Murray, London, 1815. Reprinted Greenhill Books, London, 1988.

Roessler, Alfred von, *Geschichte des K. Pr. 1. Nassauischen Infanterie-Regiments Nr 87 und seines Stammes des Hzgl. Nass. 1. IR 1809–1874*, E. S. Mittler und Sohn, Berlin, 1882.

Roessler, Ph. von, *Die Geschichte der Herzoglich Nassauischen Truppen*, Adolph Stein, Wiesbaden 1863. Excellent for Nassau regiments in Spain 1808–1813.

Rousset, Camille, *Les Volontaires 1791–1794*, Librarie Académique, Paris, 1874.

Rüstow, Wilhelm, *Der Krieg von 1805 in Deutschland und Italien*, Zürich, 1859.

Sabron, Frederik H. A., *De oorlog van 1794–1795 op ed van de Republik der Vereenigde Nederlanden*, Breda, 1892–93. Very good for Dutch troops 1794–95.

Schäfer, Ernst, 'Mecklenburgs Militärwesen vor und in den Freiheitskriegen' (*Jahrbücher des Vereins für Mecklenburgischen Geschichte und Altertumskunde, Jahrgang LXXX*), 1915.

Schneidawind, F. J. A., *Der Feldzug der Franzosen gegen die Verbündeten in Italien in den Jahren 1798 und 1799*, Darmstadt, 1836.

Schreckenstein, Roth von, General Freiherr, *Die Kavallerie in der Schlacht an der Moskwa*, Münster, 1858. Excellent for allied cavalry at Borodino, 1812.

Schüler, *Geschichte des Schwarzburg-Rudolstätdischen Contingents in den Kriegsjahren von 1807–bis 1815*, Bock, Rudolstadt, 1883. Very good for the Schwarzburg-Rudolstadt contingent 1807–15.

Schulz, Gustav von, *Geschichte des Krieges im Jahre 1805*, Posen und Bromberg, 1847.

— *Geschichte der Kriege in Europa seit dem Jahr 1792 als Folgen der Staatsveränderung in Frankreich unter König Ludwig XVI*, F. A. Brockhaus, Leipzig, 1847. Very good, very broad-based coverage of the revolutionary wars 1792–1800 and the 1805 campaign.

Schuster O. and Franke F. A., *Geschichte der Sächsischen Armee*, Leipzig, 1885. Very good for the Saxon army.

Schwertfeger, Bernhard, *Geschicht der Königl. Deutschen Legion 1803–1816*, Hannover, 1907. Excellent for the King's German Legion.

Siborne, Captain W., *History of the Waterloo Campaign*, Boone, London, 1844, and Greenhill Books, 1990. Excellent for Ligny, Quatre-Bras and Waterloo, 1815.

Sichart, A. von, *Geschichte der Königl. Hannoverschen Armee*, Hannover 1898. Excellent for the Hanoverian army 1792–1803 and 1813–1815.

Soden, Franz Ludwig Freiherr von, *Beytrag zur Geschichte des Krieges 1812 und 1813 besonders in Bezug des 6. Rheinbund-Regiments der damaligen Fürsten-Division usw*, Arnstadt, 1821. Excellent for the 6th Regiment, Confederation of the Rhine, 1812 and 1813.

Specht, F. A. K. von, *Das Königreich Westphalen und seine Armee im Jahre 1813*, Kassel, 1848. Excellent for the Westfalian Army, 1813.

Sporschil, Johann, *Die Grosse Chronik. Geschichte des Krieges des Verbündeten Europas gegen Napoleon Bonaparte in den Jahren 1813, 1814 und 1815*, Georg Westermann, Braunschweig, 1841. Excellent for the campaigns of 1813, 1814 and 1815 in northern Europe.

Stadlinger, L. J. von, *Geschichte des Württembergischen Kriegswesens von der frühesten bis zur neuesten Zeit*, Guttenberg, Stuttgart, 1856. Very good for Württemberg throughout the period.

— *Militär-Handbuch des Königreichs Württemberg*, Beck und Fränkel, Stuttgart, 1836.

Starklof, R., *Geschichte des Königl. Württembergischen Vierten Reiter-Regiments Königin Olga 1805-1866*, Stuttgart, 1867.

Stenzel, A., *Seekriegsgeschichte*, Hahnsche Verlag, Hannover, 1907-1921. Naval historical overview.

Strack von Weissenbach, *Geschichte der Königlich Württembergischen Artillerie*, W. Kohlhammer, Stuttgart, 1882. Excellent for Württemberg artillery participation.

Strobl, Adolf, *Aspern und Wagram*, Wien, 1897. Very good for the battles of Aspern and Wagram, 1809.

Strengschwerd, Karl, *Rechtliches Gutachten die Übergabe der Festung Mannheim an den Reichsfeind Betreffend*, Regensburg, 1795.

Susane, Louis, General, *Histoire de l'Infanterie Française*, Paris 1867; reprinted 1985.

Sussmilch, *Geschichte des 2. Königl. Sächsischen Husaren-Regiments Nr 19*, Brockhaus, Leipzig, 1882.

Tarnow, Gerhard, 'Die Aufstellung des Mecklenburg-Strelitz Rheinbund Kontingents und des Vaterländischen Husaren Regiments 1808-1817'. (*Mecklenburg-Strelitzer Geschichtsblätter, Jahrgang XIXI*). Neustrelitz, 1935. Excellent for Mecklenburg 1808-15.

Treskow, Albert C. von, *Der Feldzug der Preussen im Jahre 1794*, Berlin, 1837. Very good for Prussian participation 1794.

Vaudoncourt, F. Guillaume, General Baron, *Histoire des Campagnes d'Italie en 1813 et 1814*, Booth and Egerton, London 1817.

Veltzé, Alois, Hauptmann, *Der Krieg gegen Neapel 1815*, Wien, 1914.

— *Kriegsbilder aus Polen, Steiermark und Ungarn aus dem Kriegsjahr 1809 in Einzeldarstellungen*, Wien. Very good for Austrian participation in Poland, Steyermark and Hungary 1809.

Voigt, Günther, *Deutschlands Heere bis 1918*, Biblio-Verlag, Osnabrück, 1983, 11 volumes.

Wagner, August, *Der Feldzug der Königlich Preussischen Armee am Rhein im Jahre 1793*, Berlin, 1831 and Wiesbaden, 1981.

Walter, Friedrich, *Mannheim in Vergangenheit und Gegenwart*, Vol 1, Mannheim, 1907 and 1977.

Welden, Ludwig, Freiherr von, *Der Krieg 1809 zwischen Österreich und Frankreich*, Wien, 1872. Very good for Austria, 1809.

Weltmann, Hauptmann, *Geschichte des Infanterie-Regiments von Horn (3. Rheinisches Nr 29)*, Lintz Verlag, Trier, 1894.

Wisnar, Julius, Regierungsrat: 'Die Schlacht bei Znaim im Jahre 1809', from the *Jahresbericht des k. k. Gymnasiums in Znaim für das Schuljahr 1909/1910*, Znaim, 1910. Very good for the battle of Znaim, 1809.

Witzleben, August von, *Prinz Friedrich Josias von Coburg-Saalfeld*, Berlin, 1859. Königl. Geheime Ober-Hofdruckerei. Excellent for 1792, 1793, the Netherlands campaigns, particularly the Austrians, Prussians, British, etc. Not so good for the French.

Woinovich, Emil von, General, *Kämpfe in der Lika, in Kroatien und Dalmatien 1809*, C. W. Stern, Wien, 1906. Excellent for Lika, Croatia and Dalmatia, 1809.

Woinovich, Emil von, General, *Kulm, Leipzig, Hanau 1813*, Edlinger, Wien and Leipzig, 1911.

Wrede, Alphons, Freiherr von, *Geschichte der K. u. K. Wehrmacht*, Wien, 1898-1905. Very good (but very brief) for the entire Austrian army 1792-1815.

Wrochem, Paul von, *Geschichte des Grossherz. Mecklenburgischen Füsilier-Regiments Nr 90*, E. S. Mittler und Sohn, Berlin, 1888. Excellent for Mecklenburg 1806-15.

Zech, Karl von and Porbeck, Freiherr von, *Geschichte der Badischen Truppen 1809*, Carl Winter, Heidelberg, 1909. Excellent for the Baden contingent's participation in 1809.

Zelle, Walter, Doctor, *Geschichte der Freiheitskriege 1812-1815*, Richard Sattlers Verlag, Leipzig, 1907. Good for 1813-15.

Zimmermann, Rittmeister, *Geschichte des Grossherzogl. Hess. Dragoner-Regiments (Garde-Dragoner-Regiment) Nr 23*, Part 1 (1790-1860). Arnold Bergsträssler, Darmstadt, 1878. Very good for Hessen-Darmstadt's cavalry 1792-1815.

The publications *Zeitschrift für Heereskunde* by Dr Arnold Wirtgen provide an excellent source covering all armies and periods.

INDEX OF ACTIONS